2023
EDITION

Essentials of
FEDERAL
INCOME TAXATION
For Individuals and Business

ROBERT W. JAMISON, Ph.D., CPA
Professor Emeritus of Accounting

TERESA STEPHENSON, Ph.D., CMA
Professor of Accounting

 Wolters Kluwer

EDITORIAL STAFF

Production: Jennifer Schencker, Manjula Mahalingam, Prabhu Menakshisundaram
Editorial: Barbara L. Post J.D.
Cover Design: Laila Gaidulis

ISBN: 978-0-8080-5714-7

List of acronyms used:

AAA—Accumulated Adjustments Account
ABLE—Achieving a Better Life Experience
ACA—(Patient Protection and) Affordable Care Act
ACRS—Accelerated Cost Recovery System
ACV—Amortized Carrying Value
ADS—Alternate Depreciation System
AFR—Applicable Federal Rate
AGI—Adjusted Gross Income
AMT—Alternative Minimum Tax
AMTI—Alternative Minimum Tax Income
AOTC—American Opportunity Tax Credit
ARP—American Rescue Plan Act of 2021
AVD—Alternative Valuation Date
CAA—Consolidated Appropriations Act of 2021
CD—Certificate of Deposit
CDE—Community Development Entity
CPA— Certified Public Accountant
CPE—Continuing Professional Education
CPI—Consumer Price Index
CTC—Child Tax Credit
DB—Declining Balance
DOMA—Defense of Marriage Act
DRD—Dividend Received Deduction
EA—Enrolled Agent
E&P—Earnings and Profits
EIC—Earned Income Credit
EIN—Employer Identification Number
EIP—Economic Impact Payment
FICA—Federal Insurance Contributions Act
FMV—Fair Market Value
FSA—Flexible Spending Account
FTE—Full-time Equivalent
FUTA—Federal Unemployment Tax Act
HI—Hospital Insurance
HOH—Head of Household
HSA—Health Savings Account
IRA—Individual Retirement Arrangement
IRS—Internal Revenue Service
LLC—Limited Liability Company
LLP—Limited Liability Partnership
MACRS—Modified Accelerated Cost Recovery System
MFJ—Married Filing Jointly
MFS—Married Filing Separately
NII—Net Investment Income
NOL—Net Operating Loss
OASDI—Old Age, Survivors, and Disability Insurance
OID—Original Issue Discount
PSC—Personal Service Corporation
PTC—Premium Tax Credit
PTIN—Preparer Tax Identification Number
QBI—Qualified Business Income
QIP—Qualified Improvement Property
SEP—Simplified Employee Pension
SIMPLE—Savings Incentive Match Plan for Employees
SL—Straight-line
SSN—Social Security Number
TI—Taxable Income
TIN—Taxpayer Identification Number
WOTC—Work Opportunity Tax Credit

Preface

WHY STUDY FEDERAL INCOME TAXATION?

Essentials of Federal Income Taxation for Individuals and Business, 2023 Edition, covers the taxation of individuals for the 2022 tax year. It provides complete coverage in an easy-to-read and easy-to-understand format for your first course in taxation. This practical text helps you understand the tax laws and improve the reporting quality of your tax returns. The coverage does not assume that you have had an introductory accounting course. If you are interested in learning how to prepare tax returns, including your own, studying this text and mastering its content will help you solve actual tax problems and succeed in preparing your own tax returns. At press time, the *2023 Edition* contains the latest information and tax forms available for the 2022 tax year. It also contains the latest information for the 2023 tax planning process.

LOADED WITH OUTSTANDING FEATURES

Many outstanding features make the *2023 Edition* the main reference for completing 2022 federal income tax returns. Before you start reading *Essentials of Federal Income Taxation for Individuals and Business, 2023 Edition,* you are encouraged to spend a little time looking over the next few pages. The *2023 Edition* benefits from the helpful comments and suggestions contributed by instructors and students who have taught and learned federal income taxation from previous editions.

BUSINESS ENTITY OPTION

While this text focuses on the income taxation of individuals, it also makes available an optional course of study that examines the taxation of income earned by corporations and partnerships, as well as sole proprietorships. This option is included in response to the growing number of instructors who believe that an introductory tax course should compare and contrast the tax challenges facing the different forms of business organizations.

Those who choose to place more attention on the taxation of business entities are encouraged to study the chapters in the following sequence: 1, 2, 14, 15, 16, 3, 4, 5, 6, 7, 8, 9, 10, 11, 12, and 13. Chapters 1 and 2 cover the basic tax structure for individuals. Chapters 14, 15, and 16 introduce the students to the taxation of C corporations, S corporations, and partnerships. All subsequent chapters (3–13) include at least one special business entity problem. These problems require students to relate the material covered in the chapter to the different forms of business.

The business entity problems are located near the end of each chapter's QUESTIONS AND PROBLEMS. The solutions to the business entity problems generally require information from Chapters 14, 15, and 16. Consequently, students will be reviewing these chapters on a regular basis throughout the course. The business entity problems are indicated by the business folder icon (shown here in the left margin).

OTHER SPECIAL FEATURES

- The information icon (shown here in the left margin) next to a shaded box highlights tax tips, planning opportunities, general observations, and fun facts designed to enrich the learning experience.

- The computer mouse icon (shown here in the left margin) indicates homework problems suitable for completion using tax preparation software.

- Some provisions discussed in this textbook are set to expire at some date in the future or have temporarily expired under the Tax Cuts and Jobs Act. These changes have been incorporated into the chapters, and any information that concerns future tax years is discussed in shaded boxes and is identified with the new developments icon shown here in the left margin.

  Feature: This textbook presents the tax laws that will assist you in preparing tax returns for the 2022 tax year. Additional information that may affect a later tax year is discussed separately in a legislative developments box identified with the icon shown here to the left of the shaded box.

  Benefit: The material presented in the legislative developments box will provide you with that information, which, in turn, will assist you in tax planning for the current and future tax years.

- Line-by-line instructions describing how to complete tax forms and schedules are illustrated throughout the chapters. These illustrations are found next to the filled-in forms icon shown here in the left margin.

  Feature: Each filled-in tax form is supported by information provided from the taxpayer's records and receipts. References to specific line numbers where the taxpayer's information is entered have been provided for each filled-in form and schedule presented in the chapter. The line number references shown in the textbook correspond to the line numbers on the tax forms and schedules included in the textbook, including draft versions of 2022 tax forms, when necessary.

  Benefit: This concise presentation makes it easier for you to relate tax data to the tax form. The format presents information supplied by the taxpayer highlighted in bold. Once this data has been entered on the appropriate line(s) of the tax form, the rest of the lines on the form can be completed by following the instructions provided on the form. This approach helps you see how information is used to complete each tax form and schedule introduced in the chapter.

- COMPREHENSIVE PROBLEMS are included in most chapters; many include two versions of the problem.

  Feature: These problems incorporate many concepts introduced in the chapter. Many of these involve completing a tax return or portions of a tax return.

  Benefit: This learning application integrates and summarizes the concepts covered in the chapter. Completing the comprehensive problems will help you see how the concepts from the chapter are reported on the tax return. By including multiple versions of the problem, students have more opportunities to solve real-world tax problems, as well as complete real-world tax returns.

- CUMULATIVE PROBLEMS are included in this textbook.

  Feature: Comprehensive problems focus primarily on the concepts introduced in the chapter. Cumulative problems, on the other hand, not only incorporate the concepts from the current chapter, but also include concepts studied in prior chapters. Many of these involve using the taxpayer's information to complete the entire income tax return.

  Benefit: These learning applications integrate and summarize concepts from multiple chapters to give students the opportunity to step back and see the big picture. Also, by completing the Cumulative Problems, you will gain a greater sense of what is involved in preparing a real-world income tax return.

- Tax questions and problems requiring the use of the IRS website are included at the end of the chapter. These problems are identified by the icon shown to the left here.

  Feature: The answers to these questions and problems are found in the information contained in IRS tax forms and schedules, the instructions to IRS forms and schedules, or IRS publications.

  Benefit: You will learn how to find answers to tax questions from IRS publications available on the Internet. You will also learn how to find needed tax forms, fill them out while on the Internet, and print out copies of the completed forms. These learning applications provide you the opportunity to obtain knowledge about tax law using information outside of the textbook.

HELPFUL INFORMATION INCLUDED IN THE 2023 EDITION

- Frequently used tax facts are provided.
  Feature: Handy Tax Facts appear on the inside front cover. Included are the 2022 tax rate schedules and standard mileage rates, standard deduction and exemption deduction amounts for 2022, and OASDI base amounts for 2022.
  Benefit: This helpful page provides a quick and easy reference source for frequently used tax facts.

- Commonly used AGI threshold amounts and phase-out ranges are provided.
  Feature: These amounts and ranges appear on the inside back cover.
  Benefit: This helpful page provides a quick and easy reference to some of the more commonly-used AGI thresholds and phase-out ranges.

- Paragraph referencing system.
  Feature: All major headings and subheadings in the chapter have been referenced using a paragraph referencing system.
  Benefit: Paragraph references provide an additional method of indexing the material in each chapter. When referring to information in a chapter, students and instructors can refer to either the page number on the page or the paragraph number where the material can be found. Paragraph references also are used throughout the chapters to cross-reference material discussed elsewhere in the textbook.

- Learning objectives are provided at the beginning of each chapter.
  Feature: The major learning objectives for each chapter have been provided and referenced in the homework problems.
  Benefit: Each homework problem is linked to a learning objective. This helps students make sure that they have mastered all major learning objectives before proceeding to the next chapter.

- Numerous examples are provided.
  Feature: Every chapter includes numerous easy-to-follow examples.
  Benefit: These examples show you how tax laws are applied in a variety of real-life situations.

- Step-by-step instructions on how to access IRS forms and publications from the IRS website are given.
  Feature: Information on how to obtain forms and publications from the IRS through the Internet appears in Appendix A after Chapter 16.
  Benefit: This information will help you access the most up-to-date forms, instructions to forms, and IRS publications referenced in the text.

- Appendix of commonly-used blank tax forms.
  Feature: Blank copies of selected tax forms and schedules are provided in Appendix B.
  Benefit: The selected forms and schedules provided are some of the more commonly-used forms and schedules. Having these forms and schedules in one place will help students visualize the flow of tax information on the tax return. The tax forms and schedules included in Appendix B are the most recent ones available at the time the *2023 Edition* was sent to press.

OTHER SUCCESSFUL FEATURES OF ESSENTIALS OF FEDERAL INCOME TAXATION FOR INDIVIDUALS AND BUSINESS, 2023 EDITION

- Comprehensive coverage of self-employed taxpayers
- Detailed coverage of business entities, including C corporations, partnerships, and S corporations
- Almost 50 filled-in forms, schedules, and worksheets are illustrated, each including details regarding the line numbers where data is initially entered by the taxpayer or tax preparer
- Multiple versions (a./b.) for many comprehensive problems, allowing students the opportunity to work two different problems using the same tax forms
- A table referencing the filled-in tax forms, schedules, and worksheets follows the Table of Contents
- A detailed Table of Contents of headings and subheadings for each chapter is located at the end of this Preface
- Tax tips are provided throughout the textbook to assist with tax planning and tax reduction
- Problems at the end of chapters designated for a tax software solution
- Assignments that provide actual application and check students' understanding
- Acronym list on the copyright page (that precedes this Preface) provides actual words for the acronyms used in this textbook

SPECIAL NOTE REGARDING FINAL TAX FORMS AND SCHEDULES FOR THE 2022 TAX YEAR

One of the user-friendly features of *Essentials of Federal Taxation for Individuals and Business* is the filled-in forms that follow the discussion of the tax topic. To illustrate how the relevant tax form is completed, the information needed to complete the form is provided. Line number references and calculations are then provided to help you see how to prepare the form. This technique enhances your learning experience and gives you the tools necessary to prepare the real-world tax return problems found at the end of the chapter. To this end, the *2023 Edition* includes the most up-to-date tax forms and schedules available at the time the textbook was sent to press. When final forms were not available, draft versions of the form were included in the textbook. When a draft version of the current year's tax form had not been released, the final version of the prior year's form was used. Usually, the use of draft forms or the prior year's tax forms does not pose much of a problem, as many tax forms do not change much from year to year.

When completing tax return problems at the end of the chapters, it is recommended that the final version of each form and schedule be used. However, please keep in mind that the line number references might change should the final version of the form differ in any way from the form that appears in the textbook.

Final tax forms and schedules can be downloaded from the IRS website. Appendix A includes step-by-step instructions on how to use the IRS website to download tax forms and IRS Publications.

About the Authors

ROBERT W. JAMISON, PH.D., CPA

Bob Jamison received his doctorate in Accounting from The University of Texas at Austin. He is Professor Emeritus of Accounting at Indiana University, Purdue University, Indianapolis (IUPUI). His principal area of specialization is S Corporations. He is the sole author of *S Corporation Taxation* and co-author of *Multistate Tax Guide to Pass-Through Entities*, both of which are published annually by CCH, a Wolters Kluwer business. He is curator of Wolters Kluwer Answerconnect Topic "S Corporations" and subtopics thereunder. He has contributed to Land Grant University Tax Education Foundation, Inc. National Income Tax Workbook and has contributed to Federal Tax Workshop. He presents advanced and updated S Corporation seminars for various states' CPA societies and other professional organizations. Bob resides in Leesburg, Virginia. He is a member of the AICPA S Corporation Technical Resource Panel and the Washington, DC-based S Corporation Study Group. He consults on S corporation and other business entity problems and has secured private letter rulings from the IRS on behalf of clients. He is the author of three CCH Incorporated guides to the Tax Cuts and Jobs Act of 2017:
Tax Cuts and Jobs Act Impact—Guide to Pass-Through Entities
Tax Cuts and Jobs Act Impact—Guide to Choice of Entity
Tax Cuts and Jobs Act Impact—Guide to Small Business
His articles have appeared in *Taxes: The Tax Magazine, The Tax Adviser, Journal of Passthrough Entities, Practical Tax Strategies, The ATA Journal of Legal Tax Research, Journal of Accountancy, and other professional and academic journals.*
His testimony before the IRS has contributed to proposed and final regulations.

TERESA STEPHENSON, PH.D., CMA

Teresa Stephenson is a Professor of Accounting at the University of Alaska Anchorage. She completed her doctorate at the University of Kentucky in 2006. In 2000, she earned a Master of Professional Accountancy at Indiana University. Prior to her doctoral work, she worked as an independent consultant and tax preparer for small business managers and owners. She has taught accounting and taxation at several schools, including the University of Alaska Anchorage (where she received the *CBPP Senior Undergraduate Teacher of the Year* award), University of South Dakota, University of Wyoming, Indiana University, University of Kentucky, Sullivan University, and Ivy Tech. Over the years, she has won several awards related to teaching and service, including the *"Top Prof" award* given by the University of Wyoming's Cap and Gown Chapter of the Mortar Board Society, the College of Business Advisory Board's *Faculty Award*, and the Sparky Turner *Raise the Bar* service award.

She is a co-author of *Multistate Tax Guide to Pass-Through Entities*, which is published annually by CCH, a Wolters Kluwer business. She has over 30 article publications appearing in journals such as *The CPA Journal, Accounting Horizons, Advances in Taxation, Tax Notes, Practical Tax Strategies, Journal of Legal, Ethical, and Regulatory Issues, Journal of Business Ethics,* and *Journal of Accounting Education.* Research-related awards include the *CBPP Research Award* from the University of Alaska Anchorage, the *Beacom Faculty Excellence Award in Research* at the University of South Dakota, the University of Wyoming's College of Business *Outstanding Junior Research Award*, the American Society of Business Publication Editors' (ASBPE) *Northeast Regional Gold Award* for best feature series in *Strategic Finance* (with Jason Porter), and the *Lybrand Certificate of Merit* for a second series in *Strategic Finance* (again with Jason Porter). She is also a co-author of two supplemental textbooks that introduce Excel to business students, the latest edition of which was published in 2022. She also serves on the Board of Directors for the Alaska Chapter of the IMA and is an editorial board member of IMA's Educational Case Journal.

Acknowledgments

For many years, Professor Linda Johnson (one of Bob's former students) developed this excellent entry-level tax primer. Even though she has retired from authorship, her contributions will have lasting positive impacts on this book. The authors wish to express gratitude to Senior Developmental Editor Barbara Post. Her patience with us while keeping us to a schedule is a balancing act of commendable proportions.

Contents

FILLED-IN TAX FORMS AND SCHEDULES

Form	Title	Paragraph
941	Employer's QUARTERLY Federal Tax Return	1306.03
1040	U.S. Individual Income Tax Return	403.01, 512.02
	Schedule 1: Additional Income and Adjustments to Income	403.01, 512.02
	Schedule 3: Additional Credits and Payments	403.01
	Schedule A: Itemized Deductions	502, 512.01
	Schedule B: Interest and Ordinary Dividends	308.10, 309.05
	Schedule C: Profit or Loss From Business (Sole Proprietorship)	705, 705.05, 705.06
	Schedule D: Capital Gains and Losses	1101.05
	Schedule E: Supplemental Income and Loss	903.01, 905.06
	Schedule EIC: Earned Income Credit	204.12
	Schedule SE: Self-Employment Tax	706.02, 706.03
	Schedule 8812: Credits for Qualifying Children and Other Dependents	204.08
1040-X	Amended U.S. Individual Income Tax Return	1313.01
1065	U.S. Return of Partnership Income	1502.09
	Schedule K-1 (Form 1065): Partner's Share of Income, Deductions, Credits, etc.	1502.13
	Schedule K-2 (Form 1065): Partners' Distributive Share Items—International	1502.12
	Schedule K-3 (Form 1065): Partner's Share of Income, Deductions, Credits, etc.—International	1502.14
1120	U.S. Corporation Income Tax Return	1403.04
	Schedule G (Form 1120): Information on Certain Persons Owning the Corporation's Voting Stock	1403.04
1120-S	U.S. Income Tax Return for an S Corporation	1603.08

Form	Title	Paragraph
	Schedule K-1 (Form 1120-S): Shareholder's Share of Income, Deductions, Credits, etc.	1603.09
	Schedule K-2 (Form 1120-S): Shareholders' Pro Rata Share Items—International	1603.08
	Schedule K-3 (Form 1120-S): Shareholder's Share of Income, Deductions, Credits, etc.—International	1603.09
1125-A	Cost of Goods Sold	1403.04
2441	Child and Dependent Care Expenses	204.03
2553	Election by a Small Business Corporation	1602.03
4562	Depreciation and Amortization	602.06, 602.08, 604

Form	Title	Paragraph
4684	Casualties and Thefts	1103.02
4797	Sales of Business Property	1103.04
6251	Alternative Minimum Tax—Individuals	1203.06
7203	S Corporation Shareholder Stock and Debt Basis Limitations	1603.04
8582	Passive Activity Loss Limitations	905.06
8615	Tax for Certain Children Who Have Unearned Income	314.01
8812	Credits for Qualifying Children and other Dependents	204.08
8815	Exclusion of Interest From Series EE and I U.S. Savings Bonds Issued After 1989	401.03
8829	Expenses for Business Use of Your Home	705.04, 603.05
8863	Education Credits(American Opportunity and Lifetime Learning Credits)	204.05
8949	Sales and Other Dispositions of Capital Assets	1101.05

Table of Contents

Chapter

1

Overview of the Tax Structure

CHAPTER CONTENTS

LEARNING OBJECTIVES

After completing Chapter 1, you should be able to:

1. Describe how taxable income is computed.
2. Distinguish between the concepts of gross income, deductions, and tax credits.
3. Compute a taxpayer's total standard deduction.
4. Determine the number of persons the taxpayer can claim as a dependent.
5. Determine a taxpayer's filing status.
6. Explain a taxpayer's filing requirements and responsibilities.
7. Explain how Congress uses the tax laws to meet certain objectives and how taxpayers can use tax planning to their advantage.

CHAPTER OVERVIEW

This textbook provides an introduction of the U.S. income tax system as it pertains to individuals and their businesses. Prior to the Civil War, government revenues came mainly from sales taxes and tariffs. In 1862, Congress enacted the first income tax to pay for the costs of the Civil War. After ten years, the war was paid for and the income tax went away. In 1894, the government found itself in need of more revenue, prompting Congress to reenact the income tax. A year later, the U.S. Supreme Court ruled that the individual income tax was unconstitutional, as the Constitution required a direct tax to be "apportioned according to the population of each state." Thus, the only way to impose an individual income tax was for Congress to amend the Constitution. In 1913, Congress passed the 16th Amendment to the Constitution, which allowed the income tax to become a permanent part of the U.S. tax system.

The newness of the tax law, along with the rapidly changing conditions of the first half of the twentieth century required frequent revisions to the substance and the structure of the law. By the end of the twentieth century, the primary statutory authority for the federal income tax system was Title 26, U.S. Code, also known as the Internal Revenue Code (IRC, or Code), or Internal Revenue Code of 1986. There are hundreds of provisions in the law. There are also many subdivisions, such as subtitles, chapters within subtitles, subchapters within chapters and a few others. However, the most important segment of information is the *Section*. Many tax publications, including this text, use the term "I.R.C. §" to designate a section of the Code. One of the advantages of the section numbering scheme is that each section is unique to the entire Code. All Code sections begin with an Arabic numeral. They vary from one to five digits. In some cases there is a capital letter at the end of the section. For example, I.R.C. §1 contains the rate structures for individuals. There is only one §1 in the entire Code. This text refers to the Code by Section (§). Many tax credits, discussed in Chapter 2 at ¶204, are designated in this fashion.

Although the Code is the primary statutory authority for the tax law, there are other federal statutes that override the Code. These are usually limited in scope or duration. In 2020, several laws were introduced, most importantly the CARES Act of 2020 (P.L. 116-136), that affect several of the rules discussed in this book. Although this act amended some Code provisions, some of its rules do not appear in the Code. Any citations to these non-Code provisions use the notation "CARES Act of 2020, P.L. 116-136, §….." The section numbering in the CARES Act does not reflect the numbering rules of the Code.

Congress writes and adopts the Code, subject to signature by the U.S. President. The Executive Branch has the responsibility of enforcing laws. Most tax laws are within the jurisdiction of the Treasury Department. Within this Department, the Internal Revenue Service (IRS) is the agency charged with enforcing the income tax. To aid in enforcement, the IRS publishes regulations to guide taxpayers on issues of general importance. These regulations are usually indexed to Code sections. For example, §1 of the Code imposes an income tax on individuals. One of the regulations explains the status of persons as U.S. citizens or residents, who are subject to the income tax. The particular regulation that accomplishes this tax is Regulations Section (Reg. §) 1.1-1. The indexing rules are:

[Chapter of Code].[Section].[ordinal number under code section]

Deconstructing Reg. §1.1-1 tells the reader:

Chapter 1 (income tax). Section 1-First regulation in series

For more specific applications, the IRS issues Revenue Rulings and Revenue Procedures. A Revenue Ruling (Rev. Rul.) provides guidance on a narrow issue. Many of these are issued in response to requests for specific information from a taxpayer. Others address routine, but important issues. The IRS designates Revenue Rulings by year, and ordinal number within the year. Thus, Rev. Rul. 2022-1 is the first ruling effective in calendar year 2022.

Revenue Procedures address some issues of widespread importance, but little complexity. Revenue Procedures (Rev. Procs.) have the same designation scheme as Revenue Rulings. The only distinction is the designation "Rev. Rul." for rulings and "Rev. Proc." for procedures. For example, Rev. Proc. 2022-45 was the 45th Revenue Procedure issued in 2022.

Various federal courts also contribute to the tax law. One of these is an administrative court within the Treasury Department named the U.S. Tax Court. It only hears tax cases. When the IRS discovers an issue on a tax return and the taxpayer and the IRS cannot reach an agreement, the taxpayer can appeal to the Tax Court, without first paying the tax. The court decides which of its cases are important and worthy of publication. The court publishes these in volumes. When one volume reaches capacity, the court starts a new volume. For example, the case of *Kevin Dewitt Skaggs v. Commissioner* appears as 148 T.C. No. 15. This is the 15th case in volume 148 of cases published by the court. These published decisions, also known as "Tax Court Regular" decisions, do not indicate the year of the decision. This case, decided in 2017, determined that an inmate in a mental hospital was not entitled to the earned income credit (see ¶204.11 for more information about the earned income credit). Mr. Skaggs filed his tax return claiming this credit, which is not allowable for persons incarcerated in penal institutions. The Tax Court determined that he was not entitled to the credit. Since the Tax Court believed that this case set precedent, the court chose to publish it as a "regular" decision. Most Tax Court decisions are concerned with matters that are unique to the case, such as dates on which events occurred, values, or positions for which there is established case law. The court does not publish these cases, known as "Memorandum Decisions." Wolters Kluwer (CCH Incorporated) and other publishers compile these cases. The Tax Court numbers these cases chronologically by the year of decision. For instance, *Randy G Sellers v. Commissioner*, TC Memo 2020-84, was the 84th Memorandum Decision issued in 2020. In this case, Mr. Sellers had claimed a deduction for self-employed health insurance (see ¶402.07 for more information about the self-employed health insurance deduction) but offered no documentation to support the deduction. The court held that he could not deduct the purported cost.

The Tax Court also offers an option with substantially reduced court costs. These are known as "small cases" and involve controversies where the tax issue is $50,000 or less. These cases are not appealable. These decisions, known as "Summary Opinions," are not usable as precedents for any other taxpayer.

Courts within the judicial branch of the federal government are also available to resolve disputes. Any person with a claim against the U.S. government may bring an action in the Court of Federal Claims. Some tax cases originate in this court. Alternatively, a person may file a claim against the federal government in the U.S. district court that has jurisdiction in the taxpayer's place of residence. To bring an action in the Court of Federal Claims or in a district court, the taxpayer must pay the tax in question and file for a refund. If the IRS denies the refund claim, the taxpayer sues for a refund.

Except for small case decisions of the Tax Court, the taxpayer or the government may appeal a decision. If the case originated in the Court of Federal Claims, the Court of Appeals for the Federal Circuit hears the appeal. For any district court case or tax court case, the appellant files with the Circuit Court of Appeals that has jurisdiction over the taxpayer's place of residence. Ultimately, some tax cases wind up in the U.S. Supreme Court. This court's decision is final, with respect to the law as it existed for the year of the controversy.

Various publishers, including Wolters Kluwer (CCH Incorporated), compile volumes of the district and appellate courts as well as the Supreme Court. Wolters Kluwer (CCH Incorporated) publishes these decisions, as they relate to federal tax cases, in its series United States Tax Cases, or USTC (not to be confused with the U.S. Tax Court). District Court decisions may or may not be published, depending on the wishes of the court. Wolters Kluwer (CCH Incorporated) publishes two volumes per year. Before 1999, Wolters Kluwer (CCH Incorporated) designated these cases as [yy]-[volume] USTC [¶####]. Beginning in 1999, Wolters Kluwer (CCH Incorporated) designates these cases as [yyyy]-[volume] USTC [¶####].

A well-known case, *James v. United States of America*, concerned the taxation of embezzled income. A district court (unpublished opinion) had held that embezzled funds were not taxable, since the embezzler was obligated to repay the amount. The Seventh Circuit upheld the district court decision, in *U.S. v. James*, 60-1 USTC ¶9158. However, the Supreme Court reversed the decision and held that the income was taxable to Mr. James. See *James v. U.S.*, 61-1 USTC ¶9449. The citations indicate that the circuit decided its case in 1960, and Wolters Kluwer (CCH Incorporated) included this case in Volume 1 of the year's compilation. The Supreme Court reached its conclusion in 1961, and Wolters Kluwer (CCH Incorporated) included this case in the first volume for that year.

The federal government uses a progressive tax rate structure to tax income. This means that as income rises, the tax rate increases. Back in 1913, an individual's income was taxed at a 1% rate. When income reached $20,000, a surtax was imposed. This surtax started at 1% and gradually increased to 6% for taxable income above $500,000. Today, tax rates range from 10% to 37%. [I.R.C. §1] The current rate schedules appear on the Handy Tax Facts page on the inside front cover of this textbook.

Our current tax system, like the original one, requires taxpayers to determine their own taxes. It also requires that each taxpayer file a tax return and pay any tax due the government by certain deadlines. Taxpayers that fail to meet these requirements face possible fines, penalties, and in extreme cases, jail time. In addition, the IRS charges interest on unpaid taxes.

Many taxpayers seek help from tax professionals, who prepare about half of all filed tax returns. Although many taxpayers hire tax preparers to prepare their tax returns, every taxpayer should have a basic understanding of the tax laws. This understanding will help them prepare their own returns or anticipate the information tax professionals need to prepare their clients' returns. This basic knowledge also will help them review a professionally prepared return before filing it with the IRS. Finally, an understanding of the tax laws can help taxpayers recognize potential problems before taxable events take place. Through proper planning, taxpayers can reduce the amount of taxes they owe.

The first part of this chapter provides an overview of our current income tax system. The last section presents basic tax planning guidelines.

¶101   Income Tax Objectives

The federal income tax system raises money (tax revenues) to help cover the government's annual operating costs. The U.S. Constitution gives Congress the power to enact and change federal tax laws. Thus, it is Congress that decides what amount to tax and what tax rates to use in raising tax revenues. However, Congress also uses the tax law to achieve various economic, political, and social goals. These include redistributing the country's wealth, encouraging economic growth and full employment, and encouraging or discouraging certain behaviors.

For example, if the government's goal is to increase employment, Congress can lower taxes, thereby giving taxpayers more money to spend. Increased spending by taxpayers would create more demand for products and services, and result in a need for an increased number of workers to make the products and provide the services. An example of Congress' use of the tax laws to discourage certain behavior is the excise tax added to the cost of cigarettes. With an added cost, the desired result is a decrease in demand for tobacco.

¶102 Basic Tax Formula

Governments levy taxes by assessing a tax rate to a tax base. In the income tax system, the tax base is taxable income. Simply put, "taxable income" is the difference between the amount of income the government decides to tax and the deductions it allows to be subtracted from this income.

Anything that causes wealth to increase generally is regarded as income. However, not all items that increase one's wealth are taxed. Income that the government taxes is called "gross income." Most deductions involve expenses that the government allows as reductions of gross income. However, some deductions are not tied to expenditures. Gross income is discussed in Chapters 3 and 4. Tax deductions are discussed later in this chapter and in Chapters 4 through 11.

Basic Taxable Income Formula

	Income from all sources
−	Exempt income
=	Gross income
−	Deductions
=	Taxable income

For purposes of this textbook, a "taxpayer" is any person or entity required to file an income tax return with the IRS. Regular corporations (called "C corporations") are business entities that pay tax each year on their taxable income. In this regard, they are similar to individual taxpayers. Corporations are the focus of Chapter 14.

However, not all taxpayers pay income taxes. Flow-through entities report gross income and deductions to the IRS. However, it is the owners of these entities that pay taxes on their respective shares of the entity's taxable income. Partnerships and S corporations are examples of flow-through entities. They are the focus of Chapters 15 and 16.

Although the focus of this textbook begins with the individual taxpayer, the taxation of businesses is presented in this textbook as well. Many of the tax laws described in this textbook apply equally to all types of taxpayers. However, special rules sometimes apply only to one group of taxpayers. For example, the basic formula for computing taxable income presented above is the same for both corporations and individuals. However, individuals are entitled to more types of deductions and, thus, use an expanded taxable income formula (described in ¶103).

For purposes of this textbook, when the term "taxpayer" is used while discussing a tax law, it applies to all types of taxpayers, including corporations, individuals, and flow-through entities, unless from the discussion it is clear that use of the term "taxpayer" refers to a particular type of taxpayer (for example, an individual or a corporation). If a tax law is unique to one type of taxpayer, then the title of the section or the discussion itself will state the type of taxpayer to which that particular tax law applies.

After C corporations and individuals compute taxable income, they compute their tax liability using the tax rates set by Congress. Although different tax rates may apply, the federal income tax rates are progressive, which means that as taxable income increases, so too does the tax rate. After 2017, the progressive system applies to individuals, estates and trusts. In contrast, C corporations are subject to a flat rate, often termed a "proportional" tax. Taxpayers may owe other taxes in addition to income taxes. Individuals may owe self-employment taxes, penalties for early distributions from retirement accounts, net investment income tax, additional Medicare tax, or alternative minimum tax (AMT) in addition to the regular income tax.

Individuals and C corporations may also be entitled to subtract tax credits from these taxes to arrive at their taxes owed (or refund due) at the end of the year. Tax credits can be business-related or personal in nature. The former applies to all types of businesses. The latter applies only to individual taxpayers. Tax credits generated by flow-through entities are passed through to the owners, who then report the tax credits on their income tax returns.

Calculation of Taxes Owed (To Be Refunded)

	Taxable income
×	Tax rate
=	Income tax liability
+	Additional taxes
−	Tax credits and prepayments
=	Final tax due (refund)

¶102.01 DEDUCTIONS VERSUS CREDITS

The distinction between a deduction and a credit is important:

- Tax deductions reduce the taxpayer's taxable income by the amount of the deduction.
- Tax credits reduce the taxpayer's taxes by the amount of the credit.

Deductions reduce the taxpayer's taxes by the amount of the deduction times the taxpayer's tax rate. For example, a $100 deduction reduces taxable income by $100. This saves $15 in taxes if the tax rate is 15% ($100 × 15%), but saves $35 if the tax rate is 35% ($100 × 35%). A $100 tax credit, on the other hand, reduces the taxpayer's taxes by $100 regardless of the taxpayer's tax rate.

¶103 Individual Taxpayers

Although there are a variety of types of income, the concept of gross income is the same for all taxpayers. That is, the government taxes some income, while other types of income are not subject to income tax. The tax laws also allow a variety of deductions in the calculation of taxable income. Individual taxpayers can reduce their taxable income by a mix of business and personal deductions. Accordingly, the tax laws separate the deductions available to individuals into two categories: deductions for adjusted gross income (AGI) and deductions from AGI. Deductions from AGI are often personal in nature, as opposed to business or investment-related. They are introduced in this chapter and are the focus of Chapter 5.

The tax rate that individual taxpayers apply to taxable income depends on their filing status. A person's filing status depends on whether they are married on the last day of the tax year, along with other factors. More about the rules for each filing status will be presented later in the chapter at ¶112. The five filing statuses are: (1) married filing jointly (MFJ); (2) married filing separately (MFS); (3) qualifying widow(er) (QW); (4) head of household (HOH); and (5) single.

Tax Formula for Individuals

	Income from all sources
−	Exempt income
=	Gross income
−	Deductions for AGI (adjusted gross income)
=	AGI
−	Deductions from AGI
	Itemized deductions or standard deduction
	Qualified business income deduction
=	Taxable income
×	Tax rate

=	Income tax liability
+	Additional taxes
–	Tax credits and prepayments
=	Final tax due (refund)

Individual taxpayers who are required to file an income tax return file Form 1040, U.S. Individual Income Tax Return.

Form 1040 is revised annually, and some revisions are more substantial than others. The 2017 version was a two-page form. There were simplified versions of the form available for taxpayers with certain income characteristics. In 2018, the IRS completely redesigned Form 1040 to have a smaller size but with six additional schedules. In 2019, the IRS redesigned the basic form again, and reduced the number of schedules. Beginning with the 2019 taxable year, an individual who is age 65 or older has another option, the Form 1040-SR, U.S. Tax Return for Seniors. In 2021, the IRS redesigned Schedules 1, 2 and 3. These forms were much more detailed than they were in 2020, and now have specific lines on which to report specific types of income, deductions, credits and other taxes. In 2022, the IRS modified Form 1040 to include specific types on income in addition to W-2 income on line 1.

¶104   Gross Income

Taxpayers must be able to compute their gross income. The Internal Revenue Code (the Code) is the source of tax law written by Congress. The Code defines gross income as all wealth that flows to a taxpayer from whatever source derived. It then exempts some income from taxation. The Code lists the following different gross income sources (and implies that others exist):

1. Compensation for services, including salary, wages, fees, commissions, fringe benefits, etc.
2. Gross income from a business
3. Gains from the disposal of property
4. Interest
5. Rents
6. Royalties
7. Dividends
8. Alimony and separate maintenance payments received pursuant to divorce or separation agreements executed prior to 2019 and not modified after 2018
9. Annuities
10. Income generated from life insurance proceeds
11. Pensions
12. Income from forgiveness of debt
13. Share of distributive partnership income and pro rata share of S Corporation income
14. Income in respect of a decedent
15. Income from an interest in an estate or trust

To determine gross income, taxpayers generally examine their various sources of income (items that increase their wealth) and subtract out exempt income. Regardless of the form or name of an income item, proper authority must exist to exclude the item from gross income. Taxpayers may find such authority in the tax laws, which include the Code, Treasury Regulations, IRS rulings, or case law. From gross income, taxpayers subtract allowed deductions to arrive at taxable income.

¶104.01   IMPORTANCE OF GROSS INCOME

It is important that taxpayers correctly compute their gross income. When gross income exceeds a certain amount, taxpayers must file an income tax return (see ¶113.02). Failure to file a proper return on time can result in tax penalties. Also, when a taxpayer accidentally understates gross income by more than 25%, the IRS is given more time to audit the taxpayer's return (see ¶115.01). Finally, individuals may be allowed or denied a deduction for claiming another person as a dependent based on the amount of that other person's gross income (discussed at ¶109.03).

¶105   Deductions for Individual Taxpayers

Individual taxpayers have two broad groups of deductions: deductions for AGI and deductions from AGI. Taxpayers subtract deductions for AGI from gross income to arrive at AGI. They then subtract deductions from AGI to arrive at taxable income.

There are two types of deductions from AGI. One is the *greater of* a taxpayer's itemized deductions or standard deduction. The other is a qualified business income deduction. Prior to 2018, personal exemptions were also deducted from AGI. For tax years 2018 through 2025, the deduction for personal and dependency exemptions is temporarily repealed. [I.R.C. §152] Personal exemptions will come back in 2026 unless this provision is extended by Congress or made permanent. In 2020 and 2021, certain charitable contributions were also allowed as deductions from AGI for taxpayers that do not itemize. As of this writing, this provision has not been extended by Congress. Corporations, partnerships, estates, and trusts do not compute AGI.

¶105.01   DEDUCTIONS FOR AGI

The Code defines an individual's AGI as gross income less certain deductions. [I.R.C. §62(a)] Deductions for AGI, (also termed "deductions in arriving at AGI", or "above the line") are covered in Chapters 4 and 7–11. Some of the major deductions include:

1. Trade and business deductions for business owners
2. Losses on the disposal of business or investment property
3. Deductions related to rental and royalty income
4. Certain contributions to retirement plans of self-employed individuals
5. Certain contributions to traditional Individual Retirement Accounts (IRAs)
6. Penalties for early withdrawals from certificates of deposits
7. Alimony paid pursuant to divorce or separation agreements executed before 2019 and not modified after 2018
8. One-half of self-employment tax
9. Health insurance premiums paid by self-employed persons
10. Individual contributions to a medical savings or health savings accounts
11. Interest paid on student loans
12. Certain educator expenses
13. Moving expense for members of the Armed Forces
14. Certain business expenses of reservists, performing artists, and fee basis government officials.

There are other deductions for AGI. This book discusses some of these in the relevant chapters.

¶105.02   DEDUCTIONS FROM AGI

After computing AGI, individuals subtract out the *greater of* their itemized deductions or their total standard deduction. [I.R.C. §63] Relative to deductions for AGI, itemized deductions are expenses that typically are more personal in nature. Itemized deductions are the focus of Chapter 5. They include:

1. Medical expenses
2. State, local, foreign taxes

3. Home mortgage interest
4. Charitable contributions
5. Casualty and theft losses
6. Other miscellaneous deductions

¶106   # Standard Deduction

The standard deduction is a deduction from AGI that only applies to individual taxpayers. It consists of two amounts: the basic standard deduction and the additional standard deduction. Both amounts are adjusted for inflation each year (a process described in ¶202). Also, when spouses file separate returns, both spouses must either itemize deductions or take the standard deduction. Thus, if one spouse itemizes, the other spouse must also itemize.

¶106.01   ## BASIC STANDARD DEDUCTION

There are four basic standard deduction amounts. [I.R.C. §63(c)] Filing status determines which amount applies. A special rule applies to persons who are claimed as a dependent of another taxpayer (as discussed later in ¶106.03).

Basic Standard Deduction Amounts for 2022

Filing Status	Amount
Married filing jointly (MFJ)	$25,900
Qualifying widow(er)	25,900
Head of household (HOH)	19,400
Single	12,950
Married filing separately (MFS)	12,950

¶106.02   ## ADDITIONAL STANDARD DEDUCTION

Blind and elderly taxpayers may claim an additional standard deduction amount. This additional deduction is available only for the taxpayer, which includes both spouses when a joint return is filed. A taxpayer cannot claim an additional standard deduction for an elderly or blind dependent. There are two additional standard deduction amounts. The taxpayer's filing status determines which amount is used.

Additional Standard Deduction Amounts for 2022

MFJ, MFS and qualifying widow(er)	$1,400
Single and head of household	1,750

For a taxpayer to get an additional standard deduction, their status as elderly or blind must exist at the end of the tax year (or at death). For tax purposes, individuals age the day before their calendar birthday, and elderly is defined as having reached age 65. Thus, a taxpayer who turns 65 on January 1 is 65 for tax purposes as of December 31 of the preceding year.

A taxpayer may claim the additional deduction for blindness either by failing a visual ability or field of vision test. For the visual ability test, sight in either eye cannot exceed 20/200 with a corrective lens. For the field of vision test, the person's field of vision cannot exceed 20 degrees.

The taxpayer supports the additional deduction for blindness with a certified statement from an eye doctor.

Each incidence of age and blindness carries with it an additional deduction. In the case of married taxpayers, each spouse is eligible for both deductions. Thus, if both spouses are age 65, the total additional standard deduction is $2,800 (2 × $1,400). If both spouses are age 65 and one is blind, the extra deduction is $4,200 (3 × $1,400). For a single person, age 65 and blind, the extra deduction is $3,500 (2 × $1,750).

EXAMPLE 1	Pam is 70 and blind. Her filing status is single. Pam's 2022 total standard deduction equals $16,450 ($12,950 + ($1,750 × 2)).

EXAMPLE 2	Don and Dina Miner are married and file a joint return (MFJ) in 2022. As of December 31, 2022, Don is 67 and Dina is 64. Neither has any problems with vision. The Miners add to their $25,900 basic standard deduction for MFJ an additional $1,400 for Don's age. Their total standard deduction equals $27,300. If the Miners' itemized deductions exceed this amount, they will itemize. Otherwise they will subtract $27,300 from their AGI when computing their 2022 taxable income.

¶106.03   STANDARD DEDUCTION FOR DEPENDENTS

For 2022, a person who qualifies as a dependent of another taxpayer computes the basic standard deduction as the *greater of* (i) $1,150 or (ii) earned income plus $350. The deduction cannot exceed the basic standard deduction for the dependent's filing status. Any additional standard deduction for which the dependent qualifies is added to the basic standard deduction.

Special rules apply to married persons who file separate returns. If either spouse is claimed as a dependent by another taxpayer, each spouse's basic standard deduction is limited to the *greater of*

  (i) $1,150 or
  (ii) earned income plus $350.

However, if one spouse itemizes deductions, the total standard deduction for the other spouse is $0.

For purposes of computing a dependent's basic standard deduction, earned income includes salaries, tips, professional fees, and other compensation received for personal services rendered. It also includes taxable scholarships and net profit from self-employment activities.

EXAMPLE 3	Sue, single and age 74, has no earned income and is claimed as a dependent on her son's tax return. Her 2022 basic standard deduction is limited to $1,150 (the greater of (i) $1,150 or (ii) $0 earned income + $350). Her additional standard deduction is $1,750. Sue deducts $2,900 ($1,150 + $1,750) from AGI when computing her 2022 taxable income.

¶106.04   STANDARD DEDUCTION WORKSHEET FOR DEPENDENTS

 ### INFORMATION FOR FIGURE 1-1:

Figure 1-1 presents a filled-in Standard Deduction Worksheet for 16-year-old Gloria Moore. Gloria's parents claim her as a dependent. Gloria has perfect vision. She earned $1,400 working part-time during the year. Her standard deduction of $1,750 is computed as follows.

Figure 1-1: Standard Deduction Worksheet For Dependents		
1. Enter your earned income plus $350	1.	1,750
2. Enter $1,150 (minimum amount)	2.	1,150
3. Enter the larger of line 1 or line 2	3.	1,750
4. Enter $12,950 for single	4.	12,950
5. a. Enter the lesser of line 3 or line 4	5a.	1,750
b. If 65 or older or blind, multiply $1,750 by the number of incidences of age and blindness	5b.	0
c. Add lines 5a and 5b. This is your standard deduction	5c.	1,750

¶107 Exemptions

The exemption deduction, like the standard deduction, reduces AGI. For tax years 2018 through 2025, the deduction for personal and dependency exemptions is temporarily repealed. [I.R.C. §152] No deduction may be claimed for personal and dependency exemptions during these years, but the rules for determining who is a dependent of the taxpayer are applicable for claiming other tax benefits (e.g., child tax credit). In determining who is a dependent for these other tax benefits, the exemption amount is $4,400 for 2022.

¶108 Qualifying Child

One group of persons who may qualify as a dependent includes those who meet the rules of a qualifying child. The first rule is that a qualifying child must be younger than the taxpayer. (This is not a typo. Due to the definitions of "child" it is possible, though rare, that a "parent" may be younger than a "child.") On a joint return, the qualifying child need only be younger than one of the spouses. Determining if a dependent is a qualifying child is important for the taxpayer's filing status and determining certain credits (child tax credit and credit for other dependents). In addition, a **qualifying child** must pass each of the following six tests.

1. Relationship test for qualifying child
2. Age test
3. Residency test
4. Support test for qualifying child
5. Joint return test
6. Citizenship test

¶108.01 RELATIONSHIP TEST FOR QUALIFYING CHILD

Each of the following persons passes the relationship test for a qualifying child:

- Taxpayer's natural child, stepchild, adopted child, eligible foster child, or descendants of any of these children (the taxpayer's grandchildren, great-grandchildren, etc.). An eligible foster child is a child placed with the taxpayer by an authorized agency or by a court order.
- Taxpayer's brothers and sisters, half-brothers and half-sisters, stepbrothers and stepsisters, or descendants of these siblings (the taxpayer's nieces and nephews).

EXAMPLE 4	Marie's household includes her son, her son's daughter (Marie's granddaughter), her younger sister, her sister's son (Marie's nephew), her younger stepbrother, and her stepbrother's daughter (her step-niece). Each of these persons is younger than Marie and passes the relationship test with respect to Marie. Thus, if the other five tests are passed, these persons would qualify as Marie's dependents using the qualifying child rules.

¶108.02   AGE TEST

The age test does not apply to persons who are permanently and totally disabled. For all others, a qualifying child must be either under the age of 19 or a full-time student under the age of 24. A full-time student is a person who meets the institution's full-time enrollment standard and attends classes during some part of each of five calendar months during the year. The institution must have a full-time faculty and course offerings plus a regular body of attending students; a school offering *only* online courses does not qualify. Enrollment in correspondence or employment training courses will not qualify a person as a full-time student.

¶108.03   RESIDENCY TEST

A qualifying child must have the same residence as the taxpayer for more than half of the year. Temporary absences, such as those due to illness, education, business, military service, or vacations, are ignored. Also, special rules apply to children of divorced or separated parents.

¶108.04   SUPPORT TEST FOR QUALIFYING CHILD

A qualifying child must not provide over 50% of his or her own support. Support includes amounts paid for food, clothing, education, medical and dental care, entertainment, transportation, and lodging. It does not include funeral costs or payments of life insurance premiums.

Support also does not include scholarships received from educational institutions. For example, assume a child who receives a $4,500 college scholarship in a year in which the parent provides $3,800 for the child's support. If no other sources of support exist, the parent meets the support requirements to claim the child as a dependent because the tax law ignores the $4,500 scholarship. Thus, the parent is treated as having provided all $3,800 of the child's total support.

Usually the status and source of support funds make no difference. Social Security income, student loans and welfare payments count if the dependent uses them to buy support items. However, the definition of support excludes amounts a state pays for training and educating a handicapped or mentally ill child.

¶108.05   JOINT RETURN TEST

To qualify as the dependent of another taxpayer, a married person cannot file a joint return. However, an exception applies when the IRS treats a married couple's joint return as strictly means for claiming a refund of all prepaid taxes during the year. This occurs when all three of the following conditions are met:

1. Neither spouse is required to file a tax return (see discussion at ¶113),
2. A separate return filed by either spouse would not result in any tax liability, and
3. The only reason for filing a return is to get a refund of all federal income taxes withheld.

EXAMPLE 5

Amy provides 75% of her married daughter's support. For the year, her daughter earns $3,100 working part-time. Amy's son-in-law receives $4,000 of nontaxable interest. The couple lives with Amy for over half of the year. To get a refund of the income taxes withheld from the daughter's wages, the couple files a joint return. Because their combined gross income is only $3,100, the tax law does not require them to file a tax return (see ¶113). Also, both the daughter and son-in-law would have a zero tax liability if they filed separate tax returns. Thus, both the daughter and son-in-law pass the joint return test.

¶108.06   CITIZENSHIP TEST

A dependent must be a citizen of the United States, or resident of Canada or Mexico. However, an exception exists for foreign-born children adopted by U.S. citizens living abroad. These children may qualify as dependents, but only if they live with the taxpayer the entire year.

Children not classified as a "qualifying child" because they fail to meet one or more of the rules described at ¶108 may still qualify as dependents under the "qualifying relative" rules (see ¶109).

Taxpayers use the qualifying child rules in ¶108 to determine their eligibility for: head of household filing status (discussed at ¶112.04); the earned income credit (discussed at ¶204.11); the child tax credit (discussed at ¶204.07); and the child and dependent care credit (discussed at ¶204.02).

When using the term "entire year," we shorten the year that includes the death or birth of a dependent to that period during which they were alive. Also, temporary absences due to illness, school, vacation, work, or military service continue to count as time living with the taxpayer. Indefinite nursing home stays to receive constant medical care may also be considered temporary.

¶109   Qualifying Relatives

A second group of persons who can be claimed as a dependent are qualifying relatives of the taxpayer. [I.R.C. §152(d)] A qualifying relative is anyone who meets the following five tests, but does not meet the requirements to be a qualifying child. Determining a qualifying relative is important for the taxpayer's filing status and determining certain credits (child tax credit and credit for other dependents).

1. Relationship test for qualifying relatives
2. Support test for qualifying relatives
3. Gross income test
4. Joint return test
5. Citizenship test

The rules for the joint return and citizenship tests are the same as those for a qualifying child (¶108.05 and ¶108.06). The three remaining tests are discussed in the sections that follow.

¶109.01   RELATIONSHIP TEST FOR QUALIFYING RELATIVES

The relationship test for qualifying relatives requires that the person be a relative of the taxpayer. It is not necessary that a relative live with the taxpayer to qualify as a dependent. For income tax purposes, the Code specifies that the following persons qualify as a taxpayer's relatives.

- Brother, sister, half-brother, half-sister, stepbrother, or stepsister and any of their descendants (nephews and nieces)
- Child, grandchild or other descendant of the taxpayer, including a legally adopted child Stepchild of the taxpayer, but not the stepchild's descendants
- Parent, grandparent, or other direct ancestor, and stepmother or stepfather (but not a foster parent, foster grandparent, etc.)
- Father-in-law, mother-in-law, son-in-law, daughter-in-law, brother-in-law, or sister-in-law (but only if related by blood, not by marriage)
- Uncle or aunt (but only if related by blood, not by marriage)
- Any other person that lived with the taxpayer as a member of the household for the entire year (other than the taxpayer's spouse and as long as the relationship does not violate local law).

At the time of a couple's marriage, the tax law sets up permanent legal relationships with the in-laws that continue after the couple divorces or a spouse's death. Thus, a husband may claim an exemption for his mother-in-law after his wife's death (provided the other four tests for qualifying relatives are met). Aunts, uncles, nieces, and nephews are relatives only if their relationship to the taxpayer is established by blood (not through marriage). On a joint return, relatives of either spouse may qualify as dependents. Thus, even though the aunt of one's spouse does not qualify as one's relative, on a joint return the aunt is a relative of the spouse and may qualify as the couple's dependent.

EXAMPLE 6	Linda's mother has two sisters, Linda's Aunt Jane and her Aunt Reva. Jane's husband is Linda's Uncle Jim. Jane and Jim have a son, Bruce, who is Linda's cousin. For tax purposes, Linda's aunts qualify as her relatives since they are related to her by blood. Her Uncle Jim is not a relative since his relationship to Linda was established by his marriage to her Aunt Jane. Cousins are not included in the definition of a relative; thus, the Code does not count Bruce as Linda's relative.

EXAMPLE 7	Margaret and Ken adopted Rachel in 2016. Rachel and her lineal descendants (children, grandchildren, etc.) are forever relatives of both Margaret and Ken.

EXAMPLE 8	Dan and April were married in 2016. At the time of their marriage, April's parents permanently became Dan's mother-in-law and a father-in-law. Thus, they will always be Dan's relatives, even if he and April divorce or should April die.

EXAMPLE 9	For the past two years, Darcy lived with her younger cousin Mary. In January, Darcy moved to a nursing home. The doctor informed Mary that Darcy must stay in the nursing home indefinitely so that she can receive her required medical care. For tax purposes, Darcy still lives with Mary. Thus, if the other dependency tests are met, Mary can claim Darcy as a dependent. The fact that Darcy is older than Mary is irrelevant. The rule that the dependent be younger than the taxpayer only applies to a qualifying child.

¶109.02   SUPPORT TEST FOR QUALIFYING RELATIVES

The support test for a qualifying relative is different than for a qualifying child. For a qualifying relative to pass the support test, the taxpayer usually must provide more than 50% of the person's total support during the tax year. On a joint return, support coming from either spouse counts. Support includes food, clothing, education, medical and dental care, entertainment, transportation, and lodging.

When a taxpayer furnishes a relative's lodging, the IRS treats the fair rental value of the lodging as support. Fair rental value is the rent a taxpayer could expect to receive from a stranger for the same lodging. Fair rental value covers the use of one room or a proportionate share of a house. Capital items such as cars and furniture count as support if given to (or bought for) a relative. Support also includes costs paid for a relative's wedding.

Support does not include scholarships received from educational institutions, and the status and source of support funds generally makes no difference. Also, payments for life insurance premiums and funeral costs do not count as support. These rules are the same as used to define support for a qualifying child (¶108.04).

To determine if a taxpayer provides over 50% of a relative's support, the taxpayer calculates the relative's total support, which consists of three amounts:

1. Fair rental value of lodging provided to the relative
2. The relative's share of household expenses (such as food, but not lodging) unrelated to any specific household members
3. Other support-related expenses incurred or paid directly to or for the relative

EXAMPLE 10

Martha's parents live with her. Martha's parents do not pay any rent. The fair rental value of the lodging she provides is $4,200 for each parent. Martha's father receives nontaxable social security income of $9,600, which he spent equally on support items for himself and for his wife. Dental expenses for Martha's mother total $3,200. Martha paid $700 of these expenses; Martha's brother paid $2,500. Martha's parents eat all of their meals in her home. The cost of all meals consumed in the home was $5,400 ($1,800 per person). Support for Martha's parents for the year is as follows:

	Mother	Father	Total
Lodging (provided by Martha)	$4,200	$4,200	$8,400
Social security spent by parents	4,800	4,800	9,600
Dental expense	3,200	0	3,200
Share of food provided by Martha	1,800	1,800	3,600
Total	$14,000	$10,800	$24,800

In order for Martha to claim her mother as a dependent, she must provide more than half of her mother's total support. Martha provided $6,700 toward her mother's support during the year ($4,200 lodging + $700 dental + $1,800 for food). Since this amount does not exceed $7,000 ($14,000 of the mother's total support × 50%), the support test has not been met with respect to the mother. However, Martha provided $6,600 toward her father's support during the year ($4,800 lodging + $1,800 for food). Since this amount exceeds $5,400 ($10,800 of the father's total support × 50%), the support test has been met with respect to the father.

Multiple Support Agreements

Sometimes, a group of people (e.g., children) together provide for a dependent's (e.g., parent) support, but no one person (including the dependent) provides over 50% of the support. To qualify, the group member must:

1. Provide more than 10% of the dependent's support,
2. Provide, with the other group members, more than 50% of the dependent's support, and
3. Be able to otherwise claim the person as a dependent.

EXAMPLE 11

Elaine, a U.S. citizen, lives with Logan for the entire year. Elaine is single and has no gross income. Logan, Marty, Nan, Michael, and Lilly provide 100% of Elaine's support. Each person's relationship to Elaine, plus the amounts of support they provided are as follows.

	Amounts	Percentage
Logan (Elaine's son)	$1,000	10%
Marty (Elaine's son-in-law)	2,500	25%
Nan (Elaine's stepdaughter)	2,500	25%
Michael (Elaine's brother)	2,500	25%
Lilly (Elaine's friend)	1,500	15%
Total	$10,000	100%

Eligible group members include Marty, Nan, and Michael. Logan and Lilly cannot be eligible group members. Since Elaine is not one of Lilly's relatives, for Elaine to pass the relationship test, she would have to live with Lilly the entire year. Instead, Elaine lives with Logan. Logan cannot be an eligible group member because he does not provide more than 10% of Elaine's support. Elaine qualifies as a relative to Marty, Nan, and Michael. Thus, each passes the relationship test. Marty, Nan, and Michael must decide which of them will claim Elaine as a dependent.

¶109.03   GROSS INCOME TEST

To pass the gross income test, the person's gross income must be less than the exemption amount. Although the deductible exemption amount for 2018 through 2025 is zero, the gross income limitation definition of a qualified child or qualified relative for other tax benefits is $4,400 in 2022. In addition to wages, dividends, and taxable interest, gross income includes gross receipts from rental property before expenses are deducted. To compute the gross income of a business, cost of goods sold is subtracted from net sales and any miscellaneous income is added to the difference. Gross income includes only the income that the government taxes. The calculation of gross income is the focus of Chapters 3 and 4.

¶110   Tax Base Formula—Another View

Below is another view of the tax base formula. It should enhance the meaning of new tax terms and concepts.

Income from all sources:		
Rent from tenants	$12,550	
Salary	16,200	
Dividends on common stock	720	
Interest from savings account	80	
Tax-exempt bond interest	30	$29,580
Gross income exclusions:		
Tax-exempt bond interest		(30)
Gross income		$29,550
Deductions for AGI:		
Expenses of apartment (rental property)		(1,400)
AGI		$28,150
Deductions from AGI:		
Standard deduction (single person)	$12,950	
Exemptions (one personal exemption)	0	(12,950)
Taxable Income		$15,200

¶111   Filing Status

Any individual who files a return falls into one of five filing status groups. [I.R.C. §1] The filing status determines the standard deduction amount used in computing taxable income and the tax rates used in calculating the tax liability.

Married couples generally have two filing options: married filing jointly or married filing separately. Head of household status is available to married taxpayers in certain cases (see the Abandoned Spouse rules at ¶111.04). The filing statuses available to unmarried persons include qualifying widow(er), head of household, and single. Both married filing jointly and qualifying widow(er) share the most favorable tax rates, followed by head of household, and then single. The least favorable of the tax rates apply to taxpayers who file married filing separately. Whenever possible, taxpayers would like to qualify for the most favorable tax rate possible for their marital status.

¶111.01   MARRIED FILING JOINTLY

For tax purposes, a taxpayer's marital status is determined on the last day of the tax year. Thus, a person who is married on the last day of the tax year may file a joint return with his or her spouse. Likewise, a person who is legally divorced or separated before the end of the year may not file a joint return. When the divorce or legal separation has not been finalized at year-end, the couple is still legally married for tax purposes and, as such, may file a joint return.

A married couple can file a joint return even if only one spouse has income. Both spouses must sign a jointly filed tax return, thereby making each spouse liable for the entire tax liability. The IRS's authority to collect any taxes owed against either spouse continues even if the couple divorces.

Year of Death

Marital status is also determined at the date of death in the event that a spouse dies. The tax law requires a final income tax return to be filed on behalf of the decedent. A widow(er) may file a joint return with the deceased spouse in the year the spouse dies. The surviving spouse should enter the word *deceased*, the name of the deceased spouse, and the date of death across the top of the return. When signing the return, the survivor should enter *filing as surviving spouse* on the spouse's signature line. When someone other than the widow(er) is the personal representative of the deceased, that person's signature should appear in the deceased's signature line along with the words *personal representative.*

If a widowed person remarries before the end of the year, the widow(er) may file a joint return with the new spouse. A remarried widow(er) cannot file a joint return with the deceased spouse, even if the survivor's new spouse files as married filing separately.

¶111.02   MARRIED FILING SEPARATELY

When spouses have their own income, they may pay less taxes as a couple by filing separate returns. Taxpayers should compute their tax liabilities using both the joint and separate return statuses to see which one yields the least tax liability.

Filing Separate Returns in Community Property States

The laws of the state where the taxpayer lives control whether property is considered community property or separate property. There are currently nine community property states. In a community property state, all property acquired during a marriage (other than gifts or inheritances) is considered jointly-owned property, regardless of which spouse legally owns the property. Community property laws can be complex, and vary by state.

Election to File Joint or Separate Return

An election to file a joint or separate return for one year does not carry over to future years. Each year stands alone. After a couple files a joint return, they cannot change to separate returns after the due date of the tax return. However, spouses who file separately may change to a joint return even after the due date passes. An amended return must be filed within three years. Chapter 13 (at ¶1313) covers the filing of amended returns.

¶111.03 QUALIFYING WIDOW(ER)

For two tax years following the year of a spouse's death, special status as a qualifying widow(er) may apply to the survivor. Persons filing as a qualifying widow(er) use the married filing jointly tax rates to compute their tax liability. They also use the married filing jointly basic and additional standard deduction amounts. Even though qualifying widows(ers) use the joint return tax rates and other amounts, they do not file a joint return. Qualifying widow(er) status is not available to a spouse who remarries. A widow(er) who remarries files a joint or separate return with the new spouse.

To qualify for qualifying widow(er) status, a widow(er) must pay over 50% of the household costs where the widow(er) and a dependent son or daughter live for the entire year. This child may be the taxpayer's qualifying foster, adopted, natural, or stepchild. Temporary absences from the household do not affect the ability to file as a qualifying widow(er). Thus, a son or daughter who attends a boarding school and returns home during vacation periods remains a member of the widow(er)'s household. Hospital stays receive the same treatment.

EXAMPLE 12

Ron maintains a household where he and his 12-year-old dependent daughter live. Ron's wife died in 2021. Ron filed a joint return in 2021. Assuming Ron does not remarry and continues to claim his daughter as a dependent, he files his tax returns for 2022 and 2023 using qualifying widow(er) filing status.

¶111.04 HEAD OF HOUSEHOLD

Head of household status can be used by certain unmarried persons. The tax rates for head of household are lower than for single taxpayers, but are higher than for those who file married filing jointly. Head of household status does not apply to persons who can file as a qualifying widow(er), as these taxpayers should file using the more favorable filing status.

To qualify for head of household status, the taxpayer must pay more than half the cost of maintaining a household where a "qualifying child" (see ¶108) or "qualifying relative" (see ¶109) lives with the taxpayer for more than half of the year. A dependent parent need not live with the taxpayer. However, the taxpayer must pay over 50% of the parent's household costs for the year. Also, a married "qualifying child" or a married child who is not a qualifying child must pass each of the five dependency tests for a "qualifying relative" (see ¶109). When a paid tax preparer determines that a taxpayer qualifies for the head of household status, they should complete Form 8867, Paid Preparer's Due Diligence Checklist, and file it with the taxpayer's tax return.

When a dependent child is used to obtain head of household status, custodial parents do not lose head of household status when they give away their right to claim their child as a dependent.

Maintaining a household means that the taxpayer pays more than 50% of the household costs for the year, which usually covers payments for the mutual benefit of household occupants. These costs include amounts paid for food, utilities, and repairs. They do not include the value of services provided by the taxpayer or household members.

EXAMPLE 13

Candy is single and maintains a household where she and her 25-year-old unmarried son live. Candy provides all of her son's support during the year. The son is a full-time student and has no gross income. Because of his age, the son is not a qualifying child. He does, however, pass all five tests for a qualifying relative. Thus, Candy claims her son as a dependent and files as head of household.

EXAMPLE 14	Tom and Drew divorced in 2016. Together they share custody of their nine-year-old son, Mark, for more than six months of the year and provide over half of his support. Tom has custody of Mark; however, he has given away his right to claim Mark as a dependent. For purposes of filing as head of household, Mark is a qualifying child for Tom, but not for Drew. Thus, Tom files as head of household even though he does not claim Mark as a dependent. Drew's filing status is single and he claims Mark as a dependent.

EXAMPLE 15	Pat's husband died in 2021. Pat maintains a household where she lives with her married son and his wife. Neither the son nor the daughter-in-law qualifies as Pat's dependent. Thus, neither the son nor his wife qualify Pat for head of household filing status. However, Pat also pays over half of the costs to maintain a separate home for her aging mother, who qualifies as Pat's dependent. Pat files as head of household because she maintains a household for her dependent mother. A dependent parent is the only person who can qualify a taxpayer for head of household filing status without having to live with the taxpayer.

EXAMPLE 16	Same facts as in Example 15, except that Pat's unmarried son, who is 18 and a full-time student, lives with her. The son is a qualifying child to Pat, and accordingly, she is entitled to claim him as a dependent. Assuming Pat can continue to claim her son as a dependent, she will file as a qualifying widow(er) in 2022 and 2023, the two tax years that follow the year of her husband's death.

Abandoned Spouses (Married Persons Who Live Apart)

Married persons who do not live with their spouses during the last six months of the year may qualify as abandoned spouses. For tax purposes, abandoned spouses are treated as not married and thus can qualify for head of household filing status. The other spouse must file as married filing separately. To qualify as an abandoned spouse, a married taxpayer must meet these five requirements.

1. The taxpayer does not file a joint return.
2. For more than six months of the year, the taxpayer lives with a son or daughter who is the taxpayer's natural, step, adopted, or qualifying foster child.
3. During the year, the taxpayer pays more than 50% of the costs of maintaining the home.
4. At least one son or daughter qualifies as a dependent of the taxpayer. This rule does not apply if the taxpayer passes each of the tests to claim the exemption but has agreed to give the exemption to the noncustodial parent.
5. The taxpayer did not live with his or her spouse at any time during the last six months of the tax year.

EXAMPLE 17	Jim and Danielle Nova are legally separated. They have not lived together since March, 2022. In 2022, Danielle pays more than half of the costs to maintain the home where she and her two children live. However, Danielle has agreed to allow Jim to claim the children as dependents. As of the end of 2022, the Novas' divorce had not been finalized. Even though Danielle cannot claim the children as dependents, she qualifies as an abandoned spouse. Her filing status for 2022 is head of household. Jim will claim the two children as his dependents, but he must file as married filing separately.

¶111.05   SINGLE

An unmarried person who does not qualify to file as qualifying widow(er) or as head of household must file as a single taxpayer. A person legally separated, but not yet divorced, files as a single taxpayer unless head of household filing status applies. Likewise, in the years following a spouse's death, a widow(er) who has not remarried files as a single taxpayer unless the rules for filing as qualifying widow(er) or as head of household are met.

¶112   Filing Requirements for Individuals

Under our self-reporting tax system, persons who meet certain conditions must file an income tax return. Current filing requirements depend primarily on the taxpayer's:

1. Net earnings from self-employment, or
2. Gross income and filing status.

The filing requirements apply to all U.S. citizens and resident aliens. Resident aliens are non-U.S. citizens who pay U.S. tax on their worldwide income. These requirements can apply to nonresident aliens married to U.S. citizens. Nonresident aliens are non-U.S. citizens who only pay U.S. tax on their U.S. income.

¶112.01   SELF-EMPLOYMENT INCOME THRESHOLD

Persons with self-employment income must file a tax return when net earnings from self-employment is $400 or more. Net earnings from self-employment is 92.35% of the self-employment profits.

EXAMPLE 18	Antoine's only source of income is $1,000 of gross income from self-employment. His business deductions total $580. Self-employment profit is $420 ($1,000 − $580), and net earnings from self-employment is $388 ($420 × 92.35%). Since this amount does not exceed $400, Antoine is not required to file a tax return.

¶112.02   GROSS INCOME THRESHOLD

Persons who are claimed as a dependent on another taxpayer's return must file a 2022 tax return when their gross income exceeds greater of (i) $1,150 or (ii) their earned income plus $350 (not to exceed $12,950). Any additional standard deductions for age and blindness that apply increase this threshold. However, dependents who have unearned income (interest, dividends, etc.), must file a tax return when the amount of their unearned income exceeds $1,150 plus any amounts for additional standard deductions. A married dependent whose spouse files separately and deducts itemized deductions must file a tax return when gross income is $5 or more.

EXAMPLE 19	Toddra is claimed as a dependent on her son's tax return. Toddra is widowed and 68 years old. She earned $2,900 during the year from a part-time job and has $300 of interest income. Toddra's $300 of unearned income does not exceed the $2,900 threshold ($1,150 + $1,750 additional standard deduction). Likewise, her $3,200 of gross income ($2,900 + $300) does not exceed the $5,000 threshold ($2,900 earned income + $350 + $1,750). Thus, Toddra is not required to file a return for 2022.

Higher thresholds generally apply to persons who are not claimed as dependents on another's return. Married persons filing separately must file a return when gross income exceeds the applicable standard deduction ($12,950 for 2022). All other persons must file a return when their combined gross income exceeds the applicable standard deduction, and additional standard deduction for age, but not the additional standard deduction for blindness. On a joint tax return, the deductions for both spouses count. Thus, for a married couple filing jointly, where one spouse is 65 and the other is blind, the filing requirement is $27,300. This represents a combination of the standard deduction of $25,900 plus the $1,400 additional standard deduction for age. [I.R.C. §6012(f)]

Figure 1-2: Who Must File a Tax Return—Rules for Nondependents

Gross income thresholds for 2022:

1.	Single	$12,950	
	65 or over	$14,700	($12,950 + $1,750)
2.	Married filing jointly	$25,900	
	One 65 or over	$27,300	($25,900 + $1,400)
	Both 65 or over	$28,700	($25,900 + $2,800)
3.	Married filing separately	$5	
4.	Head of household	$19,400	
	65 or over	$21,150	($19,400 + $1,750)
5.	Qualifying widow(er)	$25,900	
	65 or over	$27,300	($25,900 + $1,400)

In determining whether a dependent must file a tax return, the additional standard deduction for both age and blindness increases the gross income threshold. For example, the threshold for a blind, 65-year-old, single person claimed as a dependent on another's return is $4,650 in 2022 if the dependent has no earned income ($1,150 basic standard deduction + $1,750 for age + $1,750 for blindness).

¶113   Tax Year

Although most individuals use the calendar year for tax reporting, a few use a fiscal year. Some corporations and partnerships use a fiscal year. A fiscal year consists of any 12-month period that ends on the last day of a calendar month other than December. Unless otherwise stated, this textbook assumes that all taxpayers use the calendar year.

Tax returns for individuals are due on or before the 15th day of the fourth month following the close of the tax year. For calendar year taxpayers, this is April 15 of the following year. However, if this date falls on Saturday, Sunday, or a legal holiday, the due date is the next business day. A taxpayer files a timely return when the return is postmarked on or before the due date and it is properly addressed and has the correct amount of postage.

¶114   Taxpayer Responsibilities

Under our self-reporting tax system, the law requires taxpayers to compute their tax liabilities, file proper returns on time, and pay the taxes when due. Taxpayers who do not meet these responsibilities face possible fines, penalties, and imprisonment. In addition, the IRS charges interest on unpaid taxes. The IRS wants taxpayers to file their returns electronically but taxpayers have the option of mailing them to the proper IRS service center.

¶114.01 MAINTAINING GOOD RECORDS

Taxpayers need to keep good records to support all items reported on the tax return. Taxpayers should develop and maintain an organized tax record system. This system should allow easy access to the nature, purpose, and amount of old transactions. The underlying files should contain invoices, canceled checks, payment receipts, property titles, and copies of old tax returns. An orderly indexing system helps taxpayers find stored documents. A good record-keeping system helps prevent taxpayers from overlooking deductions at tax time. These records and receipts need to be kept until the closing date of the tax return.

The normal closing date (last chance for the IRS to initiate an audit) is three years after the *later of* (i) the return's due date (including extensions) or (ii) the date when the return was filed. For example, if the taxpayer files a return for the 2022 tax year before its April 15, 2023 due date, then the exposure for the 2022 tax year closes on April 15, 2026.

The closing date for a tax return that omits more than 25% of the gross income for the year is six years after the *later of* (i) the return's due date (including extensions) or (ii) the actual filing date. Thus, if a taxpayer files a return for the year 2022 before its April 15, 2023 due date, and the inadvertent omission rule for gross income applies, the taxpayer's 2022 tax year closes on April 15, 2028. There is no statutory limit for assessing the additional taxes on a fraudulent return.

Taxpayers should keep records showing the cost of property longer. This includes items like stocks, homes, and other investments. Taxpayers must report gain (and sometimes loss) when they dispose of property. Thus, all documents used in computing cost basis should be kept until the closing date of the tax return on which the disposal is reported. A copy of the tax return and tax calculations should also be retained.

¶115 Reducing the Tax Bite

All taxpayers have the right to use all legal means to avoid or postpone paying taxes. Through proper tax planning, taxpayers may be able to reduce the tax bite. As a basic goal, taxpayers should try to reduce current and future taxes. Often, it is a good idea to defer taxes to future years, if possible.

¶115.01 ACQUIRE A WORKING KNOWLEDGE OF THE TAX LAWS

The tax laws contain an overwhelming number of rules covering a multitude of personal, business, and investment situations. The average taxpayer should not expect to develop even a general familiarity with all aspects of these laws. However, the "game of life" happens to involve taxation, and it is difficult to play the game without a working knowledge of the basic rules. Taxpayers should focus on those laws that impact their particular personal and business situations. Developing a working knowledge of these rules is most beneficial in reducing current and future taxes. It will improve tax problem recognition skills. It will also lead to improved record keeping and reduced time for tax return preparation. For taxpayers who use computer tax software, knowledge of the tax laws will provide some assurance that the software produces proper results.

Although taxpayers may hire tax advisers to prepare their returns, knowledge of the tax laws should help minimize the adviser's fee. Most advisers base their fees on the time spent preparing the client's tax return and the time spent advising the client. With a more knowledgeable taxpayer, the adviser will not have to charge for explaining basic tax rules.

¶115.02 ADVANCED PLANNING TO REDUCE TAXES

The way the law taxes most completed events or transactions is fairly clear. Consequently, it is important for taxpayers to plan their transactions in advance. Once an action is taken, the tax consequences are usually locked in. Proper planning of the action can produce desirable tax results.

Taxpayers need to be aware of those available deductions and tax credits that will benefit their particular situations. To facilitate planning, taxpayers should become familiar with methods that will:

1. Accelerate or postpone the recognition of revenue.
2. Accelerate or postpone the recognition of expenses.

Taxpayers whose total itemized deductions are about the same as their standard deduction amount can use the bunching process to slow down or speed up their itemized deduction payments. By using the bunching process, taxpayers influence the year in which an itemized deduction falls. Taxpayers who use this process itemize their deductions in one year and take the standard deduction in the next. The timing of payments for charitable contributions, medical expenses, property taxes, and state income taxes are among the easiest to control.

Couples might arrange their wedding date (December versus January) to reduce the tax bite. Taxpayers with dependents under the multiple support rules (¶109.02) can use the bunching process. By controlling the amount they pay to support other persons, they can control the number of dependents they can claim. To some degree, taxpayers can control their tax credits. Usually, taxpayers want to claim their credits as early as possible to generate cash (tax) savings sooner rather than later.

EXAMPLE 20	Bruno files as a single taxpayer. Bruno's total itemized deductions are usually around $11,000 (less than the standard deduction amount). However, the $11,000 includes $1,500 of charitable contributions he makes to his church each December. For 2022, the greater of Bruno's standard deduction or itemized deductions would be the $12,950 standard deduction for single taxpayers. If Bruno were to delay making the $1,500 charitable contribution for 2022 until early 2023, he would still deduct $12,950 in 2022. However, his 2023 itemized deductions of $14,000 ($11,000 + $1,500 held over from 2022 and $1,500 for 2023) would exceed his 2023 standard deduction. By using this bunching strategy, Bruno would get a greater deduction from AGI in 2023. However, for 2022 only, Bruno could take advantage of a special rule that allows any individual to claim up to $300 of charitable deductions below AGI if he does not itemize deductions. See Chapter 4, at ¶402.11, and Chapter 5, at ¶506, for discussion of this temporary rule.

Although tax planning is advantageous for everyone, most tax benefits favor business owners and taxpayers who itemize. People who have their own businesses stand to gain the most through tax planning. Current trends show an increasing number of people starting their own businesses. Thus, a greater number of taxpayers will benefit from comprehensive tax planning. For business owners, greater deduction possibilities exist. They can convert many expenses that are normally itemized deductions or nondeductible items into deductions from gross income. Knowledge of these situations is highly beneficial, and many are presented in this textbook.

Timing the recognition of revenues and expenses is more easily done in a business setting. For example, taxpayers in service businesses who use the cash method of accounting can control end-of-year income. They might increase income by accelerating billings or postpone it by delaying them. Other taxpayers who use the cash method of accounting (most persons) can control end-of-year gains and losses by advancing or delaying the closing dates on the sales of property they own. Taxpayers who control the timing of their transactions can adjust their income and deductions to take full advantage of the tax laws.

As indicated before, taxpayers can reduce their taxes through careful planning. Some tax plans cover a short-term period, while others cover a long-term period. A short-term plan tries to reduce taxes over the next few years; a long-term plan tries to reduce them over a longer time span. Long-term plans usually involve complex techniques beyond the scope of this textbook. They include selecting retirement plans and developing estate, gift, and trust strategies. A taxpayer with stable income, deductions, exemptions, and credits usually develops a short-term tax plan covering one to three years. When uncertainty exists, the taxpayer should consider aggressive, conservative, and middle-of-the-road assumptions. In all cases, the plan should be updated annually.

¶115.03   MAXIMIZE UNREALIZED INCOME

Some taxpayers want more after-tax dollars so they can spend it on consumable items. Others prefer to accumulate wealth. For those who want the latter, maximizing unrealized income is important. Taxpayers can generally accumulate more wealth by investing in assets that produce income that is not currently taxable. Such income can then grow without being taxed each year. Making contributions to tax-free or tax-deferred retirement accounts is one way to meet this goal. The tax advantages of contributing to retirement accounts are discussed in Chapters 3, 4, and 7 (see ¶305, ¶402.10, and ¶801).

The tax laws operate under the **realization principle**, where gains from property are not taxed until realized (the property is disposed of). Thus, taxpayers that invest in property that appreciates in value (e.g., stocks or real estate) can defer (delay) the tax on the unrealized gain (i.e., the appreciation).

Watch for Tax Opportunities

As taxpayers learn more about the tax laws, they can spot planning opportunities more quickly. Remember the basic goal: reduce current and future taxes. As you study each chapter, keep this goal in mind and watch for tax-reducing suggestions.

1

Name:

Section:

Date: _____

QUESTIONS AND PROBLEMS

1. **Income Tax Objectives.** (Obj. 7) The primary objective of the U.S. income tax system is to raise revenues to cover government spending. Name some of the other objectives of our income tax system.

2. **Taxable Income Formula.** (Obj. 1) Is the basic taxable income formula the same for all taxpayers? What is the difference between the basic formula and the expanded formula used by individuals?

3. **Gross Income.** (Obj. 2) The Code lists a number of different gross income sources. When a taxpayer receives something that is not one of the listed items, is it exempt from tax? Explain your answer.

4. **Itemized Deductions.** (Obj. 2) Itemized deductions fall into one of six groups. Two of the groups are (1) casualty and theft losses and (2) other miscellaneous deductions. What are the other four groups?

5. **Standard Deduction.** (Obj. 3) Under what circumstances is a person's standard deduction $0?

6. **Itemized Deductions.** (Obj. 2) Explain when itemized deductions are used in computing taxable income.

7. **Standard Deduction.** (Obj. 3) Who qualifies for the additional standard deduction? What additional amount is available?

8. **Standard Deduction.** (Obj. 3) Compute each taxpayer's 2022 total standard deduction.

    a. Bryce, age 20, is a full-time student. His parents claim him as a dependent. Bryce has interest income of $320 and wages from a part-time job of $3,800.

    b. Same as in Part a., except that Bryce's wages are $6,500.

    c. Heather, age 66, is married and files a separate return. Her husband also uses the standard deduction on his return.

    d. Juliet, age 19, is blind and claimed as a dependent by her parents. Her only income is $5,200 of taxable interest.

9. **Taxable Income.** (Objs. 1 and 4) John and Jamie Kerr (ages 67 and 64, respectively) do not claim any dependents on their joint tax return. Both have good vision. Compute their 2022 taxable income if the Kerrs use the standard deduction and their AGI is $365,880.

10. **Taxable Income.** (Objs. 1 and 4) In 2022, Terry (age 48 with good vision) uses qualifying widow(er) as his filing status. Compute Terry's taxable income if his AGI is $330,540 and he uses the standard deduction.

11. **Dependents.** (Obj. 4) Indicate by inserting an **X** in the proper column which of the following persons pass, with respect to the taxpayer, (1) the relationship test for a qualifying child or (2) the relationship test for a qualifying relative. The taxpayer is 46 years old and unmarried.

		Qualifying Child?	*Qualifying Relative?*
a.	Taxpayer's 31-year-old cousin	———	———
b.	Taxpayer's father	———	———
c.	Taxpayer's 67-year-old foster mother	———	———
d.	Taxpayer's 50-year-old stepsister	———	———
e.	Taxpayer's 45-year-old brother-in-law	———	———
f.	Taxpayer's grandchild	———	———
g.	Taxpayer's 42-year-old half-brother	———	———
h.	Taxpayer's 21-year-old nephew (sister's son)	———	———
i.	Father (age 62) of taxpayer's former spouse	———	———
j.	Uncle (age 59) of taxpayer's deceased spouse	———	———
k.	Taxpayer's 29-year-old son-in-law	———	———
l.	Taxpayer's grandfather	———	———
m.	Taxpayer's mother-in-law (taxpayer's spouse deceased)	———	———

12. **Filing Status.** (Obj. 5) Indicate the proper filing status for each of the following taxpayers.

    a. Unmarried; divorced last year; no dependents

    b. Married; spouse has been properly claimed as a dependent on another taxpayer's return

    c. Married on December 31, no dependents

    d. Widower; spouse died last year; has a dependent six-year-old child; has not remarried

    e.   Divorce finalized on December 30; has no dependents

    f.   Married; maintains a household for more than six months of the year for self and an adopted four-year-old child who qualifies as a dependent; spouse left home on February 15 of the current year and has not been seen since

    g.   Unmarried; maintains a home for the entire year for self and his eight-year-old grandchild, whom the taxpayer claims as a dependent

    h.   Married; has $15,000 of gross income; spouse has filed a separate return

    i.   Widower; spouse died January 16 last year; has not remarried; maintained parent's home for the entire year; parent qualifies as a dependent

13. **Filing Status.** (Obj. 5) Grace provides 52% of the household costs for her widowed mother during the year. Grace claims her mother as a dependent. Can Grace file a return as head of household if her mother does not live with her? Explain the reason for your answer.

14. **Filing Requirements.** (Obj. 6) For each of the following situations, determine whether the taxpayer must file a tax return for 2022. Provide a full explanation for your answer, including which threshold was used in making your determination.

    a.   Andy, age 17, is claimed as a dependent on his parents' tax return. He earned $3,190 from his paper route and other after-school jobs. Andy deposits most of his earnings in a savings account at the local bank. His interest income was $400.

    b.   Marla, age 25, is claimed as a dependent on her parents' tax return. She received a $5,000 tax-free academic scholarship during the year. Marla had interest income of $125 and $515 of net earnings from self-employment.

    c.   Todd, age 22 and single, graduated from college last year. He has not been able to find a full-time job. Todd had wages from a part-time job of $5,000 and taxable interest income of $1,000. Although he used some of his earned income for support items, the majority of Todd's support came from his parents.

15. Fiscal Year. (Obj. 6) Most individual taxpayers use the calendar year for reporting their taxable income. However, a few use the fiscal year. What is a fiscal year?

16. Tax Years. (Obj. 6) The date a tax year closes is an important date from a taxpayer's point of view because it stops the IRS from assessing a tax deficiency on a closed tax year. It is an important date from the government's point of view because it stops a taxpayer from making a refund claim on a closed tax year.

    a.   If a taxpayer files her tax return for 2022 on April 1, 2023, on what specific date does her 2022 tax year close under the normal closing rule?

    b.   If a taxpayer inadvertently (mistakenly) omits too much gross income from his or her income tax return, the normal closing of a tax year is extended by three years. What percentage of the taxpayer's gross income must be omitted from his or her income tax return in order for the closing year to be extended? As part of your answer, explain exactly how this percentage is applied.

17. Standard Deduction and Filing Requirements. (Obj. 6) For each of the following individuals, determine (1) their total standard deduction and (2) the amount of their gross income threshold (and unearned income threshold for dependents) they use to determine whether they must file an income tax return for 2022.

    a.   Steve is 36 years old. His filing status is single and he has 20/20 vision.

    b.   Maggie is a 70 years old widow. Her son claims her as a dependent. Maggie is permanently blind. Her gross income includes investment income, but no earned income.

   c.   Same as in Part b., except that Maggie is not claimed a dependent on her son's return.

   d.   Jeannie and Tom file a joint tax return. Jennie turned 65 on January 1, 2022; Tom turned 69 on March 8, 2022. Neither have any vision problems.

   e.   Sally files a separate tax return from her husband. She is 40 years old and blind.

   f.   Joe's wife died in 2022. Joe is 70 years old and has good eyesight. At the time of her death, Joe's wife was 60 and had good eyesight. Joe does not itemize.

18. Tax Laws. (Obj. 7) Wendy engages a local tax professional to prepare her tax return each year. She sees no reason to learn more about the tax laws. After she files her return each year, she just wants to forget the whole thing. Explain to Wendy why it would be her advantage to know more about the tax laws.

19. Tax Planning. (Obj. 7)

   a.   Define the concept of tax planning and distinguish between short-term and long-term tax planning.

   b.   What is the primary reason for tax planning?

   c.   Identify three tax-planning principles that will help a taxpayer achieve a tax-planning objective.

   d.   Under what circumstances should a taxpayer plan to control the timing of payments that are deductible as itemized deductions?

Chapter

2

Tax Determination, Payments, and Reporting Procedures

CHAPTER CONTENTS

LEARNING OBJECTIVES

After completing Chapter 2, you should be able to:

1. Compute a taxpayer's tax liability using the appropriate tax table or tax rate schedule.
2. List out the various personal tax credits and compute the amount of each credit.
3. Learn about the impact of the American Rescue Plan Act of 2021 (ARP) on filing an individual income tax return.
4. Complete the various tax forms and schedules introduced in the chapter, including Form 2441, Schedule 8812, Form 8863, Schedule EIC, and Form 8962.

CHAPTER OVERVIEW

Chapter 1 presented the tax structure and the process for computing taxable income. Chapter 2 shows how individual taxpayers compute the amount of their tax liability. It reviews the role of tax payments and personal tax credits in determining the final amount due to or from the government.

¶201 Individual Income Tax Rates

The Internal Revenue Code (Code) dictates the tax rates taxpayers apply to taxable income to compute their tax liability. The current income tax rate structure is a progressive structure—the higher the income, the higher the tax rate that applies. For individual taxpayers, the seven rates currently used are 10%, 12%, 22%, 24%, 32%, 35%, and 37%. The Internal Revenue Service (IRS) presents these rates in **Tax Rate Schedules** and a **Tax Table**.

To determine their tax, taxpayers first must know their taxable income and filing status. Taxpayers with $100,000 or more of taxable income must use the Tax Rate Schedules. The tax rate schedules are found on the inside front cover of this textbook. Those with less than $100,000 of taxable income must use the Tax Table. The Tax Tables can be found in Appendix T at the back of the textbook.

¶201.01 TAX RATE SCHEDULES

There are four tax rate schedules—one for each filing status (married filing jointly and qualifying widow(er) use the same tax rates). Taxpayers using a tax rate schedule must compute their tax. The Tax Table requires no tax calculations.

Example 1 shows how to compute a tax liability from the tax rate schedules using these steps:

1. Select the correct tax rate schedule (based on filing status).
2. Locate the proper income range and take note of both the dollar amount and the tax rate applicable to taxable income in that range.
3. Subtract the lowest amount in that income range from taxable income.
4. Multiply the difference from Step 3 by the tax rate noted in Step 2.
5. Add the amount from Step 4 to the dollar amount noted in Step 2 to arrive at the tax on taxable income.

EXAMPLE 1

Four taxpayers each have $100,000 of taxable income. The following list shows their filing status and income tax for 2022 as computed using Schedules X, Y-1, Y-2, and Z, which can be found on the inside front cover of the textbook.

Filing Status	Tax Liability
Married filing jointly	$13,234
Head of household	$16,117
Single	$17,617
Married filing separately	$17,617

Using Schedule Y-1, the tax calculation for married couples that file jointly is shown below.

Taxable income (TI)	$100,000	
Less	−83,550*	$9,615
TI taxed at 22% rate	$ 16,450	
Multiply by rate	× 22%	$3,619
Tax on TI of $100,000		$13,234

*The 10% rate and the 12% rate combined produce a tax of $9,615 on $83,550 of TI [($20,550 × 10%) + ($63,000 × 12%)]. The 22% rate applies only to the last $16,450 of TI. Total tax on $100,000 of TI equals the sum of the taxes on these two amounts.

¶201.02   TAX TABLE

The tax law requires that taxpayers with less than $100,000 of taxable income use the Tax Table to determine their tax. Taxpayers simply locate their tax from the table using their taxable income and filing status.

The Tax Table contains separate columns for each filing status. A qualifying widow(er) uses the same column as married filing jointly.

To determine the Tax Table amounts, the IRS uses the tax rate schedules to compute the tax on the midpoint of each income range. For a single taxpayer with $21,000 of taxable income, the Tax Table shows a tax of $2,318. This amount represents the tax on $21,025 – the midpoint of $21,000 and $21,050. The table shows this amount on the line that includes taxable income of at least $21,000, but less than $21,050. Since the taxpayer is single, the proper tax appears at the intersection of the row for the income range and the "Single" column.

If line 15 (taxable income) is—		And you are—			
At least	But less than	Single	Married filing jointly *	Married filing sepa-rately	Head of a house-hold
			Your tax is—		
21,000					
21,000	21,050	2,318	2,112	2,318	2,230
21,050	21,100	2,324	2,118	2,324	2,236
21,100	21,150	2,330	2,124	2,330	2,242
21,150	21,200	2,336	2,130	2,336	2,248
21,200	21,250	2,342	2,136	2,342	2,254

¶201.03   BASIC INDIVIDUAL TAX FORMS

Form 1040 is the central form for computation of income tax by individuals. This form has been in existence since 1913, the first year of the current income taxing system. It has undergone many changes in the past century, and there have been some variations. Figure 2-1 shows the basic two-page Form 1040 for 2022. Later chapters introduce the other supplemental schedules to the basic form, as well as numerous other schedules and forms that may be necessary to complete a tax return properly.

Form 1040
Department of the Treasury—Internal Revenue Service
U.S. Individual Income Tax Return **2022** OMB No. 1545-0074 | IRS Use Only—Do not write or staple in this space.

Filing Status
Check only one box.
☐ Single ☐ Married filing jointly ☐ Married filing separately (MFS) ☐ Head of household (HOH) ☐ Qualifying widow(er) (QW)
If you checked the MFS box, enter the name of your spouse. If you checked the HOH or QW box, enter the child's name if the qualifying person is a child but not your dependent:

Your first name and middle initial	Last name	Your social security number

If joint return, spouse's first name and middle initial	Last name	Spouse's social security number

Home address (number and street). If you have a P.O. box, see instructions.		Apt. no.	**Presidential Election Campaign**

City, town, or post office. If you have a foreign address, also complete spaces below.	State	ZIP code	Check here if you, or your spouse if filing jointly, want $3 to go to this fund. Checking a box below will not change your tax or refund.

Foreign country name	Foreign province/state/county	Foreign postal code	☐ You ☐ Spouse

At any time during 2022, did you: (a) receive (as a reward, award, or compensation); or (b) sell, exchange, gift, or otherwise dispose of a digital asset (or a financial interest in a digital asset)? (See instructions.) . . ☐ Yes ☐ No

Standard Deduction
Someone can claim: ☐ You as a dependent ☐ Your spouse as a dependent
☐ Spouse itemizes on a separate return or you were a dual-status alien

Age/Blindness **You:** ☐ Were born before January 2, 1958 ☐ Are blind **Spouse:** ☐ Was born before January 2, 1958 ☐ Is blind

Dependents (see instructions):

(1) First name Last name	(2) Social security number	(3) Relationship to you	(4) Check the box if qualifies for (see instructions): Child tax credit	Credit for other dependents
If more than four dependents, see instructions and check here . . ☐				☐	☐
			☐	☐
			☐	☐
			☐	☐

Income

Attach Form(s) W-2 here. Also attach Forms W-2G and 1099-R if tax was withheld.

If you did not get a Form W-2, see instructions.

Attach Sch. B if required.

1a	Total amount from Form(s) W-2, box 1 (see instructions)	1a	
b	Household employee wages not reported on Form(s) W-2	1b	
c	Tip income not reported on line 1a (see instructions)	1c	
d	Medicaid waiver payments not reported on Form(s) W-2 (see instructions) .	1d	
e	Taxable dependent care benefits from Form 2441, line 26	1e	
f	Employer-provided adoption benefits from Form 8839, line 29	1f	
g	Wages from Form 8919, line 6	1g	
h	Other earned income (see instructions)	1h	
i	Nontaxable combat pay election (see instructions) 1i		
z	Add lines 1a through 1h	1z	
2a	Tax-exempt interest . . . 2a	b Taxable interest	2b	
3a	Qualified dividends . . . 3a	b Ordinary dividends	3b	
4a	IRA distributions 4a	b Taxable amount	4b	
5a	Pensions and annuities . . 5a	b Taxable amount	5b	
6a	Social security benefits . . 6a	b Taxable amount	6b	

Standard Deduction for—
• Single or Married filing separately, $12,950
• Married filing jointly or Qualifying widow(er), $25,900
• Head of household, $19,400
• If you checked any box under *Standard Deduction*, see instructions.

c	If you elect to use the lump-sum election method, check here (see instructions) . . . ☐		
7	Capital gain or (loss). Attach Schedule D if required. If not required, check here . . . ☐	7	
8	Other income from Schedule 1, line 10	8	
9	Add lines 1z, 2b, 3b, 4b, 5b, 6b, 7, and 8. This is your **total income**	9	
10	Adjustments to income from Schedule 1, line 26	10	
11	Subtract line 10 from line 9. This is your **adjusted gross income**	11	
12	**Standard deduction or itemized deductions** (from Schedule A)	12	
13	Qualified business income deduction from Form 8995 or Form 8995-A	13	
14	Add lines 12 and 13	14	
15	Subtract line 14 from line 11. If zero or less, enter -0-. This is your **taxable income** . .	15	

For Disclosure, Privacy Act, and Paperwork Reduction Act Notice, see separate instructions. Cat. No. 11320B Form **1040** (2022)

¶201.03

Version A, Cycle 7

Form 1040 (2022)   Page **2**

Tax and Credits	16	**Tax** (see instructions). Check if any from Form(s): 1 ☐ 8814 2 ☐ 4972 3 ☐		16	
	17	Amount from Schedule 2, line 3		17	
	18	Add lines 16 and 17		18	
	19	Child tax credit or credit for other dependents from Schedule 8812		19	
	20	Amount from Schedule 3, line 8		20	
	21	Add lines 19 and 20		21	
	22	Subtract line 21 from line 18. If zero or less, enter -0-		22	
	23	Other taxes, including self-employment tax, from Schedule 2, line 21		23	
	24	Add lines 22 and 23. This is your **total tax**		24	
Payments	25	Federal income tax withheld from:			
	a	Form(s) W-2	25a		
	b	Form(s) 1099	25b		
	c	Other forms (see instructions)	25c		
	d	Add lines 25a through 25c		25d	
If you have a qualifying child, attach Sch. EIC.	26	2022 estimated tax payments and amount applied from 2021 return		26	
	27	Earned income credit (EIC)	27		
	28	Additional child tax credit from Schedule 8812	28		
	29	American opportunity credit from Form 8863, line 8	29		
	30	Reserved for future use	30		
	31	Amount from Schedule 3, line 15	31		
	32	Add lines 27, 28, 29, and 31. These are your **total other payments and refundable credits**		32	
	33	Add lines 25d, 26, and 32. These are your **total payments**		33	
Refund	34	If line 33 is more than line 24, subtract line 24 from line 33. This is the amount you **overpaid**		34	
	35a	Amount of line 34 you want **refunded to you**. If Form 8888 is attached, check here ☐		35a	
Direct deposit? See instructions.	b	Routing number	c Type: ☐ Checking ☐ Savings		
	d	Account number			
	36	Amount of line 34 you want **applied to your 2023 estimated tax**	36		
Amount You Owe	37	Subtract line 33 from line 24. This is the **amount you owe.** For details on how to pay, go to *www.irs.gov/Payments* or see instructions		37	
	38	Estimated tax penalty (see instructions)	38		

Third Party Designee	Do you want to allow another person to discuss this return with the IRS? See instructions	**Yes.** Complete below. ☐	☐ **No**
	Designee's name	Phone no.	Personal identification number (PIN)

Sign Here	Under penalties of perjury, I declare that I have examined this return and accompanying schedules and statements, and to the best of my knowledge and belief, they are true, correct, and complete. Declaration of preparer (other than taxpayer) is based on all information of which preparer has any knowledge.			
	Your signature	Date	Your occupation	If the IRS sent you an Identity Protection PIN, enter it here (see inst.)
Joint return? See instructions. Keep a copy for your records.	Spouse's signature. If a joint return, **both** must sign.	Date	Spouse's occupation	If the IRS sent your spouse an Identity Protection PIN, enter it here (see inst.)
	Phone no.	Email address		

Paid Preparer Use Only	Preparer's name	Preparer's signature	Date	PTIN	Check if: ☐ Self-employed
	Firm's name			Phone no.	
	Firm's address			Firm's EIN	

Go to *www.irs.gov/Form1040* for instructions and the latest information.   Form **1040** (2022)

Form 1040-SR is an option to Form 1040. This form requires no different inputs than those required for Form 1040 and even uses the same line numbers for income and deduction items. It is available for "Seniors," defined as persons who are 65 or older. Figure 2-2 shows this form, which has larger type and wider spacing than Form 1040.

However, these features cause the Form 1040-SR to use three pages, rather than the two on the standard Form 1040.

Form 1040-SR Department of the Treasury—Internal Revenue Service
U.S. Tax Return for Seniors | 2022 | OMB No. 1545-0074 | IRS Use Only—Do not write or staple in this space.

Filing Status
Check only one box.

☐ Single ☐ Married filing jointly ☐ Married filing separately (MFS)
☐ Head of household (HOH) ☐ Qualifying surviving spouse (QSS)

If you checked the MFS box, enter the name of your spouse. If you checked the HOH or QSS box, enter the child's name if the qualifying person is a child but not your dependent:

Your first name and middle initial | Last name | Your social security number

If joint return, spouse's first name and middle initial | Last name | Spouse's social security number

Home address (number and street). If you have a P.O. box, see instructions. | Apt. no.

City, town, or post office. If you have a foreign address, also complete spaces below. | State | ZIP code

Foreign country name | Foreign province/state/county | Foreign postal code

Presidential Election Campaign
Check here if you, or your spouse if filing jointly, want $3 to go to this fund. Checking a box below will not change your tax or refund. ☐ You ☐ Spouse

Digital Assets
At any time during 2022, did you: (a) receive (as a reward, award, or payment for property or services); or (b) sell, exchange, gift, or otherwise dispose of a digital asset (or a financial interest in a digital asset)? (See instructions.) ☐ Yes ☐ No

Standard Deduction
Someone can claim: ☐ You as a dependent ☐ Your spouse as a dependent
☐ Spouse itemizes on a separate return or you were a dual-status alien

Age/Blindness {
You: ☐ Were born before January 2, 1958 ☐ Are blind
Spouse: ☐ Was born before January 2, 1958 ☐ Is blind
}

Dependents (see instructions):
If more than four dependents, see instructions and check here ☐

(1) First name Last name	(2) Social security number	(3) Relationship to you	(4) Check the box if qualifies for (see instructions):	
			Child tax credit	Credit for other dependents
			☐	☐
			☐	☐
			☐	☐
			☐	☐

Income

Attach Form(s) W-2 here. Also attach Forms W-2G and 1099-R if tax was withheld.

If you did not get a Form W-2, see instructions.

1a	Total amount from Form(s) W-2, box 1 (see instructions)	1a
b	Household employee wages not reported on Form(s) W-2	1b
c	Tip income not reported on line 1a (see instructions)	1c
d	Medicaid waiver payments not reported on Form(s) W-2 (see instructions)	1d
e	Taxable dependent care benefits from Form 2441, line 26	1e
f	Employer-provided adoption benefits from Form 8839, line 29	1f
g	Wages from Form 8919, line 6	1g
h	Other earned income (see instructions)	1h
i	Nontaxable combat pay election (see instructions) . 1i	
z	Add lines 1a through 1h	1z

Attach Schedule B if required.

2a	Tax-exempt interest .	2a		b	Taxable interest . .	2b
3a	Qualified dividends . .	3a		b	Ordinary dividends .	3b
4a	IRA distributions . . .	4a		b	Taxable amount . .	4b
5a	Pensions and annuities	5a		b	Taxable amount . .	5b
6a	Social security benefits .	6a		b	Taxable amount . .	6b

c If you elect to use the lump-sum election method, check here (see instructions) . . . . ☐

7 Capital gain or (loss). Attach Schedule D if required. If not required, check here . . . . ☐ | 7

For Disclosure, Privacy Act, and Paperwork Reduction Act Notice, see separate instructions.   Cat. No. 71930F   Form **1040-SR** (2022)

¶201.03

	8	Other income from Schedule 1, line 10	8	
	9	Add lines 1z, 2b, 3b, 4b, 5b, 6b, 7, and 8. This is your **total income** . .	9	
	10	Adjustments to income from Schedule 1, line 26	10	
	11	Subtract line 10 from line 9. This is your **adjusted gross income** . . .	11	
Standard Deduction See *Standard Deduction Chart* on the last page of this form.	12	**Standard deduction or itemized deductions** (from Schedule A) .	12	
	13	Qualified business income deduction from Form 8995 or Form 8995-A .	13	
	14	Add lines 12 and 13	14	
	15	Subtract line 14 from line 11. If zero or less, enter -0-. This is your **taxable income**	15	
Tax and Credits	16	**Tax** (see instructions). Check if any from: 1 ☐ Form(s) 8814 2 ☐ Form(s) 4972 3 ☐ _____	16	
	17	Amount from Schedule 2, line 3	17	
	18	Add lines 16 and 17	18	
	19	Child tax credit or credit for other dependents from Schedule 8812 . .	19	
	20	Amount from Schedule 3, line 8	20	
	21	Add lines 19 and 20	21	
	22	Subtract line 21 from line 18. If zero or less, enter -0-	22	
	23	Other taxes, including self-employment tax, from Schedule 2, line 21 . .	23	
	24	Add lines 22 and 23. This is your **total tax**	24	
Payments	25	Federal income tax withheld from:		
	a	Form(s) W-2	25a	
	b	Form(s) 1099	25b	
	c	Other forms (see instructions)	25c	
	d	Add lines 25a through 25c	25d	
	26	2022 estimated tax payments and amount applied from 2021 return . .	26	
If you have a qualifying child, attach Sch. EIC.	27	Earned income credit (EIC)	27	
	28	Additional child tax credit from Schedule 8812 . . .	28	
	29	American opportunity credit from Form 8863, line 8 .	29	
	30	Reserved for future use	30	
	31	Amount from Schedule 3, line 15	31	
	32	Add lines 27, 28, 29, and 31. These are your **total other payments and refundable credits**	32	
	33	Add lines 25d, 26, and 32. These are your **total payments**	33	

Form 1040-SR (2022)   Page **2**

Go to *www.irs.gov/Form1040SR* for instructions and the latest information.   Form **1040-SR** (2022)

DRAFT AS OF September 21, 2022 DO NOT FILE

Form 1040-SR (2022)   Page **3**

Refund	**34**	If line 33 is more than line 24, subtract line 24 from line 33. This is the amount you **overpaid**	**34**	
	35a	Amount of line 34 you want **refunded to you.** If Form 8888 is attached, check here . . . . ☐	**35a**	
Direct deposit? See instructions.	**b**	Routing number		**c** Type: ☐ Checking ☐ Savings
	d	Account number		
	36	Amount of line 34 you want **applied to your 2023** estimated tax	**36**	
Amount You Owe	**37**	Subtract line 33 from line 24. This is the **amount you owe.** For details on how to pay, go to *www.irs.gov/Payments* or see instructions	**37**	
	38	Estimated tax penalty (see instructions)	**38**	

| **Third Party Designee** | Do you want to allow another person to discuss this return with the IRS? See instructions . . . . ☐ **Yes.** Complete below. ☐ **No** | | |
| | Designee's name | Phone no. | Personal identification number (PIN) |

Sign Here	Under penalties of perjury, I declare that I have examined this return and accompanying schedules and statements, and to the best of my knowledge and belief, they are true, correct, and complete. Declaration of preparer (other than taxpayer) is based on all information of which preparer has any knowledge.			
	Your signature	Date	Your occupation	If the IRS sent you an Identity Protection PIN, enter it here (see inst.)
Joint return? See instructions. Keep a copy for your records.	Spouse's signature. If a joint return, **both** must sign.	Date	Spouse's occupation	If the IRS sent your spouse an Identity Protection PIN, enter it here (see inst.)
	Phone no.		Email address	

Paid Preparer Use Only	Preparer's name	Preparer's signature		Date	PTIN	Check if: ☐ Self-employed
	Firm's name					Phone no.
	Firm's address					Firm's EIN

Go to *www.irs.gov/Form1040SR* for instructions and the latest information.   Form **1040-SR** (2022)

¶201.03

¶201.04   REDUCED TAX RATE ON QUALIFIED DIVIDENDS AND NET CAPITAL GAIN

A reduced tax rate applies to qualified dividends and net capital gain included in individual taxpayers' taxable income. The reduced rate is 0% for taxpayers whose taxable income is less than $83,350 (MFJ/QW), $55,800 (HoH), or $41,675 (single and MFS). It is 20% for taxpayers with income above $517,200 (MFJ/QW), $488,500 (HoH), $459,750 (single), or 258,600 (MFS). It is 15% for all other taxpayers. Dividends are distributions of earnings and profits (E&P) that corporations pay to their owners (called shareholders). Not all dividends paid to shareholders are qualified dividends, and only qualified dividends are taxed at the reduced rate. Dividend income is covered in Chapter 3 (¶309).

When taxpayers sell property that they own, they realize a gain or loss measured by the difference between the amount realized from the sale and their adjusted basis (net investment) in the property sold. The three types of property taxpayers can own include business property, investment property, and personal-use property. Investment property and personal-use property are called capital assets. Sales of capital assets result in capital gains or capital losses.

The tax laws usually tax all capital gains, but only allow taxpayers to offset capital gains with capital losses from the sale of investment property. Capital losses from personal-use property cannot be used to offset capital gains. Net capital gain results when the net gains from the sale of capital assets held for more than a year (net long-term capital gains) exceed the net losses on the sale of capital assets held for less than one year (net short-term capital losses). Chapter 11 (¶1101.03) describes the calculation of net capital gain in greater detail, and explains how a taxpayer's tax liability is computed when net capital gain or qualified dividends are included in taxable income.

¶201.05   ADDITIONAL TAX ON INVESTMENT INCOME

Certain taxpayers may be subject to a higher tax rate on investment income, which includes interest, dividends, capital gains, rents and royalties (topics discussed in ¶¶308-311). First, dependent children with investment (unearned) income may find some of their unearned income taxed at their parents' marginal rate. Second, some higher-income taxpayers whose taxable income includes net investment income (NII) are subject to an additional tax on at least some, if not all, of their NII. Both the "kiddie tax" and the NII tax are discussed in Chapter 3 (see ¶¶314-315).

¶202   Indexing for Inflation

The tax laws specify that certain amounts be adjusted each year for inflation. These include the basic and additional standard deduction amounts, the personal and dependency exemption deductions, and the brackets (taxable income ranges) in the tax rate schedules. Various other amounts introduced in this textbook are also subject to annual inflation adjustments. For tax years beginning after 2017, the calculation of annual inflation adjustments will be made using the Chained Consumer Price Index for All Urban Consumers (C-CPI-U). For example, the inflation-adjusted amounts for the 2022 tax year are based on the C-CPI-U for the period September 1, 2020—August 31, 2021.

¶203   Paying the Tax Liability

When it comes to paying tax liabilities, individual taxpayers generally pay their taxes through the tax withholding system imposed on them by their employers. All taxpayers also may make estimated tax payments. Other factors that affect the amount due with a tax return include tax credits, prior year overpayments, excess payroll taxes withheld, and payments mailed with taxpayers' requests to extend the filing deadline of their tax returns. Taxpayers subtract these items from their tax liability to determine the net amount due to or from the government.

¶203.01   FEDERAL TAXES WITHHELD

The tax law requires employers to withhold income and FICA taxes from wages they pay their employees. FICA taxes consist of (1) social security taxes (also called Old Age, Survivors, and Disability Insurance (OASDI)) and (2) Medicare taxes. To help employers determine the correct amount of federal income tax to withhold, the IRS publishes tax withholding tables. Employers use these tables in conjunction with personal data provided by their employees on Form W-4, Employee's Withholding Allowance Certificate (discussed in Chapter 13). By cross-referencing the information on the two documents, employers determine the proper amount of federal income tax to withhold.

Before February 1 of each year, employers inform employees of their previous year's earnings and tax withholdings. They use Form W-2, Wage and Tax Statement, to communicate this information to employees. When preparing their federal income tax returns, employees enter their federal income tax withholdings in the "Payments" section on their tax returns.

¶203.02   ESTIMATED TAX PAYMENTS

The tax withholding system only applies to certain types of income. In addition to wages, those paying interest, dividends and pensions are able to withhold taxes on the payee's behalf if the payee requests it. The taxes associated with all other types of income must be paid to the IRS through quarterly estimated tax payments. Like federal income tax withheld, estimated payments are reported in the "Payments" section. Estimated payments are discussed in Chapter 13.

¶203.03   EXCESS FICA WITHHOLDING

In addition to withholding income taxes, employers withhold FICA taxes from their employees' wages. The amount of FICA taxes employers are required to withhold is set by law. When an employee ends up having too much FICA tax withheld, the excess is returned to the employee. In 2022, employers must withhold 6.2% of the first $147,000 of each employee's social security (OASDI) wages. When an employee works for more than one employer during the year and total OASDI wages exceed $147,000, the employee will end up having too much OASDI taxes withheld. In 2022, the maximum OASDI tax an employee is required to pay is $9,114 ($147,000 × 6.2%). If the employee ends up paying more than this amount because FICA tax is withheld from multiple employers, the excess is returned by reporting the excess in the "Payments" section on the employee's tax return (Form 1040).

The second part of FICA tax is the Medicare tax. For unmarried taxpayers, a 1.45% tax rate applies to the first $200,000 of Medicare wages. An additional 0.9% surtax applies to Medicare wages in excess of $200,000 for a combined rate of 2.35% on these wages. For married taxpayers who file a joint tax return, the 2.35% tax rate applies once the couple's combined Medicare wages exceed $250,000. For married taxpayers who file separately from their spouses, the higher rate applies to Medicare wages in excess of $125,000.

The tax laws require employers to withhold 1.45% of the first $200,000 of each employee's Medicare wages, and 2.35% of Medicare wages in excess of $200,000. This rule applies to all employees, regardless of the employee's marital status or whether the employee is employed elsewhere during the year. Consequently, it is possible that an employee's Medicare taxes withheld may differ from the employee's actual Medicare tax liability. Employees who end up having too much Medicare taxes withheld report the excess in the "Payments" section on Form 1040, Schedule 3. FICA taxes are discussed in greater detail in Chapter 13 (see ¶1302).

¶203.04   TAX CREDITS

Tax credits reduce a taxpayer's tax liability dollar-for-dollar which make them more valuable than tax deductions which only reduce taxable income. Some tax credits are refundable, but most are nonrefundable. **Refundable credits** not only offset income tax liability, but also entitle the taxpayer to a payment from the government when the amount of these credits exceeds the taxpayer's tax liability. **Nonrefundable credits**, in contrast, can only offset the taxpayer's total income tax liability. A taxpayer's total income tax liability is the sum of the taxpayer's regular income tax liability (¶201) and alternative minimum tax (discussed in Chapter 12).

Calculation of Taxes Owed (To Be Refunded)

	Total income tax liability (regular income tax and alternative minimum tax)
−	Nonrefundable tax credits (not to exceed total income tax liability)
+	Additional taxes (for example, self-employment tax)
=	Remaining tax liability
−	Refundable tax credits, prepaid income taxes, and overwithheld FICA taxes
=	Final tax due to (or refund from) the government

¶203.05   RECOVERY REBATE CREDIT

In 2020 and 2021, taxpayers other than those with high income, were eligible for economic impact payments (EIP) authorized by Congress as a reaction to the COVID-19 pandemic. While many taxpayers received the correct payments during the year, the taxpayer's tax return reconciled what taxpayers were eligible for and what they actually received. If the EIPs received were less than what the taxpayer was eligible for, a refundable credit is calculated on the tax return. In general, taxpayers that received too much EIP did not have to repay the excess; however, taxpayers that received an EIP that they were ineligible for were required to return or repay that amount.

¶204   Personal Tax Credits

Some tax credits are personal in nature. Others relate to business activities. This chapter covers personal tax credits. Chapter 12 covers the business tax credits.

¶204.01   FOREIGN TAX CREDIT

The foreign tax credit applies to both individuals and corporations. U.S. citizens, U.S. residents, and domestic corporations are taxed on their worldwide income. Because of this, foreign income might be taxed twice—once by the foreign country and once by the United States. The foreign tax credit reduces the U.S. income tax by the taxes paid to foreign countries. Thus, it prevents foreign income from being taxed twice. The foreign tax credit cannot exceed the portion of U.S. taxes related to the foreign income reported in taxable income. Form 1116, Foreign Tax Credit, is used by individuals to compute the amount of foreign tax credit. As an alternative, individuals can deduct foreign taxes paid as an itemized deduction on Schedule A (discussed at ¶504.04 in Chapter 5).

¶204.02   CHILD AND DEPENDENT CARE CREDIT

A nonrefundable child and dependent care credit is available to individual taxpayers who pay someone to care for a qualifying person while they work. [I.R.C. §21] The American Rescue Plan Act of 2021 (ARP), enacted March 11, 2021, increased the amount of work-related expenses taken into account, the percentage of allowed work-related expenses, and the income limitations. It also made the credit refundable for a taxpayer who lives in one of the 50 states or the District of Columbia for more than half the year in 2021. [I.R.C. §21(g)]

However, these rules were not extended to include the 2022 taxable year. The credit reverted to the rules that were in effect for 2020.

The credit equals a percentage of the qualified expenses incurred for the care of one or more qualifying persons. The percentage used in computing the credit ranges from 20% to 35%, depending on the taxpayer's AGI.

Taxpayers with AGI up to $15,000 compute their credit by multiplying their qualified expenses by 35%. For each $2,000 of AGI over $15,000, this percentage drops by 1% until it reaches 20% for taxpayers with AGI in excess of $43,000. Figure 2-3 shows the percentages that apply for each level of AGI.

Figure 2-3: Child and Dependent Care Credit

Amount of AGI	Applicable Percentage	Amount of AGI	Applicable Percentage
Up to $15,000	35%	$29,001–31,000	27%
$15,001–17,000	34%	31,001–33,000	26%
17,001–19,000	33%	33,001–35,000	25%
19,001–21,000	32%	35,001–37,000	24%
21,001–23,000	31%	37,001–39,000	23%
23,001–25,000	30%	39,001–41,000	22%
25,001–27,000	29%	41,001–43,000	21%
27,001–29,000	28%	43,001 and over	20%

Qualifying Person

To claim the child and dependent care credit, at least one qualifying person must live with the taxpayer for more than half of the year. For purposes of this credit, a *qualifying person* includes:

1. A "qualifying child" (defined at ¶108) under age 13 whom the taxpayer can claim as a dependent,
2. A dependent (of any age) physically or mentally unable to provide self-care, or
3. A spouse physically or mentally unable to provide self-care.

For parents who are divorced or separated, only the custodial parent can claim the child as a qualifying person. The custodial parent is the one with whom the child lived for the greater number of nights during the year. If the child spent an even number of nights with each parent, the one with the higher adjusted gross income is the custodial parent. Even when the custodial parent allows the noncustodial parent to claim the dependency exemption, the noncustodial parent cannot claim the child as a qualifying person (since the child will not have lived with the parent for more than half of the year). When both parents share custody of a child, the parent having custody for the longer period during the year can claim the child as a qualifying person.

Qualified Expenses

For purposes of the child and dependent care credit, qualified expenses are the amounts taxpayers spend for child and dependent care so that they can work, look for work, or go to school. The costs can include payments for household services such as cooking and housekeeping, as long as the main reason for the cost was to provide care for a qualifying person.

The qualified expenses can be for services provided in the taxpayer's home or for out-of-home care. Payments to a relative count toward the credit unless the taxpayer claims the relative as a dependent. However, payments to the taxpayer's child who will not reach the age of 19 by the end of the year, never count as qualified expenses. Likewise, payments to the taxpayer's spouse are not qualified expenses.

Payments for overnight camp or private kindergarten or higher-grade-level classes do not qualify as work-related expenses. Payments for before or after school care are qualified expenses as long as all other conditions are met.

EXAMPLE 2

> While Jerry works, he pays his 22-year-old daughter, Frances, to watch his four-year-old son, Adam. Jerry claims Adam, but not Frances, as a dependent. Payments to Frances for Adam's care are qualified expenses. Had Frances not reached the age of 19 by December 31, or had Jerry been able to claim Frances as a dependent, the payments would not count as qualified expenses.

Qualified expenses must be reduced by nontaxable reimbursements the taxpayer receives from an employer's dependent care assistance plan. Dependent care assistance plans are a fringe benefit discussed in Chapter 4 (see ¶401.05).

EXAMPLE 3

> During the year, Al and Lisa Sherman paid a childcare provider $6,000 to look after their sons (ages four and six) while they worked. Al received a $2,500 nontaxable reimbursement from his employer's dependent care assistance plan. The Shermans' qualified expenses are $3,500 ($6,000 – $2,500).

Limitations on Qualified Expenses

The Code initially limits the amount of qualified expenses to $3,000 for one qualifying person ($6,000 for two or more qualifying persons). These dollar amounts are reduced by nontaxable reimbursements that the taxpayer receives from an employer's dependent care assistance plan. The Code further limits these amounts to the taxpayer's earned income. If the taxpayer is married, the maximum qualified expenses are limited to the earned income of the spouse with the lower amount of earned income. Thus, the **maximum qualified expenses** in 2022 are the *lesser of* (i) the taxpayer's qualified expenses reduced by nontaxable reimbursements from a dependent care assistance plan, (ii) the dollar limits ($3,000/$6,000) reduced by the nontaxable reimbursements, or (iii) the taxpayer's earned income.

EXAMPLE 4

> Marlin paid $2,100 in qualified expenses for the care of his seven-year-old son in 2022. Marlin's earned income is $15,500. His maximum qualified expenses are $2,100 [the *lesser of* (i) qualified expenses of $2,100, (ii) $3,000 limit for one qualifying person, or (iii) earned income of $15,500].

EXAMPLE 5

Same facts as in Example 4, except that during the year Marlin received a $1,700 nontaxable reimbursement from his employer's dependent care assistance plan. Marlin's maximum qualified expenses are $400 [the *lesser of* (i) $400 of qualified expenses ($2,100 – $1,700), (ii) $1,300 limit for one qualifying person ($3,000 – $1,700), or (iii) earned income of $15,500].

A married couple must file a joint return to be able to take the child and dependent care credit. Usually a taxpayer's spouse must be gainfully employed for the couple to be eligible for the child and dependent care credit. However, a special rule applies to spouses who are either disabled or full-time students. This rule assigns a fictitious amount of earned income to the spouse for purposes of calculating the earned income limitation. The amount "deemed" earned is $250 per month when the couple has one qualifying person and $500 when the couple has two or more qualifying persons. The amount is "deemed" earned only for those months that the spouse is a full-time student or incapable of self-care.

EXAMPLE 6

Paul and Kim Foxx have two children, ages 3 and 5. During 2022, Paul worked full-time. Kim did not work, but she attended college full-time ten months out of the year. The Foxxes paid $6,600 in qualified childcare expenses. Since the Foxxes' childcare expenses exceed the $6,000 limit for two or more qualifying persons, the Foxxes' qualified expenses are initially limited to $6,000. Even though Kim does not work, she is "deemed" to be employed for ten months of the year with earnings of $5,000 ($500 × 10 months). Since Kim's "deemed" earnings of $5,000 are less than $6,000, the Foxxes' maximum qualified expenses for purposes of computing the child and dependent care credit are $5,000.

Giving a full-time student spouse who does not work "deemed" earned income allows the couple to claim the child and dependent care credit. Without this special rule, the lesser of qualified expenses, the dollar limit, and earned income would be $0 in situations where the full-time student spouse did not work. However, these "deemed" earnings are not taxable income and are not included in the calculation of the couple's taxable income.

To compute the child and dependent care credit, taxpayers multiply their maximum qualified expenses by the applicable percentage (from Figure 2-3).

EXAMPLE 7

Assume that in Example 6, the Foxxes' only source of gross income is Paul's wages of $29,500. Taxpayers with AGI between $29,001 and $31,000 multiply their maximum qualified expenses by 27% (Figure 2-3). Thus, the Foxxes' nonrefundable child and dependent care credit would equal $1,350 ($5,000 × 27%). Although Kim's "deemed" wages of $5,000 were used in determining the couple's maximum qualified expenses, they are not real wages. Accordingly, they are not used in computing the couple's $29,500 of AGI.

Claiming the Credit

Taxpayers who file Form 1040 claim their credit on Form 2441, Child and Dependent Care Expenses. Form 2441 is illustrated in Figure 2-4. The child and dependent care credit is a nonrefundable credit. The amount of the credit is limited to the taxpayer's total tax liability, minus any foreign tax credit taken by the taxpayer. Any unused amounts cannot be used in any other tax year.

¶204.03   FILLED-IN FORM 2441

To assist your learning on how to complete the various forms and schedules illustrated in this textbook, amounts in bold come from either the taxpayer's tax records or from other tax forms, schedules, or worksheets that already have been completed. Once the information in bold has been entered on the form, all that is left is to follow the instructions provided for the rest of the lines on the tax form.

INFORMATION FOR FIGURE 2-4:

Patricia and Clyde Smith live and work in Chicago. They resided in the U.S. for all of 2022. Patricia works full-time and earns **$30,000**. Clyde works part time during the year and earns **$10,500**. The Smiths have no other sources of income and have no deductions for AGI. They claim their six-year-old son as a dependent. For the year, the Smiths paid **Lucy Burke $8,200** to care for their son after school until the Smiths got home from work.

Line #

3: The **$3,000** limit for one qualifying person applies
7: AGI, **$40,500** ($30,000 + $10,500)
8: Decimal amount from table, **.22** (based on AGI of $40,500)
9a: Decimal amount x allowable costs, **$660**
10: Tax liability limit, **$1,463**
11: Credit, **$660**

Figure 2-4: Filled-In Form 2441 (Page 1)

Form **2441**	**Child and Dependent Care Expenses**	OMB No. 1545-0074
Department of the Treasury Internal Revenue Service	Attach to Form 1040, 1040-SR, or 1040-NR. Go to *www.irs.gov/Form2441* for instructions and the latest information.	**2022** Attachment Sequence No. **21**

Name(s) shown on return

Patricia and Clyde Smith

Your social security number

376-00-7371

A You can't claim a credit for child and dependent care expenses if your filing status is married filing separately unless you meet the requirements listed in the instructions under *Married Persons Filing Separately*. If you meet these requirements, check this box . . ☐

B If you or your spouse was a student or was disabled during 2022 and you're entering deemed income of $250 or $500 a month on Form 2441 based on the income rules listed in the instructions under *If You or Your Spouse Was a Student or Disabled*, check this box ☐

Part I   **Persons or Organizations Who Provided the Care**—You **must** complete this part.
If you have more than three care providers, see the instructions and check this box . . . . ☐

1 (a) Care provider's name	**(b)** Address (number, street, apt. no., city, state, and ZIP code)	**(c)** Identifying number (SSN or EIN)	**(d)** Was the care provider your household employee in 2022? For example, this generally includes nannies but not daycare centers. (see instructions)	**(e)** Amount paid (see instructions)
Lucy Burke	1606 N Elm St Address	677-00-6605	☐ Yes ☑ No	8,200
			☐ Yes ☐ No	
			☐ Yes ☐ No	

Did you receive **dependent care benefits?**	**No** —— Complete only Part II below.
	Yes —— Complete Part III on page 2 next.

Caution: If the care provider is your household employee, you may owe employment taxes. For details, see the Instructions for Schedule H (Form 1040). If you incurred care expenses in 2022 but didn't pay them until 2023, or if you prepaid in 2022 for care to be provided in 2023, don't include these expenses in column (d) of line 2 for 2022. See the instructions.

Part II   **Credit for Child and Dependent Care Expenses**

2 Information about your **qualifying person(s)**. If you have more than three qualifying persons, see the instructions and check this box ☐

(a) Qualifying person's name		**(b)** Qualifying person's social security number	**(c)** Check here if the qualifying person was over age 12 and was disabled. (see instructions)	**(d)** Qualified expenses you incurred and paid in 2022 for the person listed in column (a)
First	Last			
Michael	Smith	569-00-8793	☐	8,200
			☐	
			☐	

3	Add the amounts in column (d) of line 2. **Don't** enter more than $3,000 if you had one qualifying person or $6,000 if you had two or more persons. If you completed Part III, enter the amount from line 31	**3**	3,000
4	Enter your **earned income**. See instructions	**4**	30,000
5	If married filing jointly, enter your spouse's earned income (if you or your spouse was a student or was disabled, see the instructions); **all others**, enter the amount from line 4	**5**	10,500
6	Enter the **smallest** of line 3, 4, or 5	**6**	3,000
7	Enter the amount from Form 1040, 1040-SR, or 1040-NR, line 11 **7** 40,500		
8	Enter on line 8 the decimal amount shown below that applies to the amount on line 7.		

If line 7 is:			If line 7 is:			If line 7 is:		
Over	But not over	Decimal amount is	Over	But not over	Decimal amount is	Over	But not over	Decimal amount is
$0—15,000		.35	$25,000—27,000		.29	$37,000—39,000		.23
15,000—17,000		.34	27,000—29,000		.28	39,000—41,000		.22
17,000—19,000		.33	29,000—31,000		.27	41,000—43,000		.21
19,000—21,000		.32	31,000—33,000		.26	43,000—No limit		.20
21,000—23,000		.31	33,000—35,000		.25			
23,000—25,000		.30	35,000—37,000		.24			

		8	X. 22
9a	Multiply line 6 by the decimal amount on line 8	**9a**	660
b	If you paid 2021 expenses in 2022, complete Worksheet A in the instructions. Enter the amount from line 13 of the worksheet here. Otherwise, enter -0- on line 9b and go to line 9c	**9b**	
c	Add lines 9a and 9b and enter the result	**9c**	660
10	Tax liability limit. Enter the amount from the Credit Limit Worksheet in the instructions **10** 1,463		
11	**Credit for child and dependent care expenses.** Enter the **smaller** of line 9c or line 10 here and on Schedule 3 (Form 1040), line 2	**11**	660

For Paperwork Reduction Act Notice, see your tax return instructions.   Cat. No. 11862M   Form **2441** (2022)

¶204.04   Higher Education Credits

Education credits are available for persons who pay qualified education expenses during the year on behalf of themselves or eligible students. There are two types of education credits: the American opportunity credit and the lifetime learning credit. Taxpayers cannot claim both credits in the same year for the same student. However, they can claim both credits in the same year, but for different students. These credits are not available once a taxpayer's AGI exceeds a certain level. Married persons that file separately are not allowed to claim the education credits.

To qualify for the credit, the tuition normally must be paid in the same year as the year in which the semester or quarter begins. However, tuition paid in one year for a course that starts within three months of the next year, qualifies for the credit in the year it is paid. Thus, tuition paid in 2021 for classes that begin before April 1, 2022, count toward the 2021 education credit.

Only "adjusted qualified education expenses" are used to compute either education credit. These are the taxpayer's out-of-pocket amounts paid for tuition, fees, and course-related books, supplies, and equipment. Therefore, any costs paid for with nontaxable scholarships and other tax-free educational benefits cannot be used to compute the credit. This includes amounts received from an employer's educational assistance plan (a type of fringe benefit discussed in Chapter 4, see ¶401.05).

American Opportunity Tax Credit

The American opportunity tax credit (AOTC) provides taxpayers with a maximum $2,500 tax credit for *each* eligible student. [I.R.C. §25A] *Eligible students* for purposes of this credit are students enrolled in their first four years of post-secondary education. The student must also be enrolled at least half of full-time credit hours during one semester or quarter during the year.

Post-secondary education is the stage of learning that takes place after high school. Students receive a post-secondary education when they attend universities, academies, colleges, seminaries, technical institutes, vocational or trade schools, and other institutions that award academic degrees or professional certifications.

To compute the amount of the credit, taxpayers add 100% of the first $2,000 of adjusted qualified education expenses paid during the tax year to 25% of the *lesser of* (i) $2,000 or (ii) those expenses in excess of $2,000. The maximum credit is $2,500 [(100% × $2,000) + (25% × $2,000)].

EXAMPLE 8

On December 22, 2021, Brad paid $800 for his son's tuition for the Spring 2022 semester. The son attends college full-time and is a freshman during the Spring semester. On August 15, 2022, Brad paid $840 for his son's Fall 2022 tuition. Brad's AOTC for 2022, equals $840. The $800 paid in 2021 for classes that began before April 1, 2022, qualified for the AOTC in 2021.

Taxpayers whose filing status is single, head of household, or qualifying widow(er), and whose AGI exceeds $80,000, must reduce their AOTC. Married couples who file a joint return must reduce their credit if AGI exceeds $160,000. (Married taxpayers who file separately (MFS) cannot take the education credit.) The reduction in the credit equals:

$$\text{AOTC} \quad \times \quad \frac{[\text{AGI} - \$80{,}000^*]}{\$10{,}000^{**}}$$

* **$160,000 for married couples filing a joint return**
** **$20,000 for married couples filing a joint return**

The phase-out range is $10,000 for taxpayers filing as single, head of household or qualifying widow(er). Thus, when AGI for these taxpayers exceeds $90,000 ($80,000 + $10,000), the AOTC is reduced to $0. The phase-out range is $20,000 for married couples filing a joint return, so when the couple's AGI exceeds $180,000 ($160,000 + $20,000), their AOTC is fully phased out.

EXAMPLE 9

Betty reports AGI of $82,330 on her tax return. During the year, Betty paid $3,000 in tuition and fees for her dependent son, who is a full-time student attending his fourth year of college. Betty's initial AOTC is $2,250 [($2,000 × 100%) + ($1,000 × 25%)]. However, because her AGI exceeds the $80,000 threshold for unmarried taxpayers, Betty must reduce her credit by $524 [$2,250 × ($82,330 – $80,000)/$10,000]. Betty's AOTC is $1,726 ($2,250 – $524).

For most taxpayers, 40% of their AOTC is a refundable tax credit. [I.R.C. §25A(i)] The remaining 60% is a nonrefundable credit, which only can be used to offset a taxpayer's total income tax liability. For example, in Example 9, Betty would report $690 as a refundable credit ($1,726 × 40%), and $1,036 as a nonrefundable credit ($1,726 – $690).

Lifetime Learning Credit

The lifetime learning credit provides taxpayers with a maximum tax credit of $2,000 each year per tax return (i.e., a married couple filing jointly may take a total of $2,000 regardless of the number of eligible students). [I.R.C. §25A(c)] This differs from the AOTC where the maximum credit is $2,500 for each eligible student per year. Other differences between the two credits are as follows.

1. A student can attend less than half-time and qualify for the lifetime learning credit, but not the AOTC.
2. Tuition and course-related items paid for education that extends beyond the first four years of college qualify for the lifetime learning credit, but not the AOTC.
3. The lifetime learning credit is nonrefundable; the AOTC is partially refundable for most taxpayers.
4. As of 2021, the same AGI thresholds apply to reduce the lifetime learning credit for higher-income taxpayers than for the AOTC.
5. Students do not need to be pursuing a degree or recognized credential for the lifetime learning credit, but need to be doing so for the AOTC.
6. Anyone convicted of a felony drug charge for possessing or distributing a controlled substance is ineligible for the AOTC, but may still be eligible for the lifetime learning credit.
7. Tuition and required enrollment fees are qualified expenses for both of them, but for the lifetime learning credit, course-related expenses such as books, supplies, or equipment are *required* to be paid to the institution, whereas for the AOTC, required materials may be purchased anywhere.

To compute the lifetime learning credit, taxpayers multiply 20% by the *lesser of* (i) $10,000 or (ii) adjusted qualified education expenses for the year.

EXAMPLE 10

On August 10, 2022, Becky paid $3,000 to cover her tuition for the Fall semester. Becky is a graduate student in the nursing program at Arizona State University. Becky's lifetime learning credit for 2022 equals $600 ($3,000 × 20%).

EXAMPLE 11

On December 16, 2022, the Johnsons paid $6,000 for their daughter's and $7,000 for their son's Spring 2023 tuition. The Spring semester began on January 16, 2023. Both children attend college less than half-time. The Johnsons' lifetime learning credit for 2022 equals $2,000 [(*lesser of* $10,000 or $13,000) × 20%]. The maximum lifetime learning credit is $2,000 per tax return each year.

Taxpayers whose filing status is single, head of household, or qualifying widow(er), and whose AGI in 2022 exceeds $80,000, must reduce the amount of their lifetime learning credit. The AGI threshold is $160,000 for couples filing a joint return. (The education credit is not allowed if a married taxpayer files MFS.) For 2022, the reduction in the credit equals:

$$\text{AOTC} \quad \times \quad \frac{[\text{AGI} - \$80,000^*]}{\$10,000^{**}}$$

* $160,000 for married couples filing a joint return
** $20,000 for married couples filing a joint return

As with the AOTC, the phase-out range for the lifetime learning credit is $10,000 for taxpayers whose filing status is single, head of household or qualifying widow(er).

EXAMPLE 12

The Steins' AGI is $194,000. In 2022, the Steins paid $8,000 for their son's tuition. Their son is in his first year of college, but he does not attend college at least half-time, so the Steins cannot claim the AOTC. The Steins' initial lifetime learning credit is $1,600 ($8,000 × 20%). Because AGI exceeds the $180,000 threshold for MFJ, their lifetime learning credit is reduced to $480.

Initial lifetime learning credit		$1,600
AGI	$ 194,000	
Less AGI threshold	(180,000)	
Excess AGI	$ 14,000	
	÷ $20,000	
	70%	
	× $1,600	(1120)
Lifetime learning credit		$ 480

The AGI thresholds for the lifetime learning credit are adjusted annually for inflation, using the method described earlier in the chapter (see ¶202). This differs from the AGI thresholds for the AOTC which are fixed in amount and will not change unless Congress specifically changes them.

Claiming the Credit

Taxpayers claim the education credit on Form 8863, Education Credits (American Opportunity and Lifetime Learning Credits). They start by completing a separate Part III (found on page 2 of the form) for each student for whom the taxpayer is claiming an education credit. In Part III, taxpayers provide the student's name (line 20) and social security number (line 21). They also provide information about the educational institution the student attended and whether the student received a scholarship that was reported to the IRS by the institution on Form 1098-T (line 22). They then answer questions (lines 23–26) that determine whether the taxpayer can claim the AOTC or the lifetime learning credit for the student.

If the student identified in Part III qualifies the taxpayer for the AOTC, the adjusted qualified education expenses are entered on line 27, and the initial credit (before any reduction due to excess AGI) is computed by following the instructions on lines 28–30. If the student qualifies the taxpayer for the lifetime learning credit, adjusted qualified education expenses are entered on line 31.

Once page 2 of Form 8863 has been completed for each student, the taxpayer adds up all adjusted qualified expenses for each credit and enters the total for the AOTC on Part I (line 1). The total for the lifetime learning credit is then entered on Part II (line 10).

If the taxpayer is claiming the AOTC, the taxpayer follows the directions on lines 2 through 7 to reduce the amount of the credit when AGI exceeds $80,000 ($160,000 if married filing jointly). Any credit remaining on line 7 is multiplied by 40%. This is the refundable portion of the taxpayer's education credit. The nonrefundable portion (60%) is entered in Part II (line 9), and gets added to the taxpayer's nonrefundable lifetime learning credit.

If the taxpayer is claiming the lifetime learning credit, they complete Part II. On line 11, the initial lifetime learning credit is limited to the lesser of the total adjusted qualified expenses or $10,000. Twenty percent of the amount from line 11 is entered on line 12. This amount represents the taxpayer's initial lifetime learning credit. The taxpayer follows the directions on lines 13 through 18 to reduce the amount of the credit when AGI exceeds $59,000 ($119,000 if married filing jointly). The taxpayer's nonrefundable education credit is the *lesser of* (i) the taxpayer's tax liability, minus the foreign tax credit, child and dependent care credit, and elderly or disabled credit, or (ii) the taxpayer's total nonrefundable education credits. This determination is done on a Credit Limit Worksheet found in the instructions for Form 8863. The final step is to transfer any refundable credit (from line 8) and nonrefundable credit (from line 19) to their respective lines on the taxpayer's tax return (Form 1040).

EXAMPLE 13	In 2022, Ed and Sue Reese pay $3,500 for their daughter, Mary's, tuition at Flathead Community College, in Kalispell, MT. Mary is a freshman attending college full-time. Mary did not receive any scholarship income, and the Reeses' 2022 AGI is $174,660. The Reeses' initial AOTC is $2,375 [($2,000 × 100%) + ($1,500 × 25%)]. Because their AGI exceeds $160,000, they must reduce their credit by $1,741 [$2,375 × ($14,660 excess AGI/$20,000 for MFJ)]. The Reeses' education credit for 2022 is $634 ($2,375 − $1,741), of which 40%, or $254, is refundable and the rest, or $380, is nonrefundable.

¶204.05 FILLED-IN FORM 8863

INFORMATION FOR FIGURE 2-5:

Figure 2-5 shows a completed Form 8863, Education Credits (American Opportunity and Lifetime Learning Credits), for the Reeses from Example 13. The Reeses first complete Part III (lines 20–26). It is here that they answer questions about Mary and her educational institution. They then enter the amounts shown below in bold on the designated lines.

Line #
- 3: AGI, **$174,660**
- 19: Nonrefundable education credits (from the Credit Limit Worksheet, which makes sure the nonrefundable portion of the credit does not exceed the taxpayer's tax liability minus any foreign tax credit, child and dependent care credit and elderly or disabled credit), **$380**.
- 22: Box (2) is marked **YES** because Mary received Form 1098-T, Tuition Statement, from the college. Box (3) is marked **NO** because box 7 on the form was not checked.
- 27: Adjusted qualified education expenses, up to $4,000, **$3,500**

Starting with lines 27–30, the Reeses compute their initial AOTC. The Reeses transfer the amount from line 30 to Part I (line 1). They then follow the instructions for the remaining lines on the form to compute the refundable and nonrefundable portions of their education credit. These amounts are transferred to the Reeses' Form 1040.

Figure 2-5: Filled-In Form 8863 (Page 1)

Form **8863**	**Education Credits**	OMB No. 1545-0074
Department of the Treasury Internal Revenue Service	**(American Opportunity and Lifetime Learning Credits)** Attach to Form 1040 or 1040-SR. Go to *www.irs.gov/Form8863* for instructions and the latest information.	20**22** Attachment Sequence No. **50**

Name(s) shown on return	Your social security number
Edward L and Susan L Reese	839 00 2576

⚠ **CAUTION** *Complete a separate Part III on page 2 for each student for whom you're claiming either credit before you complete Parts I and II.*

Part I   Refundable American Opportunity Credit

1	After completing Part III for each student, enter the total of all amounts from all Parts III, line 30 . .	**1**	2,375
2	Enter: $180,000 if married filing jointly; $90,000 if single, head of household, or qualifying widow(er) **2** 180,000		
3	Enter the amount from Form 1040 or 1040-SR, line 11. If you're filing Form 2555 or 4563, or you're excluding income from Puerto Rico, see Pub. 970 for the amount to enter **3** 174,660		
4	Subtract line 3 from line 2. If zero or less, **stop**; you can't take any education credit **4** 5,340		
5	Enter: $20,000 if married filing jointly; $10,000 if single, head of household, or qualifying widow(er) **5** 20,000		
6	If line 4 is: • Equal to or more than line 5, enter 1.000 on line 6 . . . . } • Less than line 5, divide line 4 by line 5. Enter the result as a decimal (rounded to at least three places)	**6**	.267
7	Multiply line 1 by line 6. **Caution:** If you were under age 24 at the end of the year **and** meet the conditions described in the instructions, you **can't** take the refundable American opportunity credit; skip line 8, enter the amount from line 7 on line 9, and check this box . . . . ☐	**7**	634
8	**Refundable American opportunity credit.** Multiply line 7 by 40% (0.40). Enter the amount here and on Form 1040 or 1040-SR, line 29. Then go to line 9 below.	**8**	254

Part II   Nonrefundable Education Credits

9	Subtract line 8 from line 7. Enter here and on line 2 of the Credit Limit Worksheet (see instructions) .	**9**	380
10	After completing Part III for each student, enter the total of all amounts from all Parts III, line 31. If zero, skip lines 11 through 17, enter -0- on line 18, and go to line 19	**10**	
11	Enter the smaller of line 10 or $10,000	**11**	
12	Multiply line 11 by 20% (0.20)	**12**	
13	Enter: $180,000 if married filing jointly; $90,000 if single, head of household, or qualifying widow(er) **13**		
14	Enter the amount from Form 1040 or 1040-SR, line 11. If you're filing Form 2555 or 4563, or you're excluding income from Puerto Rico, see Pub. 970 for the amount to enter **14**		
15	Subtract line 14 from line 13. If zero or less, skip lines 16 and 17, enter -0- on line 18, and go to line 19 . . . . **15**		
16	Enter: $20,000 if married filing jointly; $10,000 if single, head of household, or qualifying widow(er) **16**		
17	If line 15 is: • Equal to or more than line 16, enter 1.000 on line 17 and go to line 18 • Less than line 16, divide line 15 by line 16. Enter the result as a decimal (rounded to at least three places)	**17**	.0
18	Multiply line 12 by line 17. Enter here and on line 1 of the Credit Limit Worksheet (see instructions) .	**18**	
19	**Nonrefundable education credits.** Enter the amount from line 7 of the Credit Limit Worksheet (see instructions) here and on Schedule 3 (Form 1040), line 3	**19**	380

For Paperwork Reduction Act Notice, see your tax return instructions.	Cat. No. 25379M	Form **8863** (2022)

Figure 2-5: Filled-In Form 8863 (Page 2)

Form 8863 (2022)

Page **2**

Name(s) shown on return	Your social security number
Edward L and Susan L Reese	839 00 2576

> **!** **CAUTION** *Complete Part III for each student for whom you're claiming either the American opportunity credit or lifetime learning credit. Use additional copies of page 2 as needed for each student.*

Part III **Student and Educational Institution Information.** See instructions.

20 Student name (as shown on page 1 of your tax return)
Mary Reese

21 Student social security number (as shown on page 1 of your tax return)
399 00 1120

22 Educational institution information (see instructions)

a. Name of first educational institution
Flathead Community College

b. Name of second educational institution (if any)

(1) Address. Number and street (or P.O. box). City, town or post office, state, and ZIP code. If a foreign address, see instructions.
Kalispell, MT

(1) Address. Number and street (or P.O. box). City, town or post office, state, and ZIP code. If a foreign address, see instructions.

(2) Did the student receive Form 1098-T from this institution for 2022? ☐ Yes ☐ No

(2) Did the student receive Form 1098-T from this institution for 2022? ☐ Yes ☐ No

(3) Did the student receive Form 1098-T from this institution for 2021 with box 7 checked? ☐ Yes ☐ No

(3) Did the student receive Form 1098-T from this institution for 2021 with box 7 checked? ☐ Yes ☐ No

(4) Enter the institution's employer identification number (EIN) if you're claiming the American opportunity credit or if you checked "Yes" in **(2)** or **(3)**. You can get the EIN from Form 1098-T or from the institution.
7 0 – 2 0 0 0 3 9 0

(4) Enter the institution's employer identification number (EIN) if you're claiming the American opportunity credit or if you checked "Yes" in **(2)** or **(3)**. You can get the EIN from Form 1098-T or from the institution.
— —— ————

23 Has the American opportunity credit been claimed for this student for any 4 tax years before 2022?
☐ Yes — **Stop!** Go to line 31 for this student. ☐ No — Go to line 24.

24 Was the student enrolled at least half-time for at least one academic period that began or is treated as having begun in 2022 at an eligible educational institution in a program leading towards a postsecondary degree, certificate, or other recognized postsecondary educational credential? See instructions.
☐ Yes — Go to line 25. ☐ No — **Stop!** Go to line 31 for this student.

25 Did the student complete the first 4 years of postsecondary education before 2022? See instructions.
☐ Yes — **Stop!** Go to line 31 for this student. ☐ No — Go to line 26.

26 Was the student convicted, before the end of 2022, of a felony for possession or distribution of a controlled substance?
☐ Yes — **Stop!** Go to line 31 for this student. ☐ No — Complete lines 27 through 30 for this student.

> **!** **CAUTION** *You **can't** take the American opportunity credit and the lifetime learning credit for the **same student** in the same year. If you complete lines 27 through 30 for this student, don't complete line 31.*

American Opportunity Credit

27 Adjusted qualified education expenses (see instructions). **Don't enter more than $4,000**	**27**	3,500
28 Subtract $2,000 from line 27. If zero or less, enter -0-.	**28**	1,500
29 Multiply line 28 by 25% (0.25)	**29**	375
30 If line 28 is zero, enter the amount from line 27. Otherwise, add $2,000 to the amount on line 29 and enter the result. Skip line 31. Include the total of all amounts from all Parts III, line 30, on Part I, line 1 .	**30**	2,375

Lifetime Learning Credit

31 Adjusted qualified education expenses (see instructions). Include the total of all amounts from all Parts III, line 31, on Part II, line 10	**31**	

Form **8863** (2022)

¶204.06   RETIREMENT SAVINGS CONTRIBUTIONS CREDIT

Certain taxpayers may take a nonrefundable tax credit for contributions (including amounts with-held from their paychecks) to retirement savings plans. [I.R.C. §25B] The credit is in addition to any deduction or exclusion relating to the retirement plan contributions. The credit applies to contributions made to traditional and Roth IRAs and other qualified retirement plans such as 401(k) plans, 403(b) annuities, 457 plans, SIMPLE and SEP plans.

The credit for 2022 is determined by multiplying the contributions (not to exceed $2,000 per taxpayer) by a percentage taken from Figure 2-6. On a joint tax return, the credit can be based on a $4,000 maximum contribution, provided both spouses make at least a $2,000 contribution to a retirement plan during the year. The percentages used to compute the credit depend on the taxpayer's filing status and AGI.

Figure 2-6: Retirement Savings Contributions Credit						Applicable %
Married Filing Jointly		Head of Household		All Others		
AGI Over	Not Over	AGI Over	Not Over	AGI Over	Not Over	
$0	$41,000	$0	$30,750	$0	$20,500	50%
41,000	44,000	30,750	33,000	20,500	22,000	20
44,000	68,000	33,000	51,000	22,000	34,000	10
68,000	—	51,000	—	34,000	—	0

Taxpayers must be at least 18 years old to qualify for the credit. Also, no credit is available for persons claimed as dependents or those who are full-time students. As Figure 2-6 shows, no credit is available in 2022 for joint filers with AGI in excess of $68,000; head of households filers with AGI over $51,000, or for all other filers with AGI in excess of $34,000 (which includes taxpayers whose filing status is single, married filing separately, or qualifying widow(er)).

Claiming the Credit

The retirement savings contributions credit is computed on Form 8880, Credit for Qualified Retirement Savings Contributions. The credit is then reported on Form 1040 along with the taxpayer's other nonrefundable tax credits. The amount of the credit is limited to the taxpayer's total tax liability after subtracting out the following nonrefundable tax credits: foreign tax credit, child and dependent care credit, elderly or disabled credit, and education credit.

EXAMPLE 14

Dave and Sue Orr report $42,000 of AGI on their 2022 joint return. During the year, Dave contributed $5,000 to his Roth IRA. Sue did not make any contributions during the year. The Orrs' retirement savings contributions credit equals $400 ($2,000 per taxpayer maximum × 20% from the table in Figure 2-6). Assuming the Orrs do not have any other nonrefundable tax credits for the year, they report this amount on Form 1040.

EXAMPLE 15

Same facts as in Example 14, except that in addition to the retirement savings contributions credit, the Orrs claim a $1,200 education credit and a child care credit of $200. The Orrs' total tax liability for 2022 is $1,610. Once the Orrs reduce their tax liability by the $1,400 education and child care credits, only $210 of tax liability remains. Their retirement savings contributions credit will be limited to $210. Since the retirement savings contributions credit is nonrefundable, the Orrs receive no tax benefit from the $190 ($400 – $210) unused portion of the credit.

¶204.07   CHILD TAX CREDIT (CTC)

Before 2018, taxpayers claimed an exemption deduction for each dependent. For taxpayers with modest incomes, there was also a child tax credit (CTC). In 2018, Congress repealed the exemption deduction. As compensation for taxpayers with children, it also increased the CTC and expanded its availability.

Taxpayers may be able to claim a $2,000 tax credit for each "qualifying child" (defined at ¶108). The child must be under the age of 17 as of the end of the tax year and claimed as a dependent on the taxpayer's tax return. For divorced or separated parents, the CTC can be taken only by the parent who claims the child as a dependent. [I.R.C. §24]

A $500 other dependent credit (ODC) may be claimed for each dependent who is not a qualifying child. A dependent is a qualifying relative and must be a U.S. citizen, national, or resident of the United States. To claim a qualifying child, the dependent must have a valid a Social Security Number (SSN). A qualifying child who does not have an SSN may be claimed for the $500 ODC credit instead. Further, to claim the nonrefundable $500 credit, the dependent must have an SSN, or taxpayer identification number (TIN) or adoption identification number (ATIN).

For years beginning after 2017 and before 2026 (except for 2021), the principal rules are:

1. The credit amount is $2,000 per child.
2. The full credit is available for married taxpayers filing jointly with AGI of no more than $400,000 and unmarried taxpayers with AGI of no more than $200,000. When AGI exceeds the applicable threshold, the taxpayer must reduce the credit by $50 for each $1,000 (or fraction thereof) of the excess.

For 2021, the American Rescue Plan Act expanded the CTC. For this year only, the rules were:

1. The credit amount was $3,600 per child under the age of six and $3,000 for children between six and 17 years old (adding an extra year of eligible age).
2. The full credit was available for married taxpayers filing jointly with AGI of no more than $150,000, heads of household with AGI of no more than $112,500, and unmarried taxpayers with AGI of no more than $75,000. When AGI exceeded the applicable threshold, the taxpayer reduced the credit by $50 for each $1,000 (or fraction thereof) of the excess down to the normal $2,000 per child amounts.
3. The normal phase-outs applied to the $2,000 per child amounts.

Additionally, for 2021, the government sent advance CTC payments to some taxpayers as part of the COVID-19 pandemic stimulus efforts. Taxpayers that received advance CTC payments reconciled what they were eligible for against what they had already received when completing their 2022 tax returns. If the payments received were less than the CTC on the 2021 tax return, the taxpayers received a credit, but if the payments received were more than the CTC, then they needed to repay some or all of the excess payments received. Some lower-income taxpayers were protected from repayment.

None of the special rules for 2021 continued into 2022.

EXAMPLE 16

For 2022, Tom and Carol Normand file a joint tax return. They claim their two children, ages 8 and 9, as dependents. Because the Normands' AGI of $406,400 exceeds the $400,000 threshold for MFJ, they are not entitled to the full $4,000 CTC.

Their $3,650 CTC is calculated below.

Initial CTC ($2,000 × 2 qualifying children)		$4,000
AGI	$406,400	
Less: AGI threshold for MFJ	(400,000)	
Excess AGI	$ 6,400	
	÷ $1,000	
	6.4	
Number of $1,000 intervals (or portion thereof)	7	
	× $50	(350)
Child tax credit		$3,650

EXAMPLE 17

In 2022, John files as head of household and claims his ten-year-old nephew as a dependent. John's AGI is $77,430. Since a nephew is not a qualifying child, but a qualifying relative, John claims the $500 ODC.

Claiming the Credit

In many situations, the credit is nonrefundable. The taxpayer adds the child credit to the credit for child and dependent care expenses, the education credit, the retirement savings contribution credit, and the residential energy credit and reduces the tax liability accordingly. However, a portion of the credit may be refundable. The refundable portion is subject to several complexities.

First, a partial credit, due to the phasedown for excess AGI, is not refundable. The refundable portion is the least of three amounts:

- $2,000 per child less the nonrefundable credit.
- $1,500 per child.
- 15% of the excess of the taxpayer's earned income over $2,500.

Before computing the refundable portion of the CTC, taxpayers must first compute the nonrefundable amount. This is done on the Child Tax Credit Worksheet found in the instructions for Form 1040. This worksheet subtracts from the taxpayer's total tax liability the following nonrefundable personal credits: foreign tax credit, child and dependent care credit, nonrefundable education credit, elderly or disabled credit, and retirement savings contributions credit. The *lesser of* (i) the remaining tax liability or (ii) the taxpayer's CTC represents the nonrefundable portion of the credit. Taxpayers report their nonrefundable CTC with their other nonrefundable tax credits on Form 1040. The result of this is that it reduces the tax liability down to a minimum of zero, but not less than zero. Leftover CTC becomes refundable unless otherwise limited.

EXAMPLE 18

The Stewarts file a joint return. They claim their three children (all under age 17) as dependents. The Stewarts' AGI is $62,000 and their total tax liability is $6,124. They are only entitled to one tax credit—the CTC. Since the Stewarts' AGI is less than $400,000, they do not lose any of their $6,000 CTC ($2,000 × 3 qualifying children) due to excess AGI. The Stewarts can only claim up to $1,400 per qualifying child as refundable credit.

Calculation of Additional Child Tax Credit

The amount of the taxpayer's CTC that cannot be taken as a nonrefundable credit is refundable up to $1,400 per qualifying child. Taxpayers compute the refundable portion of the CTC on Schedule 8812, Additional Child Tax Credit, and report this amount with their other refundable tax credits on Form 1040.

For 2021 only, the CTC (but not the other dependent credit) is fully refundable if the taxpayer claiming the credit meets one of two conditions:

- The taxpayer had a principal place of abode in the United States for at least one-half of the tax year; or
- The taxpayer was a bona fide resident of Puerto Rico for the tax year. [I.R.C. §24(i)(1)]

EXAMPLE 19

Joel and Ruth Floyd file a joint return. They claim their two children, ages 8 and 10, as dependents. The Floyds' 2022 AGI is $43,830, which includes their combined wages (earned income) of $41,200. Because their AGI is less than $400,000, they are potentially eligible for the full $6,000 CTC. They were citizens and residents of the United States for the entire year.

The Floyds' tax liability before credits is $1,793, and they are entitled to a $600 child and dependent care credit. After subtracting this credit from their taxes, the Floyds' remaining tax liability is $1,193 ($1,793 – $600). The credit is nonrefundable.

¶204.08   FILLED-IN SCHEDULE 8812

INFORMATION FOR FIGURE 2-7:

Figure 2-7 shows a completed Schedule 8812, Additional Child Tax Credit, for the Floyds from Example 19. Amounts shown in bold below are entered on the lines indicated. The form is then completed by following the instructions provided for the rest of the lines on the form.

Line #
- 1 & 3: AGI, $43,830
- 4: Number of children, 2
- 5: Since AGI is less than the threshold for either the basic $200 credit or the additional $1,000 credit, this is $2,000 times the number of children, $4,000
- 8: Credit before phaseout, $4,000
- 9: AGI phaseout floor for basic credit for joint filers $400,000
- 10, 11 &12: All blank since AGI is under phaseout
- 13: Tax liability after child care credit, $1,193
- 14: Credit, $1,193

Figure 2-7: Filled-In Schedule 8812 (Page 1)

SCHEDULE 8812 (Form 1040) Department of the Treasury Internal Revenue Service	**Credits for Qualifying Children and Other Dependents** Attach to Form 1040, 1040-SR, or 1040-NR. Go to *www.irs.gov/Schedule8812* for instructions and the latest information.	OMB No. 1545-0074 20**22** Attachment Sequence No. **47**

Name(s) shown on return
Joel and Ruth Floyd

Your social security number
376-00-4930

Part I **Child Tax Credit and Credit for Other Dependents**

1	Enter the amount from line 11 of your Form 1040, 1040-SR, or 1040-NR		**1**	43,830
2a	Enter income from Puerto Rico that you excluded	2a		
b	Enter the amounts from lines 45 and 50 of your Form 2555	2b		
c	Enter the amount from line 15 of your Form 4563	2c		
d	Add lines 2a through 2c		**2d**	
3	Add lines 1 and 2d		**3**	43,830
4	Number of qualifying children under age 17 with the required social security number	4 ⟶ 2		
5	Multiply line 4 by $2,000		**5**	4,000
6	Number of other dependents, including any qualifying children who are not under age 17 or who do not have the required social security number	6		
	Caution: Do not include yourself, your spouse, or anyone who is not a U.S. citizen, U.S. national, or U.S. resident alien. Also, do not include anyone you included on line 4.			
7	Multiply line 6 by $500		**7**	
8	Add lines 5 and 7		**8**	4,000
9	Enter the amount shown below for your filing status. • Married filing jointly—$400,000 • All other filing statuses—$200,000		**9**	400,000
10	Subtract line 9 from line 3. • If zero or less, enter -0-. • If more than zero and not a multiple of $1,000, enter the next multiple of $1,000. For example, if the result is $425, enter $1,000; if the result is $1,025, enter $2,000, etc.		**10**	
11	Multiply line 10 by 5% (0.05)		**11**	
12	Is the amount on line 8 more than the amount on line 11?		**12**	
	☐ **No. STOP.** You cannot take the child tax credit, credit for other dependents, or additional child tax credit. Skip Parts II-A and II-B. Enter -0- on lines 14 and 27. ☐ **Yes.** Subtract line 11 from line 8. Enter the result.			
13	Enter the amount from the **Credit Limit Worksheet A**		**13**	1,793
14	Enter the smaller of line 12 or 13. **This is your child tax credit and credit for other dependents**. Enter this amount on Form 1040, 1040-SR, or 1040-NR, line 19.		**14**	1,793

If the amount on line 12 is more than the amount on line 14, you may be able to take the **additional child tax credit** on Form 1040, 1040-SR, or 1040-NR, line 28. Complete your Form 1040, 1040-SR, or 1040-NR through line 27 (also complete Schedule 3, line 11) before completing Part II-A.

For Paperwork Reduction Act Notice, see your tax return instructions.   Cat. No. 59761M   Schedule 8812 (Form 1040) 2022

¶204.09   RESIDENTIAL ENERGY EFFICIENT PROPERTY CREDIT

The **residential energy efficient property credit** encourages taxpayers to make energy efficient improvements to their principal residence. Examples of qualified improvements include adding insulation and installing energy efficient doors, windows, water heaters, and heating and air conditioning systems. [I.R.C. §25C] The credit equals 10% of the cost of the qualified property, subject to a $500 lifetime maximum credit (of which $200 can come from installing energy efficient windows and $150 from installing an energy efficient furnace or boiler). The credit is available for property placed in service before January 1, 2022, although that date may be extended by Congress.

 Taxpayers claim the nonbusiness energy property credit on Form 5695, Residential Energy Credits.

¶204.10   ADOPTION CREDIT

Taxpayers can take a nonrefundable tax credit for qualified adoption expenses. For adoptions of U.S. citizens or residents, the credit is taken in the year the expenses are paid only if the adoption is finalized in that year or was finalized in a prior year. Otherwise the credit is taken in the year after the year in which the expenses are paid. This is often called the one-year delay rule. When the adoption expenses are spread over more than one year, the limits in effect in the year the adoption is finalized are used in computing the credit. For adoptions of U.S. citizens or residents, the adoption credit can be taken even if the adoption is never finalized. For adoptions of a foreign child, the adoption credit can only be taken if the adoption is finalized.

For 2022, the amount of the adoption credit is limited to the first $14,890 of qualified adoption expenses for each eligible adoption. The amount of the credit is cumulative. Thus, if expenses are paid over 2021 and 2022 for an adoption finalized in 2022, the $14,890 limit would apply. The amount of the 2022 adoption credit is further limited for taxpayers with modified AGI in excess of $223,410. Those with excess modified AGI (AGI plus any foreign earned income exclusion, discussed at ¶401.14) reduce their credit by:

$$\text{(the } \textit{lesser of } \$14{,}890 \text{ or qualified expenses)} \quad \times \quad \text{(excess modified AGI} \div \$40{,}000)$$

EXAMPLE 20	In 2021, the Holdens paid $15,000 in qualified adoption expenses. The adoption was finalized in 2022. The Holdens' modified AGI in 2021 was $169,450. It was $225,000 in 2022. Since the adoption was not finalized in 2021, the Holdens claim a $14,298 adoption credit in 2022 (under the one-year-delay rule).

Lesser of (i) $14,890 or (ii) $15,000 of qualified adoption expenses	$14,890
Less phase-out of credit [$14,890 × (($225,000 − $223,410) ÷ $40,000)]	(592)
Adoption credit	$14,298

Qualified adoption expenses include the expenses directly related to the legal adoption of a child who is either under the age of 18 at the time of the adoption, or physically or mentally incapable of self-care. Such costs include reasonable and necessary adoption fees, court costs, and attorney's fees. Both the qualified adoption expenses and the $14,890 limit must be reduced by nontaxable reimbursements that the taxpayer receives from an employer's adoption assistance plan (another nontaxable fringe benefit discussed in Chapter 4, see ¶401.05).

EXAMPLE 21

Same facts as in Example 20, except that the Holdens receive a $2,000 nontaxable reimbursement from an employer adoption assistance plan. The Holdens' credit would be $12,378.

Initial credit, *lesser of* ($14,890 – $2,000) or ($15,000 – $2,000)	12,890
Less phase-out of credit [$12,890 × (($225,000 – $223,410) ÷ $40,000)]	(512)
Adoption credit	$12,378

The full $14,890 initial credit is allowed for the adoption of a special needs child regardless of the amount actually paid for qualified adoption expenses. This amount is reduced by nontaxable amounts received from an employer adoption assistance plan or when the taxpayer's modified AGI exceeds the threshold.

Claiming the Credit

Taxpayers claiming the adoption credit complete Form 8839, Qualified Adoption Expenses. They then include their adoption credit on Form 1040, along with their other nonrefundable credits. They also must attach proof documenting their expenses paid. Taxpayers unable to benefit from the full amount of their adoption credit (due to the fact it is a nonrefundable credit) can carry over the unused credit for five years.

¶204.11   EARNED INCOME CREDIT

The earned income credit (EIC) is a refundable tax credit that provides tax relief to lower-paid workers. [I.R.C. §32] Taxpayers reporting a small amount of earned income may receive more money back from the government than they had withheld by claiming the EIC. This happens when the amount of their EIC exceeds their tax liability.

Congress designed the EIC to encourage people to become part of the workforce. Within limits, as a person's earned income (wages) goes up, the amount of the EIC increases. The purpose of the EIC is to encourage people to seek employment (see discussion of income tax objectives in ¶101).

Taxpayers Qualifying for the Credit

The EIC is not available to married persons using married filing separately filing status, or to anyone claimed as a dependent. Also, taxpayers with disqualified income in excess of $10,000 in 2022 cannot take the EIC. Disqualified income includes dividends, taxable and tax-exempt interest, net rental income, and capital gains. Taxpayers who qualify for the EIC must either:

1. Be at least 25 and younger than 65 as of the end of the tax year and have lived in the U.S. over half of the year, or
2. Have a "qualifying child."

A qualifying child must be younger than the taxpayer. Taxpayers claiming the EIC for a qualifying child must provide the child's name, age and social security number (SSN). If any of these are not provided, the EIC will be denied with respect to that child. In Chapter 1, a qualifying child was defined as a person that passes six tests: relationship, age, residency, support, joint return, and citizenship (see ¶108). For purposes of the EIC, a "qualifying child" must meet only the first three of these tests (relationship, age, and residency).

To be a qualifying child for purposes of the EIC, an unmarried person does not have to be the taxpayer's dependent, but a married person does. However, the custodial parent may claim a married child as a qualifying child (and claim the EIC for that child) when the dependency exemption for a married child has been given to the noncustodial parent.

If the parents are divorced or separated and the child is a qualifying child for both parents, the child is treated as a qualifying child of the custodial parent. If there is no custodial parent, then the parent with the highest AGI gets to claim the EIC for the child. In other situations where the child may be a qualifying child for more than one taxpayer, the credit goes to the child's parent. If neither person is the child's parent, then the taxpayer with the highest AGI gets to claim the EIC for the child. These tie-break rules are the same as those used in determining which person can claim the dependency exemption for a qualifying child.

There are special exceptions for when a grandparent and parent live in the same house and can both claim the dependent child as a qualifying child. For more information about tiebreaker rules, refer to IRS Publication 596, *Earned Income Credit (EIC)*.

EXAMPLE 22

Jake and his five-year-old son live with Jake's father, Frank, for the whole year. Jake's AGI is $25,000, and Frank's AGI is $20,000. The son is a qualifying child to both Jake and Frank. Since Jake is the parent AND has the higher income, he claims the EIC.

Credit Rates and Dollar Amounts

The EIC increases as earned income increases, then caps at a certain level of income, and begins phasing out. This phaseout is based on the higher of earned income or AGI. Taxpayers use the Earned Income Credit Worksheet (shown in ¶204.12) to compute the proper EIC using the Earned Income Credit tables (found in Appendix E at the back of this textbook). Taxpayers keep this worksheet for their records. However, those with qualifying children must also complete and attach Schedule EIC, Earned Income Credit, to their tax returns.

For purposes of the EIC, earned income includes all types of taxable compensation, as well as net earnings from self-employment. It does not include nontaxable employee compensation such as salary deferrals under retirement plans, salary reductions under cafeteria plans, or any dependent care, adoption or educational assistance benefits. Earned income also does not include retirement income, social security income, unemployment benefits, or alimony.

¶204.12   FILLED-IN EIC WORKSHEET

INFORMATION FOR FIGURE 2-8:

James Williams earned $19,665 in wages in 2022. His employer withheld no income taxes from his pay. Sarah Williams earned $12,100 in wages. Her employer withheld no income taxes. The Williamses also earned $150 of interest on their joint savings account.

The Williamses file a joint tax return. They claim their two qualifying children as dependents. Figure 2-9 shows the Williamses' filled-in Schedule EIC. They claim a $4,971 EIC on their tax return and attach Schedule EIC to their return.

Figure 2-8: Filled-In EIC Worksheet		
1. Enter your earned income. ($19,665 + $12,100)	1.	31,765
2. Look up the EIC on the amount on line 1 above in the EIC Table. Enter the credit here.	2.	5,003
3. Enter your AGI. ($31,765 + $150)	3.	31,915
4. Are the amounts on lines 1 and 3 the same?		
Yes. Skip line 5; enter the amount from line 2 on line 6		
No. Go to line 5.		
5. If you have:		
a. No qualifying children, is the amount on line 3 less than $8,500 ($14,200 if married filed jointly)?		
b. One or more qualifying children, is the amount on line 3 less than $18,700 ($24,350 if married filed jointly)?		
Yes. Leave line 5 blank; enter the amount from line 2 on line 6		
No. Look up the EIC on the amount on line 3 above in the EIC Table. Enter the credit here.	5.	4,971
6. Your earned income credit (the smaller of line 2 or line 5).	6.	4,971

As the EIC worksheet shows, the earned income credit is the smaller of two amounts from the EIC Table. The first amount is found using the taxpayer's earned income; the second amount using the taxpayer's AGI. For 2022, taxpayers will have at least $1 of earned income credit as long as they have earned income and their earned income or AGI (whichever is greater) does not exceed the amounts shown in the table that follows.

	Married Filing Jointly	All Other Taxpayers
No children	$22,610	$16,480
One qualifying child	$49,622	$43,492
Two qualifying children	$55,529	$49,399
Three or more qualifying children	$59,187	$53,057

Figure 2-9: Filled-In Schedule EIC

SCHEDULE EIC
(Form 1040)

Department of the Treasury
Internal Revenue Service

Earned Income Credit
Qualifying Child Information

Complete and attach to Form 1040 or 1040-SR only if you have a qualifying child.
Go to *www.irs.gov/ScheduleEIC* for the latest information.

OMB No. 1545-0074

2022

Attachment
Sequence No. **43**

Name(s) shown on return
James and Sarah Williams

Your social security number
282-00

If you are separated from your spouse, filing a separate return, and meet the requirements to claim the EIC (see instructions), check here ☐

Before you begin:
- See the instructions for Form 1040, line 27, to make sure that (**a**) you can take the EIC, and (**b**) you have a qualifying child.
- Be sure the child's name on line 1 and social security number (SSN) on line 2 agree with the child's social security card. Otherwise, at the time we process your return, we may reduce your EIC. If the name or SSN on the child's social security card is not correct, call the Social Security Administration at 800-772-1213.
- If you have a child who meets the conditions to be your qualifying child for purposes of claiming the EIC, but that child doesn't have an SSN as defined in the instructions for Form 1040, line 27, see the instructions.

⚠ **CAUTION**
- *You can't claim the EIC for a child who didn't live with you for more than half of the year.*
- *If your child doesn't have an SSN as defined in the instructions for Form 1040, line 27, see the instructions.*
- *If you take the EIC even though you are not eligible, you may not be allowed to take the credit for up to 10 years. See the instructions for details.*
- *It will take us longer to process your return and issue your refund if you do not fill in all lines that apply for each qualifying child.*

Qualifying Child Information	Child 1	Child 2	Child 3
1 Child's name If you have more than three qualifying children, you have to list only three to get the maximum credit.	First name / Last name **Martha Williams**	First name / Last name **Kyle Williams**	First name / Last name
2 Child's SSN The child must have an SSN as defined in the instructions for Form 1040, line 27, unless the child was born and died in 2022 or you are claiming the self-only EIC; see instructions. If your child was born and died in 2022 and did not have an SSN, enter "Died" on this line and attach a copy of the child's birth certificate, death certificate, or hospital medical records showing a live birth.	**520-00-1120**	**520-00-3412**	
3 Child's year of birth	Year **2 0 1 4** *If born after 2003 and the child is younger than you (or your spouse, if filing jointly), skip lines 4a and 4b; go to line 5.*	Year **2 0 1 6** *If born after 2003 and the child is younger than you (or your spouse, if filing jointly), skip lines 4a and 4b; go to line 5.*	Year ___ *If born after 2003 and the child is younger than you (or your spouse, if filing jointly), skip lines 4a and 4b; go to line 5.*
4a Was the child under age 24 at the end of 2022, a student, and younger than you (or your spouse, if filing jointly)?	☐ Yes. ✔ No. *Go to line 5.* / *Go to line 4b.*	☐ Yes. ✔ No. *Go to line 5.* / *Go to line 4b.*	☐ Yes. ☐ No. *Go to line 5.* / *Go to line 4b.*
b Was the child permanently and totally disabled during any part of 2022?	✔ Yes. ☐ No. *Go to line 5.* / The child is not a qualifying child.	✔ Yes. ☐ No. *Go to line 5.* / The child is not a qualifying child.	☐ Yes. ☐ No. *Go to line 5.* / The child is not a qualifying child.
5 Child's relationship to you (for example, son, daughter, grandchild, niece, nephew, eligible foster child, etc.)	Daughter	Son	
6 Number of months child lived with you in the United States during 2022 • If the child lived with you for more than half of 2022 but less than 7 months, enter "7." • If the child was born or died in 2022 and your home was the child's home for more than half the time he or she was alive during 2022, enter "12."	**12** months *Do not enter more than 12 months.*	**12** months *Do not enter more than 12 months.*	___ months *Do not enter more than 12 months.*

For Paperwork Reduction Act Notice, see your tax return instructions.   Cat. No. 13339M   Schedule EIC (Form 1040) 2022

¶204.13   PREMIUM TAX CREDIT (PTC)

Taxpayers buy health insurance from an insurance company or from a government exchange (Marketplace). Taxpayers who buy their insurance through the government's health insurance "Marketplace" may be eligible for federal government subsidy to help pay for a portion of their premiums. For some taxpayers, this subsidy may be in the form of reduced monthly payments. For others, it comes in the form of a refundable tax credit, called the premium tax credit (PTC).

The amount of the premium reduction (advance subsidy) is based on household income and family size reported by the taxpayer at the time of enrollment. Since the taxpayer's actual household income for the year will likely differ from the self-reported amount provided at the time of enrollment, taxpayers who receive subsidies during the year need to reconcile their advanced subsidies (total premium reduction) with the amounts to which they were entitled based on actual household income. Taxpayers whose actual subsidies they received during the year were greater than their entitled subsidies must repay the excess by reporting additional tax on their tax returns. Taxpayers who did not receive the subsidies they were entitled to during the year claim a refundable PTC for the difference. The American Rescue Plan Act suspends the requirement that taxpayers increase their tax liability by all or a portion of their excess advance payments.

Taxpayers Who Qualify for the PTC

Only taxpayers whose household income is at least 100%, but no more than 400%, of the federal poverty line can claim the PTC. Taxpayers who qualify for Medicare or Medicaid, or who are eligible to get insurance under an employer-sponsored plan, self-funded student health plan, or through high-risk pools offered by the state government, cannot claim the PTC. Married taxpayers must file a joint tax return in order to claim the PTC, and taxpayers claimed as a dependent on another person's return are not eligible for this credit.

Computing the PTC

Using the taxpayer's total household income and family size, the government determines the maximum amount each taxpayer should have to pay for health insurance. The term the IRS uses to describe this amount is "annual contribution for health care." The government also determines what the taxpayer's annual premiums would be for its silver plan (the second lowest cost plan offered by the Marketplace). The taxpayer's PTC is the *lesser of* (i) the taxpayer's actual premiums (prior to any subsidy), or (ii) the difference between the cost of the silver plan and the taxpayer's annual contribution for health care.

 Form 1095-A, Health Insurance Marketplace Statement, is an information return sent out to Marketplace participants after the end of each year. This form informs participants of the cost of the premiums (prior to any subsidies) for the policy in which they enrolled, as well as what their cost would have been had they chosen the silver plan.

EXAMPLE 23   Duke buys his health insurance through the federal Marketplace. Duke selects a bronze plan, which is the least costly of the four types of plans offered by the Marketplace. Total annual premiums for his plan are $3,000. Had Duke selected the silver plan, his premiums would have been $5,600. Based on Duke's household income and family size, the government has determined that Duke's annual contribution for health care is $1,700. Duke's PTC is $3,000, which is the *lesser of* (i) $3,000 total premiums for the plan Duke enrolled in, or (ii) $3,900 ($5,600 premiums under the silver plan – $1,700 annual contribution for health care).

| EXAMPLE 24 | Same facts as in Example 23, except that Duke selects a platinum (most expensive) plan, and his premiums are $8,000. Duke's PTC is $3,900, which is the *lesser of* (i) $8,000, or (ii) $3,900 ($5,600 – $1,700). |

From looking at how the PTC is calculated, the government has concluded that every individual is entitled to receive the benefits offered by the Marketplace's silver plan. For taxpayers whom the government does not believe have enough household income to pay for these benefits (based on the ratio of household income to the federal poverty line), it is willing to provide help up to the difference between the silver plan premiums and the taxpayer's annual contribution limit (as shown in Example 24). Taxpayers who decide to go with a less expensive (bronze) plan will find their PTC limited to the cost of premiums under that plan (as shown in Example 23).

The taxpayer's annual contribution for health care represents what the government has determined should be the maximum amount that the taxpayer should have to pay for health insurance premiums. It is based on total household income and the number of exemptions the taxpayer claims. Household income is the sum of the modified AGI for all exemptions (personal and dependency) claimed on the taxpayer's return. For purposes of the PTC, "modified AGI" is AGI plus any tax-exempt interest income (¶401.03), nontaxable social security benefits (¶307), and foreign earned income exclusion (¶401.14).

| EXAMPLE 25 | Jim and Cathy Thompson live in Missouri. They file a joint tax return and claim their three children as dependents. The Thompsons are not eligible for health insurance through their work, so they purchase their insurance through the Marketplace. On their joint tax return, the Thompsons report $500 of tax-exempt interest income and $57,097 of AGI. The Thompsons' son earned $2,000 working part-time during the year. The Thompsons' household income equals $59,597. This amount is the sum of the couples' $57,597 of modified AGI ($57,097 + $500) and their dependent child's $2,000 of modified AGI. |

Once the taxpayer's household income has been computed, the taxpayer uses an IRS-provided table to find the federal poverty line that corresponds to the total number of (personal and dependency) exemptions the taxpayer claimed. For purposes of computing the PTC in 2022, the poverty line thresholds for most taxpayers are provided in Figure 2-10. [Source: (https://www.govinfo.gov/content/pkg/FR-2021-02-01/pdf/2021-01969.pdf)] There are different amounts for taxpayers living in Alaska and Hawaii. This information can also be found in the Instructions to Form 8962.

Figure 2-10: Federal Poverty Line Thresholds used for 2022	
Total Exemptions Claimed	**Threshold**
1	$13,590
2	17,420
3	21,960
4	26,500
5	31,040
6	35,580
7	40,120
8	44,660

EXAMPLE 26	Continuing with Example 25, the Thompsons use Figure 2-10 to look up the federal poverty amount for taxpayers claiming five total exemptions. This amount is $31,040.

The next step in the process of determining the taxpayer's annual contribution for health care is to divide household income by the federal poverty line threshold. Only taxpayers whose household income falls between 100% and 400% of the threshold qualify for the PTC.

EXAMPLE 27	Continuing with Example 26, the Thompsons divide their $59,597 of household income by $31,040. The 1.92 result means that the Thompsons' household income is 192% of the federal poverty line. Because this percentage falls between 100% and 400%, the Thompsons qualify for the PTC.

Once it has been determined that the taxpayer qualifies for the PTC, the taxpayer's annual contribution for health care can be computed. This is done by multiplying the taxpayer's household income by the taxpayer's "applicable figure" from an IRS-provided table in the instructions for Form 8962 (reproduced in Appendix C at the back of the textbook). The applicable figure is the number from the table that corresponds to the percentage previously calculated (household income divided by the federal poverty line).

EXAMPLE 28	Continuing with Example 27, the Thompsons go to the table in Appendix C and find that the applicable figure for .192 is .0618. They multiply this number by their $59,597 of household income to arrive at their annual contribution for health care ($59,597 × .0611 = $3,683). This amount represents the maximum amount the government has determined the Thompsons should have to pay for health insurance premiums.

After the annual contribution for health care has been computed, taxpayers can use the information reported to them on Form 1095-A to compute their PTC. This amount is the *lesser of* (i) the taxpayer's actual premiums (prior to any subsidy), or (ii) the difference between the cost of the silver plan and the taxpayer's annual contribution for health care.

EXAMPLE 29	Continuing with Example 28, the Thompsons' Form 1095-A shows that their annual premiums for the policy they enrolled in was $7,000, and that their premiums would have been $6,600 had they enrolled in the silver plan. The Thompsons' PTC equals $2,959. This is the *lesser of* (i) the $7,000 cost of premiums for the plan they enrolled in, or (ii) $2,917 (the $6,600 cost for premiums under the silver plan minus their $3,683 annual contribution for health care).

For taxpayers who did not receive any premium reductions during the year, the PTC is reported as a refundable tax credit on Form 1040, Schedule 5 (line 70, "Net premium tax credit"). Taxpayers receiving premium reductions (advance payment of PTC) need to reconcile the difference between their advance payment and their PTC.

Reconciling Advance Payment of PTC and Actual PTC

In addition to providing taxpayers with the cost of their insurance premiums under both the plan they enrolled in and the silver plan, Form 1095-A also provides taxpayers with the amount of premium reductions they received during the year. This amount represents their advance payment of PTC. Taxpayers compare their PTC to their advance payment of PTC. If the taxpayer's PTC exceeds their advance payment, the difference ("net PTC") is reported as a refundable tax credit on Form 1040.

EXAMPLE 30	June and Jim Rosen compute their PTC to be $4,500. The Rosens' Form 1095-A shows that they received advance payments totaling $3,850 during the year. The Rosens reduce their PTC by their advance payments and report the $650 net PTC ($4,500 – $3,850) as a refundable tax credit on Form 1040.

Excess Advance PTC Repayment

When the taxpayer's advance payment of PTC exceeds their PTC, at least some of the excess must usually be paid back to the government. The American Rescue Plan Act suspends this requirement for 2021 only. Normally, this repayment is done by having the taxpayer report an additional tax on Form 1040, Schedule 2 (line 46). The amount that must be repaid is the *lesser of* (i) the excess of the advance payment over the PTC, or (ii) the amount from the table below that corresponds to the taxpayer's filing status. Thus, the amounts in the table serve as a maximum repayment for taxpayers receiving advanced payments.

Taxpayer's Household Income as a Percentage of Federal Poverty Line:	Taxpayer's Filing Status	
	Single	All Others
Less than 200%	$ 300	$ 600
At least 200% but less than 300%	750	1,500
At least 300% but less than 400%	1,275	2,550

EXAMPLE 31

Continuing with Example 29, assume that the Thompsons' Form 1095-A shows that they received $4,000 of advance payment of PTC. This amount exceeds the Thompsons' PTC by $1,083 ($4,000 – $2,917). From the above table, the amount that corresponds to MFJ taxpayers whose household income as a percentage of the federal poverty line is 192% is $600. Since the $1,083 of excess is more than this amount, the Thompsons report no additional tax on their Form 1040.

Form 8962

Form 8962, Premium Tax Credit (PTC), is a two-page tax form that calculates the taxpayer's PTC. For taxpayers who received advanced payment of PTC (through reduced premiums), the taxpayer's net PTC (not enough subsidies) or excess advance PTC repayment (too much subsidy) is also calculated on this form. These calculations are performed in Parts I–III of Form 8962 (page 1). Parts IV and V involve complex situations that are beyond the scope of this discussion.

In Part I, taxpayers compute their annual contribution for health care. In Part II, taxpayers report the information provided to them on Form 1095-A and calculate their PTC. Net PTC is also calculated in Part II. Taxpayers receiving advanced payment of PTC during the year in excess of their PTC compute their required repayment in Part III.

¶204.14   FILLED-IN FORM 8962

INFORMATION FOR FIGURE 2-11:

The Thompsons (from Examples 25–29, and Example 31) compute their net PTC or repayment amount by entering on the form the information provided below in bold font. The Thompsons then follow the instructions on Form 8962 to compute their $600 excess advance premium tax credit repayment. They report this amount as an additional tax on Form 1040 (line 46).

Line #
- 1: Family size, **5** (2 personal + 3 dependency exemptions)
- 2a: Modified AGI reported on the Thompsons' tax return, **($57,097 + $500)**, provided in Example 25)

2b: Modified AGI of the Thompsons' dependents, **$2,000** (provided in Example 25)

4: Federal poverty line, **$31,040** (source: Figure 2-10, see Example 26)

6: The Thompsons check **No.** because the 193% reported on line 5 does not exceed 400%.

7: Applicable Figure, **.0172** (source: see Example 28)

11(a): Premium Amount, **$7,000** (source: Form 1095-A, line 33A. This is the total cost of the premiums (before subsidies) of the insurance plan the Thompsons enrolled in).

11(b): Annual Premium Amount of SLCSP, **$6,600** (source: Form 1095-A, line 33B. This is the total cost of the premiums for the second lowest cost silver plan).

11(f): Annual Advance Payment of PTC, **$4,000** (source: Form 1095-A, line 33C. This is the amount of the Thompsons' health care premiums that the government paid on their behalf.)

Figure 2-11: Filled-In Form 8962 (Page 1)

Version A, Cycle 4

Form **8962**

Premium Tax Credit (PTC)

OMB No. 1545-0074

2022

Department of the Treasury
Internal Revenue Service

Attach to Form 1040, 1040-SR, or 1040-NR.
Go to *www.irs.gov/Form8962* for instructions and the latest information.

Attachment Sequence No. **73**

Name shown on your return: Jim and Kathy Thompson

Your social security number: 859-00-4466

A. You cannot take the PTC if your filing status is married filing separately unless you qualify for an exception. See instructions. If you qualify, check the box ☐

Part I   Annual and Monthly Contribution Amount

1	Tax family size. Enter your tax family size. See instructions	1	5
2a	Modified AGI. Enter your modified AGI. See instructions	2a 57,597	
b	Enter the total of your dependents' modified AGI. See instructions	2b 2,000	
3	Household income. Add the amounts on lines 2a and 2b. See instructions	3	59,977
4	Federal poverty line. Enter the federal poverty line amount from Table 1-1, 1-2, or 1-3. See instructions. Check the appropriate box for the federal poverty table used. a ☐ Alaska b ☐ Hawaii c ☑ Other 48 states and DC	4	31,040
5	Household income as a percentage of federal poverty line (see instructions)	5	193 %
6	Reserved for future use		
7	Applicable figure. Using your line 5 percentage, locate your "applicable figure" on the table in the instructions	7	.0172
8a	Annual contribution amount. Multiply line 3 by line 7. Round to nearest whole dollar amount **8a** 1,032	**b** Monthly contribution amount. Divide line 8a by 12. Round to nearest whole dollar amount **8b**	86

Part II   Premium Tax Credit Claim and Reconciliation of Advance Payment of Premium Tax Credit

9   Are you allocating policy amounts with another taxpayer or do you want to use the alternative calculation for year of marriage? See instructions.
☐ **Yes.** Skip to Part IV, Allocation of Policy Amounts, or Part V, Alternative Calculation for Year of Marriage.   ☐ **No.** Continue to line 10.

10   See the instructions to determine if you can use line 11 or must complete lines 12 through 23.
☐ **Yes.** Continue to line 11. Compute your annual PTC. Then skip lines 12–23 and continue to line 24.   ☐ **No.** Continue to lines 12–23. Compute your monthly PTC and continue to line 24.

Annual Calculation	(a) Annual enrollment premiums (Form(s) 1095-A, line 33A)	(b) Annual applicable SLCSP premium (Form(s) 1095-A, line 33B)	(c) Annual contribution amount (line 8a)	(d) Annual maximum premium assistance (subtract (c) from (b); if zero or less, enter -0-)	(e) Annual premium tax credit allowed (smaller of (a) or (d))	(f) Annual advance payment of PTC (Form(s) 1095-A, line 33C)
11 Annual Totals	7,000	6,600	1,032	5,568	5,568	4,000

Monthly Calculation	(a) Monthly enrollment premiums (Form(s) 1095-A, lines 21–32, column A)	(b) Monthly applicable SLCSP premium (Form(s) 1095-A, lines 21–32, column B)	(c) Monthly contribution amount (amount from line 8b or alternative marriage monthly calculation)	(d) Monthly maximum premium assistance (subtract (c) from (b); if zero or less, enter -0-)	(e) Monthly premium tax credit allowed (smaller of (a) or (d))	(f) Monthly advance payment of PTC (Form(s) 1095-A, lines 21–32, column C)
12 January						
13 February						
14 March						
15 April						
16 May						
17 June						
18 July						
19 August						
20 September						
21 October						
22 November						
23 December						

24	Total premium tax credit. Enter the amount from line 11(e) or add lines 12(e) through 23(e) and enter the total here	24	5,568
25	Advance payment of PTC. Enter the amount from line 11(f) or add lines 12(f) through 23(f) and enter the total here	25	4,000
26	Net premium tax credit. If line 24 is greater than line 25, subtract line 25 from line 24. Enter the difference here and on Schedule 3 (Form 1040), line 9. If line 24 equals line 25, enter -0-. Stop here. If line 25 is greater than line 24, leave this line blank and continue to line 27	26	1,568

Part III   Repayment of Excess Advance Payment of the Premium Tax Credit

27	Excess advance payment of PTC. If line 25 is greater than line 24, subtract line 24 from line 25. Enter the difference here	27	
28	Repayment limitation (see instructions)	28	
29	Excess advance premium tax credit repayment. Enter the smaller of line 27 or line 28 here and on Schedule 2 (Form 1040), line 2	29	

For Paperwork Reduction Act Notice, see your tax return instructions.   Cat. No. 37784Z   Form **8962** (2022)

Figure 2-11: Filled-In Form 8962 (Page 2)

Form 8962 (2022)   Page **2**

Part IV — Allocation of Policy Amounts

Complete the following information for up to four policy amount allocations. See instructions for allocation details.

Allocation 1

30	**(a)** Policy Number (Form 1095-A, line 2)	**(b)** SSN of other taxpayer	**(c)** Allocation start month	**(d)** Allocation stop month

	Allocation percentage applied to monthly amounts	**(e)** Premium Percentage	**(f)** SLCSP Percentage	**(g)** Advance Payment of the PTC Percentage

Allocation 2

31	**(a)** Policy Number (Form 1095-A, line 2)	**(b)** SSN of other taxpayer	**(c)** Allocation start month	**(d)** Allocation stop month

	Allocation percentage applied to monthly amounts	**(e)** Premium Percentage	**(f)** SLCSP Percentage	**(g)** Advance Payment of the PTC Percentage

Allocation 3

32	**(a)** Policy Number (Form 1095-A, line 2)	**(b)** SSN of other taxpayer	**(c)** Allocation start month	**(d)** Allocation stop month

	Allocation percentage applied to monthly amounts	**(e)** Premium Percentage	**(f)** SLCSP Percentage	**(g)** Advance Payment of the PTC Percentage

Allocation 4

33	**(a)** Policy Number (Form 1095-A, line 2)	**(b)** SSN of other taxpayer	**(c)** Allocation start month	**(d)** Allocation stop month

	Allocation percentage applied to monthly amounts	**(e)** Premium Percentage	**(f)** SLCSP Percentage	**(g)** Advance Payment of the PTC Percentage

34 Have you completed all policy amount allocations?

☐ **Yes.** Multiply the amounts on Form 1095-A by the allocation percentages entered by policy. Add all allocated policy amounts and non-allocated policy amounts from Forms 1095-A, if any, to compute a combined total for each month. Enter the combined total for each month on lines 12–23, columns (a), (b), and (f). Compute the amounts for lines 12–23, columns (c)–(e), and continue to line 24.

☐ **No.** See the instructions to report additional policy amount allocations.

Part V — Alternative Calculation for Year of Marriage

Complete line(s) 35 and/or 36 to elect the alternative calculation for year of marriage. For eligibility to make the election, see the instructions for line 9. To complete line(s) 35 and/or 36 and compute the amounts for lines 12–23, see the instructions for this Part V.

		(a) Alternative family size	**(b)** Alternative monthly contribution amount	**(c)** Alternative start month	**(d)** Alternative stop month
35	Alternative entries for your SSN				
36	Alternative entries for your spouse's SSN				

Form **8962** (2022)

¶205   Shared Responsibility Payment

Taxpayers who failed to comply with the ACA mandate during any portion of the year used to include a shared responsibility payment on their income tax returns. The mandate to carry minimum essential health care coverage extended not only to the taxpayer, but to the taxpayer's spouse (when filing a joint return) as well as to all dependents listed on the taxpayer's return. However, Congress repealed this requirement, and it is no longer in effect.

¶206   Electronic Filing

The IRS encourages electronic filing of tax returns. Electronic filing reduces the IRS's processing costs and speeds up the time it takes taxpayers to get their refunds. Taxpayers who file their returns electronically and have their refunds deposited directly into their bank accounts can receive their refunds much faster than returns filed by mail. IRS statistics for fiscal year 2020 shows almost 152 million individual income tax returns were filed electronically (*https://www.efile.com/efile-tax-return-direct-deposit-statistics/*).

Persons who e-file their tax returns and have their refunds deposited directly to their checking or savings accounts should expect to receive their refunds within 1–3 weeks. The processing of refunds takes a little longer during peak tax filing season. Taxpayers interested in checking on the status of their federal income tax refunds can call 1-800-829-4477, where they will reach an automated information line. Alternatively, taxpayers can check online the status of their federal tax refunds (as well as the state tax refunds for many states) at: *https://www.IRS.gov/refunds*. Or, taxpayers can download the *IRS2Go* app to their mobile device.

¶207   IRS Website

The IRS provides lots of useful information through its Internet home page (*http://www.irs.gov*). This is a good source of forms, publications, and other material that may be downloaded. Appendix A (located at the back of this textbook) provides instructions on how to use the IRS website.

¶208   Extension of Time to File

Taxpayers that cannot file their tax returns on time can get an extension of time to file. Individual taxpayers wanting an automatic six month extension file Form 4868, Application for Automatic Extension of Time To File U.S. Individual Income Tax Return, no later than the due date of their tax return (April 15). Filing an extension provides taxpayers with more time to file their tax returns, but does not give them more time to pay their taxes. Taxpayers must pay their taxes by original due date for their returns even when they file an extension. Amounts paid to the IRS when filing an extension are reported in the "Payments" section when the tax return is prepared at a later date. Interest is charged on any unpaid amounts and penalties may be assessed as well.

2

QUESTIONS AND PROBLEMS

1. **Using the Tax Rate Schedules.** (Obj. 1) The IRS publishes tax rate schedules and a Tax Table. When must taxpayers use the tax rate schedules instead of the Tax Table to compute their income tax liability?

2. **Comparison of Tax Tables and Tax Rate Schedules.** (Obj. 1) Matteo (unmarried) files his tax return using head of household filing status. His taxable income is $60,550.

    a. What is Matteo's tax liability using the Tax Table?

    b. Compute Matteo's tax liability using the tax rate schedule. Explain any difference in your answers to Parts a. and b.

3. **Tax Computation.** (Obj. 1) Barb, age 25, files as a single taxpayer. She is employed at a monthly salary of $2,150. She claims no dependents. Her employer withheld $1,600 from her wages for income taxes for 12 months of work. Compute Barb's taxable income and income tax due to or from the IRS.

4. **Tax Computations.** (Obj. 1) Compute the taxable income and income tax liability (before credits) for each of the following taxpayers. Each taxpayer uses the standard deduction.

   a. A widowed taxpayer, age 30, has one dependent. Her filing status is qualifying widow(er); AGI is $46,400.

   b. An unmarried taxpayer, age 74, has no dependents and AGI of $19,590.

   c. A taxpayer, age 40, is married but files a separate return from his spouse. The taxpayer is the noncustodial parent of his eight-year-old child. His wife has signed Form 8332 giving him the right to claim their daughter as a dependent. AGI is $130,580.

   d. An unmarried taxpayer, age 72, is claimed as a dependent on her son's return. Her AGI consists solely of $3,150 of taxable interest.

   e. A married couple, ages 67 and 66, file a joint return. They claim one dependent. AGI is $161,555.

5. **Tax Credits vs. Tax Deductions.** (Obj. 1) What is the difference between a tax credit and a tax deduction? If a taxpayer with a marginal tax rate of 15% has a $1,000 deduction, how much tax will she save? How much tax will she save with a $1,000 tax credit?

6. **Child and Dependent Care Credit.** (Obj. 2) Bud and Katie Milner file a joint return. During the year, they paid $11,000 to their nanny to look after their three children, ages 2, 9, and 11. Bud and Katie both work and earned $24,000 and $31,000, respectively. The wages are the Milners' only source of income, and they have no deductions for AGI.

   a. Compute the Milners' child and dependent care credit.

   b. Compute the Milners' child and dependent care credit assuming Katie received a $4,000 nontaxable reimbursement from her employer's dependent care assistance plan.

7. **Child and Dependent Care Credit.** (Obj. 2) Todd and Jo Mendin pay their 17-year-old daughter, Erin, $5,000 to look after their ten-year-old son, TJ. The Mendins file a joint return and claim Erin and TJ as their dependents. The Mendlins' AGI is $84,000. Both spouses work and each has wages in excess of $30,000.

    a. Compute the Mendlins' child and dependent care credit.

    b. How, if at all, would your answer to Part a. change if Erin were 22 years old, but still claimed as a dependent on her parents' return?

    c. How, if at all, would your answer to Part a. change if the Mendins paid Todd's mother to look after TJ?

8. **Child and Dependent Care Credit and Form 2441.** (Objs. 2 and 4) Denise (SSN 182-00-0113) and Marcus Anders claim their two children, David (SSN 392-00-7417, age 7) and Stacy (SSN 813-00-4444, age 11), as dependents. During the year, Denise worked full-time and earned $38,200. Marcus was a full-time student at the local college for 9 months during the year. The Anders paid Tanya McCully (SSN 921-00-0122) $5,500 for qualified childcare expenses that allowed Denise to work and Marcus to attend college. Tanya lives at 130 N. Main Street, Unit B, Memphis, TN 37501.

    a. Compute the Anders's child and dependent care credit if their AGI is $38,710.

    b. How, if at all, would your answer to Part a. change if Marcus attended college full-time for five months during the spring semester, but only took classes part-time in the fall?

    c. Prepare Form 2441 for the Anders from Part b. The Anders's tax liability limit is $981.

(Use for Problem 8.)

Form **2441**	**Child and Dependent Care Expenses**	OMB No. 1545-0074
Department of the Treasury Internal Revenue Service	Attach to Form 1040, 1040-SR, or 1040-NR. Go to *www.irs.gov/Form2441* for instructions and the latest information.	**2022** Attachment Sequence No. **21**
Name(s) shown on return		Your social security number

A You can't claim a credit for child and dependent care expenses if your filing status is married filing separately unless you meet the requirements listed in the instructions under *Married Persons Filing Separately*. If you meet these requirements, check this box . . ☐

B If you or your spouse was a student or was disabled during 2022 and you're entering deemed income of $250 or $500 a month on Form 2441 based on the income rules listed in the instructions under *If You or Your Spouse Was a Student or Disabled*, check this box ☐

Part I   Persons or Organizations Who Provided the Care—You **must** complete this part.
If you have more than three care providers, see the instructions and check this box . . . . ☐

1 (a) Care provider's name	(b) Address (number, street, apt. no., city, state, and ZIP code)	(c) Identifying number (SSN or EIN)	(d) Was the care provider your household employee in 2022? For example, this generally includes nannies but not daycare centers. (see instructions)	(e) Amount paid (see instructions)
			☐ Yes ☐ No	
			☐ Yes ☐ No	
			☐ Yes ☐ No	

Did you receive **dependent care benefits?**	**No** ——— Complete only Part II below.
	Yes ——— Complete Part III on page 2 next.

Caution: If the care provider is your household employee, you may owe employment taxes. For details, see the Instructions for Schedule H (Form 1040). If you incurred care expenses in 2022 but didn't pay them until 2023, or if you prepaid in 2022 for care to be provided in 2023, don't include these expenses in column (d) of line 2 for 2022. See the instructions.

Part II   Credit for Child and Dependent Care Expenses

2 Information about your **qualifying person(s)**. If you have more than three qualifying persons, see the instructions and check this box ☐

(a) Qualifying person's name		(b) Qualifying person's social security number	(c) Check here if the qualifying person was over age 12 and was disabled. (see instructions)	(d) Qualified expenses you incurred and paid in 2022 for the person listed in column (a)
First	Last			
			☐	
			☐	
			☐	

3	Add the amounts in column (d) of line 2. **Don't** enter more than $3,000 if you had one qualifying person or $6,000 if you had two or more persons. If you completed Part III, enter the amount from line 31	**3**	
4	Enter your **earned income**. See instructions	**4**	
5	If married filing jointly, enter your spouse's earned income (if you or your spouse was a student or was disabled, see the instructions); **all others**, enter the amount from line 4	**5**	
6	Enter the **smallest** of line 3, 4, or 5	**6**	
7	Enter the amount from Form 1040, 1040-SR, or 1040-NR, line 11 . . .	**7**	
8	Enter on line 8 the decimal amount shown below that applies to the amount on line 7.		

If line 7 is:		Decimal amount is	If line 7 is:		Decimal amount is	If line 7 is:		Decimal amount is
Over	But not over		Over	But not over		Over	But not over	
$0—15,000		.35	$25,000—27,000		.29	$37,000—39,000		.23
15,000—17,000		.34	27,000—29,000		.28	39,000—41,000		.22
17,000—19,000		.33	29,000—31,000		.27	41,000—43,000		.21
19,000—21,000		.32	31,000—33,000		.26	43,000—No limit		.20
21,000—23,000		.31	33,000—35,000		.25			
23,000—25,000		.30	35,000—37,000		.24			

Line 8: **X .**

9a	Multiply line 6 by the decimal amount on line 8	**9a**	
b	If you paid 2021 expenses in 2022, complete Worksheet A in the instructions. Enter the amount from line 13 of the worksheet here. Otherwise, enter -0- on line 9b and go to line 9c	**9b**	
c	Add lines 9a and 9b and enter the result	**9c**	
10	Tax liability limit. Enter the amount from the Credit Limit Worksheet in the instructions **10**		
11	**Credit for child and dependent care expenses.** Enter the **smaller** of line 9c or line 10 here and on Schedule 3 (Form 1040), line 2	**11**	

For Paperwork Reduction Act Notice, see your tax return instructions.   Cat. No. 11862M   Form **2441** (2022)

9.   **Education Tax Credit and Form 8863.** (Objs. 2 and 4) In 2022 , Jean Loptein (SSN 169-00-2903) paid $3,300 for her son's fall tuition. Her son, Robert Loptein (SSN 399-00-1120), is a full-time student and a freshman at the University of Georgia (212 Carlton Street, Athens, GA 30602). Jean files as head of household.

a.   Compute Jean's education tax credit if her AGI is $32,800. How much of her credit is refundable versus nonrefundable?

b.   Same as in Part a., except that Jean's AGI is $84,700.

c.   Prepare Form 8863 for Jean in Part b. Robert received a Form 1098-T from the University of Georgia, whose employer identification number is 70-2226900. Box 7 on the form was not checked. Robert has not been convicted of a felony.

10. **Education Tax Credit.** (Obj. 2) Curt and Kathy Norton paid $3,200 of tuition for their son, who attends college less than half-time. Of this amount, $1,500 was paid on December 28, 2021, for the Spring 2022 semester, and $1,700 was paid on August 4, 2022, for the Fall 2022 semester.

a.   Compute the Nortons' 2022 education tax credit if their AGI is $71,900. How much of their credit is refundable versus nonrefundable?

b.   Same as in Part a., except that the Nortons' AGI is $122,816.

11. **Education Tax Credit.** (Obj. 2) In 2022, Paul and Karen Mitchell pay $12,000 for their daughter's tuition for the Spring and Fall semesters. Their daughter is a full-time graduate student. The Mitchells also paid $3,800 for their son's tuition for the Spring and Fall semesters. In the Fall of 2022, their son, Ron began his sophomore year of college. The son attends college full-time.

a.   Compute the Mitchells' 2022 education tax credit if their AGI is $124,600. How much of their credit is refundable versus nonrefundable?

b.   Same as in Part a., except that the Mitchells' AGI is $174,360.

(Use for Problem 9.)

Form **8863**		Education Credits		OMB No. 1545-0074
Department of the Treasury Internal Revenue Service		**(American Opportunity and Lifetime Learning Credits)** Attach to Form 1040 or 1040-SR. Go to *www.irs.gov/Form8863* for instructions and the latest information.		**2022** Attachment Sequence No. **50**

Name(s) shown on return   **Your social security number**

> ⚠ **CAUTION** *Complete a separate Part III on page 2 for each student for whom you're claiming either credit before you complete Parts I and II.*

Part I — Refundable American Opportunity Credit

1	After completing Part III for each student, enter the total of all amounts from all Parts III, line 30	**1**
2	Enter: $180,000 if married filing jointly; $90,000 if single, head of household, or qualifying widow(er)	**2**
3	Enter the amount from Form 1040 or 1040-SR, line 11. If you're filing Form 2555 or 4563, or you're excluding income from Puerto Rico, see Pub. 970 for the amount to enter	**3**
4	Subtract line 3 from line 2. If zero or less, **stop**; you can't take any education credit	**4**
5	Enter: $20,000 if married filing jointly; $10,000 if single, head of household, or qualifying widow(er)	**5**
6	If line 4 is: • Equal to or more than line 5, enter 1.000 on line 6 • Less than line 5, divide line 4 by line 5. Enter the result as a decimal (rounded to at least three places)	**6**
7	Multiply line 1 by line 6. **Caution:** If you were under age 24 at the end of the year **and** meet the conditions described in the instructions, you **can't** take the refundable American opportunity credit; skip line 8, enter the amount from line 7 on line 9, and check this box ☐	**7**
8	**Refundable American opportunity credit.** Multiply line 7 by 40% (0.40). Enter the amount here and on Form 1040 or 1040-SR, line 29. Then go to line 9 below.	**8**

Part II — Nonrefundable Education Credits

9	Subtract line 8 from line 7. Enter here and on line 2 of the Credit Limit Worksheet (see instructions)	**9**
10	After completing Part III for each student, enter the total of all amounts from all Parts III, line 31. If zero, skip lines 11 through 17, enter -0- on line 18, and go to line 19	**10**
11	Enter the smaller of line 10 or $10,000	**11**
12	Multiply line 11 by 20% (0.20)	**12**
13	Enter: $180,000 if married filing jointly; $90,000 if single, head of household, or qualifying widow(er)	**13**
14	Enter the amount from Form 1040 or 1040-SR, line 11. If you're filing Form 2555 or 4563, or you're excluding income from Puerto Rico, see Pub. 970 for the amount to enter	**14**
15	Subtract line 14 from line 13. If zero or less, skip lines 16 and 17, enter -0- on line 18, and go to line 19	**15**
16	Enter: $20,000 if married filing jointly; $10,000 if single, head of household, or qualifying widow(er)	**16**
17	If line 15 is: • Equal to or more than line 16, enter 1.000 on line 17 and go to line 18 • Less than line 16, divide line 15 by line 16. Enter the result as a decimal (rounded to at least three places)	**17**
18	Multiply line 12 by line 17. Enter here and on line 1 of the Credit Limit Worksheet (see instructions)	**18**
19	**Nonrefundable education credits.** Enter the amount from line 7 of the Credit Limit Worksheet (see instructions) here and on Schedule 3 (Form 1040), line 3	**19**

For Paperwork Reduction Act Notice, see your tax return instructions.   Cat. No. 25379M   Form **8863** (2022)

DRAFT AS OF October 3, 2022 DO NOT FILE

(Use for Problem 9.)

Form 8863 (2022)		Page **2**
Name(s) shown on return		Your social security number

> ⚠️ **CAUTION** *Complete Part III for each student for whom you're claiming either the American opportunity credit or lifetime learning credit. Use additional copies of page 2 as needed for each student.*

Part III Student and Educational Institution Information. See instructions.

20 Student name (as shown on page 1 of your tax return)	**21** Student social security number (as shown on page 1 of your tax return)

22 Educational institution information (see instructions)

a. Name of first educational institution	**b.** Name of second educational institution (if any)
(1) Address. Number and street (or P.O. box). City, town or post office, state, and ZIP code. If a foreign address, see instructions.	**(1)** Address. Number and street (or P.O. box). City, town or post office, state, and ZIP code. If a foreign address, see instructions.
(2) Did the student receive Form 1098-T from this institution for 2022? ☐ Yes ☐ No	**(2)** Did the student receive Form 1098-T from this institution for 2022? ☐ Yes ☐ No
(3) Did the student receive Form 1098-T from this institution for 2021 with box 7 checked? ☐ Yes ☐ No	**(3)** Did the student receive Form 1098-T from this institution for 2021 with box 7 checked? ☐ Yes ☐ No
(4) Enter the institution's employer identification number (EIN) if you're claiming the American opportunity credit or if you checked "Yes" in **(2)** or **(3)**. You can get the EIN from Form 1098-T or from the institution. ___ ___ - ___ ___ ___ ___ ___ ___ ___	**(4)** Enter the institution's employer identification number (EIN) if you're claiming the American opportunity credit or if you checked "Yes" in **(2)** or **(3)**. You can get the EIN from Form 1098-T or from the institution. ___ ___ - ___ ___ ___ ___ ___ ___ ___

23	Has the American opportunity credit been claimed for this student for any 4 tax years before 2022?	☐ Yes — **Stop!** Go to line 31 for this student. ☐ No — Go to line 24.
24	Was the student enrolled at least half-time for at least one academic period that began or is treated as having begun in 2022 at an eligible educational institution in a program leading towards a postsecondary degree, certificate, or other recognized postsecondary educational credential? See instructions.	☐ Yes — Go to line 25. ☐ No — **Stop!** Go to line 31 for this student.
25	Did the student complete the first 4 years of postsecondary education before 2022? See instructions.	☐ Yes — **Stop!** Go to line 31 for this student. ☐ No — Go to line 26.
26	Was the student convicted, before the end of 2022, of a felony for possession or distribution of a controlled substance?	☐ Yes — **Stop!** Go to line 31 for this student. ☐ No — Complete lines 27 through 30 for this student.

> ⚠️ **CAUTION** You **can't** take the American opportunity credit and the lifetime learning credit for the **same student** in the same year. If you complete lines 27 through 30 for this student, don't complete line 31.

American Opportunity Credit

27	Adjusted qualified education expenses (see instructions). **Don't enter more than $4,000**	**27**	
28	Subtract $2,000 from line 27. If zero or less, enter -0-.	**28**	
29	Multiply line 28 by 25% (0.25)	**29**	
30	If line 28 is zero, enter the amount from line 27. Otherwise, add $2,000 to the amount on line 29 and enter the result. Skip line 31. Include the total of all amounts from all Parts III, line 30, on Part I, line 1 .	**30**	

Lifetime Learning Credit

31	Adjusted qualified education expenses (see instructions). Include the total of all amounts from all Parts III, line 31, on Part II, line 10	**31**	

Form **8863** (2022)

12. **Retirement Savings Contributions Credit.** (Obj. 2) Tom and Meg Wherry's joint tax return for 2022 shows $46,000 of AGI. During the year, Tom contributed $3,000 to his IRA and Meg contributed $1,500 to her IRA. What amount of tax credit is available for these contributions?

13. **Child Tax Credit.** (Obj. 2) Compute the child tax credit for each of the following taxpayers.

    a. Jett is married but does not file a joint return with his spouse. Jett claims his six-year-old son as a dependent and files as head of household under the abandoned spouse rules. Jett's AGI is $85,440.

    b. Eren is divorced. She and her ex-husband share custody of their four children, ages 2-8, but Eren is the custodial parent. She has not signed away her right to claim the children as dependents. She files as a head of household. Her AGI is $95,694.

    c. Michelle is 43 years old and a single parent. She claims her three children, ages 9, 14 and 17, as dependents. She files as a head of household. Her AGI is $123,639.

    d. Randy and Tammy O'Brien file a joint return. Tammy's 16-year-old sister lives with them the entire year. They claim the sister and their two-year-old daughter as dependents. The O'Briens' AGI is $145,800.

14. **Child Tax Credit.** (Obj. 2) Compute the child tax credit for each of the following taxpayers.

    a. Jay and Marie Stockton file a joint return and claim their three children, all under age 17, as dependents. The Stocktons' AGI is $121,400.

    b. DJ files as head of household. He claims his twin sons, age 4, as dependents. DJ's AGI is $80,340.

   c. Jenn files as head of household. She claims her 12-year-old daughter as a dependent. Jenn's AGI is $78,450.

15. **Refundable Child Tax Credit.** (Obj. 2) Pat and Diedra Donovan file a joint tax return for 2022. The Donovans' AGI is $30,900, of which $27,300 is taxable wages. The Donovans take the standard deduction and claim as dependents their two teenage children, ages 13 and 15. Other than the child tax credit, the Donovans do not claim any nonrefundable personal tax credits. Compute the Donovans' nonrefundable and refundable child tax credit.

16. **Nonbusiness Energy Property Credit.** (Obj. 2) During 2022, Maureen paid $5,500 to install qualified energy efficient improvements in her principal residence. What amount can Maureen claim as a tax credit on her 2022 tax return?

17. **Adoption Credit.** (Obj. 2) Jon and Mary Hoppe paid $15,000 in qualified adoption expenses of a healthy child. The adoption was finalized in 2022. The Hoppes' modified AGI is $228,312. In addition, Jon received $3,000 from an employer adoption assistance plan. Compute the Hoppes' adoption credit.

18. **Adoption Credit.** (Obj. 2) In 2021, a married couple paid $6,000 in qualified adoption expenses to adopt a child that is a U.S. citizen. In 2022, they paid an additional $4,200 in qualified adoption expenses. The adoption was finalized in 2022.

   a. Compute the couples' adoption credit if their modified AGI in both years is $115,000. In what year(s) is the credit taken?

   b. How would your answer to Part a. change if the couples' modified AGI was $234,940 in both years?

   c. How would your answer to Part a. change if the couple adopted a child with special needs?

   d. How would your answer to Part a. change if the adoption fell through?

19. **Adoption Credit.** (Obj. 2) In 2021, a married couple paid $14,000 in qualified adoption expenses to adopt a child that is a U.S. citizen. The adoption was finalized in 2022.

    a. Compute the adoption credit if the couple's modified AGI is $202,600 in 2021 and $217,890 in 2022. In what year(s) is the credit taken?

    b. How, if at all, would your answer to Part a. change if the couple adopted a foreign child?

    c. How, if at all, would your answer to Part b. change if the adoption fell through?

20. **Earned Income Credit.** (Obj. 2) For each of the following situations, compute the taxpayer's 2022 earned income credit.

    a. Patty and Ron Barnett file a joint return, claiming their two sons, ages 3 and 5, as dependents. The Barnetts' AGI is $14,400, which consists entirely of Ron's wages.

    b. Joseph is a 25-year-old graduate student. His gross income consists of $5,000 of wages, and $80 in interest from a savings account. Joseph files as single and claims no dependents.

    c. Suzanne and Vernon Zimmerman file a joint return, claiming their six-year-old daughter as a dependent. The Zimmermans' AGI consists of Vernon's $26,375 in wages, and $400 in dividend income.

    d. Sarah files as head of household, claiming her two-year-old son as a dependent. Sarah's AGI consists of $18,000 in wages and $3,620 in interest income.

21. **Earned Income Credit.** (Obj. 2) For each of the following situations, determine under the tie-break rules the person entitled to claim the qualifying child for purpose of the earned income credit.

   a. Kate (age 30) and her son, Jimmy (age 3), live with Kate's father, Fred, the entire year. Jimmy is a qualifying child to both Kate and Fred. Kate's AGI is $20,000; Fred's is $64,000.

   b. Ned and Tammy are divorced. They share custody of their twin sons, age 13. The boys live with Ned half of the year and with Tammy the other half of the year. Tammy lives with her parents. The twins are qualifying children to Ned, Tammy, and Tammy's parents. Ned's AGI is $45,000, Tammy's AGI is $20,200, and the parents' AGI is $36,900.

   c. Same as in Part b., except that the boys spend more days with Tammy during the year.

   d. Same as in Part b., except that the boys spend more days with Ned during the year.

   e. Darcy's parents are both deceased. Darcy is 15 and is being raised by her aunt. Her grandparents also participate in her upbringing and support. Darcy is a qualifying child for both her aunt and her grandparents. The aunt's AGI is $21,500. The grandparents' AGI is $45,300.

22. **Premium Tax Credit.** (Objs. 2 and 3) During all of 2022, each of the following taxpayers fully comply with the ACA mandate to carry minimum essential (health care) coverage. Compute each taxpayer's premium tax credit.

   a. John, who is single, buys his health insurance through the federal Marketplace. He selects the bronze plan, and his premiums for the year are $2,500. Had John selected the silver plan, his premiums would have been $4,000. Based on his household income and family size, the government has determined that John's annual contribution for health care is $1,400.

b.   Same as in part a., except that John's premiums under the bronze plan were $3,000.

c.   The Wagners purchase a bronze plan through the federal Marketplace. The Wagners file a joint tax return, and their premiums for 2022 were $5,000. Had the Wagners selected the silver plan, their premiums would have been $8,000. Based on their household income and family size, the government has determined that the Wagners' annual contribution for health care is $6,400.

d.   Same as in part c., except that the Wagners' annual contribution for health care is $2,200.

23. **Tax Planning**. (Obj. 1) Mary and Chuck, unmarried individuals, are both 29 years of age. For 2022, Mary and Chuck will earn wages of $60,000 and $35,000, respectively. This will be their only source of income. They are considering getting married in either December 2022 or January 2023. Before setting a wedding date, they want to know how much they will save in federal income taxes if they get married in December and file a joint return. They ask you to compare their combined federal income taxes as single individuals with their taxes as a married couple filing jointly. Neither taxpayer has any dependents. Also, no other taxpayer can claim either of them as a dependent. Regardless of their marital status, they will claim the standard deduction.

24. **Internet Problem: Filling out Form 4868**. (Obj. 4)
Cheryl Bier needs more time to file her 2022 tax return. Cheryl expects her total tax liability to be $16,500. She had $15,800 withheld from her wages. Cheryl (SSN 678-00-1234) lives at 829 North Broadway, Garden Grove, CA 92842.
Go to the IRS website and locate Form 4868, Application for Automatic Extension of Time To File U.S. Individual Income Tax Return. Using the computer, fill in the form for Cheryl and print out a completed copy.
See Appendix A for instructions on use of the IRS website.

COMPREHENSIVE PROBLEM

25. Toni Tornan is a single parent. During 2022 she earned wages $26,750. Her employer did not withhold federal income taxes from her pay. Toni claims her two children, age 5 and 8, as dependents. The wages are Toni's only source of gross income. Compute Toni's taxable income and her taxes due to (or from) the government when she files her 2022 tax return.

CUMULATIVE PROBLEM 1 (CHAPTERS 1-2)

Jack Bennett is married but does not file a joint return with his spouse. He is 36 years of age and has excellent vision. Jack and his wife share custody of their ten-year-old son. They have lived in separate households since May 2022. Jack is not the custodial parent, but his wife has signed Form 8332, allowing Jack to claim their son as a dependent. Jack's AGI is $63,440 (all from wages) and he uses the standard deduction. His employer withheld $8,000 for federal income taxes during the year. Compute Jack's 2022 taxable income and taxes owed (to be refunded).

CUMULATIVE PROBLEM 2 (CHAPTERS 1-2)

Emily and David Chen claim their three children, ages 5-10, as dependents. During 2022, Emily worked full-time and earned $39,850. Her employer withheld nothing for federal income taxes. David attended college full-time for the entire year. Other than Emily's wages, the couple's only other source of earned income is $800 of taxable interest. (David received a tax-free scholarship that paid for his college tuition, book, and fees.) The Chens paid $2,500 in qualified childcare expenses so that Emily could work and David could attend college. Compute the couple's taxable income and taxes owed (to be refunded) on their 2022 joint tax return. The couple uses the standard deduction. They are both under age 65 and have no problems with their vision.

Chapter

3

Gross Income Inclusions

CHAPTER CONTENTS

LEARNING OBJECTIVES

After completing Chapter 3, you should be able to:

1. Recognize the various types of income and determine in what tax year income should be reported.
2. Describe how pensions, annuities, IRA distributions, and social security benefits are taxed.
3. Explain how the tax laws treat the income from original issue discount (OID) bonds, market discount bonds, and below market loans.
4. Explain the tax treatment of distributions from corporations and mutual funds, including ordinary dividends, return of capital distributions, and capital gain distributions.
5. Determine how investment income is taxed for certain children and higher-income taxpayers.
6. Prepare the forms and schedules introduced in the chapter, including Schedule B, and Form 8615.

CHAPTER OVERVIEW

Chapters 1 and 2 presented an overview of the basic tax and reporting structure. They illustrated several tax forms, schedules, and worksheets, including the simplest tax return. The next few chapters focus on particular segments of the taxable income formula, starting with gross income.

As was discussed in Chapter 1, the amount of gross income determines whether an individual must file a tax return and whether a person qualifies as a dependent. Strangely, though, nowhere on Form 1040 do taxpayers report their gross income.

Chapter 3 and the first half of Chapter 4 examine the two components of gross income, namely "income" and "exclusions" from gross income. Chapter 3 starts off the discussion of gross income by examining items of income that, with few exceptions, remain in gross income. This includes sources of earned income (like wages and business income), retirement income (like social security and pension benefits), and investment income (like interest, dividends, and rental income). Chapter 4 continues the discussion of gross income by examining the most common types of exclusions, which are items of income subtracted from total income in arriving at gross income.

¶301   General Recognition Guidelines

Gross income is all income from every source, except those sources specifically excluded by tax law. [I.R.C. §61(a)] Thus, taxpayers face two problems:

1. Determining income, and
2. Identifying exclusions (income that is not taxed).

Although the Internal Revenue Code (Code) does not define income, it generally includes any increase in wealth (assets minus liabilities). Taxpayers usually report income only in the year it is realized as determined by their accounting method. There are two principal overall accounting methods [I.R.C. §446]:

1. The cash method, and
2. The accrual method.

Cash basis taxpayers report income in the year money, property, or services are actually or constructively received in an income-producing event. **Constructive receipt** takes place when assets are credited or made available to the taxpayer without restriction (e.g., interest credited to the taxpayer's bank account.) Taxpayers report as income the amount of money or the value of property and services they receive.

Accrual basis taxpayers normally report income in the year they earn it, regardless of when they receive the cash. They report service revenue in income in the year they perform the services. They report interest in income in the year the interest accrues. They report the revenues from the sale of goods in the year the sale occurs.

Although appreciation in property values may cause an increase in wealth, the tax law does not recognize mere appreciation of assets as income. Instead, taxpayers must convert the property into cash or other property before realizing a gain. Furthermore, only the excess of the amount realized over the taxpayer's investment in the property (known as "basis") counts as income.

¶301.01   EXCEPTIONS

Accrual basis taxpayers normally report income in the year they earn it. However, certain advanced payments are taxed in the year received. [Reg. §1.451-1(a)] This includes payments for interest income and for warranty services offered by third parties. It also includes most prepaid rent.

There is a special rule that permits deferral of warranty income when the seller of a product provides the warranty. [Rev. Proc. 97-38, 1997-2 C.B. 479] This rule allows the seller to prorate the warranty over its period. This rule does not apply to third-party warranty providers.

EXAMPLE 1

On November 2, 2021, Jenny buys an appliance from ASE, a local retailer. She pays ASE $900 for a warranty that will cover all repair costs for the first two years. ASE uses a calendar tax year and the accrual method. Since the seller (not a third party) offered the warranty, ASE prorates the income over two years. In 2021, ASE reports income of $75 ($900/24 × 2 months). ASE reports the rest ($900 − $75 = $825) in 2022. Even though the warranty extends into 2023, ASE cannot defer (delay) the income beyond the second tax year.

EXAMPLE 2

Same facts as in Example 1, except that Jenny buys the warranty from a third party. The third party must include the $900 in income in 2021. The rule that allows the deferral of income to the next tax year does not apply to warranties offered by third parties.

Accrual method taxpayers may report certain advance payments over two tax years. Income earned in the year the payment is received is reported as income in that year. The rest is reported as income in the next year. This rule holds even if the payment is for goods and services that extend beyond the second year. [I.R.C. §451(c)]

EXAMPLE 3	On August 1, 2021, an accrual basis taxpayer, Dance Studio, received $1,800 for 36 dance lessons. Eight lessons are given in 2021. On its 2021 tax return, Dance Studio reports $400 ($1,800/36 × 8). It reports the rest ($1,800 − $400 = $1,400) in 2022.

EXAMPLE 4	On April 6, 2021, accrual basis taxpayer, Golf World, received $2,400 for 48 golf lessons under a two-year contract. Ten lessons are given in 2021, 20 were given in 2022, and 15 were given in 2023. The customer forfeited the last three lessons. On its 2021 tax return, Golf World reports income of $500 ($2,400/48 × 10). It reports the rest ($2,400 − $500 = $1,900) in 2022. The fact that some of the services were provided in 2023 (or never provided at all) does not affect the timing of when the $1,900 is reported in gross income.

¶302   Employee Compensation

Employee compensation includes wages, salaries, commissions, bonuses, and tips. Employers inform their employees of their taxable compensation for the year on Form W-2. Employees include the amount reported in the box labeled "Wages, tips, other compensation" from Form W-2 on their tax returns. Employees report compensation on Form 1040. Students who receive scholarships add the taxable amount to their wages. Thus, these too can be reported on any of the three tax returns. The tax laws that govern scholarship income are discussed in ¶401.07. Form W-2 is illustrated in Figure 13-3 (¶1303.03).

¶302.01   FEES, BONUSES, COMMISSIONS, SALARIES, AND WAGES

Compensation is something received in exchange for services rendered. Most compensation is taxable, regardless of the form it takes. When a person receives compensation in the form of property, the Code taxes its fair market value (FMV). For example, when a person speaks at a conference and is paid by being given free merchandise, the speaker includes the FMV of the merchandise in gross income.

 Fair market value (FMV) is the price that a willing buyer will pay and a willing seller will accept. FMV assumes that neither the buyer nor the seller <u>must</u> buy or sell. It also assumes that the buyer and the seller have reasonable knowledge of all necessary facts. In the absence of an actual sale or exchange, FMV can be determined by an expert appraisal or other supporting evidence.

Unless an exclusion applies, an employee who provides services and receives something of value in return has taxable compensation. Taxpayers include as compensation amounts withheld from their pay for social security, Medicare, and income taxes. Compensation also includes amounts withheld to pay insurance premiums, union dues, etc. Unless specifically exempt by the tax laws, compensation includes all employee fringe benefits (additional compensation provided by employers, discussed in the next chapter at ¶401.05).

¶302.02   TIPS

The Code taxes tips as other compensation. This includes cash tips and credit card tips received from customers or other employees. Taxpayers who receive tips must follow special reporting rules.

Reporting Tips to the Employer

Employees are expected to file tip reports with their employers by the 10th day of the month that follows the month in which they receive the tips. However, employers may require more frequent reporting. Employers add reported tip income to wages on the employee's Form W-2. Thus, employees who receive tips in December 2021 and report the tips to their employers in January 2022 will have these tips added to the wages reported on their 2022 Form W-2. When employees fail to turn in tip reports, they must add their unreported tips to their wages in the year they receive the tips.

Tips of Less than $20

Employees who receive less than $20 in tips during the month while working for one employer do not need to tell the employer about that month's tips. Although employees must add these tips to their wages on their tax returns, they do not pay social security or Medicare taxes on these tips.

EXAMPLE 5	Rodney works for a hotel. Sometimes, hotel guests give him tips. However, his total tips are always less than $20 a month. Rodney's tips for the year total $165. He adds this amount to his taxable wages when he files his tax return. Although Rodney pays income tax on his tip income, he does not pay social security or Medicare taxes on the $165.

Tips of $20 or More

An employee who receives $20 or more in tips during the month while working for one employer must report that month's tips to the employer. The employer adds reported tips to the employee's wages and withholds social security and Medicare taxes, as well as income taxes on the reported amounts. [I.R.C. §6053]

Employees who have monthly tips of $20 or more but fail to report them to their employers add the unreported tips to their wages on Form 1040. Employees then compute social security and Medicare taxes on their unreported tips on Form 4137, Social Security and Medicare Tax on Unreported Tip Income. These social security and Medicare taxes are added to the employee's other taxes on page 2 of Form 1040. Employees must attach Form 4137 to their tax returns. [I.R.C. §1041]

Allocating Tips to Employees

The government assumes that food and beverage servers earn tips equal to at least 8% of gross sales. When employees of certain large restaurants and bars report less than this amount to their employers, the employers must pay their employees the difference and report it as additional income on the employees' Form W-2. These "allocated tips" appear on Form W-2 as a separate item. Employers do not report them with wages and reported tips. Thus, employers do not withhold income, social security, or Medicare taxes on these amounts. Employees add their allocated tips to their taxable wages on Form 1040. They then complete and attach Form 4137 to their tax return to pay social security and Medicare taxes on their allocated tip income.

 Allocating tips usually applies to businesses that employ more than ten persons on a typical business day. Only businesses that serve food or beverages on the premises and have regular tipping customers are subject to this rule. Cafeterias and fast-food restaurants are exempt from this rule.

¶303   Business Activities

Amounts independent contractors and business owners receive for their goods and services are reported as business income on Schedule C, Profit or Loss From Business (Sole Proprietorship). Deductible business expenses are also reported on Schedule C. Schedule C is the focus of Chapter 7. Special rules apply to farming because of the unique activities associated with growing crops, raising animals, and maintaining land and other resources. Thus, income and expenses from farming activities are reported on Schedule F, Profit or Loss From Farming, rather than Schedule C.

¶304   Divorce and Separation Agreements

When a married couple gets a divorce or becomes legally separated, three financial issues arise:

1. Division of marital property (property settlement),
2. Spousal support (alimony), and
3. Support of the children (child support).

¶304.01   PROPERTY SETTLEMENT

A property settlement involves the transfer of cash and other property between spouses or former spouses during the process of splitting up marital assets. Neither party reports income or deductions on these transfers. The transferee's investment ("tax basis") in the property received is the same as that of the transferor. [I.R.C. §1041]

EXAMPLE 6

Tim and Cher Hudsen's divorce was finalized during the year. As part of the divorce decree, Tim transferred to Cher title to the couple's vacation home. At the time of the transfer, the home was worth $250,000. Tim bought the home prior to their marriage. He paid $110,000 for the home. Cher does not report gross income on the transfer. Her tax basis in the home is $110,000. Cher uses this to determine her taxable gain when she later sells the home.

¶304.02   ALIMONY

Spousal support (alimony) is taxable to the recipient and deductible by the payer. A person receiving spousal support reports it as "Alimony received" on Form 1040, if the alimony is received pursuant to a divorce decreed or modified before 2019. The payer deducts the same amount for AGI and provides the IRS with the recipient's social security number (SSN). The IRS charges the taxpayer $50 for failure to report the recipient's SSN.

The deduction for alimony and separate maintenance payments, as well as the inclusion of the payments in gross income, are repealed for divorce or separation instruments executed or modified after 2018.

For separations and divorces that occur after 1984, payments to a spouse or former spouse must meet several conditions in order to qualify as alimony: [I.R.C. §215] [**Note.** Although I.R.C. §215 was repealed, it remains in effect for alimony payments from pre-2019 divorces.]

1. The payment must be made in cash.
2. The payment cannot be for child support.
3. The payment must be required under a legal divorce decree or a separate maintenance or divorce instrument.
4. The governing decree or instrument must not label payments as something other than alimony.
5. The payer must not be required to make payments after the recipient's death.
6. The parties cannot be living in the same household at the time of the payment.

A different set of rules applies to divorces and separations occurring before 1985. These rules can be found in IRS Publication 504, *Divorced or Separated Individuals*.

¶304.03   CHILD SUPPORT

The Code excludes child support payments from gross income. [I.R.C. §71(c)] [**Note.** Although I.R.C. §71 was repealed, it remains in effect for alimony payments from pre-2019 divorces.] The exclusion applies to payments clearly labeled as child support as well as those that can be implied as child support. For example, if payments to a former spouse decline when the child reaches age 18, the tax law treats the amount of the reduction as child support. When the total alimony and child support payments are less than the required amount, payments first apply toward child support.

EXAMPLE 7	Bud and Suzie divorced in 2015. As part of the divorce decree, Bud is to pay Suzie $1,600 each month. The agreement states that $700 represents support for their eight-year-old son. During the year, Bud pays Suzie $19,200 ($1,600 × 12). Suzie reports in gross income the $10,800 she received that represents alimony ($1,600 – $700 = $900 × 12). Bud deducts this same amount for AGI on his tax return and gives the IRS Suzie's SSN.

EXAMPLE 8	Same facts as in Example 7, except that the divorce decree states that the entire $1,600 payment represents alimony. However, Bud's payments drop to $900 once the son turns 18. The tax laws treat the $700 reduction in payments as child support. Since $8,400 of the total payments ($700 × 12) is considered nontaxable child support, Suzie reports $10,800 ($19,200 – $8,400) in gross income as alimony. Bud deducts this same $10,800 for AGI on his tax return and gives the IRS Suzie's SSN.

EXAMPLE 9	Same facts as in Example 7, except that Bud fails to make two of his required payments during the year. Suzie receives $16,000 ($1,600 × 10 monthly payments) during the year. Of this amount, $8,400 is considered to be child support ($700 × 12). Suzie reports $7,600 ($16,000 – $8,400) in gross income as alimony. Bud deducts this same $7,600 for AGI on his tax return and gives the IRS Suzie's SSN.

EXAMPLE 10	Same facts as in Example 7, except that the divorce occurred in 2019. Bud receives no deduction and Suzie has no gross income resulting from these payments.

¶305   Distributions from Traditional IRAs

Persons who stop working often pay their expenses during their retirement from a variety of sources, including amounts saved and invested during their working years. Common sources of income retirees may receive include social security benefits, distributions from retirement plans, and earnings from investments. The tax laws regarding these types of income are discussed below and in the sections that follow, through ¶311.

Individual retirement arrangements (IRAs) are a type of retirement account. Unlike pension plans that are offered through and often funded by an employer, IRAs are set up and funded by the worker. There are two types of IRAs: traditional IRAs and Roth IRAs. The most attractive feature of IRAs is that earnings from these accounts are not taxed when earned. [I.R.C. §408] Instead, these earnings are either taxed when withdrawn (traditional IRAs) or excluded from income (Roth IRAs).

Persons with earned income can contribute to an IRA. Earned income includes wages, net income from self-employment, and alimony. Some people can deduct amounts they contribute to a traditional IRA, whereas contributions to a Roth IRA are never deductible. Those who cannot make deductible contributions to their traditional IRAs can still make nondeductible contributions. The rules regarding the deductibility of contributions to traditional IRAs are discussed in Chapter 4 (¶402.10). Because the earnings taken out of Roth IRAs are excluded from gross income, the tax laws regarding contributions to and distributions from Roth IRAs are discussed along with other gross income exclusions in Chapter 4 (¶401.09). The discussion that follows pertains solely to distributions from traditional IRAs.

Deductible contributions to an IRA are made with "pre-tax" dollars, which means that these amounts have yet to be taxed. Nondeductible contributions, on the other hand, are made with "after-tax" dollars. To illustrate this distinction, assume a person with $10,000 of wages contributes $2,000 to an IRA. If the $2,000 is deducted for AGI, the person's AGI from those wages is $8,000 ($10,000 – $2,000). Deductible contributions are made with what is called "pre-tax" dollars, as only $8,000 of the $10,000 has been taxed at this point. In contrast, AGI would include the entire $10,000 if the $2,000 contribution were not deductible. Hence, nondeductible contributions are made with taxable dollars, usually referred to as "after-tax" dollars.

When a taxpayer withdraws amounts from a traditional IRA, only the amount that has not been previously taxed is included in gross income. If no nondeductible contributions were ever made, then the entire distribution came entirely from a combination of deductible contributions and earnings. Thus, all amounts withdrawn would be taxable. However, if nondeductible contributions were made, then the portion of the distribution that represents nondeductible contributions is not taxed again. Taxpayers use the following formula to compute the nontaxable portion of their distributions.

$$\frac{\text{Balance of nondeductible contributions}}{\text{Value of the IRA}} \times \text{Distribution} = \text{Nontaxable distribution}$$

The numerator in the fraction represents the amount of nondeductible contributions that remain in the IRA account. Right before the very first distribution from the account is made, this amount is the total of all nondeductible contributions the taxpayer made over the years. Once distributions begin, this amount is reduced each year by the nontaxable portion of the distribution (as computed using the formula above). Thus, it is up to the taxpayer to keep track of the nondeductible contributions that are still left in the IRA account. The denominator in the fraction is the value in the IRA account, which is measured as account balance at the end of the year plus the withdrawals made during the year.

EXAMPLE 11	Over the years, Peter made nondeductible contributions to his traditional IRA. At the beginning of the year, he had yet to withdraw $40,000 of his nondeductible contributions. At the end of the year, the value of the assets in the IRA was $120,000. During the year, Peter withdrew $30,000 from the account. Therefore, the value of the IRA was $150,000 ($120,000 + $30,000). Using the above formula, Peter computes his $8,000 nontaxable distribution ($40,000/$150,000 × $30,000). Only $22,000 of the distribution is included in Peter's gross income ($30,000 – $8,000).

EXAMPLE 12	Same facts as in Example 11, except that all of Peter's contributions were deductible. Peter includes the entire $30,000 distribution in his gross income.

¶305.01   AVOIDING PENALTIES

The timing of distributions from a traditional IRA is important, as penalties are imposed on withdrawals taken either too early or too late. A 10% penalty is imposed on taxpayers who take a distribution before reaching age 59½. [I.R.C. §4974(c)] This penalty can be avoided if the early distribution is:

1.   Due to the IRA owner's death or disability,
2.   Made as part of a series of equal periodic payments over the owner's life expectancy (or the joint life expectancies of the owner and the owner's spouse),
3.   Used to pay unreimbursed qualified medical expenses in excess of the AGI floor,
4.   Used by an unemployed IRA owner to buy health insurance for the owner, the owner's spouse, or the owner's dependents,
5.   Used to pay qualified higher education expenses,
6.   Used to pay expenses as a qualified first-time homebuyer ($10,000 lifetime limit), or
7.   Made as part of a qualified distribution by a military reservist called up to active duty.

A penalty is also imposed if the taxpayer waits too long before starting to take (and paying taxes on) distributions. Taxpayers are required to start taking distributions from their traditional IRAs when they reach a certain age. [I.R.C. §401(a)(9)] Before 2020, the law required each person with a balance in a traditional IRA or other qualified retirement plan to begin receiving distributions in the year in which he or she reached age 70½. Beginning in 2020, that age increased to 72.

A taxpayer may defer the first distribution until as late as April 1 of the next year. This exception only applies to the first distribution. If a taxpayer chooses to defer the first distribution to the year after they turn 72, they must make both the first and second year distributions. For example, a taxpayer who reaches age 72 in 2021 has until April 1, 2022 to make the first required distribution. The taxpayer then has until December 31, 2022 to make the second required distribution. Alternatively, the taxpayer can take the first distribution prior to the end of 2021 and spread out the first two distributions over two tax years. At the time distributions are required to start, the taxpayer may choose to withdraw the entire balance in the account, or start receiving periodical distributions over the taxpayer's life expectancy. Failure to make the required minimum distributions results in a penalty equal to 50% of the shortage.

Taxpayers who reached age 70½ in 2019 and received a distribution in 2020 before the law changed were allowed to return the distribution and avoid tax liability. This was a rule unique to 2020.

¶305.02   REPORTING TRADITIONAL IRA DISTRIBUTIONS

Taxpayers who receive distributions from IRAs receive Form 1099-R, Distributions From Pensions, Annuities, Retirement or Profit-Sharing Plans, IRAs, Insurance Contracts, etc. This form shows the total distributions received during the year from that payor, and sometimes provides the taxable amount. The taxable amount is the total distribution minus the nontaxable amount computed using the formula from ¶305.

Taxpayers report their distributions from traditional IRAs on Form 1040, including the 10% early withdrawal penalty if one is imposed. Taxpayers report on the tax return both their total distribution and the taxable amount.

¶306   Pensions and Annuities

Two other common sources of a retiree's income are pension benefits and annuity income. Each of these is discussed in the sections that follow.

¶306.01   PENSIONS

Retired workers receive a pension if they participated in their employer's pension plan during their working years. Persons receiving a pension get a series of cash payments (benefits) that last for the rest of their lives. Many pensions pay benefits for the lives of the retiree's spouse as well. Often, contributions to the employee's pension plan were made either by the employee with pre-tax amounts or by the employer. The pension benefits from these plans have never been taxed and are 100% taxable when paid to the retiree. However, if any of the employee's contributions were made with after-tax dollars, a formula similar to that used to compute the nontaxable portion of IRA withdrawals must be used to determine the nontaxable pension benefits.

Each year, employers send retirees a Form 1099-R. This form shows the total benefits paid during the year. Often the employer is able to provide the retiree with both the taxable and non-taxable portions of those benefits. Persons who started receiving their pensions from a qualified retirement plan after November 18, 1996, use the following formula to compute the nontaxable portion of their monthly pension benefits.

$$\frac{\textbf{After-tax contributions}}{\textbf{Number of monthly payments}} = \textbf{Nontaxable amount}$$

If the number of payments is fixed, the number of payments is used as the denominator. However, most pension benefits are paid for the rest of the retiree's life, and thus, the number of expected monthly payments is used in the denominator. [I.R.C. §72(d)] The number of expected monthly payments is based on the retiree's age when payments begin and determined from Table 3-1:

Table 3-1 Expected Number of Monthly Payments, Single Life	
Age as of the Starting Date	**Number of Expected Monthly Payments**
55 and under	360
56–60	310
61–65	260
66–70	210
71 and over	160

When benefits are paid over the lives of both the retiree and the retiree's spouse, the number of expected monthly payments is determined by the couple's combined ages using Table 3-2.

Table 3-2 Expected Number of Monthly Payments, Joint Lives	
Combined Age as of the Starting Date	**Number of Expected Monthly Payments**
110 and under	410
111–120	360
121–130	310
131–140	260
141 and over	210

When the payments are not made on a monthly basis, the numbers from these tables must be adjusted. For example, if the payments are quarterly, the number of payments from the table is divided by four.

These procedures apply only to qualified pension plans where some or all of the taxpayer's contributions have already been taxed. If no taxes have been paid on any of the contributions into the plan, all payments (benefits) are taxed.

¶306.01

EXAMPLE 13	On July 1, 2021, Jason (age 65) retired and started receiving $4,000 a month from his employer's pension plan. Based on his age, Jason is expected to receive 260 payments over his lifetime. Over the years, Jason had contributed $124,800 to the plan with after-tax dollars. Each month, the nontaxable portion of Jason's payment is $480 ($124,800/260 payments). Thus, for 2021 his total benefits are $24,000 ($4,000 × 6). His taxable amount is $21,120 ($24,000 − ($480 × 6)). He includes the $21,120 in gross income. For 2022, Jason's total benefits are $48,000 ($4,000 × 12). His taxable amount is $42,240 ($48,000 − ($480 × 12)). He includes the $42,240 in his gross income for 2022.

EXAMPLE 14	Same facts as in Example 13, except that Jason is married and his wife is age 62 at the time he begins receiving his pension. The pension benefits will continue for both Jason and his wife's lives. Based on their combined age of 127, this is expected to be 310 months. Each month, the nontaxable portion of the payment is $402.58 ($124,800/310). Thus, for 2021, taxable amount of their pension benefits is $21,585 ($24,000 − ($402.58 × 6)). For 2022, the taxable amount is $43,169 ($48,000 − ($402.58 × 12)).

Taxpayers report both the total and taxable pension benefits on Form 1040.

Because the formula for determining the nontaxable pension payments uses life expectancy tables, it is possible that the payments will continue beyond the expected number of payments. Likewise, they could stop before the full amount of the after-tax contributions has been recovered. For pensions starting after November 18, 1996, any payments received beyond the number of payments used in the formula are fully taxable. If payments stop before the last of the number of payments used in the formula, any unrecovered contribution amounts are taken as an itemized deduction on the final income tax return of the deceased.

EXAMPLE 15	Going back to the facts in Example 13, assume that Jason dies on April 9, 2029. At the time of his death, Jason had received 94 of the 260 payments he was expected to receive over his lifetime. For 2029, Jason's final income tax return shows total pension benefits of $16,000 ($4,000 × 4) and taxable benefits of $14,080 ($16,000 − ($480 × 4)). The $14,080 is included in gross income. The unrecovered contributions of $79,680 ($124,800 − ($480 × 94)) are taken as an itemized deduction on Jason's 2029 final tax return.

¶306.02   ANNUITIES

Recipients of annuity payments pay for the right to receive cash payments for the rest of their lives (life annuity) or for a set period of time (term annuity). The amount paid for this right is typically made with after-tax dollars. Thus, the portion of each annuity payment that comes from these previously taxed amounts is not taxed again. These amounts are a return of the recipient's previously taxed investment in the annuity. The formula used to determine the nontaxable portion of the annuity payments is as follows:

$$\frac{\text{Amount paid for the annuity}}{\text{Total expected return}} \times \text{Amount received} = \text{Nontaxable proceeds}$$

When computing the total expected return for a life annuity, life expectancy tables are used to estimate how long the recipient is expected to live (and how many payments are estimated to be made). For a term annuity, the term of the annuity is used to compute the expected return. Once determined, the ratio in the formula does not change. For annuities starting after 1986, this ratio is used each year until the recipient has recovered the entire investment in the annuity. After that, all payments are subject to tax. If the payments are based on the recipient's life expectancy, and the recipient dies before recovering his or her entire investment, the tax laws allow the unrecovered amounts to be deducted as an itemized deduction on the deceased's final tax return. For annuities that started before 1987, the formula is used until the payments cease, and no deduction is allowed for any unrecovered amounts.

EXAMPLE 16	Late last year, Sally purchased a life annuity for $72,000. The annuity pays equal annual installments of $8,000 beginning January 1 of the current year. Sally's life expectancy is 12 years. She computes the taxable portion of each payment as follows:

Investment in contract	$72,000
Expected return ($8,000 × 12 years)	÷ $96,000
Exclusion percentage	75%
Amount received during a year	$8,000
Less: Exclusion ($8,000 × 75%)	(6,000)
Taxable portion	$2,000

For the first 12 years, Sally includes $2,000 in gross income from the annuity. After the 12th year, she includes all $8,000 in gross income each year. If Sally should die before receiving the 12th payment, she would deduct the unrecovered portion of her $72,000 investment in the annuity as an itemized deduction on her final tax return.

¶307   Social Security Benefits

Nine out of every ten persons age 65 or older receive social security benefits. Dependents of these persons also receive social security benefits until they turn 18. Other persons who receive social security benefits are disabled workers and dependents of disabled workers until they turn 18.

Many social security recipients are not taxed on the benefits they receive. Some, however, must include a portion of their social security benefits in gross income. [I.R.C. §86] Depending on the amount of the taxpayer's "modified AGI," they can be taxed on 50% to 85% of their social security benefits. Examples 17–19 show how the taxable portion of social security benefits is computed.

To determine if social security is taxable, a taxpayer compares a base amount with a modified AGI amount. If the modified AGI is larger than the base amount, then a portion of the social security benefits are taxable. For purposes of social security, taxpayers are either considered (1) single, which includes head of household, qualifying widow(er), and married filing separately if the taxpayer lived away from their spouse all year, (2) married filing jointly, or (3) married filing separately and did not live away from their spouse. For single taxpayers, the base amount is $25,000; for married taxpayers, it is $32,000; and for married filing separate taxpayers, the base amount is zero. Modified AGI for this purpose is computed as ½ of social security benefits plus taxable income including wages, pensions, interest, ordinary dividends, and capital gains, plus tax-exempt interest.

Taxpayers whose modified AGI exceeds the base amount are subject to tax on 50% of their social security benefits or 50% of the amount by which their modified AGI exceeds the base amount, whichever is less. Once taxpayers reach a second threshold, that amount increases to 85% of social security or 85% of the amount by which their modified AGI exceeds the second threshold plus the lessor of 50% of social security or $4,500 if single, or $6,000 if married. The second threshold for single taxpayers is $34,000 and for married taxpayers, it is $44,000. Let's go through a couple of examples.

EXAMPLE 17	Derrick May is unmarried. His adjusted gross income (AGI) is $31,500, not including $13,500 of social security benefits. Derrick also has $3,500 of tax-exempt interest.

1. AGI before social security	$31,500
2. Plus: 50% of social security benefits (50% × $13,500)	6,750
3. Plus: Tax-exempt interest	3,500
4. Modified AGI	$41,750
5. Less: Base amount*	(25,000)

    * *$32,000 MFJ; $0 MFS and lived with spouse during part of the year; $25,000 all others*

6. Excess modified AGI	$16,750
7. 50% of excess modified AGI (from line 6)	$ 8,375
8. Tentative taxable social security benefits (lesser of line 2 or line 7)	$ 6,750

If modified AGI (line 4) does not exceed the threshold amount ($44,000 for MFJ; $0 for MFS taxpayers who lived with spouse during part of the year; $34,000 for all others), the amount on line 8 equals the taxable social security benefits. If modified AGI exceeds the threshold amount, the following calculations are required.

9. The lesser of the amount from line 8 or a set amount ($6,000 for MFJ; $0 for MFS and lived with spouse any part of the year; $4,500 for all others)	$ 4,500
10. Plus: 85% × ($41,750 modified AGI − $34,000 threshold for unmarried taxpayers)	6,588
11. Sum of lines 9 and 10	$11,088
12. 85% of social security benefits (85% × $13,500)	$11,475
13. Taxable social security benefits (lesser of line 11 or line 12)	$11,088

EXAMPLE 18	Same facts as in Example 17, except Derrick is married and files a joint return with his wife.

1. AGI before social security	$31,500
2. Plus: 50% of social security benefits	6,750
3. Plus: Tax-exempt interest	3,500
4. Modified AGI	$41,750
5. Less: Base amount ($32,000 for MFJ)	(32,000)
6. Excess modified AGI	$ 9,750
7. 50% of excess modified AGI (from line 6)	$ 4,875
8. Tentative taxable social security benefits (lesser of line 2 or line 7)	$ 4,875

Since the Mays' modified AGI (line 4) does not exceed the $44,000 threshold for MFJ taxpayers, the Mays' taxable social security benefits equal the $4,875 from line 8.

EXAMPLE 19	Same facts as in Example 18, except that Derrick files separately from his wife, whom he lived with during part of the year. Derrick computes his $11,475 of taxable social security benefits as follows.	
	1. AGI before social security	$31,500
	2. Plus: 50% of social security benefits	6,750
	3. Plus: Tax-exempt interest	3,500
	4. Modified AGI	$41,750
	5. Less: Base amount ($0 since MFS and lived with spouse part of the year)	(0)
	6. Excess modified AGI	$41,750
	7. 50% of excess modified AGI (from line 4)	$20,875
	8. Tentative taxable social security benefits (lesser of line 2 or line 7)	$ 6,750
	Since Derrick's modified AGI (line 4) exceeds the $0 threshold for MFS taxpayers who lived with spouse during part of the year, he must complete lines 9–13.	
	9. The lesser of line 8 or $0 threshold	$ 0
	10. Plus: 85% × ($41,750 Modified AGI – $0 threshold)	35,488
	11. Sum of lines 9 and 10	$35,488
	12. 85% of social security benefits	$11,475
	13. Taxable social security benefits (lesser of line 11 or line 12)	$11,475

Taxpayers who receive social security benefits report both the gross and taxable amounts on Form 1040.

¶308   Interest Income

Interest represents a charge for the use of money. Gross income includes interest received on bank deposits, notes, mortgages, corporate bonds, and U.S. savings bonds. Gross income also includes interest on income tax refunds. In some cases, the IRS requires taxpayers to impute interest income on low interest or no interest loans. Unless an exception applies, all interest is included in gross income. One example of an exception is the interest from municipal bonds, which the tax laws exempt from gross income. Other exclusions are discussed in Chapter 4.

In the case of higher income taxpayers, interest income may also be a component of net investment income. See ¶315.

¶308.01   SAVINGS ACCOUNTS AND CERTIFICATES

Gross income includes interest taxpayers receive from banks. This includes interest received on checking accounts, savings accounts, certificates of deposit (CDs), and so forth. When a bank credits a taxpayer's account with interest, a cash basis taxpayer includes the interest in gross income under the constructive receipt rule (¶301). Once the interest has been credited to the account, it belongs to the taxpayer and is taxable at that time.

¶308.02   U.S. SAVINGS BONDS

The federal government issues U.S. savings bonds. Investors can buy Series EE savings bonds by paying a fraction of their face value (amount paid at maturity). They then redeem the bonds for full face value at maturity. The difference between the cost of the bond and its face value represents interest (the amount paid to investors for the use of their money). Investors can also buy Series I savings bonds from the government. These bonds are purchased at face value. Interest on Series I bonds accrues every three months. The accrued interest is added to the redemption value of the bond.

The tax laws allow cash-basis investors two options for reporting the interest on U.S. savings bonds. The first option is to wait until they redeem the bonds to report all accrued (accumulated) interest. Under this option, the difference between the redemption amount (which includes accrued interest) and the amount paid for the bonds would be included in gross income. Under the second option, investors can elect to report the interest in gross income as it accrues each year. The accrued interest is the difference between in the bond's redemption value at end and the start of the year. If the taxpayer elects to report the accrued interest each year, the taxpayer's investment in the bonds increases by the amounts reported in income. Whichever method is selected, it must be used for all U.S. savings bonds the taxpayer owns.

EXAMPLE 20	Carl buys Series EE U.S. savings bonds for $500 during 2021. The face value of the bonds is $1,000. At the end of 2021, the redemption value of the bonds is $520; at the end of 2022, it is $543. Carl has two options for reporting the interest on the bonds. He can wait until he redeems the bonds to report the interest. For example, if Carl waits to redeem the bonds for their $1,000 face value, he will report $500 ($1,000 − $500 purchase price) of interest in gross income in the redemption year. Alternatively, if he elects to report the accrued interest each year, Carl will include $20 in gross income ($520 − $500) in 2021 and $23 ($543 − $520) in gross income in 2022. Carl increases his basis in the bonds by the amounts he includes in gross income.

¶308.03 U.S. TREASURY BILLS, NOTES, AND BONDS

In addition to savings bonds, the U.S. government also issues Treasury bills, Treasury notes and Treasury bonds. Treasury bills are short-term and mature in 4-, 13-, or 26-weeks. They are issued at a discount (for less than face value) in multiples of $1,000. The difference between the discounted price investors pay and the face value is interest income. Investors report the interest in gross income in the year the Treasury bill matures.

Treasury notes have maturity periods ranging from one to ten years. Treasury bonds have maturity periods of more than ten years. Both Treasury notes and bonds are issued in multiples of $1,000. Both pay interest every six months (semiannually). Cash basis investors report interest in gross income in the year it is paid to them. When the notes or bonds mature, investors redeem them for face value.

Sometimes Treasury notes and bonds are issued at a discount (less than face value). The difference between issue price and face value is called **original issue discount**. This amount represents additional interest income the investor earns over the life of the bond. Unless the discount is *de minimis* (small in amount), the investor reports the OID in gross income as it accrues over the life of the bond (see discussion on OID at ¶308.05). The OID reported in income is then added to the investor's basis (investment) in the bond. When the bond matures, the investor will have reported all OID in gross income and the investor's basis in the bond will equal its face value.

¶308.04 ACCRUED INTEREST

When a taxpayer buys a bond between interest dates, the accrued interest up to the purchase date belongs to the seller. The buyer pays this interest to the seller at the time of purchase and subtracts it from the first interest payment received. The buyer then includes all future interest on the bond in gross income.

EXAMPLE 21	On October 1, 2023, a cash basis investor pays $10,134 for bonds. The bonds were originally issued on December 1, 2021 at their $10,000 face value. The bonds pay $200 interest on June 1 and December 1. Included in the purchase price is $134 of interest that had accrued from June 1, 2023 – October 1, 2023. On December 1, 2023, the corporation (issuer of the bonds) pays the investor $200. The investor reports $66 ($200 – $134) in gross income on his 2023 tax return. The following year, the investor will receive two $200 payments and will include all $400 on their tax return.

¶308.05   ORIGINAL ISSUE DISCOUNT (OID) BONDS

Taxpayers that use the cash method include the interest from bonds in gross income when they receive it. However, when a corporation issues its bonds at a discount, a different situation arises for the purchasing bondholder. Because bondholders receive the full face value at maturity, they must recognize the discount (face value minus issue price) as income. One issue that arises is when this income should be reported. Another issue is whether to treat the income as ordinary interest or capital gain.

To answer these questions, the taxpayer must first determine the amount of original issue discount (OID). [I.R.C. §1272] The Code defines OID as the difference between a bond's face value and its (original) issue price.

EXAMPLE 22	A corporation issues a 20-year, $100,000 bond for $12,861. Thus, an investor pays the corporation $12,861 for the right to receive $100,000 20 years from now. The OID equals $87,139 ($100,000 – $12,861).

The Code treats the amount of OID as $0 when the amount is *de minimis* (a small amount). The Code defines **de minimis** OID as less than one-fourth of 1% (0.0025) of the face value times the number of full years to maturity. When the *de minimis* rule applies, the holder includes the discount in income when the bond is sold or redeemed. If the bond is held as an investment (i.e., capital asset), the bondholder reports the income as a capital gain.

EXAMPLE 23	A corporation issues a ten-year, $100,000 bond for $98,000. Although the true amount of OID equals $2,000, the Code treats it as $0. The $2,000 discount falls below the OID threshold of $2,500 (.0025 × $100,000 face value of bond × 10 years to maturity). The investor's tax basis (investment) in the bond stays at $98,000. If the investor holds the bond to maturity, at that time the $2,000 will be reported as capital gain ($100,000 face value – $98,000 basis in the bond).

When the amount of the discount exceeds the *de minimis* threshold, the taxpayer recognizes the OID as income over the life of the bond by including a portion of it in gross income each year. For OID bonds issued after April 3, 1993, taxpayers use the *effective interest rate method* to determine the interest earned. In making this computation, a taxpayer multiplies his investment (basis) in the bond by the interest rate, which is the rate needed to produce the desired yield. The interest must be compounded semiannually (twice a year). The taxpayer reports the difference between the resulting product and the interest actually paid on the bond as ordinary income. This amount reduces the remaining OID and increases the taxpayer's basis in the bonds. This timing rule is an exception to the cash basis method of accounting because the taxpayer must recognize income before receiving the cash.

EXAMPLE 24	On January 1, 2021, a corporation issues a 30-year, $1,000,000 zero-coupon bond for $169,700. The annual yield to maturity equals 6%. Interest is compounded semiannually (June 30 and December 31). The bond's original issue discount equals $830,300 ($1,000,000 − $169,700). Earned interest for 2021 is as follows:

January 1, 2021 through June 30, 2021 ([6% × $169,700] × 6/12)	$ 5,091
July 1, 2021 through December 31, 2021 ([6% × ($169,700 + $5,091 accrued interest)] × 6/12)	5,244
	$10,335

At the end of 2021, the investor's basis in the bond is $180,035 ($169,700 + $10,335). Over the 30 years, the investor writes off the discount and recognizes interest income of $830,300. At the end of 30 years, the carrying value of the bond will equal its $1,000,000 face value ($169,700 + $830,300).

Using the method shown in Example 24, companies that issue OID bonds compute for investors the amount of OID to be included in income each year. They report this amount on Form 1099-OID, Original Issue Discount. In Example 24, the corporation issues to the investor of the $1,000,000 bond a Form 1099-OID for 2021. On this form, the investor is told of the $10,335 of OID. This amount is reported as interest income on the investor's 2021 tax return.

For OID bonds issued before April 4, 1993, different write-off rules apply. Also, original issue discount rules do not apply to U.S. Savings Bonds.

¶308.06   MARKET DISCOUNT BONDS

A market discount arises when an investor buys a bond from an existing bondholder (rather than from the issuing corporation) for less than its amortized carrying value. **Amortized carrying value (ACV)** equals a bond's (original) issue price plus all OID previously included in gross income. Taxpayers purchasing a market discount bond may elect to include some of the discount as interest income each year, or wait until the bond is sold/redeemed and recognize the entire market discount as interest income at that time.

Some bondholders must deal with both OID and market discount. An investor must accrue the OID income over the life of the bond using the effective interest rate method. Bondholders with market discount who elect to amortize the interest may choose either the effective rate method or the straight-line method to accrue the interest. [I.R.C. §1276]

EXAMPLE 25	On January 1, 2022, Ron pays $9,320 for 30-year corporate bonds. The bonds were originally issued on January 1, 2003, for $9,200 and have a $10,000 face value. They mature on January 1, 2033. At the time the bonds were issued, the OID was $800 ($10,000 − $9,200). This amount exceeds the $750 threshold for *de minimis* OID ($10,000 × .0025 × 30 years to maturity). Thus, the prior owner(s) included $210 of the OID in gross income each year. The amortized OID was added to the bond's ACV. As of January 1, 2022, the ACV of the bond is $9,410 ($9,200 original issue price plus $210 recognized OID).
	Ron purchased the bonds at a $90 market discount ($9,320 − $9,410 ACV). Ron can elect to include a share of this amount in gross income each year from 2022-2033. The amount would be taxed as interest income and would increase his basis in the bonds. His other choice is to wait until he sells the bonds or until they mature to report the $90 as interest income. As of January 1, 2022, the bond had remaining OID of $590 ($10,000 − $9,410). Each year, the corporation will issue Ron a Form 1099-OID to let him know how much of this OID he must include in gross income. Ron will increase his tax basis (investment) in the bonds by the amount of OID he includes in gross income.

¶308.07   BOND PREMIUMS ON TAXABLE BONDS

Taxpayers who purchase taxable bonds at a premium (an amount in excess of face value) can choose to offset interest income by a portion of the bond's premium each year and decrease the basis of the bond by the premium written off. [I.R.C. §171] Taxpayers may also choose not to write off bond premiums and report more interest income each year. This would result in a higher basis in the bonds upon sale or redemption, which translates into less gain or more loss when the bonds are sold or redeemed. The taxpayer's choice must be applied to all bonds the taxpayer owns.

EXAMPLE 26

Donna pays $102,000 for bonds that have a face value of $100,000. Donna has two options for dealing with the $2,000 premium she paid for these bonds. She can amortize the premium over the life of the bonds and reduce the amount of interest income she reports in gross income each year. If she does this, Donna will decrease her basis in the bonds by the amortized amount. At maturity, her basis would equal the face value of the bonds. Her second option is to not reduce the amount of interest she reports in gross income and keep her basis in the bonds at $102,000. If Donna holds the bonds to maturity she will report a long-term capital loss when the bonds are redeemed. If she sells the bonds prior to maturity, the difference between the amount realized from the sale and $102,000 will result in a gain or loss.

¶308.08   IMPUTED INTEREST ON BELOW-MARKET LOANS

The IRS may impute interest on loans made with no interest or too low of an interest rate. This means the lender must recognize interest income equal to the imputed interest, and the borrower has an implied interest payment to the lender. [I.R.C. §7872] To impute the interest, the IRS uses the applicable federal rate (AFR) at the time the loan is made, compounded semiannually. The difference between the interest using the AFR and the interest actually paid on the loan is the amount of imputed interest.

Published Applicable Federal Rates (AFRs)

Each month the IRS publishes AFRs for short-term, mid-term, and long-term loans. Taxpayers use the short-term rates for demand loans (loans that are due upon the lender's demand) and loans with a maturity date of three years or less. They use the mid-term rates for loans with more than three-year, but no more than nine-year maturities, and long-term rates for loans maturing in more than nine years.

Potential Below-Market Loan Situations

1. Tax-avoidance loans
2. Gift loans (for example, a loan from a parent to a child)
3. Compensation-related loans between employer and employee
4. Loans between a corporation and its shareholder

Gift Loans

Loans to family members and friends (gift loans) fall under the imputed interest rules. Unless an exception applies, the IRS imputes interest on a gift loan when the interest charged is less than the AFR. The lender includes the imputed interest in gross income. Under certain conditions, the borrower may deduct the imputed interest payment as investment interest expense (discussed at ¶505.03). In addition, since the lender never actually takes possession of this interest, the tax laws assume that the lender makes annual gifts to the borrower equal to the imputed interest. Depending on the amount of the gifts, the lender may have to a file a gift tax return.

Interest is always imputed on gift loans made for tax avoidance reasons. However, for all other gift loans, the amount of imputed interest may be limited or be $0 in certain situations. The three exceptions to the imputed interest rule on gift loans are as follows.

1. No interest is imputed on gift loans of $10,000 or less, as long as the loan proceeds are not used to purchase income-producing property (like stocks, bonds, and similar property).
2. No interest is imputed on a gift loan of $100,000 or less if the borrower's net investment income for the year does not exceed $1,000. Net investment income includes taxable interest, dividends and capital gains from investments minus any deductible investment-related expenses.
3. The amount of imputed interest on a gift loan cannot exceed the borrower's net investment income for the year when the borrower's net investment income exceeds $1,000 and the amount of the loan between the individuals does not exceed $100,000.

EXAMPLE 27	Bob and Sandra Grady are saving to buy a house. Sandra's parents offer them a $10,000 interest-free loan, provided Bob and Sandra sign a ten-year note. Bob and Sandra agree to these terms. If the Gradys use the loan proceeds to make the down payment (and not to buy income-producing property), the IRS will not impute interest on the $10,000 gift loan (see Exception 1).
EXAMPLE 28	Marilyn and Rod Lange are having trouble saving enough for a down payment on a home. Marilyn's parents offer to loan them $10,000. No interest would be charged on the loan. The $10,000 would be due at the end of ten years. The Langes intend to use the proceeds to invest in stock and bonds. Their plan is to let the balance grow until they have enough for a down payment. Normally, gift loans of $10,000 or less are not subject to the imputed interest rules. However, since the proceeds were used to buy income-producing property, this exception does not apply (see Exception 1). The amount of the gift loan does not exceed $100,000. Thus, no imputed interest will be charged as long as the Langes' net investment income (NII) does not exceed $1,000 (Exception 2). If their NII exceeds $1,000, then the imputed interest is limited to the amount of the Langes' NII (Exception 3). For example, if the Langes' NII for the year is $900, no imputed interest would be charged (see Exception 2). If, however, their NII is $1,100, then the amount of imputed interest could not exceed $1,100 (see Exception 3). Imputed interest would be the interest charged using the long-term AFR (for loans longer than nine years) less the $0 of interest the Langes are paying Marilyn's parents. Should the imputed interest rules apply, the IRS treats the Langes as having paid Marilyn's parents this amount as interest. The parents report the imputed interest in gross income. Because the proceeds were used to purchase investments, the Langes may be able to deduct this amount as investment interest expense (an itemized deduction, see ¶505.03). The parents are then deemed to make a gift to the Langes for the amount of imputed interest.
EXAMPLE 29	Same facts as in Example 28, except that the Langes do not buy income-producing property with the $10,000. Since the amount of the loan does not exceed $10,000, no interest would be imputed (see Exception 1).
EXAMPLE 30	Same facts as in Example 29, except that the parents loan the Langes $10,001. The exception for gift loans of $10,000 or less does not apply. The same reasoning as presented in Example 28 holds. Thus, as long as the Langes' NII does not exceed $1,000, no interest would be imputed (see Exception 2). However, if their NII exceeds $1,000, the amount of imputed interest cannot exceed their NII since the loan amount does not exceed $100,000 (see Exception 3).

Compensation-Related Loans

When an employer loans money to one of its employees and charges no interest or too low of an interest rate, the imputed interest rules apply if either the loan exceeds $10,000, or the loan was made for tax avoidance reasons. As with all below-market loans, the amount of imputed interest is the difference between the amount of interest computed semiannually using the AFR at the time of the loan and the actual interest paid.

In a compensation-related loan, the employee is deemed to pay the imputed interest to the employer. The employer reports the interest in gross income. Since the employee does not actually pay interest to the employer, to square things up, the employer is deemed to pay wages to the employee for the same amount. These deemed wages are included in the employee's gross income, and are deducted as wage expense on the employer's tax return. If the proceeds from the loan were used for personal reasons, the interest would be nondeductible personal interest to the employee. However, if the proceeds were used to purchase an investment, the employee may be able to deduct the interest as an itemized deduction (see discussion at ¶505.03).

EXAMPLE 31

On January 1, Backe & Co. loans $20,000 to its employee, Ross. The terms of the note require no interest to be paid and for the $20,000 to be repaid at the end of five years. At the time the loan was made, the current annual mid-term AFR (for loans between three and nine years) was 3% (1.5% semiannually). Imputed interest for the first year is $604.50 – $0 interest paid]. Backe & Co. includes the $604.50 of interest in gross income. Whether Ross will be able to deduct the $604.50 depends on how he used the loan proceeds. Backe & Co. is then deemed to pay wages to Ross for $604.50 and deducts this amount as wage expense on its tax return. Ross includes the additional $604.50 of wages in his gross income.

First half of year		
Principal	$20,000	
Interest	0.015	$300.00
Second half of year		
Principal	20,300	
Interest	0.015	304.50
Total for year		$604.50

Corporation-Shareholder Loans

When an employer makes a loan to one of its shareholders and charges interest below the AFR, the imputed interest rules apply if either the loan exceeds $10,000, or the loan was made for tax avoidance reasons. When the imputed interest rules apply, the shareholder is deemed to pay the imputed interest to the corporation. The corporation includes the interest in gross income. The shareholder may or may not deduct the interest expense depending on how the proceeds from the loan are used. To even things up, the corporation is deemed to pay a dividend to the shareholder for the same amount. The deemed dividends are reported as dividend income on the shareholder's tax return. There is no deduction to the corporation for dividends paid.

EXAMPLE 32

Same facts as in Example 31, except that Ross is a shareholder, instead of an employee, of Backe & Co. At the end of the year, Ross is deemed to have paid $604.50 of interest to Backe & Co. In turn, Backe & Co. is deemed to pay a $604.50 dividend to Ross. Backe & Co. includes the deemed interest in its gross income. Ross reports the deemed dividend on his tax return. Since a dividend is not a deductible business expense, Backe & Co. has no deduction to offset its gross income.

EXAMPLE 33	Same facts as in Example 32, except that the terms of the loan required Ross to pay 2% simple interest annually. Ross now pays $400 interest to Backe & Co. annually ($20,000 × 2%). At the end of the first year, Ross is deemed to have paid additional interest to Backe & Co. of $204.50 ($604.50 − $400). The imputed amount is taxed as interest income to Backe & Co. and as dividend income to Ross.

Summary of Below Market Loans

Type of Loan	Tax Consequences to the Lender	Tax Consequences to the Borrower
Gift loan	Interest income Gift tax (perhaps)	Interest expense (perhaps)
Employer-employee loan	Interest income Wage expense	Interest expense (perhaps) Wage income
Corporation-shareholder loan	Interest income	Interest expense (perhaps) Dividend income

¶308.09   REPORTING INTEREST INCOME

Taxpayers report taxable interest income on Form 1040. The IRS also wants to see the amount of tax-exempt interest on these forms. Normally, a taxpayer receiving interest income of $10 or more receives a Form 1099-INT, Interest Income, from the payer. This form identifies taxable interest and any state or federal tax withholding that might have taken place. Copies of Form 1099-INT go to the payee and the IRS. Taxpayers do not file this form with their returns unless tax was withheld that they are claiming as a tax payment on their tax returns. Taxpayers should keep copies of Form 1099-INT with their tax records.

Taxpayers who withdraw certificate of deposit (CD) funds before the due date pay a penalty. This penalty is a deduction for AGI (see discussion at ¶402.08). Taxpayers with an early withdrawal penalty will want to file Form 1040 to deduct the penalty.

Form 1040 is also used to report the following types of taxable interest.

1. When the taxpayer includes in gross income OID other than the amount reported on Form 1099-OID.
2. When the taxpayer has accrued interest on bonds bought between interest dates.
3. When the taxpayer elects to reduce interest income by writing off a bond premium.

Form 1040

There are no restrictions on the amount or type of interest income that a person may report on Form 1040. Tax-exempt interest is reported on Form 1040 (line 2a). Taxable interest appears on Line 2b. When taxable interest income exceeds $1,500, the taxpayer lists each item of taxable interest income separately on Schedule B, Part I.

¶308.10   FILLED-IN SCHEDULE B, PART I

INFORMATION FOR FIGURE 3-1:

Ruth Baker uses Part I on Schedule B to report her interest income. Ruth receives **$700** from **Erie Lake Distributing Company**, **$250** from **Buckeye Lake Brewing Company**, **$1,505** from **Franklin Company**, and **$1,010** of tax-exempt interest from **City of Madison bonds**. Ruth transfers the

$2,455 of taxable interest to Form 1040 (line 2b). She reports the $1,010 of tax-exempt interest on Form 1040 (line 2a).

Figure 3-1: Filled-In Schedule B, Part I

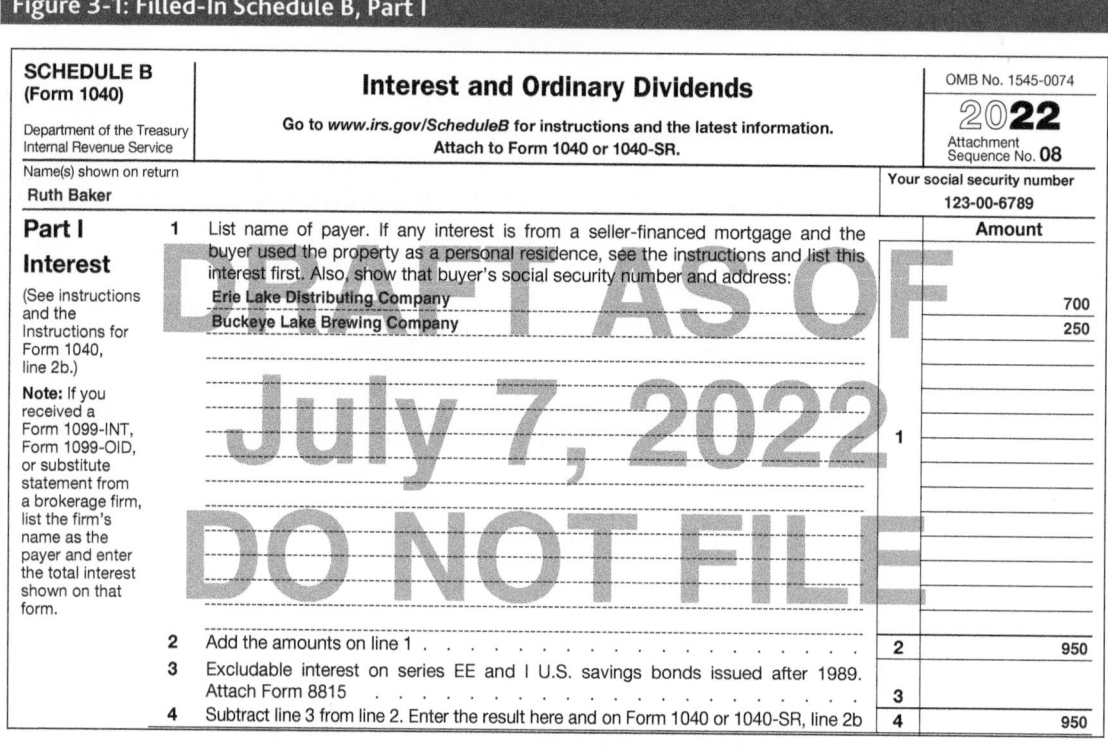

¶309   Dividend Income

Corporations can distribute to their shareholders cash and noncash property, as well as rights to purchase more of the corporation's stock. Each year, corporations report the value of these distributions to shareholders on Form 1099-DIV, Dividends and Distributions. Distributions of a corporation's earnings and profits (E&P) are taxed to the shareholders as ordinary dividends. [I.R.C. §301] Any distribution in excess of E&P is treated as a return of capital to the shareholders. Mutual funds that generate income pass along each investor's share of income on Form 1099-DIV. Such income may include ordinary dividends, qualified dividends included in ordinary dividends, as well as capital gain distributions.

In the case of higher income taxpayers, dividend income may also be a component of net investment income. See ¶315.

 By definition, dividends represent a distribution of a corporation's profits to its owners (shareholders). E&P keeps a running total of a corporation's undistributed profits. When a corporation distributes cash or property in excess of its E&P, the excess is treated as a return of the shareholder's investment (basis) in the stock of the corporation (known as a return of capital distribution).

¶309.01   ORDINARY DIVIDENDS

Both cash and accrual basis shareholders include ordinary dividends in gross income in the year received. When a corporation distributes noncash property to its shareholders from its E&P, the shareholder increases gross income by the FMV of the distributed property.

Most ordinary dividends received by individual taxpayers are taxed at a reduced rate. A rate of 0%, 15%, or 20% applies, based upon the amount of an individual taxpayer's taxable income. These are the same rates that apply to net long-term capital gains. See Chapter 11.

Taxable incomes below or above certain "breakpoints" cause these dividends to be taxed at different rates. The "breakpoints" are adjusted annually for inflation. These dividends, called **qualified dividends**, are taxed using the same rates that apply to net long-term capital gains. Some dividends (nonqualified dividends) are not eligible for these reduced rates and are taxed at the taxpayers ordinary rates. Shortly after the end of the year, corporations issue a Form 1099-DIV to each of its shareholders. On that form, the corporation reports the shareholder's total ordinary dividends and the amount of ordinary dividends that are qualified dividends.

Figure 3-2 shows the taxable income levels for which the long-term capital gain rates are effective. The breakpoints vary depending on the taxpayer's filing status. These rates are subject to indexation each year.

Figure 3-2: Tax Rates Imposed on Long-Term Capital Gains and Qualified Dividends

Rate	Taxable Income Range Married Filing Jointly And Surviving Spouses	Heads Of Household	Single	Married Filing Separately
0%	0 – 83,350	0 – 55,800	0 – 41,675	0 – 41,675
15%	83,351 – 517,200	55,801 – 488,500	41,676 – 459,750	41,676 – 258,600
20%	Above 517,200	Above 488,500	Above 459,750	Above 258,600

EXAMPLE 34 James is single. His taxable income is $49,000, which includes $5,000 of qualified dividends. For 2022, the breakpoints for single taxpayers are $41,675 for the 0% rate and $459,751 for the 20% rate. James' taxable income falls between these breakpoints, so a 15% rate applies to his qualified dividends.

¶309.02   DIVIDEND REINVESTMENT PLANS

Some corporations offer shareholders dividend reinvestment plans. Under these plans, the dividends paid to the shareholder are used to buy more shares of stock in the same corporation. After the dividend, the shareholder owns more shares of stock in the corporation. The taxpayer's investment (basis) in the new shares is the amount of the taxable dividend.

EXAMPLE 35 Mona owns 300 shares of stock in ABX. Mona participates in ABX's dividend reinvestment plan. During the year, ABX pays its shareholders a $.50 dividend at a time when the stock was selling for $40 a share. Mona includes the $150 of dividends paid (300 shares owned × $.50) in her gross income. This $150 is then used to purchase 3.75 more shares of stock in ABX ($150/$40). After the dividend, Mona owns 303.75 shares of ABX stock. The $150 of qualified dividends is reported to Mona on Form 1099-DIV.

¶309.03   RETURN OF CAPITAL DISTRIBUTIONS

Distributions of cash or noncash property in excess of E&P are treated as a return of shareholders' basis in the stock. These "return-of-capital" distributions are not taxed as dividends. Instead they reduce a shareholder's tax basis in the stock until it reaches zero. Once the stock's basis has been reduced to zero, the Code taxes any additional distribution as a capital gain. The gain is long-term or short-term, depending on how long the taxpayer has owned the stock. See Chapter 11.

EXAMPLE 36

> Doc Hinder is the sole shareholder in DH Corporation. Doc has owned the stock for two years. At the beginning of the year, DH has E&P of $22,000 and Doc's basis in his shares of DH was $5,000. During the year, DH distributes $30,000 to Doc. The first $22,000 is taxed as ordinary dividends (to the extent of E&P). The next $5,000 (to the extent of Doc's tax basis) is treated as a nontaxable return of capital. The last $3,000 ($30,000 – $22,000 – $5,000) is taxed as long-term capital gain.

¶309.04   REPORTING DIVIDEND INCOME

Individual taxpayers use Form 1040 to report dividend income. Form 1040 has separate lines for ordinary dividends (those included in gross income) and for qualified dividends (those taxed at a reduced rate). When the taxpayer's taxable dividends exceed $1,500, Schedule B must be completed. Figure 3-3 illustrates Schedule B, Part II, where dividend income is reported. Capital gains distributions are usually reported on Schedule D (Form 1040), Capital Gains and Losses.

¶309.05   FILLED-IN SCHEDULE B, PART II

INFORMATION FOR FIGURE 3-3:

Jackie Heard uses Part II on Schedule B to report the ordinary dividends she received during the year. Jackie received dividends of **$530** from **Bay Weaving Company** and **$1,340** from **Pike Moving Company**. She transfers the $1,870 of ordinary dividends to her tax return (Form 1040 (line 3b)). She then enters the amount of qualified dividends included in the $1,870 on her tax return (Form 1040 (line 3a)). This amount is reported to her on Form 1099-DIV, Dividends and Distributions. Jackie had no interest in or signatory authority over a foreign bank account. She did not receive a distribution from any foreign trust and was not a grantor of a foreign trust.

Figure 3-3: Filled-In Schedule B, Part II

			Amount
Note: If line 4 is over $1,500, you must complete Part III.			
Part II **Ordinary Dividends** (See instructions and the Instructions for Form 1040, line 3b.) **Note:** If you received a Form 1099-DIV or substitute statement from a brokerage firm, list the firm's name as the payer and enter the ordinary dividends shown on that form.	**5** List name of payer: **Bay Weaving Company** **Pike Moving Company**	**5**	530
			1,340
	6 Add the amounts on line 5. Enter the total here and on Form 1040 or 1040-SR, line 3b	**6**	1,870
	Note: If line 6 is over $1,500, you must complete Part III.		

Part III **Foreign Accounts and Trusts** **Caution:** If required, failure to file FinCEN Form 114 may result in substantial penalties. Additionally, you may be required to file Form 8938, Statement of Specified Foreign Financial Assets. See instructions.	You must complete this part if you **(a)** had over $1,500 of taxable interest or ordinary dividends; **(b)** had a foreign account; or **(c)** received a distribution from, or were a grantor of, or a transferor to, a foreign trust.	Yes	No
	7a At any time during 2022, did you have a financial interest in or signature authority over a financial account (such as a bank account, securities account, or brokerage account) located in a foreign country? See instructions		✔
	If "Yes," are you required to file FinCEN Form 114, Report of Foreign Bank and Financial Accounts (FBAR), to report that financial interest or signature authority? See FinCEN Form 114 and its instructions for filing requirements and exceptions to those requirements		
	b If you are required to file FinCEN Form 114, list the name(s) of the foreign country(-ies) where the financial account(s) are located: _____		
	8 During 2022, did you receive a distribution from, or were you the grantor of, or transferor to, a foreign trust? If "Yes," you may have to file Form 3520. See instructions		✔

For Paperwork Reduction Act Notice, see your tax return instructions.   Cat. No. 17146N   Schedule B (Form 1040) 2022

¶310   # Gains and Losses

When taxpayers sell or exchange property, a gain or loss results. As a rule, taxpayers report on their tax returns all gains, but they report losses only from sales or exchanges of investment or business property.

In theory, recognized gains are included in gross income and recognized losses are deducted for AGI. On the tax return, gain and losses are netted against one another and only the net gain or loss appears on the tax return. However, an individual can only deduct up to $3,000 of capital losses in excess of capital gains each year. Chapters 10 and 11 describe the calculation of gains and losses, as well as the tax forms where they appear.

¶311   # Rents and Royalties

Gross income includes rent and royalty income. The tax law allows ordinary, necessary, and reasonable rental expenses to offset rental income on the tax return. However, limits on the deductions may apply. The rules governing rental property are discussed in Chapter 9.

¶312   # Unemployment Compensation

Unemployed workers may receive unemployment compensation. Unemployment compensation is taxable and reported on Schedule 1 (Form 1040), line 19. [I.R.C. §85] For 2020 only, an individual excluded up to $10,200 of unemployment compensation if AGI was less than $150,000.

¶313   # Other Sources of Income

The topics discussed thus far in the chapter are not an exhaustive list of income items. Recall that income is any item that increases the taxpayer's net worth. Examples of other items of income include certain state and local refunds, illegal income, and gambling winnings.

¶313.01   ## STATE AND LOCAL INCOME TAX REFUNDS

When taxpayers get back amounts they deducted in a prior tax year, the amounts they are refunded may be subject to tax. The **tax benefit rule** gets its name because the amounts refunded are included in gross income if the taxpayer benefited from deducting these amounts in a prior tax year. [I.R.C. §111] A "benefit" results if the deduction reduced the taxpayer's taxes in that year. In years in which taxpayers report negative taxable income, normally there is no tax benefit. When the deduction involves an itemized deduction, the amount recovered is not taxable if the taxpayer took the standard deduction in the prior year. Even when the taxpayer itemized, the recovered amounts are taxable only to the extent that they resulted in less taxes paid.

The tax benefit rule applies to refunds of state and local income taxes. Taxpayers deduct as an itemized deduction amounts they pay during the year for state or local income taxes. This includes amounts employers withhold from their pay, as well as any other payments for state and local income taxes that they make during the year. Amounts withheld from employees' paychecks in 2021 to cover their state and local income taxes owed for the 2021 tax year are deducted as itemized deductions on their 2021 federal income tax return.

Like the federal income tax return, taxpayers file their state and local tax returns in the next tax year. Thus, a taxpayer's 2021 state income tax return is not due until 2022. As a result, taxpayers that overpay their 2021 income taxes do not receive their refunds until the next tax year. The tax benefit rule requires that a refund of state or local income taxes be included in gross income in the year received if the taxpayer "benefited" from taking a deduction for the amount in a prior tax year. In the year, a taxpayer receives a state or local income tax refund, the amount included in gross income is the *lesser of* (i) the amount refunded or (ii) the taxpayer's excess itemized deductions.

EXAMPLE 37	Rory, age 46 and single, deducted $4,260 for state income taxes on his 2021 federal income tax return. Rory has excellent vision. In 2022, he received a state income tax refund of $700. On his 2021 tax return, Rory deducted itemized deductions of $15,613. His excess itemized deductions were $3,063 ($15,613 − $12,550 standard deduction for single taxpayers in 2021). Thus, he includes in gross income the lesser of (i) the $700 refunded amount, or (ii) his $3,063 of excess itemized deductions. Rory includes $700 in gross income in 2022.

¶313.02   ILLEGAL INCOME

Income from illegal activities is included in gross income. Taxpayers may deduct the ordinary and necessary business expenses (rents, wages, utilities, etc.) required to produce this income. However, illegal payments (bribes to police and judges) are not deductible, regardless of whether the business is legal or illegal. In the case of illegal drug trafficking, the cost of goods sold reduces gross receipts to yield gross income, but no other costs are deductible.

EXAMPLE 38	Riley operates an illegal gambling business. During the year, he generated $93,000 of income. His ordinary and necessary expenses related to his business totaled $32,000. Riley is required to report the $61,000 of profits from his business on his tax return. If he fails to report this amount to the IRS, he faces stiff penalties imposed on tax evaders.

Many states have legalized the sale of marijuana for medical or recreational use. However, it remains a controlled substance, the dealing of which is illegal under federal law. There is a special rule that denies any deduction for expenses in connection with illegal drugs. This rule does not apply to other illegal activities.

EXAMPLE 39	Jordan operates a legal marijuana dispensary. During the year, he generated $93,000 of income. His ordinary and necessary expenses related to his business totaled $32,000. Jordan is required to report the $93,000 of income from his business on his tax return. He cannot deduct any portion of the $32,000 expenses. If he fails to report the income to the IRS, he faces stiff penalties imposed on tax evaders.

¶313.03   GAMBLING WINNINGS

Gross income includes gambling winnings. Casual gamblers may claim an itemized deduction for gambling losses and certain expenses up to the amounts of their winnings. Professional gamblers can deduct their gambling losses (to the extent of their winnings) for AGI.

EXAMPLE 40	An amateur poker player wins $1.2 million at a poker event in Las Vegas. During the same year, the taxpayer can document $230,000 of gambling losses. On his tax return, the taxpayer includes the $1.2 million on Schedule 1 (Form 1040) as "Other income." He then deducts $230,000 of gambling losses as an itemized deduction.

EXAMPLE 41	Same facts as in Example 40, except that the taxpayer's documented gambling losses total $1.5 million. The taxpayer still includes the $1.2 million on Schedule 1 (Form 1040) as "Other income." He deducts $1.2 million as an itemized deduction.

¶313.04 OTHER INCOME

Gross income includes amounts taxpayers receive from contests, raffles, and similar promotions. It also includes the value of door prizes and employee awards. A limited exclusion (up to $400) exists for awards employees receive for length of service and safety achievement. These awards must be in the form of personal property (not cash). Unless *de minimis* rules apply (see ¶401.05), gross income includes all other awards or prizes from employers. Taxpayers include noncash prizes and awards in gross income at their FMV.

Gross income includes awards in recognition of past religious, charitable, scientific, educational, artistic, literary, or civic achievements. Such awards include the Pulitzer Prize and the Nobel Peace Prize. [I.R.C. §74(a)] The only way these types of prizes can avoid being taxed is if the recipient immediately assigns the award to a qualified governmental unit or tax-exempt charity. [I.R.C. §74(b)]

Taxpayers who enter into a business with the intent to make a profit usually report the activities from the business on Schedule C (¶303). However, sometimes the activity does not rise to the level of a bona fide business, and is instead treated as a hobby. Since all sources of income are taxable unless the tax laws state otherwise, hobby income must be reported in gross income. Hobby income is reported on the line designated as "Other income" on Schedule 1 (Form 1040).

¶314 "Kiddie Tax"

Certain children with unearned income may find some of that income taxed at a higher tax rate than would apply to the child. Unearned income is basically investment income from sources such as dividends, interest, capital gains, rents, royalties, and annuities.

Under current rules, income above a certain level is to be taxed at the child's parents' marginal rates. [I.R.C. §1(g)] If the parents are married and file a joint return, the marginal rate is based on the parents' hypothetical taxable income if it included the income of all children subject to the kiddie tax. This amount determines the marginal rate. If the parents are not married or do not file a joint return, and one is the custodial parent, that parent's marginal rate determines the child's rate. In other cases, the appropriate rate is that of the parent with the highest taxable income.

This "kiddie tax" does not apply to children who do not have at least one living parent or step-parent. It also does not apply to married children who file a joint tax return with their spouse. For all others, the kiddie tax applies in 2022 to children under age 18 who have unearned income of more than $2,300. It also applies to children who are 18 years old or full-time students between the ages of 19 and 23 who have unearned income in excess of $2,300 and whose earned income does not exceed 50% of their total support for the year. The kiddie tax is calculated on Form 8615, Tax for Certain Children Who Have Unearned Income (see Figure 3-4).

EXAMPLE 42	During 2022, Betsy, age 17, is a full-time student with interest income of $3,200 and wages of $4,000. Betsy's parents claim Betsy as a dependent on their joint tax return. Total support for Betsy during the year was $7,600 as originally stated.			
	Interest		3,200	
	Wages		4,000	
	Gross income		7,200	
	Standard deduction			
	Standard amount	$400	(4,400)	
	plus earned income	$4,000		
	Taxable income		2,800	
	"Net" unearned income			
	Interest	3,200		
	Allowed	(2,300)	900	Taxed at parents' rates
	Earned taxable income		1,900	Taxed at single rates

EXAMPLE 43	Same facts as Example 42, except that Betsy is 18 years old. Although Betsy's unearned income exceeds $2,300, her earned income ($4,000) exceeds one-half of her total support for the year ($7,600 × 50% = $3,800). Therefore, Betsy is not subject to the kiddie tax. She will pay tax on her $2,800 taxable income using the column in the tax table for single taxpayers.

EXAMPLE 44	During 2022, Tim, age 21, has interest income of $3,600 and wages of $3,000. Tim was a full-time student during the year. His parents claim Tim as a dependent on their joint tax return. Support from all sources during the year for Tim was $7,000. Tim's taxable income is $3,200 ($6,600 AGI – $3,400 standard deduction for dependents). Tim is between the ages of 19 and 24 and a full-time student with unearned income in excess of $2,300. His earned income ($3,000) does not exceed one-half of his total support for the year ($7,000 × 50% = $3,500). Thus, Tim is subject to the kiddie tax. He will pay tax on his $1,300 of net unearned income ($3,600 – $1,150 – $1,150) using tax rate applicable to his parents, his custodial parent, or the parent with the highest taxable income, as circumstances dictate. The tax on the remaining $1,900 ($3,200 – $1,300) will be found in the tax table (using the column for single taxpayers).

EXAMPLE 45	During 2022, Ray, age 13, has interest income of $3,700 and no earned income. Ray's parents are deceased. He lives with his grandmother, who claims Ray as a dependent on her tax return. Since Ray does not have at least one living parent or stepparent, he is not subject to the kiddie tax. He will file a tax return and use the tax table to compute tax on his $2,600 of taxable income ($3,700 – $1,150 standard deduction for dependents).

Under certain conditions, parents can choose to report their child's income on their tax returns. For this reporting, parents must file Form 8814 with their Form 1040. When parents choose this reporting option, the child does not file a return. However, any unearned income of the child reported on the parents' tax return is considered to be the parents' investment income for purposes of the net investment income tax (see ¶315).

¶314.01   FILLED-IN FORM 8615

INFORMATION FOR FIGURE 3-4:

Helen Wong, age 16, receives $3,650 of interest from her investments. Helen has no other income and no itemized deductions. Her parents, George and Amy Wong, file a joint return. Their taxable income is $280,000. They have no other dependents. Thus, Helen's net unearned income is $1,350 ($3,650 – $1,150 – $1,150). This amount is taxed at her parents' ordinary tax rate. Helen's $439 tax liability is computed on Form 8615 by entering the following information on the appropriate lines and then following the instructions on the form.

Figure 3-4: Filled-In Form 8615

Form **8615**	**Tax for Certain Children Who Have Unearned Income**	OMB No. 1545-0074
Department of the Treasury Internal Revenue Service	Attach only to the child's Form 1040 or 1040-NR. Go to *www.irs.gov/Form8615* for instructions and the latest information.	**20**22 Attachment Sequence No. **33**

Child's name shown on return	Child's social security number
Helen Wong	987-65-4321

A Parent's name (first, initial, and last). **Caution:** See instructions before completing.   **B** Parent's social security number

George & Amy Wong   876-54-3219

C Parent's filing status (check one):
☐ Single   ☑ Married filing jointly   ☐ Married filing separately   ☐ Head of household   ☐ Qualifying widow(er)

Part I   Child's Net Unearned Income

1	Enter the child's unearned income. See instructions	**1**	3,650
2	If the child **did not** itemize deductions on **Schedule A** (Form 1040) or **Schedule A** (Form 1040-NR), enter $2,300. Otherwise, see instructions	**2**	2,300
3	Subtract line 2 from line 1. If zero or less, **stop;** do not complete the rest of this form but do attach it to the child's return	**3**	1,350
4	Enter the child's **taxable income** from Form 1040 or 1040-NR, line 15. If the child files Form 2555, see the instructions	**4**	2,500
5	Enter the **smaller** of line 3 or line 4. If zero, **stop;** do not complete the rest of this form but **do** attach it to the child's return	**5**	1,350

Part II   Tentative Tax Based on the Tax Rate of the Parent

6	Enter the parent's **taxable income** from Form 1040 or 1040-NR, line 15. If zero or less, enter -0-. If the parent files Form 2555, see the instructions	**6**	280,000
7	Enter the total, if any, from Forms 8615, line 5, of **all other** children of the parent named above. **Do not** include the amount from line 5 above	**7**	
8	Add lines 5, 6, and 7. See instructions	**8**	281,350
9	Enter the tax on the amount on line 8 based on the **parent's** filing status above. See instructions. If the Qualified Dividends and Capital Gain Tax Worksheet, Schedule D Tax Worksheet, or Schedule J (Form 1040) is used to figure the tax, check here ☐	**9**	55,195
10	Enter the parent's tax from Form 1040 or 1040-NR, line 16, minus any alternative minimum tax. **Do not** include any tax from **Form 4972** or **Form 8814,** or any tax from the recapture of an education credit. If the parent files Form 2555, see the instructions. If the Qualified Dividends and Capital Gain Tax Worksheet, Schedule D Tax Worksheet, or Schedule J (Form 1040) was used to figure the tax, check here ☐	**10**	54,871
11	Subtract line 10 from line 9 and enter the result. If line 7 is blank, also enter this amount on line 13 and go to **Part III**	**11**	324
12a	Add lines 5 and 7 . . . . . **12a**	1,350	
b	Divide line 5 by line 12a. Enter the result as a decimal (rounded to at least three places)	**12b**	× . 1.000
13	Multiply line 11 by line 12b	**13**	324

Part III   Child's Tax—If lines 4 and 5 above are the same, enter -0- on line 15 and go to line 16.

14	Subtract line 5 from line 4 . . . . . **14**	1,150	
15	Enter the tax on the amount on line 14 based on the **child's** filing status. See instructions. If the Qualified Dividends and Capital Gain Tax Worksheet, Schedule D Tax Worksheet, or Schedule J (Form 1040) is used to figure the tax, check here ☐	**15**	115
16	Add lines 13 and 15	**16**	439
17	Enter the tax on the amount on line 4 based on the **child's** filing status. See instructions. If the Qualified Dividends and Capital Gain Tax Worksheet, Schedule D Tax Worksheet, or Schedule J (Form 1040) is used to figure the tax, check here ☐	**17**	250
18	Enter the **larger** of line 16 or line 17 here and on the **child's** Form 1040 or 1040-NR, line 16. If the child files Form 2555, see the instructions	**18**	439

For Paperwork Reduction Act Notice, see your tax return instructions.   Cat. No. 64113U   Form **8615** (2022)

¶315   NET INVESTMENT INCOME (NII) TAX

Higher-income taxpayers must pay an additional tax on some, if not all, of their net investment income (NII). [I.R.C. §1411] Investment income includes taxable interest (¶308), dividends (¶309), taxable gains on the sale of investment property (¶310, ¶1101), rents and royalties (¶311), and the earnings portion of amounts withdrawn from nonqualified annuities (annuities purchased with after-tax dollars, ¶306.02). NII is investment income minus expenses properly allocated to items included in investment income. Examples include rental expenses, investment interest expense, and various investment expenses.

The amount subject to the 3.8% additional tax is the *lesser of* (i) NII, or (ii) modified AGI in excess of the amounts shown in Figure 3-5. Modified AGI for this purpose is AGI with any foreign earned income exclusion (¶401.14) added back. Taxpayers compute their NII tax on Form 8960, Net Investment Income Tax—Individuals, Estates, and Trusts. The NII tax is then reported on Schedule 4 (Form 1040), line 62. Estates and trusts' amounts are subject to indexation. Individuals do not adjust income levels.

Figure 3-5: Modified AGI Thresholds for Additional 3.8% NII Tax	
Married filing jointly (MFJ) and qualifying widow(er)	$250,000
Single and head of household (HOH)	200,000
Married filing separately (MFS)	125,000

EXAMPLE 46

Suzy and Marv Dion file a joint tax return. Their modified AGI is $278,776. Included in this amount is $39,505 of NII. The Dion's modified AGI exceeds the $250,000 threshold for MFJ taxpayers. Their NII tax is $1,093 [3.8% × (*lesser of* (i) $39,505 NII or (ii) $28,776 excess modified AGI)]. This tax is owed in addition to the income taxes owed on taxable income.

EXAMPLE 47

Amarilis Rose (SSN 481-00-5250) files her tax return using head of household filing status. Amarilis's modified AGI is $203,883. Included in this amount is $4,460 of interest and 5,500 of dividends. Amarilis's modified AGI exceeds the $200,000 threshold for taxpayers who file as head of household. She computes her NII tax on Form 8960 [3.8% × (*lesser of*

(i) $9,960 NII or
(ii) $3,883 excess modified AGI) = $148].

She reports her $148 NII tax on Schedule 2 of her Form 1040, Schedule 3 and attaches Form 8960 to her tax return.

Amarilis's $148 tax liability is computed on Form 8960 by entering the following information on the appropriate lines and then following the instructions on the form.

Figure 3-5: Filled-In Form 8960

Form **8960**	Net Investment Income Tax—	OMB No. 1545-2227
Department of the Treasury Internal Revenue Service	**Individuals, Estates, and Trusts** Attach to your tax return. Go to *www.irs.gov/Form8960* for instructions and the latest information.	20**22** Attachment Sequence No. **72**

Name(s) shown on your tax return	Your social security number or EIN
Amarilis Rose	481-00-5250

Part I   Investment Income   ☐ Section 6013(g) election (see instructions)
☐ Section 6013(h) election (see instructions)
☐ Regulations section 1.1411-10(g) election (see instructions)

1	Taxable interest (see instructions)	1	4,460
2	Ordinary dividends (see instructions)	2	5,500
3	Annuities (see instructions)	3	
4a	Rental real estate, royalties, partnerships, S corporations, trusts, etc. (see instructions)	4a	
b	Adjustment for net income or loss derived in the ordinary course of a non-section 1411 trade or business (see instructions)	4b	
c	Combine lines 4a and 4b	4c	
5a	Net gain or loss from disposition of property (see instructions)	5a	
b	Net gain or loss from disposition of property that is not subject to net investment income tax (see instructions)	5b	
c	Adjustment from disposition of partnership interest or S corporation stock (see instructions)	5c	
d	Combine lines 5a through 5c	5d	
6	Adjustments to investment income for certain CFCs and PFICs (see instructions)	6	
7	Other modifications to investment income (see instructions)	7	
8	Total investment income. Combine lines 1, 2, 3, 4c, 5d, 6, and 7	8	9,960

Part II   Investment Expenses Allocable to Investment Income and Modifications

9a	Investment interest expenses (see instructions)	9a	
b	State, local, and foreign income tax (see instructions)	9b	
c	Miscellaneous investment expenses (see instructions)	9c	
d	Add lines 9a, 9b, and 9c	9d	
10	Additional modifications (see instructions)	10	
11	Total deductions and modifications. Add lines 9d and 10	11	

Part III   Tax Computation

12	Net investment income. Subtract Part II, line 11, from Part I, line 8. Individuals, complete lines 13–17. Estates and trusts, complete lines 18a–21. If zero or less, enter -0-	12	9,960
	Individuals:		
13	Modified adjusted gross income (see instructions)	13	203,883
14	Threshold based on filing status (see instructions)	14	200,000
15	Subtract line 14 from line 13. If zero or less, enter -0-	15	3,883
16	Enter the smaller of line 12 or line 15	16	3,883
17	Net investment income tax for individuals. Multiply line 16 by 3.8% (0.038). **Enter here and include on your tax return** (see instructions)	17	148
	Estates and Trusts:		
18a	Net investment income (line 12 above)	18a	
b	Deductions for distributions of net investment income and deductions under section 642(c) (see instructions)	18b	
c	Undistributed net investment income. Subtract line 18b from line 18a (see instructions). If zero or less, enter -0-	18c	
19a	Adjusted gross income (see instructions)	19a	
b	Highest tax bracket for estates and trusts for the year (see instructions)	19b	
c	Subtract line 19b from line 19a. If zero or less, enter -0-	19c	
20	Enter the smaller of line 18c or line 19c	20	
21	Net investment income tax for estates and trusts. Multiply line 20 by 3.8% (0.038). **Enter here and include on your tax return** (see instructions)	21	

For Paperwork Reduction Act Notice, see your tax return instructions.	Cat. No. 59474M	Form **8960** (2022)

3

Name:

Section:

Date:

QUESTIONS AND PROBLEMS

1. **Receipt of advanced payments.** (Obj. 1) On May 1, 2021, an insurance company sells a three-year insurance policy to one of its customers. The cost of the premiums is $1,200. The insurance company uses the accrual basis and a calendar year.

    a. What amount of the $1,200 must the company include in its gross income during each year of the policy (2021 – 2024)?

    b. Would your answer change if the company used the cash basis? Explain.

2. **Compensation.** (Obj. 1) Mark Wellaby, M.D., practices medicine. During the year he received the following items in payment for his services: cash of $48,000; farm produce worth $1,000; common stock with a total par value of $300; and a $485, 90-day noninterest-bearing note dated December 1. The stock at the time of receipt had a fair market value of $500. On December 31, the fair market value of the stock had dropped to $100. Compute Dr. Wellaby's gross income.

3. **Tips.** (Obj. 1) The following questions involve tip income. Answer each question by inserting an **X** in the proper column.

		True	*False*
a.	Employees receiving less than $20 in monthly tips while working for one employer need not report them to the employer.	_____	_____
b.	Employees receiving less than $20 in monthly tips do not pay social security and Medicare taxes on their tips.	_____	_____
c.	Employees receiving less than $20 in monthly tips do not pay income taxes on their tips.	_____	_____
d.	The IRS normally assumes that food and beverage servers make at least 10% of gross sales in tips.	_____	_____
e.	When tips reported to employers are less than the IRS's assumed tipping rate, some employers must report the difference as additional income on the employee's Form W-2.	_____	_____
f.	"Allocated tips" are subject to withholding for income, social security, and Medicare taxes.	_____	_____

4. **Tips.** (Obj. 1) Marge is a hostess at a local diner. As a hostess, Marge normally does not receive tips. However, on occasion she will help out with an order and the waitress will give Marge part of her tips. During the current year, Marge's total tips were $200.

   a. Discuss the tax consequences of the tip income if Marge did not receive more than $20 in tips in any one month during the year.

   b. How would your answer to Part a. differ if she received more than $20 in tips during the month of May?

5. **Property Settlements, Alimony, and Child Support.** (Obj. 1) Distinguish between the three types of payments former spouses may make to one another and discuss the tax treatment to both the paying spouse and the recipient spouse of each type of payment.

6. **Alimony.** (Obj. 1) For a divorce or legal separation after 1984 and before 2019, alimony payments are deducted by the payer and included in the payee's gross income. However, to be considered alimony, the payments must meet six conditions. What are these conditions?

1. _____

2. _____

3. _____

4. _____

5. _____

6. _____

7. **Alimony and Child Support.** (Obj. 1) Under the terms of their divorce finalized in 2018, Henry is to pay Winona $1,000 a month. The terms of the agreement specify that $550 of each payment is to be for child support. The $550 payment will stop when the child turns 18.

a. If Henry makes all of his required payments during the current year, how much must Winona include in gross income? What amount can Henry deduct?

b. How, if at all, would your answer to Part a. change if the agreement were silent as to how much of each payment constituted child support?

c. How, if at all, would your answer to Part a. change if Henry only makes 8 of the 12 required payments during the year?

8. **Property Settlements, Alimony, and Child Support.** (Obj. 1) Under the terms of a divorce agreement, Gary is to pay $300 per month as child support to Judy who has custody of their 12-year-old child. Judy is also to receive alimony of $1,200 per month for 12 years, but this payment will change to $1,000 per month when the child reaches age 18. Gary is also to transfer stock to Judy. The stock cost $20,000 and has a fair market value of $50,000. The divorce is finalized on May 1, 2018. In the first year under the agreement, Judy receives the stock and 8 months of cash payments.

    a. How do these transfers affect Judy's gross income and Gary's AGI?

    b. How, if at all, would your answer to Part a. change if during the first year Gary only made payments totaling $9,000 during the year?

9. **Traditional IRA Distributions.** (Obj. 2) Over the years, Jen made nondeductible contributions to her traditional IRA. At the beginning of the year, she had yet to withdraw $56,420 of her nondeductible contributions. At the end of the year, the value of the assets in the IRA was $225,850. During the year, Jen withdrew $42,000 from the account.

    a. Describe the tax consequences to Jen assuming Jen is 61 years old at the time of the distribution.

    b. Same as in Part a., except that Jen is 56 years old, and does not meet one of the penalty-free exceptions for making early withdrawals from her IRA.

10. **Pension Benefits.** (Obj. 2) On August 10, 2021, Don turned 65 and received his first pension payment. Over the years, he had contributed $68,900 to his employer's qualified retirement plan. Taxes were paid on $24,700 of this amount. The remaining $44,200 was contributed after the law was changed to permit pre-tax contributions to the plan. Don is to receive monthly benefits of $425 on the same day every month for the remainder of his life.

   a. From the 5 monthly payments Don receives in 2021, what amount is included in gross income?

   b. If Don receives 12 payments in 2022, what amount does he include in gross income?

   c. If Don lives longer than his expected 260 payments, how much of each month's $425 payment will be included in his gross income?

   d. How would your answer to Parts a. - c. change if Don were married and his pension benefits were to continue for both his and his wife's lives? Don's wife is 61 as of August 10, 2021.

11. **Annuity Income.** (Obj. 2) Gregg purchased an annuity contract for $92,400. The contract stated that he would receive $550 a month for life, starting on January 1, 2013. On that date, Gregg's remaining life expectancy was 20 years. For 2022, how much of the $6,600 of annuity payments can Gregg exclude from gross income?

12. **Social Security Benefits.** (Obj. 2) Taxpayers A through C received social security (SS) benefits during the year. Taxpayer C lived with his spouse part of the year. Follow the instructions and fill in the blank lines in the table below for each taxpayer. On line p. show the amount of taxable social security benefits for each taxpayer.

		A Single	B MFJ	C MFS
	Social Security benefits received	$ 7,800	$12,900	$11,000
	First-Tier Formula			
a.	AGI before SS	$50,000	$48,000	$ 5,000
b.	50% SS benefits	3,900	6,450	5,500
c.	Tax-exempt interest	500	400	400
d.	Modified AGI	$ _____	$ _____	$ _____
e.	Less: Base amount	(25,000)	(32,000)	(0)
f.	Excess modified AGI	$ _____	$ _____	$ _____
g.	50% of line f.	$ _____	$ _____	$ _____
h.	Tentative taxable SS benefits (lesser of line g. or b.)	$ _____	$ _____	$ _____
	Second-Tier Formula			
i.	Modified AGI (line d.)	$ _____	$ _____	$ _____
j.	Less: Threshold amount	(34,000)	(44,000)	(0)
k.	Excess	$ _____	$ _____	$ _____
l.	Line k. × 85%	$ _____	$ _____	$ _____
m.	Lesser of line h. or q.	$ _____	$ _____	$ _____
n.	Line l. + line m.	$ _____	$ _____	$ _____
o.	SS benefits × 85%	$ _____	$ _____	$ _____
p.	Taxable benefits (lesser of line n. or o.)	$ _____	$ _____	$ _____
	Threshold amount (line j)	$34,000	$44,000	$ 0
	Less base amount (line e.)	(25,000)	(32,000)	(0)
	Difference	$ 9,000	$12,000	$ 0
q.	50% of the difference	$ 4,500	$ 6,000	$ 0

13. **Social Security Benefits.** (Obj. 2) Taxpayers D through G receive social security (SS) benefits during the year. Taxpayer F did not live with his spouse at all during the year. Information used to determine the taxable amount of their benefits is provided below. Fill in blank lines e. through h. for each taxpayer. On line h., determine the amount of the taxable social security benefits included in gross income for each taxpayer.

Taxpayer status		*D* Single	*E* MFJ	*F* MFS	*G* MFJ
a.	Social security benefits	$ 7,800	$ 9,400	$ 6,200	$11,000
b.	AGI before SS benefits	25,000	32,300	12,000	24,000
c.	50% SS benefits	3,900	4,700	3,100	5,500
d.	Tax-exempt interest	500	0	0	400
e.	Modified AGI	$ _____	$ _____	$ _____	$ _____
f.	Less base amount	(_____)	(_____)	(_____)	(_____)
g.	Excess modified AGI	$ _____	$ _____	$ _____	$ _____
h.	Taxable SS benefits (lesser of line c. or 50% of g.)	$ _____	$ _____	$ _____	$ _____

14. **Series EE U.S. Savings Bonds.** (Obj. 3) Norma, age 30 and single, is considering investing $2,000 in Series EE U.S. Savings Bonds. Discuss the options Norma has with respect to reporting the interest income from these bonds.

15. **Series EE U.S. Savings Bonds.** (Obj. 3) Following are the issue (purchase) price, original face (maturity) value, and selected redemption values of Series EE bonds purchased by Grady in 2022.

Issue (Purchase) Price	Face (Maturity) Value	Redemption Value	
		As of 12/31/22	As of 12/31/23
$ 600	$ 1,200	$ 638	$ 673
200	400	233	261
1,000	2,000	1,025	1,051
50	100	54	58
150	300	156	162

Grady elects to report the increase in redemption value each year on Series EE bonds. At the election date he owned no other U.S. savings bonds. What amount does Grady include in gross income from these bonds in 2022 and 2023?

16. **Accrued Interest on Bonds.** (Obj. 3) Ramona purchased a $40,000 par value bond of DPQ Corporation. She paid the seller $40,533 ($40,000 par value + $533 accrued interest). The 8% bond pays interest semiannually on June 30 and December 31. Ramona received the first semiannual interest payment of $1,600 on December 31, 2022. Discuss how much interest income Ramona must include in gross income in 2022.

17. **Original Issue Discount.** (Obj. 3) On January 1, 2022, a cash basis taxpayer paid $32,870 for a 25-year, zero-coupon bond with a face value of $100,000. The annual yield to maturity is 4.5%.

    a. What is the OID on the bond?

    b. What portion of the OID would be included in taxable interest income for 2022?

    c. What portion of the OID would be included in taxable interest income for 2023?

18. **Original Issue Discount.** (Obj. 3) A 30-year bond with a face value of $100,000 is issued at a discount. How large can the discount be and still be treated as *de minimis* OID? Discuss the tax consequences to the purchaser of a bond with *de minimis* OID.

19. **Market Discount.** (Obj. 3) On January 1, 2022, Dolly pays $9,380 for corporate bonds. The bonds were originally issued on January 1, 2014 for $9,330 and have a $10,000 face value. They mature on January 1, 2040. The bond's amortized carrying value (ACV) on January 1, 2022 was $9,450. What portion of the $620 difference between the $9,380 Dolly paid for the bonds and their $10,000 face value is OID? What portion is market discount? Discuss how Dolly treats these amounts on her tax return.

20. **Bond Premium.** (Obj. 3) Dean pays $104,700 for bonds with a face value of $100,000. Describe the tax consequences to Dean of buying bonds at a premium.

21. **Below Market Loans.** (Obj. 3) Under what circumstances do the below market loan rules apply? Describe the tax consequences of making a below market loan. Be sure to discuss the consequences to both the borrower and the lender.

22. **Imputed Interest.** (Obj. 3)

    a.   What are applicable federal rates (AFRs)? What purpose do they serve?

    b.   How is the imputed interest on a below market loan computed?

23. **Gift Loans.** (Obj. 3) Janet's parents lend Janet and her husband $125,000 to buy a new home. The loan is for ten years with no interest.

    a.   Must interest be imputed on the loan? If so, how would the amount of imputed interest be determined?

    b.   If the loan amount were $100,000, would interest have to be imputed? If so, how would the amount of imputed interest be determined?

    c.   If the loan amount were $10,000, would interest have to be imputed?

24. **Compensation-Related Loans.** (Obj. 3) On January 1, a company loans its employee, Liz Kittner, $50,000. The terms of the note require that Liz pay interest annually based on a 1.5% annual rate of interest. In addition, Liz is to repay the $50,000 at the end of three years. At the time the loan was made, the current annual AFR short-term, mid-term and long-term rates were 2%, 3% and 4%, respectively. Determine the tax consequences of this loan to both the company and to Liz in the first year.

25. **Corporation-Shareholder Loans.** (Obj. 3) On January 1, a corporation loans its shareholder, Lynda Matsen, $120,000. The terms of the loan require that Lynda pay interest annually based on a 2.0% annual rate of interest. In addition, Lynda is to repay the $120,000 at the end of six years. At the time the loan was made, the current annual AFR short-term, mid-term and long-term rates were 2%, 3% and 4%, respectively. Determine the tax consequences of this loan to both the corporation and to Lynda in the first year.

26. **Dividend Income.** (Obj. 4) What are dividends and how are qualified dividends taxed differently from nonqualified dividends?

27. **Dividend Income.** (Obj. 4) Susan owns shares of stock in a corporation. In January 2023, she received a 1099-DIV reporting the following for 2022:

Total ordinary dividends	$526
Qualified dividends included in total dividends	450

How are these dividends reported on Susan's tax return?

28. **Kiddie Tax.** (Obj. 5) Dee Evans (SSN 842-00-6940), age 10, received taxable interest of $4,600 during 2022. She has no other income, and no itemized deductions related to investment income. Compute Dee's tax liability by completing Dee's Form 8615. Her father Robert's SSN is 490-00-9919. Her father files as a head of household. He has no other dependents. His taxable income is $90,000.

(Use for Problem 28.)

Form **8615** Department of the Treasury Internal Revenue Service	**Tax for Certain Children Who Have Unearned Income** Attach only to the child's Form 1040 or 1040-NR. Go to *www.irs.gov/Form8615* for instructions and the latest information.	OMB No. 1545-0074 **2022** Attachment Sequence No. **33**

Child's name shown on return | Child's social security number

A Parent's name (first, initial, and last). **Caution:** See instructions before completing. | **B** Parent's social security number

C Parent's filing status (check one):
☐ Single ☐ Married filing jointly ☐ Married filing separately ☐ Head of household ☐ Qualifying widow(er)

Part I Child's Net Unearned Income

1 Enter the child's unearned income. See instructions **1**

2 If the child **did not** itemize deductions on **Schedule A** (Form 1040) or **Schedule A** (Form 1040-NR), enter $2,300. Otherwise, see instructions **2**

3 Subtract line 2 from line 1. If zero or less, **stop**; do not complete the rest of this form but **do** attach it to the child's return **3**

4 Enter the child's **taxable income** from Form 1040 or 1040-NR, line 15. If the child files Form 2555, see the instructions **4**

5 Enter the **smaller** of line 3 or line 4. If zero, **stop**; do not complete the rest of this form but **do** attach it to the child's return **5**

Part II Tentative Tax Based on the Tax Rate of the Parent

6 Enter the parent's **taxable income** from Form 1040 or 1040-NR, line 15. If zero or less, enter -0-. If the parent files Form 2555, see the instructions **6**

7 Enter the total, if any, from Forms 8615, line 5, of **all other** children of the parent named above. **Do not** include the amount from line 5 above **7**

8 Add lines 5, 6, and 7. See instructions **8**

9 Enter the tax on the amount on line 8 based on the **parent's** filing status above. See instructions. If the Qualified Dividends and Capital Gain Tax Worksheet, Schedule D Tax Worksheet, or Schedule J (Form 1040) is used to figure the tax, check here . . . . . . ☐ **9**

10 Enter the parent's tax from Form 1040 or 1040-NR, line 16, minus any alternative minimum tax. **Do not** include any tax from **Form 4972** or **Form 8814**, or any tax from the recapture of an education credit. If the parent files Form 2555, see the instructions. If the Qualified Dividends and Capital Gain Tax Worksheet, Schedule D Tax Worksheet, or Schedule J (Form 1040) was used to figure the tax, check here . . . . . . ☐ **10**

11 Subtract line 10 from line 9 and enter the result. If line 7 is blank, also enter this amount on line 13 and go to **Part III** **11**

12a Add lines 5 and 7 . . . . **12a**

b Divide line 5 by line 12a. Enter the result as a decimal (rounded to at least three places) . . . . . **12b** × .

13 Multiply line 11 by line 12b **13**

Part III Child's Tax—If lines 4 and 5 above are the same, enter -0- on line 15 and go to line 16.

14 Subtract line 5 from line 4 . . . . **14**

15 Enter the tax on the amount on line 14 based on the **child's** filing status. See instructions. If the Qualified Dividends and Capital Gain Tax Worksheet, Schedule D Tax Worksheet, or Schedule J (Form 1040) is used to figure the tax, check here . . . . . . ☐ **15**

16 Add lines 13 and 15 . . . . **16**

17 Enter the tax on the amount on line 4 based on the **child's** filing status. See instructions. If the Qualified Dividends and Capital Gain Tax Worksheet, Schedule D Tax Worksheet, or Schedule J (Form 1040) is used to figure the tax, check here . . . . . . ☐ **17**

18 Enter the **larger** of line 16 or line 17 here and on the **child's** Form 1040 or 1040-NR, line 16. If the child files Form 2555, see the instructions **18**

For Paperwork Reduction Act Notice, see your tax return instructions. Cat. No. 64113U Form **8615** (2022)

29. **Net Investment Income (NII) Tax.** (Obj. 5) Compute the net investment income (NII) tax for each of the following taxpayers.

    a.   A married couple files a joint return. Their modified AGI is $316,990, and they have net investment income of $19,965.

    b.   A taxpayer files as head of household. His modified AGI is $270,888, and he has net investment income of $60,640.

    c.   A married taxpayer files separately from his spouse. His modified AGI is $306,408, and he has net investment income of $213,049.

    d.   An unmarried taxpayer files as single. Her modified AGI is $189,640, and she has net investment income of $14,233.

    e.   A taxpayer files his tax return using qualified widow(er) filing status. His modified AGI is $263,815, and he has net investment income of $34,588.

30. **Tax Benefit Rule.** (Obj. 1) Explain the tax benefit rule as it applies to refunds of state and local income taxes, as well as federal income taxes.

31. **Tax Benefit Rule.** (Obj. 1) In 2021, Lou, age 35 and single, deducted $5,325 on his federal income tax return for state income taxes withheld during the year. Lou has excellent vision. In 2022, Lou received an $875 refund from the state. For 2021, Lou deducted $17,254 in itemized deductions. After these deductions, Lou's taxable income was $100,000. The 2021 standard deduction for a single taxpayer was $12,550. How much of the refund must Lou include in his 2022 gross income?

32. **Internet Problem: Filling out Schedule B.** (Obj. 6)

Joyce Mayer (SSN 234-00-7891) receives two 1099s for the year. Form 1099-DIV from Fidelity Investments reports $10,290 of ordinary dividends. Form 1099-INT from State Bank reports interest income of $2,655. Joyce files as single and does not have any foreign bank accounts.

Go to the IRS website and locate Schedule B. Using the computer, fill in Schedule B for Joyce Mayer and print out a completed copy.

See Appendix A for instructions on use of the IRS website.

33. **Business Entity Problem:** This problem is designed for those using the "business entity" approach. **The solution may require information from Chapters 14–16.** Please answer the following true and false questions in the space provided.

		True	*False*
a.	Corporations owning less than 80% of another corporation are generally taxed on at least a portion of the dividends they receive from that company.	_____	_____
b.	Corporations receiving dividends from another corporation are taxed on 60% of the dividend income if they own 10% of the other company.	_____	_____
c.	S corporations receiving a dividend from another corporation do not pay taxes on the dividend.	_____	_____
d.	Partnerships receiving dividends from a corporation must include the dividends in the calculation of "ordinary income."	_____	_____
e.	A shareholder receiving a property distribution from a corporation must recognize the property distribution at its fair market value (FMV) on the distribution date.	_____	_____
f.	A partner receiving a property distribution from the partnership must recognize the property distribution at its fair market value (FMV) on the distribution date.	_____	_____

34. **Business Entity Problem:** This problem is designed for those using the "business entity" approach. **The solution may require information from Chapter 14.**

Jason owns 100% of the stock in a C corporation. On December 31, the end of the corporation's tax year, the company has earnings and profits of $20,000 before consideration of any distribution to the owner. On December 31, the company distributes property with a market value of $50,000 to Jason. The basis of the property is $30,000.

a. What are the tax implications to the corporation?

b. What are the tax implications to Jason if his basis in the stock prior to the distribution is $27,000?

COMPREHENSIVE PROBLEMS

 35. Schedule B. (Obj. 6)

a. Neale D. (SSN 394-00-7584) and Judith L. (SSN 746-00-4457) Hamilton file a joint Form 1040. The Hamiltons have no foreign accounts or trusts. During the year, they received interest and dividends. Using the information provided below, prepare the Hamiltons' Schedule B (Form 1040), Interest and Ordinary Dividends.

Amounts Reported on Form 1099-INT	Amount
U.S. Treasury bond	$ 600
Ace Manufacturing Company note	50
AT&T debenture bond	60
Bank of America	90
State of Michigan municipal (tax-exempt) bond	75
City of Meadowood municipal (tax-exempt) bond	160

Interest Not Reported on Form 1099-INT	Amount
Interest on the mortgage of Mr. and Mrs. K. J. Roe	$ 732
K. R. Smith, personal note	115

Amounts Reported on Form 1099-DIV	Amount
Red Corporation dividend on preferred stock	$ 280
USC Corporation dividend on common stock	1,341
Dow Chemical Company dividend on common stock	185

b. Albert B. Kennedy (SSN 664-22-7857) receives various Form 1099s during the year. He has no foreign accounts or trusts. From the information provided below, prepare Albert's Schedule B (Form 1040), Interest and Ordinary Dividends.

Amounts Reported on Form 1099-INT	Amount
Bryce Corporation bonds	$3,830
Canyon Enterprises corporate bonds	490
State of Illinois municipal (tax-exempt) bonds	1,750

Amounts Reported on Form 1099-DIV	Amount
Exxon Mobil common stock	$ 975
UCB Corporation dividend on preferred stock	280
GE dividend reinvested in common stock through GE's dividend reinvestment plan	108

Chapter

Gross Income Exclusions and Deductions for AGI

CHAPTER CONTENTS

LEARNING OBJECTIVES

After completing Chapter 4, you should be able to:

1. Describe the items of income that can be excluded from gross income and compute the amount of the exclusion.
2. Recognize the various types of fringe benefits that employees might receive from their employers and if they are excluded from income.
3. Describe the deductions for AGI specifically listed on Form 1040 and compute the amount of the deduction.
4. Compare and contrast Roth IRAs and traditional IRAs, including the limits imposed on contributions to each type of IRA and the rules that govern distributions from these two types of IRAs.
5. Describe the various tax deductions and exclusions available for education-related expenses.
6. Prepare the tax forms and schedules introduced in the chapter, including Form 8815, Form 3903, and Form 1040.

CHAPTER OVERVIEW

Chapter 3 started the discussion of the calculation of gross income by describing some of the more common types of gross income inclusions. The first part of Chapter 4 continues that discussion by introducing items included in income that are specifically excluded from gross income. The latter part of the chapter introduces the details behind the deductions from gross income (commonly called "deductions for AGI") that are reported directly on the tax return. The chapter concludes with an illustration of Form 1040.

¶401 Exclusions from Gross Income

Income includes all wealth that flows to a taxpayer. Gross income is all income that the government taxes. Exclusions are amounts of income not subject to tax. This section describes many of the items of income that are entirely or partially exempt from gross income, but not all of them. [I.R.C. §§101-140]

¶401.01 LIFE INSURANCE PROCEEDS

Usually, life insurance proceeds paid because of the insured's death are tax-free. [I.R.C. §101] However, gross income results when an insurance company holds on to the proceeds of the policy and pays out the interest to the beneficiary. Under such an arrangement, gross income includes the interest when it becomes available to the beneficiary (e.g., credited to the beneficiary's account).

¶401.02 GIFTS AND INHERITANCES

The recipient of a gift or inheritance excludes from gross income the value of the gifted or inherited property. [I.R.C. §102] The donor of gifted property may be subject to gift tax. However, the recipient is not taxed on these transfers. After the transfer, any subsequent income the property earns is taxed to the recipient under the normal tax laws described in this textbook.

¶401.03 TAX-EXEMPT INTEREST

Interest received on general obligation bonds of a state, territory, or the District of Columbia is not taxable. [I.R.C. §103] This exclusion also applies to bonds issued by cities, counties, and school districts. Although it is not taxable, taxpayers report the amount of tax-exempt interest separately on their returns as an information item. This tax-exempt interest is included in some tax calculations, such as the calculation for determining taxable Social Security benefits (see ¶307).

Educational Savings Bonds, Series EE and I

You may recall from Chapter 3 that the interest on savings bonds is not taxed until the bonds are redeemed (see ¶308.02). Under certain conditions, taxpayers can exclude the interest on Series EE and I U.S. Savings Bonds they redeem during the year. [I.R.C. §135] The exclusion applies when the taxpayer uses the proceeds to pay for qualified educational expenses at an eligible institution. When there are proceeds left over after the educational expenses are paid, some of the interest is taxed. Also, when the taxpayer's income rises above a certain level, the exclusion is phased out. This exclusion applies only to bonds purchased after 1989.

To qualify for the exclusion, the taxpayer (or spouse, if filing jointly) must be the registered owner of the bond. Married taxpayers must file a joint return to qualify for the exclusion. Bonds issued to persons under age 24 do not qualify for the exclusion, unless they received the bonds upon the death of the registered owner. Taxpayers use Form 8815, Exclusion of Interest From Series EE and I U.S. Savings Bonds Issued After 1989, to compute the excluded interest.

Eligible institutions include public and nonprofit higher education schools, as well as postsecondary institutions. They do not include proprietary schools. **Qualified educational expenses** include tuition and fees paid to an eligible institution for the taxpayer, the taxpayer's spouse, and the taxpayer's dependents. Such expenses do not include payments for room and board. The taxpayer must reduce qualified expenses by certain nontaxable benefits received during the year. These benefits include scholarships awarded to the student and amounts received from an employer-provided educational assistance plan. Expenses used in computing the education tax credit for the student also reduce qualified expenses.

Taxpayers use the following formula to determine the interest exclusion before applying the phase-out rules.

Bonds Interest Exclusion Before Phase-Out

$$\text{Initial Exclusion} \;=\; \text{Interest Portion of the Proceeds} \;\times\; \frac{\text{Qualified Education Expenses – Nontaxable Education Benefits – Expenses Used in Computing Education Credits}}{\text{Redemption Proceeds}}$$

After using the above formula to determine the initial exclusion amount, taxpayers compute their modified AGI. This amount is AGI computed without the educational savings bond interest exclusion (currently being calculated) and the foreign earned income exclusion (see ¶401.14). They then compare this amount with the $85,800 threshold ($128,650 for MFJ or qualifying widow(er)) applicable for 2022. If modified AGI exceeds this threshold, the phase-out applies. The interest exclusion phases out proportionately over a range of $15,000 ($30,000 for MFJ or qualifying widow(er)). The phase-out threshold is adjusted each year for inflation (see ¶202). The exclusion is not available to a married taxpayer filing a separate return.

Phase-Out of Bond Interest Exclusion

$$\text{Initial Exclusion} \;\times\; \frac{\text{Modified AGI} - \$85,800^{*}}{\$15,000^{**}} \;=\; \text{Reduction in Interest Exclusion}$$

* $128,650 for MFJ or qualifying widow(er)
** $30,000 for MFJ or qualifying widow(er)

EXAMPLE 1

Fred and Ida Smith file a joint return. They claim their daughter, Inez, as a dependent. During the year, the Smiths paid $5,000 for Inez's tuition at Kent State University, where Inez is a full-time student. During the year, Inez received a $1,000 nontaxable scholarship. In September, the Smiths redeemed $10,000 of Series EE bonds. Of the cash received, $1,500 is interest and $8,500 is principal. The Smiths' modified AGI is $133,950, consisting of $132,450 of salary and the $1,500 interest that we are calculating the exclusion for.

Qualified education expenses for the year were $4,000 ($5,000 – $1,000 nontaxable scholarship). Because the Smiths did not use the entire $10,000 of proceeds on qualified education expenses, a portion of the $1,500 of interest income does not qualify for the exclusion. Their initial exclusion is $600 ($1,500 × $4,000/$10,000). However, since the Smiths' modified AGI exceeds the $128,650 MFJ threshold, they must further reduce the amount of their exclusion. The amount of the reduction is $106 ($600 initial exclusion × ($133,950 modified AGI – $128,650 MFJ threshold)/$30,000). Thus, $494 ($600 – $106) of the interest is excluded from gross income.

Filled-In Form 8815

INFORMATION FOR FIGURE 4-1:

The Smiths (from Example 1) complete Form 8815 to compute their educational savings bond interest exclusion. They enter the amounts in bold from below on the appropriate lines on the form. They then follow the instructions on the form to complete the rest of the form. After the Smiths report all $1,500 as interest income on Schedule B (line 1), they enter $548 on Schedule B (line 3) to subtract out their "Excludable interest on series EE and I U.S. savings bonds."

¶401.03

Line #

   2: Qualified higher education expenses paid in 2022, **$5,000**
   3: Inez's nontaxable scholarship, **$1,000**
   4: Expenses less scholarship, **$4,000**
   5: Proceeds from Series EE bonds, **$10,000**
   6: Interest associated with EE bonds, **$1,500**
   9: Modified AGI, **$133,950**

Figure 4-1: Filled-In Form 8815 (Page 1)

Form **8815**	**Exclusion of Interest From Series EE and I U.S. Savings Bonds Issued After 1989** (For Filers With Qualified Higher Education Expenses) Go to *www.irs.gov/Form8815* for the latest information. Attach to Form 1040 or 1040-SR.	OMB No. 1545-0074 **2022**
Department of the Treasury Internal Revenue Service		Attachment Sequence No. **167**

Name(s) shown on return
Fred and Ida Smith

Your social security number
376-00-7371

1	**(a)** Name of person (you, your spouse, or your dependent) who was enrolled at or attended an eligible educational institution	**(b)** Name and address of eligible educational institution
	Inez Smith	**Kent State University** Kent, OH 442342

If you need more space, attach a statement.

2	Enter the total qualified higher education expenses you paid in 2022 for the person(s) listed in column (a) of line 1. See the instructions to find out which expenses qualify	2	5,000
3	Enter the total of any nontaxable educational benefits (such as nontaxable scholarship or fellowship grants) received for 2022 for the person(s) listed in column (a) of line 1. See instructions	3	1,000
4	Subtract line 3 from line 2. If zero or less, **stop.** You **cannot** take the exclusion	4	4,000
5	Enter the total proceeds (principal and interest) from all series EE and I U.S. savings bonds **issued after 1989** that you **cashed during 2022**	5	
6	Enter the interest included on line 5. See instructions	6	
7	If line 4 is equal to or more than line 5, enter "1.000." If line 4 is less than line 5, divide line 4 by line 5. Enter the result as a decimal (rounded to at least three places)	7	× . 040
8	Multiply line 6 by line 7	8	600
9	Enter your modified adjusted gross income. See instructions	9	133,950		

Note: If line 9 is $100,800 or more if single, head of household, or qualifying widow(er); or $158,650 or more if married filing jointly, **stop.** You **cannot** take the exclusion.

10	Enter: $85,800 if single, head of household, or qualifying widow(er); $128,650 if married filing jointly	10	128,650		
11	Subtract line 10 from line 9. If zero or less, skip line 12, enter -0- on line 13, and go to line 14	11	5,300		
12	Divide line 11 by: $15,000 if single, head of household, or qualifying widow(er); $30,000 if married filing jointly. Enter the result as a decimal (rounded to at least three places)			12	× . 177
13	Multiply line 8 by line 12			13	106
14	**Excludable savings bond interest.** Subtract line 13 from line 8. Enter the result here and on Schedule B (Form 1040), line 3			14	494

For Paperwork Reduction Act Notice, see your tax return instructions.   Cat. No. 10822S   Form **8815** (2022)

DRAFT AS OF August 10, 2022 DO NOT FILE

¶401.04   COMPENSATION FOR PHYSICAL INJURY AND SICKNESS

Persons who are harmed on or off the job will sometimes receive payments related to their injuries. These payments can vary from workers' compensation, damage awards, and payments from an accident or health insurance plan. Under the general rule, these payments are all types of income to the recipient. Whether any of these payments can be excluded from gross income depends on the type of payment, and in some cases, the type of injury.

Cause	Taxable	Excludable
Physical injury	Reimbursed medical expense that were deducted in prior years (under the tax benefit rule). Punitive damages awarded due to the injury.	Compensation for the injury. Reimbursement for medical expenses related to the injury.
Emotional injury or distress	Compensation for emotional or nonphysical injuries not directly related to a physical injury. Punitive damages awarded due to the injury.	Compensation only if the emotional injury is a result of a physical injury (i.e., emotional trauma as a result of a serious physical accident).
Payments from accident or health insurance	Payments received by the taxpayer in excess of actual expense.	Reimbursed medical expenses disbursed under a policy paid for by the taxpayer or the taxpayer's (or spouse's) employer.

WORKERS' COMPENSATION

Workers' compensation is paid to an injured employee to cover lost wages and to pay the employee's medical expenses. [I.R.C. §104(a)] In exchange, the employee gives up the right to sue the employer for negligence. Taxpayers who receive workers' compensation exclude it from gross income, even though the payments are meant to replace wages that would have been taxed if earned on the job.

COMPENSATORY PAYMENTS AND MEDICAL REIMBURSEMENTS

Payments a person receives to compensate them for a physical injury or sickness are excluded from gross income. [I.R.C. §104(a)] Such payments are awarded to injured parties to make them whole again. Compensatory payments may cover lost wages or profits, which normally would be taxed had they been earned. Although emotional distress is not a physical injury, when payments for emotional distress are received *as a result of a physical injury or sickness*, they too are excluded from gross income. The reasoning is that the emotional distress is considered a part of the physical injury or sickness.

Also excluded from gross income are reimbursements for medical expenses stemming from a physical injury or sickness. However, if in a prior tax year the taxpayer had deducted and received a tax benefit for the medical expenses being reimbursed, then to the extent of the tax benefit received, the taxpayer reports that amount as "Other income" on Form 1040. (See ¶313.01 for a discussion of the tax benefit rule.)

Compensatory payments awarded for nonphysical injuries are always taxable. Examples of nonphysical injuries for which someone might be awarded payments include harassment, discrimination, wrongful termination, libel, slander, and invasion of privacy. Even though these compensatory payments are made to make the injured person whole again, payments received for nonphysical injuries are taxable to the person receiving them.

As a rule, it does not matter if the amounts awarded stem from a lawsuit or an out-of-court settlement. It also does not matter if the amount awarded is received in a lump sum or a series of payments.

Amounts awarded by the courts for punitive damages are taxable, even if they stem from a physical injury or sickness. [I.R.C. §104(a)(2)] Punitive damages are meant to punish the wrongdoer, rather than to compensate the victim. They often are awarded when the party that caused the harm was negligent or did something illegal.

PAYMENTS FROM AN ACCIDENT OR HEALTH INSURANCE PLAN

When the injured person receives payments from an accident or health insurance plan, whether those payments are excluded from gross income depends on who paid the premiums and the relationship of the amounts received to the actual medical expenses. Insurance payments for medical care are excludable from the patient's gross income if the patient or the employer paid the premiums on the policy. [I.R.C. §105(b)]

However, if any part of the payment received is a reimbursement for medical costs, the rules discussed earlier in this section (for compensatory payments) apply. Non-medical payments received from the plan are included in the employee's gross income to the extent that the employer paid the premiums. Thus, if 75% of the premiums are paid by the employer and 25% by the employee, only 25% of the non-medical payments received will be excluded from gross income. If the employee pays all of the premiums, then all payments are excluded from gross income. If the employer pays all of the premiums, then the employee is taxed on all payments received in excess of the medical expenses incurred.

¶401.05   ## FRINGE BENEFITS

A fringe benefit is a type of compensation employees receive. It is often in the form of goods or services given to them by their employers. When an employer provides fringe benefits, the employee often avoids paying the costs for these goods or services themselves. Thus, fringe benefits are a source of wealth to employees, and as such, are income. A fringe benefit is taxable unless the tax laws exclude it from gross income. Many tax laws exist that exclude fringe benefits. In the discussion that follows, some of the more common nontaxable fringe benefits are discussed.

Fringe Benefits Discussed in this Chapter

- Accident and health insurance
- Adoption assistance
- Athletic facilities
- Dependent care assistance
- *De minimis* benefits
- Educational assistance
- Employee discounts
- Group-term life insurance
- Meals and lodging provided on the employer's premises
- Military—Certain expenses and items of income
- No-additional-cost services
- Retirement planning services
- Transportation benefits
- Tuition reduction
- Working condition fringe benefits

Although fringe benefits may be excluded from an employee's gross income, the discrimination rule taxes key and highly paid employees on the value of most fringe benefits they receive when the benefit plan favors them. The discrimination rule applies to all fringe benefits discussed in this chapter, except for *de minimis* benefits, transportation benefits, and working condition fringe benefits. However, any benefits included as part of a collective bargaining agreement (union contract) are not considered to favor key or highly paid employees (and therefore, not subject to the discrimination rule).

For 2022, a **key employee** is (1) an officer of the company whose annual pay exceeds $200,000; (2) an employee who owns at least 5% of the company; or (3) an employee who owns at least 1% of the company and whose pay exceeds $150,000. **Highly paid employees** are employees, their spouses and dependents who (1) are an officer of the company; (2) own more than 5% of the voting stock in the company; or (3) are highly paid. [I.R.C. §416] The tax laws for defining what is considered "highly paid" vary depending on the type of fringe benefit. These rules are beyond the scope of this discussion and can be found in IRS Publication 15-B, *Employer's Tax Guide to Fringe Benefits*.

The Internal Revenue Code (Code) denies an exclusion to both key and highly paid employees when the benefit plan favors them. However, it continues to allow all other employees to exclude the benefits from gross income. The discrimination rule is intended to encourage employers to provide benefits to all of their employees, not just those who are officers, shareholders, or highly paid.

Accident and Health Insurance

Employers often offer their employees health insurance coverage. Employees exclude from gross income the cost of coverage employers pay on their behalf. [I.R.C. §106] Employees also exclude any insurance reimbursements they receive for medical care. However, the discrimination rule denies this exclusion to key employees and highly paid employees for benefits in excess of the benefits provided to other employees.

The nondiscrimination rule applies for employers that reimburse medical costs out of their own pockets, and for employers providing reimbursement or group coverage through a cafeteria plan. Historically, the nondiscrimination rule has not applied to employer group coverage purchased from an insurer unless it is offered through a cafeteria plan. The Affordable Care Act extends the nondiscrimination rule to such plans, but the IRS has postponed enforcement until it issues guidance. As of early 2022, it has not done so.

Under the Affordable Care Act, employers are limited in their ability to reimburse employees for the purchase of their own individual coverage. Violation of the rules may result in a $100 per day, per affected employee. These limits do not affect the deduction, exclusion and nondis- crimination rules, however.

EXAMPLE 2

Santex, Inc. provides its employees with health insurance coverage. During the year, it pays $8,000 to cover each of its employees. As long as Santex's plan does not favor key or highly paid employees, none of the employees are taxed on the $8,000 of insurance premiums. However, if the plan discriminates in favor of these employees, the IRS could require that the employer add the applicable amounts to the taxable wages of its key and highly paid employees (but not its other employees). As of early 2022, there is no such requirement. If Santex provided medical reimbursements that are not offered through an insurance plan, it would need to add the reimbursements to the taxable wages of the key employees.

Adoption Assistance

Under an adoption assistance program, employers pay or reimburse employees for qualified adoption costs. [I.R.C. §137] For 2022, employees exclude from gross income up to $14,890 of such costs. This amount is phased out when the employee's AGI falls between $223,410 and $263,410. These amounts are the same as those used in computing the adoption credit (¶204.10). Note that filing status does not matter; married and unmarried taxpayers have the same limits. Amounts excluded from gross income reduce the amount eligible for the adoption credit.

EXAMPLE 3	Joe's employer offers an adoption assistance program. During 2022, Joe is reimbursed $8,000 for adoption costs incurred during the year. Joe's AGI is $120,000. Since his AGI is less than the $223,410 AGI threshold, and the amount reimbursed is less than the cap of $14,890, the entire $8,000 is excluded from Joe's gross income.

Athletic Facilities

Employees exclude from gross income the value of the use of athletic facilities provided on the employer's property. These services include tennis courts, swimming pools, weight rooms, etc. To qualify for the exclusion, substantially all of the facility's use must be by employees, their spouses, and their dependent children.

Dependent Care Assistance

An employee can exclude from gross income up to $5,000 of amounts employers pay to provide dependent care for their employees under a dependent care assistance program. [I.R.C. §129] Only an employee's children and dependents can receive such care. Also, the care must be provided so that the employee can work. Instead of making payments to outsiders, an employer can provide care at the work site.

The annual exclusion cannot exceed the lesser of (i) $5,000 ($2,500 for married persons filing separately) or (ii) the employee's earned income. If the employee is married, then the earned income of the spouse with the lesser earnings is used. Special rules (similar to those discussed in ¶204.02) apply if the taxpayer or the taxpayer's spouse is either a full-time student or incapable of self-care. Taxpayers who use the exclusion must reduce their child and dependent care payments by the excluded amount when computing the child and dependent care credit (¶204.02).

Instead of providing dependent care for their employees, employers can set up plans that allow employees to be reimbursed for their dependent care costs from accounts that employees fund with their own wages. These accounts are commonly known as dependent care flexible spending accounts (FSAs). [I.R.C. §125] A dependent care FSA allows employees to set aside each year up to $5,000 of their wages from which they can pay qualified dependent care costs. Employers withhold FSA contribution amounts from employees' pay. Amounts withheld are excluded from employees' taxable wages. Thus, contributions to FSAs are made with pre-tax dollars. As employees pay for qualified dependent care costs, they submit receipts to their plan administrator for reimbursement from their FSA accounts.

EXAMPLE 4	Janet's employer offers a dependent care FSA. This year, Janet contributes $5,000 of her $45,000 wages to her FSA. As Janet pays for dependent care, she will submit her receipts to the plan administrator for reimbursement from her account. The $5,000 Janet uses to fund her FSA is excluded from gross income. This will be reflected on her W-2, which will report $40,000 of taxable wages. Because of her FSA contribution (and reduced taxable wages), Janet will pay less taxes this year. Hence, Janet's total out-of-pocket costs for dependent care are actually less than the $5,000 she paid to the child care provider.

De Minimis Benefits

Employees exclude from gross income benefits of a small (*de minimis*) value that they receive from employers. [I.R.C. §132(e)] Examples include occasional personal use of copy machines and office supplies. They also may include occasional tickets to entertainment and sporting events and office parties. Employees also exclude small holiday gifts, such as turkeys and hams.

    The discrimination rule does not apply to *de minimis* fringe benefits. Thus, key employees can exclude the value of occasional tickets to a sporting event, even if such tickets are only offered to key employees. [I.R.C. §132]

Educational Assistance

Under an educational assistance plan, employers pay or reimburse employees for qualified education costs. [I.R.C. §127] Each year, employees can exclude up to $5,250. The exclusion covers amounts paid for tuition, fees, books and supplies. Both graduate and undergraduate courses are included.

EXAMPLE 5

Leon's employer offers an educational assistance program. During the year, Leon was reimbursed $4,000 for tuition, books and fees for courses he took at the local college. Since this amount is less than the $5,250 maximum exclusion, the $4,000 is excluded from Leon's gross income.

Employee Discounts

Employees may exclude from gross income discounts they receive from their employers on goods and services. To qualify for the exclusion, the employee must work in the part of the employer's business giving the discount. For example, airline employees cannot exclude discounts they receive at a hotel owned by the airline company. For services, the amount of the discount cannot exceed 20% of the price charged to nonemployees. For goods, the discount cannot exceed the employer's gross profit percentage times the price charged to nonemployees. [I.R.C. §132(c)(1)]

EXAMPLE 6

A department store's gross profit percentage is 40%. The store's policy is to offer all its employees a 60% discount. The 20% excess discount times the sales price charged to nonemployees would be taxed as additional wages to employees who take advantage of the employee discount.

EXAMPLE 7

A clothing store offers a 15% discount to regular employees. It gives a 25% discount to highly paid employees. The store's gross profit percentage is 35%. Although neither discount exceeds the store's 35% gross profit percentage, the difference in discounts shows that the plan favors highly paid employees. Thus, the entire 25% discount to employees in the favored group is added to their gross income. Regular employees are not affected. They still exclude their 15% discount.

Group-Term Life Insurance

Sometimes an employer buys life insurance for employees under a group-term plan, where the employees name their beneficiaries. For each employee, the employer can purchase up to $50,000 of insurance without increasing the employee's gross income. [I.R.C. §79] When the coverage exceeds $50,000, the employee adds to gross income the cost associated with the excess insurance coverage. To determine this cost, the employer uses a uniform premium table (Figure 4-2).

Figure 4-2: Uniform Premium Table

Age at Year-End	Taxable Amount Each Month for $1,000 of Excess Coverage
Under 25	$.05
25–29	.06
30–34	.08
35–39	.09
40–44	.10
45–49	.15
50–54	.23
55–59	.43
60–64	.66
65–69	1.27
70 and over	2.06

To compute the employee's taxable amount, first determine the excess coverage under the plan. Next, divide the excess by $1,000, and round the result to the nearest tenth. The uniform premium table (Figure 4-2) lists the insurance rates by age. The employer determines an employee's age on the last day of the year and looks up the monthly rate for the employee's age. The employer then multiplies the monthly rate by the number of $1,000 increments. Finally, the employer multiplies this amount by the number of months of insurance coverage. The formula used is as follows:

Taxable Amount	=	Monthly Rate from Figure 4-2	×	Number of $1,000 Increments of Excess Coverage (rounded to the nearest tenth)	×	Number of Months of Coverage

When the employee pays part of the premiums, the employer subtracts *all* of the employee's payments from the (calculated) cost of the excess insurance. When the cost exceeds an employee's payments, the excess is included in the employee's gross income as additional taxable wages on Form W-2. When an employee's payments exceed the cost of the excess insurance, the employee has no additional gross income.

EXAMPLE 8

Bow Company pays an annual premium for $94,700 of life insurance for Harry Socket, age 56. Bow shares the cost with Harry, who pays Bow $12.50 a month through payroll deductions. With these payments, Harry gets 12 months of group-term life insurance protection. For Harry's age, the table in Figure 4-2 shows a monthly cost of $0.43. Bow adds $80.65 to Harry's taxable wages, as computed below.

Group-term life insurance coverage	$94,700
Less exempt coverage	(50,000)
Taxable coverage	$44,700
Cost subject to gross income inclusion [$44,700/$1,000 = 44.7; 44.7 × $0.43 × 12]	$230.65
Less payments by Harry ($12.50 × 12)	(150.00)
Gross income	$80.65

Employers whose plan favors key or highly paid employees must include in these favored employees' gross income the full cost of group-term life insurance provided to them (not just the excess over $50,000). The taxable amount for these favored employees is the *greater of* (i) the actual premiums paid, or (ii) the amount computed using the table in Figure 4-2.

EXAMPLE 9

> Tom is 45 years old and a key employee at his firm. The employer provides Tom with $200,000 of group life insurance coverage. The employer's actual cost for this coverage is $800; Tom pays nothing. If the employer's plan favors key or highly paid employees, Tom's employer would add $800 to Tom's taxable wages on Form W-2. This amount is the *greater of* (i) the employer's $800 actual cost, or (ii) $360, as determined using the monthly amounts in Figure 4-2 ($.15 × 200 increments based on $200,000 of coverage × 12 months). If the plan does not favor key or highly paid employees, the employer adds $270 to Tom's taxable wages ($150,000 excess coverage ÷ $1,000 = 150 increments × $.15 × 12).

Meals and Lodging Provided on the Employer's Premises

Employees exclude the value of meals and lodging provided by their employer when provided on the employer's premises for the convenience of the employer as a condition of employment. [I.R.C. §119] For example, nurses and doctors may be allowed to eat in the hospital cafeteria free-of-charge so that they can be reached, if needed in an emergency. Likewise, resident advisors of college dorms may exclude the value of the room and board provided to them free-of-charge if the college requires them to live in the dorm as a condition of their employment.

If the meals and lodging provided by the employer do not meet these qualifications, they are taxable compensation to the employee. The employer reports the fair market value of these benefits on the W-2 as non-cash compensation. See Chapter 13 at ¶1303 for additional explanation.

Military—Certain Expenses and Items of Income

Military personnel can exclude certain retirement pay, certain benefits, and certain moving expense reimbursements from income. [I.R.C. §§122, 132, and 134]

No-Additional-Cost Services

Employees exclude from gross income the value of services that do not cause large added costs or lost revenues to the employer. Examples of no-additional-cost services are the use of vacant hotel rooms, as well as unsold seats on airlines, buses and trains. To get the exclusion, the employee must work in the line of business providing the services. [I.R.C. §132]

Retirement Planning Services

Employees exclude from gross income the value of any qualified retirement plan services provided to them or their spouses by their employers. [I.R.C. §132] Note that this is the planning services, not the monetary contributions to retirement plans.

Transportation Benefits

In 2022, employees exclude from gross income up to $280 a month for employer-provided qualified parking or for employer-provided qualified transportation. **Qualified parking** includes parking provided near the employer's business or near the place where the employee commutes to work using mass transit or carpools. **Qualified transportation** includes transit passes and transportation to the employer's workplace in a commuter vehicle.

Unlike many of the other fringe benefits, the discrimination rule does not apply to transportation benefits. Thus, key employees and highly paid employees can exclude the value of these benefits, even when the benefit plan favors them. [I.R.C. §132]

EXAMPLE 10	Quinn's employer provides free monthly parking to its employees. The parking is valued at $330. The maximum monthly benefit for 2022 is $280. Thus, the employer includes an additional $600 ($50 excess × 12 months) in Quinn's 2022 taxable wages.

Tuition Reduction

Colleges and universities can exclude from their employees' wages the value of a qualified tuition reduction they give their employees. [I.R.C. §117(d)] A tuition reduction for graduate education qualifies for the exclusion if it is for the education of a graduate student who performs teaching or research activities for the institution. For undergraduate courses, the exclusion is allowed if the education is for one of the following persons:

1. A current employee.
2. A former employee who retired or left on disability.
3. A widow(er) of a person who died while working as an employee.
4. A widow(er) of a former employee who retired or left on disability.
5. A dependent child or spouse of any person listed above.

Working Condition Fringe Benefits

Usually employees deduct their job-related expenses as an itemized deduction. [I.R.C. §132(d)] When an employer pays for these costs, employees exclude their value from gross income. This includes amounts that qualify as deductible education costs that exceed the $5,250 fringe benefit under an employer's educational assistance plan.

The discrimination rule does not apply to working condition fringe benefits. Thus, key employees and highly paid employees can exclude the value of working condition fringe benefits, even when the benefit plan favors them. [I.R.C. §132]

EXAMPLE 11	Lenny's employer offers a qualifying educational assistance program. Lenny is reimbursed $8,400 for tuition, books, and fees for courses he took at the local college. If not reimbursed, the $8,400 would have been deductible as an employee business expense. Lenny excludes $5,250 under the educational assistance program. He excludes the rest ($8,400 – $5,250 = $3,150) as a working condition fringe benefit.

¶401.06   DISCHARGE OF DEBT

When a taxpayer's debt is forgiven, the decrease in debt causes the taxpayer's net worth to increase, thereby resulting in income. Usually, the amount of forgiven debt is included in gross income; however, if the taxpayer is bankrupt or insolvent at the time that debt is forgiven, the forgiven debt is excluded from gross income. [I.R.C. §108] As a tradeoff for the exclusion, the debtor must reduce certain tax aspects, such as net operating loss carryforwards. There are other discharge of debt provisions for business and farming properties.

 A provision in the Code temporarily allows taxpayers to exclude up to $2 million of income resulting from the discharge of debt on the taxpayer's principal residence. At the time the textbook was sent to the printer, this tax law has been extended through 2025.

¶401.07   SCHOLARSHIPS AND FELLOWSHIPS

A student excludes from gross income the portion of scholarships and fellowship grants used to pay tuition and course-required fees, books, supplies, and equipment. [I.R.C. §117] Only degree candidates get this exclusion. Degree candidates include undergraduate and graduate students who pursue studies aimed at getting an academic or professional degree. Postdoctoral fellowship students do not get this exclusion.

Graduate students who get paid to teach or do research at their degree-granting institutions can exclude tuition waivers they receive. They cannot reduce their taxable wages by amounts spent on books, supplies, and equipment.

 The exclusion for scholarships does not apply to compensation for services rendered, even if all candidates for the degree are required to perform the services.

Students with taxable scholarships report this amount as additional wages on Form 1040. The student writes in the words **SCH =** and the taxable amount in the space to the left of where taxable wages are reported. Thus, these amounts count as earned income for purposes of computing the standard deduction for those claimed as a dependent on another's return (¶106.03).

EXAMPLE 12

Mandy is awarded a $10,000 scholarship to attend State College. Mandy is claimed as a dependent on her parents' return. Her tuition and course-required books and fees for the year are $6,000. The rest of the scholarship is used to cover room and board. Mandy excludes $6,000 of the scholarship from gross income. On her tax return she writes in "SCH = $4,000" and adds the $4,000 to her taxable wages. This amount is part of her earned income used to compute her limited standard deduction (the *lesser of* (i) $1,100 or (ii) earned income + $350; see ¶106.03).

¶401.08   EXCLUSION OF SALE OF PRINCIPAL RESIDENCE

Taxpayers can exclude some or all of the gain on the sale of their principal residence under certain conditions. [I.R.C. §121] This exclusion is up to $250,000 for single taxpayers and $500,000 for those married filing jointly. The exclusion of the gain on the sale of principal residence is covered in Chapter 10.

¶401.09   ROTH IRAS

Another source of tax-free income comes from investing in a Roth IRA. Taxpayers make non-deductible contributions to Roth IRAs and in return, the earnings grow tax-free. [I.R.C. §408A] Taxpayers make withdrawals tax and penalty-free if the distribution is made after the Roth IRA has been open for five tax years and any one of the following conditions exists.

1. The distribution is made after the taxpayer reaches age 59½.
2. The distribution is made to a beneficiary as a result of the taxpayer's death.
3. The distribution is made on account of the taxpayer's disability.
4. The distribution is used to pay first-time homebuyer expenses (subject to a $10,000 lifetime limit).

Amounts withdrawn from a Roth IRA are considered to come first from contributions, and then earnings. When distributions do not meet at least one of the above criteria, amounts received in excess of the taxpayer's contributions are included in gross income. A 10% early withdrawal penalty also applies to the amount taxed. However, taxpayers can withdraw their contributions at any time and for any reason without tax or penalty. Since contributions to a Roth IRA are not deductible, there is never any tax when only the taxpayer's contributions are taken from a Roth IRA. However, once the taxpayer has withdrawn amounts from a Roth IRA, they cannot be returned to the Roth IRA to grow tax-free.

EXAMPLE 13	After making contributions of $4,500 over a three-year period, Ben (age 35) withdraws $5,400 from his Roth IRA to buy a new car. Of this amount, $4,500 is a tax-free withdrawal of his contributions. Ben must pay income tax on the earnings of $900. He also pays a nondeductible early withdrawal penalty of $90 (10% × $900).

For 2022, the maximum contribution to a Roth IRA is the *lesser of* (i) $6,000 or (ii) 100% of the taxpayer's earned income. Taxpayers at least 50 years old may contribute another $1,000. When a married couple files a joint tax return, the amount increases to $12,000 (plus $1,000 for each spouse who is 50 or older). However, the couple must have enough combined earnings to match the total contribution. Each spouse must establish a separate Roth IRA. Also, the amount that can be contributed to either spouse's Roth IRA cannot exceed $6,000 ($7,000 if age 50 or older). The taxpayer's maximum contribution is proportionally phased out when AGI falls within the following ranges:

Single, head of household, and MFS but did not live with spouse at any time during the year: $129,000–$144,000 [$15,000 range]
    MFJ and qualifying widow(er): $204,000–$214,000 [$10,000 range]
    MFS and lived with spouse at some point during the year: $0–$10,000 [$10,000 range]

Taxpayers round their reduced contribution up to the nearest $10. If their reduced contribution is more than $0, but less than $200, they increase the amount to $200. Examples 14 and 15 show how the reduced contribution is computed for taxpayers whose AGI falls in the phase-out range.

EXAMPLE 14	Grace is single and 43 years old. She wants to contribute the most she can to a Roth IRA. Her AGI is $131,250. She is $2,250 over the $129,000 threshold. For 2022, Grace may contribute $5,100 [$6,000 maximum − ($2,250/$15,000 phase-out range × 6,000)].

EXAMPLE 15	Kathy and Adam Keck are both age 60. Since both are age 50 or older, their initial Roth IRA limit increases to $7,000 ($6,000 + $1,000). However, their AGI is $212,105 (most of which comes from taxable wages). This is $8,105 over the $204,000 threshold. The maximum each of them can contribute to their respective Roth IRA for 2022 is $1,330 [$7,000 maximum − ($8,105/$10,000 phase-out range × $7,000) then rounded up to nearest $10].

Taxpayers filing MFJ with over $214,000 of AGI ($10,000 for MFS and living with their spouse; $144,000 for all others) cannot contribute to a Roth IRA for 2022. They may, however, contribute to a traditional IRA (discussed at ¶402.10).

The deadline for making contributions to a Roth IRA for 2022 is April 15, 2023. The IRS charges a 6% penalty on excess contributions made to an IRA. In addition to the penalty, when the excess amounts are withdrawn, the earnings withdrawn are subject to income tax and a 10% early withdrawal penalty.

¶401.10   ROTH 401(K) PLANS

An employer's 401(k) plan may let employees make designated Roth 401(k) contributions. [I.R.C. §402A] **Designated Roth contributions** are made with post-tax wages. This means that that amounts designated as Roth contributions do not reduce the employee's taxable wages. However, as with Roth IRAs, qualified distributions from Roth 401(k) plans are tax-free once the account has been around for five years. Like with Roth IRAs, the part of a nonqualified distribution that is earnings is included in gross income and subject to a 10% early withdrawal penalty. Although Roth 401(k) plans are similar to Roth IRAs, the two differ in several ways.

1. There is no income limit on who can make designated Roth contributions.
2. In 2022, employees can contribute up to $20,500 of their wages (plus $6,00 if age 50 or older) to a Roth 401(k).
3. Qualified distributions are the same as those used for Roth IRAs. However, withdrawing amounts for first-time home purchases is a nonqualified distribution from a Roth 401(k).

¶401.11   COVERDELL EDUCATION SAVINGS ACCOUNTS

An education savings account (ESA) is a tax-advantaged way to save for a child's education. [I.R.C. §530] The contributor opens an ESA and names the child as the beneficiary. Often the contributor is the child's parent or grandparent. However, there is no rule that contributor be related to the child. Contributions to an ESA are not deductible and must be made prior to the child's 18th birthday. Otherwise a 6% penalty is assessed. There is no age restriction for a child with special needs.

An annual $2,000 contribution limit applies to all ESAs where the child is the named the beneficiary. A 6% penalty is assessed if combined contributions for a child during any year exceed $2,000. Since $2,000 is a per beneficiary limit, a taxpayer can contribute to multiple ESAs for different children, as long as the $2,000 per beneficiary limit (by all contributors) is not exceeded.

EXAMPLE 16	Three years ago, Grandpa Joe opened an ESA for his grandson, Kyle. The next year, Kyle's father opened a second ESA in his son's name. These are the only two ESAs where Kyle is the beneficiary. If in the current year Grandpa Joe contributes $700 to the first ESA, the most Kyle's father can contribute to the second ESA is $1,300 ($2,000 per beneficiary limit – $700). If Kyle's father mistakenly contributes $2,000 during the year, a 6% penalty will be assessed on the $700 excess.

Married taxpayers who file MFJ and have modified AGI in excess of $220,000 ($110,000 for all other taxpayers) cannot contribute to an ESA. A reduced contribution is allowed for MFJ taxpayers with modified AGI that falls between $190,000–$220,000 ($95,000–$110,000 for all other taxpayers). For most taxpayers, modified AGI is the same as their AGI.

EXAMPLE 17	Same as in Example 16, except that Grandpa Joe, who is widowed, has modified AGI of $115,000. Since Grandpa Joe's modified AGI exceeds $110,000, he is not allowed to make any ESA contributions this year. If he mistakenly contributes to an ESA, a 6% penalty will be assessed on his contribution.

The tax-advantaged feature of these accounts is that earnings distributed from an ESA are excluded from the child's gross income as long as the child uses the amounts to pay for qualified education expenses before the child's 30th birthday. When distributions during the year exceed the amount of qualified higher education expenses, the law treats some of the excess as a distribution of earnings and taxes it.

Qualified education expenses include tuition, fees, books, supplies, equipment, and room and board. For room and board to qualify, the student must attend school on at least a half-time basis in a program leading to a recognized educational credential. It does not matter whether the qualified expenses are paid for the student's elementary (grade school), secondary (junior high and high school), or post-secondary (college) education.

When the beneficiary reaches age 30, any unused amount in the account must be distributed to the beneficiary. Any earnings included in the distribution will be added to the beneficiary's gross income and taxed. A 10% penalty on the earnings also will be assessed. To avoid this situation, the unused amount may be rolled over into an ESA of a sibling or child of the beneficiary and escape both income taxes and the 10% penalty.

 The beneficiary can make a tax-free distribution from a Coverdell ESA in the same year part of the beneficiary's education costs are paid for with tax-free educational assistance. A tax-free distribution can also be made in a year in which an education tax credit is claimed on behalf of the beneficiary. However, the same educational expenses cannot be used for more than one purpose. Thus, in computing qualified education expenses from the ESA, the beneficiary must first reduce the education costs by amounts paid for with tax-free educational assistance from an employer's fringe benefit plan. Any remaining costs then must be reduced by expenses taken into account in computing the American opportunity or lifetime learning tax credit.

¶401.12   529 PLANS

Many states, colleges, and brokerage firms have set up qualified tuition programs from which taxpayers can later pay a beneficiary's college expenses. [I.R.C. §529] In most cases, the beneficiary is the taxpayer's child or grandchild; however, there is no rule that the beneficiary be related to the taxpayer (contributor). The more common name for these accounts is **529 plans**.

Contributions to 529 plans are not deductible, but the earnings from these accounts remain tax free if the funds are later used to pay qualified education expenses for the beneficiary. Qualified expenses include tuition, fees, books, and supplies, as well as room and board. However, these amounts must be reduced by any tax-free assistance the student uses to pay for these costs. For example, if the student receives a nontaxable scholarship, qualified expenses are computed net of the scholarship. Likewise, if a parent is reimbursed amounts from an employer's educational assistance plan, qualified expenses are computed net of the reimbursement.

EXAMPLE 18   Starting in 2007, Paul has contributed each year to a 529 plan for his daughter, Susan. At the end of last year, the balance in the plan is $30,000. In the fall of this year, $6,000 is withdrawn from the account to pay for Susan's tuition and fees at Northwest College. None of the $6,000 is taxable. The balance left in the account can be used in the future to pay more of Susan's qualified education expenses.

If amounts withdrawn from a 529 plan are not used to pay the beneficiary's qualified education expenses, a portion of the earnings withdrawn are included in the beneficiary's gross income. The taxable earnings equal the earnings withdrawn times the ratio of the nonqualified distribution to the total amount withdrawn from the 529 plan. A 10% penalty is assessed on the taxable earnings.

EXAMPLE 19   Same facts as in Example 18, except that Susan received a $4,500 scholarship to cover her tuition. Qualified expenses would be reduced to $1,500 ($6,000 – $4,500), leaving the excess of $4,500 withdrawn as a nonqualified distribution. If $1,000 of the $6,000 withdrawn is earnings, then 75% ($4,500 nonqualified distribution ÷ $6,000 withdrawn) of the $1,000, or $750, would be included in Susan's gross income.

If the beneficiary ends up not going to college, the plan refunds the amount in the account to the contributor. Any portion returned that is earnings is taxed to the contributor as interest income, and is subject to a 10% penalty. To avoid this situation, the unused amount may be rolled over into a 529 plan of the beneficiary's spouse or family member (as defined in the Code).

The earnings on amounts withdrawn from a 529 plan that are not used for qualified education expenses are taxed to the beneficiary. However, when the beneficiary does not attend college, the 529 plan funds revert to the contributor and the earnings are taxed to the contributor. This is different from the way education savings accounts (ESAs) work. With an ESA, if the beneficiary does not attend college, the earnings from the account are taxed to the beneficiary, unless they are rolled over into an ESA of the beneficiary's sibling or child.

Beginning in 2018, 529 plans may distribute up to $10,000 in tuition expenses incurred during the tax year for designated beneficiaries enrolled at a public, private, or religious elementary or secondary school. The limitation applies on a per-student, not per-account basis. Any distribution in excess of $10,000 would be taxable.

EXAMPLE 20   Matthew goes to Saint Viator High School and his tuition is $14,000 a year. His mom, Priscilla has a 529 plan which Matthew is a beneficiary. His grandma, Allison has a 529 which Matthew is also a beneficiary. In June 2022, Priscilla had a distribution of $6,000 to pay for Matthew's tuition. In August 2022, Allison had a distribution of $6,000 to also pay for Matthew's tuition. Since only $10,000 is allowed, Priscilla and Allison must come to an agreement as to who will be taxed on the $2,000 excess distribution.

¶401.13   ABLE ACCOUNTS

ABLE accounts were enacted by Congress late in 2014 as part of the Achieving a Better Life Experience (ABLE) Act. [I.R.C. §529A] ABLE accounts are similar to 529 plans in that contributions are not deductible (made with after-tax dollars). Likewise, the earnings are never taxed as long as the amounts from the account are used to pay for qualified expenses.

The account owner and beneficiary of an ABLE account is a person who became disabled before turning 26 and who receives social security benefits as a result of that disability. Eligible persons can have only one ABLE account, and the account must be one offered by the state where the disabled person lives. Total contributions to an ABLE account (from all contributors) are limited each year. The limit for 2022 is $16,000. Excess contributions are subject to a 6% penalty.

Distributions from ABLE accounts are tax-free as long as the amounts are used to pay the beneficiary's "qualified disability expenses." Earnings withdrawn as part of a nonqualified distribution are included in the beneficiary's gross income and subject to a 10% penalty. Qualified disability expenses are those related to the beneficiary's blindness or disability, as well as those that help the disabled person maintain or improve health, independence, and quality of life. Examples include costs related to housing, education, transportation, health care, job training, and personal support services.

An individual is allowed to roll over amounts from a 529 plan to an ABLE account if the ABLE account is owned by the same designated beneficiary of the 529 plan or a member of the designated beneficiary's family. However, any rolled-over amounts count toward the overall limitation on amounts that can be contributed to an ABLE account within a tax year. [I.R.C. §529A]

¶401.14   FOREIGN EARNED INCOME EXCLUSION

For 2021, U.S. citizens and residents may elect to exclude up to $108,700 of income earned while working in foreign countries. [I.R.C. §911] For 2022, the maximum exclusion is $112,000. To qualify for this exclusion, the taxpayer must either (1) be a bona fide resident of a foreign country for the entire tax year or (2) be physically present in a foreign country for 330 full days during a 12-month period.

When the taxpayer qualifies for the exclusion, but resides in a foreign country only part of the year, the exclusion must be prorated. For example, if a taxpayer resides in France for the last 210 days of 2021 and the first 300 days in 2022, the taxpayer's 510 days of physical presence easily meets the 330-days in a 12-month-period requirement. Thus, the taxpayer qualifies for the foreign earned income exclusion in each year. The maximum exclusion must be prorated as shown below:

$$2021: (210/365) \times \$108,700 \quad = \quad \$62,540 \text{ maximum exclusion}$$

$$2022: (300/365) \times \$112,000 \quad = \quad \$92,055 \text{ maximum exclusion}$$

As an alternative to the exclusion, taxpayers may elect to include all foreign income in gross income and take a tax credit for the income taxes paid to foreign countries. The foreign tax credit is discussed in ¶204.01.

EXAMPLE 21   On June 5, 2021, Jane's employer sends her to work in the Paris office. She is there until October 27, 2022. Jane's annual pay is $144,000 for both 2021 and 2022. Her earnings while working in France were $80,548 in 2021 and $115,068 in 2022. Jane was not present in France for the entire year in 2021 or 2022, but lived there at least 330 days during a 12-month period. (She lived in France 510 days from June 5, 2021 – October 27, 2022. (Count both the first and the last day.) She can reduce her AGI by $62,540 in 2021 and by $92,055 in 2022 (see calculations above). Her other option is to include the salary in AGI and use the rules from Chapter 2 to take a foreign tax credit for the income taxes she pays to the French government.

EXAMPLE 22   Same facts as in Example 21, except that Jane works in France until February 15, 2023. Her annual pay remains at $144,000, with $100,000 earned while working in Paris in 2022. The maximum foreign earned income exclusion for 2022 would be $112,000. In 2023, her maximum foreign earned income exclusion (using the 2022 limit) is $14,115 (46 days/365 × $112,000).

   The purpose of the foreign earned income exclusion and the foreign tax credit is to give tax relief to U.S. citizens and residents of the U.S. who might end up paying income taxes to both the U.S. and the foreign country where they work. The maximum exclusion is adjusted each year to reflect changes in the cost of living (see ¶202 for discussion of indexing for inflation).

¶402   Deductions for AGI

Not all deductions for AGI are deducted directly on Form 1040. Some deductions offset gross income on supporting forms and schedules, with the net result shown in the income section of Form 1040. For example, a sole proprietor's deductible business expenses reduce gross income from the business on Schedule C. Only the net profit (or loss) appears on Form 1040 and is included in calculation of the taxpayer's AGI.

Common Deductions Reported Elsewhere
1. Trade or business deductions, Schedule C (Chapter 7)
2. Losses from property sales, Schedule D (Chapter 11)
3. Rent and royalty expenses, Schedule E (Chapter 9)

Figure 4-3 lists out all deductions for which there are separate lines on Schedule 1 (Form 1040). The taxpayer can also write in the foreign earned income exclusion (¶401.14) on the dotted portion of the last line before entering the total deductions.

Figure 4-3: Deductions Listed on Form 1040, Schedule 1	Line
1. Educator expenses	11
2. Certain business expenses of reservists, performing artists, and fee-basis government officials	12
3. Health savings account deduction	13
4. Moving expenses for members of the Armed Forces	14
5. Deductible part of self-employment tax	15
6. Self-employed SEP, SIMPLE, and qualified plans	16
7. Self-employed health insurance deduction	17
8. Penalty on early withdrawal of savings	18
9. Alimony paid	19a
10. Individual Retirement Account (IRA) deduction	20
11. Student loan interest deduction	21

For 2020 and 2021 only, an individual who did not itemize their deductions could claim a for AGI deduction for qualified charitable contributions. [See Chapter 5 for itemized deductions.] However, the individual reported the deduction on Form 1040, line 10b, rather than on Schedule 1. [I.R.C. §§62(a)(22) and 62(f)(1)]

¶402.01   EDUCATOR EXPENSES

A deduction for AGI of up to $300 is available to elementary through high school educational workers for their out-of-pocket classroom expenses. [I.R.C. §62(a)(2)(D)] On a joint return, a deduction up to $600 is allowed if both spouses are eligible for the deduction and each spouse spends at least $300 on classroom expenses.

¶402.02   CERTAIN BUSINESS EXPENSES OF RESERVISTS, PERFORMING ARTISTS, AND FEE-BASIS GOVERNMENT OFFICIALS

Armed Forces reservists, performing artists, and fee-basis government officials may deduct vehicle expenses, parking fees, tolls, transportation expenses, travel expenses, other business expenses, and 50% of meals that were incurred in the course of their employment, but not reimbursed by their employer. To do so, they use Form 2106, Employee Business Expenses, and the final amount is transferred to Schedule 1.

To claim a deduction for AGI, married taxpayers must file jointly unless the spouses lived apart at all times during the year.

Certain performing artists may qualify to deduct their employee business expenses as deduction for AGI. [I.R.C. §62(a)(2)(B)] To do so, they need to meet these three requirements:

1. During the year, the artist performs services in the performing arts for at least two employers, each of whom pay the artist at least $200,
2. Business expenses must exceed 10% of gross income from the performing arts, and
3. AGI (before deducting these expenses) does not exceed $16,000. [I.R.C. §62(b)(1)]

¶402.03   HEALTH SAVINGS ACCOUNT DEDUCTION

Taxpayers deduct for AGI contributions they make to their **health savings accounts** (HSAs). [I.R.C. §62(a)(19)] HSAs can be used by individuals who have high-deductible health care plans. They allow taxpayers to save money to pay for their medical costs. In 2022, the maximum that can be contributed to an HSA is $3,650 for single coverage ($7,300 for family coverage).

Taxpayers 55 and older can contribute an additional $1,000. Unlike IRAs, there is no rule that HSAs be funded with earned income. All contributions for the current year must be made by April 15 of the next tax year. Once a taxpayer turns 65, contributions to an HSA must stop, if the individual is eligible for Medicare. [I.R.C. §223(b)(7)] Amounts contributed to HSAs in excess of the allowed amounts are subject to a 6% excise tax. Taxpayers claiming HSA deductions complete Form 8889, Health Savings Accounts (HSAs), and include it with their tax returns; the final amount is transferred to Schedule 1. For 2022, a **high-deductible health plan** is one that has at least a $1,400 deductible for single coverage and a $2,800 deductible for family coverage. Maximum out-of-pocket costs are $7,050 for single coverage ($14,100 for family coverage). Eligible taxpayers cannot also be covered under a health care plan offering the same coverage that does not qualify as a high-deductible plan.

Amounts withdrawn from an HSA to pay for medical costs are excluded from gross income. Any balance in an HSA at the end of the year stays in the account to pay medical costs in future years. Amounts withdrawn and not used to pay medical expenses are included in gross income and subject to a 20% penalty. However, when withdrawn after the taxpayer turns 65, the amounts are included in gross income but avoid the penalty. Since the earnings on amounts put in an HSA are not taxed until withdrawn, taxpayers can accumulate a sizeable sum in their HSAs over the years.

EXAMPLE 23	During 2022, Hope contributes the maximum $7,300 for family coverage to her employer's health care plan at work. The deductible for her family plan is $2,800, which makes it a high-deductible plan. During the year, Hope withdraws $1,000 from the HSA to pay unreimbursed medical costs for her family. At the end of the year, the balance in the account is $6,350 ($7,300 contributed − $1,000 withdrawn + $50 earnings). Hope is not taxed on either the $1,000 withdrawn or the $50 of earnings. The $6,350 balance carries forward to 2023 where it can be used to pay medical costs in that year or continue to earn tax-free income.

¶402.04 MOVING EXPENSES FOR MEMBERS OF THE ARMED FORCES

Members of the Armed Forces on active duty that move due to a military order and permanent change of station (PCS) may deduct the unreimbursed cost of moving. Deductible costs include moving charges for household goods and personal effects, storage and traveling expenses (including lodging) to a new home. No deduction is allowed for meals. Taxpayers claiming moving deductions complete Form 3903, Moving Expenses, and include it with their tax returns; the final amount is transferred to Schedule 1.

¶402.05 DEDUCTIBLE PART OF SELF-EMPLOYMENT TAX

Self-employed persons pay self-employment tax on their net earnings from self-employment. [I.R.C. §164(f)] The self-employment tax consists of the employer and employee shares of FICA taxes (see discussion in ¶706). Self-employed persons deduct the employer's (one-half) share of this tax for AGI on Form 1040. Self-employed taxpayers are also required to deduct one-half of the total self-employment taxes when calculating their qualified business income deduction (QBI). Self-employment tax (¶706) and QBI (¶802) are discussed in more detail in Chapters 7 and 8.

¶402.06 SELF-EMPLOYED SEP, SIMPLE, AND QUALIFIED PLANS

Self-employed taxpayers may make deductible contributions to a variety of plans including Keogh, SIMPLE, and simplified employee pension (SEP) plans. [I.R.C. §62(a)(6)] A taxpayer deducts the contributions as a deduction for AGI on Schedule 1, Additional Income and Adjustments to Income. Taxpayers are required to deduct contributions to these plans from QBI. Retirement plans for the self-employed (¶801) and QBI (¶802) are discussed in more detail in Chapter 8.

¶402.07   SELF-EMPLOYED HEALTH INSURANCE DEDUCTION

Self-employed taxpayers deduct their health insurance premiums for AGI. [I.R.C. §162(l)] The deduction equals the *lesser of* (i) 100% of the eligible health insurance premiums or (ii) net profit from the taxpayer's business reduced by any retirement plan contributions. The taxpayer treats any nondeductible premiums for health insurance as a medical expense (see ¶503.02 in Chapter 5).

Eligible health insurance premiums include amounts paid to insure the taxpayer, the taxpayer's spouse, the taxpayer's dependents, and the taxpayer's children under the age of 27. Self-employed persons cannot take this deduction for any month in which they (or their spouses) are eligible to participate in an employer's health care plan. Also, a self-employed taxpayer with employees cannot take the deduction when the plan favors the taxpayer.

Taxpayers are also required to deduct qualified self-employment health insurance when calculating QBI (see ¶802 in Chapter 8).

EXAMPLE 24	Pete Douglas is self-employed. His wife, Emma, works full-time for five months during the year. During those months, Emma is eligible for health insurance coverage through her employer. However, due to Emma's unsteady work, the Douglases chose to pay for their own health insurance coverage through Pete's business. During the current year, they paid $1,200 a month for family coverage ($14,400 for the year). Since Emma was eligible for health insurance through her employer for five months during the year, the Douglases can only deduct $8,400 in the current year ($1,200 × 7 months). They deduct this amount for AGI on Form 1040, page 1. The rest of the cost ($14,400 − $8,400 = $6,000) can be deducted as a medical expense on Schedule A. See Chapter 5 at ¶503.

¶402.08   PENALTY ON EARLY WITHDRAWAL OF SAVINGS

Money invested in certificates of deposit (CDs) usually earns a higher rate of interest than normal savings accounts. Banks offer higher rates for funds that remain on deposit until maturity. CDs can have maturities ranging anywhere from 1-month to 10-years. Usually, the longer the term, the higher the interest rate. In return for these higher rates, banks impose a large penalty if the investor cashes in the CD early. A taxpayer who cashes in the CD early includes the full interest income in gross income and then deducts the lost interest as a deduction for AGI on the line, "Penalty on early withdrawal of savings." [I.R.C. §62(a)(7)]

EXAMPLE 25	In 2018, Arthur invested $50,000 in a 5-year CD. In return, the bank promised to pay him an annual interest rate of 3% on his $50,000 investment. In 2022, Arthur decides to cash in his CD. He receives a check from the bank for $53,606, even though at the time of the withdrawal, the balance in his account was $55,231. The difference between these two amounts was the penalty for early withdrawal. After the end of the year, the bank will issue Arthur a Form 1099-INT reporting interest paid to him in the amount of $5,231 ($55,231 − $50,000) and his $1,625 early withdrawal penalty ($55,231 − $53,606). Arthur will report the full amount of interest income on Schedule B. He will then deduct the penalty as a deduction for AGI on Form 1040, Schedule 1. Only the net of these two amounts ($5,231 − $1,625 = $3,606) will increase his AGI in 2022.

¶402.09   ALIMONY PAID

As discussed in Chapter 3 (¶304.02), a person who pays alimony deducts it for AGI, and the recipient includes the same amount in gross income. This deduction is not available if it is pursuant to a divorce decree after 2018.

¶402.10   INDIVIDUAL RETIREMENT ARRANGEMENT (IRA) DEDUCTION

Working taxpayers can contribute to a traditional Individual Retirement Arrangement (IRA). Like the Roth IRA, this savings program allows the earnings to accumulate tax-free. However, unlike Roth IRAs, the earnings from a traditional IRA are taxed when withdrawn (as discussed in ¶305). Certain taxpayers can also deduct from gross income their contributions to a traditional IRA. For these people, the contributions and the earnings are tax-free until funds are withdrawn from the account.

IRA Contribution Limits

Contributions to an IRA must come from earned income. The tax law treats alimony as earned income, but only if it is includible in gross income. [Prop. Reg. §1.219(a)-6(d)] Interest, dividends, and other types of investment income are not earned income.

For 2022, the maximum contribution to an IRA is the *lesser of* (i) $6,000 or (ii) 100% of the taxpayer's earned income. Taxpayers at least 50 years old may contribute another $1,000. When a married couple files a joint tax return, the amount increases to $12,000 (plus $1,000 for each spouse who is 50 or older), as long as the couple has enough combined earnings to match the contribution. Each spouse must establish a separate (traditional) IRA. Also, the amount that can be contributed to either spouse's IRA cannot exceed $6,000 ($7,000 if age 50 or older).

The maximum contribution rules for (traditional) IRAs are the same as those for contributing to Roth IRAs (¶401.09). All taxpayers with enough earned income can contribute to a traditional IRA, regardless of their level of AGI. The maximum contribution to a Roth IRA is reduced for certain higher income taxpayers (see ¶401.09).

The deadline for contributing to an IRA for the current year is April 15 of the next year. If April 15 falls on a weekend day or legal holiday, the taxpayer has until the next business day to make the contribution. In the year, a taxpayer reaches age 70½, no further contributions usually are allowed.

EXAMPLE 26	Jim and Jeanette (both age 45) file a joint return. During 2022, Jim earns $50,000 at his job. Jeanette does not work. Jim and Jeanette can each contribute up to $6,000 to their respective IRAs. They have until April 15, 2023, to make their respective contributions. [I.R.C. §219(f)(3)]

EXAMPLE 27	Same facts as in Example 26, except that Jim is age 50. Jim can contribute up to $7,000 to his IRA. He can contribute up to $6,000 to Jeanette's IRA.

IRA contributions made between January 1 and April 15 could be considered contributions for either the current or previous tax year. Most IRA trustees assume a contribution made in this time frame is for the current year. If the taxpayer wants the contribution to count toward the prior year, then the taxpayer should inform the IRA trustee of this (preferably in writing) at the time the contribution is made.

Excess Contributions to IRAs

When contributions to all IRAs (Roth and traditional combined) exceed the allowed limit, the IRS assesses a 6% excise tax on the excess. This excise tax is not assessed if the taxpayer withdraws the excess (plus any related earnings) before the due date of the taxpayer's tax return. Withdrawn earnings are taxable and may be assessed a 10% early withdrawal penalty.

The maximum contribution taxpayers under age 50 can make to all IRAs during the year (includes both Roth and traditional) is the lesser of $6,000 or the taxpayer's earned income. Thus, qualifying taxpayers cannot contribute $6,000 to a traditional IRA and another $6,000 to a Roth IRA. Doing this will result in a 6% excise tax on the excess $6,000 contribution.

Limitation on IRA Deductions

Taxpayers who are not active participants in an employer-sponsored retirement plan can deduct up to $6,000 ($7,000 if 50 or older) for contributions made to a traditional IRA for 2022. Anyone participating in an employer-sponsored retirement plan may see their deduction reduced if "modified AGI" exceeds a certain amount. However, a nonparticipating taxpayer (filing MFJ) whose spouse is a participant in an employer plan can still receive a full IRA deduction as long as the couple's modified AGI does not exceed $204,000.

Employer Plans

The AGI phase-out limits come into play only when the taxpayer (or the taxpayer's spouse for MFJ taxpayers) is a participant in an employer-sponsored retirement plan. Employer plans include qualifying pension plans, profit-sharing plans, 401(k) plans, SIMPLE plans, and simplified employee pension (SEP) plans. Keoghs and other retirement plans of self-employed taxpayers also count as employer plans.

For participants in an employer-sponsored retirement plan, the reduction takes place proportionally when modified AGI falls within the following ranges:

Single and head of household	$68,000–$78,000
Married filing jointly and qualifying widow(er)	$109,000–$129,000
Married filing separately and not living with spouse any part of the year	$68,000–$78,000
Married filing separately and living with spouse part of the year	$0–$10,000
Nonparticipating spouse who files MFJ with participating spouse	$204,000–$214,000

When modified AGI exceeds the upper amounts in these ranges, no deduction is allowed. For purposes of the IRA deduction, "modified AGI" is AGI without any deduction for IRAs (currently being computed) or student loan interest (see ¶402.11). Also, any amounts the taxpayer excluded for interest from series EE and I educational savings bonds (¶401.03), foreign-earned income (¶401.14), or adoption assistance (¶401.05) are added back in computing modified AGI. A participant in a qualified plan whose modified AGI is within the phase-out range must compute a reduced IRA deduction. The maximum deduction is reduced proportionately for each dollar of modified AGI that falls within the phase out range ($20,000 for MFJ and qualifying widow(er); $10,000 for all others). However, for a nonparticipating spouse who files jointly with a participating spouse, the phase-out range is $10,000. Taxpayers round their reduced deductions up to the nearest $10. If their deduction is more than $0, but less than $200, they increase the deduction to $200.

EXAMPLE 28

Stan Decker, age 48, is married and files a joint return with his wife, Dorothy, age 52. They both want to make the largest possible deductible contributions to their IRAs. Their modified AGI is $110,250. Stan is an active participant in his employer's retirement plan. Dorothy does not have a retirement plan at work. Because the Deckers' modified AGI is $1,250 above the $109,000 threshold for MFJ and Stan is in a retirement plan at work, his maximum deductible contribution is limited. He will only be able to deduct $5,630 [$6,000 − ($1,250 excess/$20,000 phase-out range × $6,000) = $375, which rounded up to the nearest $10 is $5,630]. If he chooses to contribute the full $6,000, he will have to track the remaining amount as a non-deductible contribution of $370 ($6,000 - $5,630). In contrast, Dorothy does not participate in an employer-sponsored retirement plan, and because the Deckers' modified AGI does not exceed $214,000, she can contribute and deduct $7,000 (includes $1,000 for being age 50 or older).

EXAMPLE 29	Same facts as in Example 28, except that the Deckers' modified AGI is $210,000. Stan may contribute up to $6,000 but he cannot deduct any of his contribution because modified AGI exceeds the $129,000 ceiling for MFJ active participants. Because Dorothy is not an active participant, her modified AGI threshold is $204,000 and their AGI exceeds that by $6,000 [$210,000 – $204,000]. Thus, Dorothy's maximum deduction is $2,800 [$7,000 – ($6,000 excess/$10,000 phase-out range × $7,000)]. If she contributes the maximum $7,000, she will only be able to deduct $2,800.

EXAMPLE 30	Laura, age 38, is single and has modified AGI of $70,450. Included in this amount is $50,000 of wage income. She participates in an employer-sponsored retirement plan. Her threshold is $66,000 and her modified AGI exceeds that by $2,450 [$70,450 - $68,000]. Laura can contribute up to $6,000 to an IRA for 2022. However, the maximum that she can deduct is $4,530 [$6,000 – ($2,450 excess/$10,000 phase-out range × $6,000)]. If Laura contributes more than $4,530, up to the maximum $6,000, to her IRA, the excess over $4,530 will be a nondeductible contribution .

EXAMPLE 31	Same facts as in Example 30, except that Laura's modified AGI is $76,000. She can still contribute up to $6,000 to an IRA for 2022, but will only be able to deduct $1,200 [$6,000 – ($8,000 excess/$10,000 phase-out range × $6,000)].

Nondeductible Contributions

Taxpayers who do not qualify to deduct their contributions to an IRA can still make nondeductible contributions to their IRAs. Taxpayers who make both deductible and nondeductible contributions to the same IRA should keep good records to show the amount of their nondeductible contributions, which are tax-free when withdrawn (as discussed in ¶305). To help with this task, the IRS provides Form 8606, Nondeductible IRAs. Taxpayers who make nondeductible IRA contributions should file Form 8606 with the IRS, even if they do not file a tax return.

¶402.11 STUDENT LOAN INTEREST DEDUCTION

Each year, taxpayers may deduct for AGI up to $2,500 of interest they paid on money borrowed to pay qualified higher education expenses for themselves, their spouses, and dependents. [I.R.C. §221] No deduction is allowed for persons who are claimed as a dependent on another person's tax return. Qualified education expenses include tuition, books, supplies, and room and board. These expenses must be paid on behalf of a student enrolled at least half-time in a program leading to a recognized credential at a qualified institution of higher education.

The interest deduction is phased out evenly as "modified AGI" increases from $70,000 to $85,000 ($15,000 to $175,000 for MFJ taxpayers). For purposes of this deduction, "modified AGI" is AGI plus any foreign earned income exclusion (¶401.14) and without the deductions for student loan interest (currently being computed). Also, married taxpayers must file a joint return to claim the deduction.

EXAMPLE 32	Danny paid $800 interest on a qualified student loan. Danny files a joint return with his wife. Their modified AGI is $166,000 which exceeds the $145,000 threshold by $21,000. Danny and his wife are limited to a deduction $240 [$800 – ($21,000 excess/$30,000 phase-out range × $800)] for AGI on their joint tax return.

EXAMPLE 33

Avery paid interest of $2,620 on a qualified student loan; however, the maximum deduction is $2,500. Avery is not married. His modified AGI is $81,400 which exceeds the $70,000 threshold by $11,400. Avery deducts $600 [$2,500 maximum – ($11,400 excess/$15,000 phase-out range × $2,500 maximum)] for AGI on his tax return.

¶403   Form 1040

Form 1040, U.S. Individual Income Tax Return, is a two-page tax form filed by almost all taxpayers. This form begins with information about the taxpayer including filing status, social security numbers, age/blindness, and dependents. It then works down the basic tax formula (¶102.01) starting with various types of income finishing with **total income**, then deductions allowed for AGI ending with **AGI**, followed by deductions from AGI ending with **taxable income**. On the next page, the first line is the income tax amount. Next, other taxes and nonrefundable credits ending with **total tax**. After that, taxes withheld or paid and refundable credits determine **total payments**. Finally, total payments are compared to total tax and an amount due or overpaid is calculated. Taxpayers may choose to have overpayments refunded or applied to their next year's tax return. Additional schedules and forms are likely to be required to be prepared and filed with the Form 1040 in order to fully calculate these amounts for all but the simplest tax situation. Form 1040 has no limits on the types of income, deductions, credits or additional taxes that can be reported.

Figure 4-4 shows the completed Form 1040 for Karl and Jill Cook.

¶403.01   FILLED-IN FORM 1040

INFORMATION FOR FIGURE 4-4:

Karl and Jill Cook (ages 40 and 39, respectively) file a joint tax return. They claim their seven-year-old daughter, Nan, as a dependent. The payroll data from their Forms W-2 is shown below.

	Taxable Wages	Federal Income Tax Withheld	FICA Taxes Withheld	Net Pay
Karl E. Cook	$ 96,200	$ 17,316	$ 7,359	$ 71,525
Jillian R. Cook	45,950	3,569	3,515	38,866
Totals	$142,150	$20,885	$10,874	$110,391

Although the Cooks' take-home pay was $110,391, they include their gross wages of $142,150 on Form 1040. FICA taxes are withheld from an employee's pay, but are not deductible on the tax return.

On April 3, 2023, Karl and Jill contribute to their respective IRAs the maximum allowed for 2022 ($6,000 for persons under the age of 50). Karl has a pension plan at work; Jill does not. Because the Cooks' AGI exceeds $129,000, Karl (an active participant) cannot deduct any of his IRA contribution. However, because AGI does not exceed $214,000, Jill (who is not an active participant, but files a joint return with Karl, who is an active participant) will be allowed to deduct her entire $6,000 IRA contribution (¶402.10).

The Cooks had NOL virtual currency transactions in 2022.

Line #

Page 1: The box in column (4) is checked to indicate that Nan is a qualifying child for purposes of the child tax credit

1: Taxable wages, **$142,150** (source: Karl and Jill's W-2s)

2b: Taxable interest, **$3,640** (source: Schedule B)

10: IRA deduction, **$6,000** (Jill's contribution) (source: Schedule 1)

12: Standard deduction for MFJ, **$25,900**

16: Tax, **$16,290** (source: tax rate Schedule Y-1 for MFJ taxpayers)

19: Nonrefundable child tax credit, **$2,000** (source: Form 8812 page 1)

25a: Federal income tax withheld, **$20,885** (source: Karl and Jill's W-2s)

25d: Total withholding, **$20,885**

34: Amount refunded to the Cooks, **$6,595** (the Cooks chose to receive a refund for their overpayment (line 35a), rather than apply the excess to their 2023 tax liability)

By not providing information about their bank or bank account on Form 1040 (lines 35b, 35d), the Cooks have decided to have the IRS mail them their refund check.

Figure 4-4: Filled-In Form 1040 (Page 1)

Form 1040

Department of the Treasury—Internal Revenue Service

U.S. Individual Income Tax Return　**2022**　OMB No. 1545-0074　IRS Use Only—Do not write or staple in this space.

Filing Status
Check only one box.

☐ Single　☑ Married filing jointly　☐ Married filing separately (MFS)　☐ Head of household (HOH)　☐ Qualifying widow(er) (QW)

If you checked the MFS box, enter the name of your spouse. If you checked the HOH or QW box, enter the child's name if the qualifying person is a child but not your dependent:

Your first name and middle initial **Karl**	Last name **Cook**	Your social security number 2 6 9 0 0 9 0 9 2
If joint return, spouse's first name and middle initial **Jillian**	Last name **Cook**	Spouse's social security number 1 6 9 0 0 2 9 0 7

Home address (number and street). If you have a P.O. box, see instructions. **400 Deadwood Dr**　Apt. no.

City, town, or post office. If you have a foreign address, also complete spaces below. **Rapid City**　State **SD**　ZIP code **57702**

Foreign country name　Foreign province/state/county　Foreign postal code

Presidential Election Campaign
Check here if you, or your spouse if filing jointly, want $3 to go to this fund. Checking a box below will not change your tax or refund.　☐ You　☐ Spouse

At any time during 2022, did you: (a) receive (as a reward, award, or compensation); or (b) sell, exchange, gift, or otherwise dispose of a digital asset (or a financial interest in a digital asset)? (See instructions.)　☐ Yes　☑ No

Standard Deduction
Someone can claim: ☐ You as a dependent　☐ Your spouse as a dependent
☐ Spouse itemizes on a separate return or you were a dual-status alien

Age/Blindness　You: ☐ Were born before January 2, 1958　☐ Are blind　**Spouse:** ☐ Was born before January 2, 1958　☐ Is blind

Dependents (see instructions):
If more than four dependents, see instructions and check here ☐

(1) First name　Last name	(2) Social security number	(3) Relationship to you	(4) Check the box if qualifies for (see instructions): Child tax credit	Credit for other dependents
Nan Cook	3 9 9 0 0 1 1 2 0	Daughter	☑	☐
			☐	☐
			☐	☐

Income

Attach Form(s) W-2 here. Also attach Forms W-2G and 1099-R if tax was withheld.

If you did not get a Form W-2, see instructions.

Attach Sch. B if required.

Standard Deduction for—
• Single or Married filing separately, $12,950
• Married filing jointly or Qualifying widow(er), $25,900
• Head of household, $19,400
• If you checked any box under Standard Deduction, see instructions.

1a	Total amount from Form(s) W-2, box 1 (see instructions)	1a	142,150
b	Household employee wages not reported on Form(s) W-2	1b	
c	Tip income not reported on line 1a (see instructions)	1c	
d	Medicaid waiver payments not reported on Form(s) W-2 (see instructions)	1d	
e	Taxable dependent care benefits from Form 2441, line 26	1e	
f	Employer-provided adoption benefits from Form 8839, line 29	1f	
g	Wages from Form 8919, line 6	1g	
h	Other earned income (see instructions)	1h	
i	Nontaxable combat pay election (see instructions)　1i		
z	Add lines 1a through 1h	1z	142,150
2a	Tax-exempt interest　2a	b Taxable interest　2b	3,640
3a	Qualified dividends　3a	b Ordinary dividends　3b	
4a	IRA distributions　4a	b Taxable amount　4b	
5a	Pensions and annuities　5a	b Taxable amount　5b	
6a	Social security benefits　6a	b Taxable amount　6b	
c	If you elect to use the lump-sum election method, check here (see instructions) ☐		
7	Capital gain or (loss). Attach Schedule D if required. If not required, check here ☐	7	
8	Other income from Schedule 1, line 10	8	
9	Add lines 1z, 2b, 3b, 4b, 5b, 6b, 7, and 8. This is your **total income**	9	145,790
10	Adjustments to income from Schedule 1, line 26	10	6,000
11	Subtract line 10 from line 9. This is your **adjusted gross income**	11	139,790
12	**Standard deduction or itemized deductions** (from Schedule A)	12	25,900
13	Qualified business income deduction from Form 8995 or Form 8995-A	13	
14	Add lines 12 and 13	14	25,900
15	Subtract line 14 from line 11. If zero or less, enter -0-. This is your **taxable income**	15	113,890

For Disclosure, Privacy Act, and Paperwork Reduction Act Notice, see separate instructions.　Cat. No. 11320B　Form **1040** (2022)

Figure 4-4: Filled-In Form 1040 (Page 2)

Version A, Cycle 7

Form 1040 (2022)

Page **2**

Tax and Credits	16	**Tax** (see instructions). Check if any from Form(s): **1** ☐ 8814 **2** ☐ 4972 **3** ☐ _____	16	16,290
	17	Amount from Schedule 2, line 3	17	
	18	Add lines 16 and 17	18	16,290
	19	Child tax credit or credit for other dependents from Schedule 8812	19	2,000
	20	Amount from Schedule 3, line 8	20	
	21	Add lines 19 and 20	21	2,000
	22	Subtract line 21 from line 18. If zero or less, enter -0-	22	14,290
	23	Other taxes, including self-employment tax, from Schedule 2, line 21	23	
	24	Add lines 22 and 23. This is your **total tax**	24	14,290

Payments	25	Federal income tax withheld from:			
	a	Form(s) W-2	25a	20,885	
	b	Form(s) 1099	25b		
	c	Other forms (see instructions)	25c		
	d	Add lines 25a through 25c		25d	20,885
If you have a qualifying child, attach Sch. EIC.	26	2022 estimated tax payments and amount applied from 2021 return		26	
	27	Earned income credit (EIC)	27		
	28	Additional child tax credit from Schedule 8812	28		
	29	American opportunity credit from Form 8863, line 8	29		
	30	Reserved for future use	30		
	31	Amount from Schedule 3, line 15	31		
	32	Add lines 27, 28, 29, and 31. These are your **total other payments and refundable credits**		32	
	33	Add lines 25d, 26, and 32. These are your **total payments**		33	20,885

Refund	34	If line 33 is more than line 24, subtract line 24 from line 33. This is the amount you **overpaid**	34	6,595
	35a	Amount of line 34 you want **refunded to you.** If Form 8888 is attached, check here ☐	35a	6,595
Direct deposit? See instructions.	b	Routing number |_|_|_|_|_|_|_|_|_| c Type: ☐ Checking ☐ Savings		
	d	Account number |_|_|_|_|_|_|_|_|_|		
	36	Amount of line 34 you want **applied to your 2023 estimated tax** ... 36		

Amount You Owe	37	Subtract line 33 from line 24. This is the **amount you owe.** For details on how to pay, go to *www.irs.gov/Payments* or see instructions	37	
	38	Estimated tax penalty (see instructions) ... 38		

Third Party Designee	Do you want to allow another person to discuss this return with the IRS? See instructions ☐ **Yes.** Complete below. ☐ **No**
	Designee's name _____ Phone no. _____ Personal identification number (PIN) |_|_|_|_|_|

Sign Here

Joint return? See instructions. Keep a copy for your records.

Under penalties of perjury, I declare that I have examined this return and accompanying schedules and statements, and to the best of my knowledge and belief, they are true, correct, and complete. Declaration of preparer (other than taxpayer) is based on all information of which preparer has any knowledge.

Your signature	Date	Your occupation	If the IRS sent you an Identity Protection PIN, enter it here (see inst.) |_|_|_|_|_|_|
Spouse's signature. If a joint return, **both** must sign.	Date	Spouse's occupation	If the IRS sent your spouse an Identity Protection PIN, enter it here (see inst.) |_|_|_|_|_|_|
Phone no.		Email address	

Paid Preparer Use Only	Preparer's name	Preparer's signature	Date	PTIN	Check if: ☐ Self-employed
	Firm's name			Phone no.	
	Firm's address			Firm's EIN	

Figure 4-4: Filled-In Form 1040, Schedule 1 (Page 1)

SCHEDULE 1 (Form 1040) Department of the Treasury Internal Revenue Service	**Additional Income and Adjustments to Income** Attach to Form 1040, 1040-SR, or 1040-NR. Go to *www.irs.gov/Form1040* for instructions and the latest information.	OMB No. 1545-0074 2022 Attachment Sequence No. **01**

Name(s) shown on Form 1040, 1040-SR, or 1040-NR Karl and Jillian Cook	Your social security number 269-00-9092

Part I　Additional Income

1	Taxable refunds, credits, or offsets of state and local income taxes	**1**	
2a	Alimony received	**2a**	
b	Date of original divorce or separation agreement (see instructions):		
3	Business income or (loss). Attach Schedule C	**3**	
4	Other gains or (losses). Attach Form 4797	**4**	
5	Rental real estate, royalties, partnerships, S corporations, trusts, etc. Attach Schedule E	**5**	
6	Farm income or (loss). Attach Schedule F	**6**	
7	Unemployment compensation	**7**	
8	Other income:		
a	Net operating loss	**8a** ( )	
b	Gambling	**8b**	
c	Cancellation of debt	**8c**	
d	Foreign earned income exclusion from Form 2555	**8d** ( )	
e	Income from Form 8853	**8e**	
f	Income from Form 8889	**8f**	
g	Alaska Permanent Fund dividends	**8g**	
h	Jury duty pay	**8h**	
i	Prizes and awards	**8i**	
j	Activity not engaged in for profit income	**8j**	
k	Stock options	**8k**	
l	Income from the rental of personal property if you engaged in the rental for profit but were not in the business of renting such property	**8l**	
m	Olympic and Paralympic medals and USOC prize money (see instructions)	**8m**	
n	Section 951(a) inclusion (see instructions)	**8n**	
o	Section 951A(a) inclusion (see instructions)	**8o**	
p	Section 461(l) excess business loss adjustment	**8p**	
q	Taxable distributions from an ABLE account (see instructions)	**8q**	
r	Scholarship and fellowship grants not reported on Form W-2	**8r**	
s	Nontaxable amount of Medicaid waiver payments included on Form 1040, line 1a or 1d	**8s** ( )	
t	Pension or annuity from a nonqualifed deferred compensation plan or a nongovernmental section 457 plan	**8t**	
u	Wages earned while incarcerated	**8u**	
z	Other income. List type and amount: _____	**8z**	
9	Total other income. Add lines 8a through 8z	**9**	
10	Combine lines 1 through 7 and 9. Enter here and on Form 1040, 1040-SR, or 1040-NR, line 8	**10**	

For Paperwork Reduction Act Notice, see your tax return instructions.　Cat. No. 71479F　Schedule 1 (Form 1040) 2022

Figure 4-4: Filled-In Form 1040, Schedule 1 (Page 2)

Schedule 1 (Form 1040) 2022 — Page **2**

Part II Adjustments to Income

11	Educator expenses	11	
12	Certain business expenses of reservists, performing artists, and fee-basis government officials. Attach Form 2106	12	
13	Health savings account deduction. Attach Form 8889	13	
14	Moving expenses for members of the Armed Forces. Attach Form 3903	14	
15	Deductible part of self-employment tax. Attach Schedule SE	15	
16	Self-employed SEP, SIMPLE, and qualified plans	16	
17	Self-employed health insurance deduction	17	
18	Penalty on early withdrawal of savings	18	
19a	Alimony paid	19a	
b	Recipient's SSN		
c	Date of original divorce or separation agreement (see instructions):		
20	IRA deduction	20	6,000
21	Student loan interest deduction	21	
22	Reserved for future use	22	
23	Archer MSA deduction	23	
24	Other adjustments:		
a	Jury duty pay (see instructions)	24a	
b	Deductible expenses related to income reported on line 8l from the rental of personal property engaged in for profit	24b	
c	Nontaxable amount of the value of Olympic and Paralympic medals and USOC prize money reported on line 8m	24c	
d	Reforestation amortization and expenses	24d	
e	Repayment of supplemental unemployment benefits under the Trade Act of 1974	24e	
f	Contributions to section 501(c)(18)(D) pension plans	24f	
g	Contributions by certain chaplains to section 403(b) plans	24g	
h	Attorney fees and court costs for actions involving certain unlawful discrimination claims (see instructions)	24h	
i	Attorney fees and court costs you paid in connection with an award from the IRS for information you provided that helped the IRS detect tax law violations	24i	
j	Housing deduction from Form 2555	24j	
k	Excess deductions of section 67(e) expenses from Schedule K-1 (Form 1041)	24k	
z	Other adjustments. List type and amount:	24z	
25	Total other adjustments. Add lines 24a through 24z	25	
26	Add lines 11 through 23 and 25. These are your **adjustments to income**. Enter here and on Form 1040 or 1040-SR, line 10, or Form 1040-NR, line 10a	26	6,000

Schedule 1 (Form 1040) 2022

Figure 4-4: Filled-In Schedule 8812, page 1

SCHEDULE 8812 (Form 1040)	**Credits for Qualifying Children and Other Dependents**	OMB No. 1545-0074
Department of the Treasury Internal Revenue Service	Attach to Form 1040, 1040-SR, or 1040-NR. Go to *www.irs.gov/Schedule8812* for instructions and the latest information.	20**22**
		Attachment Sequence No. **47**

Name(s) shown on return
Karl and Jillian Cook

Your social security number
269-00-9092

Part I   Child Tax Credit and Credit for Other Dependents

1	Enter the amount from line 11 of your Form 1040, 1040-SR, or 1040-NR	**1**	139,790
2a	Enter income from Puerto Rico that you excluded	2a	
b	Enter the amounts from lines 45 and 50 of your Form 2555 . . .	2b	
c	Enter the amount from line 15 of your Form 4563	2c	
d	Add lines 2a through 2c	2d	
3	Add lines 1 and 2d	**3**	139,790
4	Number of qualifying children under age 17 with the required social security number	4	1	
5	Multiply line 4 by $2,000	**5**	2,000
6	Number of other dependents, including any qualifying children who are not under age 17 or who do not have the required social security number	6	
	Caution: Do not include yourself, your spouse, or anyone who is not a U.S. citizen, U.S. national, or U.S. resident alien. Also, do not include anyone you included on line 4.		
7	Multiply line 6 by $500	**7**	
8	Add lines 5 and 7	**8**	2,000
9	Enter the amount shown below for your filing status. • Married filing jointly—$400,000 • All other filing statuses—$200,000	**9**	400,000
10	Subtract line 9 from line 3. • If zero or less, enter -0-. • If more than zero and not a multiple of $1,000, enter the next multiple of $1,000. For example, if the result is $425, enter $1,000; if the result is $1,025, enter $2,000, etc.	**10**	
11	Multiply line 10 by 5% (0.05)	**11**	
12	Is the amount on line 8 more than the amount on line 11?	**12**	
	☐ **No. STOP.** You cannot take the child tax credit, credit for other dependents, or additional child tax credit. Skip Parts II-A and II-B. Enter -0- on lines 14 and 27.		
	☐ **Yes.** Subtract line 11 from line 8. Enter the result.		
13	Enter the amount from the **Credit Limit Worksheet A**	**13**	16,290
14	Enter the smaller of line 12 or 13. **This is your child tax credit and credit for other dependents** . . . . . **Enter this amount on Form 1040, 1040-SR, or 1040-NR, line 19.**	**14**	2,000

If the amount on line 12 is more than the amount on line 14, you may be able to take the **additional child tax credit** on Form 1040, 1040-SR, or 1040-NR, line 28. Complete your Form 1040, 1040-SR, or 1040-NR through line 27 (also complete Schedule 3, line 11) before completing Part II-A.

For Paperwork Reduction Act Notice, see your tax return instructions.   Cat. No. 59761M   Schedule 8812 (Form 1040) 2022

4

Name:

Section:

Date:

QUESTIONS AND PROBLEMS

1. **Foreign Earned Income Exclusion.** (Obj. 1) From March 9, 2021, until August 15, 2022, Eva is sent to London, England, on a temporary work assignment. Eva's salary during 2021 is $120,000, of which $94,000 is earned while working in London. Her salary during 2022 is $125,000, of which $77,000 is earned while working in London.

    a. How much of Eva's salary is taxed in 2021 and 2022?

    b. Besides taking the exclusion for foreign earned income, what other options are available to Eva?

2. **Foreign Earned Income Exclusion.** (Obj. 1) From October 6, 2021, until September 5, 2022, Jack was sent to work at his employer's office in Rome, Italy. Jack's salary during 2021 was $72,000. Of this amount, $18,000 was earned while working in Rome.

    a. How much of Jack's salary can be excluded from gross income in 2021?

    b. How, if at all, would your answer to Part a. differ if Jack's assignment lasted until August 7, 2022?

3. **Fringe Benefits.** (Obj. 2) The discrimination rule applies to certain fringe benefits, but not to others.

    a. For each category of fringe benefits given, state whether the discrimination rule applies, and give two examples of specific fringe benefits in that category.

Fringe Benefit Category	Discrimination Rule Applies?	Examples of Specific Benefits in Each Category
De minimis fringe benefits	_____	_____
		_____
Qualified employee discounts	_____	_____
		_____
Working condition fringe benefits	_____	_____
		_____
No-additional-cost services	_____	_____
		_____
On-premise athletic facilities	_____	_____
		_____

    b. What are the tax consequences of violating the discrimination rule?

4. **Group-Term Life Insurance.** (Obj. 2) Paine Distributing pays an annual premium for $90,000 for nondiscriminatory group-term life insurance coverage on its president, Fred J. Noble. Fred is 44 years of age. His wife, Melanie, is the policy's beneficiary. For this group-term life insurance, Fred pays the company $0.20 per year for each $1,000 of coverage. His share of the insurance premium is deducted from his gross salary under Paine's payroll deduction plan. What portion of the group-term life insurance cost is included in Fred's gross income for the year?

5. **Group-Term Life Insurance.** (Obj. 2) Remix, Inc. provides group-term life insurance coverage for each of its employees. The amount of coverage is equal to one year's salary. Remix pays 100% of the cost for the premiums. Tony and Ruth are employees of Remix. Tony is 46 years old; his salary for the year is $85,000. Ruth is 52 years old; her salary for the year is $120,000. Ruth is a key employee of Remix; Tony is not.

   a. Discuss the consequences to Tony and Ruth if Remix's plan does not favor key and highly paid employees.

   b. Discuss the consequences to Tony and Ruth if Remix's plan favors key or highly paid employees.

6. **Employer-Provided Health Insurance.** (Obj. 2) Monix Enterprises provides its employees with health insurance coverage. During the year, it pays $7,500 of insurance premiums for each of its employees. Randy is a highly paid employee of Monix. Jon is not one of Monix's highly paid employees.

   a. Discuss the consequences to Randy and Jon if the plan favors highly paid employees.

   b. Discuss the consequences to Randy and Jon if the plan does not favor key or highly paid employees.

7. **Fringe Benefits.** (Obj. 2) A retailer gives a 20% discount to its full-time employees; key employees are entitled to a 30% discount. The retailer's gross profit percentage on the goods it sells is 35%. During the year, two full-time employees, Fritz and Tad, each buy goods that sell for $2,000. Fritz is a key employee; Tad is not. Discuss the tax consequences to Fritz and Tad of the discounts they each received during the year.

8. **Bond Interest.** (Obj. 1) A single taxpayer owns five different bonds listed below. During the current year she received the interest amounts shown. In the space provided for each bond, state the amount of interest to be included in or excluded from gross income. If excluded, state why.

Bond	Issuer	Date Purchased	Interest
A	Racer Tannery	12–10–06	$ 276
B	City of Austin	7–1–09	800
C	U.S. Treasury	2–1–12	600
D	Matured Series EE U.S. Savings	11–1–14	1,000
E	Kingsville School District	7–10–15	500

Bond	Interest Includable	Interest Excludable and Why
A	_____	_____
B	_____	_____
C	_____	_____
D	_____	_____
E	_____	_____

9. **Form 8815.** (Obj. 6) Michael J. Dugan (SSN 372-00-6729) and his wife, Rachel, received $15,000 ($12,000 principal and $3,000 interest) from the redemption of a Series EE U.S. Savings Bond. They used the proceeds to pay university tuition and fees totaling $8,250 for their two dependent children, Colleen R. Dugan and Patrick T. Dugan. Colleen is 21 years of age; Patrick is 20. With the exception of temporary absences from home to attend the University of Michigan in Ann Arbor, Michigan full-time, they live with their parents. During the year, Colleen and Patrick each received a tax-exempt university scholarship of $2,250. Michael's salary is $127,000. The salary and interest from the bonds are the Dugans' only sources of income. Prepare Form 8815 to be attached to the Dugans' 2022 joint tax return.

10. **Exclusion for Series EE and I U.S. Savings Bonds.** (Obj. 5) Irina cashes in Series I Savings Bonds during 2022. She receives $18,755, of which $15,000 was principal and the rest interest. Irina uses the proceeds to pay out-of-state tuition and fees totaling $16,500 for her son, who is a full-time student during the year. She uses the rest of the proceeds to pay for her son's room and board. Irina's filing status is head of household. Irina's only other source of income is her $83,300 salary. Compute Irina's exclusion for Series EE and I interest.

(Use for Problem 9.)

Form **8815**	Exclusion of Interest From Series EE and I	OMB No. 1545-0074
Department of the Treasury Internal Revenue Service	**U.S. Savings Bonds Issued After 1989** (For Filers With Qualified Higher Education Expenses) Go to *www.irs.gov/Form8815* for the latest information. **Attach to Form 1040 or 1040-SR.**	20**22** Attachment Sequence No. **167**

Name(s) shown on return   Your social security number

1		(a) Name of person (you, your spouse, or your dependent) who was enrolled at or attended an eligible educational institution	(b) Name and address of eligible educational institution

DRAFT AS OF August 10, 2022 DO NOT FILE

If you need more space, attach a statement.

2	Enter the total qualified higher education expenses you paid in 2022 for the person(s) listed in column (a) of line 1. See the instructions to find out which expenses qualify	2	
3	Enter the total of any nontaxable educational benefits (such as nontaxable scholarship or fellowship grants) received for 2022 for the person(s) listed in column (a) of line 1. See instructions	3	
4	Subtract line 3 from line 2. If zero or less, **stop.** You **cannot** take the exclusion	4	
5	Enter the total proceeds (principal and interest) from all series EE and I U.S. savings bonds **issued after 1989** that you **cashed during 2022**	5	
6	Enter the interest included on line 5. See instructions	6	
7	If line 4 is equal to or more than line 5, enter "1.000." If line 4 is less than line 5, divide line 4 by line 5. Enter the result as a decimal (rounded to at least three places)	7	× .
8	Multiply line 6 by line 7	8	
9	Enter your modified adjusted gross income. See instructions	9	
	Note: If line 9 is $100,800 or more if single, head of household, or qualifying widow(er); or $158,650 or more if married filing jointly, **stop.** You **cannot** take the exclusion.		
10	Enter: $85,800 if single, head of household, or qualifying widow(er); $128,650 if married filing jointly	10	
11	Subtract line 10 from line 9. If zero or less, skip line 12, enter -0- on line 13, and go to line 14	11	
12	Divide line 11 by: $15,000 if single, head of household, or qualifying widow(er); $30,000 if married filing jointly. Enter the result as a decimal (rounded to at least three places)	12	× .
13	Multiply line 8 by line 12	13	
14	**Excludable savings bond interest.** Subtract line 13 from line 8. Enter the result here and on Schedule B (Form 1040), line 3	14	

For Paperwork Reduction Act Notice, see your tax return instructions.   Cat. No. 10822S   Form **8815** (2022)

11. **Scholarships.** (Obj. 5) On August 1, 2022, Rob was granted a $5,400 scholarship for each of four academic years (nine months each year) to earn a degree from Birdhaven University. The scholarship grant includes $3,600 for tuition, fees, and books and $1,800 for room and board. Payment is one-ninth each month, starting September 10, 2022, and is made on the tenth of each month thereafter.

    a. How much of the scholarship payments can Rob exclude from gross income in 2022? Why?

    b. If Rob is not a degree candidate, is there any limitation to the amount of his exclusion? Explain.

12. **Gross Income Exclusions.** (Obj. 1) Indicate, by placing an **X** in the proper column, whether each of the following items is includable in or excludable from gross income.

Item	Includable	Excludable
a. Life insurance proceeds paid because of insured's death	_____	_____
b. Workers' compensation for a physical injury	_____	_____
c. Employer-paid health insurance premiums paid to a non-key, non-highly paid employee	_____	_____
d. FMV of automobile won on television game show	_____	_____
e. Free parking in employer's lot (valued at $100/month)	_____	_____
f. A nonbankrupt taxpayer is forgiven of $1,000 of credit card debt	_____	_____
g. Gold necklace received as a gift	_____	_____
h. Health resort fee paid for taxpayer by employer	_____	_____

13. **Physical Injury and Sickness Payments.** (Obj. 1) For each taxpayer, discuss how much (if any) of the payments received during the year are included in gross income.

    a. Anne sued her employer for discrimination and was awarded $50,000.

    b. Todd was physically injured on the job. He is reimbursed $16,400 for medical expenses he paid as a result of his injuries. Todd's employer paid 100% of the premiums on his health insurance policy.

    c. Meg was physically injured on the job. She received $12,000 of workers' compensation.

    d. Sandra had an adverse reaction to the drug her doctor prescribed. She sued the drug company and was awarded $12 million. Of this amount, $11.5 million was for punitive damages.

14. **Roth IRAs.** (Obj. 4) Kenya and Carl Reed are ages 48 and 50, respectively. Their 2022 AGI is $209,480, most of which stems from taxable wages. Compute the maximum amounts Kenya and Carl can contribute to their respective Roth IRAs for this year.

15. **Roth IRA.** (Obj. 4) Kathy, age 40, is single and wants to contribute to a Roth IRA in 2022. Her AGI is $129,500. Compute the maximum contribution that Kathy may make to her Roth IRA.

16. **Deductions for AGI.** (Obj. 3) For each statement, check *true* or *false*.

		True	*False*

a. Reservists who travel 100 miles or less from home to perform services as a member of the reserves deduct their travel expenses as a miscellaneous itemized deduction.   _____   _____

b. Qualified performing artists may deduct their business expenses from gross income to arrive at AGI.   _____   _____

c. To receive the tax benefits of a "performing artist," the individual's AGI cannot exceed $14,000 before deducting business expenses.   _____   _____

d. State and local government officials paid on a fee basis report their business expenses on Form 2106.   _____   _____

e. Taxpayers 55-years-old may contribute an additional $1,000 to their health savings accounts.   _____   _____

f. Retired taxpayers over age 64 may continue to make deductible contributions to a health savings account.   _____   _____

g. Withdrawals from a health savings account that are not used for medical expenses may be subject to a 6% penalty tax.   _____   _____

17. **Health Savings Accounts.** (Obj. 3) Mari's employer offers an HSA plan.

a. Discuss the tax consequences to Mari if she participates in the plan. Mari is 44-years-old, unmarried, and does not claim any dependents on her tax return.

b. Same as in Part a., except that Mari is 56 years old.

18. **Self-Employed Health Insurance Deduction.** (Obj. 3) Ashley is a self-employed artist. Her self-employment earnings in the current year are $25,000. She pays $650 a month for health insurance coverage through her business. From August 1 through October 31, Ashley worked 30 hours a week for an ad agency and received W-2 wages of $12,000. During that three-month period, she was eligible for her employer's health insurance, but opted not to enroll in it.

    a. How much of the $7,800 in health insurance premiums can Ashley deduct?

    b. Where on her tax return does she take this deduction?

19. **Self-Employed Health Insurance Deduction.** (Obj. 3)

    a. What is the maximum self-employed health insurance deduction that can be claimed as a deduction for AGI?

    b. Under what conditions would a taxpayer **not** be eligible for the self-employed health insurance deduction?

20. **IRA Contributions.** (Obj. 4) Joyce and Barry Bright are both employed and 56 years of age. In 2022, Barry earned wages of $2,500; Joyce earned wages of $86,530. Joyce is an active participant in her employer-maintained pension plan. The Brights plan to file a joint tax return. Their modified AGI is $115,782.

    a. What is the latest date by which an IRA contribution must be made in order for it to be claimed on the Brights' 2022 return?

    b. What is the maximum amount Joyce and Barry can each contribute to an IRA and be able to deduct for this year?

    c. Are the earnings from the IRA subject to federal income taxes in 2022? Explain.

21. **IRA Deduction.** (Obj. 4) Fred and Diane Workman file a joint return. Neither taxpayer is covered by a retirement plan at work. Fred's wages are $37,900; Diane's are $31,500. Between January 1, 2022 and April 15, 2023, Diane and Fred contributed the following amounts to their respective traditional IRAs:

Diane:	April 26, 2022	$ 750
	July 1, 2022	750
	October 3, 2022	750
	January 4, 2023	750
Fred:	June 16, 2022	$1,500
	February 3, 2023	1,500

Earnings credited to their IRAs during 2022 were $890 for Diane and $340 for Fred. Discuss the tax implications of the contributions to and the earnings from the IRAs as they pertain to the Workmans' 2022 tax return.

22. **Traditional IRA Characteristics.** (Obj. 4) For each statement, check *true* or *false*.

		True	False
a.	Contributions to a nonworking spouse's IRA must be equal to the IRA contributions of the working spouse.	_____	_____
b.	Contributions to a traditional IRA are deductible in the computation of AGI for a single employee whose only income is wages of $25,000.	_____	_____
c.	Contributions to a traditional IRA generally must stop in the year the IRA account owner reaches age 70½.	_____	_____
d.	The earnings of a traditional IRA are taxed to the employee in the year earned.	_____	_____
e.	The income earned on nondeductible traditional IRA contributions is not taxable until it is withdrawn.	_____	_____
f.	The maximum deductible IRA contributions in 2022 is $6,000 for a married couple of which only one spouse works and earns $25,000.	_____	_____

23. Nondeductible IRA Contributions. (Obj. 4) Mike and Marg Sweeney, both age 42, each want to set aside the maximum amount for their retirement using an individual retirement account. They prefer to make deductible contributions. Mike and Marg have $75,000 and $48,000 of earned income, respectively. Their modified AGI is $130,000. Marg is covered by an employer-maintained retirement plan. Mike's employer has no such plan.

a. Discuss the tax consequences if the Sweeneys use traditional IRAs to save for retirement.

b. Can you suggest a better plan? If so, what would it be?

c. How would your responses to Parts a. and b. change if Marg's earned income was $106,000, Mike's was $88,000, and the Sweeney's modified AGI was $210,000?

24. Student Loan Interest. (Obj. 5) Larry paid $580 interest on a qualified student loan. Larry files his tax return as a single taxpayer. His modified AGI is $75,810. Compute Larry's deduction for AGI for the interest paid on his student loan.

25. Miscellaneous Questions. (Obj. 3) For each statement, check *true* or *false*.

		True	*False*
a.	Withdrawals from a Roth IRA may be subject to a 6% early withdrawal penalty.	_____	_____
b.	Regardless of the number of children, a taxpayer may contribute only $2,000 each year to a Coverdell Education Savings Account.	_____	_____
c.	Contributions to an ABLE account are deductible for AGI.	_____	_____
d.	Contributions to a Coverdell Education Savings Account (ESA) must be for a person under age 18.	_____	_____
e.	The student loan interest deduction is available only for the first 60 months of interest payments.	_____	_____

		True	*False*
f.	In 2022, employees may exclude up to $275 a month for parking provided by the employer, even if the parking privilege is discriminatory.	____	____
g.	Under a qualified tuition program (529 plan), if the child does not go to college, a refund is made to the child who must pay taxes on the interest income included in the refund.	____	____
h.	Some employers provide meals to their employees. For the value of the meals to be tax-free, the meals must be served on the premises of the employer for the employer's convenience.	____	____

26. **Miscellaneous Questions.** (Obj. 3)

a.   Explain the deduction for the penalty on early withdrawal of savings.

b.   What are the tax consequences of purchasing a new truck with funds from a Roth IRA for a taxpayer of age 50?

c.   What are the tax consequences of purchasing a new truck with funds from a traditional IRA for a taxpayer of age 50?

27. **Internet Problem: Filling out Form 3903.** (Obj. 6)

Charles Randall (SSN 567-00-1234), an active member of the Armed Services, was ordered to move from Cleveland, Ohio, to Kansas City, Missouri. He moved on September 16. As part of the move, Charles drove his car 971 miles and paid the following amounts. The government reimbursed Charles for 75% of his qualified moving expenses.

House hunting trip expenses	$1,600
Moving van	3,300
Cost of meals end-route	85
Lodging en route	120

Go to the IRS website and locate Form 3903. Using the computer, fill in the form for Charles Randall and print out a completed copy.

See Appendix A for instructions on use of the IRS website.

28. Business Entity Problem: This problem is designed for those using the "business entity" approach. **The solution may require information from Chapters 14–16.** For each statement, check *true* or *false*.

		True	*False*
a.	Self-employed persons may deduct 50% of their self-employment tax for AGI.	_____	_____
b.	Companies reimbursing their employees for house hunting and temporary living expenses do not report these reimbursements as income on the employee's W-2.	_____	_____
c.	When a company provides "free meals" as part of the employee's compensation package, the company includes the value of the meals as taxable wages on the employee's W-2.	_____	_____
d.	In 2022, a company pays $305 per month to provide its CEO with a parking space. The company must include $3,660 on the CEO's W-2 as taxable wages.	_____	_____
e.	When a company reimburses an employee for nondeductible moving expenses, it must report the reimbursement as additional taxable wages on the employee's W-2.	_____	_____
f.	Employers may annually provide up to $5,250 of tax-free educational assistance to their employees to pursue a Master's Degree.	_____	_____
g.	When a company provides over $50,000 of group-term life insurance to an employee, it must add the taxable portion of the premiums to wages on the employee's W-2.	_____	_____
h.	A self-employed person who provides health insurance for himself, but not his three full-time employees, may deduct the premiums for AGI.	_____	_____

COMPREHENSIVE PROBLEM

29. Use the information below to compute the 2022 taxable income and tax liability for an unmarried taxpayer (age 52 with no dependents). Prepare an analysis showing each item and amount under the appropriate headings of (1) economic betterment, (2) gross income exclusions, (3) total gross income, (4) deductions for AGI, (5) AGI, (6) deductions from AGI, (7) taxable income, and (8) tax liability.

Cash Received

Interest on savings account	$ 1,728
Gift of money from parent	1,000
Rent from farmland owned	30,000
Proceeds of life insurance policy received upon parent's death	40,000
Nondegree candidate fellowship, granted 8/20/2022, of $450 per month for four months	1,800
Net pay received (Gross salary of $33,000 less $7,440 state and federal income taxes, $2,046 social security taxes, and $479 Medicare taxes)	23,035
Employer's share of health insurance premiums, $4,260	0
De minimis employee fringe benefits valued at $25	0
Company provided parking costing employer $300/month for 12 months	
Total cash received	$97,563

Cash Payments

Expenses of farmland rental (real estate taxes)	$ 1,750
Personal living expenses	26,600
Total cash payments	$28,350

CUMULATIVE PROBLEM 1 (CHAPTERS 1–4)

 Use the following information to prepare Erica Hansen's tax return. Use Form 1040, Schedule 1, Schedule 3, Schedule EIC, Schedule 8812, and Form 8880. This problem is suitable for manual preparation or computer software application.

Erica L. Hansen (SSN 376-00-4930), age 42, is a single parent with three children. She resides at 19 Sunset Road, Normal, Illinois 61761. She chooses to support the Presidential campaign fund.

Her household includes Randall L. Hansen, her 19-year-old son (SSN 369-00-3418), Tiffany A. Hansen, her 12-year-old daughter (SSN 396-00-6439), and Donna M. Hansen, her 14-year-old daughter (SSN 653-00-8177). Erica provides over half of the support of each child.

Donna has no income of her own, but Randall earns $4,200 during the year delivering papers and mowing lawns. All children lived in the household for 12 months. Randall is a full-time student at Heartland College in Normal, Illinois.

Erica works as an office manager for Universal Development Corporation. Information from her W-2, as well as other relevant information follows.

Gross wages	$39,500
Social security tax withheld	2,449
Medicare tax withheld	573
Federal income tax withheld	0
State income tax withheld	819
Interest received:	
First Federal Savings Bank	$775
Olympic Savings—certificate of deposit cashed in	175
State of Maryland bonds	300

Erica gets her family health care coverage through her work. Erica is a participant in an employer-sponsored retirement plan. However, she wants to make the largest possible deductible contribution to her traditional IRA. If Erica has overpaid her taxes, she prefers to receive a refund. She signs and dates her return on April 5, 2023.

Retirement Savings Contributions Credit:

Compute the amount of the credit using the information presented in ¶204.06.

EIC Calculation:

Look up the amount in the EIC Tables for both earned income and AGI.

Additional Child Tax Credit:

Enter on Schedule 8812 (line 1) $1,400 for each qualifying child.

CUMULATIVE PROBLEM 2 (CHAPTERS 1–4)

 Use the following information to prepare the tax return for Bryan Connel. Use Form 1040, Schedule 1, Schedule 3, Schedule B, and Form 8863. This problem is suitable for manual preparation or computer software application.

Bryan Connel (SSN 573-00-5878) works as a manager for an oil company. His taxable wages for 2022 were $132,900, from which his employer withheld $9,450 and $1,900, respectively for federal and state income taxes.

During 2022, Bryan paid $6,000 for tuition for his dependent daughter, April Connel (SSN 549-00-5584). This amount was reported in box 2 on Form 1098-T, Tuition Statement, that April received early in 2023. Box 7 on 1098-T was not checked. April (age 20) attends the University of Houston full-time. She entered her sophomore year during 2022. April lives with Bryan when she is not in school. The University of Houston is located at 4800 Calhoun Road, Houston, Texas 77004. The employer identification number for the university is 51-2000390.

Bryan is divorced. The divorce was finalized in 2017. During 2022, he paid alimony totaling $50,000 to his ex-wife, Anne Connel (SSN 558-00-5377). His only other income includes $4,250 of interest from a Texas Commerce Bank certificate of deposit and $1,840 of interest from State of Iowa government bonds. He does not have an interest in any foreign accounts or trusts. Bryan lives at 1143 W. Adams Ave., Wichita, KS 76300. Bryan uses the standard deduction, is under age 65, and has good eyesight. He does not want $3 to go to the Presidential election campaign fund. Bryan signs and dates his return on April 10, 2023.

(Use for Cumulative Problem 1.)

Form 1040   Department of the Treasury—Internal Revenue Service
U.S. Individual Income Tax Return   **2022**   OMB No. 1545-0074   IRS Use Only—Do not write or staple in this space.

Filing Status
Check only one box.

☐ Single ☐ Married filing jointly ☐ Married filing separately (MFS) ☐ Head of household (HOH) ☐ Qualifying widow(er) (QW)

If you checked the MFS box, enter the name of your spouse. If you checked the HOH or QW box, enter the child's name if the qualifying person is a child but not your dependent:

Your first name and middle initial	Last name	Your social security number

If joint return, spouse's first name and middle initial	Last name	Spouse's social security number

Home address (number and street). If you have a P.O. box, see instructions.	Apt. no.	**Presidential Election Campaign**

Check here if you, or your spouse if filing jointly, want $3 to go to this fund. Checking a box below will not change your tax or refund.

City, town, or post office. If you have a foreign address, also complete spaces below.	State	ZIP code

Foreign country name	Foreign province/state/county	Foreign postal code

☐ You ☐ Spouse

At any time during 2022, did you: (a) receive (as a reward, award, or compensation); or (b) sell, exchange, gift, or otherwise dispose of a digital asset (or a financial interest in a digital asset)? (See instructions.)   ☐ Yes ☐ No

Standard Deduction

Someone can claim: ☐ You as a dependent ☐ Your spouse as a dependent

☐ Spouse itemizes on a separate return or you were a dual-status alien

Age/Blindness   You: ☐ Were born before January 2, 1958 ☐ Are blind   **Spouse:** ☐ Was born before January 2, 1958 ☐ Is blind

Dependents (see instructions):

(1) First name Last name	(2) Social security number	(3) Relationship to you	(4) Check the box if qualifies for (see instructions):
			Child tax credit Credit for other dependents

If more than four dependents, see instructions and check here ☐

Income

Attach Form(s) W-2 here. Also attach Forms W-2G and 1099-R if tax was withheld.

If you did not get a Form W-2, see instructions.

1a	Total amount from Form(s) W-2, box 1 (see instructions)	1a
b	Household employee wages not reported on Form(s) W-2	1b
c	Tip income not reported on line 1a (see instructions)	1c
d	Medicaid waiver payments not reported on Form(s) W-2 (see instructions)	1d
e	Taxable dependent care benefits from Form 2441, line 26	1e
f	Employer-provided adoption benefits from Form 8839, line 29	1f
g	Wages from Form 8919, line 6	1g
h	Other earned income (see instructions)	1h
i	Nontaxable combat pay election (see instructions) 1i	
z	Add lines 1a through 1h	1z

Attach Sch. B if required.

2a	Tax-exempt interest	2a	b Taxable interest	2b
3a	Qualified dividends	3a	b Ordinary dividends	3b
4a	IRA distributions	4a	b Taxable amount	4b
5a	Pensions and annuities	5a	b Taxable amount	5b
6a	Social security benefits	6a	b Taxable amount	6b
c	If you elect to use the lump-sum election method, check here (see instructions) ☐			
7	Capital gain or (loss). Attach Schedule D if required. If not required, check here ☐			7

Standard Deduction for—

- Single or Married filing separately, $12,950
- Married filing jointly or Qualifying widow(er), $25,900
- Head of household, $19,400
- If you checked any box under *Standard Deduction,* see instructions.

8	Other income from Schedule 1, line 10	8
9	Add lines 1z, 2b, 3b, 4b, 5b, 6b, 7, and 8. This is your **total income**	9
10	Adjustments to income from Schedule 1, line 26	10
11	Subtract line 10 from line 9. This is your **adjusted gross income**	11
12	**Standard deduction or itemized deductions** (from Schedule A)	12
13	Qualified business income deduction from Form 8995 or Form 8995-A	13
14	Add lines 12 and 13	14
15	Subtract line 14 from line 11. If zero or less, enter -0-. This is your **taxable income**	15

For Disclosure, Privacy Act, and Paperwork Reduction Act Notice, see separate instructions.   Cat. No. 11320B   Form **1040** (2022)

(Use for Cumulative Problem 1.)

Version A, Cycle 7

Form 1040 (2022)   Page **2**

Tax and Credits	16	**Tax** (see instructions). Check if any from Form(s): 1 ☐ 8814 2 ☐ 4972 3 ☐ _____	16	
	17	Amount from Schedule 2, line 3	17	
	18	Add lines 16 and 17	18	
	19	Child tax credit or credit for other dependents from Schedule 8812	19	
	20	Amount from Schedule 3, line 8	20	
	21	Add lines 19 and 20	21	
	22	Subtract line 21 from line 18. If zero or less, enter -0-	22	
	23	Other taxes, including self-employment tax, from Schedule 2, line 21	23	
	24	Add lines 22 and 23. This is your **total tax**	24	
Payments	25	Federal income tax withheld from:		
	a	Form(s) W-2	25a	
	b	Form(s) 1099	25b	
	c	Other forms (see instructions)	25c	
	d	Add lines 25a through 25c	25d	
If you have a qualifying child, attach Sch. EIC.	26	2022 estimated tax payments and amount applied from 2021 return	26	
	27	Earned income credit (EIC)	27	
	28	Additional child tax credit from Schedule 8812	28	
	29	American opportunity credit from Form 8863, line 8	29	
	30	Reserved for future use	30	
	31	Amount from Schedule 3, line 15	31	
	32	Add lines 27, 28, 29, and 31. These are your **total other payments and refundable credits**	32	
	33	Add lines 25d, 26, and 32. These are your **total payments**	33	
Refund	34	If line 33 is more than line 24, subtract line 24 from line 33. This is the amount you **overpaid**	34	
	35a	Amount of line 34 you want **refunded to you**. If Form 8888 is attached, check here ☐	35a	
Direct deposit? See instructions.	b	Routing number _____ c Type: ☐ Checking ☐ Savings		
	d	Account number _____		
	36	Amount of line 34 you want **applied to your 2023 estimated tax**	36	
Amount You Owe	37	Subtract line 33 from line 24. This is the **amount you owe**. For details on how to pay, go to *www.irs.gov/Payments* or see instructions	37	
	38	Estimated tax penalty (see instructions)	38	

Third Party Designee	Do you want to allow another person to discuss this return with the IRS? See instructions . . . . ☐ **Yes.** Complete below. ☐ **No**
	Designee's name _____ Phone no. _____ Personal identification number (PIN) ☐☐☐☐☐☐

Sign Here

Under penalties of perjury, I declare that I have examined this return and accompanying schedules and statements, and to the best of my knowledge and belief, they are true, correct, and complete. Declaration of preparer (other than taxpayer) is based on all information of which preparer has any knowledge.

Joint return? See instructions. Keep a copy for your records.

Your signature	Date	Your occupation	If the IRS sent you an Identity Protection PIN, enter it here (see inst.) ☐☐☐☐☐☐
Spouse's signature. If a joint return, **both** must sign.	Date	Spouse's occupation	If the IRS sent your spouse an Identity Protection PIN, enter it here (see inst.) ☐☐☐☐☐☐
Phone no. _____		Email address _____	

Paid Preparer Use Only

Preparer's name	Preparer's signature	Date	PTIN	Check if: ☐ Self-employed
Firm's name			Phone no.	
Firm's address			Firm's EIN	

Go to *www.irs.gov/Form1040* for instructions and the latest information.   Form **1040** (2022)

(Use for Cumulative Problem 1.)

SCHEDULE 1 (Form 1040)	Additional Income and Adjustments to Income	OMB No. 1545-0074
Department of the Treasury Internal Revenue Service	Attach to Form 1040, 1040-SR, or 1040-NR. Go to *www.irs.gov/Form1040* for instructions and the latest information.	2022 Attachment Sequence No. 01

Name(s) shown on Form 1040, 1040-SR, or 1040-NR	Your social security number

Part I Additional Income

1	Taxable refunds, credits, or offsets of state and local income taxes	1
2a	Alimony received	2a
b	Date of original divorce or separation agreement (see instructions):	
3	Business income or (loss). Attach Schedule C	3
4	Other gains or (losses). Attach Form 4797	4
5	Rental real estate, royalties, partnerships, S corporations, trusts, etc. Attach Schedule E	5
6	Farm income or (loss). Attach Schedule F	6
7	Unemployment compensation	7
8	Other income:	
a	Net operating loss	8a ( )
b	Gambling	8b
c	Cancellation of debt	8c
d	Foreign earned income exclusion from Form 2555	8d ( )
e	Income from Form 8853	8e
f	Income from Form 8889	8f
g	Alaska Permanent Fund dividends	8g
h	Jury duty pay	8h
i	Prizes and awards	8i
j	Activity not engaged in for profit income	8j
k	Stock options	8k
l	Income from the rental of personal property if you engaged in the rental for profit but were not in the business of renting such property	8l
m	Olympic and Paralympic medals and USOC prize money (see instructions)	8m
n	Section 951(a) inclusion (see instructions)	8n
o	Section 951A(a) inclusion (see instructions)	8o
p	Section 461(l) excess business loss adjustment	8p
q	Taxable distributions from an ABLE account (see instructions)	8q
r	Scholarship and fellowship grants not reported on Form W-2	8r
s	Nontaxable amount of Medicaid waiver payments included on Form 1040, line 1a or 1d	8s ( )
t	Pension or annuity from a nonqualifed deferred compensation plan or a nongovernmental section 457 plan	8t
u	Wages earned while incarcerated	8u
z	Other income. List type and amount: _____	8z
9	Total other income. Add lines 8a through 8z	9
10	Combine lines 1 through 7 and 9. Enter here and on Form 1040, 1040-SR, or 1040-NR, line 8	10

For Paperwork Reduction Act Notice, see your tax return instructions.   Cat. No. 71479F   Schedule 1 (Form 1040) 2022

DRAFT AS OF July 27, 2022 DO NOT FILE

(Use for Cumulative Problem 1.)

Part II   Adjustments to Income

11	Educator expenses	11
12	Certain business expenses of reservists, performing artists, and fee-basis government officials. Attach Form 2106	12
13	Health savings account deduction. Attach Form 8889	13
14	Moving expenses for members of the Armed Forces. Attach Form 3903	14
15	Deductible part of self-employment tax. Attach Schedule SE	15
16	Self-employed SEP, SIMPLE, and qualified plans	16
17	Self-employed health insurance deduction	17
18	Penalty on early withdrawal of savings	18
19a	Alimony paid	19a
b	Recipient's SSN	
c	Date of original divorce or separation agreement (see instructions): _____	
20	IRA deduction	20
21	Student loan interest deduction	21
22	Reserved for future use	22
23	Archer MSA deduction	23
24	Other adjustments:	
a	Jury duty pay (see instructions)	24a
b	Deductible expenses related to income reported on line 8l from the rental of personal property engaged in for profit	24b
c	Nontaxable amount of the value of Olympic and Paralympic medals and USOC prize money reported on line 8m	24c
d	Reforestation amortization and expenses	24d
e	Repayment of supplemental unemployment benefits under the Trade Act of 1974	24e
f	Contributions to section 501(c)(18)(D) pension plans	24f
g	Contributions by certain chaplains to section 403(b) plans	24g
h	Attorney fees and court costs for actions involving certain unlawful discrimination claims (see instructions)	24h
i	Attorney fees and court costs you paid in connection with an award from the IRS for information you provided that helped the IRS detect tax law violations	24i
j	Housing deduction from Form 2555	24j
k	Excess deductions of section 67(e) expenses from Schedule K-1 (Form 1041)	24k
z	Other adjustments. List type and amount: _____ _____	24z
25	Total other adjustments. Add lines 24a through 24z	25
26	Add lines 11 through 23 and 25. These are your **adjustments to income**. Enter here and on Form 1040 or 1040-SR, line 10, or Form 1040-NR, line 10a	26

(Use for Cumulative Problem 1.)

SCHEDULE 3 (Form 1040)	**Additional Credits and Payments**	OMB No. 1545-0074
Department of the Treasury Internal Revenue Service	Attach to Form 1040, 1040-SR, or 1040-NR. Go to *www.irs.gov/Form1040* for instructions and the latest information.	**2022** Attachment Sequence No. **03**

Name(s) shown on Form 1040, 1040-SR, or 1040-NR | Your social security number

Part I   Nonrefundable Credits

1	Foreign tax credit. Attach Form 1116 if required	**1**
2	Credit for child and dependent care expenses from Form 2441, line 11. Attach Form 2441	**2**
3	Education credits from Form 8863, line 19	**3**
4	Retirement savings contributions credit. Attach Form 8880	**4**
5	Residential energy credits. Attach Form 5695	**5**
6	Other nonrefundable credits:	
a	General business credit. Attach Form 3800	**6a**
b	Credit for prior year minimum tax. Attach Form 8801	**6b**
c	Adoption credit. Attach Form 8839	**6c**
d	Credit for the elderly or disabled. Attach Schedule R	**6d**
e	Alternative motor vehicle credit. Attach Form 8910	**6e**
f	Qualified plug-in motor vehicle credit. Attach Form 8936	**6f**
g	Mortgage interest credit. Attach Form 8396	**6g**
h	District of Columbia first-time homebuyer credit. Attach Form 8859	**6h**
i	Qualified electric vehicle credit. Attach Form 8834	**6i**
j	Alternative fuel vehicle refueling property credit. Attach Form 8911	**6j**
k	Credit to holders of tax credit bonds. Attach Form 8912	**6k**
l	Amount on Form 8978, line 14. See instructions	**6l**
z	Other nonrefundable credits. List type and amount: _____	**6z**
7	Total other nonrefundable credits. Add lines 6a through 6z	**7**
8	Add lines 1 through 5 and 7. Enter here and on Form 1040, 1040-SR, or 1040-NR, line 20	**8**

(continued on page 2)

For Paperwork Reduction Act Notice, see your tax return instructions.   Cat. No. 71480G   Schedule 3 (Form 1040) 2022

DRAFT AS OF September 21, 2022 DO NOT FILE

(Use for Cumulative Problem 1.)

Schedule 3 (Form 1040) 2022   Page **2**

Part II   Other Payments and Refundable Credits

9	Net premium tax credit. Attach Form 8962	**9**	
10	Amount paid with request for extension to file (see instructions)	**10**	
11	Excess social security and tier 1 RRTA tax withheld	**11**	
12	Credit for federal tax on fuels. Attach Form 4136	**12**	
13	Other payments or refundable credits:		
a	Form 2439 . . . . **13a**		
b	Credit for qualified sick and family leave wages paid in 2022 from Schedule(s) H for leave taken before April 1, 2021 . . . . . **13b**		
c	Reserved for future use **13c**		
d	Credit for repayment of amounts included in income from earlier years **13d**		
e	Reserved for future use **13e**		
f	Deferred amount of net 965 tax liability (see instructions) . . . **13f**		
g	Reserved for future use **13g**		
h	Credit for qualified sick and family leave wages paid in 2022 from Schedule(s) H for leave taken after March 31, 2021, and before October 1, 2021 . . . . **13h**		
z	Other payments or refundable credits. List type and amount: _____ **13z**		
14	Total other payments or refundable credits. Add lines 13a through 13z	**14**	
15	Add lines 9 through 12 and 14. Enter here and on Form 1040, 1040-SR, or 1040-NR, line 31	**15**	

Schedule 3 (Form 1040) 2022

(Use for Cumulative Problem 1.)

SCHEDULE 8812
(Form 1040)

Department of the Treasury
Internal Revenue Service

**Credits for Qualifying Children
and Other Dependents**

Attach to Form 1040, 1040-SR, or 1040-NR.
Go to *www.irs.gov/Schedule8812* for instructions and the latest information.

OMB No. 1545-0074

2022

Attachment
Sequence No. **47**

Name(s) shown on return

Your social security number

Part I	**Child Tax Credit and Credit for Other Dependents**		
1	Enter the amount from line 11 of your Form 1040, 1040-SR, or 1040-NR		**1**
2a	Enter income from Puerto Rico that you excluded	**2a**	
b	Enter the amounts from lines 45 and 50 of your Form 2555	**2b**	
c	Enter the amount from line 15 of your Form 4563	**2c**	
d	Add lines 2a through 2c		**2d**
3	Add lines 1 and 2d		**3**
4	Number of qualifying children under age 17 with the required social security number	**4**	
5	Multiply line 4 by $2,000		**5**
6	Number of other dependents, including any qualifying children who are not under age 17 or who do not have the required social security number	**6**	
	Caution: Do not include yourself, your spouse, or anyone who is not a U.S. citizen, U.S. national, or U.S. resident alien. Also, do not include anyone you included on line 4.		
7	Multiply line 6 by $500		**7**
8	Add lines 5 and 7		**8**
9	Enter the amount shown below for your filing status. • Married filing jointly—$400,000 • All other filing statuses—$200,000		**9**
10	Subtract line 9 from line 3. • If zero or less, enter -0-. • If more than zero and not a multiple of $1,000, enter the next multiple of $1,000. For example, if the result is $425, enter $1,000; if the result is $1,025, enter $2,000, etc.		**10**
11	Multiply line 10 by 5% (0.05)		**11**
12	Is the amount on line 8 more than the amount on line 11?		**12**
	☐ **No. STOP.** You cannot take the child tax credit, credit for other dependents, or additional child tax credit. Skip Parts II-A and II-B. Enter -0- on lines 14 and 27.		
	☐ **Yes.** Subtract line 11 from line 8. Enter the result.		
13	Enter the amount from the **Credit Limit Worksheet A**		**13**
14	Enter the smaller of line 12 or 13. **This is your child tax credit and credit for other dependents**		**14**
	Enter this amount on Form 1040, 1040-SR, or 1040-NR.		

If the amount on line 12 is more than the amount on line 14, you may be able to take the **additional child tax credit** on Form 1040, 1040-SR, or 1040-NR, line 28. Complete your Form 1040, 1040-SR, or 1040-NR through line 27 (also complete Schedule 3, line 11) before completing Part II-A.

For Paperwork Reduction Act Notice, see your tax return instructions.   Cat. No. 59761M   Schedule 8812 (Form 1040) 2022

(Use for Cumulative Problem 1.)

Schedule 8812 (Form 1040) 2022   Page **2**

Part II-A   Additional Child Tax Credit for All Filers

Caution: If you file Form 2555, you cannot claim the additional child tax credit.

15	Check this box if you **do not** want to claim the additional child tax credit. Skip Parts II-A and II-B. Enter -0- on line 27 . . . . . ☐	
16a	Subtract line 14 from line 12. If zero, **stop here**; you cannot take the additional child tax credit. Skip Parts II-A and II-B. Enter -0- on line 27	**16a**
b	Number of qualifying children under 17 with the required social security number: _____ x $1,500.	
	Enter the result. If zero, **stop here**; you cannot claim the additional child tax credit. Skip Parts II-A and II-B. Enter -0- on line 27	**16b**
	TIP: The number of children you use for this line is the same as the number of children you used for line 4.	
17	Enter the **smaller** of line 16a or line 16b	**17**
18a	Earned income (see instructions) **18a**	
b	Nontaxable combat pay (see instructions) **18b**	
19	Is the amount on line 18a more than $2,500?	
	☐ **No.** Leave line 19 blank and enter -0- on line 20.	
	☐ **Yes.** Subtract $2,500 from the amount on line 18a. Enter the result . . . **19**	
20	Multiply the amount on line 19 by 15% (0.15) and enter the result	**20**
	Next. On line 16b, is the amount $4,500 or more?	
	☐ **No.** If you are a bona fide resident of Puerto Rico, go to line 21. Otherwise, skip Part II-B and enter the **smaller** of line 17 or line 20 on line 27.	
	☐ **Yes.** If line 20 is equal to or more than line 17, skip Part II-B and enter the amount from line 17 on line 27. Otherwise, go to line 21.	

Part II-B   Certain Filers Who Have Three or More Qualifying Children and Bona Fide Residents of Puerto Rico

21	Withheld social security, Medicare, and Additional Medicare taxes from Form(s) W-2, boxes 4 and 6. If married filing jointly, include your spouse's amounts with yours. If your employer withheld or you paid Additional Medicare Tax or tier 1 RRTA taxes, see instructions **21**	
22	Enter the total of the amounts from Schedule 1 (Form 1040), line 15; Schedule 2 (Form 1040), line 5; Schedule 2 (Form 1040), line 6; and Schedule 2 (Form 1040), line 13 . **22**	
23	Add lines 21 and 22 . . . . **23**	
24	**1040 and**	
	1040-SR filers: Enter the total of the amounts from Form 1040 or 1040-SR, line 27, and Schedule 3 (Form 1040), line 11. ⎫	
	1040-NR filers: Enter the amount from Schedule 3 (Form 1040), line 11. ⎭ **24**	
25	Subtract line 24 from line 23. If zero or less, enter -0-	**25**
26	Enter the **larger** of line 20 or line 25	**26**
	Next, enter the **smaller** of line 17 or line 26 on line 27.	

Part II-C   Additional Child Tax Credit

27	**This is your additional child tax credit. Enter this amount on Form 1040, 1040-SR, or 1040-NR, line 28** . .	**27**

Schedule 8812 (Form 1040) 2022

(Use for Cumulative Problem 1.)

SCHEDULE EIC (Form 1040)	Earned Income Credit	OMB No. 1545-0074
	Qualifying Child Information	2022
Department of the Treasury Internal Revenue Service	Complete and attach to Form 1040 or 1040-SR only if you have a qualifying child. Go to www.irs.gov/ScheduleEIC for the latest information.	Attachment Sequence No. 43

Name(s) shown on return	Your social security number

If you are separated from your spouse, filing a separate return, and meet the requirements to claim the EIC (see instructions), check here ☐

Before you begin:
- See the instructions for Form 1040, line 27, to make sure that (**a**) you can take the EIC, and (**b**) you have a qualifying child.
- Be sure the child's name on line 1 and social security number (SSN) on line 2 agree with the child's social security card. Otherwise, at the time we process your return, we may reduce your EIC. If the name or SSN on the child's social security card is not correct, call the Social Security Administration at 800-772-1213.
- If you have a child who meets the conditions to be your qualifying child for purposes of claiming the EIC, but that child doesn't have an SSN as defined in the instructions for Form 1040, line 27, see the instructions.

⚠ CAUTION
- *You can't claim the EIC for a child who didn't live with you for more than half of the year.*
- *If your child doesn't have an SSN as defined in the instructions for Form 1040, line 27, see the instructions.*
- *If you take the EIC even though you are not eligible, you may not be allowed to take the credit for up to 10 years. See the instructions for details.*
- *It will take us longer to process your return and issue your refund if you do not fill in all lines that apply for each qualifying child.*

Qualifying Child Information	Child 1	Child 2	Child 3
1 Child's name If you have more than three qualifying children, you have to list only three to get the maximum credit.	First name _____ Last name _____	First name _____ Last name _____	First name _____ Last name _____
2 Child's SSN The child must have an SSN as defined in the instructions for Form 1040, line 27, unless the child was born and died in 2022 or you are claiming the self-only EIC; see instructions. If your child was born and died in 2022 and did not have an SSN, enter "Died" on this line and attach a copy of the child's birth certificate, death certificate, or hospital medical records showing a live birth.			
3 Child's year of birth	Year _____ *If born after 2003 and the child is younger than you (or your spouse, if filing jointly), skip lines 4a and 4b; go to line 5.*	Year _____ *If born after 2003 and the child is younger than you (or your spouse, if filing jointly), skip lines 4a and 4b; go to line 5.*	Year _____ *If born after 2003 and the child is younger than you (or your spouse, if filing jointly), skip lines 4a and 4b; go to line 5.*
4a Was the child under age 24 at the end of 2022, a student, and younger than you (or your spouse, if filing jointly)?	☐ **Yes.** *Go to line 5.* ☐ **No.** *Go to line 4b.*	☐ **Yes.** *Go to line 5.* ☐ **No.** *Go to line 4b.*	☐ **Yes.** *Go to line 5.* ☐ **No.** *Go to line 4b.*
b Was the child permanently and totally disabled during any part of 2022?	☐ **Yes.** *Go to line 5.* ☐ **No.** The child is not a qualifying child.	☐ **Yes.** *Go to line 5.* ☐ **No.** The child is not a qualifying child.	☐ **Yes.** *Go to line 5.* ☐ **No.** The child is not a qualifying child.
5 Child's relationship to you (for example, son, daughter, grandchild, niece, nephew, eligible foster child, etc.)			
6 Number of months child lived with you in the United States during 2022 • If the child lived with you for more than half of 2022 but less than 7 months, enter "7." • If the child was born or died in 2022 and your home was the child's home for more than half the time he or she was alive during 2022, enter "12."	_____ months *Do not enter more than 12 months.*	_____ months *Do not enter more than 12 months.*	_____ months *Do not enter more than 12 months.*

For Paperwork Reduction Act Notice, see your tax return instructions.　　Cat. No. 13339M　　Schedule EIC (Form 1040) 2022

(Use for Cumulative Problem 1.)

Form **8880**	**Credit for Qualified Retirement Savings Contributions**	OMB No. 1545-0074
Department of the Treasury Internal Revenue Service	Attach to Form 1040, 1040-SR, or 1040-NR. Go to *www.irs.gov/Form8880* for the latest information.	**2022** Attachment Sequence No. **54**

Name(s) shown on return   Your social security number

CAUTION You **cannot** take this credit if **either** of the following applies.
- The amount on Form 1040, 1040-SR, or 1040-NR, line 11, is more than $34,000 ($51,000 if head of household; $68,000 if married filing jointly).
- The person(s) who made the qualified contribution or elective deferral (a) was born after January 1, 2005; (b) is claimed as a dependent on someone else's 2022 tax return; or (c) was a **student** (see instructions).

		(a) You	(b) Your spouse
1	Traditional and Roth IRA contributions, and ABLE account contributions by the designated beneficiary for 2022. **Do not** include rollover contributions . . . **1**		
2	Elective deferrals to a 401(k) or other qualified employer plan, voluntary employee contributions, and 501(c)(18)(D) plan contributions for 2022 (see instructions) . **2**		
3	Add lines 1 and 2 . . . . **3**		
4	Certain distributions received **after** 2019 and **before** the due date (including extensions) of your 2022 tax return (see instructions). If married filing jointly, include **both** spouses' amounts in **both** columns. See instructions for an exception . **4**		
5	Subtract line 4 from line 3. If zero or less, enter -0- **5**		
6	In each column, enter the **smaller** of line 5 or $2,000 . . . . . **6**		
7	Add the amounts on line 6. If zero, **stop**; you can't take this credit	**7**	
8	Enter the amount from Form 1040, 1040-SR, or 1040-NR, line 11* **8**		
9	Enter the applicable decimal amount from the table below.		

If line 8 is—		And your filing status is—		
Over—	But not over—	Married filing jointly	Head of household	Single, Married filing separately, or Qualifying surviving spouse
		Enter on line 9—		
---	$20,500	0.5	0.5	0.5
$20,500	$22,000	0.5	0.5	0.2
$22,000	$30,750	0.5	0.5	0.1
$30,750	$33,000	0.5	0.2	0.1
$33,000	$34,000	0.5	0.1	0.1
$34,000	$41,000	0.5	0.1	0.0
$41,000	$44,000	0.2	0.1	0.0
$44,000	$51,000	0.1	0.1	0.0
$51,000	$68,000	0.1	0.0	0.0
$68,000	---	0.0	0.0	0.0

9 x 0.

Note: If line 9 is zero, **stop**; you can't take this credit.

10	Multiply line 7 by line 9	**10**	
11	Limitation based on tax liability. Enter the amount from the Credit Limit Worksheet in the instructions	**11**	
12	**Credit for qualified retirement savings contributions.** Enter the **smaller** of line 10 or line 11 here and on Schedule 3 (Form 1040), line 4	**12**	

* See Pub. 590-A for the amount to enter if you claim any exclusion or deduction for foreign earned income, foreign housing, or income from Puerto Rico or for bona fide residents of American Samoa.

For Paperwork Reduction Act Notice, see your tax return instructions.   Cat. No. 33394D   Form **8880** (2022)

(Use for Cumulative Problem 1.)

Section references are to the Internal Revenue Code unless otherwise noted.

Future Developments

For the latest information about developments related to Form 8880 and its instructions, such as legislation enacted after they were published, go to *www.irs.gov/Form8880*.

Reminder

Contributions by a designated beneficiary to an Achieving a Better Life Experience (ABLE) account. A retirement savings contribution credit may be claimed for the amount of contributions you, as the designated beneficiary of an ABLE account, make before January 1, 2026, to the ABLE account. See Pub. 907, Tax Highlights for Persons With Disabilities, for more information.

General Instructions

Purpose of Form

Use Form 8880 to figure the amount, if any, of your retirement savings contributions credit (also known as the saver's credit).

 This credit can be claimed in addition to any IRA deduction claimed on Schedule 1 (Form 1040), line 20.

Who Can Take This Credit

You may be able to take this credit if you, or your spouse if filing jointly, made (a) contributions (other than rollover contributions) to a traditional or Roth IRA; (b) elective deferrals to a 401(k), 403(b), governmental 457(b), SEP, SIMPLE, or to the federal Thrift Savings Plan (TSP); (c) voluntary employee contributions to a qualified retirement plan, as defined in section 4974(c) (including the federal TSP); (d) contributions to a 501(c)(18)(D) plan; or (e) contributions, as a designated beneficiary of an ABLE account, to the ABLE account, as defined in section 529A.

However, you can't take the credit if either of the following applies.

• The amount on Form 1040, 1040-SR, or 1040-NR, line 11, is more than $34,000 ($51,000 if head of household; $68,000 if married filing jointly).

• The person(s) who made the qualified contribution or elective deferral (a) was born after January 1, 2005; (b) is claimed as a dependent on someone else's 2022 tax return; or (c) was a student.

 You'll need to refigure the amount on Form 1040 or 1040-SR, line 11, if you're filing Form 2555 or Form 4563 or you're excluding income from Puerto Rico. See Pub. 590-A at www.irs.gov/Pub590A for details.

You were a student if during any part of 5 calendar months of 2022 you:

• Were enrolled as a full-time student at a school; or

• Took a full-time, on-farm training course given by a school or a state, county, or local government agency.

A school includes technical, trade, and mechanical schools. It doesn't include on-the-job training courses, correspondence schools, or schools offering courses only through the Internet.

Specific Instructions

Column (b)

Complete column (b) only if you're filing a joint return.

Line 2

Include on line 2 any of the following amounts.

• Elective deferrals (including designated Roth contributions under section 402A, if applicable) to a 401(k), 403(b), governmental 457(b), SEP, SIMPLE, or to the federal TSP.

• Voluntary employee contributions to a qualified retirement plan, as defined in section 4974(c) (including the federal TSP).

• Contributions to a 501(c)(18)(D) plan.

These amounts may be shown in box 12 of your Form(s) W-2 for 2022.

Note: Contributions designated under section 414(h)(2) are treated as employer contributions and, as such, they aren't voluntary contributions made by the employee. They don't qualify for the credit and shouldn't be included on line 2.

Line 4

Enter the total amount of distributions you, and your spouse if filing jointly, received after 2019 and before the due date of your 2022 return (including extensions) from any of the following types of plans.

• Traditional or Roth IRAs, or ABLE accounts.

• 401(k), 403(b), governmental 457(b), 501(c)(18)(D), SEP, SIMPLE, or the federal TSP.

• Qualified retirement plans, as defined in section 4974(c).

Don't include any of the following.

• Distributions not taxable as the result of a rollover or a trustee-to-trustee transfer.

• Distributions that are taxable as the result of an in-plan rollover to your designated Roth account.

• Distributions from your eligible retirement plan (other than a Roth IRA) rolled over or converted to your Roth IRA.

• Loans from a qualified employer plan treated as a distribution.

• Distributions of excess contributions or deferrals (and income allocable to such contributions or deferrals).

• Distributions of contributions made to an IRA during a tax year and returned (with any income allocable to such contributions) on or before the due date (including extensions) for that tax year.

• Distributions of dividends paid on stock held by an employee stock ownership plan under section 404(k).

• Distributions from a military retirement plan (other than the federal TSP).

• Distributions from an inherited IRA by a nonspousal beneficiary.

If you're filing a joint return, include both spouses' amounts in both columns.

Exception. Don't include your spouse's distributions with yours when entering an amount on line 4 if you and your spouse didn't file a joint return for the year the distribution was received.

Example. You received a distribution of $5,000 from a qualified retirement plan in 2022. Your spouse received a distribution of $2,000 from a Roth IRA in 2020. You and your spouse file a joint return in 2022, but didn't file a joint return in 2020. You would include $5,000 in column (a) and $7,000 in column (b).

Line 7

Add the amounts from line 6, columns (a) and (b), and enter the total.

Line 11

Before you complete the following worksheet, figure the amount of any credit for the elderly or the disabled you're claiming on Schedule 3 (Form 1040), line 6d. See Schedule R (Form 1040) to figure the credit.

Credit Limit Worksheet

Complete this worksheet to figure the amount to enter on line 11.

1. Enter the amount from Form 1040, 1040-SR, or 1040-NR, line 18 . . . .   1._____

2. Enter the total of your credits from Schedule 3, lines 1 through 3, 6d, and 6l . . . . . .   2._____

3. Subtract line 2 from line 1. Also enter this amount on Form 8880, line 11. But if zero or less, **stop**; you can't take the credit—don't file this form .   3._____

(Use for Cumulative Problem 2.)

Form 1040 — Department of the Treasury—Internal Revenue Service — U.S. Individual Income Tax Return — 2022

OMB No. 1545-0074 | IRS Use Only—Do not write or staple in this space.

Filing Status
Check only one box.
☐ Single ☐ Married filing jointly ☐ Married filing separately (MFS) ☐ Head of household (HOH) ☐ Qualifying widow(er) (QW)

If you checked the MFS box, enter the name of your spouse. If you checked the HOH or QW box, enter the child's name if the qualifying person is a child but not your dependent:

Your first name and middle initial | Last name | Your social security number

If joint return, spouse's first name and middle initial | Last name | Spouse's social security number

Home address (number and street). If you have a P.O. box, see instructions. | Apt. no.

City, town, or post office. If you have a foreign address, also complete spaces below. | State | ZIP code

Foreign country name | Foreign province/state/county | Foreign postal code

Presidential Election Campaign
Check here if you, or your spouse if filing jointly, want $3 to go to this fund. Checking a box below will not change your tax or refund.
☐ You ☐ Spouse

At any time during 2022, did you: (a) receive (as a reward, award, or compensation); or (b) sell, exchange, gift, or otherwise dispose of a digital asset (or a financial interest in a digital asset)? (See instructions.) . . ☐ Yes ☐ No

Standard Deduction
Someone can claim: ☐ You as a dependent ☐ Your spouse as a dependent
☐ Spouse itemizes on a separate return or you were a dual-status alien

Age/Blindness **You:** ☐ Were born before January 2, 1958 ☐ Are blind **Spouse:** ☐ Was born before January 2, 1958 ☐ Is blind

Dependents (see instructions):

(1) First name Last name	(2) Social security number	(3) Relationship to you	(4) Check the box if qualifies for (see instructions): Child tax credit	Credit for other dependents
			☐	☐
			☐	☐
			☐	☐
			☐	☐

If more than four dependents, see instructions and check here . . ☐

Income

Attach Form(s) W-2 here. Also attach Forms W-2G and 1099-R if tax was withheld.

If you did not get a Form W-2, see instructions.

1a	Total amount from Form(s) W-2, box 1 (see instructions)	1a
b	Household employee wages not reported on Form(s) W-2	1b
c	Tip income not reported on line 1a (see instructions)	1c
d	Medicaid waiver payments not reported on Form(s) W-2 (see instructions) . . .	1d
e	Taxable dependent care benefits from Form 2441, line 26	1e
f	Employer-provided adoption benefits from Form 8839, line 29	1f
g	Wages from Form 8919, line 6	1g
h	Other earned income (see instructions)	1h
i	Nontaxable combat pay election (see instructions) 1i	
z	Add lines 1a through 1h	1z

Attach Sch. B if required.

2a	Tax-exempt interest . . .	2a	b	Taxable interest	2b
3a	Qualified dividends . . .	3a	b	Ordinary dividends	3b
4a	IRA distributions	4a	b	Taxable amount	4b
5a	Pensions and annuities . .	5a	b	Taxable amount	5b
6a	Social security benefits . .	6a	b	Taxable amount	6b

Standard Deduction for—
• Single or Married filing separately, $12,950
• Married filing jointly or Qualifying widow(er), $25,900
• Head of household, $19,400
• If you checked any box under *Standard Deduction,* see instructions.

c	If you elect to use the lump-sum election method, check here (see instructions) . ☐	
7	Capital gain or (loss). Attach Schedule D if required. If not required, check here . . . ☐	7
8	Other income from Schedule 1, line 10	8
9	Add lines 1z, 2b, 3b, 4b, 5b, 6b, 7, and 8. This is your **total income** . . .	9
10	Adjustments to income from Schedule 1, line 26	10
11	Subtract line 10 from line 9. This is your **adjusted gross income**	11
12	**Standard deduction or itemized deductions** (from Schedule A)	12
13	Qualified business income deduction from Form 8995 or Form 8995-A	13
14	Add lines 12 and 13	14
15	Subtract line 14 from line 11. If zero or less, enter -0-. This is your **taxable income**	15

For Disclosure, Privacy Act, and Paperwork Reduction Act Notice, see separate instructions.   Cat. No. 11320B   Form **1040** (2022)

(Use for Cumulative Problem 2.)

Version A, Cycle 7

Form 1040 (2022) — Page **2**

Tax and Credits	16	**Tax** (see instructions). Check if any from Form(s): **1** ☐ 8814 **2** ☐ 4972 **3** ☐ _____	16
	17	Amount from Schedule 2, line 3	17
	18	Add lines 16 and 17	18
	19	Child tax credit or credit for other dependents from Schedule 8812	19
	20	Amount from Schedule 3, line 8	20
	21	Add lines 19 and 20	21
	22	Subtract line 21 from line 18. If zero or less, enter -0-	22
	23	Other taxes, including self-employment tax, from Schedule 2, line 21	23
	24	Add lines 22 and 23. This is your **total tax**	24
Payments	25	Federal income tax withheld from:	
	a	Form(s) W-2	25a
	b	Form(s) 1099	25b
	c	Other forms (see instructions)	25c
	d	Add lines 25a through 25c	25d
If you have a qualifying child, attach Sch. EIC.	26	2022 estimated tax payments and amount applied from 2021 return	26
	27	Earned income credit (EIC)	27
	28	Additional child tax credit from Schedule 8812	28
	29	American opportunity credit from Form 8863, line 8	29
	30	Reserved for future use	30
	31	Amount from Schedule 3, line 15	31
	32	Add lines 27, 28, 29, and 31. These are your **total other payments and refundable credits**	32
	33	Add lines 25d, 26, and 32. These are your **total payments**	33
Refund	34	If line 33 is more than line 24, subtract line 24 from line 33. This is the amount you **overpaid**	34
	35a	Amount of line 34 you want **refunded to you**. If Form 8888 is attached, check here ☐	35a
Direct deposit? See instructions.	b	Routing number ___ **c** Type: ☐ Checking ☐ Savings	
	d	Account number ___	
	36	Amount of line 34 you want **applied to your 2023 estimated tax**	36
Amount You Owe	37	Subtract line 33 from line 24. This is the **amount you owe**. For details on how to pay, go to *www.irs.gov/Payments* or see instructions	37
	38	Estimated tax penalty (see instructions)	38

Third Party Designee

Do you want to allow another person to discuss this return with the IRS? See instructions . . . ☐ **Yes.** Complete below. ☐ **No**

Designee's name ___ Phone no. ___ Personal identification number (PIN) ___

Sign Here

Under penalties of perjury, I declare that I have examined this return and accompanying schedules and statements, and to the best of my knowledge and belief, they are true, correct, and complete. Declaration of preparer (other than taxpayer) is based on all information of which preparer has any knowledge.

Your signature	Date	Your occupation	If the IRS sent you an Identity Protection PIN, enter it here (see inst.)

Joint return? See instructions. Keep a copy for your records.

Spouse's signature. If a joint return, **both** must sign.	Date	Spouse's occupation	If the IRS sent your spouse an Identity Protection PIN, enter it here (see inst.)

Phone no. ___ Email address ___

Paid Preparer Use Only

Preparer's name	Preparer's signature	Date	PTIN	Check if: ☐ Self-employed
Firm's name			Phone no.	
Firm's address			Firm's EIN	

Go to *www.irs.gov/Form1040* for instructions and the latest information. Form **1040** (2022)

(Use for Cumulative Problem 2.)

SCHEDULE 1 (Form 1040)

Additional Income and Adjustments to Income

Department of the Treasury
Internal Revenue Service

Attach to Form 1040, 1040-SR, or 1040-NR.
Go to *www.irs.gov/Form1040* for instructions and the latest information.

OMB No. 1545-0074

2022

Attachment Sequence No. 01

Name(s) shown on Form 1040, 1040-SR, or 1040-NR

Your social security number

DRAFT AS OF July 27, 2022 DO NOT FILE

Part I — Additional Income

Line	Description		Amount
1	Taxable refunds, credits, or offsets of state and local income taxes	1	
2a	Alimony received	2a	
b	Date of original divorce or separation agreement (see instructions):		
3	Business income or (loss). Attach Schedule C	3	
4	Other gains or (losses). Attach Form 4797	4	
5	Rental real estate, royalties, partnerships, S corporations, trusts, etc. Attach Schedule E	5	
6	Farm income or (loss). Attach Schedule F	6	
7	Unemployment compensation	7	
8	Other income:		
a	Net operating loss	8a	( )
b	Gambling	8b	
c	Cancellation of debt	8c	
d	Foreign earned income exclusion from Form 2555	8d	( )
e	Income from Form 8853	8e	
f	Income from Form 8889	8f	
g	Alaska Permanent Fund dividends	8g	
h	Jury duty pay	8h	
i	Prizes and awards	8i	
j	Activity not engaged in for profit income	8j	
k	Stock options	8k	
l	Income from the rental of personal property if you engaged in the rental for profit but were not in the business of renting such property	8l	
m	Olympic and Paralympic medals and USOC prize money (see instructions)	8m	
n	Section 951(a) inclusion (see instructions)	8n	
o	Section 951A(a) inclusion (see instructions)	8o	
p	Section 461(l) excess business loss adjustment	8p	
q	Taxable distributions from an ABLE account (see instructions)	8q	
r	Scholarship and fellowship grants not reported on Form W-2	8r	
s	Nontaxable amount of Medicaid waiver payments included on Form 1040, line 1a or 1d	8s	( )
t	Pension or annuity from a nonqualifed deferred compensation plan or a nongovernmental section 457 plan	8t	
u	Wages earned while incarcerated	8u	
z	Other income. List type and amount: _____	8z	
9	Total other income. Add lines 8a through 8z	9	
10	Combine lines 1 through 7 and 9. Enter here and on Form 1040, 1040-SR, or 1040-NR, line 8	10	

For Paperwork Reduction Act Notice, see your tax return instructions.   Cat. No. 71479F   Schedule 1 (Form 1040) 2022

(Use for Cumulative Problem 2.)

	Schedule 1 (Form 1040) 2022	Page **2**
Part II	**Adjustments to Income**	
11	Educator expenses	11
12	Certain business expenses of reservists, performing artists, and fee-basis government officials. Attach Form 2106	12
13	Health savings account deduction. Attach Form 8889	13
14	Moving expenses for members of the Armed Forces. Attach Form 3903 . . .	14
15	Deductible part of self-employment tax. Attach Schedule SE . . .	15
16	Self-employed SEP, SIMPLE, and qualified plans	16
17	Self-employed health insurance deduction	17
18	Penalty on early withdrawal of savings	18
19a	Alimony paid	19a
b	Recipient's SSN	
c	Date of original divorce or separation agreement (see instructions):	
20	IRA deduction	20
21	Student loan interest deduction	21
22	Reserved for future use	22
23	Archer MSA deduction	23
24	Other adjustments:	
a	Jury duty pay (see instructions) 24a	
b	Deductible expenses related to income reported on line 8l from the rental of personal property engaged in for profit 24b	
c	Nontaxable amount of the value of Olympic and Paralympic medals and USOC prize money reported on line 8m 24c	
d	Reforestation amortization and expenses 24d	
e	Repayment of supplemental unemployment benefits under the Trade Act of 1974 . . . . 24e	
f	Contributions to section 501(c)(18)(D) pension plans 24f	
g	Contributions by certain chaplains to section 403(b) plans 24g	
h	Attorney fees and court costs for actions involving certain unlawful discrimination claims (see instructions) 24h	
i	Attorney fees and court costs you paid in connection with an award from the IRS for information you provided that helped the IRS detect tax law violations 24i	
j	Housing deduction from Form 2555 . . . . 24j	
k	Excess deductions of section 67(e) expenses from Schedule K-1 (Form 1041) 24k	
z	Other adjustments. List type and amount: _____ 24z	
25	Total other adjustments. Add lines 24a through 24z	25
26	Add lines 11 through 23 and 25. These are your **adjustments to income**. Enter here and on Form 1040 or 1040-SR, line 10, or Form 1040-NR, line 10a	26
		Schedule 1 (Form 1040) 2022

(Use for Cumulative Problem 2.)

SCHEDULE 3 (Form 1040) Department of the Treasury Internal Revenue Service	**Additional Credits and Payments** Attach to Form 1040, 1040-SR, or 1040-NR. Go to *www.irs.gov/Form1040* for instructions and the latest information.	OMB No. 1545-0074 20**22** Attachment Sequence No. **03**

Name(s) shown on Form 1040, 1040-SR, or 1040-NR | Your social security number

Part I   Nonrefundable Credits

1	Foreign tax credit. Attach Form 1116 if required	1
2	Credit for child and dependent care expenses from Form 2441, line 11. Attach Form 2441	2
3	Education credits from Form 8863, line 19	3
4	Retirement savings contributions credit. Attach Form 8880	4
5	Residential energy credits. Attach Form 5695	5
6	Other nonrefundable credits:	
a	General business credit. Attach Form 3800	6a
b	Credit for prior year minimum tax. Attach Form 8801	6b
c	Adoption credit. Attach Form 8839	6c
d	Credit for the elderly or disabled. Attach Schedule R	6d
e	Alternative motor vehicle credit. Attach Form 8910	6e
f	Qualified plug-in motor vehicle credit. Attach Form 8936	6f
g	Mortgage interest credit. Attach Form 8396	6g
h	District of Columbia first-time homebuyer credit. Attach Form 8859	6h
i	Qualified electric vehicle credit. Attach Form 8834	6i
j	Alternative fuel vehicle refueling property credit. Attach Form 8911	6j
k	Credit to holders of tax credit bonds. Attach Form 8912	6k
l	Amount on Form 8978, line 14. See instructions	6l
z	Other nonrefundable credits. List type and amount:	6z
7	Total other nonrefundable credits. Add lines 6a through 6z	7
8	Add lines 1 through 5 and 7. Enter here and on Form 1040, 1040-SR, or 1040-NR, line 20	8

(continued on page 2)

For Paperwork Reduction Act Notice, see your tax return instructions.   Cat. No. 71480G   Schedule 3 (Form 1040) 2022

(Use for Cumulative Problem 2.)

Schedule 3 (Form 1040) 2022
Page **2**

Part II   **Other Payments and Refundable Credits**

9	Net premium tax credit. Attach Form 8962	**9**	
10	Amount paid with request for extension to file (see instructions)	**10**	
11	Excess social security and tier 1 RRTA tax withheld	**11**	
12	Credit for federal tax on fuels. Attach Form 4136	**12**	
13	Other payments or refundable credits:		
a	Form 2439	**13a**	
b	Credit for qualified sick and family leave wages paid in 2022 from Schedule(s) H for leave taken before April 1, 2021	**13b**	
c	Reserved for future use	**13c**	
d	Credit for repayment of amounts included in income from earlier years	**13d**	
e	Reserved for future use	**13e**	
f	Deferred amount of net 965 tax liability (see instructions) . . .	**13f**	
g	Reserved for future use	**13g**	
h	Credit for qualified sick and family leave wages paid in 2022 from Schedule(s) H for leave taken after March 31, 2021, and before October 1, 2021	**13h**	
z	Other payments or refundable credits. List type and amount:		
	_____	**13z**	
14	Total other payments or refundable credits. Add lines 13a through 13z	**14**	
15	Add lines 9 through 12 and 14. Enter here and on Form 1040, 1040-SR, or 1040-NR, line 31	**15**	

Schedule 3 (Form 1040) 2022

(Use for Cumulative Problem 2.)

SCHEDULE B
(Form 1040)

Department of the Treasury
Internal Revenue Service

Interest and Ordinary Dividends

Go to *www.irs.gov/ScheduleB* for instructions and the latest information.
Attach to Form 1040 or 1040-SR.

OMB No. 1545-0074

2022

Attachment
Sequence No. **08**

Name(s) shown on return

Your social security number

				Amount
Part I **Interest** (See instructions and the Instructions for Form 1040, line 2b.) **Note:** If you received a Form 1099-INT, Form 1099-OID, or substitute statement from a brokerage firm, list the firm's name as the payer and enter the total interest shown on that form.	**1**	List name of payer. If any interest is from a seller-financed mortgage and the buyer used the property as a personal residence, see the instructions and list this interest first. Also, show that buyer's social security number and address:	**1**	
	2	Add the amounts on line 1	**2**	
	3	Excludable interest on series EE and I U.S. savings bonds issued after 1989. Attach Form 8815	**3**	
	4	Subtract line 3 from line 2. Enter the result here and on Form 1040 or 1040-SR, line 2b	**4**	

Note: If line 4 is over $1,500, you must complete Part III.

				Amount
Part II **Ordinary Dividends** (See instructions and the Instructions for Form 1040, line 3b.) **Note:** If you received a Form 1099-DIV or substitute statement from a brokerage firm, list the firm's name as the payer and enter the ordinary dividends shown on that form.	**5**	List name of payer:	**5**	
	6	Add the amounts on line 5. Enter the total here and on Form 1040 or 1040-SR, line 3b	**6**	

Note: If line 6 is over $1,500, you must complete Part III.

Part III

Foreign Accounts and Trusts

Caution: If required, failure to file FinCEN Form 114 may result in substantial penalties. Additionally, you may be required to file Form 8938, Statement of Specified Foreign Financial Assets. See instructions.

You must complete this part if you **(a)** had over $1,500 of taxable interest or ordinary dividends; **(b)** had a foreign account; or **(c)** received a distribution from, or were a grantor of, or a transferor to, a foreign trust.

		Yes	No
7a	At any time during 2022, did you have a financial interest in or signature authority over a financial account (such as a bank account, securities account, or brokerage account) located in a foreign country? See instructions		
	If "Yes," are you required to file FinCEN Form 114, Report of Foreign Bank and Financial Accounts (FBAR), to report that financial interest or signature authority? See FinCEN Form 114 and its instructions for filing requirements and exceptions to those requirements		
b	If you are required to file FinCEN Form 114, list the name(s) of the foreign country(-ies) where the financial account(s) are located:		
8	During 2022, did you receive a distribution from, or were you the grantor of, or transferor to, a foreign trust? If "Yes," you may have to file Form 3520. See instructions		

For Paperwork Reduction Act Notice, see your tax return instructions.   Cat. No. 17146N   Schedule B (Form 1040) 2022

(Use for Cumulative Problem 2.)

Form 8863

Department of the Treasury
Internal Revenue Service

Education Credits
(American Opportunity and Lifetime Learning Credits)
Attach to Form 1040 or 1040-SR.
Go to *www.irs.gov/Form8863* for instructions and the latest information.

OMB No. 1545-0074

2022

Attachment
Sequence No. **50**

Name(s) shown on return

Your social security number

⚠️ **CAUTION** *Complete a separate Part III on page 2 for each student for whom you're claiming either credit before you complete Parts I and II.*

DRAFT AS OF
October 3, 2022
DO NOT FILE

Part I	Refundable American Opportunity Credit	
1	After completing Part III for each student, enter the total of all amounts from all Parts III, line 30	**1**
2	Enter: $180,000 if married filing jointly; $90,000 if single, head of household, or qualifying widow(er)	**2**
3	Enter the amount from Form 1040 or 1040-SR, line 11. If you're filing Form 2555 or 4563, or you're excluding income from Puerto Rico, see Pub. 970 for the amount to enter	**3**
4	Subtract line 3 from line 2. If zero or less, **stop**; you can't take any education credit	**4**
5	Enter: $20,000 if married filing jointly; $10,000 if single, head of household, or qualifying widow(er)	**5**
6	If line 4 is: • Equal to or more than line 5, enter 1.000 on line 6 • Less than line 5, divide line 4 by line 5. Enter the result as a decimal (rounded to at least three places)	**6**
7	Multiply line 1 by line 6. **Caution:** If you were under age 24 at the end of the year **and** meet the conditions described in the instructions, you **can't** take the refundable American opportunity credit; skip line 8, enter the amount from line 7 on line 9, and check this box ☐	**7**
8	**Refundable American opportunity credit.** Multiply line 7 by 40% (0.40). Enter the amount here and on Form 1040 or 1040-SR, line 29. Then go to line 9 below.	**8**

Part II	Nonrefundable Education Credits	
9	Subtract line 8 from line 7. Enter here and on line 2 of the Credit Limit Worksheet (see instructions)	**9**
10	After completing Part III for each student, enter the total of all amounts from all Parts III, line 31. If zero, skip lines 11 through 17, enter -0- on line 18, and go to line 19	**10**
11	Enter the smaller of line 10 or $10,000	**11**
12	Multiply line 11 by 20% (0.20)	**12**
13	Enter: $180,000 if married filing jointly; $90,000 if single, head of household, or qualifying widow(er)	**13**
14	Enter the amount from Form 1040 or 1040-SR, line 11. If you're filing Form 2555 or 4563, or you're excluding income from Puerto Rico, see Pub. 970 for the amount to enter	**14**
15	Subtract line 14 from line 13. If zero or less, skip lines 16 and 17, enter -0- on line 18, and go to line 19	**15**
16	Enter: $20,000 if married filing jointly; $10,000 if single, head of household, or qualifying widow(er)	**16**
17	If line 15 is: • Equal to or more than line 16, enter 1.000 on line 17 and go to line 18 • Less than line 16, divide line 15 by line 16. Enter the result as a decimal (rounded to at least three places)	**17**
18	Multiply line 12 by line 17. Enter here and on line 1 of the Credit Limit Worksheet (see instructions)	**18**
19	**Nonrefundable education credits.** Enter the amount from line 7 of the Credit Limit Worksheet (see instructions) here and on Schedule 3 (Form 1040), line 3	**19**

(Use for Cumulative Problem 2.)

For Paperwork Reduction Act Notice, see your tax return instructions.   Cat. No. 25379M   Form **8863** (2022)

(Use for Cumulative Problem 2.)

Form 8863 (2022)   Page **2**

Name(s) shown on return   Your social security number

⚠ **CAUTION** *Complete Part III for each student for whom you're claiming either the American opportunity credit or lifetime learning credit. Use additional copies of page 2 as needed for each student.*

Part III   Student and Educational Institution Information. See instructions.

20 Student name (as shown on page 1 of your tax return)   **21** Student social security number (as shown on page 1 of your tax return)

22 Educational institution information (see instructions)

a. Name of first educational institution	b. Name of second educational institution (if any)
(1) Address. Number and street (or P.O. box). City, town or post office, state, and ZIP code. If a foreign address, see instructions.	**(1)** Address. Number and street (or P.O. box). City, town or post office, state, and ZIP code. If a foreign address, see instructions.
(2) Did the student receive Form 1098-T from this institution for 2022? ☐ Yes ☐ No	**(2)** Did the student receive Form 1098-T from this institution for 2022? ☐ Yes ☐ No
(3) Did the student receive Form 1098-T from this institution for 2021 with box 7 checked? ☐ Yes ☐ No	**(3)** Did the student receive Form 1098-T from this institution for 2021 with box 7 checked? ☐ Yes ☐ No
(4) Enter the institution's employer identification number (EIN) if you're claiming the American opportunity credit or if you checked "Yes" in **(2)** or **(3)**. You can get the EIN from Form 1098-T or from the institution. ___ ___ - ___ ___ ___ ___ ___ ___ ___	**(4)** Enter the institution's employer identification number (EIN) if you're claiming the American opportunity credit or if you checked "Yes" in **(2)** or **(3)**. You can get the EIN from Form 1098-T or from the institution. ___ ___ - ___ ___ ___ ___ ___ ___ ___

23 Has the American opportunity credit been claimed for this student for any 4 tax years before 2022?   ☐ Yes — **Stop!** Go to line 31 for this student.   ☐ No — Go to line 24.

24 Was the student enrolled at least half-time for at least one academic period that began or is treated as having begun in 2022 at an eligible educational institution in a program leading towards a postsecondary degree, certificate, or other recognized postsecondary educational credential? See instructions.   ☐ Yes — Go to line 25.   ☐ No — **Stop!** Go to line 31 for this student.

25 Did the student complete the first 4 years of postsecondary education before 2022? See instructions.   ☐ Yes — **Stop!** Go to line 31 for this student.   ☐ No — Go to line 26.

26 Was the student convicted, before the end of 2022, of a felony for possession or distribution of a controlled substance?   ☐ Yes — **Stop!** Go to line 31 for this student.   ☐ No — Complete lines 27 through 30 for this student.

⚠ **CAUTION** *You **can't** take the American opportunity credit and the lifetime learning credit for the **same student** in the same year. If you complete lines 27 through 30 for this student, don't complete line 31.*

American Opportunity Credit

27	Adjusted qualified education expenses (see instructions). **Don't enter more than $4,000**	**27**
28	Subtract $2,000 from line 27. If zero or less, enter -0-.	**28**
29	Multiply line 28 by 25% (0.25)	**29**
30	If line 28 is zero, enter the amount from line 27. Otherwise, add $2,000 to the amount on line 29 and enter the result. Skip line 31. Include the total of all amounts from all Parts III, line 30, on Part I, line 1 .	**30**

Lifetime Learning Credit

31	Adjusted qualified education expenses (see instructions). Include the total of all amounts from all Parts III, line 31, on Part II, line 10	**31**

Form **8863** (2022)

Chapter

5

Personal Itemized Deductions

CHAPTER CONTENTS

LEARNING OBJECTIVES

After completing Chapter 5, you should be able to:

1. Identify and describe the five types of itemized deductions that are the focus of this chapter.
2. Describe the various types of expenses deductible as medical and dental expenses.
3. List the various types of taxes taxpayers pay and identify the ones deductible as itemized deductions.
4. Identify the types of interest expense that taxpayers can deduct as itemized deductions.
5. Understand how to compute a taxpayer's charitable contribution deduction, including the deduction for gifts of ordinary income property and capital gain property.
6. Compute a taxpayer's personal casualty and theft loss deduction.
7. Describe the various types of deductible business.
8. Distinguish between expenditures deductible for AGI, deductible from AGI, and not deductible.
9. List the factors that may classify an activity as a hobby instead of a trade or business, and explain how the expenses of each are treated on the taxpayer's tax return.
10. Prepare Schedule A.

CHAPTER OVERVIEW

The tax laws usually do not allow individuals to deduct personal expenses on their tax returns. There are, however, exceptions. Several types of personal expenses can be deducted as **itemized deductions**. As an alternative to itemizing, taxpayers may choose to take the standard deduction (usually if that amount is greater) or be required to do so (such as when married filing separately and one's spouse takes the standard deduction).

Individuals have two basic types of deductions. One type reduces gross income to yield adjusted gross income (AGI). Expenses incurred in a trade or business are examples of this type of deduction. Deductions for AGI were discussed in the last chapter. The other type of deduction (which includes itemized deductions) reduces AGI yielding taxable income. This is referred to as from AGI deduction.

Deductions for AGI are the most desirable deductions. One reason for this is that the tax law uses AGI as a base to limit some deductions from AGI. As examples, medical expenses are deductible only to the extent that they exceed 7.5% of AGI. Personal casualty losses are deductible only to the extent they exceed 10% of AGI. Thus, the lower the AGI, the larger these types of deductions are. Another reason deductions for AGI are preferred is that over two-thirds of all taxpayers use the standard deduction in lieu of itemizing deductions. Taxpayers deducting the standard deduction do not benefit from having expenses that are deductible as itemized deductions. Thus, taxpayers should look for ways to maximize their deductions for AGI.

Chapter 5 presents itemized deductions, which taxpayers report on Schedule A. This chapter explains when these deductions can be taken and how the deduction is calculated. It describes the most common personal deductions available on Schedule A, which includes medical expenses, taxes, interest, charitable contributions, casualty or theft losses, gambling losses, and miscellaneous deductions as well as some deductions that are no longer allowed such as hobby- and job-related deductions. The chapter also describes the reduction in total itemized deductions that higher-income taxpayers are usually required to make.

For those who itemize, the tax laws generally allow taxpayers only to deduct their own expenses that they pay from their own funds. Only in limited cases is it possible for taxpayers to take deductions for expenses they pay on behalf of other people. These exceptions are pointed out in the chapter.

¶501   # Reporting Itemized Deductions

Taxpayers usually deduct the larger of either the standard deduction or the total amount of itemized deductions. However, recall from Chapter 1 that when spouses file separately and one spouse itemizes deductions, the other spouse must also itemize, even if that amount is $0 (see ¶106), or else both spouses must take the standard deduction.

Taxpayers that itemize show their deductions on Schedule A. For some deductions, an extra form must be completed to support the amount reported on Schedule A. Examples include Form 4952 (Investment Interest Expense Deduction), Form 8283 (Noncash Charitable Contributions), and Form 4684 (Casualties and Thefts).

¶502   # Filled-In Schedule A

INFORMATION FOR FIGURE 5-1:

Steven T. and Laurie R. Neal report AGI of $374,864 on their joint tax return, which includes $7,600 of taxable investment income. The Neals compute their itemized deductions on Schedule A (Figure 5-1) by entering the amounts shown below in bold font on the appropriate lines. They then follow the instructions on the form to complete Schedule A. They transfer their total itemized deductions to the "Itemized Deductions" line (line 12) on Form 1040, page 2. How the Neals came up with each deduction reported on Schedule A is explained in numerous examples throughout the chapter.

Line #
- 1: Medical and dental expenses, **$16,952** (Example 5)
- 2: AGI, **$374,864** (source: Form 1040, page 1)
- 5a: State and local income taxes, **$13,050** (Example 7)
- 5b: Real estate taxes, **$10,483** (Example 10)
- 5c: Personal property taxes, **$667** (Example 11)
    However, the limit for all of these taxes is $10,000
- 8a: Home mortgage interest, **$16,435** (Example 12)
- 9: Investment interest expense, **$5,457**
- 11: Gifts by cash or check, **$3,725** (Example 21)
- 12: Noncash gifts, **$4,345** [$720 (Example 24), $125 (Example 25), $3,500 (Example 26)]
- 17: Total itemized deductions, **$39,962**

Figure 5-1: Filled-In Schedule A

SCHEDULE A
(Form 1040)

Department of the Treasury
Internal Revenue Service

Itemized Deductions

Go to *www.irs.gov/ScheduleA* for instructions and the latest information.

Attach to Form 1040 or 1040-SR.

Caution: If you are claiming a net qualified disaster loss on Form 4684, see the instructions for line 16.

OMB No. 1545-0074

2022

Attachment
Sequence No. **07**

Name(s) shown on Form 1040 or 1040-SR
Steven T and Laurie R Neal

Your social security number
268-00-9092

Medical and Dental Expenses	**Caution:** Do not include expenses reimbursed or paid by others.		
	1 Medical and dental expenses (see instructions)	**1** 16,952	
	2 Enter amount from Form 1040 or 1040-SR, line 11 **2** 374,864		
	3 Multiply line 2 by 7.5% (0.075)	**3** 28,115	
	4 Subtract line 3 from line 1. If line 3 is more than line 1, enter -0-	**4**	0
Taxes You Paid	5 State and local taxes.		
	a State and local income taxes or general sales taxes. You may include either income taxes or general sales taxes on line 5a, but not both. If you elect to include general sales taxes instead of income taxes, check this box . . . ☐	**5a** 13,050	
	b State and local real estate taxes (see instructions)	**5b** 10,483	
	c State and local personal property taxes	**5c** 667	
	d Add lines 5a through 5c	**5d** 24,200	
	e Enter the smaller of line 5d or $10,000 ($5,000 if married filing separately)	**5e** 10,000	
	6 Other taxes. List type and amount:	**6**	
	7 Add lines 5e and 6	**7**	10,000
Interest You Paid	8 Home mortgage interest and points. If you didn't use all of your home mortgage loan(s) to buy, build, or improve your home, see instructions and check this box . . . ☐		
Caution: Your mortgage interest deduction may be limited. See instructions.	a Home mortgage interest and points reported to you on Form 1098. See instructions if limited	**8a** 16,435	
	b Home mortgage interest not reported to you on Form 1098. See instructions if limited. If paid to the person from whom you bought the home, see instructions and show that person's name, identifying no., and address	**8b**	
	c Points not reported to you on Form 1098. See instructions for special rules	**8c**	
	d Reserved for future use	**8d**	
	e Add lines 8a through 8c	**8e** 16,435	
	9 Investment interest. Attach Form 4952 if required. See instructions	**9** 5,457	
	10 Add lines 8e and 9	**10**	21,892
Gifts to Charity	11 Gifts by cash or check. If you made any gift of $250 or more, see instructions	**11** 3,725	
Caution: If you made a gift and got a benefit for it, see instructions.	12 Other than by cash or check. If you made any gift of $250 or more, see instructions. You **must** attach Form 8283 if over $500.	**12** 4,345	
	13 Carryover from prior year	**13**	
	14 Add lines 11 through 13	**14**	8,070
Casualty and Theft Losses	15 Casualty and theft loss(es) from a federally declared disaster (other than net qualified disaster losses). Attach Form 4684 and enter the amount from line 18 of that form. See instructions	**15**	
Other Itemized Deductions	16 Other—from list in instructions. List type and amount:	**16**	
Total Itemized Deductions	17 Add the amounts in the far right column for lines 4 through 16. Also, enter this amount on Form 1040 or 1040-SR, line 12	**17**	39,962
	18 If you elect to itemize deductions even though they are less than your standard deduction, check this box . . . ☐		

For Paperwork Reduction Act Notice, see the Instructions for Form 1040.   Cat. No. 17145C   Schedule A (Form 1040) 2022

¶503 Medical and Dental Expenses

Most taxpayers cannot take advantage of the medical and dental deduction. To be deductible, unreimbursed medical expenses normally must exceed 7.5% of the taxpayer's AGI. [I.R.C. §213(a)].

Taxpayers normally cannot deduct expenses they pay on behalf of others. However, the Internal Revenue Code (Code) allows taxpayers to deduct medical and dental expenses they pay on behalf of their dependents (as defined in ¶108–¶109). They also can deduct medical and dental expenses they pay for other persons whom they do not claim as dependents, provided that the person either (1) passes the citizenship, relationship, and support tests, or (2) passes the citizenship and relationship tests for a qualifying child (see ¶108 and ¶109). Thus, a taxpayer can deduct amounts paid for her father's prescription drugs whom the taxpayer supports, but cannot claim as a dependent because the father's gross income exceeds $12,200. Likewise, a taxpayer can deduct the medical bills paid on behalf of the taxpayer's sister, whom the taxpayer cannot claim as a dependent because the sister provides over half of her own support for the year. (Recall from ¶108.01 that siblings pass the relationship test for a qualifying child).

When one spouse receives extensive medical care, the couple should consider filing separate returns. The 7.5% AGI floor applies to the lower AGI amount when only one spouse's income is reported on the return.

¶503.01 PRESCRIPTION DRUGS AND INSULIN

Only prescription drugs are deductible as medical expenses. Even when prescribed, most over-the-counter items do not qualify as a deductible medical expense. Some commonly used over-the-counter (nondeductible) prescribed items include iron and calcium supplements, gluten-free foods, cold medicines, aspirin, allergy medications, and antacid tablets. Insulin is deductible even if not prescribed.

EXAMPLE 1

For Steven Neal's cold and fever, a doctor prescribed an antibiotic and an over-the-counter cold remedy. Steven's co-pay for the antibiotic was $25. The insurance company paid the rest. The cold remedy cost $5. Only the $25 Steven paid for the antibiotic may be deducted.

¶503.02 MEDICAL AND DENTAL INSURANCE PREMIUMS

Medical expenses include insurance premiums paid for medical and dental care, including amounts paid through payroll deductions at work. Also deductible are Medicare premiums withheld from the taxpayer's monthly social security checks, as well as amounts social security recipients pay to supplement their Medicare coverage. Long-term care insurance premiums are also deductible, with limitations. Self-employed taxpayers deduct for AGI insurance premiums paid for months when the taxpayer (and the taxpayer's spouse, if married) is not eligible for an employer's medical plan (¶402.07). Any premiums paid by self-employed taxpayers not deductible for AGI are deductible as a medical expense on Schedule A (line 1).

Amounts that are not deductible as a medical expense include premiums paid on the medical portion of auto insurance, life insurance premiums, and premiums paid for insurance that covers lost earnings or loss of a limb or sight. Taxpayers also cannot deduct insurance premiums employers pay on their behalf.

<table>
<tr><td>EXAMPLE 2</td><td>The Neals' medical and dental insurance premiums for the year total $24,930. Steven paid $9,972 of this amount through payroll deductions. His employer paid the rest. During the year, the Neals also paid $1,200 for life insurance and $600 for disability insurance. Only the $9,972 of health insurance premiums Steven paid counts as a medical deduction. The $14,958 of premiums paid by the employer is a tax-free fringe benefit (¶401.05).</td></tr>
</table>

¶503.03   OTHER MEDICAL EXPENSES

Taxpayers can deduct payments made directly to medical providers, such as doctors, dentists, nurses, hospitals, and clinics. Deductible payments also include those made to authorized Christian Science practitioners, chiropractors, osteopaths, and therapists. Deductible forms of medical care include lab work, medical procedures, X-rays, CAT scans, and MRIs.

Some treatments designed to help patients stop smoking also qualify as a medical expense deduction. This includes participation in a stop-smoking program. It also includes the purchase of drugs requiring a physician's prescription to lessen the effects of nicotine withdrawal. Taxpayers can deduct the cost of a weight-loss program only if weight loss is the treatment for a specific disease diagnosed by a doctor (e.g., obesity, hypertension, or heart disease). They cannot deduct the cost of a weight-loss program when the reason for the weight loss is the improvement of appearance, general health, or sense of well-being.

Cosmetic surgery is deductible only when it is necessary for medical reasons, such as correction of a birth defect or to repair of damage from injury or disease. The cost of cosmetic surgery undergone for personal (vanity) reasons is not deductible.

Nursing Home Care

Depending on the condition of a nursing home resident and the types of services offered by the home, the entire amount paid to the facility may be deductible. When the main purpose of the stay relates to a medical condition, the taxpayer deducts all expenses, even the cost of food and lodging. Some conditions that qualify for 100% medical treatment include Alzheimer's disease, paralysis, alcoholism, drug rehabilitation, and a physical injury or handicap. If the main reason for living in the home relates to personal care or family convenience, the taxpayer deducts only the amount paid for medical expenses. However, amounts paid for qualified long-term care are deductible when such services are required by a chronically ill person.

School for the Handicapped

Amounts paid to send a mentally or physically handicapped spouse or disabled dependent to a special school or facility are deductible medical costs. The school's main focus must be to help the student compensate or overcome problems in order to function better.

Travel and Transportation

Taxpayers can deduct the costs of traveling to seek medical care. This includes the cost for bus, train, and airline tickets, as well as taxi fares, and the costs for rental cars and ambulance services. The travel costs for a nurse also are deductible when paid to accompany a sick person who is unable to travel alone. This rule also applies to the travel costs for a parent when accompanying a child seeking medical care. When overnight travel is required, the Code limits the deduction for lodging to $50 per night for each person. The cost of meals while traveling for medical reasons is not deductible.

Taxpayers who use their personal car in seeking medical care may use either a standard mileage rate or their actual costs to compute their medical deduction. For 2022, the standard mileage rate for medical expenses is $.18 per mile. The costs of tolls and parking are added to this amount. Although individuals may deduct their actual expenses, the standard mileage rate is easier to use. When choosing to use the actual expense method, taxpayers may deduct only out-of-pocket expenses. Taxpayers must keep a log showing the mileage and expenses, as well as receipts for all items paid.

Capital Expenditures

Home improvements and special equipment installed in a home may be deducted when prescribed by a medical provider as part of a specific treatment. Three common improvements are swimming pools, air conditioners, and elevators. When the improvement increases the value of the home by more than the cost of the improvement, no medical deduction is allowed. The reasoning is that the taxpayer will be repaid when the home is later sold for more money. However, when the cost exceeds the increase in value of the home, the excess is deducted as a medical expense.

EXAMPLE 3	Under a doctor's prescription for a medical condition, the Neals (from Figure 5-1) pay $7,000 for a hot tub. The hot tub increases the value of the home by $4,000. The Neals can deduct the $3,000 difference. They add this amount to their other unreimbursed medical expenses on Schedule A (line 1).

An exception exists for improvements that make it possible for a physically handicapped individual to live independently. Examples include constructing ramps, widening hallways and doorways for wheelchair use, installing support bars and railings, and adjusting outlets and fixtures. The IRS treats the costs of these types of improvements as adding no value to the home for tax purposes. Thus, the entire cost of the improvement is deductible.

EXAMPLE 4	Robin (age 36) is confined to a wheelchair. In order to live alone, Robin pays $10,000 to have entrance ramps, bars and railings installed in her home. Although these features are estimated to add as much as $2,000 to the value of her home, the IRS treats their added value as $0. This allows Robin to deduct the full $10,000 as a medical expense deduction. She adds this to her other unreimbursed medical expenses. She then reduces the total by 7.5% of her AGI.

Other Expenditures

Other commonly deductible medical expenses include eye exams, eyeglasses, contact lenses, noncosmetic dental work (crowns, dentures, braces, etc.), crutches, canes, wheelchairs, and guide dogs. Common nondeductible medical items include health club memberships, massages, burial and funeral costs, and illegal drugs or operations.

¶503.04   REIMBURSEMENTS

A taxpayer's medical and dental expense deduction equals the sum of all qualified medical expenses minus any reimbursements received during the year related to those expenses. This net amount is reported on Schedule A (line 1).

EXAMPLE 5	In addition to the $25 prescription medicine (Example 1), $9,972 of health insurance premiums (Example 2), and $3,000 for the (doctor-prescribed) hot tub (Example 3), the Neals (from Figure 5-1) also paid $28,375 of deductible medical costs during the year. The Neals were reimbursed $24,420 by their insurance company. The Neals enter the $16,952 difference ($25 + $9,972 + $3,000 + $28,375 − $24,420) on Schedule A (line 1). They reduce this amount by $28,115 ($374,864 AGI × 7.5%), leaving them with a $0 medical expense deduction on Schedule A (line 4).

Two situations occur that make medical reimbursements taxable. First, when an employer-paid insurance policy provides reimbursements greater than the medical expenses actually paid, the excess is taxable. (When the employee pays the premium, the excess is not taxable.) Second, when the taxpayer takes a medical deduction and receives a reimbursement in the following year, all or part of that reimbursement may be taxable under the tax benefit rule described in Chapter 3. This rule requires that taxpayers report the reimbursement in gross income only when they benefited from deducting medical expenses in an earlier year (see discussion of the tax benefit rule in ¶313.01).

EXAMPLE 6	Terri pays $5,000 of medical expenses in 2021. Although this amount exceeds the AGI floor, Terri's standard deduction is higher than her total itemized deductions in 2021. Early in 2022, Terri's insurance company reimburses her $2,000 for medical costs paid in 2021. Terri does not include any of the $2,000 in gross income in 2022. Because Terri's income taxes were not lowered by the $5,000 of medical costs in 2021, she did not receive a tax benefit from the amounts reimbursed.

¶504   State, Local and Foreign Taxes

Individuals who itemize deductions include certain state, local and foreign taxes in this calculation. [I.R.C. §164] However, there are several limits on this deduction.

The tax law limits the types of taxes that are deductible. Income taxes and property taxes qualify as itemized deductions, but only when levied by an agency other than the federal government. Qualifying taxes must meet two conditions before a deduction is available. First, the taxpayer must actually pay the taxes. Second, the taxes paid must be those owed by the taxpayer. Amounts the taxpayer pays for someone else's taxes cannot be deducted.

Other nondeductible taxes include federal income taxes; FICA (social security and Medicare) taxes; federal and state estate, gift or inheritance taxes; use and excise taxes (taxes imposed on gasoline, tobacco, and alcohol). The remainder of this section describes the types of taxes that can be deducted as an itemized deduction on Schedule A.

¶504.01   DEDUCTION FOR STATE AND LOCAL INCOME TAXES OR GENERAL SALES TAXES

Taxpayers have the option of deducting either (i) the state and local income taxes they paid during the year, or (ii) general sales taxes paid during the year. The deduction by individuals for state, local, and foreign property taxes, and state and local income taxes, and general sales taxes paid or accrued during the tax year is limited for tax years 2018 through 2025 to only $10,000 or $5,000 for married taxpayer filing a separate return.

Taxpayers who itemize check box 5a on Schedule A if they choose to deduct their general sales taxes. They then enter the amount of their deduction (either state and local income taxes or general sales taxes) on Schedule A (line 5).

Taxpayers living in states that impose an income tax often find that the amount of state and local income taxes paid during the year exceeds the general sales tax deduction. There are three ways of paying state and local income taxes. These are: (1) through W-2 (paycheck) withholdings, (2) by making estimated tax payments in the current tax year, and (3) by paying additional taxes (excluding interest and penalties) for the current or previous years.

EXAMPLE 7	The Neals are subject to the $10,000 deduction cap for taxes. They enter $10,000 on Schedule A (line 5e).

State income tax withheld during 2022	$10,420
Estimated state income tax paid during 2022	2,400
State income tax paid with 2021 return filed in April 2022	175
Additional tax assessed on 2020 state income tax paid in May 2022	55
Total deduction for state income taxes, before limit	$13,050

Taxpayers who live in one of the states that do not impose an income tax can deduct their sales taxes paid during the year. Taxpayers compute their general sales tax deduction using either actual sales receipts or by estimating their amount using an IRS-provided table. The IRS-provided sales tax table uses the tax rate of the state where the taxpayer lives, the taxpayer's available income, and the number of exemptions claimed by the taxpayer to estimate the amount of general sales taxes the taxpayer paid during the year. When using the IRS table, taxpayers add to this amount any sales tax paid on motor vehicles, boats, and aircraft.

Refund of State and Local Income Taxes

A refund of prior year's state or local income taxes does not reduce the amount of taxes paid during the year. Instead, when the refund stems from taxes deducted in a prior tax year, the amount is reported on Schedule 1 (Form 1040) (line 1) as "Taxable refunds, credits, or offsets of state and local income taxes" in accordance with the tax benefit rule (discussed at ¶313.01).

EXAMPLE 8	During 2021, Jason's employer withheld $3,600 for state income taxes from his wages. Jason's itemized deductions in 2021 exceeded his standard deduction by $8,000. In April of 2022, Jason files his state income tax return. Two months later he receives a $700 refund. Since Jason's tax liability was lowered in 2021 when he deducted the $3,600 as an itemized deduction, he reports the $700 in gross income in 2022. The tax benefit rule taxes Jason on the *lesser of* (i) the $700 refund, (ii) the $8,000 excess of his 2021 itemized deductions over his standard deduction amount, or (iii) the $3,600 state income taxes included in itemized deductions during 2021.

¶504.02 REAL ESTATE TAXES

The tax laws allow individuals to deduct from AGI ad valorem taxes they pay to state and local governments. **Ad valorem taxes** are taxes imposed on the value of the property. Local governments levy real estate taxes on the owners of real property based on the property's value. Thus, the owners can deduct state and local real estate taxes as an itemized deduction. They also can deduct real estate taxes paid to foreign governments. This deduction, which includes all state and local income, sales and property taxes, is limited to $10,000 ($5,000 for married filing separately).

When real estate is sold during the year, the seller is responsible for the real estate taxes up until the day of the sale. The buyer's responsibility starts on the day of the sale. Real estate taxes are normally assessed once a year. The tax bill is sent to the property owner. The tax laws allow taxpayers to deduct expenses that they both pay and are responsible for. When real estate is sold during the year, the party that pays the real estate tax bill may not be the one responsible for all of the taxes being paid. In these situations, only the portion of the taxes that the owner is responsible for can be deducted. To ensure no deductions are lost, at the time real estate is sold, sellers need to remit to the buyers their share of real estate taxes up to the date of the sale. Standard language to this effect is found in most sales contracts.

EXAMPLE 9	On May 11, 2021, Jill sells her home to the Ryans for $200,000. Real estate taxes on the home are expected to be $3,000 for 2021. At the closing, Jill pays the Ryans $1,068 ($3,000 × 130/365). This amount is her share of the real estate taxes for the 130 days she owned the home during 2021. In turn, Jill deducts this amount as real estate taxes on Schedule A in 2021. At the end of the year, the local government sends the Ryans the tax bill for 2021. Although they will pay the entire amount due, the Ryans' out-of-pocket costs will be the amount paid minus the $1,068 they received from Jill at the closing. This net amount is the Ryans' share of the real estate taxes. They deduct this amount as real estate taxes on Schedule A in 2021.

Condominium and cooperative housing owners may deduct their shares of real estate taxes paid on these properties. When the homeowners association pays real estate taxes, it must identify the actual pass-through of property taxes to provide owners with the documentation for the tax deduction. "Special assessments" added to the property tax bill for local improvements like streets, sidewalks, and sewers do not qualify as deductible taxes. Instead, these amounts are added to the owner's basis (investment) in the property.

EXAMPLE 10	During the year, the Neals (from Figure 5-1) paid real estate taxes on their main home ($6,405), their vacation home ($3,322), and on a vacant lot they own as an investment ($756). They report $10,483 of total real estate taxes paid on Schedule A (line 5b). The tax law does not limit the number of properties on which real estate taxes can be deducted. However, state and local taxes are subject to the $10,000 deduction limit.

¶504.03   PERSONAL PROPERTY TAXES

Real estate is not the only type of property where a property tax is imposed. Some states levy taxes on personal property. For tax purposes, "personal property" is all property that is not real estate. This means that all property that is neither land nor buildings is called personal property. Individuals and businesses can own personal property. Individuals can own personal property that they use in their personal lives or hold for investment. This would include clothing, home furnishings, artwork, and shares of stock. Examples of personal property businesses might own include automobiles, trucks, office furniture, and machinery.

Personal property should not be confused with the property that individuals own and use in their personal lives. This type of property is personal-use property. Other uses of property include business and investment-use. State and local personal property taxes are deductible if the tax base used is the value of the personal property. Also, the tax must be charged on an annual basis, even if it is collected more or less often.

Personal property can be tangible or intangible. Tangible property has physical characteristics. Intangible property does not. Examples of tangible personal property include automobiles, books, clothing, and equipment. Examples of intangible property include patents, copyrights, goodwill, trademarks, etc. The tax law also considers stocks, bonds, mutual funds, and money market accounts to be intangible property. Almost all states that impose a tax on intangible property impose a tax on these latter intangibles. If the amount of tax depends on the property's value, the tax is deductible.

States that impose a tax on tangible personal property generally tax property that the owners register with the state (e.g. motor vehicles, boats, and aircraft). This allows the tax to be included as part of the annual registration fee charged to owners, or it may be billed separately. In states where the annual registration fee is based on the property's value, individuals can deduct that portion of the fee as an itemized deduction. Any added fees not based on the property's value cannot be deducted.

EXAMPLE 11	The Neals (from Figure 5-1) paid the Department of Motor Vehicles $717 for the annual cost to register their two cars. The fee includes a $50 tag renewal fee. The rest of the fee is based on the value of the car. The Neals report $667 ($717 – $50) as personal property tax on Schedule A (line 5c).

¶504.04   OTHER TAXES

Taxpayers with foreign sources of income may pay foreign income taxes. Individual taxpayers have two options on how to handle foreign income taxes paid during the year. First, they can take the taxes as a foreign tax credit (¶204.01). Second, they can deduct the foreign taxes as an itemized deduction. When deducting foreign taxes, taxpayers write "Foreign income taxes" and the amount on the "Other taxes" line on Schedule A. Foreign income taxes are not subject to the $10,000 or $5,000 limit. When a taxpayer has state and local income or sales, and property taxes that exceed $10,000 (or $5,000), he or she adds deductible foreign income taxes to the limit.

¶505   Interest on Nonbusiness Debts

Most personal interest is not deductible. However, home mortgage interest, points, and investment interest may qualify as itemized deductions. In contrast, interest on student loans is not an itemized deduction. Eligible taxpayers deduct student loan interest for AGI on Schedule 1 (Form 1040) (¶402.11).

¶505.01   HOME MORTGAGE INTEREST

Taxpayers deduct interest paid on qualified home loans, which include debt on the taxpayer's principal residence (main home) plus a second home. [I.R.C. §163(h)(3)] A vacation home qualifies as a second home. Houses, condos, and mobile homes all count as personal homes. Sometimes, boats and motorhomes qualify as well. To take the mortgage interest deduction, the one paying the interest must also own the home.

Persons who own three or more homes can deduct the mortgage interest paid on only their main home plus one other home of their choosing. When allowing others to use a home, the home will qualify as a second home if the taxpayer uses the home during the year for more than the *greater of* (i) 14 days or (ii) 10% of the total days rented.

EXAMPLE 12   The Neals (from Figure 5-1) make mortgage payments on their main home and their vacation home. The interest paid on these properties was $13,215 and $3,220, respectively. The Neals deduct $16,435 ($13,215 + $3,220) as home mortgage interest on Schedule A.

EXAMPLE 13   The Friedlands live most of the year in Dallas, Texas. They vacation in Phoenix, Arizona and Park City, Utah. They own homes in all three locations and have mortgages on all three homes. In the current year, the Friedlands paid interest expense on the Dallas, Phoenix, and Park City mortgages of $6,000, $10,000, and $18,500, respectively. When preparing Schedule A, the Friedlands can deduct the $6,000 interest paid on the loan used to finance their main home (in Dallas). They also can deduct the $18,500 paid on the mortgage of their Park City home. The $10,000 paid on their other vacation home is nondeductible personal interest.

Acquisition Indebtedness

One type of qualifying home interest is **acquisition indebtedness** (acquisition debt). This includes money borrowed to buy, build, or substantially improve the taxpayer's main or second home. Only the interest paid on up to $1,000,000 of acquisition debt can be deducted ($500,000 for married couples filing MFS). This **limit** is reduced to $750,000 ($375,000 if married filing separately) for mortgages acquired after December 15, 2017. No interest deduction limits exist on debt incurred before October 13, 1987, although there are few, if any, of these loans still outstanding as this book goes to press. Still, a sizable loan on the main home may limit the interest deduction on a second home acquired after this date. Special rules limit the deduction when refinancing the original debt. If the new loan has a balance higher than the old loan, the amount of new debt that replaces the old debt qualifies as acquisition debt. Also, any portion of the excess debt used to buy or improve the taxpayer's main or second home qualifies as acquisition debt. Any remaining new debt is not acquisition debt, but may qualify as home equity debt. However, home equity debt interest is not deductible between 2018 and 2025.

EXAMPLE 14	The Tremlins own a home in Evanston, Illinois. They paid $1.5 million for the home many years ago. On January 31, 2022, the mortgage on the home was $700,000, and the value of their home was $1.7 million, and the Tremlins refinanced their mortgage. Their new mortgage is for $1.3 million. The Tremlins did not use any of the loan proceeds to improve their home. Interest paid on $700,000 of the new loan is deductible as acquisition debt. Some of the interest paid on the rest of the debt would qualify as home equity debt in a year in which the law permits this deduction (see discussion to follow). Any interest paid on the excess borrowed that is not home equity debt is nondeductible personal interest.

EXAMPLE 15	Same facts as in Example 14, except that the Tremlins used $120,000 of the loan proceeds to remodel their kitchen. The Tremlins can deduct interest on $750,000 ($700,000 + $120,000, but limited to $750,000) of the $1.3 million mortgage as acquisition debt.

EXAMPLE 16	Same facts as in Example 15, except that in addition to using $120,000 to improve their home, the Tremlins spent $200,000 to buy a second home. The Tremlins can deduct interest on $750,000 of the mortgage as acquisition debt. Interest on the excess debt is not deductible unless the second home is security for the debt.

Home Equity Debt

For tax years 2018 through 2025, a taxpayer may not claim an itemized deduction for mortgage interest paid or accrued on any home equity debt on any qualified residence unless it is used to buy, build, or substantially improve a qualified residence. However, for taxable years beginning after 2025, this deduction may be allowed again. Total home equity debt cannot exceed $100,000 ($50,000 for married couples who file MFS). Such debt, plus the balance of any acquisition debt, cannot exceed the fair market value (FMV) of the home.

EXAMPLE 17	Continuing with Example 16, $300,000 of the $1.3 million mortgage that did not count as acquisition debt qualifies as home equity debt. However, the Code prohibits the Tremlins' deduction of interest on $100,000 of such debt after 2017. Thus, they will be allowed to deduct interest related to $750,000 of their debt as home mortgage interest on Schedule A. Once the Tremlins' loan balance falls below $750,000, their interest deduction will not be limited.

EXAMPLE 18	In 2004, the Hoffmans bought a home for $600,000 and took out $400,000 of acquisition debt. By February 10, 2022, the loan had a balance of $180,000, and the FMV of the home was $1,000,000. The Hoffmans took out a second mortgage of $20,000 and used the money to buy a car and take a trip. Since this money was not used to improve the home, it falls under the rules for home equity debt.
	On August 15, 2022, the Hoffmans decided to add a pool and a patio, which cost $25,000. The builder financed the work. The property secures the builder's loan, along with the other loans. This loan to finance improvements to the Hoffmans' main home qualifies as acquisition debt. Interest on this loan is $1,000 for 2022. Total interest associated with their house payments is $18,800 ($17,000 on their acquisition debt + $800 on their home equity debt + 1,000 on the home improvement debt). The Hoffmans deduct $18,000 as home mortgage interest.

Mortgage Insurance Premiums

For a limited period, homeowners who pay mortgage insurance premiums can treat those payments as interest. [I.R.C. §163(h)(3)(E)] However, this deduction is limited to persons whose AGI does not exceed $100,000 ($50,000 if married filing separately). When AGI exceeds the limit, the taxpayer must reduce the deduction by 10% of each $1,000 excess of AGI over $100,000 (10% of each $500 excess over $50,000 if married filing separately). In addition, the mortgage must have been issued after 2006. This rule expires after 2021, unless Congress reinstates it, as it has done several times in the past.

Reporting Home Mortgage Interest

Most taxpayers who have a mortgage receive from their lender Form 1098, Mortgage Interest Statement. This form reports to taxpayers the amount of mortgage interest paid during the year. Mortgage interest reported on Form 1098 is shown on a different line on Schedule A, from any home mortgage interest paid during the year not reported on Form 1098.

¶505.02   POINTS

Also called "loan origination fees" or "loan fees," **points** are a type of prepaid interest. In exchange for paying points (interest) up front, the borrower gets a lower interest rate over the term of the loan. One point equals 1% of the loan amount. The more points paid, the lower the interest rate. Taxpayers may deduct points as interest. However, not all loan costs qualify as deductible points. For example, fees charged for loan services provided by the lender are not deductible. To be deductible, the points must meet these three conditions:

1. Paying points on borrowed money is an established business practice in the area.
2. The amount charged does not exceed the amount usually charged in the area.
3. Funds to pay the points must come from the borrower's own money, not from the lender's funds.

As a rule, taxpayers deduct prepaid expenses over the periods to which they apply. Since points are the same as prepaying interest, they usually must be deducted (amortized) evenly over the life of the loan. However, when the proceeds of the loan are used to buy or improve the taxpayer's main home, cash basis taxpayers can deduct points in the year paid. [Reg. §1.163-10T(j)(2)] This special rule only applies to cash basis taxpayers who take out loans to buy or improve their main homes. It does not extend to vacation homes, second homes or to refinancing of loans. It also does not apply to accrual basis taxpayers.

A special situation arises when the property is sold or the loan is refinanced. If the property is sold, any unamortized (not yet deducted) points are deducted in the year of the sale. If the loan is refinanced, then the unamortized points plus any new points paid with the refinancing are deducted over the life of the new loan. However, if a part of the proceeds from refinancing a main home are used to improve the home, cash basis taxpayers can deduct a portion of the points in the year paid. The rest are deducted evenly over the term of the loan.

EXAMPLE 19

In 2020, Carrey (cash basis taxpayer) took out a mortgage to buy his main home. In 2022, Carrey refinanced his mortgage with a 30-year, $150,000 loan. To get a lower interest rate, he paid three points ($150,000 × 3% = $4,500). Two points ($3,000) were for prepaid interest. One point ($1,500) was charged for services provided by the lender. The payment of points is an established practice in the area. The 2% charged is not more than the amount typically charged for points. Carrey's first payment on the new loan was due May 1, 2022.

Since the proceeds from the new loan were not used to buy or improve his main home, Carrey cannot deduct all of the points in 2022. Instead, he deducts the $3,000 evenly over the life of the loan. The $1,500 for the other one point cannot be deducted. In 2022, Carrey's deduction is $67 [($3,000/360 months in a 30-year loan) × 8 payments made in 2022].

Reporting Points

When points are paid on the purchase of the taxpayer's principal residence, the amount of points paid should be reported on Form 1098. The points are fully deductible in the year paid and are added to any home mortgage interest reported on Form 1098. The deductible portion of points not reported on Form 1098 are reported on the line designated "Points not reported to you on Form 1098," on Schedule A.

¶505.03   INVESTMENT INTEREST

An individual itemizes deductions and is allowed a limited deduction for interest on loans used to acquire or hold certain investment property. [I.R.C. §163(d)]

Investment interest includes interest paid on a loan to buy or hold on to taxable investments, which include stocks, taxable bonds, vacant land, gemstones, and artwork. The tax law does not allow deductions for expenses related to nontaxable income. Therefore, interest paid on amounts borrowed to buy or hold onto nontaxable investments (like municipal bonds) is not deductible. Some investments are considered "passive" investments. The tax law does not treat interest expense related to a passive investment as investment interest. This interest is deducted elsewhere on the tax return. For instance, interest expense on rental property (a passive investment) belongs on Schedule E, not on Schedule A. Passive investments are discussed in Chapter 9.

The **investment interest limitation** limits the deduction of investment interest to the amount of the taxpayer's net investment income. Any investment interest not deducted because of this limit may be carried over and used in future years. When carried to the next year, it acts just like that year's investment interest and faces the same limits.

Investment income includes taxable interest, nonqualified dividends, and some royalties. It may also include qualified dividends and the gain from the sale of investments. If the taxpayer chooses to tax qualified dividends and net capital gain at the lower tax rates (¶201.04, ¶1101.03), then these amounts cannot count as investment income. However, if the taxpayer elects to pay the normal tax rates on qualified dividends and net capital gain, then these amounts count as investment income. This second option may allow the taxpayer to take a higher deduction for investment interest in the current year.

<table>
<tr><td>EXAMPLE 20</td><td>Joel borrows $30,000 to purchase taxable investments. He pays $2,800 of interest on the loan during the year. Joel is in the 32% tax bracket. During the year, his investments produce $1,600 in taxable interest, $600 in qualified dividends, $240 in nonqualified dividends, and $1,600 in net capital gain. The $1,840 of taxable interest and nonqualified dividends counts as investment income. However, the $2,200 of qualified dividends and net capital gain only counts as investment income if Joel elects to tax these amounts at his normal (32%) tax rate.

Joel's options regarding the investment interest are as follows. First, he can choose to tax the $2,200 of qualified dividends and net capital gain at the lower 15% tax rate. This will result in his investment interest expense being limited to his $1,840 of investment income. He would carry over the $960 excess ($2,800 − $1,840) to the next tax year. Joel's second option is to elect to tax $960 of the qualified dividends and net capital gain at the 32% tax rate. If he does this, then his investment income will increase to $2,800 ($1,840 + $960). This will allow him to deduct the entire $2,800 of investment interest in the current year. He will then be allowed to tax the remaining $1,240 of qualified dividends and net capital gain ($2,200 − $960) at the lower 15% tax rate.</td></tr>
</table>

Net investment income is the excess of the taxpayer's investment income over the amount of investment expenses actually included in the taxpayer's total itemized deductions. These expenses include fees paid to an investment advisor, safe deposit box rental fees, and the costs of investment publications. However, for tax years 2018–2025 deductibility of miscellaneous itemized deduction is suspended, therefore the net investment income is simply the investment income. Taxpayers file Form 4952, Investment Interest Expense Deduction, to support their investment interest deduction on Schedule A.

Interest paid on debts used to acquire or own tax-exempt securities is nondeductible. It is not carried forward to any tax year, but is disallowed permanently.

¶506 Gifts to Charity

Individuals can deduct as an itemized deduction both cash and noncash property they donate to a qualified charity. [I.R.C. §170] The most that can be deducted in any one year depends on the amount of the taxpayer's AGI. Any deductions limited due to AGI carry over to the next five tax years.

¶506.01 GIFTS BY CASH OR CHECK

Deductible gifts (donations) must be made to qualified charitable organizations. To deduct gifts to foreign countries for disaster relief and other causes, taxpayers must make the donation to qualified U.S. nonprofit organizations.

Gifts may be made by cash, check, or credit card. When taxpayers use their car for charitable purposes, they may deduct actual car expenses or a standard rate of $.14 per mile. This allowance is statutory and is not subject to automatic adjustments for inflation. Car expenses are treated as cash gifts. As a rule, donations are deducted in the year that they are made, regardless of whether the taxpayer uses the cash or accrual method. Taxpayers must keep receipts to support their deduction. If the charity gave the taxpayer any gifts or services in return for the donation, the amount of the deduction must be reduced by the value of what the taxpayer received in return for the donation.

<table>
<tr><td>EXAMPLE 21</td><td>The Neals (from Figure 5-1) paid $400 a plate for a YMCA benefit and made a cash donation of $3,000 at the banquet. The YMCA's cost for the dinner was $20 per person. The Neals could have bought the same two meals at a bistro for $75. The charitable contribution deduction is $3,725, the difference between the amount donated and the value of the dinner ($3,000 cash donation + $800 meals − $75 value). The Neals do not take the YMCA's cost into account. The Neals enter $3,725 on the "Gifts by cash or check" line on Schedule A.</td></tr>
</table>

Taxpayers may only deduct gifts made to qualified non-profit organizations. All other gifts are not deductible. Handouts to needy people may be generous, but they are not deductible.

EXAMPLE 22	The Neals have a widowed neighbor to whom they gave $200 each month for groceries over a four-month period. The Neals' gifts to the widow are not deductible.

 Qualified charities are nonprofit organizations that are exempt from tax under Section 501(c)(3) of the Internal Revenue Code. They include organizations that operate solely for religious, scientific, charitable, literary, or educational purposes. They also include organizations that promote the arts or to prevent cruelty to children or animals. This is only a partial list of the types of organizations that qualify as 501(c)(3) organizations. A complete list of qualified charities can be found on the IRS website.

Donations with the Right to Buy Collegiate Athletic Tickets

A special rule applies to certain donations to a college or university. When the taxpayer's donation provides the taxpayer with the right to buy tickets to athletic events, no charitable deduction is allowed. [I.R.C. §170(l)(2)(B)]

EXAMPLE 23	Waylon donates $1,000 to his alma mater. His gift allows him to buy season tickets to the university's football and basketball games. The tax law treats $0 as deductible.

¶506.02   NONCASH GIFTS

Special rules apply to donations of property that fall in either of these two categories: (1) ordinary income property (includes all property held for one year or less) or (2) capital gain property held more than one year. Donations in both categories may include real estate, tangible personal property, or intangible personal property.

Tangible personal property consists of most tangible property that a taxpayer owns that is not real estate. The usual items contributed under this category include clothing, toys, furniture, appliances, and books. Normally, the FMV of these items is less than the taxpayer's basis. The FMV of household goods and clothing is their thrift shop or garage sale value. "Blue book" value is a common source for valuing vehicles. The charity cannot determine the FMV of donated items.

Intangible assets most commonly donated include stocks, bonds, and mutual funds. For the most part, these assets are widely traded and their FMV is easy to determine.

Generally, the deduction for noncash gifts is equal to the FMV of the property at the time of donation. This holds true when the FMV is less than the taxpayer's basis (investment) in the property. However, when the FMV is greater than the basis, the amount of the deduction depends on whether the item takes the form of (1) ordinary income property or long-term capital gain property and (2) how the charity uses the property.

When the total deduction for noncash items exceeds $500, the donor provides information about each noncash donation on Form 8283, Noncash Charitable Contributions. For any noncash donation, a receipt from the qualifying organization must specify how the organization uses the property.

Taxpayers who donate vehicles to charities that then sell the vehicles can only deduct what the charity gets from the sale. The charity may incur penalties if it does not report the sales price to both the donor and the IRS.

EXAMPLE 24

The Neals (from Figure 5-1) make several noncash donations during the year. Even though the amounts paid for the donated items were far greater than their value at the time of the donations, their deduction is limited to the FMV of the donated items. The Neals got receipts from the charities for each of their donations, and use documented thrift store value to arrive at their $720 deduction.

Ordinary Income Property

Ordinary income property is property that, if sold, would generate income taxed at the regular (ordinary) tax rates. It includes such items as business inventory and investments held for one year or less. When a taxpayer donates ordinary income property, the tax law limits the value of the contribution to the taxpayer's basis (investment) in the property. Most often, this is the amount the taxpayer paid for the property. No deduction is allowed for the value of personal services rendered to a charity.

EXAMPLE 25

Steven Neal (from Figure 5-1) built a bookcase and donated it to the local public high school. The bookcase was appraised at $800. Steven spent $125 on materials. The Neals deduct only the $125 cost of materials, as the bookcase would be ordinary income property if they had sold it. They receive no deduction for the value of Steven's time in constructing the bookcase.

Capital Gain Property

Capital gain property consists of certain appreciated assets held for more than one year that, if sold, would produce long-term capital gain. This category includes stocks, bonds, and real estate. It also includes most investments and an individual's personal belongings. FMV at the time of the donation determines the value of the gift. Taxpayers can get written appraisals or stock market quotes to establish the value. Taxpayers who have decided to make donations to qualifying charities have a tax incentive when the FMV of the item exceeds the taxpayer's basis. The donor avoids reporting the increased value as income. In addition to avoiding paying taxes on the increase in the asset's value, the donor gets to deduct the higher FMV amount.

EXAMPLE 26

The Neals (from Figure 5-1) donated shares of IBM stock to their church. They paid $2,000 for the stock many years ago. On the date of the donation, the stock was worth $3,500. The Neals' deduction for noncash contributions total $4,220 ($720 from Example 24 + $3,500 FMV of the stock). Since this amount exceeds $500, the Neals complete Form 8283 to provide details of their noncash donations. They attach Form 8283 to their tax return and enter $4,345, ($4,220 value of shares plus the $125 cost of the bookcase) on the "Other than by cash or check" line on Schedule A.

The Code allows taxpayers to deduct only their basis in appreciated tangible personal property when such property is not used by the charity directly for its tax exempt purpose. This rule only applies to gifts of appreciated tangible personal property. Thus, the reduced deduction does not apply to gifts of capital gain property that is intangible property or real estate.

EXAMPLE 27	Ray, an art collector, donates a painting worth $25,000 to the local hospital. Ray paid $3,000 for the painting years ago. The painting is tangible personal property held long-term. Thus, it is capital gain property. However, since the hospital cannot use the painting in relation to its exempt purpose (treating patients), Ray's charitable deduction is limited to $3,000.
EXAMPLE 28	Same facts as in Example 27, except that Ray donates the painting to a local art museum. Since the painting will be put to use in the museum's tax-exempt purpose, Ray can deduct the full $25,000 FMV of the painting.
EXAMPLE 29	Same facts as in Example 28, except that Ray purchased the painting nine months earlier. Since the painting was not held for more than one year at the time it was donated, if it had been sold it would have produced short-term capital gain taxed at Ray's regular (ordinary) tax rate. Thus, the painting is ordinary income property. The Code limits the deduction of such property to Ray's $3,000 basis.
EXAMPLE 30	Same facts as in Example 27, except that the donated property was stock in a corporation. Stock is intangible property and Ray held it for more than one year prior to donating it. Thus, the stock is capital gain property, and the Code allows Ray to deduct the $25,000 FMV of the stock.
EXAMPLE 31	Same facts as in Example 27, except that the property donated was land held as an investment. The hospital uses the land to expand its facilities. Since land is real property that Ray held it for more than one year, it is capital gain property and Ray deducts the $25,000 FMV of the land.
EXAMPLE 32	Same facts as in Example 27, except that Ray paid $25,000 for the painting and at the time it was donated, it was worth $3,000. Since the painting declined in value since Ray bought it, it is not capital gain (appreciated) property. The general rule allows Ray to deduct the ($3,000) FMV of the property.

¶506.03   NONDEDUCTIBLE GIFTS

Taxpayers should verify a charity's status as a 501(c)(3) organization prior to making a gift. This information can be found on the IRS website, shown above at ¶506.01. Many fund-raising groups may look like qualified charities, but are not. Donations to lobbying or political action groups of qualified organizations may not be deductible. Other contributions that cannot be deducted include dues to clubs or lodges and tuition paid to private or religious schools. Also, the cost of raffle tickets is not deductible.

¶506.04   LIMITATIONS

For most years after 2017, the Code limits a taxpayer's total charitable contribution deduction each year to 60%, 30%, or 20% of the taxpayer's AGI. However, for 2020 and 2021 only, there were special rules:

1. The percentage of AGI limits did not apply in 2020 or 2021. In effect, a taxpayer could deduct contributions up to 100% of AGI. [This is an unusual law, which is not in the Internal Revenue Code. It appears in the **CARES Act of 2020, P.L. 116-136 at §2205DivA**]

2. For 2020 only, a taxpayer who did not itemize deductions may claim a charitable contribution deduction for AGI. [I.R.C. §62(a)(22)] The taxpayer reports this directly on page 1 of Form 1040. The limit for this deduction is $300 ($150 for married taxpayers filing separately).

3. For 2021 only, a taxpayer who did not itemize deductions may claim a charitable contribution deduction from AGI. The limit for this deduction is $300 ($600 for married taxpayers filing jointly).

For all other years, the percentage limitation that applies depends on the type of contribution being made and the nature of the charity. The deduction of contributions of cash and property to most organizations may never exceed 60% of AGI, although this limit is scheduled to become 50% of AGI after 2025. The deduction for appreciated capital gain property when the (higher) FMV is deducted can never exceed 30% of AGI. Taxpayers can avoid the 30% AGI limit on the contribution of appreciated capital gain property by reducing the amount of the donation of the appreciated capital gain property to the taxpayer's basis. The 60% limit applies. The 30% limit also applies to donations of cash and ordinary income property to certain private nonoperating foundations. When taxpayers contribute capital gain property to certain private foundations not operating for the benefit of the public at large, the contribution is limited to 20% of AGI.

When the 60%, 30%, and 20% AGI limits reduce a taxpayer's contribution deduction, the taxpayer carries forward any unused contributions for up to five years. When carried forward, the same 60%, 30%, and 20% AGI limits apply to the contributions. For example, an unused contribution subject to the 30% AGI limit in 2022 is subject to the same 30% AGI limit when carried over to 2023. Taxpayers report the deductible amount of contributions carried over from a prior tax year on the "Carryover from prior year" line on Schedule A.

EXAMPLE 33

In 2022, Jackie donates stock worth $35,000 to the local university. Jackie paid $25,000 for the stock three years ago. In 2022, Jackie's AGI is $60,000. If Jackie reports a $35,000 FMV donation for the stock, she will only be able to deduct $18,000 ($60,000 × 30%). She carries over the $17,000 excess to 2023-2027. When preparing her tax returns for 2023-2027, the same 30% AGI limit will apply to the $17,000 deduction carried forward.

If the year were 2020 or 2021, Jackie could have claimed the entire $35,000 contribution as a deduction carried forward.

EXAMPLE 34

Same facts as in Example 33, except that Jackie elects to report her donation using her $25,000 basis in the stock, and apply the 60% AGI limit. Jackie will be able to deduct the full $25,000 on Schedule A in 2021. Since she elected to reduce the amount of her deduction, the $10,000 difference between FMV and her basis in the stock will never be deducted. This is the "price" Jackie paid to be able to use the higher 60% AGI limit. In 2020 or 2021, this election would provide no tax benefit to Jackie.

¶507 Casualty and Theft Losses

Individuals are allowed to deduct losses they incur when their personal belongings are stolen or damaged in a casualty. [I.R.C. §165] They measure each casualty (or theft) loss as the *lesser of* (i) the difference between the FMV before and after the casualty (or theft) or (ii) the basis of the property. They reduce this amount first, by any insurance or other reimbursements they receive, and then, by $100 per event (not per item). Taxpayers then total the net loss from each casualty event that occurs during the year. From this total they subtract 10% of AGI. Only the remaining amount is deductible on Schedule A.

For tax years 2018 through 2025, the deduction for personal casualty and theft losses is limited only to losses attributable to federally declared disasters. [I.R.C. §165(h)(5)] A taxpayer may still claim personal casualty and theft losses not attributable federally declared disasters to the extent of any personal casualty and theft gains.

Loans taken out to cover the loss do not count as reimbursements. When an individual has insurance coverage but declines to report the incident in order to avoid raising insurance premiums, no personal casualty loss deduction results for the amount of insurance benefits given up.

All of these rules make losses from personal casualties hard to deduct. Personal casualty deductions rarely take place without a major uninsured disaster. Lesser casualties generally result in losses below the 10% of AGI threshold and result in no tax benefits. Taxpayers compute their casualty loss deduction on Form 4684, Casualties and Thefts, and then enter the net loss in excess of 10% of AGI on Schedule A. If more than one casualty takes place during the year, the IRS requires that taxpayers fill out a separate Form 4684 for each event.

EXAMPLE 35

Roy wrecked his personal automobile that originally cost $30,000. This was his only casualty for the year. The vehicle had an FMV of $25,855 before the accident. The estimated FMV after the accident was $1,000, resulting in a $24,855 change in value ($25,855 – $1,000). Roy collected $16,355 of insurance proceeds. His AGI of $52,090 reduces the casualty loss deduction to $3,191.

Lesser of (i) $24,855 change in FMV or (ii) $30,000 basis	$24,855
Less insurance proceeds	(16,355)
Less $100 reduction	(100)
Less 10% of AGI	(5,209)
Net casualty loss, not less than $0:	$ 3,191

Deductible only if Roy is in a federally declared disaster area.

Taxpayers may be able to exclude from gross income reimbursements they receive to cover additional living expenses they incur as a result of a casualty. Such amounts are nontaxable to the extent that they compensate the taxpayer for a temporary increase in living expenses. Reimbursements in excess of actual costs are taxable, as are reimbursements that cover normal expenses. While often associated with casualties, these reimbursements do not affect the casualty loss deduction.

EXAMPLE 36

A casualty damages a couple's home. While repairing the home, the couple lives in another house, costing them $3,500 per month. The couple's normal living expenses before the storm were $1,500 per month. They continue to pay all of their normal living expenses in addition to the $3,500 each month. The insurance company reimburses the couple $4,000 per month. They include $500 per month in gross income for the reimbursement they receive in excess of the $3,500 increase in living expenses. This amount is reported as "Other income" on Schedule 1 (Form 1040) (line 21).

¶507.01   CASUALTY EVENTS

The IRS defines a **casualty** as a sudden, unexpected, or unusual event [Rev. Rul. 75-592]. Events creating casualty losses include accidents, fires, storms, earthquakes, floods, hurricanes, thefts, and other disasters [I.R.C. §165(c)(3)]. Many irritating events, although expensive and inconvenient, do not qualify as casualties because they are not considered sudden, unexpected, or unusual. Some examples include long-term termite or moth damage, plant disease, property value reduction due to a landslide on a nearby lot, or loss of a diamond ring dropped down a drain. No deduction is allowed for items deliberately destroyed or damaged by willful neglect.

Also, deductions are allowed only for damage to the taxpayer's own property. Therefore, if a driver hits and destroys the neighbor's fence, the cost of repairing the neighbor's fence cannot be deducted as a casualty loss on the driver's tax return.

¶507.02   PROOF

The mere loss of an item does not create a casualty. The taxpayer must prove that a theft, accident, or disaster took place. Taxpayers should report any loss to the police or other government authority to get a written report for their files. The taxpayer must also establish the amount of the casualty loss. "Before" and "after" pictures can help prove the extent of the damage. Objective appraisals of the property both before and after the event provide evidence of the loss suffered. The IRS generally will accept the cost of repairing the property as the amount of the loss. However, the cost of repairs cannot be used if the repairs restore the property to a better condition and a higher value than before the loss.

¶507.03   YEAR OF DEDUCTION

The general rule allows a casualty loss deduction only in the year the casualty occurs. A theft loss is deducted in the year the taxpayer discovers the theft. However, the taxpayer can elect to deduct a loss occurring in a federally-declared disaster area in the year of the disaster or in the previous tax year. This special rule makes it possible for taxpayers to get disaster-based tax refunds sooner. [I.R.C. §165(i)]

¶508   Job Expenses and Certain Miscellaneous Deductions (Pre-2018)

Before 2018, there was a category of miscellaneous deductions that could be taken on Schedule A, subject to a 2% of AGI floor. Beginning in 2018, taxpayers are no longer allowed any miscellaneous itemized deductions. [I.R.C. §67(g)] These deductions are scheduled to return after 2025 unless Congress permanently removes them or extends the window for nondeductibility.

Unreimbursed employee expenses were costs employees incur in connection with their employment such as employer-required physicals, union dues, licenses, travel expenses, job search expenses, and so forth. Any amount that was reimbursed to the employee through their employer was not deductible. Note that job expenses incurred by self-employed persons or statutory employees are for AGI deductions that are reported on Schedule C. **Statutory employees** include full-time employees in the following occupations: outside salespersons, life insurance sales agents, some agent/commission-based drivers, and home-based piece-goods workers (see ¶705.01).

Tax preparation fees and amounts paid to produce or collect taxable income, and to manage or protect property held for earning income were also included in this category. Examples were certain legal and accounting fees and investment expenses.

Taxpayers added these costs together, subtracted 2% of AGI from the total, and deducted the excess on Schedule A. However, for tax years 2018 through 2025, an individual may not claim any miscellaneous itemized deduction subject to the 2% AGI limit. These deductions are scheduled to return after 2025 unless Congress permanently removes them or extends the window for nondeductibility. (See ¶601 and ¶602.)

¶508.01   HOBBY LOSSES

When an activity has elements of both personal pleasure and profit, the question often arises as to whether the taxpayer had a profit motive. The presence of a profit motive affects the amount of expenses taxpayers deduct as well as where on the tax return they deduct them. Taxpayers who enter into an activity expecting to make a profit can deduct all expenses from the activity as a deduction for AGI using Schedule C (see ¶703). In contrast, expenses from an activity in which the taxpayer did not have a profit motive (a hobby) used to be deducted to the extent of income from the activity as a miscellaneous itemized deduction (subject to the 2% AGI floor). [I.R.C. §183(b)] However, along with other miscellaneous itemized deductions, the hobby loss deduction is disallowed for years 2018 through 2025.

Taxpayers continue to deduct expenses that they would otherwise be able to deduct even if the activity did not exist, including home mortgage interest, property taxes, and casualty losses. Other expenses, like supplies, utilities, insurance, and depreciation are deductible only because of tax laws that allow taxpayers to deduct them against hobby income. Because these expenses are no longer deductible, the income from hobbies is included in gross income; no deduction for expenses is allowable. Any disallowed expenses are lost and cannot be carried over to future years.

EXAMPLE 37

Rob paints as a hobby. Rob does his painting in a separate studio located in his home. During the year, Rob sold some paintings for $2,300. His expenses totaled $3,025 and consisted of $400 for real estate taxes on the studio, $1,125 for utilities, and $1,500 for painting supplies. He computes his hobby income and expense as follows:

Gross income	$2,300
Less real estate taxes deductible elsewhere on Schedule A	(400)
Limit on deduction for "other expenses"	$1,900
"Other expenses" related to the hobby:	
Utilities	$1,125
Painting supplies	1500
Total "other expenses"	$2,625
Deductible "other expenses"*	(1,900)
Net hobby income	$0

* Before 2018 or after 2025

For years in which the hobby loss deduction is allowed, Rob reports $2,300 of gross income from the hobby as "Other income" on Form 1040. On Schedule A, Rob deducts $400 as real estate taxes and the remaining $1,900 of "other expenses" as a miscellaneous itemized deduction. He adds the $1,900 to his other miscellaneous deductions, and reduces the total by 2% of AGI. Rob cannot deduct the $725 of painting supplies and utilities that exceed $1,900 ($2,625 − $1,900 = $725).

For years in which the hobby loss deduction is disallowed, Rob reports $2,300 of gross income. He combines the property tax with his other itemized deductions for tax, subject to the $10,000 (or $5,000) cap. He cannot claim a deduction for any of the other expenses.

Unlike hobby losses, losses from a profit activity can be used to offset other income. The drawback of having an activity treated as a hobby should help explain why taxpayers should make every effort to be able to treat an activity as a business. The fact that a taxpayer enjoys an activity does not prevent it from being profitable. The burden of proving whether an activity is engaged in for profit generally rests with the taxpayer. However, the burden of proof shifts to the IRS for an activity that shows a profit in any three of five consecutive years (two of seven for activities involving horses). [I.R.C. §183(d)] When this happens, it is assumed that a profit motive exists, and it is up to the IRS to prove that the activity is a hobby.

Taxpayers involved in an activity for less than three years may elect to postpone any challenge from the IRS until after the first five years. This gives taxpayers the opportunity to show a profit in three of those years and shift the burden of proof to the IRS. However, filing such an election may alert the IRS to a possible hobby activity. Factors used to decide whether an activity is a business or a hobby include:

1. The taxpayer's expertise in the area;
2. Whether the taxpayer keeps separate books and records for the activity;
3. Whether the activity showed profits in some years and losses in others;
4. The amount of occasional profits the taxpayer earned from the activity;
5. The relative amount of pleasure the taxpayer derives from the activity;
6. The extent to which the taxpayer depends on the activity for financial support;
7. The time and effort the taxpayer devotes to the activity;
8. The taxpayer's past success with other activities; and
9. The taxpayer's expectation that the property used in the activity will rise in value. [Reg. §1.183-2]

¶509 Other Miscellaneous Deductions

Taxpayers report the following expenses on Schedule A in the "Other Itemized Deductions" section (these deductions are not reduced by 2% of AGI):

- Gambling losses to the extent of gambling income;
- Casualty losses from investment property (see ¶507);
- Federal estate taxes on income in respect of a decedent;
- Repayment under the claim of right doctrine;
- Unrecovered costs in pensions and annuities (¶306.01, ¶306.02); and
- Impairment-related work expenses of disabled persons (see ¶509.02 below).

¶509.01 GAMBLING LOSSES

Taxpayers report all gambling winnings on Schedule 1 (Form 1040) as "Other income." They may deduct their gambling losses up to the amount of their reported winnings as an itemized deduction on Schedule A in the "Other Itemized Deductions" section. Thus, taxpayers who do not itemize lose the gambling deduction, but are still taxed on their gambling winnings. Beginning in 2018, gambling losses include any deduction in carrying on any wagering transaction, and not just the actual costs of wagers. [I.R.C. §165(d)]

EXAMPLE 38

In several trips to Las Vegas, Newman lost $8,000 playing blackjack and poker. However, he won $4,500 from the state lottery. Newman reports the $4,500 lottery winnings as "Other income" on Schedule 1 (Form 1040). He reports only $4,500 as gambling losses as "Other itemized deductions" on Schedule A (line 16). He cannot deduct the other $3,500 of gambling losses. Newman cannot take advantage of any deduction for the gambling loss unless his total itemized deductions exceed his total standard deduction amount.

¶509.02 IMPAIRMENT-RELATED WORK EXPENSES

An impairment is a physical or mental disability that limits a taxpayer's employment. Impairments include those limiting vision, hearing, or movement. When impaired taxpayers purchase special tools or devices to make it possible to work as an employee, they deduct the costs directly on Schedule A. [I.R.C. §67(b)(6)] They are not required to depreciate these special purchases. Deductible expenses include modifications to computers, special listening devices, and reading devices. Self-employed persons deduct their impairment-related work expenses on Schedule C.

¶510 Nondeductible Expenses

Over the years, some taxpayers have illegally taken deductions for expenses that are not deductible. Below is a sample of nondeductible expenses, but there are many more costs that taxpayers have unsuccessfully tried to deduct. In some cases, both the taxpayers and the tax preparers have faced severe penalties. (See Chapter 13 at ¶1308.)

- Funeral costs, including the lot;
- Political contributions, illegal bribes, and kickbacks;
- Parking tickets and fines, even if related to business;
- Costs of clothing used in work, but suitable for normal use; and
- Personal living expenses, like rent, insurance, utilities, and life insurance.

¶511 Reduction in Itemized Deductions for Higher-Income Taxpayers

Prior to 2018, higher-income taxpayers reduced their total itemized deductions by up to 3% of AGI in excess of a specified threshold. The threshold amounts vary by filing status. They are the same amounts used in computing the phase-out of the exemption deduction.

The phase-out or overall limitation on itemized deductions is temporarily repealed for tax years 2018 through 2025.

¶512 Schedule A and Form 1040 Revisited

Figures 5-2 and 5-3 show how the information flows from Schedule A to Form 1040.

¶512.01 FILLED-IN SCHEDULE A

 ### INFORMATION FOR FIGURE 5-2:

Arthur and Drea McBurney have **$90,517** of AGI. The McBurneys use the information shown below to compute their itemized deductions on Schedule A.

Line #
- 1: Unreimbursed medical and dental expenses, **$9,754**
- 2: AGI, **$90,517** (given)
- 5a: State of Wisconsin income taxes, **$5,640**
- 5b: Real estate taxes, **$6,224**
- 5c: Personal (ad valorem) property taxes, **$96**
- 8a: Home mortgage interest, **$14,426**
- 11: Gifts by cash or check, **$1,287** cash and check
- 12: Noncash gifts, **$181** ($160 used clothing + (150 miles × $.14 = $21))
- 13: Charitable contribution carryover from a prior year, **$200**

Figure 5-2: Filled-In Schedule A

SCHEDULE A (Form 1040)	**Itemized Deductions**	OMB No. 1545-0074

Itemized Deductions

SCHEDULE A (Form 1040)

Department of the Treasury
Internal Revenue Service

Go to *www.irs.gov/ScheduleA* for instructions and the latest information.
Attach to Form 1040 or 1040-SR.
Caution: If you are claiming a net qualified disaster loss on Form 4684, see the instructions for line 16.

OMB No. 1545-0074
2022
Attachment Sequence No. **07**

Name(s) shown on Form 1040 or 1040-SR
Arthur and Drea McBurney

Your social security number
392-00-6811

Medical and Dental Expenses

Caution: Do not include expenses reimbursed or paid by others.

1	Medical and dental expenses (see instructions)	**1**	9,754	
2	Enter amount from Form 1040 or 1040-SR, line 11 **2** 90,517			
3	Multiply line 2 by 7.5% (0.075)	**3**	6,789	
4	Subtract line 3 from line 1. If line 3 is more than line 1, enter -0-		**4**	2,965

Taxes You Paid

5 State and local taxes.

a State and local income taxes or general sales taxes. You may include either income taxes or general sales taxes on line 5a, but not both. If you elect to include general sales taxes instead of income taxes, check this box . . . . ☐ **5a** 5,540

b State and local real estate taxes (see instructions) **5b** 6,224

c State and local personal property taxes **5c** 96

d Add lines 5a through 5c **5d** 11,960

e Enter the smaller of line 5d or $10,000 ($5,000 if married filing separately) **5e** 10,000

6 Other taxes. List type and amount: _____
_____ **6**

7 Add lines 5e and 6 . . . . **7** 10,000

Interest You Paid

Caution: Your mortgage interest deduction may be limited. See instructions.

8 Home mortgage interest and points. If you didn't use all of your home mortgage loan(s) to buy, build, or improve your home, see instructions and check this box . . . . ☐

a Home mortgage interest and points reported to you on Form 1098. See instructions if limited **8a** 14,426

b Home mortgage interest not reported to you on Form 1098. See instructions if limited. If paid to the person from whom you bought the home, see instructions and show that person's name, identifying no., and address **8b**
_____

c Points not reported to you on Form 1098. See instructions for special rules **8c**

d Reserved for future use **8d**

e Add lines 8a through 8c **8e** 14,426

9 Investment interest. Attach Form 4952 if required. See instructions . **9**

10 Add lines 8e and 9 . . . . **10** 14,426

Gifts to Charity

Caution: If you made a gift and got a benefit for it, see instructions.

11 Gifts by cash or check. If you made any gift of $250 or more, see instructions **11** 1,287

12 Other than by cash or check. If you made any gift of $250 or more, see instructions. You **must** attach Form 8283 if over $500. . . . **12** 181

13 Carryover from prior year **13** 200

14 Add lines 11 through 13 . . . . **14** 1,668

Casualty and Theft Losses

15 Casualty and theft loss(es) from a federally declared disaster (other than net qualified disaster losses). Attach Form 4684 and enter the amount from line 18 of that form. See instructions **15**

Other Itemized Deductions

16 Other—from list in instructions. List type and amount: _____
_____ **16**

Total Itemized Deductions

17 Add the amounts in the far right column for lines 4 through 16. Also, enter this amount on Form 1040 or 1040-SR, line 12 . . . . **17** 29,059

18 If you elect to itemize deductions even though they are less than your standard deduction, check this box . . . . ☐

For Paperwork Reduction Act Notice, see the Instructions for Form 1040. Cat. No. 17145C Schedule A (Form 1040) 2022

¶512.02   FILLED-IN FORM 1040

INFORMATION FOR FIGURE 5-3:

Arthur and Drea McBurney (from Figure 5-2) claim their two minor children and Arthur's mother (widowed, with no income) as dependents. Arthur, age 35, is a teacher and Drea, age 27, is a secretary.

Arthur's social security number is 392-00-6811, and Drea's is 392-00-6800.

Victor McBurney, 684-00-1111, son, age 8

Caroline McBurney, 684-00-1110, daughter, age 5

Vivian McBurney, 684-00-1109, mother, age 68

Neither Arthur nor Drea is a participant in an employer's pension program. Figure 5-3 shows the McBurneys' completed Form 1040, which is based on the information shown below, as well as Schedule A from Figure 5-2. They had no interests in any foreign bank accounts or trusts. They resided in the U.S. for the entire year. They received no advance payments of the child credit in 2022. They each want $3 to go the Presidential Election Campaign. Neither spouse acquired or disposed of any interest in a digital asset during the year. If they overpaid, they will ask for a cash refund.

Form 1040

Line #

1a: Wages, **$94,000** (Arthur, $55,000 + Drea, $39,000, source: Form W-2)
2b: Taxable interest, **$1,913** (source: Schedule B)
7: Short-term capital gain, **$1,250** (source: Schedule D)
8: Other income, **$5,354** (source: Schedule 1, Line 10)
9: Total income, **$102,517** (lines 1 through 8)
10: Adjustments to income, **$12,000** (source: Schedule 1, Line 26)
11: Adjusted gross income, **$90,517**
12: Standard deduction or itemized deductions, **$29,059** (source: Schedule A, see Figure 5-2)
15: Taxable income **$61,457**
16: Tax, **$6,966** (source: MFJ tax table)
19: Nonrefundable Child tax credit/credit for other dependents, **$4,500**
25a: Federal income tax withheld, **$4,200** (source: Forms W-2 and 1099)
33: Total payments, **$4,200**
34: Overpayment, **$1,734**
35a: Refund **$1,734**

Schedule 1

Line #

1: Taxable state income tax refund, **$251** (source: Form 1099-G from 2021 state income tax return)
5: Net rent from apartments, **$4,303** (source: Schedule E). This income is not qualified business income (See Chapter 6.)
8i: Door prize, **$800** (source: Form 1099-MISC)
10: Combined income on Schedule 1, **$5,354**
20: IRA deduction, **$12,000** (neither taxpayer is an active participant in an employer-sponsored plan)
26: Adjustments to income, **$12,000**

Figure 5-3: Filled-In Form 1040 (Page 1)

Form 1040 — Department of the Treasury—Internal Revenue Service
U.S. Individual Income Tax Return — **2022** — OMB No. 1545-0074 — IRS Use Only—Do not write or staple in this space.

Filing Status
Check only one box.
☐ Single ☑ Married filing jointly ☐ Married filing separately (MFS) ☐ Head of household (HOH) ☐ Qualifying widow(er) (QW)
If you checked the MFS box, enter the name of your spouse. If you checked the HOH or QW box, enter the child's name if the qualifying person is a child but not your dependent:

Your first name and middle initial: Arthur	Last name: McBurney	Your social security number: 3 9 2 0 0 6 8 1 1
If joint return, spouse's first name and middle initial: Drea	Last name: McBurney	Spouse's social security number: 3 9 2 0 0 6 8 0 0

Home address (number and street). If you have a P.O. box, see instructions. **1432 E. 2nd St.** — Apt. no.

City, town, or post office. If you have a foreign address, also complete spaces below. **Verona** — State **WI** — ZIP code **89434**

Foreign country name — Foreign province/state/county — Foreign postal code

Presidential Election Campaign
Check here if you, or your spouse if filing jointly, want $3 to go to this fund. Checking a box below will not change your tax or refund.
☑ You ☑ Spouse

At any time during 2022, did you: (a) receive (as a reward, award, or compensation); or (b) sell, exchange, gift, or otherwise dispose of a digital asset (or a financial interest in a digital asset)? (See instructions.) ☐ Yes ☑ No

Standard Deduction
Someone can claim: ☐ You as a dependent ☐ Your spouse as a dependent
☐ Spouse itemizes on a separate return or you were a dual-status alien

Age/Blindness You: ☐ Were born before January 2, 1958 ☐ Are blind **Spouse:** ☐ Was born before January 2, 1958 ☐ Is blind

Dependents (see instructions):
If more than four dependents, see instructions and check here ☐

(1) First name Last name	(2) Social security number	(3) Relationship to you	(4) Child tax credit	Credit for other dependents
Victor McBurney	6 8 4 0 0 1 1 1 1	son	☑	☐
Caroline McBurney	6 8 4 0 0 1 1 1 0	daughter	☑	☐
Vivian McBurney	6 8 4 0 0 1 1 0 9	mother	☐	☑
			☐	☐

Income

Attach Form(s) W-2 here. Also attach Forms W-2G and 1099-R if tax was withheld.
If you did not get a Form W-2, see instructions.

Attach Sch. B if required.

Standard Deduction for—
• Single or Married filing separately, $12,950
• Married filing jointly or Qualifying widow(er), $25,900
• Head of household, $19,400
• If you checked any box under Standard Deduction, see instructions.

1a	Total amount from Form(s) W-2, box 1 (see instructions)	1a 94,000
b	Household employee wages not reported on Form(s) W-2	1b
c	Tip income not reported on line 1a (see instructions)	1c
d	Medicaid waiver payments not reported on Form(s) W-2 (see instructions)	1d
e	Taxable dependent care benefits from Form 2441, line 26	1e
f	Employer-provided adoption benefits from Form 8839, line 29	1f
g	Wages from Form 8919, line 6	1g
h	Other earned income (see instructions)	1h
i	Nontaxable combat pay election (see instructions) . . . 1i	
z	Add lines 1a through 1h	1z 94,000
2a	Tax-exempt interest . . . 2a	b Taxable interest 2b 1,913
3a	Qualified dividends . . . 3a	b Ordinary dividends 3b
4a	IRA distributions 4a	b Taxable amount 4b
5a	Pensions and annuities . . 5a	b Taxable amount 5b
6a	Social security benefits . . 6a	b Taxable amount 6b
c	If you elect to use the lump-sum election method, check here (see instructions) ☐	
7	Capital gain or (loss). Attach Schedule D if required. If not required, check here ☐	7 1,250
8	Other income from Schedule 1, line 10	8 5,354
9	Add lines 1z, 2b, 3b, 4b, 5b, 6b, 7, and 8. This is your **total income**	9 102,517
10	Adjustments to income from Schedule 1, line 26	10 12,000
11	Subtract line 10 from line 9. This is your **adjusted gross income**	11 90,517
12	**Standard deduction or itemized deductions** (from Schedule A)	12 29,059
13	Qualified business income deduction from Form 8995 or Form 8995-A	13
14	Add lines 12 and 13	14 29,059
15	Subtract line 14 from line 11. If zero or less, enter -0-. This is your **taxable income**	15 61,457

For Disclosure, Privacy Act, and Paperwork Reduction Act Notice, see separate instructions. Cat. No. 11320B Form **1040** (2022)

Figure 5-3: Filled-In Form 1040 (Page 2)

Version A, Cycle 7

Form 1040 (2022)   Page **2**

Section	Line	Description		Amount
Tax and Credits	16	Tax (see instructions). Check if any from Form(s): 1 ☐ 8814 2 ☐ 4972 3 ☐ _____	16	6,966
	17	Amount from Schedule 2, line 3	17	
	18	Add lines 16 and 17	18	6,966
	19	Child tax credit or credit for other dependents from Schedule 8812	19	4,500
	20	Amount from Schedule 3, line 8	20	
	21	Add lines 19 and 20	21	4,500
	22	Subtract line 21 from line 18. If zero or less, enter -0-	22	2,466
	23	Other taxes, including self-employment tax, from Schedule 2, line 21	23	
	24	Add lines 22 and 23. This is your **total tax**	24	2,466
Payments	25	Federal income tax withheld from:		
	a	Form(s) W-2	25a 4,200	
	b	Form(s) 1099	25b	
	c	Other forms (see instructions)	25c	
	d	Add lines 25a through 25c	25d	4,200
If you have a qualifying child, attach Sch. EIC.	26	2022 estimated tax payments and amount applied from 2021 return	26	
	27	Earned income credit (EIC)	27	
	28	Additional child tax credit from Schedule 8812	28	
	29	American opportunity credit from Form 8863, line 8	29	
	30	Reserved for future use	30	
	31	Amount from Schedule 3, line 15	31	
	32	Add lines 27, 28, 29, and 31. These are your **total other payments and refundable credits**	32	
	33	Add lines 25d, 26, and 32. These are your **total payments**	33	4,200
Refund	34	If line 33 is more than line 24, subtract line 24 from line 33. This is the amount you **overpaid**	34	1,734
	35a	Amount of line 34 you want **refunded to you**. If Form 8888 is attached, check here ☐	35a	1,734
Direct deposit? See instructions.	b	Routing number _____ c Type: ☐ Checking ☐ Savings		
	d	Account number _____		
	36	Amount of line 34 you want **applied to your 2023 estimated tax**	36	
Amount You Owe	37	Subtract line 33 from line 24. This is the **amount you owe**. For details on how to pay, go to *www.irs.gov/Payments* or see instructions	37	
	38	Estimated tax penalty (see instructions)	38	

Third Party Designee

Do you want to allow another person to discuss this return with the IRS? See instructions . . . . ☐ **Yes.** Complete below.   ☐ **No**

Designee's name	Phone no.	Personal identification number (PIN)	

Sign Here

Under penalties of perjury, I declare that I have examined this return and accompanying schedules and statements, and to the best of my knowledge and belief, they are true, correct, and complete. Declaration of preparer (other than taxpayer) is based on all information of which preparer has any knowledge.

Joint return? See instructions. Keep a copy for your records.

Your signature	Date	Your occupation	If the IRS sent you an Identity Protection PIN, enter it here (see inst.)
		Teacher	
Spouse's signature. If a joint return, **both** must sign.	Date	Spouse's occupation	If the IRS sent your spouse an Identity Protection PIN, enter it here (see inst.)
		Secretary	
Phone no.		Email address	

Paid Preparer Use Only

Preparer's name	Preparer's signature	Date	PTIN	Check if: ☐ Self-employed
Firm's name			Phone no.	
Firm's address			Firm's EIN	

Go to *www.irs.gov/Form1040* for instructions and the latest information.   Form **1040** (2022)

Figure 5-3: Filled-In Schedule 1 (Page 1)

SCHEDULE 1 (Form 1040)	Additional Income and Adjustments to Income	OMB No. 1545-0074
Department of the Treasury Internal Revenue Service	Attach to Form 1040, 1040-SR, or 1040-NR. Go to *www.irs.gov/Form1040* for instructions and the latest information.	2022 Attachment Sequence No. 01

Name(s) shown on Form 1040, 1040-SR, or 1040-NR	Your social security number
Arthur and Drea McBurney	392-00-6811

Part I   Additional Income

1	Taxable refunds, credits, or offsets of state and local income taxes	**1**	251
2a	Alimony received	**2a**	
b	Date of original divorce or separation agreement (see instructions):		
3	Business income or (loss). Attach Schedule C	**3**	
4	Other gains or (losses). Attach Form 4797	**4**	
5	Rental real estate, royalties, partnerships, S corporations, trusts, etc. Attach Schedule E	**5**	4,303
6	Farm income or (loss). Attach Schedule F	**6**	
7	Unemployment compensation	**7**	
8	Other income:		
a	Net operating loss	**8a** ( )	
b	Gambling	**8b**	
c	Cancellation of debt	**8c**	
d	Foreign earned income exclusion from Form 2555	**8d** ( )	
e	Income from Form 8853	**8e**	
f	Income from Form 8889	**8f**	
g	Alaska Permanent Fund dividends	**8g**	
h	Jury duty pay	**8h**	
i	Prizes and awards	**8i** 800	
j	Activity not engaged in for profit income	**8j**	
k	Stock options	**8k**	
l	Income from the rental of personal property if you engaged in the rental for profit but were not in the business of renting such property	**8l**	
m	Olympic and Paralympic medals and USOC prize money (see instructions)	**8m**	
n	Section 951(a) inclusion (see instructions)	**8n**	
o	Section 951A(a) inclusion (see instructions)	**8o**	
p	Section 461(l) excess business loss adjustment	**8p**	
q	Taxable distributions from an ABLE account (see instructions)	**8q**	
r	Scholarship and fellowship grants not reported on Form W-2	**8r**	
s	Nontaxable amount of Medicaid waiver payments included on Form 1040, line 1a or 1d	**8s** ( )	
t	Pension or annuity from a nonqualifed deferred compensation plan or a nongovernmental section 457 plan	**8t**	
u	Wages earned while incarcerated	**8u**	
z	Other income. List type and amount: _____	**8z**	
9	Total other income. Add lines 8a through 8z	**9**	800
10	Combine lines 1 through 7 and 9. Enter here and on Form 1040, 1040-SR, or 1040-NR, line 8	**10**	5,354

For Paperwork Reduction Act Notice, see your tax return instructions.   Cat. No. 71479F   Schedule 1 (Form 1040) 2022

DRAFT AS OF July 27, 2022 DO NOT FILE

¶512.02

Figure 5-3: Filled-In Schedule 1 (Page 2)

Schedule 1 (Form 1040) 2022   Page **2**

Part II Adjustments to Income

Line	Description	No.	Amount
11	Educator expenses	11	
12	Certain business expenses of reservists, performing artists, and fee-basis government officials. Attach Form 2106	12	
13	Health savings account deduction. Attach Form 8889	13	
14	Moving expenses for members of the Armed Forces. Attach Form 3903	14	
15	Deductible part of self-employment tax. Attach Schedule SE	15	
16	Self-employed SEP, SIMPLE, and qualified plans	16	
17	Self-employed health insurance deduction	17	
18	Penalty on early withdrawal of savings	18	
19a	Alimony paid	19a	
b	Recipient's SSN		
c	Date of original divorce or separation agreement (see instructions):		
20	IRA deduction	20	12,000
21	Student loan interest deduction	21	
22	Reserved for future use	22	
23	Archer MSA deduction	23	
24	Other adjustments:		
a	Jury duty pay (see instructions)	24a	
b	Deductible expenses related to income reported on line 8l from the rental of personal property engaged in for profit	24b	
c	Nontaxable amount of the value of Olympic and Paralympic medals and USOC prize money reported on line 8m	24c	
d	Reforestation amortization and expenses	24d	
e	Repayment of supplemental unemployment benefits under the Trade Act of 1974	24e	
f	Contributions to section 501(c)(18)(D) pension plans	24f	
g	Contributions by certain chaplains to section 403(b) plans	24g	
h	Attorney fees and court costs for actions involving certain unlawful discrimination claims (see instructions)	24h	
i	Attorney fees and court costs you paid in connection with an award from the IRS for information you provided that helped the IRS detect tax law violations	24i	
j	Housing deduction from Form 2555	24j	
k	Excess deductions of section 67(e) expenses from Schedule K-1 (Form 1041)	24k	
z	Other adjustments. List type and amount: _____	24z	
25	Total other adjustments. Add lines 24a through 24z	25	
26	Add lines 11 through 23 and 25. These are your **adjustments to income**. Enter here and on Form 1040 or 1040-SR, line 10, or Form 1040-NR, line 10a	26	12,000

Schedule 1 (Form 1040) 2022

5

Name:

Section:

Date:

QUESTIONS AND PROBLEMS

1. **Medical Expense Deduction.** (Obj. 2) Ian and Bella Brown (ages 55 and 54, respectively) maintain a home where they live with their disabled daughter, Brenda, who is 24. The Browns' AGI is $60,000. Unreimbursed amounts paid for medical and dental expenses during the year follow:

	Brenda	The Browns
R. J. Stone, M.D.	$ 260	$ 250
G. O. Wright, D.D.S.	220	200
Hearing aid		525
Premium on health insurance		1,240
Eyeglasses		130
Toothpaste	20	35
Prescription drugs	3,275	125
Total	$3,775	$2,505

Compute the Browns' medical and dental expense deduction on their 2022 joint tax return.

2. **Medical Expense Deduction.** (Obj. 2) Mei (age 40, unmarried, no dependents) paid various expenses during the year.

a. In the space after each unreimbursed item, indicate whether or not the item is deductible as a medical expense, and if so, enter the deductible amount (without regard to the AGI floor).

Item	Deductible?	Deductible Amount
1. Premium on health insurance, $386	_____	_____
2. Premium on life insurance, $275	_____	_____
3. Premium on automobile accident insurance, $610	_____	_____
4. Acne cream, $30	_____	_____
5. Prescription medication, $300	_____	_____
6. Prescribed vitamins, $60	_____	_____
7. Cosmetics, $150	_____	_____
8. Dr. Wall, dentist, $120	_____	_____
9. Dues to health spa, $325	_____	_____
10. X-ray examination, $60	_____	_____
11. City Hospital, room and services, $375	_____	_____
12. Eyeglasses, $125	_____	_____
13. Cemetery plot, $600	_____	_____
14. Miles driven for medical in May—1,176	_____	_____
15. Illegal drugs, $135	_____	_____
16. Vacation recommended by doctor to improve general health, $875	_____	_____
17. Dr. Root, minor surgery, $350	_____	_____
18. Used wheelchair, $275	_____	_____
19. Dr. Spencer for false teeth, $480, and fittings, $100	_____	_____

b. If Mei's AGI is $24,290, compute her medical and dental expense deduction.

3. **Medical Reimbursements.** (Obj. 2) A taxpayer receives a reimbursement for a medical expense of $455 in the current year. What is the proper tax treatment of the $455 if:

    a. The reimbursed expense was paid in the current year.

    b. The reimbursed expense was paid last year. The taxpayer took the standard deduction last year.

    c. The reimbursed expense was paid last year, and last year the taxpayer's total itemized deductions exceeded the standard deduction by $2,000 and medical expenses in excess of the AGI floor were $840.

    d. Same as in Part c. except that medical expenses in excess of the AGI floor were $350.

    e. The total reimbursement includes $75 in excess of the taxpayer's medical expenses for the current year. The taxpayer paid the premiums on the policy.

    f. Same as in Part e., except that the employer paid the premiums on the policy, which were treated as a tax-free fringe benefit to the taxpayer.

4. **Physical Exams.** (Obj. 2) If an employee pays for a periodic medical checkup required by an employer, can the amount paid be deducted, and if so, is there any limitation? Explain.

5. **Medical Deduction.** (Obj. 2) Tracey suffers from severe arthritis. His doctor has prescribed that he install a hot tub at his home to help relieve the pain. Tracey pays $7,500 to have a hot tub installed. The hot tub is expected to increase the value of his home by $3,000. What amount, if any, can Tracey deduct as a medical expense on his tax return?

6. **State and Local Income Taxes.** (Obj. 3) In April 2023, Jose filed his 2022 federal and state income tax returns. He paid $800 with his federal return and $450 when he filed his state income tax return. During 2022, Jose's employer withheld $6,600 and $3,100, respectively for federal and state income taxes. Jose files as single.

   a. What amount can Jose deduct as an itemized deduction on his 2022 tax return?

   b. When Jose files his 2022 tax returns early in 2023, he receives a $90 refund from the federal government and $120 back from the state. Discuss the tax consequences to Jose of receiving refunds totaling $210. Jose's other itemized deductions in 2022 totaled $13,150.

   c. Same as in Part b. except that Jose's other itemized deductions total $1,000.

7. **Estimated State and Local Income Taxes.** (Obj. 3) Ivy is self-employed and a cash basis taxpayer. For the 2021 and 2022 tax years, she makes quarterly estimated tax payments to the state, as shown below. When she files her 2021 tax return in April 2022, she receives a $300 refund from the state. When she files her 2022 tax return in April 2023, she owes $650 to the state. Compute Ivy's 2022 state and local income tax deduction.

	Date Paid	Amount Paid
1st installment	April 15, 2021	$220
2nd installment	June 15, 2021	220
3rd installment	September 15, 2021	250
4th installment	January 15, 2022	250
1st installment	April 15, 2022	$300
2nd installment	June 15, 2022	300
3rd installment	September 15, 2022	275
4th installment	January 15, 2023	250

8. **Personal Property Taxes.** (Obj. 3) Jan lives in a state that imposes a property tax on the value on motor vehicles. Karl lives in a state that imposes a flat $55 renewal fee for license tags. Jan pays the state $430 to renew her license tags. Included in this amount is a $25 license plate fee. The rest is an ad valorem tax. Discuss the tax consequences to each of these taxpayers on their federal income tax returns.

9. **Home Mortgage Interest.** (Obj. 4) The Hemphills own three homes, all acquired after 2018. Their main home is located in Pittsburg. They also own condos in Las Vegas and Tampa. The amount of acquisition debt and interest paid on each property is shown below.

Location of Home	Acquisition Debt	Interest Paid
Pittsburg	$140,000	$8,330
Las Vegas	440,000	21,555
Tampa	400,000	23,443

   a. Compute the Hemphills' home mortgage interest deduction.

   b. How would your answer to Part a. change if the Pittsburg home were fully paid for, and the Hemphills only had mortgages on the two vacation homes?

10. **Home Mortgage Interest.** (Obj. 4) The Stephens own a home in Boston. They paid $780,000 for the home in 2016. Their current balance on their mortgage is $660,000. At the time that their home was worth $900,000, they refinanced their mortgage. Their new mortgage is for $800,000. In addition to the home in Boston, the Stephens also own a vacation home in Florida. They paid $350,000 for the home in 2014, and the current mortgage on the second home is $195,000.

   a. Discuss how much interest the Stephens are allowed to deduct if the excess proceeds from the refinancing are used to buy or improve their main home.

   b. Same as in Part a. except that the excess proceeds from the loan are used to buy a new car and take a vacation to Europe.

11. **Points.** (Obj. 4) During 2022, Lee borrowed money on two different occasions from the local bank. She took out the first loan on March 1 to purchase land for a place to graze horses and livestock as an investment activity. Lee paid $33,000 for the land, making a down payment of $6,000 and borrowing $27,000 for ten years at 9% interest. To obtain a lower interest rate on the loan, she was required to pay two points, totaling $540 (2% × $27,000). In August, Lee bought a new house that she uses as her main home. Her mortgage was $48,000 at 4% for 20 years. Lee paid the lender one point, or $480 (1% × $48,000) to get a lower interest rate.

   a. Determine the amount of points Lee may use as a 2022 interest deduction in connection with the two loans.

   b. What happens to any amount of points not deducted in 2022?

12. **Points.** (Obj. 4) Years ago, the Devons took out a 30-year mortgage on their vacation home. When they originally took out the loan, they paid the lender $24,000 in points. On September 1 of the current year, the Devons refinanced their $650,000 balance of the mortgage with another 30-year mortgage. To get a lower interest rate, the Devons paid the lender points totaling $13,000. At the time of the refinancing, the Devons had unamortized points from the first loan of $18,000. How much can the Devons deduct as points on their tax return for the current year?

13. **Investment Interest.** (Obj. 4) In 2014, the Edlins borrowed money to purchase stocks and taxable corporate bonds. During 2022, the Edlins paid $11,900 of interest in conjunction with this loan. Their investment income for 2022 consists of $5,000 of qualified dividend income, $2,400 of taxable interest income, and $3,300 of net capital gain. How much of the $11,900 can the Edlins deduct on their 2022 Schedule A? Be sure to discuss all options available to the Edlins.

14. **Interest Deduction.** (Obj. 4) Indicate the correct treatment for each listed item by placing an **X** in the appropriate column.

Description	Deductible	Nondeductible
a. Al took out a $20,000 home equity loan to buy an airplane. Al paid interest of $1,750.	_____	_____
b. Betty paid $300 in credit card interest, including $30 in late fees.	_____	_____
c. Charles borrowed $50,000 to buy City of Austin bonds. The interest he paid was $3,000. His net investment interest income was $2,500.	_____	_____
d. David constructed a new home for $175,000. He borrowed $157,500 as a construction loan. The interest on the new mortgage was $8,500.	_____	_____
e. Ed paid $80 in interest on back state taxes due.	_____	_____
f. Fred took out a loan to buy a vacation home. The lender charged Fred $350 to process his loan.	_____	_____
g. Gabe borrowed $60,000 to buy corporate bonds. He paid $4,000 interest on this loan. The corporation paid Gabe $5,000 of interest.	_____	_____

15. **Interest Deduction.** (Obj. 4) The Greenfields' 2022 AGI is $98,500, which includes $620 of taxable interest income. They incurred the following interest expenses during the year.

Credit card interest	$ 79
Automobile loan interest (on their older car)	337
Mortgage interest on their main home prior to refinancing	6,300
Mortgage interest on their main home after refinancing	7,200
Points paid on main home refinancing ($190,000 × 3%)	5,700
Mortgage interest on vacation home	13,080
Investment interest expense on a loan to purchase corporate stocks	543
Investment interest expense on a loan to purchase tax-exempt bonds	381

The Greenfields originally paid $260,000 for their main home. At the beginning of 2022, the home was worth $300,000 and the balance on the mortgage on their main home was $138,000. On May 1, the Greenfields refinanced the mortgage on their main home with a $190,000, ten-year loan. They used the extra proceeds to buy a new car, take a vacation, and consolidate other loans. Compute the Greenfields' interest expense deduction on Schedule A.

16. **Charitable Contribution Deduction.** (Obj. 5) Place an **X** in the proper column to indicate whether each of the following gifts or other expenditures is (i) deductible as a charitable contribution, (ii) deductible but not as a charitable contribution, or (iii) not deductible. Assume that the taxpayer has a receipt from the charity for the donation.

Item	Deductible Contribution	Deductible, Not a Contribution	Not Deductible
a. Cash to American Red Cross	_____	_____	_____
b. Pledge to make a gift to one's church	_____	_____	_____
c. Auto expense of church employee	_____	_____	_____
d. Cash to Girl Scouts of America	_____	_____	_____
e. Inherited land to American Legion	_____	_____	_____
f. Cash to political party	_____	_____	_____
g. Cash to public library	_____	_____	_____
h. Clothing to Salvation Army	_____	_____	_____
i. Common stock to St. Mary's Church	_____	_____	_____
j. Cash to Brigham Young University	_____	_____	_____
k. U.S. bonds to Mayo Clinic	_____	_____	_____
l. Reading at The Braille Institute (value of services rendered, $35)	_____	_____	_____
m. Auto expense of a volunteer worker while running errands for a local food bank	_____	_____	_____

17. **Charitable Contribution—Benefit Event.** (Obj. 5) A professional concert is played for the benefit of the American Heart Association each year. The admission charge is $32 per ticket, which is also the usual admission price for a professional concert. One-half of the purchase price goes directly to the American Heart Association. Clark buys four tickets at a total cost of $128. Clark itemizes deductions.

a. How much can Clark deduct per ticket as a charitable contribution?

b. How would your answer to Part a. differ if Clark had no intention of going to the concert and in fact did not go, leaving the tickets unused?

c. How would your answer be different if Clark paid $32 for each ticket, when the usual admission charge per ticket was $20?

18. **Charitable Contribution Deduction.** (Obj. 5) Jeanne has AGI of $60,000. During the year the taxpayer makes the following contributions.

Item	FMV	Cost
Check to the Greek Orthodox Church		$4,000
Used clothing to Children's Hospital	$100	380
Cash to University of Cal State Fullerton		1,200
Check to Mayor Fred's election campaign		300
Used camping equipment to the Boy Scouts of America	300	1,200
Cash to homeless father for his children's clothing		150

a. Compute her charitable contribution deduction if she itemizes deductions.

b. Compute her charitable contribution deduction if she does **not** itemize deductions and the year is 2022.

c. Compute her charitable contribution deduction if she does **not** itemize deductions and the year is 2020 or 2021.

19. **Charitable Contribution—Appreciated Property.** (Obj. 5) Vic contributed land worth $190,000 to the City General Hospital. The land has been held for five years and had a basis of $72,000. His AGI is $389,200.

a. What amount can Vic deduct as a charitable gift, if the year is 2022?

b. What amount could Vic have deducted as a charitable gift, if the year was 2021?

c. What amount can Vic deduct in 2022 if the land had been held for eight months instead of five years?

20. **Charitable Contribution—Appreciated Property.** (Obj. 5) Tony has an AGI of $49,000 and donates common stock with a market value of $15,000 to an educational institution to be sold and used for scholarships. The basis in the stock is $3,575, and it was purchased six years ago.

    a. What amount may be claimed as an itemized deduction resulting from this contribution if the year is 2020?

    b. What amount may be claimed as an itemized deduction resulting from this contribution if the year is 2022?

    c. How would your answer to Part a. change if the stock had been purchased 6 months ago?

21. **Charitable Contributions.** (Obj. 5) Toni occasionally donates her services as an attorney to a qualified charitable organization. During the current year, Toni spent 45 hours working for the charity. Her normal billing rate is $250 an hour. Toni drove 115 miles going to and from the offices for the charity. She also spent $160 for supplies necessary in conjunction with providing her services. Compute Toni's charitable deduction.

22. **Casualty Loss.** (Obj. 6) The Wildes' home was damaged by a severe storm in 2022. The home had been purchased in 2000 for $73,000, excluding the cost of the land. The building's FMV just before the storm was $97,000, and its FMV after the storm was estimated at $79,000. The Wildes collected $15,000 in insurance proceeds, and their AGI is $22,000. This was their only casualty loss during the year.

    a. Determine the amount that the Wildes can report as a casualty loss deduction, assuming that the home is in a federally declared disaster area, and the year or years in which they can claim the deduction.

    b. Determine the amount that the Wildes can report as a casualty loss deduction, assuming that the home is not in a federally declared disaster area, and the year or years in which they can claim the deduction.

23. Itemized Deductions. (Obj. 1) State whether each of the following payments can be deducted as an itemized deduction on Schedule A by placing an "**X**" in the appropriate *Yes* or *No* column. Assume that the amount is within any limit that applies.

Item	Yes	No
a. Payment to a nursing home for a person with Alzheimer's:		
(1) Meals	——	——
(2) Lodging	——	——
(3) Nursing care	——	——
b. Interest on amounts borrowed to buy municipal bonds	——	——
c. Supplemental Medicare insurance premiums	——	——
d. Personal Credit card interest	——	——
e. Interest on a student loan	——	——
f. Canadian income taxes paid	——	——
g. Interest paid on past due state income taxes	——	——
h. Long-term care insurance premiums	——	——

24. Deductions. (Obj. 8) Use the knowledge you have acquired from Chapters 1 through 5 to identify each of the following expenditures as **(A)** deductible for AGI, **(B)** deductible from AGI, or **(C)** not deductible. Ignore any AGI limitations.

a. State inheritance taxes   _____

b. Safe deposit box rental (used to store stock investments)   _____

c. CPA examination registration fee   _____

d. IRS penalty for late filing   _____

e. Fee paid to an accountant to prepare the personal property tax return on rental property   _____

f. Loss on bookstore operations (Schedule C is used)   _____

g. Auto registration for business vehicle   _____

25. **Deductions.** (Obj. 8) Use the knowledge you have acquired from Chapters 1 through 5 to identify each of the following expenditures as **(A)** deductible for AGI, **(B)** deductible from AGI, or **(C)** not deductible. Ignore any AGI limitations.

   a.   Purchase of uniforms for work suitable for street wear   _____

   b.   Homeowner's insurance on the taxpayer's main home   _____

   c.   Union dues paid by a steelworker   _____

   d.   Unreimbursed employee business travel expense   _____

   e.   Mortgage interest on rental property   _____

   f.   Unreimbursed storm damage to trees in main home's yard in federally declared disaster area   _____

   g.   Loss on sale of the taxpayer's personal car not in federally declared disaster area   _____

   h.   Repairs to friend's car for damage caused when taxpayer's car hit friend's car   _____

26. **Deductions.** (Obj. 8) Use the knowledge you have acquired from Chapters 1 through 5 to identify each of the following expenditures as **(A)** deductible for AGI, **(B)** deductible from AGI, or **(C)** not deductible. Ignore any AGI limitations.

   a.   Loss on sale of stock held as an investment   _____

   b.   Interest on loan to pay for family vacation   _____

   c.   Interest on loan used to buy stock   _____

   d.   Depreciation on rental property   _____

   e.   Charitable contributions to a university   _____

   f.   Sole proprietor's cost for continuing education seminar   _____

   g.   Storm damage to rental property   _____

27. **Gambling Losses.** (Obj. 8) During the year, Mark won $1,400 from football bets. He lost $750 from basketball wagering. Mark also lost $1,150 at the track.

   a.   How do these gambling activities affect Mark's gross income and his deductible expenses?

   b.   Where would the appropriate income and expenses be entered on Mark's income tax return?

28. **Hobby Losses.** (Obj. 4) Russ is retired from his regular work and now spends his time painting landscapes in a studio set up in his home that he rents during the year. The studio occupies 12% of the living space in his home. During the year, Russ sold some of his paintings for the first time. Russ is not certain whether he is required to file a tax return and, if so, whether he will be required to pay any taxes on his painting as a business. The revenue from sales of paintings was $2,300. Russ's expenses for the year were as follows:

Rent payments	$12,000
Painting supplies	$1,750
Electricity for the home	$2,400
Gas heat for the home	$2,900

    a.   How much can Russ deduct of the above expenses if his painting activity is treated as a business? Show your calculations.

    b.   Same as in Part a., except that the painting activity is treated as a hobby.

    c.   Explain what Russ might do in the way of tax planning to further support a claim that his painting is a business activity.

29. **Total Itemized Deductions.** (Obj. 7 and 8)

    a.   Brian Pido (SSN 476-00-3477) is 42 years old and files his tax return as a single taxpayer. Brian's AGI is $173,702, including $15,000 of taxable interest. Brian has the following itemized deductions for 2022. Compute Brian's total itemized deductions and complete his Schedule A.

Amount paid to the state with 2021 income tax return	$ 425
Charitable contributions	5,000
Investment interest expense	12,000
Mortgage interest	11,880
Real estate taxes	6,898
State and local income taxes withheld from wages	3,583
Unreimbursed medical	3,200

    b.   Randy (SSN 937-00-8266) and Misty Moore file a joint tax return. Randy and Misty are ages 39 and 40, respectively. Their AGI for 2022 is $184,583, including $1,800 of taxable interest income. They report the following itemized deductions for 2022. Compute the Moores' total itemized deductions and complete their Schedule A.

Amount paid to the state with 2021 income tax return	$ 888
Charitable contributions	13,540
Investment interest expense	2,600
Mortgage interest	17,559
Real estate taxes	4,582
State and local income taxes withheld from wages	6,682
Unreimbursed medical	20,414

(Use for Problem 29.)

SCHEDULE A (Form 1040)	Itemized Deductions	OMB No. 1545-0074
Department of the Treasury Internal Revenue Service	Go to *www.irs.gov/ScheduleA* for instructions and the latest information. **Attach to Form 1040 or 1040-SR.** **Caution:** If you are claiming a net qualified disaster loss on Form 4684, see the instructions for line 16.	**2022** Attachment Sequence No. **07**

Name(s) shown on Form 1040 or 1040-SR | Your social security number

Medical and Dental Expenses	**Caution:** Do not include expenses reimbursed or paid by others.	
	1 Medical and dental expenses (see instructions)	**1**
	2 Enter amount from Form 1040 or 1040-SR, line 11 **2**	
	3 Multiply line 2 by 7.5% (0.075) **3**	
	4 Subtract line 3 from line 1. If line 3 is more than line 1, enter -0-	**4**
Taxes You Paid	**5** State and local taxes.	
	a State and local income taxes or general sales taxes. You may include either income taxes or general sales taxes on line 5a, but not both. If you elect to include general sales taxes instead of income taxes, check this box ☐	**5a**
	b State and local real estate taxes (see instructions)	**5b**
	c State and local personal property taxes	**5c**
	d Add lines 5a through 5c	**5d**
	e Enter the smaller of line 5d or $10,000 ($5,000 if married filing separately)	**5e**
	6 Other taxes. List type and amount: _____	**6**
	7 Add lines 5e and 6	**7**
Interest You Paid **Caution:** Your mortgage interest deduction may be limited. See instructions.	**8** Home mortgage interest and points. If you didn't use all of your home mortgage loan(s) to buy, build, or improve your home, see instructions and check this box . . . . ☐	
	a Home mortgage interest and points reported to you on Form 1098. See instructions if limited	**8a**
	b Home mortgage interest not reported to you on Form 1098. See instructions if limited. If paid to the person from whom you bought the home, see instructions and show that person's name, identifying no., and address . . . . _____ _____	**8b**
	c Points not reported to you on Form 1098. See instructions for special rules	**8c**
	d Reserved for future use	**8d**
	e Add lines 8a through 8c	**8e**
	9 Investment interest. Attach Form 4952 if required. See instructions .	**9**
	10 Add lines 8e and 9	**10**
Gifts to Charity **Caution:** If you made a gift and got a benefit for it, see instructions.	**11** Gifts by cash or check. If you made any gift of $250 or more, see instructions	**11**
	12 Other than by cash or check. If you made any gift of $250 or more, see instructions. You **must** attach Form 8283 if over $500. . . .	**12**
	13 Carryover from prior year	**13**
	14 Add lines 11 through 13	**14**
Casualty and Theft Losses	**15** Casualty and theft loss(es) from a federally declared disaster (other than net qualified disaster losses). Attach Form 4684 and enter the amount from line 18 of that form. See instructions	**15**
Other Itemized Deductions	**16** Other—from list in instructions. List type and amount: _____ _____	**16**
Total Itemized Deductions	**17** Add the amounts in the far right column for lines 4 through 16. Also, enter this amount on Form 1040 or 1040-SR, line 12	**17**
	18 If you elect to itemize deductions even though they are less than your standard deduction, check this box . . . . ☐	

For Paperwork Reduction Act Notice, see the Instructions for Form 1040.   Cat. No. 17145C   Schedule A (Form 1040) 2022

30. Internet Problem: Researching Instructions to Form 4684. (Obj. 6)

If a taxpayer experiences a loss from a deposit in a credit union that became financially insolvent, what options are available for recognizing this loss on the tax return?

Go to the IRS website. Locate the Instructions for Form 4684 and find the solution to the above question.

See Appendix A for instructions on use of the IRS website.

31. Internet Problem: Filling out Form 8283. (Obj. 5)

Jacob R. (SSN 846-00-7922) and Brenda Tyler made the following noncash contributions during 2022. On May 5, they donated two bags of clothing (consisting of 22 items) valued at $120. On July 8, they donated a TV worth $50. On October 5, they donated a 5-piece queen bedroom set valued at $440. All items were donated to Goodwill, Industries (147 W. 53rd Street, Mesa, AZ 85203). The Tylers used thrift store value to value their items.

Go to the IRS website and locate Form 8283, Noncash Charitable Contributions. Fill out Form 8283 for the Tylers that they will attach to their 2022 tax return.

See Appendix A for instructions on use of the IRS website.

32. Business Entity Problem: This problem is designed for those using the "business entity" approach. **The solution may require information from Chapters 14–16.**

a. A corporation has $350,000 of taxable income before consideration of charitable contributions. If the corporation donates $50,000 to a qualified charity, what amount can it deduct if the current year is 2022?

b. By what date must the corporation make its donation?

c. What amount can it deduct if the current year is 2021?

d. Same as in Part a., except that the business is an S corporation.

e. Same as in Part a., except that the business is a partnership.

COMPREHENSIVE PROBLEMS

 33. Schedule A. (Obj. 8)

a. Marcus (SSN 397-00-8399) and Debra Cross own three homes. Information regarding the amount of acquisition debt, as well as interest and taxes paid on each home during the year is as follows.

	Acquisition Debt	Interest Paid	Taxes Paid
Main home	$240,000	$18,330	$2,400
Vacation home #1	300,000	18,583	2,800
Vacation home #2	350,000	19,044	3,400

During 2022, the Crosses made cash gifts totaling $12,000 to various qualified public charities. The Crosses gifted 150 shares of stock to their church during 2022. They purchased 100 shares of the stock for $10 a share in 2010. The other 50 shares were purchased earlier in 2022 for $18 a share. At the time the shares were donated to the church, their fair market value was $24 a share. The Crosses' only other itemized deductions were $4,240 that their employers withheld from their paychecks for state income taxes. The Crosses' AGI is $216,952. Compute the Crosses' total itemized deductions and prepare their Schedule A.

b. Maurice Prior (SSN 839-00-9222) is married, but files separately from his spouse. Below is a summary of expenditures that Maurice has made. In addition, Maurice's employer withheld $3,967 and $13,550 in state and federal income taxes in 2022. His employer also withheld $6,300 in social security and Medicare taxes. Maurice's AGI is $167,667. Maurice made the following quarterly estimated payments taxes for 2021 and 2022.

Date Paid	Amount Paid to the State	Amount Paid to the IRS
April 15, 2021	$ 700	$3,500
June 15, 2021	700	3,500
September 15, 2021	800	3,500
January 15, 2022	800	3,500
April 15, 2022	1,200	5,000
June 15, 2022	1,200	5,000
September 15, 2022	1,200	5,000
January 15, 2023	1,200	5,000

Other taxes Maurice paid during 2022 include $3,290 in real estate taxes; $296 for ad valorem taxes on his boat; and $800 for a special assessment for a new sidewalk. Maurice paid home mortgage interest totaling $16,940 during 2022, and he gave cash totaling $1,500 to his church. Compute Maurice's total itemized deductions and prepare his Schedule A.

c. Daniel Saad (SSN 432-00-7809) and his wife Marion (ages 52 and 51, respectively) file a joint return. Their 2022 AGI is $167,900, consisting of wages of $164,200 and interest income of $3,700. The Saads put together the following list of expenses. Compute the Saads' total itemized deductions and prepare their Schedule A.

Unreimbursed medical expenses	$27,743
Jacuzzi for John's aching back (not prescribed)	2,500
Real estate taxes	4,400
Homeowners association assessment for street repairs	1,200
State and local income taxes withheld	4,800
Federal income tax	22,300
General sales tax	785
Mortgage interest	15,200
Credit card interest	945
Investment interest	5,000
Charitable contributions (cash)	6,400
Uninsured damage to auto from accident	3,300

d. Charlie P. (SSN 367-00-9403) and Maggie S. Church (ages 32 and 33, respectively) file a joint tax return. Their AGI is $74,105. The Churchs' expenses follow. Unless otherwise stated, they have canceled checks or receipts for each item. Prepare the Churchs' Schedule A.

Mortgage interest on main home	$14,200
Cash contributions to church	2,500
Hunting license	90
Marriage license	16
Cash to homeless person begging for money (no receipt)	50
Cash contribution to American Red Cross	300
Paid to United Way (no canceled check or receipt)	310
Property tax on main home	6,450
R.K. Snell, physician (unreimbursed by insurance)	2,980
E.I. Newman, dentist (unreimbursed by insurance)	1,290
G.R. Gross, veterinarian (unreimbursed by insurance)	125
Medical insurance premiums	2,556
Safe deposit box rental (storing securities)	22
Paid to Evanston Drug for over-the-counter medications	160
State income taxes withheld	3,890

e. Roberto (SSN 123-00-6789) and Lena Gomez, both engineers, and both 53 years old, file a joint return reporting AGI of $383,531. This amount includes $326,500 in wages, $38,051 in interest income, and $18,980 in nonqualified dividends. They have receipts for the following deductions.

Federal income tax withholding	$72,000
Unreimbursed medical expenses	$12,000
Unreimbursed employee job expenses	10,610
State income taxes	14,500
Real estate taxes on main home	8,000
Mortgage interest on main home	17,000
Investment interest expense	2,000
Investment fees and expenses	2,800
Tax preparation fees	550
Charitable contributions (all cash)	6,400

a. Prepare the Gomezes' Schedule A.

b. Assuming Roberto and Lena claim their 10-year-old son Leon as a dependent, compute the Gomezes' taxable income. They resided in the U.S. for the entire year.

(Use for Problem 33.)

SCHEDULE A **(Form 1040)** Department of the Treasury Internal Revenue Service	**Itemized Deductions** Go to *www.irs.gov/ScheduleA* for instructions and the latest information. **Attach to Form 1040 or 1040-SR.** **Caution:** If you are claiming a net qualified disaster loss on Form 4684, see the instructions for line 16.	OMB No. 1545-0074 **2022** Attachment Sequence No. **07**

Name(s) shown on Form 1040 or 1040-SR | Your social security number

Medical and Dental Expenses

Caution: Do not include expenses reimbursed or paid by others.

1 Medical and dental expenses (see instructions) **1**

2 Enter amount from Form 1040 or 1040-SR, line 11 | **2**

3 Multiply line 2 by 7.5% (0.075) **3**

4 Subtract line 3 from line 1. If line 3 is more than line 1, enter -0- **4**

Taxes You Paid

5 State and local taxes.

a State and local income taxes or general sales taxes. You may include either income taxes or general sales taxes on line 5a, but not both. If you elect to include general sales taxes instead of income taxes, check this box . . . . ☐ **5a**

b State and local real estate taxes (see instructions) **5b**

c State and local personal property taxes **5c**

d Add lines 5a through 5c **5d**

e Enter the smaller of line 5d or $10,000 ($5,000 if married filing separately) **5e**

6 Other taxes. List type and amount: _____

_____ **6**

7 Add lines 5e and 6 . . . . **7**

Interest You Paid

Caution: Your mortgage interest deduction may be limited. See instructions.

8 Home mortgage interest and points. If you didn't use all of your home mortgage loan(s) to buy, build, or improve your home, see instructions and check this box . . . . ☐

a Home mortgage interest and points reported to you on Form 1098. See instructions if limited **8a**

b Home mortgage interest not reported to you on Form 1098. See instructions if limited. If paid to the person from whom you bought the home, see instructions and show that person's name, identifying no., and address **8b**

_____

_____

c Points not reported to you on Form 1098. See instructions for special rules **8c**

d Reserved for future use **8d**

e Add lines 8a through 8c **8e**

9 Investment interest. Attach Form 4952 if required. See instructions . **9**

10 Add lines 8e and 9 . . . . **10**

Gifts to Charity

Caution: If you made a gift and got a benefit for it, see instructions.

11 Gifts by cash or check. If you made any gift of $250 or more, see instructions **11**

12 Other than by cash or check. If you made any gift of $250 or more, see instructions. You **must** attach Form 8283 if over $500. . . . . **12**

13 Carryover from prior year **13**

14 Add lines 11 through 13 . . . . **14**

Casualty and Theft Losses

15 Casualty and theft loss(es) from a federally declared disaster (other than net qualified disaster losses). Attach Form 4684 and enter the amount from line 18 of that form. See instructions **15**

Other Itemized Deductions

16 Other—from list in instructions. List type and amount: _____

_____ **16**

Total Itemized Deductions

17 Add the amounts in the far right column for lines 4 through 16. Also, enter this amount on Form 1040 or 1040-SR, line 12 . . . . **17**

18 If you elect to itemize deductions even though they are less than your standard deduction, check this box . . . . ☐

For Paperwork Reduction Act Notice, see the Instructions for Form 1040. | Cat. No. 17145C | Schedule A (Form 1040) 2022

CUMULATIVE PROBLEM (CHAPTERS 1–5)

Use the following information to prepare the joint income tax return of Frank and Sandra Anderson. Use Form 1040, Schedule 1, Schedule 3, Schedule A, Form 2441, and Schedule 8812. All parties sign and date the return on April 1, 2023. This problem is suitable for manual preparation or computer software application.

Frank A. (SSN 811-00-3717) and Sandra K. (SSN 820-00-0231) Anderson (ages 48 and 51, respectively) reside at 2121 Century Avenue, Middleton, CA 92657, with their three children whom they fully support: Mandy (age 9, SSN 998-00-5246), Charles (age 11, SSN 998-00-5247), and Carol (age 14, SSN 998-00-1827).

The Andersons file a joint return, and neither elects to have $3 go to the Presidential election campaign fund. Frank is employed as a customer service representative. Sandra is employed as a computer operator. Details of their salaries and withholdings, are as follows:

	Gross Wages	State Income Tax Withheld	Federal Income Tax Withheld	Social Security Tax Withheld	Medicare Tax Withheld
Frank	$66,500	$4,792	$6,700	$4,123	$964
Sandra	40,343	3,087	2,980	2,501	585

Frank's employer provides him with full family health care coverage as a tax-free employee benefit. Part of Frank's compensation package also includes group-term life insurance equal to 75% of his annual salary. The cost to the company for the premium was $240.

In August, Sandra earned $400 of interest when she cashed in a certificate of deposit from State Bank. The Middleton Farmers Bank credited $300 of interest to the Andersons' joint savings account during the year. The Andersons overpaid their 2021 state income taxes by $142. They received their refund in June. The Andersons' itemized deductions exceeded the standard deduction by $2,300 last year.

Since they both work outside the home, they are unable to be there when their children return home from school. This year the Andersons paid a neighbor, Gloria Dryden (SSN 992-00-4270), $4,100 to care for Mandy and Charles in her home after school hours and during the summer vacation period while the Andersons were at work. Gloria's address is 2132 Century Avenue, Middleton, CA 92657.

During the year, Sandra received unemployment compensation of $6,000. Frank is covered by a qualified pension plan at work; Sandra is not. The Andersons are interested in contributing to their respective traditional IRAs the maximum that they can deduct on their 2022 tax return. Both contributions take place before April 15, 2023.

Cancelled checks, receipts, and paid bills support the following expenditures:

Orlo T. Miller, M.D. (not covered by insurance)	$ 818
Qualified stop smoking program for Sandra	175
Alex B. Kramer, D.V.M. (treatment of Fritz, the Andersons' dog)	168
Life insurance premiums on Frank's life (Sandra is the beneficiary)	1,200
Kathryn R. Smith, dentist (not covered by insurance)	459
Weight loss program for Frank (cosmetic purposes)	180
Martin R. Jones, optometrist (not covered by insurance)	50
Eyeglasses for Mandy (not covered by insurance)	175
Driver's license renewal for Sandra	32
Fishing license for Frank	12
Credit card interest	275
Home mortgage interest on the main home	15,690
Real estate taxes on the main home	6,851
Trash pickup fees	120
Home repairs and improvements	620
Homeowner's insurance	500
General sales taxes paid during the year	2,572
State excise taxes	98
Cash gift to First Unity Church (with receipt)	2,200
Value of Frank's time volunteered to the Girl Scouts	300
Political contributions	50
Bingo and lottery tickets	260
Rental for safe deposit box to store investment items	67
Legal fees paid for preparation of the Andersons' personal wills	875

In addition, on April 24, 2022, the Andersons paid $600 to Homer P. Gill for preparation of their 2021 tax return.

When Frank's father died on Christmas Day, Frank inherited his father's savings account. The account balance was $20,000.

In March, Sandra's best friend, Nancy, moved to Sweden. Nancy's 17-year-old daughter, Inga, stayed with the Andersons for the rest of the year. Inga had a part-time job after school and earned $4,120. The Andersons provided over half of Inga's support.

(Use for Cumulative Problem.)

Form 1040

Department of the Treasury—Internal Revenue Service

U.S. Individual Income Tax Return | **2022** | OMB No. 1545-0074 | IRS Use Only—Do not write or staple in this space.

Filing Status
Check only one box.

☐ Single ☐ Married filing jointly ☐ Married filing separately (MFS) ☐ Head of household (HOH) ☐ Qualifying widow(er) (QW)

If you checked the MFS box, enter the name of your spouse. If you checked the HOH or QW box, enter the child's name if the qualifying person is a child but not your dependent:

Your first name and middle initial	Last name	Your social security number

If joint return, spouse's first name and middle initial	Last name	Spouse's social security number

Home address (number and street). If you have a P.O. box, see instructions.	Apt. no.

Presidential Election Campaign
Check here if you, or your spouse if filing jointly, want $3 to go to this fund. Checking a box below will not change your tax or refund.
☐ You ☐ Spouse

City, town, or post office. If you have a foreign address, also complete spaces below.	State	ZIP code

Foreign country name	Foreign province/state/county	Foreign postal code

At any time during 2022, did you: (a) receive (as a reward, award, or compensation); or (b) sell, exchange, gift, or otherwise dispose of a digital asset (or a financial interest in a digital asset)? (See instructions.) ☐ Yes ☐ No

Standard Deduction

Someone can claim: ☐ You as a dependent ☐ Your spouse as a dependent

☐ Spouse itemizes on a separate return or you were a dual-status alien

Age/Blindness **You:** ☐ Were born before January 2, 1958 ☐ Are blind **Spouse:** ☐ Was born before January 2, 1958 ☐ Is blind

Dependents (see instructions):

If more than four dependents, see instructions and check here . . ☐

(1) First name Last name	(2) Social security number	(3) Relationship to you	(4) Check the box if qualifies for (see instructions):	
			Child tax credit	Credit for other dependents
			☐	☐
			☐	☐
			☐	☐
			☐	☐

Income

Attach Form(s) W-2 here. Also attach Forms W-2G and 1099-R if tax was withheld.

If you did not get a Form W-2, see instructions.

Attach Sch. B if required.

Standard Deduction for—
• Single or Married filing separately, $12,950
• Married filing jointly or Qualifying widow(er), $25,900
• Head of household, $19,400
• If you checked any box under *Standard Deduction,* see instructions.

1a	Total amount from Form(s) W-2, box 1 (see instructions)			**1a**	
b	Household employee wages not reported on Form(s) W-2			**1b**	
c	Tip income not reported on line 1a (see instructions)			**1c**	
d	Medicaid waiver payments not reported on Form(s) W-2 (see instructions)			**1d**	
e	Taxable dependent care benefits from Form 2441, line 26			**1e**	
f	Employer-provided adoption benefits from Form 8839, line 29			**1f**	
g	Wages from Form 8919, line 6			**1g**	
h	Other earned income (see instructions)			**1h**	
i	Nontaxable combat pay election (see instructions)	**1i**			
z	Add lines 1a through 1h			**1z**	
2a	Tax-exempt interest	**2a**	**b** Taxable interest	**2b**	
3a	Qualified dividends	**3a**	**b** Ordinary dividends	**3b**	
4a	IRA distributions	**4a**	**b** Taxable amount	**4b**	
5a	Pensions and annuities	**5a**	**b** Taxable amount	**5b**	
6a	Social security benefits	**6a**	**b** Taxable amount	**6b**	
c	If you elect to use the lump-sum election method, check here (see instructions) ☐				
7	Capital gain or (loss). Attach Schedule D if required. If not required, check here ☐			**7**	
8	Other income from Schedule 1, line 10			**8**	
9	Add lines 1z, 2b, 3b, 4b, 5b, 6b, 7, and 8. This is your **total income**			**9**	
10	Adjustments to income from Schedule 1, line 26			**10**	
11	Subtract line 10 from line 9. This is your **adjusted gross income**			**11**	
12	**Standard deduction or itemized deductions** (from Schedule A)			**12**	
13	Qualified business income deduction from Form 8995 or Form 8995-A			**13**	
14	Add lines 12 and 13			**14**	
15	Subtract line 14 from line 11. If zero or less, enter -0-. This is your **taxable income**			**15**	

For Disclosure, Privacy Act, and Paperwork Reduction Act Notice, see separate instructions. | Cat. No. 11320B | Form **1040** (2022)

(Use for Cumulative Problem.)

Form 1040 (2022)			Page **2**

Tax and Credits	16	**Tax** (see instructions). Check if any from Form(s): **1** ☐ 8814 **2** ☐ 4972 **3** ☐ _____	16	
	17	Amount from Schedule 2, line 3	17	
	18	Add lines 16 and 17	18	
	19	Child tax credit or credit for other dependents from Schedule 8812	19	
	20	Amount from Schedule 3, line 8	20	
	21	Add lines 19 and 20	21	
	22	Subtract line 21 from line 18. If zero or less, enter -0-	22	
	23	Other taxes, including self-employment tax, from Schedule 2, line 21	23	
	24	Add lines 22 and 23. This is your **total tax**	24	
Payments	25	Federal income tax withheld from:		
	a	Form(s) W-2	25a	
	b	Form(s) 1099	25b	
	c	Other forms (see instructions)	25c	
	d	Add lines 25a through 25c	25d	
If you have a qualifying child, attach Sch. EIC.	26	2022 estimated tax payments and amount applied from 2021 return	26	
	27	Earned income credit (EIC)	27	
	28	Additional child tax credit from Schedule 8812	28	
	29	American opportunity credit from Form 8863, line 8	29	
	30	Reserved for future use	30	
	31	Amount from Schedule 3, line 15	31	
	32	Add lines 27, 28, 29, and 31. These are your **total other payments and refundable credits**	32	
	33	Add lines 25d, 26, and 32. These are your **total payments**	33	
Refund	34	If line 33 is more than line 24, subtract line 24 from line 33. This is the amount you **overpaid**	34	
	35a	Amount of line 34 you want **refunded to you**. If Form 8888 is attached, check here ☐	35a	
Direct deposit? See instructions.	b	Routing number	**c** Type: ☐ Checking ☐ Savings	
	d	Account number		
	36	Amount of line 34 you want **applied to your 2023 estimated tax**	36	
Amount You Owe	37	Subtract line 33 from line 24. This is the **amount you owe**. For details on how to pay, go to *www.irs.gov/Payments* or see instructions	37	
	38	Estimated tax penalty (see instructions)	38	

Third Party Designee	Do you want to allow another person to discuss this return with the IRS? See instructions	☐ **Yes.** Complete below. ☐ **No**
	Designee's name	Phone no.	Personal identification number (PIN)

Sign Here	Under penalties of perjury, I declare that I have examined this return and accompanying schedules and statements, and to the best of my knowledge and belief, they are true, correct, and complete. Declaration of preparer (other than taxpayer) is based on all information of which preparer has any knowledge.			
	Your signature	Date	Your occupation	If the IRS sent you an Identity Protection PIN, enter it here (see inst.)
Joint return? See instructions. Keep a copy for your records.	Spouse's signature. If a joint return, **both** must sign.	Date	Spouse's occupation	If the IRS sent your spouse an Identity Protection PIN, enter it here (see inst.)
	Phone no.		Email address	

Paid Preparer Use Only	Preparer's name	Preparer's signature		Date	PTIN	Check if: ☐ Self-employed
	Firm's name					Phone no.
	Firm's address					Firm's EIN

Go to *www.irs.gov/Form1040* for instructions and the latest information. Form **1040** (2022)

(Use for Cumulative Problem.)

SCHEDULE 1 (Form 1040)	Additional Income and Adjustments to Income	OMB No. 1545-0074
Department of the Treasury Internal Revenue Service	Attach to Form 1040, 1040-SR, or 1040-NR. Go to *www.irs.gov/Form1040* for instructions and the latest information.	**2022** Attachment Sequence No. **01**

Name(s) shown on Form 1040, 1040-SR, or 1040-NR	Your social security number

Part I   Additional Income

1	Taxable refunds, credits, or offsets of state and local income taxes	**1**	
2a	Alimony received	**2a**	
b	Date of original divorce or separation agreement (see instructions):		
3	Business income or (loss). Attach Schedule C	**3**	
4	Other gains or (losses). Attach Form 4797	**4**	
5	Rental real estate, royalties, partnerships, S corporations, trusts, etc. Attach Schedule E	**5**	
6	Farm income or (loss). Attach Schedule F	**6**	
7	Unemployment compensation	**7**	
8	Other income:		
a	Net operating loss	**8a** ( )	
b	Gambling	**8b**	
c	Cancellation of debt	**8c**	
d	Foreign earned income exclusion from Form 2555	**8d** ( )	
e	Income from Form 8853	**8e**	
f	Income from Form 8889	**8f**	
g	Alaska Permanent Fund dividends	**8g**	
h	Jury duty pay	**8h**	
i	Prizes and awards	**8i**	
j	Activity not engaged in for profit income	**8j**	
k	Stock options	**8k**	
l	Income from the rental of personal property if you engaged in the rental for profit but were not in the business of renting such property . . .	**8l**	
m	Olympic and Paralympic medals and USOC prize money (see instructions)	**8m**	
n	Section 951(a) inclusion (see instructions)	**8n**	
o	Section 951A(a) inclusion (see instructions)	**8o**	
p	Section 461(l) excess business loss adjustment	**8p**	
q	Taxable distributions from an ABLE account (see instructions) . . .	**8q**	
r	Scholarship and fellowship grants not reported on Form W-2 . . .	**8r**	
s	Nontaxable amount of Medicaid waiver payments included on Form 1040, line 1a or 1d	**8s** ( )	
t	Pension or annuity from a nonqualifed deferred compensation plan or a nongovernmental section 457 plan	**8t**	
u	Wages earned while incarcerated	**8u**	
z	Other income. List type and amount: _____ _____	**8z**	
9	Total other income. Add lines 8a through 8z	**9**	
10	Combine lines 1 through 7 and 9. Enter here and on Form 1040, 1040-SR, or 1040-NR, line 8	**10**	

For Paperwork Reduction Act Notice, see your tax return instructions.   Cat. No. 71479F   Schedule 1 (Form 1040) 2022

(Use for Cumulative Problem.)

Schedule 1 (Form 1040) 2022   Page **2**

Part II Adjustments to Income

11	Educator expenses	**11**
12	Certain business expenses of reservists, performing artists, and fee-basis government officials. Attach Form 2106	**12**
13	Health savings account deduction. Attach Form 8889	**13**
14	Moving expenses for members of the Armed Forces. Attach Form 3903	**14**
15	Deductible part of self-employment tax. Attach Schedule SE	**15**
16	Self-employed SEP, SIMPLE, and qualified plans	**16**
17	Self-employed health insurance deduction	**17**
18	Penalty on early withdrawal of savings	**18**
19a	Alimony paid	**19a**
b	Recipient's SSN	
c	Date of original divorce or separation agreement (see instructions): _____	
20	IRA deduction	**20**
21	Student loan interest deduction	**21**
22	Reserved for future use	**22**
23	Archer MSA deduction	**23**
24	Other adjustments:	
a	Jury duty pay (see instructions)	**24a**
b	Deductible expenses related to income reported on line 8l from the rental of personal property engaged in for profit	**24b**
c	Nontaxable amount of the value of Olympic and Paralympic medals and USOC prize money reported on line 8m	**24c**
d	Reforestation amortization and expenses	**24d**
e	Repayment of supplemental unemployment benefits under the Trade Act of 1974	**24e**
f	Contributions to section 501(c)(18)(D) pension plans	**24f**
g	Contributions by certain chaplains to section 403(b) plans	**24g**
h	Attorney fees and court costs for actions involving certain unlawful discrimination claims (see instructions)	**24h**
i	Attorney fees and court costs you paid in connection with an award from the IRS for information you provided that helped the IRS detect tax law violations	**24i**
j	Housing deduction from Form 2555	**24j**
k	Excess deductions of section 67(e) expenses from Schedule K-1 (Form 1041)	**24k**
z	Other adjustments. List type and amount: _____	**24z**
25	Total other adjustments. Add lines 24a through 24z	**25**
26	Add lines 11 through 23 and 25. These are your **adjustments to income**. Enter here and on Form 1040 or 1040-SR, line 10, or Form 1040-NR, line 10a	**26**

Schedule 1 (Form 1040) 2022

(Use for Cumulative Problem.)

SCHEDULE 3 (Form 1040)	**Additional Credits and Payments**	OMB No. 1545-0074
Department of the Treasury Internal Revenue Service	Attach to Form 1040, 1040-SR, or 1040-NR. Go to *www.irs.gov/Form1040* for instructions and the latest information.	2022 Attachment Sequence No. 03

Name(s) shown on Form 1040, 1040-SR, or 1040-NR | Your social security number

Part I   Nonrefundable Credits

1	Foreign tax credit. Attach Form 1116 if required	1
2	Credit for child and dependent care expenses from Form 2441, line 11. Attach Form 2441	2
3	Education credits from Form 8863, line 19	3
4	Retirement savings contributions credit. Attach Form 8880	4
5	Residential energy credits. Attach Form 5695	5
6	Other nonrefundable credits:	
a	General business credit. Attach Form 3800	6a
b	Credit for prior year minimum tax. Attach Form 8801	6b
c	Adoption credit. Attach Form 8839	6c
d	Credit for the elderly or disabled. Attach Schedule R	6d
e	Alternative motor vehicle credit. Attach Form 8910	6e
f	Qualified plug-in motor vehicle credit. Attach Form 8936	6f
g	Mortgage interest credit. Attach Form 8396	6g
h	District of Columbia first-time homebuyer credit. Attach Form 8859	6h
i	Qualified electric vehicle credit. Attach Form 8834	6i
j	Reserved for future use	6j
k	Credit to holders of tax credit bonds. Attach Form 8912	6k
l	Amount on Form 8978, line 14. See instructions	6l
z	Other nonrefundable credits. List type and amount:	6z
7	Total other nonrefundable credits. Add lines 6a through 6z	7
8	Add lines 1 through 5 and 7. Enter here and on Form 1040, 1040-SR, or 1040-NR, line 20	8

(continued on page 2)

For Paperwork Reduction Act Notice, see your tax return instructions.   Cat. No. 71480G   Schedule 3 (Form 1040) 2022

(Use for Cumulative Problem.)

SCHEDULE 8812 (Form 1040)	Credits for Qualifying Children and Other Dependents	OMB No. 1545-0074
	Attach to Form 1040, 1040-SR, or 1040-NR.	**2022**
Department of the Treasury Internal Revenue Service	Go to *www.irs.gov/Schedule8812* for instructions and the latest information.	Attachment Sequence No. **47**

Name(s) shown on return	Your social security number

Part I   Child Tax Credit and Credit for Other Dependents

1	Enter the amount from line 11 of your Form 1040, 1040-SR, or 1040-NR		**1**	
2a	Enter income from Puerto Rico that you excluded	**2a**		
b	Enter the amounts from lines 45 and 50 of your Form 2555	**2b**		
c	Enter the amount from line 15 of your Form 4563	**2c**		
d	Add lines 2a through 2c		**2d**	
3	Add lines 1 and 2d		**3**	
4	Number of qualifying children under age 17 with the required social security number	**4**		
5	Multiply line 4 by $2,000		**5**	
6	Number of other dependents, including any qualifying children who are not under age 17 or who do not have the required social security number	**6**		
	Caution: Do not include yourself, your spouse, or anyone who is not a U.S. citizen, U.S. national, or U.S. resident alien. Also, do not include anyone you included on line 4.			
7	Multiply line 6 by $500		**7**	
8	Add lines 5 and 7		**8**	
9	Enter the amount shown below for your filing status. • Married filing jointly—$400,000 • All other filing statuses—$200,000		**9**	
10	Subtract line 9 from line 3. • If zero or less, enter -0-. • If more than zero and not a multiple of $1,000, enter the next multiple of $1,000. For example, if the result is $425, enter $1,000; if the result is $1,025, enter $2,000, etc.		**10**	
11	Multiply line 10 by 5% (0.05)		**11**	
12	Is the amount on line 8 more than the amount on line 11?		**12**	
	☐ **No. STOP.** You cannot take the child tax credit, credit for other dependents, or additional child tax credit. Skip Parts II-A and II-B. Enter -0- on lines 14 and 27. ☐ **Yes.** Subtract line 11 from line 8. Enter the result.			
13	Enter the amount from the **Credit Limit Worksheet A**		**13**	
14	Enter the smaller of line 12 or 13. **This is your child tax credit and credit for other dependents** Enter this amount on Form 1040, 1040-SR, or 1040-NR, line 19.		**14**	

If the amount on line 12 is more than the amount on line 14, you may be able to take the **additional child tax credit** on Form 1040, 1040-SR, or 1040-NR, line 28. Complete your Form 1040, 1040-SR, or 1040-NR through line 27 (also complete Schedule 3, line 11) before completing Part II-A.

For Paperwork Reduction Act Notice, see your tax return instructions.	Cat. No. 59761M	Schedule 8812 (Form 1040) 2022

(Use for Cumulative Problem.)

SCHEDULE A (Form 1040) Department of the Treasury Internal Revenue Service	**Itemized Deductions** Go to *www.irs.gov/ScheduleA* for instructions and the latest information. **Attach to Form 1040 or 1040-SR.** **Caution:** If you are claiming a net qualified disaster loss on Form 4684, see the instructions for line 16.	OMB No. 1545-0074 20**22** Attachment Sequence No. **07**

Name(s) shown on Form 1040 or 1040-SR | Your social security number

Medical and Dental Expenses			
	Caution: Do not include expenses reimbursed or paid by others.		
	1 Medical and dental expenses (see instructions)	**1**	
	2 Enter amount from Form 1040 or 1040-SR, line 11 **2**		
	3 Multiply line 2 by 7.5% (0.075)	**3**	
	4 Subtract line 3 from line 1. If line 3 is more than line 1, enter -0-		**4**

Taxes You Paid			
	5 State and local taxes.		
	a State and local income taxes or general sales taxes. You may include either income taxes or general sales taxes on line 5a, but not both. If you elect to include general sales taxes instead of income taxes, check this box ☐	**5a**	
	b State and local real estate taxes (see instructions)	**5b**	
	c State and local personal property taxes	**5c**	
	d Add lines 5a through 5c	**5d**	
	e Enter the smaller of line 5d or $10,000 ($5,000 if married filing separately)	**5e**	
	6 Other taxes. List type and amount: _____	**6**	
	7 Add lines 5e and 6		**7**

Interest You Paid			
Caution: Your mortgage interest deduction may be limited. See instructions.	**8** Home mortgage interest and points. If you didn't use all of your home mortgage loan(s) to buy, build, or improve your home, see instructions and check this box ☐		
	a Home mortgage interest and points reported to you on Form 1098. See instructions if limited	**8a**	
	b Home mortgage interest not reported to you on Form 1098. See instructions if limited. If paid to the person from whom you bought the home, see instructions and show that person's name, identifying no., and address _____	**8b**	
	c Points not reported to you on Form 1098. See instructions for special rules	**8c**	
	d Reserved for future use	**8d**	
	e Add lines 8a through 8c	**8e**	
	9 Investment interest. Attach Form 4952 if required. See instructions	**9**	
	10 Add lines 8e and 9		**10**

Gifts to Charity			
Caution: If you made a gift and got a benefit for it, see instructions.	**11** Gifts by cash or check. If you made any gift of $250 or more, see instructions	**11**	
	12 Other than by cash or check. If you made any gift of $250 or more, see instructions. You **must** attach Form 8283 if over $500.	**12**	
	13 Carryover from prior year	**13**	
	14 Add lines 11 through 13		**14**

Casualty and Theft Losses			
	15 Casualty and theft loss(es) from a federally declared disaster (other than net qualified disaster losses). Attach Form 4684 and enter the amount from line 18 of that form. See instructions		**15**

Other Itemized Deductions		
	16 Other—from list in instructions. List type and amount: _____	**16**

Total Itemized Deductions		
	17 Add the amounts in the far right column for lines 4 through 16. Also, enter this amount on Form 1040 or 1040-SR, line 12	**17**
	18 If you elect to itemize deductions even though they are less than your standard deduction, check this box ☐	

For Paperwork Reduction Act Notice, see the Instructions for Form 1040.	Cat. No. 17145C	Schedule A (Form 1040) 2022

(Use for Cumulative Problem.)

Form 2441

Department of the Treasury
Internal Revenue Service

Child and Dependent Care Expenses

Attach to Form 1040, 1040-SR, or 1040-NR.
Go to *www.irs.gov/Form2441* for instructions and the latest information.

OMB No. 1545-0074

2022

Attachment
Sequence No. **21**

Name(s) shown on return

Your social security number

A You can't claim a credit for child and dependent care expenses if your filing status is married filing separately unless you meet the requirements listed in the instructions under *Married Persons Filing Separately*. If you meet these requirements, check this box . . ☐

B If you or your spouse was a student or was disabled during 2022 and you're entering deemed income of $250 or $500 a month on Form 2441 based on the income rules listed in the instructions under *If You or Your Spouse Was a Student or Disabled*, check this box . ☐

Part I **Persons or Organizations Who Provided the Care**—You **must** complete this part.
If you have more than three care providers, see the instructions and check this box . . . . ☐

1 (a) Care provider's name	(b) Address (number, street, apt. no., city, state, and ZIP code)	(c) Identifying number (SSN or EIN)	(d) Was the care provider your household employee in 2022? For example, this generally includes nannies but not daycare centers. (see instructions)	(e) Amount paid (see instructions)
			☐ Yes ☐ No	
			☐ Yes ☐ No	
			☐ Yes ☐ No	

Did you receive **dependent care benefits**?

— **No** — Complete only Part II below.
— **Yes** — Complete Part III on page 2 next.

Caution: If the care provider is your household employee, you may owe employment taxes. For details, see the Instructions for Schedule H (Form 1040). If you incurred care expenses in 2022 but didn't pay them until 2023, or if you prepaid in 2022 for care to be provided in 2023, don't include these expenses in column (d) of line 2 for 2022. See the instructions.

Part II **Credit for Child and Dependent Care Expenses**

2 Information about your **qualifying person(s)**. If you have more than three qualifying persons, see the instructions and check this box ☐

(a) Qualifying person's name First / Last	(b) Qualifying person's social security number	(c) Check here if the qualifying person was over age 12 and was disabled. (see instructions)	(d) Qualified expenses you incurred and paid in 2022 for the person listed in column (a)
		☐	
		☐	
		☐	

3	Add the amounts in column (d) of line 2. **Don't** enter more than $3,000 if you had one qualifying person or $6,000 if you had two or more persons. If you completed Part III, enter the amount from line 31	**3**	
4	Enter your **earned income**. See instructions	**4**	
5	If married filing jointly, enter your spouse's earned income (if you or your spouse was a student or was disabled, see the instructions); **all others**, enter the amount from line 4	**5**	
6	Enter the **smallest** of line 3, 4, or 5	**6**	
7	Enter the amount from Form 1040, 1040-SR, or 1040-NR, line 11 . . .	**7**			
8	Enter on line 8 the decimal amount shown below that applies to the amount on line 7.		

If line 7 is: Over	But not over	Decimal amount is	If line 7 is: Over	But not over	Decimal amount is	If line 7 is: Over	But not over	Decimal amount is
$0—15,000		.35	$25,000—27,000		.29	$37,000—39,000		.23
15,000—17,000		.34	27,000—29,000		.28	39,000—41,000		.22
17,000—19,000		.33	29,000—31,000		.27	41,000—43,000		.21
19,000—21,000		.32	31,000—33,000		.26	43,000—No limit		.20
21,000—23,000		.31	33,000—35,000		.25			
23,000—25,000		.30	35,000—37,000		.24			

8 X.

9a	Multiply line 6 by the decimal amount on line 8	**9a**	
b	If you paid 2021 expenses in 2022, complete Worksheet A in the instructions. Enter the amount from line 13 of the worksheet here. Otherwise, enter -0- on line 9b and go to line 9c	**9b**	
c	Add lines 9a and 9b and enter the result	**9c**	
10	Tax liability limit. Enter the amount from the Credit Limit Worksheet in the instructions	**10**		
11	**Credit for child and dependent care expenses.** Enter the **smaller** of line 9c or line 10 here and on Schedule 3 (Form 1040), line 2	**11**	

For Paperwork Reduction Act Notice, see your tax return instructions. Cat. No. 11862M Form **2441** (2022)

Chapter

6

Depreciation and Amortization

CHAPTER CONTENTS

LEARNING OBJECTIVES

After completing Chapter 6, you should be able to:

1. Compute a taxpayer's depreciation expense deduction for personal and real property.
2. Determine how much Section 179 a taxpayer can elect to expense for the year and how that affects the taxpayer's total depreciation expense for the year.
3. Understand the special tax rules that govern the amount of depreciation allowed on luxury automobiles, leased vehicles, and listed property.
4. Understand which intangible assets are subject to amortization and how to calculate the amount of a taxpayer's amortization expense deduction.
5. Prepare Form 4562.

CHAPTER OVERVIEW

Chapter 7 covers the reporting requirements for sole proprietors. Sole proprietors report most of their business activities on Schedule C. The filled-in Schedule Cs shown in Chapter 7 (Figures 7-1 and 7-4) reported amounts for depreciation expense. This chapter presents the depreciation rules for business property and shows how to compute the depreciation expense deduction. This chapter also introduces Form 4562, Depreciation and Amortization, which supports the amount deducted for depreciation and amortization on Schedule C. The same Form 4562 is also used by corporations and partnerships to support their deductions for depreciation and amortization expense.

¶601 Depreciation of Business Property

When taxpayers buy business property with a useful life of more than one year, they recover the cost over several years by taking annual deductions from gross income. These annual deductions, called **depreciation expense,** represent the portion of the property's cost written off each year because of wear and tear, deterioration, and normal obsolescence. How quickly taxpayers depreciate business property depends on (1) whether the property is real property or tangible personal property and (2) when the property is placed in service.

Taxpayers recover the costs of tangible personal property more quickly than the costs of real property. Also, they can use more accelerated methods to depreciate tangible personal property. **Real property** includes all real estate, such as office buildings, apartment buildings, manufacturing plants, and warehouses. Land is not depreciated, even though it is real property. **Tangible personal property** includes tangible property other than real estate, such as furniture, machinery, equipment, and vehicles. The depreciation methods taxpayers can use depend on when the property was placed in service.

The depreciation rules in effect when the asset is placed in service continue to apply during the entire time the taxpayer owns the property. For example, to compute the 2022 depreciation expense on a building placed in service in 2014, the taxpayer uses the rules that applied to property placed in service in 2014.

Taxpayers need to understand how to depreciate property correctly. Depreciation expense reduces a property's adjusted basis, even if the taxpayer fails to deduct it on the tax return. Thus, the adjusted basis must be reduced by the *greater of* depreciation "allowed or allowable." This refers to depreciation that is deducted or that which the taxpayer is entitled to deduct. A taxpayer can claim overlooked depreciation expense by filing an amended return within three years of the due date of the tax return on which the expense went unclaimed. After three years, overlooked depreciation cannot be claimed, but it still reduces the taxpayer's basis in the property. (See ¶1313 for more discussion on how to file an amended tax return.)

This chapter focuses on the rules that apply to the depreciation of property placed in service after 1986, since property placed in service before 1987 has been fully depreciated. Those interested in learning more about pre-1986 depreciation rules should refer to IRS Publication 534, *Depreciating Property Placed in Service Before 1987.* The depreciation rules for tangible personal property are presented first, followed by the rules for real property.

 Sole proprietors deduct depreciation expense on their business property on Schedule C. Depreciation expense taken on rental property is reported on Schedule E.

¶602 Depreciation of Tangible Personal Property

Normally taxpayers deduct the cost of long-lived assets over several years, thereby requiring them to wait several years to recognize the full tax benefits from taking depreciation deductions. Occasionally, tax laws are passed that speed up the recovery process by allowing taxpayers to deduct extra amounts (and get greater tax benefits) in the first year. These practices are done to encourage taxpayers to buy more business property, often in hopes of stimulating the economy. Section 179 immediate expensing (discussed later in the chapter at ¶602.05) is one such method. Another method used is first-year "bonus" depreciation.

¶602.01   "BONUS" FIRST-YEAR DEPRECIATION

In an effort to jump-start a sluggish economy after the events of 9-11, Congress enacted first-year **bonus depreciation** for purchases of new personal property used for business or investment acquired after September 10, 2001 and placed in service by December 31, 2004. Taxpayers were required to deduct bonus depreciation for all eligible purchases unless they made an election not to take it. After deducting bonus depreciation from the cost of the property, taxpayers depreciated the remaining cost (known as "MACRS basis") using the MACRS rules presented in ¶602.02. For property placed in service between September 11, 2001 and May 5, 2003, the bonus percentage was 30% of the cost of the property. After May 5, 2003, the percentage increased to 50%.

Until 2018, purchases of new property with a recovery period of 20 years or less (tangible personal property) were eligible for 50% bonus depreciation. The bonus percentage rate now is increased to 100% for property acquired and placed in service after September 27, 2017, and before January 1, 2023. Used property, films, television shows, and theatrical productions are also eligible for bonus depreciation. Bonus depreciation is claimed on Form 4562 (line 14).

| EXAMPLE 1 | On August 1, 2022, Victor paid $20,000 for new personal property to be used in his business. Victor deducts $20,000 ($20,000 × 100%) of bonus depreciation in 2022. |

| EXAMPLE 2 | Same facts as in Example 1, except that Victor purchases used personal property in August 2017 but did not place the property in service until 2020. Victor does not deduct bonus depreciation in 2020 because bonus depreciation can only be claimed on used personal property that is acquired after September 27, 2017. |

Since originally enacted in 2001, bonus depreciation has only been allowed to expire in 2015 and 2016. In 2018, Congress increased bonus depreciation to 100% for property acquired and placed in service after September 27, 2017, and before January 1, 2023. The rate phases down 20% per year beginning in 2023. However, the laws are likely to change occasionally, if not frequently.

¶602.02   MODIFIED ACCELERATED COST RECOVERY SYSTEM (MACRS)

MACRS [I.R.C. §168] is a statutory classification system for depreciable assets. Instead of a "facts and circumstances" criterion to determine the depreciation life and rate of any asset, there are stated lives and methods.

To calculate depreciation expense using MACRS, taxpayers multiply the MACRS basis of the property by a percentage taken from an IRS-provided table. Under MACRS, personal property is assigned a regular recovery period of 3, 5, 7, 10, or 15 years, regardless of its actual useful life. MACRS assigns the more common properties a 5-year or 7-year recovery period. The 5-year property class includes vehicles, certain types of office equipment, and cell phones. 5-year office equipment includes copiers, fax machines, computers, printers, and the like. The 7-year property class includes office furniture and equipment not described above.

MACRS uses the 200% declining balance method to recover the costs of the 3-, 5-, 7-, and 10-year property classes. The 150% declining balance method is used for 15-year property. MACRS switches to the straight-line method when straight-line depreciation yields a greater deduction.

MACRS ignores salvage value. Instead, taxpayers multiply the percentage from the table by the property's MACRS basis to compute their MACRS deduction. Computing MACRS basis begins with the unadjusted basis in the property, which is the taxpayer's total cost of the property for use at its operating location. It includes the purchase price, sales tax, plus any delivery and installation costs. However, Section 179, discussed at ¶602.05, preempts MACRS. This provision is elective.

Any Section 179 expense or bonus depreciation taken in the first year is subtracted from the unadjusted basis to compute the taxpayer's MACRS basis. The unadjusted basis is reduced by any section 179 allowance before computing bonus depreciation and regular depreciation deductions.

The unadjusted basis of nonbusiness property that a taxpayer converts to business or investment use equals the *lesser of* (i) the taxpayer's adjusted basis in the property, or (ii) its fair market value (FMV) on the conversion date. Special rules also apply to property acquired by exchange, gift, or inheritance. These rules are discussed in Chapter 10.

¶602.03 AVERAGING CONVENTIONS

Two averaging conventions determine the date on which taxpayers can begin depreciating personal property. These two conventions are the half-year convention and the mid-quarter convention. The half-year convention applies when at least 60% of the basis of personal property placed in service during the year is placed in service during the first nine months of the year. The mid-quarter convention applies when more than 40% of the basis of personal property placed in service during the year is placed in service during the last three months of the year.

Half-Year Convention

When at least 60% of all personal property placed in service during the year is placed in service during the first nine months of the year, all personal property placed in service during that year is depreciated using the half-year convention. When using the half-year convention, the actual date on which personal property is placed in service is ignored. Instead, the **half-year convention** assumes that taxpayers place personal property in service halfway through the tax year. The half-year convention also assumes that taxpayers dispose of (e.g., sell) property halfway through the tax year. Thus, under the half-year convention, taxpayers get one-half year's depreciation in the first and last years, regardless of how long the taxpayer actually owned the property in those years.

Figure 6-1 shows the MACRS percentages for 5- and 7-year classes under the half-year convention. To compute MACRS on property depreciated under the half-year convention, taxpayers multiply these percentages by the MACRS basis of the property (as described in ¶602.02).

Figure 6-1: MACRS Table for 5- and 7-Year Classes Using the Half-Year Convention		
	Recovery Period	
Year	**5-Year**	**7-Year**
1	20.00%	14.29%
2	32.00	24.49
3	19.20	17.49
4	11.52*	12.49
5	11.52	8.93*
6	5.76	8.92
7		8.93
8		4.46

*Switching to straight-line results in the maximum depreciation deduction.

The Year 1 percentages from Figure 6-1 reflect a half year of depreciation. Using the 200% declining balance method, taxpayers should deduct 40% of the cost of 5-year property in the first year (1/5 × 200%). However, because the half-year convention assumes taxpayers place property in service halfway through the year, the MACRS percentage for Year 1 is one-half of the full-year percentage, or 20% for 5-year property. Starting in Year 2, the percentages shown in Figure 6-1 reflect a full year of depreciation under the 200% declining balance method. An asterisk shows the switch to the straight-line method when straight-line yields a greater deduction. Figure 6-1 also shows that the rest of the first year's depreciation is deducted in the year after the recovery period ends. This is the sixth year for 5-year property and the eighth year for 7-year property.

EXAMPLE 3	On March 2, 2022, Caroline placed new 5-year property costing $10,100 in service. She deducted 100% of this as bonus depreciation.

Except in the last year of the recovery period, when using the half-year convention, taxpayers multiply the MACRS percentage from the table by one-half in the year they dispose of the property. In the last year of the recovery period (for example, year 6 for 5-year property), taxpayers use the full MACRS percentage to compute depreciation expense on the property, even if they dispose of the property in that year. The table percentage for the last year already reflects the half-year convention.

EXAMPLE 4

On April 10, 2019, Kate placed in service 5-year property costing $10,000. She elects not to claim bonus depreciation for this property. On November 30, 2022, Kate sells the property. Under the half-year convention, the annual depreciation for the property is shown below.

Year	MACRS	Calculation
2019	$2,000	$10,000 × 20%
2020	3,200	$10,000 × 32%
2021	1,920	$10,000 × 19.2%
2022	576	$10,000 × 11.52% × ½
Total	$7,696	

It does not matter when in 2022 Kate actually sells the property. The half-year convention assumes that she sells the property on June 30, 2022, halfway through the tax year.

Mid-Quarter Convention

During the first few years after the half-year convention was enacted, many taxpayers took advantage of it by purchasing assets near the end of the year. This allowed them to take a half-year's depreciation in the first year, even though they owned the property for less than half of the year. To counter this strategy, the government now imposes a mid-quarter convention on all personal property placed in service during the year for taxpayers that purchase over 40% of their depreciable personal property (non-real-estate) during the last quarter of the year.

Like the half-year convention, the mid-quarter convention ignores the actual date personal property is placed in service. Instead, the **mid-quarter convention** assumes that taxpayers placed their personal property in service in the middle of the quarter. Thus, taxpayers that place personal property in service between January 1 and March 31 are assumed to place it in service on February 15. This means that, in the first year, they can depreciate the property from February 15 until December 31 (10.5 months). Figure 6-2 shows the four mid-quarter tables for 5- and 7-year classes.

Figure 6-2: MACRS Table for 5- and 7-Year Classes Using the Mid-Quarter Convention

Placed in Service in	Years							
1st quarter	1	2	3	4	5	6	7	8
5-year	35.00%	26.00%	15.60%	11.01%	11.01%	1.38%		
7-year	25.00	21.43	15.31	10.93	8.75	8.74	8.75%	1.09%
2nd quarter								
5-year	25.00	30.00	18.00	11.37	11.37	4.26		
7-year	17.85	23.47	16.76	11.97	8.87	8.87	8.87	3.34
3rd quarter								
5-year	15.00	34.00	20.40	12.24	11.30	7.06		
7-year	10.71	25.51	18.22	13.02	9.30	8.85	8.86	5.53
4th quarter								
5-year	5.00	38.00	22.80	13.68	10.94	9.58		
7-year	3.57	27.55	19.68	14.06	10.04	8.73	8.73	7.64

The Year 1 percentages in Figure 6-2 reflect the portion of the year in which the property is assumed to be in service. For property placed in service in the first quarter, depreciation on the property begins on February 15. For 5-year property, the first-year percentage equals 35% (1/5 × 200% × 10.5/12). For 7-year property placed in service in the fourth quarter (deemed placed in service on November 15), the first-year percentage equals 3.57% (1/7 × 200% × 1.5/12). Starting in Year 2, the percentages reflect a full year of depreciation under the 200% declining balance method, switching to straight-line when straight-line results in a greater deduction.

When property is being depreciated using the mid-quarter convention, the tax laws assume that taxpayers dispose of property halfway through the quarter. Thus, all personal property sold during October, November, and December is deemed to have been sold on November 15, regardless of the quarter in which the property was purchased. Likewise, all personal property sold during April, May, and June is deemed sold on May 15. Except in the last year of the recovery period, in the year taxpayers dispose of personal property, the percentage from the table must be reduced to reflect the portion of the year the property was assumed to be in service. When using the mid-quarter convention, this would be from January 1 until the middle of the quarter in which the property is sold.

EXAMPLE 5

In March 2020, Ed placed in service new 7-year property that cost $20,000. Ed elected out of bonus depreciation in 2020. Ed sold the property in June 2022. Under the mid-quarter convention, depreciation taken on the property is as follows.

Year	Depreciation	Calculation
2020	$5,000	($20,000 MACRS basis × 25%)
2021	4,286	$20,000 MACRS basis × 21.43%
2022	1,148	$20,000 MACRS basis × 15.31% × 4.5/12
Total	$10,434	

The MACRS first-quarter percentages apply since Ed placed the property in service during the first quarter. Although Ed actually sold the property in June, the property is deemed sold halfway through the second quarter (May 15). Ed multiplies the Year 3 MACRS percentage by 4.5/12 to reflect the property's depreciation from January 1 through May 15. Notice that Ed uses the percentages for 7-year property placed in service in the 1st quarter for all years that he depreciates the property. At the date of sale, Ed's adjusted basis in the property is $12,084 ($20,000 – $7,916 accumulated depreciation).

Each year taxpayers must determine whether the half-year or mid-quarter convention applies to personal property placed in service that year. If the mid-quarter convention applies, taxpayers may need to use four different tables to compute depreciation on personal property placed in service that year. (Under the half-year convention, taxpayers use one table to depreciate all personal property placed in service during the year.) The mid-quarter convention applies when the taxpayer placed in service in the fourth quarter more than 40% of the total depreciable personal property placed in service that year. Otherwise, the half-year convention applies. Thus, the relevant percentage is fourth quarter depreciable personal property placed in service divided by total depreciable personal property placed in service during the year. Only the cost of personal property after subtracting out all Section 179 expenses elected on the properties is used in this calculation. Neither the cost of real property placed in service during the year, nor bonus depreciation taken on personal property, are considered in making this calculation.

EXAMPLE 6

On June 21, 2021, Nelson placed in service 7-year property that costs $40,000. On October 10, 2021, he placed in service 5-year property that costs $30,000. These are the only properties placed in service in 2021. Section 179 was not taken on either property. Nelson is considered to have placed in service 42.9% ($30,000/$70,000) of the personal property in the fourth quarter. Thus, the mid-quarter convention applies to all personal property placed in service in 2021. Nelson uses the mid-quarter tables to compute depreciation on the MACRS basis. He continues to use the same mid-quarter tables to depreciate these properties in future tax years.

EXAMPLE 7

Same facts as in Example 6, except that Nelson placed the 5-year property in service on September 30, 2021. Since at least 60% of the personal property placed in service in 2021 was placed in service in the first three quarters (less than 40%), the half-year convention applies to both properties.

¶602.04   ELECTION CHOICES

Taxpayers that do not wish to use either bonus or the regular MACRS (accelerated) method can elect to use either straight-line MACRS or the Alternative Depreciation System (ADS).

Straight-line MACRS

Straight-line MACRS uses the straight-line method instead of the accelerated method. Straight-line depreciation spreads the cost evenly over the MACRS recovery period. When the taxpayer elects the straight-line method, the recovery periods and averaging conventions continue to apply.

EXAMPLE 8

On June 5, 2021, a taxpayer places in service 5-year property costing $10,000. The half-year convention applies to all personal property placed in service that year. The taxpayer sells the property on January 14, 2024. A comparison of regular (accelerated) MACRS and straight-line MACRS follows. An election not to claim bonus depreciation on 5-year property was made.

Year	Regular MACRS		Straight-line MACRS	
2021	$10,000 × 20%	$2,000	$10,000 × 1/5 × ½	$1,000
2022	$10,000 × 32%	3,200	$10,000 × 1/5	2,000
2023	$10,000 × 19.2%	1,920	$10,000 × 1/5	2,000
2024	$10,000 × 11.52% × ½	576	$10,000 × 1/5 × ½	1,000
Total		$7,696		$6,000

EXAMPLE 9

Same facts as in Example 8, except that the mid-quarter convention applies to all personal property placed in service during 2021.

Year	Regular MACRS		Straight-line MACRS	
2021	$10,000 × 25%	$2,500	$10,000 × 1/5 × 7.5/12	$1,250
2022	$10,000 × 30%	3,000	$10,000 × 1/5	2,000
2023	$10,000 × 18%	1,800	$10,000 × 1/5	2,000
2024	$10,000 × 11.37% × 1.5/12	142	$10,000 × 1/5 × 1.5/12	250
Total		$7,442		$5,500

Under the mid-quarter convention, the taxpayer begins depreciating the property in the middle of the quarter in which it is placed in service. In this case, that would be on May 15 (the middle of the second quarter). Thus, in the first year, depreciation is allowed for 7.5 months (built into the MACRS tables). This property was sold in the first quarter. Thus, depreciation in 2024 is allowed until the middle of the first quarter (February 15, or 1.5 months (not built into the MACRS tables)).

The election to use the straight-line method can be made annually for each class of property. For example, a taxpayer that elects the straight-line method in 2022 for 5-year property must use the straight-line method to depreciate all 5-year property placed in service in 2022. However, the taxpayer can use the regular (accelerated) MACRS for 7-year property purchased in 2022. This is called an election on a **class-by-class basis.** A taxpayer that uses the straight-line method to depreciate 5-year property placed in service in one year does not have to use it to depreciate 5-year property placed in service in any other year. Elections out of bonus depreciation are also made on a class-by-class basis.

EXAMPLE 10

Jones Company placed in service the following properties during 2021.

- Equipment (7-year personal property)
- Furniture (7-year personal property)
- Delivery van (5-year personal property)
- Warehouse (commercial real property)
- Office building (commercial real property)

If Jones wants to use straight-line MACRS to depreciate the equipment, it must use the straight-line method to depreciate all 7-year property placed in service during 2021 (i.e., the furniture). Jones's decision to use straight-line MACRS to depreciate the 7-year property placed in service during 2021 does not affect the depreciation method it uses to depreciate the 5-year property or any real property placed in service during 2021. Also, its decision to use straight-line MACRS to depreciate the 7-year property placed in service during in 2021 does not affect the depreciation method it uses to depreciate 7-year property placed in service in 2022 or any future tax year.

Alternative Depreciation System (ADS)

The **Alternative Depreciation System (ADS)** differs from MACRS in that most properties have longer recovery periods. In addition, the straight-line method applies. The half-year and mid-quarter conventions apply to personal property depreciated under the ADS method. Separate depreciation tables are available for this method. These tables can be found in IRS Publication 946, *How to Depreciate Property*. The following table compares the recovery periods of a few sample assets under MACRS and ADS.

	MACRS	ADS
Office furniture, fixtures, and equipment	7 years	10 years
Automobiles, light general-purpose trucks, computers, and printers	5 years	5 years
Copiers, calculators, and typewriters	5 years	6 years
Heavy general purpose trucks	5 years	6 years

Personal property with no designated class life has a recovery period of 12 years under ADS. The taxpayer makes the election to use ADS annually on a class-by-class basis. Once a taxpayer elects to depreciate a specific class of property using ADS, that election for that class of property cannot be revoked. Straight-line ADS must be used to depreciate "listed" property used 50% or less for business (discussed later in the chapter at ¶602.07). It also is used to compute a corporation's "earnings and profits" (discussed at ¶1405.02). Example 11 shows the four different options available for depreciating personal property.

In addition to electing ADS for a particular class of property, a taxpayer may elect the MACRS straight-line method for a class of property (discussed above). This election differs from the ADS election in that the ADS recovery period will typically be longer. The straight-line election recovery period is the same as the regular recovery period.

Another election available on a property class basis, is the MACRS 150% declining balance method election. This election may be made for a property class which is otherwise depreciated under MACRS using the 200% declining balance method. The regular depreciation period also applies.

EXAMPLE 11

Natalie places a desk in service. To recover the cost of the desk and all other 7-year property placed in service during the year, Natalie can choose from the following methods:

Bonus
100%

MACRS:
- 200% declining balance over 7 years (regular MACRS)
- 150% declining balance over 7 years (elective on property class basis)
- Straight-line over 7 years (straight-line MACRS) (elective on property class basis)

ADS:
- Straight-line over ten years (elective on property class basis)

No matter which method Natalie selects, the percentage of all personal property placed in service in the fourth quarter will determine whether the half-year or mid-quarter convention applies. Also, the method Natalie selects will apply to all 7-year property placed in service during the year. Regardless of which depreciation method Natalie selects, she must continue to depreciate the desk (plus all other 7-year property placed in service during the year) using that method in all future years.

It is often assumed that the taxpayer should take the maximum deduction allowed at the earliest possible time. However, a taxpayer currently in a low tax bracket may expect to be in a higher tax bracket in future years. This particular taxpayer may benefit more by delaying depreciation deductions until the higher tax bracket years. This can be accomplished by electing straight-line MACRS or ADS to depreciate property.

¶602.05 SECTION 179 EXPENSE ELECTION

Taxpayers that qualify can elect to take an up-front deduction in the year certain personal property is placed in service. Taxpayers can expense up to $1,080,000 of Section 179 property placed in service in tax years beginning in 2022. The Internal Revenue Code (Code) defines **Section 179 property** as *tangible section 1245 property and "qualified real property" placed in service by the taxpayer and predominantly used in a trade or business.* Thus, depreciable personal property used for investment is not Section 179 property. However, both new and used property that the taxpayer buys for use in the taxpayer's business is eligible for Section 179 expensing.

For years in which 100% bonus depreciation is in effect, Section 179 has limited appeal. However, there are a few assets, such as certain building components, that qualify for Section 179 but not for bonus depreciation. Some states' income tax rules also prohibit bonus depreciation but allow all or a part of a Section 179 deduction. Finally, the bonus depreciation rules are "all or nothing" for any taxable year. By opting out of bonus depreciation a taxpayer may elect to expense a portion of qualifying property and manage income accordingly. Therefore, the Section 179 election plays an important but limited role in tax planning. However, as the following discussion indicates, there are several obstacles and pitfalls in the Section 179 election that are not present in bonus depreciation.

The property must be used more than 50% in a trade or business. Only the basis attributable to business use may be expensed. If business use falls below this level during the recovery period that applies to the asset, the Section 179 deduction is recaptured.

In 2018 and later tax years, qualified real property consists of an improvement to the interior of nonresidential real property (e.g., improvements made by the owner or a tenant of an office building) made by the taxpayer after the building was first placed in service. It also includes replacement roofs and replacement air conditioning/heating/and ventilation systems (HVACS) on nonresidential real property. Prior to 2018, qualified real property consisted only of improvements to the interior of nonresidential real property if made pursuant to a lease and interior improvements to retail and restaurant buildings whether or not the building was leased.

The amount of Section 179 property that taxpayers can expense in the first year is reduced dollar-for-dollar when more than $2,700,000 of Section 179 property is placed in service during 2022. This rule is referred to as the "investment limitation." For example, taxpayers who place in service $3,200,000 of Section 179 property during 2022 would be allowed to expense up to $500,000 [$1,000,000 – ($3,200,000 – $2,700,000)] of the Section 179 property in that year. Married couples who file married filing separately can each claim one-half of the couples' allowed Section 179 amount (taking into account the investment limitation), or they can agree to split the allowed amount in any other manner. Taxpayers compute the maximum Section 179 expense they can take each year on Form 4562, Part I (lines 1 to 5).

Taxpayers can elect Section 179 expense only in the year they place the section 179 property in service. Taxpayers must identify on the tax return the property (or properties) they elect to expense under Section 179. The election to expense may be made for all or a portion of the cost of a particular section 179 property. Taxpayers make this election on Form 4562, Part I (line 6). After selecting the section 179 property (or properties) to expense under Section 179, they can recover the rest of the unadjusted basis of the property (or properties) using bonus depreciation (when allowed), and MACRS depreciation deductions.

EXAMPLE 12	On February 10, 2022, Lowe Enterprises placed in service equipment that costs $2,800,000. The equipment is 7-year MACRS property. Since Lowe placed in service more than $2,700,000 of Section 179 property during the year, it can elect to expense up to $980,000 under Section 179 [$1,080,000 – ($2,800,000 – $2,700,000)]. Lowe elects not to claim bonus depreciation. The remaining $1,820,000 of equipment is depreciated under MACRS using the half-year convention.

Section 179 expense deduction for the tax year cannot exceed a taxpayer's combined taxable income from the active conduct of any trade or business. This amount is called the "business income limitation" on Form 4562 (line 11). Taxpayers can carry over to the next tax year any Section 179 expense disallowed because of the business income limitation. However, this carryover is subject to the Section 179 limit that applies to the next year(s). For purposes of MACRS, taxpayers must reduce the basis in the property by the total amount they *elect* to expense under Section 179 even if a portion of the elected expense is deferred as a carryforward under the business income limitation.

EXAMPLE 13	Same facts as in Example 12, except that Lowe's business income limitation (taxable income from the business after all other depreciation has been deducted) is $67,143 after depreciation on the $1,820,000 of equipment not expensed under Section 179. Although Lowe can elect up to $980,000 of Section 179 expense, only $67,143 can be deducted in 2022. The $912,857 of disallowed expense can be carried over to 2023 and later years (if necessary), subject to the taxable income limitation in the carryforward years.

¶602.06   FILLED-IN FORM 4562, PART I

INFORMATION FOR FIGURE 6-3:

Lowe Enterprises from Example 13 computes the maximum amount it can elect to expense under Section 179. Lowe enters the amounts shown below in bold on Form 4562 and then follows the instructions on the form to determine that $67,143 of Section 179 expense that can be deducted in the current year and $912,857 must be carried over to next years.

Line #

1: Maximum amount, $1,080,000
2: Total cost of section 179 property placed in service, **$2,800,000**
3: Threshold cost of section 179 property before reduction in limitation, **$2,700,000**
4: Reduction in limitation, **$100,000** ($2,800,000 – $2,700,000)
5: Dollar limitation (maximum Section 179 that can be elected), **$980,000** ($1,080,000 – $100,000)
6(a): Description of property, **Equipment**
6(b): Cost (business use only), **$2,800,000**
6(c): Elected cost (to be expensed under Section 179), **$980,000**
8: Total cost of elected §179 property, **$980,000**
9: Tentative deduction, **$980,000**
11: Business income limitation, the smaller of business income of $67,143 or line 5 ($980,000), **$67,143**
12: Section 179 expense deduction, **$67,143**
13: Carryover to 2023, **$912,857**
19c: Property placed in service in excess of the Section 179 deduction ($2,800,000 - $980,000), **$1,820,000**

Figure 6-3: Filled-In Form 4562, Part I

Form **4562**	**Depreciation and Amortization**	OMB No. 1545-0172
Department of the Treasury Internal Revenue Service	(Including Information on Listed Property) Attach to your tax return. Go to *www.irs.gov/Form4562* for instructions and the latest information.	**2022** Attachment Sequence No. **179**

Name(s) shown on return	Business or activity to which this form relates	Identifying number
Lowe Enterprises	Lowe Enterprises	--

Part I   Election To Expense Certain Property Under Section 179
Note: If you have any listed property, complete Part V before you complete Part I.

1	Maximum amount (see instructions)	**1**	1,080,000
2	Total cost of section 179 property placed in service (see instructions)	**2**	2,800,000
3	Threshold cost of section 179 property before reduction in limitation (see instructions)	**3**	2,700,000
4	Reduction in limitation. Subtract line 3 from line 2. If zero or less, enter -0-	**4**	100,000
5	Dollar limitation for tax year. Subtract line 4 from line 1. If zero or less, enter -0-. If married filing separately, see instructions	**5**	980,000

6	(a) Description of property	(b) Cost (business use only)	(c) Elected cost	
	Equipment	2,800,000	980,000	

7	Listed property. Enter the amount from line 29	**7**	
8	Total elected cost of section 179 property. Add amounts in column (c), lines 6 and 7	**8**	980,000
9	Tentative deduction. Enter the **smaller** of line 5 or line 8	**9**	980,000
10	Carryover of disallowed deduction from line 13 of your 2021 Form 4562	**10**	
11	Business income limitation. Enter the smaller of business income (not less than zero) or line 5. See instructions	**11**	67,143
12	Section 179 expense deduction. Add lines 9 and 10, but don't enter more than line 11	**12**	67,143
13	Carryover of disallowed deduction to 2023. Add lines 9 and 10, less line 12	**13**	912,857

Note: Don't use Part II or Part III below for listed property. Instead, use Part V.

Part II   Special Depreciation Allowance and Other Depreciation (Don't include listed property. See instructions.)

14	Special depreciation allowance for qualified property (other than listed property) placed in service during the tax year. See instructions	**14**	
15	Property subject to section 168(f)(1) election	**15**	
16	Other depreciation (including ACRS)	**16**	

Part III   MACRS Depreciation (Don't include listed property. See instructions.**)**

Section A

17	MACRS deductions for assets placed in service in tax years beginning before 2022	**17**	
18	If you are electing to group any assets placed in service during the tax year into one or more general asset accounts, check here ☐		

Section B—Assets Placed in Service During 2022 Tax Year Using the General Depreciation System

(a) Classification of property	(b) Month and year placed in service	(c) Basis for depreciation (business/investment use only—see instructions)	(d) Recovery period	(e) Convention	(f) Method	(g) Depreciation deduction
19a 3-year property						
b 5-year property						
c 7-year property		1,820,000	7	hy	2	260,000
d 10-year property						
e 15-year property						
f 20-year property						
g 25-year property			25 yrs.		S/L	
h Residential rental property			27.5 yrs.	MM	S/L	
			27.5 yrs.	MM	S/L	
i Nonresidential real property			39 yrs.	MM	S/L	
				MM	S/L	

Section C—Assets Placed in Service During 2022 Tax Year Using the Alternative Depreciation System

(a) Classification of property	(b)	(c)	(d)	(e)	(f)	(g)
20a Class life					S/L	
b 12-year			12 yrs.		S/L	
c 30-year			30 yrs.	MM	S/L	
d 40-year			40 yrs.	MM	S/L	

Part IV   Summary (See instructions.)

21	Listed property. Enter amount from line 28	**21**	220
22	**Total.** Add amounts from line 12, lines 14 through 17, lines 19 and 20 in column (g), and line 21. Enter here and on the appropriate lines of your return. Partnerships and S corporations—see instructions	**22**	327,363
23	For assets shown above and placed in service during the current year, enter the portion of the basis attributable to section 263A costs	**23**	

For Paperwork Reduction Act Notice, see separate instructions.   Cat. No. 12906N   Form **4562** (2022)

¶602.07   LISTED PROPERTY LIMITATIONS

Special rules apply to certain types of property *suitable for personal use.* Such property, referred to as **listed property,** commonly includes vehicles, computers, and printers. Computers and related peripheral equipment were listed property effective for property placed in service before 2018. Listed property that the taxpayer does not use more than 50% of the time for business does not qualify for regular (accelerated) MACRS, bonus depreciation, or Section 179 first-year expense. Instead, such property must be depreciated under ADS using the straight-line method. The half-year and mid-quarter provisions apply to listed property.

Any property that must be depreciated using ADS, such as listed property not used predominantly in a trade or business, does not qualify for bonus depreciation. The section 179 allowance may be claimed on mandatory ADS property with the exception of listed property used 50% or less for business purposes and property used predominantly outside of the U.S.

Property Suitable for Personal Use

Property used for transportation
- Passenger automobiles and motorcycles
- Trucks, buses, boats, and airplanes

Property used for entertainment, recreation, or amusement
- Cameras and VCRs
- Communication and stereo equipment

For property used for transportation (like automobiles), the 50% test should be based on *miles used for business* in relation to total miles used. For other types of listed property, taxpayers should use the appropriate *units of time* (hours) to allocate between business use and other use. Although any investment use of the property is not eligible for expensing and is not considered in meeting the more-than-50% business use test, taxpayers can depreciate the portion of the property's cost that involves investment use regardless of the percentage of business and investment use. Bonus depreciation may only be claimed on listed property that is used more than 50% for business purposes. Bonus, however, unlike the section 179 expense allowance applies to the investment use portion of the listed property if business use exceeds 50%.

Taxpayers must be able to substantiate the amount, time, place, and business purpose of transportation expenses. For automobiles and other vehicles, they must establish both the business/investment miles and total miles the vehicle was driven during the year. They do this by keeping adequate records or by producing evidence that supports statements they prepare.

Part V of Form 4562 is where taxpayers report the depreciation of listed property. In Part V, taxpayers confirm that they have written evidence to support the business or investment use of the property. They then separate the listed property used more than 50% of the time for business from property used 50% or less for business. Only listed property used more than 50% for business can be expensed under Section 179 and depreciated using bonus depreciation (when applicable) and regular (accelerated) MACRS. When Section 179 or bonus depreciation is taken on listed property placed in service during the year, taxpayers report Section 179 expense on line 26(i) and bonus depreciation on line 25(h). Only the remaining (MACRS) basis is reported on line 26(e).

EXAMPLE 14

On August 9, 2022, Tom placed in service new video recording equipment with a regular recovery period of 5 years and a 9-year ADS recovery period that costs $4,000. This is the only property Tom placed in service in 2022, so the half-year convention applies. Tom uses the equipment 60% of the time for business, 15% of the time for investment purposes, and 25% of the time for personal use. Since the business use of the equipment exceeds 50%, accelerated depreciation methods can be used to depreciate the 75% combined business and investment use ($4,000 × 75% = $3,000 business/investment basis). If an election out of 100% bonus depreciation is not made, Tom may claim a $3,000 bonus deduction for the basis attributable to investment and business use. ADS is not required because business use exceeded 50%. Assume Tom elects out of bonus depreciation. Since business use exceeds 50%, Tom could have elected to expense $2,400 ($4,000 × 60%) under Section 179 and used MACRS to depreciate the $600 investment basis ($4,000 × 15%). Investment basis does not qualify for expensing. Depreciation on the investment basis is $120 ($600 × 20% first-year table percentage for 5-year property subject to half-year convention).

EXAMPLE 15

Same facts as in Example 14, except that Tom uses the video equipment 40% for business, 15% for investment purposes, and 45% for personal use. Because business use does not exceed 50%, Section 179 cannot be elected and Tom cannot take bonus depreciation in 2022 or any year thereafter, even if business use increases to more than 50%. Instead, he must use straight-line ADS and the half-year convention to depreciate the 55% combined business/investment basis. Tom's 2022 depreciation on the equipment would be $122 ($2,200 basis × 5.56% first-year ADS table percentage for property with a 9-year ADS recovery period). His 2023 depreciation would be $244 ($2,200 × 11.11 second-year ADS depreciation table percentage).

If the business usage of listed property drops at or below 50% in a future year and the taxpayer has used Section 179, bonus depreciation, or regular (accelerated) MACRS to depreciate the property, the taxpayer must permanently switch to the straight-line ADS method. Also, the taxpayer must recompute what depreciation would have been in all prior years for that property using only straight-line ADS to depreciate the listed property. The difference between accumulated depreciation taken on the property (including any bonus depreciation and Section 179 expense) and what accumulated depreciation would have been using straight-line ADS must be included in the taxpayer's income in the year business usage drops at or below 50%. "Recapture" is the term used to describe the inclusion of the excess amount in gross income.

EXAMPLE 16

Fred paid $3,000 for video equipment on April 3, 2021. It has a 5-year regular recovery period and a 6-year ADS recovery period. He used the computer 60% for business and 40% for personal use during both 2021 and 2022. Fred elected out of taking bonus depreciation, but used regular (accelerated) MACRS and the half-year convention to depreciate the computer. On his 2021 and 2022 tax returns, Fred deducted $360 ($3,000 × 60% × 20%) and $576 ($3,000 × 60% × 32%), respectively. Twenty percent and 32% are the depreciation table percentages for 5-year property depreciated using the 200 percent declining balance method and half-year convention. In 2023, Fred's business usage drops to 45%.

Beginning in 2023, Fred must permanently switch to straight-line ADS. His 2023 depreciation expense deduction is $225 ($3,000 × 45% × 16.67% ADS third-year table percentage for property with a 6-year ADS recovery period). In addition, Fred must compute what his depreciation expense would have been in 2021 and 2022 using straight-line ADS. His depreciation would have been $150 ($3,000 × 60% × 8.33% ADS first-year table percentage) in 2020 and $300 ($3,000 × 60% × 16.67% ADS second-year table percentage) in 2023. Fred must include in his gross income the $486 difference between the $936 ($360 + $576) he deducted in 2021 and 2022 and the $450 ($150 + $300) that he would have deducted had he used straight-line ADS from the beginning.

¶602.07

¶602.08   FILLED-IN FORM 4562, PART V

INFORMATION FOR FIGURE 6-4:

Tom from Example 15 uses Form 4562, Part V, to report the depreciation on his video equipment. Tom has written evidence to support his 40% business use and 15% investment use so he marks **YES** on lines 24a and 24b. He enters the information for the equipment on line 27 because his business use alone does not exceed 50%. The depreciation deduction on line 27(h) reflects straight-line ADS depreciation using the half-year convention.

Line #

27(a): Type of property, **Video equipment**
27(b): Date placed in service, **8-19-2022**
27(c): Business/investment use percentage, **55%**
27(d): Cost or other basis, **$4,000**
27(e): Basis for depreciation, **$2,200** ($4,000 cost × 55% business/investment percentage)
27(f): Recovery period, **5 yr.**
27(g): Convention, **HY**, half-year convention applies
27(h): Depreciation deduction, **$220** ($4,000 basis × .55%)
  28: All deduction for listed property **$220**

Figure 6-4: Filled-In Form 4562, Part V

Form 4562 (2022)   Page **2**

Part V **Listed Property** (Include automobiles, certain other vehicles, certain aircraft, and property used for entertainment, recreation, or amusement.)

Note: For any vehicle for which you are using the standard mileage rate or deducting lease expense, complete **only** 24a, 24b, columns (a) through (c) of Section A, all of Section B, and Section C if applicable.

Section A—Depreciation and Other Information (Caution: See the instructions for limits for passenger automobiles.)

24a Do you have evidence to support the business/investment use claimed? ☐ **Yes** ☐ **No**   **24b** If "Yes," is the evidence written? ☐ **Yes** ☐ **No**

(a) Type of property (list vehicles first)	(b) Date placed in service	(c) Business/ investment use percentage	(d) Cost or other basis	(e) Basis for depreciation (business/investment use only)	(f) Recovery period	(g) Method/ Convention	(h) Depreciation deduction	(i) Elected section 179 cost
25 Special depreciation allowance for qualified listed property placed in service during the tax year and used more than 50% in a qualified business use. See instructions .					**25**			
26 Property used more than 50% in a qualified business use:								
		%						
		%						
		%						
27 Property used 50% or less in a qualified business use:								
Video Equipment	08-19-2022	55.000 %	4,000	2,200	5	S/L – S/L	220	
		%				S/L –		
		%				S/L –		
28 Add amounts in column (h), lines 25 through 27. Enter here and on line 21, page 1 .						**28**	220	
29 Add amounts in column (i), line 26. Enter here and on line 7, page 1								**29**

Section B—Information on Use of Vehicles

Complete this section for vehicles used by a sole proprietor, partner, or other "more than 5% owner," or related person. If you provided vehicles to your employees, first answer the questions in Section C to see if you meet an exception to completing this section for those vehicles.

	(a) Vehicle 1		(b) Vehicle 2		(c) Vehicle 3		(d) Vehicle 4		(e) Vehicle 5		(f) Vehicle 6	
30 Total business/investment miles driven during the year (**don't** include commuting miles) .												
31 Total commuting miles driven during the year												
32 Total other personal (noncommuting) miles driven												
33 Total miles driven during the year. Add lines 30 through 32												
34 Was the vehicle available for personal use during off-duty hours?	Yes	No	Yes	No	Yes	No	Yes	No	Yes	No	Yes	No
35 Was the vehicle used primarily by a more than 5% owner or related person? . .												
36 Is another vehicle available for personal use?												

Section C—Questions for Employers Who Provide Vehicles for Use by Their Employees

Answer these questions to determine if you meet an exception to completing Section B for vehicles used by employees who **aren't** more than 5% owners or related persons. See instructions.

		Yes	No
37	Do you maintain a written policy statement that prohibits all personal use of vehicles, including commuting, by your employees?		
38	Do you maintain a written policy statement that prohibits personal use of vehicles, except commuting, by your employees? See the instructions for vehicles used by corporate officers, directors, or 1% or more owners . .		
39	Do you treat all use of vehicles by employees as personal use?		
40	Do you provide more than five vehicles to your employees, obtain information from your employees about the use of the vehicles, and retain the information received?		
41	Do you meet the requirements concerning qualified automobile demonstration use? See instructions		

Note: If your answer to 37, 38, 39, 40, or 41 is "Yes," don't complete Section B for the covered vehicles.

Part VI **Amortization**

(a) Description of costs	(b) Date amortization begins	(c) Amortizable amount	(d) Code section	(e) Amortization period or percentage	(f) Amortization for this year
42 Amortization of costs that begins during your 2022 tax year (see instructions):					
43 Amortization of costs that began before your 2022 tax year				**43**	
44 **Total.** Add amounts in column (f). See the instructions for where to report				**44**	

Form **4562** (2022)

¶602.09   LUXURY AUTOMOBILE LIMITS

The tax laws limit the depreciation of vehicles used for business, even those used 100% for business. These limits apply to all types of depreciation, including Section 179 expenses and bonus depreciation. The limits are referred to as the "luxury car" caps but they actually apply to most vehicles. Figure 6-5 shows the depreciation limits for cars (other than trucks or vans) placed in service from 2018–2022. Slightly higher limits apply to trucks and vans. See Rev. Proc. 2022-17 for the limits on vehicles placed in service in 2022.

Figure 6-5: Luxury Car Depreciation Limits for the Years 2018–2022				
	Placed in Service During	Placed in Service During	Placed in Service During	Placed in Service During
Year	2018	2019-2020	2021	2022
1	$10,000 ($18,000 if bonus claimed)	$10,100 ($18,100 if bonus claimed)	$10,200 ($18,200 if bonus claimed)	$11,200 ($19,200 if bonus claimed)
2	$16,000	$16,100	$16,400	$18,000
3	$9,600	$16,100	$9,800	$10,800
4 and on	$5,760	$5,760	$9,800	$6,460

The first-year depreciation cap on a luxury passenger vehicle is increased by $8,000 if bonus depreciation is claimed. For example, the $11,200 first-year cap for 2022 is increased by $8,000 to $19,200 if bonus is claimed.

The limits in Figure 6-5 apply only to passenger automobiles. A passenger automobile is any four-wheeled vehicle made primarily for use on public streets, roads, and highways and whose gross vehicle weight rating (GVWR) is 6,000 pounds or less. GVWR is the combined unloaded weight of the vehicle and the maximum cargo weight (including passengers). Ambulances, hearses, taxis, and limousines are not subject to the luxury automobile rules. Neither are trucks and vans if they have been modified so that they are not likely to be used for personal use.

Since many sports utility vehicles (SUVs) have a GVWR over 6,000 pounds, taxpayers found they could avoid the luxury automobile limits by purchasing these "heavy" SUVs and using them in their businesses. This allowed them to expense the entire SUV's cost under Section 179 (assuming 100% business use).

Congress addressed this issue by enacting tax rules that now limit the amount of Section 179 expense allowed on heavy SUVs to a maximum of $25,000. Amounts not expensed under Section 179 are depreciated using the MACRS rules discussed in this chapter. The $25,000 limitation (inflation adjusted to $27,000 for tax years beginning in 2022) also applies to heavy pick-up trucks with a cargo-bed length less than 6 feet long and certain heavy passenger vans.

The luxury automobile limits, like those shown for cars in Figure 6-5, are the limits imposed for vehicles used 100% of the time for business. Taxpayers must reduce the limits when the vehicle is used less than 100% for business. For vehicles used partially for business, taxpayers must combine the rules for listed property with those for luxury automobiles.

EXAMPLE 17

On August 2, 2020, Paula placed in service a new car that cost $40,000. The half-year convention applies to personal property Paula placed in service in 2020. Paula uses the car 70% of the time for business. Thus, her business-use cost of the car is $28,000 ($40,000 × 70%). Since business use exceeds 50%, bonus depreciation and regular MACRS were taken on the car. Paula uses the "2020" column from Figure 6-5 to compute her luxury car limits. Her depreciation calculations are:

2020	$12,740	(lesser of 100% × 28,000 or 70% × 18,200)
2021	$15,260	(lesser of 100% × (28,000 – 12,740) or 16,400)
2022	$0	All basis is recovered

EXAMPLE 18

On July 15, 2019, Anne placed in service a used car that cost $52,000. The half-year convention applies to personal property Anne placed in service in 2019. Anne uses the car 80% of the time for business. She uses the "2019" column from Figure 6-5 to compute her luxury car limits. Anne elects out of bonus depreciation. Anne's depreciation calculations are:

Cost	$52,000	80.00%	$41,600		
	Basis	MACRS %	MACRS	Limit	Lesser
2019	$41,600	20.00%	$8,320	$10,000	$8,320
2020	33,280	32.00%	13,312	16,000	13,312
2021	19,968	19.20%	7,987	9,600	7,987
2022	$11,981	11.52%	$1,380	$5,760	$1,380

EXAMPLE 19

On April 5, 2021, Phil placed in service a used European luxury car costing $175,000. Phil elects out of bonus depreciation for the year. Phil uses the car 100% for business and uses straight-line ADS to depreciate the car. The ADS recovery period for the car is same as the regular recovery period—5 years. The half-year convention applies. Phil elected not to claim bonus depreciation on the vehicle. Phil's first-year ADS depreciation on the car is $17,500 ($175,000 × 1/5 × ½). However, this amount exceeds the $10,000 first-year limit for cars placed in service during 2021. Thus, Phil's deduction is limited to $10,000. In 2022, ADS depreciation would be $35,000 ($175,000 × 1/5). However, this amount exceeds the $16,400 year 2 limit for cars placed in service during 2021. Thus, Phil's 2022 depreciation deduction is limited to $16,400.

Leased Vehicles

Taxpayers leasing cars and other vehicles can either use the standard mileage rate or deduct the business portion of their lease payments. To prevent taxpayers from getting around the luxury automobile limits by leasing (rather than buying) expensive cars, the government reduces the amount taxpayers can deduct for their lease payments. They do this by reducing the taxpayer's car expense deduction by an "inclusion amount." The inclusion amount is based on the FMV of the vehicle. Taxpayers multiply the inclusion amount from the IRS table by the business-use percentage. In the first and last years of the lease, the amount is further reduced to reflect the portion of the year the car was leased. In the last year of the lease, the inclusion amount is determined by reference to the table amount for the preceding (penultimate) year. See Example 21. The inclusion amounts for leased cars can be found Appendix A of IRS Publication 463, *Travel, Gift, and Car Expenses*. Publication 463 contains a series of tables based on the year that the vehicle was first leased. Figure 6-6 shows the portion of the table for cars with a FMV between $60,000 and $70,000 that were first leased during 2022. Inclusion amounts for trucks and vans are slightly lower.

Figure 6-6: Inclusion Amounts for Cars First Leased in 2022						
Fair Market Value		Tax Year of Lease				
Over	Not Over	1st	2nd	3rd	4th	5th and later
60,000	62,000	6	13	20	23	28
62,000	64,000	9	19	27	34	38
64,000	66,000	11	24	36	43	50
66,000	68,000	14	30	43	53	61
68,000	70,000	16	35	52	63	72

EXAMPLE 20

On September 1, 2022, Lane began leasing a car for $700 a month. The lease term is four years. Lane leased the car for 122 days during 2022 (September 1 to December 31). The FMV of the car was $62,200 and Lane's business usage is 70%. In 2022, Lane's initial deduction equals 70% of her lease payments, or $1,960 ($700 × 4 × 70%). From Figure 6-6, the inclusion amount for 2022 (1st year of the lease) for a car valued at $62,200, is $9. Lane reduces her 2022 lease expense deduction by $2 ($19 × 70% × 122/365) and deducts $1,958 ($1,960 – $2) on Schedule C (line 20a). In 2023, Lane's lease expense deduction is $5,867 [$5,880 for her lease payments ($700 × 12 × 70%) – $13 ($19 inclusion amount × 70%)]. Lane will also need to compute lease inclusion amounts for the remaining years of the lease.

EXAMPLE 21

On March 2, 2022, Michelle entered into a 36-month lease. The FMV of the car she leased is $64,500. Michelle drives the car 75% for business each year. To compute her $7 inclusion amount in 2022, Michelle multiplies the $11 first-year inclusion amount from Figure 6-6 by 75% and then by 305/365 (the portion of 2021 that she leased the car). For 2023 and 2024, she multiplies the $24 and $36 inclusion amounts by 75% to compute her inclusion amount in those years. In 2025 (the last year of the lease), Michelle multiplies the $36 third-year inclusion amount by both 75% and 60/365 (the portion of the fourth year that she leased the car during 2025). In the last year of the lease, the inclusion amount is based on the table amount for the preceding year of the lease.

¶603 Depreciation of Real Property

¶603.01 MODIFIED ACRS (MACRS)

Under MACRS, taxpayers depreciate real property using the straight-line method. The recovery period for real property under MACRS depends on whether the property is residential or nonresidential real property. Taxpayers recover the cost of residential rental property over 27.5 years. Real property is residential rental realty if the building is used as a place where people live. Examples of residential realty include apartment buildings and rental vacation homes. The recovery period for nonresidential (commercial and industrial) real estate, such as office buildings, manufacturing plants, and warehouses, is 31.5 years if placed in service before May 13, 1993. For nonresidential property placed in service after May 12, 1993, the recovery period is 39 years. Although land is real property, it is not depreciated.

There are some special rules for "qualified improvement property." The term "qualified improvement property" means any improvement made by a taxpayer to an interior portion of a building which is nonresidential real property if such improvement is placed in service after the date such building was first placed in service. [I.R.C. §168(e)(6)]. This class of property has a 15-year life, and a 150% declining balance method. Unlike other real property, it is subject to the half-year convention or mid-quarter convention, discussed in ¶602.03. The ADS period is 20 years.

EXAMPLE 22

In 2021, Loretta acquires a building for use in her restaurant business. The building cost is $250,000. In early 2022, she incurs $400,000 of costs in order to convert the property from a hardware store to an upscale bar and restaurant. She must depreciate the $250,000 acquisition cost over 39 years using the straight-line method. However, she uses a 15-year, 150% declining balance method to recover the $400,000 renovation cost incurred in 2022.

The **mid-month convention** applies to real property depreciated under MACRS. The mid-month convention assumes taxpayers place real property in service in the middle of the month they actually place it in service. The mid-month convention also assumes that taxpayers dispose of real property in the middle of a month.

EXAMPLE 23

On March 1, 1997, Vicky placed in service residential real property that cost $100,000. Vicky sells the property on December 5, 2022. Vicky's annual cost recovery for the property follows.

Year	Calculation	MACRS
1997	$100,000 × 1/27.5 = $3,636 × 9.5/12 =	$ 2,879
1998–2021	$100,000 × 1/27.5 = $3,636 × 24 years =	87,264
2022	$100,000 × 1/27.5 = $3,636 × 11.5/12 =	3,485
Total		$93,628

EXAMPLE 24

Same facts as in Example 23, except that Vicky placed the nonresidential real property in service on July 1, 1996. In this scenario, nonresidential real property is placed in service after May 12, 1993 , so a 39-year recovery period applies. Also, the property is now placed in service in July, so Vicky starts depreciating the building on July 15.

Year	Calculation	MACRS
1996	$100,000 × 1/39 = $2,564 × 5.5/12 =	$ 1,175
1996–2021	$100,000 × 1/39 = $2,564 × 24 years =	61,536
2022	$100,000 × 1/39 = $2,564 × 11.5/12 =	2,457
Total		$65,168

EXAMPLE 25

Chuck operates a business out of his home. In the current year, Chuck began using one room in his home exclusive as an office where he regularly meets with clients. Although the rest of the home is where Chuck lives, the room where Chuck conducts his business is used solely for work. Thus, the home office is nonresidential realty. Under MACRS, the home office is depreciated over 39 years using the straight-line method.

¶603.02   ALTERNATIVE DEPRECIATION SYSTEM (ADS)

Instead of using MACRS recovery periods of 27.5 (for residential realty) or 31.5 or 39 years (for nonresidential realty), taxpayers can elect under the Alternative Depreciation System (ADS) to depreciate both residential and nonresidential realty. The ADS period for nonresidential real property is 40 years. The ADS period for residential rental property is 30 years. [I.R.C. §168(g)(2)(C)] Those who elect ADS continue to use the straight-line method and the mid-month convention. Taxpayers can elect to use the ADS recovery period on a **property-by-property** basis. This allows them to depreciate one piece of real property over the ADS period and another over the regular MACRS recovery period.

¶603.02

EXAMPLE 26	During the year, a taxpayer places in service an office building and a warehouse. The taxpayer can elect to use the regular 39-year MACRS recovery period to depreciate one of the buildings and the 40-year ADS recovery period to depreciate the other. Regardless of which depreciation method is used to depreciate the buildings, the mid-month convention applies to both the first and last years.

¶603.03   DEPRECIATION FOR BUSINESS USE OF A HOME

Persons who use part of their home for business purposes can depreciate the business portion of the home. Chapter 7 discussed the rules regarding deductions for the business use of the home (¶705.03). To compute the depreciation deduction, taxpayers first determine the percentage of the total square footage of the home used for business. If the rooms are all of approximately equal size, they can divide the number of rooms used for business by the total number of rooms in the home. The business-use percentage of the home is used to compute depreciation on the home.

The depreciable basis for the home is the *lesser of* (i) the home's adjusted basis or (ii) its FMV at the time the home office was placed in service. In determining the depreciable basis, the cost of the land must be removed from the adjusted basis. Likewise, the value of the land cannot be included when computing the FMV of the home. Taxpayers report the allowable depreciation deduction for a business in the home for a sole proprietor on Form 8829, Expenses for Business Use of Your Home, Part III. Figure 6-7 shows the calculation of the depreciation deduction.

Chapter 7 (¶705.03) discussed the order in which taxpayers deduct home office expenses:

1. All non–home office expenses from Schedule C. This amount includes depreciation on personal and real property (other than the home office).
2. The portion of mortgage interest, real estate taxes, and casualty losses taken on Form 8829 that relates to the home office.
3. The portion of operating expenses that relates to the business use of the home. These amounts include repairs, maintenance, utilities, and insurance.
4. The business portion of depreciation on the home.

Expenses listed in items 3 and 4 cannot create or increase a business loss. The disallowed expenses may be carried forward and included on Form 8829 in the following year. Home office expenses that carry over to the next year are reported on Form 8829, Part IV.

EXAMPLE 27	In 2022, Mack reports $1,600 as tentative profit on Schedule C. He uses 10% of his home exclusively as an office. Expenses for the 10% business portion of the home include mortgage interest and real estate taxes of $420, operating expenses (insurance, maintenance, and utilities) of $1,000, and depreciation of $650. Mack's deduction on Form 8829 for the business use of his home follows:

Tentative profit	$ 1,600
Less interest and taxes	(420)
Net income derived from the business	$ 1,180
Less allowable operating expenses	(1,000)
Limit placed on depreciation expense	$ 180
Depreciation expense	(650)
Depreciation expense not deductible in 2022 (show on line 43 and carry forward to 2023)	($ 470)

All business expenses except the $470 of depreciation offset 2022 income. Since Mack cannot deduct the entire depreciation in 2022, he reduces the basis of the home office by the $180 deducted in 2022. The basis in the home will be reduced for the rest of the depreciation in the year he deducts it.

Optional Safe Harbor. As an alternative to calculating actual home office expenses, a taxpayer may elect a simplified safe harbor method to compute the home office deduction without having to substantiate, calculate, and allocate deductible home office expenses. Under the safe harbor, the deduction is equal to $5 per square foot of the home office, up to a maximum of 300 square feet. Thus, the maximum deduction is $1,500. The deduction cannot exceed the taxpayer's gross income from the business nor can the excess be carried forward to the next year. Further, if home office expenses are reimbursed by an employer, safe harbor cannot be used.

¶603.04   QUALIFIED IMPROVEMENT PROPERTY

For taxable years beginning after 2017, there is a new class of real property. One of the changes that relates closely to the expensing rules was the creation of a new class of "qualified improvement property." [I.R.C. §168(e)(6)] This new category combines several types of property. Before the Tax Cuts and Jobs Act of 2017 (TCJA), there were several classes of 15-year MACRS real property:

- Qualified leasehold improvement property was any improvement to an interior portion of a nonresidential building if the improvements were made by a lessee or lessor subject to a lease agreement.
- Qualified restaurant property was a building or improvement thereto if more than 50% of the building's square footage was used for meal preparation and seating.
- Qualified retail improvement property was any improvement to an interior portion of a retail establishment, but only if the improvement is placed in service more than three years after the date the building was first placed in service.

The TCJA eliminated the separate definitions of qualified leasehold improvement, qualified restaurant, and qualified retail improvement property, and provides a general 15-year recovery period for qualified improvement property, and a 20-year ADS recovery period for such property. See Rev. Proc. 2017-33, §4.02, for comprehensive definitions of qualified improvement property. Since qualified improvement property has a MACRS life of less than 20 years, it qualifies for bonus depreciation.

¶603.05   FILLED-IN FORM 8829

INFORMATION FOR FIGURE 6-7:

In 2007, Darryl Collins bought a home for $320,000 (includes $80,000 for the land). On March 1, 2010, when the FMV of the home was $340,000 (includes $80,000 for the land), Darryl began using one room exclusively as a business office. The square footage of the office is **200**; the total square footage of the home is **4,000**. Since Darryl uses the business portion of the home as an office, it meets the definition of nonresidential real property. A 2.564% depreciation percentage is used (straight-line over 39 years applies to nonresidential realty placed in service after May 12, 1993).

Darryl computes the depreciation on the home office in Part III (lines 37-42). He then enters this amount on line 30 to include it as part of his deduction for the business use of his home.

Line #
- 37: Smaller of home's adjusted basis or fair market value, **$320,000**
- 38: Value of land included on line 37, **$80,000**
- 41: Depreciation percentage, **2.564** (1/39)

Figure 6-7: Filled-In Form 8829

This Form is Overset by 2 Lines

Form 8829

Department of the Treasury
Internal Revenue Service

Expenses for Business Use of Your Home

File only with Schedule C (Form 1040). Use a separate Form 8829 for each home you used for business during the year.
Go to *www.irs.gov/Form8829* for instructions and the latest information.

OMB No. 1545-0074

2022

Attachment
Sequence No. **176**

Name(s) of proprietor(s): Darryl Collins

Your social security number: 508-00-5925

Part I — Part of Your Home Used for Business

1	Area used regularly and exclusively for business, regularly for daycare, or for storage of inventory or product samples (see instructions)	1	200
2	Total area of home	2	4,000
3	Divide line 1 by line 2. Enter the result as a percentage	3	5.000 %

For daycare facilities not used exclusively for business, go to line 4. All others, go to line 7.

4	Multiply days used for daycare during year by hours used per day	4	hr.
5	If you started or stopped using your home for daycare during the year, see instructions; otherwise, enter 8,760	5	hr.
6	Divide line 4 by line 5. Enter the result as a decimal amount	6	
7	Business percentage. For daycare facilities not used exclusively for business, multiply line 6 by line 3 (enter the result as a percentage). All others, enter the amount from line 3	7	5.000 %

Part II — Figure Your Allowable Deduction

8	Enter the amount from Schedule C, line 29, **plus** any gain derived from the business use of your home, **minus** any loss from the trade or business not derived from the business use of your home. See instructions.	8	

See instructions for columns (a) and (b) before completing lines 9–22.

		(a) Direct expenses	(b) Indirect expenses		
9	Casualty losses (see instructions)	9			
10	Deductible mortgage interest (see instructions)	10			
11	Real estate taxes (see instructions)	11			
12	Add lines 9, 10, and 11	12			
13	Multiply line 12, column (b), by line 7		13		
14	Add line 12, column (a), and line 13			14	
15	Subtract line 14 from line 8. If zero or less, enter -0-			15	
16	Excess mortgage interest (see instructions)	16			
17	Excess real estate taxes (see instructions)	17			
18	Insurance	18			
19	Rent	19			
20	Repairs and maintenance	20			
21	Utilities	21			
22	Other expenses (see instructions)	22			
23	Add lines 16 through 22	23			
24	Multiply line 23, column (b), by line 7		24		
25	Carryover of prior year operating expenses (see instructions)		25		
26	Add line 23, column (a), line 24, and line 25			26	
27	Allowable operating expenses. Enter the **smaller** of line 15 or line 26			27	
28	Limit on excess casualty losses and depreciation. Subtract line 27 from line 15			28	
29	Excess casualty losses (see instructions)		29		
30	Depreciation of your home from line 42 below		30	308	
31	Carryover of prior year excess casualty losses and depreciation (see instructions)		31		
32	Add lines 29 through 31			32	308
33	Allowable excess casualty losses and depreciation. Enter the **smaller** of line 28 or line 32			33	
34	Add lines 14, 27, and 33			34	
35	Casualty loss portion, if any, from lines 14 and 33. Carry amount to **Form 4684**. See instructions			35	
36	**Allowable expenses for business use of your home.** Subtract line 35 from line 34. Enter here and on Schedule C, line 30. If your home was used for more than one business, see instructions			36	

Part III — Depreciation of Your Home

37	Enter the **smaller** of your home's adjusted basis or its fair market value. See instructions	37	320,000
38	Value of land included on line 37	38	80,000
39	Basis of building. Subtract line 38 from line 37	39	240,000
40	Business basis of building. Multiply line 39 by line 7	40	12,000
41	Depreciation percentage (see instructions)	41	2.564 %
42	Depreciation allowable (see instructions). Multiply line 40 by line 41. Enter here and on line 30 above	42	308

Part IV — Carryover of Unallowed Expenses to 2023

43	Operating expenses. Subtract line 27 from line 26. If less than zero, enter -0-	43	
44	Excess casualty losses and depreciation. Subtract line 33 from line 32. If less than zero, enter -0-	44	308

For Paperwork Reduction Act Notice, see your tax return instructions.

Cat. No. 13232M

Form **8829** (2022)

¶603.05

¶604   Filled-In Form 4562

 ### INFORMATION FOR FIGURE 6-8:

Let's work with Harold's Hardware Store, which will appear again in Chapter 7. Figure 6-8 shows how Harold's Hardware Store computes depreciation. The amounts in the third column are the cost (for 2022 purchases) or MACRS basis (for pre-2022 purchases) of the property. The half-year convention applies to all personal property. Harold has written evidence to support the business use of the computer. All properties were purchased new.

Figure 6-8: Depreciation for Harold's Hardware Store

Property	Date Acquired	Cost or MACRS Basis	Recovery Period	% or Method	Depreciation in 2022
Cash register and card reader	6/30/2022	1,191	5	Bonus	1,191
Shelving*	3/1/2020	10,430	7	200% DB	1,824
Tool cabinet*	07/21/2020	1,715	7	200% DB	300
Tools**	05/01/2021	1,750	5	Bonus	0
Tools saw***	03/01/2018	950	5	200% DB	55
Storage shed	04/01/2016	12,450	39	SL	319
Total		28,486			$3,689

*   Elected out of bonus depreciation in 2020
**   Claimed bonus depreciation in 2021
*** Claimed 50 % bonus depreciation in 2018

Figure 6-9: Filled-In Form 4562

Form **4562**	**Depreciation and Amortization** (Including Information on Listed Property) Attach to your tax return. Go to *www.irs.gov/Form4562* for instructions and the latest information.	OMB No. 1545-0172
Department of the Treasury Internal Revenue Service		2022 Attachment Sequence No. **179**

Name(s) shown on return	Business or activity to which this form relates	Identifying number
Harold R. Wilson	Harold's Hardware Store	272-00-8855

Part I   **Election To Expense Certain Property Under Section 179**

Note: If you have any listed property, complete Part V before you complete Part I.

1	Maximum amount (see instructions)	1	1,080,000
2	Total cost of section 179 property placed in service (see instructions)	2	
3	Threshold cost of section 179 property before reduction in limitation (see instructions)	3	1,080,000
4	Reduction in limitation. Subtract line 3 from line 2. If zero or less, enter -0-	4	
5	Dollar limitation for tax year. Subtract line 4 from line 1. If zero or less, enter -0-. If married filing separately, see instructions	5	1,080,000

6	(a) Description of property	(b) Cost (business use only)	(c) Elected cost

7	Listed property. Enter the amount from line 29 7		
8	Total elected cost of section 179 property. Add amounts in column (c), lines 6 and 7	8	
9	Tentative deduction. Enter the **smaller** of line 5 or line 8	9	
10	Carryover of disallowed deduction from line 13 of your 2021 Form 4562	10	
11	Business income limitation. Enter the smaller of business income (not less than zero) or line 5. See instructions	11	
12	Section 179 expense deduction. Add lines 9 and 10, but don't enter more than line 11	12	
13	Carryover of disallowed deduction to 2023. Add lines 9 and 10, less line 12 13		

Note: Don't use Part II or Part III below for listed property. Instead, use Part V.

Part II   **Special Depreciation Allowance and Other Depreciation (Don't** include listed property. See instructions.)

14	Special depreciation allowance for qualified property (other than listed property) placed in service during the tax year. See instructions	14	1,191
15	Property subject to section 168(f)(1) election	15	
16	Other depreciation (including ACRS)	16	

Part III   **MACRS Depreciation (Don't** include listed property. See instructions.)

Section A

17	MACRS deductions for assets placed in service in tax years beginning before 2022	17	2,498
18	If you are electing to group any assets placed in service during the tax year into one or more general asset accounts, check here ☐		

Section B—Assets Placed in Service During 2022 Tax Year Using the General Depreciation System

(a) Classification of property	(b) Month and year placed in service	(c) Basis for depreciation (business/investment use only—see instructions)	(d) Recovery period	(e) Convention	(f) Method	(g) Depreciation deduction
19a 3-year property						
b 5-year property						
c 7-year property						
d 10-year property						
e 15-year property						
f 20-year property						
g 25-year property			25 yrs.		S/L	
h Residential rental property			27.5 yrs.	MM	S/L	
			27.5 yrs.	MM	S/L	
i Nonresidential real property			39 yrs.	MM	S/L	
				MM	S/L	

Section C—Assets Placed in Service During 2022 Tax Year Using the Alternative Depreciation System

20a Class life					S/L	
b 12-year			12 yrs.		S/L	
c 30-year			30 yrs.	MM	S/L	
d 40-year			40 yrs.	MM	S/L	

Part IV   **Summary** (See instructions.)

21	Listed property. Enter amount from line 28	21	
22	**Total.** Add amounts from line 12, lines 14 through 17, lines 19 and 20 in column (g), and line 21. Enter here and on the appropriate lines of your return. Partnerships and S corporations—see instructions	22	3,689
23	For assets shown above and placed in service during the current year, enter the portion of the basis attributable to section 263A costs 23		

For Paperwork Reduction Act Notice, see separate instructions.	Cat. No. 12906N	Form **4562** (2022)

¶605   Amortization of Intangible Property

Depreciation applies to the cost recovery of tangible personal and real property. Amortization applies to the cost recovery of intangible personal property. Tangible property differs from intangible property in that the former has physical traits, whereas the latter does not. Amortization recovers the cost of intangible property through annual deductions over a fixed period of time (similar to the straight-line method).

The Code requires that Section 197 intangibles used in a trade or business or for the production of income be amortized over 15 years (180 months). The 15-year amortization period applies to all Section 197 intangibles, even those that have shorter or longer actual useful lives. Franchises, trademarks, and trade names are always Section 197 intangibles, regardless of how they are acquired. Also, amounts paid for licenses, permits, or other rights granted by a government agency are Section 197 intangibles. All other Section 197 intangibles are acquired when the taxpayer buys a business and pays more than the value of its tangible property (minus any debt owed by the business). The excess paid is to purchase Section 197 intangibles, which may include:

- Goodwill, going concern, and the business's existing work force,
- Business books and records, operating systems, or any other data base (including customer lists),
- Patents, copyrights, formulas, designs, computer software, or similar items,
- Customer-based or supplier-based intangibles, and
- Covenants not to compete.

The Code allows taxpayers to write off the cost of other intangible property (those that are not Section 197 intangibles) that have an ascertainable value and a limited life that can be determined with reasonable accuracy. Patents, copyrights, and covenants not-to-compete acquired separately (not as part of the purchase of a business) are examples of intangibles other than Section 197 intangibles. The cost of intangibles other than those covered under Section 197 is amortized over their useful lives. In the case of computer software, the Code specifies that its useful life is 36 months.

 The amortization only applies to purchased intangibles. Although self-created goodwill provides value to the business, there is no cost or other basis to amortize.

EXAMPLE 28   Kataran Corporation pays $75,000 to a departing executive in exchange for his promise not to compete with the corporation for the next four years. The covenant not to compete is not a Section 197 intangible (it was not acquired in connection with the acquisition of a business). Thus, Kataran will write-off (expense) the $75,000 over the next four years.

EXAMPLE 29   On June 1, 2022, Blake Industries acquired all of the assets of Fontaine, Inc. Of the $10 million purchase price, $2 million is allocated to goodwill. Since purchased goodwill is a Section 197 intangible (it was acquired in a purchase of a business), the $2 million cost basis for the goodwill must be amortized using the straight-line method over 15 years beginning on June 1, 2022. If Blake uses a calendar year-end, it can deduct $77,778 ($2,000,000/180 months × 7 months) on its 2022 tax return. From 2023-2034, it will deduct $133,333 ($2,000,000/180 × 12 months). In 2037, Blake will deduct the last of the goodwill ($55,556).

EXAMPLE 30   On February 1, 2022, Amicable Company paid $12,000 for off-the-shelf computer software. Because the software was not part of the purchase of a business, it is not a Section 197 intangible. If Amicable elects out of bonus depreciation, it deducts $3,667 ($12,000/36 × 11 months) in 2022. It will deduct $4,000 ($12,000/36 × 12) in both 2023 and 2024, and $333 ($12,000/36 × 1 month) in 2025.

6

Name:

Section:

Date:

QUESTIONS AND PROBLEMS

1. **MACRS Recovery Periods.** (Obj. 1) For each of the following types of properties, state the MACRS recovery period, depreciation method, and averaging convention(s) that are used to depreciate the property under regular MACRS.

	Recovery Period	Depreciation Method	Averaging Convention
Automobiles			
Light trucks			
Computers			
Furniture and fixtures			
Commercial building (pre-5/13/93)			
Commercial buildings (post 5/12/93)			
Residential buildings			

2. **Mid-Quarter vs. Half-Year Convention.** (Obj. 1) A calendar-year taxpayer acquired four new machines in 2022 on the dates shown below. Section 179 is not elected, but regular MACRS is used to depreciate the machines. The machines have a recovery period of 7 years. The taxpayer elects out of taking bonus depreciation.

February 1	$50,000
April 1	70,000
October 1	60,000
December 1	80,000

a. Compute total MACRS depreciation expense for 2022 that would be reported on Schedule C, using the appropriate averaging convention.

b. Same as in Part a., except that the third machine was acquired on September 30 (instead of October 1). Comment on the significance of the difference between this amount and your answer to Part a.

3. **MACRS.** (Obj. 1) Florence placed in service the following properties during 2022. Compute Florence's total depreciation expense for 2022 and 2023, assuming that she elects to expense 50% of the cost of qualifying property using Section 179. She elects out of bonus depreciation. The machine, equipment, and furniture are 7-year property.

Type of Property	Cost	Date Placed in Service
Machine	$130,000	March 3, 2022
Equipment	110,000	June 8, 2022
Furniture	48,000	August 15, 2022
Office building	200,000	October 4, 2022

4. **MACRS, Year of Sale.** (Obj. 1) Bradford Company sold the following properties. Compute the allowable depreciation deduction for 2022 for each property.

Property	Date Acquired	MACRS Basis*	Depreciation Method	Averaging Convention	Date of Sale
Computer	7-1-20	$ 4,200	DDB	HY	8-5-22
Automobile	4-1-19	12,000	DDB	MQ	3-1-22
Furniture	7-10-18	24,000	DDB	MQ	7-1-22

*After subtracting bonus depreciation from the original cost

5. **MACRS, Year of Sale.** (Obj. 1) Judson Company sold the following properties. Compute the allowable depreciation deduction for 2022 for each property. This machine is 7-year property.

Property	Date Acquired	MACRS Basis*	Depreciation Method	Averaging Convention	Date of Sale
Machine	6-1-2018	$44,000	DDB	MQ	12-9-2022
Furniture	8-8-2021	12,000	DDB	HY	3-21-2022
Computer	1-6-2020	24,000	DDB	MQ	9-30-2022

*After subtracting bonus depreciation from the original cost

6. **ADS and MACRS.** (Obj. 1) Peter purchased the following new properties to use in his business.

   Equipment: Acquired in April, 2016 at a cost of $144,000
   Furniture: Acquired in March, 2020 at a cost of $84,000
   Computer: Acquired in July, 2022 at a cost of $10,000

   a. Compute Peter's 2022 depreciation expense. Peter has never elected Section 179, nor has he ever elected out of taking bonus depreciation. Peter elects ADS straight-line method with a ten-year life to depreciate the equipment. He uses regular (accelerated) MACRS to depreciate the furniture and computer. The half-year convention applies to all three properties.

   b. Same as in Part a., except that the mid-quarter convention applied to all personal property placed in service in 2020.

   c. Same as in Part a. except that Peter purchased each of these properties in 2022 and elected out of bonus depreciation. Compute depreciation for each of these properties for 2022 using the regular MACRS depreciation allowed for each property without electing Section 179. The equipment is 7-year property and ADS is not elected.

7. **MACRS.** (Obj. 1) Marv uses the following properties in his business.

   Computer: Acquired new in August 24, 2020 at a cost of $32,000
   Machine: Acquired new on October 11, 2017 at a cost of $120,000
   Furniture: Acquired new on January 16, 2014 at a cost of $42,000

   a. Compute Marv's 2022 depreciation expense. Marv has never elected Section 179, but took bonus depreciation. He uses regular (accelerated) MACRS to depreciate these properties. The mid-quarter convention applies to property placed in service during 2013 and 2017. The half-year convention applied to property placed in service in 2020. The machine is 7-year property.

   b. Same as in Part a., except that Marv purchased each of these properties in 2022 and elected out of bonus depreciation. Compute depreciation for each of these properties for 2022 using regular MACRS depreciation. Assume Marv does not elect to take Section 179 on any of the three properties. Also assume these were the only properties placed in service during the year for purposes of determining the applicable convention.

8. **Section 179.** (Obj. 2) Sand Corporation buys one asset in 2022—machinery costing $32,300,000. The machine was placed in service on June 2, 2022. Sand wants to elect the maximum Section 179 possible, even if some must be carried over to 2023. Sand's 2022 business income limitation (taxable income before Section 179 expense, but after all other expenses, including depreciation) is $167,000.

   a. Compute the maximum Section 179 Sand can elect to expense in 2022, the actual allowed 2022 expense deduction, and the Section 179 carryover to 2023.

   b. What is the regular depreciation deduction on the machine (7-year property; half-year convention) after taking into account the maximum Section 179 deduction and assuming no bonus depreciation is claimed?

   c. What is the maximum bonus depreciation that Sand could claim in 2022?

9. **Section 179.** (Obj. 2) In May 2022, Riddick Enterprises placed in service new 7-year property costing $1,100,000 and new 5-year property costing $1,100,000. These are the only two properties Riddick placed in service during the year. Riddick elects out of bonus depreciation.

   a. Compute Riddick's total depreciation expense deduction assuming Riddick uses regular MACRS and elects to take the maximum Section 179 expense on the 5-year property.

   b. Compute Riddick's total depreciation expense deduction assuming Riddick uses regular MACRS and elects to take the maximum Section 179 expense on the 7-year property.

   c. Which choice results in the largest total depreciation deduction? Comment on your answers to Parts a. and b.

10. **MACRS, Section 179.** (Objs. 1 and 2) The Redwood Company, a calendar-year corporation, acquired the following new properties.

Item	Cost	Date Acquired
Copier	$28,000	March 1, 2022
Furniture	84,000	June 1, 2022
Equipment	540,000	June 30, 2022
Warehouse	110,250	July 9, 2022

a. Compute the maximum depreciation deduction that Redwood can take in 2022 and 2023 on each of these properties assuming one-half of the cost of each qualifying property was expensed under section 179 and an election out of bonus depreciation was made for each property class. Assume the equipment is 7-year property.

b. Assume that Redwood elects the maximum allowed Section 179 expense on the equipment acquired on June 30, 2022, and that the equipment costs $1,200,000. The company uses bonus depreciation and regular MACRS to depreciate the rest of the cost. Redwood's business income limitation (taxable income before Section 179 expense, but after all other expenses, including depreciation) is $950,000. Compute the maximum total depreciation deduction (179, bonus, and regular depreciation) for the equipment for 2022.

11. **Listed Property, Section 179.** (Objs. 2 and 3) Terrell is a self-employed personal financial adviser. In March 2022, Terrell purchased video equipment, 5-year listed property, for $2,800. This was his only purchase of depreciable property in 2022. He uses the computer 75% of the time in providing financial advice to clients, 15% of the time managing his own investments, and the rest of the time for personal use. Terrell elects out of bonus depreciation.

a. Compute Terrell's maximum depreciation expense deduction in 2022 for the video equipment assuming he does not elect Section 179 in 2022.

b. Same as in Part a., except that Terrell elects the maximum Section 179 expense.

c. Where on his tax return does Terrell deduct this depreciation expense?

12. **Listed Property.** (Obj. 3) During 2022, Simon (self-employed) pays $34,500 for a new car that he uses 45% of the time for business, 25% of the time for investment purposes, and 30% of the time for personal use. The half-year convention applies to the car. How much depreciation is Simon entitled to deduct in 2022?

13. **Luxury Automobiles.** (Obj. 3) Charlotte purchased a used car on March 1, 2018, for $66,000 and uses it 80% of the time for business purposes. Prepare a schedule that shows the maximum depreciation she will be entitled to take in each of the years 2018 through 2022, assuming that she uses the automobile 80% of the time for business each year, and the half year convention applies to all 2018 purchases of personal property. Assume that the car was purchased from a related party and does not qualify for bonus depreciation.

14. **Luxury Automobiles.** (Obj. 3) On September 13, 2022, Debi places in service a new car costing $25,000 (her only acquisition during the year). She uses the car 90% of the time for business. Compute Debi's maximum depreciation deduction (including bonus) for 2022.

15. **Leased Vehicles.** (Obj. 3) On March 1, 2022, Casey enters into a 36-month lease for a car valued at $63,800. Her monthly lease payment is $960, and she uses the car 75% for business. What amount will Casey deduct in 2022 and 2023?

16. **Leased Vehicles.** (Obj. 3) Bart operates his business as a sole proprietorship. On October 1, 2022, Bart enters into a 24-month lease on a car valued at $65,800. His monthly payments are $800. Bart uses the car 85% for business each year. Compute Bart's lease deduction and inclusion amounts for 2022–2024.

17. **MACRS and Averaging Conventions.** (Obj. 1) Jan purchased the following properties during 2022.

Description	Date Placed in Service	Cost
New Computer	March 9, 2022	$ 6,000
Used Machinery	July 17, 2022	70,000
Used Office building	September 6, 2022	270,000
New Equipment	December 27, 2022	84,000

Compute Jan's depreciation for each of these properties for 2022 and 2023. Assume that Jan elected to expense 50% of the cost of each item of qualified property and elected out of bonus depreciation. The machine and equipment are 7-year property.

18. **MACRS and Averaging Conventions.** (Objs. 1, 3, 5) Howard (SSN 748-29-4631) operates the H.B. Fields Company as a sole proprietorship. H.B. Fields has the following depreciable property. The automobile is used 100% for business. Howard has written evidence of the business use, which was 19,280 miles in 2022. He has another vehicle he uses for personal use. No Section 179 allowance was claimed on any qualifying property. Using this information, prepare Howard's 2022 Form 4562, Depreciation and Amortization. A blank form is located below.

Date of Acquisition	Item	Cost	Averaging Convention
January 30, 2020	Used car	$24,000	HY
March 10, 2021	Garage for auto	39,000	MM
August 6, 2021	New machine	12,460	HY
December 1, 2019	Used desk	1,910	MQ

19. **MACRS, Real Property.** (Obj. 1) In February 2022, a taxpayer purchased an office building for $320,000 and an apartment building for $400,000. These amounts include only the buildings, not the land. Compute the 2022 MACRS expense for each building.

20. **MACRS and ADS, Real Property.** (Obj. 1) Drew operates a business as a sole proprietorship. On January 3, 2022, Drew placed in service a warehouse costing $650,000. On November 25, 2022, he placed in service an apartment complex costing $990,000.

    a. Compute Drew's 2022 depreciation expense on each building. Drew uses MACRS to depreciate the warehouse and elects to use ADS to depreciate the apartment building.

    b. Same as in Part a., except that Drew elects to depreciate the warehouse using ADS and uses MACRS to depreciate the apartment building.

    c. Same as in Part a., except that Drew uses MACRS to depreciate both buildings.

    d. Same as in Part a., except that Drew elects to use ADS to depreciate both buildings.

(Use for Problem 18.)

Form **4562**	**Depreciation and Amortization** **(Including Information on Listed Property)** Attach to your tax return. Go to *www.irs.gov/Form4562* for instructions and the latest information.	OMB No. 1545-0172 20**22** Attachment Sequence No. **179**

Department of the Treasury
Internal Revenue Service

Name(s) shown on return	Business or activity to which this form relates	Identifying number

Part I **Election To Expense Certain Property Under Section 179**
Note: If you have any listed property, complete Part V before you complete Part I.

1	Maximum amount (see instructions)	1	
2	Total cost of section 179 property placed in service (see instructions)	2	
3	Threshold cost of section 179 property before reduction in limitation (see instructions)	3	
4	Reduction in limitation. Subtract line 3 from line 2. If zero or less, enter -0-	4	
5	Dollar limitation for tax year. Subtract line 4 from line 1. If zero or less, enter -0-. If married filing separately, see instructions	5	

6	(a) Description of property	(b) Cost (business use only)	(c) Elected cost

7	Listed property. Enter the amount from line 29 7		
8	Total elected cost of section 179 property. Add amounts in column (c), lines 6 and 7	8	
9	Tentative deduction. Enter the **smaller** of line 5 or line 8	9	
10	Carryover of disallowed deduction from line 13 of your 2021 Form 4562	10	
11	Business income limitation. Enter the smaller of business income (not less than zero) or line 5. See instructions	11	
12	Section 179 expense deduction. Add lines 9 and 10, but don't enter more than line 11	12	
13	Carryover of disallowed deduction to 2023. Add lines 9 and 10, less line 12 . 13		

Note: Don't use Part II or Part III below for listed property. Instead, use Part V.

Part II **Special Depreciation Allowance and Other Depreciation (Don't** include listed property. See instructions.)

14	Special depreciation allowance for qualified property (other than listed property) placed in service during the tax year. See instructions	14	
15	Property subject to section 168(f)(1) election	15	
16	Other depreciation (including ACRS)	16	

Part III **MACRS Depreciation (Don't** include listed property. See instructions.)

Section A

17	MACRS deductions for assets placed in service in tax years beginning before 2022	17	
18	If you are electing to group any assets placed in service during the tax year into one or more general asset accounts, check here . . . . ☐		

Section B—Assets Placed in Service During 2022 Tax Year Using the General Depreciation System

(a) Classification of property	(b) Month and year placed in service	(c) Basis for depreciation (business/investment use only—see instructions)	(d) Recovery period	(e) Convention	(f) Method	(g) Depreciation deduction
19a 3-year property						
b 5-year property						
c 7-year property						
d 10-year property						
e 15-year property						
f 20-year property						
g 25-year property			25 yrs.		S/L	
h Residential rental property			27.5 yrs.	MM	S/L	
			27.5 yrs.	MM	S/L	
i Nonresidential real property			39 yrs.	MM	S/L	
				MM	S/L	

Section C—Assets Placed in Service During 2022 Tax Year Using the Alternative Depreciation System

20a Class life					S/L	
b 12-year			12 yrs.		S/L	
c 30-year			30 yrs.	MM	S/L	
d 40-year			40 yrs.	MM	S/L	

Part IV **Summary** (See instructions.)

21	Listed property. Enter amount from line 28	21	
22	**Total.** Add amounts from line 12, lines 14 through 17, lines 19 and 20 in column (g), and line 21. Enter here and on the appropriate lines of your return. Partnerships and S corporations—see instructions	22	
23	For assets shown above and placed in service during the current year, enter the portion of the basis attributable to section 263A costs 23		

For Paperwork Reduction Act Notice, see separate instructions.   Cat. No. 12906N   Form **4562** (2022)

(Use for Problem 18.)

Form 4562 (2022)

Page **2**

Part V　Listed Property (Include automobiles, certain other vehicles, certain aircraft, and property used for entertainment, recreation, or amusement.)

Note: For any vehicle for which you are using the standard mileage rate or deducting lease expense, complete **only** 24a, 24b, columns (a) through (c) of Section A, all of Section B, and Section C if applicable.

Section A—Depreciation and Other Information (Caution: See the instructions for limits for passenger automobiles.)

24a Do you have evidence to support the business/investment use claimed? ☐ Yes ☐ No **24b** If "Yes," is the evidence written? ☐ Yes ☐ No

(a) Type of property (list vehicles first)	(b) Date placed in service	(c) Business/ investment use percentage	(d) Cost or other basis	(e) Basis for depreciation (business/investment use only)	(f) Recovery period	(g) Method/ Convention	(h) Depreciation deduction	(i) Elected section 179 cost
25 Special depreciation allowance for qualified listed property placed in service during the tax year and used more than 50% in a qualified business use. See instructions . **25**								
26 Property used more than 50% in a qualified business use:								
		%						
		%						
		%						
27 Property used 50% or less in a qualified business use:								
		%				S/L –		
		%				S/L –		
		%				S/L –		
28 Add amounts in column (h), lines 25 through 27. Enter here and on line 21, page 1 . **28**								
29 Add amounts in column (i), line 26. Enter here and on line 7, page 1							**29**	

Section B—Information on Use of Vehicles

Complete this section for vehicles used by a sole proprietor, partner, or other "more than 5% owner," or related person. If you provided vehicles to your employees, first answer the questions in Section C to see if you meet an exception to completing this section for those vehicles.

	(a) Vehicle 1		(b) Vehicle 2		(c) Vehicle 3		(d) Vehicle 4		(e) Vehicle 5		(f) Vehicle 6	
30 Total business/investment miles driven during the year (**don't** include commuting miles) .												
31 Total commuting miles driven during the year .												
32 Total other personal (noncommuting) miles driven												
33 Total miles driven during the year. Add lines 30 through 32												
34 Was the vehicle available for personal use during off-duty hours?	Yes	No	Yes	No	Yes	No	Yes	No	Yes	No	Yes	No
35 Was the vehicle used primarily by a more than 5% owner or related person? . .												
36 Is another vehicle available for personal use?												

Section C—Questions for Employers Who Provide Vehicles for Use by Their Employees

Answer these questions to determine if you meet an exception to completing Section B for vehicles used by employees who **aren't** more than 5% owners or related persons. See instructions.

	Yes	No
37 Do you maintain a written policy statement that prohibits all personal use of vehicles, including commuting, by your employees?		
38 Do you maintain a written policy statement that prohibits personal use of vehicles, except commuting, by your employees? See the instructions for vehicles used by corporate officers, directors, or 1% or more owners . .		
39 Do you treat all use of vehicles by employees as personal use?		
40 Do you provide more than five vehicles to your employees, obtain information from your employees about the use of the vehicles, and retain the information received?		
41 Do you meet the requirements concerning qualified automobile demonstration use? See instructions		

Note: If your answer to 37, 38, 39, 40, or 41 is "Yes," don't complete Section B for the covered vehicles.

Part VI　Amortization

(a) Description of costs	(b) Date amortization begins	(c) Amortizable amount	(d) Code section	(e) Amortization period or percentage	(f) Amortization for this year
42 Amortization of costs that begins during your 2022 tax year (see instructions):					
43 Amortization of costs that began before your 2022 tax year **43**					
44 Total. Add amounts in column (f). See the instructions for where to report **44**					

Form **4562** (2022)

21. **MACRS, Real Property.** (Obj. 1) On April 3, 1994, a taxpayer purchased land and an office building for $350,000 ($75,000 of the $350,000 is allocated to the land). On August 2, 2022, the taxpayer sold the office building. Compute MACRS on the building for 2022, and the taxpayer's adjusted basis in the office building at the time of the sale.

22. **MACRS and ADS, Real Property.** (Obj. 1) On April 29, 2014, Conley, Inc. placed in service an office building costing $450,000. Conley depreciates the office building using ADS. It sold the building on January 4, 2022. Compute Conley's depreciation expense on the building for 2013–2022 and its adjusted basis on January 4, 2022.

23. **MACRS, Realty.** (Obj. 1) What depreciation method and useful life are used to depreciate a home office placed in service in 2022? Explain.

24. **Amortization of Intangibles.** (Obj. 4) For the intangibles listed, which can be amortized, what method should be used to amortize them, and how quickly can they be amortized?

    a. Goodwill purchased as part of a business acquired during the year.

    b. A copyright purchased separately for use in the taxpayer's business.

    c. Same as in Part b., except that the copyright is purchased as part of the acquisition of a business.

    d. Covenant not to compete entered into as part of an acquisition of a business.

    e. Same as in Part d., except that the covenant is not part of the purchase of a business.

f.   Compute software not purchased as part of the acquisition of a business.

g.   Same as in Part f., except that the software is part of the purchase of a business.

 25. **Internet Problem: Researching IRS Publication 463.** (Obj. 3)

On August 29, 2019, Renee entered into a 60-month lease for a car valued at $60,220. Renee's monthly lease payment is $790. She uses the car 65% for business.

a.   What affect does this lease arrangement have on the amount Renee can deduct in 2022?

b.   How much of the lease payment can be deducted?

c.   How is this information presented on the tax return?

Go to the IRS website. Locate IRS Publication 463 and find the appropriate page in Appendix A to answer the above question regarding Renee's inclusion amount. Print out a copy of the page where you found your answer. Underline or highlight the pertinent information.

See Appendix A for instructions on use of the IRS website.

 26. **Business Entity Problem.** This problem is designed for those using the "business entity" approach. **The solution may require information from Chapter 14.**

MSO Corporation owns a residential apartment building that it depreciates over 27.5 years. The building originally cost $550,000.

a.   How much depreciation expense can the company claim on its tax return in the fifth year of ownership?

b.   Earnings and profits serve as the source of taxable dividends. By what amount does depreciation reduce the corporation's earnings and profits in the fifth year of ownership?

Chapter

7

Self-Employment

CHAPTER CONTENTS

LEARNING OBJECTIVES

After completing Chapter 7, you should be able to:

1. Compare and contrast the reporting of income and deductions for cash vs. accrual basis taxpayers.
2. Distinguish between self-employment income and income not from self-employment.
3. Recognize the expenses deducted on Schedule C and compute the amount of the deduction.
4. Understand when the home office deduction can be taken and compute the amount of the deduction.
5. Compute a sole proprietor's self-employment tax.
6. Prepare the forms and schedules introduced in this chapter, including Schedule C, Schedule SE, and Form 8829.

CHAPTER OVERVIEW

Chapters 1 through 5 presented the basic structure for reporting income and deductions. Chapter 6 covered income tax depreciation, one of the foundations of business taxation for all activities that use real or personal property. This chapter focuses on tax reporting for self-employed taxpayers. It shows how they compute their self-employment profits or losses and self-employment taxes.

Sole proprietors report income and expenses on Schedule C, Profit or Loss From Business (Sole Proprietorship). They then compute the self-employment tax on their profits on Schedule SE, Self-Employment Tax. After they complete Schedules C and SE, they can compute the amount they can contribute (and deduct for AGI) to their retirement plans.

To understand the reporting process for self-employed taxpayers, it is important to realize that tax and financial accounting rules may differ. Thus, profits reported on Schedule C may not be the same as the net income reflected on the "books" of the business. For example, self-employed taxpayers who sell business property do not report the gain or loss on Schedule C. Instead, they report it on Form 4797, Sales of Business Property, discussed in Chapter 11. However, for financial accounting purposes, they include the gain or loss in computing "book" net income. With the exception of the section on self-employment tax and retirement plans for self-employed taxpayers, the scope of this chapter is limited to income and expense items reported on Schedule C.

¶701 Accounting Methods

All businesses must keep records to support the calculation of taxable income. Most taxpayers use either the cash or accrual method of accounting. Taxpayers using the cash method to report income must also use it to deduct expenses. Likewise, those who deduct expenses using the accrual method must use the accrual method to report income. Some taxpayers use one method for tax purposes and another for their financial statements.

Taxpayers may use the accrual method to compute business profits and the cash method for their nonbusiness items. Those with more than one business may use different accounting methods for each separate and distinct business. Most businesses with gross receipts in excess of $25 million must use the accrual method. For taxable years beginning after 2018, the threshold is indexed for inflation. For 2022, the indexed value is $27 million.

¶701.01 CASH METHOD

Under the cash method, taxpayers report income when they actually or constructively receive it. Taxpayers constructively receive income when it is credited to their accounts or made available to them without restrictions. Constructive receipt has little to do with when the taxpayer actually takes possession of the cash. Instead, it has to do with when the taxpayer is entitled to the cash.

EXAMPLE 1	On December 31, 2021, Carson receives a check for $200 in payment of fees earned. Carson constructively receives the $200 in 2021, even if the check cannot be cashed until January 2, 2022. Thus, Carson reports the $200 as income in 2021.

EXAMPLE 2	On December 30, 2021, Jamie receives a check for $500 as payment for services rendered. The customer informs Jamie that the check will bounce if cashed before January 2, 2022. Because the funds are not available until 2022, Jamie has not constructively received the $500 in 2021. Jamie reports the $500 as income in 2022 and documents the customer's assertion.

Taxpayers who sell services rather than merchandise often use the cash method of accounting. For example, lawyers who use the cash method will keep logs of fees charged to clients but record the fees as income only upon receipt of the cash. Taxpayers who receive income other than cash report as income the fair market value (FMV) of the property or services received.

EXAMPLE 3	Scott receives ten shares of stock in exchange for services rendered. The market value of a share of stock is $28. Scott reports income of $280 ($28 × 10 shares).

Under the cash method, taxpayers deduct expenses when they pay the cash, but only if the expenses relate to the current or a previous tax year. Taxpayers usually deduct prepaid amounts in the year the prepaid item is used in their businesses. Thus, cash basis taxpayers who prepay rent, insurance, etc., must wait until it is used in their businesses before they deduct it.

EXAMPLE 4	On September 23, 2021, Ming pays $36,000 for two years' insurance coverage that begins on October 1, 2021. Although Ming is a cash basis taxpayer, she cannot deduct the $36,000 payment in 2021. Instead she deducts $4,500 ($36,000/24 × 3) in 2021. Ming will deduct $18,000 ($36,000/24 × 12) in 2022 and the rest ($36,000/24 × 9 = $13,500) in 2023.

¶701.02   ACCRUAL METHOD

Under the accrual method, income includes amounts earned or accrued but not received. Expenses include liabilities incurred but not paid. The accrual method is based on the right to receive the revenue rather than the actual receipt of cash. It is based on the use of the asset or service rather than the actual cash payment.

EXAMPLE 5	On January 3, 2022, an employer pays salaries that its employees earned for the week ended December 31, 2021. Under the accrual method, the employer reports the salaries as an expense in 2021. Under the cash method, the employer reports the expense in 2022.

Taxpayers account for prepaid expenses the same way under both the cash and accrual methods. That is, they deduct only the amounts properly allocable to a given year and carry forward the rest to the next year. In Example 4, the amount deducted each year would be the same had Ming used the accrual method of accounting.

The tax law generally requires taxpayers using the accrual method to recognize prepaid income in the year they receive it. However, when the taxpayer sells goods or performs services that extend beyond the current tax year, most prepaid income can be spread over the current tax year and the next tax year. Also, many accrual-method taxpayers do not have to accrue service revenue that their experience tells them will not be collectible. These taxpayers include those who perform certain services (like health, law, consulting) and whose businesses had average annual gross receipts of $26 million or less (adjusted annually for inflation) for the last three years.

EXAMPLE 6	Kent is in the business of selling and repairing televisions. On April 1, 2021, Kent receives $1,200 from one of his customers for a two-year warranty contract. Kent spreads his prepaid income over two tax years. He reports $450 ($1,200 × 9 months/24 months) on his 2021 tax return, and the rest ($1,200 – $450 = $750) on his 2022 tax return. Kent must report the entire $1,200 on his 2021 and 2022 tax returns, even though some of the services extend into 2023.

The exception that allows accrual method taxpayers to spread out prepaid income over two tax years does not extend to prepaid interest and most prepaid rent. It also does not extend to prepaid warranty income received by third parties. A third-party provider is one who did not sell the goods being warranted to the customer to whom the warranty is sold. Taxpayers who receive these types of prepaid items report the full amounts in income in the year they receive it.

EXAMPLE 7	Same facts as in Example 6, except that Kent offers the warranty contract as a third-party provider. Kent must report the entire $1,200 in gross income in 2021.

Reporting Business Profit or Loss

There are several forms in which businesses can operate. One of the most popular and easiest to start is the sole proprietorship. As the name implies, this type of business can only have a single owner, who must be an individual. When a business is operated as a sole proprietorship, all activities of the business are reported on the owner's tax return. The details of reporting the profit and loss of self-employed persons (sole proprietors) are the focus of this chapter.

Partnerships and corporations are other means through which businesses can operate. Partnerships and corporations are entities separate from their owners and must file separate income tax returns. The details of these businesses' tax returns are discussed in Chapters 14–16.

A self-employed taxpayer who owns a business reports net profit or (loss) on Form 1040. Schedule C, Profit or Loss From Business (Sole Proprietorship), summarizes the revenues and expenses of sole proprietors. Only self-employment income and related expenses are reported on Schedule C.

Income reported on Schedule C comes from revenues earned while operating a business as a sole proprietorship. It can result from part-time or full-time activities. Self-employment income includes gross receipts from sales (for businesses that sell goods), as well as fees earned by service providers, clergy members, and Christian Science practitioners. Also reported on Schedule C are fees earned by serving on the Board of Directors for a corporation (director's fees), fees earned by professional executors (those whose business is managing estates), and commissions earned by real estate agents.

Sometimes determining whether earnings are reported as self-employment income depends on where the services are rendered. For example, fees charged by a childcare provider (babysitter) are reported on Schedule C only if the services are provided outside of the parent's home. Other times it is the party who employs the worker that determines whether the earnings are reported on Schedule C. For instance, when a registered nurse or licensed practicing nurse is employed directly by the patient, the earnings are reported on the nurse's Schedule C. However, if the nurse is employed by an agency, doctor, or a hospital to care for a patient, the nurse's earnings are considered wages.

There are many items of income that are not reported on Schedule C. For instance, interest earned on the taxpayer's investments is not business income. Instead, it is reported as a separate line item on the tax return (see discussion at ¶308.09). However, interest earned on business accounts (from customer balances or the business bank account) is reported as other income on Schedule C.

Rental income from real estate holdings is not reported on Schedule C unless the taxpayer's business involves rental real estate. Many rental activities are considered passive activities and are reported on Schedule E, Supplemental Income and Loss. Rental activities and Schedule E are the focus of Chapter 9.

Gains and losses from the sale of business property (other than inventory) are not reported as part of business profit or loss on Schedule C. These gains and losses are reported on Form 4797, Sales of Business Property, and appear on a separate line item from business profits on Schedule 1 (Form 1040 or 1040-SR). The sale of business property is discussed in Chapter 11.

¶703 Reporting Net Profit (or Loss) by Sole Proprietorships

Net profit derived from a business operated as a sole proprietorship is taxable. A net loss is deducted in arriving at adjusted gross income. In computing the amount of net profit (or loss), sole proprietors subtract from business income the cost of goods sold and all deductible business expenses. To be deductible, expenses from a business must be *ordinary and necessary* for its operation. Also, the expenses must be *reasonable* in amount. An expense is ordinary if it is customary or usual in the taxpayer's line of business. An expense is necessary if it helps the taxpayer's business. The costs of capital expenditures (assets lasting more than one year), such as trucks, office machinery, and buildings, are deducted over several years through annual depreciation deductions. Depreciation is the focus of Chapter 6.

Sole proprietorships report net profit on Schedule C, Profit or Loss From Business (Sole Proprietorship). Sole proprietorships reporting a net loss must also file Schedule C. This chapter focuses on completing Schedule C.

¶704 Structure of Schedule C

Schedule C, Profit or Loss From Business (Sole Proprietorship), is a two-page schedule that reports the net profit or (loss) from a business operated as a sole proprietorship. A sole proprietor must pay self-employment tax on Schedule C profits. When a married couple files a joint return, and each spouse owns a business, each spouse must file a Schedule C. If only one spouse owns a business, only the owner's name appears on Schedule C. If a proprietor owns more than one business, a separate Schedule C must be filed for each business.

Schedule C (Figure 7-1) supports the amount shown on Schedule 1 (Form 1040), line 12. Page 1 of Schedule C focuses on the calculation of net profit (or loss). It also requests general information about the business. Page 2 provides the supporting data for cost of goods sold, vehicle expenses, and other expenses reported on page 1.

¶704.01   FILLED-IN SCHEDULE C

INFORMATION FOR FIGURE 7-1:

Monroe L. Peters is the owner of Monroe L. Peters, Consulting (line C). Monroe operates the business out of his home, which is located at 1712 Market Street, Cincinnati, Ohio 45227-9193 (line E). He uses the cash method (line F) and materially participates in the operation of his consulting business (line G). The principal business code for consulting is 541600 (line B), which is found in the instructions to Schedule C. Because Monroe is required to withhold and pay payroll taxes on behalf of his employees, he has an Employer ID number, which he reports on Schedule C (line D).

¶705 Item-by-Item Reporting on Schedule C

This section explains each line item shown on Schedule C. The amounts reported relate to Monroe Peters's filled-in Schedule C from Figure 7-1.

Figure 7-1: Filled-In Schedule C (Page 1)

SCHEDULE C (Form 1040)	Profit or Loss From Business (Sole Proprietorship)	OMB No. 1545-0074
Department of the Treasury Internal Revenue Service	Go to www.irs.gov/ScheduleC for instructions and the latest information. Attach to Form 1040, 1040-SR, 1040-NR, or 1041; partnerships must generally file Form 1065.	2022 Attachment Sequence No. 09

Name of proprietor	Social security number (SSN)
Monroe L. Peters	268-00-9092

A Principal business or profession, including product or service (see instructions)
Consulting

B Enter code from instructions: 5 4 1 6 0 0

C Business name. If no separate business name, leave blank.
Monroe L. Peters Consulting

D Employer ID number (EIN) (see instr.): 7 0 1 2 3 4 5 6 9

E Business address (including suite or room no.) 1712 Market St
City, town or post office, state, and ZIP code Cincinnati, OH 45227

F Accounting method: **(1)** ☐ Cash **(2)** ☐ Accrual **(3)** ☐ Other (specify)

G Did you "materially participate" in the operation of this business during 2022? If "No," see instructions for limit on losses ☐ Yes ☐ No

H If you started or acquired this business during 2022, check here ☐

I Did you make any payments in 2022 that require you to file Form(s) 1099? See instructions ☐ Yes ☐ No

J If "Yes," did you or will you file required Form(s) 1099? ☐ Yes ☐ No

Part I Income

1	Gross receipts or sales. See instructions for line 1 and check the box if this income was reported to you on Form W-2 and the "Statutory employee" box on that form was checked ☐	1	156,921
2	Returns and allowances	2	
3	Subtract line 2 from line 1	3	156,921
4	Cost of goods sold (from line 42)	4	
5	**Gross profit.** Subtract line 4 from line 3	5	156,921
6	Other income, including federal and state gasoline or fuel tax credit or refund (see instructions)	6	
7	**Gross income.** Add lines 5 and 6	7	156,921

Part II Expenses. Enter expenses for business use of your home only on line 30.

8	Advertising	8	492	18	Office expense (see instructions)	18	1,640
9	Car and truck expenses (see instructions)	9	2,940	19	Pension and profit-sharing plans	19	
10	Commissions and fees	10		20	Rent or lease (see instructions):		
11	Contract labor (see instructions)	11		a	Vehicles, machinery, and equipment	20a	
12	Depletion	12		b	Other business property	20b	1,200
13	Depreciation and section 179 expense deduction (not included in Part III) (see instructions)	13	1,619	21	Repairs and maintenance	21	1,389
				22	Supplies (not included in Part III)	22	1,642
				23	Taxes and licenses	23	7,210
				24	Travel and meals:		
14	Employee benefit programs (other than on line 19)	14		a	Travel	24a	842
15	Insurance (other than health)	15	742	b	Deductible meals (see instructions)	24b	215
16	Interest (see instructions):			25	Utilities	25	3,600
a	Mortgage (paid to banks, etc.)	16a		26	Wages (less employment credits)	26	40,616
b	Other	16b		27a	Other expenses (from line 48)	27a	780
17	Legal and professional services	17	310	b	Reserved for future use	27b	

28	**Total expenses** before expenses for business use of home. Add lines 8 through 27a	28	65,237
29	Tentative profit or (loss). Subtract line 28 from line 7	29	91,684
30	Expenses for business use of your home. Do not report these expenses elsewhere. Attach Form 8829 unless using the simplified method. See instructions. **Simplified method filers only:** Enter the total square footage of (a) your home: _____ and (b) the part of your home used for business: _____ . Use the Simplified Method Worksheet in the instructions to figure the amount to enter on line 30	30	1,084
31	**Net profit or (loss).** Subtract line 30 from line 29. • If a profit, enter on both **Schedule 1 (Form 1040), line 3,** and on **Schedule SE, line 2.** (If you checked the box on line 1, see instructions.) Estates and trusts, enter on **Form 1041, line 3.** • If a loss, you **must** go to line 32.	31	90,600
32	If you have a loss, check the box that describes your investment in this activity. See instructions. • If you checked 32a, enter the loss on both **Schedule 1 (Form 1040), line 3,** and on **Schedule SE, line 2.** (If you checked the box on line 1, see the line 31 instructions.) Estates and trusts, enter on **Form 1041, line 3.** • If you checked 32b, you **must** attach **Form 6198.** Your loss may be limited.	32a ☐ All investment is at risk. 32b ☐ Some investment is not at risk.	

For Paperwork Reduction Act Notice, see the separate instructions. Cat. No. 11334P Schedule C (Form 1040) 2022

Figure 7-1: Filled-In Schedule C (Page 2)

Schedule C (Form 1040) 2022   Page **2**

Part III   **Cost of Goods Sold** (see instructions)

33   Method(s) used to value closing inventory: **a** ☐ Cost   **b** ☐ Lower of cost or market   **c** ☐ Other (attach explanation)

34   Was there any change in determining quantities, costs, or valuations between opening and closing inventory? If "Yes," attach explanation . . . . ☐ **Yes**   ☐ **No**

35   Inventory at beginning of year. If different from last year's closing inventory, attach explanation . . | **35** |

36   Purchases less cost of items withdrawn for personal use . . . . | **36** |

37   Cost of labor. Do not include any amounts paid to yourself . . . . | **37** |

38   Materials and supplies . . . . | **38** |

39   Other costs . . . . | **39** |

40   Add lines 35 through 39 . . . . | **40** |

41   Inventory at end of year . . . . | **41** |

42   **Cost of goods sold.** Subtract line 41 from line 40. Enter the result here and on line 4 . . . . . . | **42** |

Part IV   **Information on Your Vehicle.** Complete this part **only** if you are claiming car or truck expenses on line 9 and are not required to file Form 4562 for this business. See the instructions for line 13 to find out if you must file Form 4562.

43   When did you place your vehicle in service for business purposes? (month/day/year)   _____ / _____ / _____

44   Of the total number of miles you drove your vehicle during 2022, enter the number of miles you used your vehicle for:

a   Business _____   **b** Commuting (see instructions) _____   **c** Other _____

45   Was your vehicle available for personal use during off-duty hours? . . . . ☐ **Yes**   ☐ **No**

46   Do you (or your spouse) have another vehicle available for personal use? . . . . ☐ **Yes**   ☐ **No**

47a   Do you have evidence to support your deduction? . . . . ☐ **Yes**   ☐ **No**

b   If "Yes," is the evidence written? . . . . ☐ **Yes**   ☐ **No**

Part V   **Other Expenses.** List below business expenses not included on lines 8–26 or line 30.

Education	780

48   **Total other expenses.** Enter here and on line 27a . . . . | **48** | 780 |

Schedule C (Form 1040) 2022

¶705.01   SCHEDULE C, PART I: INCOME

Total Gross Receipts, $156,921 (Line 1)

In addition to gross receipts from the business, statutory employees report their W-2 wages on Schedule C (line 1). **Statutory employees** include full-time employees in the following occupations: outside salespersons, life insurance sales agents, some agent/commission-based drivers, and home-based piece-goods workers. As for all employees, the wages of these workers are reported to them on Form W-2. However, the tax law treats statutory employees as self-employed for purposes of reporting their income and expenses. Thus, statutory employees report their W-2 wages and deduct all work-related expenses on Schedule C. However, self-employment taxes do not apply to statutory employees, as both the employer and the employee each pay FICA taxes through the tax withholding system. The employer alerts the IRS of this situation by checking the "Statutory Employee" box on Form W-2.

Monroe, owner of Monroe L. Peters, Consulting, uses the cash method and works from home. He reports the $156,921 actually and constructively received during the year.

Returns and Allowances, $0 (Line 2) and Net Sales

Taxpayers subtract returns and allowances (line 2) from total gross receipts, resulting in net sales (line 3). Since Monroe operates a service business, he had no returns or allowances.

Cost of Goods Sold, $0 (Line 4) and Gross Profit

Taxpayers report their cost of goods sold on Schedule C (line 4) and subtract it from the amount on Schedule C (line 3) to arrive at their gross profit (line 5). Taxpayers calculate cost of goods sold on Schedule C, Part III (covered later in the chapter). Since Monroe's business does not involve selling products, he does not complete Part III. Monroe's gross profit (line 5) is $156,921.

Other Income and Gross Income, $156,921 (Line 7)

Gross income equals other income (line 6) plus gross profit (line 5). Other income includes interest income earned by the business.

¶705.02   SCHEDULE C, PART II: EXPENSES

Sole proprietors generally deduct all ordinary, necessary, and reasonable expenses of operating a business. Schedule C, Part II lists a number of separate expenses that sole proprietors can deduct.

Advertising, $492 (Line 8)

Taxpayers generally can deduct advertising expenses related to their businesses. They cannot, however, deduct advertising for purposes of influencing legislation.

Car and Truck Expenses, $2,940 (Line 9)

Taxpayers use either the standard mileage rate or actual expenses to deduct the business use of a vehicle. Under both methods, taxpayers keep track of:

- Date the vehicle was first used for work
- Total miles driven during the year

■ Total work-related miles driven during the year
■ Commuting miles driven during the year

Taxpayers provide this information for each vehicle driven for business. The IRS also requires employees to answer four specific questions on Schedule C, part IV, or Form 4562 (see Chapter 6). Responding "No" to the third or fourth question may trigger an audit. Also, the lack of written evidence can result in the loss of deductions.

1. Was the vehicle available for personal use?
2. Does the taxpayer (or the taxpayer's spouse) have another vehicle available for personal use?
3. Does the taxpayer have evidence to support the deduction?
4. Is the evidence written?

The tax laws for computing the deduction an employer takes when reimbursing an employee's transportation expense are the same ones self-employed taxpayers use to compute their car and truck expense deduction on Schedule C (line 9). Taxpayers use either the standard mileage rate or the business portion of their actual expenses and add to that amount their business parking and tolls.

When using the actual expenses method, taxpayers must keep records of their car expenses, total miles, and total business miles driven during the year. The deductible amount equals the total car expenses times the percentage of business use during the year. Car expenses include amounts paid for gas, insurance, repairs, maintenance, tags and licenses, garage rent, and depreciation.

Taxpayers compute depreciation using the methods described in Chapter 6. These methods include accelerated depreciation methods, which allow taxpayers to take more depreciation in the earlier years of the vehicle's life. However, once taxpayers deduct their car expenses using the actual expenses that include the use of an accelerated depreciation method, they can no longer use the standard mileage rate method for that car in later years. Instead, they must continue to use the actual expenses method to compute their car expense deduction.

At the beginning of 2022, the standard mileage rate was $0.58 per mile. The IRS increased this rate to $0.625 for miles driven after June 30, 2022. [Announcement 2022-13, 2022-26 I.R.B. 1185] The taxpayer must prove the business miles driven for all vehicles by keeping a detailed log.

When leasing a car, taxpayers may elect to use the standard mileage rate, or they may elect to deduct the entire business portion of the monthly lease payments. For more expensive cars, the IRS limits the amount of the deduction. The deduction for leased cars is covered in Chapter 6 (¶602.09).

Self-employed taxpayers that are not required to file Form 4562, Depreciation and Amortization, must complete Schedule C, Part IV to support their deductions. Monroe uses the standard mileage rate method. Monroe drove a total of 4,910 business miles in 2022. 2,861 of those miles were driven before July 1.

His car and truck expense deduction equals:

Dates	Deduction	Miles	Rate
Before July	$1,659	2,861	0.58
After June	$1,281	2,049	0.625
Total	$2,940	4,910	

EXAMPLE 8

In 2022, Terry drove 6,000 business miles and 20,000 total miles. He drove half of those miles in each half of the year. In 2022, Terry had used the actual cost method and accelerated depreciation to deduct expenses related to the business use of his car. Terry's expenses for the car in 2022 are as follows.

Business parking and tolls	$ 100
Depreciation	4,000
Gas	1,000
Insurance	450
License tags	50
Oil change	20
Total	$5,620

Under the actual cost method, Terry deducts $1,756 [($5,520 × 6,000/20,000) + $100 business parking and tolls]. Since Terry used an accelerated depreciation method in 2021, he must use the actual cost method in 2022. Had Terry been able to use the standard mileage rate method, his deduction would have been $3,615.

Dates	Deduction	Miles	Rate
Before July	$1,740	3,000	0.58
After June	$1,875	3,000	0.625
Total	$3,615	6,000	

In addition to expenses directly related to the car, taxpayers can deduct business-related parking, tolls, and other transportation expenses, regardless of whether the standard rate or the actual expenses method is used. Deductible transportation expenses include cab, bus, and train fares.

EXAMPLE 9

Harvey uses his personal car for his proprietorship. In 2022, Harvey drove 8,300 work-related miles and 21,430 total miles. He drove half of those miles in each half of the year. His car expenses are as follows. In addition to these amounts, Harvey paid $253 in business-related parking and tolls.

Depreciation	$ 1,875
Gas	2,670
Insurance	1,540
License tags	75
Repairs and maintenance	850
Total	$7,010

Under the actual expenses method, Harvey deducts $2,968 [($7,010 × 8,300/21,430) + $253]. Using the standard mileage method, his deduction would be $5,254:

Dates	Deduction	Miles	Rate
Before July	$2,407	4,150	0.58
After June	$2,594	4,150	0.625
Total	$5,001	8,300	
Tolls	253		
Total	$5,254		

Under both methods, the business parking and tolls are deducted in addition to the deduction for other car-related expenses. Based on these calculations, Harvey would be better off using the standard mileage method to deduct his car expenses. He can use this method as long as he has not depreciated the car using an accelerated depreciation method in a previous tax year.

Commissions and Fees, $0 (Line 10)

Taxpayers can deduct commissions and fees paid for business purposes on Schedule C (line 10).

Contract Labor, $0 (Line 11)

Taxpayers deduct amounts paid for contract labor on Schedule C (line 11). Contract labor includes amounts paid to workers who are independent contractors. It does not include wages paid to employees. Wages paid to employees are reported on Schedule C (line 26).

Depletion, $0 (Line 12)

Taxpayers operating a business that owns a natural resource, such as an oil well, a coal mine, or a gold mine, may claim a depletion deduction. **Depletion** is the process that allows taxpayers to deduct the cost of natural resources as units from the resource are sold (under the accrual method) or sold and payment is received (under the cash method). The two methods for computing the depletion deduction are the cost method and the percentage depletion method. Each year the taxpayer may use whichever method produces the greatest deduction.

The *cost method* allows taxpayers to deduct the costs of natural resources as the resource units are recovered and sold. The cost of the natural resource is divided by the number of units expected to be recovered. This provides depletion per unit. The per-unit cost is then multiplied by the number of units sold during the year.

Under the *percentage depletion method,* taxpayers multiply a set percentage by the gross income generated by the resource during the year. The government specifies the percentages used, which range from 5% for sand and gravel to 22% for lead, zinc, tin, and sulfur. A 15% rate applies to copper, gold, silver, iron, oil, and gas. The percentage depletion method has a distinct advantage over cost depletion in that the taxpayer can continue to take the percentage depletion deduction even after the entire cost invested in the natural resource has been fully recovered through annual depletion deductions.

Depreciation and Section 179 Expense Deduction, $1,619 (Line 13)

Monroe completes and attaches Form 4562, Depreciation and Amortization, to support the depreciation and Section 179 expense deduction. See Chapter 6. In 2022, Monroe purchased $1,619 of computer equipment. He used the first-year allowance "bonus" depreciation to deduct the total cost in 2022, which he reports on Schedule C (line 13).

Employee Benefit Programs, $0 (Line 14)

Employers generally can deduct the costs of benefits they provide for their employees. For example, employers can deduct life insurance premiums paid for policies on employees' lives, but only for policies that do not list the employer as the beneficiary. Employers also deduct the cost of health insurance premiums paid on behalf of their employees. Other examples include the costs of adoption assistance, childcare, parking, and transportation provided to employees.

Insurance, $742 (Line 15)

Self-employed persons deduct malpractice and other professional insurance. Taxpayers deduct insurance premiums on business property, including real estate, furniture, machinery, and equipment. Employers deduct premiums paid for medical and life insurance for their employees as employee benefits (line 14). As mentioned earlier in the chapter (¶701.01), cash method taxpayers cannot deduct advance payments on policies that cover more than one tax year. They can

Figure 7-2: Filled-In Form 4562 (Page 1)

Form **4562**	**Depreciation and Amortization** (Including Information on Listed Property) Attach to your tax return. Go to www.irs.gov/Form4562 for instructions and the latest information.	OMB No. 1545-0172 **2022** Attachment Sequence No. **179**
Department of the Treasury Internal Revenue Service		

Name(s) shown on return	Business or activity to which this form relates	Identifying number
Monroe L. Peters	Monroe L. Peters Consulting	268-00-9092

Part I   Election To Expense Certain Property Under Section 179
Note: If you have any listed property, complete Part V before you complete Part I.

1	Maximum amount (see instructions)	**1** 1,080,000
2	Total cost of section 179 property placed in service (see instructions)	**2**
3	Threshold cost of section 179 property before reduction in limitation (see instructions)	**3** 2,700,000
4	Reduction in limitation. Subtract line 3 from line 2. If zero or less, enter -0-	**4**
5	Dollar limitation for tax year. Subtract line 4 from line 1. If zero or less, enter -0-. If married filing separately, see instructions	**5** 2,700,000

6	(a) Description of property	(b) Cost (business use only)	(c) Elected cost

7	Listed property. Enter the amount from line 29 . . . **7**	
8	Total elected cost of section 179 property. Add amounts in column (c), lines 6 and 7	**8**
9	Tentative deduction. Enter the **smaller** of line 5 or line 8	**9**
10	Carryover of disallowed deduction from line 13 of your 2021 Form 4562	**10**
11	Business income limitation. Enter the smaller of business income (not less than zero) or line 5. See instructions	**11**
12	Section 179 expense deduction. Add lines 9 and 10, but don't enter more than line 11	**12**
13	Carryover of disallowed deduction to 2023. Add lines 9 and 10, less line 12 **13**	

Note: Don't use Part II or Part III below for listed property. Instead, use Part V.

Part II   Special Depreciation Allowance and Other Depreciation (Don't include listed property. See instructions.)

14	Special depreciation allowance for qualified property (other than listed property) placed in service during the tax year. See instructions	**14** 1,619
15	Property subject to section 168(f)(1) election	**15**
16	Other depreciation (including ACRS)	**16**

Part III   MACRS Depreciation (Don't include listed property. See instructions.)

Section A

17	MACRS deductions for assets placed in service in tax years beginning before 2022	**17**
18	If you are electing to group any assets placed in service during the tax year into one or more general asset accounts, check here ☐	

Section B—Assets Placed in Service During 2022 Tax Year Using the General Depreciation System

(a) Classification of property	(b) Month and year placed in service	(c) Basis for depreciation (business/investment use only—see instructions)	(d) Recovery period	(e) Convention	(f) Method	(g) Depreciation deduction
19a 3-year property						
b 5-year property						
c 7-year property						
d 10-year property						
e 15-year property						
f 20-year property						
g 25-year property			25 yrs.		S/L	
h Residential rental property			27.5 yrs.	MM	S/L	
			27.5 yrs.	MM	S/L	
i Nonresidential real property			39 yrs.	MM	S/L	
				MM	S/L	

Section C—Assets Placed in Service During 2022 Tax Year Using the Alternative Depreciation System

20a Class life					S/L	
b 12-year			12 yrs.		S/L	
c 30-year			30 yrs.	MM	S/L	
d 40-year			40 yrs.	MM	S/L	

Part IV   Summary (See instructions.)

21	Listed property. Enter amount from line 28	**21**
22	**Total.** Add amounts from line 12, lines 14 through 17, lines 19 and 20 in column (g), and line 21. Enter here and on the appropriate lines of your return. Partnerships and S corporations—see instructions	**22** 1,619
23	For assets shown above and placed in service during the current year, enter the portion of the basis attributable to section 263A costs **23**	

For Paperwork Reduction Act Notice, see separate instructions.   Cat. No. 12906N   Form **4562** (2022)

deduct only the premiums that apply to the current or previous years. Monroe deducted $742 for insurance on Schedule C (line 15).

Interest, $0 (Lines 16a and 16b)

Business interest includes interest on mortgages (line 16a) and other business loans (line 16b). If the taxpayer borrows money and uses the loan proceeds partly for nonbusiness purposes, then only the interest related to the business-use portion of the borrowed funds can be deducted. The business interest deduction may be limited unless the taxpayer (1) has average annual gross receipts of $25 million or less (this amount is indexed for inflation and is $27 million in 2022) for the three prior tax years or (2) meets one of the other filing exceptions listed in the Instructions for Form 8990, Limitation on Business Interest Expense Under Section 163(j).

EXAMPLE 10   Jay borrows funds secured by business property. Jay uses 25% of the funds to buy a personal car. He uses the rest in his business. Jay deducts 75% of the interest on Schedule C. Personal interest is not deductible.

Legal and Professional Services, $310 (Line 17)

Taxpayers can deduct legal and professional fees, including the portion of tax preparation fees that relate to the preparation of Schedule C. They cannot deduct legal fees incurred to acquire business property. Instead, these amounts are added to the amount the taxpayer pays for the property. Monroe deducts $310 for legal services on Schedule C (line 17).

Office Expense, $1,640 (Line 18)

Office expense includes postage, stationery, and other general expenses of operating a business office. Monroe deducts $1,640 for office expense on Schedule C (Line 18).

Pension and Profit-Sharing Plans, $0 (Line 19)

Sole proprietors deduct on Schedule C amounts they contribute to their employees' qualified pension and profit-sharing plans. See Chapter 8.

Rent or Lease, $0 (Line 20a) and $1,200 (Line 20b)

Rent or lease expense is the amount paid for the use of property not owned by the taxpayer. If the taxpayer will receive title to the property at the end of the lease, then the amount paid is not rent expense. Instead, these payments are included in the purchase price of the property.

Taxpayers can deduct rent on property used in their trade or business. Those that pay rent in advance only deduct the amount that applies to the current or a previous tax year. They deduct the rest in the year or years to which the rent applies.

EXAMPLE 11   Katy leases property for three years beginning June 1, 2021. On June 1, 2021, Katy pays $12,000 for 12 months' rent but can deduct only $7,000 in 2021 ($12,000/12 × 7) under both the cash and the accrual methods. On June 1, 2022, she pays $13,200 for another 12 months' rent. In 2022, Katy will deduct the remaining $5,000 paid in 2021, and $7,700 ($13,200/12 × 7) of the $13,200 paid on June 1, 2022.

Taxpayers who lease a car deduct the costs related to the business-use portion of the lease. Taxpayers must spread any advance lease payments over the entire term of the lease. Payments made to buy a car are not deductible as rent, even if they are described as lease payments. Chapter 6 describes the rules for leased cars. Monroe reports a $1,200 deduction for rental of other business property on Schedule C (line 20b).

Repairs and Maintenance, $1,389 (Line 21)

Taxpayers can deduct the costs of keeping business property in its normal operating condition. Repair costs must be distinguished from capital expenditures. Taxpayers capitalize (increase their basis in the property) any costs that either add to the value or usefulness of the property or significantly extend its useful life. Repairs and maintenance allocable to the cost of goods sold are deducted on Schedule C, Part III when calculating cost of goods sold, not in Part II. Monroe deducts $1,389 for repairs on Schedule C (line 21).

Supplies, $1,642 (Line 22)

Taxpayers can deduct the cost of supplies that they normally use within one year. The cost of supplies not expected to be used within one year is deducted in the year the supplies are used. Monroe deducts $1,642 for supplies on Schedule C (line 22).

Taxes and Licenses, $7,210 (Line 23)

Sole proprietors can deduct property taxes paid on business property. They also can deduct their (the employer's) share of social security and Medicare taxes paid for employees plus amounts paid for state and federal unemployment taxes. Deductible licenses include business licenses required by state and local governments for operating the taxpayer's trade or business. Nursing licenses, hair stylist licenses, health department certifications, and any other professional licenses are also deductible. Monroe deducts $7,210 for taxes and licenses on Schedule C (line 23).

Travel, $842 (Line 24a)

The tax law permits self-employed persons to deduct costs related to business travel. Employees are no longer able to deduct these costs, although an accountable expense plan may allow employees to exclude reimbursements for employment-related travel expenses. For the self-employed person, there are several categories of costs that have special rules.

Deductible travel expenses include amounts paid when a self-employed person is temporarily away from home overnight for work-related reasons. "Temporary" absences from home are those not exceeding one year. Travel expenses usually cannot be deducted when the absence exceeds one year. The IRS defines "home" as the principal workplace, regardless of where the taxpayer lives. Travel expenses include all transportation costs, plus lodging and the incidental costs incurred while away from home. Self-employed persons can deduct meals purchased while traveling (subject to the 50% limit). A spouse's travel expenses are deducted only when the spouse actually works for the business during the bulk of the trip.

After 2017, entertainment expenses are no longer deductible. Amounts owners pay for business-related travel and meals on behalf of themselves or their employees are deductible on Schedule C. When an owner reimburses an employee for work-related expenses, the amount of the deduction and its location on Schedule C depends on whether the reimbursement was paid from an "accountable" or "nonaccountable" plan.

An accountable plan requires the employee to (1) adequately report the expenses to the employer and (2) return any excess reimbursements to the employer. Owners with an accountable plan deduct the reimbursements under "Travel and meals" but can deduct only 50% of the amounts reimbursed for meals.

When the reimbursement is made from a nonaccountable plan (one that does not meet both criteria for an accountable plan), the reimbursement is treated as "Wages" and is deductible as such on Schedule C. Employees are taxed on these additional wages. For 2018 through 2025, employees cannot deduct their work-related expenses at all. Before 2018 and after 2025, deductible work-related meals are limited to 50% of the cost of the meals, added to any other work-related expenses, and other allowable miscellaneous itemized deductions which are then subject to a 2% AGI floor.

However, for 2021 and 2022 only, business meals are fully deductible if they are provided by a restaurant. [I.R.C. §274(n)(2)(D)]

EXAMPLE 12

Gene is self-employed. In 2022, he reimburses an employee $10,000 for travel expenses and $2,000 for meals under an accountable plan. Gene deducts $10,000 as travel on Schedule C (line 24a) and $2,000 as deductible meals (line 24b). The employee reports no gross income and claims no deduction for these items. After 2022, his meal deduction would be limited to $1,000 (50% × $2,000).

EXAMPLE 13

Same facts as in Example 12, except that Gene has a nonaccountable plan. Gene deducts all $12,000 as wages on Schedule C (line 26). The employee is taxed on the $12,000 but cannot deduct the travel and meal expenses as a miscellaneous itemized deduction subject to the 2% AGI floor as those deductions are suspended for tax years 2018-2025.

If it were 2026, the employee could deduct $10,000 of travel expenses plus $1,000 ($2,000 × 50%) of meals as miscellaneous itemized deductions, which, along with any other allowable items, would be reduced by 2% of the employee's AGI.

Deductible Travel Expenses

- Air, rail, and bus transportation, including transportation to and from the airport and the hotel
- Baggage handling charges
- Dry cleaning and laundry
- Lodging
- Meals (subject to limitations)
- Car expenses, including car rental
- Telephone, internet, and fax costs
- Tips related to travel

Some employers use the "per diem" approach to reimburse employees for the costs of meals and lodging. Employers deduct a reimbursement based on a per diem amount as "Travel and meals" but deduct only 50% of the per diem meal allowance. The rules regarding the use of per diems in lieu of actual expenses for meals also apply to sole proprietors. However, the per diem for lodging can only be used for purposes of reimbursing employees. When the owner of the business is away from home overnight on business, the owner must deduct the actual costs for lodging.

The U.S. General Services Administration (GSA) sets the rates for the coming calendar year on October 1 of the preceding year. For 2022 and later years, there is an interactive chart. See https://www.gsa.gov/travel/plan-book/per-diem-rates.

Self-employed persons who combine business and pleasure on the same trip face limits on the amount they can deduct. Different rules apply to trips within the United States and foreign travel. When traveling in the United States on a trip primarily for business (more than 50% work-related), deduct 100% of the expenses traveling to and from the destination. Once at their destination, they deduct only their work-related expenses (lodging, meals, and local transportation for work days only). For domestic travel that is 50% or less work-related, self-employed persons can only deduct their work-related expenses while at the business destination. They cannot deduct any airfare or other costs of traveling to and from their destination (like cab fare to and from the airport).

EXAMPLE 14	Blake attends a three-day seminar in Boston. After the seminar, he stays five more days in Boston to visit friends. Blake spent $450 on airfare, $250 a night for lodging, and $100 a day for meals. Because Blake's (domestic) trip was not primarily for business, the cost of his airfare is not deductible. He can, however, deduct the hotel expenses and 50% of the cost of his meals for the three days he spent conducting business.

EXAMPLE 15	Mandy is self-employed. During the year, Mandy takes a business trip to Boston. She is gone a total of six days (five nights), four of which were spent conducting business. Her travel costs include $600 for airfare, $220 for transportation to and from the airport, $250 a night for lodging, and $70 a day for meals. The per diem for Boston was $376, which includes 305 for lodging and $71 for meals and incidentals. Because her trip is primarily for business (4/6 > 50%), Mandy can deduct the $820 she spent for traveling to and from the destination ($600 + $220). The $71 daily per diem rate for meals exceeds her actual costs for meals. Thus, she is allowed to deduct $142 ($71 × 4 days × 50%) for business meals. She also can deduct $750 for lodging ($250 × 3 nights). Although the nightly per diem for lodging ($305) exceeds her actual daily lodging costs ($250), sole proprietors cannot use the per diem rates for lodging. They must deduct their actual lodging costs.

EXAMPLE 16	Lucas is self-employed. During the year, Lucas sends his employee on a business trip to Boston. The employee is gone four days (three nights), all of which were spent conducting business. The employee's actual travel costs include $600 for airfare, $220 for transportation to and from the airport, $250 a night for lodging, and $60 a day for meals. The per diem for Boston was $376, which includes $305 for lodging and $71 for meals and incidentals. Lucas reimburses the employee $2,019 under an accountable reimbursement plan. This amount includes $820 for traveling to and from the destination ($600 + $220), $915 for lodging ($305 × 3), and $284 ($71 × 4) for meals. The employee is not taxed on the $2,019 reimbursement. On his Schedule C, Lucas deducts $1,735 ($820 + $915) for travel (line 24a) and $284 for meals (line 24b). After 2022, his meal deduction is limited to $142 ($284 × 50%).

EXAMPLE 17	Same facts as Example 16, except that Lucas advances the employee $2,000 before the trip and does not require the employee to turn in receipts for amounts spent on the trip. Lucas now has made a reimbursement from a nonaccountable plan. He adds the $2,000 to the employee's taxable wages on Form W-2. He then deducts the $2,000 as wage expense on Schedule C (line 26). (For 2018 through 2025, the employee cannot deduct his travel expenses as miscellaneous itemized deductions subject to the 2% AGI floor.)

On trips involving travel outside the United States, the self-employed person must separate the costs for the business and personal portions of the trip. The taxpayer divides the business and personal costs based on the time devoted to each activity. For instance, trips comprised of 40% personal activities permit the self-employed person to deduct only 60% of the total travel expenses. However, any of the following three conditions eliminates the need to allocate the cost of traveling to and from the destination: (1) the taxpayer has no control over arranging the trip, and there is no significant element of vacation present; (2) they are away from home for fewer than eight days; or (3) the personal portion of the trip is less than 25% of the total days away from home.

For purposes of determining whether an employee's trip lasts for less than eight days (see (2) above), the day the employee returns home from the trip is counted, but the day of departure is not. Thus, if an employee leaves on a business trip on a Saturday and returns home the following Saturday, the employee is considered to have been away from home for seven days (Sunday through Saturday). Since the trip is deemed to have lasted for less than eight days, the employee would be able to deduct all costs of traveling to and from the foreign destination. Ignoring the day of departure only applies for purposes of determining whether the employee's trip lasts for eight days or less. When counting business versus personal days for purposes of allocating the costs of a business trip between business and nonbusiness, both the day of departure and day the employee returns home count as business days (see the discussion that follows).

Allocating expenses between business and nonbusiness activities requires separating the days spent away from home between business and personal days. When separating business days from personal days, both travel days count as business days. Weekends and holidays on which no significant business is conducted count as business days if a business day precedes and follows the weekend or holiday. Otherwise, the weekend or holiday counts as a personal day.

EXAMPLE 18

Edward attends a trade show in Paris, France, that begins on Tuesday and ends on Friday, with no meetings on Wednesday or Thursday. Edward travels to the trade show on Monday and returns home on Saturday. The trip lasts less than eight days. Therefore, for this (outside the U.S.) trip, all qualified travel expenses to and from his home and the trade show are deductible. The rest of the expenses must be allocated between the four business days (Monday, Tuesday, Friday, Saturday) and the two personal days (Wednesday, Thursday). Monday and Saturday count as business days because, for purposes of allocating expenses between business and personal activities, both days spent traveling count as business days. Neither Wednesday nor Thursday counts as a business day because Wednesday is not followed by a business day, and Thursday is not preceded by a business day.

EXAMPLE 19

Toddra is a panelist in a training seminar in London, England. She is gone for a total of 11 days, of which eight count as business days. Since none of the three exceptions apply, Toddra must allocate all of her travel costs between business and personal days. Of her travel costs, 72.73% (8/11) are deductible; 27.27% are nondeductible personal expenses. If Toddra's employer reimburses her for her trip, she subtracts the amount of the reimbursement from the deductible portion of her travel costs.

Special rules apply for travel outside of North America (which includes the United States and its possessions, the Trust Territories, Canada, and Mexico). For an employee to deduct expenses for traveling to conventions outside North America, the meeting must satisfy the following two conditions:

1. The convention must be directly related to the person's business, and
2. It must be as reasonable to hold the meeting outside North America as it would be to hold it in North America.

Monroe deducts $842 for business travel on Schedule C (line 24a).

Deductible Meals, $215 (Line 24b)

For meals to be deductible, the taxpayer must be present. Paying for a dinner meeting and not attending it does not qualify as a deductible expense. Moreover, only the business portion of the meals is deductible. Also, no deduction is allowed for lavish costs.

EXAMPLE 20

Janet spent $250 on meals while away from home overnight on a business trip. Included in that amount is $100 she spent on meals with family members. Janet reports $150 ($250 − $100) as business meals and entertainment expense. Assuming that all of the meals were consumed in restaurants, her deduction would be $150 in 2021 or 2022. In other years, the 50% limitation would apply. Janet deducts the meals on Schedule C.

Utilities, $3,600 (Line 25)

Utilities include the costs for heat, power, water, and telephone. Taxpayers can deduct the costs for utilities to the extent the costs are not incurred for personal use. Taxpayers deduct utilities for an office located in their home on Form 8829, Expenses for Business Use of Your Home (covered later in the chapter at ¶705.03).

Wages, $40,616 (Line 26)

Employers deduct amounts paid as wages to employees. They also deduct amounts paid to employees as bonuses, vacation pay, taxable employee achievement awards, and reimbursements under nonaccountable plans. The amount shown for wages on Schedule C (line 26) does not include wages included in cost of goods sold or withdrawals the owner makes from the business.

Other Expenses, $780 (Line 27a)

Other expenses are amounts not deductible elsewhere on Schedule C. Sole proprietors deducting other expenses list the type and amount of each expense on Schedule C, page 2, Part V. Total other expenses from Part V are transferred to Schedule C, Part II (line 27(a)). Four common other expenses sole proprietors may have are education expenses, business gifts, dues and subscriptions, and bad debts.

Taxpayers can deduct dues they pay to the Chamber of Commerce or to civic and public service organizations, like the Lions, Kiwanis, or Rotary clubs. They also can deduct dues to professional organizations, provided the dues are an ordinary and necessary expense of the taxpayer's business or employment. Examples would include dues a certified public accountant (CPA) pays to the American Institute of CPAs or dues a doctor pays to belong to the American Medical Association. However, the tax law does not allow taxpayers to deduct dues they pay to various business, social, athletic, sporting, or airline clubs. This rule applies, even if the taxpayer joined the club solely as a means to meet or entertain clients or customers. Although club dues are never deductible, taxpayers can deduct the cost of meals charged while dining with business clients at the club (subject to the 50% limit).

Self-employed taxpayers can deduct professional dues and subscriptions related to their line of business. They also can deduct the ordinary and necessary costs incurred to educate and train employees in operating the business. Deductible education expenses include tuition, books, transportation, meals (subject to the 50% rule), and lodging. In addition, sole proprietors can deduct amounts spent on their own education as long as it does not (1) prepare them to meet the minimum education requirements of their present profession or (2) qualify them for a new trade or business. Assuming neither of these situations apply, to deduct these costs, sole proprietors must show that the education (1) maintains or improves the skills required in their business or (2) is required by law to keep their status in the profession. Monroe deducts $780 for educational courses taken during the year.

| EXAMPLE 21 | Raines is a self-employed tax accountant. Raines holds a Bachelor of Science degree in accounting. He is currently taking night classes in pursuit of his law degree. During the year, his education costs include $2,500 for tuition, $620 for books, and $220 for transportation. Since getting a law degree will allow him to enter a new profession (the practice of law), the costs of his education are not deductible on Schedule C. The fact that the content of the courses will enable him to be a better tax accountant is irrelevant if the courses are part of a program of study that will enable him to enter into a new (different) profession. |

EXAMPLE 22

> Same facts as in Example 21, except that the classes Raines is taking are in pursuit of a Masters of Taxation degree. Since completion of this degree prepares Raines to be a tax accountant (which he already is), the education is not preparing him to enter into a new profession. Instead, the courses help him improve his skills in his existing profession. Thus, Raines can deduct $3,340 ($2,500 + $620 + $220) as another expense on Schedule C, Part V.

Sole proprietors can deduct the costs of business gifts to customers and clients. The maximum deduction cannot exceed $25 for business gifts given to any one person during the tax year. Gifts not subject to the $25 limit include:

1. A widely distributed item costing $4 or less on which the donor's company name is permanently imprinted. Examples include pens and key chains.
2. Signs, display racks, and other promotional material used on the recipient's business premises.
3. Incidental costs, such as engraving, packaging, insuring, and mailing the gift.

> Before 2018, employees were able to deduct the costs of business gifts to clients and customers using these same rules. They could deduct the cost of gifts they make to people who work for them. They cannot deduct the cost of gifts to people they work for (their bosses). However, for 2018 through 2025, employees cannot deduct work-related expenses as miscellaneous itemized deductions subject to the 2% AGI floor.

Any item that can be considered either a gift or entertainment generally is considered entertainment. A taxpayer who gives a business client tickets to an event but does not attend the event with the client can treat the tickets either as a gift or as entertainment. However, if the taxpayer goes with the client to the event, the tickets must be treated as entertainment. Note that business expense deductions are eliminated for most entertainment expenses, including expenses for a facility used in connection with entertainment, that are paid or incurred after 2017.

Employers also may deduct property valued at up to $400 given to employees for their length of service or safety achievement.

Taxpayers deduct bad debts that result from business operations. Bad debts may result from credit sales to customers. They also may result from loans to suppliers, clients, employees, or distributors. Sole proprietors deduct bad debts when a receivable, or a portion of a receivable, becomes uncollectible (known as the direct write-off method). The tax law does not permit the use of the "reserve" method, which is an acceptable financial accounting practice. For a bad debt to be deductible, a true creditor-debtor relationship must exist between the taxpayer (the creditor) and the debtor. Also, the taxpayer must incur an actual loss of money or have previously reported the amount owed in gross income. Thus, a cash basis taxpayer who renders services cannot take a bad debt deduction when a customer's receivable becomes uncollectible because no income was ever reported.

To deduct a business bad debt, the taxpayer must show a valid business reason for making the loan or sale. Only the uncollectible portion of a receivable qualifies as a business bad debt. A business bad debt is deductible in the year it becomes partially or completely worthless. Should the IRS challenge the bad debt deduction, the taxpayer must prove that the debt is worthless and will remain worthless. Doing so may involve going to court, which taxpayers can avoid by showing that the court would rule that the receivable was uncollectible. This usually occurs in the case of a bankrupt debtor.

EXAMPLE 23

> Tim is self-employed. During 2021, Tim loans his friend $5,000 so that his friend can start his own business. In 2023, the friend files for bankruptcy, and Tim is told that he should expect to receive $.15 on the dollar. Since the purpose of the loan was not related to Tim's business, the bad debt is a nonbusiness bad debt. The tax treatment for nonbusiness bad debts is discussed in ¶1101.07.

EXAMPLE 24	Same facts as in Example 23, except that Tim's loan is to his business supplier. The reason for the loan is to keep the supplier in business and prevent the delivery of Tim's inventory from being delayed. Because the purpose of the loan is related to Tim's business, Tim can begin taking a bad debt deduction in 2023 when the debt becomes partially worthless. He reports $4,250 ($5,000 − ($5,000 × $.15)) as an other expense on Schedule C, Part V.

EXAMPLE 25	Continuing with Example 24, assume that in 2024, the bankruptcy proceedings are finalized, and Tim receives $300 for his $5,000 loan. Tim's total bad debt deduction is $4,700 ($5,000 − $300). Since Tim deducted $4,250 in 2023, he deducts $450 ($4,700 − $4,250) as another expense on his 2024 Schedule C.

EXAMPLE 26	Same facts as in Example 25, except that Tim receives $1,000 (instead of $300) from the bankruptcy court. Tim's total bad debt deduction is now $4,000 ($5,000 − $1,000). Because Tim deducted $4,250 in 2023, the tax benefit rule (see ¶313.01) requires that he include $250 as other income on his 2024 Schedule C (line 6).

Total Expenses, $65,237 (Line 28)

Monroe subtracts total expenses from gross income (line 7) to arrive at a tentative profit (loss) of $91,704 (line 29).

¶705.03   BUSINESS USE OF THE HOME

Sole proprietors normally can deduct expenses related to an office located in the home only if they use that part of the home regularly and exclusively as either (1) the principal place of business, or (2) a place to meet or deal with patients, clients, or customers in the normal course of business. However, they are allowed to deduct expenses for using part of the home as a day-care facility or as a place to store inventory, even if sometimes that part of the home is used for personal purposes.

To claim a home office deduction, the taxpayer usually must be able to demonstrate that, relative to the work done outside the office, the work done in the office is more important to the business. However, this rule does not apply to those who use their home office exclusively and regularly for administrative or management activities and have no other location to perform these duties. For example, a self-employed plumber who spends several hours each week scheduling appointments and preparing invoices qualifies for the home office deduction, provided that the office is used regularly and exclusively for administrative and management activities.

EXAMPLE 27	Stan, a self-employed writer, uses an office located in his home exclusively and regularly to write. Stan conducts most of his interviews outside of the office. He also spends many hours doing research at the library. Although doing research and conducting interviews are important to the business, the most important part is the actual writing. Since Stan does his writing at the office located in his home, he qualifies for the home office deduction.

EXAMPLE 28	Robyn is a self-employed physical therapist who works at three different hospitals. Robyn uses one room in her two-bedroom apartment exclusively as a home office. She uses the office to schedule and confirm appointments. She also uses it to prepare and file medical insurance claims for her patients. None of the hospitals provide her with an office to perform these tasks. Although the most important aspect of her job is treating patients (which is done at the hospital), she must perform these administrative tasks in order to make a living. Since the home office is used regularly and exclusively to perform these administrative tasks and there is no other place for her to do this, Robyn qualifies for the home office deduction.

EXAMPLE 29	Same facts as in Example 28, except that one of the hospitals provides its contractors with an office to perform their administrative tasks. Robyn, however, prefers to do these tasks in the comfort of her own home. Because she has been given another place to perform her administrative duties, Robyn cannot take the home office deduction.

Sole proprietors who qualify to take the home office deduction can choose each year between one of two methods allowed to compute the deduction. The first method uses the actual costs of operating the home. Some of the more common operating costs are home mortgage interest, real estate taxes, insurance, utilities, repairs, and depreciation. Only the business-use portion of these costs is used in computing the deduction.

To allocate expenses to the home office, taxpayers divide the square feet of the home office by the total square feet of the home. Taxpayers who use part of their home exclusively as a childcare facility also use this method to allocate a portion of their expenses of the home to the childcare business. However, for areas of the home not used on an exclusive basis, the deductible costs must be reduced by the ratio of hours the area is used for day care to the total hours in the year. Total hours in 2022 are 8,760 (24 hours × 365 days).

EXAMPLE 30	Jennifer provides childcare in her home. The area of the home used in her childcare business is 40% of the total area of the home. For 50 weeks, Jennifer provides childcare services ten hours a day, five days a week, for a total of 2,500 hours (10 × 5 × 50). Jennifer can deduct 11.42% (40% × 2,500/8,760) of the expenses of her home against the income she earns providing childcare in 2022.

The second method for computing the home office deduction is the safe harbor method (also called the simplified method). Taxpayers using this method multiply the square footage of the home office (up to 300 square feet) by $5. The safe harbor method can be used by renters, as well as homeowners. Sole proprietors using the safe harbor method enter the square footage of both the home office and the entire home, plus the amount of the deduction, on Schedule C (line 30).

¶705.04   FILLED-IN FORM 8829

Sole proprietors who use their actual operating costs of the home to compute their home office deduction must complete Form 8829, Expenses for Business Use of Your Home, to support their deduction. On Form 8829, Part I, proprietors determine the business percentage of the home. Using this percentage, in Part II, they compute their home office deduction. The depreciation expense deduction reported on Form 8829 (line 30) is computed in Form 8829, Part III. It is here in Part III that only the business portion of the home itself (excluding the land) is depreciated using the depreciation methods described in Chapter 6 (see ¶603.03). Figure 7-3 shows a completed Form 8829 for Monroe Peters (from Figure 7-1).

INFORMATION FOR FIGURE 7-3:

Monroe Peters (from Figure 7-1) enters the amounts shown below in bold on the appropriate lines of Form 8829. He then follows the instructions on the form to compute his home office deduction. Monroe enters the deduction from Form 8829 (line 36) on Schedule C (line 30).

Line #
- 1: Area used regularly and exclusively for business, **240**
- 2: Total area of home, **2,400**
- 8: Tentative profit from Schedule C, line 29, **$91,684** (from Figure 7-1)
- 10(b): Mortgage interest, **$4,300**
- 11(b): Real estate taxes, **$1,500**
- 18(b): Insurance, **$280**
- 20(b): Repairs and maintenance, **$950**
- 21(b): Utilities, **$1,810**
- 37: Smaller of the home's adjusted basis ($90,000) or its FMV ($128,000), **$90,000**
- 38: Value of land included on line 37, **$12,000**
- 41: Depreciation percentage, **2.564** (1/39 years, explained in Chapter 6)

In Figure 7-3, the income from the business activity exceeded both the business expenses reported on Schedule C, Part II, and the expenses related to the office in the home. With the exception of the business portion of home mortgage interest, real estate taxes, and casualty losses, home office expenses cannot create a loss on Schedule C. Specifically, taxpayers can deduct these other types of home office expenses only to the extent of net income derived from the business. **Net income derived from the business** equals tentative profit shown on Schedule C (line 29) minus the home office expenses for home mortgage interest, real estate taxes, and casualty losses. Any disallowed expenses carry over to the next year.

EXAMPLE 31

Morgan conducts a business in his home. The business portion equals 20% of the total square footage of the home. Expenses of operating the home include utilities, $3,500; real estate taxes, $5,000; mortgage interest, $6,000; insurance, $800; general home repairs, $2,000; and depreciation, $4,500. The tentative profit from the business is $3,300. Morgan computes net income derived from the business as follows.

Tentative profit	$3,300
Less business portion of mortgage interest and real estate taxes [20% × ($6,000 + $5,000)]	(2,200)
Net income derived from the business	$1,100

After deducting the business portion of mortgage interest, real estate taxes, and casualty losses, taxpayers deduct the other home office expenses (to the extent of net income derived from the business) in the following order:

1. The business portion of expenses (other than depreciation) incurred in operating the business in the home. These expenses include repairs, maintenance, insurance, and utilities.
2. The depreciation on the business portion of the home.

Any home office expenses in excess of net income derived from the business carry over to the next year.

Figure 7-3: Filled-In Form 8829

This Form is Overset by 2 Lines

Form **8829**	**Expenses for Business Use of Your Home**	OMB No. 1545-0074
Department of the Treasury Internal Revenue Service	File only with Schedule C (Form 1040). Use a separate Form 8829 for each home you used for business during the year. Go to *www.irs.gov/Form8829* for instructions and the latest information.	20**22** Attachment Sequence No. **176**

Name(s) of proprietor(s)	Your social security number
Monroe L. Peters	268-00-9092

Part I   Part of Your Home Used for Business

1	Area used regularly and exclusively for business, regularly for daycare, or for storage of inventory or product samples (see instructions)	**1**	240
2	Total area of home	**2**	2,400
3	Divide line 1 by line 2. Enter the result as a percentage	**3**	10.000 %
	For daycare facilities not used exclusively for business, go to line 4. All others, go to line 7.		
4	Multiply days used for daycare during year by hours used per day **4** hr.		
5	If you started or stopped using your home for daycare during the year, see instructions; otherwise, enter 8,760 **5** hr.		
6	Divide line 4 by line 5. Enter the result as a decimal amount **6**		
7	Business percentage. For daycare facilities not used exclusively for business, multiply line 6 by line 3 (enter the result as a percentage). All others, enter the amount from line 3	**7**	10.000 %

Part II   Figure Your Allowable Deduction

8	Enter the amount from Schedule C, line 29, **plus** any gain derived from the business use of your home, **minus** any loss from the trade or business not derived from the business use of your home. See instructions.	**8**	91,684

See instructions for columns (a) and (b) before completing lines 9–22.

			(a) Direct expenses	(b) Indirect expenses		
9	Casualty losses (see instructions)	**9**				
10	Deductible mortgage interest (see instructions)	**10**		4,300		
11	Real estate taxes (see instructions)	**11**		1,500		
12	Add lines 9, 10, and 11	**12**		5,800		
13	Multiply line 12, column (b), by line 7	**13**		580		
14	Add line 12, column (a), and line 13				**14**	580
15	Subtract line 14 from line 8. If zero or less, enter -0-				**15**	91,104
16	Excess mortgage interest (see instructions)	**16**				
17	Excess real estate taxes (see instructions)	**17**				
18	Insurance	**18**		280		
19	Rent	**19**				
20	Repairs and maintenance	**20**		950		
21	Utilities	**21**		1,810		
22	Other expenses (see instructions)	**22**				
23	Add lines 16 through 22	**23**		3,040		
24	Multiply line 23, column (b), by line 7	**24**		304		
25	Carryover of prior year operating expenses (see instructions)	**25**				
26	Add line 23, column (a), line 24, and line 25				**26**	304
27	Allowable operating expenses. Enter the **smaller** of line 15 or line 26				**27**	304
28	Limit on excess casualty losses and depreciation. Subtract line 27 from line 15				**28**	90,800
29	Excess casualty losses (see instructions)	**29**				
30	Depreciation of your home from line 42 below	**30**		200		
31	Carryover of prior year excess casualty losses and depreciation (see instructions)	**31**				
32	Add lines 29 through 31				**32**	200
33	Allowable excess casualty losses and depreciation. Enter the **smaller** of line 28 or line 32				**33**	200
34	Add lines 14, 27, and 33				**34**	1,084
35	Casualty loss portion, if any, from lines 14 and 33. Carry amount to **Form 4684**. See instructions				**35**	
36	**Allowable expenses for business use of your home.** Subtract line 35 from line 34. Enter here and on Schedule C, line 30. If your home was used for more than one business, see instructions				**36**	1,084

Part III   Depreciation of Your Home

37	Enter the **smaller** of your home's adjusted basis or its fair market value. See instructions	**37**	90,000
38	Value of land included on line 37	**38**	12,000
39	Basis of building. Subtract line 38 from line 37	**39**	78,000
40	Business basis of building. Multiply line 39 by line 7	**40**	7,800
41	Depreciation percentage (see instructions)	**41**	2.564 %
42	Depreciation allowable (see instructions). Multiply line 40 by line 41. Enter here and on line 30 above	**42**	200

Part IV   Carryover of Unallowed Expenses to 2023

43	Operating expenses. Subtract line 27 from line 26. If less than zero, enter -0-	**43**	
44	Excess casualty losses and depreciation. Subtract line 33 from line 32. If less than zero, enter -0-	**44**	

For Paperwork Reduction Act Notice, see your tax return instructions.   Cat. No. 13232M   Form **8829** (2022)

EXAMPLE 32	Continuing with Example 31, Morgan computes the rest of the home office deduction and the expenses carried over to the next year as follows.

Utilities, insurance, repairs (20% × $6,300)	$1,260
Depreciation on the home office (20% × $4,500)	900
Total other home office expenses	$2,160
Deductible expenses limited to net income derived from the business	(1,100)
Home office expenses carried forward to next year	$1,060

The $1,100 of deductible home office expenses comes from the home office portion of expenses for utilities, insurance, and repairs. The $1,060 of expenses carried over consists of $160 ($1,260 − $1,100) of utilities, insurance, and repairs, and $900 of depreciation (since depreciation is the last home office expense that is deducted).

Although the one drawback of the safe harbor method is the $1,500 limit placed on the deduction, the safe harbor method has its advantages. In addition to being an easier deduction to compute, taxpayers who use the safe harbor method do not have to complete Form 8829. Instead, they report their home office deduction directly on Schedule C (line 30). Second, in the years the safe harbor method is used, taxpayers do not have to keep receipts for the various expenses related to the home. Third, the depreciation component in the $5 per square foot amount is assumed to be $0. Thus, in years in which the safe harbor method is used, taxpayers do not reduce the basis in their homes by any depreciation taken for the home office.

¶705.05   SCHEDULE C, PART III: COST OF GOODS SOLD

Inventory is a major part of manufacturing, wholesale, and retail businesses. For sole proprietors, the calculation of cost of goods sold is done on Schedule C, Part III. Cost of goods sold equals beginning inventory plus the cost of net purchases, labor, materials, and other costs for the year minus ending inventory. Cost of goods sold should include only expenses directly related to getting or producing the goods sold.

For merchants, beginning inventory consists of products held for sale. For manufacturers, beginning inventory is the sum of raw materials, work in process, and finished goods. Beginning inventory of one year should be the same as ending inventory of the prior year.

For merchants, purchases include all goods bought for sale during the year. For manufacturers, purchases of raw materials include all materials bought during the year to be used in making the finished products. Any freight paid is added to the costs of purchases. The cost of goods returned reduces total purchases. Cash discounts can either be credited to separate discount accounts (as other income) or deducted from total purchases. The method for handling cash discounts must be used consistently from year to year. Figure 7-5 shows a filled-in Schedule C for a taxpayer in the retail business.

¶705.06   FILLED-IN SCHEDULE C

INFORMATION FOR FIGURE 7-5:

Harold R. Wilson is the owner of Harold's Hardware Store. Harold operates his business as a sole proprietorship. Figure 7-4 shows Harold's income statement. He completes Schedule C using this information. His business code is 444130. This code can be found in the instructions to Schedule C. Harold enters this code on line B. Harold materially participates in the business, so he checks the Yes box on line G. He uses the accrual method of accounting (box 2, line F) and the cost method to value inventory (box a, line 33). Because Harold has employees, he has an Employer ID Number (EIN) that he reports on line D.

Net income from Harold's income statement is $147,496. Schedule C, however, shows a net profit of $148,805. Part of the $1,893 difference ($148,805 – $147,496) relates to the $460 of charitable contributions. Although the business paid this amount, the tax laws require charitable contributions of a sole proprietor to be deducted as an itemized deduction on Schedule A. The $584 of interest income is reported on Schedule B. The rest of the $175 difference is due to reducing meals by 50% on Schedule C (assuming the meals were not consumed in restaurants).

Figure 7-4: Income Statement for Harold's Hardware Store

HAROLD'S HARDWARE STORE
Income Statement
For Year Ended December 31, 2022

Operating revenue:			
Sales		$384,280	
Less: Sales returns and allowances		(2,751)	
Net sales			$381,529
Cost of merchandise sold:			
Merchandise inventory, beginning of period		$ 131,216	
Purchases	$180,716		
Less: Purchases discount	(3,614)		
Net purchases	$ 177,102		
Less: Merchandise withdrawn for personal use	(400)	176,702	
Merchandise available for sale		$ 307,918	
Less: Merchandise inventory end of period		(167,546)	
Cost of merchandise sold			(140,372)
Gross profit on sales			$ 241,157
Operating expenses:			
Advertising expense		$ 5,437	
Charitable contributions		460	
Depreciation expense		3,689	
Meals expense		350	
Insurance expense		2,250	
Legal and professional services		4,137	
Miscellaneous expense		15	
Payroll taxes		8,845	
Personal property taxes		1,192	
Rent expense		10,200	
Repairs to store equipment		2,125	
Supplies expense		3,400	
Telephone expense		1,258	
Travel		184	
Truck rental expense		2,498	
Utilities expense		3,908	
Wage expense		44,297	
Total operating expenses			(94,245)
Operating income			$ 146,912
Other income:			
Interest income			584
Net income			$ 147,496

Figure 7-5: Filled-In Schedule C (Page 1)

SCHEDULE C (Form 1040)	Profit or Loss From Business	OMB No. 1545-0074
Department of the Treasury Internal Revenue Service	(Sole Proprietorship) Go to *www.irs.gov/ScheduleC* for instructions and the latest information. **Attach to Form 1040, 1040-SR, 1040-NR, or 1041; partnerships must generally file Form 1065.**	2022 Attachment Sequence No. **09**

Name of proprietor	Social security number (SSN)
Harold R. Wilson	272-00-8855

A Principal business or profession, including product or service (see instructions)
Retail Hardware

B Enter code from instructions: 4 4 4 1 3 0

C Business name. If no separate business name, leave blank.
Harold's Hardware Store

D Employer ID number (EIN) (see instr.): 7 0 0 6 2 4 4 3 1

E Business address (including suite or room no.) 21 Main St.
City, town or post office, state, and ZIP code Madison, WI 53593

F Accounting method: (1) ☐ Cash (2) ☑ Accrual (3) ☐ Other (specify)

G Did you "materially participate" in the operation of this business during 2022? If "No," see instructions for limit on losses ☑ Yes ☐ No

H If you started or acquired this business during 2022, check here ☐

I Did you make any payments in 2022 that would require you to file Form(s) 1099? See instructions ☑ Yes ☐ No

J If "Yes," did you or will you file required Form(s) 1099? ☑ Yes ☐ No

Part I   Income

1	Gross receipts or sales. See instructions for line 1 and check the box if this income was reported to you on Form W-2 and the "Statutory employee" box on that form was checked ☐	1	384,280
2	Returns and allowances	2	2,751
3	Subtract line 2 from line 1	3	381,529
4	Cost of goods sold (from line 42)	4	140,372
5	**Gross profit.** Subtract line 4 from line 3	5	241,157
6	Other income, including federal and state gasoline or fuel tax credit or refund (see instructions)	6	
7	**Gross income.** Add lines 5 and 6	7	241,157

Part II   Expenses. Enter expenses for business use of your home **only** on line 30.

8	Advertising	**8**	5,437	18	Office expense (see instructions)	**18**	
9	Car and truck expenses (see instructions)	**9**		19	Pension and profit-sharing plans	**19**	
10	Commissions and fees	**10**		20	Rent or lease (see instructions):		
11	Contract labor (see instructions)	**11**		a	Vehicles, machinery, and equipment	**20a**	2,498
12	Depletion	**12**		b	Other business property	**20b**	10,200
13	Depreciation and section 179 expense deduction (not included in Part III) (see instructions)	**13**	3,689	21	Repairs and maintenance	**21**	2,125
				22	Supplies (not included in Part III)	**22**	3,400
				23	Taxes and licenses	**23**	10,037
14	Employee benefit programs (other than on line 19)	**14**		24	Travel and meals:		
				a	Travel	**24a**	184
15	Insurance (other than health)	**15**	2,250	b	Deductible meals (see instructions)	**24b**	175
16	Interest (see instructions):			25	Utilities	**25**	3,908
a	Mortgage (paid to banks, etc.)	**16a**		26	Wages (less employment credits)	**26**	44,297
b	Other	**16b**		27a	Other expenses (from line 48)	**27a**	1,273
17	Legal and professional services	**17**	4,137	b	Reserved for future use	**27b**	

28	**Total expenses** before expenses for business use of home. Add lines 8 through 27a	28	93,610
29	Tentative profit or (loss). Subtract line 28 from line 7	29	147,547
30	Expenses for business use of your home. Do not report these expenses elsewhere. Attach Form 8829 unless using the simplified method. See instructions. **Simplified method filers only:** Enter the total square footage of (a) your home: _____ and (b) the part of your home used for business: _____ . Use the Simplified Method Worksheet in the instructions to figure the amount to enter on line 30	30	
31	**Net profit or (loss).** Subtract line 30 from line 29. • If a profit, enter on both **Schedule 1 (Form 1040), line 3,** and on **Schedule SE, line 2.** (If you checked the box on line 1, see instructions.) Estates and trusts, enter on **Form 1041, line 3.** • If a loss, you **must** go to line 32.	31	147,547
32	If you have a loss, check the box that describes your investment in this activity. See instructions. • If you checked 32a, enter the loss on both **Schedule 1 (Form 1040), line 3,** and on **Schedule SE, line 2.** (If you checked the box on line 1, see the line 31 instructions.) Estates and trusts, enter on **Form 1041, line 3.** • If you checked 32b, you **must** attach **Form 6198.** Your loss may be limited.	32a ☐ All investment is at risk. 32b ☐ Some investment is not at risk.	

For Paperwork Reduction Act Notice, see the separate instructions.   Cat. No. 11334P   Schedule C (Form 1040) 2022

¶705.06

Figure 7-5: Filled-In Schedule C (Page 2)

Schedule C (Form 1040) 2022   Page **2**

Part III   **Cost of Goods Sold** (see instructions)

33	Method(s) used to value closing inventory: **a** ☑ Cost **b** ☐ Lower of cost or market **c** ☐ Other (attach explanation)		
34	Was there any change in determining quantities, costs, or valuations between opening and closing inventory? If "Yes," attach explanation . . . . ☐ Yes ☑ No		
35	Inventory at beginning of year. If different from last year's closing inventory, attach explanation . .	35	131,216
36	Purchases less cost of items withdrawn for personal use	36	176,702
37	Cost of labor. Do not include any amounts paid to yourself	37	
38	Materials and supplies	38	
39	Other costs	39	
40	Add lines 35 through 39	40	307,918
41	Inventory at end of year	41	167,546
42	**Cost of goods sold.** Subtract line 41 from line 40. Enter the result here and on line 4	42	140,372

Part IV   **Information on Your Vehicle.** Complete this part **only** if you are claiming car or truck expenses on line 9 and are not required to file Form 4562 for this business. See the instructions for line 13 to find out if you must file Form 4562.

43   When did you place your vehicle in service for business purposes? (month/day/year) _____ / _____ / _____

44   Of the total number of miles you drove your vehicle during 2022, enter the number of miles you used your vehicle for:

a Business _____ **b** Commuting (see instructions) _____ **c** Other _____

45	Was your vehicle available for personal use during off-duty hours?	☐ Yes	☐ No
46	Do you (or your spouse) have another vehicle available for personal use?	☐ Yes	☐ No
47a	Do you have evidence to support your deduction?	☐ Yes	☐ No
b	If "Yes," is the evidence written?	☐ Yes	☐ No

Part V   **Other Expenses.** List below business expenses not included on lines 8–26 or line 30.

Misc	15
Telephone	1,258
48 **Total other expenses.** Enter here and on line 27a	48 1,273

Schedule C (Form 1040) 2022

¶706   Self-Employment Tax

For the government to generate enough funds to pay social security and Medicare benefits, taxpayers who work must pay social security and Medicare taxes (FICA). Employees pay FICA taxes through withholdings from their wages. Employers make matching FICA contributions on behalf of their employees. Employers then send all FICA contributions to the government. Employers deduct as a payroll tax expense their share of FICA taxes paid.

FICA consists of two parts: (1) social security or OASDI (Old-Age, Survivors, and Disability Insurance) and (2) Medicare or HI (Hospital Insurance). The OASDI tax rate is 6.2% for employees (12.4% after employer matching). The Medicare rate is 1.45% (2.9% after employer matching). For 2022, the first $147,000 of a taxpayer's earnings is subject to OASDI taxes. All earnings are subject to Medicare taxes.

The self-employment tax is similar to FICA taxes withheld from employees' wages. However, instead of having the tax withheld from their wages, self-employed taxpayers pay the tax with their (quarterly) estimated payments. They make up any balance due when they file their tax return. Because there is no employer to make matching contributions, self-employed taxpayers must pay both the employee's and the employer's shares of the FICA tax. These two shares combined make up the 15.3% self-employment tax. Self-employed taxpayers deduct the employer's (one-half) share of self-employment taxes paid. This amount is reported on Schedule 1 (Form 1040 or 1040-SR), not on Schedule C. The taxpayer then uses this amount to determine AGI on Form 1040.

Self-employed taxpayers pay self-employment tax on their *net earnings from self-employment*. Net earnings from self-employment is 92.35% of self-employment net profit (reported on Schedule C, line 31). This calculation provides a substitute for the sole proprietor's net earnings after deducting the employer's share of the OASDI and Medicare taxes (100% − 6.2% OASDI tax − 1.45% Medicare tax = 92.35%).

Only taxpayers with $400 or more of net earnings from self-employment owe self-employment tax. Taxpayers with a net loss from self-employment do not pay self-employment tax. Computing self-employment net profit involves combining net profit (or loss) from all activities.

EXAMPLE 33	Jessica owns two businesses. Jessica uses a separate Schedule C to report the net profit (or loss) from each business. Net profit from the first business is $45,000; net profit from the second business is $5,000. Jessica's self-employment net profit is $50,000.

EXAMPLE 34	Same facts as in Example 33, except that Jessica reports a net loss of $5,000 from the second business. Jessica's self-employment net profit is $40,000.

EXAMPLE 35	Same facts as in Example 34, except that Jessica is married and her spouse owns the second business. Jessica's self-employment net profit is $45,000. Because her spouse reports a net loss, he pays no self-employment tax. Jessica pays self-employment tax on her $41,558 of net earnings from self-employment ($45,000 × 92.35%).

The full self-employment tax rate is 15.3% (12.4% for OASDI taxes + 2.9% for Medicare taxes). The full rate applies until the taxpayer's OASDI earnings reach the limit for the year ($147,000 for 2022). After that, the OASDI component goes away, and the self-employment tax rate drops to the 2.9% Medicare tax component.

EXAMPLE 36

Avery Garza reports $10,000 of self-employment net profit. Avery's net earnings from self-employment equals $9,235 ($10,000 × 92.35%). His self-employment tax is $1,413 ($9,235 × 15.3%). The deductible portion of the tax is $707 ($1,413 × ½). Avery reports this amount on Schedule 1 (Form 1040 or 1040-SR), then uses it to calculate AGI on Form 1040, page 1, line 8a.

For self-employed taxpayers who are also employees, their wages subject to social security (OASDI) tax reduce the maximum earnings subject to the 12.4% OASDI tax.

EXAMPLE 37

Same facts as in Example 36, except that in addition to the $10,000 of self-employment net profit, Avery has FICA taxes withheld on $139,200 of wages earned as an employee in 2022. The first $147,000 of earnings is subject to OASDI taxes. Through withholding on wages, Avery has paid OASDI taxes on $139,200. All $9,235 of net earnings from self-employment is subject to Medicare taxes, but only $7,800 ($147,000 – $139,200) is subject to the OASDI tax. Avery's self-employment tax equals $1,235 [($7,800 × 12.4%) + ($9,235 × 2.9%)]. Avery reports $618 ($1,235 × ½) on Schedule 1 (Form 1040 or 1040-SR), then uses that amount to calculate AGI on Form 1040, page 1, line 8a.

The employee portion of the Medicare tax rate is normally 1.45% of Medicare earnings (which includes net earnings from self-employment). The employee's Medicare tax rate increases to 2.35% once a taxpayer's Medicare earnings reach a certain threshold (the employer's Medicare rate remains at 1.45%). This additional 0.9% Medicare tax is not part of the self-employment tax calculation. Instead, taxpayers whose Medicare earnings exceed the specified threshold complete Form 8959, Additional Medicare Tax. They then report their additional Medicare tax separately on Schedule 2 (Form 1040 or 1040-SR). The additional Medicare tax is discussed in Chapter 13 (¶1302.02).

¶706.01   SCHEDULE SE

Taxpayers compute self-employment tax on Schedule SE. Self-employed taxpayers first compute their self-employment net profit and their net earnings from self-employment. They then report the amount of their wages for the year subject to social security tax withholding. If this amount exceeds the OASDI limit ($147,000 in 2022), the taxpayer is not subject to the 12.4% OASDI on the net earnings from self-employment. If the amount does not exceed the OASDI limit, then the taxpayer multiplies 12.4% by the *lesser of* the difference or net earnings from self-employment. The taxpayer adds this amount to 2.9% of net earnings from self-employment to compute the self-employment tax. The taxpayer reports the tax on Schedule 2 (Form 1040). The taxpayer then calculates the employer's (one-half) share of the tax, enters the amount on Schedule 1 (Form 1040), and uses the amount to determine AGI on Form 1040.

On a joint return, only the name and social security number of the person with self-employment income is shown on Schedule SE. If both spouses have self-employment income, each must complete a separate Schedule SE.

¶706.02   FILLED-IN SCHEDULE SE

A taxpayer whose self-employment income exceeds a threshold amount is subject to an additional .9% (.009) tax. The threshold is $250,000 for married filing jointly, $125,000 for married filing separately, and $200,000 for all others. This tax does not appear on Schedule SE. Form 8959 serves this purpose. No portion of this additional tax is allowable as a deduction.

INFORMATION FOR FIGURE 7-6:

Monroe L. Peters (from Figure 7-1) computes his self-employment tax on Schedule SE.

Line #

2: Net profit from Schedule C, line 31, **$90,600**

4: Net earnings from self-employment, **$83,669** ($90,600 × 92.35%)

10: Retirement portion of self-employment tax **$10,375** ($83.669 × 12.4%, since $83,669 < $147,000)

11: Medicare portion of self-employment tax, **$2,426** ($83,669 × 2.9%)

12: Self-employment tax, **$12,801** ($10,375 + 2,426)

13: Deduction for one-half of self-employment tax, **$6,401** ($12,801 × ½)

Figure 7-6: Filled-In Schedule SE

SCHEDULE SE (Form 1040) Department of the Treasury Internal Revenue Service	**Self-Employment Tax** Go to *www.irs.gov/ScheduleSE* for instructions and the latest information. Attach to Form 1040, 1040-SR, or 1040-NR.	OMB No. 1545-0074 20**22** Attachment Sequence No. **17**
Name of person with self-employment income (as shown on Form 1040, 1040-SR, or 1040-NR) Monroe L. Peters	Social security number of person with **self-employment** income	268-00-9092

Part I Self-Employment Tax

Note: If your only income subject to self-employment tax is **church employee income,** see instructions for how to report your income and the definition of church employee income.

A   If you are a minister, member of a religious order, or Christian Science practitioner **and** you filed Form 4361, but you had $400 or more of **other** net earnings from self-employment, check here and continue with Part I . . . . ☐

Skip lines 1a and 1b if you use the farm optional method in Part II. See instructions.

1a	Net farm profit or (loss) from Schedule F, line 34, and farm partnerships, Schedule K-1 (Form 1065), box 14, code A	**1a**	
b	If you received social security retirement or disability benefits, enter the amount of Conservation Reserve Program payments included on Schedule F, line 4b, or listed on Schedule K-1 (Form 1065) box 20, code AH	**1b**	( )

Skip line 2 if you use the nonfarm optional method in Part II. See instructions.

2	Net profit or (loss) from Schedule C, line 31; and Schedule K-1 (Form 1065), box 14, code A (other than farming). See instructions for other income to report or if you are a minister or member of a religious order	**2**	90,600
3	Combine lines 1a, 1b, and 2	**3**	90,600
4a	If line 3 is more than zero, multiply line 3 by 92.35% (0.9235). Otherwise, enter amount from line 3 .	**4a**	83,669
	Note: If line 4a is less than $400 due to Conservation Reserve Program payments on line 1b, see instructions.		
b	If you elect one or both of the optional methods, enter the total of lines 15 and 17 here	**4b**	
c	Combine lines 4a and 4b. If less than $400, **stop;** you don't owe self-employment tax. **Exception:** If less than $400 and you had **church employee income,** enter -0- and continue	**4c**	
5a	Enter your **church employee income** from Form W-2. See instructions for definition of church employee income **5a**		
b	Multiply line 5a by 92.35% (0.9235). If less than $100, enter -0-	**5b**	
6	Add lines 4c and 5b	**6**	83,669
7	Maximum amount of combined wages and self-employment earnings subject to social security tax or the 6.2% portion of the 7.65% railroad retirement (tier 1) tax for 2022	**7**	147,000
8a	Total social security wages and tips (total of boxes 3 and 7 on Form(s) W-2) and railroad retirement (tier 1) compensation. If $147,000 or more, skip lines 8b through 10, and go to line 11 . . . . **8a**		
b	Unreported tips subject to social security tax from Form 4137, line 10 . . . **8b**		
c	Wages subject to social security tax from Form 8919, line 10 . . . . . . **8c**		
d	Add lines 8a, 8b, and 8c	**8d**	
9	Subtract line 8d from line 7. If zero or less, enter -0- here and on line 10 and go to line 11	**9**	147,000
10	Multiply the **smaller** of line 6 or line 9 by 12.4% (0.124)	**10**	10,375
11	Multiply line 6 by 2.9% (0.029)	**11**	2,426
12	**Self-employment tax.** Add lines 10 and 11. Enter here and on **Schedule 2 (Form 1040), line 4** . .	**12**	12,801
13	**Deduction for one-half of self-employment tax.** Multiply line 12 by 50% (0.50). Enter here and on **Schedule 1 (Form 1040), line 15** **13** 6,401		

Part II Optional Methods To Figure Net Earnings (see instructions)

Farm Optional Method. You may use this method **only** if **(a)** your gross farm income[1] wasn't more than $9,060, **or (b)** your net farm profits[2] were less than $6,540.

14	Maximum income for optional methods	**14**	6,040
15	Enter the **smaller** of: two-thirds (⅔) of gross farm income[1] (not less than zero) **or** $6,040. Also, include this amount on line 4b above	**15**	

Nonfarm Optional Method. You may use this method **only** if **(a)** your net nonfarm profits[3] were less than $6,540 and also less than 72.189% of your gross nonfarm income,[4] **and (b)** you had net earnings from self-employment of at least $400 in 2 of the prior 3 years. **Caution:** You may use this method no more than five times.

16	Subtract line 15 from line 14	**16**	
17	Enter the **smaller** of: two-thirds (⅔) of gross nonfarm income[4] (not less than zero) **or** the amount on line 16. Also, include this amount on line 4b above	**17**	

[1] From Sch. F, line 9; and Sch. K-1 (Form 1065), box 14, code B.
[2] From Sch. F, line 34; and Sch. K-1 (Form 1065), box 14, code A—minus the amount you would have entered on line 1b had you not used the optional method.
[3] From Sch. C, line 31; and Sch. K-1 (Form 1065), box 14, code A.
[4] From Sch. C, line 7; and Sch. K-1 (Form 1065), box 14, code C.

For Paperwork Reduction Act Notice, see your tax return instructions.   Cat. No. 11358Z   Schedule SE (Form 1040) 2022

¶706.03   FILLED-IN SCHEDULE SE

INFORMATION FOR FIGURE 7-7:

Avery Garza from Example 37 completes Schedule SE to compute his self-employment tax. He transfers the $1,235 of self-employment tax to Schedule 2 (Form 1040 or 1040-SR). He computes the deductible portion on Schedule SE (line 13) and enters the amount on Schedule 1 (Form 1040 or 1040-SR). Avery then uses that amount to determine AGI on Form 1040.

Line #

2: Net profit from Schedule C, line 31, **$10,000**

4a: Net earnings from self-employment, **$9,235** ($10,000 × 92.35%)

8a: Total social security wages, **$139,200** (Source: box 3 on Form W-2)

12: Total OASDI taxes, **$1,235** ((smaller of line 6 ($9,235) or line 9 ($7,800) multiplied by 12.4% OASDI rate, $7,800 × 12.4% = $967)) plus $9,235 multiplied by 2.9% Medicare tax)

13: Deduction for one-half of the self-employment tax, **$618** ($1,235 from line 12 × ½)

Figure 7-7: Filled-In Schedule SE

SCHEDULE SE
(Form 1040)

Department of the Treasury
Internal Revenue Service

Self-Employment Tax

Go to *www.irs.gov/ScheduleSE* for instructions and the latest information.
Attach to Form 1040, 1040-SR, or 1040-NR.

OMB No. 1545-0074

2022

Attachment
Sequence No. **17**

Name of person with self-employment income (as shown on Form 1040, 1040-SR, or 1040-NR)	Social security number of person with **self-employment** income
Avery Garza	692-00-1922

Part I Self-Employment Tax

Note: If your only income subject to self-employment tax is **church employee income**, see instructions for how to report your income and the definition of church employee income.

A   If you are a minister, member of a religious order, or Christian Science practitioner **and** you filed Form 4361, but you had $400 or more of **other** net earnings from self-employment, check here and continue with Part I . . . . ☐

Skip lines 1a and 1b if you use the farm optional method in Part II. See instructions.

1a	Net farm profit or (loss) from Schedule F, line 34, and farm partnerships, Schedule K-1 (Form 1065), box 14, code A	**1a**	
b	If you received social security retirement or disability benefits, enter the amount of Conservation Reserve Program payments included on Schedule F, line 4b, or listed on Schedule K-1 (Form 1065), box 20, code AH	**1b** (	)

Skip line 2 if you use the nonfarm optional method in Part II. See instructions.

2	Net profit or (loss) from Schedule C, line 31; and Schedule K-1 (Form 1065), box 14, code A (other than farming). See instructions for other income to report or if you are a minister or member of a religious order	**2**	10,000
3	Combine lines 1a, 1b, and 2	**3**	10,000
4a	If line 3 is more than zero, multiply line 3 by 92.35% (0.9235). Otherwise, enter amount from line 3	**4a**	9,235
	Note: If line 4a is less than $400 due to Conservation Reserve Program payments on line 1b, see instructions.		
b	If you elect one or both of the optional methods, enter the total of lines 15 and 17 here . .	**4b**	
c	Combine lines 4a and 4b. If less than $400, **stop**; you don't owe self-employment tax. **Exception:** If less than $400 and you had **church employee income**, enter -0- and continue	**4c**	
5a	Enter your **church employee income** from Form W-2. See instructions for definition of church employee income **5a**		
b	Multiply line 5a by 92.35% (0.9235). If less than $100, enter -0-	**5b**	
6	Add lines 4c and 5b	**6**	9,235
7	Maximum amount of combined wages and self-employment earnings subject to social security tax or the 6.2% portion of the 7.65% railroad retirement (tier 1) tax for 2022	**7**	147,000
8a	Total social security wages and tips (total of boxes 3 and 7 on Form(s) W-2) and railroad retirement (tier 1) compensation. If $147,000 or more, skip lines 8b through 10, and go to line 11 . . . . **8a** 139,200		
b	Unreported tips subject to social security tax from Form 4137, line 10 . . . **8b**		
c	Wages subject to social security tax from Form 8919, line 10 . . . . . . **8c**		
d	Add lines 8a, 8b, and 8c	**8d**	139,200
9	Subtract line 8d from line 7. If zero or less, enter -0- here and on line 10 and go to line 11	**9**	7,800
10	Multiply the **smaller** of line 6 or line 9 by 12.4% (0.124)	**10**	967
11	Multiply line 6 by 2.9% (0.029)	**11**	268
12	**Self-employment tax.** Add lines 10 and 11. Enter here and on **Schedule 2 (Form 1040), line 4** . .	**12**	1,235
13	**Deduction for one-half of self-employment tax.** Multiply line 12 by 50% (0.50). Enter here and on **Schedule 1 (Form 1040), line 15** **13** 618		

Part II Optional Methods To Figure Net Earnings (see instructions)

Farm Optional Method. You may use this method only if **(a)** your gross farm income[1] wasn't more than $9,060, **or (b)** your net farm profits[2] were less than $6,540.

14	Maximum income for optional methods	**14**	6,040
15	Enter the **smaller** of: two-thirds (²/₃) of gross farm income[1] (not less than zero) **or** $6,040. Also, include this amount on line 4b above	**15**	

Nonfarm Optional Method. You may use this method only if **(a)** your net nonfarm profits[3] were less than $6,540 and also less than 72.189% of your gross nonfarm income,[4] **and (b)** you had net earnings from self-employment of at least $400 in 2 of the prior 3 years. **Caution:** You may use this method no more than five times.

16	Subtract line 15 from line 14	**16**	
17	Enter the **smaller** of: two-thirds (²/₃) of gross nonfarm income[4] (not less than zero) **or** the amount on line 16. Also, include this amount on line 4b above	**17**	

[1] From Sch. F, line 9; and Sch. K-1 (Form 1065), box 14, code B.
[2] From Sch. F, line 34; and Sch. K-1 (Form 1065), box 14, code A—minus the amount you would have entered on line 1b had you not used the optional method.
[3] From Sch. C, line 31; and Sch. K-1 (Form 1065), box 14, code A.
[4] From Sch. C, line 7; and Sch. K-1 (Form 1065), box 14, code C.

For Paperwork Reduction Act Notice, see your tax return instructions.   Cat. No. 11358Z   Schedule SE (Form 1040) 2022

7

Name: _____

Section: _____

Date: _____

QUESTIONS AND PROBLEMS

1. **Cash vs. Accrual Method.** (Obj. 1) Lis is a self-employed CPA. She wants to know how reporting each of the following items would differ under the cash method versus the accrual method. In the space provided, enter the correct amount that would be reported on Schedule C under each method. If there is no amount to be reported, enter **0**.

			Cash Method	*Accrual Method*
a.	Repaid loan at bank:			
	Principal	$1,000	$_____	$_____
	Interest	60	_____	_____
b.	Paid contribution pledged to church	1,000	_____	_____
c.	Paid for supplies used last year	150	_____	_____
d.	Paid for supplies used during current year	850	_____	_____
e.	Paid two-year subscription for professional journals on January 1	200	_____	_____
f.	Supplies not used during current year and not yet paid for	40	_____	_____
g.	Paid for a new computer	1,564	_____	_____

2. **Cash vs. Accrual Method. (Obj. 1)** Taylor is a self-employed dentist. He wants to know how reporting each of the following items would differ under the cash method versus the accrual method. In the space provided, enter the correct amount that would be reported on Schedule C under each method. If there is no amount to be reported, enter **0**.

			Cash Method	*Accrual Method*
a.	Salary paid to receptionist	$12,500	$_____	$_____
b.	Paid for long-distance phone charges made during last year	4	_____	_____
c.	Written-off client billing for fees; work performed in current year	150	_____	_____
d.	Written-off client billing for fees; work performed last year	135	_____	_____
e.	Paid annual subscription to magazines for the office waiting room	50	_____	_____
f.	Paid life insurance premium on the owner's life	516	_____	_____

3. **Prepaid Income. (Obj. 1)** Scott operates a fitness center as a sole proprietorship. On May 1, 2022, Scott sells a 24-month membership for $1,200.

   a. How much of the $1,200 must Scott report on his 2022-2024 tax returns if he uses the accrual method of accounting?

   b. How would your answer to Part a. change if Scott uses the cash method?

4. **Prepaid Income. (Obj. 1)** Cliff uses the accrual method for the business he runs as a sole proprietorship. Cliff fixes and sells major appliances. He also sells warranty contracts. On April 1, 2022, Cliff collects $480 for a 36-month warranty contract. How much of the $480 must he include in gross income in 2022-2024?

5. **Prepaid Expenses. (Obj. 1)** On August 1, 2022, a sole proprietor pays $24,000 for two years' rent.

   a. How much of the $24,000 can be deducted in 2022 if the cash method is used?

   b. How much of the $24,000 can be deducted in 2022 if the accrual method is used?

6. **Prepaid Expenses.** (Obj. 1) A sole proprietor who operates a warehouse buys insurance for his building and equipment in three-year increments to get a good insurance premium rate. The insurance policy was acquired on October 1, 2022, for $4,800 and will be in effect until September 30, 2025. The premium on this policy was paid on July 1, 2022.

    a. Compute the amount of insurance premium that can be deducted on Schedule C in 2022–2025, assuming the taxpayer uses the cash method of accounting.

    b. Same as Part a., except that the taxpayer uses the accrual method.

7. **Self-Employment Income.** (Obj. 2) Indicate with **Y** (yes) or **N** (no) if the following items are amounts subject to self-employment tax.

    _____   a.   Net rentals from an apartment building

    _____   b.   Net profit from an accounting practice

    _____   c.   Interest income on a loan to a friend

    _____   d.   Consulting fees

    _____   e.   Fees earned for services as a minister

    _____   f.   Dividends from U.S. corporations

8. **Self-Employment Income.** (Obj. 2) Indicate with **Y** (yes) or **N** (no) if the following items are amounts subject to self-employment tax.

    _____   a.   Gross rent received on an office building

    _____   b.   Net profit from a doctor's practice

    _____   c.   Prize for winning an essay contest

    _____   d.   Salary for a secretary

    _____   e.   Net gain on the sale of business property

    _____   f.   Director's fees

9. **Self-Employment Income.** (Obj. 2) Indicate whether each statement is *true* or *false*.

   _____ a. Interest on accounts receivable received by a trade or business is treated as self-employment income.

   _____ b. Babysitters who provide childcare in the parents' homes treat their earnings as self-employment income.

   _____ c. Registered nurses who are hired directly by patients to provide private nursing services are treated as self-employed.

   _____ d. Real estate agents' commissions are considered self-employment income.

   _____ e. A 16-year-old newspaper delivery boy's earnings are not considered self-employment income.

   _____ f. All executors of estates are treated as self-employed.

10. **Car and Truck Expense.** (Obj. 3) Keith is self-employed. In 2022, he drove his car a total of 9,169 miles for work. He drove 4,669 of the business miles before July 1. He drove a total of 21,468 miles during the year. His car expenses for the year were as follows.

Business parking and tolls	$ 360
Depreciation	1,475
Gas	2,557
Insurance	940
License tags	50
Repairs and maintenance	52
	$5,434

    a. Compute Keith's car expense deduction using the standard mileage rate.

    b. Compute Keith's car expense deduction using the actual cost method.

11. **Travel Expense.** (Obj. 3) Andre is self-employed. In October, he attends a three-day seminar. Andre is out of town for five days and four nights. He spends the two extra days visiting friends and sightseeing. His travel costs are as follows.

Airfare	$ 850
Transportation to and from the airport	150
Hotel ($170 a night for 4 nights — 2 for business)	680
Meals ($42 a day for 5 days — 3 for business)	210
	$1,890

   a. Compute Andre's travel expense deduction, assuming the seminar was held in Texas.

   b. Compute his travel expense deduction, assuming the seminar was held in Germany.

12. **Education Expenses.** (Obj. 3) For each situation described in Parts a. through d., determine whether the taxpayer meets the criteria for the education expense deduction (True or False).

   a. A self-employed accountant pays $525 for accounting courses to meet the state's continuing professional education (CPE) requirement.

   b. A CPA pays $3,500 for tuition and books for courses he is enrolled in law school. The courses count in meeting the state's CPE requirements.

c. A high school teacher pays tuition of $2,700. The teacher is enrolled in graduate school and is taking classes in order to meet the state law requirements that will allow her to renew her teaching certificate.

d. A company executive pays $8,000 for tuition, books, and transportation to attend an executive MBA program to improve his business management and employee relations skills.

13. **Accountable vs. Nonaccountable Plans.** (Obj. 3) Amanda operates her business as a sole proprietorship. Amanda has two full-time employees. She reimburses each employee $250 per month for meals and entertainment ($6,000 per year) without any specific accounting. Assuming that the employees incur meal expenses of $2,000 and entertainment expenses of $4,900, answer the following questions about the way the $6,000 should be reported on Amanda's tax return.

a. How much and where on Schedule C should Amanda deduct the reimbursements?

b. How would your answer to Part a. differ if Amanda required her employees to make an adequate accounting of their meals and entertainment expenses and also required them to return any excess reimbursement?

14. **Education Expense.** (Obj. 3) Aimee is a self-employed CPA. She holds both a bachelor's and a master's degree in accounting. Each year she takes two graduate courses at the local university to satisfy her continuing education requirements, as required by state law to keep her CPA license. Her coursework will not lead to her getting another degree. During 2022, Aimee spent $2,400 for tuition and $600 for books. She also drove her personal car 600 miles to get to and from her classes. What amount can Aimee deduct as an education expense on Schedule C?

15. **Business Gifts.** (Obj. 3) Dabny operates his business as a sole proprietorship. During the year, he sends holiday gifts to 20 of his clients. Each gift cost $55. What amount can Dabny deduct as business gifts on Schedule C?

16. **Business Gifts and Entertainment.** (Obj. 3) Stu is self-employed. During the year, Stu paid $60 for a concert ticket. He gave the ticket to a client.

    a. What amount can Stu deduct on Schedule C if he did not attend the event with the client?

    b. What amount can Stu deduct if he were to attend the event with his client?

17. **Bad Debt Expense.** (Obj. 3) Mickey is self-employed. In 2020, Mickey loaned a business associate $10,000 so that the associate could stay in business. Mickey's business would suffer if his associate went out of business. In 2022, the business associate filed for bankruptcy, and Mickey was told that he might not receive more than $1,000 back from the loan. In 2023, Mickey receives $800 from the bankruptcy court. Discuss the tax consequences of the loan to Mickey, including the amount and year in which he can take a bad debt deduction.

18. **Schedule C.** (Obj. 3) Robert works as a cost accountant. He also works nights and weekends preparing tax returns for some regular clients. He does not have a regular office in his home, so he does not take a deduction for a home office. However, he prepares Schedule C to reflect the income from his tax practice. Robert has asked you to review his Schedule C to determine whether he is properly reporting the operating expenses of his business in relation to other aspects of his tax return. Robert has included the following expenses on Schedule C.

Supplies and postage	$ 72
Professional dues paid to AICPA tax division	120
Professional dues to the Institute of Management Accountants (IMA)	175
Meals ($80) and entertainment ($120) of tax clients	200
Automobile expenses for tax clients (using the standard mileage rate)	110
Contribution to New York State Society's Political Action Committee	100
CPE course fees to meet the annual requirements to be a member of the AICPA and the New York State Society of CPAs	600
Cost of a new printer for use with tax clients (shown as a repair)	650
Interest paid on bank loan used to buy a computer for tax and personal use (used for tax clients 60% of the time during the tax year)	400

Of these expenses, indicate what amounts, if any, cannot be deducted on Schedule C and explain why in each case.

19. **Home Office Expense.** (Obj. 4) Rita operates a childcare service in her home. The rooms used for this purpose constitute 30% of the total living space of the home. Expenses of operating the home during the year included electricity, $3,600; water, $340; gas heating, $480; property taxes, $4,000; and home repairs, $800. The depreciation on the rooms used for childcare was $1,800. What is the total amount of expenses that Rita can deduct for using her own home to provide childcare services if she uses these rooms 2,000 hours in 2022 for her childcare business?

20. Form 8829. (Obj. 4) Elaine Gerber (SSN 802-00-4903) conducts a business in her home. The tentative profit from Schedule C (line 29) was $9,600. The following information relates to her expenses.

Square footage of home	3,000
Used for business	240
Basis of home, including land	160,000
Basis of land	30,000
Deductible mortgage interest	11,800
Deductible real estate tax	2,500
Nondeductible real estate tax	500
Utilities	1,750

a. Follow the instructions on Form 8829 on the following page to compute Elaine's home office deduction.

b. How, if at all, would your answer to Part a. change if Elaine elects to use the safe harbor method to compute her home office deduction?

c. How, if at all, would your answer to Part b. change if the square footage of the areas used for business was 340 instead of 240 square feet?

21. Schedule C, Part III, Cost of Goods Sold. (Obj. 8) Roger operates a novelty shop as a sole proprietor. You have been asked to compute the Cost of Goods Sold section of Schedule C for his 2022 income tax return since he is unfamiliar with detailed accounting concepts. You have been given the following information from his records to help meet his request:

Sales revenue	$200,000
Purchases	80,000
Cash operating expenses	40,000
Depreciation expense	15,000
Beginning inventory	60,000
Ending inventory	54,000
Bad debts written off	3,200

Using the appropriate information from Roger's books, prepare the Cost of Goods Sold section of Schedule C. Roger uses the cost method to value inventory.

(Use for Problem 20.a.)

This Form is Overset by 2 Lines

Form 8829

Department of the Treasury
Internal Revenue Service

Expenses for Business Use of Your Home

File only with Schedule C (Form 1040). Use a separate Form 8829 for each home you used for business during the year.
Go to *www.irs.gov/Form8829* for instructions and the latest information.

OMB No. 1545-0074

2022

Attachment
Sequence No. **176**

Name(s) of proprietor(s)

Your social security number

Part I — Part of Your Home Used for Business

1	Area used regularly and exclusively for business, regularly for daycare, or for storage of inventory or product samples (see instructions)	1	
2	Total area of home	2	
3	Divide line 1 by line 2. Enter the result as a percentage	3	%

For daycare facilities not used exclusively for business, go to line 4. All others, go to line 7.

4	Multiply days used for daycare during year by hours used per day	4		hr.
5	If you started or stopped using your home for daycare during the year, see instructions; otherwise, enter 8,760	5		hr.
6	Divide line 4 by line 5. Enter the result as a decimal amount	6		
7	Business percentage. For daycare facilities not used exclusively for business, multiply line 6 by line 3 (enter the result as a percentage). All others, enter the amount from line 3	7		%

Part II — Figure Your Allowable Deduction

8   Enter the amount from Schedule C, line 29, **plus** any gain derived from the business use of your home, **minus** any loss from the trade or business not derived from the business use of your home. See instructions.   **8**

See instructions for columns (a) and (b) before completing lines 9–22.

			(a) Direct expenses	(b) Indirect expenses	
9	Casualty losses (see instructions)	9			
10	Deductible mortgage interest (see instructions)	10			
11	Real estate taxes (see instructions)	11			
12	Add lines 9, 10, and 11	12			
13	Multiply line 12, column (b), by line 7	13			
14	Add line 12, column (a), and line 13				14
15	Subtract line 14 from line 8. If zero or less, enter -0-				15
16	Excess mortgage interest (see instructions)	16			
17	Excess real estate taxes (see instructions)	17			
18	Insurance	18			
19	Rent	19			
20	Repairs and maintenance	20			
21	Utilities	21			
22	Other expenses (see instructions)	22			
23	Add lines 16 through 22	23			
24	Multiply line 23, column (b), by line 7	24			
25	Carryover of prior year operating expenses (see instructions)	25			
26	Add line 23, column (a), line 24, and line 25				26
27	Allowable operating expenses. Enter the **smaller** of line 15 or line 26				27
28	Limit on excess casualty losses and depreciation. Subtract line 27 from line 15				28
29	Excess casualty losses (see instructions)	29			
30	Depreciation of your home from line 42 below	30			
31	Carryover of prior year excess casualty losses and depreciation (see instructions)	31			
32	Add lines 29 through 31				32
33	Allowable excess casualty losses and depreciation. Enter the **smaller** of line 28 or line 32				33
34	Add lines 14, 27, and 33				34
35	Casualty loss portion, if any, from lines 14 and 33. Carry amount to **Form 4684**. See instructions				35
36	**Allowable expenses for business use of your home.** Subtract line 35 from line 34. Enter here and on Schedule C, line 30. If your home was used for more than one business, see instructions				36

Part III — Depreciation of Your Home

37	Enter the **smaller** of your home's adjusted basis or its fair market value. See instructions	37	
38	Value of land included on line 37	38	
39	Basis of building. Subtract line 38 from line 37	39	
40	Business basis of building. Multiply line 39 by line 7	40	
41	Depreciation percentage (see instructions)	41	%
42	Depreciation allowable (see instructions). Multiply line 40 by line 41. Enter here and on line 30 above	42	

Part IV — Carryover of Unallowed Expenses to 2023

43	Operating expenses. Subtract line 27 from line 26. If less than zero, enter -0-	43	
44	Excess casualty losses and depreciation. Subtract line 33 from line 32. If less than zero, enter -0-	44	

For Paperwork Reduction Act Notice, see your tax return instructions.   Cat. No. 13232M   Form **8829** (2022)

DRAFT AS OF July 21, 2022 DO NOT FILE

22. **Self-Employment Tax.** (Obj. 5) Determine the self-employment tax that would be paid for 2022 by each of the following taxpayers. If there is no self-employment tax, explain why.

   a. Net business profit, $39,000; dividend income, $300; wages subject to social security, $5,000; gross rental income, $6,000; net rental income, $1,500.

   b. Net business profit, $29,000; dividend income, $500; wages subject to social security, $60,000.

   c. Net business profit, $70,000; dividend income, $200.

   d. Net business profit, $15,000; dividend income, $100; wages subject to social security, $138,000.

   e. Net business profit, $3,000; dividend income, $450; net rental loss, $500.

   f. Net business profit, $420; dividend income, $50; wages subject to social security, $400.

23. **Self-Employment Tax.** (Obj. 5) Rosemary is employed as an attorney and also operates a consulting business on the side. If her net profit reported on Schedule C was $425, how much self-employment tax would Rosemary pay?

24. **Self-Employment Tax.** (Obj. 5) Connor has a Schedule C net profit of $10,000. Compute Connor's 2022 self-employment tax if his salary as a CPA was $140,400.

25. **Self-Employment Tax.** (Obj. 5) Theodore Williams (SSN 327-00-8119) reports $150,000 of net profit on Schedule C. Complete Theodore's 2022 Schedule SE if his salary subject to social security taxes for the year was $89,200.

(Use for Problem 25.)

SCHEDULE SE (Form 1040) Department of the Treasury Internal Revenue Service	Self-Employment Tax Go to *www.irs.gov/ScheduleSE* for instructions and the latest information. **Attach to Form 1040, 1040-SR, or 1040-NR.**	OMB No. 1545-0074 20**22** Attachment Sequence No. **17**
Name of person with self-employment income (as shown on Form 1040, 1040-SR, or 1040-NR)		Social security number of person with **self-employment** income

| **Part I** | **Self-Employment Tax** |

Note: If your only income subject to self-employment tax is **church employee income**, see instructions for how to report your income and the definition of church employee income.

A	If you are a minister, member of a religious order, or Christian Science practitioner **and** you filed Form 4361, but you had $400 or more of **other** net earnings from self-employment, check here and continue with Part I . . . . ▶ ☐

Skip lines 1a and 1b if you use the farm optional method in Part II. See instructions.

1a	Net farm profit or (loss) from Schedule F, line 34, and farm partnerships, Schedule K-1 (Form 1065), box 14, code A . . .	**1a**	
b	If you received social security retirement or disability benefits, enter the amount of Conservation Reserve Program payments included on Schedule F, line 4b, or listed on Schedule K-1 (Form 1065), box 20, code AH	**1b**	( )

Skip line 2 if you use the nonfarm optional method in Part II. See instructions.

2	Net profit or (loss) from Schedule C, line 31; and Schedule K-1 (Form 1065), box 14, code A (other than farming). See instructions for other income to report or if you are a minister or member of a religious order	**2**	
3	Combine lines 1a, 1b, and 2	**3**	
4a	If line 3 is more than zero, multiply line 3 by 92.35% (0.9235). Otherwise, enter amount from line 3	**4a**	
	Note: If line 4a is less than $400 due to Conservation Reserve Program payments on line 1b, see instructions.		
b	If you elect one or both of the optional methods, enter the total of lines 15 and 17 here	**4b**	
c	Combine lines 4a and 4b. If less than $400, **stop;** you don't owe self-employment tax. **Exception:** If less than $400 and you had **church employee income,** enter -0- and continue	**4c**	
5a	Enter your **church employee income** from Form W-2. See instructions for definition of church employee income	**5a**	
b	Multiply line 5a by 92.35% (0.9235). If less than $100, enter -0-	**5b**	
6	Add lines 4c and 5b	**6**	
7	Maximum amount of combined wages and self-employment earnings subject to social security tax or the 6.2% portion of the 7.65% railroad retirement (tier 1) tax for 2022	**7**	147,000
8a	Total social security wages and tips (total of boxes 3 and 7 on Form(s) W-2) and railroad retirement (tier 1) compensation. If $147,000 or more, skip lines 8b through 10, and go to line 11	**8a**	
b	Unreported tips subject to social security tax from Form 4137, line 10 . . .	**8b**	
c	Wages subject to social security tax from Form 8919, line 10	**8c**	
d	Add lines 8a, 8b, and 8c	**8d**	
9	Subtract line 8d from line 7. If zero or less, enter -0- here and on line 10 and go to line 11	**9**	
10	Multiply the **smaller** of line 6 or line 9 by 12.4% (0.124)	**10**	
11	Multiply line 6 by 2.9% (0.029)	**11**	
12	**Self-employment tax.** Add lines 10 and 11. Enter here and on **Schedule 2 (Form 1040), line 4** . .	**12**	
13	**Deduction for one-half of self-employment tax.** Multiply line 12 by 50% (0.50). Enter here and on **Schedule 1 (Form 1040), line 15** **13**		

| **Part II** | **Optional Methods To Figure Net Earnings** (see instructions) |

Farm Optional Method. You may use this method **only** if **(a)** your gross farm income[1] wasn't more than $9,060, **or (b)** your net farm profits[2] were less than $6,540.

14	Maximum income for optional methods	**14**	6,040
15	Enter the **smaller** of: two-thirds (⅔) of gross farm income[1] (not less than zero) **or** $6,040. Also, include this amount on line 4b above	**15**	

Nonfarm Optional Method. You may use this method **only** if **(a)** your net nonfarm profits[3] were less than $6,540 and also less than 72.189% of your gross nonfarm income,[4] **and (b)** you had net earnings from self-employment of at least $400 in 2 of the prior 3 years. **Caution:** You may use this method no more than five times.

16	Subtract line 15 from line 14	**16**	
17	Enter the **smaller** of: two-thirds (⅔) of gross nonfarm income[4] (not less than zero) **or** the amount on line 16. Also, include this amount on line 4b above	**17**	

[1] From Sch. F, line 9; and Sch. K-1 (Form 1065), box 14, code B.
[2] From Sch. F, line 34; and Sch. K-1 (Form 1065), box 14, code A—minus the amount you would have entered on line 1b had you not used the optional method.
[3] From Sch. C, line 31; and Sch. K-1 (Form 1065), box 14, code A.
[4] From Sch. C, line 7; and Sch. K-1 (Form 1065), box 14, code C.

For Paperwork Reduction Act Notice, see your tax return instructions.   Cat. No. 11358Z   Schedule SE (Form 1040) 2022

26. **Business Entity Problem:** This problem is designed for those using the "business entity" approach. **The solution may require information from Chapters 15 and 16.**

    Tom is a general partner in a partnership that reports an ordinary income of $80,000. His distributive share of partnership ordinary income is $40,000. During the year, his guaranteed payments were $30,000, and he withdrew $25,000 from the partnership.

    a. What amount would be subject to social security and Medicare taxes? Explain.

    b. Is the partnership responsible for withholding income taxes and FICA taxes on the partner's earnings? Explain how these taxes are paid to the government.

    c. How would your answers to Parts a. and b. change if the business was operated as an S corporation?

Chapter

8

Self-Employed Retirement Plans and Qualified Business Income Deductions

CHAPTER CONTENTS

LEARNING OBJECTIVES

After completing Chapter 8, you should be able to:

1. Understand the various types of retirement plans available to self-employed persons.
2. Calculate the QBI deduction.
3. Prepare the forms and schedules introduced in this chapter, including Forms 8995 and 8995-A.

CHAPTER OVERVIEW

Chapters 1 through 5 presented the basic structure for reporting income and deductions. Chapter 6 began the coverage of business and rental income with the introduction of the tax depreciation rules. Chapter 7 focused on tax reporting for self-employed taxpayers. It showed how they compute their self-employment profits or losses and self-employment taxes. This chapter covers retirement plans available to self-employed persons. It also covers the important and complicated Qualified Business Income deduction which began with the 2018 taxable year.

¶801

Retirement Plans for the Self-Employed

Sole proprietors deduct on Schedule C amounts they contribute to their employees' qualified pension and profit-sharing plans. Under a qualified plan, the employer must offer the plan to all eligible full-time employees. Two common qualified plans are defined benefit and defined contribution plans.

A **defined benefit plan** focuses on the annual benefits at retirement. Employers must contribute annually to the plan so that the promised benefits will be available at retirement. The benefit formula used in computing the annual contribution considers employees' compensation levels and years of service. This calculation usually requires professional help.

In contrast, a **defined contribution plan** focuses on annual contributions. The amount contributed is usually a percentage of the employee's compensation. Unlike a defined benefit plan, this type of plan promises no predetermined benefits. Instead, annual contributions are made to individual employee accounts. Employees then receive whatever benefits accumulate in their respective accounts.

A **simplified employee pension (SEP) plan** is a defined contribution plan employers can establish for their employees. In 2022, the maximum contribution an employer can make to an employee's SEP is the *lesser of* (i) $61,000 or (ii) 25% of the employee's compensation. For SEP plans established after 1986, only employers (not employees) can make contributions to an employee's SEP. An alternative to a SEP is a 401(k). The main advantage to a 401(k) over a SEP is that employees can make pre-tax contributions to their 401(k)s, thereby reducing their taxable wages. In 2022, employees can contribute up to $20,500 to a 401(k). Employees age 50 and older can contribute up to $27,000. Employers may contribute to their employees' 401(k)s but are not required to do so. A common practice for employers is to match 50% of the employee's contributions, up to a certain percentage of the employee's wages. Employers deduct only the matching contributions they make on Schedule C (line 19).

In recent years, some employers have begun offering Roth 401(k)s to their employees. Employees' contributions to a Roth 401(k) are made with after-tax funds. This means that the wages used to contribute to a Roth 401(k) are reported as taxable wages on the employee's Form W-2. Only the employee can contribute to a Roth 401(k). Employer contributions are not allowed. Although contributions to a Roth 401(k) are made with after-tax dollars, all amounts in a Roth 401(k) grow tax-free. Thus, when qualified distributions are eventually made from a Roth 401(k), both employee contributions and the accumulated earnings are exempt from tax. Roth 401(k)s are subject to the same contribution limits that apply to 401(k) plans, including catch-up provisions for participants age 50 or older. The $20,500 limit ($27,000 for age 50 and older) applies to all 401(k) contributions made during 2022.

EXAMPLE 1	Bobby is 42 years old. He participates in a 401(k) plan at work. His employer offers both a standard 401(k) and a Roth 401(k). In 2022, Bobby designates that $13,000 of his pre-tax wages be designated to his 401(k). This allows him to designate up to another $6,500 as an after-tax contribution to his Roth 401(k). His taxable wages will be reduced by the $13,000 that he contributes to his (standard) 401(k).

EXAMPLE 2	Same facts as in Example 1, except that Bobby is 51 years old. Bobby can contribute up to $13,000 ($27,000 maximum contribution – $13,000) of his after-tax wages to his Roth 401(k).

Employers that have 100 or fewer employees who earned $5,000 or more in the prior year can adopt a **savings incentive match plan for employees (SIMPLE).** Employers can set up SIMPLE plans using either IRAs or 401(k)s. Employees who earned at least $5,000 in any two prior years and expect to earn at least $5,000 in the current year would be allowed to contribute up to $14,000 of their salaries to the plan for 2022. Employees age 50 and older can contribute up to $17,000. Employers generally are required to make matching contributions up to 3% of the employee's compensation. Only the employer's contribution is deductible on Schedule C.

Sole proprietors can establish retirement plans for themselves and include the contributions as adjustments to income reported on Schedule 1 (Form 1040 or 1040-SR). Any contributions sole proprietors make to their own retirement plans do not reduce their Schedule C net profits but will reduce their AGI. Only deductions reported on Schedule C reduce a sole proprietor's self-employment tax. Thus, sole proprietors' contributions to their own retirement plans will reduce their income tax liability but have no impact on their self-employment tax. Sole proprietors who set up retirement plans for themselves also may have to provide retirement plans for eligible employees. They deduct any contributions they make to their employees' retirement plans on Schedule C (line 19).

Self-employed taxpayers have several retirement plan options. They can set up qualified defined benefit and defined contribution plans. When set up for self-employed taxpayers, these plans are commonly referred to as "Keoghs." They can also set up SEP, 401(k), and SIMPLE plans. Whichever retirement plan they choose, they must also make it available to all eligible employees.

¶801.01   KEOGH PLANS

The same contribution limits that apply to employees apply to sole proprietors. For defined contribution plans, the maximum contribution for 2022 is the *lesser of* (i) $61,000 or (ii) 25% of the participant's compensation. **Compensation** for a self-employed taxpayer equals self-employment net profit minus both the deduction for one-half of the self-employment tax and the contribution made to the retirement plan.

In computing their maximum allowable contribution, self-employed taxpayers first complete Schedule C to determine net profit. They then compute their self-employment tax on Schedule SE and deduct one-half of this tax from their net profit. Self-employed taxpayers may contribute up to 20% of the remaining amount to a defined contribution plan. This percentage is less than the 25% maximum contribution limit that is allowed for employees because of how a sole proprietor's "compensation" is computed. Example 3 shows how the 20% is determined.

EXAMPLE 3

Lloyd, a self-employed taxpayer, has a Schedule C net profit of $60,000. His Keogh plan requires a 25% contribution each year. Net earnings from self-employment is $55,410 ($60,000 × 92.35%). Self-employment tax is $8,478 ($55,410 × 15.3%). Lloyd reports $4,239 ($8,478 × ½) as an adjustment to income on Schedule 1 (Form 1040 or 1040-SR).

Using the required percentage of 25% of his compensation, Lloyd sets up a formula to solve for the required contribution (C): **25% × (Schedule C net profit – ½ of SE tax – C) = C**

For Lloyd, this equation is: **25% × ($60,000 – $4,239 – C) = C**

Solving for C: **25% × ($55,761 – C) = C**
            $13,940 = 125% × C
            $11,152 = C

Lloyd contributes $11,152 to his Keogh. He deducts this amount for AGI on Schedule 1 (Form 1040 or 1040-SR).

As shown in Example 3, 20% of the Schedule C net profit minus the employer's share of the self-employment tax [20% × ($60,000 – $4,239) = $11,152] is the same as 25% of the Schedule C net profit minus one-half of the self-employment tax and the contribution [25% × ($60,000 – $4,239 – $11,152) = $11,152]. Another way to compute the 20% is to divide the required percentage by the sum of 100% and the required percentage (25%/125% = 20%). This shortcut is used in Example 4.

EXAMPLE 4

Same facts as in Example 3, except that the plan requires a 10% contribution. Using the short cut approach, Lloyd computes his deductible contribution: **10%/110% = .0909 × $55,761 = $5,069**.

Keogh Requirements

1. The plan must be established before the end of the tax year.
2. The plan must be in writing, and employees must be provided a summary description, including the rules on discrimination and vesting.
3. The plan should be intended as a permanent plan.
4. The plan must have a designated trustee.
5. The contribution must be made by the due date of the tax return (including extensions).

Taxpayers can make contributions to qualified retirement plans until the due date of the tax return (including extensions). The big benefit of a Keogh plan is the ability to deduct the contributions each year plus postpone paying taxes on the accrued earnings until the funds are withdrawn. For this reason, the sooner the taxpayer contributes to the plan, the sooner the contributions begin earning tax-deferred (postponed) income.

To illustrate, on January 2, 2022, a self-employed taxpayer makes a $30,000 contribution to a Keogh plan. During 2022, $2,000 of earnings accrue on the $30,000. The income tax on that $2,000 is postponed until the funds are withdrawn after retirement. Had the taxpayer held the $30,000 in a taxable investment account and waited until December 31, 2022, to make the Keogh contribution, the $2,000 earned by the taxable investment during 2022 would be included in gross income on the taxpayer's 2022 tax return.

¶801.02 SIMPLIFIED EMPLOYEE PENSION (SEP) PLANS

Another retirement plan option for sole proprietors is a SEP. A SEP is a defined contribution plan. The maximum contribution self-employed taxpayers can make to a SEP in 2022 is the *lesser of* (i) $61,000 or (ii) 25% of the participant's compensation. This is the same as the *lesser of* (i) $61,000 or (ii) 20% of self-employment net profit after it is reduced by one-half of the self-employment tax.

The IRS provides an alternative calculation on the limit. The maximum compensation that may be taken into account is $305,000. Therefore, the maximum contribution is $61,000 (20% × $305,000).

As with a Keogh, self-employed taxpayers may contribute to a SEP until the due date of the return, including extensions. However, unlike a Keogh, a SEP does not need to be set up before the end of the tax year. Self-employed taxpayers have until the due date of their tax returns (including extensions) to set up a SEP plan. SEP plans have another advantage—they have no annual reporting requirements. Keoghs have annual reporting requirements, even if the taxpayer is the only participant. (These requirements are beyond the scope of this textbook).

EXAMPLE 5

Vince is self-employed and has a SEP. During 2022, he reports Schedule C net profits of $49,520. His self-employment tax is $6,997 ($49,520 × 92.35% × 15.3%), and his deduction for one-half of the self-employment tax is $3,499 ($6,997 × ½). Vince's maximum SEP contribution is $9,204.

25%/125% = 20% × ($49,520 − $3,499 deduction for SE tax) = $9,204

EXAMPLE 6

Kallie, a single taxpayer, is self-employed and has an SEP. During 2022, she reports Schedule C net profits of $334,559. Her basic self-employment tax on this amount is:

Component	Amount	Percentage	Result
Retirement	147,000	12.4	18,228
Medicare (334.559 × .9235)	308,965	2.9	8,960
Total basic			27,188
Deduction	27,188	50	13,594

Self-employment income	$334,559
Less self-employment tax deduction	(13,594)
Net	$320,965
Percent	20
Maximum per formula	$64,193

Although the formula shows a maximum contribution of $64,193, her contribution is limited to $61,000 in 2022. Kallie is also subject to the additional tax on self-employment income since her income exceeds $200,000. However, this tax does not contribute to the self-employment tax deduction and has no effect on her contribution limit.

> **SEP Requirements**
> 1. Each employee has an individual account.
> 2. Contributions must be made for all full-time employees who are at least age 21, have worked for the employer for three of the last five years, and have received at least $650 of wages during 2022.
> 3. Contributions are made under a written allocation formula.
> 4. The SEP cannot discriminate in favor of highly paid employees.
> 5. Employees must be able to withdraw the employer's contributions without restriction.

¶801.03 SAVINGS INCENTIVE MATCH PLAN FOR EMPLOYEES (SIMPLE)

Sole proprietors can set up a SIMPLE plan for themselves and their employees. The maximum that sole proprietors can contribute to their own SIMPLE plan in 2022 is the *lesser of* (i) $14,000 or (ii) 100% of their compensation. Sole proprietors age 50 and older can contribute up to $3,000 more, for a total of $17,000 (assuming they have at least $17,000 of compensation). An advantage to having a SIMPLE plan is that it is not subject to the nondiscrimination and top-heavy rules associated with other retirement plans. A disadvantage is that employer matching is required with a SIMPLE plan. Neither of these are issues for sole proprietors with no employees. Due to the $14,000 ($17,000) limit, sole proprietors with no employees may want to consider a SEP plan, which has a higher contribution limit.

> **SIMPLE Requirements**
> 1. There must be 100 or fewer employees in the previous year.
> 2. The SIMPLE plan is the only retirement plan offered.
> 3. All employees who had at least $5,000 of compensation in the previous year and expect to have at least $5,000 of compensation in the current year must be allowed to participate.

> The choice of a retirement plan will depend on the extent of compliance requirements, administrative and other costs, contribution limits, and flexibility. Sole proprietors considering setting up a retirement plan should carefully review the requirements and limitations of each type of plan and determine the type of plan best suited to their needs. Since most plans require that all eligible employees be allowed to participate, sole proprietors with employees may want to consider the potential costs of required employer (matching) contributions when deciding on a retirement plan for themselves.

¶802 QUALIFIED BUSINESS INCOME (QBI) DEDUCTION

For tax years beginning after 2017 and before 2026, a self-employed taxpayer may be entitled to claim a deduction for qualified business income (QBI), in addition to the standard or itemized deductions. The QBI deduction allows the taxpayer to deduct up to 20% of their QBI from a qualified trade or business, plus 20% of the aggregate amount of qualified real estate investment trust (REIT) dividends and qualified publicly traded partnership (PTP) income. The deduction is subject to a number of limitations, including limits based on the type of trade or business, the taxpayer's taxable income, the amount of W-2 wages paid in the qualified trade or business, and the unadjusted basis of qualified property held by the trade or business. The taxpayer claims the QBI deduction on Form 1040, not on Schedule C.

The deduction is 20% of the qualifying income but is limited to 20% of the individual's taxable income, reduced for items taxed as net capital gains (long-term capital gains and qualified dividends). The deduction is taken from AGI and is available in full for taxpayers who itemize or use the standard deduction.

EXAMPLE 7	Tracy has $150,000 of AGI in 2022. $50,000 qualifies for the QBI deduction. She is single and does not itemize her deductions. Her taxable income is:	
	AGI	$ 150,000
	Standard deduction	(12,950)
	QBI deduction ($50,000 × 20%)	(10,000)
	Taxable income	$ 127,050

¶802.01   REIT AND PTP RULES

A REIT is taxable as a corporation, except that it deducts the dividends paid to its owners. The owners include the dividends from the REIT as gross income. Some of the dividends may be treated as capital gains and others as ordinary income.

A PTP exists when interests in the partnership are traded on an established securities market or secondary market. A PTP is treated as a corporation unless 90% or more of its gross income is from "passive-type" sources. These sources are interest, dividends, real property rents, gains from the disposition of real property, income from oil, gas, mineral, and other natural resources, and gains from the disposition of any assets used in these income-producing activities.

A distribution from a REIT qualifies for the 20% deduction if it is not treated as a capital gain or qualified dividend. Similarly, an individual's share of income from a PTP that is not taxed as a corporation qualifies for the 20% deduction, to the extent that the income of the PTP is from one or more of the income classifications that qualify for the QBI deduction. The shareholder or partner deduction for QBI from a REIT or PTP does not depend on the W-2 wages or qualified property of the entity.

¶802.02   RULES FOR PROPRIETORS AND OWNERS OF INTERESTS IN PASS-THROUGH ENTITIES

For business income other than from REITs and PTPs, there are several requirements, some of which depend upon the taxpayer's level of income. Rules that do not fluctuate with the taxpayer's income level include:

- The income must be effectively connected with a U.S. trade or business;
- Certain income is not QBI, even if it is effectively connected with a U.S. trade or business;
- Each taxpayer must compute QBI separately for each trade or business.

Provisions that vary with the taxpayer's income are:

- The deduction is generally limited to 20% of the taxable income if taxable income is less than the taxpayer's QBI.
- Income from a specified service business may or may not be part of the base for the QBI deduction, depending on the amount of taxable income and the taxpayer's filing status.
- The amount of the deduction may depend on the qualified business's W-2 wages and basis in qualified property, depending on the amount of taxable income and the taxpayer's filing status.

¶802.03   INCOME NOT TREATED AS QUALIFIED BUSINESS INCOME

Certain income is not QBI, even if it is effectively connected with a U.S. trade or business. These items include:

- Long-term and short-term capital gains and losses;
- Dividends and equivalents (other than patronage dividends from cooperatives);
- Interest (other than that properly allocable to a qualified trade or business); and
- Annuities (unless properly allocable to a qualified trade or business).

In addition, wage or salary income received from the activity does not constitute QBI for an S corporation shareholder-employee. However, deductions such as self-employed retirement plan contributions and medical insurance of the self-employed are elements of QBI.

¶802.04   TAXABLE INCOME LIMIT

If the taxpayer's taxable income is less than the QBI, the deduction limit is 20% of taxable income. For this purpose, taxable income does not include anything taxed at capital gain rates. This includes long-term capital gains, discussed in Chapter 11, and qualified dividends (see ¶201.03). Taxable income is calculated without regard to the QBI deduction itself.

EXAMPLE 8

Virgil has $150,000 of AGI in 2022. All $150,000 qualifies for the QBI deduction. He is single and does not itemize deductions. Based only on his QBI, his deduction would be $30,000.

His taxable income, before the QBI deduction, is:

AGI	$150,000
Standard deduction	(12,950)
Taxable income before QBI deduction	$137,050

Since Virgil's taxable income is less than his QBI, the deduction is 20% of his taxable income, or $27,410.

EXAMPLE 9

Dale and Doris are married and file a joint return. In 2022, Dale has 120,000 of income from a qualifying business. Doris has $100,000 of qualified dividends. They have $12,000 of self-employed health insurance deduction and $45,000 of itemized deductions. Their taxable income, before the QBI deduction, is:

Qualified business income	$120,000
Qualified dividends	100,000
Self-employed health insurance deduction	(12,000)
AGI	208,000

Dale and Doris are below the 2022 threshold for married taxpayers filing jointly, so they are not limited by wages paid by Dale's business or qualified property of the business (see below). If no other limit applied, the QBI would be $108,000 ($120,000 – 12,000 self-employed health insurance deduction). This would yield a deduction of $21,600. However, they must consider the taxable income limitation.

AGI	$ 208,000
less itemized deductions	(45,000)
less qualified dividend	(100,000)
	63,000
20% of taxable income	12,600

¶802.05 TAXABLE INCOME THRESHOLD RULES

Some of the most important tax planning needs to focus on increasing or decreasing taxable income to get certain results for the QBI deduction. Important limits apply to individual taxpayers based on their levels of taxable income.

- If taxable income is below a certain threshold, income from specified services can be qualified business income. If the income is above the threshold, this income does not qualify for the QBI deduction.
- If income is below the threshold, the deduction for income from a trade or business is not dependent upon the W-2 wages paid by the business or the qualified property held by the business. If the taxpayer's income exceeds the threshold, the deduction for QBI is limited by one or both of these factors.

When income exceeds the threshold, there is a phase-out range. When taxable income exceeds the threshold but is within the phase-out range, the limits apply in part. When taxable income exceeds the threshold plus the phase-out range, the limits apply in full. The threshold rules depend on the taxpayer's filing status. The thresholds, but not the phase-out ranges, are indexed after 2018.

2022 Taxable Year

Filing status	Single, Head of household	Married Filing Separate	Married Filing Joint
Threshold	$170,050	$170,050	$340,100
Phase-out for wage and property limit and service income	50,000	50,000	100,000
End of phase-out	$220,050	$220,050	$440,100

¶802.06 SPECIFIED SERVICE TRADE OR BUSINESS RULES

The qualified business income legislation was not intended to cover professional services. However, for persons of moderate income levels, amounts derived from service professions may qualify for the deduction. Any taxpayer whose taxable income exceeds the threshold plus phase-out is not able to claim a deduction for income from a "specified service trade or business" (SSTB). However, any taxpayer whose income is below the threshold shown above may claim the deduction in whole or in part. The following activities are SSTBs:

- health
- law
- accounting
- actuarial science
- performing arts
- consulting
- athletics
- financial services
- brokerage services
- investing and investment management
- trading, or dealing in securities, partnership interests, or commodities
- any trade or business where the principal asset is the reputation or skill of one or more of its employees.

EXAMPLE 10

Steve is an attorney. He is married and files a joint return. In 2022, Steve's income from his law practice was $250,000. Their other income was $70,000 and itemized deductions for the year were $40,000. Since their combined taxable income, before the QBI deduction, did not exceed $340,100, Steve's law practice income qualifies for a QBI deduction of $50,000.

EXAMPLE 11

Laura is a partner in an international CPA firm. In 2022, her income from the practice was $800,000, and her taxable income, before any QBI deduction, was $1,050,000. None of Laura's income from the accounting practice qualifies for the QBI deduction.

When a professional's income is between the threshold and the end of the phase-out range, there is a proportionate disallowance. Income within this range leads to some of the more complicated calculations since the W-2 wages and qualified property limits (discussed below) also apply.

¶802.07   OTHER TRADE OR BUSINESS RULES

U.S. source business income other than specified service business income is subject to the QBI deduction even for taxpayers whose incomes exceed the threshold. However, there are some special limitations that affect this deduction, which are dependent upon the relationship of the taxpayer's taxable income to the thresholds and phase-outs.

When taxable income is below the threshold, the wage and property limits do not apply. The QBI deduction is 20% of the qualifying income, limited to 20% of taxable income, before the QBI deduction and without including any long-term capital gains of qualified dividends.

W-2 Wage Limitation

In general, a taxpayer's QBI deduction is limited to 50% of W-2 wages paid by qualified businesses. However, there are some exceptions to this rule. First, the limit does not apply to any taxpayer whose taxable income (before the Section 199A deduction) is less than the threshold amount. The threshold and phase-ins are the same as those discussed above. Second, a taxpayer with substantial depreciable property may qualify for the combined W-2 wage and property limitation.

EXAMPLE 12

Martha is a self-employed architect. In 2022, she is single. Her earnings from her brokerage in 2022, after self-employment tax, self-employed health insurance deduction, and retirement plan contributions, were $156,000. She paid $30,000 of wages to her employees and properly reported these on Form W-2. She had $22,000 of interest income and claimed $18,000 of itemized deductions. Her taxable income before the QBI deduction is:

Income as architect	$156,000
Interest	22,000
AGI	178,000
Itemized deductions	(18,000)
Taxable income before QBI deduction	160,000

Since Martha's taxable income is less than the single taxpayer's threshold for 2022, her deduction does not depend on W-2 wages paid. She claims a QBI deduction of $31,200 since her QBI is less than her taxable income.

When taxable income exceeds the threshold plus the phase-out range, the QBI deduction is 50% of the W-2 wages paid by the business, unless the qualified property limit (discussed below) produces a higher limit.

EXAMPLE 13

Martha, from Example 12, had $122,000 of interest income and claimed $18,000 of itemized deductions. Her business did not have any substantial qualified property. Her taxable income before the QBI deduction is:

Income as architect	$156,000
Interest	122,000
AGI	278,000
Itemized deductions	(18,000)
Taxable income before QBI deduction	260,000

Since Martha's taxable income exceeds the single taxpayer's threshold plus phase-out range for 2022, her deduction is limited to 50% W-2 wages paid. She claims a QBI deduction of $15,000 since this amount is less than 20% of her QBI.

When taxable income before the QBI deduction exceeds the threshold but is within the phase-out range, there is a proportional application of the limit. In essence, the QBI deduction equals 20% of the income from the activity, less a percentage of the difference between 20% of the income and 50% of the W-2 wages. The proportion is the amount by which the taxable income exceeds the threshold, divided by the phase-out range ($100,000 for married taxpayers filing jointly and $50,000 for all others).

EXAMPLE 14

Martha, from Example 12, had $60,000 of interest income and claimed $18,000 of itemized deductions. Her business did not have any substantial qualified property. Her taxable income before the QBI deduction is:

Income as architect	$156,000
Interest	60,000
AGI	216,000
Itemized deductions	(18,000)
Taxable income before QBI deduction	198,000

Since Martha's taxable income exceeds the single taxpayer's threshold but the excess is less than the phase-out range of $50,000, she must compute a percentage. She applies this percentage to the excess of 20% of the income over 50% of the W-2 wages.

Her percentage is:

Taxable income before QBI deduction	$198,000
Less threshold	(170,050)
Excess income	$27,950
Excess income as % of $50,000	55.9
20% of qualified business income	31,200
50% of W-2 wages	(15,000)
Excess of 20% income over 50% wages	16,200
Excess times percentage (55.9)	9,056
Deduction (31,200 – 9,056)	22,144

Since $22,144 is less than 20% of her taxable income, she claims that as her deduction. Her taxable income after the QBI deduction is:

Taxable income before QBI deduction	198,000
Less QBI deduction	(22,144)
Taxable income	$175,856

Wage and Property Limitation

As an alternative to the wage limitation, a taxpayer may claim a limit based on W-2 wages plus a percentage of the basis of certain property. The first component is 25% of the W-2 wage base. The second component is based on the unadjusted basis immediately after acquisition (UBIA) of certain qualified property that the qualified business holds at the end of the year.

Qualified property has several requirements as described below:

- Only tangible and depreciable property qualifies (thus, land and intangibles do not qualify);
- The property must be held and available for use at the end of the year;
- The property must have been used for production of QBI during the year;

■ The "depreciable period" of the property must not have ended at the close of the year. There are some special rules relating to the depreciable period of property, as the term applies to QBI:
  – If the property's MACRS life exceeds ten years (see Chapter 8), the depreciable period is the last full year of MACRS life;
  – For other property, the depreciable period is ten years.

UBIA is the basis of property before any reduction for depreciation. See Chapter 11 for basis rules and Chapter 6 for depreciation.

EXAMPLE 15

Victor owns an equipment rental company. In 2022, his net income, after self-employment tax, self-employed health insurance deduction, and contributions to his Keogh plan, is $650,000. His AGI exceeds the threshold plus phase-out range for 2022. The business had one employee and paid $66,000 of W-2 wages during the year. The company's UBIA at the end of the year was $1,500,000.

Victor computes his QBI deduction.

1.	20% of income	$130,000
2.	Limit, greater of:	
	50% of W-2 wages	$ 33,000
	25% W-2 wages	$ 16,500
	2.5% UBIA	$ 37,500
	Sum of 25% W-2 wages + 2.5% UBIA	$ 54,000
QBI deduction		$ 54,000

LIMIT PER TRADE OR BUSINESS

This limitation applies to each separate trade or business. The business owners may not use the W-2 wages or qualified property of one business to support the QBI deduction.

REPORTING REQUIREMENTS

Persons whose income does not exceed the threshold use Form 8995. Others use Form 8995-A.

¶802.08   FILLED-IN FORM 8995

INFORMATION FOR FIGURE 8-1:

Monroe Peters, from Chapter 7, Figure 7-1, is single in 2022. His taxable income from all sources, after subtracting all deductions except QBI, is $140,000, none of which is capital gain or qualified dividend. Monroe's income is less than the threshold for single persons in 2022. Therefore, his income, which is from a specified service trade or business (consulting), qualifies for the QBI deduction, and the wage and qualified property limits do not apply. He has no income from REITs or PTPs.

Monroe calculates his net qualified business income as:

Income from Schedule C	$ 90,600
Less self-employment tax deduction	(6,401)
Net qualified business income	$ 84,199

Since his income does not exceed the threshold, he uses Form 8995 to report the QBI deduction of $16,992. He would also enter this on Line 10 of Form 1040.

Figure 8-1: Filled-In Form 8995

Form **8995**	**Qualified Business Income Deduction** **Simplified Computation**	OMB No. 1545-2294
Department of the Treasury Internal Revenue Service	▶ Attach to your tax return. ▶ Go to *www.irs.gov/Form8995* for instructions and the latest information.	**2021** Attachment Sequence No. **55**

Name(s) shown on return	Your taxpayer identification number
Monroe L. Peters	268-00-9092

Note. *You can claim the qualified business income deduction **only** if you have qualified business income from a qualified trade or business, real estate investment trust dividends, publicly traded partnership income, or a domestic production activities deduction passed through from an agricultural or horticultural cooperative. See instructions.*
Use this form if your taxable income, before your qualified business income deduction, is at or below $164,900 ($164,925 if married filing separately; $329,800 if married filing jointly), and you aren't a patron of an agricultural or horticultural cooperative.

1	(a) Trade, business, or aggregation name	(b) Taxpayer identification number	(c) Qualified business income or (loss)
i	Monroe L. Peters Consulting	70-1234569	84,199
ii			
iii			
iv			
v			

2	Total qualified business income or (loss). Combine lines 1i through 1v, column (c)	**2**	84,199	
3	Qualified business net (loss) carryforward from the prior year	**3** (	)	
4	Total qualified business income. Combine lines 2 and 3. If zero or less, enter -0-	**4**	84,199	
5	Qualified business income component. Multiply line 4 by 20% (0.20)			**5** 16,840
6	Qualified REIT dividends and publicly traded partnership (PTP) income or (loss) (see instructions)	**6**		
7	Qualified REIT dividends and qualified PTP (loss) carryforward from the prior year	**7** (	)	
8	Total qualified REIT dividends and PTP income. Combine lines 6 and 7. If zero or less, enter -0-	**8**		
9	REIT and PTP component. Multiply line 8 by 20% (0.20)			**9**
10	Qualified business income deduction before the income limitation. Add lines 5 and 9			**10** 16,840
11	Taxable income before qualified business income deduction (see instructions)	**11**	140,000	
12	Net capital gain (see instructions)	**12**		
13	Subtract line 12 from line 11. If zero or less, enter -0-	**13**	140,000	
14	Income limitation. Multiply line 13 by 20% (0.20)			**14** 28,000
15	Qualified business income deduction. Enter the smaller of line 10 or line 14. Also enter this amount on the applicable line of your return (see instructions) . . . . ▶			**15** 16,840
16	Total qualified business (loss) carryforward. Combine lines 2 and 3. If greater than zero, enter -0- . .			**16** ( )
17	Total qualified REIT dividends and PTP (loss) carryforward. Combine lines 6 and 7. If greater than zero, enter -0-			**17** ( )

For Privacy Act and Paperwork Reduction Act Notice, see instructions.	Cat. No. 37806C	Form **8995** (2021)

¶802.09   FILLED-IN FORM 8995-A

 ## INFORMATION FOR FIGURE 8-2:

Harold R. Wilson, from Chapter 7, Figure 7-4, is eligible for the QBI deduction. He and his wife Wendy file a joint return for 2022. Their combined taxable income before the QBI deduction consists of the following:

Income from hardware store	$ 147,547
Wendy's salary	264,000
Interest	39,250
Qualified dividends	40,000
Self-employment tax deduction	(10,424)
AGI	480,373
Itemized deductions	(35,500)
Taxable income before QBI deduction	$444,873

Since the Wilsons' taxable income exceeds the threshold for married taxpayers filing jointly in 2022, they must use Form 8995-A to compute the QBI deduction.

Line #

    1A: Harold's Hardware 70-0624331

    2:   Schedule C income of $147,547 less self-employment tax deduction of $10,424 = $137,123

    3:   20% of $137,123 = 27,425

    4:   wages of $44,297

    5:   50% of wages = 22,149

    6:   25% of wages = 11,074

    7:   Harold's Hardware has $24,846 of unadjusted basis immediately after acquisition in qualified property. See Figure 6-8 in Chapter 6.

    8:   2.5% of the UBIA is $621

    9:   $11,695, 25% W-2 wages + 2.5% UBIA

    10:   greater of line 5 or line 9, $22,149

    11:   smaller of 20% of income, or limitation $22,149

         No entry on Line 12, since taxable income exceeds phase-out range

    13:   $22,149

    14:   only applies to patrons of agricultural cooperatives

    15:   $22,149

    16:   $22,149

Part III lines 17-26 are only necessary for a taxpayer whose income is between the threshold and the end of the phase-out range. Harold and Wendy are above this range.

Figure 8-2: Filled-In Form 8995-A (Page 1)

Form **8995-A**	**Qualified Business Income Deduction**	OMB No. 1545-2294

Department of the Treasury
Internal Revenue Service

Attach to your tax return.
Go to www.irs.gov/Form8995A for instructions and the latest information.

2022
Attachment
Sequence No. **55A**

Name(s) shown on return
Harold R. Wilson

Your taxpayer identification number
272-00-8855

Note: You can claim the qualified business income deduction **only** if you have qualified business income from a qualified trade or business, real estate investment trust dividends, publicly traded partnership income, or a domestic production activities deduction passed through from an agricultural or horticultural cooperative. See instructions.

Use this form if your taxable income, before your qualified business income deduction, is above $170,050 ($340,100 if married filing jointly), or you're a patron of an agricultural or horticultural cooperative.

Part I   Trade, Business, or Aggregation Information

Complete Schedules A, B, and/or C (Form 8995-A), as applicable, before starting Part I. Attach additional worksheets when needed. See instructions.

1	(a) Trade, business, or aggregation name	(b) Check if specified service	(c) Check if aggregation	(d) Taxpayer identification number	(e) Check if patron
A	Harold's Hardware Store	☐	☐	70-0624431	☐
B		☐	☐		☐
C		☐	☐		☐

Part II   Determine Your Adjusted Qualified Business Income

			A	B	C
2	Qualified business income from the trade, business, or aggregation. See instructions	2	137,123		
3	Multiply line 2 by 20% (0.20). If your taxable income is $170,050 or less ($340,100 if married filing jointly), skip lines 4 through 12 and enter the amount from line 3 on line 13	3	27,425		
4	Allocable share of W-2 wages from the trade, business, or aggregation	4	44,297		
5	Multiply line 4 by 50% (0.50)	5	22,149		
6	Multiply line 4 by 25% (0.25)	6	11,074		
7	Allocable share of the unadjusted basis immediately after acquisition (UBIA) of all qualified property	7	24,846		
8	Multiply line 7 by 2.5% (0.025)	8	621		
9	Add lines 6 and 8	9	11,695		
10	Enter the greater of line 5 or line 9	10	22,149		
11	W-2 wage and UBIA of qualified property limitation. Enter the smaller of line 3 or line 10	11	22,149		
12	Phased-in reduction. Enter the amount from line 26, if any	12	21,897		
13	Qualified business income deduction before patron reduction. Enter the greater of line 11 or line 12	13	22,149		
14	Patron reduction. Enter the amount from Schedule D (Form 8995-A), line 6, if any. See instructions	14			
15	Qualified business income component. Subtract line 14 from line 13	15	22,149		
16	Total qualified business income component. Add all amounts reported on line 15	16	22,149		

For Privacy Act and Paperwork Reduction Act Notice, see separate instructions.   Cat. No. 71661B   Form **8995-A** (2022)

Figure 8-2: Filled-In Form 8995-A (Page 2)

Form 8995-A (2022) Page **2**

Part III Phased-in Reduction

Complete Part III only if your taxable income is more than $170,050 but not $220,050 ($340,100 and $440,100 if married filing jointly) and line 10 is less than line 3. Otherwise, skip Part III.

			A	B	C
17	Enter the amounts from line 3	17	27,425		
18	Enter the amounts from line 10	18	22,149		
19	Subtract line 18 from line 17	19	5,276		
20	Taxable income before qualified business income deduction	20 444,873			
21	Threshold. Enter $170,050 ($340,100 if married filing jointly)	21 340,100			
22	Subtract line 21 from line 20	22 104,773			
23	Phase-in range. Enter $50,000 ($100,000 if married filing jointly)	23 100,000			
24	Phase-in percentage. Divide line 22 by line 23	24 1 %			
25	Total phase-in reduction. Multiply line 19 by line 24	25	5,528		
26	Qualified business income after phase-in reduction. Subtract line 25 from line 17. Enter this amount here and on line 12, for the corresponding trade or business	26	21,897		

Part IV Determine Your Qualified Business Income Deduction

27	Total qualified business income component from all qualified trades, businesses, or aggregations. Enter the amount from line 16	27	22,149	
28	Qualified REIT dividends and publicly traded partnership (PTP) income or (loss). See instructions	28		
29	Qualified REIT dividends and PTP (loss) carryforward from prior years	29 (	)	
30	Total qualified REIT dividends and PTP income. Combine lines 28 and 29. If less than zero, enter -0-	30		
31	REIT and PTP component. Multiply line 30 by 20% (0.20)	31		
32	Qualified business income deduction before the income limitation. Add lines 27 and 31	32	22,149	
33	Taxable income before qualified business income deduction	33	444,873	
34	Net capital gain. See instructions	34		
35	Subtract line 34 from line 33. If zero or less, enter -0-	35	444,873	
36	Income limitation. Multiply line 35 by 20% (0.20)	36	88,975	
37	Qualified business income deduction before the domestic production activities deduction (DPAD) under section 199A(g). Enter the smaller of line 32 or line 36	37	22,149	
38	DPAD under section 199A(g) allocated from an agricultural or horticultural cooperative. Don't enter more than line 33 minus line 37	38		
39	Total qualified business income deduction. Add lines 37 and 38	39	22,149	
40	Total qualified REIT dividends and PTP (loss) carryforward. Combine lines 28 and 29. If zero or greater, enter -0-	40 (	)	

Form **8995-A** (2022)

¶802.09

8

Name:

Section:

Date: _____

QUESTIONS AND PROBLEMS

1. **Pension Plans.** (Obj. 3) Three common pension plans employers can provide to their employees are SEP, 401(k), and SIMPLE plans. For each of the following statements, identify the plan or plans having the described characteristics.

    _____ a. This plan allows employees under age 50 to contribute up to $14,000 of their wages to their plan in 2022.

    _____ b. This plan allows only employers to make contributions to employees' plans.

    _____ c. Employers are required to make matching contributions to this plan.

    _____ d. The maximum contribution to this plan is the *lesser of* $56,000 or 25% of the employee's compensation.

    _____ e. Employees can contribute pre-tax earnings to this plan.

2. **Retirement Plans.** (Obj. 1).

    a. Assume that Liz Bell (SSN 304-00-1059) had $14,000 of net profit from self-employment in 2022 and wants to make the maximum contribution to a SEP. Prepare Schedule SE to determine the amount of self-employment tax that Liz owes on her self-employment profits.

    b. What is the maximum Liz can contribute to a SEP plan that would be fully deducted from gross income on her 2022 income tax return? Where on the tax return is the deduction claimed?

    c. If Liz wants to contribute to a SEP plan, by what date must she make a contribution for 2022?

3. **Retirement Plans.** (Obj. 1) Diana has a consulting practice. She has no employees. For the 2022 tax year, Diana's gross consulting revenue was $155,000, and her operating expenses, not including retirement plan contributions, were $10,000. In addition to her consulting income, Diana also received $5,000 in 2022 for writing a chapter in a book about management consulting. In 2022, Diana established a defined contribution (Keogh) plan. The plan stipulates a fixed percentage of 10% of compensation as the amount of the required annual contribution.

    a.   What is the amount of self-employment tax that Diana must pay for 2022?

    b.   What is the required dollar contribution that Diana must make to her Keogh for 2022?

    c.   By what date must the Keogh be established in order for Diana to take a deduction for the contributions on her 2022 tax return?

    d.   By what date must the contributions be paid into the Keogh plan in order for Diana to take a deduction on her 2022 tax return?

4. **QBI deduction** (Obj. 2) Teresa has $140,000 of AGI in 2022. $60,000 qualifies for the QBI deduction. She is single and does not itemize her deductions.

    a.   Compute her QBI deduction

    b.   Compute her taxable income

5. **QBI deduction** (Obj. 2) Carl and Jeanne are married and file a joint return. In 2022, Jeanne has $138,000 of income from a qualifying business. They have $90,000 of qualified dividends. They have $12,000 of deductible contributions to IRAs, $6,000 of which is attributable to Jeanne's business, and $42,000 of itemized deductions.

   a. Their taxable income, before the QBI deduction, is:

   b. The deduction based on Jeanne's income, without considering the taxable income limitation, is:

   c. The taxable income limitation is:

   d. The QBI deduction is:

   e. Taxable income after all deductions is:

6. **QBI deduction** (Obj. 2) Linda is a self-employed CPA. She is single in 2022. Discuss the eligibility of her income from her accounting practice for the QBI deduction under the following alternatives. State whether or not the wages she paid to employees or the unadjusted basis in qualified property would affect your answer.

   a. Her taxable income, before any QBI deduction, is $160,000

   b. Her taxable income, before any QBI deduction, is $360,000

   c. Her taxable income, before any QBI deduction, is $190,000

7. **QBI deduction** (Obj. 2) Ken and Penny, husband and wife, file a joint return in 2022. They own a truck repair center. Their income from the business was $480,000 after subtracting all deductions attributable to the business. They had taxable interest income of $55,000 and itemized deductions of $36,000. The business paid W-2 wages of $124,000 during the year and owned qualified property with UBIA of $1,750,000 at the end of the year.

    a. Determine whether or not the limits bases on W-2 wages and qualified property apply, based on the level of taxable income.

    b. Determine the limit based solely on W-2 wages paid.

    c. Determine the limit based on W-2 wages paid and qualified property.

    d. Compute the QBI deduction.

8. **Internet Problem: Researching the Instructions to Form 5329.** (Obj. 6)

    Normally a 10% penalty is assessed when employees and self-employed taxpayers take distributions from a retirement plan before reaching age 59½. However, exceptions do exist. Describe the various circumstances under which individuals can take early distributions from the various retirement plans do not have to pay the 10% penalty.

    Go to the IRS website. Locate the Instructions for Form 5329, and find the answer to the above question regarding exceptions to the 10% penalty. Print out a copy of the page(s) where you found your answer. Underline or highlight the pertinent information.

    See Appendix A for instructions on using the IRS website.

9. **Tax Ethics Case.*** The date is April 14, and Helen Baldwin, a CPA tax practitioner, sits at her desk, pondering the tax return before her. Helen has spent plenty of time pondering during the past year since moving from her home in a large eastern city to set up her new tax practice in a small western town. Clients in this small town have not exactly beaten a path to Helen's door to take advantage of her services. Building a client base has proven much more difficult than she had anticipated.

    The return in front of Helen was completed on behalf of her newest client, Billy Joe Carter, who owns Honest Bill's Used Car Lot. He is a cousin of half of the members of the town council and is very influential in the local business community. Establishing a client relationship with Billy is the break that Helen has been looking for. In fact, Billy has made it clear that if Helen can complete and file his return before the April 15 deadline, Helen will receive his tax return business, as well as that of his family, for years to come.

Of concern to Helen, however, are several items on Billy's return. Billy insists that he is entitled to a business deduction for his new four-wheel-drive truck since he uses it 100% of the time for business errands (such as traveling to car auctions, picking up parts, etc.). Helen thinks she has seen Billy driving the truck a number of times on what appeared to be personal trips. Also, Billy insists that the expenses associated with several trips to Las Vegas are deductible since the trips were "primarily of a business nature." Billy also claims several other large deductions without offering what Helen would consider "substantial documentation." As if anticipating Helen's skepticism, Billy said, "I don't know how things were in the big city where you came from, but around here, people believe that a person's word is worth something. You'll just have to trust good old 'Honest Bill' this year, and next year I'll try to keep some better records."

a. What are the ethical issues in this case?

b. Who and what are the stakeholders who will be affected directly or indirectly by an inappropriate decision on Helen's part?

c. What are Helen's options in this situation?

d. What do you recommend that Helen do?

*   *Case adapted from ethics cases prepared for publication by the American Accounting Association.*

10. Maria A. Solo owns and operates the Reliable Drug Store. Chapter 7 Cumulative Problem 2 required preparation of Form 1040, Schedules 1, 2, C, SE, and Form 8812. Her income is Qualified Business Income.

a.   Should Maria prepare Form 8995 or Form 8995-A?

b.   Fill out the appropriate form for Maria to claim her Qualified Business Income deduction. (SSN 318-01-6921) lives at 190 Glenn Drive, Grand Rapids, Michigan 49527-2005. Maria (age 45 and single) claims her aunt, Selda Ray (SSN 282-61-4011), as a dependent. Selda lives with Maria. Maria owns and operates the Reliable Drug Store at 1816 First Street in Grand Rapids, Michigan 49503-1902, in which she materially participates the entire year. Her EIN is 38-9654321. Employer quarterly payroll tax returns were filed as required, and Maria values her inventory at cost. The income statement for 2021 is reproduced on the next page. Maria reports on the accrual method but uses the "direct write-off" method to compute bad debt expense. Her business code is 446110. She does not deduct expenses for an office in her home.

An examination of Maria's business records reveals that the depreciable property includes furniture and fixtures, a delivery truck, and store equipment. The depreciation expense shown on the 2021 income statement meets the income tax requirements for depreciation for using the mentioned assets during 2021. Maria rounds calculations to the nearest dollar. Miscellaneous expenses include the following:

Contributions to the Red Cross and United Way	$350
Chamber of Commerce dues	125
Personal electric bill for August	80
Total miscellaneous expenses	$555

Other income for Maria includes a salary of $100 each month for her services as a member of a working committee of the Drug Association. Her Form W-2 from the association shows gross wages of $1,200 and federal income tax withheld of $296.

Maria also earned $320 in taxable interest. Maria made federal estimated tax payments totaling $5,000. This amount is reported on Schedule 3 (Form 1040 or 1040-SR) and on line 18 of Form 1040, page 2.

Prepare Form 1040, Schedules 1, 2, 8812, C, and SE, and Form 8995 for Maria Solo using the forms provided on the pages that follow. Maria does not want $3 to go to the Presidential election campaign fund. She signs her return on April 15, 2021.

RELIABLE DRUG STORE
Income Statement

For the Year Ended December 31, 2021

Operating revenue:

Sales		$324,200
Less sales returns and allowances		(3,390)
Net sales		$320,810

cost of merchandise sold:

Merchandise inventory, beginning	$ 68,920	
Purchases	$198,240	
Less purchases returns and allowances	(8,100)	
Net purchases	$190,140	
Merchandise available for sale	$259,060	
Less merchandise inventory, ending	(69,185)	
Cost of merchandise sold		(189,875)
Gross profit on sales		$130,935

Operating expenses:

Advertising expense	$ 6,541	
Bad debt expense (direct write off method)	850	
Car and truck expense	7,967[1]	
Depreciation expense	3,396	
Insurance expense (other than health)	644	
Miscellaneous expense	125	
Payroll taxes	3,471	
Rent expense (other business property)	12,000	
Telephone and utilities expense	2,395	
Travel expense	256	
Meals expense	70	
Wages expense	62,500	
Total operating expenses		(100,215)
Net income		$ 30,720

Maria drove her personal automobile for 13,163 business miles during the year. 7,304 of the business miles were before July 1. Total miles for the year were 32,815. There were 1,300 commuting miles. This is Maria's only car. She has kept a written log documenting her business miles. Maria first used the car in her business on May 4, 2020. She uses the standard mileage method.

(Use for Comprehensive Problem.)

Form 1040 — U.S. Individual Income Tax Return (2022)

Form 1040   Department of the Treasury—Internal Revenue Service

U.S. Individual Income Tax Return   **2022**   OMB No. 1545-0074   IRS Use Only—Do not write or staple in this space.

Filing Status
Check only one box.

☐ Single ☐ Married filing jointly ☐ Married filing separately (MFS) ☐ Head of household (HOH) ☐ Qualifying widow(er) (QW)

If you checked the MFS box, enter the name of your spouse. If you checked the HOH or QW box, enter the child's name if the qualifying person is a child but not your dependent:

Your first name and middle initial	Last name	Your social security number

If joint return, spouse's first name and middle initial	Last name	Spouse's social security number

Home address (number and street). If you have a P.O. box, see instructions.		Apt. no.

City, town, or post office. If you have a foreign address, also complete spaces below.	State	ZIP code

Foreign country name	Foreign province/state/county	Foreign postal code

Presidential Election Campaign
Check here if you, or your spouse if filing jointly, want $3 to go to this fund. Checking a box below will not change your tax or refund.   ☐ You   ☐ Spouse

At any time during 2022, did you: (a) receive (as a reward, award, or compensation); or (b) sell, exchange, gift, or otherwise dispose of a digital asset (or a financial interest in a digital asset)? (See instructions.)   ☐ Yes ☐ No

Standard Deduction

Someone can claim: ☐ You as a dependent   ☐ Your spouse as a dependent
☐ Spouse itemizes on a separate return or you were a dual-status alien

Age/Blindness   **You:** ☐ Were born before January 2, 1958   ☐ Are blind   **Spouse:** ☐ Was born before January 2, 1958   ☐ Is blind

Dependents (see instructions):
If more than four dependents, see instructions and check here ☐

(1) First name Last name	(2) Social security number	(3) Relationship to you	(4) Check the box if qualifies for (see instructions): Child tax credit	Credit for other dependents
			☐	☐
			☐	☐
			☐	☐
			☐	☐

Income

Attach Form(s) W-2 here. Also attach Forms W-2G and 1099-R if tax was withheld.

If you did not get a Form W-2, see instructions.

Attach Sch. B if required.

1a	Total amount from Form(s) W-2, box 1 (see instructions)	1a
b	Household employee wages not reported on Form(s) W-2	1b
c	Tip income not reported on line 1a (see instructions)	1c
d	Medicaid waiver payments not reported on Form(s) W-2 (see instructions)	1d
e	Taxable dependent care benefits from Form 2441, line 26	1e
f	Employer-provided adoption benefits from Form 8839, line 29	1f
g	Wages from Form 8919, line 6	1g
h	Other earned income (see instructions)	1h
i	Nontaxable combat pay election (see instructions) 1i	
z	Add lines 1a through 1h	1z
2a	Tax-exempt interest . . . 2a b Taxable interest	2b
3a	Qualified dividends . . . 3a b Ordinary dividends	3b
4a	IRA distributions . . . . 4a b Taxable amount	4b
5a	Pensions and annuities . . 5a b Taxable amount	5b
6a	Social security benefits . . 6a b Taxable amount	6b
c	If you elect to use the lump-sum election method, check here (see instructions) . . ☐	
7	Capital gain or (loss). Attach Schedule D if required. If not required, check here . . ☐	7
8	Other income from Schedule 1, line 10	8
9	Add lines 1z, 2b, 3b, 4b, 5b, 6b, 7, and 8. This is your **total income**	9
10	Adjustments to income from Schedule 1, line 26	10
11	Subtract line 10 from line 9. This is your **adjusted gross income**	11
12	**Standard deduction or itemized deductions** (from Schedule A)	12
13	Qualified business income deduction from Form 8995 or Form 8995-A	13
14	Add lines 12 and 13	14
15	Subtract line 14 from line 11. If zero or less, enter -0-. This is your **taxable income**	15

Standard Deduction for—
- Single or Married filing separately, $12,950
- Married filing jointly or Qualifying widow(er), $25,900
- Head of household, $19,400
- If you checked any box under *Standard Deduction,* see instructions.

For Disclosure, Privacy Act, and Paperwork Reduction Act Notice, see separate instructions.   Cat. No. 11320B   Form **1040** (2022)

(Use for Comprehensive Problem.)

Form 1040 (2022)   Page **2**

Tax and Credits	16	**Tax** (see instructions). Check if any from Form(s): **1** ☐ 8814 **2** ☐ 4972 **3** ☐ _____ . .	16	
	17	Amount from Schedule 2, line 3	17	
	18	Add lines 16 and 17	18	
	19	Child tax credit or credit for other dependents from Schedule 8812	19	
	20	Amount from Schedule 3, line 8	20	
	21	Add lines 19 and 20	21	
	22	Subtract line 21 from line 18. If zero or less, enter -0-	22	
	23	Other taxes, including self-employment tax, from Schedule 2, line 21	23	
	24	Add lines 22 and 23. This is your **total tax** . . . . ▶	24	
Payments	25	Federal income tax withheld from:		
	a	Form(s) W-2	25a		
	b	Form(s) 1099	25b		
	c	Other forms (see instructions)	25c		
	d	Add lines 25a through 25c	25d	
If you have a qualifying child, attach Sch. EIC.	26	2022 estimated tax payments and amount applied from 2021 return	26	
	27	Earned income credit (EIC)	27		
	28	Additional child tax credit from Schedule 8812	28		
	29	American opportunity credit from Form 8863, line 8	29		
	30	Reserved for future use	30		
	31	Amount from Schedule 3, line 15	31		
	32	Add lines 27, 28, 29, and 31. These are your **total other payments and refundable credits** . . ▶	32	
	33	Add lines 25d, 26, and 32. These are your **total payments** . . . . ▶	33	
Refund	34	If line 33 is more than line 24, subtract line 24 from line 33. This is the amount you **overpaid** . .	34	
	35a	Amount of line 34 you want **refunded to you.** If Form 8888 is attached, check here . . . . ☐	35a	
Direct deposit? See instructions.	b	Routing number ⬚⬚⬚⬚⬚⬚⬚⬚⬚ **c** Type: ☐ Checking ☐ Savings		
	d	Account number ⬚⬚⬚⬚⬚⬚⬚⬚⬚⬚⬚⬚⬚⬚⬚⬚⬚		
	36	Amount of line 34 you want **applied to your 2023 estimated tax** . . .	36		
Amount You Owe	37	Subtract line 33 from line 24. This is the **amount you owe.** For details on how to pay, go to *www.irs.gov/Payments* or see instructions . . . . ▶	37	
	38	Estimated tax penalty (see instructions)	38		

Third Party Designee	Do you want to allow another person to discuss this return with the IRS? See instructions . . . . ▶ ☐ **Yes.** Complete below. ☐ **No**
	Designee's name	Phone no.	Personal identification number (PIN) ⬚⬚⬚⬚⬚

Sign Here	Under penalties of perjury, I declare that I have examined this return and accompanying schedules and statements, and to the best of my knowledge and belief, they are true, correct, and complete. Declaration of preparer (other than taxpayer) is based on all information of which preparer has any knowledge.
	Your signature	Date	Your occupation	If the IRS sent you an Identity Protection PIN, enter it here (see inst.) ⬚⬚⬚⬚⬚⬚
Joint return? See instructions. Keep a copy for your records.	Spouse's signature. If a joint return, **both** must sign.	Date	Spouse's occupation	If the IRS sent your spouse an Identity Protection PIN, enter it here (see inst.) ⬚⬚⬚⬚⬚⬚
	Phone no.	Email address		

Paid Preparer Use Only	Preparer's name	Preparer's signature	Date	PTIN	Check if: ☐ Self-employed
	Firm's name				Phone no.
	Firm's address				Firm's EIN

Go to *www.irs.gov/Form1040* for instructions and the latest information.   Form **1040** (2022)

(Use for Comprehensive Problem.)

SCHEDULE 1 (Form 1040)	Additional Income and Adjustments to Income	OMB No. 1545-0074
Department of the Treasury Internal Revenue Service	Attach to Form 1040, 1040-SR, or 1040-NR. Go to *www.irs.gov/Form1040* for instructions and the latest information.	2022 Attachment Sequence No. 01

Name(s) shown on Form 1040, 1040-SR, or 1040-NR | Your social security number

Part I — Additional Income

1	Taxable refunds, credits, or offsets of state and local income taxes	1
2a	Alimony received	2a
b	Date of original divorce or separation agreement (see instructions):	
3	Business income or (loss). Attach Schedule C	3
4	Other gains or (losses). Attach Form 4797	4
5	Rental real estate, royalties, partnerships, S corporations, trusts, etc. Attach Schedule E	5
6	Farm income or (loss). Attach Schedule F	6
7	Unemployment compensation	7
8	Other income:	
a	Net operating loss	8a ( )
b	Gambling	8b
c	Cancellation of debt	8c
d	Foreign earned income exclusion from Form 2555	8d ( )
e	Income from Form 8853	8e
f	Income from Form 8889	8f
g	Alaska Permanent Fund dividends	8g
h	Jury duty pay	8h
i	Prizes and awards	8i
j	Activity not engaged in for profit income	8j
k	Stock options	8k
l	Income from the rental of personal property if you engaged in the rental for profit but were not in the business of renting such property	8l
m	Olympic and Paralympic medals and USOC prize money (see instructions)	8m
n	Section 951(a) inclusion (see instructions)	8n
o	Section 951A(a) inclusion (see instructions)	8o
p	Section 461(l) excess business loss adjustment	8p
q	Taxable distributions from an ABLE account (see instructions)	8q
r	Scholarship and fellowship grants not reported on Form W-2	8r
s	Nontaxable amount of Medicaid waiver payments included on Form 1040, line 1a or 1d	8s ( )
t	Pension or annuity from a nonqualifed deferred compensation plan or a nongovernmental section 457 plan	8t
u	Wages earned while incarcerated	8u
z	Other income. List type and amount: _____	8z
9	Total other income. Add lines 8a through 8z	9
10	Combine lines 1 through 7 and 9. Enter here and on Form 1040, 1040-SR, or 1040-NR, line 8	10

For Paperwork Reduction Act Notice, see your tax return instructions.   Cat. No. 71479F   Schedule 1 (Form 1040) 2022

(Use for Comprehensive Problem.)

	Schedule 1 (Form 1040) 2022			Page **2**
Part II	**Adjustments to Income**			
11	Educator expenses	**11**		
12	Certain business expenses of reservists, performing artists, and fee-basis government officials. Attach Form 2106	**12**		
13	Health savings account deduction. Attach Form 8889	**13**		
14	Moving expenses for members of the Armed Forces. Attach Form 3903	**14**		
15	Deductible part of self-employment tax. Attach Schedule SE	**15**		
16	Self-employed SEP, SIMPLE, and qualified plans	**16**		
17	Self-employed health insurance deduction	**17**		
18	Penalty on early withdrawal of savings	**18**		
19a	Alimony paid	**19a**		
b	Recipient's SSN			
c	Date of original divorce or separation agreement (see instructions): _____			
20	IRA deduction	**20**		
21	Student loan interest deduction	**21**		
22	Reserved for future use	**22**		
23	Archer MSA deduction	**23**		
24	Other adjustments:			
a	Jury duty pay (see instructions)	**24a**		
b	Deductible expenses related to income reported on line 8l from the rental of personal property engaged in for profit	**24b**		
c	Nontaxable amount of the value of Olympic and Paralympic medals and USOC prize money reported on line 8m	**24c**		
d	Reforestation amortization and expenses	**24d**		
e	Repayment of supplemental unemployment benefits under the Trade Act of 1974	**24e**		
f	Contributions to section 501(c)(18)(D) pension plans	**24f**		
g	Contributions by certain chaplains to section 403(b) plans	**24g**		
h	Attorney fees and court costs for actions involving certain unlawful discrimination claims (see instructions)	**24h**		
i	Attorney fees and court costs you paid in connection with an award from the IRS for information you provided that helped the IRS detect tax law violations	**24i**		
j	Housing deduction from Form 2555	**24j**		
k	Excess deductions of section 67(e) expenses from Schedule K-1 (Form 1041)	**24k**		
z	Other adjustments. List type and amount: _____	**24z**		
25	Total other adjustments. Add lines 24a through 24z	**25**		
26	Add lines 11 through 23 and 25. These are your **adjustments to income**. Enter here and on Form 1040 or 1040-SR, line 10, or Form 1040-NR, line 10a	**26**		
				Schedule 1 (Form 1040) 2022

(Use for Comprehensive Problem.)

SCHEDULE 3 (Form 1040)	Additional Credits and Payments	OMB No. 1545-0074
Department of the Treasury Internal Revenue Service	Attach to Form 1040, 1040-SR, or 1040-NR. Go to *www.irs.gov/Form1040* for instructions and the latest information.	2022 Attachment Sequence No. 03

Name(s) shown on Form 1040, 1040-SR, or 1040-NR | Your social security number

Part I **Nonrefundable Credits**

1	Foreign tax credit. Attach Form 1116 if required	**1**	
2	Credit for child and dependent care expenses from Form 2441, line 11. Attach Form 2441	**2**	
3	Education credits from Form 8863, line 19	**3**	
4	Retirement savings contributions credit. Attach Form 8880	**4**	
5	Residential energy credits. Attach Form 5695	**5**	
6	Other nonrefundable credits:		
a	General business credit. Attach Form 3800	**6a**	
b	Credit for prior year minimum tax. Attach Form 8801	**6b**	
c	Adoption credit. Attach Form 8839	**6c**	
d	Credit for the elderly or disabled. Attach Schedule R	**6d**	
e	Alternative motor vehicle credit. Attach Form 8910	**6e**	
f	Qualified plug-in motor vehicle credit. Attach Form 8936	**6f**	
g	Mortgage interest credit. Attach Form 8396	**6g**	
h	District of Columbia first-time homebuyer credit. Attach Form 8859	**6h**	
i	Qualified electric vehicle credit. Attach Form 8834	**6i**	
j	Reserved for future use	**6j**	
k	Credit to holders of tax credit bonds. Attach Form 8912	**6k**	
l	Amount on Form 8978, line 14. See instructions	**6l**	
z	Other nonrefundable credits. List type and amount:		
		6z	
7	Total other nonrefundable credits. Add lines 6a through 6z	**7**	
8	Add lines 1 through 5 and 7. Enter here and on Form 1040, 1040-SR, or 1040-NR, line 20	**8**	

(continued on page 2)

For Paperwork Reduction Act Notice, see your tax return instructions. | Cat. No. 71480G | Schedule 3 (Form 1040) 2022

(Use for Comprehensive Problem.)

Schedule 3 (Form 1040) 2022				Page **2**
Part II	**Other Payments and Refundable Credits**			
9	Net premium tax credit. Attach Form 8962	**9**		
10	Amount paid with request for extension to file (see instructions)	**10**		
11	Excess social security and tier 1 RRTA tax withheld	**11**		
12	Credit for federal tax on fuels. Attach Form 4136	**12**		
13	Other payments or refundable credits:			
a	Form 2439	**13a**		
b	Credit for qualified sick and family leave wages paid in 2022 from Schedule(s) H for leave taken before April 1, 2021	**13b**		
c	Reserved for future use	**13c**		
d	Credit for repayment of amounts included in income from earlier years	**13d**		
e	Reserved for future use	**13e**		
f	Deferred amount of net 965 tax liability (see instructions) . . .	**13f**		
g	Reserved for future use	**13g**		
h	Credit for qualified sick and family leave wages paid in 2022 from Schedule(s) H for leave taken after March 31, 2021, and before October 1, 2021	**13h**		
z	Other payments or refundable credits. List type and amount: _____	**13z**		
14	Total other payments or refundable credits. Add lines 13a through 13z	**14**		
15	Add lines 9 through 12 and 14. Enter here and on Form 1040, 1040-SR, or 1040-NR, line 31	**15**		

Schedule 3 (Form 1040) 2022

(Use for Comprehensive Problem.)

SCHEDULE C (Form 1040)	**Profit or Loss From Business** (Sole Proprietorship)	OMB No. 1545-0074
Department of the Treasury Internal Revenue Service	Go to *www.irs.gov/ScheduleC* for instructions and the latest information. **Attach to Form 1040, 1040-SR, 1040-NR, or 1041; partnerships must generally file Form 1065.**	**2022** Attachment Sequence No. **09**

Name of proprietor | Social security number (SSN)

A Principal business or profession, including product or service (see instructions) | **B** Enter code from instructions

C Business name. If no separate business name, leave blank. | **D** Employer ID number (EIN) (see instr.)

E Business address (including suite or room no.)
City, town or post office, state, and ZIP code

F Accounting method: **(1)** ☐ Cash **(2)** ☐ Accrual **(3)** ☐ Other (specify)

G Did you "materially participate" in the operation of this business during 2022? If "No," see instructions for limit on losses   ☐ Yes ☐ No

H If you started or acquired this business during 2022, check here   ☐

I Did you make any payments in 2022 that would require you to file Form(s) 1099? See instructions   ☐ Yes ☐ No

J If "Yes," did you or will you file required Form(s) 1099?   ☐ Yes ☐ No

Part I   Income

1	Gross receipts or sales. See instructions for line 1 and check the box if this income was reported to you on Form W-2 and the "Statutory employee" box on that form was checked ☐	**1**	
2	Returns and allowances	**2**	
3	Subtract line 2 from line 1	**3**	
4	Cost of goods sold (from line 42)	**4**	
5	**Gross profit.** Subtract line 4 from line 3	**5**	
6	Other income, including federal and state gasoline or fuel tax credit or refund (see instructions)	**6**	
7	**Gross income.** Add lines 5 and 6	**7**	

Part II   Expenses. Enter expenses for business use of your home **only** on line 30.

8	Advertising	**8**		18	Office expense (see instructions)	**18**	
9	Car and truck expenses (see instructions)	**9**		19	Pension and profit-sharing plans	**19**	
10	Commissions and fees	**10**		20	Rent or lease (see instructions):		
11	Contract labor (see instructions)	**11**		a	Vehicles, machinery, and equipment	**20a**	
12	Depletion	**12**		b	Other business property	**20b**	
13	Depreciation and section 179 expense deduction (not included in Part III) (see instructions)	**13**		21	Repairs and maintenance	**21**	
				22	Supplies (not included in Part III)	**22**	
				23	Taxes and licenses	**23**	
				24	Travel and meals:		
14	Employee benefit programs (other than on line 19)	**14**		a	Travel	**24a**	
15	Insurance (other than health)	**15**		b	Deductible meals (see instructions)	**24b**	
16	Interest (see instructions):			25	Utilities	**25**	
a	Mortgage (paid to banks, etc.)	**16a**		26	Wages (less employment credits)	**26**	
b	Other	**16b**		27a	Other expenses (from line 48)	**27a**	
17	Legal and professional services	**17**		b	**Reserved for future use**	**27b**	

28	**Total expenses** before expenses for business use of home. Add lines 8 through 27a	**28**	
29	Tentative profit or (loss). Subtract line 28 from line 7	**29**	
30	Expenses for business use of your home. Do not report these expenses elsewhere. Attach Form 8829 unless using the simplified method. See instructions. **Simplified method filers only:** Enter the total square footage of (a) your home: _____ and (b) the part of your home used for business: _____ . Use the Simplified Method Worksheet in the instructions to figure the amount to enter on line 30	**30**	
31	**Net profit or (loss).** Subtract line 30 from line 29. • If a profit, enter on both **Schedule 1 (Form 1040), line 3,** and on **Schedule SE, line 2.** (If you checked the box on line 1, see instructions.) Estates and trusts, enter on **Form 1041, line 3.** • If a loss, you **must** go to line 32.	**31**	
32	If you have a loss, check the box that describes your investment in this activity. See instructions. • If you checked 32a, enter the loss on both **Schedule 1 (Form 1040), line 3,** and on **Schedule SE, line 2.** (If you checked the box on line 1, see the line 31 instructions.) Estates and trusts, enter on **Form 1041, line 3.** • If you checked 32b, you **must** attach **Form 6198.** Your loss may be limited.	**32a** ☐ All investment is at risk. **32b** ☐ Some investment is not at risk.	

For Paperwork Reduction Act Notice, see the separate instructions.   Cat. No. 11334P   Schedule C (Form 1040) 2022

(Use for Comprehensive Problem.)

Schedule C (Form 1040) 2022   Page **2**

Part III   **Cost of Goods Sold** (see instructions)

33   Method(s) used to
     value closing inventory: **a** ☐ Cost   **b** ☐ Lower of cost or market   **c** ☐ Other (attach explanation)

34   Was there any change in determining quantities, costs, or valuations between opening and closing inventory?
     If "Yes," attach explanation . . . . ☐ Yes   ☐ No

35   Inventory at beginning of year. If different from last year's closing inventory, attach explanation . . | **35** |

36   Purchases less cost of items withdrawn for personal use . . . . | **36** |

37   Cost of labor. Do not include any amounts paid to yourself . . . . | **37** |

38   Materials and supplies . . . . | **38** |

39   Other costs . . . . | **39** |

40   Add lines 35 through 39 . . . . | **40** |

41   Inventory at end of year . . . . | **41** |

42   **Cost of goods sold.** Subtract line 41 from line 40. Enter the result here and on line 4 . . . . . | **42** |

Part IV   **Information on Your Vehicle.** Complete this part **only** if you are claiming car or truck expenses on line 9 and are not required to file Form 4562 for this business. See the instructions for line 13 to find out if you must file Form 4562.

43   When did you place your vehicle in service for business purposes? (month/day/year) _____ / ___ / _____

44   Of the total number of miles you drove your vehicle during 2022, enter the number of miles you used your vehicle for:

     a   Business _____   **b** Commuting (see instructions) _____   **c** Other _____

45   Was your vehicle available for personal use during off-duty hours? . . . . ☐ Yes   ☐ No

46   Do you (or your spouse) have another vehicle available for personal use? . . . . ☐ Yes   ☐ No

47a Do you have evidence to support your deduction? . . . . ☐ Yes   ☐ No

  b   If "Yes," is the evidence written? . . . . ☐ Yes   ☐ No

Part V   **Other Expenses.** List below business expenses not included on lines 8–26 or line 30.

----

48   **Total other expenses.** Enter here and on line 27a . . . . | **48** |

Schedule C (Form 1040) 2022

(Use for Comprehensive Problem.)

SCHEDULE SE (Form 1040)	Self-Employment Tax	OMB No. 1545-0074
Department of the Treasury Internal Revenue Service	Go to *www.irs.gov/ScheduleSE* for instructions and the latest information. Attach to Form 1040, 1040-SR, or 1040-NR.	2022 Attachment Sequence No. 17

Name of person with self-employment income (as shown on Form 1040, 1040-SR, or 1040-NR)	Social security number of person with **self-employment** income

Part I　Self-Employment Tax

Note: If your only income subject to self-employment tax is **church employee income,** see instructions for how to report your income and the definition of church employee income.

A　If you are a minister, member of a religious order, or Christian Science practitioner **and** you filed Form 4361, but you had $400 or more of **other** net earnings from self-employment, check here and continue with Part I . . . . ☐

Skip lines 1a and 1b if you use the farm optional method in Part II. See instructions.

| **1a** | Net farm profit or (loss) from Schedule F, line 34, and farm partnerships, Schedule K-1 (Form 1065), box 14, code A . . . . | **1a** | |
| **b** | If you received social security retirement or disability benefits, enter the amount of Conservation Reserve Program payments included on Schedule F, line 4b, or listed on Schedule K-1 (Form 1065), box 20, code AH | **1b** | ( ) |

Skip line 2 if you use the nonfarm optional method in Part II. See instructions.

2	Net profit or (loss) from Schedule C, line 31; and Schedule K-1 (Form 1065), box 14, code A (other than farming). See instructions for other income to report or if you are a minister or member of a religious order	**2**	
3	Combine lines 1a, 1b, and 2	**3**	
4a	If line 3 is more than zero, multiply line 3 by 92.35% (0.9235). Otherwise, enter amount from line 3	**4a**	
	Note: If line 4a is less than $400 due to Conservation Reserve Program payments on line 1b, see instructions.		
b	If you elect one or both of the optional methods, enter the total of lines 15 and 17 here	**4b**	
c	Combine lines 4a and 4b. If less than $400, **stop;** you don't owe self-employment tax. **Exception:** If less than $400 and you had **church employee income,** enter -0- and continue	**4c**	
5a	Enter your **church employee income** from Form W-2. See instructions for definition of church employee income **5a**		
b	Multiply line 5a by 92.35% (0.9235). If less than $100, enter -0-	**5b**	
6	Add lines 4c and 5b	**6**	
7	Maximum amount of combined wages and self-employment earnings subject to social security tax or the 6.2% portion of the 7.65% railroad retirement (tier 1) tax for 2022	**7**	147,000
8a	Total social security wages and tips (total of boxes 3 and 7 on Form(s) W-2) and railroad retirement (tier 1) compensation. If $147,000 or more, skip lines 8b through 10, and go to line 11 . . . . **8a**		
b	Unreported tips subject to social security tax from Form 4137, line 10 . . . **8b**		
c	Wages subject to social security tax from Form 8919, line 10 . . . . . . **8c**		
d	Add lines 8a, 8b, and 8c	**8d**	
9	Subtract line 8d from line 7. If zero or less, enter -0- here and on line 10 and go to line 11	**9**	
10	Multiply the **smaller** of line 6 or line 9 by 12.4% (0.124)	**10**	
11	Multiply line 6 by 2.9% (0.029)	**11**	
12	**Self-employment tax.** Add lines 10 and 11. Enter here and on **Schedule 2 (Form 1040), line 4** . .	**12**	
13	**Deduction for one-half of self-employment tax.** Multiply line 12 by 50% (0.50). Enter here and on **Schedule 1 (Form 1040), line 15** **13**		

Part II　Optional Methods To Figure Net Earnings (see instructions)

Farm Optional Method. You may use this method **only** if **(a)** your gross farm income[1] wasn't more than $9,060, **or (b)** your net farm profits[2] were less than $6,540.

| **14** | Maximum income for optional methods . . . . | **14** | 6,040 |
| **15** | Enter the **smaller** of: two-thirds ($\frac{2}{3}$) of gross farm income[1] (not less than zero) **or** $6,040. Also, include this amount on line 4b above . . . . | **15** | |

Nonfarm Optional Method. You may use this method **only** if **(a)** your net nonfarm profits[3] were less than $6,540 and also less than 72.189% of your gross nonfarm income,[4] **and (b)** you had net earnings from self-employment of at least $400 in 2 of the prior 3 years. **Caution:** You may use this method no more than five times.

| **16** | Subtract line 15 from line 14 . . . . | **16** | |
| **17** | Enter the **smaller** of: two-thirds ($\frac{2}{3}$) of gross nonfarm income[4] (not less than zero) **or** the amount on line 16. Also, include this amount on line 4b above . . . . | **17** | |

[1] From Sch. F, line 9; and Sch. K-1 (Form 1065), box 14, code B.
[2] From Sch. F, line 34; and Sch. K-1 (Form 1065), box 14, code A—minus the amount you would have entered on line 1b had you not used the optional method.
[3] From Sch. C, line 31; and Sch. K-1 (Form 1065), box 14, code A.
[4] From Sch. C, line 7; and Sch. K-1 (Form 1065), box 14, code C.

For Paperwork Reduction Act Notice, see your tax return instructions.　　Cat. No. 11358Z　　Schedule SE (Form 1040) 2022

(Use for Comprehensive Problem, if it is the appropriate form.)

Form **8995**	**Qualified Business Income Deduction Simplified Computation**	OMB No. 1545-2294
Department of the Treasury Internal Revenue Service	Attach to your tax return. Go to *www.irs.gov/Form8995* for instructions and the latest information.	**2022** Attachment Sequence No. **55**
Name(s) shown on return		Your taxpayer identification number

Note. *You can claim the qualified business income deduction **only** if you have qualified business income from a qualified trade or business, real estate investment trust dividends, publicly traded partnership income, or a domestic production activities deduction passed through from an agricultural or horticultural cooperative. See instructions.*
Use this form if your taxable income, before your qualified business income deduction, is at or below $170,050 ($340,100 if married filing jointly), and you aren't a patron of an agricultural or horticultural cooperative.

1	(a) Trade, business, or aggregation name	(b) Taxpayer identification number	(c) Qualified business income or (loss)
i			
ii			
iii			
iv			
v			

2	Total qualified business income or (loss). Combine lines 1i through 1v, column (c)	**2**		
3	Qualified business net (loss) carryforward from the prior year	**3**	( )	
4	Total qualified business income. Combine lines 2 and 3. If zero or less, enter -0-	**4**		
5	Qualified business income component. Multiply line 4 by 20% (0.20)			**5**
6	Qualified REIT dividends and publicly traded partnership (PTP) income or (loss) (see instructions)	**6**		
7	Qualified REIT dividends and qualified PTP (loss) carryforward from the prior year	**7**	( )	
8	Total qualified REIT dividends and PTP income. Combine lines 6 and 7. If zero or less, enter -0-	**8**		
9	REIT and PTP component. Multiply line 8 by 20% (0.20)			**9**
10	Qualified business income deduction before the income limitation. Add lines 5 and 9			**10**
11	Taxable income before qualified business income deduction (see instructions)	**11**		
12	Net capital gain (see instructions)	**12**		
13	Subtract line 12 from line 11. If zero or less, enter -0-	**13**		
14	Income limitation. Multiply line 13 by 20% (0.20)			**14**
15	Qualified business income deduction. Enter the smaller of line 10 or line 14. Also enter this amount on the applicable line of your return (see instructions)			**15**
16	Total qualified business (loss) carryforward. Combine lines 2 and 3. If greater than zero, enter -0- . .			**16** ( )
17	Total qualified REIT dividends and PTP (loss) carryforward. Combine lines 6 and 7. If greater than zero, enter -0-			**17** ( )

For Privacy Act and Paperwork Reduction Act Notice, see instructions.   Cat. No. 37806C   Form **8995** (2022)

(Use for Comprehensive Problem, if it is the appropriate form.)

Form **8995-A** Department of the Treasury Internal Revenue Service	**Qualified Business Income Deduction** Attach to your tax return. Go to *www.irs.gov/Form8995A* for instructions and the latest information.	OMB No. 1545-2294 20**22** Attachment Sequence No. **55A**

Name(s) shown on return	Your taxpayer identification number

Note: You can claim the qualified business income deduction **only** if you have qualified business income from a qualified trade or business, real estate investment trust dividends, publicly traded partnership income, or a domestic production activities deduction passed through from an agricultural or horticultural cooperative. See instructions.

Use this form if your taxable income, before your qualified business income deduction, is above $170,050 ($340,100 if married filing jointly), or you're a patron of an agricultural or horticultural cooperative.

Part I   Trade, Business, or Aggregation Information

Complete Schedules A, B, and/or C (Form 8995-A), as applicable, before starting Part I. Attach additional worksheets when needed. See instructions.

1	(a) Trade, business, or aggregation name	(b) Check if specified service	(c) Check if aggregation	(d) Taxpayer identification number	(e) Check if patron
A		☐	☐		☐
B		☐	☐		☐
C		☐	☐		☐

Part II   Determine Your Adjusted Qualified Business Income

			A	B	C
2	Qualified business income from the trade, business, or aggregation. See instructions	2			
3	Multiply line 2 by 20% (0.20). If your taxable income is $170,050 or less ($340,100 if married filing jointly), skip lines 4 through 12 and enter the amount from line 3 on line 13	3			
4	Allocable share of W-2 wages from the trade, business, or aggregation	4			
5	Multiply line 4 by 50% (0.50)	5			
6	Multiply line 4 by 25% (0.25)	6			
7	Allocable share of the unadjusted basis immediately after acquisition (UBIA) of all qualified property	7			
8	Multiply line 7 by 2.5% (0.025)	8			
9	Add lines 6 and 8	9			
10	Enter the greater of line 5 or line 9	10			
11	W-2 wage and UBIA of qualified property limitation. Enter the smaller of line 3 or line 10	11			
12	Phased-in reduction. Enter the amount from line 26, if any . . .	12			
13	Qualified business income deduction before patron reduction. Enter the greater of line 11 or line 12	13			
14	Patron reduction. Enter the amount from Schedule D (Form 8995-A), line 6, if any. See instructions	14			
15	Qualified business income component. Subtract line 14 from line 13	15			
16	Total qualified business income component. Add all amounts reported on line 15	16			

For Privacy Act and Paperwork Reduction Act Notice, see separate instructions.	Cat. No. 71661B	Form **8995-A** (2022)

(Use for Comprehensive Problem, if it is the appropriate form.)

Form 8995-A (2022)   Page **2**

Part III Phased-in Reduction

Complete Part III only if your taxable income is more than $170,050 but not $220,050 ($340,100 and $440,100 if married filing jointly) and line 10 is less than line 3. Otherwise, skip Part III.

			A	B	C
17	Enter the amounts from line 3	17			
18	Enter the amounts from line 10	18			
19	Subtract line 18 from line 17	19			
20	Taxable income before qualified business income deduction	20			
21	Threshold. Enter $170,050 ($340,100 if married filing jointly)	21			
22	Subtract line 21 from line 20	22			
23	Phase-in range. Enter $50,000 ($100,000 if married filing jointly)	23			
24	Phase-in percentage. Divide line 22 by line 23	24 %			
25	Total phase-in reduction. Multiply line 19 by line 24	25			
26	Qualified business income after phase-in reduction. Subtract line 25 from line 17. Enter this amount here and on line 12, for the corresponding trade or business	26			

Part IV Determine Your Qualified Business Income Deduction

27	Total qualified business income component from all qualified trades, businesses, or aggregations. Enter the amount from line 16	27	
28	Qualified REIT dividends and publicly traded partnership (PTP) income or (loss). See instructions	28	
29	Qualified REIT dividends and PTP (loss) carryforward from prior years	29 ( )	
30	Total qualified REIT dividends and PTP income. Combine lines 28 and 29. If less than zero, enter -0-	30	
31	REIT and PTP component. Multiply line 30 by 20% (0.20)	31	
32	Qualified business income deduction before the income limitation. Add lines 27 and 31		32
33	Taxable income before qualified business income deduction	33	
34	Net capital gain. See instructions	34	
35	Subtract line 34 from line 33. If zero or less, enter -0-		35
36	Income limitation. Multiply line 35 by 20% (0.20)		36
37	Qualified business income deduction before the domestic production activities deduction (DPAD) under section 199A(g). Enter the smaller of line 32 or line 36		37
38	DPAD under section 199A(g) allocated from an agricultural or horticultural cooperative. Don't enter more than line 33 minus line 37		38
39	Total qualified business income deduction. Add lines 37 and 38		39
40	Total qualified REIT dividends and PTP (loss) carryforward. Combine lines 28 and 29. If zero or greater, enter -0-		40 ( )

Form **8995-A** (2022)

CUMULATIVE PROBLEM 1 (CHAPTERS 1–8)

 Use the following information to prepare the tax return of Robert E. Dunkin using Form 1040, Schedule 1, Schedule 2, Schedule A, Schedule C, Schedule SE, and Forms 8829 and 8995. This problem is suitable for manual preparation or computer software application.

Robert E. Dunkin (SSN 392-00-6844) operates a consulting business out of his home located at 293 E. Main Street, Lafayette, LA 70503. The IRS business code (Schedule C, line B) is 541600. He uses the cash basis and materially participates in the business. During 2022, his business generated income of $55,088, and he had the following expenses: advertising, $150; depreciation expense, $1,630; office expense, $695; and supplies, $450. Rob drove his personal automobile 500 business miles during 2022, all during the last half of the year. He uses the standard mileage rate method.

Rob uses one of the rooms in his house regularly and exclusively as a home office. The size of the room used as an office is 224 square feet. The total square footage of his home is 2,800 square feet. The expenses of operating the home during the year included utilities, $3,500; insurance, $250; home mortgage interest, $8,500; and real estate taxes, $3,205. The depreciable basis in the home is $110,840 ($130,840 minus $20,000 for the land). His depreciation percentage (Form 8829, line 41) is 2.564%.

a. Complete Schedule C and Form 8829 for Rob Dunkin. Then complete Rob's Schedule SE.

b. Based on your answers to Part a., what is the maximum amount Rob can contribute to a SEP plan for 2022?

c. How long does Rob have to set up a SEP and make his 2022 SEP contribution?

d. Complete Rob's Form 8995.

e. Complete Rob's Form 1040, assuming that he makes the maximum contribution allowed to his SEP for 2022. Rob files as single with no dependents. He is 47 years old and made $10,000 of estimated federal income tax payments for the 2022 tax year. This amount is reported on Schedule 3 (Form 1040). Rob's only other source of gross income is $1,120 of taxable interest, and his only other deduction for AGI is $3,600 that he pays during the year for health insurance.

In addition to the non-home office portion of the interest and taxes on his home, his other itemized deductions include $2,000 of state income taxes paid during the year, $1,300 of cash contributions to his alma mater, and $150 of noncash contributions to Goodwill. Rob does not want $3 to go to the Presidential election campaign fund. He signs and dates his return on April 11, 2022.

(Use for Cumulative Problem 1.)

Form **1040** Department of the Treasury—Internal Revenue Service
U.S. Individual Income Tax Return 20**22** OMB No. 1545-0074 | IRS Use Only—Do not write or staple in this space.

Filing Status
Check only one box.
☐ Single ☐ Married filing jointly ☐ Married filing separately (MFS) ☐ Head of household (HOH) ☐ Qualifying widow(er) (QW)
If you checked the MFS box, enter the name of your spouse. If you checked the HOH or QW box, enter the child's name if the qualifying person is a child but not your dependent:

Your first name and middle initial	Last name	Your social security number

If joint return, spouse's first name and middle initial	Last name	Spouse's social security number

Home address (number and street). If you have a P.O. box, see instructions.	Apt. no.	**Presidential Election Campaign** Check here if you, or your spouse if filing jointly, want $3 to go to this fund. Checking a box below will not change your tax or refund. ☐ You ☐ Spouse

City, town, or post office. If you have a foreign address, also complete spaces below.	State	ZIP code

Foreign country name	Foreign province/state/county	Foreign postal code

At any time during 2022, did you: (a) receive (as a reward, award, or compensation); or (b) sell, exchange, gift, or otherwise dispose of a digital asset (or a financial interest in a digital asset)? (See instructions.) . . ☐ Yes ☐ No

Standard Deduction
Someone can claim: ☐ You as a dependent ☐ Your spouse as a dependent
☐ Spouse itemizes on a separate return or you were a dual-status alien

Age/Blindness **You:** ☐ Were born before January 2, 1958 ☐ Are blind **Spouse:** ☐ Was born before January 2, 1958 ☐ Is blind

Dependents (see instructions):
If more than four dependents, see instructions and check here . . ☐

(1) First name Last name	(2) Social security number	(3) Relationship to you	(4) Check the box if qualifies for (see instructions):	
			Child tax credit	Credit for other dependents
			☐	☐
			☐	☐
			☐	☐

Income

Attach Form(s) W-2 here. Also attach Forms W-2G and 1099-R if tax was withheld.

If you did not get a Form W-2, see instructions.

Attach Sch. B if required.

Standard Deduction for—
- Single or Married filing separately, $12,950
- Married filing jointly or Qualifying widow(er), $25,900
- Head of household, $19,400
- If you checked any box under Standard Deduction, see instructions.

1a	Total amount from Form(s) W-2, box 1 (see instructions)	1a
b	Household employee wages not reported on Form(s) W-2	1b
c	Tip income not reported on line 1a (see instructions)	1c
d	Medicaid waiver payments not reported on Form(s) W-2 (see instructions)	1d
e	Taxable dependent care benefits from Form 2441, line 26	1e
f	Employer-provided adoption benefits from Form 8839, line 29	1f
g	Wages from Form 8919, line 6	1g
h	Other earned income (see instructions)	1h
i	Nontaxable combat pay election (see instructions) 1i	
z	Add lines 1a through 1h	1z
2a	Tax-exempt interest . . . 2a	b Taxable interest	2b
3a	Qualified dividends . . . 3a	b Ordinary dividends	3b
4a	IRA distributions . . . 4a	b Taxable amount	4b
5a	Pensions and annuities . . 5a	b Taxable amount	5b
6a	Social security benefits . . 6a	b Taxable amount	6b
c	If you elect to use the lump-sum election method, check here (see instructions) . . . ☐	
7	Capital gain or (loss). Attach Schedule D if required. If not required, check here . . . ☐	7
8	Other income from Schedule 1, line 10	8
9	Add lines 1z, 2b, 3b, 4b, 5b, 6b, 7, and 8. This is your **total income**	9
10	Adjustments to income from Schedule 1, line 26	10
11	Subtract line 10 from line 9. This is your **adjusted gross income**	11
12	**Standard deduction or itemized deductions** (from Schedule A)	12
13	Qualified business income deduction from Form 8995 or Form 8995-A	13
14	Add lines 12 and 13	14
15	Subtract line 14 from line 11. If zero or less, enter -0-. This is your **taxable income**	15

For Disclosure, Privacy Act, and Paperwork Reduction Act Notice, see separate instructions.   Cat. No. 11320B   Form **1040** (2022)

(Use for Cumulative Problem 1.)

Version A, Cycle 7

Form 1040 (2022)

Page **2**

Tax and Credits	16	**Tax** (see instructions). Check if any from Form(s): 1 ☐ 8814 2 ☐ 4972 3 ☐ _____	16	
	17	Amount from Schedule 2, line 3	17	
	18	Add lines 16 and 17	18	
	19	Child tax credit or credit for other dependents from Schedule 8812	19	
	20	Amount from Schedule 3, line 8	20	
	21	Add lines 19 and 20	21	
	22	Subtract line 21 from line 18. If zero or less, enter -0-	22	
	23	Other taxes, including self-employment tax, from Schedule 2, line 21	23	
	24	Add lines 22 and 23. This is your **total tax**	24	

Payments	25	Federal income tax withheld from:			
	a	Form(s) W-2	25a		
	b	Form(s) 1099	25b		
	c	Other forms (see instructions)	25c		
	d	Add lines 25a through 25c		25d	
If you have a qualifying child, attach Sch. EIC.	26	2022 estimated tax payments and amount applied from 2021 return		26	
	27	Earned income credit (EIC)	27		
	28	Additional child tax credit from Schedule 8812	28		
	29	American opportunity credit from Form 8863, line 8	29		
	30	Reserved for future use	30		
	31	Amount from Schedule 3, line 15	31		
	32	Add lines 27, 28, 29, and 31. These are your **total other payments and refundable credits**		32	
	33	Add lines 25d, 26, and 32. These are your **total payments**		33	

Refund	34	If line 33 is more than line 24, subtract line 24 from line 33. This is the amount you **overpaid**		34	
	35a	Amount of line 34 you want **refunded to you**. If Form 8888 is attached, check here ☐		35a	
Direct deposit? See instructions.	b	Routing number _____ **c** Type: ☐ Checking ☐ Savings			
	d	Account number _____			
	36	Amount of line 34 you want **applied to your 2023 estimated tax**	36		

Amount You Owe	37	Subtract line 33 from line 24. This is the **amount you owe**. For details on how to pay, go to *www.irs.gov/Payments* or see instructions		37	
	38	Estimated tax penalty (see instructions)	38		

Third Party Designee	Do you want to allow another person to discuss this return with the IRS? See instructions	☐ **Yes.** Complete below.	☐ **No**
	Designee's name _____ Phone no. _____	Personal identification number (PIN) ☐☐☐☐☐	

Sign Here

Joint return? See instructions. Keep a copy for your records.

Under penalties of perjury, I declare that I have examined this return and accompanying schedules and statements, and to the best of my knowledge and belief, they are true, correct, and complete. Declaration of preparer (other than taxpayer) is based on all information of which preparer has any knowledge.

Your signature	Date	Your occupation	If the IRS sent you an Identity Protection PIN, enter it here (see inst.) ☐☐☐☐☐☐
Spouse's signature. If a joint return, **both** must sign.	Date	Spouse's occupation	If the IRS sent your spouse an Identity Protection PIN, enter it here (see inst.) ☐☐☐☐☐☐
Phone no.		Email address	

Paid Preparer Use Only	Preparer's name	Preparer's signature	Date	PTIN	Check if: ☐ Self-employed
	Firm's name			Phone no.	
	Firm's address			Firm's EIN	

Go to *www.irs.gov/Form1040* for instructions and the latest information.

Form **1040** (2022)

(Use for Cumulative Problem 1.)

SCHEDULE 1 (Form 1040) Department of the Treasury Internal Revenue Service	**Additional Income and Adjustments to Income** Attach to Form 1040, 1040-SR, or 1040-NR. Go to *www.irs.gov/Form1040* for instructions and the latest information.	OMB No. 1545-0074 20**22** Attachment Sequence No. **01**

Name(s) shown on Form 1040, 1040-SR, or 1040-NR	Your social security number

Part I Additional Income

1	Taxable refunds, credits, or offsets of state and local income taxes	**1**	
2a	Alimony received	**2a**	
b	Date of original divorce or separation agreement (see instructions):		
3	Business income or (loss). Attach Schedule C	**3**	
4	Other gains or (losses). Attach Form 4797	**4**	
5	Rental real estate, royalties, partnerships, S corporations, trusts, etc. Attach Schedule E	**5**	
6	Farm income or (loss). Attach Schedule F	**6**	
7	Unemployment compensation	**7**	
8	Other income:		
a	Net operating loss	**8a** ( )	
b	Gambling	**8b**	
c	Cancellation of debt	**8c**	
d	Foreign earned income exclusion from Form 2555	**8d** ( )	
e	Income from Form 8853	**8e**	
f	Income from Form 8889	**8f**	
g	Alaska Permanent Fund dividends	**8g**	
h	Jury duty pay	**8h**	
i	Prizes and awards	**8i**	
j	Activity not engaged in for profit income	**8j**	
k	Stock options	**8k**	
l	Income from the rental of personal property if you engaged in the rental for profit but were not in the business of renting such property	**8l**	
m	Olympic and Paralympic medals and USOC prize money (see instructions)	**8m**	
n	Section 951(a) inclusion (see instructions)	**8n**	
o	Section 951A(a) inclusion (see instructions)	**8o**	
p	Section 461(l) excess business loss adjustment	**8p**	
q	Taxable distributions from an ABLE account (see instructions)	**8q**	
r	Scholarship and fellowship grants not reported on Form W-2	**8r**	
s	Nontaxable amount of Medicaid waiver payments included on Form 1040, line 1a or 1d	**8s** ( )	
t	Pension or annuity from a nonqualifed deferred compensation plan or a nongovernmental section 457 plan	**8t**	
u	Wages earned while incarcerated	**8u**	
z	Other income. List type and amount: _____	**8z**	
9	Total other income. Add lines 8a through 8z	**9**	
10	Combine lines 1 through 7 and 9. Enter here and on Form 1040, 1040-SR, or 1040-NR, line 8	**10**	

For Paperwork Reduction Act Notice, see your tax return instructions.   Cat. No. 71479F   Schedule 1 (Form 1040) 2022

DRAFT AS OF July 27, 2022 DO NOT FILE

(Use for Cumulative Problem 1.)

Schedule 1 (Form 1040) 2022   Page **2**

Part II   Adjustments to Income

11	Educator expenses	**11**
12	Certain business expenses of reservists, performing artists, and fee-basis government officials. Attach Form 2106	**12**
13	Health savings account deduction. Attach Form 8889	**13**
14	Moving expenses for members of the Armed Forces. Attach Form 3903	**14**
15	Deductible part of self-employment tax. Attach Schedule SE	**15**
16	Self-employed SEP, SIMPLE, and qualified plans	**16**
17	Self-employed health insurance deduction	**17**
18	Penalty on early withdrawal of savings	**18**
19a	Alimony paid	**19a**
b	Recipient's SSN	
c	Date of original divorce or separation agreement (see instructions): _____	
20	IRA deduction	**20**
21	Student loan interest deduction	**21**
22	Reserved for future use	**22**
23	Archer MSA deduction	**23**

24   Other adjustments:

a	Jury duty pay (see instructions)	**24a**
b	Deductible expenses related to income reported on line 8l from the rental of personal property engaged in for profit	**24b**
c	Nontaxable amount of the value of Olympic and Paralympic medals and USOC prize money reported on line 8m	**24c**
d	Reforestation amortization and expenses	**24d**
e	Repayment of supplemental unemployment benefits under the Trade Act of 1974	**24e**
f	Contributions to section 501(c)(18)(D) pension plans	**24f**
g	Contributions by certain chaplains to section 403(b) plans	**24g**
h	Attorney fees and court costs for actions involving certain unlawful discrimination claims (see instructions)	**24h**
i	Attorney fees and court costs you paid in connection with an award from the IRS for information you provided that helped the IRS detect tax law violations	**24i**
j	Housing deduction from Form 2555	**24j**
k	Excess deductions of section 67(e) expenses from Schedule K-1 (Form 1041)	**24k**
z	Other adjustments. List type and amount: _____ _____	**24z**

25	Total other adjustments. Add lines 24a through 24z	**25**
26	Add lines 11 through 23 and 25. These are your **adjustments to income**. Enter here and on Form 1040 or 1040-SR, line 10, or Form 1040-NR, line 10a	**26**

Schedule 1 (Form 1040) 2022

(Use for Cumulative Problem 1.)

SCHEDULE 2 (Form 1040) Department of the Treasury Internal Revenue Service	**Additional Taxes** Attach to Form 1040, 1040-SR, or 1040-NR. Go to *www.irs.gov/Form1040* for instructions and the latest information.	OMB No. 1545-0074 2022 Attachment Sequence No. 02
Name(s) shown on Form 1040, 1040-SR, or 1040-NR		Your social security number

Part I   Tax

1	Alternative minimum tax. Attach Form 6251	**1**	
2	Excess advance premium tax credit repayment. Attach Form 8962	**2**	
3	Add lines 1 and 2. Enter here and on Form 1040, 1040-SR, or 1040-NR, line 17 . .	**3**	

Part II   Other Taxes

4	Self-employment tax. Attach Schedule SE		**4**	
5	Social security and Medicare tax on unreported tip income. Attach Form 4137	**5**		
6	Uncollected social security and Medicare tax on wages. Attach Form 8919	**6**		
7	Total additional social security and Medicare tax. Add lines 5 and 6		**7**	
8	Additional tax on IRAs or other tax-favored accounts. Attach Form 5329 if required. If not required, check here . . . . ☐		**8**	
9	Household employment taxes. Attach Schedule H		**9**	
10	Repayment of first-time homebuyer credit. Attach Form 5405 if required		**10**	
11	Additional Medicare Tax. Attach Form 8959		**11**	
12	Net investment income tax. Attach Form 8960		**12**	
13	Uncollected social security and Medicare or RRTA tax on tips or group-term life insurance from Form W-2, box 12		**13**	
14	Interest on tax due on installment income from the sale of certain residential lots and timeshares		**14**	
15	Interest on the deferred tax on gain from certain installment sales with a sales price over $150,000		**15**	
16	Recapture of low-income housing credit. Attach Form 8611		**16**	

(continued on page 2)

For Paperwork Reduction Act Notice, see your tax return instructions.   Cat. No. 71478U   Schedule 2 (Form 1040) 2022

(Use for Cumulative Problem 1.)

Schedule 2 (Form 1040) 2022   Page **2**

Part II   **Other Taxes** *(continued)*

17   Other additional taxes:

   a   Recapture of other credits. List type, form number, and amount:

     _____ | **17a** |

   b   Recapture of federal mortgage subsidy, if you sold your home see instructions . . . . | **17b** |

   c   Additional tax on HSA distributions. Attach Form 8889 . . . | **17c** |

   d   Additional tax on an HSA because you didn't remain an eligible individual. Attach Form 8889 . . . . | **17d** |

   e   Additional tax on Archer MSA distributions. Attach Form 8853 . | **17e** |

   f   Additional tax on Medicare Advantage MSA distributions. Attach Form 8853 . . . . | **17f** |

   g   Recapture of a charitable contribution deduction related to a fractional interest in tangible personal property . . . . . | **17g** |

   h   Income you received from a nonqualified deferred compensation plan that fails to meet the requirements of section 409A . . . | **17h** |

   i   Compensation you received from a nonqualified deferred compensation plan described in section 457A . . . . | **17i** |

   j   Section 72(m)(5) excess benefits tax . . . . | **17j** |

   k   Golden parachute payments . . . . | **17k** |

   l   Tax on accumulation distribution of trusts . . . . | **17l** |

   m Excise tax on insider stock compensation from an expatriated corporation . . . . | **17m** |

   n   Look-back interest under section 167(g) or 460(b) from Form 8697 or 8866 . . . . | **17n** |

   o   Tax on non-effectively connected income for any part of the year you were a nonresident alien from Form 1040-NR . . . . | **17o** |

   p   Any interest from Form 8621, line 16f, relating to distributions from, and dispositions of, stock of a section 1291 fund . . . . | **17p** |

   q   Any interest from Form 8621, line 24 . . . . | **17q** |

   z   Any other taxes. List type and amount: _____

     _____ | **17z** |

18   Total additional taxes. Add lines 17a through 17z . . . . | **18** |

19   Reserved for future use . . . . | **19** |

20   Section 965 net tax liability installment from Form 965-A . . . | **20** |

21   Add lines 4, 7 through 16, and 18. These are your **total other taxes.** Enter here and on Form 1040 or 1040-SR, line 23, or Form 1040-NR, line 23b . . . . | **21** |

Schedule 2 (Form 1040) 2022

(Use for Cumulative Problem 1.)

SCHEDULE A (Form 1040)	**Itemized Deductions**	OMB No. 1545-0074
Department of the Treasury Internal Revenue Service	Go to *www.irs.gov/ScheduleA* for instructions and the latest information. **Attach to Form 1040 or 1040-SR.** **Caution:** If you are claiming a net qualified disaster loss on Form 4684, see the instructions for line 16.	**20**22 Attachment Sequence No. **07**

Name(s) shown on Form 1040 or 1040-SR | Your social security number

Medical and Dental Expenses	**Caution:** Do not include expenses reimbursed or paid by others.		
	1 Medical and dental expenses (see instructions)	**1**	
	2 Enter amount from Form 1040 or 1040-SR, line 11 | **2** |		
	3 Multiply line 2 by 7.5% (0.075)	**3**	
	4 Subtract line 3 from line 1. If line 3 is more than line 1, enter -0-		**4**
Taxes You Paid	**5** State and local taxes.		
	a State and local income taxes or general sales taxes. You may include either income taxes or general sales taxes on line 5a, but not both. If you elect to include general sales taxes instead of income taxes, check this box . . . . ▢	**5a**	
	b State and local real estate taxes (see instructions) . . .	**5b**	
	c State and local personal property taxes	**5c**	
	d Add lines 5a through 5c	**5d**	
	e Enter the smaller of line 5d or $10,000 ($5,000 if married filing separately)	**5e**	
	6 Other taxes. List type and amount: _____ _____	**6**	
	7 Add lines 5e and 6		**7**
Interest You Paid **Caution:** Your mortgage interest deduction may be limited. See instructions.	**8** Home mortgage interest and points. If you didn't use all of your home mortgage loan(s) to buy, build, or improve your home, see instructions and check this box . . . . ▢		
	a Home mortgage interest and points reported to you on Form 1098. See instructions if limited	**8a**	
	b Home mortgage interest not reported to you on Form 1098. See instructions if limited. If paid to the person from whom you bought the home, see instructions and show that person's name, identifying no., and address . . . . _____ _____	**8b**	
	c Points not reported to you on Form 1098. See instructions for special rules	**8c**	
	d Reserved for future use	**8d**	
	e Add lines 8a through 8c	**8e**	
	9 Investment interest. Attach Form 4952 if required. See instructions .	**9**	
	10 Add lines 8e and 9		**10**
Gifts to Charity **Caution:** If you made a gift and got a benefit for it, see instructions.	**11** Gifts by cash or check. If you made any gift of $250 or more, see instructions	**11**	
	12 Other than by cash or check. If you made any gift of $250 or more, see instructions. You **must** attach Form 8283 if over $500. . . .	**12**	
	13 Carryover from prior year	**13**	
	14 Add lines 11 through 13		**14**
Casualty and Theft Losses	**15** Casualty and theft loss(es) from a federally declared disaster (other than net qualified disaster losses). Attach Form 4684 and enter the amount from line 18 of that form. See instructions		**15**
Other Itemized Deductions	**16** Other—from list in instructions. List type and amount: _____ _____		**16**
Total Itemized Deductions	**17** Add the amounts in the far right column for lines 4 through 16. Also, enter this amount on Form 1040 or 1040-SR, line 12		**17**
	18 If you elect to itemize deductions even though they are less than your standard deduction, check this box . . . . ▢		

For Paperwork Reduction Act Notice, see the Instructions for Form 1040. | Cat. No. 17145C | **Schedule A (Form 1040) 2022**

(Use for Cumulative Problem 1.)

SCHEDULE C (Form 1040)	**Profit or Loss From Business** (Sole Proprietorship)	OMB No. 1545-0074
Department of the Treasury Internal Revenue Service	Go to *www.irs.gov/ScheduleC* for instructions and the latest information. **Attach to Form 1040, 1040-SR, 1040-NR, or 1041; partnerships must generally file Form 1065.**	**20**22 Attachment Sequence No. **09**

Name of proprietor _____ Social security number (SSN) _____

A	Principal business or profession, including product or service (see instructions)	**B** Enter code from instructions
C	Business name. If no separate business name, leave blank.	**D** Employer ID number (EIN) (see instr.)
E	Business address (including suite or room no.) City, town or post office, state, and ZIP code	

F Accounting method: **(1)** ☐ Cash **(2)** ☐ Accrual **(3)** ☐ Other (specify) _____
G Did you "materially participate" in the operation of this business during 2022? If "No," see instructions for limit on losses . ☐ **Yes** ☐ **No**
H If you started or acquired this business during 2022, check here . . . . ☐
I Did you make any payments in 2022 that would require you to file Form(s) 1099? See instructions . . . . . ☐ **Yes** ☐ **No**
J If "Yes," did you or will you file required Form(s) 1099? . . . . ☐ **Yes** ☐ **No**

Part I   Income

1	Gross receipts or sales. See instructions for line 1 and check the box if this income was reported to you on Form W-2 and the "Statutory employee" box on that form was checked . . . . ▶ ☐	**1**	
2	Returns and allowances	**2**	
3	Subtract line 2 from line 1	**3**	
4	Cost of goods sold (from line 42)	**4**	
5	**Gross profit.** Subtract line 4 from line 3	**5**	
6	Other income, including federal and state gasoline or fuel tax credit or refund (see instructions) . . .	**6**	
7	**Gross income.** Add lines 5 and 6 . . . . ▶	**7**	

Part II   Expenses. Enter expenses for business use of your home **only** on line 30.

8	Advertising	**8**		18	Office expense (see instructions) .	**18**
9	Car and truck expenses (see instructions)	**9**		19	Pension and profit-sharing plans .	**19**
10	Commissions and fees .	**10**		20	Rent or lease (see instructions):	
11	Contract labor (see instructions)	**11**		a	Vehicles, machinery, and equipment	**20a**
12	Depletion	**12**		b	Other business property . . .	**20b**
13	Depreciation and section 179 expense deduction (not included in Part III) (see instructions)	**13**		21	Repairs and maintenance . . .	**21**
				22	Supplies (not included in Part III) .	**22**
				23	Taxes and licenses	**23**
				24	Travel and meals:	
14	Employee benefit programs (other than on line 19) .	**14**		a	Travel	**24a**
15	Insurance (other than health)	**15**		b	Deductible meals (see instructions)	**24b**
16	Interest (see instructions):			25	Utilities	**25**
a	Mortgage (paid to banks, etc.)	**16a**		26	Wages (less employment credits)	**26**
b	Other	**16b**		27a	Other expenses (from line 48) . .	**27a**
17	Legal and professional services	**17**		b	Reserved for future use . . .	**27b**

28	**Total expenses** before expenses for business use of home. Add lines 8 through 27a . . . . ▶	**28**	
29	Tentative profit or (loss). Subtract line 28 from line 7	**29**	
30	Expenses for business use of your home. Do not report these expenses elsewhere. Attach Form 8829 unless using the simplified method. See instructions. **Simplified method filers only:** Enter the total square footage of (a) your home: _____ and (b) the part of your home used for business: _____ . Use the Simplified Method Worksheet in the instructions to figure the amount to enter on line 30	**30**	
31	**Net profit or (loss).** Subtract line 30 from line 29. • If a profit, enter on both **Schedule 1 (Form 1040), line 3,** and on **Schedule SE, line 2.** (If you checked the box on line 1, see instructions.) Estates and trusts, enter on **Form 1041, line 3.** • If a loss, you **must** go to line 32.	**31**	
32	If you have a loss, check the box that describes your investment in this activity. See instructions. • If you checked 32a, enter the loss on both **Schedule 1 (Form 1040), line 3,** and on **Schedule SE, line 2.** (If you checked the box on line 1, see the line 31 instructions.) Estates and trusts, enter on **Form 1041, line 3.** • If you checked 32b, you **must** attach Form 6198. Your loss may be limited.	**32a** ☐ All investment is at risk. **32b** ☐ Some investment is not at risk.	

For Paperwork Reduction Act Notice, see the separate instructions.   Cat. No. 11334P   Schedule C (Form 1040) 2022

(Use for Cumulative Problem 1.)

Schedule C (Form 1040) 2022   Page **2**

Part III **Cost of Goods Sold** (see instructions)

33 Method(s) used to
    value closing inventory: **a** ☐ Cost   **b** ☐ Lower of cost or market   **c** ☐ Other (attach explanation)

34 Was there any change in determining quantities, costs, or valuations between opening and closing inventory?
    If "Yes," attach explanation . . . . ☐ Yes   ☐ No

35 Inventory at beginning of year. If different from last year's closing inventory, attach explanation . . | **35** |

36 Purchases less cost of items withdrawn for personal use . . . . | **36** |

37 Cost of labor. Do not include any amounts paid to yourself . . . . | **37** |

38 Materials and supplies . . . . | **38** |

39 Other costs . . . . | **39** |

40 Add lines 35 through 39 . . . . | **40** |

41 Inventory at end of year . . . . | **41** |

42 **Cost of goods sold.** Subtract line 41 from line 40. Enter the result here and on line 4 . . . . | **42** |

Part IV **Information on Your Vehicle.** Complete this part **only** if you are claiming car or truck expenses on line 9 and are not required to file Form 4562 for this business. See the instructions for line 13 to find out if you must file Form 4562.

43 When did you place your vehicle in service for business purposes? (month/day/year) ____ / ____ / ____

44 Of the total number of miles you drove your vehicle during 2022, enter the number of miles you used your vehicle for:

 a Business _____   **b** Commuting (see instructions) _____   **c** Other _____

45 Was your vehicle available for personal use during off-duty hours? . . . . ☐ Yes   ☐ No

46 Do you (or your spouse) have another vehicle available for personal use? . . . . ☐ Yes   ☐ No

47a Do you have evidence to support your deduction? . . . . ☐ Yes   ☐ No

 b If "Yes," is the evidence written? . . . . ☐ Yes   ☐ No

Part V **Other Expenses.** List below business expenses not included on lines 8–26 or line 30.

48 **Total other expenses.** Enter here and on line 27a . . . . | **48** |

Schedule C (Form 1040) 2022

(Use for Cumulative Problem 1.)

SCHEDULE SE (Form 1040) Department of the Treasury Internal Revenue Service	**Self-Employment Tax** Go to *www.irs.gov/ScheduleSE* for instructions and the latest information. Attach to Form 1040, 1040-SR, or 1040-NR.	OMB No. 1545-0074 **2022** Attachment Sequence No. **17**

Name of person with self-employment income (as shown on Form 1040, 1040-SR, or 1040-NR)	Social security number of person with **self-employment** income

Part I   **Self-Employment Tax**

Note: If your only income subject to self-employment tax is **church employee income**, see instructions for how to report your income and the definition of church employee income.

A	If you are a minister, member of a religious order, or Christian Science practitioner **and** you filed Form 4361, but you had $400 or more of **other** net earnings from self-employment, check here and continue with Part I . . . . ▶ ☐		

Skip lines 1a and 1b if you use the farm optional method in Part II. See instructions.

| **1a** | Net farm profit or (loss) from Schedule F, line 34, and farm partnerships, Schedule K-1 (Form 1065), box 14, code A . . . | **1a** | |
| **b** | If you received social security retirement or disability benefits, enter the amount of Conservation Reserve Program payments included on Schedule F, line 4b, or listed on Schedule K-1 (Form 1065), box 20, code AH | **1b** | ( ) |

Skip line 2 if you use the nonfarm optional method in Part II. See instructions.

2	Net profit or (loss) from Schedule C, line 31; and Schedule K-1 (Form 1065), box 14, code A (other than farming). See instructions for other income to report or if you are a minister or member of a religious order	**2**	
3	Combine lines 1a, 1b, and 2	**3**	
4a	If line 3 is more than zero, multiply line 3 by 92.35% (0.9235). Otherwise, enter amount from line 3	**4a**	
	Note: If line 4a is less than $400 due to Conservation Reserve Program payments on line 1b, see instructions.		
b	If you elect one or both of the optional methods, enter the total of lines 15 and 17 here	**4b**	
c	Combine lines 4a and 4b. If less than $400, **stop;** you don't owe self-employment tax. **Exception:** If less than $400 and you had **church employee income**, enter -0- and continue	**4c**	
5a	Enter your **church employee income** from Form W-2. See instructions for definition of church employee income **5a**		
b	Multiply line 5a by 92.35% (0.9235). If less than $100, enter -0-	**5b**	
6	Add lines 4c and 5b	**6**	
7	Maximum amount of combined wages and self-employment earnings subject to social security tax or the 6.2% portion of the 7.65% railroad retirement (tier 1) tax for 2022	**7**	147,000
8a	Total social security wages and tips (total of boxes 3 and 7 on Form(s) W-2) and railroad retirement (tier 1) compensation. If $147,000 or more, skip lines 8b through 10, and go to line 11 . . . . **8a**		
b	Unreported tips subject to social security tax from Form 4137, line 10 . . . **8b**		
c	Wages subject to social security tax from Form 8919, line 10 . . . . . . **8c**		
d	Add lines 8a, 8b, and 8c	**8d**	
9	Subtract line 8d from line 7. If zero or less, enter -0- here and on line 10 and go to line 11	**9**	
10	Multiply the **smaller** of line 6 or line 9 by 12.4% (0.124)	**10**	
11	Multiply line 6 by 2.9% (0.029)	**11**	
12	**Self-employment tax.** Add lines 10 and 11. Enter here and on **Schedule 2 (Form 1040), line 4** . .	**12**	
13	**Deduction for one-half of self-employment tax.** Multiply line 12 by 50% (0.50). Enter here and on **Schedule 1 (Form 1040), line 15** **13**		

Part II   **Optional Methods To Figure Net Earnings** (see instructions)

Farm Optional Method. You may use this method **only** if **(a)** your gross farm income[1] wasn't more than $9,060, **or (b)** your net farm profits[2] were less than $6,540.

| **14** | Maximum income for optional methods . . . . | **14** | 6,040 |
| **15** | Enter the **smaller** of: two-thirds (⅔) of gross farm income[1] (not less than zero) **or** $6,040. Also, include this amount on line 4b above . . . . | **15** | |

Nonfarm Optional Method. You may use this method **only** if **(a)** your net nonfarm profits[3] were less than $6,540 and also less than 72.189% of your gross nonfarm income,[4] **and (b)** you had net earnings from self-employment of at least $400 in 2 of the prior 3 years. **Caution:** You may use this method no more than five times.

| **16** | Subtract line 15 from line 14 . . . . | **16** | |
| **17** | Enter the **smaller** of: two-thirds (⅔) of gross nonfarm income[4] (not less than zero) **or** the amount on line 16. Also, include this amount on line 4b above . . . . | **17** | |

[1] From Sch. F, line 9; and Sch. K-1 (Form 1065), box 14, code B.
[2] From Sch. F, line 34; and Sch. K-1 (Form 1065), box 14, code A—minus the amount you would have entered on line 1b had you not used the optional method.
[3] From Sch. C, line 31; and Sch. K-1 (Form 1065), box 14, code A.
[4] From Sch. C, line 7; and Sch. K-1 (Form 1065), box 14, code C.

For Paperwork Reduction Act Notice, see your tax return instructions.   Cat. No. 11358Z   Schedule SE (Form 1040) 2022

DRAFT AS OF July 28, 2022 DO NOT FILE

(Use for Cumulative Problem 1.)

This Form is Overset by 2 Lines

Form **8829**

Department of the Treasury
Internal Revenue Service

Expenses for Business Use of Your Home

File only with Schedule C (Form 1040). Use a separate Form 8829 for each home you used for business during the year.
Go to *www.irs.gov/Form8829* for instructions and the latest information.

OMB No. 1545-0074

2022

Attachment Sequence No. **176**

Name(s) of proprietor(s)

Your social security number

Part I Part of Your Home Used for Business

1 Area used regularly and exclusively for business, regularly for daycare, or for storage of inventory or product samples (see instructions) **1**

2 Total area of home **2**

3 Divide line 1 by line 2. Enter the result as a percentage . . . . **3** %

For daycare facilities not used exclusively for business, go to line 4. All others, go to line 7.

4 Multiply days used for daycare during year by hours used per day . . **4** hr.

5 If you started or stopped using your home for daycare during the year, see instructions; otherwise, enter 8,760 . . . . **5** hr.

6 Divide line 4 by line 5. Enter the result as a decimal amount . . . **6**

7 Business percentage. For daycare facilities not used exclusively for business, multiply line 6 by line 3 (enter the result as a percentage). All others, enter the amount from line 3 . . . . **7** %

Part II Figure Your Allowable Deduction

8 Enter the amount from Schedule C, line 29, **plus** any gain derived from the business use of your home, **minus** any loss from the trade or business not derived from the business use of your home. See instructions. **8**

See instructions for columns (a) and (b) before completing lines 9–22.

		(a) Direct expenses	(b) Indirect expenses		
9	Casualty losses (see instructions)	**9**			
10	Deductible mortgage interest (see instructions)	**10**			
11	Real estate taxes (see instructions)	**11**			
12	Add lines 9, 10, and 11	**12**			
13	Multiply line 12, column (b), by line 7		**13**		
14	Add line 12, column (a), and line 13			**14**	
15	Subtract line 14 from line 8. If zero or less, enter -0-			**15**	
16	Excess mortgage interest (see instructions)	**16**			
17	Excess real estate taxes (see instructions)	**17**			
18	Insurance	**18**			
19	Rent	**19**			
20	Repairs and maintenance	**20**			
21	Utilities	**21**			
22	Other expenses (see instructions)	**22**			
23	Add lines 16 through 22	**23**			
24	Multiply line 23, column (b), by line 7		**24**		
25	Carryover of prior year operating expenses (see instructions)		**25**		
26	Add line 23, column (a), line 24, and line 25			**26**	
27	Allowable operating expenses. Enter the **smaller** of line 15 or line 26			**27**	
28	Limit on excess casualty losses and depreciation. Subtract line 27 from line 15			**28**	
29	Excess casualty losses (see instructions)		**29**		
30	Depreciation of your home from line 42 below		**30**		
31	Carryover of prior year excess casualty losses and depreciation (see instructions)		**31**		
32	Add lines 29 through 31			**32**	
33	Allowable excess casualty losses and depreciation. Enter the **smaller** of line 28 or line 32			**33**	
34	Add lines 14, 27, and 33			**34**	
35	Casualty loss portion, if any, from lines 14 and 33. Carry amount to **Form 4684.** See instructions			**35**	
36	**Allowable expenses for business use of your home.** Subtract line 35 from line 34. Enter here and on Schedule C, line 30. If your home was used for more than one business, see instructions			**36**	

Part III Depreciation of Your Home

37	Enter the **smaller** of your home's adjusted basis or its fair market value. See instructions	**37**	
38	Value of land included on line 37	**38**	
39	Basis of building. Subtract line 38 from line 37	**39**	
40	Business basis of building. Multiply line 39 by line 7	**40**	
41	Depreciation percentage (see instructions)	**41**	%
42	Depreciation allowable (see instructions). Multiply line 40 by line 41. Enter here and on line 30 above	**42**	

Part IV Carryover of Unallowed Expenses to 2023

43	Operating expenses. Subtract line 27 from line 26. If less than zero, enter -0-	**43**	
44	Excess casualty losses and depreciation. Subtract line 33 from line 32. If less than zero, enter -0-	**44**	

For Paperwork Reduction Act Notice, see your tax return instructions. Cat. No. 13232M Form **8829** (2022)

(Use for Cumulative Problem 1.)

Form **8995** Department of the Treasury Internal Revenue Service	**Qualified Business Income Deduction** **Simplified Computation** Attach to your tax return. Go to *www.irs.gov/Form8995* for instructions and the latest information.	OMB No. 1545-2294 20**22** Attachment Sequence No. **55**
Name(s) shown on return		Your taxpayer identification number

Note. You can claim the qualified business income deduction **only** if you have qualified business income from a qualified trade or business, real estate investment trust dividends, publicly traded partnership income, or a domestic production activities deduction passed through from an agricultural or horticultural cooperative. See instructions.

Use this form if your taxable income, before your qualified business income deduction, is at or below $170,050 ($340,100 if married filing jointly), and you aren't a patron of an agricultural or horticultural cooperative.

1		(a) Trade, business, or aggregation name	(b) Taxpayer identification number	(c) Qualified business income or (loss)
i				
ii				
iii				
iv				
v				

2	Total qualified business income or (loss). Combine lines 1i through 1v, column (c)	2		
3	Qualified business net (loss) carryforward from the prior year	3	( )	
4	Total qualified business income. Combine lines 2 and 3. If zero or less, enter -0-	4		
5	Qualified business income component. Multiply line 4 by 20% (0.20)			5
6	Qualified REIT dividends and publicly traded partnership (PTP) income or (loss) (see instructions)	6		
7	Qualified REIT dividends and qualified PTP (loss) carryforward from the prior year	7	( )	
8	Total qualified REIT dividends and PTP income. Combine lines 6 and 7. If zero or less, enter -0-	8		
9	REIT and PTP component. Multiply line 8 by 20% (0.20)			9
10	Qualified business income deduction before the income limitation. Add lines 5 and 9			10
11	Taxable income before qualified business income deduction (see instructions)	11		
12	Net capital gain (see instructions)	12		
13	Subtract line 12 from line 11. If zero or less, enter -0-	13		
14	Income limitation. Multiply line 13 by 20% (0.20)			14
15	Qualified business income deduction. Enter the smaller of line 10 or line 14. Also enter this amount on the applicable line of your return (see instructions)			15
16	Total qualified business (loss) carryforward. Combine lines 2 and 3. If greater than zero, enter -0- . .			16 ( )
17	Total qualified REIT dividends and PTP (loss) carryforward. Combine lines 6 and 7. If greater than zero, enter -0-			17 ( )

For Privacy Act and Paperwork Reduction Act Notice, see instructions.   Cat. No. 37806C   Form **8995** (2022)

CUMULATIVE PROBLEM 2 (CHAPTERS 1–8)

Patrick A. and Danielle R. Beckman file a joint return for 2022. The Beckmans rent a three-bedroom apartment located at 529 W. Maywood, #4, Aurora, IL 60505. They provide over half of the support for Danielle's mother, Ellen Tyler (SSN 384-00-7338), who qualifies as their dependent. Ellen lives in a nursing home in Peoria, Illinois. The Beckmans claim their 20-year-old daughter, Tara (SSN 487-00-3957) as a dependent. Tara lives with the Beckmans while attending college full-time.

Danielle (SSN 394-00-3948) works full-time for an advertising firm. Through her employer, Danielle gets full health care insurance coverage for her family. In 2022, Danielle's taxable wages were $59,000, from which her employer withheld $6,000 in federal income taxes, $3,869 in social security taxes, $905 in Medicare taxes, and $1,020 in state income taxes. Danielle is an active participant in her employer's 401(k). During the year, Danielle contributed $3,400 to her 401(k). Danielle and Patrick each contributed $1,500 to their respective traditional IRAs for 2022.

Patrick (SSN 549-00-2497) is self-employed. He began his carpet cleaning business in 2016. The business code for Schedule C (line B) is 812990. Patrick uses the spare bedroom in the apartment solely and exclusively as a home office to perform administrative tasks. The bedroom is 220 square feet in size. The square footage of the entire apartment is 1,800 square feet. Patrick elects to use the safe harbor method to compute his home office deduction. Patrick uses the cash method. During the year, his business income was $18,000, and he paid $1,828 for cleaning chemicals and supplies, $300 for advertising, and $50 for office expenses.

On September 10, 2020, Patrick purchased carpet-cleaning equipment for $14,762. This was the only depreciable property placed in service in 2020. The equipment is 5-year property. Patrick did not elect Section 179 in 2020. He did take bonus depreciation and uses regular MACRS to depreciate the equipment. On June 8, 2022, Patrick purchased video equipment for $2,000. Assume this equipment is 5-year property also with a 5-year ADS period. Patrick uses the video equipment 40% for business and 60% for personal use. Patrick has written evidence to support the 40% business use. The video equipment was Patrick's only acquisition in 2022.

Patrick uses his van to get to and from customers' homes. During the year, Patrick drove his van 1,845 miles for business. 800 miles were between January 1 and June 30. He keeps a written log as evidence of these miles. Total miles for the year on the van were 10,540. He drove 4,800 of those miles before July 1. Danielle has her own car that she uses to get to and from work. Patrick bought the van on March 5, 2014. He used the standard mileage method in 2022. Patrick incurred no business-related parking or tolls in 2022.

Prepare the Beckmans' Form 1040 and accompanying Schedule 1, Schedule 2, Schedule 8812, Schedules C and SE, Form 4562, Form 8880, and Form 8995. Be sure to complete lines 30–36 on Form 4562. Neither Patrick nor Danielle wants $3 to go to the Presidential election campaign fund. The Beckmans sign their return on April 15, 2023.

(Use for Cumulative Problem 2.)

Form 1040   Department of the Treasury—Internal Revenue Service
U.S. Individual Income Tax Return   **2022**   OMB No. 1545-0074   IRS Use Only—Do not write or staple in this space.

Filing Status Check only one box.
☐ Single ☐ Married filing jointly ☐ Married filing separately (MFS) ☐ Head of household (HOH) ☐ Qualifying widow(er) (QW)

If you checked the MFS box, enter the name of your spouse. If you checked the HOH or QW box, enter the child's name if the qualifying person is a child but not your dependent:

Your first name and middle initial	Last name		Your social security number
If joint return, spouse's first name and middle initial	Last name		Spouse's social security number

Home address (number and street). If you have a P.O. box, see instructions.   Apt. no.

City, town, or post office. If you have a foreign address, also complete spaces below.   State   ZIP code

Foreign country name   Foreign province/state/county   Foreign postal code

Presidential Election Campaign
Check here if you, or your spouse if filing jointly, want $3 to go to this fund. Checking a box below will not change your tax or refund. ☐ You ☐ Spouse

At any time during 2022, did you: (a) receive (as a reward, award, or compensation); or (b) sell, exchange, gift, or otherwise dispose of a digital asset (or a financial interest in a digital asset)? (See instructions.) . . ☐ Yes ☐ No

Standard Deduction
Someone can claim: ☐ You as a dependent ☐ Your spouse as a dependent
☐ Spouse itemizes on a separate return or you were a dual-status alien

Age/Blindness You: ☐ Were born before January 2, 1958 ☐ Are blind   **Spouse:** ☐ Was born before January 2, 1958 ☐ Is blind

Dependents (see instructions):

(1) First name Last name	(2) Social security number	(3) Relationship to you	(4) Check the box if qualifies for (see instructions):	
			Child tax credit	Credit for other dependents
			☐	☐
			☐	☐
			☐	☐
			☐	☐

If more than four dependents, see instructions and check here . . ☐

Income

Attach Form(s) W-2 here. Also attach Forms W-2G and 1099-R if tax was withheld.

If you did not get a Form W-2, see instructions.

Attach Sch. B if required.

1a	Total amount from Form(s) W-2, box 1 (see instructions)	1a	
b	Household employee wages not reported on Form(s) W-2	1b	
c	Tip income not reported on line 1a (see instructions)	1c	
d	Medicaid waiver payments not reported on Form(s) W-2 (see instructions) . .	1d	
e	Taxable dependent care benefits from Form 2441, line 26	1e	
f	Employer-provided adoption benefits from Form 8839, line 29	1f	
g	Wages from Form 8919, line 6	1g	
h	Other earned income (see instructions)	1h	
i	Nontaxable combat pay election (see instructions) 1i		
z	Add lines 1a through 1h	1z	

2a	Tax-exempt interest . . .	2a		b Taxable interest	2b	
3a	Qualified dividends . . .	3a		b Ordinary dividends	3b	
4a	IRA distributions . . .	4a		b Taxable amount	4b	
5a	Pensions and annuities . .	5a		b Taxable amount	5b	
6a	Social security benefits . .	6a		b Taxable amount	6b	

Standard Deduction for—
• Single or Married filing separately, $12,950
• Married filing jointly or Qualifying widow(er), $25,900
• Head of household, $19,400
• If you checked any box under Standard Deduction, see instructions.

c	If you elect to use the lump-sum election method, check here (see instructions) . . . . . ☐		
7	Capital gain or (loss). Attach Schedule D if required. If not required, check here . . . . . ☐	7	
8	Other income from Schedule 1, line 10	8	
9	Add lines 1z, 2b, 3b, 4b, 5b, 6b, 7, and 8. This is your **total income**	9	
10	Adjustments to income from Schedule 1, line 26	10	
11	Subtract line 10 from line 9. This is your **adjusted gross income**	11	
12	**Standard deduction or itemized deductions** (from Schedule A)	12	
13	Qualified business income deduction from Form 8995 or Form 8995-A	13	
14	Add lines 12 and 13	14	
15	Subtract line 14 from line 11. If zero or less, enter -0-. This is your **taxable income**	15	

For Disclosure, Privacy Act, and Paperwork Reduction Act Notice, see separate instructions.   Cat. No. 11320B   Form **1040** (2022)

(Use for Cumulative Problem 2.)

Version A, Cycle 7

Form 1040 (2022)   Page **2**

Tax and Credits	16	Tax (see instructions). Check if any from Form(s): 1 ☐ 8814 2 ☐ 4972 3 ☐ _____	16	
	17	Amount from Schedule 2, line 3	17	
	18	Add lines 16 and 17	18	
	19	Child tax credit or credit for other dependents from Schedule 8812	19	
	20	Amount from Schedule 3, line 8	20	
	21	Add lines 19 and 20	21	
	22	Subtract line 21 from line 18. If zero or less, enter -0-	22	
	23	Other taxes, including self-employment tax, from Schedule 2, line 21	23	
	24	Add lines 22 and 23. This is your **total tax**	24	
Payments	25	Federal income tax withheld from:		
	a	Form(s) W-2	25a	
	b	Form(s) 1099	25b	
	c	Other forms (see instructions)	25c	
	d	Add lines 25a through 25c	25d	
If you have a qualifying child, attach Sch. EIC.	26	2022 estimated tax payments and amount applied from 2021 return	26	
	27	Earned income credit (EIC)	27	
	28	Additional child tax credit from Schedule 8812	28	
	29	American opportunity credit from Form 8863, line 8	29	
	30	Reserved for future use	30	
	31	Amount from Schedule 3, line 15	31	
	32	Add lines 27, 28, 29, and 31. These are your **total other payments and refundable credits**	32	
	33	Add lines 25d, 26, and 32. These are your **total payments**	33	
Refund	34	If line 33 is more than line 24, subtract line 24 from line 33. This is the amount you **overpaid**	34	
	35a	Amount of line 34 you want **refunded to you**. If Form 8888 is attached, check here ☐	35a	
Direct deposit? See instructions.	b	Routing number ⬚⬚⬚⬚⬚⬚⬚⬚⬚ c Type: ☐ Checking ☐ Savings		
	d	Account number ⬚⬚⬚⬚⬚⬚⬚⬚⬚⬚⬚⬚⬚⬚⬚⬚⬚		
	36	Amount of line 34 you want **applied to your 2023 estimated tax** 36		
Amount You Owe	37	Subtract line 33 from line 24. This is the **amount you owe**. For details on how to pay, go to *www.irs.gov/Payments* or see instructions	37	
	38	Estimated tax penalty (see instructions) 38		

Third Party Designee	Do you want to allow another person to discuss this return with the IRS? See instructions ☐ **Yes.** Complete below. ☐ **No**		
	Designee's name	Phone no.	Personal identification number (PIN) ⬚⬚⬚⬚⬚

Sign Here	Under penalties of perjury, I declare that I have examined this return and accompanying schedules and statements, and to the best of my knowledge and belief, they are true, correct, and complete. Declaration of preparer (other than taxpayer) is based on all information of which preparer has any knowledge.			
	Your signature	Date	Your occupation	If the IRS sent you an Identity Protection PIN, enter it here (see inst.) ⬚⬚⬚⬚⬚⬚
Joint return? See instructions. Keep a copy for your records.	Spouse's signature. If a joint return, **both** must sign.	Date	Spouse's occupation	If the IRS sent your spouse an Identity Protection PIN, enter it here (see inst.) ⬚⬚⬚⬚⬚⬚
	Phone no.	Email address		

Paid Preparer Use Only	Preparer's name	Preparer's signature	Date	PTIN	Check if: ☐ Self-employed
	Firm's name			Phone no.	
	Firm's address			Firm's EIN	

Go to *www.irs.gov/Form1040* for instructions and the latest information.   Form **1040** (2022)

(Use for Cumulative Problem 2.)

SCHEDULE 1 (Form 1040)	Additional Income and Adjustments to Income	OMB No. 1545-0074
Department of the Treasury Internal Revenue Service	Attach to Form 1040, 1040-SR, or 1040-NR. Go to *www.irs.gov/Form1040* for instructions and the latest information.	2022 Attachment Sequence No. 01

Name(s) shown on Form 1040, 1040-SR, or 1040-NR   Your social security number

Part I   Additional Income

1	Taxable refunds, credits, or offsets of state and local income taxes	1	
2a	Alimony received	2a	
b	Date of original divorce or separation agreement (see instructions):		
3	Business income or (loss). Attach Schedule C	3	
4	Other gains or (losses). Attach Form 4797	4	
5	Rental real estate, royalties, partnerships, S corporations, trusts, etc. Attach Schedule E	5	
6	Farm income or (loss). Attach Schedule F	6	
7	Unemployment compensation	7	
8	Other income:		
a	Net operating loss	8a ( )	
b	Gambling	8b	
c	Cancellation of debt	8c	
d	Foreign earned income exclusion from Form 2555	8d ( )	
e	Income from Form 8853	8e	
f	Income from Form 8889	8f	
g	Alaska Permanent Fund dividends	8g	
h	Jury duty pay	8h	
i	Prizes and awards	8i	
j	Activity not engaged in for profit income	8j	
k	Stock options	8k	
l	Income from the rental of personal property if you engaged in the rental for profit but were not in the business of renting such property	8l	
m	Olympic and Paralympic medals and USOC prize money (see instructions)	8m	
n	Section 951(a) inclusion (see instructions)	8n	
o	Section 951A(a) inclusion (see instructions)	8o	
p	Section 461(l) excess business loss adjustment	8p	
q	Taxable distributions from an ABLE account (see instructions)	8q	
r	Scholarship and fellowship grants not reported on Form W-2	8r	
s	Nontaxable amount of Medicaid waiver payments included on Form 1040, line 1a or 1d	8s ( )	
t	Pension or annuity from a nonqualifed deferred compensation plan or a nongovernmental section 457 plan	8t	
u	Wages earned while incarcerated	8u	
z	Other income. List type and amount: _____	8z	
9	Total other income. Add lines 8a through 8z	9	
10	Combine lines 1 through 7 and 9. Enter here and on Form 1040, 1040-SR, or 1040-NR, line 8	10	

For Paperwork Reduction Act Notice, see your tax return instructions.   Cat. No. 71479F   Schedule 1 (Form 1040) 2022

(Use for Cumulative Problem 2.)

Schedule 1 (Form 1040) 2022 Page **2**

Part II Adjustments to Income

11	Educator expenses	11	
12	Certain business expenses of reservists, performing artists, and fee-basis government officials. Attach Form 2106	12	
13	Health savings account deduction. Attach Form 8889	13	
14	Moving expenses for members of the Armed Forces. Attach Form 3903	14	
15	Deductible part of self-employment tax. Attach Schedule SE	15	
16	Self-employed SEP, SIMPLE, and qualified plans	16	
17	Self-employed health insurance deduction	17	
18	Penalty on early withdrawal of savings	18	
19a	Alimony paid	19a	
b	Recipient's SSN		
c	Date of original divorce or separation agreement (see instructions):		
20	IRA deduction	20	
21	Student loan interest deduction	21	
22	Reserved for future use	22	
23	Archer MSA deduction	23	
24	Other adjustments:		
a	Jury duty pay (see instructions)	24a	
b	Deductible expenses related to income reported on line 8l from the rental of personal property engaged in for profit	24b	
c	Nontaxable amount of the value of Olympic and Paralympic medals and USOC prize money reported on line 8m	24c	
d	Reforestation amortization and expenses	24d	
e	Repayment of supplemental unemployment benefits under the Trade Act of 1974	24e	
f	Contributions to section 501(c)(18)(D) pension plans	24f	
g	Contributions by certain chaplains to section 403(b) plans	24g	
h	Attorney fees and court costs for actions involving certain unlawful discrimination claims (see instructions)	24h	
i	Attorney fees and court costs you paid in connection with an award from the IRS for information you provided that helped the IRS detect tax law violations	24i	
j	Housing deduction from Form 2555	24j	
k	Excess deductions of section 67(e) expenses from Schedule K-1 (Form 1041)	24k	
z	Other adjustments. List type and amount:	24z	
25	Total other adjustments. Add lines 24a through 24z	25	
26	Add lines 11 through 23 and 25. These are your **adjustments to income**. Enter here and on Form 1040 or 1040-SR, line 10, or Form 1040-NR, line 10a	26	

Schedule 1 (Form 1040) 2022

(Use for Cumulative Problem 2.)

SCHEDULE 2 (Form 1040) Department of the Treasury Internal Revenue Service	Additional Taxes Attach to Form 1040, 1040-SR, or 1040-NR. Go to *www.irs.gov/Form1040* for instructions and the latest information.	OMB No. 1545-0074 2022 Attachment Sequence No. 02

Name(s) shown on Form 1040, 1040-SR, or 1040-NR | Your social security number

Part I   Tax

1	Alternative minimum tax. Attach Form 6251	**1**	
2	Excess advance premium tax credit repayment. Attach Form 8962	**2**	
3	Add lines 1 and 2. Enter here and on Form 1040, 1040-SR, or 1040-NR, line 17 . .	**3**	

Part II   Other Taxes

4	Self-employment tax. Attach Schedule SE	**4**	
5	Social security and Medicare tax on unreported tip income. Attach Form 4137	**5**	
6	Uncollected social security and Medicare tax on wages. Attach Form 8919	**6**	
7	Total additional social security and Medicare tax. Add lines 5 and 6 . . .	**7**	
8	Additional tax on IRAs or other tax-favored accounts. Attach Form 5329 if required. If not required, check here . . . . ☐	**8**	
9	Household employment taxes. Attach Schedule H	**9**	
10	Repayment of first-time homebuyer credit. Attach Form 5405 if required	**10**	
11	Additional Medicare Tax. Attach Form 8959	**11**	
12	Net investment income tax. Attach Form 8960	**12**	
13	Uncollected social security and Medicare or RRTA tax on tips or group-term life insurance from Form W-2, box 12	**13**	
14	Interest on tax due on installment income from the sale of certain residential lots and timeshares	**14**	
15	Interest on the deferred tax on gain from certain installment sales with a sales price over $150,000	**15**	
16	Recapture of low-income housing credit. Attach Form 8611	**16**	

(continued on page 2)

For Paperwork Reduction Act Notice, see your tax return instructions.   Cat. No. 71478U   Schedule 2 (Form 1040) 2022

(Use for Cumulative Problem 2.)

Schedule 2 (Form 1040) 2022   Page **2**

Part II   **Other Taxes** *(continued)*

17	Other additional taxes:		
a	Recapture of other credits. List type, form number, and amount:		
	_____	**17a**	
b	Recapture of federal mortgage subsidy, if you sold your home see instructions	**17b**	
c	Additional tax on HSA distributions. Attach Form 8889 . . .	**17c**	
d	Additional tax on an HSA because you didn't remain an eligible individual. Attach Form 8889	**17d**	
e	Additional tax on Archer MSA distributions. Attach Form 8853	**17e**	
f	Additional tax on Medicare Advantage MSA distributions. Attach Form 8853	**17f**	
g	Recapture of a charitable contribution deduction related to a fractional interest in tangible personal property	**17g**	
h	Income you received from a nonqualified deferred compensation plan that fails to meet the requirements of section 409A . . .	**17h**	
i	Compensation you received from a nonqualified deferred compensation plan described in section 457A	**17i**	
j	Section 72(m)(5) excess benefits tax	**17j**	
k	Golden parachute payments	**17k**	
l	Tax on accumulation distribution of trusts	**17l**	
m	Excise tax on insider stock compensation from an expatriated corporation	**17m**	
n	Look-back interest under section 167(g) or 460(b) from Form 8697 or 8866	**17n**	
o	Tax on non-effectively connected income for any part of the year you were a nonresident alien from Form 1040-NR	**17o**	
p	Any interest from Form 8621, line 16f, relating to distributions from, and dispositions of, stock of a section 1291 fund	**17p**	
q	Any interest from Form 8621, line 24	**17q**	
z	Any other taxes. List type and amount: _____		
	_____	**17z**	
18	Total additional taxes. Add lines 17a through 17z	**18**	
19	Reserved for future use	**19**	
20	Section 965 net tax liability installment from Form 965-A . . .	**20**	
21	Add lines 4, 7 through 16, and 18. These are your **total other taxes**. Enter here and on Form 1040 or 1040-SR, line 23, or Form 1040-NR, line 23b	**21**	

Schedule 2 (Form 1040) 2022

(Use for Cumulative Problem 2.)

SCHEDULE 8812 **(Form 1040)** Department of the Treasury Internal Revenue Service	**Credits for Qualifying Children** **and Other Dependents** Attach to Form 1040, 1040-SR, or 1040-NR. Go to *www.irs.gov/Schedule8812* for instructions and the latest information.	OMB No. 1545-0074 **2022** Attachment Sequence No. **47**

Name(s) shown on return | Your social security number

Part I Child Tax Credit and Credit for Other Dependents

1	Enter the amount from line 11 of your Form 1040, 1040-SR, or 1040-NR		**1**
2a	Enter income from Puerto Rico that you excluded	**2a**	
b	Enter the amounts from lines 45 and 50 of your Form 2555	**2b**	
c	Enter the amount from line 15 of your Form 4563	**2c**	
d	Add lines 2a through 2c		**2d**
3	Add lines 1 and 2d		**3**
4	Number of qualifying children under age 17 with the required social security number	**4**	
5	Multiply line 4 by $2,000		**5**
6	Number of other dependents, including any qualifying children who are not under age 17 or who do not have the required social security number	**6**	
	Caution: Do not include yourself, your spouse, or anyone who is not a U.S. citizen, U.S. national, or U.S. resident alien. Also, do not include anyone you included on line 4.		
7	Multiply line 6 by $500		**7**
8	Add lines 5 and 7		**8**
9	Enter the amount shown below for your filing status. • Married filing jointly—$400,000 • All other filing statuses—$200,000		**9**
10	Subtract line 9 from line 3. • If zero or less, enter -0-. • If more than zero and not a multiple of $1,000, enter the next multiple of $1,000. For example, if the result is $425, enter $1,000; if the result is $1,025, enter $2,000, etc.		**10**
11	Multiply line 10 by 5% (0.05)		**11**
12	Is the amount on line 8 more than the amount on line 11?		**12**
	☐ **No. STOP.** You cannot take the child tax credit, credit for other dependents, or additional child tax credit. Skip Parts II-A and II-B. Enter -0- on lines 14 and 27. ☐ **Yes.** Subtract line 11 from line 8. Enter the result.		
13	Enter the amount from the **Credit Limit Worksheet A**		**13**
14	Enter the smaller of line 12 or 13. **This is your child tax credit and credit for other dependents**		**14**
	Enter this amount on Form 1040, 1040-SR, or 1040-NR, line 19.		

If the amount on line 12 is more than the amount on line 14, you may be able to take the **additional child tax credit** on Form 1040, 1040-SR, or 1040-NR, line 28. Complete your Form 1040, 1040-SR, or 1040-NR through line 27 (also complete Schedule 3, line 11) before completing Part II-A.

For Paperwork Reduction Act Notice, see your tax return instructions. | Cat. No. 59761M | Schedule 8812 (Form 1040) 2022

(Use for Cumulative Problem 2.)

SCHEDULE C (Form 1040)

Department of the Treasury
Internal Revenue Service

Profit or Loss From Business
(Sole Proprietorship)

Go to *www.irs.gov/ScheduleC* for instructions and the latest information.
Attach to Form 1040, 1040-SR, 1040-NR, or 1041; partnerships must generally file Form 1065.

OMB No. 1545-0074

2022

Attachment Sequence No. **09**

Name of proprietor

Social security number (SSN)

A Principal business or profession, including product or service (see instructions)

B Enter code from instructions

C Business name. If no separate business name, leave blank.

D Employer ID number (EIN) (see instr.)

E Business address (including suite or room no.)

City, town or post office, state, and ZIP code

F Accounting method: (1) ☐ Cash (2) ☐ Accrual (3) ☐ Other (specify)

G Did you "materially participate" in the operation of this business during 2022? If "No," see instructions for limit on losses . ☐ Yes ☐ No

H If you started or acquired this business during 2022, check here . ☐

I Did you make any payments in 2022 that would require you to file Form(s) 1099? See instructions . ☐ Yes ☐ No

J If "Yes," did you or will you file required Form(s) 1099? . ☐ Yes ☐ No

Part I Income

1	Gross receipts or sales. See instructions for line 1 and check the box if this income was reported to you on Form W-2 and the "Statutory employee" box on that form was checked . ☐	**1**
2	Returns and allowances .	**2**
3	Subtract line 2 from line 1 .	**3**
4	Cost of goods sold (from line 42) .	**4**
5	**Gross profit.** Subtract line 4 from line 3 .	**5**
6	Other income, including federal and state gasoline or fuel tax credit or refund (see instructions) .	**6**
7	**Gross income.** Add lines 5 and 6 .	**7**

Part II Expenses. Enter expenses for business use of your home **only** on line 30.

8	Advertising .	8		18	Office expense (see instructions) .	18
9	Car and truck expenses (see instructions) .	9		19	Pension and profit-sharing plans .	19
10	Commissions and fees .	10		20	Rent or lease (see instructions):	
11	Contract labor (see instructions)	11		a	Vehicles, machinery, and equipment	20a
12	Depletion .	12		b	Other business property .	20b
13	Depreciation and section 179 expense deduction (not included in Part III) (see instructions) .	13		21	Repairs and maintenance .	21
				22	Supplies (not included in Part III) .	22
				23	Taxes and licenses .	23
				24	Travel and meals:	
14	Employee benefit programs (other than on line 19) .	14		a	Travel .	24a
15	Insurance (other than health)	15		b	Deductible meals (see instructions) .	24b
16	Interest (see instructions):			25	Utilities .	25
a	Mortgage (paid to banks, etc.)	16a		26	Wages (less employment credits)	26
b	Other .	16b		27a	Other expenses (from line 48) .	27a
17	Legal and professional services	17		b	**Reserved for future use** .	27b

28	**Total expenses** before expenses for business use of home. Add lines 8 through 27a .	28
29	Tentative profit or (loss). Subtract line 28 from line 7 .	29
30	Expenses for business use of your home. Do not report these expenses elsewhere. Attach Form 8829 unless using the simplified method. See instructions. **Simplified method filers only:** Enter the total square footage of (a) your home: _____ and (b) the part of your home used for business: _____ . Use the Simplified Method Worksheet in the instructions to figure the amount to enter on line 30 .	30
31	**Net profit or (loss).** Subtract line 30 from line 29. • If a profit, enter on both **Schedule 1 (Form 1040), line 3,** and on **Schedule SE, line 2.** (If you checked the box on line 1, see instructions.) Estates and trusts, enter on **Form 1041, line 3.** • If a loss, you **must** go to line 32.	31
32	If you have a loss, check the box that describes your investment in this activity. See instructions. • If you checked 32a, enter the loss on both **Schedule 1 (Form 1040), line 3,** and on **Schedule SE, line 2.** (If you checked the box on line 1, see the line 31 instructions.) Estates and trusts, enter on **Form 1041, line 3.** • If you checked 32b, you **must** attach **Form 6198.** Your loss may be limited.	32a ☐ All investment is at risk. 32b ☐ Some investment is not at risk.

For Paperwork Reduction Act Notice, see the separate instructions.   Cat. No. 11334P   Schedule C (Form 1040) 2022

(Use for Cumulative Problem 2.)

Schedule C (Form 1040) 2022 · · · · · · · · · · · Page **2**

Part III　**Cost of Goods Sold** (see instructions)

33　Method(s) used to value closing inventory:　**a** ☐ Cost　**b** ☐ Lower of cost or market　**c** ☐ Other (attach explanation)

34　Was there any change in determining quantities, costs, or valuations between opening and closing inventory? If "Yes," attach explanation . . . . ☐ Yes　☐ No

35　Inventory at beginning of year. If different from last year's closing inventory, attach explanation . . | **35** |

36　Purchases less cost of items withdrawn for personal use . . . . | **36** |

37　Cost of labor. Do not include any amounts paid to yourself . . . . | **37** |

38　Materials and supplies . . . . | **38** |

39　Other costs . . . . | **39** |

40　Add lines 35 through 39 . . . . | **40** |

41　Inventory at end of year . . . . | **41** |

42　**Cost of goods sold.** Subtract line 41 from line 40. Enter the result here and on line 4 . . . . . . | **42** |

Part IV　**Information on Your Vehicle.** Complete this part **only** if you are claiming car or truck expenses on line 9 and are not required to file Form 4562 for this business. See the instructions for line 13 to find out if you must file Form 4562.

43　When did you place your vehicle in service for business purposes? (month/day/year) ____/____/____

44　Of the total number of miles you drove your vehicle during 2022, enter the number of miles you used your vehicle for:

a　Business _____　**b** Commuting (see instructions) _____　**c** Other _____

45　Was your vehicle available for personal use during off-duty hours? . . . . ☐ Yes　☐ No

46　Do you (or your spouse) have another vehicle available for personal use? . . . . ☐ Yes　☐ No

47a　Do you have evidence to support your deduction? . . . . ☐ Yes　☐ No

b　If "Yes," is the evidence written? . . . . ☐ Yes　☐ No

Part V　**Other Expenses.** List below business expenses not included on lines 8–26 or line 30.

48　**Total other expenses.** Enter here and on line 27a . . . . | **48** |

(Use for Cumulative Problem 2.)

SCHEDULE SE
(Form 1040)

Department of the Treasury
Internal Revenue Service

Self-Employment Tax

Go to *www.irs.gov/ScheduleSE* for instructions and the latest information.

Attach to Form 1040, 1040-SR, or 1040-NR.

OMB No. 1545-0074

2022

Attachment
Sequence No. **17**

Name of person with self-employment income (as shown on Form 1040, 1040-SR, or 1040-NR)

Social security number of person with **self-employment** income

Part I   Self-Employment Tax

Note: If your only income subject to self-employment tax is **church employee income**, see instructions for how to report your income and the definition of church employee income.

A	If you are a minister, member of a religious order, or Christian Science practitioner **and** you filed Form 4361, but you had $400 or more of **other** net earnings from self-employment, check here and continue with Part I . . . . ☐	

Skip lines 1a and 1b if you use the farm optional method in Part II. See instructions.

1a	Net farm profit or (loss) from Schedule F, line 34, and farm partnerships, Schedule K-1 (Form 1065), box 14, code A	**1a**	
b	If you received social security retirement or disability benefits, enter the amount of Conservation Reserve Program payments included on Schedule F, line 4b, or listed on Schedule K-1 (Form 1065), box 20, code AH	**1b**	( )

Skip line 2 if you use the nonfarm optional method in Part II. See instructions.

2	Net profit or (loss) from Schedule C, line 31; and Schedule K-1 (Form 1065), box 14, code A (other than farming). See instructions for other income to report or if you are a minister or member of a religious order	**2**	
3	Combine lines 1a, 1b, and 2	**3**	
4a	If line 3 is more than zero, multiply line 3 by 92.35% (0.9235). Otherwise, enter amount from line 3 .	**4a**	
	Note: If line 4a is less than $400 due to Conservation Reserve Program payments on line 1b, see instructions.		
b	If you elect one or both of the optional methods, enter the total of lines 15 and 17 here	**4b**	
c	Combine lines 4a and 4b. If less than $400, **stop**; you don't owe self-employment tax. **Exception:** If less than $400 and you had **church employee income**, enter -0- and continue	**4c**	
5a	Enter your **church employee income** from Form W-2. See instructions for definition of church employee income **5a**		
b	Multiply line 5a by 92.35% (0.9235). If less than $100, enter -0-	**5b**	
6	Add lines 4c and 5b	**6**	
7	Maximum amount of combined wages and self-employment earnings subject to social security tax or the 6.2% portion of the 7.65% railroad retirement (tier 1) tax for 2022	**7**	147,000
8a	Total social security wages and tips (total of boxes 3 and 7 on Form(s) W-2) and railroad retirement (tier 1) compensation. If $147,000 or more, skip lines 8b through 10, and go to line 11 **8a**		
b	Unreported tips subject to social security tax from Form 4137, line 10 . . . **8b**		
c	Wages subject to social security tax from Form 8919, line 10 . . . . . . **8c**		
d	Add lines 8a, 8b, and 8c	**8d**	
9	Subtract line 8d from line 7. If zero or less, enter -0- here and on line 10 and go to line 11	**9**	
10	Multiply the **smaller** of line 6 or line 9 by 12.4% (0.124)	**10**	
11	Multiply line 6 by 2.9% (0.029)	**11**	
12	**Self-employment tax.** Add lines 10 and 11. Enter here and on **Schedule 2 (Form 1040), line 4** . .	**12**	
13	**Deduction for one-half of self-employment tax.** Multiply line 12 by 50% (0.50). Enter here and on **Schedule 1 (Form 1040), line 15** **13**		

Part II   Optional Methods To Figure Net Earnings (see instructions)

Farm Optional Method. You may use this method **only** if (a) your gross farm income[1] wasn't more than $9,060, **or (b)** your net farm profits[2] were less than $6,540.

14	Maximum income for optional methods	**14**	6,040
15	Enter the **smaller** of: two-thirds (2/3) of gross farm income[1] (not less than zero) **or** $6,040. Also, include this amount on line 4b above	**15**	

Nonfarm Optional Method. You may use this method **only** if (a) your net nonfarm profits[3] were less than $6,540 and also less than 72.189% of your gross nonfarm income,[4] **and (b)** you had net earnings from self-employment of at least $400 in 2 of the prior 3 years. **Caution:** You may use this method no more than five times.

16	Subtract line 15 from line 14	**16**	
17	Enter the **smaller** of: two-thirds (2/3) of gross nonfarm income[4] (not less than zero) **or** the amount on line 16. Also, include this amount on line 4b above	**17**	

[1] From Sch. F, line 9; and Sch. K-1 (Form 1065), box 14, code B.

[2] From Sch. F, line 34; and Sch. K-1 (Form 1065), box 14, code A—minus the amount you would have entered on line 1b had you not used the optional method.

[3] From Sch. C, line 31; and Sch. K-1 (Form 1065), box 14, code A.

[4] From Sch. C, line 7; and Sch. K-1 (Form 1065), box 14, code C.

For Paperwork Reduction Act Notice, see your tax return instructions.   Cat. No. 11358Z   Schedule SE (Form 1040) 2022

(Use for Cumulative Problem 2.)

Form **4562**	**Depreciation and Amortization**	OMB No. 1545-0172
Department of the Treasury Internal Revenue Service	**(Including Information on Listed Property)** Attach to your tax return. Go to *www.irs.gov/Form4562* for instructions and the latest information.	**2022** Attachment Sequence No. **179**

Name(s) shown on return	Business or activity to which this form relates	Identifying number

Part I **Election To Expense Certain Property Under Section 179**
Note: If you have any listed property, complete Part V before you complete Part I.

1	Maximum amount (see instructions)	**1**	
2	Total cost of section 179 property placed in service (see instructions)	**2**	
3	Threshold cost of section 179 property before reduction in limitation (see instructions)	**3**	
4	Reduction in limitation. Subtract line 3 from line 2. If zero or less, enter -0-	**4**	
5	Dollar limitation for tax year. Subtract line 4 from line 1. If zero or less, enter -0-. If married filing separately, see instructions	**5**	

6	(a) Description of property	(b) Cost (business use only)	(c) Elected cost

7	Listed property. Enter the amount from line 29	**7**	
8	Total elected cost of section 179 property. Add amounts in column (c), lines 6 and 7	**8**	
9	Tentative deduction. Enter the **smaller** of line 5 or line 8	**9**	
10	Carryover of disallowed deduction from line 13 of your 2021 Form 4562 . . .	**10**	
11	Business income limitation. Enter the smaller of business income (not less than zero) or line 5. See instructions	**11**	
12	Section 179 expense deduction. Add lines 9 and 10, but don't enter more than line 11	**12**	
13	Carryover of disallowed deduction to 2023. Add lines 9 and 10, less line 12 .	**13**	

Note: Don't use Part II or Part III below for listed property. Instead, use Part V.

Part II **Special Depreciation Allowance and Other Depreciation (Don't include listed property. See instructions.)**

14	Special depreciation allowance for qualified property (other than listed property) placed in service during the tax year. See instructions	**14**	
15	Property subject to section 168(f)(1) election	**15**	
16	Other depreciation (including ACRS)	**16**	

Part III **MACRS Depreciation (Don't include listed property. See instructions.)**

Section A

17	MACRS deductions for assets placed in service in tax years beginning before 2022	**17**	
18	If you are electing to group any assets placed in service during the tax year into one or more general asset accounts, check here . . . . ☐		

Section B—Assets Placed in Service During 2022 Tax Year Using the General Depreciation System

(a) Classification of property	(b) Month and year placed in service	(c) Basis for depreciation (business/investment use only—see instructions)	(d) Recovery period	(e) Convention	(f) Method	(g) Depreciation deduction
19a 3-year property						
b 5-year property						
c 7-year property						
d 10-year property						
e 15-year property						
f 20-year property						
g 25-year property			25 yrs.		S/L	
h Residential rental property			27.5 yrs.	MM	S/L	
			27.5 yrs.	MM	S/L	
i Nonresidential real property			39 yrs.	MM	S/L	
				MM	S/L	

Section C—Assets Placed in Service During 2022 Tax Year Using the Alternative Depreciation System

20a Class life					S/L	
b 12-year			12 yrs.		S/L	
c 30-year			30 yrs.	MM	S/L	
d 40-year			40 yrs.	MM	S/L	

Part IV **Summary (See instructions.)**

21	Listed property. Enter amount from line 28	**21**	
22	**Total.** Add amounts from line 12, lines 14 through 17, lines 19 and 20 in column (g), and line 21. Enter here and on the appropriate lines of your return. Partnerships and S corporations—see instructions .	**22**	
23	For assets shown above and placed in service during the current year, enter the portion of the basis attributable to section 263A costs	**23**	

For Paperwork Reduction Act Notice, see separate instructions.   Cat. No. 12906N   Form **4562** (2022)

(Use for Cumulative Problem 2.)

Form 4562 (2022)   Page **2**

Part V   **Listed Property**   (Include automobiles, certain other vehicles, certain aircraft, and property used for entertainment, recreation, or amusement.)

Note: For any vehicle for which you are using the standard mileage rate or deducting lease expense, complete **only** 24a, 24b, columns (a) through (c) of Section A, all of Section B, and Section C if applicable.

Section A—Depreciation and Other Information (Caution: See the instructions for limits for passenger automobiles.**)**

24a Do you have evidence to support the business/investment use claimed? ☐ **Yes** ☐ **No** | **24b** If "Yes," is the evidence written? ☐ **Yes** ☐ **No**

(a) Type of property (list vehicles first)	(b) Date placed in service	(c) Business/ investment use percentage	(d) Cost or other basis	(e) Basis for depreciation (business/investment use only)	(f) Recovery period	(g) Method/ Convention	(h) Depreciation deduction	(i) Elected section 179 cost
25 Special depreciation allowance for qualified listed property placed in service during the tax year and used more than 50% in a qualified business use. See instructions .				**25**				
26 Property used more than 50% in a qualified business use:								
		%						
		%						
		%						
27 Property used 50% or less in a qualified business use:								
		%				S/L –		
		%				S/L –		
		%				S/L –		
28 Add amounts in column (h), lines 25 through 27. Enter here and on line 21, page 1 .						**28**		
29 Add amounts in column (i), line 26. Enter here and on line 7, page 1							**29**	

Section B—Information on Use of Vehicles

Complete this section for vehicles used by a sole proprietor, partner, or other "more than 5% owner," or related person. If you provided vehicles to your employees, first answer the questions in Section C to see if you meet an exception to completing this section for those vehicles.

	(a) Vehicle 1		(b) Vehicle 2		(c) Vehicle 3		(d) Vehicle 4		(e) Vehicle 5		(f) Vehicle 6	
30 Total business/investment miles driven during the year (**don't** include commuting miles) .												
31 Total commuting miles driven during the year												
32 Total other personal (noncommuting) miles driven												
33 Total miles driven during the year. Add lines 30 through 32												
34 Was the vehicle available for personal use during off-duty hours?	Yes	No	Yes	No	Yes	No	Yes	No	Yes	No	Yes	No
35 Was the vehicle used primarily by a more than 5% owner or related person? . .												
36 Is another vehicle available for personal use?												

Section C—Questions for Employers Who Provide Vehicles for Use by Their Employees

Answer these questions to determine if you meet an exception to completing Section B for vehicles used by employees who **aren't** more than 5% owners or related persons. See instructions.

	Yes	No
37 Do you maintain a written policy statement that prohibits all personal use of vehicles, including commuting, by your employees?		
38 Do you maintain a written policy statement that prohibits personal use of vehicles, except commuting, by your employees? See the instructions for vehicles used by corporate officers, directors, or 1% or more owners . .		
39 Do you treat all use of vehicles by employees as personal use?		
40 Do you provide more than five vehicles to your employees, obtain information from your employees about the use of the vehicles, and retain the information received?		
41 Do you meet the requirements concerning qualified automobile demonstration use? See instructions		

Note: If your answer to 37, 38, 39, 40, or 41 is "Yes," don't complete Section B for the covered vehicles.

Part VI   **Amortization**

(a) Description of costs	(b) Date amortization begins	(c) Amortizable amount	(d) Code section	(e) Amortization period or percentage	(f) Amortization for this year
42 Amortization of costs that begins during your 2022 tax year (see instructions):					
43 Amortization of costs that began before your 2022 tax year				**43**	
44 **Total.** Add amounts in column (f). See the instructions for where to report				**44**	

Form **4562** (2022)

(Use for Cumulative Problem 2.)

Form 8880

Department of the Treasury
Internal Revenue Service

Credit for Qualified Retirement Savings Contributions

Attach to Form 1040, 1040-SR, or 1040-NR.
Go to *www.irs.gov/Form8880* for the latest information.

OMB No. 1545-0074

2022

Attachment Sequence No. **54**

Name(s) shown on return

Your social security number

⚠️ **CAUTION**

You **cannot** take this credit if **either** of the following applies.

- The amount on Form 1040, 1040-SR, or 1040-NR, line 11, is more than $34,000 ($51,000 if head of household; $68,000 if married filing jointly).
- The person(s) who made the qualified contribution or elective deferral **(a)** was born after January 1, 2005; **(b)** is claimed as a dependent on someone else's 2022 tax return; or **(c)** was a **student** (see instructions).

		(a) You	(b) Your spouse
1	Traditional and Roth IRA contributions, and ABLE account contributions by the designated beneficiary for 2022. **Do not** include rollover contributions . . . **1**		
2	Elective deferrals to a 401(k) or other qualified employer plan, voluntary employee contributions, and 501(c)(18)(D) plan contributions for 2022 (see instructions) **2**		
3	Add lines 1 and 2 . . . . **3**		
4	Certain distributions received **after** 2019 and **before** the due date (including extensions) of your 2022 tax return (see instructions). If married filing jointly, include **both** spouses' amounts in **both** columns. See instructions for an exception **4**		
5	Subtract line 4 from line 3. If zero or less, enter -0- **5**		
6	In each column, enter the **smaller** of line 5 or $2,000 . . . . **6**		

7 Add the amounts on line 6. If zero, **stop**; you can't take this credit **7**

8 Enter the amount from Form 1040, 1040-SR, or 1040-NR, line 11* **8**

9 Enter the applicable decimal amount from the table below.

If line 8 is—		And your filing status is—		
Over—	But not over—	Married filing jointly	Head of household	Single, Married filing separately, or Qualifying widow(er)
		Enter on line 9—		
---	$20,500	0.5	0.5	0.5
$20,500	$22,000	0.5	0.5	0.2
$22,000	$30,750	0.5	0.5	0.1
$30,750	$33,000	0.5	0.2	0.1
$33,000	$34,000	0.5	0.1	0.1
$34,000	$41,000	0.5	0.1	0.0
$41,000	$44,000	0.2	0.1	0.0
$44,000	$51,000	0.1	0.1	0.0
$51,000	$68,000	0.1	0.0	0.0
$68,000	---	0.0	0.0	0.0

9 x 0.

Note: If line 9 is zero, **stop**; you can't take this credit.

10 Multiply line 7 by line 9 . . . . **10**

11 Limitation based on tax liability. Enter the amount from the Credit Limit Worksheet in the instructions **11**

12 **Credit for qualified retirement savings contributions.** Enter the **smaller** of line 10 or line 11 here and on Schedule 3 (Form 1040), line 4 . . . . **12**

* See Pub. 590-A for the amount to enter if you claim any exclusion or deduction for foreign earned income, foreign housing, or income from Puerto Rico or for bona fide residents of American Samoa.

For Paperwork Reduction Act Notice, see your tax return instructions.   Cat. No. 33394D   Form **8880** (2022)

(Use for Cumulative Problem 2.)

Form **8995**	**Qualified Business Income Deduction** **Simplified Computation** Attach to your tax return. Go to *www.irs.gov/Form8995* for instructions and the latest information.	OMB No. 1545-2294 **2022** Attachment Sequence No. **55**
Department of the Treasury Internal Revenue Service		

Name(s) shown on return	Your taxpayer identification number

Note. You can claim the qualified business income deduction **only** if you have qualified business income from a qualified trade or business, real estate investment trust dividends, publicly traded partnership income, or a domestic production activities deduction passed through from an agricultural or horticultural cooperative. See instructions.
Use this form if your taxable income, before your qualified business income deduction, is at or below $170,050 ($340,100 if married filing jointly), and you aren't a patron of an agricultural or horticultural cooperative.

1	**(a)** Trade, business, or aggregation name	**(b)** Taxpayer identification number	**(c)** Qualified business income or (loss)
i			
ii			
iii			
iv			
v			

2	Total qualified business income or (loss). Combine lines 1i through 1v, column (c)	**2**	
3	Qualified business net (loss) carryforward from the prior year	**3** ( )	
4	Total qualified business income. Combine lines 2 and 3. If zero or less, enter -0-	**4**	
5	Qualified business income component. Multiply line 4 by 20% (0.20)		**5**
6	Qualified REIT dividends and publicly traded partnership (PTP) income or (loss) (see instructions)	**6**	
7	Qualified REIT dividends and qualified PTP (loss) carryforward from the prior year	**7** ( )	
8	Total qualified REIT dividends and PTP income. Combine lines 6 and 7. If zero or less, enter -0-	**8**	
9	REIT and PTP component. Multiply line 8 by 20% (0.20)		**9**
10	Qualified business income deduction before the income limitation. Add lines 5 and 9		**10**
11	Taxable income before qualified business income deduction (see instructions)	**11**	
12	Net capital gain (see instructions)	**12**	
13	Subtract line 12 from line 11. If zero or less, enter -0-	**13**	
14	Income limitation. Multiply line 13 by 20% (0.20)		**14**
15	Qualified business income deduction. Enter the smaller of line 10 or line 14. Also enter this amount on the applicable line of your return (see instructions)		**15**
16	Total qualified business (loss) carryforward. Combine lines 2 and 3. If greater than zero, enter -0- . .		**16** ( )
17	Total qualified REIT dividends and PTP (loss) carryforward. Combine lines 6 and 7. If greater than zero, enter -0-		**17** ( )

For Privacy Act and Paperwork Reduction Act Notice, see instructions.	Cat. No. 37806C	Form **8995** (2022)

Chapter

9

Rental Activities

CHAPTER CONTENTS

LEARNING OBJECTIVES

After completing Chapter 9, you should be able to:

1. Compute the amount of rental income and expenses reported in the calculation of taxable income.
2. Determine the amount of expenses taxpayers can deduct against rental income when renting out a vacation home.
3. Understand how the at-risk and passive activity loss rules may limit the taxpayer's deductions in the current year and compute any carryover to future tax years.
4. Prepare Schedule E and Form 8582.

CHAPTER OVERVIEW

In addition to earning income from their jobs, many individuals earn income from property they own. For instance, taxpayers who own stocks often earn dividend income. Likewise, those who own bonds earn interest income. Taxpayers also can earn income by renting out property that they own. Chapters 3 and 4 described the tax rules for reporting interest and dividend income. This chapter focuses on the income and expenses from rental activities. Taxpayers report rental income and expenses on Schedule E (Form 1040), Supplemental Income and Loss. However, in cases where rental expenses exceed rental income, the vacation home rules, at-risk rules, or passive loss rules may limit the losses taxpayers can deduct on Form 1040. The chapter begins with a discussion of rental income and expenses. The focus then shifts to the areas of the tax law that may limit deductions for losses from rental activities.

¶901   Rental Income and Expenses

Although taxpayers can rent both personal and real property, this chapter focuses on the tax aspects of owning residential rental property. **Residential rental property** is rental property where at least 80% of the income comes from the rental of dwelling units. A **dwelling unit** is property that provides the basic living accommodations—kitchen, sleeping, and toilet facilities. Examples of dwelling units include houses, apartments, condominiums, mobile homes, motor homes, yachts, and boats. Hotels, motels, and similar establishments are not considered dwelling units.

¶901.01   RENTAL INCOME

Rental income includes the payments taxpayers receive for allowing others to use or occupy their property. Usually rent payments are received in cash. However, when a tenant performs services in exchange for the use of the taxpayer's property, rental income includes the value of those services. Rental income includes payments a tenant makes to cancel a lease. It also includes the value of improvements a tenant makes to the taxpayer's property in place of rent.

EXAMPLE 1	Brent rents property he owns to a tenant for $500 a month. In November, the tenant installs a ceiling fan valued at $100. Brent reduces the tenant's December rent by $100. Brent's rental income equals $6,000 ($500 × 11 months + $400 for December + $100 improvement in lieu of rent). Brent then capitalizes and depreciates the ceiling fan.

Cash basis taxpayers report rental income in the year they receive it, even when it applies to a prior or future tax year. Accrual basis taxpayers usually report rental income in the year it is due to them, but must report rent received in advance in the year they receive it. Therefore, if on December 26, 20x1, the taxpayer receives $600 from a tenant for January 20x2 rent, the $600 would be reported as rental income in 20x1 under both the cash and accrual methods.

A security deposit is considered rent received in advance when the deposit represents the tenant's final rent payment. It is not considered rent received in advance if the taxpayer intends to return the deposit at the end of the lease. However, should the tenant forfeit any part of the deposit in a future year (for example, to cover late charges), the forfeited amount is rental income to the taxpayer in the year the tenant forfeits it.

EXAMPLE 2	Connie enters into a 5-year lease to rent property she owns. On July 1, 20x1, Connie receives $6,000 for the first year's rent and $6,000 of rent in advance for the final year of the lease. Connie also receives a $1,000 security deposit that she intends to return to the tenant at the end of the lease. Connie's 20x1 rental income equals $12,000, regardless of whether she uses the cash or accrual method of accounting.

¶901.02   RENTAL EXPENSES

Taxpayers can deduct against rental income all ordinary expenses related to the rental property. Examples of common rental expenses include advertising, cleaning, utilities, real estate taxes, mortgage interest, insurance premiums, management fees, and necessary travel and transportation. Other rental expenses include repairs, maintenance, and depreciation. Accrual basis taxpayers take deductions in the year that services are received, or assets are used. Cash basis taxpayers deduct rental expenses in the year the expenses are paid, except for prepaid expenses, which are spread over the periods benefited.

Repairs and maintenance keep rental property in good operating condition. Examples include painting the property (both inside and out), fixing a leak, and repairing a screen. Taxpayers deduct the costs of repairs and maintenance to rental property as a rental expense. Repairs are different from improvements, which are costs that add value to the property or prolong its useful life. Examples include adding a bathroom, installing new appliances, or replacing the roof. Taxpayers recover the cost of improvements through annual depreciation deductions.

Improvements made to residential rental property are depreciated using the straight-line method over 27.5 years (MACRS) or 30 years (ADS). Taxpayers use MACRS or ADS to depreciate rental furnishings. These include furniture, appliances, and carpeting. Bonus depreciation is allowed in the first year on new rental furnishings placed in service during a year in which bonus depreciation is allowed. If MACRS is used, rental furnishings are 5-year property. If ADS is elected, the furnishings have a nine-year recovery period (see ¶802.04 for more on ADS).

Often, telling the difference between a repair and an improvement is easy. For example, fixing a leaky roof is a repair; replacing the roof is an improvement. However, sometimes it is difficult to draw the line where an expense becomes an improvement instead of a repair. For example, when a major leak in the roof results in having to replace a large portion of the roof, the question becomes whether the cost to replace part of the roof is a deductible expense or something that must be depreciated.

The IRS has taken some of the guesswork out of this question by issuing final "repairs regs" that can be used by smaller taxpayers. [Reg. §1.263(a)-3] Under the repair regs, taxpayers can use a *de minimis* rule to expense items costing $2,500 or less ($5,000 if they have "applicable financial statements," which in essence, are audited financial statements). Small taxpayers are those who either (1) have assets (at the beginning of the year) that do not exceed $10 million, or (2) had no more than $10 million in annual gross receipts for each distinct business they own for the past three years.

The repair regs also allows certain landlords to use a safe harbor to deduct costs that otherwise might be considered improvements. The safe harbor rules can only be used as long as the unadjusted basis of the building (original cost-plus improvements) does not exceed $1 million. The $1 million limit is applied to each rental building the landlord owns. Also, the safe harbor rules can be used only if the cost does exceed the *lesser of* (i) $10,000, or (ii) 2% of the unadjusted basis of the building. The $10,000/2% limit is applied separately to each building. Thus, if the taxpayer owns four rental properties (each with an unadjusted basis of $1 million or less), depending on the amount of expenses incurred for each building, the taxpayer may be able to use the safe harbor rule to expense all of the expenses for some of the buildings, but not others.

Taxpayers wanting to take advantage of either the *de minimis* or safe harbor rules must attach an election stating their intent to a timely filed tax return. Once an election is made, it cannot be revoked.

| EXAMPLE 3 | Vince rents out a condo that he once used as his main home. Vince's unadjusted basis in the home is $80,000. During the year, Vince paid $200 to replace a screen door and $1,000 to replace the furnace. Vince can use the safe harbor under the repair regs because his unadjusted basis in the home does not exceed $1 million, and the $1,200 he spent during the year does not exceed $1,600 ($80,000 × 2%). By attaching a statement to his return that he intends to use the safe harbor to deduct the entire $1,200 as a rental expense, Vince does not have to worry about whether any of the costs might instead be considered an improvement, rather than a repair. |

¶901.03   SPECIAL RULES WHEN ONLY PART OF THE PROPERTY IS RENTED

The rules just described assume that the rental property is used exclusively by or is available for use by rent-paying tenants. Sometimes, an individual rents only part of the property, as is the case when an owner of a duplex rents one unit and lives in the other. In such instances, the taxpayer must allocate expenses between rental and personal use. The taxpayer then deducts the rental portion of each expense against rental income and can deduct the personal portion of the mortgage interest and real estate taxes as itemized deductions.

Some expenses are easy to split between rental and personal use. For example, taxpayers can fully deduct the cost of repairs performed on rental units but cannot deduct the cost to repair their own personal units. Other expenses, like real estate taxes and depreciation, are harder to divide between rental and personal use. For these expenses, taxpayers can use any reasonable method to divide expenses between the two uses. The number of rooms or the relative square footage are two widely used methods for allocating these types of expenses.

EXAMPLE 4	Marvin rents one room in his home. The area of the rented room is 140 square feet. The area of the entire home is 1,400 square feet. Marvin deducts against rental income 10% (140/1,400) of the expenses related to the home during the year. Thus, if Marvin's real estate taxes are $2,000, he can deduct $200 against rental income and the rest ($1,800) as an itemized deduction. The itemized portion is subject to the $10,000 cap on all taxes claimed as itemized deductions. The $200 allocated to rental is not subject to this cap.

¶901.04   CONVERTING A PERSONAL HOME TO RENTAL USE

When taxpayers convert a personal home to rental property, they must divide the expenses from the conversion year between the two uses. Rental use begins when the property is first offered for rent. Taxpayers deduct the rental portion of these expenses against rental income. They can deduct the personal portion of the mortgage interest and real estate taxes up to $10,000 as itemized deductions. (See ¶504.02 for more on the deductibility of real estate taxes.) For depreciation purposes, the basis is the lesser of the cost of the building or the fair market value of the building on the date that business use commences. [Reg. §1.167(g)-1]

EXAMPLE 5	In September, Sylvia moved out of her home. Sylvia listed her home for rent on October 1, and on November 1, she entered into a two-year lease. Sylvia can deduct 25% (October–December) of the annual expenses (real estate taxes, insurance, depreciation) against the rental income she receives during the year. She also can deduct any other expenses (mortgage interest, utilities, etc.) allocated to the last three months of the year. Sylvia can deduct the personal portion (75%) of the interest and taxes as itemized deductions.

¶902   Rental of Vacation Homes

Special rules apply when taxpayers rent out their homes for part of the year and personally use the property during other parts of the year. The tax treatment of this type of rental activity depends on the number of rental and personal days during the year.

¶902.01   PROPERTY RENTED LESS THAN 15 DAYS

When individual taxpayers rent their main homes or vacation homes for less than 15 days during the year, they do not report the rental income and do not deduct any rental expenses. [I.R.C. §280A(d)(1)(A)] However, home mortgage interest (but only for the taxpayer's main home or second home), real estate taxes (up to $10,000 total for all properties), and casualty losses may be deducted as itemized deductions. (See ¶504.02 for more on the deductibility of real estate taxes.)

EXAMPLE 6	

Benton rents his vacation home for 12 days during the year and personally uses it for 80 days. The rest of the year the home sits vacant. Benton collects rents of $3,000 and incurs the following expenses.

Home mortgage interest	$ 6,000
Real estate taxes	1,800
Utilities	400
Depreciation	2,000
Total expenses	$10,200

Since Benton rents the property for less than 15 days, he does not report the $3,000 of rental income. Benton can deduct as itemized deductions the $6,000 of home mortgage interest (as his second home) and the $1,800 of real estate taxes.

¶902.02　PROPERTY RENTED MORE THAN 14 DAYS

Taxpayers who rent their main homes or vacation homes for more than 14 days during the year report the rental income on their personal tax returns. Expenses related solely to rental activities (like advertising or commissions) can be deducted against rental income. All other expenses must be allocated between rental and personal use. Taxpayers can then deduct the rental portion of these the expenses.

The Internal Revenue Code (Code) requires taxpayers to allocate expenses other than interest, taxes, and casualty losses on the basis of the days the property is used during the year. [I.R.C. §280A(e)(1)] To compute the rental portion of expenses like utilities, repairs, and depreciation, taxpayers multiply the expense by the ratio of the number of days rented for a fair rental price to the number of days of use during the year.

$$\text{Percent allocated to rental activity} \ = \ \frac{\text{Number of fair rental days}}{\text{Number of days used during the year}}$$

The Code does not address how to allocate interest, taxes, and casualty losses between rental and personal use. In IRS Publication 527, the IRS suggests that taxpayers use the same method used to allocate other expenses. The courts, however, have allowed interest and taxes to be allocated based on the days rented to the number of days in the year. For purposes of this chapter, the same ratio (days rented/days used) is used to allocate all expenses between rental and personal use.

EXAMPLE 7	

Wally rents out his vacation home for 120 days during the year. He personally uses it for 80 days. Wally collects rents of $12,000 and incurs the following expenses.

Home mortgage interest	$ 8,000
Real estate taxes	2,500
Utilities	800
Depreciation	3,000
Total expenses	$14,300

Wally allocates 60% of the expenses (120 rental days/200 total days used during the year) to rental use. He deducts $8,580 ($14,300 × 60%) as rental expense. Wally can potentially deduct the rest of the real estate taxes ($2,500 × 40% = $1,000) as an itemized deduction (see ¶504.02 for more on the deductibility of real estate taxes). He may be able to deduct the rest of the home mortgage interest ($8,000 × 40% = $3,200) if the home is selected as Wally's second home.

A rental day is any day the taxpayer rents the property for a fair rental price, even if rented to a friend or relative. Days that the property is offered for rental, but not actually rented, do not count as days rented at a fair rental price.

> **What Is a Fair Rental Price?**
>
> A fair rental price is the amount of rent that an *unrelated person* would be willing to pay to use the property. If the rent charged is substantially less than the rents received on *similar* properties, it might not be considered a fair rental price. The following questions can be used to determine whether two properties are *similar:*
>
> ■ Are the properties used for the same purpose?
>
> ■ Are the properties about the same size?
>
> ■ Are the properties in about the same condition?
>
> ■ Do the properties have similar furnishings?
>
> ■ Are the properties in similar locations?
>
> Generally, answering "No" to any of these questions means that the two properties are not similar.

Expenses Limited for Certain Vacation Homes

When the property is considered a "residence," rental expenses are deductible only to the extent of rental income. Disallowed expenses carry over to offset rental income in future tax years. A vacation home qualifies as a **residence** if the number of personal days exceeds the *greater of* (i) 14 days or (ii) 10% of the fair rental days. Thus, if the taxpayer's personal days exceed *both* (i) 14 days and (ii) 10% of the number of fair rental days, then the property is considered a residence. When the property is treated as a residence, the personal portion of the mortgage interest can be deducted as an itemized deduction if the property is chosen as the taxpayer's second home. When the property does not qualify as a residence, the personal portion of the interest cannot be deducted.

In order to properly determine whether the taxpayer's home qualifies as a residence, it is important to understand what days count as personal days. Personal use includes days when the taxpayer donates use of the property to a charitable organization. Personal use also includes days when the property is used by:

1. The owner, unless the owner is working full-time to repair or maintain the property.
2. A member of an owner's family, unless the family member pays a fair rental price **and** the family member uses the property as his or her main home. Family members include siblings (brothers and sisters), ancestors (parents, grandparents, etc.), and lineal descendants (children, grandchildren, etc.).
3. Anyone who has a reciprocal agreement that allows the owner to use some other dwelling unit (e.g., home exchanges).
4. Anyone who pays less than a fair rental price to use the property.

EXAMPLE 8

> Ella owns a house that she rents to her son. The son pays a fair rental price to use the house as his main home. Ella does not consider the son's use of the house personal days since the son is paying a fair rental price to use the house as his main home.

EXAMPLE 9

June and Jay Linden own a vacation home that they personally use 24 days during the year. During part of the year, the following occupants used the home. The home was vacant during the rest of the year. Fair rental price is $125 a night.

Occupant	Number of Days
June's parents, who pay no rent	32
Friends of the Lindens, who paid rent of $2,000	40
Jay's brother, who paid rent of $875	7
Unrelated persons, who paid rent of $7,500	60

The 60 days the home was used by unrelated persons are not personal days, since the tenants paid $125 a night (fair rental price). Although Jay's brother paid a fair rental price, his seven days count as personal days since he is a family member and he did not use the home as his main home. The parents did not pay a fair rental price, nor did they use the home as their main home. Thus, their 32 days count as personal days. The 40 days that the home is used by the Lindens' friends count as personal days since they did not pay a fair rental price to use the home. The Lindens' total personal days equal 103 (24 + 32 + 40 + 7). Since the 103 personal days exceed both 14 days and 6.7 days (10% of the 67 fair rental days), the vacation home qualifies as a residence. Thus, rental expenses will be limited to rental income.

EXAMPLE 10

Same facts as in Example 9, except that five of the days the Linden spent at the vacation home were spent making repairs to the property. These five days no longer count as personal days. The Lindens' personal days are reduced to 98 (103 – 5). However, the home still qualifies as a residence.

EXAMPLE 11

Bruce rents his vacation home for 200 days during the year. On 40 of the 200 days, Bruce's sister paid a fair rental price to use the house. The other 160 days also were rented at a fair rental price. Bruce treats the days his sister rents the house as personal days, since she is a relative and does not use the house as her main home. The 40 personal days exceed the *greater of* (i) 14 days, or (ii) 10% of the 200 fair rental days. Thus, the vacation home qualifies as a residence. Accordingly, even though 100% of the rental expenses are deductible (since all 200 days the home was used during the year were rented at a fair rental price), Bruce can only deduct the rental expenses to the extent of rental income.

EXAMPLE 12

From June 1 through October 31 (153 days), Denise rents her cabin (used as a vacation home) and receives a fair rental price. Denise uses the cabin five days during the year. Denise's parents stayed at the cabin for 12 days in May. In deciding whether the cabin qualifies as a residence, personal days include days the parents used the cabin (12 days). Thus, the total number of personal days equals 17 (5 + 12).

Denise treats the cabin as a residence since her 17 personal days exceed the *greater of* (i) 14 days or (ii) 15.3 days (10% of the 153 days rented at fair rental). Thus, Denise can deduct the rental portion of the expenses on the cabin only to the extent of rental income. She carries over any excess rental expense to the next year. In allocating expenses between rental and personal use, Denise allocates 90% (153 rental days/170 days used) of the expenses to the rental activity.

Because the cabin qualifies as a residence, Denise can deduct the personal portion of the mortgage interest (10%) as an itemized deduction if she selects the cabin as her second home. Denise can deduct 10% of the real estate taxes on the cabin as an itemized deduction, if her total state and local tax deductions do not exceed $10,000 (see ¶504.02 for more on the deductibility of real estate taxes).

If the rental property qualifies as a residence and the taxpayer's rental expenses exceed rental income, the taxpayer deducts the expenses against the rental income in the following order:

1. Home mortgage interest, real estate taxes, casualty and theft losses, and rental expenses not directly related to the rental property (management fees, advertising, etc.)
2. All other rental expenses other than depreciation on the rental property
3. Depreciation of the rental property

EXAMPLE 13

Marilyn rents her vacation home at a fair rental price to an unrelated party for 35 days during the year. Marilyn personally uses the home for 15 days. The property is not used during any other time. During the year, Marilyn collects $6,000 in rents and has the following expenses:

Home mortgage interest	$ 6,000
Real estate taxes	1,500
Utilities	300
Depreciation	3,000
Total expenses	$10,800

Marilyn allocates 70% (35 rental days/50 total days used) of the expenses to the rental use. The rental portion of the expenses related to the home equals $7,560 ($10,800 × 70%). Because Marilyn's personal use (15 days) exceeds the *greater of* (i) 14 days or (ii) 10% of the fair rental days (35 × 10% = 3.5), the vacation home is treated as a residence. Thus, Marilyn's rental expenses cannot exceed rental income. Marilyn deducts the rental expenses in the following order:

Rental income	$6,000
Less rental portion of interest and taxes ($7,500 × 70%)	(5,250)
Rental income left to cover rent expenses other than interest and taxes	$ 750
Less rent expenses other than depreciation ($300 × 70%)	(210)
Rental income left to cover depreciation expense	$ 540
Less depreciation ($3,000 × 70% = $2,100)	(540)
Net rental income	$ 0

Marilyn can deduct only $540 of the $2,100 of depreciation allocated to rental use. Marilyn carries over the disallowed depreciation of $1,560 ($2,100 − $540) to the next year. She adds this amount to next year's depreciation expense.

Since the home qualifies as a residence, Marilyn can select the vacation home as her second home and deduct the $1,800 ($6,000 × 30%) personal portion of the home mortgage interest as an itemized deduction. Marilyn can deduct the $450 personal portion of the real estate taxes, if her total state and local tax deductions do not exceed $10,000 (see ¶504.02 for more on the deductibility of real estate taxes).

When renting out a vacation home, the owner's personal use of the property will determine whether the limitation rules apply. These rules cannot take effect until the owner's personal days exceed 14. Thus, to avoid having the tax law limit the deduction for rental expenses, owners might consider limiting their personal usage of the home to two weeks a year.

¶903   Reporting Rental Activities on Schedule E

Taxpayers use Schedule E (Form 1040), Supplemental Income and Loss, to report income and expenses from rental activities. In Part I (line 1a), taxpayers provide the address for each property. In Part I (line 1b), they state the type of property being rented from the list provided (1 = single-family residence, 2 = multi-family residence, 3 = vacation/short-term rental, etc.). In Part I (line 2), taxpayers provide the number of fair rental days and the number of personal use days. These numbers are used to determine whether the property qualifies as a residence. Taxpayers also report in Part I rental income and expenses used in computing their overall income or loss from the rental activity.

¶903.01   FILLED-IN SCHEDULE E

INFORMATION FOR FIGURE 9-1:

During 2022, Kurt F. and Heather M. Reding received rents from an eight-unit apartment complex. The Redings paid $600,000 for the apartment building in 2010, which includes $200,000 for the land. They depreciate the building using ADS.

The Redings also own a condominium in Naples, Florida that they used for 30 days in 2022. They rented the condo for 90 days and received a fair rental price. None of the tenants were members of the Redings' family. The Redings paid $295,000 for the condo in 2012 and depreciate it using MACRS.

The Redings report their rental income and expenses on Schedule E, Supplemental Income and Loss. They enter the amounts shown in bold on the appropriate lines on the schedule. They then transfer their $210 of net rental income to Form 1040, Schedule 1 (line 5).

Line #

1aA: Physical address: **1500 Vanderbilt Beach Road, Naples, FL 34110**
1aB: Physical address: **505 West Street, Verona, WI 53593**
1bA: Type of Property, **2** (Vacation/Short-Term Rental)
1bB: Type of Property, **3** (Multi-Family Residence)
2A: Fair rental days, **90**; Personal use days, **30**
2B: Fair rental days, **365**; Personal use days, **0**
3A: Rents received, **$15,000**
3B: Rents received, **$48,168**
5A: Advertising, **$75** (no allocation necessary since all related to rental activities)
5B: Advertising, **$250** (no allocation necessary since no personal use)
7A: Cleaning and maintenance, **$375** (100% related to rental activities)
7B: Cleaning and maintenance, **$2,500** (no allocation necessary since no personal use)
9A: Insurance, **$225** (90/120 × $300)
9B: Insurance, **$1,227** (no allocation necessary since no personal use)
10B: Legal and other professional fees, **$300** (no allocation necessary since no personal use)
12A: Mortgage interest, **$6,900** (90/120 × $9,200)
12B: Mortgage interest, **$14,329** (no allocation necessary since no personal use)
14B: Repairs, **$3,262** (no allocation necessary since no personal use)
16A: Taxes, **$2,550** (90/120 × $3,400)
16B: Taxes, **$4,290** (no allocation necessary since no personal use)
17A: Utilities, **$750** (90/120 × $1,000)
17B: Utilities, **$1,800** (no allocation necessary since no personal use)
18A: Depreciation expense, **$4,125** ($295,000/27.5 × 90/120 = $8,045; however, property A is considered a residence. Thus, total rental expenses cannot exceed the $15,000 of rental income. Since expenses other than depreciation total $10,875, depreciation is limited to $4,125).
18B: Depreciation expense, **$10,000** (($600,000 – $200,000)/40 years under ADS)

Figure 9-1: Filled-In Schedule E

SCHEDULE E (Form 1040)	Supplemental Income and Loss	OMB No. 1545-0074
Department of the Treasury Internal Revenue Service	(From rental real estate, royalties, partnerships, S corporations, estates, trusts, REMICs, etc.) **Attach to Form 1040, 1040-SR, 1040-NR, or 1041.** Go to *www.irs.gov/ScheduleE* for instructions and the latest information.	**2022** Attachment Sequence No. **13**

Name(s) shown on return	Your social security number
Kurt F. and Heather M. Reding	392-00-6811

Part I Income or Loss From Rental Real Estate and Royalties

Note: If you are in the business of renting personal property, use **Schedule C**. See instructions. If you are an individual, report farm rental income or loss from **Form 4835** on page 2, line 40.

A Did you make any payments in 2022 that would require you to file Form(s) 1099? See instructions . . . . ☑ **Yes** ☐ **No**

B If "Yes," did you or will you file required Form(s) 1099? . . . . ☑ **Yes** ☐ **No**

1a Physical address of each property (street, city, state, ZIP code)

A	1500 Vanderbilt Beach Road, Naples, FL 34110
B	505 West Street, Verona, WI 53593
C	

1b Type of Property (from list below)	2 For each rental real estate property listed above, report the number of fair rental and personal use days. Check the QJV box only if you meet the requirements to file as a qualified joint venture. See instructions.		Fair Rental Days	Personal Use Days	QJV
A	3	A	90	30	☐
B	2	B	365		☐
C		C			☐

Type of Property:

1 Single Family Residence   3 Vacation/Short-Term Rental   5 Land   7 Self-Rental

2 Multi-Family Residence   4 Commercial   6 Royalties   8 Other (describe) _____

			Properties:		
			A	B	C
Income:					
3	Rents received	3	15,000	48,168	
4	Royalties received	4			
Expenses:					
5	Advertising	5	75	250	
6	Auto and travel (see instructions)	6			
7	Cleaning and maintenance	7	375	2,500	
8	Commissions	8			
9	Insurance	9	225	1,227	
10	Legal and other professional fees	10		300	
11	Management fees	11			
12	Mortgage interest paid to banks, etc. (see instructions)	12	6,900	14,329	
13	Other interest	13			
14	Repairs	14		3,262	
15	Supplies	15			
16	Taxes	16	2,550	4,290	
17	Utilities	17	750	1,800	
18	Depreciation expense or depletion	18	4,125	10,000	
19	Other (list) _____	19			
20	Total expenses. Add lines 5 through 19	20	15,000	37,958	
21	Subtract line 20 from line 3 (rents) and/or 4 (royalties). If result is a (loss), see instructions to find out if you must file **Form 6198**	21		10,210	
22	Deductible rental real estate loss after limitation, if any, on **Form 8582** (see instructions)	22	( )( )( )( )		

23a	Total of all amounts reported on line 3 for all rental properties	23a	63,168	
b	Total of all amounts reported on line 4 for all royalty properties	23b		
c	Total of all amounts reported on line 12 for all properties	23c	21,229	
d	Total of all amounts reported on line 18 for all properties	23d	14,125	
e	Total of all amounts reported on line 20 for all properties	23e	52,958	

24	**Income.** Add positive amounts shown on line 21. **Do not** include any losses	24	10,210
25	**Losses.** Add royalty losses from line 21 and rental real estate losses from line 22. Enter total losses here	25	( )
26	**Total rental real estate and royalty income or (loss).** Combine lines 24 and 25. Enter the result here. If Parts II, III, IV, and line 40 on page 2 do not apply to you, also enter this amount on Schedule 1 (Form 1040), line 5. Otherwise, include this amount in the total on line 41 on page 2 .	26	10,210

For Paperwork Reduction Act Notice, see the separate instructions.   Cat. No. 11344L   Schedule E (Form 1040) 2022

¶904   At-Risk Rules

When rental expenses exceed rental income and the rental property is considered a "residence," the tax laws limit the amount of rental expenses taxpayers can deduct against rental income. For rental property not considered a "residence," two other sets of rules may affect the taxpayer's ability to deduct losses arising from rental activities: the at-risk rules and the passive activity loss rules. These rules not only affect rental activities, but also can affect losses arising from any trade, business, or income-producing activity. The at-risk rules are discussed first, followed by the passive activity loss rules (in ¶905).

The at-risk rules limit a taxpayer's loss to the amount the taxpayer could actually lose (that is, be out-of-pocket for) from the activity. This is known as the amount the taxpayer is "at-risk." The at-risk rules apply to any activity carried on as a trade or business (reported on Schedule C) or for the production of income (reported on Schedule E). A taxpayer's risk in any activity equals the following:

1. The money and adjusted basis (cost + improvements – accumulated depreciation) of any property contributed to the activity, **plus**
2. Amounts borrowed for use in the activity if the taxpayer either is personally liable for the loan or pledges personal assets to back up the loan.

Taxpayers that suffer a loss from an at-risk activity determine their deductible loss on Form 6198, At-Risk Limitations. Taxpayers can only deduct losses to the extent they have amounts at-risk. Taxpayers' amount at-risk decreases when they deduct losses from the activity on their tax returns and when they take withdrawals from the activity. In years when the taxpayer's loss is less than the amount at-risk, the taxpayer can deduct the entire loss, and the amount at-risk is reduced by the loss deducted. This (reduced) at-risk amount becomes the taxpayer's amount at-risk for the start of the next year.

EXAMPLE 14	In 20x1, William starts his own business by contributing $10,000 cash from his personal funds and by getting a $100,000 interest-only loan. William uses his personal assets to secure the loan. William's initial amount at-risk is $110,000. During 20x1, the business suffers a $60,000 loss. William can deduct the entire $60,000 loss on his tax return. His amount at-risk is reduced to $50,000.

In years when the amount of the loss exceeds the taxpayer's amount at-risk, the taxpayer's loss deduction is limited to the amount at-risk. Any disallowed loss carries over to the next year. Since the amount at-risk has been reduced to zero, no future losses will be allowed until the taxpayer gets a positive amount at-risk. This can be done through a variety of means. For example, the taxpayer could make additional investments in the activity, or have the activity take out a loan for which the taxpayer is personally responsible.

EXAMPLE 15	Continuing with Example 14, in 20x2, William's business suffers another $60,000 loss. Since William's amount at-risk is $50,000, he will only be allowed to deduct $50,000 of his 20x2 losses. He carries over the $10,000 disallowed loss to 20x3.

¶905   Passive Activity Losses

After applying the at-risk rules, taxpayers must consider the passive activity loss rules. Losses generated by activities of a passive nature can only offset income and gains generated from passive activities. Taxpayers carry over excess passive losses to offset passive income in future tax years. When the taxpayer disposes of the entire interest in a passive activity, any suspended losses left from that activity are fully deductible in that year.

¶905.01   PASSIVE ACTIVITY INCOME DEFINED

The passive activity rules classify all income and losses as coming from one of three types of activities: active, portfolio, or passive. **Active income** consists of wages, salaries, and income from material participation in a trade or business. **Portfolio income** comes from investments that generate dividends and interest. Portfolio income also includes gains from the sale of securities (stocks and bonds). **Passive income** generally comes from (1) a trade or business in which the taxpayer does not materially participate, (2) rental activities, and (3) limited partnerships.

Any of these three types of activities may produce losses. Losses from the sale of portfolio investments are capital losses. However, losses not classified as portfolio are either active or passive. The distinction is important, as taxpayers can offset losses from active activities against both portfolio and passive income. They can only offset losses from passive activities against income from other passive activities.

Material participation in a trade or business produces active income and losses. **Material participation** occurs when the taxpayer is involved in the operations of the activity on a regular, continuous, and substantial basis. Except for rental real estate activities (which must meet a stricter test, discussed later at ¶905.02), the material participation requirement can be met if the taxpayer participates in the activity for more than 500 hours during the year. (For purposes of the 500-hour test, participation by the owner's spouse is considered participation by the owner.) Another way to meet this requirement is for the taxpayer to participate in the activity for more than 100 hours during the year and for the taxpayer's participation to be at least as much as the participation of any other individual, including employees. IRS Publication 925 describes other ways to meet the material participation requirement.

EXAMPLE 16	Ginny and Barry jointly own and work for a business that does not involve rental realty. Ginny also works part-time as an employee. Ginny and Barry are not married to each other. During the year she works 425 hours for the business, and 600 hours as an employee. Barry is not employed elsewhere and spends 40 hours a week working for the business. Because his hours of participation exceed 500, Barry materially participates in the business. Ginny does not participate in the business more than 500 hours, and although her hours exceed 100, her hours do not equal Barry's hours. Thus, unless she can meet the material participation requirements another way, the passive activity loss rules would apply to Ginny with respect to this activity. If Barry and Ginny were husband and wife, each would be able to count the participation of the other. The total participation of the couple would be Barry's 2080 (40 × 52) hours plus Ginny's 425.

EXAMPLE 17	Same facts as in Example 16, except that Ginny averages ten hours a week working for the business. Since Ginny's 520 hours (10 × 52 weeks) exceed 500, she materially participates in the activity. Thus, the business would not be considered a passive activity for Ginny.

The tax laws treat most rental activities as passive activities. However, exceptions do exist. One exception applies to taxpayers involved in the business of renting real property. This situation is described in ¶905.02. Three other exceptions include rental activities where: (1) the average rental period is less than eight days (e.g., a tool rental store); (2) the average rental period is less than 31 days and significant personal services are provided (e.g., motels and hotels); and (3) the rental activity is incidental to the taxpayer's business. Unless one of these four exceptions applies, losses from the rental activity will be considered passive losses.

¶905.02   RENTAL REAL ESTATE LOSSES

Rental real estate activities usually are treated as passive, even if one of the seven ways for meeting the material participation requirement has been met. However, a rental real estate activity may qualify as an active trade or business if the taxpayer satisfies both of the following:

1. More than 50% of the personal services rendered during the year are performed in a trade or business involving real estate, **and**
2. At a minimum, the taxpayer performs more than 750 hours of personal service in the real property trade or business. [I.R.C. §469(c)(7)]

If the taxpayer passes both tests, then the rental real estate activity is not considered passive, and any losses from the activity would be fully deductible against ordinary income (subject to the at-risk limits described in ¶904). A married couple passes the two tests only if one spouse separately satisfies both conditions. In other words, couples cannot pool their time and efforts in meeting the two conditions for rental real estate activities. If these conditions are not met, then the rental real estate activity is considered a passive activity.

EXAMPLE 18	Same facts as in Example 17, except that Ginny and Barry's business involves rental realty. Barry performs more than 750 hours of personal services in businesses involving real property. In addition, this work is more than 50% of his total hours of personal services rendered during the year. Thus, Barry materially participates in the rental realty business. Ginny's hours, on the other hand, do not exceed 750. Thus, Ginny is not a material participant in the business. Accordingly, the business is a passive activity to Ginny.

EXAMPLE 19	A husband and wife each work 400 hours in a rental realty business. Although as a couple they work more than 750 hours in the rental realty business, the tax laws require that at least one spouse meet the two conditions for material participation. Thus, the rental activity is a passive activity to the couple.

The taxpayer has the burden of providing proof that any personal service tests have been met. To do this, taxpayers should keep a daily log of their hours spent on the activity to prove their hours of participation in the activity.

$25,000 Special Deduction for Active Participants

Taxpayers who are not in a "real estate trade or business" and have losses from rental real estate activities may be able to deduct up to $25,000 of rental real estate losses from active and portfolio income. [I.R.C. §469(i)] The deduction limit is $12,500 for married taxpayers filing separately and living apart at all times during the year. No special deduction is allowed for married taxpayers filing separately if the couple lived together at any time during the year. To qualify for this special deduction, the taxpayer must meet both of the following requirements:

1. The taxpayer actively participates in the rental real estate activity, **and**
2. The taxpayer owns at least 10% of the value of all interests in the activity throughout the entire year.

Active participation and material participation are two different concepts. **Active participation** requires less involvement than material participation. Active participation does not require regular, continuous, and substantial involvement. However, it does require that the taxpayer participate in management decisions in a significant and real sense. Examples of this level of involvement include approving new tenants, deciding on rental terms, approving improvements or repairs, or arranging for others to provide services such as repairs.

EXAMPLE 20

> Going back to Example 18, although Ginny's hours do not constitute material participation, they do indicate active participation in the rental realty business. Since Ginny owns at least 10% of the business, she qualifies for the $25,000 special deduction. Thus, in years in which the activity produces a net loss, Ginny may be able to deduct up to $25,000 of her share of the loss against her active and portfolio income.

The $25,000 annual deduction is reduced by 50% of the taxpayer's modified AGI in excess of $100,000 ($50,000 for married taxpayers who file separately). Thus, the deduction is completely phased out when modified AGI reaches $150,000 ($75,000 for married taxpayers filing separately). In computing modified AGI, passive losses cannot exceed passive income. Modified AGI is any passive activity loss of taxpayers in a real property business, without the following items:

1. passive income or loss;
2. rental real estate loss allowed to real estate professionals;
3. any overall loss from a publicly traded partnership;
4. the taxable amount of social security and railroad retirement benefits (¶307);
5. deductible contributions to IRAs and certain pension plans (¶402.10);
6. the deduction for foreign-derived intangible income and global intangible low-taxed income;
7. the exclusion from income of interest from series EE and I U.S. savings bonds (¶401.03);
8. the exclusion of amounts received under an employer's adoption assistance program (¶401.05);
9. the student loan interest deduction (¶402.11);
10. the tuition and fees deduction; or
11 The deduction for self-employment tax.

EXAMPLE 21

Rachel, a single taxpayer, earned $110,000 from her job, $15,000 of passive income from a non–real estate activity, and $20,000 of interest income. Rachel also incurred a $50,000 loss from a rental real estate activity in which she actively participates. Rachel made a $6,000 deductible IRA contribution in 2022. Under the general rule, passive losses usually can offset only passive income. Therefore, Rachel can use $15,000 of her $50,000 rental real estate loss to offset the $15,000 of the income from the non–real estate passive activity. Because Rachel is actively involved in the rental real estate activities, she may be able to deduct more than $15,000 of her loss. Rachel computes the additional deduction and passive loss carryover as follows.

Wages	$110,000
Interest income	20,000
Modified AGI	$130,000
Less AGI threshold for the phase-out	(100,000)
Amount subject to phase-out	$ 30,000
	× 50%
Amount of deduction lost due to phase-out	$ 15,000

Because Rachel's modified AGI exceeds $100,000 by $30,000, she must reduce the $25,000 deduction for active participants by one-half of the excess, or $15,000. Thus, Rachel's additional passive loss deduction is $10,000 ($25,000 limit – $15,000 reduction in limit).

Excess passive loss from rental real estate ($50,000 – $15,000)	$ 35,000
Additional passive loss deduction for active participation in rental real estate	(10,000)
Passive loss carried forward to 2023	$ 25,000

Modified AGI does not include the $6,000 IRA deduction or the $35,000 of passive losses in excess of passive income. Rachel will deduct a total of $25,000 of passive activity losses ($15,000 under the general rule and $10,000 special deduction). Of that amount, $15,000 will offset passive activity income, and the excess $10,000 loss will reduce Rachel's active and portfolio income.

¶905.03   SUSPENDED LOSSES

Passive activity losses not deducted in the current tax year carry forward to the next year. Passive losses that are carried forward must be allocated among the various activities that produced the loss. When multiple passive activities exist, taxpayers must determine the suspended loss for each separate activity using the following formula.

$$\text{Total disallowed loss} \quad \times \quad \frac{\text{Loss from separate activity}}{\text{Sum of all losses}}$$

EXAMPLE 22	Denny reports the following income and losses from his four passive activities for 20x1.

Activity A	($40,000)
Activity B	30,000
Activity C	(32,000)
Activity D	(8,000)
Net passive loss	($50,000)

Denny allocates his $50,000 net passive loss to activities A, C, and D (the activities producing a total of $80,000 of losses) as follows:

Activity A ($50,000 × $40,000/$80,000)	($25,000)
Activity C ($50,000 × $32,000/$80,000)	(20,000)
Activity D ($50,000 × $8,000/$80,000)	(5,000)
Total suspended losses	($50,000)

These suspended losses carry forward indefinitely as deductions associated with the activity to which each relates. Thus, the $25,000 passive loss carryover associated with Activity A is added to/netted against any passive income (loss) generated by Activity A in 20x2. This net amount becomes Denny's passive income (loss) from Activity A for 20x2. The same process is applied to Activities C and D.

¶905.04 DISPOSING OF A PASSIVE ACTIVITY

When taxpayers dispose of a passive activity, any suspended losses relating to that activity are deductible in full. To qualify for this treatment, taxpayers must dispose of their entire interest in the activity in a fully taxable transaction. Also, the new property owner cannot be the taxpayer's sibling (sister or brother), ancestor (parent, grandparent, etc.), or descendant (child, grandchild, etc.). Special rules apply when taxpayers dispose of a passive activity by way of gift or inheritance. These rules are beyond the scope of this textbook.

The gain or loss from the sale of a passive activity receives special treatment. If a loss results, the loss is either an ordinary loss or capital loss depending on the circumstances. The loss is not treated as a passive loss, so it is not limited to offsetting just passive income. Chapter 11 explains the difference between ordinary and capital losses in greater detail.

EXAMPLE 23	Continuing with Example 22, if Denny sells Activity A in 20x2, any part of the $25,000 passive loss carryover from 20x1 that is not utilized in 20x2 to offset passive income and gains is deducted against Denny's active and portfolio income.

¶905.05 REPORTING PASSIVE ACTIVITY LOSSES

Taxpayers with income or loss from passive activities complete Form 8582, Passive Activity Loss Limitations, to compute the amount of passive loss allowed from such activities. Taxpayers then report the passive loss allowed on the appropriate tax form or schedule. For example, taxpayers report the passive loss allowed from rental activities on Schedule E.

Regardless of the number or complexity of passive activities, taxpayers file only one Form 8582. Taxpayers prepare Form 8582 to determine whether the passive loss rules disallow any of the losses reported on those other forms and schedules.

Form 8582 consists of three parts. In Part I, taxpayers report net income (line 1a), net loss (line 1b), and prior year carryforwards (line 1c) from rental real estate activities with active participation. They also report in Part I net income (line 3a), net loss (line 3b), and prior year carryforwards (line 3c) from all other passive activities. Taxpayers then combine their passive income and losses (line 4). If net income results, taxpayers enter the net amount on the appropriate tax form or schedule to which the activity relates (for example, Schedule E for rental real estate). If a net loss results, then taxpayers proceed to Part II to see whether they can utilize any of the $25,000 special allowance for active participation in rental real estate activities.

In Part II, taxpayers determine the amount of net loss available for the $25,000 special allowance. They then compute their modified adjusted gross income and determine the amount of phase-out, if any, that applies (lines 6–9). In Part IV, taxpayers compute the passive income and loss reported on that year's tax return. Deductible passive losses (line 16) equal the total passive income (from lines 1a and 3a) plus the special allowance amount from Part II (line 10). Figure 9-2 shows a completed Form 8582 for a taxpayer who actively participates in a rental real estate activity.

¶905.06   FILLED-IN FORM 8582

INFORMATION FOR FIGURE 9-2:

Robert France earned $117,000 from his job, $15,000 of interest income, $10,000 net income from a passive activity (non–real estate), and a $25,000 loss from a rental real estate activity in which he actively participates (see accompanying Schedule E). Robert has no other income and no passive loss carryovers from prior years. Form 8582 (line 16) shows that Robert can deduct $19,000 of his passive losses. He deducts this amount on Schedule E (line 22). Robert's passive loss carryover to 2023 is $6,000 ($25,000 – $19,000).

Line #
- 1b: Activities with net loss (rental real estate activities with active participation), **$25,000**
- 3a: Activities with net income (all other passive activities), **$10,000**
- 4: Excess of total passive losses over total passive income, (**$15,000**) ($25,000 passive losses – $10,000 passive income)
- 5: The smaller of the loss on line 1d or the loss on line 4, **$15,000** (entered as a positive amount as per the instructions for Part II)
- 7: Modified adjusted gross income, **$132,000** [$117,000 + $15,000 + $10,000 (non–real estate passive net income) – $10,000 (rental real estate passive loss to the extent of passive net income)]
- 16: Total passive losses allowed in the current year, **$19,000** ($10,000 allowed to offset passive income + $9,000 special allowance for active participation in rental real estate activities)

Figure 9-2: Filled-In Form 8582

Form **8582**	**Passive Activity Loss Limitations** — OMB No. 1545-1008

Form **8582**
Department of the Treasury
Internal Revenue Service

Passive Activity Loss Limitations
See separate instructions.
Attach to Form 1040, 1040-SR, or 1041.
Go to *www.irs.gov/Form8582* for instructions and the latest information.

OMB No. 1545-1008
2022
Attachment Sequence No. **858**

Name(s) shown on return
Robert France

Identifying number
421-00-5546

Part I 2022 Passive Activity Loss

Caution: Complete Parts IV and V before completing Part I.

Rental Real Estate Activities With Active Participation (For the definition of active participation, see *Special Allowance for Rental Real Estate Activities* in the instructions.)

1a	Activities with net income (enter the amount from Part IV, column (a))	**1a**	10,000
b	Activities with net loss (enter the amount from Part IV, column (b))	**1b** (	25,000)
c	Prior years' unallowed losses (enter the amount from Part IV, column (c))	**1c** (	)
d	Combine lines 1a, 1b, and 1c	**1d**	(15,000)

All Other Passive Activities

2a	Activities with net income (enter the amount from Part V, column (a))	**2a**	
b	Activities with net loss (enter the amount from Part V, column (b))	**2b** (	)
c	Prior years' unallowed losses (enter the amount from Part V, column (c))	**2c** (	)
d	Combine lines 2a, 2b, and 2c	**2d**	

3	Combine lines 1d and 2d. If this line is zero or more, stop here and include this form with your return; all losses are allowed, including any prior year unallowed losses entered on line 1c or 2c. Report the losses on the forms and schedules normally used	**3**	(15,000)

If line 3 is a loss and: • Line 1d is a loss, go to Part II.
                          • Line 2d is a loss (and line 1d is zero or more), skip Part II and go to line 10.

Caution: If your filing status is married filing separately and you lived with your spouse at any time during the year, **do not** complete Part II. Instead, go to line 10.

Part II Special Allowance for Rental Real Estate Activities With Active Participation

Note: Enter all numbers in Part II as positive amounts. See instructions for an example.

4	Enter the **smaller** of the loss on line 1d or the loss on line 3	**4**	15,000
5	Enter $150,000. If married filing separately, see instructions	**5** 150,000	
6	Enter modified adjusted gross income, but not less than zero. See instructions	**6** 132,000	
	Note: If line 6 is greater than or equal to line 5, skip lines 7 and 8 and enter -0- on line 9. Otherwise, go to line 7.		
7	Subtract line 6 from line 5	**7** 18,000	
8	Multiply line 7 by 50% (0.50). **Do not** enter more than $25,000. If married filing separately, see instructions	**8**	9,000
9	Enter the **smaller** of line 4 or line 8	**9**	9,000

Part III Total Losses Allowed

10	Add the income, if any, on lines 1a and 2a and enter the total	**10**	10,000
11	**Total losses allowed from all passive activities for 2022.** Add lines 9 and 10. See instructions to find out how to report the losses on your tax return	**11**	19,000

Part IV Complete This Part Before Part I, Lines 1a, 1b, and 1c. See instructions.

Name of activity	Current year		Prior years	Overall gain or loss	
	(a) Net income (line 1a)	**(b)** Net loss (line 1b)	**(c)** Unallowed loss (line 1c)	**(d)** Gain	**(e)** Loss
1802 Eighth St. #207, Danville, IL 60560		25,000			25,000
Others	10,000			10,000	
Total. Enter on Part I, lines 1a, 1b, and 1c	10,000	25,000			

For Paperwork Reduction Act Notice, see instructions.   Cat. No. 63704F   Form **8582** (2022)

Figure 9-2: Schedule E to Accompany Filled-In Form 8582

SCHEDULE E (Form 1040) Department of the Treasury Internal Revenue Service	**Supplemental Income and Loss** (From rental real estate, royalties, partnerships, S corporations, estates, trusts, REMICs, etc.) Attach to Form 1040, 1040-SR, 1040-NR, or 1041. Go to *www.irs.gov/ScheduleE* for instructions and the latest information.	OMB No. 1545-0074 20**22** Attachment Sequence No. **13**

Name(s) shown on return	Your social security number
Robert France	421-00-5546

Part I   Income or Loss From Rental Real Estate and Royalties

Note: If you are in the business of renting personal property, use **Schedule C**. See instructions. If you are an individual, report farm rental income or loss from **Form 4835** on page 2, line 40.

A	Did you make any payments in 2022 that would require you to file Form(s) 1099? See instructions	☑ Yes ☐ No
B	If "Yes," did you or will you file required Form(s) 1099?	☑ Yes ☐ No

1a   Physical address of each property (street, city, state, ZIP code)

A	1802 Eighth St. #207, Danville, IL 60560
B	
C	

1b	Type of Property (from list below)	2	For each rental real estate property listed above, report the number of fair rental and personal use days. Check the QJV box only if you meet the requirements to file as a qualified joint venture. See instructions.		Fair Rental Days	Personal Use Days	QJV
A	2			A	365	0	☐
B				B			☐
C				C			☐

Type of Property:
1 Single Family Residence   3 Vacation/Short-Term Rental   5 Land   7 Self-Rental
2 Multi-Family Residence   4 Commercial   6 Royalties   8 Other (describe) _____

			Properties:		
Income:			**A**	**B**	**C**
3	Rents received	3	7,800		
4	Royalties received	4			
Expenses:					
5	Advertising	5			
6	Auto and travel (see instructions)	6			
7	Cleaning and maintenance	7	1,600		
8	Commissions	8			
9	Insurance	9	140		
10	Legal and other professional fees	10			
11	Management fees	11			
12	Mortgage interest paid to banks, etc. (see instructions)	12	14,700		
13	Other interest	13			
14	Repairs	14	3,100		
15	Supplies	15			
16	Taxes	16	2,950		
17	Utilities	17	1,620		
18	Depreciation expense or depletion	18	4,810		
19	Other (list) _____	19	3,880		
20	Total expenses. Add lines 5 through 19	20	32,800		
21	Subtract line 20 from line 3 (rents) and/or 4 (royalties). If result is a (loss), see instructions to find out if you must file **Form 6198**	21	(25,000)	0	
22	Deductible rental real estate loss after limitation, if any, on **Form 8582** (see instructions)	22	(19,000)(	)(	)

23a	Total of all amounts reported on line 3 for all rental properties	23a	7,800
b	Total of all amounts reported on line 4 for all royalty properties	23b	
c	Total of all amounts reported on line 12 for all properties	23c	14,700
d	Total of all amounts reported on line 18 for all properties	23d	4,810
e	Total of all amounts reported on line 20 for all properties	23e	32,800
24	**Income.** Add positive amounts shown on line 21. **Do not** include any losses	24	
25	**Losses.** Add royalty losses from line 21 and rental real estate losses from line 22. Enter total losses here	25	(19,000)
26	**Total rental real estate and royalty income or (loss).** Combine lines 24 and 25. Enter the result here. If Parts II, III, IV, and line 40 on page 2 do not apply to you, also enter this amount on Schedule 1 (Form 1040), line 5. Otherwise, include this amount in the total on line 41 on page 2 .	26	(19,000)

For Paperwork Reduction Act Notice, see the separate instructions.	Cat. No. 11344L	Schedule E (Form 1040) 2022

Qualified Business Income

A rental activity is eligible for the QBI deduction if the owner's activities are sufficient for the enterprise to be treated as a trade or business under general tax laws. Many cases have held that an owner who actively manages rental properties, even one single-family home, is carrying on a trade or business. On the other hand, the owner of property subject to a "triple-net" lease, in which the tenant pays for maintenance, insurance and all other necessary costs, is not engaged in a trade or business, but holds the property as a mere investment. It is not necessary to qualify as a real estate professional to claim the QBI deduction on rental income. Nor is it necessary to meet the standard of material participation that would cause the operation to be nonpassive if it were not a rental activity.

 ## INFORMATION FOR FIGURE 9-3:

Kurt and Heather Reding, from Figure 9-1, incurred numerous expenses, other than interest, taxes and depreciation, on their property at 505 West Street, Verona, WI 53593. These expenses indicate their active management of the property. Accordingly, they treat it as a business and claim the QBI deduction. Their combined taxable income, before the QBI deduction, is $185,000. Therefore, they are beneath the threshold at which the W-2 wages and qualified property limit the deduction. Figure 9-3 shows their filled-in Form 8995.

Figure 9-3: Filled-In Form 8995

Form **8995**	**Qualified Business Income Deduction** **Simplified Computation**	OMB No. 1545-2294
Department of the Treasury Internal Revenue Service	► Attach to your tax return. ► Go to *www.irs.gov/Form8995* for instructions and the latest information.	**2021** Attachment Sequence No. **55**

Name(s) shown on return	Your taxpayer identification number
Kurt F. and Heather M. Reding	392-00-6811

Note. You can claim the qualified business income deduction **only** if you have qualified business income from a qualified trade or business, real estate investment trust dividends, publicly traded partnership income, or a domestic production activities deduction passed through from an agricultural or horticultural cooperative. See instructions.

Use this form if your taxable income, before your qualified business income deduction, is at or below $164,900 ($164,925 if married filing separately; $329,800 if married filing jointly), and you aren't a patron of an agricultural or horticultural cooperative.

1	(a) Trade, business, or aggregation name	(b) Taxpayer identification number	(c) Qualified business income or (loss)
i	505 West Street, Verona, WI 53593	-	10,210
ii		-	
iii			
iv			
v			

2	Total qualified business income or (loss). Combine lines 1i through 1v, column (c)	**2** 10,210	
3	Qualified business net (loss) carryforward from the prior year	**3** ( )	
4	Total qualified business income. Combine lines 2 and 3. If zero or less, enter -0-	**4** 10,210	
5	Qualified business income component. Multiply line 4 by 20% (0.20)	**5**	2,042
6	Qualified REIT dividends and publicly traded partnership (PTP) income or (loss) (see instructions)	**6**	
7	Qualified REIT dividends and qualified PTP (loss) carryforward from the prior year	**7** ( )	
8	Total qualified REIT dividends and PTP income. Combine lines 6 and 7. If zero or less, enter -0-	**8**	
9	REIT and PTP component. Multiply line 8 by 20% (0.20)	**9**	
10	Qualified business income deduction before the income limitation. Add lines 5 and 9	**10**	2,042
11	Taxable income before qualified business income deduction (see instructions)	**11** 185,000	
12	Net capital gain (see instructions)	**12**	
13	Subtract line 12 from line 11. If zero or less, enter -0-	**13** 185,000	
14	Income limitation. Multiply line 13 by 20% (0.20)	**14**	37,000
15	Qualified business income deduction. Enter the smaller of line 10 or line 14. Also enter this amount on the applicable line of your return (see instructions) ►	**15**	2,042
16	Total qualified business (loss) carryforward. Combine lines 2 and 3. If greater than zero, enter -0-	**16** ( )	
17	Total qualified REIT dividends and PTP (loss) carryforward. Combine lines 6 and 7. If greater than zero, enter -0-	**17** ( )	

For Privacy Act and Paperwork Reduction Act Notice, see instructions.   Cat. No. 37806C   Form **8995** (2021)

9

Name:

Section:

Date: _____

QUESTIONS AND PROBLEMS

1. **Rental Income.** (Obj. 1) State the amount of rental income that must be reported on Schedule E for 2022 by each of the following taxpayers.

Taxpayer	Description	Amount
A	On November 30, 2022, the taxpayer receives $1,500 a security deposit, $1,000 for the December rent, and an advance payment of $5,000 for an additional five months' rent.	$_____
B	The taxpayer normally receives rent of $300 per month on the first of each month. In 2022, the tenant made $600 of improvements in lieu of two months' rent.	$_____
C	Rent of $1,200 is received when the taxpayer rents a personal residence to friends for 12 days during the Mardi Gras festivities.	$_____

2. **Rental Expenses.** (Obj. 1) State the maximum amount of rental expenses attributable to the property that can be claimed by each of the following taxpayers.

Taxpayer	Description	Amount
A	A dwelling unit is rented to a friend for $100 per month for two months and to an unrelated party for $275 per month for three months. Fair rental price is $275/month.	$_____
B	A personal residence rented for 12 days during the year, for a total of $300.	$_____

3. **Net Rental Income.** (Obj. 1) Quentin owns a two-family home. He rents out the first floor and resides on the second floor. Each floor is of equal size. Quentin received $6,400 in rental income during the year, and incurred the following expenses attributable to the building.

	Entire Building	Expenses For	
		First Floor	Second Floor
Depreciation	$4,000		
Real estate taxes	2,000		
Mortgage interest	1,600		
Utilities	1,200		
Repairs		$500	
Painting			$400

a. What amount of expenses can Quentin deduct on Schedule E?

b. What amount of the expenses can Quentin deduct on Schedule A?

4. **Net Rental Income.** (Obj. 1) Sandee, a cash basis taxpayer, owns a house with two identical units. Sandee resides in one unit and rents out the other. The tenant made timely monthly rental payments of $500 for the months of January through November 2022. The tenant paid rents for December 2022 and January 2023 on January 5, 2023. During the year, Sandee paid $3,600 for utilities and $600 for insurance. These expenses were for the entire house. She paid $400 for maintenance and repairs on the rental unit. Depreciation on the entire house equals $3,000. Compute Sandee's 2022 net rental income.

5. **Vacation Homes.** (Obj. 2) Dari owns a vacation home that she personally uses 14 days during the year. The rest of the year the following occupants used the home. Fair rental price is $125 a night.

Occupant	Number of Days
Dari's best friend, who paid no rent	8
Dari's brother, who paid a fair rental price	21
Couple who won a charity auction	7
Unrelated persons, who paid rent of $7,500	60

Dari's expenses related to the vacation home were as follows:

Mortgage interest	$ 6,700
Real estate taxes	3,300
Utilities and repairs	2,540
Depreciation	6,650
	$19,190

a. Compute the number of (1) days the property was rented at a fair rental price; (2) total days the property was used during the year; and (3) personal days. Discuss the significance of these three numbers as they pertain to the vacation home rules.

b. Compute Dari's net rental income and any expenses that she must carry over to the next year.

6. **Vacation Homes.** (Obj. 2) Henry owns a fishing cabin in Wisconsin. Henry offered the cabin for rent from June 1 through September 30, except for 16 days in August when his family used it. Henry was unable to rent the cabin for two weeks (14 days) during the remaining rental period. At all other times, the cabin was rented at a fair rental price to unrelated persons.

a. Will Henry's cabin be treated as a residence? Explain.

b. For purposes of allocating expenses, how many fair rental days does Henry have?

7. **Vacation Homes.** (Obj. 2)

a. What is the tax advantage to having a vacation home treated as a residence?

b. What is the disadvantage to having a vacation home considered a residence?

8. **Vacation Homes.** (Obj. 2) During the year, Carlin Barone (SSN 839-00-1444) rents his vacation home for 90 days and spends 60 days there. The vacation home is a townhome located at 610 Oak St. in Boulder, Colorado 80302. Gross rental income from the property totals $6,000. Carlin's expenses for the property are shown below. Using this information, complete Carlin Barone's Schedule E.

Mortgage interest	$3,000
Real estate taxes	1,500
Utilities	800
Maintenance	900
Depreciation	4,000

9. **At-risk.** (Obj. 3)

   a. Discuss the significance of the at-risk rules.

   b. What activities are subject to the at-risk loss rules?

   c. What happens to losses that are disallowed by the at-risk rules?

10. **Passive Activities.** (Obj. 3)

   a. What types of trade or business activities are considered passive activities?

   b. Distinguish between material participation and active participation in rental activities. Explain the significance of this difference.

   c. Under the passive activity loss rules, how are dividend income and interest income treated? Can passive losses offset dividend and interest income?

(Use for Problem 8.)

SCHEDULE E (Form 1040)

Department of the Treasury
Internal Revenue Service

Supplemental Income and Loss

(From rental real estate, royalties, partnerships, S corporations, estates, trusts, REMICs, etc.)

Attach to Form 1040, 1040-SR, 1040-NR, or 1041.

Go to *www.irs.gov/ScheduleE* for instructions and the latest information.

OMB No. 1545-0074

2022

Attachment Sequence No. **13**

Name(s) shown on return

Your social security number

Part I — Income or Loss From Rental Real Estate and Royalties

Note: If you are in the business of renting personal property, use **Schedule C**. See instructions. If you are an individual, report farm rental income or loss from **Form 4835** on page 2, line 40.

A Did you make any payments in 2022 that would require you to file Form(s) 1099? See instructions . . . . . ☐ Yes ☐ No

B If "Yes," did you or will you file required Form(s) 1099? . . . . ☐ Yes ☐ No

1a Physical address of each property (street, city, state, ZIP code)

A
B
C

1b Type of Property (from list below)

2 For each rental real estate property listed above, report the number of fair rental and personal use days. Check the QJV box only if you meet the requirements to file as a qualified joint venture. See instructions.

	1b Type of Property		Fair Rental Days	Personal Use Days	QJV
A		A			☐
B		B			☐
C		C			☐

Type of Property:

1 Single Family Residence   3 Vacation/Short-Term Rental   5 Land   7 Self-Rental

2 Multi-Family Residence   4 Commercial   6 Royalties   8 Other (describe) _____

		Properties:		
		A	B	C
Income:				
3	Rents received	3			
4	Royalties received	4			
Expenses:					
5	Advertising	5			
6	Auto and travel (see instructions)	6			
7	Cleaning and maintenance	7			
8	Commissions	8			
9	Insurance	9			
10	Legal and other professional fees	10			
11	Management fees	11			
12	Mortgage interest paid to banks, etc. (see instructions)	12			
13	Other interest	13			
14	Repairs	14			
15	Supplies	15			
16	Taxes	16			
17	Utilities	17			
18	Depreciation expense or depletion	18			
19	Other (list) _____	19			
20	Total expenses. Add lines 5 through 19	20			
21	Subtract line 20 from line 3 (rents) and/or 4 (royalties). If result is a (loss), see instructions to find out if you must file **Form 6198**	21			
22	Deductible rental real estate loss after limitation, if any, on **Form 8582** (see instructions)	22	( )	( )	( )

23a	Total of all amounts reported on line 3 for all rental properties	23a	
b	Total of all amounts reported on line 4 for all royalty properties	23b	
c	Total of all amounts reported on line 12 for all properties	23c	
d	Total of all amounts reported on line 18 for all properties	23d	
e	Total of all amounts reported on line 20 for all properties	23e	
24	**Income.** Add positive amounts shown on line 21. **Do not** include any losses	24	
25	**Losses.** Add royalty losses from line 21 and rental real estate losses from line 22. Enter total losses here	25	( )
26	**Total rental real estate and royalty income or (loss).** Combine lines 24 and 25. Enter the result here. If Parts II, III, IV, and line 40 on page 2 do not apply to you, also enter this amount on Schedule 1 (Form 1040), line 5. Otherwise, include this amount in the total on line 41 on page 2 .	26	

For Paperwork Reduction Act Notice, see the separate instructions.   Cat. No. 11344L   Schedule E (Form 1040) 2022

11. **Material vs. Active Participation.** (Obj. 3) For each of the following independent situations, discuss whether (**A**) the taxpayer materially participates in the activity or (**B**) the activity is a passive activity. In activities involving rental real estate, discuss whether the special deduction for active participation would apply.

    a. The taxpayer works 900 hours in a nonrental real estate activity and 1,000 hours as an employee (not involving rental real estate).

    b. The taxpayer works 650 hours in a rental real estate activity and 500 hours as an employee (not involving rental real estate).

    c. The taxpayer works in an activity (not involving rental real estate) 150 hours during the year. The taxpayer is retired, so this is the only activity he works for during the year.

    d. Both spouses participate in an activity (not involving rental real estate). The husband works 300 hours; the wife works 250 hours. Both spouses work full-time for companies that have nothing to do with rental real estate.

    e. Both spouses participate in a rental real estate activity. The husband works 400 hours; the wife works 520 hours. Both spouses also work full-time as employees for companies that have nothing to do with rental real estate.

    f. Same as in Part e. except that the wife's hours are 800 instead of 520.

12. **Passive Activities.** (Obj. 3) A taxpayer owned four passive activities. Net income (loss) for each activity is shown below.

Passive Activity	Gross Income	Deductions	Net Income (or Loss)
A	$12,000	$ 8,000	$ 4,000
B	20,000	32,000	(12,000)
C	3,000	6,000	(3,000)
D	14,000	12,000	2,000

a. What is the amount of passive loss that can offset passive income in the current year?

b. What is the amount of passive loss that is carried forward for each activity?

13. **Passive Activities.** (Obj. 3) A taxpayer owns three passive activities. Net income (loss) for each activity is shown below.

Passive Activity	Net Income (or Loss)
1	$26,000
2	(13,500)
3	(18,000)

a. Compute the amount of passive loss that can offset passive income in the current year.

b. Determine the amount of passive loss that is carried forward to each activity.

14. **Rental Real Estate.** (Obj. 3) The Warrens incur a $22,000 loss from rental real estate activities in which they actively participate. The Warrens own more than 10% of the activity. Their only other source of income for the year is $130,000 of wages. What amount of the loss can the Warrens deduct on their joint tax return?

15. **Rental Real Estate.** (Obj. 3) Martin actively participates in three different rental real estate activities. His ownership in each activity exceeds 10%. Martin's income and losses from these activities are shown below. Martin's only other source of income is $80,000 of wages. Calculate Martin's loss allowed and suspended loss.

Activity	Income (or Loss)
X	($10,000)
Y	(30,000)
Z	9,000

16. **Passive Activities.** (Obj. 3) A taxpayer owns three passive activities, none of which involve rental real estate. Suspended losses at the beginning of the year and income (or loss) generated by each activity during 2022 are shown below. Explain how the results of these activities should be reported on the taxpayer's 2022 tax return.

Activity	Suspended Losses	Current Year Income (Loss)
X	($20,000)	$10,000
Y	(30,000)	(10,000)
Z	0	20,000

17. **Rental Real Estate, Active Participation.** (Obj. 4)

a. In 2011, Tyler Tomey (548-00-9234) paid $135,000 for a condominium that he uses as rental property. In 2018, he spent $18,500 furnishing the condo. He uses regular (accelerated) MACRS to depreciate the furnishings. He elected not to use bonus depreciation. The half-year convention applies to the furnishings. During 2022, Tyler received $15,000 in rental income and paid the following expenses:

Association dues	$2,800
Insurance	350
Mortgage interest	7,460
Real estate taxes	1,400
Repairs	760
Utilities	360

The property is located at 5505 West End Road, #5, Farmington, IN 46883. Tyler actively participates in the rental activity. His AGI before considering the above income and expenses is $141,400. He depreciates the condominium using MACRS. Prepare Schedule E and Form 8582 for Tyler Tomey.

b. In 2001, Jeremy L. Schultz (SSN 678-00-5244) paid $90,000 for a townhouse purchased as an investment. The townhouse is located at 812 E. Locust, Springfield, MO 65807. During 2022, Jeremy received $9,600 in rental income from the tenants and paid the following expenses:

Association dues	$ 400
Depreciation	3,273
Insurance	130
Mortgage interest	6,200
Real estate taxes	1,100
Repairs	320
Utilities	440

Jeremy actively participates in the rental of the town home. His AGI before considering the income and expenses from the rental property is $140,000. He depreciates the townhouse using MACRS. Prepare Jeremy Schultz's Schedule E and Form 8582.

(Use for Problem 17.)

SCHEDULE E (Form 1040)

Supplemental Income and Loss

(From rental real estate, royalties, partnerships, S corporations, estates, trusts, REMICs, etc.)

Department of the Treasury
Internal Revenue Service

Attach to Form 1040, 1040-SR, 1040-NR, or 1041.
Go to www.irs.gov/ScheduleE for instructions and the latest information.

OMB No. 1545-0074

2022

Attachment Sequence No. **13**

Name(s) shown on return

Your social security number

Part I — Income or Loss From Rental Real Estate and Royalties

Note: If you are in the business of renting personal property, use **Schedule C**. See instructions. If you are an individual, report farm rental income or loss from **Form 4835** on page 2, line 40.

A Did you make any payments in 2022 that would require you to file Form(s) 1099? See instructions . . ☐ Yes ☐ No
B If "Yes," did you or will you file required Form(s) 1099? . . . . ☐ Yes ☐ No

1a Physical address of each property (street, city, state, ZIP code)

A
B
C

1b Type of Property (from list below)

A
B
C

2 For each rental real estate property listed above, report the number of fair rental and personal use days. Check the QJV box only if you meet the requirements to file as a qualified joint venture. See instructions.

	Fair Rental Days	Personal Use Days	QJV
A			☐
B			☐
C			☐

Type of Property:
1 Single Family Residence 3 Vacation/Short-Term Rental 5 Land 7 Self-Rental
2 Multi-Family Residence 4 Commercial 6 Royalties 8 Other (describe)

			Properties: A	B	C
Income:					
3	Rents received	3			
4	Royalties received	4			
Expenses:					
5	Advertising	5			
6	Auto and travel (see instructions)	6			
7	Cleaning and maintenance	7			
8	Commissions	8			
9	Insurance	9			
10	Legal and other professional fees	10			
11	Management fees	11			
12	Mortgage interest paid to banks, etc. (see instructions)	12			
13	Other interest	13			
14	Repairs	14			
15	Supplies	15			
16	Taxes	16			
17	Utilities	17			
18	Depreciation expense or depletion	18			
19	Other (list)	19			
20	Total expenses. Add lines 5 through 19	20			
21	Subtract line 20 from line 3 (rents) and/or 4 (royalties). If result is a (loss), see instructions to find out if you must file **Form 6198**	21			
22	Deductible rental real estate loss after limitation, if any, on **Form 8582** (see instructions)	22	( )	( )	( )

23a	Total of all amounts reported on line 3 for all rental properties	23a	
b	Total of all amounts reported on line 4 for all royalty properties	23b	
c	Total of all amounts reported on line 12 for all properties	23c	
d	Total of all amounts reported on line 18 for all properties	23d	
e	Total of all amounts reported on line 20 for all properties	23e	
24	**Income.** Add positive amounts shown on line 21. **Do not** include any losses	24	
25	**Losses.** Add royalty losses from line 21 and rental real estate losses from line 22. Enter total losses here	25	( )
26	**Total rental real estate and royalty income or (loss).** Combine lines 24 and 25. Enter the result here. If Parts II, III, IV, and line 40 on page 2 do not apply to you, also enter this amount on Schedule 1 (Form 1040), line 5. Otherwise, include this amount in the total on line 41 on page 2	26	

For Paperwork Reduction Act Notice, see the separate instructions.   Cat. No. 11344L   Schedule E (Form 1040) 2022

(Use for Problem 17.)

Form 8582

Department of the Treasury
Internal Revenue Service

Passive Activity Loss Limitations

See separate instructions.
Attach to Form 1040, 1040-SR, or 1041.
Go to *www.irs.gov/Form8582* for instructions and the latest information.

OMB No. 1545-1008

2022

Attachment
Sequence No. **858**

Name(s) shown on return | Identifying number

Part I	**2022 Passive Activity Loss**

Caution: Complete Parts IV and V before completing Part I.

Rental Real Estate Activities With Active Participation (For the definition of active participation, see *Special Allowance for Rental Real Estate Activities* in the instructions.)

1a	Activities with net income (enter the amount from Part IV, column (a)) . . .	**1a**
b	Activities with net loss (enter the amount from Part IV, column (b))	**1b** ( )
c	Prior years' unallowed losses (enter the amount from Part IV, column (c)) . .	**1c** ( )
d	Combine lines 1a, 1b, and 1c	**1d**

All Other Passive Activities

2a	Activities with net income (enter the amount from Part V, column (a)) . . .	**2a**
b	Activities with net loss (enter the amount from Part V, column (b))	**2b** ( )
c	Prior years' unallowed losses (enter the amount from Part V, column (c)) . .	**2c** ( )
d	Combine lines 2a, 2b, and 2c	**2d**

3 Combine lines 1d and 2d. If this line is zero or more, stop here and include this form with your return; all losses are allowed, including any prior year unallowed losses entered on line 1c or 2c. Report the losses on the forms and schedules normally used **3**

If line 3 is a loss and: • Line 1d is a loss, go to Part II.
• Line 2d is a loss (and line 1d is zero or more), skip Part II and go to line 10.

Caution: If your filing status is married filing separately and you lived with your spouse at any time during the year, **do not** complete Part II. Instead, go to line 10.

Part II	**Special Allowance for Rental Real Estate Activities With Active Participation**

Note: Enter all numbers in Part II as positive amounts. See instructions for an example.

4	Enter the **smaller** of the loss on line 1d or the loss on line 3	**4**
5	Enter $150,000. If married filing separately, see instructions	**5**
6	Enter modified adjusted gross income, but not less than zero. See instructions	**6**
	Note: If line 6 is greater than or equal to line 5, skip lines 7 and 8 and enter -0- on line 9. Otherwise, go to line 7.	
7	Subtract line 6 from line 5	**7**
8	Multiply line 7 by 50% (0.50). **Do not** enter more than $25,000. If married filing separately, see instructions	**8**
9	Enter the **smaller** of line 4 or line 8	**9**

Part III	**Total Losses Allowed**

10	Add the income, if any, on lines 1a and 2a and enter the total	**10**
11	**Total losses allowed from all passive activities for 2022.** Add lines 9 and 10. See instructions to find out how to report the losses on your tax return	**11**

Part IV	**Complete This Part Before Part I, Lines 1a, 1b, and 1c.** See instructions.

Name of activity	Current year		Prior years	Overall gain or loss	
	(a) Net income (line 1a)	**(b)** Net loss (line 1b)	**(c)** Unallowed loss (line 1c)	**(d)** Gain	**(e)** Loss
Total. Enter on Part I, lines 1a, 1b, and 1c					

For Paperwork Reduction Act Notice, see instructions.   Cat. No. 63704F   Form **8582** (2022)

18. **Internet Problem: Researching IRS Publication 925.** (Obj. 3)

The chapter discussed two ways to meet the material participation test: (1) participate in the activity for more than 500 hours during the year, and (2) participate in the activity for more than 100 hours during the year and have that participation be at least as much as the participation by all other individuals, including employees. There are five other ways in which to meet the material participation test.

Go to the IRS website. Locate IRS Publication 925 and find the appropriate page that lists all the various ways to meet the material participation test. Print out a copy of the page where you found your answer. Underline or highlight the pertinent information.

See Appendix A for instructions on use of the IRS website.

19. **Business Entity Problem:** This problem is designed for those using the "business entity" approach. **The solution may require information from Chapters 14–16.**

The Hampton-Lewis Partnership owns an apartment building. Gross income from the apartments was $200,000. Total deductions were $260,000. The two partners share profits and losses equally.

a.   How will the partnership report the resulting $60,000 loss?

b.   If Hampton-Lewis was an S corporation (with two shareholders who each own 50% of the stock), how would the loss be reported?

c.   If Hampton-Lewis was a regular C corporation (with two shareholders who each own 50% of the stock), how would the loss be reported?

COMPREHENSIVE PROBLEM

20. (Obj. 4) On January 2, 2002, Cecily J. Cook (SSN 344-00-5768) purchased a two-unit apartment building at 1626 Flat Street, Ritzville, Washington, 99270-8224. The costs of the land and building were $20,000 and $82,500, respectively. Both apartments are the same size, with one on the ground floor and the other upstairs. Cecily has lived in the upstairs apartment since she acquired the building. The tenant in the ground-floor apartment at the time the building was purchased has continued to rent from Cecily. The tenant pays $350 a month in rent. On June 30, the tenant moved out. The apartment was vacant until August 1, even though Cecily advertised and attempted to rent it. On August 1, a new tenant moved in, paying rent of $400 per month. Rent is due on the first day of the month. Cecily uses MACRS to depreciate the rental portion of the building. Information on the apartment follows:

Revenue

Rent from the first tenant (6 months × $350)	$2,100
Rent from the second tenant (5 months × $400)	2,000
Total revenue	$4,100

Expenses
Entire house:

Real estate taxes	$1,700
Janitor and yard work	160
Electricity and water	440
Repairs	300
Heat (gas)	800
Interest on mortgage	1,100
Insurance	376
Expenses other than depreciation	$4,876

Ground-floor apartment:

Advertising	100
Cleaning and maintenance	420
Repairs	70
	$590

Upstairs apartment:

Repairs	$ 90
Cleaning and maintenance	480
	$570

In addition to the rental property, Cecily works as an administrative assistant and earned $17,600 in wages. From this amount, $660 of federal income tax was withheld. Cecily also earned $147 in interest from Bank of America. Cecily is single, has no dependents, and is legally blind. Prepare Cecily Cook's tax return. Cecily does not want $3 to go to the Presidential election campaign fund. She signs her return on April 10, 2023.

Prepare Form 1040, Form 1040 Schedule 1, Schedule E and Form 8582 for 2022. No other forms or schedules are necessary.

(Use for Problem 20.)

| Form **1040** | Department of the Treasury—Internal Revenue Service **U.S. Individual Income Tax Return** | **2022** | OMB No. 1545-0074 | IRS Use Only—Do not write or staple in this space. |

Filing Status
Check only one box.

☐ Single ☐ Married filing jointly ☐ Married filing separately (MFS) ☐ Head of household (HOH) ☐ Qualifying widow(er) (QW)

If you checked the MFS box, enter the name of your spouse. If you checked the HOH or QW box, enter the child's name if the qualifying person is a child but not your dependent.

| Your first name and middle initial | Last name | Your social security number |
| If joint return, spouse's first name and middle initial | Last name | Spouse's social security number |

Home address (number and street). If you have a P.O. box, see instructions.		Apt. no.	**Presidential Election Campaign** Check here if you, or your spouse if filing jointly, want $3 to go to this fund. Checking a box below will not change your tax or refund.
City, town, or post office. If you have a foreign address, also complete spaces below.	State	ZIP code	
Foreign country name	Foreign province/state/county	Foreign postal code	☐ You ☐ Spouse

At any time during 2022, did you: (a) receive (as a reward, award, or compensation); or (b) sell, exchange, gift, or otherwise dispose of a digital asset (or a financial interest in a digital asset)? (See instructions.) . . ☐ Yes ☐ No

Standard Deduction

Someone can claim: ☐ You as a dependent ☐ Your spouse as a dependent
☐ Spouse itemizes on a separate return or you were a dual-status alien

Age/Blindness **You:** ☐ Were born before January 2, 1958 ☐ Are blind **Spouse:** ☐ Was born before January 2, 1958 ☐ Is blind

Dependents (see instructions):
If more than four dependents, see instructions and check here . . ☐

(1) First name　Last name	(2) Social security number	(3) Relationship to you	(4) Check the box if qualifies for (see instructions):
			Child tax credit	Credit for other dependents
			☐	☐
			☐	☐
			☐	☐
			☐	☐

Income

Attach Form(s) W-2 here. Also attach Forms W-2G and 1099-R if tax was withheld.

If you did not get a Form W-2, see instructions.

Attach Sch. B if required.

1a	Total amount from Form(s) W-2, box 1 (see instructions)	1a	
b	Household employee wages not reported on Form(s) W-2	1b	
c	Tip income not reported on line 1a (see instructions)	1c	
d	Medicaid waiver payments not reported on Form(s) W-2 (see instructions)	1d	
e	Taxable dependent care benefits from Form 2441, line 26	1e	
f	Employer-provided adoption benefits from Form 8839, line 29	1f	
g	Wages from Form 8919, line 6	1g	
h	Other earned income (see instructions)	1h	
i	Nontaxable combat pay election (see instructions)	1i	
z	Add lines 1a through 1h	1z	
2a	Tax-exempt interest . . .	2a		b Taxable interest	2b	
3a	Qualified dividends . . .	3a		b Ordinary dividends	3b	
4a	IRA distributions . . .	4a		b Taxable amount	4b	
5a	Pensions and annuities . .	5a		b Taxable amount	5b	
6a	Social security benefits . .	6a		b Taxable amount	6b	
c	If you elect to use the lump-sum election method, check here (see instructions) . . ☐		
7	Capital gain or (loss). Attach Schedule D if required. If not required, check here . . ☐	7	
8	Other income from Schedule 1, line 10	8	
9	Add lines 1z, 2b, 3b, 4b, 5b, 6b, 7, and 8. This is your **total income** . . .	9	
10	Adjustments to income from Schedule 1, line 26	10	
11	Subtract line 10 from line 9. This is your **adjusted gross income** . . .	11	
12	**Standard deduction or itemized deductions** (from Schedule A)	12	
13	Qualified business income deduction from Form 8995 or Form 8995-A . .	13	
14	Add lines 12 and 13	14	
15	Subtract line 14 from line 11. If zero or less, enter -0-. This is your **taxable income** . . .	15	

Standard Deduction for—
- Single or Married filing separately, $12,950
- Married filing jointly or Qualifying widow(er), $25,900
- Head of household, $19,400
- If you checked any box under *Standard Deduction,* see instructions.

For Disclosure, Privacy Act, and Paperwork Reduction Act Notice, see separate instructions.　Cat. No. 11320B　Form **1040** (2022)

(Use for Problem 20.)

Form 1040 (2022)   Page **2**

Tax and Credits	16	**Tax** (see instructions). Check if any from Form(s): 1 ☐ 8814 2 ☐ 4972 3 ☐ ____	16
	17	Amount from Schedule 2, line 3	17
	18	Add lines 16 and 17	18
	19	Child tax credit or credit for other dependents from Schedule 8812	19
	20	Amount from Schedule 3, line 8	20
	21	Add lines 19 and 20	21
	22	Subtract line 21 from line 18. If zero or less, enter -0-	22
	23	Other taxes, including self-employment tax, from Schedule 2, line 21	23
	24	Add lines 22 and 23. This is your **total tax**	24
Payments	25	Federal income tax withheld from:	
	a	Form(s) W-2	25a
	b	Form(s) 1099	25b
	c	Other forms (see instructions)	25c
	d	Add lines 25a through 25c	25d
If you have a qualifying child, attach Sch. EIC.	26	2022 estimated tax payments and amount applied from 2021 return	26
	27	Earned income credit (EIC)	27
	28	Additional child tax credit from Schedule 8812	28
	29	American opportunity credit from Form 8863, line 8	29
	30	Reserved for future use	30
	31	Amount from Schedule 3, line 15	31
	32	Add lines 27, 28, 29, and 31. These are your **total other payments and refundable credits**	32
	33	Add lines 25d, 26, and 32. These are your **total payments**	33
Refund	34	If line 33 is more than line 24, subtract line 24 from line 33. This is the amount you **overpaid**	34
	35a	Amount of line 34 you want **refunded to you**. If Form 8888 is attached, check here ☐	35a
Direct deposit? See instructions.	b	Routing number c Type: ☐ Checking ☐ Savings	
	d	Account number	
	36	Amount of line 34 you want **applied to your 2023 estimated tax**	36
Amount You Owe	37	Subtract line 33 from line 24. This is the **amount you owe**. For details on how to pay, go to *www.irs.gov/Payments* or see instructions	37
	38	Estimated tax penalty (see instructions)	38

Third Party Designee   Do you want to allow another person to discuss this return with the IRS? See instructions   ☐ **Yes.** Complete below.   ☐ **No**

Designee's name   Phone no.   Personal identification number (PIN)

Sign Here

Under penalties of perjury, I declare that I have examined this return and accompanying schedules and statements, and to the best of my knowledge and belief, they are true, correct, and complete. Declaration of preparer (other than taxpayer) is based on all information of which preparer has any knowledge.

Joint return? See instructions. Keep a copy for your records.

Your signature   Date   Your occupation   If the IRS sent you an Identity Protection PIN, enter it here (see inst.)

Spouse's signature. If a joint return, **both** must sign.   Date   Spouse's occupation   If the IRS sent your spouse an Identity Protection PIN, enter it here (see inst.)

Phone no.   Email address

Paid Preparer Use Only

Preparer's name   Preparer's signature   Date   PTIN   Check if: ☐ Self-employed

Firm's name   Phone no.

Firm's address   Firm's EIN

Go to *www.irs.gov/Form1040* for instructions and the latest information.   Form **1040** (2022)

(Use for Problem 20.)

SCHEDULE 1 (Form 1040)	Additional Income and Adjustments to Income	OMB No. 1545-0074
Department of the Treasury Internal Revenue Service	Attach to Form 1040, 1040-SR, or 1040-NR. Go to *www.irs.gov/Form1040* for instructions and the latest information.	2022 Attachment Sequence No. 01

Name(s) shown on Form 1040, 1040-SR, or 1040-NR — Your social security number

Part I   Additional Income

1	Taxable refunds, credits, or offsets of state and local income taxes	**1**	
2a	Alimony received	**2a**	
b	Date of original divorce or separation agreement (see instructions):		
3	Business income or (loss). Attach Schedule C	**3**	
4	Other gains or (losses). Attach Form 4797	**4**	
5	Rental real estate, royalties, partnerships, S corporations, trusts, etc. Attach Schedule E	**5**	
6	Farm income or (loss). Attach Schedule F	**6**	
7	Unemployment compensation	**7**	
8	Other income:		
a	Net operating loss	**8a** ( )	
b	Gambling	**8b**	
c	Cancellation of debt	**8c**	
d	Foreign earned income exclusion from Form 2555	**8d** ( )	
e	Income from Form 8853	**8e**	
f	Income from Form 8889	**8f**	
g	Alaska Permanent Fund dividends	**8g**	
h	Jury duty pay	**8h**	
i	Prizes and awards	**8i**	
j	Activity not engaged in for profit income	**8j**	
k	Stock options	**8k**	
l	Income from the rental of personal property if you engaged in the rental for profit but were not in the business of renting such property	**8l**	
m	Olympic and Paralympic medals and USOC prize money (see instructions)	**8m**	
n	Section 951(a) inclusion (see instructions)	**8n**	
o	Section 951A(a) inclusion (see instructions)	**8o**	
p	Section 461(l) excess business loss adjustment	**8p**	
q	Taxable distributions from an ABLE account (see instructions)	**8q**	
r	Scholarship and fellowship grants not reported on Form W-2	**8r**	
s	Nontaxable amount of Medicaid waiver payments included on Form 1040, line 1a or 1d	**8s** ( )	
t	Pension or annuity from a nonqualifed deferred compensation plan or a nongovernmental section 457 plan	**8t**	
u	Wages earned while incarcerated	**8u**	
z	Other income. List type and amount: _____	**8z**	
9	Total other income. Add lines 8a through 8z	**9**	
10	Combine lines 1 through 7 and 9. Enter here and on Form 1040, 1040-SR, or 1040-NR, line 8	**10**	

For Paperwork Reduction Act Notice, see your tax return instructions.   Cat. No. 71479F   Schedule 1 (Form 1040) 2022

(Use for Problem 20.)

Schedule 1 (Form 1040) 2022   Page **2**

Part II   Adjustments to Income

11	Educator expenses	**11**	
12	Certain business expenses of reservists, performing artists, and fee-basis government officials. Attach Form 2106	**12**	
13	Health savings account deduction. Attach Form 8889	**13**	
14	Moving expenses for members of the Armed Forces. Attach Form 3903 . . .	**14**	
15	Deductible part of self-employment tax. Attach Schedule SE	**15**	
16	Self-employed SEP, SIMPLE, and qualified plans	**16**	
17	Self-employed health insurance deduction	**17**	
18	Penalty on early withdrawal of savings	**18**	
19a	Alimony paid	**19a**	
b	Recipient's SSN		
c	Date of original divorce or separation agreement (see instructions): _____		
20	IRA deduction	**20**	
21	Student loan interest deduction	**21**	
22	Reserved for future use	**22**	
23	Archer MSA deduction	**23**	
24	Other adjustments:		
a	Jury duty pay (see instructions)	**24a**	
b	Deductible expenses related to income reported on line 8l from the rental of personal property engaged in for profit	**24b**	
c	Nontaxable amount of the value of Olympic and Paralympic medals and USOC prize money reported on line 8m	**24c**	
d	Reforestation amortization and expenses	**24d**	
e	Repayment of supplemental unemployment benefits under the Trade Act of 1974	**24e**	
f	Contributions to section 501(c)(18)(D) pension plans	**24f**	
g	Contributions by certain chaplains to section 403(b) plans	**24g**	
h	Attorney fees and court costs for actions involving certain unlawful discrimination claims (see instructions)	**24h**	
i	Attorney fees and court costs you paid in connection with an award from the IRS for information you provided that helped the IRS detect tax law violations	**24i**	
j	Housing deduction from Form 2555	**24j**	
k	Excess deductions of section 67(e) expenses from Schedule K-1 (Form 1041)	**24k**	
z	Other adjustments. List type and amount: _____	**24z**	
25	Total other adjustments. Add lines 24a through 24z	**25**	
26	Add lines 11 through 23 and 25. These are your **adjustments to income**. Enter here and on Form 1040 or 1040-SR, line 10, or Form 1040-NR, line 10a	**26**	

Schedule 1 (Form 1040) 2022

(Use for Problem 20.)

SCHEDULE E (Form 1040) Department of the Treasury Internal Revenue Service	Supplemental Income and Loss (From rental real estate, royalties, partnerships, S corporations, estates, trusts, REMICs, etc.) Attach to Form 1040, 1040-SR, 1040-NR, or 1041. Go to www.irs.gov/ScheduleE for instructions and the latest information.	OMB No. 1545-0074 2022 Attachment Sequence No. 13

Name(s) shown on return _____   Your social security number _____

Part I   Income or Loss From Rental Real Estate and Royalties

Note: If you are in the business of renting personal property, use **Schedule C**. See instructions. If you are an individual, report farm rental income or loss from **Form 4835** on page 2, line 40.

A Did you make any payments in 2022 that would require you to file Form(s) 1099? See instructions . . ☐ Yes ☐ No
B If "Yes," did you or will you file required Form(s) 1099? . . . . ☐ Yes ☐ No

1a Physical address of each property (street, city, state, ZIP code)

A	
B	
C	

1b Type of Property (from list below)	2 For each rental real estate property listed above, report the number of fair rental and personal use days. Check the QJV box only if you meet the requirements to file as a qualified joint venture. See instructions.		Fair Rental Days	Personal Use Days	QJV
A		A			☐
B		B			☐
C		C			☐

Type of Property:
1 Single Family Residence   3 Vacation/Short-Term Rental   5 Land   7 Self-Rental
2 Multi-Family Residence   4 Commercial   6 Royalties 8 Other (describe) _____

		Properties:		
		A	B	C
Income:				
3	Rents received	3			
4	Royalties received	4			
Expenses:				
5	Advertising	5			
6	Auto and travel (see instructions)	6			
7	Cleaning and maintenance	7			
8	Commissions	8			
9	Insurance	9			
10	Legal and other professional fees	10			
11	Management fees	11			
12	Mortgage interest paid to banks, etc. (see instructions)	12			
13	Other interest	13			
14	Repairs	14			
15	Supplies	15			
16	Taxes	16			
17	Utilities	17			
18	Depreciation expense or depletion	18			
19	Other (list) _____	19			
20	Total expenses. Add lines 5 through 19	20			
21	Subtract line 20 from line 3 (rents) and/or 4 (royalties). If result is a (loss), see instructions to find out if you must file **Form 6198**	21			
22	Deductible rental real estate loss after limitation, if any, on **Form 8582** (see instructions)	22	( )	( )	( )
23a	Total of all amounts reported on line 3 for all rental properties	23a		
b	Total of all amounts reported on line 4 for all royalty properties	23b		
c	Total of all amounts reported on line 12 for all properties	23c		
d	Total of all amounts reported on line 18 for all properties	23d		
e	Total of all amounts reported on line 20 for all properties	23e		
24	**Income.** Add positive amounts shown on line 21. **Do not** include any losses	24	
25	**Losses.** Add royalty losses from line 21 and rental real estate losses from line 22. Enter total losses here	25	( )
26	**Total rental real estate and royalty income or (loss).** Combine lines 24 and 25. Enter the result here. If Parts II, III, IV, and line 40 on page 2 do not apply to you, also enter this amount on Schedule 1 (Form 1040), line 5. Otherwise, include this amount in the total on line 41 on page 2 .	26	

For Paperwork Reduction Act Notice, see the separate instructions.   Cat. No. 11344L   Schedule E (Form 1040) 2022

(Use for Problem 20.)

Form **8582** Department of the Treasury Internal Revenue Service	**Passive Activity Loss Limitations** See separate instructions. Attach to Form 1040, 1040-SR, or 1041. Go to *www.irs.gov/Form8582* for instructions and the latest information.	OMB No. 1545-1008 **2022** Attachment Sequence No. **858**

Name(s) shown on return | Identifying number

Part I   2022 Passive Activity Loss
Caution: Complete Parts IV and V before completing Part I.

Rental Real Estate Activities With Active Participation (For the definition of active participation, see *Special Allowance for Rental Real Estate Activities* in the instructions.)

1a	Activities with net income (enter the amount from Part IV, column (a)) . . .	**1a**
b	Activities with net loss (enter the amount from Part IV, column (b)) . . .	**1b** ( )
c	Prior years' unallowed losses (enter the amount from Part IV, column (c)) .	**1c** ( )
d	Combine lines 1a, 1b, and 1c	**1d**

All Other Passive Activities

2a	Activities with net income (enter the amount from Part V, column (a)) . . .	**2a**
b	Activities with net loss (enter the amount from Part V, column (b))	**2b** ( )
c	Prior years' unallowed losses (enter the amount from Part V, column (c)) . .	**2c** ( )
d	Combine lines 2a, 2b, and 2c	**2d**

3   Combine lines 1d and 2d. If this line is zero or more, stop here and include this form with your return; all losses are allowed, including any prior year unallowed losses entered on line 1c or 2c. Report the losses on the forms and schedules normally used   .   .   .   . | **3**

If line 3 is a loss and: • Line 1d is a loss, go to Part II.
   • Line 2d is a loss (and line 1d is zero or more), skip Part II and go to line 10.

Caution: If your filing status is married filing separately and you lived with your spouse at any time during the year, **do not** complete Part II. Instead, go to line 10.

Part II   Special Allowance for Rental Real Estate Activities With Active Participation
Note: Enter all numbers in Part II as positive amounts. See instructions for an example.

4	Enter the **smaller** of the loss on line 1d or the loss on line 3		**4**
5	Enter $150,000. If married filing separately, see instructions	**5**	
6	Enter modified adjusted gross income, but not less than zero. See instructions	**6**	
	Note: If line 6 is greater than or equal to line 5, skip lines 7 and 8 and enter -0- on line 9. Otherwise, go to line 7.		
7	Subtract line 6 from line 5	**7**	
8	Multiply line 7 by 50% (0.50). **Do not** enter more than $25,000. If married filing separately, see instructions		**8**
9	Enter the **smaller** of line 4 or line 8		**9**

Part III   Total Losses Allowed

10	Add the income, if any, on lines 1a and 2a and enter the total	**10**
11	**Total losses allowed from all passive activities for 2022.** Add lines 9 and 10. See instructions to find out how to report the losses on your tax return	**11**

Part IV   Complete This Part Before Part I, Lines 1a, 1b, and 1c. See instructions.

Name of activity	Current year		Prior years	Overall gain or loss	
	(a) Net income (line 1a)	**(b)** Net loss (line 1b)	**(c)** Unallowed loss (line 1c)	**(d)** Gain	**(e)** Loss
Total. Enter on Part I, lines 1a, 1b, and 1c					

For Paperwork Reduction Act Notice, see instructions. | Cat. No. 63704F | Form **8582** (2022)

CUMULATIVE PROBLEM (CHAPTERS 1-9)

Merv R. Baldwin (age 39, SSN 550-00-7400) and Melanie A. Baldwin (age 36, SSN 598-00-3775) live at 515 W. 35th Ave., Provo, Utah 84200. They claim their nine-year-old son, Adam (SSN 458-00-9330) as their only dependent. Merv works as a computer analyst; Melanie is employed as a manager. Details from their respective W-2s are shown below. In order to allow them both to work, the Baldwins paid Anna Furlough (Melanie's mother, SSN 583-00-9991) $3,600 during the year for after-school childcare. Anna lives down the street at 735 W. 35th Ave.

	Gross Wages	State Income Tax Withheld	Federal Income Tax Withheld	Social Security Tax Withheld	Medicare Tax Withheld
Merv	$176,500	$8,466	$36,100	$7,886	$2,559
Melanie	75,605	6,644	24,064	4,688	1,096

During 2022, the Baldwins received $33,667 from the rental of their cabin in Park City, Utah. The cabin is located at 1900 Mountain View Lane, Park City, Utah 85068. The cabin was rented out for 104 days during the year, and the Baldwins personally used the cabin for 20 days during the summer. The Baldwins paid $319,000 for the cabin in 1997, of which $50,000 was allocated to the land. They depreciate the cabin using MACRS. Expenses related to the cabin include:

Cleaning and maintenance	$ 700
Commissions*	12,400
Insurance	522
Mortgage interest	7,230
Real estate taxes	5,900
Repairs	240
Utilities	4,800

* Paid to a leasing company to help them identify and screen potential tenants, collect rents, and schedule necessary repairs and cleaning services.

The Baldwins also have receipts for the following income and expenses during the year.

Income:

City of Ogden bond interest	$12,200
Key Bank CD interest	40,750
Zion Bank interest	29,794

Expenses:

Home mortgage interest (on main home)	$15,909
Real estate taxes (on main home)	5,525
Cash contributions to a qualified charity	2,000
Noncash contributions to a qualified charity	150
Amount paid when filing 2021 state tax return	429
Amount paid when filing 2021 federal tax return	2,440
Tax preparation fees	275

Prepare the Baldwins' joint tax return (Form 1040, Schedule 3, Schedule A, Schedule B, Schedule E, Form 2441, Form 8812 and Form 8960). The Baldwins get full health care coverage through Merv's employer. The Baldwins did not have any interest in a foreign account or trust. They sign their return on April 15, 2023, and both want to contribute $3 to the Presidential campaign fund.

(Use for Cumulative Problem.)

Form **1040**	Department of the Treasury—Internal Revenue Service **U.S. Individual Income Tax Return**	**2022**	OMB No. 1545-0074	IRS Use Only—Do not write or staple in this space.

Filing Status
Check only one box.

☐ Single ☐ Married filing jointly ☐ Married filing separately (MFS) ☐ Head of household (HOH) ☐ Qualifying widow(er) (QW)

If you checked the MFS box, enter the name of your spouse. If you checked the HOH or QW box, enter the child's name if the qualifying person is a child but not your dependent:

Your first name and middle initial	Last name		**Your social security number**
If joint return, spouse's first name and middle initial	Last name		**Spouse's social security number**
Home address (number and street). If you have a P.O. box, see instructions.		Apt. no.	**Presidential Election Campaign**
City, town, or post office. If you have a foreign address, also complete spaces below.	State	ZIP code	Check here if you, or your spouse if filing jointly, want $3 to go to this fund. Checking a box below will not change your tax or refund.
Foreign country name	Foreign province/state/county	Foreign postal code	☐ You ☐ Spouse

At any time during 2022, did you: (a) receive (as a reward, award, or compensation); or (b) sell, exchange, gift, or otherwise dispose of a digital asset (or a financial interest in a digital asset)? (See instructions.) . . ☐ Yes ☐ No

Standard Deduction

Someone can claim: ☐ You as a dependent ☐ Your spouse as a dependent
☐ Spouse itemizes on a separate return or you were a dual-status alien

Age/Blindness **You:** ☐ Were born before January 2, 1958 ☐ Are blind **Spouse:** ☐ Was born before January 2, 1958 ☐ Is blind

Dependents (see instructions):
If more than four dependents, see instructions and check here . . ☐

(1) First name Last name	(2) Social security number	(3) Relationship to you	(4) Check the box if qualifies for (see instructions):	
			Child tax credit	Credit for other dependents
			☐	☐
			☐	☐
			☐	☐
			☐	☐

Income

Attach Form(s) W-2 here. Also attach Forms W-2G and 1099-R if tax was withheld.

If you did not get a Form W-2, see instructions.

Attach Sch. B if required.

Standard Deduction for—
• Single or Married filing separately, $12,950
• Married filing jointly or Qualifying widow(er), $25,900
• Head of household, $19,400
• If you checked any box under *Standard Deduction*, see instructions.

1a	Total amount from Form(s) W-2, box 1 (see instructions)	1a
b	Household employee wages not reported on Form(s) W-2	1b
c	Tip income not reported on line 1a (see instructions)	1c
d	Medicaid waiver payments not reported on Form(s) W-2 (see instructions)	1d
e	Taxable dependent care benefits from Form 2441, line 26	1e
f	Employer-provided adoption benefits from Form 8839, line 29	1f
g	Wages from Form 8919, line 6	1g
h	Other earned income (see instructions)	1h
i	Nontaxable combat pay election (see instructions) 1i	
z	Add lines 1a through 1h	1z
2a	Tax-exempt interest . . . 2a	b Taxable interest	2b
3a	Qualified dividends . . . 3a	b Ordinary dividends	3b
4a	IRA distributions . . . 4a	b Taxable amount	4b
5a	Pensions and annuities . . 5a	b Taxable amount	5b
6a	Social security benefits . . 6a	b Taxable amount	6b
c	If you elect to use the lump-sum election method, check here (see instructions) ☐	
7	Capital gain or (loss). Attach Schedule D if required. If not required, check here . . ☐	7
8	Other income from Schedule 1, line 10	8
9	Add lines 1z, 2b, 3b, 4b, 5b, 6b, 7, and 8. This is your **total income**	9
10	Adjustments to income from Schedule 1, line 26	10
11	Subtract line 10 from line 9. This is your **adjusted gross income**	11
12	**Standard deduction or itemized deductions** (from Schedule A) . . .	12
13	Qualified business income deduction from Form 8995 or Form 8995-A . .	13
14	Add lines 12 and 13	14
15	Subtract line 14 from line 11. If zero or less, enter -0-. This is your **taxable income**	15

For Disclosure, Privacy Act, and Paperwork Reduction Act Notice, see separate instructions.   Cat. No. 11320B   Form **1040** (2022)

(Use for Cumulative Problem.)

Version A, Cycle 7

Form 1040 (2022)   Page **2**

Tax and Credits	16	**Tax** (see instructions). Check if any from Form(s): 1 ☐ 8814 2 ☐ 4972 3 ☐ _____	16	
	17	Amount from Schedule 2, line 3	17	
	18	Add lines 16 and 17	18	
	19	Child tax credit or credit for other dependents from Schedule 8812	19	
	20	Amount from Schedule 3, line 8	20	
	21	Add lines 19 and 20	21	
	22	Subtract line 21 from line 18. If zero or less, enter -0-	22	
	23	Other taxes, including self-employment tax, from Schedule 2, line 21	23	
	24	Add lines 22 and 23. This is your **total tax**	24	
Payments	25	Federal income tax withheld from:		
	a	Form(s) W-2	25a	
	b	Form(s) 1099	25b	
	c	Other forms (see instructions)	25c	
	d	Add lines 25a through 25c		25d
If you have a qualifying child, attach Sch. EIC.	26	2022 estimated tax payments and amount applied from 2021 return		26
	27	Earned income credit (EIC)	27	
	28	Additional child tax credit from Schedule 8812	28	
	29	American opportunity credit from Form 8863, line 8	29	
	30	Reserved for future use	30	
	31	Amount from Schedule 3, line 15	31	
	32	Add lines 27, 28, 29, and 31. These are your **total other payments and refundable credits**		32
	33	Add lines 25d, 26, and 32. These are your **total payments**		33
Refund	34	If line 33 is more than line 24, subtract line 24 from line 33. This is the amount you **overpaid**		34
	35a	Amount of line 34 you want **refunded to you.** If Form 8888 is attached, check here ☐		35a
Direct deposit? See instructions.	b	Routing number _____ c Type: ☐ Checking ☐ Savings		
	d	Account number _____		
	36	Amount of line 34 you want **applied to your 2023 estimated tax**	36	
Amount You Owe	37	Subtract line 33 from line 24. This is the **amount you owe**. For details on how to pay, go to *www.irs.gov/Payments* or see instructions		37
	38	Estimated tax penalty (see instructions)	38	

| **Third Party Designee** | Do you want to allow another person to discuss this return with the IRS? See instructions | ☐ **Yes.** Complete below. | ☐ **No** | |
| | Designee's name _____ | Phone no. _____ | Personal identification number (PIN) _____ | |

Sign Here

Under penalties of perjury, I declare that I have examined this return and accompanying schedules and statements, and to the best of my knowledge and belief, they are true, correct, and complete. Declaration of preparer (other than taxpayer) is based on all information of which preparer has any knowledge.

Joint return? See instructions. Keep a copy for your records.

Your signature	Date	Your occupation	If the IRS sent you an Identity Protection PIN, enter it here (see inst.) _____
Spouse's signature. If a joint return, **both** must sign.	Date	Spouse's occupation	If the IRS sent your spouse an Identity Protection PIN, enter it here (see inst.) _____
Phone no.		Email address	

Paid Preparer Use Only

Preparer's name	Preparer's signature	Date	PTIN	Check if: ☐ Self-employed
Firm's name			Phone no.	
Firm's address			Firm's EIN	

Go to *www.irs.gov/Form1040* for instructions and the latest information.   Form **1040** (2022)

(Use for Cumulative Problem.)

SCHEDULE 3 (Form 1040) Department of the Treasury Internal Revenue Service	**Additional Credits and Payments** Attach to Form 1040, 1040-SR, or 1040-NR. Go to *www.irs.gov/Form1040* for instructions and the latest information.	OMB No. 1545-0074 20**22** Attachment Sequence No. **03**
Name(s) shown on Form 1040, 1040-SR, or 1040-NR		Your social security number

Part I   Nonrefundable Credits

1	Foreign tax credit. Attach Form 1116 if required	**1**	
2	Credit for child and dependent care expenses from Form 2441, line 11. Attach Form 2441	**2**	
3	Education credits from Form 8863, line 19	**3**	
4	Retirement savings contributions credit. Attach Form 8880	**4**	
5	Residential energy credits. Attach Form 5695	**5**	
6	Other nonrefundable credits:		
a	General business credit. Attach Form 3800	**6a**	
b	Credit for prior year minimum tax. Attach Form 8801 . . .	**6b**	
c	Adoption credit. Attach Form 8839	**6c**	
d	Credit for the elderly or disabled. Attach Schedule R	**6d**	
e	Alternative motor vehicle credit. Attach Form 8910	**6e**	
f	Qualified plug-in motor vehicle credit. Attach Form 8936 . . .	**6f**	
g	Mortgage interest credit. Attach Form 8396	**6g**	
h	District of Columbia first-time homebuyer credit. Attach Form 8859	**6h**	
i	Qualified electric vehicle credit. Attach Form 8834	**6i**	
j	Reserved for future use	**6j**	
k	Credit to holders of tax credit bonds. Attach Form 8912 . . .	**6k**	
l	Amount on Form 8978, line 14. See instructions	**6l**	
z	Other nonrefundable credits. List type and amount: _____		
		6z	
7	Total other nonrefundable credits. Add lines 6a through 6z	**7**	
8	Add lines 1 through 5 and 7. Enter here and on Form 1040, 1040-SR, or 1040-NR, line 20	**8**	

(continued on page 2)

For Paperwork Reduction Act Notice, see your tax return instructions.   Cat. No. 71480G   Schedule 3 (Form 1040) 2022

(Use for Cumulative Problem.)

Schedule 3 (Form 1040) 2022   Page **2**

Part II   **Other Payments and Refundable Credits**

9	Net premium tax credit. Attach Form 8962	**9**	
10	Amount paid with request for extension to file (see instructions)	**10**	
11	Excess social security and tier 1 RRTA tax withheld	**11**	
12	Credit for federal tax on fuels. Attach Form 4136	**12**	
13	Other payments or refundable credits:		
a	Form 2439	**13a**	
b	Credit for qualified sick and family leave wages paid in 2022 from Schedule(s) H for leave taken before April 1, 2021	**13b**	
c	Reserved for future use	**13c**	
d	Credit for repayment of amounts included in income from earlier years	**13d**	
e	Reserved for future use	**13e**	
f	Deferred amount of net 965 tax liability (see instructions) . . .	**13f**	
g	Reserved for future use	**13g**	
h	Credit for qualified sick and family leave wages paid in 2022 from Schedule(s) H for leave taken after March 31, 2021, and before October 1, 2021	**13h**	
z	Other payments or refundable credits. List type and amount: _____	**13z**	
14	Total other payments or refundable credits. Add lines 13a through 13z	**14**	
15	Add lines 9 through 12 and 14. Enter here and on Form 1040, 1040-SR, or 1040-NR, line 31	**15**	

Schedule 3 (Form 1040) 2022

(Use for Cumulative Problem.)

SCHEDULE A (Form 1040)

Department of the Treasury
Internal Revenue Service

Itemized Deductions

Go to *www.irs.gov/ScheduleA* for instructions and the latest information.

Attach to Form 1040 or 1040-SR.

Caution: If you are claiming a net qualified disaster loss on Form 4684, see the instructions for line 16.

OMB No. 1545-0074

2022

Attachment Sequence No. **07**

Name(s) shown on Form 1040 or 1040-SR

Your social security number

Medical and Dental Expenses	**Caution:** Do not include expenses reimbursed or paid by others.	
	1 Medical and dental expenses (see instructions)	1
	2 Enter amount from Form 1040 or 1040-SR, line 11 ⬚2	
	3 Multiply line 2 by 7.5% (0.075)	3
	4 Subtract line 3 from line 1. If line 3 is more than line 1, enter -0-	4
Taxes You Paid	5 State and local taxes.	
	a State and local income taxes or general sales taxes. You may include either income taxes or general sales taxes on line 5a, but not both. If you elect to include general sales taxes instead of income taxes, check this box ⬚	5a
	b State and local real estate taxes (see instructions)	5b
	c State and local personal property taxes	5c
	d Add lines 5a through 5c	5d
	e Enter the smaller of line 5d or $10,000 ($5,000 if married filing separately)	5e
	6 Other taxes. List type and amount: _____	6
	7 Add lines 5e and 6	7
Interest You Paid **Caution:** Your mortgage interest deduction may be limited. See instructions.	8 Home mortgage interest and points. If you didn't use all of your home mortgage loan(s) to buy, build, or improve your home, see instructions and check this box ⬚	
	a Home mortgage interest and points reported to you on Form 1098. See instructions if limited	8a
	b Home mortgage interest not reported to you on Form 1098. See instructions if limited. If paid to the person from whom you bought the home, see instructions and show that person's name, identifying no., and address	8b
	_____	
	c Points not reported to you on Form 1098. See instructions for special rules	8c
	d Reserved for future use	8d
	e Add lines 8a through 8c	8e
	9 Investment interest. Attach Form 4952 if required. See instructions	9
	10 Add lines 8e and 9	10
Gifts to Charity **Caution:** If you made a gift and got a benefit for it, see instructions.	11 Gifts by cash or check. If you made any gift of $250 or more, see instructions	11
	12 Other than by cash or check. If you made any gift of $250 or more, see instructions. You **must** attach Form 8283 if over $500	12
	13 Carryover from prior year	13
	14 Add lines 11 through 13	14
Casualty and Theft Losses	15 Casualty and theft loss(es) from a federally declared disaster (other than net qualified disaster losses). Attach Form 4684 and enter the amount from line 18 of that form. See instructions	15
Other Itemized Deductions	16 Other—from list in instructions. List type and amount: _____	16
Total Itemized Deductions	17 Add the amounts in the far right column for lines 4 through 16. Also, enter this amount on Form 1040 or 1040-SR, line 12	17
	18 If you elect to itemize deductions even though they are less than your standard deduction, check this box ⬚	

For Paperwork Reduction Act Notice, see the Instructions for Form 1040.

Cat. No. 17145C

Schedule A (Form 1040) 2022

(Use for Cumulative Problem.)

SCHEDULE B (Form 1040)	Interest and Ordinary Dividends	OMB No. 1545-0074
Department of the Treasury Internal Revenue Service	Go to *www.irs.gov/ScheduleB* for instructions and the latest information. Attach to Form 1040 or 1040-SR.	2022 Attachment Sequence No. 08

Name(s) shown on return | Your social security number

Part I

Interest

(See instructions and the Instructions for Form 1040, line 2b.)

Note: If you received a Form 1099-INT, Form 1099-OID, or substitute statement from a brokerage firm, list the firm's name as the payer and enter the total interest shown on that form.

		Amount
1	List name of payer. If any interest is from a seller-financed mortgage and the buyer used the property as a personal residence, see the instructions and list this interest first. Also, show that buyer's social security number and address:	1
2	Add the amounts on line 1	2
3	Excludable interest on series EE and I U.S. savings bonds issued after 1989. Attach Form 8815	3
4	Subtract line 3 from line 2. Enter the result here and on Form 1040 or 1040-SR, line 2b	4

Note: If line 4 is over $1,500, you must complete Part III.

Part II

Ordinary Dividends

(See instructions and the Instructions for Form 1040, line 3b.)

Note: If you received a Form 1099-DIV or substitute statement from a brokerage firm, list the firm's name as the payer and enter the ordinary dividends shown on that form.

		Amount
5	List name of payer:	5
6	Add the amounts on line 5. Enter the total here and on Form 1040 or 1040-SR, line 3b	6

Note: If line 6 is over $1,500, you must complete Part III.

Part III

Foreign Accounts and Trusts

Caution: If required, failure to file FinCEN Form 114 may result in substantial penalties. Additionally, you may be required to file Form 8938, Statement of Specified Foreign Financial Assets. See instructions.

You must complete this part if you (**a**) had over $1,500 of taxable interest or ordinary dividends; (**b**) had a foreign account; or (**c**) received a distribution from, or were a grantor of, or a transferor to, a foreign trust.

		Yes	No
7a	At any time during 2022, did you have a financial interest in or signature authority over a financial account (such as a bank account, securities account, or brokerage account) located in a foreign country? See instructions		
	If "Yes," are you required to file FinCEN Form 114, Report of Foreign Bank and Financial Accounts (FBAR), to report that financial interest or signature authority? See FinCEN Form 114 and its instructions for filing requirements and exceptions to those requirements		
b	If you are required to file FinCEN Form 114, list the name(s) of the foreign country(-ies) where the financial account(s) are located:		
8	During 2022, did you receive a distribution from, or were you the grantor of, or transferor to, a foreign trust? If "Yes," you may have to file Form 3520. See instructions		

For Paperwork Reduction Act Notice, see your tax return instructions.	Cat. No. 17146N	Schedule B (Form 1040) 2022

(Use for Cumulative Problem.)

SCHEDULE E (Form 1040) Department of the Treasury Internal Revenue Service	Supplemental Income and Loss (From rental real estate, royalties, partnerships, S corporations, estates, trusts, REMICs, etc.) Attach to Form 1040, 1040-SR, 1040-NR, or 1041. Go to *www.irs.gov/ScheduleE* for instructions and the latest information.	OMB No. 1545-0074 2022 Attachment Sequence No. 13
Name(s) shown on return		Your social security number

Part I   **Income or Loss From Rental Real Estate and Royalties**

Note: If you are in the business of renting personal property, use **Schedule C**. See instructions. If you are an individual, report farm rental income or loss from **Form 4835** on page 2, line 40.

A   Did you make any payments in 2022 that would require you to file Form(s) 1099? See instructions . . . .   ☐ Yes ☐ No

B   If "Yes," did you or will you file required Form(s) 1099? . . . .   ☐ Yes ☐ No

1a   Physical address of each property (street, city, state, ZIP code)

A	
B	
C	

1b	Type of Property (from list below)	2	For each rental real estate property listed above, report the number of fair rental and personal use days. Check the QJV box only if you meet the requirements to file as a qualified joint venture. See instructions.		Fair Rental Days	Personal Use Days	QJV
A				A			☐
B				B			☐
C				C			☐

Type of Property:

1 Single Family Residence   3 Vacation/Short-Term Rental   5 Land   7 Self-Rental

2 Multi-Family Residence   4 Commercial   6 Royalties   8 Other (describe) _____

			Properties:		
Income:			**A**	**B**	**C**
3	Rents received	3			
4	Royalties received	4			
Expenses:					
5	Advertising	5			
6	Auto and travel (see instructions)	6			
7	Cleaning and maintenance	7			
8	Commissions	8			
9	Insurance	9			
10	Legal and other professional fees	10			
11	Management fees	11			
12	Mortgage interest paid to banks, etc. (see instructions)	12			
13	Other interest	13			
14	Repairs	14			
15	Supplies	15			
16	Taxes	16			
17	Utilities	17			
18	Depreciation expense or depletion	18			
19	Other (list) _____	19			
20	Total expenses. Add lines 5 through 19	20			
21	Subtract line 20 from line 3 (rents) and/or 4 (royalties). If result is a (loss), see instructions to find out if you must file **Form 6198**	21			
22	Deductible rental real estate loss after limitation, if any, on **Form 8582** (see instructions)	22	( )	( )	( )

23a	Total of all amounts reported on line 3 for all rental properties	23a	
b	Total of all amounts reported on line 4 for all royalty properties	23b	
c	Total of all amounts reported on line 12 for all properties	23c	
d	Total of all amounts reported on line 18 for all properties	23d	
e	Total of all amounts reported on line 20 for all properties	23e	
24	**Income.** Add positive amounts shown on line 21. **Do not** include any losses	24	
25	**Losses.** Add royalty losses from line 21 and rental real estate losses from line 22. Enter total losses here	25	( )
26	**Total rental real estate and royalty income or (loss).** Combine lines 24 and 25. Enter the result here. If Parts II, III, IV, and line 40 on page 2 do not apply to you, also enter this amount on Schedule 1 (Form 1040), line 5. Otherwise, include this amount in the total on line 41 on page 2 .	26	

For Paperwork Reduction Act Notice, see the separate instructions.   Cat. No. 11344L   Schedule E (Form 1040) 2022

(Use for Cumulative Problem.)

Form **2441** Department of the Treasury Internal Revenue Service	**Child and Dependent Care Expenses** Attach to Form 1040, 1040-SR, or 1040-NR. Go to *www.irs.gov/Form2441* for instructions and the latest information.	OMB No. 1545-0074 2022 Attachment Sequence No. **21**
Name(s) shown on return		Your social security number

A You can't claim a credit for child and dependent care expenses if your filing status is married filing separately unless you meet the requirements listed in the instructions under *Married Persons Filing Separately*. If you meet these requirements, check this box ☐

B If you or your spouse was a student or was disabled during 2022 and you're entering deemed income of $250 or $500 a month on Form 2441 based on the income rules listed in the instructions under *If You or Your Spouse Was a Student or Disabled*, check this box ☐

Part I   Persons or Organizations Who Provided the Care—You **must** complete this part.

If you have more than three care providers, see the instructions and check this box . . . . ☐

1 (a) Care provider's name	(b) Address (number, street, apt. no., city, state, and ZIP code)	(c) Identifying number (SSN or EIN)	(d) Was the care provider your household employee in 2022? For example, this generally includes nannies but not daycare centers. (see instructions)	(e) Amount paid (see instructions)
			☐ Yes ☐ No	
			☐ Yes ☐ No	
			☐ Yes ☐ No	

Did you receive **dependent care benefits?**	— No — Complete only Part II below.
	— Yes — Complete Part III on page 2 next.

Caution: If the care provider is your household employee, you may owe employment taxes. For details, see the Instructions for Schedule H (Form 1040). If you incurred care expenses in 2022 but didn't pay them until 2023, or if you prepaid in 2022 for care to be provided in 2023, don't include these expenses in column (d) of line 2 for 2022. See the instructions.

Part II   Credit for Child and Dependent Care Expenses

2 Information about your **qualifying person(s)**. If you have more than three qualifying persons, see the instructions and check this box ☐

(a) Qualifying person's name		(b) Qualifying person's social security number	(c) Check here if the qualifying person was over age 12 and was disabled. (see instructions)	(d) Qualified expenses you incurred and paid in 2022 for the person listed in column (a)
First	Last			
			☐	
			☐	
			☐	

3	Add the amounts in column (d) of line 2. **Don't** enter more than $3,000 if you had one qualifying person or $6,000 if you had two or more persons. If you completed Part III, enter the amount from line 31	**3**	
4	Enter your **earned income**. See instructions	**4**	
5	If married filing jointly, enter your spouse's earned income (if you or your spouse was a student or was disabled, see the instructions); **all others**, enter the amount from line 4	**5**	
6	Enter the **smallest** of line 3, 4, or 5	**6**	
7	Enter the amount from Form 1040, 1040-SR, or 1040-NR, line 11 . . .	**7**	

8 Enter on line 8 the decimal amount shown below that applies to the amount on line 7.

If line 7 is:			If line 7 is:			If line 7 is:		
Over	But not over	Decimal amount is	Over	But not over	Decimal amount is	Over	But not over	Decimal amount is
$0—15,000		.35	$25,000—27,000		.29	$37,000—39,000		.23
15,000—17,000		.34	27,000—29,000		.28	39,000—41,000		.22
17,000—19,000		.33	29,000—31,000		.27	41,000—43,000		.21
19,000—21,000		.32	31,000—33,000		.26	43,000—No limit		.20
21,000—23,000		.31	33,000—35,000		.25			
23,000—25,000		.30	35,000—37,000		.24			

Line 8: X.

9a	Multiply line 6 by the decimal amount on line 8	**9a**	
b	If you paid 2021 expenses in 2022, complete Worksheet A in the instructions. Enter the amount from line 13 of the worksheet here. Otherwise, enter -0- on line 9b and go to line 9c	**9b**	
c	Add lines 9a and 9b and enter the result	**9c**	
10	Tax liability limit. Enter the amount from the Credit Limit Worksheet in the instructions	**10**	
11	**Credit for child and dependent care expenses.** Enter the **smaller** of line 9c or line 10 here and on Schedule 3 (Form 1040), line 2	**11**	

For Paperwork Reduction Act Notice, see your tax return instructions.   Cat. No. 11862M   Form **2441** (2022)

(Use for Cumulative Problem.)

Form 2441 (2022)   Page **2**

Part III   **Dependent Care Benefits**

12	Enter the total amount of **dependent care benefits** you received in 2022. Amounts you received as an employee should be shown in box 10 of your Form(s) W-2. **Don't** include amounts reported as wages in box 1 of Form(s) W-2. If you were self-employed or a partner, include amounts you received under a dependent care assistance program from your sole proprietorship or partnership	**12**
13	Enter the amount, if any, you carried over from 2020 or 2021 and used in 2022. See instructions	**13**
14	If you forfeited or carried over to 2023 any of the amounts reported on line 12 or 13, enter the amount. See instructions	**14** ( )
15	Combine lines 12 through 14. See instructions	**15**
16	Enter the total amount of **qualified expenses** incurred in 2022 for the care of the **qualifying person(s)**	**16**	
17	Enter the **smaller** of line 15 or 16	**17**	
18	Enter your **earned income**. See instructions	**18**	
19	Enter the amount shown below that applies to you.		
	• If married filing jointly, enter your spouse's earned income (if you or your spouse was a student or was disabled, see the instructions for line 5).	**19**	
	• If married filing separately, see instructions.		
	• All others, enter the amount from line 18.		
20	Enter the **smallest** of line 17, 18, or 19	**20**	
21	Enter $5,000 ($2,500 if married filing separately **and** you were required to enter your spouse's earned income on line 19). If you entered an amount on line 13, add it to the $5,000 or $2,500 amount you enter on line 21. However, don't enter more than the maximum amount allowed under your dependent care plan. If your dependent care plan uses a non-calendar plan year, see instructions	**21**	
22	Is any amount on line 12 or 13 from your sole proprietorship or partnership?		
	☐ **No.** Enter -0-.		
	☐ **Yes.** Enter the amount here	**22**	
23	Subtract line 22 from line 15	**23**	
24	**Deductible benefits.** Enter the **smallest** of line 20, 21, or 22. Also, include this amount on the appropriate line(s) of your return. See instructions	**24**
25	**Excluded benefits.** If you checked "No" on line 22, enter the smaller of line 20 or 21. Otherwise, subtract line 24 from the smaller of line 20 or line 21. If zero or less, enter -0-	**25**
26	**Taxable benefits.** Subtract line 25 from line 23. If zero or less, enter -0-. Also, enter this amount on Form 1040, 1040-SR, or 1040-NR, line 1e	**26**

To claim the child and dependent care credit,
complete lines 27 through 31 below.

27	Enter $3,000 ($6,000 if two or more qualifying persons)	**27**
28	Add lines 24 and 25	**28**
29	Subtract line 28 from line 27. If zero or less, **stop.** You can't take the credit. **Exception.** If you paid 2021 expenses in 2022, see the instructions for line 9b	**29**
30	Complete line 2 on page 1 of this form. **Don't** include in column (d) any benefits shown on line 28 above. Then, add the amounts in column (d) and enter the total here	**30**
31	Enter the **smaller** of line 29 or 30. Also, enter this amount on line 3 on page 1 of this form and complete lines 4 through 11	**31**

Form **2441** (2022)

(Use for Cumulative Problem.)

Form 8960 — Net Investment Income Tax—Individuals, Estates, and Trusts

Department of the Treasury Internal Revenue Service (99)

▶ Attach to your tax return.
▶ Go to www.irs.gov/Form8960 for instructions and the latest information.

OMB No. 1545-2227
2021
Attachment Sequence No. 72

Name(s) shown on your tax return

Your social security number or EIN

Part I Investment Income
- ☐ Section 6013(g) election (see instructions)
- ☐ Section 6013(h) election (see instructions)
- ☐ Regulations section 1.1411-10(g) election (see instructions)

1	Taxable interest (see instructions)	1
2	Ordinary dividends (see instructions)	2
3	Annuities (see instructions)	3
4a	Rental real estate, royalties, partnerships, S corporations, trusts, etc. (see instructions)	4a
b	Adjustment for net income or loss derived in the ordinary course of a non-section 1411 trade or business (see instructions)	4b
c	Combine lines 4a and 4b	4c
5a	Net gain or loss from disposition of property (see instructions)	5a
b	Net gain or loss from disposition of property that is not subject to net investment income tax (see instructions)	5b
c	Adjustment from disposition of partnership interest or S corporation stock (see instructions)	5c
d	Combine lines 5a through 5c	5d
6	Adjustments to investment income for certain CFCs and PFICs (see instructions)	6
7	Other modifications to investment income (see instructions)	7
8	Total investment income. Combine lines 1, 2, 3, 4c, 5d, 6, and 7	8

Part II Investment Expenses Allocable to Investment Income and Modifications

9a	Investment interest expenses (see instructions)	9a
b	State, local, and foreign income tax (see instructions)	9b
c	Miscellaneous investment expenses (see instructions)	9c
d	Add lines 9a, 9b, and 9c	9d
10	Additional modifications (see instructions)	10
11	Total deductions and modifications. Add lines 9d and 10	11

Part III Tax Computation

12	Net investment income. Subtract Part II, line 11, from Part I, line 8. Individuals, complete lines 13–17. Estates and trusts, complete lines 18a–21. If zero or less, enter -0-	12
Individuals:		
13	Modified adjusted gross income (see instructions)	13
14	Threshold based on filing status (see instructions)	14
15	Subtract line 14 from line 13. If zero or less, enter -0-	15
16	Enter the smaller of line 12 or line 15	16
17	Net investment income tax for individuals. Multiply line 16 by 3.8% (0.038). **Enter here and include on your tax return** (see instructions)	17
Estates and Trusts:		
18a	Net investment income (line 12 above)	18a
b	Deductions for distributions of net investment income and deductions under section 642(c) (see instructions)	18b
c	Undistributed net investment income. Subtract line 18b from line 18a (see instructions). If zero or less, enter -0-	18c
19a	Adjusted gross income (see instructions)	19a
b	Highest tax bracket for estates and trusts for the year (see instructions)	19b
c	Subtract line 19b from line 19a. If zero or less, enter -0-	19c
20	Enter the smaller of line 18c or line 19c	20
21	Net investment income tax for estates and trusts. Multiply line 20 by 3.8% (0.038). **Enter here and include on your tax return** (see instructions)	21

For Paperwork Reduction Act Notice, see your tax return instructions.   Cat. No. 59474M   Form **8960** (2021)

Chapter

10

Property: Basis and Nontaxable Exchanges

CHAPTER CONTENTS

LEARNING OBJECTIVES

After completing Chapter 10, you should be able to:

1. Distinguish between realized and recognized gains and losses and calculate the realized gain or loss on the sale or exchange of property.
2. Understand when the wash sale rules apply and distinguish between realized and recognized losses on the sale of stocks and bonds involved in a wash sale.
3. Know what constitutes a related party and the rules that govern sales between related parties.
4. Understand what is involved in a like-kind exchange, and compute both the realized and recognized gain or loss resulting from a like-kind exchange, as well as the basis in the like-kind property received.
5. Recognize the various types of involuntary conversions and compute the realized and recognized gain or loss on property involved in an involuntary conversion.

CHAPTER OVERVIEW

When taxpayers sell or otherwise dispose of property, a gain or loss usually results. This chapter explains how taxpayers compute those gains and losses. It also explains which gains and losses taxpayers report on the tax return. The chapter begins by presenting the formula used to compute realized gains and losses when disposing of property. Realized gains and losses reflect the taxpayer's economic gain or loss from the transaction. They are the difference between the amount realized from the transaction and the taxpayer's adjusted basis in the property. When the amount realized exceeds the adjusted basis, a realized gain results. A realized loss occurs when the amount realized is less than the adjusted basis. The rules for computing amount realized and adjusted basis are presented in the chapter.

Although disposing of property results in a realized gain or loss, not all realized gains and losses are reported on the tax return. As a rule, taxpayers are taxed on all realized gains but can deduct only realized losses that result from disposing of investment or business property. One exception to this rule involves property destroyed in a theft or a federal disaster. Although the general rule does not allow taxpayers to deduct losses from the disposal of personal-use property, Chapter 5 presented the rules for the (itemized) deduction for nonbusiness theft and federal disaster losses. Other exceptions are introduced in this chapter.

¶1001   Realized Gain or Loss

Realized gains or losses occur when taxpayers sell, exchange, or otherwise dispose of property. They also occur when the government exercises its right to take the taxpayer's property in exchange for fair compensation (a process known as condemnation). When the amount realized from the transaction exceeds the adjusted basis in the property given up, the difference is a **realized gain**. When the adjusted basis exceeds the amount realized, the difference is a **realized loss**. Stated another way,

Realized gain (loss)   =   Amount realized   –   Adjusted basis

¶1001.01   AMOUNT REALIZED

The **amount realized** equals the sales price minus selling expenses. [I.R.C. §1001(b), Reg. §1.263(a)-1(e)] Selling expenses include commissions, legal fees, and other costs related to the sale. The sales price is the sum of the fair market value (FMV) of the property (which includes cash) and services received in return for the property given up. It also includes any debt of the taxpayer (seller) that the buyer assumes. [Reg. §1.1001-2] (When the buyer assumes the seller's debt, it is similar to the buyer giving the seller cash that the seller uses to pay off the debt. Also, see ¶302.01 for an explanation of how to determine FMV.)

EXAMPLE 1	Howard sells stock for $12,000 cash plus a car valued at $5,000. Howard's amount realized is $17,000 ($12,000 + $5,000).

EXAMPLE 2	Marta exchanges land for a building that has a FMV of $90,000. The land is subject to a $50,000 mortgage, which the other party assumes. Marta's amount realized is $140,000 ($90,000 + $50,000).

¶1001.02   ADJUSTED BASIS

When disposing of property, the tax laws allow taxpayers to recover their investment in property tax free. **Basis** is the term used to describe the taxpayer's investment in property. Taxpayers realize a gain when the amount realized exceeds their basis in the property. If the entire basis is not recovered, taxpayers realize a loss for the unrecovered amount.

Between the time taxpayers acquire property and the time they dispose of it, events may occur that require taxpayers to adjust their basis in property. **Adjusted basis** is the term for the taxpayer's investment in property after making those adjustments. Adjusted basis can be stated as follows:

Adjusted basis   =   Initial basis in property   +   Capital additions   –   Capital recoveries

The initial basis of purchased property usually is its cost. However, taxpayers can acquire property in other ways, such as through gift or inheritance. The initial basis of a property depends on how the taxpayer acquired it. The rules for computing initial basis are presented later in the chapter at ¶1002.

Capital Additions

Capital additions include costs incurred in transferring or defending title to the property. Examples of such costs include commissions and legal fees. Capital additions also include the cost of improvements that increase the property's value, lengthen its useful life, or convert it to a different use. Improvements have a useful life that exceeds one year. Maintenance and repairs are not improvements since they are routine and recurring costs.

Examples of Improvements

- Installing a new furnace or roof
- Putting up a fence
- Paving a driveway
- Rebuilding a car engine
- Landscaping
- Building a recreation room in an unfinished basement
- Paying special assessments for sidewalks, roads, etc.
- Adding a room onto a house or other building

EXAMPLE 3

Years ago, Leroy paid $125,000 for a house that he uses as a vacation home. Over the years, Leroy has paid $35,000 to remodel the kitchen, $5,000 to install a wooden fence around the property, and $3,000 to reshingle the roof. He also has paid $13,800 to keep the property in good condition. Leroy's adjusted basis in the home is $168,000 ($125,000 + $35,000 + $5,000 + $3,000). Since the vacation home is a personal belonging, the $13,800 spent on repairs and maintenance is a nondeductible personal expense. If Leroy were to sell the home, his realized gain or loss would be the difference between the amount realized from the sale and his $168,000 adjusted basis in the home.

Capital Recoveries

Capital recoveries are a return of the taxpayer's investment in property. They occur when taxpayers receive money or take tax deductions in connection with the property. Any time taxpayers recover part of their investment in property prior to disposing of it, they must reduce their basis in the property accordingly. When property is damaged in a casualty, taxpayers reduce their basis in the property by amounts they receive from the insurance company. The same basis reduction rule applies to amounts taxpayers receive from the government in exchange for the government's right to use part of their property (known as an easement). The amounts taxpayers receive from the insurance company or from the government represent a return of their initial investment in the property. After receiving these amounts, the taxpayer has less invested in the property. Thus, the taxpayer's basis (investment) in the property must be reduced accordingly.

EXAMPLE 4

Several years ago, Ralph paid $120,000 for land. In the current year, Ralph receives $20,000 from the government in exchange for the right to use part of the land. Ralph must reduce his basis in the land by $20,000. Although Ralph initially paid $120,000 for the land, after receiving $20,000 from the government, his net investment in the land is $100,000. Ralph's adjusted basis in the land equals $100,000 ($120,000 initial basis − $20,000 capital recovery).

Taxpayers also reduce the basis in property by amounts deducted on their tax returns in connection with the property. This includes amounts deducted for casualty or theft losses. It also includes amounts deducted for depreciation, which includes bonus depreciation and Section 179 expense.

EXAMPLE 5

Jennie is a sole proprietor. During the year, Jennie placed in service equipment costing $24,000. She elected to expense the entire amount under Section 179. Jennie's adjusted basis in the equipment is $0. Thus, the entire amount realized on the sale of the equipment will result in realized gain.

EXAMPLE 6	In 2014, Lee paid $62,000 for a building. Lee spent $10,000 in 2018 for a new roof. In 2019, a federal disaster damaged the building. The insurance company paid Lee $20,000 for the loss. Lee claimed a $10,000 loss deduction on her 2019 tax return for the unreimbursed portion of the loss. In 2022, Lee spent $29,000 to rebuild the part of the building destroyed in the disaster. Over the years, Lee has deducted $22,000 for depreciation on the building. Lee computes the adjusted basis in the building as follows.

Initial basis in the building		$62,000
Plus capital additions		
Improvements	$10,000	
Restoration costs	29,000	39,000
Less capital recoveries		
Depreciation deductions	$22,000	
Insurance proceeds	20,000	
Casualty loss deduction	10,000	(52,000)
Adjusted basis in the building		$49,000

¶1002 Initial Basis

When computing their adjusted basis in property, taxpayers start with the initial basis. The initial basis of purchased property is its cost. However, taxpayers can acquire property through other means, such as through gifts, inheritances, and divorce settlements.

¶1002.01 PROPERTY ACQUIRED BY PURCHASE

The initial basis of purchased property is its cost (what the taxpayer gives up to buy the property). [I.R.C. §1012] It includes amounts taxpayers borrow to buy the property. It also includes any costs incurred to obtain clear title or make the property ready for use. Examples of such costs include:

- Sales or excise taxes paid on the purchase
- Title insurance and survey costs
- Expenses paid to deliver, install, and test the property
- Recording, legal, and accounting fees

EXAMPLE 7	Burt buys real estate, paying $50,000 cash and assuming the seller's $75,000 mortgage on the property. Burt's initial basis is $125,000 ($50,000 + $75,000).

EXAMPLE 8	Kelly buys a machine for $10,000. She pays $600 in sales tax and $400 for delivery and installation. Kelly's initial basis in the machine equals $11,000 ($10,000 + $600 + $400).

When the taxpayer performs services in exchange for property, the initial basis in the property is the value of the services the taxpayer includes in income.

EXAMPLE 9	Sal received ten shares of stock in exchange for services he rendered. The market value of the shares is $300. Sal is taxed on $300 for his services. His initial basis in the shares is $300.

Bargain Purchases

Sometimes companies sell goods or other property to their employees for less than FMV. Often, the employee is taxed on the difference between the FMV and the purchase price. In these cases, the employee's initial basis ends up the same as the FMV of the property, since the initial basis includes amounts taxed as income. If the employee does not have to report any income from the bargain purchase (as in a qualified employee discount, see ¶401.05), then the employee's initial basis equals the amount paid for the property.

EXAMPLE 10	Morgan pays $60 for property from a company where he is an employee. The FMV of the property is $100. Morgan reports the $40 difference between FMV and the purchase price as income on his tax return. Morgan's initial basis in the property equals $100 ($60 purchase price + $40 reported in income).

Basket Purchases

Sometimes a single purchase price buys more than one property. As we learned in Chapter 8, different depreciation rules can apply to different properties. Also, taxpayers may sell the properties at various times in the future. For these reasons, the purchase price must be allocated among the properties acquired. [I.R.C. §1060] Taxpayers allocate the purchase price among the properties on the basis of their relative FMVs. The amount allocated to one property equals the purchase price times the ratio of the FMV of that property to the total FMV of all properties.

$$\text{Initial basis} \ = \ \text{Purchase price} \ \times \ \frac{\text{FMV of the property}}{\text{FMV of all properties}}$$

EXAMPLE 11	Devon pays $90,000 for land and a building. At the time of the purchase, the FMV of the land and building are $80,000 and $40,000, respectively. Devon's basis in the land equals $60,000 [$90,000 × ($80,000/$120,000)]. His basis in the building equals $30,000 [$90,000 × ($40,000/$120,000)].

¶1002.02   PROPERTY RECEIVED FROM A SPOUSE

When a taxpayer receives property from a spouse, the spouse's adjusted basis in the property carries over to the taxpayer. [I.R.C. §1041] No tax consequences occur when property is transferred between spouses (or former spouses when the transfer is part of a divorce settlement).

EXAMPLE 12	As part of a divorce settlement, Drew transferred to April title to his mountain cabin. Drew paid $80,000 for the cabin six years prior to his marriage to April. Over the years, he spent $23,500 on improvements to the cabin. At the time of the transfer, the cabin was worth $240,000. April's basis in the home equals Drew's adjusted basis in the home $103,500 ($80,000 + $23,500). If April were to sell the home for its current fair market value, her realized gain would be $136,500 ($240,000 – $103,500).

¶1002.03   INHERITED PROPERTY

When a person dies, an executor is assigned to distribute the decedent's property (known as the estate). Before distributing the estate to the decedent's heirs, the executor first computes the estate tax due. Estate tax is computed on the total FMV of the decedent's estate (net of liabilities). Estate tax is due only when the value of the estate exceeds a certain amount.

In computing the estate tax, the executor usually values the estate on the date of the decedent's death (DOD). [I.R.C. §1014(a)] An heir's initial basis in the inherited property is the property's FMV on the DOD. However, under certain conditions, the executor can elect to value the estate six months later (known as the alternative valuation date, or AVD). [I.R.C. §2032] When the executor values the estate on the AVD, the heir's initial basis in the inherited property is its FMV on the AVD or on the date it is distributed to the heir, whichever occurs first.

EXAMPLE 13	Rhonda inherited land from her grandfather, who died on November 5, 2020. On that day, the land was valued at $45,000. On May 5, 2022, its value was $42,000. The land was distributed to Rhonda on July 2, 2022. Rhonda's basis in the land is $45,000 if DOD is used to value the grandfather's estate. If the AVD is used, Rhonda's basis is $42,000 (since the AVD occurs before the date of distribution).

EXAMPLE 14	Same facts as in Example 13, except that the land was distributed to Rhonda on March 10, 2022, when its value was $43,000. If DOD is used to value the grandfather's estate, Rhonda's basis in the land is still $45,000. If the AVD is used, Rhonda's basis is $43,000 (since the distribution date occurs first).

In 2010, there was no estate tax and "modified carryover basis" rules could apply to property inherited from decedents dying in 2010. Under the modified carryover basis rules, the decedent's adjusted basis in the property (not its FMV) is used as the starting point in determining the heir's basis in inherited property. Those interested in learning more about the modified carryover basis rules that were in effect for 2010 only, should refer to IRS Publication 4895, *Tax Treatment of Property Acquired from a Decedent Dying in 2010*. Although these rules only applied for one year, the basis rules will attach to the property as long as the person who received the property is still the owner.

¶1002.04   GIFTED PROPERTY

Two sets of rules apply to property received as a gift. One set applies when, at the time of the gift, the FMV of the property is less than the donor's adjusted basis in the property. Another set applies when the FMV exceeds the donor's adjusted basis in the property.

FMV Less Than Donor's Basis

When at the time of the gift the FMV of the property is less than the donor's (adjusted) basis, the donee's basis in the property is not known until the donee (the person receiving the gift) disposes of the property. Upon disposal, the donee computes gain or loss first using the FMV of the property at the time of the gift as the donee's initial basis. If loss results, then the donee's initial basis is the FMV at the time of the gift. [I.R.C. §1015(a)] If a gain results, then the donor's basis usually is the donee's initial basis. However, if the second calculation does not result in a gain, then there is no gain or loss and the donee's adjusted basis equals the amount realized.

EXAMPLE 15	Joan receives stock valued at $15,000 as a gift. The donor paid $20,000 for the stock. Joan later sells the stock for $23,000. Since Joan sells the stock for more than the donor's basis, her basis in the stock is $20,000. Joan realizes a $3,000 gain ($23,000 amount realized – $20,000 basis).

EXAMPLE 16	Same facts as in Example 15, except that Joan sells the stock for $13,000. Joan sells the stock for less than the $15,000 FMV. Thus, her basis in the stock is $15,000, and she realizes a $2,000 loss ($13,000 amount realized – $15,000 basis).

EXAMPLE 17	Same facts as in Example 15, except that Joan sells the stock for $17,000. When Joan uses the $15,000 FMV ("loss basis") to compute her loss, a $2,000 gain results. When she uses the donor's $20,000 adjusted basis ("gain basis"), a $3,000 loss results. Thus, Joan recognizes neither a gain nor a loss. Her basis in the stock equals $17,000 (the amount realized from the sale).

When the gifted property is depreciable property to the donee, the donee uses the donor's basis to compute depreciation expense.

FMV Exceeds Donor's Basis

If at the time of the gift the FMV of the property exceeds the donor's basis, the donee takes over the donor's basis. [I.R.C. §1015(a)] If the donor paid gift tax on the transfer, then the donee adds a portion of the gift tax to the basis. For gifts made prior to 1977, 100% of the gift tax is added to the donee's basis. [I.R.C. §1015(d)(2)] For gifts made after 1976, only a fraction of the gift tax is added to the donee's basis. [I.R.C. §1015(d)(6)] This fraction equals the ratio of the amount the property increased in value while owned by the donor (FMV at the time of the gift – donor's basis) to the taxable value of the gift. In both cases, the donee's basis cannot exceed the FMV of the property at the time of the gift.

EXAMPLE 18	In 1993, Millie received property from her uncle worth $75,000. The uncle paid $15,000 in gift tax on the transfer. The uncle's adjusted basis in the property was $30,000. Since the FMV exceeds the uncle's basis, Millie takes her uncle's $30,000 basis. While her uncle owned the property, it went up in value by $45,000 ($75,000 – $30,000). If the taxable value of the gift is $75,000, Millie adds 60% ($45,000 ÷ $75,000) of the gift tax to her basis. Millie's initial basis in the gifted property would be $39,000 [$30,000 + (60% × $15,000)].

EXAMPLE 19	Same facts as in Example 18, except that the gift occurred in 1973. Millie still takes her uncle's basis in the property, but adds 100% of the gift tax to arrive at her initial basis in the property. Millie's initial basis would be $45,000 ($30,000 + $15,000), as this amount is less than the $75,000 FMV of the gifted property.

Donee's Initial Basis in Gifted Property

When FMV at time of gift < donor's basis and donee disposes of the property for

- A gain: donee's initial basis = donor's basis
- A loss: donee's initial basis = FMV at time of gift
- No gain or loss: donee's adjusted basis = amount realized

When FMV at time of gift > donor's basis and no gift tax is paid, donee's initial basis = donor's basis

When FMV at time of gift > donor's basis and gift tax is paid, the donee's initial basis is the *lesser of*

- Pre-1977 gifts: FMV at time of gift or (donor's basis + 100% of the gift tax paid)
- Post-1976 gifts: FMV at time of gift or (donor's basis + the gift tax attributable to the increase in value)

¶1002.05   PROPERTY CONVERTED TO BUSINESS OR RENTAL USE

Instead of buying new property to use in a business or rental activity, taxpayers can convert their personal belongings to such use. For example, taxpayers can convert their homes to rental property, or they can start using their personal cars or computers in their businesses. As with gifted property, two sets of rules apply to the basis of converted property. The first set applies if the FMV of the property at the time of conversion exceeds the taxpayer's adjusted basis in the property. Another set applies if the FMV is less than the taxpayer's adjusted basis.

FMV Exceeds Adjusted Basis (Appreciated Property)

When taxpayers convert appreciated property, they use the general rule to compute the adjusted basis: Initial basis + Capital additions – Capital recoveries. If the converted property is depreciable property, they use the adjusted basis at the time of conversion to compute depreciation expense.

EXAMPLE 20	On May 4, 2022, Donna converted her home into rental property. Donna paid $93,630 for the home in 2021. Over the years, she has made improvements to the home totaling $25,300. Thus, her adjusted basis in the home is $118,930 ($93,630 + $25,300). On May 4, 2022, the home is worth $155,300. Donna's adjusted basis in the rental property is $118,930, since the FMV at the time of the conversion exceeds that amount. Donna uses this amount (minus the cost of the land) to compute her depreciation expense in 2022.

FMV Less Than Adjusted Basis

When taxpayers convert property that has declined in value, the adjusted basis of the property is determined at the time they dispose of it. To compute realized gains, taxpayers use the general rule for computing adjusted basis: Initial basis + all capital additions – all capital recoveries. To compute realized losses, they use: FMV at conversion + post conversion capital additions – post conversion capital recoveries. If the converted property is depreciable property, taxpayers use the FMV of property at the time of the conversion to compute depreciation expense. [Reg. §1.167(g)-1]

EXAMPLE 21	On January 1, 2019, Emily converted her home to rental property. At the time of the conversion, the FMV of the home was $50,000. Emily paid $56,000 for the home and made $4,000 of capital improvements prior to 2019. After converting the property, Emily deducted $6,000 for depreciation and made $3,000 in capital improvements. Emily sells the property for $59,000. Since at the time of conversion the $50,000 FMV was less than $60,000 the adjusted basis ($56,000 + $4,000 pre-conversion improvements), Emily computes an adjusted basis for gain and an adjusted basis for loss. Emily also uses the $50,000 FMV, minus the FMV of the land, as her basis for depreciating the home.

Initial basis	$56,000
Plus all capital additions ($4,000 + $3,000)	7,000
Less all capital recoveries	(6,000)
Adjusted basis for gain	$57,000
FMV at conversion	$50,000
Plus post conversion capital additions	3,000
Less post conversion capital recoveries	(6,000)
Adjusted basis for loss	$47,000

Because the amount realized exceeds the adjusted basis for gain, Emily sells the property for a gain. Using an adjusted basis of $57,000, Emily realizes a $2,000 gain ($59,000 – $57,000). Had Emily sold the property for a loss (an amount realized less than $47,000), her adjusted basis would have been $47,000. Had the amount realized been between $47,000 and $57,000, Emily would have realized no gain or loss, and her adjusted basis would be the amount realized.

¶1002.05

Adjusted Basis in Converted Property

When at conversion FMV > adjusted basis,

- Adjusted basis = Initial basis + all capital additions − all capital recoveries
- Depreciable basis = Adjusted basis (minus the cost of the land, if any)

When at conversion FMV < adjusted basis,

- Adjusted basis for gains = Initial basis + all capital additions − all capital recoveries
- Adjusted basis for losses = FMV at conversion + post conversion capital additions − post conversion capital recoveries
- Depreciable basis = FMV at conversion (minus the FMV of the land, if any)

¶1002.06   SPECIAL RULES FOR STOCK OWNERSHIP

When taxpayers buy stock, their basis in the shares equals the purchase price plus commissions or transfer fees paid. If taxpayers acquire stock through other means (gift, inheritance, etc.), the rules presented earlier in the chapter for computing adjusted basis apply.

Identification of Shares

Taxpayers can acquire identical shares of stock in the same company at various times for different amounts. When taxpayers sell stock in that company, they should identify which shares they are selling at the time of the sale. If no identification is made, the Internal Revenue Code (Code) requires taxpayers to use the first-in, first-out method. [Reg. §1.1012-1(c)(1)(i).]

EXAMPLE 22   In 2011, Hugh paid $10,000 for 1,000 shares of common stock in ABC corporation. In 2012, he paid $12,500 for another 1,000 shares. During the current year, Hugh sells 1,000 of his shares in ABC for $11,000. If he does not specify which 1,000 were sold, the tax laws require him to use the $10,000 basis in the earliest shares he purchased. This would result in a $1,000 realized gain ($11,000 amount realized − $10,000 adjusted basis). However, if at the time of the sale, Hugh were to tell his stockbroker that he wanted to sell the 1,000 shares that he purchased in 2012, he would have a realized loss of $1,500 ($11,000 − $12,500).

To identify shares sold, taxpayers should deliver the stock certificates to the broker or agent. If a broker or agent holds the stock certificates, then taxpayers should instruct the broker in writing which shares they wish to sell. Taxpayers should request confirmation from the broker as proof that the instructions were followed.

Stock Splits

Taxpayers owning stock may later acquire additional shares either through a stock split or a stock dividend. In a stock split, the corporation distributes to its shareholders a ratable portion of additional shares. This results in every shareholder getting more shares without affecting any shareholder's percentage ownership in the company. With a stock split, no income is realized. Taxpayers simply allocate their adjusted basis in the original shares to all shares held after the split. [I.R.C. §307]

EXAMPLE 23	Years ago, Portia paid $14,000 for 1,000 shares of stock in ABCO ($14 a share). During the current year, ABCO declared a two-for-one stock split. Each shareholder received two shares of stock for every one share they returned to ABCO. The shareholders of ABCO are not taxed on the split. After the split, Portia owns 2,000 shares of ABCO stock. Her adjusted basis in those shares is her original $14,000 adjusted basis in the stock. Thus, Portia's basis in each share of stock has been reduced to $7 ($14,000/2,000 shares).

Stock Dividends

Shareholders receive a stock dividend when the corporation pays them a dividend with shares of stock in the corporation, instead of cash. If shareholders have the option to receive either a stock or a cash dividend, then the cash or FMV of the stock (whichever they choose) must be included as income on the tax return. If they choose to receive a stock dividend, then the FMV of the stock becomes their basis in the newly acquired shares. [I.R.C. §305(b)(1)]

When the corporation pays shareholders a stock dividend on common stock without giving them the option of a cash dividend, it is a nontaxable event. [I.R.C. §305(a)] As with stock splits, taxpayers must allocate some basis from the original shares to the shares acquired in the nontaxable stock dividend. When the stock dividend is of the same class, the taxpayer prorates the original basis among the total number of shares. An example of a *same class of stock* dividend would be a common stock shareholder receiving a common stock dividend. When the stock dividend is not of the same class, the taxpayer allocates the basis in the original shares using the relative FMV of the total shares. Taxpayers use the same formula used to allocate the purchase price among properties acquired in a basket purchase. An example of a stock dividend *not of the same class* would be a common stock shareholder receiving a preferred stock dividend.

EXAMPLE 24	Dean paid $1,100 for 50 shares of common stock. This year Dean received five shares of common stock as a nontaxable stock dividend. Dean's basis in 55 shares of common stock is $1,100, or $20 a share.

¶1002.07   RETURN-OF-CAPITAL

Corporations pay dividends from earnings and profits (E&P). E&P is roughly the same as retained earnings on the corporate balance sheet. When a corporation with no E&P distributes property (including cash) to its shareholders, the distribution is treated as a return of the shareholder's investment. The amount distributed is not taxable, but as with other capital recoveries, the shareholder reduces the basis in the stock by the amount distributed. [I.R.C. §301(c)(2)] If the amount distributed exceeds the shareholder's basis in the stock, then the shareholder realizes a gain for the excess amount. [I.R.C. §301(c)(3)]

 Corporations report distributions to their shareholders on Form 1099-DIV. On this form, corporations report taxable dividends paid to the shareholder during the year (distributions from E&P), as well as distributions that represent a return of the shareholder's investment.

¶1003   Recognized Gains and Losses

Recognized gains and losses are realized gains and losses taxpayers report on their tax returns. Not all realized gains and losses result in taxable gains and losses. As a general rule, taxpayers recognize all realized gains but recognize losses only from the disposal of business or investment property. Chapter 5 described an exception to this rule that allows taxpayers to deduct federal disaster losses on personal-use property. This chapter covers six more exceptions to the general rule.

- Losses involving wash sales
- Losses from sales between related parties
- Gains from the sale of qualified small business stock
- Gains and losses from like-kind exchanges
- Most gains from the sale of a principal residence
- Certain gains from involuntary conversions

¶1004   Wash Sales

Because securities (stocks and bonds) are an investment, the taxpayer usually recognizes any realized loss on the sale of securities. However, no loss is allowed when the taxpayer re-purchases "substantially identical" securities within 30 days before or 30 days after the sale. [I.R.C. §1091(a)] The term used to describe these sales and repurchases is **wash sales.**

Substantially identical securities are securities *in the same company* that have similar features. For stocks, substantially identical would be the same class of stock with the same voting rights. For bonds, substantially identical would be bonds with similar interest rates and maturity dates. If the taxpayer repurchases only a fraction of the securities within the 61-day period surrounding the sale, then only that fraction of the loss is denied.

EXAMPLE 25

On January 5, 2022, Tom sold 1,000 shares of common stock in Omega Co. for $5,000. Tom's purchases of Omega common stock are shown below.

1,000 shares on June 6, 2013	$8,000
600 shares on November 6, 2021	4,500
250 shares on December 17, 2021	2,000
350 shares on January 10, 2022	3,000

Assuming Tom does not identify which shares were sold, he is assumed to have sold the 1,000 shares purchased on June 6, 2013 (see discussion at ¶1002.06). The sale results in a $3,000 realized loss ($5,000 − $8,000), which normally would be recognized for tax purposes. However, since Tom repurchased 600 (250 + 350) of the 1,000 shares between December 6, 2021, and February 4, 2022 (61 days surrounding January 5, 2022), 60% (600 ÷ 1,000) of the loss is disallowed ($3,000 × 60% = $1,800). Tom recognizes a $1,200 loss ($3,000 − $1,800) on the 400 shares sold and not repurchased.

Any disallowed loss due to a wash sale is merely postponed and will be allowed when the tax-payer later sells the (repurchased) shares. To postpone the loss, the taxpayer adds the disallowed loss to the basis of the repurchased shares. [I.R.C. §1091(d)]

EXAMPLE 26

In Example 25, Tom allocates the $1,800 disallowed loss among the 600 shares that caused the wash sale ($1,800 ÷ 600 = $3 a share). The basis in the 250 shares purchased on December 17, 2021, equals $2,750 [$2,000 + ($3 × 250)]. The basis in the 350 shares purchased on January 10, 2022, equals $4,050 [$3,000 + ($3 × 350)]. The basis in the 600 shares purchased on November 6, 2021, is their $4,500 cost since the shares were not involved in the wash sale.

¶1005   Sales Between Related Parties

Taxpayers usually can recognize a loss on the sale of investment or business property for less than its adjusted basis. However, taxpayers cannot recognize losses when they sell property to a related party. [I.R.C. §267(a)(1)] For tax purposes, individuals and their family members are considered to be related parties. **Family members** include spouses, siblings (brothers and sisters), descendants (children, grandchildren, etc.), and ancestors (parents, grandparents, etc.). Unlike the wash sales, the disallowed loss does not increase the (related) buyer's basis in the property. Instead, the buyer can use the disallowed loss to offset any realized gain when the property is later sold. The buyer cannot use the disallowed loss to create or increase a loss. [I.R.C. §267(d)]

EXAMPLE 27

Pete sold stock to his son, Stan, for $10,000. Pete bought the stock several years ago for $16,000. Although stock is investment property, Pete cannot recognize the $6,000 realized loss ($10,000 – $16,000) since he sold the stock to a related party. Stan's basis in the stock is $10,000, the amount he paid for it.

If Stan later sells the stock for $12,000, Stan's realized gain is $2,000 ($12,000 – $10,000). Stan can use $2,000 of Pete's disallowed loss to offset this gain. Thus, Stan's recognized gain is $0. Since the disallowed loss can only reduce realized gains and cannot create a loss, the rest of Pete's disallowed loss will never be used.

EXAMPLE 28

Same facts as in Example 27, except that Stan sells the stock for $9,000. Stan realizes a $1,000 loss ($9,000 – $10,000). Since a disallowed loss cannot create or increase a loss, Stan cannot use any of Pete's disallowed loss. Stan recognizes the $1,000 loss from the sale, and Pete's entire $6,000 disallowed loss is gone.

Besides individuals and their family members, related parties also involve individuals and corporations when an individual owns more than 50% of the voting stock in the corporation. [I.R.C. §267(b)] Stock owned by family members counts as stock owned by the individual. This indirect ownership of stock is known as **constructive ownership**. [I.R.C. §267(c)]

EXAMPLE 29

Henry owns 30% of Alpha Corporation. The following people own the rest of the stock:

Henry's aunt	35%
Henry's brother	25%
Henry's father	10%

Henry owns 30% of Alpha outright. He constructively owns the 25% owned by his brother and the 10% owned by his father. Henry's actual plus constructive ownership exceeds 50%.

EXAMPLE 30

Continuing on with Example 29, in current year, Henry sells land held as an investment to Alpha Corporation for its current FMV of $75,000. Henry paid $112,000 for the land. Since Henry's actual and constructive ownership in Alpha exceeds 50%, he cannot deduct the $37,000 loss he realizes on the sale ($75,000 amount realized – $112,000 basis). Alpha's basis in the land is the $75,000 it paid for the land.

EXAMPLE 31

Continuing on with Example 30, in a future tax year Alpha sells the land for $122,000. Its realized gain is $47,000 ($122,000 – $75,000). Alpha can use Henry's $37,000 disallowed loss to reduce its recognized gain to $10,000.

A companion rule to the loss disallowance applies when a taxpayer recognizes a gain on the sale of depreciable property to a related person. [I.R.C. §1239] See Chapter 11, at ¶1101.06.

¶1006 Qualified Small Business Stock

Individuals can exclude a portion of the gain realized on the sale of Section 1202 qualified small business stock, provided the stock is held for more than five years. Inherited stock has no minimum holding period for purposes of Section 1202 exclusions. To qualify for the exclusion, the stock must have been purchased after August 10, 1993 as part of the corporation's original issuance of stock. Only certain corporations are able to issue qualified small business stock. These restrictions are beyond the scope of this discussion.

Purchases of Section 1202 qualified small business stock	Exclusion Percentage
On or before February 17, 2009	50%
Between February 18, 2009 and September 27, 2010	75%
On or after September 28, 2010	100%

EXAMPLE 32

On March 1, 2009, Marc acquires $100,000 of Section 1202 qualified small business stock. On May 1, 2022, he sells the stock for $230,000. Marc's realized gain from the sale is $130,000 ($230,000 − $100,000). However, since he bought the stock between February 18, 2009 and September 27, 2010 and held it for more than five years, Marc excludes 75% of the gain. Marc's recognized gain is $32,500 ($130,000 × 25%).

¶1007   Like-Kind Exchanges

Instead of selling property for cash, taxpayers can exchange property they own for other property. When this occurs, a realized gain or loss results from the difference between the FMV of the property received and the adjusted basis of the property given up. Under the general rule, taxpayers recognize all gains from such exchanges but recognize losses only from exchanges that involve business or investment property.

An exception to the general rule exists when the exchange involves like-kind property. In a like-kind exchange, taxpayers do not recognize gains or losses. Instead, realized gains and losses are postponed. [I.R.C. §1031] To postpone gains and losses until such time that the property is disposed of in a non-like-kind exchange, taxpayers adjust the basis of the like-kind property they receive in the exchange. This new basis is also used to compute depreciation expense on depreciable property.

$$\text{Basis of the new property} = \frac{\text{FMV of the}}{\text{new property}} + \text{Postponed loss} - \text{Postponed gain}$$

EXAMPLE 33

Jenn exchanges property with an adjusted basis of $100,000 for like-kind property valued at $60,000. Jenn realizes a $40,000 loss ($60,000 − $100,000) but does not recognize any of the loss. Jenn's basis in the new property equals $100,000 ($60,000 FMV of new property + $40,000 postponed loss). If the new property is depreciable property, she computes depreciation expense using her $100,000 basis in the property.

¶1007.01   LIKE-KIND PROPERTY

The rules just described apply only to exchanges involving like-kind property. To qualify as like-kind property, two conditions must be met.

1. A direct exchange must occur. Certain exchanges involving three parties can qualify as a direct exchange. Also, a direct exchange can occur if the property to be received is identified within 45 days and received within 180 days after the taxpayer transfers the property.
2. Both the property traded and the property received must be business or investment real property. Personal property could also be like-kind property in exchanges before 2018.

The like-kind rules are mandatory. When the conditions are met, taxpayers must postpone any realized gain or loss resulting from the like-kind exchange. Thus, to deduct a loss resulting from a like-kind exchange, the taxpayer needs to not meet one or more of the requirements. For example, the taxpayer could fail to meet the requirements for a direct exchange.

Like-Kind Exchanges of Business or Investment Real Property

The like-kind exchange rules apply only to exchanges of real property. To qualify as a like-kind exchange, real property used for business or investment must be exchanged for any other real property to be used for business or investment. Thus, unimproved land held for investment can be exchanged for a warehouse used in the taxpayer's business. Likewise, an office building used in the taxpayer's business can be exchanged for an apartment building to be held as an investment.

EXAMPLE 34	Tom exchanges his vacation home for land he plans to hold as an investment. The like-kind exchange rules do not apply to this exchange. Although both properties exchanged are real property, the vacation home is a personal belonging. For the like-kind exchange rules to apply, real property held for business or investment must be exchanged for other real property held for business or investment.

¶1007.02   BOOT

Not all like-kind exchanges involve properties of equal value. When exchanging properties of unequal value, the one receiving property of lesser value will require more property from the other party. The non-like-kind property thrown in to even up the deal is known as **boot**. Often boot involves cash, but it can involve other property. Boot occurs when one party takes over the other party's debt. The party who assumes (takes over) the debt is treated as giving boot. The party relieved of debt is treated as receiving boot. When both parties assume each other's debt, only the net (excess) liability counts as boot. The amount of gain or loss recognized on like-kind exchanges involving boot depends on whether the taxpayer gave or received boot.

EXAMPLE 35	Elaine exchanges land valued at $100,000 for Bill's building valued at $80,000. Both properties qualify as like-kind. To even up the deal, Bill agrees to assume Elaine's $20,000 liability on the land. Elaine's release from debt is similar to her receiving $20,000 cash and using it to pay off the debt. Thus, Elaine receives $20,000 boot; Bill gives $20,000 boot.

EXAMPLE 36	Sam exchanges land valued at $80,000 for Diane's building valued at $100,000. Both properties qualify as like-kind. Sam owes $40,000 on the land; Diane owes $60,000 on the building. Both parties agree to assume each other's debt. In this exchange, each party receives property worth $140,000. Sam receives a building worth $100,000 and is relieved of $40,000 of debt. Diane receives land valued at $80,000 and is relieved of $60,000 of debt. Because the parties assume each other's debt, only the net liability of $20,000 ($60,000 – $40,000) is treated as boot. Sam takes on more debt than he is relieved of; therefore, Sam gives $20,000 of boot. Diane is relieved of more debt than she assumed; therefore, Diane receives $20,000 of boot.

Receipt of Boot

Receiving boot has no effect on realized losses from the like-kind exchange. Those losses are postponed and increase the taxpayer's basis in the like-kind property received. However, the taxpayer's realized gains are recognized to the extent of the FMV of the boot received. [I.R.C. §1031(b)]

EXAMPLE 37	Ken exchanges a building with an adjusted basis of $47,000 for a building valued at $45,000 and $5,000 cash. Ken's realized gain equals $3,000 ($50,000 amount realized – $47,000 adjusted basis). Ken receives boot of $5,000; therefore, he recognizes the entire $3,000 gain. Ken's basis in the new building is its FMV of $45,000 since there is no postponed gain.

EXAMPLE 38	Same facts as in Example 37, except that Ken's adjusted basis in the old building is $42,000. Ken realizes an $8,000 gain ($50,000 – $42,000). He recognizes the gain to the extent of the boot received. Therefore, Ken reports a $5,000 gain on his tax return and postpones the rest. Ken reduces the basis in the new building by the postponed gain ($45,000 FMV – $3,000 postponed gain = $42,000).

EXAMPLE 39	Same facts as in Example 37, except that Ken's adjusted basis in the old building is $52,000. Ken realizes a $2,000 loss ($50,000 – $52,000). Since the receipt of boot has no effect on his realized losses, Ken postpones the entire loss and increases his basis in the new machine to $47,000 ($45,000 FMV + $2,000 postponed loss).

Boot Given

For the taxpayer that gives boot in a like-kind exchange, no gain or loss is recognized as long as the FMV of the boot equals the taxpayer's basis in the boot given. This occurs when the taxpayer gives cash or assumes the other party's debt. When the FMV of the boot is different from the taxpayer's basis in the boot given, the taxpayer is treated as having sold the boot to the other party and the taxpayer realizes a gain or loss for the difference between the FMV and the taxpayer's basis in the boot. Under the general rule, the taxpayer will recognize gain to the extent that the FMV of the boot exceeds its basis. However, if the FMV is less than the taxpayer's basis in the boot, the taxpayer will recognize a loss only if the boot was business or investment property. [I.R.C. §1031(d)]

¶1007.03   LIKE-KIND EXCHANGES BETWEEN RELATED PARTIES

Related parties can use the like-kind exchange rules. However, if either (related) party disposes of the like-kind property within two years after the exchange, any postponed gain or loss must be recognized in the disposal year. The basis of the like-kind property is increased by the recognized gain or reduced by the recognized loss.

EXAMPLE 40	On October 4, 2021, Bach Enterprises exchanged one parcel of land for another parcel of land with Wendell Nathan, Bach Enterprises's sole shareholder. The land that Wendell exchanged was worth $200,000, and his basis in the land was $150,000. The land that Bach Enterprises exchanged was worth $190,000, and its basis in the land was $190,000. To even up the deal, the company paid Wendell $10,000 cash.
	As a result of the like-kind exchange, Wendell realized a $50,000 gain ($200,000 FMV of the properties received – $150,000 basis in the land). He recognized a $10,000 gain (equal to the boot received), and postponed $40,000. Wendell's basis in his new land is $150,000 ($190,000 FMV of the new land – $40,000 postponed gain). Bach Enterprises, on the other hand, realized no gain or loss on the exchange ($200,000 FMV of the property received – $190,000 adjusted basis in the land – $10,000 cash paid). Its basis in the land received is its $200,000 FMV.
	On August 5, 2023, Bach Enterprises sells its new land in a non-like-kind exchange. Because the sale occurs within two years, Wendell must recognize the $40,000 of postponed gain on his 2023 tax return. Wendell's basis in the land he received in the exchange increases to $190,000 ($150,000 + $40,000 recognized gain).

¶1008 Sale of a Principal Residence

The taxpayer's principal residence (principal residence) is personal-use property. Thus, when taxpayers sell their principal residence, usually they would recognize a gain, but would not recognize a loss. However, the Code allows taxpayers to exclude up to $250,000 of the gain. Married couples that file a joint tax return can exclude up to $500,000. [I.R.C. §121] To qualify for the exclusion, taxpayers must use the home as their principal residence for two of the previous five years. Partial exclusions are available to taxpayers who fail to meet this requirement because of change in employment location, the taxpayer's health, or other specified unforeseen reasons.

If the home is used other than as a principal residence after 2008 (for example, rented out or used as a second home), the $250,000/$500,000 exclusion must be reduced by the full exclusion amount times the ratio: period of nonqualifying use / period of ownership in the last five years. For example, take an unmarried homeowner who has owned a home for 12 years, including five months of nonqualifying use during the last five years. The homeowner's exclusion would be reduced by $20,833 ($250,000 × 5/60 months). Thus, the homeowner would be allowed to exclude up to $229,167 ($250,000 – $20,833) of the gain realized from the sale.

Due to the sizable exclusion ($250,000/$500,000), many taxpayers will not report gain when selling their principal residence. However, taxpayers still want to keep track of their basis in their home to show that the gain from the sale does not exceed the exclusion amount. This involves keeping a copy of the closing statement and receipts for all improvements made to the home. Any taxable gain from the sale is considered investment income for purposes of the 3.8% net investment income (NII) tax (see ¶315).

EXAMPLE 41

The Duncans sell their principal residence of 20 years for $200,000. Selling expenses are $10,000. The Duncans paid $50,000 for the home. The Duncans do not recognize any of the $140,000 ($200,000 – $10,000 – $50,000) gain, since this amount is less than $500,000.

EXAMPLE 42

Lincoln (a single taxpayer) sells his principal residence for $450,000. Selling expenses are $25,000. Lincoln paid $115,000 for the home ten years ago. Seven years ago, he paid $15,000 to finish the basement, and six years ago, he paid $5,000 for landscaping. Of the $290,000 realized gain, Lincoln recognizes $40,000.

Sales price	$450,000
Less selling expenses	(25,000)
Amount realized	$425,000
Less adjusted basis ($115,000 + $15,000 + $5,000)	(135,000)
Realized gain	$290,000
Less $250,000 exclusion for single taxpayers	(250,000)
Recognized gain	$ 40,000

¶1009 Involuntary Conversions

Taxpayers realize a gain or loss on property involved in an involuntary conversion. The most common involuntary conversions are casualties, thefts, and condemnations.

¶1009.01   CONDEMNATION GAINS AND LOSSES

When the government exercises its right to take away the taxpayer's real property (known as a condemnation), the taxpayer is entitled to receive fair compensation in return. Most often, the taxpayer receives cash in exchange for the condemned property. Occasionally the taxpayer will receive property other than cash. Taxpayers realize a gain when the amount received from the government exceeds the adjusted basis in the condemned property. They realize a loss when the amount received is less than the adjusted basis of the property. Under the general rule, taxpayers would pay tax on all recognized gains resulting from condemnations, but deduct losses only on condemned business or investment property. There is no deduction for condemnation losses on personal-use property, even though it is an involuntary event.

¶1009.02   CASUALTY OR THEFT GAINS AND LOSSES

Taxpayers realize a casualty or theft loss when the amount of the loss exceeds the amount they are reimbursed by insurance. The amount of the loss for *personal-use property* and for *partially destroyed* business or investment property equals the *lesser of* (i) the property's adjusted basis or (ii) its decline in FMV. Decline in FMV is measured as the difference between the FMV before and after the casualty or theft. The amount of the loss for *completely destroyed (includes stolen)* business or investment property equals the adjusted basis in the property, even if the decline in FMV is less.

When the insurance proceeds exceed the amount of the loss, the taxpayer does not realize a casualty or theft loss. Instead, the taxpayer realizes a casualty or theft gain when the insurance proceeds exceed the taxpayer's adjusted basis in the property. A casualty loss that does not arise from a federally declared disaster can be used to offset a casualty gain.

EXAMPLE 43	

In March, Dirk's business auto was damaged in a federally declared disaster. In June, Dirk's business computer was stolen. Information about the properties is shown below.

	FMV Before	FMV After	Adjusted Basis	Insurance Proceeds
Auto	$22,000	$8,000	$15,000	$16,000
Computer	3,000	0	1,000	2,900

The business auto was partially destroyed; therefore, Dirk computes his casualty loss using the *lesser of* (i) the decline in value ($22,000 – $8,000 = $14,000) or (ii) the adjusted basis ($15,000). However, because the insurance proceeds ($16,000) exceed the amount of the loss ($14,000), Dirk does not incur a casualty loss on the auto. Instead, he realizes a casualty gain for the amount by which the insurance proceeds exceed Dirk's adjusted basis in the auto ($16,000 – $15,000 = $1,000).

Since the computer is completely destroyed business property, the amount of the loss is measured as Dirk's adjusted basis in the property ($1,000). However, since the insurance proceeds exceed the amount of the loss, Dirk does not incur a casualty loss on the computer. Instead, he realizes a $1,900 casualty gain ($2,900 – $1,000 adjusted basis).

Generally, taxpayers recognize both gains and losses from theft events or federally declared disasters (see ¶507).

¶1009.03   ELECTION TO POSTPONE RECOGNITION OF REALIZED GAINS

Under the general rule, taxpayers recognize gains from property involved in an involuntary conversion. However, taxpayers can postpone these gains if they invest the entire proceeds in qualified replacement property within a specified period of time. [I.R.C. §1033] This provision is elective if the taxpayer receives cash for the converted property. If the election is made, taxpayers recognize a gain (up to the amount of realized gain) for amounts not reinvested.

EXAMPLE 44	The local government condemns Craig's property. The government pays Craig $200,000 for the property. The property has an adjusted basis of $170,000. Craig can avoid recognizing the $30,000 realized gain ($200,000 – $170,000) if he reinvests at least $200,000 in qualified replacement property within the required time period.

When the election is made to postpone gains, taxpayers reduce the basis in the new property by the amount of postponed gain. Assuming Craig from Example 44 buys qualified replacement property costing $190,000, he will recognize a $10,000 gain ($200,000 – $190,000) and can elect to postpone the rest ($30,000 – $10,000 = $20,000). Craig's basis in the qualified replacement property would equal $170,000 ($190,000 cost – $20,000 postponed gain).

¶1009.04   QUALIFIED REPLACEMENT PROPERTY

For property involved in an involuntary conversion, qualified replacement property normally is property related in service or use. Thus, taxpayers usually must replace an office building with another office building. [I.R.C. §1033(a)(1)] There are four exceptions to this rule.

The first exception applies to taxpayers who lease out property involved in an involuntary conversion. Qualified replacement property for these taxpayers involves investing in other rental property. The rental property need not be of the same type. Thus, taxpayers that lease out an office building destroyed in a casualty can replace it with an apartment building or any other rental property that they lease out.

The second exception allows taxpayers to replace condemned business or investment realty with like-kind property that will be held for either purpose. The like-kind test is broader than the similar-or-related-in-use test. Taxpayers can replace a condemned office building with land to be held for investment. Alternatively, they could replace it with an apartment building, a warehouse, or any other business or investment realty.

A third exception allows any farming property to replace livestock that is converted because of weather related conditions or environmental contamination.

Finally, the replacement property requirements are relaxed when property is converted in a federally declared disaster:

1. When the converted property was held for investment or for productive use in a trade or business, replacement property includes any tangible property that the owner subsequently acquires and holds for productive use in any trade or business.
2. When the converted property was a personal residence, insurance proceeds for the house and its contents are treated as a common fund.

¶1009.05   REPLACEMENT PERIOD

Taxpayers realizing a gain from an involuntary conversion can postpone the gain by replacing the converted property within a specified period. The replacement period begins on the date the property was damaged, destroyed, or stolen. For condemned property, the period starts when the government officially threatens to condemn the property.

Taxpayers normally have two years after the close of the tax year (December 31 for calendar year taxpayers) in which they first realize any part of the gain to finish buying the qualified replacement property. Taxpayers whose business or investment real property is condemned by the government have one additional year (for a total of three years) to buy their qualified replacement property. [I.R.C. §1033(a)(2)(B)]

EXAMPLE 45	On October 19, 2022, Roland's business property was completely destroyed in a fire. At the time of the fire, the property was worth $40,000. Roland paid $80,000 for the property in 1993, and its adjusted basis at the time of the fire was $30,000. In 2022, the insurance company paid Roland $40,000. Roland's business casualty gain equals $10,000 ($40,000 – $30,000 adjusted basis). If Roland wants to postpone the entire gain, he must reinvest at least $40,000 in qualified replacement property between October 19, 2022, and December 31, 2024 (two years after 2022, the year in which Roland receives the proceeds and realizes the gain).

EXAMPLE 46	Same facts as in Example 45, except that the business property was condemned and in 2022 the government paid Roland $40,000 for the property. To avoid recognition of any of the $10,000 gain, Roland has from the date on which the government notified him of the condemnation until December 31, 2025 (three years after 2022) to buy qualified replacement property costing at least $40,000.

Taxpayers whose principal residence is destroyed in a casualty in a federally declared disaster area, are given an extra two years to reinvest in qualified replacement property. [I.R.C. §1033(h)] In essence, this gives them until December 31 of the fourth year after the year in which a gain is realized to invest in another home that they use as their principal residence.

EXAMPLE 47	The Hunters' principal residence was badly damaged by fire in a federally declared disaster. The Hunters received $820,000 from their insurance company in 2022. The Hunters' basis in the home is $270,000. In order to postpone the entire $550,000 gain realized in 2022 ($820,000 – $270,000 adjusted basis), the Hunters have until December 31, 2026 (four years after 2022, the year the proceeds were received and the gain was first realized) to use the $820,000 proceeds to buy (or build) a new principal residence.

¶1010   INVESTMENT IN QUALIFIED OPPORTUNITY FUND

The Tax Cuts and Jobs Act of 2017 added a provision to encourage investment in low income areas. The chief executive officer (governor) of the state or territory nominates the area for this status, and notifies the Secretary of the Treasury. If the Secretary approves the status, it becomes a Qualified Opportunity Zone (QOZ). [I.R.C. §1400Z-1]

Once an area has been designated as a QOZ, it becomes eligible to receive investments from a Qualified Opportunity Fund (QOF). A QOF may be a corporation, including an S corporation, or a partnership. At least 90% of the entity's assets must be in QOZ property. [I.R.C. §1400Z-2(d)]

Moreover, the QOZ business must be an activator, rather than a mere investment activity, excluding certain specified activities. No portion of the proceeds of such issue is to be used to provide (including the provision of land for) any private or commercial golf course, country club, massage parlor, hot tub facility, suntan facility, racetrack or other facility used for gambling, or any store the principal business of which is the sale of alcoholic beverages for consumption off premises. [I.R.C. §144(c)(6)(B)]

The primary tax incentive is a deferral of gain when the taxpayer selling the property invests in a QOF within 180 days of the sale or exchange. [I.R.C. §1400Z-2(a)] If the original gain is between related parties, the taxpayer is not eligible to defer. For this purpose, the related party rules as described in ¶1005 are modified, replacing the 50% general rule with a 20% threshold.

Name:

Section:

Date:

QUESTIONS AND PROBLEMS

1. **Amount Realized, Realized Gain or Loss.** (Obj. 1) Jamie sells land that has a $60,000 mortgage. In return for the land, Jamie receives cash of $40,000 and stock with an FMV of $30,000. The buyer also assumes the mortgage. Jamie's adjusted basis in the land is $80,000.

    a. What is Jamie's amount realized?

    b. What is Jamie's realized gain or loss?

    c. How would your answers to Parts a. and b. change if the buyer had not assumed the mortgage but instead had paid Jamie an additional $60,000 to pay off the mortgage?

2. **Adjusted Basis, Realized Gain or Loss.** (Obj. 1) Alexis sells for $200,000 rental property that she purchased in 2005 for $160,000. In 2007, Alexis spent $12,000 on landscaping and $2,200 on repairs. Over the years, Alexis has deducted a total of $18,440 for depreciation on the property. Compute Alexis's realized and recognized gain or loss on the sale.

3. **Basket Purchase.** (Obj. 1) Leo purchased an apartment building. Leo paid $300,000 in cash, assumed a $200,000 mortgage, and paid the following:

    Brokerage commission $35,000
    Attorney's fee to acquire title   2,000

    What is Leo's basis for depreciation on this building if the FMV of the land and building are $100,000 and $400,000, respectively?

4. **Bargain Purchase.** (Obj. 1) Dan, president of Sugarman Corporation, was given the opportunity to buy 1,000 shares of the corporation's stock for $120 per share. The par value of the stock was $100. Dan took advantage of this offer and purchased 100 shares of stock at a time when the stock was selling for $150 per share. Dan includes as income the difference between the FMV of the stock and his cost. The company also gave Dan an additional 100 shares of stock as a bonus when the stock was selling for $160 per share.

    a. What amount of income must Dan recognize as a result of these stock acquisitions?

    b. What is Dan's per-share basis in the stock he acquired?

5. **Property Received in a Divorce.** (Obj. 1) Hal and Wendy are divorced. Under the terms of the divorce agreement, Hal transferred 100 shares of Big Rig stock (cost $30,000, fair market value $45,000) to Wendy in satisfaction of Wendy's property rights. If Wendy sells the stock for $50,000, what is her recognized gain?

6. **Inherited Property.** (Obj. 1) Terry purchased 5,000 shares of Ferrero Corporation stock in 2000 for $60,000. Terry died on December 11, 2021, leaving the stock to his daughter, Debra. Debra received the stock on April 26, 2022. The FMV of the stock for various dates follows.

    | December 11, 2021 | $80,000 |
    | April 26, 2022 | 78,000 |
    | June 11, 2022 | 77,000 |

    a. Debra sells the stock for $75,000 on August 28, 2022. What is Debra's recognized gain or loss from the sale if the executor uses date of death (DOD) to value the estate?

    b. Same as in Part a. except that the executor uses the alternative valuation date (AVD).

    c. Assume instead that Debra received the stock on August 17, 2022, when the FMV of the stock was $79,000. What is Debra's recognized gain or loss if the executor uses DOD to value the estate?

    d. Same as in Part c. except that the executor uses the AVD to value the estate.

7. **Gifted Property.** (Obj. 1) Max purchased 100 shares of XQM stock in 1999 for $10,000. In 2005, Max gave the stock to his daughter, Linda, when the FMV of the stock was $8,000. No gift tax was paid.

   a. What is Linda's basis in the stock if she sells it in the current year for $11,000?

   b. What is Linda's basis in the stock if she sells it in the current year for $9,000?

   c. What is Linda's recognized gain or loss if she sells the stock in the current year for $7,000?

8. **Gifted Property.** (Obj. 1) In 1972, Tammy gave her son, Al, land worth $80,000. Tammy paid $60,000 for the land in 1970. The full $80,000 value was subject to gift tax, and Tammy paid $12,000 in gift tax on the transfer. What is Al's basis in the land?

9. **Gifted Property.** (Obj. 1) In 2021, Bruce gave Shirley a house worth $100,000. Bruce's adjusted basis in the house was $80,000. The full $100,000 value of the house was subject to gift tax, and Bruce paid $8,000 in gift tax on the transfer. What is Shirley's initial basis in the house?

10. **Gifted Property.** (Obj. 1) Darren gave stock worth $27,000 to his son. Darren paid $9,000 for the stock back in 1954. The full $27,000 value was subject to gift tax, and Darren paid $5,000 of gift tax on the transfer. In 2021, the son sold the stock for $42,000.

   a. Compute the son's recognized gain or loss assuming that the gift took place in 1970.

   b. Same as in Part a. except that the gift took place in 1985.

11. **Converted Property.** (Obj. 1) In 2007, Parker converted his personal residence to rental property. The FMV of the home at the time of conversion was $85,000. Parker paid $90,000 for the home ten years ago.

   a. If Parker sells the property for $100,000 after taking depreciation deductions of $10,000, what is his recognized gain or loss?

   b. Same as in Part a. except that Parker sells the property for $70,000.

   c. Same as in Part a. except that Parker sells the property for $78,000.

12. **Sale of Stock.** (Obj. 1) Ima had the following purchases of common stock in the same company.

2000	400 shares at $10 per share
2003	100 shares at $20 per share
2006	300 shares at $30 per share
2008	200 shares at $40 per share

   a. In 2022, Ima sold 500 shares at $35 per share. Assuming Ima did not identify which blocks of stock were sold, compute her recognized gain or loss on the sale.

   b. If Ima's objective is to minimize taxes and she could adequately identify which stock she was selling, which stock should she sell, and what is the recognized gain or loss that would result?

13. **Stock Splits.** (Obj. 1) Diane owned 100 shares of common stock in the Delta Corporation when it had a two-for-one-stock split. The original 100 shares cost $50 each, for a total cost of $5,000. After the split, Diane had 200 shares that were valued at $30 each, for a total value of $6,000. As a result of the stock split, what is Diane's basis in each share of stock, and how much income must she recognize?

14. **Stock Dividends.** (Obj. 1) In 1999, Patrick paid $1,200 for 100 shares of UPI common stock. In the current year, UPI offers Patrick the choice between a $50 cash dividend or 8 additional shares of common stock valued at $9 a share. Patrick opts for the stock dividend.

   a.   What is Patrick's basis in each of the 108 shares he now owns?

   b.   How would your answer to Part a. change if Patrick did not have the option of a cash dividend?

15. **Wash Sales.** (Obj. 2) An individual taxpayer, not a dealer or trader in securities, completed the transactions shown below for Micro Products Company common stock.

   September 15, 2022, purchased 100 shares at a cost of $4,800
   December 10, 2022, sold the above shares for $3,200
   January 4, 2023, purchased 60 shares at a cost of $1,800

   a.   Compute the recognized gain or loss from the December 10 sale and the taxpayer's basis in the stock purchased on January 4.

   b.   Same as in Part a., except that the sales price of the shares sold on December 10 was $5,300.

   c.   Compute the recognized gain or loss from the December 10 sale and the taxpayer's basis in the stock purchased on January 4 assuming that (i) the sales price of the shares sold on December 10 was $3,200 and (ii) the shares of stock sold on December 10 had been inherited by the taxpayer from the taxpayer's father on September 15, 2021. At the time of the father's death, the shares were valued at $2,500. The father had purchased the stock two months earlier for $2,000. No estate tax return was filed.

16. **Sale to a Related Party.** (Obj. 3) Fred sold stock ($12,000 cost basis) to his sister, Sara, for $9,000. Three years later Sara sold the stock for $14,000 to an unrelated party.

   a.   What was Fred's recognized loss when he sold the stock to Sara?

   b.   What is Sara's basis in the stock she purchased from Fred?

   c.   What is Sara's recognized gain or loss when she sells the stock?

   d.   If Sara had sold the stock for $11,000, what would be her recognized gain or loss?

   e.   If Sara had sold the stock for $7,000, what would be her recognized gain or loss?

17. **Sale to a Related Party.** (Obj. 3) Reed sold land to ABC company for $70,000. Reed paid $95,000 for the land three years ago. Reed owns 10% of the shares in ABC. The rest of the shares are owned by Reed's father (20%), Reed's uncle (15%), Reed's grandfather (30%), Reed's sister (10%), Reed's cousin (10%) and Reed's son (5%).

   a.   Compute Reed's realized and recognized gain or loss on the sale as well as ABC's basis in the land.

   b.   Compute ABC's realized and recognized gain or loss if it later sells the land for $85,000.

   c.   Same as in Part b., except that ABC sells the land for $115,000.

18. **Qualified Small Business Stock.** (Obj. 1) Jenson pays $30,000 for Section 1202 qualified small business stock on February 16, 2005. In October 2022, Jenson sells the stock for $80,000.

    a. Compute Jenson's realized and recognized gain on the sale.

    b. How, if at all, would your answer to Part a. change if the stock were purchased on February 16, 2018?

19. **Like-Kind Exchange.** (Obj. 4) Which of the following qualify as a like-kind exchange?

    a. Exchanging a grocery store for a rental duplex

    b. Exchanging an apartment building for a parking lot

    c. Exchanging Chrysler common stock for land to be held for investment

    d. Exchanging shares of Ford common stock for shares of GM common stock

    e. Exchanging residential rental property for a personal residence

20. Like-Kind Exchange. (Obj. 4) Which of the following qualify as a like-kind exchange?

a. Exchanging an old computer for a new computer (both used in business)

b. Exchanging inventory for a computer (used in business)

c. Exchanging an old personal auto for a new business auto

d. Exchanging office furniture for office equipment (both used in business)

e. Exchanging an automobile for machinery (both used in business)

21. Like-Kind Exchange. (Obj. 4) Dottie exchanges investment real estate for other investment real estate. The following facts relate to the exchange.

Adjusted basis of old property	$ 75,000
FMV of new property	100,000
Cash received by Dottie	10,000
Mortgage on old property assumed by other party	30,000

a. Compute Dottie's realized and recognized gain.

b. Compute Dottie's basis in the new property.

22. **Like-Kind Exchange.** (Obj. 4) For each of the following like-kind exchanges of real estate, compute the taxpayer's realized and recognized gain or loss, as well as the basis of the new property acquired.

	Basis of Old Asset	FMV of New Asset	Cash Exchanged
a.	$ 80,000	$ 50,000	$0
b.	60,000	100,000	$50,000 paid
c.	60,000	100,000	$20,000 paid
d.	100,000	70,000	$20,000 received
e.	100,000	70,000	$50,000 received
f.	100,000	110,000	$20,000 received

23. **Like-Kind Exchange.** (Obj. 4) Bufford wants Jack's farm as a site for an amusement park and offers him $200,000 for the farm. Jack does not want to sell his farm, which has a basis to Jack of $50,000. Bufford is now considering acquiring another farm for $180,000 and then offering that farm plus $20,000 to Jack in exchange for his farm. If Jack accepts this offer, what are the tax consequences?

24. **Sale of a Principal Residence.** (Obj. 1) Adam, who is single, sold his principal residence for $440,000. He paid $28,000 in selling expenses. Adam paid $107,000 for the house 17 years ago. Over the years Adam made improvements and repairs to the house totaling $42,000 and $26,000, respectively. Compute Adam's recognized gain on the sale of his home.

25. **Involuntary Conversion.** (Obj. 5) The Wholesale Dress Shop was destroyed by fire in January. The adjusted basis of the building was $150,000. In March, the insurance company paid $140,000 to cover the loss. Shortly thereafter a new building (dress shop) was purchased for $200,000.

   a. What is the Shop's recognized gain or loss?

   b. What is the basis of the new building?

26. **Involuntary Conversion.** (Obj. 5) Duffy & Co.'s warehouse, which had an adjusted basis of $1,100,000, was destroyed by fire. Duffy received $2,000,000 from the insurance company. Duffy immediately invested $1,800,000 in a new warehouse and elected to postpone as much of the gain as possible.

 a.   What is the amount of gain recognized for income tax purposes?

 b.   What is the basis of the new warehouse?

27. **Involuntary Conversion.** (Obj. 5) On February 17, 2021, Kari was notified by the state that land she owned as an investment was needed for a state park and that the land would be condemned. The state took possession of the land on January 15, 2022, and Kari received her condemnation award on January 20, 2022.

 a.   If Kari elects to postpone recognition of her gain, by what date must she purchase replacement property?

 b.   What type of property could Kari purchase and still postpone recognition of her gain?

28. **Internet Problem: Researching IRS Publication 550.** (Obj. 1)

 Beta Corporation is a C Corporation whose total gross assets have never exceeded $35 million. Trish Newton purchased stock from Beta Corporation in March 2011 as part of Beta's initial issuance. Trish is interested in selling her stock in Beta Corporation and wants to know whether Beta Corporation meets the requirements of a qualified small business corporation under Section 1202.

 Go to the IRS website. Locate IRS Publication 550, *Investment Income and Expenses,* and find the appropriate page that discusses the requirements for a qualified small business corporation under Section 1202. Print out a copy of the page where you found your answer. Underline or highlight the pertinent information. Comment on whether you can answer Trish's question with the information that has been provided.

 See Appendix A for instructions on use of the IRS website.

29. Business Entity Problem: This problem is designed for those using the "business entity" approach. **The solution may require information from Chapter 14.**

Davis converts his sole proprietorship into a regular C corporation. The basis of the assets he transfers into the corporation is $225,000. The fair market value is $265,000. In return for these assets, Davis received all of the corporation's stock—50,000 shares.

a. What is the basis of these assets to the corporation?

b. What is Davis's basis in stock he receives?

CUMULATIVE PROBLEM (CHAPTERS 6-10)

On September 29, 2022, Tripper sold rental property for $230,000. Five percent of the sales price was allocated to the furnishings. Tripper originally purchased the home (a condominium) in 1994, and used it as his principal residence. He paid $160,000 for the home and spent $35,000 on its furnishings. From 1994-2014, Tripper made improvements to the home totaling $34,000. On March 4, 2014, he converted the home to rental property. The fair market value (FMV) of the home itself at the time of the conversion was $182,000. The FMV of the furnishings were $5,000. Tripper used MACRS to depreciate both the condo and its furnishings. This was the only depreciable property Tripper placed in service during 2014. Compute Tripper's recognized gain or loss on the sale of the home and on the sale of its furnishings.

Chapter

11

Property: Capital Gains and Losses, and Depreciation Recapture

CHAPTER CONTENTS

LEARNING OBJECTIVES

After completing Chapter 11, you should be able to:

1. Distinguish between capital assets, Section 1231 property, and ordinary income property.
2. Determine the character of recognized gains and losses.
3. Understand how the netting process works, including how to determine the amount of the taxpayer's capital loss deduction, capital loss carryover, or net capital gain.
4. Compute an individual's tax liability when taxable income includes qualified dividends or net capital gain.
5. Understand the impact of depreciation recapture and unrecaptured Section 1231 losses on the taxpayer's taxable income and tax liability.
6. Compute the amount of gain to be recognized each year from an installment sale, and the character of that gain.
7. Complete the various forms and schedules introduced in this chapter, including Form 8949, Schedule D, Form 4684 (Section B), and Form 4797.

CHAPTER OVERVIEW

Chapter 10 covered the calculation of realized gains and losses from the sale, exchange, or other disposal of property. It also covered which realized gains and losses taxpayers recognize for tax purposes. This chapter examines the character of those gains and losses. Recognized gains may be capital gains or ordinary income. Recognized losses may be treated as capital losses or ordinary deductions. The distinction is important because capital gains and losses are treated differently than ordinary gains and losses. This chapter explains which gains and losses are capital and which are ordinary. It also shows where taxpayers report gains and losses on the tax return.

¶1101   Capital Gains and Losses

The tax laws treat capital gains and losses differently from ordinary gains and losses. Individual taxpayers are limited on the amount of capital losses they can deduct each year, whereas reduced tax rates may apply to capital gains. There are several ways gains and losses can be classified as capital gains and losses. The most common way is the sale or exchange of a capital asset.

¶1101.01   CAPITAL ASSETS DEFINED

All property that taxpayers own is a capital asset unless it falls into one of the following five categories:

1. Inventory held primarily for sale to customers. This includes property that will become part of inventory, such as raw materials and work-in-process.
2. Business receivables, including accounts and notes receivable.
3. Depreciable property and land used in a trade or business.
4. Copyrights; literary, musical, or artistic compositions created by the taxpayer; patents, inventions, models, designs and secret formulas or processes created by the taxpayer; or letters and memorandums created by, prepared for, or produced for the taxpayer. (However, composers of musical compositions and creators of copyrights may elect to treat their works as capital assets.)
5. U.S. government publications purchased for less than the normal sales price.

A closer look at the five categories reveals that the first three involve business property. Thus, except for items described in the last two categories, capital assets can be defined as the taxpayer's personal belongings and investment property. Common examples of capital assets include the taxpayer's clothing, residence, and automobiles (personal-use property). Other examples include stock, bonds, and land held for speculation (investment property).

Using the rules from Chapter 10, taxpayers compute the realized gains and losses that result from the sale or exchange of capital assets. Next, they determine which realized gains and losses they recognize for tax purposes. (Recall from Chapter 10 that not all realized gains and losses are recognized on the tax return.) Taxpayers then classify the recognized gains and losses as short-term or long-term capital gains and losses.

Short-term capital gains and losses result from the sale or exchange of capital assets held for one year or less. **Long-term capital gains and losses** result if the capital asset was held for more than one year. In determining whether property has been held for more than one year, the date taxpayers acquire property does not count, but the disposal date does.

EXAMPLE 1	On June 3, 2021, Thomas buys 100 shares of common stock. Thomas's holding period begins on June 4, 2021. On June 4, 2022, Thomas will have held the shares for more than one year. If Thomas sells the shares after June 3, 2022, he will recognize a long-term capital gain or loss. This, of course, assumes that neither the wash sale rules nor the related party rules from Chapter 10 prevent Thomas from recognizing a loss on the sale.

¶1101.02   HOLDING PERIODS FOR PROPERTY

Not all holding periods begin the day after the taxpayer physically acquires property. Special rules apply to inherited property and to property with a carryover basis.

Inherited Property

The holding period for property inherited from a decedent is considered to be long-term, regardless of the actual holding period. Neither the decedent's holding period nor the successor's holding period affects this rule.

EXAMPLE 2	Mariah inherited stock from her aunt. Mariah's basis in the stock is its $10,000 fair market value (FMV) on the date of her aunt's death on March 3, 2022. Mariah sold the stock for $12,400 on November 5, 2022. Although Mariah's ownership of the property did not exceed one year, she recognizes a $2,400 long-term capital gain ($12,400 – $10,000) on the sale of inherited stock.

Carryover Basis Property

When property has a carryover basis, the holding period also carries over. A carryover basis and holding period can occur one of three ways.

1. The taxpayer uses the previous owner's basis to compute the basis in property. This occurs with transfers of property between spouses, gifted property where the taxpayer uses the donor's basis, and property inherited from decedents dying in 2010 where the carryover basis rules were used. In these cases, the previous owner's holding period carries over to the taxpayer.
2. The taxpayer allocates part of the basis in existing property to the basis of newly acquired property. This happens with nontaxable stock dividends and stock splits. When these events occur, the holding period of the original shares carries over to the new shares.
3. The taxpayer adjusts the basis in property to reflect a postponed gain or loss from previously owned property. This can occur with like-kind exchanges, involuntary conversions, and wash sales. In these cases, the holding period of the old property carries over to the new property.

EXAMPLE 3	On July 11, 2022, Tara gave her nephew, Morgan, stock worth $6,000. Tara paid $7,000 for the stock on May 9, 2017. Morgan sells the stock on December 21, 2022, for $7,500.
	Recall from Chapter 10 that when the FMV of gifted property is less than the donor's basis, the donee's basis is determined when the donee disposes of the property (¶1002.04). The donee uses the donor's basis to compute gains, and the FMV of the property at the time of the gift to compute losses. Because Morgan sells the stock for a gain (more than the donor's basis), his basis in the stock is the donor's basis. Using his aunt's basis, Morgan realizes a $500 gain ($7,500 – $7,000). Since Morgan uses the donor's basis as his basis in the stock, his holding period begins on May 10, 2022 (the day after the day his aunt bought the stock). Therefore, Morgan recognizes a $500 long-term capital gain.

EXAMPLE 4	On May 7, 2022, Norm received land as part of a divorce settlement. Norm holds the land as an investment. He sells the land for $72,500 on December 4, 2022. Norm's wife paid $30,000 for the land in 2014. Norm's holding period dates back to 2014 – the date on which his spouse bought the land. The wife's basis carries over and becomes Norm's basis in the land (¶1002.02). Thus, Norm recognizes a $42,500 long-term capital gain ($72,500 – $30,000).

EXAMPLE 5	On March 10, 2022, Doug exchanges land for a building in a like-kind exchange. Doug's holding period for the land dates back to August 18, 2013. Doug's holding period in the building acquired in the like-kind exchange begins on August 18, 2013.

¶1101.03   NETTING CAPITAL GAINS AND LOSSES

The netting process begins by separating short-term gains and losses from long-term capital gains and losses. The netting process continues by offsetting the gains and losses within each of these two groups. The result is a *net short-term capital gain or loss* and a *net long-term capital gain or loss*.

EXAMPLE 6

Mandy sold the following capital assets during the year.

Description	Gain (Loss)	Group
Stock held 6 months	$ 5,000	short-term
Stock held 8 months	(7,000)	short-term
Stock held 3 years	(14,000)	long-term
Stock held 6 years	21,000	long-term

The first step in the netting process involves separating the gains and losses into two groups (see the column **Group** above). Mandy then begins netting within each group.

Short-Term	Long-Term
$5,000	($14,000)
(7,000)	21,000
($2,000)	$ 7,000

The netting process produces a $2,000 net short-term capital loss and a $7,000 net long-term capital gain.

When a net gain results in both groups, the netting process is complete. Likewise, the netting process is complete when both groups show a net loss. Otherwise, netting losses against gains between the two groups occurs. Examples 7, 8, and 9 demonstrate netting between groups.

EXAMPLE 7

Continuing with Example 6, Mandy offsets the $2,000 net short-term loss against the $7,000 net long-term gain. This leaves Mandy with a $5,000 overall net long-term capital gain.

Short-Term	Long-Term
$5,000	($14,000)
(7,000)	21,000
($2,000)	$ 7,000
	(2,000)
	$ 5,000

EXAMPLE 8

Brook sold four capital assets during the year. After separating the gains and losses into two groups, Brook nets the gains and losses within each group. This netting within groups produces a $2,000 net short-term loss and a $3,000 net long-term loss. Since both groups result in a loss, the netting process is complete.

Short-Term	Long-Term
$6,000	$ 1,000
(8,000)	(4,000)
($2,000)	$(3,000)

EXAMPLE 9

Ace sold five capital assets during the year. After separating the gains and losses into two groups, he nets the gains and losses within each group. This netting within groups results in a $5,000 net short-term capital gain, and a $1,000 net long-term capital loss. Ace uses the $1,000 net long-term capital loss to offset his net short-term gain. This leaves Ace with a $4,000 overall net short-term capital gain.

	Short-Term	Long-Term
	($13,000)	$ 3,000
	7,000	(4,000)
	11,000	
	$ 5,000	($ 1,000)
	(1,000) ◄——————	
	$ 4,000	

Once the netting process is complete, individual taxpayers with a net capital gain pay a reduced tax rate on the net capital gain. **Net capital gain** equals the excess of net long-term capital gain over net short-term capital loss. If the netting process produces a net long-term capital loss or an overall capital loss, then the taxpayer has $0 net capital gain. If the netting process produces both a net long-term capital gain and a net short-term capital gain, then net capital gain equals the net long-term capital gain.

Taxpayers with net capital gain or qualified dividends compute their tax liability by subtracting out these amounts from taxable income and computing tax on the remaining amount. They then add to this amount the tax on the net capital gain and qualified dividends. The tax rate on net capital gain and qualified dividends is 0% for taxpayers whose taxable income is less than $83,550 if married filing jointly or surviving spouse; less than $55,800 if head of household; and less than $41,775 if single or married filing separately. The rate increases to 15% if taxable income is less than $517,200 if married filing jointly or surviving spouse; $488,500 if head of household; $459,750 if single; and $258,600 if married filing separately. A 20% rate applies if taxable income is at least $517,200 if married filing jointly or surviving spouse; $488,500 if head of household; $459,750 if single; and $258,600 if married filing separately.

Recall from Chapter 5 (¶505.03) that taxpayers can deduct investment interest expense to the extent that they have net investment income. Taxpayers can elect to treat any amount of qualified dividends and net capital gain from the sale of investment property as investment income as long as they tax those amounts at the (higher) ordinary income tax rates. Thus, when this election is made, any amounts treated as investment income would be a part of ordinary taxable income when computing the taxpayer's tax liability using the method shown in Examples 10, 11 and 12.

EXAMPLE 10

Abby's taxable income for 2022 is $135,000. Abby's filing status is single. Included in taxable income is $15,000 of net capital gain. Abby's 2022 tax liability is computed as follows.

Tax on $120,000 ($135,000 – $15,000 net capital gain)	$22,636
Plus $15,000 × 15% (tax on capital gain)	2,250
Tax liability on $135,000	$24,886

EXAMPLE 11	Same facts as in Example 10, except that Abby's taxable income is $500,000.	
	Tax on $485,000 ($500,000 – $15,000)	$143,503
	Plus $15,000 × 20%	3,000
	Tax liability on $500,000	$146,503

EXAMPLE 12	Same facts as in Example 10, except that Abby's taxable income is $50,000. However, when you take out the qualified dividends ($0) and net capital gain ($15,000), taxable income drops to $35,000. The ceiling for the 15% tax rate is $41,675. Thus, only $6,775 of her net capital gain ($41,675 – $35,000) is taxed at the lowest 0% tax rate. The rest is taxed at 15%.	
	Tax on $35,000 (using the tax table for single taxpayers)	$3,998
	Plus $6,775 × 0%	0
	Plus ($15,000 – $6,675) × 15%	$1,252
	Tax liability on $50,000	$5,250

 Net capital gains from the sale of Section 1202 qualified small business stock (¶1006) and from the sale of collectibles are taxed at a higher 28% rate for taxpayers in the 28% or higher tax brackets. Collectibles include any work of art, rugs, antiques, gemstones, stamp collections and coin collections. Those interested in learning more about how gains and losses from these assets fit into the netting process should refer to the Instructions to Schedule D (Form 1040).

Net Capital Losses

When capital losses exceed capital gains, the excess is a net capital loss. Each year, individual taxpayers can use up to $3,000 of net capital losses to offset ordinary income ($1,500 for married taxpayers who file as married filing separately (MFS)). Ordinary income is income taxed at the taxpayer's regular (ordinary) tax rate. Examples of ordinary income include wages, interest, dividends, and net profit from a business.

Any net capital loss in excess of $3,000 ($1,500 for MFS) can be carried forward indefinitely. Should the netting process produce both a net short-term and a net long-term capital loss, taxpayers first use up their net short-term capital loss, and then their net long-term capital loss. For individual taxpayers, any unused long-term capital loss is carried over to the next year to offset next year's long-term capital gains. Any unused short-term capital loss is carried over to the next year to offset next year's short-term capital gains.

EXAMPLE 13

In 2022, Moe sold three capital assets that produced a $4,000 short-term gain, a $13,000 short-term capital loss, and a $2,000 long-term capital loss. Moe is married, but files as married filing separately.

	Short-Term	Long-Term
	$ 4,000	($2,000)
	(13,000)	
	($ 9,000)	($2,000)

Moe's capital losses exceed capital gains by $11,000. He uses $1,500 (limit for MFS) of the net short-term capital loss to offset ordinary income on his 2022 tax return. Moe carries over to 2023 a $7,500 short-term capital loss ($9,000 – $1,500) and a $2,000 long-term capital loss.

EXAMPLE 14

Heather is single. In 2022, she sells three capital assets that produce a $5,000 short-term gain, a $1,000 long-term gain, and a $4,000 long-term capital loss. Heather has a $6,000 short-term capital loss carryover and a $2,000 long-term capital loss carryover from 2021. She nets these amounts against her 2022 capital gains and losses as shown below.

	Short-Term	Long-Term
carryover	($6,000)	($2,000)
	5,000	1,000
		(4,000)
	($1,000)	($5,000)

Heather uses the $1,000 net short-term capital loss and $2,000 of the net long-term capital loss to offset ordinary income on her 2022 tax return. She carries over to 2022 a $3,000 long-term capital loss ($5,000 – $2,000).

EXAMPLE 15

Continuing with Example 14, Heather sells two capital assets in 2023. Those assets produce a $14,000 long-term capital gain and a $2,000 short-term capital loss. Heather's netting process in 2023 is as follows.

	Short-Term	Long-Term
carryover		($ 3,000)
	($2,000)	14,000
	($2,000)	$11,000
		(2,000)
		$ 9,000

Heather uses the $3,000 long-term capital loss carryover from 2022 to offset the $14,000 long-term capital gain generated in 2023. She then offsets the $2,000 net short-term capital loss against the net long-term capital gain. Her $9,000 net capital gain will be taxed at a reduced tax rate.

¶1101.03

EXAMPLE 16

Same facts as in Example 15, except that instead of a $14,000 long-term capital gain in 2023, Heather incurs a $14,000 long-term capital loss. In this scenario, Heather's $3,000 long-term capital loss carryover from 2022 is added to her $14,000 long-term capital loss from 2022 to produce a total $17,000 net long-term capital loss. Since the netting within the two groups results in both a net short-term loss and a net long-term capital loss, the netting process stops. Heather uses the $2,000 short-term capital loss and $1,000 of the long-term capital loss to offset her ordinary income on her 2023 tax return. This leaves Heather with a $16,000 long-term capital loss carryover ($17,000 − $1,000) to 2024.

	Short-Term	Long-Term
carryover		($ 3,000)
	($2,000)	(14,000)
	($2,000)	($17,000)

¶1101.04   FORM 8949 AND SCHEDULE D

Individual taxpayers report the details of their sales of capital assets on Form 8949, Sales and Other Dispositions of Capital Assets. They then transfer the totals to Schedule D (Form 1040), Capital Gains and Losses. On both Form 8949 and Schedule D, short-term capital gains and losses are reported in Part I, and long-term capital gains and losses are reported in Part II.

¶1101.05   FILLED-IN FORM 8949 AND SCHEDULE D

INFORMATION FOR FIGURE 11-1:

On **November 20, 2022**, Curt Stevens (single, age 40) sold **100 shares of Comco Corporation common stock** for $2,975. Curt paid a $20 commission on the sale. He purchased the stock on **June 27, 2022**, for **$750**. On **September 3, 2022**, Curt sold **100 shares of Wilcox Industries preferred stock** for $6,000. He paid a $120 commission on the sale. Curt received the stock as a gift from his father on May 8, 2011. The FMV of the stock on May 8, 2011, was $9,000. His father paid $3,192 for the stock, and the father's holding period started on February 7, 2005. The father did not pay gift tax on the transfer. Curt has a $1,000 short-term capital loss carryover from 2021.

Without regard to net capital gain and $500 in qualified dividends, Curt's taxable income is $69,112.

Curt enters the information in bold on the appropriate lines of Form 8949. Form 1099-B shows that Curt's basis in the stock was not reported to the IRS. Therefore, Curt marks boxes **(B)** and **(E)** located immediately above line 1.

Line # (Form 8949, page 1)
   1(d):   Proceeds, **$2,955** ($2,975 – $20 selling expenses)

Line # (Form 8949, page 2)
   1(b):   Date acquired, **2/7/05** (donor's holding period carries over since donor's basis is used)
   1(d):   Proceeds, **$5,880** ($6,000 – $120 selling expenses)
   1(e):   Cost or other basis, **$3,192** (donor's basis carries over since donor's basis is less than the FMV of the stock at the time of the gift)

Curt finishes filling out Form 8949 by adding up the amounts reported in columns (d)–(h) and entering the totals on line 2 at the bottom of both pages of the form.

Figure 11-1: Filled-In Form 8949 (Page 1)

Form **8949**
Department of the Treasury
Internal Revenue Service

Sales and Other Dispositions of Capital Assets
Go to *www.irs.gov/Form8949* for instructions and the latest information.
File with your Schedule D to list your transactions for lines 1b, 2, 3, 8b, 9, and 10 of Schedule D.

OMB No. 1545-0074

2022

Attachment
Sequence No. **12A**

Name(s) shown on return	Social security number or taxpayer identification number
Curt Stevens	271-00-2696

Before you check Box A, B, or C below, see whether you received any Form(s) 1099-B or substitute statement(s) from your broker. A substitute statement will have the same information as Form 1099-B. Either will show whether your basis (usually your cost) was reported to the IRS by your broker and may even tell you which box to check.

Part I **Short-Term.** Transactions involving capital assets you held 1 year or less are generally short-term (see instructions). For long-term transactions, see page 2.

Note: You may aggregate all short-term transactions reported on Form(s) 1099-B showing basis was reported to the IRS and for which no adjustments or codes are required. Enter the totals directly on Schedule D, line 1a; you aren't required to report these transactions on Form 8949 (see instructions).

You must check Box A, B, or C below. Check only one box. If more than one box applies for your short-term transactions, complete a separate Form 8949, page 1, for each applicable box. If you have more short-term transactions than will fit on this page for one or more of the boxes, complete as many forms with the same box checked as you need.

☐ **(A)** Short-term transactions reported on Form(s) 1099-B showing basis was reported to the IRS (see **Note** above)
☑ **(B)** Short-term transactions reported on Form(s) 1099-B showing basis **wasn't** reported to the IRS
☐ **(C)** Short-term transactions not reported to you on Form 1099-B

1 (a) Description of property (Example: 100 sh. XYZ Co.)	(b) Date acquired (Mo., day, yr.)	(c) Date sold or disposed of (Mo., day, yr.)	(d) Proceeds (sales price) (see instructions)	(e) Cost or other basis See the **Note** below and see *Column (e)* in the separate instructions.	(f) Code(s) from instructions	(g) Amount of adjustment	(h) Gain or (loss) Subtract column (e) from column (d) and combine the result with column (g).
100 ss Comco	06-27-2020	11-02-2020	2,955	750			2,205
2 Totals. Add the amounts in columns (d), (e), (g), and (h) (subtract negative amounts). Enter each total here and include on your Schedule D, **line 1b** (if **Box A** above is checked), **line 2** (if **Box B** above is checked), or **line 3** (if **Box C** above is checked) . .			2,955	750			2,205

Note: If you checked Box A above but the basis reported to the IRS was incorrect, enter in column (e) the basis as reported to the IRS, and enter an adjustment in column (g) to correct the basis. See *Column (g)* in the separate instructions for how to figure the amount of the adjustment.

For Paperwork Reduction Act Notice, see your tax return instructions.   Cat. No. 37768Z   Form **8949** (2022)

Figure 11-1: Filled-In Form 8949 (Page 2)

Form 8949 (2022)   Attachment Sequence No. **12A**   Page **2**

Name(s) shown on return. Name and SSN or taxpayer identification no. not required if shown on other side
Curt Stevens

Social security number or taxpayer identification number
271-00-2696

Before you check Box D, E, or F below, see whether you received any Form(s) 1099-B or substitute statement(s) from your broker. A substitute statement will have the same information as Form 1099-B. Either will show whether your basis (usually your cost) was reported to the IRS by your broker and may even tell you which box to check.

Part II **Long-Term.** Transactions involving capital assets you held more than 1 year are generally long-term (see instructions). For short-term transactions, see page 1.

Note: You may aggregate all long-term transactions reported on Form(s) 1099-B showing basis was reported to the IRS and for which no adjustments or codes are required. Enter the totals directly on Schedule D, line 8a; you aren't required to report these transactions on Form 8949 (see instructions).

You *must* check Box D, E, *or* F below. Check only one box. If more than one box applies for your long-term transactions, complete a separate Form 8949, page 2, for each applicable box. If you have more long-term transactions than will fit on this page for one or more of the boxes, complete as many forms with the same box checked as you need.

- ☐ **(D)** Long-term transactions reported on Form(s) 1099-B showing basis was reported to the IRS (see **Note** above)
- ☑ **(E)** Long-term transactions reported on Form(s) 1099-B showing basis **wasn't** reported to the IRS
- ☐ **(F)** Long-term transactions not reported to you on Form 1099-B

1 **(a)** Description of property (Example: 100 sh. XYZ Co.)	**(b)** Date acquired (Mo., day, yr.)	**(c)** Date sold or disposed of (Mo., day, yr.)	**(d)** Proceeds (sales price) (see instructions)	**(e)** Cost or other basis See the **Note** below and see *Column (e)* in the separate instructions.	Adjustment, if any, to gain or loss If you enter an amount in column (g), enter a code in column (f). See the separate instructions. **(f)** Code(s) from instructions	**(g)** Amount of adjustment	**(h)** Gain or (loss) Subtract column (e) from column (d) and combine the result with column (g).
100 ss Wilcox Industries	02-07-2005	09-03-2020	5,880	3,192			2,688
2 Totals. Add the amounts in columns (d), (e), (g), and (h) (subtract negative amounts). Enter each total here and include on your Schedule D, **line 8b** (if **Box D** above is checked), **line 9** (if **Box E** above is checked), or **line 10** (if **Box F** above is checked) . .			5,880	3,192			2,688

Note: If you checked Box D above but the basis reported to the IRS was incorrect, enter in column (e) the basis as reported to the IRS, and enter an adjustment in column (g) to correct the basis. See *Column (g)* in the separate instructions for how to figure the amount of the adjustment.

Form **8949** (2022)

Once Curt finishes filling out Form 8949, he transfers these totals from Form 8949 (line 2) to Schedule D. Because (just above line 1) Curtis checked boxes (B) and (E), he transfers the totals from Form 8949, page 1 (line 2) to Schedule D (line 2), and the totals from Form 8949, page 2 (line 2) to Schedule D (line 9). He then enters the $1,000 short-term capital loss carryover on Schedule D (line 6). Following the instructions on Schedule D, Curt computes his net short-term and net long-term capital gains.

Figure 11-1: Filled-In Schedule D (Page 1)

SCHEDULE D
(Form 1040)

Department of the Treasury
Internal Revenue Service

Capital Gains and Losses

Attach to Form 1040, 1040-SR, or 1040-NR.
Go to *www.irs.gov/ScheduleD* for instructions and the latest information.
Use Form 8949 to list your transactions for lines 1b, 2, 3, 8b, 9, and 10.

OMB No. 1545-0074

20**22**

Attachment
Sequence No. **12**

Name(s) shown on return	Your social security number
Curt Stevens	271-00-2696

Did you dispose of any investment(s) in a qualified opportunity fund during the tax year? ☐ Yes ☐ No
If "Yes," attach Form 8949 and see its instructions for additional requirements for reporting your gain or loss.

Part I Short-Term Capital Gains and Losses—Generally Assets Held One Year or Less (see instructions)

See instructions for how to figure the amounts to enter on the lines below. This form may be easier to complete if you round off cents to whole dollars.	(d) Proceeds (sales price)	(e) Cost (or other basis)	(g) Adjustments to gain or loss from Form(s) 8949, Part I, line 2, column (g)	(h) Gain or (loss) Subtract column (e) from column (d) and combine the result with column (g)
1a Totals for all short-term transactions reported on Form 1099-B for which basis was reported to the IRS and for which you have no adjustments (see instructions). However, if you choose to report all these transactions on Form 8949, leave this line blank and go to line 1b				
1b Totals for all transactions reported on Form(s) 8949 with **Box A** checked				
2 Totals for all transactions reported on Form(s) 8949 with **Box B** checked	2,955	750		2,205
3 Totals for all transactions reported on Form(s) 8949 with **Box C** checked				

4 Short-term gain from Form 6252 and short-term gain or (loss) from Forms 4684, 6781, and 8824	**4**	
5 Net short-term gain or (loss) from partnerships, S corporations, estates, and trusts from Schedule(s) K-1	**5**	
6 Short-term capital loss carryover. Enter the amount, if any, from line 8 of your **Capital Loss Carryover Worksheet** in the instructions	**6**	(1,000)
7 **Net short-term capital gain or (loss).** Combine lines 1a through 6 in column (h). If you have any long-term capital gains or losses, go to Part II below. Otherwise, go to Part III on the back	**7**	1,205

Part II Long-Term Capital Gains and Losses—Generally Assets Held More Than One Year (see instructions)

See instructions for how to figure the amounts to enter on the lines below. This form may be easier to complete if you round off cents to whole dollars.	(d) Proceeds (sales price)	(e) Cost (or other basis)	(g) Adjustments to gain or loss from Form(s) 8949, Part II, line 2, column (g)	(h) Gain or (loss) Subtract column (e) from column (d) and combine the result with column (g)
8a Totals for all long-term transactions reported on Form 1099-B for which basis was reported to the IRS and for which you have no adjustments (see instructions). However, if you choose to report all these transactions on Form 8949, leave this line blank and go to line 8b				
8b Totals for all transactions reported on Form(s) 8949 with **Box D** checked				
9 Totals for all transactions reported on Form(s) 8949 with **Box E** checked	5,880	3,192		2,688
10 Totals for all transactions reported on Form(s) 8949 with **Box F** checked				

11 Gain from Form 4797, Part I; long-term gain from Forms 2439 and 6252; and long-term gain or (loss) from Forms 4684, 6781, and 8824	**11**	
12 Net long-term gain or (loss) from partnerships, S corporations, estates, and trusts from Schedule(s) K-1	**12**	
13 Capital gain distributions. See the instructions	**13**	
14 Long-term capital loss carryover. Enter the amount, if any, from line 13 of your **Capital Loss Carryover Worksheet** in the instructions	**14**	( )
15 **Net long-term capital gain or (loss).** Combine lines 8a through 14 in column (h). Then, go to Part III on the back	**15**	2,688

For Paperwork Reduction Act Notice, see your tax return instructions.   Cat. No. 11338H   Schedule D (Form 1040) 2022

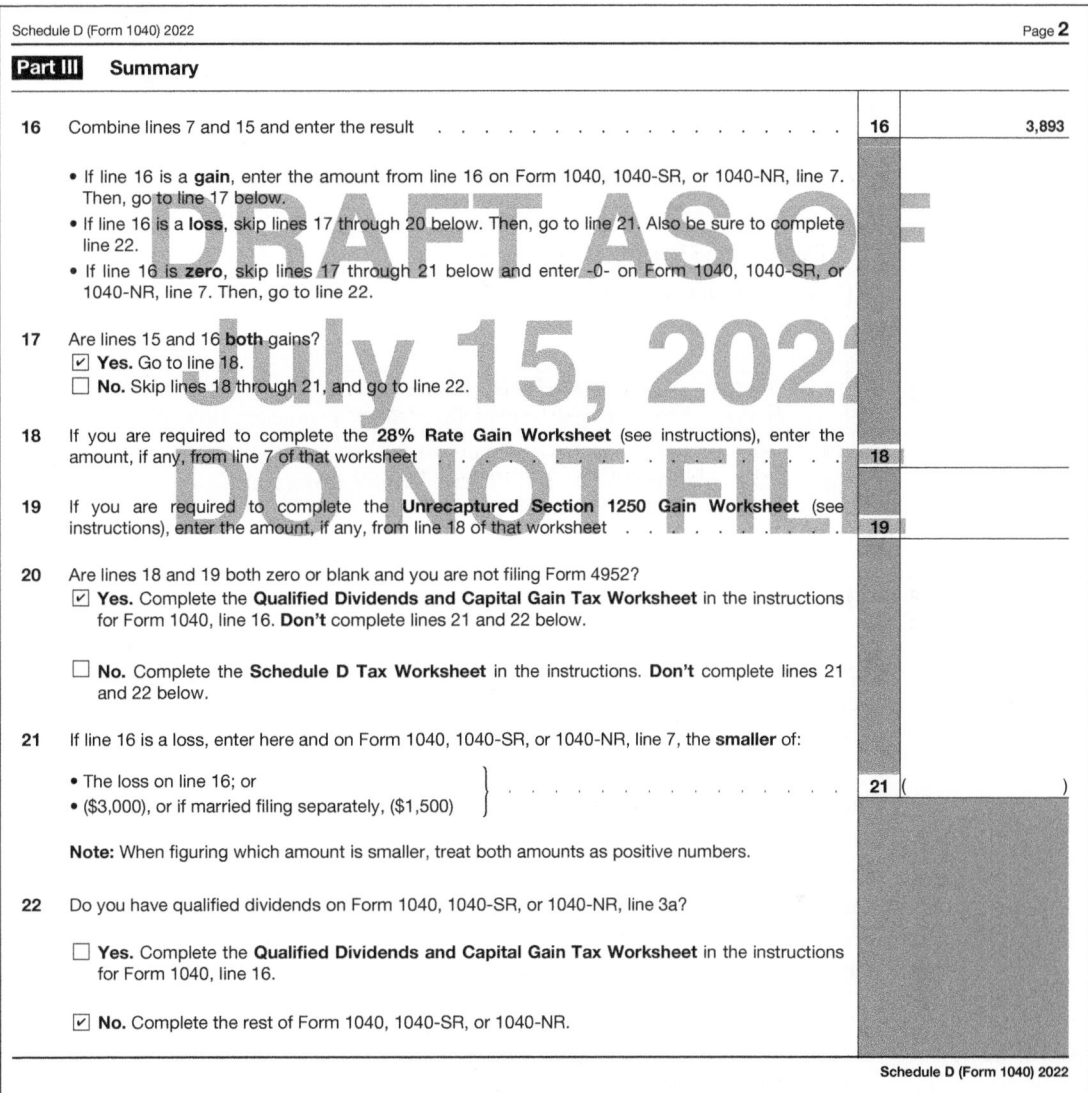

Figure 11-1: Filled-In Schedule D (Page 2)

In Part III on Schedule D (line 16), taxpayers combine the net short-term capital gain or loss (line 7) and the net long-term capital gain or loss (line 15). If combining these amounts results in an overall net loss, the taxpayer enters up to $3,000 of the net loss ($1,500 if married filing separately) on Schedule D (line 21) and transfers this amount to Form 1040. When an overall net gain results, the taxpayer completes lines 17–20, which may involve completing a worksheet to compute a reduced the tax rate on net capital gain. Even if the taxpayer does not report a net capital gain, when the taxpayer reports qualified dividends on Form 1040 (line 9b), line 22 of Schedule D is answered **YES**. The taxpayer then completes the *Qualified Dividends and Capital Gain Tax Worksheet* located in the Instructions to Form 1040 to pay a reduced tax rate on the qualified dividends. This worksheet goes through a series of calculations similar to those shown earlier in the chapter in Example 12.

Because Curt reported gains on both lines 15 (net long-term capital gain) and 16 (total capital gain), Curt marks **Yes** on line 17. He then enters the amount of his capital gains taxed at no more than 28% (**$0**) and unrecaptured Section 1250 gain taxed at no more than 25% (**$0**) on lines 18 and 19, respectively. Because both lines 18 and 19 are $0 or blank, Curt answers **Yes** to line 20. It is here that he is told that he will need to complete the *Qualified Dividends and Capital Gain Tax Worksheet* to compute his tax liability.

Curt transfers the $3,893 total capital gain from Schedule D (line 16) to Form 1040 (line 6). When Curt finishes computing his $73,505 of taxable income, he determines that included in this amount is $2,688 of net capital gain (reported on Schedule D) and $500 of qualified dividends (reported on Form 1040, line 3a). Curt then completes the *Qualified Dividends and Capital Gain Tax Worksheet* to compute his tax liability. Using the approach from Example 12, Curt's tax liability of $13,511 is computed as follows.

Tax on $70,317* (using the tax table for Single taxpayers)	$11,087
Plus $3,188 ($2,688 + $500) × 15%	478
Tax liability on $73,505 taxable income	$11,565

*($73,505 taxable income − $2,688 net capital gain − $500 qualified dividends)

In the Instructions to Form 1040, the IRS provides a *Qualified Dividends and Capital Gain Tax Worksheet* to help taxpayers compute their tax liabilities when a reduced rate applies to qualified dividends and/or net capital gain. The process used to calculate Curt's (reduced) tax liability above is very similar to the method used in the *Qualified Dividends and Capital Gain Tax Worksheet*.

¶1101.06   SPECIAL RULES

Special rules apply to losses from worthless securities and from the sale of Section 1244 stock. Special rules also apply to gains from sales between certain related parties and from sales of subdivided real estate.

Worthless Securities

In the year securities (stocks and bonds) become worthless, the taxpayer is treated as having sold the securities for $0 on the last day of the tax year. For most taxpayers, securities are capital assets. Hence, worthless securities produce a capital loss. A long-term capital loss results if, on the last day of the tax year, the taxpayer held the securities for more than one year.

EXAMPLE 17

On April 3, 2022, Rudy pays $10,000 for stock. On January 23, 2023, the stock is declared worthless. Rudy is deemed to have sold the stock for $0 on December 31, 2023. Since the period from April 4, 2022 (the day after the purchase) until December 31, 2023 (the "sales date") exceeds one year, Rudy recognizes a $10,000 long-term capital loss. He reports the loss in Part II on Form 8949 (line 1).

Section 1244 Stock

For most people, stock is an investment. A loss on the sale of an investment normally produces a capital loss. However, each year individuals can deduct as ordinary losses up to $50,000 ($100,000 on a joint return) of the loss on the sale, exchange, or worthlessness of *qualified small business stock* (also commonly called Section 1244 stock). Annual losses in excess of $50,000 ($100,000 on a joint return) are capital losses. Although both common and preferred stock qualify as Section 1244 stock, only the original owner of the stock qualifies for the ordinary loss treatment. To qualify as Section 1244 stock, the corporation issuing the stock must meet certain requirements. Two of the criteria are:

1. The corporation's contributed capital plus paid-in-surplus cannot exceed $1,000,000 at the time the stock is issued.
2. The corporation must be mainly an operating company rather than an investment company.

EXAMPLE 18	Paige, who is not married, sells Section 1244 stock for $17,000. Paige purchased the stock several years ago for $80,000. Her realized loss equals $63,000 ($17,000 – $80,000). Paige recognizes a $50,000 ordinary loss and a $13,000 long-term capital loss. She enters the long-term capital loss into the netting process and uses the ordinary loss to offset ordinary income such as wages, interest, and dividends. If Paige has no other capital gains or losses, only $3,000 of the $13,000 long-term capital loss can be used to offset ordinary income in the current year. Had the stock not qualified as Section 1244 stock, Paige would have recognized a $63,000 long-term capital loss.

Each year taxpayers are allowed up to $50,000 ($100,000 for MFJ) of ordinary losses from the sale of Section 1244 stock. Taxpayers whose Section 1244 stock has declined in value more than $50,000 ($100,000 for MFJ) from when they bought it should plan on selling their stock over more than one tax year to take advantage of the $50,000 ($100,000 for MFJ) of ordinary losses allowed each year.

Take, for example, Page from Example 18. If Page has sold just enough Section 1244 stock to produce a $53,000 loss, she would have been able to deduct the entire loss ($50,000 ordinary loss + $3,000 capital loss). She could then sell the rest of the stock next year, and deduct the (rest of) the loss as an ordinary loss from the sale of Section 1244 stock.

Gains from Sales Between Certain Related Parties

When individuals sell capital assets to a corporation for a gain, they should recognize a capital gain. However, for individuals who own (directly or constructively) more than 50% of the value of the corporation's outstanding stock, capital gain treatment does not apply if the property is depreciable property to the corporation. Instead, the individual recognizes ordinary income. The same rule applies to individuals who sell capital assets to a partnership in which they own (directly or constructively) more than a 50% interest. If the property is depreciable property to the partnership, the individual recognizes ordinary income. [I.R.C. §1239] This rule applies only to gains between these related parties. See Chapter 10 (¶1005) for rules disallowing losses between related parties, as well as the rules governing constructive ownership.

EXAMPLE 19	Aaron sells property to a corporation for a $10,000 gain. Aaron owns 60% of the stock in the corporation. The property is a capital asset to Aaron, but will be a depreciable asset in the hands of the corporation. Aaron recognizes $10,000 of ordinary income.

EXAMPLE 20	Same facts as in Example 19, except that Aaron owns 50% of the stock in the corporation. Because he does not own *more than* a 50% interest in the corporation's stock, Aaron recognizes a $10,000 capital gain on the sale of the property to the corporation.

EXAMPLE 21	Same facts as in Example 19, except that the property is land, and therefore is not depreciable property in the hands of the corporation. Aaron recognizes a $10,000 capital gain on the sale of the land.

Subdivided Property

Although a capital gain or loss usually results when investors sell parcels of land held for investment, special rules apply to gain (but not losses) on the sale of subdivided property. To receive capital gain treatment, taxpayers must first meet the following four conditions.

1. The taxpayer cannot be a dealer in real estate.
2. The taxpayer cannot be a corporation.
3. The taxpayer cannot make substantial improvements to the lots sold. Filling, draining, clearing, and leveling activities normally are not considered substantial improvements.
4. The taxpayer must hold the lots for at least five years before selling them. Inherited property has no minimum holding requirement.

Taxpayers who meet these four conditions recognize capital gain on the sale of all lots sold until the tax year in which they sell the sixth lot. [I.R.C. §1237] Starting with the tax year in which the sixth lot is sold, they recognize ordinary income for up to 5% of the sales price. Gain not taxed as ordinary income is taxed as long-term capital gain. Any selling expenses first offset any ordinary income.

EXAMPLE 22	Eric bought a tract of land in 2013. Eric, who is not a real estate dealer, subdivides the land in 2022 and sells four lots for $12,000 each. There were no selling expenses. The adjusted basis of each lot is $9,000. Eric recognizes a $3,000 long-term capital gain on the sale of each lot ($12,000 – $9,000).

EXAMPLE 23	Continuing with Example 22, in 2023, Eric sells two more lots for $12,000 each. There were no selling expenses. The adjusted basis of each lot is $9,000. Eric recognizes a $3,000 gain on the sale of each lot. Because Eric sells the sixth lot in 2023, he recognizes $600 ($12,000 × 5%) of ordinary income and $2,400 ($3,000 – $600) of long-term capital gain for each lot sold in 2023. Eric will recognize up to 5% of the sales price as ordinary income on lots sold in future years.

EXAMPLE 24	Same facts as in Example 23, except that Eric incurred $500 of selling expenses for each lot. The selling expenses reduce the recognized gain for each lot to $2,500 ($3,000 – $500). The selling expenses first offset the ordinary income. Thus, for each lot sold, Eric recognizes $100 of ordinary income ($600 – $500 selling expenses) and $2,400 of long-term capital gain ($2,500 – $100). Had the selling expenses exceeded $600, the entire recognized gain would have been long-term capital gain.

¶1101.07   OTHER WAYS OF PRODUCING CAPITAL GAINS AND LOSSES

Besides the sale or exchange of capital assets, other activities can produce capital gains and losses. These activities include nonbusiness bad debts, net casualty or theft gains on personal-use property, and certain disposals of business property.

Nonbusiness Bad Debts

Chapter 7 described the rules for deducting business bad debts (¶705.02). A nonbusiness bad debt is a bona fide debt that is not a business bad debt. A nonbusiness bad debt is reported as a short-term capital loss, regardless of how long the debt was held. This differs from business bad debts, which sole proprietors deduct on Schedule C. Also, unlike a business bad debt, taxpayers cannot deduct a nonbusiness bad debt until it becomes completely worthless.

In the year taxpayers claim a nonbusiness bad debt, they enter the name of the debtor and the words **Statement attached** on Form 8949, Part I. In the attached statement, they then include:

1. The amount of the debt and the date it was due,
2. The taxpayer's business or family relationship with the debtor,
3. The taxpayer's efforts to collect the debt, and
4. The taxpayer's reason for concluding the debt was worthless.

EXAMPLE 25

> Pam made a bona fide loan of $10,000 to her friend in 2018. In 2021, the friend filed for bankruptcy, and Pam was told to expect $.60 on the dollar for her loan. Pam received $4,500 from bankruptcy court in 2022. Pam recognizes a $5,500 ($10,000 – $4,500) short-term capital loss in 2022, the year in which the $5,500 became worthless.

Net Personal Casualty or Theft Gains

A casualty or theft gain occurs when the insurance proceeds exceed the taxpayer's adjusted basis in the property. A casualty or theft loss occurs when the amount of the loss exceeds the insurance reimbursement. For personal-use property, the amount of the loss is measured as the *lesser of* (i) the property's adjusted basis or (ii) its decline in value (¶507).

When a person has just one personal casualty or theft during the year, the taxpayer computes the gain or loss from each property damaged or destroyed in the casualty or theft. When several personal casualties and thefts occur during the year, the taxpayer first computes a net gain or loss for each casualty or theft. The taxpayer then nets the gains and losses to compute a *net personal casualty or theft gain or loss.* If the result is a net gain, then all personal casualty or theft gains and losses are treated as capital gains and losses. A net loss is not deductible unless it is attributable to a federally declared disaster, and then only to the extent it exceeds 10% of the taxpayer's adjusted gross income, and each individual disaster loss exceeds $100 (¶507).

EXAMPLE 26

> Val's home was burglarized. A family heirloom and a TV were stolen. Val's holding period in both items was long-term. Information about the items reveals the following:
>
> | | FMV Before | FMV After | Adjusted Basis | Insurance Proceeds |
> |---|---|---|---|---|
> | TV | $ 500 | $0 | $ 700 | $ 0 |
> | Heirloom | 3,000 | 0 | 1,000 | 2,900 |
>
> Since Val did not insure the TV, the theft of the TV produces a $500 casualty or theft loss (the *lesser of* (i) $700 adjusted basis or (ii) $500 decline in value). Val insured the heirloom, which results in a $1,900 casualty or theft gain ($2,900 insurance proceeds – $1,000 adjusted basis). Val's net casualty or theft gain equals $1,400 ($1,900 – $500). Val treats the $1,400 as a long-term capital gain in the netting process since both properties had been held long-term.

Taxpayers compute their net personal casualty or theft gain or loss on Form 4684 (Section A), Casualties and Thefts. If the result is a net gain, the taxpayer transfers the personal casualty or theft gains and losses to the appropriate short-term/long-term lines on Schedule D. For taxable years beginning after 2018, a net personal casualty loss is only deductible if it occurs in a federally declared disaster area.

¶1102   Business Gains and Losses

By definition, real and depreciable business property are not capital assets (see ¶1101.01). However, under certain conditions, disposing of real and depreciable business property held for over one year can result in long-term capital gain. (The disposal of real and depreciable business property held one year or less always produces ordinary income or loss). Real and depreciable business property held long-term is known as **Section 1231 property.** The sale, exchange, or condemnation of Section 1231 property produces a Section 1231 gain or loss. If Section 1231 gains for the year exceed Section 1231 losses, the net Section 1231 gain may be treated as long-term capital gain. If Section 1231 losses exceed Section 1231 gains, the net Section 1231 loss is treated as an ordinary loss.

EXAMPLE 27	For the year, Daniel reports a $12,000 Section 1231 gain and a $5,000 Section 1231 loss. Daniel's net Section 1231 gain equals $7,000 ($12,000 – $5,000). Daniel may be able to treat this amount as long-term capital gain in the netting process.

EXAMPLE 28	For the year, Morris reports a $10,000 Section 1231 gain and a $23,000 Section 1231 loss. Morris's net Section 1231 loss is $13,000 ($10,000 – $23,000). He deducts this amount from gross income as an ordinary loss.

¶1102.01   BUSINESS CASUALTY OR THEFT GAINS AND LOSSES

Chapter 10 presented the rules for computing business casualty or theft gains and losses (¶1009.02). At the end of the year, taxpayers sum all casualty or theft gains and losses from Section 1231 property (business property held long-term). When gains exceed losses, the excess is a *net business casualty or theft gain.* A net business casualty or theft gain is treated as a Section 1231 gain. When losses exceed gains, the difference is a *net business casualty or theft loss.* A net business casualty or theft loss is treated as an ordinary loss. Casualty or theft gains and losses from business property held short-term produce ordinary income and losses.

EXAMPLE 29	For the year, Leslie recognizes a $10,000 business casualty gain and a $4,000 business casualty loss from properties held long-term. She also recognizes a $2,000 Section 1231 loss. Leslie treats the $6,000 net business casualty or theft gain ($10,000 – $4,000) as a Section 1231 gain. Leslie's net Section 1231 gain is $4,000 ($6,000 – $2,000). She may be able to treat the $4,000 as a long-term capital gain in the netting process.

EXAMPLE 30	Demi has a $6,000 business casualty gain, a $13,000 business casualty loss, and a $5,000 Section 1231 gain. Demi's net business casualty or theft loss equals $7,000 ($6,000 – $13,000). She deducts the $7,000 from gross income as an ordinary loss. Demi may be able to treat the $5,000 net Section 1231 gain as a long-term capital gain.

Section 1231 provides taxpayers with the best of both situations: long-term capital gains for net Section 1231 gains and ordinary losses for net Section 1231 losses. Over the years, Congress identified two situations where taxpayers might take advantage of the favorable rules that govern Section 1231 property. The first situation involves the sale or exchange of depreciable property for a gain. The second situation involves Section 1231 losses.

¶1102.02   DEPRECIATION RECAPTURE

Depreciation expense is a deduction that reduces ordinary income. The tax benefit a taxpayer receives from deducting depreciation expense is equal to the amount of the deduction times the taxpayer's marginal tax rate. (The marginal tax rate is the tax imposed on the next dollar of taxable income. It is the taxpayer's "tax bracket.") When individual taxpayers sell property that generates long-term capital gain, such gain may be taxed at a rate that is lower than the taxpayer's marginal tax rate. The maximum tax rate individual taxpayers pay on net capital gain is 0%, 15%, or 20%, depending on which tax bracket the taxpayer's taxable income falls.

Because net Section 1231 gain can become long-term capital gain, depreciating property as quickly as possible increases the chance of recognizing long-term capital gain when the property is sold. This results in larger depreciation deductions (where the tax benefits are computed using the taxpayer's marginal tax rate) and possibly greater long-term capital gains (where net capital gain is taxed at a lower tax rate). Example 31 illustrates this point.

EXAMPLE 31	In March 2020, Wallace paid $20,000 for a machine that he used in his business. Wallace elected to expense the entire machine under Section 179, therefore his adjusted basis in the machine is $0 at the end of 2020. On October 12, 2022, Wallace sold the machine for $12,000, resulting in a $12,000 gain. If Wallace had no other Section 1231 or capital gains and losses in 2022, the entire $12,000 would be long-term capital gain, which is taxed at a reduced rate, if it were not for the depreciation recapture rules.

Had Wallace used regular MACRS with no bonus depreciation or Section 179 expensing, he would have deducted $2,858 in 2020 ($20,000 × 14.29%), $4,898 in 2021 ($20,000 × 24.49%), and $1,749 ($20,000 × 17.49% × ½) in 2022. His adjusted basis in the machine at the time of the sale would have been $10,495 ($20,000 – $9,505) and he would have recognized a $1,505 gain on the sale ($12,000 – $10,495). Because Wallace has no other Section 1231 gains or losses, the $1,505 would become long-term capital gain, if it were not for the depreciation recapture rules.

In both scenarios, Wallace's effective overall deduction equals $8,000. In the first case, Wallace deducts $20,000 for depreciation expense but reports a $12,000 gain on the sale, which nets to $8,000. In the second case, he deducts $9,505 for depreciation expense and reports gain of $1,505, which also nets to $8,000.

If Wallace's marginal tax rate in both years is 32%. In the first case, Wallace receives a $6,400 tax benefit from the depreciation expense ($20,000 × 32%). If it were not for the recapture rule he would pay tax of $1,800 ($12,000 × 15%) on the gain from the sale. The net tax benefit equals $4,600 ($6,400 – $1,800). In the second case, Wallace's tax benefit is only $3,132 [($10,495 × 32%) – ($1,505 × 15%)]. By electing Section 179, Wallace would end up saving $1,468 in taxes ($4,600 – $3,132).

As you see from Example 31, an incentive existed for taxpayers to use the fastest depreciation method possible. To limit this opportunity, Congress introduced the concept of **depreciation recapture**. Depreciation recapture requires taxpayers to tax gains as ordinary income to the extent of "excessive depreciation." Under the Section 1245 depreciation recapture rules, gains on the disposal of depreciable personal property are taxed as ordinary income to the extent of the *lesser of* (i) the gain, or (ii) all depreciation taken. Gain not taxed as ordinary income is Section 1231 gain.

For personal property, all depreciation taken (including Section 179 expense and bonus depreciation) is subject to depreciation recapture. Even when the taxpayer uses the straight-line method to depreciate personal property, the entire amount of straight-line depreciation is subject to recapture.

EXAMPLE 32	Bonnie bought a business machine on January 3, 2018, for $20,000. Bonnie sold the machine on April 25, 2022, for $21,000. In 2018–2022, Bonnie deducted depreciation totaling $14,645. Her adjusted basis in the machine equals $5,355 ($20,000 – $14,645). Bonnie recognizes a $15,645 gain ($21,000 – $5,355), of which $14,645 is treated as ordinary income and $1,000 is treated as Section 1231 gain.

Depreciation recapture only applies to real property when an accelerated depreciation method is used to depreciate the realty. Since the only depreciation method for most realty under MACRS or ADS is the straight-line method, there is no depreciation recapture on the sale of most real property placed in service after 1986. The unusual situations that still create depreciation recapture on the sale of real estate are beyond the scope of this book.

 Depreciation recapture only affects gains on the disposal of depreciable Section 1231 property. Losses on the disposal of Section 1231 property are always treated as Section 1231 losses.

¶1102.03   NONRECAPTURED SECTION 1231 LOSSES

The tax treatment of Section 1231 gains and losses gives taxpayers the opportunity to treat net Section 1231 gains as long-term capital gains and net Section 1231 losses as ordinary losses. To keep taxpayers from bunching all Section 1231 gains in one year to get long-term capital gain treatment, and then bunching Section 1231 losses in the next year to deduct them as ordinary losses, Congress introduced **nonrecaptured Section 1231 losses**. Before net Section 1231 gain can become long-term capital gain, the taxpayer must look back over its past five years and compute the amount of nonrecaptured Section 1231 losses. Nonrecaptured Section 1231 losses act like depreciation recapture. That is, net Section 1231 gain is taxed as ordinary income to the extent of nonrecaptured Section 1231 losses.

In a year in which the netting process produces a net Section 1231 gain, such gain must first be taxed (recaptured) as ordinary income to the extent of the taxpayer's nonrecaptured Section 1231 losses. Taxpayers generate nonrecaptured Section 1231 losses in years in which the netting process produces net Section 1231 losses (which are treated as ordinary deductions and used to offset ordinary income). Two events reduce the amount of nonrecaptured Section 1231 losses. First, when net Section 1231 gain is taxed (recaptured) as ordinary income, nonrecaptured Section 1231 losses are reduced by the recaptured amount. Second, any amount of nonrecaptured Section 1231 losses not recaptured within five tax years is no longer considered nonrecaptured Section 1231 losses. Thus, net Section 1231 loss is treated as nonrecaptured Section 1231 loss for five tax years or until recaptured as ordinary income, whichever occurs first.

| EXAMPLE 33 | In 2026, Jose has Section 1231 gains of $30,000 and Section 1231 losses of $12,000. Jose also has nonrecaptured Section 1231 losses from 2021-2025 of $7,000. Jose's net Section 1231 gain for 2026 equals $18,000 ($30,000 – $12,000). He reports $7,000 of this gain as ordinary income and the rest ($18,000 – $7,000 = $11,000), as long-term capital gain. Since all nonrecaptured Section 1231 losses from 2021-2025 have been "recaptured" by turning Section 1231 gain from 2026 into ordinary income, there are no nonrecaptured Section 1231 losses from 2022-2026 to apply against net Section 1231 gains in 2027. |

¶1102.04   UNRECAPTURED SECTION 1250 GAIN

When business real property placed in service after 1986 is sold at a gain, individual taxpayers treat the gain as Section 1231 gain. When Section 1231 gains exceed Section 1231 losses for the year (a net Section 1231 gain), such gain may be treated as long-term capital gain. However, the unrecaptured Section 1250 gain may be taxed at the higher 25% tax rate.

Unrecaptured Section 1250 gain equals the *lesser of* (i) the amount of gain, or (ii) allowed or allowable depreciation on the property. (Recall from Chapter 8 (¶801) that the adjusted basis of property must be reduced by the *greater of* depreciation "allowed or allowable." This refers to depreciation that the taxpayer deducts or is entitled to deduct.) Unrecaptured Section 1250 gain applies only to real property sold at a gain. It does not apply to realty sold at a loss. It also applies only to individual taxpayers, estates, and trusts and not to corporations.

EXAMPLE 34	Everett sold residential realty during 2022 for $400,000. Everett paid $520,000 for the building in 2011. Depreciation taken on the building from 2011–2022 totaled $193,818. Thus, Everett's adjusted basis in the building is $326,182 ($520,000 – $193,818). His recognized gain is $73,818 ($400,000 – $326,182). Everett's unrecaptured Section 1250 gain equals $73,818 (*lesser of* (i) the $73,818 gain, or (ii) $193,818 depreciation taken).

EXAMPLE 35	Same facts as in Example 34, except that Everett sold the property for $600,000. Unrecaptured Section 1250 gain equals $193,818 (*lesser of* (i) the $273,818 gain ($600,000 – $326,182), or (ii) $193,818 depreciation taken). When Everett goes to transfer net Section 1231 gain to long-term capital gain in the netting process, he will report the first $193,818 of the net gain as 25% long-term gain and the rest ($80,000) as long-term gain taxed at the lower (0%, 15%, or 20%) rate.

Taxpayers with unrecaptured Section 1250 gain report this gain in the netting process between the short-term and long-term columns. When unrecaptured Section 1250 gain exists, netting of gains and losses is done as follows.

1. If the amount in the 15% long-term column (which represents gain taxed at the lower 0%, 15%, or 20% rate) is a net loss, it is used first to offset any 25% long-term gain, followed by any short-term gain. If there is no net 15% long-term loss, proceed to Step 2.
2. Use any net short-term capital loss to offset any 25% long-term gain, and then any net 15% long-term gain. The netting process is complete when only all gains or all losses remain.

EXAMPLE 36	Brook and Jerry Daniels sold several assets during 2022. Their taxable income is $168,125, which does not include any qualified dividends. The netting within the groups resulted in a $2,000 net short-term loss; a $6,000 25% long-term gain; and a $7,000 net 15% long-term gain. The netting process within and between groups is as follows.

		Long-Term	
Short-Term		**25%**	**15%**
$6,000		$6,000	$18,000
(8,000)			(11,000)
($2,000)	→	(2,000)	$ 7,000
		$4,000	

Since there is no net 15% long-term loss, the Daniels skip Step 1. They begin the netting process between groups by offsetting the $2,000 net short-term loss against the 25% long-term gain (Step 2). This results in a $4,000 25% long-term gain and a $7,000 net 15% long-term gain. The Daniels compute their tax liability as follows.

Tax on $157,125 ($168,125 – $11,000 net capital gain)	$25,802
Plus $4,000 × 25%	1,000
Plus $7,000 × 15%	1,050
Tax liability on $168,125	$27,852

EXAMPLE 37

Kelli sold several capital assets during 2022. These assets produced a $9,000 net short-term loss; a $4,000 25% long-term gain; and a $13,000 net 15% long-term gain. Kelli files as head of household and her 2022 taxable income is $64,230, including net capital gains or losses, with no qualified dividends. The netting process between groups is as follows.

	Short-Term	Long-Term 25%	Long-Term 15%
	$ 6,000	$ 4,000	$14,000
	(15,000)		(1,000)
	($9,000)		$13,000
		(4,000)	(5,000)
		$ 0	$ 8,000

Because there is no net 15% long-term loss, Kelli skips Step 1. In Step 2, she uses the $9,000 net short-term loss to offset first the 25% long-term gain and then the net 15% long-term gain. Kelli is left with $8,000 net 15% long-term gain. She computes her tax liability as follows.

Tax on $56,230 ($64,230 – $8,000)	$6,488
Plus $8,000 × 15%	1,200
Tax liability on $64,230	$7,688

EXAMPLE 38

Jim and Erin Stegall sold several assets during 2022. These assets produced a $6,000 net short-term loss; a $15,000 25% long-term gain; and a $2,000 net 15% long-term loss. The Stegalls file a joint return and report taxable income of $499,230 (including $2,200 of qualified dividends). The netting process between groups is as follows.

	Short-Term	Long-Term 25%	Long-Term 15%
	($13,000)	$15,000	($3,000)
	7,000		1,000
	($ 6,000)	(2,000)	($2,000)
		$13,000	
		(6,000)	
		$ 7,000	

The Stegalls offset the net 15% long-term loss against the 25% gain (Step 1). They then use the short-term loss to offset more of the 25% gain (Step 2). The Stegalls are left with a $7,000 net 25% long-term capital gain. They compute their tax liability (including the reduced tax rates on the $7,000 net 25% long-term capital gain and the $2,200 of qualified dividends) as shown below.

Tax on $490,030 ($499,230 – $7,000 net gain – $2,200 qualified dividends)	$119,017
Plus $7,000 × 25%	1,750
Plus $2,200 × 20%	440
Tax liability on $499,230	$121,207

¶1103   Reporting Business Gains and Losses on the Tax Return

In the end, all of an individual taxpayer's recognized gains and losses appear on Form 1040. Similarly, all of a C corporation's recognized gains and losses appear on Form 1120. However, only gains and losses that appear on Schedule D, Capital Gains and Losses, receive capital gain and loss treatment. Taxpayers report the gain and loss on the sale, exchange, or condemnation of business property on Form 4797, Sales of Business Property. They report the gains and losses resulting from casualties and thefts of business property on Form 4684 (Section B), Casualties and Thefts. Net gains and losses from Form 4684 (Section B) flow through to Form 4797. Therefore, taxpayers with casualties or thefts should begin by completing Form 4684.

¶1103.01   FORM 4684 (SECTION B), CASUALTIES AND THEFTS

Taxpayers compute business casualty or theft gains and losses on Form 4684 (Section B), Casualties and Thefts. Taxpayers with more than one business casualty or theft during the year complete a separate Form 4684, Part I, for each casualty or theft. In Part II, taxpayers separate gains and losses involving Section 1231 property from gains and losses involving business property held short-term. They transfer a net business casualty or theft gain to Form 4797, Part I (line 3), and treat it as a gain from the sale of Section 1231 property. They transfer a net business casualty or theft loss to Form 4797, Part II (line 14), and deduct it as an ordinary loss. A net casualty or theft gain or loss from business property held short-term is also transferred to Form 4797, Part II (line 14), and reported as an ordinary gain or loss.

> Taxpayers also use Form 4684 (Section B) to report casualty or theft gains and losses from investment property. However, the scope of this chapter is limited to business casualties or thefts. Those interested in casualty or theft gains and losses on investment property should refer to IRS Publication 547.

¶1103.02   FILLED-IN FORM 4684 (SECTION B)

INFORMATION FOR FIGURE 11-2:

On October 15, 2022, Alan Miller's laptop **computer** and color laser poster **printer** were stolen from his office. Alan purchased both properties on **June 4, 2020**. Before the theft, the FMV of the computer and printer were $1,500 and $1,800, respectively. The insurance company reimbursed Alan $1,000 for the computer (adjusted basis, $2,200) and $2,300 for the printer (adjusted basis, $2,000).

Line #
- 20A: Adjusted basis of the computer, **$2,200**
- 20B: Adjusted basis of the printer, **$2,000**
- 21A: Insurance reimbursement for the computer, **$1,000**
- 21B: Insurance reimbursement for the printer, **$2,300**
- 23A: FMV of the computer before the theft, **$1,500**
- 24A: FMV of the computer after the theft, **$0**
- 26A: Amount from line 20 since the computer was lost in a theft (see Note: below line 26), **$2,200**

Figure 11-2: Filled-In Form 4684 (Section B)

Form 4684 (2022)	Attachment Sequence No. **26**	Page **2**

Name(s) shown on tax return. Do not enter name and identifying number if shown on other side.
Alan Miller

Identifying number
668-00-9307

SECTION B—Business and Income-Producing Property

Part I   **Casualty or Theft Gain or Loss** (Use a separate Part I for each casualty or theft.)

19 Description of properties (show type, location, and date acquired for each property). Use a separate line for each property lost or damaged from the same casualty or theft. **See instructions if claiming a loss due to a Ponzi-type investment scheme and Section C is not completed.**

Property **A**   Computer, acquired 06/04/2020
Property **B**
Property **C**
Property **D**

		Properties			
		A	B	C	D
20	Cost or adjusted basis of each property	2,200	2,000		
21	Insurance or other reimbursement (whether or not you filed a claim). See the instructions for line 3. **Note:** If line 20 is **more** than line 21, skip line 22.	1,000	2,300		
22	Gain from casualty or theft. If line 21 is **more** than line 20, enter the difference here and on line 29 or line 34, column (c), except as provided in the instructions for line 33. Also, skip lines 23 through 27 for that column. See the instructions for line 4 if line 21 includes insurance or other reimbursement you did not claim, or you received payment for your loss in a later tax year		300		
23	Fair market value **before** casualty or theft	1,500			
24	Fair market value **after** casualty or theft				
25	Subtract line 24 from line 23	1,500			
26	Enter the **smaller** of line 20 or line 25. **Note:** If the property was totally destroyed by casualty or lost from theft, enter on line 26 the amount from line 20.	2,200	2,000		
27	Subtract line 21 from line 26. If zero or less, enter -0-	1,200			

28 Casualty or theft loss. Add the amounts on line 27. Enter the total here and on line 29 **or** line 34. See instructions   **28**   1,200

Part II   **Summary of Gains and Losses** (from separate Parts I)

(a) Identify casualty or theft	(b) Losses from casualties or thefts		(c) Gains from casualties or thefts includible in income
	(i) Trade, business, rental, or royalty property	(ii) Income-producing property	

Casualty or Theft of Property Held One Year or Less

29		(	)	(	)	
		(	)	(	)	
30	Totals. Add the amounts on line 29 **30**	(	)	(	)	

31 Combine line 30, columns (b)(i) and (c). Enter the net gain or (loss) here and on Form 4797, line 14. If Form 4797 is not otherwise required, see instructions   **31**

32 Enter the amount from line 30, column (b)(ii), here. Individuals, enter the amount from income-producing property on Schedule A (Form 1040), line 16; or Schedule A (Form 1040-NR), line 7. (Do not include any loss on property used as an employee.) Estates and trusts, partnerships, and S corporations, see instructions   **32**

Casualty or Theft of Property Held More Than One Year

33	Casualty or theft gains from Form 4797, line 32			**33**	
34	Computer, acquired 06/04/2020	(1,200)	( )		
	Color laser printer, acquired 06/04/2020	( )	( )		300
35	Total losses. Add amounts on line 34, columns (b)(i) and (b)(ii) **35**	(1,200)	( )		
36	Total gains. Add lines 33 and 34, column (c)			**36**	300
37	Add amounts on line 35, columns (b)(i) and (b)(ii)			**37**	1,200

38 If the loss on line 37 is **more** than the gain on line 36:

   a Combine line 35, column (b)(i), and line 36, and enter the net gain or (loss) here. Partnerships and S corporations, see the *Note* below. All others, enter this amount on Form 4797, line 14. If Form 4797 is not otherwise required, see instructions   **38a**   900

   b Enter the amount from line 35, column (b)(ii), here. Individuals, enter the amount from income-producing property on Schedule A (Form 1040), line 16; or Schedule A (Form 1040-NR), line 7. (Do not include any loss on property used as an employee.) Estates and trusts, enter on the "Other deductions" line of your tax return. Partnerships and S corporations, see the *Note* below   **38b**

39 If the loss on line 37 is **less** than or **equal** to the gain on line 36, combine lines 36 and 37 and enter here. Partnerships, see the *Note* below. All others, enter this amount on Form 4797, line 3   **39**

   Note: Partnerships, enter the amount from line 38a, 38b, or 39 on Form 1065, Schedule K, line 11. S corporations, enter the amount from line 38a or 38b on Form 1120-S, Schedule K, line 10.

Form **4684** (2022)

Alan's computer and printer were completely lost as a result of the theft. Thus, he enters the $2,200 adjusted basis of the computer on line 26A to measure his theft loss from the computer. Because the $1,000 insurance reimbursement he received for the computer is less than the adjusted basis, Alan reports a $1,200 casualty or theft loss from the computer on line 27A. Following the instructions on line 28, he enters this amount in Part II (line 34(b)(i)) to show loss as coming from property held for more than one year.

In regards to the printer, the $2,300 insurance reimbursement Alan received for his loss exceeds his $2,000 adjusted basis in the printer. Thus, he reports a $300 casualty or theft gain on the printer on line 22B. Following the instructions from line 22, he then enters this amount on line 34(c) to show the gain as coming from property held long-term. Alan then completes the rest of Part II to arrive at a $900 net business casualty or theft loss deduction on line 38a. Following the instructions for line 38a, Alan transfers this amount to Form 4797 (line 14), where it will be added to his other ordinary losses.

¶1103.03   FORM 4797

Taxpayers use Form 4797, Sales of Business Property, to report gains and losses from the sale, exchange, or condemnation of business property. Form 4797 consists of three parts. Part I summarizes Section 1231 gains and losses. Part II summarizes ordinary gains and losses. Part III separates the gain from the sale or exchange of property subject to depreciation recapture between ordinary income and Section 1231 gain.

Part I

In Part I, taxpayers report gains and losses from Section 1231 property not subject to depreciation recapture. Also included in Part I are net business casualty gains from Form 4684 and Section 1231 gains from the sale of depreciable property reported on Form 4797, Part III. After entering all Section 1231 gains and losses in Part I, taxpayers compute their net Section 1231 gain or loss (line 7). They transfer a net Section 1231 loss to Part II (line 11) so that it can be treated as an ordinary loss. A net Section 1231 gain is first reduced by the nonrecaptured net Section 1231 losses from the past five years (line 8), and the rest is reported as a long-term capital gain on Schedule D. Taxpayers report the recaptured gain (from Part I (line 8)) as ordinary income in Part II (line 12).

Part II

Taxpayers report gains and losses from the sale, exchange, or condemnation of business property held one year or less in Part II (line 10). Taxpayers also report in Part II (line 14) net business casualty or theft losses and casualty or theft gains and losses from business property held short-term. Net Section 1231 losses and recaptured Section 1231 gains from Part I also appear in Part II. After netting the ordinary gains and losses, individual taxpayers transfer the net amount to Form 1040 (line 14).

Part III

The concept of depreciation recapture was introduced earlier in the chapter (see ¶1102.02). The recapture where gain is taxed as ordinary income to the extent of the *accumulated depreciation taken* is referred to as **Section 1245 recapture**. Section 1245 applies to tangible personal property sold for a gain. Taxpayers report property subject to Section 1245 depreciation recapture on Form 4797, Part III. On Form 4797 (lines 19-25), taxpayers provide information about the depreciable property sold and calculate their depreciation recapture.

Also in Part III, total gains from the disposition of property subject to recapture are separated between amounts recaptured as ordinary income (line 31) and Section 1231 gain (line 32). Taxpayers report the ordinary income on Part II (line 13) and the Section 1231 gain on Part I (line 6).

¶1103.04   FILLED-IN FORM 4797

INFORMATION FOR FIGURE 11-3:

On **July 3, 2018**, Jan Gordon placed in service **equipment** costing $36,000. On **May 10, 2022**, she sold the equipment for $15,000. Depreciation taken on the equipment was $26,361. On **January 3, 2022**, Jan sold **land** used in her business for **$22,800**. Commissions paid on the sale were $1,000. Jan bought the land on **February 5, 1978**, for $14,000.

In 2022, the government notified Jan that land she held for investment was to be condemned. Jan paid **$33,200** for the land on **March 5, 1983**. She received **$30,200** from the government for the land on **May 2, 2022**. Jan has $2,500 of nonrecaptured Section 1231 losses from the past five years. Jan enters the information in bold to the appropriate lines on Form 4797 and follows the instructions on the form.

Line #

1: Gross proceeds from the sale or exchange of real estate reported on Forms 1099-B or 1099-S and included on lines 2, 10, and 20, **$53,000** ($22,800 + $30,200). The proceeds on the sale of the equipment (line 20) is not included since equipment is not real estate.

2(f): Cost or other basis plus improvements and expenses of sale, **$15,000** ($14,000 + $1,000)

8: Nonrecaptured net Section 1231 losses from prior years, **$2,500**

12: Gain from line 8, **$2,500** (gain from Part I taxed as ordinary income due to nonrecaptured net Section 1231 losses from the past five years)

20: Gross sales price for the equipment, **$15,000**

21: Cost or other basis plus expenses of sale for the equipment, **$36,000**

22: Depreciation allowed or allowable, **$26,361**

Jan transfers the $2,300 of net Section 1231 gain (from Form 4797, line 9) to the long-term capital gain section of Schedule D (line 11). She transfers the $7,861 of ordinary income (from Form 4797, line 18b) to Form 1040 (line 14).

Figure 11-3: Filled-In Form 4797 (Page 1)

Form **4797**	**Sales of Business Property** (Also Involuntary Conversions and Recapture Amounts Under Sections 179 and 280F(b)(2)) **Attach to your tax return.** Go to *www.irs.gov/Form4797* for instructions and the latest information.	OMB No. 1545-0184 2022 Attachment Sequence No. **27**

Department of the Treasury
Internal Revenue Service

Name(s) shown on return	Identifying number
Jan Gordon	668-00-9307

1a	Enter the gross proceeds from sales or exchanges reported to you for 2022 on Form(s) 1099-B or 1099-S (or substitute statement) that you are including on line 2, 10, or 20. See instructions	**1a** 53,000
b	Enter the total amount of gain that you are including on lines 2, 10, and 24 due to the partial dispositions of MACRS assets	**1b**
c	Enter the total amount of loss that you are including on lines 2 and 10 due to the partial dispositions of MACRS assets	**1c**

Part I **Sales or Exchanges of Property Used in a Trade or Business and Involuntary Conversions From Other Than Casualty or Theft—Most Property Held More Than 1 Year** (see instructions)

2	(a) Description of property	(b) Date acquired (mo., day, yr.)	(c) Date sold (mo., day, yr.)	(d) Gross sales price	(e) Depreciation allowed or allowable since acquisition	(f) Cost or other basis, plus improvements and expense of sale	(g) Gain or (loss) Subtract (f) from the sum of (d) and (e)
	Land	02-05-1978	01-03-2022	22,800		15,000	7,800
	Land	03-05-1983	05-05-2022	30,200		33,200	(3,000)

3	Gain, if any, from Form 4684, line 39	**3**	
4	Section 1231 gain from installment sales from Form 6252, line 26 or 37	**4**	
5	Section 1231 gain or (loss) from like-kind exchanges from Form 8824.	**5**	
6	Gain, if any, from line 32, from other than casualty or theft	**6**	
7	Combine lines 2 through 6. Enter the gain or (loss) here and on the appropriate line as follows	**7**	4,800

Partnerships and S corporations. Report the gain or (loss) following the instructions for Form 1065, Schedule K, line 10, or Form 1120-S, Schedule K, line 9. Skip lines 8, 9, 11, and 12 below.

Individuals, partners, S corporation shareholders, and all others. If line 7 is zero or a loss, enter the amount from line 7 on line 11 below and skip lines 8 and 9. If line 7 is a gain and you didn't have any prior year section 1231 losses, or they were recaptured in an earlier year, enter the gain from line 7 as a long-term capital gain on the Schedule D filed with your return and skip lines 8, 9, 11, and 12 below.

8	Nonrecaptured net section 1231 losses from prior years. See instructions	**8**	2,500
9	Subtract line 8 from line 7. If zero or less, enter -0-. If line 9 is zero, enter the gain from line 7 on line 12 below. If line 9 is more than zero, enter the amount from line 8 on line 12 below and enter the gain from line 9 as a long-term capital gain on the Schedule D filed with your return. See instructions.	**9**	2,300

Part II **Ordinary Gains and Losses** (see instructions)

10	Ordinary gains and losses not included on lines 11 through 16 (include property held 1 year or less):		

11	Loss, if any, from line 7	**11** (	)
12	Gain, if any, from line 7 or amount from line 8, if applicable	**12**	2,500
13	Gain, if any, from line 31	**13**	5,361
14	Net gain or (loss) from Form 4684, lines 31 and 38a	**14**	
15	Ordinary gain from installment sales from Form 6252, line 25 or 36	**15**	
16	Ordinary gain or (loss) from like-kind exchanges from Form 8824	**16**	
17	Combine lines 10 through 16.	**17**	7,861
18	For all except individual returns, enter the amount from line 17 on the appropriate line of your return and skip lines a and b below. For individual returns, complete lines a and b below.		
a	If the loss on line 11 includes a loss from Form 4684, line 35, column (b)(ii), enter that part of the loss here. Enter the loss from income-producing property on Schedule A (Form 1040), line 16. (Do not include any loss on property used as an employee.) Identify as from "Form 4797, line 18a." See instructions	**18a**	
b	Redetermine the gain or (loss) on line 17 excluding the loss, if any, on line 18a. Enter here and on Schedule 1 (Form 1040), Part I, line 4	**18b**	

For Paperwork Reduction Act Notice, see separate instructions.	Cat. No. 13086I	Form **4797** (2022)

Figure 11-3: Filled-In Form 4797 (Page 2)

Form 4797 (2022)   Page **2**

Part III **Gain From Disposition of Property Under Sections 1245, 1250, 1252, 1254, and 1255** (see instructions)

19	(a) Description of section 1245, 1250, 1252, 1254, or 1255 property:		(b) Date acquired (mo., day, yr.)	(c) Date sold (mo., day, yr.)
A	Equipment		07-03-2018	05-10-2022
B				
C				
D				

These columns relate to the properties on lines 19A through 19D.		Property A	Property B	Property C	Property D
20	Gross sales price (**Note:** *See line 1a before completing.*) .	**20**	15,000			
21	Cost or other basis plus expense of sale	**21**	36,000			
22	Depreciation (or depletion) allowed or allowable . . .	**22**	26,361			
23	Adjusted basis. Subtract line 22 from line 21 . . .	**23**	9,639			
24	Total gain. Subtract line 23 from line 20	**24**	5,361			
25	**If section 1245 property:**					
a	Depreciation allowed or allowable from line 22 . .	**25a**	26,361			
b	Enter the **smaller** of line 24 or 25a.	**25b**	5,361			
26	**If section 1250 property:** If straight line depreciation was used, enter -0- on line 26g, except for a corporation subject to section 291.					
a	Additional depreciation after 1975. See instructions .	**26a**				
b	Applicable percentage multiplied by the **smaller** of line 24 or line 26a. See instructions.	**26b**				
c	Subtract line 26a from line 24. If residential rental property **or** line 24 isn't more than line 26a, skip lines 26d and 26e	**26c**				
d	Additional depreciation after 1969 and before 1976. .	**26d**				
e	Enter the **smaller** of line 26c or 26d	**26e**				
f	Section 291 amount (corporations only)	**26f**				
g	Add lines 26b, 26e, and 26f	**26g**				
27	**If section 1252 property:** Skip this section if you didn't dispose of farmland or if this form is being completed for a partnership.					
a	Soil, water, and land clearing expenses	**27a**				
b	Line 27a multiplied by applicable percentage. See instructions	**27b**				
c	Enter the **smaller** of line 24 or 27b	**27c**				
28	**If section 1254 property:**					
a	Intangible drilling and development costs, expenditures for development of mines and other natural deposits, mining exploration costs, and depletion. See instructions	**28a**				
b	Enter the **smaller** of line 24 or 28a.	**28b**				
29	**If section 1255 property:**					
a	Applicable percentage of payments excluded from income under section 126. See instructions	**29a**				
b	Enter the **smaller** of line 24 or 29a. See instructions .	**29b**				

Summary of Part III Gains. Complete property columns A through D through line 29b before going to line 30.

30	Total gains for all properties. Add property columns A through D, line 24	**30**	5,361
31	Add property columns A through D, lines 25b, 26g, 27c, 28b, and 29b. Enter here and on line 13	**31**	5,361
32	Subtract line 31 from line 30. Enter the portion from casualty or theft on Form 4684, line 33. Enter the portion from other than casualty or theft on Form 4797, line 6	**32**	

Part IV **Recapture Amounts Under Sections 179 and 280F(b)(2) When Business Use Drops to 50% or Less** (see instructions)

			(a) Section 179	(b) Section 280F(b)(2)
33	Section 179 expense deduction or depreciation allowable in prior years.	**33**		
34	Recomputed depreciation. See instructions	**34**		
35	Recapture amount. Subtract line 34 from line 33. See the instructions for where to report . .	**35**		

Form **4797** (2022)

¶1104 Installment Sales

When property is sold, the seller may collect the sales price in full at the time of sale. Alternatively, the sales price may be collected over a number of months or years. If the full sales price is collected in the year of sale, recognized gain or loss is reported in that year. When collections extend beyond the year of sale, any gain (but not loss) may be recognized on the installment method. The installment method allows taxpayers to report the gain (and pay the related taxes) as they collect payments on the installment obligation.

To use the installment sales method, at least one payment must be received in the tax year following the year of the sale. Taxpayers, however, may elect out of using the installment method. They make this election by reporting the entire gain in the year of sale. The election must be made before the due date of the return (including extensions) for the year of the sale.

The installment method is intended for casual sales of personal and real property. Thus, it cannot be used by dealers. A dealer is someone who regularly sells personal or real property in the ordinary course of a trade or business. The installment method cannot be used to report gain from the sale of publicly traded stock or securities.

¶1104.01 COMPUTING INSTALLMENT GAIN

The amount of gain that must be reported in a given tax year is computed as follows:

$$\textbf{Gain recognized} \ = \ \textbf{payments received} \ \times \ \textbf{(gross profit} \div \textbf{contract price)}$$

Payments Received

As payments on the sales price are collected, a portion of the profit is reported (recognized). Payments include cash and property the seller receives. Payments do not include notes or other obligations the seller receives from the buyer.

Gross Profit

Gross profit equals the amount realized less the adjusted basis of the property. Gross profit is the amount of gain that would be recognized in the year of sale if the installment method were not used. The amount realized includes cash and other property received. It also includes notes received from the buyer or mortgages the buyer assumes. It does not include any interest to be received from the transaction.

EXAMPLE 39

In 2021, Ellen sells land held for investment and receives $18,000. Ellen paid $11,200 for the land and over the years spent $1,400 on landscaping. Ellen's gross profit of $5,400 is determined as follows.

Amount realized		$18,000
Less adjusted basis		
Cost	$11,200	
Improvements	1,400	(12,600)
Gross profit		$ 5,400

Contract Price

The gross profit ratio is gross profit divided by the contract price. The contract price is the amount realized less mortgages the buyer assumes. It is usually the sum of the principal payments. It does not include interest that the seller expects to receive.

Taxpayers compute the current year's recognized gain by multiplying the amounts received on the principal during the year by the gross profit ratio. In Example 39, Ellen's gross profit ratio equals 30% [$5,400 (gross profit) ÷ $18,000 (contract price)]. Keep in mind that payments on notes normally include interest as well as principal. Interest received by individuals is ordinary income reported on Schedule B.

EXAMPLE 40	Assume the same facts as in Example 39, except that the purchaser gives Ellen a $4,000 down payment plus an interest-bearing note for the rest ($14,000). From this note, $12,000 of principal is due in 2021, and $2,000 is due in 2022. If the notes are paid when due, Ellen reports the gain as follows. She reports the interest income from the note on Schedule B.

2021	($4,000 + $12,000) × 30% =	$4,800
2022	$2,000 × 30% =	600
Total		$5,400

A special rule applies to the sale of nondepreciable property to a related party, which includes the taxpayer's descendant, ancestor, sibling, or spouse. If nondepreciable property is sold to a related party in an installment sale *and* the related party sells the property within two years of the sale, the rest of the installment gain is taxable to the seller in the year that the related party sells the property. Thus, the subsequent sale by a related party accelerates the gain reported by the original seller.

EXAMPLE 41	On March 1, 2021, Lucy sells land to her sister for $220,000. She accepts $20,000 down and a note that calls for four annual payments of $50,000, plus interest. The first installment is due on March 1, 2022. Lucy paid $165,000 for the land several years ago. She realizes gross profit of $55,000 on the sale.

Amount realized	$220,000
Less adjusted basis	(165,000)
Gross profit	$ 55,000

Lucy's gross profit ratio equals 25% ($55,000 gross profit ÷ $220,000 contract price). She will report the $55,000 gain from the sale as follows.

Year	Amount	
2021	$20,000 × 25% =	$ 5,000
2022	$50,000 × 25% =	12,500
2023	$50,000 × 25% =	12,500
2024	$50,000 × 25% =	12,500
2025	$50,000 × 25% =	12,500
Total		$55,000

EXAMPLE 42 Same facts as in Example 41, except that on January 25, 2023 the sister sells the land. Because the sister sold the land within two years of March 1, 2021, Lucy reports the $55,000 gain from the sale as follows.

Year	Amount	
2021	$20,000 × 25% =	$ 5,000
2022	$50,000 × 25% =	12,500
2023	rest of the gain	37,500
Total		$55,000

EXAMPLE 43 Same facts as in Example 42, except that the sister sells the land on July 25, 2023. Since the sale occurred after more than two years, the timing of the gain reported by Lucy is the same as in Example 41.

¶1104.02 DEPRECIATION RECAPTURE

If property sold as an installment sale is subject to depreciation recapture, the recapture must be recognized as ordinary income in the year of the sale, regardless of the payments received during the year. The gain reported in the first year as depreciation recapture reduces gross profit used in computing the gross profit ratio. Likewise, it reduces the amount of each installment gain to be included in income as capital gain or Section 1231 gain.

EXAMPLE 44 Jamar sells depreciable personal property for $180,000. He accepts five equal installments of $36,000 plus interest. Jamar realizes gross profit of $120,000 on the sale.

Amount realized		$180,000
Less adjusted basis		
Cost	$90,000	
Accumulated depreciation	(30,000)	(60,000)
Gross profit		$120,000

Gain on the sale of personal property is recaptured as ordinary income to the extent of depreciation taken on the property. Thus, Jamar recognizes the $30,000 of accumulated depreciation as ordinary income in the year of the sale. He also recognizes a portion of each year's receipts as Section 1231 gain. This amount is computed by reducing Jamar's gross profit by $30,000 and recalculating the gross profit ratio.

Income Recognized in Year 1

Ordinary income (depreciation recapture)	$ 30,000
Recompute the gross profit ratio:	
($120,000 – $30,000) ÷ $180,000 = 50% gross profit ratio	
Section 1231 gain reportable in Year 1 (50% × $36,000)	18,000
Total gain recognized in Year 1	$ 48,000

Income Recognized in Years 2-5

Section 1231 gain (50% × $36,000 = $18,000 × 4 years)	72,000
Total gain recognized over five years	$120,000

11

Name:

Section:

Date: _____

QUESTIONS AND PROBLEMS

1. **Capital Assets.** (Obj. 1) Indicate which of the following are capital assets.

Item	*Answer*
a. House occupied as a residence by the owner	_____
b. Delivery truck used in a contractor's business	_____
c. Corporate stocks owned by a doctor	_____
d. Valuable jewelry held for sale by Jones Jewelers	_____
e. Land held for investment by an accountant	_____
f. Automobile used for personal purposes by the owner	_____
g. Business suits worn only to work	_____
h. House used strictly as a summer residence	_____
i. Musical copyright owned by the composer	_____

2. **Capital Gains and Losses.** (Obj. 2)

   a. Distinguish between long-term capital gain and short-term capital gain for capital assets acquired January 10, 2021.

   b. If an individual has gains and losses from the sale of stocks and other investments, what form or schedule is used to support the capital gain or loss reported on Form 1040?

3. **Holding Period.** (Obj. 2) State the time when the holding period begins on capital assets acquired by the following methods:

   a. Capital asset acquired by gift, if sold at a gain

   b. Capital asset acquired by gift, if sold at a loss (assume the fair market value (FMV) of the property was less than the donor's basis at the time of the gift)

   c. Property inherited from a decedent dying in 2022

4. **Capital Gains and Losses.** (Obj. 2) For each of the following cases, determine whether the gain would be taxed as short-term capital gain, long-term capital gain taxed at 20%, long-term capital gain taxed at 15%, or long-term capital gain taxed at 0%. Assume the taxpayer files as single and this is the only capital asset sold during the year.

   a. Stock held for four years is sold for a $3,000 gain; taxable income is $25,000.

   b. Stock held for eight months is sold for a $3,000 gain; taxable income is $52,000.

   c. Stock held for four years is sold for a $2,000 gain; taxable income is $77,000.

   d. Stock held for four years is sold for a $4,000 gain; taxable income is $480,000.

   e. Stock held four months is sold for a $4,000 gain; taxable income is $410,000.

5. **Netting Capital Gains and Losses.** (Obj. 3) In each of the following cases, use the netting process between groups to determine the taxpayer's net capital gain and the tax rate paid on such gain. Assume the taxpayer files jointly and these are the only capital assets sold during the year.

    a. A $2,000 loss on the sale of a capital asset held six months; a $9,000 gain on the sale of a capital asset held for three years. Taxable income is $100,000.

    b. Same as Part a., except that taxable income is $50,000.

    c. A $6,000 gain on the sale of a capital asset held nine months; a $5,000 gain on the sale of a capital asset held four years. Taxable income is $400,000.

    d. Same as Part c., except that taxable income is $60,000.

    e. Same as in Part c., except that taxable income is $750,000.

6. **Capital Gains Tax.** (Obj. 4) During 2022, Earl, a single taxpayer, sells two capital assets. The first results in a $4,000 short-term capital gain. The second results in a $9,500 long-term capital gain. Earl's AGI without taking these two gains into consideration is $71,284 (no qualified dividends). Earl deducts the standard deduction. Compute Earl's 2022 income tax liability.

7. **Capital Gains Tax.** (Obj. 4) During 2022, Angie sells two capital assets. The first results in a $4,000 short-term capital loss. The second results in a $7,500 long-term capital gain. Angie's AGI without taking these gains and losses into consideration is $44,235 (no qualified dividends). She files as head of household and deducts the standard deduction. Compute Angie's 2022 income tax liability.

8. **Capital Gains Tax.** (Obj. 4) During 2022, Taylor sells two capital assets. The first results in a $9,000 short-term capital gain. The second results in a $2,600 long-term capital loss. Taylor's AGI without taking these gains and losses into consideration is $125,444 (no qualified dividends). Taylor files as a qualifying widow(er) and deducts the standard deduction. Compute Taylor's 2022 income tax liability.

9. **Capital Gains Tax.** (Obj. 4) In March of 2022, Shirley sold stock of the Wingate Corporation for $15,000. Shirley had acquired the stock three years earlier at a cost of $11,600. Exclusive of this gain she expects to have a taxable income of $36,000 (after deductions and exemptions) for the year. Shirley files as single. She has no qualified dividends. In December 2022, Shirley thought about selling stock of the Roberts Printing Company, which she acquired on January 15, 2020, for $18,000. It has since declined in value to $13,000.

   a. Compute Shirley's total tax liability for 2022, assuming she does not sell the Roberts stock in 2022.

   b. Compute Shirley's total tax liability for 2022, assuming she sells the Roberts stock for $13,000 in 2022. What amount of tax savings would result from the sale?

10. **Capital Losses.** (Obj. 3) Compute the capital loss deduction that can be claimed in 2022 for each of the following individual taxpayers. Also, compute the capital loss carryover to 2023 by type (short-term, long-term) of loss. If none, insert *None*. Taxpayers A and B file as single. Taxpayer C files as head of household. Taxpayer D is a married couple filing a joint tax return. Taxpayer E is a married person who is filing a separate tax return from her spouse.

Gains and Losses	A	B	C	D	E
Short-term capital gains	$ 900	$ 800	$ 0	$ 400	$ 3,200
Short-term capital losses	(6,200)	(1,200)	(400)	(2,400)	(8,600)
Long-term capital gains	800	2,200	800	1,600	1,400
Long-term capital losses	(600)	(800)	(1,150)	(4,200)	(2,600)
Capital loss deduction in 2022	$_____	$_____	$_____	$_____	$_____
Short-term loss carryover to 2023	$_____	$_____	$_____	$_____	$_____
Long-term loss carryover to 2023	$_____	$_____	$_____	$_____	$_____

11. **Stock Sales.** (Obj. 2) A taxpayer is considering selling 100 shares of stock. The current market price is $7,500. Which shares should the taxpayer instruct the broker to sell, and what are the tax consequences of this selection if the taxpayer owned the following shares in the company?

Certificate Number	Date Acquired	Number of Shares	Cost
CR642	4-11-07	300	$15,000
DO111	9-10-11	100	9,000
EA002	8-13-04	100	6,000

12. **Worthless Securities.** (Obj. 2) On July 17, 2021, Martina paid $15,000 for 4,500 shares of stock in ABC corporation. On December 29, 2021, the stock was trading for $.03 a share. On January 6, 2022, Martina's stockbroker let her know that the stock was worthless. Discuss the tax consequences of the ABC stock on Martina's 2021 and 2022 tax returns.

13. **Section 1244 Stock.** (Obj. 2)

    a. Hale sells 1,000 shares of his Section 1244 stock ("small business corporation" stock) at a loss of $200,000. If Hale and his wife file a joint return, how will this loss be treated on the tax return?

    b. If Hale were single, how would he treat the loss on his tax return?

    c. How might Hale have better planned for the sale of his Section 1244 stock?

14. **Subdivided Realty.** (Obj. 2) Juan, an investor, subdivided an unimproved tract of land that he acquired 20 years ago. In 2022, he sold four lots for $10,000 each. The basis of each lot is $2,000, and the selling expenses are $400 per lot.

    a. What is the gain or loss on these transactions, and how will it be taxed?

    b. Assuming that Juan sells five more lots in 2022 at the same price with selling expenses of $400 per lot, what will be the gain or loss, and how will it be taxed?

15. **Subdivided Realty.** (Obj. 2) Barbie, a real estate dealer, purchased two lots for $12,000 each in May 2006. On August 30, 2022, Barbie sold the tracts of land for $20,000 each. Compute the gain and describe how it will be treated on the tax return.

16. **Bad Debts.** (Obj. 2) Rita loaned her brother, Richard, $7,500 on February 14, 2018. The loan represents a bona fide loan. Richard filed for bankruptcy in 2022, and Rita learned that she could expect to receive only $.70 on the dollar on the personal loan that she had made to him. On May 17, 2023, Rita received a final settlement of $4,000.

    a. How much loss can Rita deduct in 2022?

    b. How much loss can Rita deduct in 2023?

    c. How will this loss be treated on Rita's tax return?

17. **Section 1231 and Capital Gains and Losses.** (Obj. 3) Use the following information to answer Parts a. through c.

	Period Property Was Held	Amount of Gain or Loss
Nonbusiness bad debt	Three years	($2,600)
Sale of equipment used in business	Two months	(1,500)
Sale of equipment used in business	Two years	(3,000)
Sale of corporate stock	Five years	2,500
Sale of land used in business	Four years	5,000

    a. What, if any, is the amount of net short-term capital loss?

    b. What, if any, is the amount of net Section 1231 gain or (loss)?

    c. What, if any, is the ordinary loss deduction?

18. **Nonbusiness Casualty or Theft Gains and Losses.** (Obj. 3) Blake's home was burglarized. Artwork purchased six years ago and a brand new Plasma TV were stolen. Blake had no other nonbusiness casualties or thefts during the year. Based on the information provided below about the theft, describe the tax consequences on Blake's tax return.

	FMV Before	*Adjusted Basis*	*Insurance Proceeds*
Artwork	$10,000	$5,500	$9,500
Plasma TV	1,200	2,000	1,000

19. **Business Casualty or Theft Gains and Loss.** (Obj. 3) S.R.W. Inc. had an expensive sculpture stolen from the lobby of its offices. The sculpture was insured, and S.R.W. realized an $80,000 gain from the theft. This was S.R.W.'s only casualty or theft for the year.

    a. Discuss the tax consequences of this theft on S.R.W.'s tax return if S.R.W. has $100,000 of Section 1231 gains.

    b. Same as in Part a., except that S.R.W. has $100,000 of Section 1231 losses.

20. **Nonrecaptured Section 1231 Losses.** (Obj. 5) Explain the concept of nonrecaptured Section 1231 losses and their impact a taxpayer's netting process.

21. **Sale of Business Property.** (Obj. 5) Carlotta purchased computer equipment for her business in 2018 for $60,000. In 2022, she sold the computer equipment for $35,000. Depreciation information follows:

    Regular (accelerated) MACRS deduction claimed $51,360
    Straight-line depreciation would have been $24,000

What is Carlotta's gain or loss on the sale of the computers, and how will it be treated?

22. **Unrecaptured Section 1250 Gain.** (Obj. 2) Victor purchased a warehouse in 2006 for $1,000,000. He sold the warehouse in July of 2022 for $1,200,000. Victor deducted $309,524 of depreciation during the period when he owned the building. How will this transaction be reported on the tax return? How will the gain on this transaction be taxed?

23. **Sale of Business Property.** (Obj. 7) In 2022, Virginia Banks (SSN 364-00-8153) had the following transactions involving property used in her manufacturing business.

    ■ Machinery purchased for $50,000 on August 6, 2018, was sold on April 6, 2022 for $22,000. Total depreciation taken on the machine was $31,258.
    ■ Land used in Virginia's business was sold for $23,000 on June 6, 2022. The land was purchased for $16,000 on May 3, 2005.
    ■ A small tool shed was destroyed by fire during 2022. The loss was not covered by insurance. The shed had been used for several years and had an adjusted basis of $2,500 at the time of the fire. The loss was initially reported on Form 4684. (Enter loss on Form 4797 [line 14]).
    ■ A warehouse purchased for $50,000 on August 10, 2009, was condemned by the city in order to acquire the land upon which it stood so that the state could build a new highway. Virginia was paid $45,000 for the building on May 1, 2022. Depreciation taken on the building was $10,897.
    ■ Virginia received $36,000 for the condemned land. The land had a basis of $30,000.

    Virginia will not reinvest any of the proceeds from the condemned land or building in qualified replacement property and wants to report the gain on her 2022 return. Virginia's nonrecaptured net Section 1231 losses the previous five years are $3,500. Prepare Form 4797, Sales of Business Property, using the blank form provided.

24. **Installment Sales.** (Obj. 6) Yvonne, a consulting engineer and cash basis taxpayer, decided to close her office and go back to college and study business. One of her business assets was a used car that she had purchased in 2020 for $15,000. She still owed $5,000 on the car when she sold it for $10,600 on June 10, 2022. The buyer agreed to assume the $5,000 note. Further, the buyer agreed to pay $1,600 as a down payment and pay $2,000 (plus 12% interest) on June 10, 2023, and $2,000 (plus 12% interest on the remaining balance) on June 10, 2024. Under the MACRS rules, Yvonne had correctly taken $9,240 of depreciation on the automobile. Assume that Yvonne has no other liabilities.

    a. What is the realized gain to Yvonne on the sale of the automobile?

    b. If the realized gain is reported on the installment basis, how much and what type of gain will Yvonne report as income in 2022, 2023, and 2024?

    c. How much interest income will Yvonne report in 2023 and 2024?

(Use for Problem 23.)

Form **4797**	**Sales of Business Property**	OMB No. 1545-0184
	(Also Involuntary Conversions and Recapture Amounts Under Sections 179 and 280F(b)(2))	20**22**
Department of the Treasury Internal Revenue Service	**Attach to your tax return.** Go to *www.irs.gov/Form4797* for instructions and the latest information.	Attachment Sequence No. **27**

Name(s) shown on return | Identifying number

1a Enter the gross proceeds from sales or exchanges reported to you for 2022 on Form(s) 1099-B or 1099-S (or substitute statement) that you are including on line 2, 10, or 20. See instructions **1a**

b Enter the total amount of gain that you are including on lines 2, 10, and 24 due to the partial dispositions of MACRS assets **1b**

c Enter the total amount of loss that you are including on lines 2 and 10 due to the partial dispositions of MACRS assets **1c**

Part I **Sales or Exchanges of Property Used in a Trade or Business and Involuntary Conversions From Other Than Casualty or Theft—Most Property Held More Than 1 Year** (see instructions)

2	**(a)** Description of property	**(b)** Date acquired (mo., day, yr.)	**(c)** Date sold (mo., day, yr.)	**(d)** Gross sales price	**(e)** Depreciation allowed or allowable since acquisition	**(f)** Cost or other basis, plus improvements and expense of sale	**(g)** Gain or (loss) Subtract (f) from the sum of (d) and (e)

3	Gain, if any, from Form 4684, line 39	**3**	
4	Section 1231 gain from installment sales from Form 6252, line 26 or 37	**4**	
5	Section 1231 gain or (loss) from like-kind exchanges from Form 8824	**5**	
6	Gain, if any, from line 32, from other than casualty or theft	**6**	
7	Combine lines 2 through 6. Enter the gain or (loss) here and on the appropriate line as follows	**7**	

Partnerships and S corporations. Report the gain or (loss) following the instructions for Form 1065, Schedule K, line 10, or Form 1120-S, Schedule K, line 9. Skip lines 8, 9, 11, and 12 below.

Individuals, partners, S corporation shareholders, and all others. If line 7 is zero or a loss, enter the amount from line 7 on line 11 below and skip lines 8 and 9. If line 7 is a gain and you didn't have any prior year section 1231 losses, or they were recaptured in an earlier year, enter the gain from line 7 as a long-term capital gain on the Schedule D filed with your return and skip lines 8, 9, 11, and 12 below.

| **8** | Nonrecaptured net section 1231 losses from prior years. See instructions . . . . | **8** | |
| **9** | Subtract line 8 from line 7. If zero or less, enter -0-. If line 9 is zero, enter the gain from line 7 on line 12 below. If line 9 is more than zero, enter the amount from line 8 on line 12 below and enter the gain from line 9 as a long-term capital gain on the Schedule D filed with your return. See instructions . . . . | **9** | |

Part II **Ordinary Gains and Losses** (see instructions)

10 Ordinary gains and losses not included on lines 11 through 16 (include property held 1 year or less):

11	Loss, if any, from line 7	**11** ( )
12	Gain, if any, from line 7 or amount from line 8, if applicable	**12**
13	Gain, if any, from line 31	**13**
14	Net gain or (loss) from Form 4684, lines 31 and 38a	**14**
15	Ordinary gain from installment sales from Form 6252, line 25 or 36	**15**
16	Ordinary gain or (loss) from like-kind exchanges from Form 8824	**16**
17	Combine lines 10 through 16	**17**

18 For all except individual returns, enter the amount from line 17 on the appropriate line of your return and skip lines a and b below. For individual returns, complete lines a and b below.

a If the loss on line 11 includes a loss from Form 4684, line 35, column (b)(ii), enter that part of the loss here. Enter the loss from income-producing property on Schedule A (Form 1040), line 16. (Do not include any loss on property used as an employee.) Identify as from "Form 4797, line 18a." See instructions . . . . | **18a**

b Redetermine the gain or (loss) on line 17 excluding the loss, if any, on line 18a. Enter here and on Schedule 1 (Form 1040), Part I, line 4 . . . . | **18b**

For Paperwork Reduction Act Notice, see separate instructions. | Cat. No. 13086I | Form **4797** (2022)

(Use for Problem 23.)

Form 4797 (2022)   Page **2**

Part III   Gain From Disposition of Property Under Sections 1245, 1250, 1252, 1254, and 1255 (see instructions)

19	(a) Description of section 1245, 1250, 1252, 1254, or 1255 property:		**(b)** Date acquired (mo., day, yr.)	**(c)** Date sold (mo., day, yr.)
A				
B				
C				
D				

These columns relate to the properties on lines 19A through 19D.		Property A	Property B	Property C	Property D
20	Gross sales price (**Note:** *See line 1a before completing.*) .	20				
21	Cost or other basis plus expense of sale	21				
22	Depreciation (or depletion) allowed or allowable . .	22				
23	Adjusted basis. Subtract line 22 from line 21 . . .	23				
24	Total gain. Subtract line 23 from line 20	24				
25	**If section 1245 property:**					
a	Depreciation allowed or allowable from line 22 . .	25a				
b	Enter the **smaller** of line 24 or 25a.	25b				
26	**If section 1250 property:** If straight line depreciation was used, enter -0- on line 26g, except for a corporation subject to section 291.					
a	Additional depreciation after 1975. See instructions .	26a				
b	Applicable percentage multiplied by the **smaller** of line 24 or line 26a. See instructions.	26b				
c	Subtract line 26a from line 24. If residential rental property **or** line 24 isn't more than line 26a, skip lines 26d and 26e	26c				
d	Additional depreciation after 1969 and before 1976. .	26d				
e	Enter the **smaller** of line 26c or 26d	26e				
f	Section 291 amount (corporations only)	26f				
g	Add lines 26b, 26e, and 26f	26g				
27	**If section 1252 property:** Skip this section if you didn't dispose of farmland or if this form is being completed for a partnership.					
a	Soil, water, and land clearing expenses	27a				
b	Line 27a multiplied by applicable percentage. See instructions	27b				
c	Enter the **smaller** of line 24 or 27b	27c				
28	**If section 1254 property:**					
a	Intangible drilling and development costs, expenditures for development of mines and other natural deposits, mining exploration costs, and depletion. See instructions	28a				
b	Enter the **smaller** of line 24 or 28a.	28b				
29	**If section 1255 property:**					
a	Applicable percentage of payments excluded from income under section 126. See instructions . . .	29a				
b	Enter the **smaller** of line 24 or 29a. See instructions .	29b				

Summary of Part III Gains. Complete property columns A through D through line 29b before going to line 30.

30	Total gains for all properties. Add property columns A through D, line 24	30	
31	Add property columns A through D, lines 25b, 26g, 27c, 28b, and 29b. Enter here and on line 13	31	
32	Subtract line 31 from line 30. Enter the portion from casualty or theft on Form 4684, line 33. Enter the portion from other than casualty or theft on Form 4797, line 6	32	

Part IV   Recapture Amounts Under Sections 179 and 280F(b)(2) When Business Use Drops to 50% or Less (see instructions)

			(a) Section 179	(b) Section 280F(b)(2)
33	Section 179 expense deduction or depreciation allowable in prior years.	33		
34	Recomputed depreciation. See instructions	34		
35	Recapture amount. Subtract line 34 from line 33. See the instructions for where to report . .	35		

Form **4797** (2022)

25. **Installment Sales.** (Obj. 6) Tyka sold depreciable personal property for $70,000 on August 4, 2022. The buyer agreed to pay $10,000 at the time of sale and $20,000 on August 4 in each of the next three years. In addition, interest at the current market rate will be paid on the remaining installment balance. Tyka bought the property several years ago for $43,000. Depreciation totaling $18,000 was taken on the property.

    a. Compute the total gain from the sale.

    b. How much gain and what type of gain must be reported in the year of sale?

    c. How much gain and what type of gain must be reported in each of the next three years?

26. **Internet Problem: Researching IRS Publication 537.** (Obj. 6)

    During 2021, Leo, a cash basis taxpayer, sold land at a gain to an unrelated party. Leo received part of the proceeds in 2022 and will receive the rest of the proceeds in 2022 and 2023. Leo is fairly sure he would like to elect out of the installment sales method and has asked for advice on how to accomplish this. He also wants to know if he elects out of the installment method whether he can later change his mind and use the installment method to report the gain on the sale.

    Go to the IRS website. Locate IRS Publication 537, *Installment Sales*. Print out a copy of the page where the answer to Leo's questions can be found. Underline or highlight the pertinent information. Prepare a brief discussion of the answer to Leo's questions.

    See Appendix A for instructions on use of the IRS website.

27. **Business Entity Problem.** (Obj. 2) This problem is designed for those using the "business entity" approach. **The solution may require information from Chapter 14.**

    Kenya Corporation had the following capital gains and losses for the year. Discuss how these gains and losses affect Kenya Corporation's taxable income.

Short-term capital gain	$36,000
Short-term capital loss	15,000
Long-term capital gain	16,000
Long-term capital loss	42,000

COMPREHENSIVE PROBLEMS

28. (Obj. 2) On November 10, 2022, Bev sold residential realty for $300,000. Bev purchased the realty on August 5, 2013, for $275,000. She depreciated the property over 27.5 years using the straight-line method. Compute Bev's Section 1231 gain and the amount of her unrecaptured Section 1250 gain.

 29. Form 8949, Schedule D and Form 1040. (Obj. 7)

a.   Michael L. (SSN 374-00-7774) and Joyce A. (SSN 642-00-9982) Sea, both age 38, file a joint tax return. They sold the following investments during the year. All sales were reported to the Seas on Form 1099-B. None showed the Seas' basis.

Description	Date Acquired	Adjusted Basis	Date Sold	Sales Price
20 shares Red Corp.	7-1-16	$1,661	12-6-22	$2,311
50 shares Lee Corp.	9-15-16	5,820	11-14-22	4,320
60 shares Alf Corp.	6-10-21	850	10-15-22	715
100 shares RST Corp.	5-10-97	4,600	8-8-22	2,430
$1,000 bond, TF Co.	5-5-22	800	10-15-22	900

The Seas carried over a $260 short-term capital loss and a $2,500 long-term capital loss from 2021. The Seas report taxable wages of $51,920. From this amount $1,840 was withheld for federal income taxes. The Seas's only other item of gross income during the year was $1,200 of dividend income, which does not include any qualified dividends.

Prepare the Seas' 2022 tax return. Neither want $3 to go to the Presidential election campaign fund. Use the approach from Examples 10-12 to compute the Seas' tax. The Seas live at 1319 Mayfair Drive, Champaign, IL 61821. They claim one dependent, their 13-year-old son, Tad (SSN 629-00-7881). The Seas get full health care coverage through Michael's work. The Seas sign their return on April 15, 2023.

b.   Ellen B. Ryan (SSN 392-00-6811) is unmarried with no dependents. Ellen lives at 1840 S. 200 West, Reno, Nevada 89434. She is 34 years old. During the year, she sold common stock in the following companies. All stock sales were reported to Ellen on Form 1099-B. None showed Ellen's basis.

Description	Date Acquired	Adjusted Basis	Date Sold	Sales Price
400 shares Able Co.	8-9-21	$5,175	5-11-22	$ 6,345
127 shares Tolano Corp.	3-10-21	3,929	7-15-22	3,556
690 shares Radian, Inc.	1-19-11	6,570	11-27-22	11,844

Ellen carried over a $3,500 long-term capital loss from 2021. Her taxable wages were $61,893 in 2022. Her employer withheld $7,630 for federal income taxes. Ellen also had $650 of taxable interest and $540 of tax-exempt interest. Ellen wants $3 to go to the Presidential campaign fund.

Prepare Ellen's 2022 tax return that she signs on April 11, 2023. Use the approach from Examples 10-12 to compute Ellen's tax.

(Use for Problem 29.)

Form 1040 Department of the Treasury—Internal Revenue Service
U.S. Individual Income Tax Return **2022** OMB No. 1545-0074 IRS Use Only—Do not write or staple in this space.

Filing Status
Check only one box.
☐ Single ☐ Married filing jointly ☐ Married filing separately (MFS) ☐ Head of household (HOH) ☐ Qualifying widow(er) (QW)
If you checked the MFS box, enter the name of your spouse. If you checked the HOH or QW box, enter the child's name if the qualifying person is a child but not your dependent.

Your first name and middle initial	Last name	Your social security number

If joint return, spouse's first name and middle initial	Last name	Spouse's social security number

Home address (number and street). If you have a P.O. box, see instructions.	Apt. no.	**Presidential Election Campaign**

City, town, or post office. If you have a foreign address, also complete spaces below.	State	ZIP code

Check here if you, or your spouse if filing jointly, want $3 to go to this fund. Checking a box below will not change your tax or refund.

Foreign country name	Foreign province/state/county	Foreign postal code

☐ You ☐ Spouse

At any time during 2022, did you: (a) receive (as a reward, award, or compensation); or (b) sell, exchange, gift, or otherwise dispose of a digital asset (or a financial interest in a digital asset)? (See instructions.) . . ☐ Yes ☐ No

Standard Deduction
Someone can claim: ☐ You as a dependent ☐ Your spouse as a dependent
☐ Spouse itemizes on a separate return or you were a dual-status alien

Age/Blindness You: ☐ Were born before January 2, 1958 ☐ Are blind **Spouse:** ☐ Was born before January 2, 1958 ☐ Is blind

Dependents (see instructions):

(1) First name Last name	(2) Social security number	(3) Relationship to you	(4) Check the box if qualifies for (see instructions):	
			Child tax credit	Credit for other dependents
			☐	☐
			☐	☐
			☐	☐
			☐	☐

If more than four dependents, see instructions and check here . . ☐

Income

Attach Form(s) W-2 here. Also attach Forms W-2G and 1099-R if tax was withheld.

If you did not get a Form W-2, see instructions.

1a	Total amount from Form(s) W-2, box 1 (see instructions)	1a
b	Household employee wages not reported on Form(s) W-2	1b
c	Tip income not reported on line 1a (see instructions)	1c
d	Medicaid waiver payments not reported on Form(s) W-2 (see instructions)	1d
e	Taxable dependent care benefits from Form 2441, line 26	1e
f	Employer-provided adoption benefits from Form 8839, line 29	1f
g	Wages from Form 8919, line 6	1g
h	Other earned income (see instructions)	1h
i	Nontaxable combat pay election (see instructions) . . . 1i	
z	Add lines 1a through 1h	1z

Attach Sch. B if required.

2a	Tax-exempt interest . . .	2a		b Taxable interest	2b
3a	Qualified dividends . . .	3a		b Ordinary dividends	3b
4a	IRA distributions . . .	4a		b Taxable amount	4b
5a	Pensions and annuities . .	5a		b Taxable amount	5b
6a	Social security benefits . .	6a		b Taxable amount	6b

Standard Deduction for—
- Single or Married filing separately, $12,950
- Married filing jointly or Qualifying widow(er), $25,900
- Head of household, $19,400
- If you checked any box under *Standard Deduction,* see instructions.

c	If you elect to use the lump-sum election method, check here (see instructions) . . . . ☐	
7	Capital gain or (loss). Attach Schedule D if required. If not required, check here . . . . ☐	7
8	Other income from Schedule 1, line 10	8
9	Add lines 1z, 2b, 3b, 4b, 5b, 6b, 7, and 8. This is your **total income**	9
10	Adjustments to income from Schedule 1, line 26	10
11	Subtract line 10 from line 9. This is your **adjusted gross income**	11
12	**Standard deduction or itemized deductions** (from Schedule A)	12
13	Qualified business income deduction from Form 8995 or Form 8995-A	13
14	Add lines 12 and 13	14
15	Subtract line 14 from line 11. If zero or less, enter -0-. This is your **taxable income**	15

For Disclosure, Privacy Act, and Paperwork Reduction Act Notice, see separate instructions. Cat. No. 11320B Form **1040** (2022)

(Use for Problem 29.)

Version A, Cycle 7

Form 1040 (2022)   Page **2**

Tax and Credits	16	**Tax** (see instructions). Check if any from Form(s): **1** ☐ 8814 **2** ☐ 4972 **3** ☐ _____	16	
	17	Amount from Schedule 2, line 3	17	
	18	Add lines 16 and 17	18	
	19	Child tax credit or credit for other dependents from Schedule 8812	19	
	20	Amount from Schedule 3, line 8	20	
	21	Add lines 19 and 20	21	
	22	Subtract line 21 from line 18. If zero or less, enter -0-	22	
	23	Other taxes, including self-employment tax, from Schedule 2, line 21	23	
	24	Add lines 22 and 23. This is your **total tax**	24	
Payments	25	Federal income tax withheld from:		
	a	Form(s) W-2 25a		
	b	Form(s) 1099 25b		
	c	Other forms (see instructions) 25c		
	d	Add lines 25a through 25c	25d	
If you have a qualifying child, attach Sch. EIC.	26	2022 estimated tax payments and amount applied from 2021 return	26	
	27	Earned income credit (EIC) 27		
	28	Additional child tax credit from Schedule 8812 28		
	29	American opportunity credit from Form 8863, line 8 29		
	30	Reserved for future use 30		
	31	Amount from Schedule 3, line 15 31		
	32	Add lines 27, 28, 29, and 31. These are your **total other payments and refundable credits**	32	
	33	Add lines 25d, 26, and 32. These are your **total payments**	33	
Refund	34	If line 33 is more than line 24, subtract line 24 from line 33. This is the amount you **overpaid**	34	
	35a	Amount of line 34 you want **refunded to you**. If Form 8888 is attached, check here ☐	35a	
Direct deposit? See instructions.	b	Routing number _____ **c** Type: ☐ Checking ☐ Savings		
	d	Account number _____		
	36	Amount of line 34 you want **applied to your 2023 estimated tax** 36		
Amount You Owe	37	Subtract line 33 from line 24. This is the **amount you owe**. For details on how to pay, go to *www.irs.gov/Payments* or see instructions	37	
	38	Estimated tax penalty (see instructions) 38		

Third Party Designee	Do you want to allow another person to discuss this return with the IRS? See instructions ☐ **Yes.** Complete below. ☐ **No**

	Designee's name	Phone no.	Personal identification number (PIN)

Sign Here	Under penalties of perjury, I declare that I have examined this return and accompanying schedules and statements, and to the best of my knowledge and belief, they are true, correct, and complete. Declaration of preparer (other than taxpayer) is based on all information of which preparer has any knowledge.

Joint return? See instructions. Keep a copy for your records.	Your signature Date	Your occupation	If the IRS sent you an Identity Protection PIN, enter it here (see inst.)
	Spouse's signature. If a joint return, **both** must sign. Date	Spouse's occupation	If the IRS sent your spouse an Identity Protection PIN, enter it here (see inst.)
	Phone no.	Email address	

Paid Preparer Use Only	Preparer's name	Preparer's signature	Date	PTIN Check if: ☐ Self-employed
	Firm's name			Phone no.
	Firm's address			Firm's EIN

Go to *www.irs.gov/Form1040* for instructions and the latest information.   Form **1040** (2022)

(Use for Problem 29.)

SCHEDULE D	**Capital Gains and Losses**	OMB No. 1545-0074
(Form 1040)	Attach to Form 1040, 1040-SR, or 1040-NR.	**2022**
Department of the Treasury Internal Revenue Service	Go to *www.irs.gov/ScheduleD* for instructions and the latest information. Use Form 8949 to list your transactions for lines 1b, 2, 3, 8b, 9, and 10.	Attachment Sequence No. **12**

Name(s) shown on return	Your social security number

Did you dispose of any investment(s) in a qualified opportunity fund during the tax year? ☐ Yes ☐ No
If "Yes," attach Form 8949 and see its instructions for additional requirements for reporting your gain or loss.

Part I   Short-Term Capital Gains and Losses—Generally Assets Held One Year or Less (see instructions)

See instructions for how to figure the amounts to enter on the lines below. This form may be easier to complete if you round off cents to whole dollars.	**(d)** Proceeds (sales price)	**(e)** Cost (or other basis)	**(g)** Adjustments to gain or loss from Form(s) 8949, Part I, line 2, column (g)	**(h) Gain or (loss)** Subtract column (e) from column (d) and combine the result with column (g)
1a Totals for all short-term transactions reported on Form 1099-B for which basis was reported to the IRS and for which you have no adjustments (see instructions). However, if you choose to report all these transactions on Form 8949, leave this line blank and go to line 1b				
1b Totals for all transactions reported on Form(s) 8949 with **Box A** checked				
2 Totals for all transactions reported on Form(s) 8949 with **Box B** checked				
3 Totals for all transactions reported on Form(s) 8949 with **Box C** checked				

4 Short-term gain from Form 6252 and short-term gain or (loss) from Forms 4684, 6781, and 8824 . .	**4**	
5 Net short-term gain or (loss) from partnerships, S corporations, estates, and trusts from Schedule(s) K-1	**5**	
6 Short-term capital loss carryover. Enter the amount, if any, from line 8 of your **Capital Loss Carryover Worksheet** in the instructions	**6**	( )
7 **Net short-term capital gain or (loss).** Combine lines 1a through 6 in column (h). If you have any long-term capital gains or losses, go to Part II below. Otherwise, go to Part III on the back	**7**	

Part II   Long-Term Capital Gains and Losses—Generally Assets Held More Than One Year (see instructions)

See instructions for how to figure the amounts to enter on the lines below. This form may be easier to complete if you round off cents to whole dollars.	**(d)** Proceeds (sales price)	**(e)** Cost (or other basis)	**(g)** Adjustments to gain or loss from Form(s) 8949, Part II, line 2, column (g)	**(h) Gain or (loss)** Subtract column (e) from column (d) and combine the result with column (g)
8a Totals for all long-term transactions reported on Form 1099-B for which basis was reported to the IRS and for which you have no adjustments (see instructions). However, if you choose to report all these transactions on Form 8949, leave this line blank and go to line 8b .				
8b Totals for all transactions reported on Form(s) 8949 with **Box D** checked				
9 Totals for all transactions reported on Form(s) 8949 with **Box E** checked				
10 Totals for all transactions reported on Form(s) 8949 with **Box F** checked.				

11 Gain from Form 4797, Part I; long-term gain from Forms 2439 and 6252; and long-term gain or (loss) from Forms 4684, 6781, and 8824	**11**	
12 Net long-term gain or (loss) from partnerships, S corporations, estates, and trusts from Schedule(s) K-1	**12**	
13 Capital gain distributions. See the instructions	**13**	
14 Long-term capital loss carryover. Enter the amount, if any, from line 13 of your **Capital Loss Carryover Worksheet** in the instructions	**14**	( )
15 **Net long-term capital gain or (loss).** Combine lines 8a through 14 in column (h). Then, go to Part III on the back	**15**	

For Paperwork Reduction Act Notice, see your tax return instructions.	Cat. No. 11338H	Schedule D (Form 1040) 2022

(Use for Problem 29.)

Schedule D (Form 1040) 2022   Page **2**

Part III   **Summary**

16   Combine lines 7 and 15 and enter the result . . . . | **16** |

  • If line 16 is a **gain**, enter the amount from line 16 on Form 1040, 1040-SR, or 1040-NR, line 7.
    Then, go to line 17 below.
  • If line 16 is a **loss**, skip lines 17 through 20 below. Then, go to line 21. Also be sure to complete
    line 22.
  • If line 16 is **zero**, skip lines 17 through 21 below and enter -0- on Form 1040, 1040-SR, or
    1040-NR, line 7. Then, go to line 22.

17   Are lines 15 and 16 **both** gains?
    ☐ **Yes.** Go to line 18.
    ☐ **No.** Skip lines 18 through 21, and go to line 22.

18   If you are required to complete the **28% Rate Gain Worksheet** (see instructions), enter the
      amount, if any, from line 7 of that worksheet . . . . | **18** |

19   If you are required to complete the **Unrecaptured Section 1250 Gain Worksheet** (see
      instructions), enter the amount, if any, from line 18 of that worksheet . . . . | **19** |

20   Are lines 18 and 19 both zero or blank and you are not filing Form 4952?
    ☐ **Yes.** Complete the **Qualified Dividends and Capital Gain Tax Worksheet** in the instructions
      for Form 1040, line 16. **Don't** complete lines 21 and 22 below.

    ☐ **No.** Complete the **Schedule D Tax Worksheet** in the instructions. **Don't** complete lines 21
      and 22 below.

21   If line 16 is a loss, enter here and on Form 1040, 1040-SR, or 1040-NR, line 7, the **smaller** of:

    • The loss on line 16; or   } . . . . | **21** |(   )
    • ($3,000), or if married filing separately, ($1,500) }

    Note: When figuring which amount is smaller, treat both amounts as positive numbers.

22   Do you have qualified dividends on Form 1040, 1040-SR, or 1040-NR, line 3a?

    ☐ **Yes.** Complete the **Qualified Dividends and Capital Gain Tax Worksheet** in the instructions
      for Form 1040, line 16.

    ☐ **No.** Complete the rest of Form 1040, 1040-SR, or 1040-NR.

Schedule D (Form 1040) 2022

(Use for Problem 29.)

Form **8949**	**Sales and Other Dispositions of Capital Assets**	OMB No. 1545-0074
Department of the Treasury Internal Revenue Service	Go to *www.irs.gov/Form8949* for instructions and the latest information. **File with your Schedule D to list your transactions for lines 1b, 2, 3, 8b, 9, and 10 of Schedule D.**	**2022** Attachment Sequence No. **12A**

Name(s) shown on return	Social security number or taxpayer identification number

Before you check Box A, B, or C below, see whether you received any Form(s) 1099-B or substitute statement(s) from your broker. A substitute statement will have the same information as Form 1099-B. Either will show whether your basis (usually your cost) was reported to the IRS by your broker and may even tell you which box to check.

Part I **Short-Term.** Transactions involving capital assets you held 1 year or less are generally short-term (see instructions). For long-term transactions, see page 2.

Note: You may aggregate all short-term transactions reported on Form(s) 1099-B showing basis was reported to the IRS and for which no adjustments or codes are required. Enter the totals directly on Schedule D, line 1a; you aren't required to report these transactions on Form 8949 (see instructions).

You *must* check Box A, B, or C below. Check only one box. If more than one box applies for your short-term transactions, complete a separate Form 8949, page 1, for each applicable box. If you have more short-term transactions than will fit on this page for one or more of the boxes, complete as many forms with the same box checked as you need.

- ☐ **(A)** Short-term transactions reported on Form(s) 1099-B showing basis was reported to the IRS (see **Note** above)
- ☐ **(B)** Short-term transactions reported on Form(s) 1099-B showing basis **wasn't** reported to the IRS
- ☐ **(C)** Short-term transactions not reported to you on Form 1099-B

1	**(a)** Description of property (Example: 100 sh. XYZ Co.)	**(b)** Date acquired (Mo., day, yr.)	**(c)** Date sold or disposed of (Mo., day, yr.)	**(d)** Proceeds (sales price) (see instructions)	**(e)** Cost or other basis See the **Note** below and see *Column (e)* in the separate instructions.	Adjustment, if any, to gain or loss If you enter an amount in column (g), enter a code in column (f). See the separate instructions.		**(h)** Gain or (loss) Subtract column (e) from column (d) and combine the result with column (g).
						(f) Code(s) from instructions	**(g)** Amount of adjustment	

2 Totals. Add the amounts in columns (d), (e), (g), and (h) (subtract negative amounts). Enter each total here and include on your Schedule D, **line 1b** (if **Box A** above is checked), **line 2** (if **Box B** above is checked), or **line 3** (if **Box C** above is checked) .   .

Note: If you checked Box A above but the basis reported to the IRS was incorrect, enter in column (e) the basis as reported to the IRS, and enter an adjustment in column (g) to correct the basis. See *Column (g)* in the separate instructions for how to figure the amount of the adjustment.

For Paperwork Reduction Act Notice, see your tax return instructions.	Cat. No. 37768Z	Form **8949** (2022)

(Use for Problem 29.)

Form 8949 (2022) — Attachment Sequence No. **12A** — Page **2**

Name(s) shown on return. Name and SSN or taxpayer identification no. not required if shown on other side | Social security number or taxpayer identification number

Before you check Box D, E, or F below, see whether you received any Form(s) 1099-B or substitute statement(s) from your broker. A substitute statement will have the same information as Form 1099-B. Either will show whether your basis (usually your cost) was reported to the IRS by your broker and may even tell you which box to check.

Part II **Long-Term.** Transactions involving capital assets you held more than 1 year are generally long-term (see instructions). For short-term transactions, see page 1.

Note: You may aggregate all long-term transactions reported on Form(s) 1099-B showing basis was reported to the IRS and for which no adjustments or codes are required. Enter the totals directly on Schedule D, line 8a; you aren't required to report these transactions on Form 8949 (see instructions).

You *must* check Box D, E, *or* F below. Check only one box. If more than one box applies for your long-term transactions, complete a separate Form 8949, page 2, for each applicable box. If you have more long-term transactions than will fit on this page for one or more of the boxes, complete as many forms with the same box checked as you need.

☐ **(D)** Long-term transactions reported on Form(s) 1099-B showing basis was reported to the IRS (see **Note** above)
☐ **(E)** Long-term transactions reported on Form(s) 1099-B showing basis **wasn't** reported to the IRS
☐ **(F)** Long-term transactions not reported to you on Form 1099-B

1 (a) Description of property (Example: 100 sh. XYZ Co.)	(b) Date acquired (Mo., day, yr.)	(c) Date sold or disposed of (Mo., day, yr.)	(d) Proceeds (sales price) (see instructions)	(e) Cost or other basis See the **Note** below and see *Column (e)* in the separate instructions.	Adjustment, if any, to gain or loss If you enter an amount in column (g), enter a code in column (f). See the separate instructions. (f) Code(s) from instructions	(g) Amount of adjustment	(h) Gain or (loss) Subtract column (e) from column (d) and combine the result with column (g).
2 Totals. Add the amounts in columns (d), (e), (g), and (h) (subtract negative amounts). Enter each total here and include on your Schedule D, **line 8b** (if **Box D** above is checked), **line 9** (if **Box E** above is checked), or **line 10** (if **Box F** above is checked) . .							

Note: If you checked Box D above but the basis reported to the IRS was incorrect, enter in column (e) the basis as reported to the IRS, and enter an adjustment in column (g) to correct the basis. See *Column (g)* in the separate instructions for how to figure the amount of the adjustment.

Form **8949** (2022)

Chapter

12

NOLs, EBLs, AMT, and Business Tax Credits

CHAPTER CONTENTS

LEARNING OBJECTIVES

After completing Chapter 12, you should be able to:

1. Compute a taxpayer's current year net operating loss and advise taxpayers as to their options on how to utilize the loss.
2. Understand how the alternative minimum tax affects a taxpayer's total tax liability and compute a taxpayer's alternative minimum tax.
3. Describe a variety of tax credits available to businesses through the general business credit and compute the amount of tax credit for each of these credits.
4. Complete Form 6251.

CHAPTER OVERVIEW

This chapter begins with the discussion of the net operating loss rules. These rules allow taxpayers to use certain losses generated in one tax year against income from prior and future tax years. The discussion then shifts to the alternative minimum tax, which is a second tax system that attempts to raise additional tax revenues from taxpayers who pay too little tax under the regular income tax system which has been the focus of the textbook thus far. The chapter concludes with a discussion of tax credits available to business owners.

¶1201   Net Operating Loss (NOL)

A special rule applies when individual business owners and C corporations report a loss in one year and profits in other years. It would be unfair if business profits were always taxed, but no tax relief was available when the business suffered a loss. The net operating loss (NOL) provisions allow business losses to offset income from other tax years. For taxable years beginning before 2018, the carryover rule was back two years and forward 20. For instance, an individual with a 2017 NOL would carry this loss back to 2015. He or she would recalculate the 2015 tax liability as if the deduction had been included on the original return. The recalculation would result in a refund of 2015 taxes. If the NOL exceeded the 2015 deduction, the taxpayer would recalculate 2016 income and resultant tax liability. If the NOL exceeded the amounts used in 2015 and 2016, the taxpayer would carry it forward to 2018. And future years until the income of those years had absorbed the entire NOL. An NOL incurred before 2017 can offset 100% of the taxable income in each carryback or carryforward year.

When an NOL is carried back to a prior tax year, the taxpayer completes and files Form 1045, Application for Tentative Refund, to recompute the taxpayer's tax liability in the carryback year. Alternatively, taxpayers can elect to forgo the carryback and carry forward an NOL 20 years. When carried over to another year, an individual taxpayer treats an NOL deduction as a deduction for AGI.

The Tax Cuts and Jobs Act of 2017 amended the rules. Under the new rules, an NOL generated in a tax year ending after 2017 must be carried forward indefinitely, but may not be carried back. However, the CARES Act of 2020 modified these rules, so that they do not take full effect until 2021. For losses incurred in 2018, 2019 and 2020, there is a five-year carryback period. [I.R.C. §172(b)(1)(D)]

An NOL arising in tax years beginning after 2017 is limited to 80% of taxable income, computed without regard to the NOL deduction allowed for the tax year. Any taxpayer who is carrying losses forward from 2017 and earlier years offsets up to 100% of taxable income in the deduction year. Only when all pre-2018 NOLs have been exhausted does the taxpayer claim a post-2017 loss deduction.

¶1201.01   CALCULATING NOL

An NOL is not the same as negative taxable income on Form 1040. In computing the NOL, individuals make the following adjustments to negative taxable income. [I.R.C. §172(d)]

1. Nonbusiness capital losses in excess of nonbusiness capital gains are added back. Nonbusiness capital gains and losses arise from transactions involving nonbusiness property (for example, investment property).
2. The NOL carryover of a preceding or later tax year is added back.
3. Nonbusiness deductions in excess of nonbusiness income are added back. Nonbusiness deductions include all itemized deductions except casualty and theft losses. For individuals who do not itemize, their standard deduction is a nonbusiness deduction. Nonbusiness income comes from sources other than the taxpayer's business. Examples include interest, dividends, and net gains from the sale of nonbusiness property. Salaries, net gains from the sale of business property, and rental income are treated as business income.

EXAMPLE 1

Chris and Dana Bosky are married and file a joint tax return. Chris operates a business that generated $120,000 of gross revenues and $150,000 of operating expenses during 2022. The Boskys report negative taxable income of $32,200

Salary		$ 15,000
Business loss ($120,000 – $150,000)		(30,000)
Net business capital gains		3,000
Net nonbusiness capital gains		4,000
Interest income		1,500
AGI		($ 6,500)
Less itemized deductions:		
Mortgage interest and real estate taxes	$19,500	
Casualty loss sustained in disaster area	6,200	(25,700)
Taxable income (loss)		($32,200)

Using this information, the Boskys' $18,200 NOL is computed:

Taxable loss			($22,200)
Add back:			
Net nonbusiness deductions	$19,500		
Nonbusiness income ($4,000 + $1,500)	(5,500)	14,000	4,000
NOL			($18,200)

¶1201.02   NOL DEDUCTION

Once computed, an NOL is carried forward indefinitely. When carried over to another year, an individual taxpayer treats an NOL deduction as a *deduction for* AGI. On the tax return, an NOL carried forward is entered as a negative amount on Form 1040, Schedule 1 (line 8). The taxpayer then writes "NOL" and the amount of the NOL on the dotted line after the words "Other income. List type and amount."

   From Example 1, the Boskys would report the $18,200 as a negative amount on the "Other income" line on their 2023 tax return, in the manner that the 2023 form prescribes.

¶1202   Excess Business Losses (EBLs)

The Tax Cuts and Jobs Act of 2017 introduced a limit on deductible business losses. Noncorporate taxpayers are not allowed "excess business losses" for tax years beginning after December 31, 2017, and before January 1, 2026. However, the CARES Act of 2020 retroactively deferred its applicability until taxable years beginning after 2020. Therefore, taxpayers who had filed 2018 returns with this limitation need to amend their returns to claim the maximum deduction permitted as a result of the CARES Act modifications.

   An excess business loss is the excess, if any, of:

1. a taxpayer's aggregate deductions for the tax year from the taxpayer's trades or businesses, determined without regard to whether or not such deductions are disallowed for such tax year under the excess business loss limitation; over
2. the sum of:
   a. the taxpayer's aggregate gross income or gain for the tax year from such trades or businesses, plus
   b. $250,000, adjusted annually for inflation (for a joint return, 200% of the $250,000 amount). For 2022, these limits are $270,000 and $540,000, respectively. The indexed figures for 2023 should be available in late 2022.

¶1203 Alternative Minimum Tax (AMT)

The tax law contains many exclusions, deductions, and other tax breaks that allow taxpayers to reduce their tax liabilities. Some individuals with higher incomes use these tax benefits so much that they paid little or no income tax. As a result, Congress enacted an alternative minimum tax (AMT). The AMT works with the regular income tax in an attempt to ensure that taxpayers with higher total incomes pay some amount of income tax. The AMT operates as a completely separate tax system. If subject to the AMT, the taxpayer will pay the AMT plus the regular income tax. [I.R.C. §55] Below is the formula for computing the AMT.

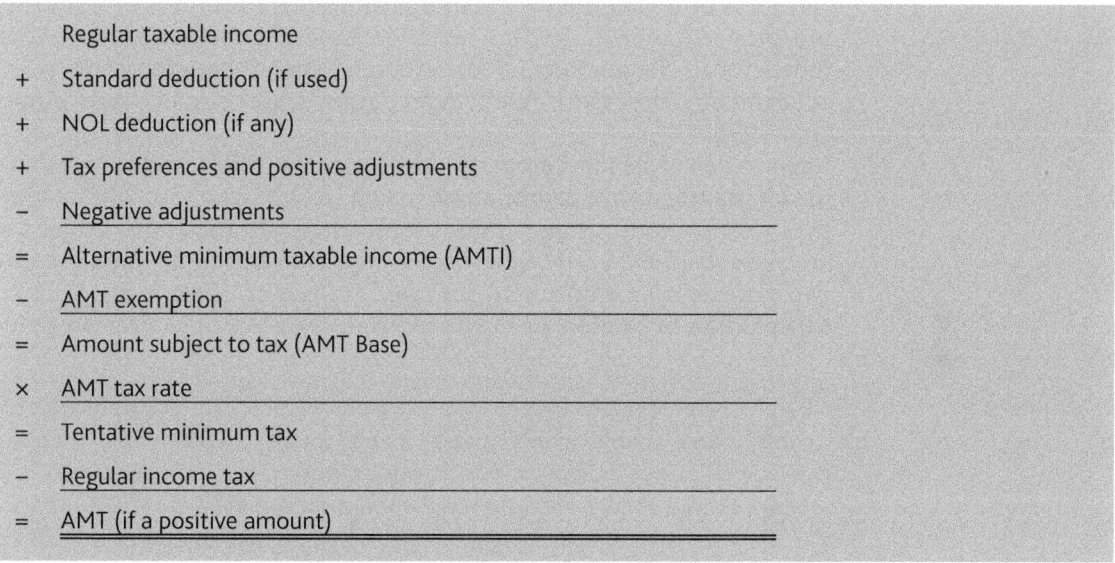

	Regular taxable income
+	Standard deduction (if used)
+	NOL deduction (if any)
+	Tax preferences and positive adjustments
−	Negative adjustments
=	Alternative minimum taxable income (AMTI)
−	AMT exemption
=	Amount subject to tax (AMT Base)
×	AMT tax rate
=	Tentative minimum tax
−	Regular income tax
=	AMT (if a positive amount)

Taxpayers who claim the QBI deduction (see Chapter 7) do not add this deduction back to compute alternative minimum taxable income. There are no adjustments required to the deduction, even though there may be adjustments to the income that created this deduction.

¶1203.01 PREFERENCES AND ADJUSTMENTS

Alternative minimum taxable income (AMTI) is regular taxable income, and then modified by the standard deduction (if used), preferences, and adjustments. Preferences and adjustments allow taxpayers to receive large exclusions and deductions in computing regular taxable income. The AMT calculation reduces the benefits of these tax incentives by limiting the exclusions or the amounts currently deductible. The amounts disallowed for AMT are added back to regular taxable income in computing AMTI.

Preference items are always added back to regular taxable income in computing AMTI. [I.R.C. §57] Thus, preferences increase income subject to AMT. Adjustments, on the other hand, can be positive or negative. [I.R.C. §56] Adjustments generally arise from timing differences. **Timing differences** occur when a deduction is allowed in computing taxable income in a year before it is allowed in computing AMTI. Thus, adjustments tend to be positive in the first years to which they apply (when the deduction allowed in computing taxable income is greater) and become negative in later years when they reverse (when the deduction allowed in computing AMTI is greater). Negative adjustments are subtracted from regular taxable income when computing AMTI.

Several adjustments and preferences used in computing AMT relate to the calculation of depreciation expense, passive losses, or tax-exempt and excluded income.

Depreciation Expense

The regular income tax system allows taxpayers to immediately expense (Section 179) and/or use an accelerated method (200% declining balance and bonus depreciation in years it is allowed) to depreciate tangible personal property. The AMT system also allows Section 179 expensing and bonus depreciation (in years bonus depreciation is allowed), but can require slower depreciation methods or longer recovery periods. Two common depreciation adjustments are:

1. **Depreciation of real property.** AMT requires that real property placed in service between 1987 and 1998 be depreciated using straight-line depreciation over 40 years. MACRS depreciates real property over 27.5, 31.5, or 39 years using the straight-line method (¶802.04). The difference in the amount of depreciation expense between these two systems is the AMT adjustment. There is no AMT depreciation adjustment for real property placed in service after 1998.

2. **Depreciation of personal property.** AMT uses the 150% declining balance (DB) method over the longer alternative depreciation system (ADS) lives. (See ¶802.04 for a discussion of ADS lives.) For computing regular taxable income, both the 200% DB and straight-line methods are allowed (¶802). The difference in the amount of depreciation expense between these two systems is an adjustment for AMT. However, there is no AMT adjustment for bonus depreciation or Section 179 deductions or the basis of subject property.

EXAMPLE 2	In 1995, Nadia and Tim Orlean paid $430,000 for a ski villa in Aspen, Colorado that they use solely as rental property. They depreciate the villa using MACRS (straight-line over 27.5 years). Each year they deduct $15,636 ($430,000 ÷ 27.5) of depreciation against their rental income when computing taxable income. For purposes of computing AMTI, depreciation allowed is $10,750 ($430,000 ÷ 40). Thus, during the years that MACRS is deducted in computing the Orleans' taxable income, they must add back to taxable income the $4,886 excess ($15,636 − $10,750) to compute AMTI. After the property is fully depreciated under MACRS, the Orleans can continue to take depreciation deductions when computing AMTI. This will result in a negative adjustment to taxable income in those years. Negative adjustments are subtracted from regular taxable income when computing AMTI.

EXAMPLE 3	Same facts as in Example 2, except that the Orleans bought the villa in 2002. For real property placed in service after 1998, there is no difference in the depreciation rules for computing taxable income and AMTI. Thus, no AMT adjustment is needed.

EXAMPLE 4	In 2022, a taxpayer buys used business personal property that costs $30,000. The half-year convention applies to the property. The recovery period is five years for regular income tax purposes. It is eight years for AMT. Depreciation for regular income tax (200% DB over 5 years) is $6,000 in year 1 ($30,000 × 20%). AMT depreciation (150% DB over 8 years) is $2,813 ($30,000 × 1/8 × 150% × ½). The $3,187 difference ($6,000 − $2,813) is added back to taxable income in computing AMTI in year 1.

The depreciation deduction adjusts the basis of the property. Since the depreciation deductions may differ between regular income tax and alternative minimum tax, each property subject to the depreciation adjustment may have a different basis for each system. Accordingly, there is often an adjustment for the gain or loss resulting from the sale of depreciated property.

Passive Losses

Neither the regular tax nor the AMT system allows for passive losses in excess of passive income to be deducted in the year they occur. Such losses carry forward and offset passive income in future years. Any losses carried forward are deducted in full when the taxpayer disposes of the entire interest in the activity (¶905.04).

While the loss recognition for both tax calculations is deferred, the amount of the loss to be deferred will usually differ. The difference occurs because the loss for AMT purposes is determined using all required AMT tax adjustments rather than the regular income tax deductions. For example, MACRS depreciates residential realty over 27.5 years using the straight-line method. For AMT, this property is depreciated over 40 years if it was placed in service before 1999. Because this difference affects the amount of passive loss carryover for regular tax versus AMT, it will affect the amount of the recognized gain when the property is sold as well as the passive loss deduction allowed.

Tax-Exempt and Excluded Income

Three other items of income may result in adjustments for AMT. First, AMTI includes interest from "specified private activity bonds" (a type of municipal bond). In computing taxable income, all municipal bond interest is exempt from gross income (¶401.03). Thus, interest from specified private activity bonds is added to taxable income in computing AMTI. Second, when exercising an incentive stock option, the excess of the fair market value (FMV) of the stock over the exercise price is income for purposes of computing AMT. Exercising an incentive stock option does not affect regular taxable income. Thus, the excess is added to taxable income in computing AMTI. Third, 7% of the excluded gain on the sale of Section 1202 small business stock is a preference item. This amount is added to taxable income to compute AMTI (recall that sometimes only a portion of the realized gain on the sale of Section 1202 stock is taxed; see ¶1006.) However, this addition is only required if the seller acquired the stock before September 28, 2010.

The tax law allows taxpayers to earn tax-free interest income when they invest in state and local government (municipal) bonds under the assumption that the bond proceeds would be used for various government projects. However, sometimes municipalities issue bonds and then loan the proceeds to private parties, or alternatively, they raise funds to construct facilities to be used for private projects. Bonds of this nature are called "private activity bonds." The interest from private activity bonds issued after August 7, 1986 and before January 1, 2009, or after 2010, is tax-exempt from regular taxable income, but taxable for purposes of computing AMTI. Such bonds are known as specified private activity bonds. Interest from specified private activity bonds is a preference item for purposes of computing AMTI.

EXAMPLE 5

Ellie owns a specified private activity bond. During the current year, the bond pays interest totaling $2,850. All interest from state and local government bonds is excluded from gross income under the regular income tax system (¶401.03). However, interest from specified private activity bonds is not an exclusion under the AMT system. Thus, in computing AMTI, Ellie adds back $2,850 to taxable income.

EXAMPLE 6

Cam paid $60 a share for 1,000 shares of stock under an incentive stock option program at work. At the time, the stock was selling for $85 a share. The excess of the value of the stock over the amount paid for the stock is excluded from Cam's gross income under the regular income tax system. However, no such exclusion is allowed in the AMT system. Thus, Cam must add back to taxable income the $25,000 excess (($85 − $60) × 1,000 shares) to taxable income when computing AMTI.

EXAMPLE 7	Lucas realized a $30,000 gain on the sale of Section 1202 stock. He had purchased the stock in 2009. Under the regular income tax system, 50% of this gain is excluded from gross income (¶1006). In computing his AMTI, Lucas adds back to taxable income 7% of the $15,000 excluded gain, or $1,050. If he had acquired the stock on or after September 28, 2010, he would have no tax preference resulting from this gain.

¶1203.02   AMT ITEMIZED DEDUCTIONS

The AMTI calculation disallows the standard deduction for taxpayers who do not itemize. For taxpayers who itemize, computing AMTI requires an adjustment to regular taxable income for certain types of itemized deductions.

Taxes

All taxes deducted on Schedule A must be added back in computing AMTI. Any state income tax refunds included in regular taxable income are not included in AMTI, and therefore must be subtracted from taxable income in computing AMTI. In taxable years beginning after 2017, this deduction is limited to $10,000 ($5,000 if married filing separately).

EXAMPLE 8	Kyle's itemized deductions exceed the standard deduction amount. Included in his itemized deductions are $4,740 of real estate taxes and $2,350 for state and local income taxes. In computing AMTI, Kyle must add back to taxable income the $7,090 deducted for taxes.

Interest

Investment interest is deductible for both regular tax and the AMT to the extent of net investment income. However, the amount of the interest deduction may vary because the amount of net investment income may not be the same for both regular tax and AMT. This is usually due to claiming private activity bond interest for AMT, thereby raising the investment interest ceiling for AMT purposes.

¶1203.03   AMT EXEMPTION

No deduction for personal and dependency exemptions is allowed in computing AMTI. Instead, a (larger) AMT exemption is intended to keep most lower- and middle-income taxpayers from being subject to the AMT. The exemption varies by taxpayer filing status, but starts to be phased out once AMTI reaches a certain level. The phase-out is 25% of AMTI above that threshold amount. Figure 12-1 shows, for each filing status, the exemption amount for 2022 and the phase-out calculation for the AMT exemption.

Figure 12-1: AMT Exemption		
	Exemption Amount	**Phase-Out Calculation**
MFJ and qualifying widow(er)	$118,100	25% × (AMTI – $1,079,800)
Single and head of household	75,900	25% × (AMTI – $539,900)
Married filing separately	59,050	25% × (AMTI – $539,900)

EXAMPLE 9	Jess files a separate tax return from his wife. During 2022, Jess's AMTI is $639,900. He computes his AMT exemption as follows.

Initial AMT exemption for MFS		$57,300
AMTI	$639,900	
Less AMTI threshold for MFS	(539,900)	
Excess	$100,000	
Phase-out percentage	× 25%	(25,000)
AMT exemption		$34,050

EXAMPLE 10	Rocky and Randi Kane file a joint tax return. Their 2022 AMTI is $1,393,000. The Kanes compute their AMT exemption as follows.

Initial AMT exemption for MFJ		$118,100
AMTI	$1,393,000	
Less AMTI threshold for MFJ	(1,079,800)	
Excess	$313,200	
Phase-out percentage	× 25%	(78,300)
AMT exemption		$39,800

¶1203.04 AMT RATES AND CREDITS

Tax Rate

A two-tiered rate schedule is used to compute the AMT. The tax rate on the first $206,100 of AMTI in excess of the allowable exemption is 26% ($103,050 for MFS). A 28% rate applies to the excess. The AMT rates do not apply to net capital gain and qualified dividends. These amounts remain taxed at the taxpayer's blended tax rate and not the zero rate that generally applies beginning in 2018.

EXAMPLE 11	Continuing with Example 10, the Kanes subtract their AMT exemption from AMTI to arrive at their AMT base ($1,393,000 – $39,800 = $1,353,200). The Kanes' tentative minimum tax equals $374,774 [($206,100 × 26%) + (($1,353,200 – $206,100) × 28%)]. If this amount exceeds their regular income tax liability, the excess is the Kanes' AMT.

Minimum Tax Credit

The portion of the AMT caused by timing differences creates a minimum tax credit in future years when the regular tax exceeds the taxpayer's tentative minimum tax. This credit can reduce the regular tax liability only in future years and may be carried forward until used. Its purpose is to help avoid double taxing of those adjustments resulting from timing differences. Those interested in learning more about the minimum tax credit should refer to the instructions to Form 8801, Credit for Prior Year Minimum Tax—Individuals, Estates, and Trusts.

¶1203.05   CALCULATING AMT

EXAMPLE 12	Jeffrey Q. Lang (single, age 47) calculates his regular tax liability for 2022 as follows.	

Salary			$95,000
Rental income		$6,000	
Rental expenses:			
Depreciation—real property	$2,400		
Depreciation—personal property	600		
Interest expense	5,000		
Property taxes	800		
Other expenses	200	(9,000)	
Net rental loss (active participation)			(3,000)
Short-term capital gain on the sale of stock			5,000
Adjusted gross income			$97,000
Less itemized deductions:			
Charitable contributions		$20,600	
Home mortgage interest		14,400	
Real estate taxes		4,400	39,400
Taxable income			$57,600
Regular tax liability (using the 2022 rate schedule)			$8,295

Jeffrey used accelerated MACRS to compute depreciation. Had he depreciated the property using the AMT depreciation rules, he would have deducted $2,200 for the real property and $450 for the personal property. Jeffrey received $41,500 in tax-exempt interest from specified private activity bonds he bought in 2004. He also paid $30,000 for $50,000 of stock through an incentive stock option plan set up by his employer. Using this information, Jeffrey's AMT is $4,181, computed as follows.

Regular taxable income		$57,600
Add: (1) Excess depreciation		
Real property ($2,400 – $2,200)	$200	
Personal property ($600 – $450)	150	350
(2) Disallowed itemized deductions:		
Real estate taxes	4,400	4,400
(3) Private activity bond interest		41,500
(4) Stock option ($50,000 – $30,000)		20,000
AMTI		$123,850
Less AMT exemption (single filing status)	$75,900	
Phase-out (does not exceed $539,900)	0	(75,900)
AMT base		47,950
AMT rate (on up to $206,100 of AMT base)		× 26%
Tentative minimum tax		$ 12,467
Less regular income tax		(8,295)
AMT		$4,172

¶1203.06   FILLED-IN FORM 6251

INFORMATION FOR FIGURE 12-2:

Jeffrey Q. Lang from Example 12 enters the amounts shown in bold on the appropriate lines of Form 6251. He then enters his AMT on Form 1040, Schedule 2, where it becomes part of his 2022 total income tax liability.

Line #
- 1: Amount from Form 1040, line 10, **$57,600** ($97,000 AGI – $39,400 itemized deductions)
- 2a: Taxes from Schedule A, line 7, **$4,400**
- 2g: Specified private activity bond interest, **$41,500**
- 2i: Adjustment for exercise of incentive stock options, **$20,000**
- 2l: Post-1986 depreciation adjustment, **$350** ($200 + $150)
- 5: Exemption amount, **$75,900**
- 10: Regular income tax from Form 1040, line 10, **$8,295**

The AMT exemption, AMTI thresholds for reducing the exemption, and threshold where the 28% AMT rate is applied, are all indexed annually for inflation (see ¶202).

Figure 12-2: Filled-In Form 6251

Form **6251**	**Alternative Minimum Tax—Individuals**	OMB No. 1545-0074
Department of the Treasury Internal Revenue Service	Go to *www.irs.gov/Form6251* for instructions and the latest information. Attach to Form 1040, 1040-SR, or 1040-NR.	**2022** Attachment Sequence No. **32**

Name(s) shown on Form 1040, 1040-SR, or 1040-NR	Your social security number
Jeffrey Q. Lang	668-00-9307

Part I   **Alternative Minimum Taxable Income** (See instructions for how to complete each line.)

1	Enter the amount from Form 1040 or 1040-SR, line 15, if more than zero. If Form 1040 or 1040-SR, line 15, is zero, subtract line 14 of Form 1040 or 1040-SR from line 11 of Form 1040 or 1040-SR and enter the result here. (If less than zero, enter as a negative amount.)	1	57,600
2a	If filing Schedule A (Form 1040), enter the taxes from Schedule A, line 7; otherwise, enter the amount from Form 1040 or 1040-SR, line 12	2a	4,400
b	Tax refund from Schedule 1 (Form 1040), line 1 or line 8z	2b	( )
c	Investment interest expense (difference between regular tax and AMT)	2c	
d	Depletion (difference between regular tax and AMT)	2d	
e	Net operating loss deduction from Schedule 1 (Form 1040), line 8a. Enter as a positive amount	2e	
f	Alternative tax net operating loss deduction	2f	( )
g	Interest from specified private activity bonds exempt from the regular tax	2g	41,500
h	Qualified small business stock, see instructions	2h	
i	Exercise of incentive stock options (excess of AMT income over regular tax income)	2i	20,000
j	Estates and trusts (amount from Schedule K-1 (Form 1041), box 12, code A)	2j	
k	Disposition of property (difference between AMT and regular tax gain or loss)	2k	
l	Depreciation on assets placed in service after 1986 (difference between regular tax and AMT)	2l	350
m	Passive activities (difference between AMT and regular tax income or loss)	2m	
n	Loss limitations (difference between AMT and regular tax income or loss)	2n	
o	Circulation costs (difference between regular tax and AMT)	2o	
p	Long-term contracts (difference between AMT and regular tax income)	2p	
q	Mining costs (difference between regular tax and AMT)	2q	
r	Research and experimental costs (difference between regular tax and AMT)	2r	
s	Income from certain installment sales before January 1, 1987	2s	( )
t	Intangible drilling costs preference	2t	
3	Other adjustments, including income-based related adjustments	3	
4	**Alternative minimum taxable income.** Combine lines 1 through 3. (If married filing separately and line 4 is more than $776,100, see instructions.)	4	123,850

Part II   **Alternative Minimum Tax (AMT)**

5	Exemption.		

IF your filing status is...	AND line 4 is not over...	THEN enter on line 5...		
Single or head of household	$ 539,900	$ 75,900		
Married filing jointly or qualifying widow(er)	1,079,800	118,100	}	
Married filing separately	539,900	59,050		5 75,900

If line 4 is **over** the amount shown above for your filing status, see instructions.

6	Subtract line 5 from line 4. If more than zero, go to line 7. If zero or less, enter -0- here and on lines 7, 9, and 11, and go to line 10.	6	
7	• If you are filing Form 2555, see instructions for the amount to enter. • If you reported capital gain distributions directly on Form 1040 or 1040-SR, line 7; you reported qualified dividends on Form 1040 or 1040-SR, line 3a; **or** you had a gain on both lines 15 and 16 of Schedule D (Form 1040) (as refigured for the AMT, if necessary), complete Part III on the back and enter the amount from line 40 here. • **All others:** If line 6 is $206,100 or less ($103,050 or less if married filing separately), multiply line 6 by 26% (0.26). Otherwise, multiply line 6 by 28% (0.28) and subtract $4,122 ($2,061 if married filing separately) from the result.	7	12,467
8	Alternative minimum tax foreign tax credit (see instructions)	8	
9	Tentative minimum tax. Subtract line 8 from line 7	9	12,467
10	Add Form 1040 or 1040-SR, line 16 (minus any tax from Form 4972), and Schedule 2 (Form 1040), line 2. Subtract from the result Schedule 3 (Form 1040), line 1 and any negative amount reported on Form 8978, line 14 (treated as a positive number). If zero or less, enter -0-. If you used Schedule J to figure your tax on Form 1040 or 1040-SR, line 16, refigure that tax without using Schedule J before completing this line. See instructions	10	8,295
11	**AMT.** Subtract line 10 from line 9. If zero or less, enter -0-. Enter here and on Schedule 2 (Form 1040), line 1	11	4,173

For Paperwork Reduction Act Notice, see your tax return instructions.   Cat. No. 13600G   Form **6251** (2022)

¶1203.06

¶1204   General Business Credit

Chapter 2 introduced the personal tax credits available to individual taxpayers. This chapter focuses on the more common tax credits available to businesses, which includes sole proprietorships, corporations and partnerships.

After all other nonrefundable credits have been offset against the taxpayer's income tax liability, taxpayers may claim the general business credit. [I.R.C. §38] This nonrefundable credit is equal to the sum of several separately computed tax credits. While some credits are beyond the scope of this textbook, the remaining sections examine the following business credits:

1. Rehabilitation credit (part of the Investment credit) [I.R.C. §§46, 47]—Form 3468
2. Disabled access credit [I.R.C. §44]—Form 8826
3. Credit for small employer health insurance premiums [I.R.C. §45R]—Form 8941
4. Credit for employer-provided childcare facilities and services [I.R.C. §45F]—Form 8882
5. Credit for small employer pension plan startup costs [I.R.C. §45E]—Form 8881
6. Work opportunity credit [I.R.C. §51]—Form 5884
7. Credit for employer differential wage payments [I.R.C. §45P]—Form 8932
8. New markets credit [I.R.C. §45D]—Form 8874

Any part of the general business credit not used in the current tax year is carried back to the previous tax year. Any remaining unused credit is then carried forward and combined with business credits generated in that year. The unused credit is carried forward until it is used up or the 20-year carryover period expires. In each carryforward year, the oldest credit is used first, but only after the current year's credit is used. This minimizes the possible expiration of any unused general business credit.

¶1204.01   REHABILITATION CREDIT

The purpose behind the rehabilitation credit is to encourage businesses to stay in economically distressed areas and to preserve historic structures. The credit equals a percentage of the costs incurred in substantially rehabilitating qualified buildings that are certified historic structures. [I.R.C. §47] A building is substantially rehabilitated when the rehabilitation costs during a 24-month period exceed the *greater of* (i) the building's adjusted basis before rehabilitation, or (ii) $5,000. Once the substantial rehabilitation test has been met, all costs to rehabilitate the property (including those before and after the 24-month period) qualify for the credit. The percentage used in computing the credit is as follows:

Type of Property Credit	Credit
Certified historic structures (both nonresidential and residential)	20%

For expenditures paid or incurred after 2017, the credit is claimed ratably over a five-year period beginning in the tax year in which the rehabilitated building is placed in service. For expenditures paid or incurred before 2018, the credit is claimed in the tax year in which the qualified rehabilitated building is placed in service. A special transition rule applies.

When taxpayers make capital expenditures to property, they normally increase their basis in the property by such costs. However, taxpayers must reduce their basis by the amount of the rehabilitation credit. This keeps them from taking depreciation deductions on the portion of the cost of the building that is taken as a tax credit.

EXAMPLE 13	Davy pays $50,000 for a certified historic structure. Over the next 18 months, he spends $60,000 to reha-bilitate the structure. Davy qualifies for the rehabilitation credit since the $60,000 spent to rehabilitate the structure exceeds $50,000 (the *greater of* (i) the $50,000 adjusted basis in the building before rehabilita-tion, or (ii) $5,000). Davy's rehabilitation credit equals $12,000 ($60,000 × 20%). His basis in the building increases by $48,000 ($60,000 – $12,000) to $98,000 ($50,000 + $48,000). Davy uses MACRS or ADS to depreciate the $98,000 basis in the building (¶803).

Taxpayers that dispose of the property within five years of taking the rehabilitation credit must recapture 20% of the credit taken for each year shy of five years. Any recaptured amount is added to the taxpayer's tax liability and to the adjusted basis of the building. For example, if Davy (from Example 13) were to sell the property after two years, he would be required to recapture (increase his tax liability by) 60% of the credit, or $7,200 ($12,000 × 60%). The amount of the recapture is 20% for each of the three years Davy is shy of holding the property for five years. Davy would increase his basis in the property at the time of sale by the $7,200 of recaptured credit.

¶1204.02   DISABLED ACCESS CREDIT

This nonrefundable credit provides an incentive to small businesses to make their buildings more accessible to disabled persons. [I.R.C. §44] The credit equals 50% of the eligible expenditures for the year that exceed $250 but do not exceed $10,250. Thus, the maximum credit is $5,000 [50% × ($10,250 – $250)]. A business qualifies for the credit if it satisfies one of the following criteria in the previous tax year:

1. The business did not have gross receipts in excess of $1 million, or
2. The business did not employ more than 30 full-time employees.

EXAMPLE 14	In the current tax year, Harvey Enterprises pays to install ramps to allow disabled persons easier access to its building. The building was first placed in service in 1982. Last year Harvey reported gross receipts of $1.2 million and employed 30 full-time workers. Harvey qualifies for the disabled access credit because it did not employ more than 30 full-time workers in the previous tax year. To qualify for the disabled access credit, a business must only satisfy one of the two criteria listed.

EXAMPLE 15	In the current tax year, Bruce Industries pays to make improvements to its office building to make it more accessible to disabled persons. The building was first placed in service in 1983. Last year Bruce reported gross receipts of $900,000 and had 35 full-time employees. Bruce qualifies for the disabled access credit because its gross receipts did not exceed $1 million.

Eligible expenditures include amounts paid to remove barriers on buildings first placed in service before November 6, 1990 that prevent businesses from being accessible to, or usable by, disabled persons. Also included are amounts paid to buy or modify equipment used by disabled persons. Other eligible expenditures include amounts paid for qualified interpreters and audio devices that help hearing-impaired persons. Likewise, amounts paid for qualified readers and other devices that help make visual materials available to visually-impaired persons are also eligible for the credit. Taxpayers claiming the disabled assess credit increase the depreciable basis of the building by the amounts spent and then reduce it by the amount of the credit.

| EXAMPLE 16 | Alana owns a small business that she reports on Schedule C. During the year, Alana pays $8,500 to make her office building more accessible to disabled persons. The building was placed in service in 1987. Alana's disabled access credit equals $4,125 [50% × ($8,500 − $250)]. Alana's basis in the building increases by $4,375 ($8,500 − $4,125). She uses the straight-line method to depreciate the $4,375 over 39 (MACRS, ¶803.01) or 40 years (ADS, ¶803.02). |

¶1204.03   CREDIT FOR SMALL EMPLOYER HEALTH INSURANCE PREMIUMS

Small employers can take a tax credit for amounts they pay for their employees' health care premiums. [I.R.C. §45R] Only premiums paid on behalf of employees enrolled in a qualified health plan (QHP) offered through the Small Business Health Options Program (SHOP) Marketplace qualify for the credit. Furthermore, this credit is only available for two consecutive years (with 2014 being the first possible year). Thus, employers who first claimed the credit in 2021 would not be entitled to a tax credit after 2022. Likewise, employers first claiming the credit in 2022 will not be entitled to take the credit after 2023.

To qualify for the credit, employers are required to pay at least half of the costs associated with providing health care coverage for each of their employees. The credit is equal to 50% of the premiums paid (35% for small tax-exempt employers). The full credit is available to employers with ten or fewer full-time equivalent (FTE) employees whose annual wages do not exceed a certain threshold amount ($27,600 in 2021 and $28,700 in 2022). The credit begins to be phased-out once the number of FTE employees exceeds ten or the employees' annual wages exceed the threshold amount. The credit is not available to sole proprietors, and certain partners and S corporation shareholders.

An employer's number of FTE employees is determined by dividing the total hours of service for its employees during the year (but not more than 2,080 hours for any employee) by 2,080. If the result is not a whole number, then the number of FTE employees does not include the fraction. For example, if the FTE formula results in an employer having 6.2 employees, then the employer is deemed to have six FTE employees.

| EXAMPLE 17 | Cole Company has seven FTE employees. Average wages paid to its FTE employees are $24,000. During 2022, Cole paid health insurance premiums totaling $63,000 on behalf of its employees. This amount was 75% of the total cost of each employee's premiums for a QHP offered through the SHOP Marketplace, and 2022 was the first year Cole bought its health insurance through the SHOP Marketplace. Cole qualifies for the full small employer health insurance credit of $31,500 ($63,000 × 50%). If Cole remains eligible to take the credit, 2023 will be the last year Cole will qualify for the credit (under the two consecutive year rule). |

For 2022, employers whose FTE employees' averages wages exceed $28,700 must reduce their credit by 3.484% for each $1,000 (or portion thereof) that exceeds $28,700. The percentage reduction per thousand is $1,000 divided by the dollar ceiling ($1,000/28,700 = 3.484%).

| EXAMPLE 18 | Same facts as in Example 17, except that Cole's employees' average wages were $31,000. Since average wages exceed $28,700, Cole must reduce its credit by 10.453% ($2,300 excess/$1,000 = 2.30, which is 3 portions thereof. Multiplying 3 × 3.484% = 10.453%). Cole's 2022 small employer health insurance credit equals $28,207 ($31,500 − ($31,500 × 10.453%)). |

Employers with more than ten FTE employees must reduce their credit by 6.667% for each FTE employee over ten. The IRS provides tables to help employers compute their reduced credit.

EXAMPLE 19

> Same facts as in Example 17, except that the $63,000 covers Cole's 12 FTE employees. Since the number of FTE employees exceeds 10, Cole must reduce its credit by 13.334% (6.667% × 2 excess FTE employees). Cole's tax credit would be $27,300 ($31,500 – ($31,500 × 13.334%)).

> Only premiums paid on behalf of employees enrolled in a QHP offered through the SHOP Marketplace qualify for the credit. Those interested in learning more about QHPs offered through the SHOP Marketplace can find this information by visiting *www.HealthCare.gov*.

¶1204.04   CREDIT FOR EMPLOYER-PROVIDED CHILDCARE FACILITIES AND SERVICES

Employers can take a tax credit for providing childcare to their employees. [I.R.C. §45F] The amount of the credit is the *sum of* (i) 25% of qualified childcare expenses plus (ii) 10% of qualified childcare resources or referral expenses. The maximum credit allowed each year is $150,000.

Qualified childcare expenses include amounts paid to acquire or construct property used as part of a qualified childcare facility. It also includes costs incurred to operate a qualified childcare facility and amounts paid to a qualified childcare facility that provides childcare services to employees. **Qualified childcare resource and referral expenses** are amounts paid under a contract to provide childcare resource and referral services to an employee. However, these services cannot discriminate in favor of key or highly paid employees (as defined in ¶401.05).

EXAMPLE 20

> In 2006, Harvey started a qualified childcare program for his employees. During 2022, he pays $7,000 in qualified childcare expenses and $1,000 in qualified childcare resource and referral expenses. Harvey's employer-provided childcare credit is $1,850 [($7,000 × 25%) + ($1,000 × 10%)]. He includes this amount as part of the General Business Credit when he prepares his 2022 tax return.

Employers are allowed a tax credit equal to 25% of the amounts paid to buy or construct a childcare facility (subject to an annual credit limit of $150,000). Employers reduce their basis in the building by any amounts taken as a credit. However, if within ten years of taking the credit, the facility is no longer used to provide childcare services for employees, some of the credit must be recaptured (added to the taxpayer's tax liability). The amount recaptured is 100% in years 1-3, and is gradually reduced to 10% by years 9 and 10. The amount recaptured is then added to the employer's adjusted basis in the building. This concept (of calculating basis and recapture) is similar to that which was described earlier in the chapter for the rehabilitation credit (see Example 13 in ¶1204.01).

¶1204.05   CREDIT FOR SMALL EMPLOYER PENSION PLAN STARTUP COSTS

Certain employers can take a tax credit equal to 50% of qualified startup costs when they establish a new defined benefit plan, defined contribution plan (including a 401(k) plan), SIMPLE plan, or SEP plan for their employees. [I.R.C. §45E] The new pension plan must cover at least one employee who is not a highly paid employee (as defined in ¶401.05). The tax credit is limited to $500 in each of the first three years the pension plan is offered. **Qualified startup costs** include amounts paid to establish or administer the new plan, as well as amounts paid to educate employees about retirement planning. Only employers that employed 100 or fewer employees earning at least $5,000 in the prior year can claim to this credit. Furthermore, the credit is available only to employers that have not maintained a qualified plan during any of the previous three tax years.

¶1204.06   WORK OPPORTUNITY TAX CREDIT (WOTC)

The work opportunity tax credit (WOTC) provides employers with a tax credit for hiring workers from one of a number of targeted groups. [I.R.C. §51] The federal government has identified ten targeted groups of individuals who may face challenges in finding work. To encourage employers to hire members from these targeted groups, Congress enacted the WOTC. The ten targeted groups of qualified workers included:

1. A member of a family receiving Temporary Assistance for Needy Families (TANF)
2. Qualified long-term unemployment recipients
3. Qualified food stamp (SNAP) recipients
4. Qualified ex-felons
5. Designated community residents
6. Qualified social security recipients
7. Disabled persons with vocational rehabilitation referrals
8. Qualified summer youth employees
9. Qualified veterans
10. Long-term family assistance program recipients

Qualified long-term unemployment recipients are persons who are unemployed for at least 27 consecutive weeks leading up to their hire date. **Designated community residents** are persons between the ages of 18 and 39 who live in federally-designated rural renewal counties or empowerment zones. **Qualified summer youth employees** are 16- and 17-year-olds that live in a federally-designated empowerment zone, and work for the employer between May 1 and September 15. Only wages paid to summer youth employees during these 4½ months while living in a designated empowerment zone can be used to compute the WOTC. Also, any person hired who is a relative, former employee, or person owning a majority interest in the company, cannot be a qualified worker, even if that person is a member of a targeted group.

Computing the Credit

The WOTC for a qualified worker equals a percentage of the *lesser of* (i) the worker's first-year wages, or (ii) a specified amount, which varies depending on the type of worker. The full 40% credit is available for new hires who work at least 400 hours for the employer during their first year. A reduced credit of 25% is allowed for those who work at least 120 hours during their first year, but do not meet the 400-hour threshold. No credit is allowed for any person working less than 120 hours during their first year.

For qualified workers from the first seven targeted groups, the maximum first-year wages that can be used in computing the WOTC is $6,000. For qualified summer youth employees, the maximum is $3,000. If the employee's first 12 months of employment spans over two of the employer's tax years, the employer can take the credit over two tax years.

Type of Qualified Worker	Maximum First-Year Wages	Maximum Credit
From one of the first seven targeted groups: worked ≥ 120 hours, but < 400 hours	$6,000	$1,500
From one of the first seven targeted groups: worked ≥ 400 hours	6,000	2,400
Qualified summer youth employees: worked ≥ 120 hours, but < 400 hours	3,000	750
Qualified summer youth employees: worked ≥ 400 hours	3,000	1,200

EXAMPLE 21

In 2022, Ranger Company hired Tanner, a qualified ex-felon. Tanner worked 180 hours for Ranger during his first year. Tanner's first-year wages were $2,700 ($1,700 paid in 2022; $1,000 paid in 2023). Since Tanner worked at least 120 hours, but less than 400 hours during his first year, Ranger uses the reduced 25% rate to compute the WOTC. Ranger's 2022 WOTC is $425 (25% × $1,700 first-year wages paid in 2022). The first $6,000 of qualified first-year wages can be used in computing the WOTC. Thus, Ranger's 2023 WOTC is $250 (25% × $1,000).

Qualified veterans are one of the ten targeted groups. They include three types of veterans of the U.S. Armed Forces. The first type is a veteran who was unemployed for at least four weeks during the one-year period leading up to the date of hire. The Internal Revenue Code (Code) refers to these veterans as "returning heroes." The second type is an unemployed veteran with service-related disabilities. For these veterans (whom the Code refers to as "wounded warriors"), there is no minimum length of unemployment required prior to their being hired. The third type includes veterans receiving food stamps.

The maximum first-year wages that can be used in computing the WOTC for qualified veterans depends on the type of veteran hired. For veterans receiving food stamps, the maximum first-year wages is $6,000. The same $6,000 applies to returning heroes who had been unemployed for less than six months (but at least four weeks) during the one year period leading up to the date they are hired. For returning heroes who had been unemployed for at least six months during that same one year period, the maximum wages increase to $14,000.

When hiring a wounded warrior who had been unemployed for less than six months during the year leading up to the hire date, up to $12,000 of first-year wages can be used in computing the WOTC. This amount doubles (to $24,000) for wounded warriors who had been unemployed for at least six months during that same one year period. The following table summarizes the maximum first-year wages and maximum credit allowed for the various types of qualified veterans.

Type of Veteran	Length of Unemployment	Maximum First-Year Wages	Maximum Credit
Food stamp recipient	not applicable	$ 6,000	$2,400
Returning hero	≥ 4 weeks, but < 6 months	6,000	2,400
Returning hero	≥ 6 months	14,000	5,600
Wounded warrior	< 6 months	12,000	4,800
Wounded warrior	≥ 6 months	24,000	9,600

EXAMPLE 22

On June 22, 2022, Estes, Inc. hired a veteran who had been unemployed for the past year. First-year wages were $21,000, of which $11,200 were paid in 2022. Estes' 2022 WOTC is $4,480 (40% × $11,200 first year wages paid in 2022). Its 2023 WOTC is $1,120 [40% × ($14,000 maximum wages – $11,200 wages paid in 2022)].

EXAMPLE 23

On July 9, 2022, Brent hired Demi, a veteran with service-related disabilities. In the year leading up to her hire date, Demi had been unemployed for three weeks. Demi's first-year wages were $15,000, of which $7,700 was paid in 2022 and $7,300 was paid in 2023. Although Demi was unemployed for only three weeks leading up to her hire date, the minimum of four weeks of unemployment does not apply to veterans with service-related disabilities (wounded warriors). The WOTC is 40% of up to $12,000 of first-year wages paid to a wounded warrior who was unemployed less than six months leading up to the hire date. Thus, Brent's 2022 WOTC equals $3,080 (40% × $7,700). His 2023 WOTC equals $1,720 (40% × $4,300). The $4,300 used in computing the 2023 WOTC represents qualified first-year wages paid in 2023 ($12,000 maximum first-year wages – $7,700 wages paid in 2022).

EXAMPLE 24	On March 19, 2022, Anthem Company hired Eugene, a veteran with service-related disabilities. In the year leading up to his hire date, Eugene had been unemployed for two years. Eugene's first-year wages were $20,000, of which $17,000 was paid in 2022 and $3,000 were paid in 2023. Anthem's 2022 WOTC equals $6,800 (40% × $17,000). Its 2023 WOTC equals $1,200 (40% × $3,000). The $3,000 used in computing the 2023 WOTC represents first-year wages paid in 2023, since first-year wages did not exceed the $24,000 maximum that can be used to compute the WOTC for hiring a wounded warrior who was unemployed for at least six months leading up to the hire date.

EXAMPLE 25	On September 4, 2022, Watney, Inc. hired a veteran with a service-related disability who had been unemployed for the last nine months. First-year wages were $28,000, of which $9,000 were paid in 2022. Watney's 2022 WOTC equals $3,600 (40% × $9,000 first year wages paid in 2022). Its 2023 WOTC equals $6,000 [40% × ($24,000 maximum first-year wages– $9,000 first-year wages paid in 2022)].

EXAMPLE 26	On October 6, 2022, Grant hired a veteran who had been receiving food stamps. First-year wages were $18,000, of which $7,000 were paid in 2022. Grant's 2022 WOTC equals $2,400 (40% × $6,000 maximum first-year wages). Since the maximum $6,000 of first-year wages were paid in 2022, Grant's 2023 WOTC for this worker is $0.

Enhanced Credit for Long-Term Family Assistance Recipients

An enhanced credit is allowed for employers that hire long-term family assistance recipients. For members of this targeted group, the amount of the credit equals 40% of up to $10,000 of first-year wages, plus 50% of up to $10,000 of second-year wages. Thus, the maximum credit for wages paid to these workers is $9,000 [($10,000 × 40%) + ($10,000 × 50%)]. If the employee's first two years of employment spans over three of the employer's tax years, the employer can take the credit over three tax years.

EXAMPLE 27	On July 29, 2021, Devry, Inc. hired Dana, a qualified long-term family assistance recipient. First-year wages paid to Dana were $9,800 of which $3,000 were paid during 2021. The rest ($6,800) were paid during 2022. Second-year wages were $10,250, of which $4,500 were paid in 2022. The rest ($5,750) were paid in 2023. Devry's WOTC for 2021–2023 is as follows.

2021 WOTC	
$3,000 qualified first-year wages × 40%	<u>$1,200</u>
2022 WOTC	
$6,800 qualified first-year wages × 40%	$2,720
$4,500 qualified second-year wages × 50%	<u>2,250</u>
	<u>$4,970</u>
2023 WOTC	
$5,500 ($10,000 maximum) qualified second-year wages × 50%	<u>$2,750</u>

Employers that claim the WOTC reduce their wage expense deduction by the amount of the credit. For example, Devry (in Example 27) would reduce its 2021 wage expense deduction by $1,200.

 The WOTC is set to expire at the end of 2025, for wages paid to persons hired after that date. This provision has expired and been reinstated several times.

¶1204.06

¶1204.07   CREDIT FOR EMPLOYER DIFFERENTIAL WAGE PAYMENTS

Employers may claim a tax credit for 20% of the first $20,000 of differential wage payments made during the year to each qualifying employee. [I.R.C. §45P] A **differential wage payment** is a payment made to an employee while the employee is on active military duty for more than 30 days when the payment takes the place of wages the employee would have earned working for the employer.

Only payments made to employees who have worked for the employer for the 91-day period immediately before the period for which any differential wage payment is made qualify for the credit. Employers claiming the credit reduce their wage expense deduction by the amount of the credit.

EXAMPLE 28	During 2022, Frye Inc. makes differential wage payments totaling $15,000 to one of its employees who was called to active military duty during the year. Frye claims a $3,000 tax credit ($15,000 × 20%) as part of its general business credit. Frye reduces its wage expense deduction by the $3,000 credit.

EXAMPLE 29	Same as Example 28, except that Frye's payments total $25,000. Since only the first $20,000 of differential wage payments can be used in computing the credit, Frye's credit is limited to $4,000 ($20,000 × 20%). Frye includes this amount as part of its general business credit and reduces its wage expense deduction by $4,000.

¶1204.08   NEW MARKETS CREDIT

The new markets tax credit was first enacted in 2000. Its objective was to spur revitalization efforts in low-income and impoverished areas in the U.S. The total credit is 39% of the taxpayer's investment, spread out over seven years.

Taxpayers that invest in a qualified community development entity may be entitled to a new markets credit. [I.R.C. §45D] A **qualified community development entity (qualified CDE)** is a domestic corporation or partnership whose primary mission is serving, or providing investment capital for, low-income communities or low-income persons. A qualified CDE must be certified as such by the federal government. During its first six years, a qualified CDE must use at least 85% of the cash it raises to make qualified low-income community investments. After the sixth year, it need only use 75% of its cash toward low-income community investments.

An equity investment in a qualified CDE is an investment in the stock of a qualified CDE (in the case of a corporation) or an investment in a capital interest of a qualified CDE (in the case of a partnership). Cash must be used to pay for the investment. However, taxpayers can borrow to get the cash needed to buy the CDE investment. The new markets credit equals a percentage times the amount invested in a qualified CDE. The percentage is 5% for the first three years. It increases to 6% for the next four years. Amounts claimed as a credit reduce the taxpayer's basis in the investment.

If at any time during the seven-year period in which the new markets credit is available, (1) the investment ceases to be a qualified CDE, (2) the taxpayer's investment is redeemed by the qualified CDE, or (3) the CDE fails to make qualified low-income community investments, the recapture rules apply. This would result in the taxpayer's taxes being increased by the amount the taxpayer's general business credit would have been reduced had there been no new markets credit.

EXAMPLE 30	On October 5, 2017, Creekside Corporation paid $200,000 for a qualified equity investment in a CDE. Creekside uses the calendar year. Its 2017 new markets credit was $10,000 (5% × $200,000). Creekside was entitled to another $10,000 credit on each of its 2018 and 2019 tax returns. It is entitled to a $12,000 (6% × $200,000) credit on each of its 2021–2022 tax returns. Creekside reduces its $200,000 initial basis in the CDE by the amounts it claims for the new markets credit.

EXAMPLE 31	Continuing with Example 30, assume that in 2020, Creekside's investment is no longer a qualified CDE. Also assume that from 2017-2019, Creekside had reduced its tax liability (via the general business credit) by $30,000 for the new markets credit ($10,000 each year). Since Creekside received a $30,000 tax benefit from the new markets credit, it increases its 2020 tax liability (and basis in the CDE) by $30,000.

	The new markets credit is set to expire at the end of 2025.

12

Name:

Section:

Date:

QUESTIONS AND PROBLEMS

1. **Net Operating Loss (NOL).** (Obj. 1)

   a. What is meant by an NOL?

   b. Can an individual who does not operate a business have an NOL? Explain.

   c. For what taxable years may an NOL created before 2018 be used as a deduction for AGI?

   d. For what taxable years may an NOL created in 2018, 2019 or 2020 be used as a deduction for AGI?

   e. For what taxable years may an NOL created in 2021 and later years be used as a deduction for AGI?

2. **Net Operating Loss.** (Obj. 1)

   a. What types of adjustments must be made in order to convert negative taxable income into an NOL?

   b. Carlos (single) reports on his 2022 tax return negative taxable income of $38,550. Included in this amount is business income of $70,000 and business deductions of $98,000. Carlos took the standard deduction. Compute Carlos's 2022 NOL assuming that no other adjustments are necessary.

   c. What would be the amount of the NOL if, in Part b., Carlos's gross income included net nonbusiness long-term capital gains of $10,000 and business income of $60,000?

   d. What carryover rules apply to this loss?

3. **Net Operating Loss (NOL).** (Obj. 1) Robin, a single taxpayer, has opened his own law office. The following summarizes the items included in Robin's 2022 negative taxable income. Compute Robin's NOL.

Business income	$54,500	
Dividends and interest	2,300	
Long-term capital gain (nonbusiness income)	1,800	
Total income		$58,600
Business deductions	$60,000	
Itemized deductions	16,150	
Total deductions		($76,150)
(Negative) taxable income		($17,550)

4. **AMT.** (Obj. 2) Explain how the alternative minimum tax (AMT) is computed under the AMT system, and how this calculation differs from the calculation of taxable income under the regular income tax system.

5. **AMT.** (Obj. 2)

    a. How must depreciation expense for real and personal property be determined in computing the alternative minimum tax (AMT)?

    b. Explain the types of adjustments and preference items that must be added to or subtracted from regular taxable income in order to compute AMTI.

6. **AMT.** (Obj. 2) A couple paid $295,000 for a villa in Florida. The villa is used solely as rental property. They depreciate the villa using the straight-line method over 27.5 years.

    a. Compute the couple's 2022 AMT adjustment if the condo was purchased in 1996.

    b. Same as in Part a., except that they purchased the condo in 2004.

7. **AMT.** (Obj. 4) James M. (SSN 346-00-4657) and Tammy S. (SSN 465-00-3647) Livingston prepared a joint income tax return for 2022 and claimed their four children, ages 3, 5, 9 and 12, as dependents. Their regular taxable income and tax liability were computed as follows:

Salaries (James)	$ 95,000	
Schedule C net profit (Tammy)	84,000	
Nonqualified dividend income	4,700	
Interest income	2,350	
Self-employment tax deduction	(5,934)	
Adjusted gross income	$180,915	
Itemized deductions	(38,497)	
QBI deduction	(15,613)	Includes $10,000 for state income and property tax (20% × (84,000 − 5,934))
Taxable income	$126,804	
Tax liability	$19,131	

The Livingstons received $25,000 of tax-exempt interest from specified private activity bonds purchased in 2005. In computing taxable income, the Livingstons took $7,000 depreciation on Schedule C, using the MACRS 200% declining balance method on property with a five-year class life. AMT allows $5,500 of depreciation for the same property. Itemized deductions include charitable contributions of $13,775, mortgage interest of $14,712, and state taxes of $10,000. They also paid $20,000 for $60,000 of stock through an incentive stock option plan set up by Tammy's employer. Complete Form 6251 for the Livingstons.

8. **General Business Tax Credit.** (Obj. 3)

    a. Which credits discussed in the chapter are combined into the general business credit?

    b. What option is available to taxpayers who are unable to use all of the general business credit from their tax liability in the current year?

    c. When the general business credit is carried to other tax years, in what year order are the carryover credits used? If general business credits from more than one year are carried over, in what order are they used?

(Use for Problem 7.)

Form **6251**	**Alternative Minimum Tax—Individuals**	OMB No. 1545-0074
Department of the Treasury Internal Revenue Service	Go to *www.irs.gov/Form6251* for instructions and the latest information. **Attach to Form 1040, 1040-SR, or 1040-NR.**	**2022** Attachment Sequence No. **32**

Name(s) shown on Form 1040, 1040-SR, or 1040-NR	Your social security number

Part I   **Alternative Minimum Taxable Income** (See instructions for how to complete each line.)

1	Enter the amount from Form 1040 or 1040-SR, line 15, if more than zero. If Form 1040 or 1040-SR, line 15, is zero, subtract line 14 of Form 1040 or 1040-SR from line 11 of Form 1040 or 1040-SR and enter the result here. (If less than zero, enter as a negative amount.)	1
2a	If filing Schedule A (Form 1040), enter the taxes from Schedule A, line 7; otherwise, enter the amount from Form 1040 or 1040-SR, line 12	2a
b	Tax refund from Schedule 1 (Form 1040), line 1 or line 8z	2b ( )
c	Investment interest expense (difference between regular tax and AMT)	2c
d	Depletion (difference between regular tax and AMT)	2d
e	Net operating loss deduction from Schedule 1 (Form 1040), line 8a. Enter as a positive amount	2e
f	Alternative tax net operating loss deduction	2f ( )
g	Interest from specified private activity bonds exempt from the regular tax	2g
h	Qualified small business stock, see instructions	2h
i	Exercise of incentive stock options (excess of AMT income over regular tax income)	2i
j	Estates and trusts (amount from Schedule K-1 (Form 1041), box 12, code A)	2j
k	Disposition of property (difference between AMT and regular tax gain or loss)	2k
l	Depreciation on assets placed in service after 1986 (difference between regular tax and AMT)	2l
m	Passive activities (difference between AMT and regular tax income or loss)	2m
n	Loss limitations (difference between AMT and regular tax income or loss)	2n
o	Circulation costs (difference between regular tax and AMT)	2o
p	Long-term contracts (difference between AMT and regular tax income)	2p
q	Mining costs (difference between regular tax and AMT)	2q
r	Research and experimental costs (difference between regular tax and AMT)	2r
s	Income from certain installment sales before January 1, 1987	2s ( )
t	Intangible drilling costs preference	2t
3	Other adjustments, including income-based related adjustments	3
4	**Alternative minimum taxable income.** Combine lines 1 through 3. (If married filing separately and line 4 is more than $776,100, see instructions.)	4

Part II   **Alternative Minimum Tax (AMT)**

5	Exemption.

IF your filing status is...	AND line 4 is not over...	THEN enter on line 5...	
Single or head of household	$ 539,900	$ 75,900	
Married filing jointly or qualifying widow(er)	1,079,800	118,100	
Married filing separately	539,900	59,050	5
If line 4 is **over** the amount shown above for your filing status, see instructions.			

6	Subtract line 5 from line 4. If more than zero, go to line 7. If zero or less, enter -0- here and on lines 7, 9, and 11, and go to line 10.	6
7	• If you are filing Form 2555, see instructions for the amount to enter. • If you reported capital gain distributions directly on Form 1040 or 1040-SR, line 7; you reported qualified dividends on Form 1040 or 1040-SR, line 3a; **or** you had a gain on both lines 15 and 16 of Schedule D (Form 1040) (as refigured for the AMT, if necessary), complete Part III on the back and enter the amount from line 40 here. • All others: If line 6 is $206,100 or less ($103,050 or less if married filing separately), multiply line 6 by 26% (0.26). Otherwise, multiply line 6 by 28% (0.28) and subtract $4,122 ($2,061 if married filing separately) from the result.	7
8	Alternative minimum tax foreign tax credit (see instructions)	8
9	Tentative minimum tax. Subtract line 8 from line 7	9
10	Add Form 1040 or 1040-SR, line 16 (minus any tax from Form 4972), and Schedule 2 (Form 1040), line 2. Subtract from the result Schedule 3 (Form 1040), line 1 and any negative amount reported on Form 8978, line 14 (treated as a positive number). If zero or less, enter -0-. If you used Schedule J to figure your tax on Form 1040 or 1040-SR, line 16, refigure that tax without using Schedule J before completing this line. See instructions	10
11	**AMT.** Subtract line 10 from line 9. If zero or less, enter -0-. Enter here and on Schedule 2 (Form 1040), line 1	11

For Paperwork Reduction Act Notice, see your tax return instructions.	Cat. No. 13600G	Form **6251** (2022)

9. **Rehabilitation Credit.** (Obj. 3) Harriet purchased an office building that is a certified historic structure. Harriet paid $100,000 for the building, and over the next 15 months, she spent an additional $150,000 to rehabilitate it.

    a. Compute Harriet's rehabilitation credit.

    b. Compute Harriet's basis in the building for depreciation purposes if she elects to take the rehabilitation credit.

10. **Disabled Access Credit.** (Obj. 3)

    a. Can a company with $5,000,000 in gross receipts qualify for the disabled access credit? Explain.

    b. Can a company with 40 full-time employees qualify for the disabled access credit? Explain.

    c. What is the maximum disabled access credit?

11. **Credit for Small Employer Health Insurance Premiums.** (Obj. 3) In 2022, Wainrite Company paid 80% of the total costs of each employee's premiums for a qualified health plan (QHP) offered through the SHOP Marketplace. The annual health care premiums for each employee are $12,000. All of Wainrite's employees work full-time.

    a. Compute Wainrite's small employer health insurance credit if it has 8 full-time employees, average employee wages of $22,300, and 2022 is its first year buying its insurance from the SHOP Marketplace.

    b. Same as in Part a., except that average wages are $30,450.

    c. Same as in Part a., except the Wainrite has 14 full-time employees.

12. **Credit for Employer-Provided Childcare Facilities and Services.** (Obj. 3) In 2016, Sarah started a qualified childcare program for her employees. During 2022, she paid $8,000 in qualified childcare expenditures and $12,000 in qualified childcare resource and referral expenses. Compute Sarah's 2022 employer-provided childcare credit.

13. **Credit for Small Employer Pension Plan Startup Costs.** (Obj. 3) Certain employers are entitled to a tax credit for costs associated with establishing a new pension plan for their employees.

    a. Which employers qualify for this credit?

    b. Are there restrictions on the types of pension plans that are eligible for this credit?

    c. How is the credit computed? For how many years can the credit be taken?

14. **Work Opportunity Tax Credit (WOTC).** (Obj. 3) During 2021, Albacross, Inc. hired Dana, Ed, and Finn, each of whom are designated community residents. During their first year, Dana worked 1,600 hours; Ed worked 300 hours, and Finn worked 115 hours. First-year wages are as follows: Dana, $19,000; Ed, $4,400; and Finn, $2,300. Of these wages, $4,000, $3,000, and $2,000, respectively, were paid in 2021. Compute Albacross's 2022 WOTC and discuss its impact on Albacross's 2022 wage expense deduction.

15. **Work Opportunity Tax Credit (WOTC).** (Obj. 3) In August of 2021, Arthur Co. hired Jan, who is a long-term family assistance program recipient. Jan's qualified first-year and second-year wages were $9,000 and $11,500, respectively. Of her $9,000 of first-year wages, $3,200 were paid in 2021, and $5,800 in 2022. Of the $11,500 of second-year wages, $4,400 were paid in 2022 and $7,100 were paid in 2023. Compute Arthur's 2021, 2022 and 2023 WOTC.

16. **Work Opportunity Tax Credit (WOTC).** (Obj. 3) On June 8, 2020, Teresa hired a veteran with service-related disabilities. First-year wages were $22,000, of which $10,000 were paid in 2020. Compute Teresa's 2022 WOTC assuming the veteran had been unemployed for two years prior to his hire date.

17. **Work Opportunity Tax Credit (WOTC).** (Obj. 3) During 2022, Hopkins, Inc. hired three veterans, Abe, Bob, and Carl. All three were unemployed veterans with service-related disabilities. Abe had been out of work for 16 weeks, Bob for 16 months, and Carl for three weeks. Total first-year wages, together with the amount of first-year wages paid during 2022 and 2023, are shown below. Using this information, compute Hopkins' 2022 and 2023 WOTC.

	Total First Year Wages	Paid in 2022	Paid in 2023
Abe	$25,000	$ 4,000	$21,000
Bob	20,000	17,000	3,000
Carl	16,000	7,000	9,000

18. **Work Opportunity Tax Credit (WOTC).** (Obj. 3) During 2020, Jay hired two veterans, Dave and Earl. During the one-year period prior to their hiring, Dave had been unemployed for eight months, and Earl had been unemployed for two weeks. Neither veteran had a service-related disability, but Earl had been receiving food stamps at the time he was hired. Both workers were paid $12,000 in first year wages, of which $4,600 was paid during 2020. Compute Jay's 2022 WOTC.

19. **New Markets Credit.** (Obj. 3)

    a. What types of investments are eligible for the new markets credit?

    b. How is the new markets credit computed, and to which years is it available?

20. **New Markets Credit.** (Obj. 3) On January 1, 2018, a taxpayer paid $350,000 for an investment in a qualified community development equity (CDE).

    a. Calculate the taxpayer's new markets credit for 2018-2021.

    b. Describe what happens if on February 10, 2022, the taxpayer's investment no longer qualifies as a CDE.

21. **Internet Problem: Researching Instructions to Form 8882.** (Obj. 3)

    The employer-provided childcare credit allows a tax credit for 25% of qualified childcare expenses, which includes amounts paid to a qualified childcare facility that provides childcare services to employees.

    Go to the IRS website and locate Form 8882, Credit for Employer-Provided Childcare Facilities and Services. Find the information immediately following the form that describes what constitutes a qualified childcare facility. Print out that page.

    See Appendix A for instructions on use of the IRS website.

22. **Business Entity Problem:** This problem is designed for those using the "business entity" approach. **The solution may require information from Chapters 14–16.**

    a. Budget Corporation, a calendar-year corporation, has a net operating loss (NOL) of $150,000 in 2022. What may the corporation do with this loss?

    b. If the business was operated as a partnership, how would the loss be treated?

    c. If Budget was an S corporation, how would the loss be treated?

COMPREHENSIVE PROBLEM

23. (Obj. 4) Theodore R. Langley (SSN 556-00-8227) lives at 118 Oxford Ave., Oak Park, IL 60725. In 2022, he has the following income and deductions.

Income:

Salary	$105,000
State of Iowa (specified private activity bonds bought in 1997)	20,000
Interest from Bank of America	10,600

Deductions:

Cash contributions to the American Red Cross	$ 4,000
Home mortgage interest	21,520
Real estate taxes	6,850
State income taxes withheld	4,820
State income taxes paid when filing his 2019 taxes	395

In addition to the above, Ted had federal income taxes withheld of $22,908 during the year. He also paid $25,000 for $47,000 worth of stock through an incentive stock option plan at work. Ted is divorced and claims his 15-year-old daughter, Teresa Langley (SSN 882-00-6648), as a dependent. Teresa lived with her father ten months during the year.

Based on this information, prepare Ted's 2022 tax return, including Form 6251 to compute his AMT. Ted does not want to contribute $3 to the Presidential election campaign fund. He does not have a foreign bank account nor did he receive a distribution from a foreign trust. Ted is a bank manager. He signs his return on April 15, 2023.

(Use for Problem 23.)

Form **1040**	Department of the Treasury—Internal Revenue Service **U.S. Individual Income Tax Return**	**2022**	OMB No. 1545-0074	IRS Use Only—Do not write or staple in this space.

Filing Status
Check only one box.

☐ Single ☐ Married filing jointly ☐ Married filing separately (MFS) ☐ Head of household (HOH) ☐ Qualifying widow(er) (QW)

If you checked the MFS box, enter the name of your spouse. If you checked the HOH or QW box, enter the child's name if the qualifying person is a child but not your dependent:

Your first name and middle initial	Last name	Your social security number

If joint return, spouse's first name and middle initial	Last name	Spouse's social security number

Home address (number and street). If you have a P.O. box, see instructions.	Apt. no.	**Presidential Election Campaign** Check here if you, or your spouse if filing jointly, want $3 to go to this fund. Checking a box below will not change your tax or refund.

City, town, or post office. If you have a foreign address, also complete spaces below.	State	ZIP code

Foreign country name	Foreign province/state/county	Foreign postal code

☐ You ☐ Spouse

At any time during 2022, did you: (a) receive (as a reward, award, or compensation); or (b) sell, exchange, gift, or otherwise dispose of a digital asset (or a financial interest in a digital asset)? (See instructions.) ☐ Yes ☐ No

Standard Deduction

Someone can claim: ☐ You as a dependent ☐ Your spouse as a dependent

☐ Spouse itemizes on a separate return or you were a dual-status alien

Age/Blindness **You:** ☐ Were born before January 2, 1958 ☐ Are blind **Spouse:** ☐ Was born before January 2, 1958 ☐ Is blind

Dependents (see instructions):

If more than four dependents, see instructions and check here . . ☐

(1) First name Last name	(2) Social security number	(3) Relationship to you	(4) Check the box if qualifies for (see instructions):	
			Child tax credit	Credit for other dependents
			☐	☐
			☐	☐
			☐	☐
			☐	☐

Income

Attach Form(s) W-2 here. Also attach Forms W-2G and 1099-R if tax was withheld.

If you did not get a Form W-2, see instructions.

Attach Sch. B if required.

Standard Deduction for—
- Single or Married filing separately, $12,950
- Married filing jointly or Qualifying widow(er), $25,900
- Head of household, $19,400
- If you checked any box under Standard Deduction, see instructions.

1a	Total amount from Form(s) W-2, box 1 (see instructions)	**1a**	
b	Household employee wages not reported on Form(s) W-2	**1b**	
c	Tip income not reported on line 1a (see instructions)	**1c**	
d	Medicaid waiver payments not reported on Form(s) W-2 (see instructions)	**1d**	
e	Taxable dependent care benefits from Form 2441, line 26	**1e**	
f	Employer-provided adoption benefits from Form 8839, line 29	**1f**	
g	Wages from Form 8919, line 6	**1g**	
h	Other earned income (see instructions)	**1h**	
i	Nontaxable combat pay election (see instructions)	**1i**	
z	Add lines 1a through 1h	**1z**	
2a	Tax-exempt interest	**2a**		**b** Taxable interest	**2b**	
3a	Qualified dividends	**3a**		**b** Ordinary dividends	**3b**	
4a	IRA distributions	**4a**		**b** Taxable amount	**4b**	
5a	Pensions and annuities	**5a**		**b** Taxable amount	**5b**	
6a	Social security benefits	**6a**		**b** Taxable amount	**6b**	
c	If you elect to use the lump-sum election method, check here (see instructions) ☐		
7	Capital gain or (loss). Attach Schedule D if required. If not required, check here ☐	**7**	
8	Other income from Schedule 1, line 10	**8**	
9	Add lines 1z, 2b, 3b, 4b, 5b, 6b, 7, and 8. This is your **total income**	**9**	
10	Adjustments to income from Schedule 1, line 26	**10**	
11	Subtract line 10 from line 9. This is your **adjusted gross income**	**11**	
12	**Standard deduction or itemized deductions** (from Schedule A)	**12**	
13	Qualified business income deduction from Form 8995 or Form 8995-A	**13**	
14	Add lines 12 and 13	**14**	
15	Subtract line 14 from line 11. If zero or less, enter -0-. This is your **taxable income**	**15**	

For Disclosure, Privacy Act, and Paperwork Reduction Act Notice, see separate instructions. Cat. No. 11320B Form **1040** (2022)

(Use for Problem 23.)

Version A, Cycle 7

Form 1040 (2022)

Page **2**

Tax and	16	**Tax** (see instructions). Check if any from Form(s): **1** ☐ 8814 **2** ☐ 4972 **3** ☐ _____		16	
Credits	17	Amount from Schedule 2, line 3		17	
	18	Add lines 16 and 17		18	
	19	Child tax credit or credit for other dependents from Schedule 8812		19	
	20	Amount from Schedule 3, line 8		20	
	21	Add lines 19 and 20		21	
	22	Subtract line 21 from line 18. If zero or less, enter -0-		22	
	23	Other taxes, including self-employment tax, from Schedule 2, line 21		23	
	24	Add lines 22 and 23. This is your **total tax**		24	
Payments	25	Federal income tax withheld from:			
	a	Form(s) W-2	25a		
	b	Form(s) 1099	25b		
	c	Other forms (see instructions)	25c		
	d	Add lines 25a through 25c		25d	
If you have a qualifying child, attach Sch. EIC.	26	2022 estimated tax payments and amount applied from 2021 return		26	
	27	Earned income credit (EIC)	27		
	28	Additional child tax credit from Schedule 8812	28		
	29	American opportunity credit from Form 8863, line 8	29		
	30	Reserved for future use	30		
	31	Amount from Schedule 3, line 15	31		
	32	Add lines 27, 28, 29, and 31. These are your **total other payments and refundable credits**		32	
	33	Add lines 25d, 26, and 32. These are your **total payments**		33	
Refund	34	If line 33 is more than line 24, subtract line 24 from line 33. This is the amount you **overpaid**		34	
	35a	Amount of line 34 you want **refunded to you.** If Form 8888 is attached, check here ☐		35a	
Direct deposit? See instructions.	b	Routing number |_|_|_|_|_|_|_|_|	**c** Type: ☐ Checking ☐ Savings		
	d	Account number			
	36	Amount of line 34 you want **applied to your 2023 estimated tax**	36		
Amount You Owe	37	Subtract line 33 from line 24. This is the **amount you owe.** For details on how to pay, go to *www.irs.gov/Payments* or see instructions		37	
	38	Estimated tax penalty (see instructions)	38		

Third Party Designee	Do you want to allow another person to discuss this return with the IRS? See instructions	☐ **Yes.** Complete below.	☐ **No**
	Designee's name	Phone no.	Personal identification number (PIN) |_|_|_|_|_|_|

Sign Here

Under penalties of perjury, I declare that I have examined this return and accompanying schedules and statements, and to the best of my knowledge and belief, they are true, correct, and complete. Declaration of preparer (other than taxpayer) is based on all information of which preparer has any knowledge.

Joint return? See instructions. Keep a copy for your records.

Your signature	Date	Your occupation	If the IRS sent you an Identity Protection PIN, enter it here (see inst.) |_|_|_|_|_|_|
Spouse's signature. If a joint return, **both** must sign.	Date	Spouse's occupation	If the IRS sent your spouse an Identity Protection PIN, enter it here (see inst.) |_|_|_|_|_|_|
Phone no.		Email address	

Paid Preparer Use Only

Preparer's name	Preparer's signature	Date	PTIN	Check if: ☐ Self-employed
Firm's name			Phone no.	
Firm's address			Firm's EIN	

Go to *www.irs.gov/Form1040* for instructions and the latest information.

Form **1040** (2022)

(Use for Problem 23.)

SCHEDULE 1
(Form 1040)

Department of the Treasury
Internal Revenue Service

Additional Income and Adjustments to Income

Attach to Form 1040, 1040-SR, or 1040-NR.
Go to *www.irs.gov/Form1040* for instructions and the latest information.

OMB No. 1545-0074

2022

Attachment
Sequence No. **01**

Name(s) shown on Form 1040, 1040-SR, or 1040-NR | Your social security number

Part I Additional Income

1	Taxable refunds, credits, or offsets of state and local income taxes	**1**
2a	Alimony received	**2a**
b	Date of original divorce or separation agreement (see instructions):	
3	Business income or (loss). Attach Schedule C	**3**
4	Other gains or (losses). Attach Form 4797	**4**
5	Rental real estate, royalties, partnerships, S corporations, trusts, etc. Attach Schedule E	**5**
6	Farm income or (loss). Attach Schedule F	**6**
7	Unemployment compensation	**7**
8	Other income:	
a	Net operating loss	**8a** ( )
b	Gambling	**8b**
c	Cancellation of debt	**8c**
d	Foreign earned income exclusion from Form 2555	**8d** ( )
e	Income from Form 8853	**8e**
f	Income from Form 8889	**8f**
g	Alaska Permanent Fund dividends	**8g**
h	Jury duty pay	**8h**
i	Prizes and awards	**8i**
j	Activity not engaged in for profit income	**8j**
k	Stock options	**8k**
l	Income from the rental of personal property if you engaged in the rental for profit but were not in the business of renting such property	**8l**
m	Olympic and Paralympic medals and USOC prize money (see instructions)	**8m**
n	Section 951(a) inclusion (see instructions)	**8n**
o	Section 951A(a) inclusion (see instructions)	**8o**
p	Section 461(l) excess business loss adjustment	**8p**
q	Taxable distributions from an ABLE account (see instructions)	**8q**
r	Scholarship and fellowship grants not reported on Form W-2	**8r**
s	Nontaxable amount of Medicaid waiver payments included on Form 1040, line 1a or 1d	**8s** ( )
t	Pension or annuity from a nonqualifed deferred compensation plan or a nongovernmental section 457 plan	**8t**
u	Wages earned while incarcerated	**8u**
z	Other income. List type and amount: _____	**8z**
9	Total other income. Add lines 8a through 8z	**9**
10	Combine lines 1 through 7 and 9. Enter here and on Form 1040, 1040-SR, or 1040-NR, line 8	**10**

For Paperwork Reduction Act Notice, see your tax return instructions. Cat. No. 71479F Schedule 1 (Form 1040) 2022

(Use for Problem 23.)

Schedule 1 (Form 1040) 2022   Page **2**

Part II   Adjustments to Income

11	Educator expenses	11
12	Certain business expenses of reservists, performing artists, and fee-basis government officials. Attach Form 2106	12
13	Health savings account deduction. Attach Form 8889	13
14	Moving expenses for members of the Armed Forces. Attach Form 3903 . . .	14
15	Deductible part of self-employment tax. Attach Schedule SE	15
16	Self-employed SEP, SIMPLE, and qualified plans	16
17	Self-employed health insurance deduction	17
18	Penalty on early withdrawal of savings	18
19a	Alimony paid	19a
b	Recipient's SSN	
c	Date of original divorce or separation agreement (see instructions): _____	
20	IRA deduction	20
21	Student loan interest deduction	21
22	Reserved for future use	22
23	Archer MSA deduction	23
24	Other adjustments:	

a	Jury duty pay (see instructions)	24a	
b	Deductible expenses related to income reported on line 8l from the rental of personal property engaged in for profit	24b	
c	Nontaxable amount of the value of Olympic and Paralympic medals and USOC prize money reported on line 8m	24c	
d	Reforestation amortization and expenses	24d	
e	Repayment of supplemental unemployment benefits under the Trade Act of 1974	24e	
f	Contributions to section 501(c)(18)(D) pension plans	24f	
g	Contributions by certain chaplains to section 403(b) plans	24g	
h	Attorney fees and court costs for actions involving certain unlawful discrimination claims (see instructions)	24h	
i	Attorney fees and court costs you paid in connection with an award from the IRS for information you provided that helped the IRS detect tax law violations	24i	
j	Housing deduction from Form 2555	24j	
k	Excess deductions of section 67(e) expenses from Schedule K-1 (Form 1041)	24k	
z	Other adjustments. List type and amount: _____ _____	24z	

25	Total other adjustments. Add lines 24a through 24z	25
26	Add lines 11 through 23 and 25. These are your **adjustments to income**. Enter here and on Form 1040 or 1040-SR, line 10, or Form 1040-NR, line 10a	26

Schedule 1 (Form 1040) 2022

(Use for Problem 23.)

SCHEDULE 2 (Form 1040) Department of the Treasury Internal Revenue Service	**Additional Taxes** Attach to Form 1040, 1040-SR, or 1040-NR. Go to *www.irs.gov/Form1040* for instructions and the latest information.	OMB No. 1545-0074 20**22** Attachment Sequence No. **02**

Name(s) shown on Form 1040, 1040-SR, or 1040-NR · Your social security number

Part I   Tax

1	Alternative minimum tax. Attach Form 6251	1	
2	Excess advance premium tax credit repayment. Attach Form 8962	2	
3	Add lines 1 and 2. Enter here and on Form 1040, 1040-SR, or 1040-NR, line 17 . .	3	

Part II   Other Taxes

4	Self-employment tax. Attach Schedule SE	4	
5	Social security and Medicare tax on unreported tip income. Attach Form 4137	5		
6	Uncollected social security and Medicare tax on wages. Attach Form 8919	6		
7	Total additional social security and Medicare tax. Add lines 5 and 6	7	
8	Additional tax on IRAs or other tax-favored accounts. Attach Form 5329 if required. If not required, check here . . . . ☐	8	
9	Household employment taxes. Attach Schedule H	9	
10	Repayment of first-time homebuyer credit. Attach Form 5405 if required	10	
11	Additional Medicare Tax. Attach Form 8959	11	
12	Net investment income tax. Attach Form 8960	12	
13	Uncollected social security and Medicare or RRTA tax on tips or group-term life insurance from Form W-2, box 12	13	
14	Interest on tax due on installment income from the sale of certain residential lots and timeshares	14	
15	Interest on the deferred tax on gain from certain installment sales with a sales price over $150,000	15	
16	Recapture of low-income housing credit. Attach Form 8611	16	

(continued on page 2)

For Paperwork Reduction Act Notice, see your tax return instructions.   Cat. No. 71478U   Schedule 2 (Form 1040) 2022

(Use for Problem 23.)

Schedule 2 (Form 1040) 2022			Page **2**

Part II   Other Taxes *(continued)*

17	Other additional taxes:			
a	Recapture of other credits. List type, form number, and amount: _____	**17a**		
b	Recapture of federal mortgage subsidy, if you sold your home see instructions	**17b**		
c	Additional tax on HSA distributions. Attach Form 8889 . . .	**17c**		
d	Additional tax on an HSA because you didn't remain an eligible individual. Attach Form 8889	**17d**		
e	Additional tax on Archer MSA distributions. Attach Form 8853 .	**17e**		
f	Additional tax on Medicare Advantage MSA distributions. Attach Form 8853	**17f**		
g	Recapture of a charitable contribution deduction related to a fractional interest in tangible personal property	**17g**		
h	Income you received from a nonqualified deferred compensation plan that fails to meet the requirements of section 409A . . .	**17h**		
i	Compensation you received from a nonqualified deferred compensation plan described in section 457A	**17i**		
j	Section 72(m)(5) excess benefits tax	**17j**		
k	Golden parachute payments	**17k**		
l	Tax on accumulation distribution of trusts	**17l**		
m	Excise tax on insider stock compensation from an expatriated corporation	**17m**		
n	Look-back interest under section 167(g) or 460(b) from Form 8697 or 8866	**17n**		
o	Tax on non-effectively connected income for any part of the year you were a nonresident alien from Form 1040-NR	**17o**		
p	Any interest from Form 8621, line 16f, relating to distributions from, and dispositions of, stock of a section 1291 fund	**17p**		
q	Any interest from Form 8621, line 24	**17q**		
z	Any other taxes. List type and amount: _____ _____	**17z**		
18	Total additional taxes. Add lines 17a through 17z		**18**	
19	Reserved for future use		**19**	
20	Section 965 net tax liability installment from Form 965-A . . .	**20**		
21	Add lines 4, 7 through 16, and 18. These are your **total other taxes.** Enter here and on Form 1040 or 1040-SR, line 23, or Form 1040-NR, line 23b		**21**	

Schedule 2 (Form 1040) 2022

(Use for Problem 23.)

SCHEDULE A (Form 1040) Department of the Treasury Internal Revenue Service	**Itemized Deductions** Go to *www.irs.gov/ScheduleA* for instructions and the latest information. **Attach to Form 1040 or 1040-SR.** **Caution:** If you are claiming a net qualified disaster loss on Form 4684, see the instructions for line 16.	OMB No. 1545-0074 20**22** Attachment Sequence No. **07**

Name(s) shown on Form 1040 or 1040-SR | Your social security number

Medical and Dental Expenses		**Caution:** Do not include expenses reimbursed or paid by others.		
	1	Medical and dental expenses (see instructions)	1	
	2	Enter amount from Form 1040 or 1040-SR, line 11	2	
	3	Multiply line 2 by 7.5% (0.075)	3	
	4	Subtract line 3 from line 1. If line 3 is more than line 1, enter -0-		4

Taxes You Paid	5	State and local taxes.		
	a	State and local income taxes or general sales taxes. You may include either income taxes or general sales taxes on line 5a, but not both. If you elect to include general sales taxes instead of income taxes, check this box ☐	5a	
	b	State and local real estate taxes (see instructions)	5b	
	c	State and local personal property taxes	5c	
	d	Add lines 5a through 5c	5d	
	e	Enter the smaller of line 5d or $10,000 ($5,000 if married filing separately)	5e	
	6	Other taxes. List type and amount: _____	6	
	7	Add lines 5e and 6		7

Interest You Paid **Caution:** Your mortgage interest deduction may be limited. See instructions.	8	Home mortgage interest and points. If you didn't use all of your home mortgage loan(s) to buy, build, or improve your home, see instructions and check this box ☐		
	a	Home mortgage interest and points reported to you on Form 1098. See instructions if limited	8a	
	b	Home mortgage interest not reported to you on Form 1098. See instructions if limited. If paid to the person from whom you bought the home, see instructions and show that person's name, identifying no., and address _____	8b	
	c	Points not reported to you on Form 1098. See instructions for special rules	8c	
	d	Reserved for future use	8d	
	e	Add lines 8a through 8c	8e	
	9	Investment interest. Attach Form 4952 if required. See instructions	9	
	10	Add lines 8e and 9		10

Gifts to Charity **Caution:** If you made a gift and got a benefit for it, see instructions.	11	Gifts by cash or check. If you made any gift of $250 or more, see instructions	11	
	12	Other than by cash or check. If you made any gift of $250 or more, see instructions. You **must** attach Form 8283 if over $500	12	
	13	Carryover from prior year	13	
	14	Add lines 11 through 13		14

Casualty and Theft Losses	15	Casualty and theft loss(es) from a federally declared disaster (other than net qualified disaster losses). Attach Form 4684 and enter the amount from line 18 of that form. See instructions		15

Other Itemized Deductions	16	Other—from list in instructions. List type and amount: _____		16

Total Itemized Deductions	17	Add the amounts in the far right column for lines 4 through 16. Also, enter this amount on Form 1040 or 1040-SR, line 12		17
	18	If you elect to itemize deductions even though they are less than your standard deduction, check this box ☐		

For Paperwork Reduction Act Notice, see the Instructions for Form 1040.   Cat. No. 17145C   Schedule A (Form 1040) 2022

(Use for Problem 23.)

SCHEDULE B (Form 1040)	Interest and Ordinary Dividends	OMB No. 1545-0074
Department of the Treasury Internal Revenue Service	Go to *www.irs.gov/ScheduleB* for instructions and the latest information. **Attach to Form 1040 or 1040-SR.**	**2022** Attachment Sequence No. **08**

Name(s) shown on return | Your social security number

Part I

Interest

(See instructions and the Instructions for Form 1040, line 2b.)

Note: If you received a Form 1099-INT, Form 1099-OID, or substitute statement from a brokerage firm, list the firm's name as the payer and enter the total interest shown on that form.

1 List name of payer. If any interest is from a seller-financed mortgage and the buyer used the property as a personal residence, see the instructions and list this interest first. Also, show that buyer's social security number and address: | Amount

DRAFT AS OF July 7, 2022 DO NOT FILE

2	Add the amounts on line 1	**2**
3	Excludable interest on series EE and I U.S. savings bonds issued after 1989. Attach Form 8815	**3**
4	Subtract line 3 from line 2. Enter the result here and on Form 1040 or 1040-SR, line 2b	**4**

Note: If line 4 is over $1,500, you must complete Part III. | Amount

Part II

Ordinary Dividends

(See instructions and the Instructions for Form 1040, line 3b.)

Note: If you received a Form 1099-DIV or substitute statement from a brokerage firm, list the firm's name as the payer and enter the ordinary dividends shown on that form.

5 List name of payer: | **5**

6	Add the amounts on line 5. Enter the total here and on Form 1040 or 1040-SR, line 3b	**6**

Note: If line 6 is over $1,500, you must complete Part III.

Part III

Foreign Accounts and Trusts

Caution: If required, failure to file FinCEN Form 114 may result in substantial penalties. Additionally, you may be required to file Form 8938, Statement of Specified Foreign Financial Assets. See instructions.

You must complete this part if you **(a)** had over $1,500 of taxable interest or ordinary dividends; **(b)** had a foreign account; or **(c)** received a distribution from, or were a grantor of, or a transferor to, a foreign trust.

		Yes	No
7a	At any time during 2022, did you have a financial interest in or signature authority over a financial account (such as a bank account, securities account, or brokerage account) located in a foreign country? See instructions		
	If "Yes," are you required to file FinCEN Form 114, Report of Foreign Bank and Financial Accounts (FBAR), to report that financial interest or signature authority? See FinCEN Form 114 and its instructions for filing requirements and exceptions to those requirements		
b	If you are required to file FinCEN Form 114, list the name(s) of the foreign country(-ies) where the financial account(s) are located:		
8	During 2022, did you receive a distribution from, or were you the grantor of, or transferor to, a foreign trust? If "Yes," you may have to file Form 3520. See instructions		

For Paperwork Reduction Act Notice, see your tax return instructions. | Cat. No. 17146N | Schedule B (Form 1040) 2022

(Use for Problem 23.)

Form **6251**	**Alternative Minimum Tax—Individuals**	OMB No. 1545-0074
Department of the Treasury Internal Revenue Service	Go to *www.irs.gov/Form6251* for instructions and the latest information. **Attach to Form 1040, 1040-SR, or 1040-NR.**	**2022** Attachment Sequence No. **32**

Name(s) shown on Form 1040, 1040-SR, or 1040-NR	Your social security number

Part I   **Alternative Minimum Taxable Income** (See instructions for how to complete each line.)

1	Enter the amount from Form 1040 or 1040-SR, line 15, if more than zero. If Form 1040 or 1040-SR, line 15, is zero, subtract line 14 of Form 1040 or 1040-SR from line 11 of Form 1040 or 1040-SR and enter the result here. (If less than zero, enter as a negative amount.)	**1**
2a	If filing Schedule A (Form 1040), enter the taxes from Schedule A, line 7; otherwise, enter the amount from Form 1040 or 1040-SR, line 12	**2a**
b	Tax refund from Schedule 1 (Form 1040), line 1 or line 8z	**2b** ( )
c	Investment interest expense (difference between regular tax and AMT)	**2c**
d	Depletion (difference between regular tax and AMT)	**2d**
e	Net operating loss deduction from Schedule 1 (Form 1040), line 8a. Enter as a positive amount	**2e**
f	Alternative tax net operating loss deduction	**2f** ( )
g	Interest from specified private activity bonds exempt from the regular tax	**2g**
h	Qualified small business stock, see instructions	**2h**
i	Exercise of incentive stock options (excess of AMT income over regular tax income) . . .	**2i**
j	Estates and trusts (amount from Schedule K-1 (Form 1041), box 12, code A)	**2j**
k	Disposition of property (difference between AMT and regular tax gain or loss)	**2k**
l	Depreciation on assets placed in service after 1986 (difference between regular tax and AMT)	**2l**
m	Passive activities (difference between AMT and regular tax income or loss)	**2m**
n	Loss limitations (difference between AMT and regular tax income or loss)	**2n**
o	Circulation costs (difference between regular tax and AMT)	**2o**
p	Long-term contracts (difference between AMT and regular tax income)	**2p**
q	Mining costs (difference between regular tax and AMT)	**2q**
r	Research and experimental costs (difference between regular tax and AMT)	**2r**
s	Income from certain installment sales before January 1, 1987	**2s** ( )
t	Intangible drilling costs preference	**2t**
3	Other adjustments, including income-based related adjustments	**3**
4	**Alternative minimum taxable income.** Combine lines 1 through 3. (If married filing separately and line 4 is more than $776,100, see instructions.)	**4**

Part II   **Alternative Minimum Tax (AMT)**

5	Exemption.	

IF your filing status is...	AND line 4 is not over...	THEN enter on line 5...	
Single or head of household	$ 539,900	$ 75,900	
Married filing jointly or qualifying widow(er)	1,079,800	118,100	
Married filing separately	539,900	59,050	**5**

If line 4 is **over** the amount shown above for your filing status, see instructions.

6	Subtract line 5 from line 4. If more than zero, go to line 7. If zero or less, enter -0- here and on lines 7, 9, and 11, and go to line 10.	**6**
7	• If you are filing Form 2555, see instructions for the amount to enter. • If you reported capital gain distributions directly on Form 1040 or 1040-SR, line 7; you reported qualified dividends on Form 1040 or 1040-SR, line 3a; **or** you had a gain on both lines 15 and 16 of Schedule D (Form 1040) (as refigured for the AMT, if necessary), complete Part III on the back and enter the amount from line 40 here. • **All others:** If line 6 is $206,100 or less ($103,050 or less if married filing separately), multiply line 6 by 26% (0.26). Otherwise, multiply line 6 by 28% (0.28) and subtract $4,122 ($2,061 if married filing separately) from the result.	**7**
8	Alternative minimum tax foreign tax credit (see instructions)	**8**
9	Tentative minimum tax. Subtract line 8 from line 7	**9**
10	Add Form 1040 or 1040-SR, line 16 (minus any tax from Form 4972), and Schedule 2 (Form 1040), line 2. Subtract from the result Schedule 3 (Form 1040), line 1 and any negative amount reported on Form 8978, line 14 (treated as a positive number). If zero or less, enter -0-. If you used Schedule J to figure your tax on Form 1040 or 1040-SR, line 16, refigure that tax without using Schedule J before completing this line. See instructions	**10**
11	**AMT.** Subtract line 10 from line 9. If zero or less, enter -0-. Enter here and on Schedule 2 (Form 1040), line 1	**11**

For Paperwork Reduction Act Notice, see your tax return instructions.   Cat. No. 13600G   Form **6251** (2022)

(Use for Problem 23.)

Form 6251 (2022)   Page **2**

Part III   **Tax Computation Using Maximum Capital Gains Rates**
Complete Part III only if you are required to do so by line 7 or by the Foreign Earned Income Tax Worksheet in the instructions.

12	Enter the amount from Form 6251, line 6. If you are filing Form 2555, enter the amount from line 3 of the worksheet in the instructions for line 7	**12**
13	Enter the amount from line 4 of the Qualified Dividends and Capital Gain Tax Worksheet in the Instructions for Form 1040 or the amount from line 13 of the Schedule D Tax Worksheet in the Instructions for Schedule D (Form 1040), whichever applies (as refigured for the AMT, if necessary). See instructions. If you are filing Form 2555, see instructions for the amount to enter	**13**
14	Enter the amount from Schedule D (Form 1040), line 19 (as refigured for the AMT, if necessary). See instructions. If you are filing Form 2555, see instructions for the amount to enter	**14**
15	If you did not complete a Schedule D Tax Worksheet for the regular tax or the AMT, enter the amount from line 13. Otherwise, add lines 13 and 14, and enter the **smaller** of that result or the amount from line 10 of the Schedule D Tax Worksheet (as refigured for the AMT, if necessary). If you are filing Form 2555, see instructions for the amount to enter	**15**
16	Enter the **smaller** of line 12 or line 15	**16**
17	Subtract line 16 from line 12	**17**
18	If line 17 is $206,100 or less ($103,050 or less if married filing separately), multiply line 17 by 26% (0.26). Otherwise, multiply line 17 by 28% (0.28) and subtract $4,122 ($2,061 if married filing separately) from the result	**18**
19	Enter: • $83,350 if married filing jointly or qualifying widow(er), • $41,675 if single or married filing separately, or • $55,800 if head of household.	**19**
20	Enter the amount from line 5 of the Qualified Dividends and Capital Gain Tax Worksheet or the amount from line 14 of the Schedule D Tax Worksheet, whichever applies (as figured for the regular tax). If you did not complete either worksheet for the regular tax, enter the amount from Form 1040 or 1040-SR, line 15; if zero or less, enter -0-. If you are filing Form 2555, see instructions for the amount to enter	**20**
21	Subtract line 20 from line 19. If zero or less, enter -0-	**21**
22	Enter the **smaller** of line 12 or line 13	**22**
23	Enter the **smaller** of line 21 or line 22. This amount is taxed at 0%	**23**
24	Subtract line 23 from line 22	**24**
25	Enter: • $459,750 if single, • $258,600 if married filing separately, • $517,200 if married filing jointly or qualifying widow(er), or • $488,500 if head of household.	**25**
26	Enter the amount from line 21	**26**
27	Enter the amount from line 5 of the Qualified Dividends and Capital Gain Tax Worksheet or the amount from line 21 of the Schedule D Tax Worksheet, whichever applies (as figured for the regular tax). If you did not complete either worksheet for the regular tax, enter the amount from Form 1040 or 1040-SR, line 15; if zero or less, enter -0-. If you are filing Form 2555, see instructions for the amount to enter	**27**
28	Add line 26 and line 27	**28**
29	Subtract line 28 from line 25. If zero or less, enter -0-	**29**
30	Enter the smaller of line 24 or line 29	**30**
31	Multiply line 30 by 15% (0.15)	**31**
32	Add lines 23 and 30	**32**
	If lines 32 and 12 are the same, skip lines 33 through 37 and go to line 38. Otherwise, go to line 33.	
33	Subtract line 32 from line 22	**33**
34	Multiply line 33 by 20% (0.20)	**34**
	If line 14 is zero or blank, skip lines 35 through 37 and go to line 38. Otherwise, go to line 35.	
35	Add lines 17, 32, and 33	**35**
36	Subtract line 35 from line 12	**36**
37	Multiply line 36 by 25% (0.25)	**37**
38	Add lines 18, 31, 34, and 37	**38**
39	If line 12 is $206,100 or less ($103,050 or less if married filing separately), multiply line 12 by 26% (0.26). Otherwise, multiply line 12 by 28% (0.28) and subtract $4,122 ($2,061 if married filing separately) from the result	**39**
40	Enter the **smaller** of line 38 or line 39 here and on line 7. If you are filing Form 2555, do not enter this amount on line 7. Instead, enter it on line 4 of the worksheet in the instructions for line 7	**40**

Form **6251** (2022)

CUMULATIVE PROBLEM (CHAPTERS 6–12)

In February 2017, Hainey paid $140,000 for a certified historic structure ($30,000 allocated to the land). During the next 14 months, Hainey spent $150,000 to rehabilitate the building. The building was placed in service as Hainey's office building on May 4, 2018. Hainey took the rehabilitation credit in that year and used MACRS to depreciate the remaining basis in the building. On July 19, 2022, he sold the building. His amount realized from the sale was $295,000, with $35,000 allocated to the land. Compute the realized and recognized gain on the sale of the building. Be sure to discuss the nature of the gain and how it is treated in the netting process.

CUMULATIVE PROBLEM (CHAPTERS 1–12)

Jerry R. (age 52, SSN 367-00-9403) and Janet K. (age 48, SSN 361-00-4098) Apps file a joint return. They reside at 410 Vernon Avenue, Carlock, Illinois 61725-1287. Use the following information to prepare the Appses' tax return. Use the approach shown in Examples 10-12 in Chapter 11 to compute the Appses' tax liability (¶1101.03). They both elect to have $3 to go to the Presidential election campaign fund and file their return on April 10, 2023.

The Appses' household includes David A. Apps, their 12-year-old son (SSN 965-00-4381), and Edwin R. Apps (SSN 157-00-2587), Jerry's 78-year-old father. Janet and Jerry provide over half of the support of both David and Edwin. David has no income of his own; Edwin received $4,500 in nontaxable social security benefits during the year.

Jerry works as a carpenter. The information on his Form W-2 is shown below. Jerry is an active participate in his employer's 401(k) plan.

Taxable wages	$52,000
Social security and Medicare tax withheld	3,978
Federal income tax withheld	4,970
State income tax withheld	2,490

Janet owns and operates J&J Networking. The principal business code is 454390. Janet has no employer ID number. She uses the accrual basis in her business and the cost method for valuing the inventory. No changes have been made in the inventory system. Janet operated her business for all 12 months and has an office in her home that she uses exclusively and regularly for business. Janet materially participates in the business. Information relating to her business operation is as follows.

Gross receipts	$60,950
Returns and allowances	900
Beginning inventory	2,700
Purchases	28,625
Ending inventory	3,825

Expenses:

Advertising	$ 400	Office expense	$ 80
Bank service charges	24	Supplies	310
		Travel	1,035
Commissions	3,200	Meals	490
Depreciation on equipment		Business seminars	1,000
placed in service in 2018	1,700	Other business taxes	560
Dues and publications	220	Miscellaneous expenses	35
Insurance (business)	650	Postage expense	110

In addition to the above expenses, Janet uses her personal car in her business. She keeps good records of her business mileage and uses the standard mileage method. The car was first used in the business on May 1, 2018. During 2022, Janet drove 8,941 miles, of which she drove 821 for business before July 1 and 329 thereafter. The rest were personal miles.

Information related to the Appses' home:

Total area of home	1,800 square feet
Area used for business	180 square feet
FMV of home, for purposes of Form 8829, line 36	$240,000
Adjusted basis of home, for purposes of Form 8829, line 36	195,000
Value of land, Form 8829, line 37	20,000
Year the home office was first placed in service	1991
Mortgage interest	$6,250
Real estate taxes	2,400
Homeowner's insurance	680
Utilities	3,200

The Appses own a four-unit apartment building that they actively manage. They paid $150,000 for the building in 1997. Of this amount, $25,000 was allocated to the land. The Appses use MACRS to depreciate the building, which is located at 19 Sunset Road in Carlock, IL 60501. All units were rented for the entire year. Information on the apartments is shown below.

Rental revenue	$33,600
Rental expenses:	
Real estate taxes	$ 4,800
Utilities	1,780
Insurance	1,550
Cleaning and maintenance	5,200
Legal and professional fees	125
Mortgage interest	7,200
Repairs	827
Supplies	325

The Appses had other income consisting of the following. Neither Jerry nor Janet had any interest in a foreign trust or bank account.

Interest from Champion Savings	$2,750
Interest on bonds from the State of Illinois	930
Qualified dividends from General Morris Corporation	425
Qualified dividends from Eagle Corporation	150
Qualified dividends from Roper Corporation	650

The Appses have a $4,950 long-term capital loss carryover from 2020. They also sold the following shares of common stock during 2022. No cost basis was provided on any of the Form 1099-Bs.

Number of Shares	Company	Date Acquired	Cost	Date Sold	Sales Price
100	Roper Corp.	5-1-11	$5,000	6-12-22	$7,500
50	Fastco Corp.	2-14-22	3,250	7-22-22	2,950
200	Eagle Corp.	3-16-13	6,200	8-10-22	8,100
100	South Corp.	3-14-21	1,500	1-24-22	6,500

A summary of the receipts for payments the Appses made during the year includes:

Medical expenses (unreimbursed):

	Jerry	Janet	David	Edwin	Total
Prescription medicines	$ 50	$ 200	$ 25	$1,000	$1,275
Doctor bills	60	500	30	200	790
Dentist bills	150	40	200	0	390
Hospital bills	0	1,800	0	2,100	3,900
Transportation	8	72	24	16	120
Eyeglasses	0	122	125	0	247
Over-the-counter medicine	0	50	30	70	150

Taxes:

Sales tax	$1,200
Balance due on 2020 state income tax return	25
Balance due on 2020 federal income tax return	725
Real estate taxes	2,400

Interest:

Mortgage interest	$6,250
Credit card interest	975

Cash contributions:

Church	$2,300
United Way	250
Presidential election campaign	50

In addition to the cash contributions, the Appses donated five shares of S&W common stock to their church on July 30. The stock had been purchased on December 15, 2018, for $2,200. The fair market value of the stock on July 30 was $6,000.

Janet and Jerry each contribute the maximum amount allowed for 2022 to their respective (traditional) IRAs. They also make the following other payments during the year:

Rental of safe deposit box for securities	$ 120
Tax preparation fee (2021 Form 1040)	524
Jerry's union dues	1,200
Automobile registration	150

(Use for Cumulative Problem.)

Form 1040 Department of the Treasury—Internal Revenue Service
U.S. Individual Income Tax Return **2022** OMB No. 1545-0074 | IRS Use Only—Do not write or staple in this space.

Filing Status
Check only one box. | ☐ Single ☐ Married filing jointly ☐ Married filing separately (MFS) ☐ Head of household (HOH) ☐ Qualifying widow(er) (QW)
If you checked the MFS box, enter the name of your spouse. If you checked the HOH or QW box, enter the child's name if the qualifying person is a child but not your dependent:

| Your first name and middle initial | Last name | Your social security number |
| If joint return, spouse's first name and middle initial | Last name | Spouse's social security number |

Home address (number and street). If you have a P.O. box, see instructions. | Apt. no. | **Presidential Election Campaign** Check here if you, or your spouse if filing jointly, want $3 to go to this fund. Checking a box below will not change your tax or refund.

City, town, or post office. If you have a foreign address, also complete spaces below. | State | ZIP code

Foreign country name | Foreign province/state/county | Foreign postal code | ☐ You ☐ Spouse

At any time during 2022, did you: (a) receive (as a reward, award, or compensation); or (b) sell, exchange, gift, or otherwise dispose of a digital asset (or a financial interest in a digital asset)? (See instructions.) . . ☐ Yes ☐ No

Standard Deduction
Someone can claim: ☐ You as a dependent ☐ Your spouse as a dependent
☐ Spouse itemizes on a separate return or you were a dual-status alien

Age/Blindness You: ☐ Were born before January 2, 1958 ☐ Are blind **Spouse:** ☐ Was born before January 2, 1958 ☐ Is blind

Dependents (see instructions):
If more than four dependents, see instructions and check here . . ☐

(1) First name Last name	(2) Social security number	(3) Relationship to you	(4) Check the box if qualifies for (see instructions):
			Child tax credit	Credit for other dependents
			☐	☐
			☐	☐
			☐	☐
			☐	☐

Income

Attach Form(s) W-2 here. Also attach Forms W-2G and 1099-R if tax was withheld.

If you did not get a Form W-2, see instructions.

1a	Total amount from Form(s) W-2, box 1 (see instructions)	1a	
b	Household employee wages not reported on Form(s) W-2	1b	
c	Tip income not reported on line 1a (see instructions)	1c	
d	Medicaid waiver payments not reported on Form(s) W-2 (see instructions)	1d	
e	Taxable dependent care benefits from Form 2441, line 26	1e	
f	Employer-provided adoption benefits from Form 8839, line 29	1f	
g	Wages from Form 8919, line 6	1g	
h	Other earned income (see instructions)	1h	
i	Nontaxable combat pay election (see instructions) 1i		
z	Add lines 1a through 1h	1z	

Attach Sch. B if required.

2a	Tax-exempt interest . . .	2a	**b** Taxable interest	2b
3a	Qualified dividends . . .	3a	**b** Ordinary dividends	3b
4a	IRA distributions . . .	4a	**b** Taxable amount	4b
5a	Pensions and annuities . .	5a	**b** Taxable amount	5b
6a	Social security benefits . .	6a	**b** Taxable amount	6b

Standard Deduction for—
- Single or Married filing separately, $12,950
- Married filing jointly or Qualifying widow(er), $25,900
- Head of household, $19,400
- If you checked any box under *Standard Deduction,* see instructions.

c	If you elect to use the lump-sum election method, check here (see instructions) . . . . . ☐	
7	Capital gain or (loss). Attach Schedule D if required. If not required, check here . . . . ☐	7
8	Other income from Schedule 1, line 10	8
9	Add lines 1z, 2b, 3b, 4b, 5b, 6b, 7, and 8. This is your **total income**	9
10	Adjustments to income from Schedule 1, line 26	10
11	Subtract line 10 from line 9. This is your **adjusted gross income**	11
12	**Standard deduction or itemized deductions** (from Schedule A)	12
13	Qualified business income deduction from Form 8995 or Form 8995-A	13
14	Add lines 12 and 13	14
15	Subtract line 14 from line 11. If zero or less, enter -0-. This is your **taxable income**	15

For Disclosure, Privacy Act, and Paperwork Reduction Act Notice, see separate instructions. | Cat. No. 11320B | Form **1040** (2022)

(Use for Cumulative Problem.)

Version A, Cycle 7

Form 1040 (2022)   Page **2**

Tax and Credits	16	Tax (see instructions). Check if any from Form(s): 1 ☐ 8814 2 ☐ 4972 3 ☐ _____		16	
	17	Amount from Schedule 2, line 3		17	
	18	Add lines 16 and 17		18	
	19	Child tax credit or credit for other dependents from Schedule 8812		19	
	20	Amount from Schedule 3, line 8		20	
	21	Add lines 19 and 20		21	
	22	Subtract line 21 from line 18. If zero or less, enter -0-		22	
	23	Other taxes, including self-employment tax, from Schedule 2, line 21		23	
	24	Add lines 22 and 23. This is your **total tax**		24	
Payments	25	Federal income tax withheld from:			
	a	Form(s) W-2	25a		
	b	Form(s) 1099	25b		
	c	Other forms (see instructions)	25c		
	d	Add lines 25a through 25c		25d	
If you have a qualifying child, attach Sch. EIC.	26	2022 estimated tax payments and amount applied from 2021 return		26	
	27	Earned income credit (EIC)	27		
	28	Additional child tax credit from Schedule 8812	28		
	29	American opportunity credit from Form 8863, line 8	29		
	30	Reserved for future use	30		
	31	Amount from Schedule 3, line 15	31		
	32	Add lines 27, 28, 29, and 31. These are your **total other payments and refundable credits**		32	
	33	Add lines 25d, 26, and 32. These are your **total payments**		33	
Refund	34	If line 33 is more than line 24, subtract line 24 from line 33. This is the amount you **overpaid**		34	
	35a	Amount of line 34 you want **refunded to you**. If Form 8888 is attached, check here ☐		35a	
Direct deposit? See instructions.	b	Routing number ☐☐☐☐☐☐☐☐☐ c Type: ☐ Checking ☐ Savings			
	d	Account number ☐☐☐☐☐☐☐☐☐☐☐☐☐☐☐☐☐			
	36	Amount of line 34 you want **applied to your 2023 estimated tax**	36		
Amount You Owe	37	Subtract line 33 from line 24. This is the **amount you owe**. For details on how to pay, go to *www.irs.gov/Payments* or see instructions		37	
	38	Estimated tax penalty (see instructions)	38		

Third Party Designee	Do you want to allow another person to discuss this return with the IRS? See instructions ☐ **Yes.** Complete below. ☐ **No**		
	Designee's name	Phone no.	Personal identification number (PIN) ☐☐☐☐☐

Sign Here	Under penalties of perjury, I declare that I have examined this return and accompanying schedules and statements, and to the best of my knowledge and belief, they are true, correct, and complete. Declaration of preparer (other than taxpayer) is based on all information of which preparer has any knowledge.			
	Your signature	Date	Your occupation	If the IRS sent you an Identity Protection PIN, enter it here (see inst.) ☐☐☐☐☐☐
Joint return? See instructions. Keep a copy for your records.	Spouse's signature. If a joint return, **both** must sign.	Date	Spouse's occupation	If the IRS sent your spouse an Identity Protection PIN, enter it here (see inst.) ☐☐☐☐☐☐
	Phone no.	Email address		

Paid Preparer Use Only	Preparer's name	Preparer's signature	Date	PTIN	Check if: ☐ Self-employed
	Firm's name			Phone no.	
	Firm's address			Firm's EIN	

Go to *www.irs.gov/Form1040* for instructions and the latest information.   Form **1040** (2022)

(Use for Cumulative Problem.)

SCHEDULE 1 (Form 1040)	**Additional Income and Adjustments to Income**	OMB No. 1545-0074
Department of the Treasury Internal Revenue Service	Attach to Form 1040, 1040-SR, or 1040-NR. Go to *www.irs.gov/Form1040* for instructions and the latest information.	**2022** Attachment Sequence No. **01**

Name(s) shown on Form 1040, 1040-SR, or 1040-NR	**Your social security number**

Part I   Additional Income

1	Taxable refunds, credits, or offsets of state and local income taxes	**1**	
2a	Alimony received	**2a**	
b	Date of original divorce or separation agreement (see instructions):		
3	Business income or (loss). Attach Schedule C	**3**	
4	Other gains or (losses). Attach Form 4797	**4**	
5	Rental real estate, royalties, partnerships, S corporations, trusts, etc. Attach Schedule E	**5**	
6	Farm income or (loss). Attach Schedule F	**6**	
7	Unemployment compensation	**7**	
8	Other income:		
a	Net operating loss	8a ( )	
b	Gambling	8b	
c	Cancellation of debt	8c	
d	Foreign earned income exclusion from Form 2555	8d ( )	
e	Income from Form 8853	8e	
f	Income from Form 8889	8f	
g	Alaska Permanent Fund dividends	8g	
h	Jury duty pay	8h	
i	Prizes and awards	8i	
j	Activity not engaged in for profit income	8j	
k	Stock options	8k	
l	Income from the rental of personal property if you engaged in the rental for profit but were not in the business of renting such property	8l	
m	Olympic and Paralympic medals and USOC prize money (see instructions)	8m	
n	Section 951(a) inclusion (see instructions)	8n	
o	Section 951A(a) inclusion (see instructions)	8o	
p	Section 461(l) excess business loss adjustment	8p	
q	Taxable distributions from an ABLE account (see instructions)	8q	
r	Scholarship and fellowship grants not reported on Form W-2	8r	
s	Nontaxable amount of Medicaid waiver payments included on Form 1040, line 1a or 1d	8s ( )	
t	Pension or annuity from a nonqualifed deferred compensation plan or a nongovernmental section 457 plan	8t	
u	Wages earned while incarcerated	8u	
z	Other income. List type and amount: _____	8z	
9	Total other income. Add lines 8a through 8z	**9**	
10	Combine lines 1 through 7 and 9. Enter here and on Form 1040, 1040-SR, or 1040-NR, line 8	**10**	

For Paperwork Reduction Act Notice, see your tax return instructions.	Cat. No. 71479F	Schedule 1 (Form 1040) 2022

(Use for Cumulative Problem.)

Schedule 1 (Form 1040) 2022 — Page **2**

Part II Adjustments to Income

11	Educator expenses	11	
12	Certain business expenses of reservists, performing artists, and fee-basis government officials. Attach Form 2106	12	
13	Health savings account deduction. Attach Form 8889	13	
14	Moving expenses for members of the Armed Forces. Attach Form 3903	14	
15	Deductible part of self-employment tax. Attach Schedule SE	15	
16	Self-employed SEP, SIMPLE, and qualified plans	16	
17	Self-employed health insurance deduction	17	
18	Penalty on early withdrawal of savings	18	
19a	Alimony paid	19a	
b	Recipient's SSN		
c	Date of original divorce or separation agreement (see instructions):		
20	IRA deduction	20	
21	Student loan interest deduction	21	
22	Reserved for future use	22	
23	Archer MSA deduction	23	
24	Other adjustments:		
a	Jury duty pay (see instructions)	24a	
b	Deductible expenses related to income reported on line 8l from the rental of personal property engaged in for profit	24b	
c	Nontaxable amount of the value of Olympic and Paralympic medals and USOC prize money reported on line 8m	24c	
d	Reforestation amortization and expenses	24d	
e	Repayment of supplemental unemployment benefits under the Trade Act of 1974	24e	
f	Contributions to section 501(c)(18)(D) pension plans	24f	
g	Contributions by certain chaplains to section 403(b) plans	24g	
h	Attorney fees and court costs for actions involving certain unlawful discrimination claims (see instructions)	24h	
i	Attorney fees and court costs you paid in connection with an award from the IRS for information you provided that helped the IRS detect tax law violations	24i	
j	Housing deduction from Form 2555	24j	
k	Excess deductions of section 67(e) expenses from Schedule K-1 (Form 1041)	24k	
z	Other adjustments. List type and amount:	24z	
25	Total other adjustments. Add lines 24a through 24z	25	
26	Add lines 11 through 23 and 25. These are your **adjustments to income**. Enter here and on Form 1040 or 1040-SR, line 10, or Form 1040-NR, line 10a	26	

Schedule 1 (Form 1040) 2022

(Use for Cumulative Problem.)

SCHEDULE 2 **(Form 1040)** Department of the Treasury Internal Revenue Service	**Additional Taxes** Attach to Form 1040, 1040-SR, or 1040-NR. Go to *www.irs.gov/Form1040* for instructions and the latest information.	OMB No. 1545-0074 20**22** Attachment Sequence No. **02**
Name(s) shown on Form 1040, 1040-SR, or 1040-NR		Your social security number

Part I   Tax

1	Alternative minimum tax. Attach Form 6251	**1**
2	Excess advance premium tax credit repayment. Attach Form 8962	**2**
3	Add lines 1 and 2. Enter here and on Form 1040, 1040-SR, or 1040-NR, line 17 . .	**3**

Part II   Other Taxes

4	Self-employment tax. Attach Schedule SE		**4**
5	Social security and Medicare tax on unreported tip income. Attach Form 4137	**5**	
6	Uncollected social security and Medicare tax on wages. Attach Form 8919	**6**	
7	Total additional social security and Medicare tax. Add lines 5 and 6		**7**
8	Additional tax on IRAs or other tax-favored accounts. Attach Form 5329 if required. If not required, check here . . . . ☐		**8**
9	Household employment taxes. Attach Schedule H		**9**
10	Repayment of first-time homebuyer credit. Attach Form 5405 if required		**10**
11	Additional Medicare Tax. Attach Form 8959		**11**
12	Net investment income tax. Attach Form 8960		**12**
13	Uncollected social security and Medicare or RRTA tax on tips or group-term life insurance from Form W-2, box 12		**13**
14	Interest on tax due on installment income from the sale of certain residential lots and timeshares		**14**
15	Interest on the deferred tax on gain from certain installment sales with a sales price over $150,000		**15**
16	Recapture of low-income housing credit. Attach Form 8611		**16**

(continued on page 2)

For Paperwork Reduction Act Notice, see your tax return instructions.   Cat. No. 71478U   Schedule 2 (Form 1040) 2022

(Use for Cumulative Problem.)

Schedule 2 (Form 1040) 2022   Page **2**

Part II **Other Taxes** *(continued)*

17 Other additional taxes:

a Recapture of other credits. List type, form number, and amount:

_____ | **17a** |

b Recapture of federal mortgage subsidy, if you sold your home
see instructions . . . . | **17b** |

c Additional tax on HSA distributions. Attach Form 8889 . . . | **17c** |

d Additional tax on an HSA because you didn't remain an eligible
individual. Attach Form 8889 . . . . | **17d** |

e Additional tax on Archer MSA distributions. Attach Form 8853 . | **17e** |

f Additional tax on Medicare Advantage MSA distributions. Attach
Form 8853 . . . . | **17f** |

g Recapture of a charitable contribution deduction related to a
fractional interest in tangible personal property . . . . . | **17g** |

h Income you received from a nonqualified deferred compensation
plan that fails to meet the requirements of section 409A . . . | **17h** |

i Compensation you received from a nonqualified deferred
compensation plan described in section 457A . . . . | **17i** |

j Section 72(m)(5) excess benefits tax . . . . | **17j** |

k Golden parachute payments . . . . | **17k** |

l Tax on accumulation distribution of trusts . . . . | **17l** |

m Excise tax on insider stock compensation from an expatriated
corporation . . . . | **17m** |

n Look-back interest under section 167(g) or 460(b) from Form
8697 or 8866 . . . . | **17n** |

o Tax on non-effectively connected income for any part of the
year you were a nonresident alien from Form 1040-NR . . . . | **17o** |

p Any interest from Form 8621, line 16f, relating to distributions
from, and dispositions of, stock of a section 1291 fund . . . . | **17p** |

q Any interest from Form 8621, line 24 . . . . | **17q** |

z Any other taxes. List type and amount: _____

_____ | **17z** |

18 Total additional taxes. Add lines 17a through 17z . . . . | **18** |

19 Reserved for future use . . . . | **19** |

20 Section 965 net tax liability installment from Form 965-A . . . | **20** |

21 Add lines 4, 7 through 16, and 18. These are your **total other taxes**. Enter here and
on Form 1040 or 1040-SR, line 23, or Form 1040-NR, line 23b . . . . | **21** |

(Use for Cumulative Problem.)

SCHEDULE A (Form 1040) Department of the Treasury Internal Revenue Service	**Itemized Deductions** Go to *www.irs.gov/ScheduleA* for instructions and the latest information. **Attach to Form 1040 or 1040-SR.** **Caution:** If you are claiming a net qualified disaster loss on Form 4684, see the instructions for line 16.	OMB No. 1545-0074 20**22** Attachment Sequence No. **07**

Name(s) shown on Form 1040 or 1040-SR	Your social security number

Medical and Dental Expenses		**Caution:** Do not include expenses reimbursed or paid by others.		
	1	Medical and dental expenses (see instructions)	**1**	
	2	Enter amount from Form 1040 or 1040-SR, line 11 | **2** |		
	3	Multiply line 2 by 7.5% (0.075)	**3**	
	4	Subtract line 3 from line 1. If line 3 is more than line 1, enter -0-		**4**
Taxes You Paid	**5**	State and local taxes.		
	a	State and local income taxes or general sales taxes. You may include either income taxes or general sales taxes on line 5a, but not both. If you elect to include general sales taxes instead of income taxes, check this box . . . . ☐	**5a**	
	b	State and local real estate taxes (see instructions)	**5b**	
	c	State and local personal property taxes	**5c**	
	d	Add lines 5a through 5c	**5d**	
	e	Enter the smaller of line 5d or $10,000 ($5,000 if married filing separately)	**5e**	
	6	Other taxes. List type and amount: _____ _____	**6**	
	7	Add lines 5e and 6		**7**
Interest You Paid **Caution:** Your mortgage interest deduction may be limited. See instructions.	**8**	Home mortgage interest and points. If you didn't use all of your home mortgage loan(s) to buy, build, or improve your home, see instructions and check this box . . . . ☐		
	a	Home mortgage interest and points reported to you on Form 1098. See instructions if limited	**8a**	
	b	Home mortgage interest not reported to you on Form 1098. See instructions if limited. If paid to the person from whom you bought the home, see instructions and show that person's name, identifying no., and address . . . . _____ _____	**8b**	
	c	Points not reported to you on Form 1098. See instructions for special rules	**8c**	
	d	Reserved for future use	**8d**	
	e	Add lines 8a through 8c	**8e**	
	9	Investment interest. Attach Form 4952 if required. See instructions .	**9**	
	10	Add lines 8e and 9		**10**
Gifts to Charity **Caution:** If you made a gift and got a benefit for it, see instructions.	**11**	Gifts by cash or check. If you made any gift of $250 or more, see instructions	**11**	
	12	Other than by cash or check. If you made any gift of $250 or more, see instructions. You **must** attach Form 8283 if over $500. . . .	**12**	
	13	Carryover from prior year	**13**	
	14	Add lines 11 through 13		**14**
Casualty and Theft Losses	**15**	Casualty and theft loss(es) from a federally declared disaster (other than net qualified disaster losses). Attach Form 4684 and enter the amount from line 18 of that form. See instructions		**15**
Other Itemized Deductions	**16**	Other—from list in instructions. List type and amount: _____ _____		**16**
Total Itemized Deductions	**17**	Add the amounts in the far right column for lines 4 through 16. Also, enter this amount on Form 1040 or 1040-SR, line 12		**17**
	18	If you elect to itemize deductions even though they are less than your standard deduction, check this box . . . . ☐		

For Paperwork Reduction Act Notice, see the Instructions for Form 1040.	Cat. No. 17145C	Schedule A (Form 1040) 2022

(Use for Cumulative Problem.)

SCHEDULE B (Form 1040)	Interest and Ordinary Dividends	OMB No. 1545-0074
Department of the Treasury Internal Revenue Service	Go to *www.irs.gov/ScheduleB* for instructions and the latest information. Attach to Form 1040 or 1040-SR.	2022 Attachment Sequence No. 08

Name(s) shown on return | Your social security number

Part I

Interest

(See instructions and the Instructions for Form 1040, line 2b.)

Note: If you received a Form 1099-INT, Form 1099-OID, or substitute statement from a brokerage firm, list the firm's name as the payer and enter the total interest shown on that form.

1 List name of payer. If any interest is from a seller-financed mortgage and the buyer used the property as a personal residence, see the instructions and list this interest first. Also, show that buyer's social security number and address:

Amount

DRAFT AS OF July 7, 2022 DO NOT FILE

2 Add the amounts on line 1	**2**
3 Excludable interest on series EE and I U.S. savings bonds issued after 1989. Attach Form 8815	**3**
4 Subtract line 3 from line 2. Enter the result here and on Form 1040 or 1040-SR, line 2b	**4**

Note: If line 4 is over $1,500, you must complete Part III.

Part II

Ordinary Dividends

(See instructions and the Instructions for Form 1040, line 3b.)

Note: If you received a Form 1099-DIV or substitute statement from a brokerage firm, list the firm's name as the payer and enter the ordinary dividends shown on that form.

5 List name of payer:

Amount

6 Add the amounts on line 5. Enter the total here and on Form 1040 or 1040-SR, line 3b	**6**

Note: If line 6 is over $1,500, you must complete Part III.

Part III

Foreign Accounts and Trusts

Caution: If required, failure to file FinCEN Form 114 may result in substantial penalties. Additionally, you may be required to file Form 8938, Statement of Specified Foreign Financial Assets. See instructions.

You must complete this part if you (**a**) had over $1,500 of taxable interest or ordinary dividends; (**b**) had a foreign account; or (**c**) received a distribution from, or were a grantor of, or a transferor to, a foreign trust.

		Yes	No
7a	At any time during 2022, did you have a financial interest in or signature authority over a financial account (such as a bank account, securities account, or brokerage account) located in a foreign country? See instructions		
	If "Yes," are you required to file FinCEN Form 114, Report of Foreign Bank and Financial Accounts (FBAR), to report that financial interest or signature authority? See FinCEN Form 114 and its instructions for filing requirements and exceptions to those requirements		
b	If you are required to file FinCEN Form 114, list the name(s) of the foreign country(-ies) where the financial account(s) are located:		
8	During 2022, did you receive a distribution from, or were you the grantor of, or transferor to, a foreign trust? If "Yes," you may have to file Form 3520. See instructions		

For Paperwork Reduction Act Notice, see your tax return instructions.   Cat. No. 17146N   Schedule B (Form 1040) 2022

(Use for Cumulative Problem.)

SCHEDULE C (Form 1040)	**Profit or Loss From Business** (Sole Proprietorship)	OMB No. 1545-0074
Department of the Treasury Internal Revenue Service	Go to *www.irs.gov/ScheduleC* for instructions and the latest information. **Attach to Form 1040, 1040-SR, 1040-NR, or 1041; partnerships must generally file Form 1065.**	**2022** Attachment Sequence No. **09**

Name of proprietor		Social security number (SSN)

A	Principal business or profession, including product or service (see instructions)	**B** Enter code from instructions
C	Business name. If no separate business name, leave blank.	**D** Employer ID number (EIN) (see instr.)
E	Business address (including suite or room no.) City, town or post office, state, and ZIP code	

F	Accounting method: **(1)** ☐ Cash **(2)** ☐ Accrual **(3)** ☐ Other (specify)		
G	Did you "materially participate" in the operation of this business during 2022? If "No," see instructions for limit on losses	☐ Yes	☐ No
H	If you started or acquired this business during 2022, check here	☐	
I	Did you make any payments in 2022 that would require you to file Form(s) 1099? See instructions	☐ Yes	☐ No
J	If "Yes," did you or will you file required Form(s) 1099?	☐ Yes	☐ No

Part I Income

1	Gross receipts or sales. See instructions for line 1 and check the box if this income was reported to you on Form W-2 and the "Statutory employee" box on that form was not checked . . . . . ☐	**1**	
2	Returns and allowances	**2**	
3	Subtract line 2 from line 1	**3**	
4	Cost of goods sold (from line 42)	**4**	
5	**Gross profit.** Subtract line 4 from line 3	**5**	
6	Other income, including federal and state gasoline or fuel tax credit or refund (see instructions)	**6**	
7	**Gross income.** Add lines 5 and 6	**7**	

Part II Expenses. Enter expenses for business use of your home **only** on line 30.

8	Advertising	**8**		18	Office expense (see instructions) .	**18**
9	Car and truck expenses (see instructions) . . .	**9**		19	Pension and profit-sharing plans .	**19**
10	Commissions and fees .	**10**		20	Rent or lease (see instructions):	
11	Contract labor (see instructions)	**11**		a	Vehicles, machinery, and equipment	**20a**
12	Depletion	**12**		b	Other business property . . .	**20b**
13	Depreciation and section 179 expense deduction (not included in Part III) (see instructions)	**13**		21	Repairs and maintenance . . .	**21**
				22	Supplies (not included in Part III) .	**22**
				23	Taxes and licenses	**23**
				24	Travel and meals:	
14	Employee benefit programs (other than on line 19) .	**14**		a	Travel	**24a**
15	Insurance (other than health)	**15**		b	Deductible meals (see instructions)	**24b**
16	Interest (see instructions):			25	Utilities	**25**
a	Mortgage (paid to banks, etc.)	**16a**		26	Wages (less employment credits) .	**26**
b	Other	**16b**		27a	Other expenses (from line 48) . .	**27a**
17	Legal and professional services	**17**		b	**Reserved for future use** . . .	**27b**

28	**Total expenses** before expenses for business use of home. Add lines 8 through 27a	**28**	
29	Tentative profit or (loss). Subtract line 28 from line 7	**29**	
30	Expenses for business use of your home. Do not report these expenses elsewhere. Attach Form 8829 unless using the simplified method. See instructions. **Simplified method filers only:** Enter the total square footage of (a) your home: _____ and (b) the part of your home used for business: _____ . Use the Simplified Method Worksheet in the instructions to figure the amount to enter on line 30	**30**	
31	**Net profit or (loss).** Subtract line 30 from line 29. • If a profit, enter on both **Schedule 1 (Form 1040), line 3,** and on **Schedule SE, line 2.** (If you checked the box on line 1, see instructions.) Estates and trusts, enter on **Form 1041, line 3.** • If a loss, you **must** go to line 32.	**31**	
32	If you have a loss, check the box that describes your investment in this activity. See instructions. • If you checked 32a, enter the loss on both **Schedule 1 (Form 1040), line 3,** and on **Schedule SE, line 2.** (If you checked the box on line 1, see the line 31 instructions.) Estates and trusts, enter on **Form 1041, line 3.** • If you checked 32b, you **must** attach **Form 6198.** Your loss may be limited.	**32a** ☐ All investment is at risk. **32b** ☐ Some investment is not at risk.	

For Paperwork Reduction Act Notice, see the separate instructions.	Cat. No. 11334P	Schedule C (Form 1040) 2022

(Use for Cumulative Problem.)

Schedule C (Form 1040) 2022   Page **2**

Part III   **Cost of Goods Sold** (see instructions)

33   Method(s) used to
     value closing inventory: **a** ☐ Cost   **b** ☐ Lower of cost or market   **c** ☐ Other (attach explanation)

34   Was there any change in determining quantities, costs, or valuations between opening and closing inventory?
     If "Yes," attach explanation . . . . ☐ **Yes**   ☐ **No**

35   Inventory at beginning of year. If different from last year's closing inventory, attach explanation . . | 35 |

36   Purchases less cost of items withdrawn for personal use . . . . | 36 |

37   Cost of labor. Do not include any amounts paid to yourself . . . . | 37 |

38   Materials and supplies . . . . | 38 |

39   Other costs . . . . | 39 |

40   Add lines 35 through 39 . . . . | 40 |

41   Inventory at end of year . . . . | 41 |

42   **Cost of goods sold.** Subtract line 41 from line 40. Enter the result here and on line 4 . . . . . . | 42 |

Part IV   **Information on Your Vehicle.** Complete this part **only** if you are claiming car or truck expenses on line 9 and are not required to file Form 4562 for this business. See the instructions for line 13 to find out if you must file Form 4562.

43   When did you place your vehicle in service for business purposes? (month/day/year) _____ / ___ / _____

44   Of the total number of miles you drove your vehicle during 2022, enter the number of miles you used your vehicle for:

 a Business _____ **b** Commuting (see instructions) _____ **c** Other _____

45   Was your vehicle available for personal use during off-duty hours? . . . . ☐ **Yes**   ☐ **No**

46   Do you (or your spouse) have another vehicle available for personal use?. . . . . ☐ **Yes**   ☐ **No**

47a Do you have evidence to support your deduction? . . . . ☐ **Yes**   ☐ **No**

 b If "Yes," is the evidence written? . . . . ☐ **Yes**   ☐ **No**

Part V   **Other Expenses.** List below business expenses not included on lines 8–26 or line 30.

-- | |

-- | |

-- | |

-- | |

-- | |

-- | |

-- | |

-- | |

48   **Total other expenses.** Enter here and on line 27a . . . . | 48 |

Schedule C (Form 1040) 2022

(Use for Cumulative Problem.)

SCHEDULE D (Form 1040) Department of the Treasury Internal Revenue Service	**Capital Gains and Losses** Attach to Form 1040, 1040-SR, or 1040-NR. Go to *www.irs.gov/ScheduleD* for instructions and the latest information. Use Form 8949 to list your transactions for lines 1b, 2, 3, 8b, 9, and 10.	OMB No. 1545-0074 2022 Attachment Sequence No. **12**

Name(s) shown on return	Your social security number

Did you dispose of any investment(s) in a qualified opportunity fund during the tax year? ☐ **Yes** ☐ **No**
If "Yes," attach Form 8949 and see its instructions for additional requirements for reporting your gain or loss.

Part I Short-Term Capital Gains and Losses—Generally Assets Held One Year or Less (see instructions)

See instructions for how to figure the amounts to enter on the lines below. This form may be easier to complete if you round off cents to whole dollars.	**(d)** Proceeds (sales price)	**(e)** Cost (or other basis)	**(g)** Adjustments to gain or loss from Form(s) 8949, Part I, line 2, column (g)	**(h) Gain or (loss)** Subtract column (e) from column (d) and combine the result with column (g)
1a Totals for all short-term transactions reported on Form 1099-B for which basis was reported to the IRS and for which you have no adjustments (see instructions). However, if you choose to report all these transactions on Form 8949, leave this line blank and go to line 1b .				
1b Totals for all transactions reported on Form(s) 8949 with **Box A** checked				
2 Totals for all transactions reported on Form(s) 8949 with **Box B** checked				
3 Totals for all transactions reported on Form(s) 8949 with **Box C** checked				

4 Short-term gain from Form 6252 and short-term gain or (loss) from Forms 4684, 6781, and 8824 . .	**4**	
5 Net short-term gain or (loss) from partnerships, S corporations, estates, and trusts from Schedule(s) K-1	**5**	
6 Short-term capital loss carryover. Enter the amount, if any, from line 8 of your **Capital Loss Carryover Worksheet** in the instructions	**6**	( )
7 **Net short-term capital gain or (loss).** Combine lines 1a through 6 in column (h). If you have any long-term capital gains or losses, go to Part II below. Otherwise, go to Part III on the back	**7**	

Part II Long-Term Capital Gains and Losses—Generally Assets Held More Than One Year (see instructions)

See instructions for how to figure the amounts to enter on the lines below. This form may be easier to complete if you round off cents to whole dollars.	**(d)** Proceeds (sales price)	**(e)** Cost (or other basis)	**(g)** Adjustments to gain or loss from Form(s) 8949, Part II, line 2, column (g)	**(h) Gain or (loss)** Subtract column (e) from column (d) and combine the result with column (g)
8a Totals for all long-term transactions reported on Form 1099-B for which basis was reported to the IRS and for which you have no adjustments (see instructions). However, if you choose to report all these transactions on Form 8949, leave this line blank and go to line 8b .				
8b Totals for all transactions reported on Form(s) 8949 with **Box D** checked				
9 Totals for all transactions reported on Form(s) 8949 with **Box E** checked				
10 Totals for all transactions reported on Form(s) 8949 with **Box F** checked				

11 Gain from Form 4797, Part I; long-term gain from Forms 2439 and 6252; and long-term gain or (loss) from Forms 4684, 6781, and 8824	**11**	
12 Net long-term gain or (loss) from partnerships, S corporations, estates, and trusts from Schedule(s) K-1	**12**	
13 Capital gain distributions. See the instructions	**13**	
14 Long-term capital loss carryover. Enter the amount, if any, from line 13 of your **Capital Loss Carryover Worksheet** in the instructions	**14**	( )
15 **Net long-term capital gain or (loss).** Combine lines 8a through 14 in column (h). Then, go to Part III on the back	**15**	

For Paperwork Reduction Act Notice, see your tax return instructions.	Cat. No. 11338H	Schedule D (Form 1040) 2022

(Use for Cumulative Problem.)

Schedule D (Form 1040) 2022   Page **2**

Part III   **Summary**

16   Combine lines 7 and 15 and enter the result . . . .   **16** |_____

- If line 16 is a **gain**, enter the amount from line 16 on Form 1040, 1040-SR, or 1040-NR, line 7. Then, go to line 17 below.
- If line 16 is a **loss**, skip lines 17 through 20 below. Then, go to line 21. Also be sure to complete line 22.
- If line 16 is **zero**, skip lines 17 through 21 below and enter -0- on Form 1040, 1040-SR, or 1040-NR, line 7. Then, go to line 22.

17   Are lines 15 and 16 **both** gains?
     ☐ **Yes.** Go to line 18.
     ☐ **No.** Skip lines 18 through 21, and go to line 22.

18   If you are required to complete the **28% Rate Gain Worksheet** (see instructions), enter the amount, if any, from line 7 of that worksheet . . . .   **18** |_____

19   If you are required to complete the **Unrecaptured Section 1250 Gain Worksheet** (see instructions), enter the amount, if any, from line 18 of that worksheet . . . .   **19** |_____

20   Are lines 18 and 19 both zero or blank and you are not filing Form 4952?
     ☐ **Yes.** Complete the **Qualified Dividends and Capital Gain Tax Worksheet** in the instructions for Form 1040, line 16. **Don't** complete lines 21 and 22 below.

     ☐ **No.** Complete the **Schedule D Tax Worksheet** in the instructions. **Don't** complete lines 21 and 22 below.

21   If line 16 is a loss, enter here and on Form 1040, 1040-SR, or 1040-NR, line 7, the **smaller** of:

     • The loss on line 16; or   } . . . .   **21** (_____)
     • ($3,000), or if married filing separately, ($1,500) }

     Note: When figuring which amount is smaller, treat both amounts as positive numbers.

22   Do you have qualified dividends on Form 1040, 1040-SR, or 1040-NR, line 3a?

     ☐ **Yes.** Complete the **Qualified Dividends and Capital Gain Tax Worksheet** in the instructions for Form 1040, line 16.

     ☐ **No.** Complete the rest of Form 1040, 1040-SR, or 1040-NR.

Schedule D (Form 1040) 2022

(Use for Cumulative Problem.)

Form **8949**	Sales and Other Dispositions of Capital Assets	OMB No. 1545-0074
Department of the Treasury Internal Revenue Service	Go to *www.irs.gov/Form8949* for instructions and the latest information. **File with your Schedule D to list your transactions for lines 1b, 2, 3, 8b, 9, and 10 of Schedule D.**	**2022** Attachment Sequence No. **12A**
Name(s) shown on return		Social security number or taxpayer identification number

Before you check Box A, B, or C below, see whether you received any Form(s) 1099-B or substitute statement(s) from your broker. A substitute statement will have the same information as Form 1099-B. Either will show whether your basis (usually your cost) was reported to the IRS by your broker and may even tell you which box to check.

Part I **Short-Term.** Transactions involving capital assets you held 1 year or less are generally short-term (see instructions). For long-term transactions, see page 2.

Note: You may aggregate all short-term transactions reported on Form(s) 1099-B showing basis was reported to the IRS and for which no adjustments or codes are required. Enter the totals directly on Schedule D, line 1a; you aren't required to report these transactions on Form 8949 (see instructions).

You *must* **check Box A, B,** *or* **C below. Check only one box.** If more than one box applies for your short-term transactions, complete a separate Form 8949, page 1, for each applicable box. If you have more short-term transactions than will fit on this page for one or more of the boxes, complete as many forms with the same box checked as you need.

☐ **(A)** Short-term transactions reported on Form(s) 1099-B showing basis was reported to the IRS (see **Note** above)
☐ **(B)** Short-term transactions reported on Form(s) 1099-B showing basis **wasn't** reported to the IRS
☐ **(C)** Short-term transactions not reported to you on Form 1099-B

1 (a) Description of property (Example: 100 sh. XYZ Co.)	(b) Date acquired (Mo., day, yr.)	(c) Date sold or disposed of (Mo., day, yr.)	(d) Proceeds (sales price) (see instructions)	(e) Cost or other basis See the **Note** below and see *Column (e)* in the separate instructions.	(f) Code(s) from instructions	(g) Amount of adjustment	(h) Gain or (loss) Subtract column (e) from column (d) and combine the result with column (g).
2 Totals. Add the amounts in columns (d), (e), (g), and (h) (subtract negative amounts). Enter each total here and include on your Schedule D, **line 1b** (if **Box A** above is checked), **line 2** (if **Box B** above is checked), or **line 3** (if **Box C** above is checked) . .							

Adjustment, if any, to gain or loss
If you enter an amount in column (g),
enter a code in column (f).
See the separate instructions.

Note: If you checked Box A above but the basis reported to the IRS was incorrect, enter in column (e) the basis as reported to the IRS, and enter an adjustment in column (g) to correct the basis. See *Column (g)* in the separate instructions for how to figure the amount of the adjustment.

For Paperwork Reduction Act Notice, see your tax return instructions.   Cat. No. 37768Z   Form **8949** (2022)

(Use for Cumulative Problem.)

Form 8949 (2022)						Attachment Sequence No. **12A**		Page **2**
Name(s) shown on return. Name and SSN or taxpayer identification no. not required if shown on other side						**Social security number or taxpayer identification number**		

Before you check Box D, E, or F below, see whether you received any Form(s) 1099-B or substitute statement(s) from your broker. A substitute statement will have the same information as Form 1099-B. Either will show whether your basis (usually your cost) was reported to the IRS by your broker and may even tell you which box to check.

Part II **Long-Term.** Transactions involving capital assets you held more than 1 year are generally long-term (see instructions). For short-term transactions, see page 1.

Note: You may aggregate all long-term transactions reported on Form(s) 1099-B showing basis was reported to the IRS and for which no adjustments or codes are required. Enter the totals directly on Schedule D, line 8a; you aren't required to report these transactions on Form 8949 (see instructions).

You *must* check Box D, E, *or* F below. Check only one box. If more than one box applies for your long-term transactions, complete a separate Form 8949, page 2, for each applicable box. If you have more long-term transactions than will fit on this page for one or more of the boxes, complete as many forms with the same box checked as you need.

- ☐ **(D)** Long-term transactions reported on Form(s) 1099-B showing basis was reported to the IRS (see **Note** above)
- ☐ **(E)** Long-term transactions reported on Form(s) 1099-B showing basis **wasn't** reported to the IRS
- ☐ **(F)** Long-term transactions not reported to you on Form 1099-B

1	(a) Description of property (Example: 100 sh. XYZ Co.)	(b) Date acquired (Mo., day, yr.)	(c) Date sold or disposed of (Mo., day, yr.)	(d) Proceeds (sales price) (see instructions)	(e) Cost or other basis See the **Note** below and see *Column (e)* in the separate instructions.	(f) Code(s) from instructions	(g) Amount of adjustment	(h) Gain or (loss) Subtract column (e) from column (d) and combine the result with column (g).

Adjustment, if any, to gain or loss — If you enter an amount in column (g), enter a code in column (f). See the separate instructions.

2 Totals. Add the amounts in columns (d), (e), (g), and (h) (subtract negative amounts). Enter each total here and include on your Schedule D, **line 8b** (if **Box D** above is checked), **line 9** (if **Box E** above is checked), or **line 10** (if **Box F** above is checked) .   .

Note: If you checked Box D above but the basis reported to the IRS was incorrect, enter in column (e) the basis as reported to the IRS, and enter an adjustment in column (g) to correct the basis. See *Column (g)* in the separate instructions for how to figure the amount of the adjustment.

Form **8949** (2022)

(Use for Cumulative Problem.)

SCHEDULE E (Form 1040)	Supplemental Income and Loss	OMB No. 1545-0074
Department of the Treasury Internal Revenue Service	(From rental real estate, royalties, partnerships, S corporations, estates, trusts, REMICs, etc.) Attach to Form 1040, 1040-SR, 1040-NR, or 1041. Go to www.irs.gov/ScheduleE for instructions and the latest information.	2022 Attachment Sequence No. 13

Name(s) shown on return   Your social security number

Part I   Income or Loss From Rental Real Estate and Royalties

Note: If you are in the business of renting personal property, use **Schedule C**. See instructions. If you are an individual, report farm rental income or loss from **Form 4835** on page 2, line 40.

A   Did you make any payments in 2022 that would require you to file Form(s) 1099? See instructions . . . . ☐ Yes ☐ No
B   If "Yes," did you or will you file required Form(s) 1099? . . . . ☐ Yes ☐ No

1a   Physical address of each property (street, city, state, ZIP code)

A
B
C

1b	Type of Property (from list below)	2	For each rental real estate property listed above, report the number of fair rental and personal use days. Check the QJV box only if you meet the requirements to file as a qualified joint venture. See instructions.		Fair Rental Days	Personal Use Days	QJV
A				A			☐
B				B			☐
C				C			☐

Type of Property:
1 Single Family Residence   3 Vacation/Short-Term Rental   5 Land   7 Self-Rental
2 Multi-Family Residence   4 Commercial   6 Royalties   8 Other (describe) _____

			Properties:		
			A	B	C
Income:					
3	Rents received	3			
4	Royalties received	4			
Expenses:					
5	Advertising	5			
6	Auto and travel (see instructions)	6			
7	Cleaning and maintenance	7			
8	Commissions	8			
9	Insurance	9			
10	Legal and other professional fees	10			
11	Management fees	11			
12	Mortgage interest paid to banks, etc. (see instructions)	12			
13	Other interest	13			
14	Repairs	14			
15	Supplies	15			
16	Taxes	16			
17	Utilities	17			
18	Depreciation expense or depletion	18			
19	Other (list) _____	19			
20	Total expenses. Add lines 5 through 19	20			
21	Subtract line 20 from line 3 (rents) and/or 4 (royalties). If result is a (loss), see instructions to find out if you must file **Form 6198**	21			
22	Deductible rental real estate loss after limitation, if any, on **Form 8582** (see instructions)	22	( )	( )	( )
23a	Total of all amounts reported on line 3 for all rental properties	23a			
b	Total of all amounts reported on line 4 for all royalty properties	23b			
c	Total of all amounts reported on line 12 for all properties	23c			
d	Total of all amounts reported on line 18 for all properties	23d			
e	Total of all amounts reported on line 20 for all properties	23e			
24	**Income.** Add positive amounts shown on line 21. **Do not** include any losses		24	
25	**Losses.** Add royalty losses from line 21 and rental real estate losses from line 22. Enter total losses here		25	( )
26	**Total rental real estate and royalty income or (loss).** Combine lines 24 and 25. Enter the result here. If Parts II, III, IV, and line 40 on page 2 do not apply to you, also enter this amount on Schedule 1 (Form 1040), line 5. Otherwise, include this amount in the total on line 41 on page 2 .		26	

For Paperwork Reduction Act Notice, see the separate instructions.   Cat. No. 11344L   Schedule E (Form 1040) 2022

(Use for Cumulative Problem.)

SCHEDULE SE **(Form 1040)** Department of the Treasury Internal Revenue Service	**Self-Employment Tax** Go to *www.irs.gov/ScheduleSE* for instructions and the latest information. Attach to Form 1040, 1040-SR, or 1040-NR.	OMB No. 1545-0074 **2022** Attachment Sequence No. **17**

Name of person with self-employment income (as shown on Form 1040, 1040-SR, or 1040-NR)	Social security number of person with **self-employment** income

Part I   **Self-Employment Tax**

Note: If your only income subject to self-employment tax is **church employee income**, see instructions for how to report your income and the definition of church employee income.

A   If you are a minister, member of a religious order, or Christian Science practitioner **and** you filed Form 4361, but you had $400 or more of **other** net earnings from self-employment, check here and continue with Part I . . . . ☐

Skip lines 1a and 1b if you use the farm optional method in Part II. See instructions.

1a	Net farm profit or (loss) from Schedule F, line 34, and farm partnerships, Schedule K-1 (Form 1065), box 14, code A	**1a**	
b	If you received social security retirement or disability benefits, enter the amount of Conservation Reserve Program payments included on Schedule F, line 4b, or listed on Schedule K-1 (Form 1065), box 20, code AH	**1b**	( )

Skip line 2 if you use the nonfarm optional method in Part II. See instructions.

2	Net profit or (loss) from Schedule C, line 31; and Schedule K-1 (Form 1065), box 14, code A (other than farming). See instructions for other income to report or if you are a minister or member of a religious order	**2**	
3	Combine lines 1a, 1b, and 2	**3**	
4a	If line 3 is more than zero, multiply line 3 by 92.35% (0.9235). Otherwise, enter amount from line 3	**4a**	
	Note: If line 4a is less than $400 due to Conservation Reserve Program payments on line 1b, see instructions.		
b	If you elect one or both of the optional methods, enter the total of lines 15 and 17 here . . .	**4b**	
c	Combine lines 4a and 4b. If less than $400, **stop;** you don't owe self-employment tax. **Exception:** If less than $400 and you had **church employee income,** enter -0- and continue	**4c**	
5a	Enter your **church employee income** from Form W-2. See instructions for definition of church employee income	**5a**	
b	Multiply line 5a by 92.35% (0.9235). If less than $100, enter -0-	**5b**	
6	Add lines 4c and 5b	**6**	
7	Maximum amount of combined wages and self-employment earnings subject to social security tax or the 6.2% portion of the 7.65% railroad retirement (tier 1) tax for 2022	**7**	147,000
8a	Total social security wages and tips (total of boxes 3 and 7 on Form(s) W-2) and railroad retirement (tier 1) compensation. If $147,000 or more, skip lines 8b through 10, and go to line 11	**8a**	
b	Unreported tips subject to social security tax from Form 4137, line 10 . . .	**8b**	
c	Wages subject to social security tax from Form 8919, line 10	**8c**	
d	Add lines 8a, 8b, and 8c	**8d**	
9	Subtract line 8d from line 7. If zero or less, enter -0- here and on line 10 and go to line 11	**9**	
10	Multiply the **smaller** of line 6 or line 9 by 12.4% (0.124)	**10**	
11	Multiply line 6 by 2.9% (0.029)	**11**	
12	**Self-employment tax.** Add lines 10 and 11. Enter here and on **Schedule 2 (Form 1040), line 4** . .	**12**	
13	**Deduction for one-half of self-employment tax.** Multiply line 12 by 50% (0.50). Enter here and on **Schedule 1 (Form 1040),** **line 15**	**13**	

Part II   **Optional Methods To Figure Net Earnings** (see instructions)

Farm Optional Method. You may use this method **only** if **(a)** your gross farm income[1] wasn't more than $9,060, **or (b)** your net farm profits[2] were less than $6,540.

14	Maximum income for optional methods	**14**	6,040
15	Enter the **smaller** of: two-thirds (²⁄₃) of gross farm income[1] (not less than zero) or $6,040. Also, include this amount on line 4b above	**15**	

Nonfarm Optional Method. You may use this method **only** if **(a)** your net nonfarm profits[3] were less than $6,540 and also less than 72.189% of your gross nonfarm income,[4] **and (b)** you had net earnings from self-employment of at least $400 in 2 of the prior 3 years. **Caution:** You may use this method no more than five times.

16	Subtract line 15 from line 14	**16**	
17	Enter the **smaller** of: two-thirds (²⁄₃) of gross nonfarm income[4] (not less than zero) **or** the amount on line 16. Also, include this amount on line 4b above	**17**	

[1] From Sch. F, line 9; and Sch. K-1 (Form 1065), box 14, code B.
[2] From Sch. F, line 34; and Sch. K-1 (Form 1065), box 14, code A—minus the amount you would have entered on line 1b had you not used the optional method.
[3] From Sch. C, line 31; and Sch. K-1 (Form 1065), box 14, code A.
[4] From Sch. C, line 7; and Sch. K-1 (Form 1065), box 14, code C.

For Paperwork Reduction Act Notice, see your tax return instructions.   Cat. No. 11358Z   Schedule SE (Form 1040) 2022

(Use for Cumulative Problem.)

Form 4562 — Depreciation and Amortization

Form **4562**

Department of the Treasury
Internal Revenue Service

Depreciation and Amortization
(Including Information on Listed Property)
Attach to your tax return.
Go to *www.irs.gov/Form4562* for instructions and the latest information.

OMB No. 1545-0172

2022

Attachment Sequence No. **179**

Name(s) shown on return | Business or activity to which this form relates | Identifying number

Part I **Election To Expense Certain Property Under Section 179**
Note: If you have any listed property, complete Part V before you complete Part I.

1 Maximum amount (see instructions) — **1**
2 Total cost of section 179 property placed in service (see instructions) — **2**
3 Threshold cost of section 179 property before reduction in limitation (see instructions) — **3**
4 Reduction in limitation. Subtract line 3 from line 2. If zero or less, enter -0- — **4**
5 Dollar limitation for tax year. Subtract line 4 from line 1. If zero or less, enter -0-. If married filing separately, see instructions — **5**

6	(a) Description of property	(b) Cost (business use only)	(c) Elected cost

7 Listed property. Enter the amount from line 29 — **7**
8 Total elected cost of section 179 property. Add amounts in column (c), lines 6 and 7 — **8**
9 Tentative deduction. Enter the **smaller** of line 5 or line 8 — **9**
10 Carryover of disallowed deduction from line 13 of your 2021 Form 4562 — **10**
11 Business income limitation. Enter the smaller of business income (not less than zero) or line 5. See instructions — **11**
12 Section 179 expense deduction. Add lines 9 and 10, but don't enter more than line 11 — **12**
13 Carryover of disallowed deduction to 2023. Add lines 9 and 10, less line 12 — **13**
Note: Don't use Part II or Part III below for listed property. Instead, use Part V.

Part II **Special Depreciation Allowance and Other Depreciation (Don't** include listed property. See instructions.)

14 Special depreciation allowance for qualified property (other than listed property) placed in service during the tax year. See instructions — **14**
15 Property subject to section 168(f)(1) election — **15**
16 Other depreciation (including ACRS) — **16**

Part III **MACRS Depreciation (Don't** include listed property. See instructions.)

Section A

17 MACRS deductions for assets placed in service in tax years beginning before 2022 — **17**
18 If you are electing to group any assets placed in service during the tax year into one or more general asset accounts, check here ☐

Section B—Assets Placed in Service During 2022 Tax Year Using the General Depreciation System

(a) Classification of property	(b) Month and year placed in service	(c) Basis for depreciation (business/investment use only—see instructions)	(d) Recovery period	(e) Convention	(f) Method	(g) Depreciation deduction
19a 3-year property						
b 5-year property						
c 7-year property						
d 10-year property						
e 15-year property						
f 20-year property						
g 25-year property			25 yrs.		S/L	
h Residential rental property			27.5 yrs.	MM	S/L	
			27.5 yrs.	MM	S/L	
i Nonresidential real property			39 yrs.	MM	S/L	
				MM	S/L	

Section C—Assets Placed in Service During 2022 Tax Year Using the Alternative Depreciation System

20a Class life					S/L	
b 12-year			12 yrs.		S/L	
c 30-year			30 yrs.	MM	S/L	
d 40-year			40 yrs.	MM	S/L	

Part IV **Summary** (See instructions.)

21 Listed property. Enter amount from line 28 — **21**
22 **Total.** Add amounts from line 12, lines 14 through 17, lines 19 and 20 in column (g), and line 21. Enter here and on the appropriate lines of your return. Partnerships and S corporations—see instructions — **22**
23 For assets shown above and placed in service during the current year, enter the portion of the basis attributable to section 263A costs — **23**

For Paperwork Reduction Act Notice, see separate instructions. Cat. No. 12906N Form **4562** (2022)

DRAFT AS OF June 9, 2022 DO NOT FILE

(Use for Cumulative Problem.)

Form 4562 (2022)   Page **2**

Part V **Listed Property** (Include automobiles, certain other vehicles, certain aircraft, and property used for entertainment, recreation, or amusement.)

Note: For any vehicle for which you are using the standard mileage rate or deducting lease expense, complete **only** 24a, 24b, columns (a) through (c) of Section A, all of Section B, and Section C if applicable.

Section A—Depreciation and Other Information (Caution: See the instructions for limits for passenger automobiles.)

24a Do you have evidence to support the business/investment use claimed? ☐ Yes ☐ No   24b If "Yes," is the evidence written? ☐ Yes ☐ No

(a) Type of property (list vehicles first)	(b) Date placed in service	(c) Business/investment use percentage	(d) Cost or other basis	(e) Basis for depreciation (business/investment use only)	(f) Recovery period	(g) Method/Convention	(h) Depreciation deduction	(i) Elected section 179 cost
25 Special depreciation allowance for qualified listed property placed in service during the tax year and used more than 50% in a qualified business use. See instructions .					25			
26 Property used more than 50% in a qualified business use:								
		%						
		%						
		%						
27 Property used 50% or less in a qualified business use:								
		%				S/L –		
		%				S/L –		
		%				S/L –		

28 Add amounts in column (h), lines 25 through 27. Enter here and on line 21, page 1 . | 28 |
29 Add amounts in column (i), line 26. Enter here and on line 7, page 1 . . . . | 29 |

Section B—Information on Use of Vehicles

Complete this section for vehicles used by a sole proprietor, partner, or other "more than 5% owner," or related person. If you provided vehicles to your employees, first answer the questions in Section C to see if you meet an exception to completing this section for those vehicles.

	(a) Vehicle 1		(b) Vehicle 2		(c) Vehicle 3		(d) Vehicle 4		(e) Vehicle 5		(f) Vehicle 6	
30 Total business/investment miles driven during the year (**don't** include commuting miles) .												
31 Total commuting miles driven during the year												
32 Total other personal (noncommuting) miles driven												
33 Total miles driven during the year. Add lines 30 through 32												
34 Was the vehicle available for personal use during off-duty hours?	Yes	No	Yes	No	Yes	No	Yes	No	Yes	No	Yes	No
35 Was the vehicle used primarily by a more than 5% owner or related person? . .												
36 Is another vehicle available for personal use?												

Section C—Questions for Employers Who Provide Vehicles for Use by Their Employees

Answer these questions to determine if you meet an exception to completing Section B for vehicles used by employees who **aren't** more than 5% owners or related persons. See instructions.

	Yes	No
37 Do you maintain a written policy statement that prohibits all personal use of vehicles, including commuting, by your employees?		
38 Do you maintain a written policy statement that prohibits personal use of vehicles, except commuting, by your employees? See the instructions for vehicles used by corporate officers, directors, or 1% or more owners . .		
39 Do you treat all use of vehicles by employees as personal use?		
40 Do you provide more than five vehicles to your employees, obtain information from your employees about the use of the vehicles, and retain the information received?		
41 Do you meet the requirements concerning qualified automobile demonstration use? See instructions		

Note: If your answer to 37, 38, 39, 40, or 41 is "Yes," don't complete Section B for the covered vehicles.

Part VI **Amortization**

(a) Description of costs	(b) Date amortization begins	(c) Amortizable amount	(d) Code section	(e) Amortization period or percentage	(f) Amortization for this year
42 Amortization of costs that begins during your 2022 tax year (see instructions):					

43 Amortization of costs that began before your 2022 tax year . . . . | 43 |
44 **Total.** Add amounts in column (f). See the instructions for where to report . . . . | 44 |

Form **4562** (2022)

(Use for Cumulative Problem.)

Form **8283** (Rev. December 2021) Department of the Treasury Internal Revenue Service	**Noncash Charitable Contributions** ► Attach one or more Forms 8283 to your tax return if you claimed a total deduction of over $500 for all contributed property. ► Go to *www.irs.gov/Form8283* for instructions and the latest information.	OMB No. 1545-0074 Attachment Sequence No. **155**
Name(s) shown on your income tax return		Identifying number

Note: Figure the amount of your contribution deduction before completing this form. See your tax return instructions.

Section A. Donated Property of $5,000 or Less and Publicly Traded Securities—List in this section **only** an item (or a group of similar items) for which you claimed a deduction of $5,000 or less. Also list publicly traded securities and certain other property even if the deduction is more than $5,000. See instructions.

Part I Information on Donated Property—If you need more space, attach a statement.

1	(a) Name and address of the donee organization	(b) If donated property is a vehicle (see instructions), check the box. Also enter the vehicle identification number (unless Form 1098-C is attached).	(c) Description and condition of donated property (For a vehicle, enter the year, make, model, and mileage. For securities and other property, see instructions.)
A		☐	
B		☐	
C		☐	
D		☐	
E		☐	

Note: If the amount you claimed as a deduction for an item is $500 or less, you do not have to complete columns (e), (f), and (g).

	(d) Date of the contribution	(e) Date acquired by donor (mo., yr.)	(f) How acquired by donor	(g) Donor's cost or adjusted basis	(h) Fair market value (see instructions)	(i) Method used to determine the fair market value
A						
B						
C						
D						
E						

Section B. Donated Property Over $5,000 (Except Publicly Traded Securities, Vehicles, Intellectual Property or Inventory Reportable in Section A)—Complete this section for one item (or a group of similar items) for which you claimed a deduction of more than $5,000 per item or group (except contributions reportable in Section A). Provide a separate form for each item donated unless it is part of a group of similar items. A qualified appraisal is generally required for items reportable in Section B. See instructions.

Part I Information on Donated Property

2   Check the box that describes the type of property donated.

a ☐ Art* (contribution of $20,000 or more)	**e** ☐ Other Real Estate	**i** ☐ Vehicles	
b ☐ Qualified Conservation Contribution	**f** ☐ Securities	**j** ☐ Clothing and household items	
c ☐ Equipment	**g** ☐ Collectibles**	**k** ☐ Other	
d ☐ Art* (contribution of less than $20,000)	**h** ☐ Intellectual Property		

* Art includes paintings, sculptures, watercolors, prints, drawings, ceramics, antiques, decorative arts, textiles, carpets, silver, rare manuscripts, historical memorabilia, and other similar objects.

** Collectibles include coins, stamps, books, gems, jewelry, sports memorabilia, dolls, etc., but not art as defined above.

Note: In certain cases, you must attach a qualified appraisal of the property. See instructions.

3	(a) Description of donated property (if you need more space, attach a separate statement)	(b) If any tangible personal property or real property was donated, give a brief summary of the overall physical condition of the property at the time of the gift.	(c) Appraised fair market value
A			
B			
C			

	(d) Date acquired by donor (mo., yr.)	(e) How acquired by donor	(f) Donor's cost or adjusted basis	(g) For bargain sales, enter amount received	(h) Amount claimed as a deduction (see instructions)	(i) Date of contribution (see instructions)
A						
B						
C						

For Paperwork Reduction Act Notice, see separate instructions.   Cat. No. 62299J   Form **8283** (Rev. 12-2021)

(Use for Cumulative Problem.)

Form 8283 (Rev. 12-2021)   Page **2**

Name(s) shown on your income tax return	Identifying number

Part II   **Partial Interests and Restricted Use Property (Other Than Qualified Conservation Contributions)—** Complete lines 4a through 4e if you gave less than an entire interest in a property listed in Section B, Part I. Complete lines 5a through 5c if conditions were placed on a contribution listed in Section B, Part I; also attach the required statement. See instructions.

4a Enter the letter from Section B, Part I that identifies the property for which you gave less than an entire interest ▶ _____
If Section B, Part II applies to more than one property, attach a separate statement.

b Total amount claimed as a deduction for the property listed in Section B, Part I: **(1)** For this tax year . . ▶ _____
          (2) For any prior tax years ▶ _____

c Name and address of each organization to which any such contribution was made in a prior year (complete only if different from the donee organization in Section B, Part V, below):
Name of charitable organization (donee)

Address (number, street, and room or suite no.)	City or town, state, and ZIP code

d For tangible property, enter the place where the property is located or kept ▶ _____
e Name of any person, other than the donee organization, having actual possession of the property ▶ _____

	Yes	No
5a Is there a restriction, either temporary or permanent, on the donee's right to use or dispose of the donated property?		
b Did you give to anyone (other than the donee organization or another organization participating with the donee organization in cooperative fundraising) the right to the income from the donated property or to the possession of the property, including the right to vote donated securities, to acquire the property by purchase or otherwise, or to designate the person having such income, possession, or right to acquire?		
c Is there a restriction limiting the donated property for a particular use?		

Part III   **Taxpayer (Donor) Statement**—List each item included in Section B, Part I above that the appraisal identifies as having a value of $500 or less. See instructions.

I declare that the following item(s) included in Section B, Part I above has to the best of my knowledge and belief an appraised value of not more than $500 (per item). Enter identifying letter from Section B, Part I and describe the specific item. See instructions.

▶ _____

Signature of taxpayer (donor) ▶ _____   Date ▶ _____

Part IV   **Declaration of Appraiser**

I declare that I am not the donor, the donee, a party to the transaction in which the donor acquired the property, employed by, or related to any of the foregoing persons, or married to any person who is related to any of the foregoing persons. And, if regularly used by the donor, donee, or party to the transaction, I performed the majority of my appraisals during my tax year for other persons.

Also, I declare that I perform appraisals on a regular basis; and that because of my qualifications as described in the appraisal, I am qualified to make appraisals of the type of property being valued. I certify that the appraisal fees were not based on a percentage of the appraised property value. Furthermore, I understand that a false or fraudulent overstatement of the property value as described in the qualified appraisal or this Form 8283 may subject me to the penalty under section 6701(a) (aiding and abetting the understatement of tax liability). I understand that my appraisal will be used in connection with a return or claim for refund. I also understand that, if there is a substantial or gross valuation misstatement of the value of the property claimed on the return or claim for refund that is based on my appraisal, I may be subject to a penalty under section 6695A of the Internal Revenue Code, as well as other applicable penalties. I affirm that I have not been at any time in the three-year period ending on the date of the appraisal barred from presenting evidence or testimony before the Department of the Treasury or the Internal Revenue Service pursuant to 31 U.S.C. 330(c).

Sign Here
Appraiser signature ▶	Date ▶
Appraiser name ▶	Title ▶

Business address (including room or suite no.)	Identifying number
City or town, state, and ZIP code	

Part V   **Donee Acknowledgment**

This charitable organization acknowledges that it is a qualified organization under section 170(c) and that it received the donated property as described in Section B, Part I, above on the following date ▶ _____
Furthermore, this organization affirms that in the event it sells, exchanges, or otherwise disposes of the property described in Section B, Part I (or any portion thereof) within 3 years after the date of receipt, it will file **Form 8282**, Donee Information Return, with the IRS and give the donor a copy of that form. This acknowledgment does not represent agreement with the claimed fair market value.
Does the organization intend to use the property for an unrelated use? . . . . ▶ ☐ Yes ☐ No

Name of charitable organization (donee)	Employer identification number
Address (number, street, and room or suite no.)	City or town, state, and ZIP code
Authorized signature	Title	Date

Form **8283** (Rev. 12-2021)

(Use for Cumulative Problem.)

Form **8995** Department of the Treasury Internal Revenue Service	**Qualified Business Income Deduction** **Simplified Computation** Attach to your tax return. Go to *www.irs.gov/Form8995* for instructions and the latest information.	OMB No. 1545-2294 20**22** Attachment Sequence No. **55**

Name(s) shown on return	Your taxpayer identification number

Note. You can claim the qualified business income deduction **only** if you have qualified business income from a qualified trade or business, real estate investment trust dividends, publicly traded partnership income, or a domestic production activities deduction passed through from an agricultural or horticultural cooperative. See instructions.
Use this form if your taxable income, before your qualified business income deduction, is at or below $170,050 ($340,100 if married filing jointly), and you aren't a patron of an agricultural or horticultural cooperative.

1	(a) Trade, business, or aggregation name	(b) Taxpayer identification number	(c) Qualified business income or (loss)
i			
ii			
iii			
iv			
v			

2	Total qualified business income or (loss). Combine lines 1i through 1v, column (c)	2	
3	Qualified business net (loss) carryforward from the prior year	3 ( )	
4	Total qualified business income. Combine lines 2 and 3. If zero or less, enter -0-	4	
5	Qualified business income component. Multiply line 4 by 20% (0.20)		5
6	Qualified REIT dividends and publicly traded partnership (PTP) income or (loss) (see instructions)	6	
7	Qualified REIT dividends and qualified PTP (loss) carryforward from the prior year	7 ( )	
8	Total qualified REIT dividends and PTP income. Combine lines 6 and 7. If zero or less, enter -0-	8	
9	REIT and PTP component. Multiply line 8 by 20% (0.20)		9
10	Qualified business income deduction before the income limitation. Add lines 5 and 9		10
11	Taxable income before qualified business income deduction (see instructions)	11	
12	Net capital gain (see instructions)	12	
13	Subtract line 12 from line 11. If zero or less, enter -0-	13	
14	Income limitation. Multiply line 13 by 20% (0.20)		14
15	Qualified business income deduction. Enter the smaller of line 10 or line 14. Also enter this amount on the applicable line of your return (see instructions)		15
16	Total qualified business (loss) carryforward. Combine lines 2 and 3. If greater than zero, enter -0-		16 ( )
17	Total qualified REIT dividends and PTP (loss) carryforward. Combine lines 6 and 7. If greater than zero, enter -0-		17 ( )

For Privacy Act and Paperwork Reduction Act Notice, see instructions.   Cat. No. 37806C   Form **8995** (2022)

Chapter

13

Payroll Taxes and Tax Compliance

CHAPTER CONTENTS

LEARNING OBJECTIVES

After completing Chapter 13, you should be able to:

1. Understand an employer's responsibilities for withholding income and payroll taxes from their employees' pay.
2. Describe how and when employers pay their employment taxes.
3. Compute a taxpayer's minimum required amount of tax prepayments for the year, and understand what happens when the minimum prepayments are not made.
4. Understand the audit and appeals processes and discuss taxpayer rights and tax preparers' responsibilities when completing and filing income tax returns.
5. Describe the various penalties that affect taxpayers and tax preparers who fail to comply with the tax laws.
6. Prepare the various forms introduced in this chapter, including Form W-2, Form W-3, Form W-4, Form 941, and Form 1040-X.

CHAPTER OVERVIEW

On January 1, 1943, the income of most wage earners became subject to *pay-as-you-go* withholding. Under this system, the government collects tax revenue by having the payer withhold taxes before distributing the income. This gives the government a steady cash flow and reduces tax collection problems. Withholding also lessens the cash burdens of taxpayers when they file their tax returns. When taxpayers do not have enough taxes withheld on their behalf during the year, they may be charged an underpayment penalty. Taxpayers can avoid this penalty by making quarterly estimated payments to cover the shortfall. This chapter provides background information about the tax withholding system and the estimated payment process.

The remainder of the chapter focuses on a variety of topics that relate to the tax compliance process. Included in this discussion are penalties imposed on taxpayers and tax preparers who do not abide by the tax laws. The chapter also describes the audit and appeals process that taxpayers may face when the IRS questions an item or items reported on the taxpayer's tax return. The chapter concludes with the discussion of filing an amended return. Taxpayers file an amended return when they discover an error or errors on a previously filed tax return.

¶1301   The Withholding System

Under the pay-as-you-go system, employers withhold taxes from employees' wages that approximate their employees' tax liabilities. Employers send in these withholdings to the government. To credit withholdings to the proper taxpayer accounts, the employer and each employee must have an identification number.

¶1301.01   IDENTIFICATION NUMBERS

The IRS uses computer programs to process withholding data and taxpayers' tax returns. Taxpayer identification numbers (TINs) provide the means to link related data. Taxpayers must report their TIN on tax returns they file with the IRS. Individual taxpayers use their social security number (SSN) as their TIN. Businesses that pay wages to employees use an employer identification number (EIN).

Individuals

Individuals who need a SSN apply for one by filing Form SS-5, Application for a Social Security Card. Individuals can get Form SS-5 from any social security office or from the Social Security administration website (*www.ssa.gov*). All U.S. citizens, including infants, should obtain a SSN. This allows them to be claimed as a dependent on another's tax return. Also, taxpayers must provide a SSN for each qualifying child in order to claim the child tax credit for that child (¶204.07).

Businesses

Employers put their EIN on payroll tax reporting forms, tax returns, and other government reports. Employers can get an EIN by calling the IRS or by filing Form SS-4, Application for Employer Identification Number, with the IRS online, by fax, or through the mail.

¶1301.02   WITHHOLDING FROM INCOME

For employees, withholding is based on the employee's gross (taxable) pay. From this amount, an employer withholds income taxes (federal, state, and local) and payroll taxes (social security and Medicare taxes).

¶1301.03   WITHHOLDING CERTIFICATE

Form W-4, Employee's Withholding Certificate, is the focal point of the income tax withholding system. The amount of income tax withheld from an employee's gross pay depends on the employee's filing status and the number of withholding allowances the employee claims on Form W-4. The more allowances claimed, the less tax withheld. Employees claim withholding allowances based on what their filing status is, whether they have income from more than one job, and what credits they expect to claim for children and other dependents for the current tax year. They also claim allowances based on certain other credits they expect to claim, as well as the deductions, adjustments, and nonwage income they expect to have for the year.

Employers request a Form W-4 from each employee. If an employee fails to furnish Form W-4, the employer withholds the maximum amount of taxes allowed for single taxpayers claiming zero allowances. Thus, married employees must complete Form W-4 to take advantage of the lower withholding rates that apply to married taxpayers.

There are up to five steps necessary to complete this form:

Step No.	Description	Mandatory (conditions) or optional
1	Personal Information	Mandatory
2	Multiple Jobs or Spouse Works	Mandatory if meet either condition
3	Claim Dependents	Mandatory if meet condition
4	Other Adjustments	Optional
5	Signature	Mandatory

Figure 13-1 shows the 2022 Form W-4, page 1. The remainder of the form consists of instructions and worksheets.

Figure 13-1: Form W-4 (Page 1)

Form **W-4**	**Employee's Withholding Certificate**	OMB No. 1545-0074
Department of the Treasury Internal Revenue Service	► Complete Form W-4 so that your employer can withhold the correct federal income tax from your pay. ► Give Form W-4 to your employer. ► Your withholding is subject to review by the IRS.	**2022**

Step 1:

Enter Personal Information

(a) First name and middle initial	Last name	(b) **Social security number**

Address

City or town, state, and ZIP code

► **Does your name match the name on your social security card?** If not, to ensure you get credit for your earnings, contact SSA at 800-772-1213 or go to *www.ssa.gov*.

(c) ☐ **Single** or **Married filing separately**

☐ **Married filing jointly** or **Qualifying widow(er)**

☐ **Head of household** (Check only if you're unmarried and pay more than half the costs of keeping up a home for yourself and a qualifying individual.)

Complete Steps 2–4 ONLY if they apply to you; otherwise, skip to Step 5. See page 2 for more information on each step, who can claim exemption from withholding, when to use the estimator at *www.irs.gov/W4App*, and privacy.

Step 2:

Multiple Jobs or Spouse Works

Complete this step if you (1) hold more than one job at a time, or (2) are married filing jointly and your spouse also works. The correct amount of withholding depends on income earned from all of these jobs.

Do **only one** of the following.

(a) Use the estimator at *www.irs.gov/W4App* for most accurate withholding for this step (and Steps 3–4); **or**

(b) Use the Multiple Jobs Worksheet on page 3 and enter the result in Step 4(c) below for roughly accurate withholding; **or**

(c) If there are only two jobs total, you may check this box. Do the same on Form W-4 for the other job. This option is accurate for jobs with similar pay; otherwise, more tax than necessary may be withheld . . ► ☐

TIP: To be accurate, submit a 2022 Form W-4 for all other jobs. If you (or your spouse) have self-employment income, including as an independent contractor, use the estimator.

Complete Steps 3–4(b) on Form W-4 for only ONE of these jobs. Leave those steps blank for the other jobs. (Your withholding will be most accurate if you complete Steps 3–4(b) on the Form W-4 for the highest paying job.)

Step 3:

Claim Dependents

If your total income will be $200,000 or less ($400,000 or less if married filing jointly):

Multiply the number of qualifying children under age 17 by $2,000 ► $ _____

Multiply the number of other dependents by $500 . . . . ► $ _____

Add the amounts above and enter the total here . . . .   **3** | $

Step 4 (optional):

Other Adjustments

(a) **Other income (not from jobs).** If you want tax withheld for other income you expect this year that won't have withholding, enter the amount of other income here. This may include interest, dividends, and retirement income . . . .   **4(a)** | $

(b) **Deductions.** If you expect to claim deductions other than the standard deduction and want to reduce your withholding, use the Deductions Worksheet on page 3 and enter the result here . . . .   **4(b)** | $

(c) **Extra withholding.** Enter any additional tax you want withheld each **pay period** . .   **4(c)** | $

Step 5:

Sign Here

Under penalties of perjury, I declare that this certificate, to the best of my knowledge and belief, is true, correct, and complete.

►
Employee's signature (This form is not valid unless you sign it.)

► **Date**

Employers Only

Employer's name and address	First date of employment	Employer identification number (EIN)

For Privacy Act and Paperwork Reduction Act Notice, see page 3.   Cat. No. 10220Q   Form **W-4** (2022)

¶1301.03

Steps 1 and 5 are self-explanatory. For step 2, there are two options. Either use the online estimator or the multiple jobs worksheet shown below.

Form W-4 (2022)   **Page 3**

Step 2(b)—Multiple Jobs Worksheet *(Keep for your records.)*

If you choose the option in Step 2(b) on Form W-4, complete this worksheet (which calculates the total extra tax for all jobs) on only **ONE** Form W-4. Withholding will be most accurate if you complete the worksheet and enter the result on the Form W-4 for the highest paying job.

Note: If more than one job has annual wages of more than $120,000 or there are more than three jobs, see Pub. 505 for additional tables; or, you can use the online withholding estimator at *www.irs.gov/W4App*.

1   **Two jobs.** If you have two jobs or you're married filing jointly and you and your spouse each have one job, find the amount from the appropriate table on page 4. Using the "Higher Paying Job" row and the "Lower Paying Job" column, find the value at the intersection of the two household salaries and enter that value on line 1. Then, **skip** to line 3 . . . .   **1** $ _____

2   **Three jobs.** If you and/or your spouse have three jobs at the same time, complete lines 2a, 2b, and 2c below. Otherwise, skip to line 3.

    a   Find the amount from the appropriate table on page 4 using the annual wages from the highest paying job in the "Higher Paying Job" row and the annual wages for your next highest paying job in the "Lower Paying Job" column. Find the value at the intersection of the two household salaries and enter that value on line 2a . . . .   **2a** $ _____

    b   Add the annual wages of the two highest paying jobs from line 2a together and use the total as the wages in the "Higher Paying Job" row and use the annual wages for your third job in the "Lower Paying Job" column to find the amount from the appropriate table on page 4 and enter this amount on line 2b . . . .   **2b** $ _____

    c   Add the amounts from lines 2a and 2b and enter the result on line 2c . . . .   **2c** $ _____

3   Enter the number of pay periods per year for the highest paying job. For example, if that job pays weekly, enter 52; if it pays every other week, enter 26; if it pays monthly, enter 12, etc. . . . . . .   **3** _____

4   **Divide** the annual amount on line 1 or line 2c by the number of pay periods on line 3. Enter this amount here and in **Step 4(c)** of Form W-4 for the highest paying job (along with any other additional amount you want withheld) . . . .   **4** $ _____

Step 3 anticipates the child credit and the other dependent credit that will reduce the employee's income tax liability for the year. Step 4 allows the employee to enter anticipated income that is not subject to withholding, as well as anticipated deductions in excess of the standard deduction into the formula. There is a worksheet for itemized deductions, as well as deductions for AGI.

	Step 4(b)—Deductions Worksheet *(Keep for your records.)*		
1	Enter an estimate of your 2022 itemized deductions (from Schedule A (Form 1040)). Such deductions may include qualifying home mortgage interest, charitable contributions, state and local taxes (up to $10,000), and medical expenses in excess of 7.5% of your income	1	$
2	Enter: { • $25,900 if you're married filing jointly or qualifying widow(er) • $19,400 if you're head of household • $12,950 if you're single or married filing separately }	2	$
3	If line 1 is greater than line 2, subtract line 2 from line 1 and enter the result here. If line 2 is greater than line 1, enter "-0-"	3	$
4	Enter an estimate of your student loan interest, deductible IRA contributions, and certain other adjustments (from Part II of Schedule 1 (Form 1040)). See Pub. 505 for more information	4	$
5	**Add** lines 3 and 4. Enter the result here and in **Step 4(b)** of Form W-4	5	$

Finally, step 5 contains the employee signature and date, and the employer information.

In 2019, the IRS introduced an online tax withholding estimator. It requires input in a Question and Answer format that incorporates all of the information that the Personal Allowances Worksheet contains. To access this program, go to: *https://apps.irs.gov/app/tax-withholding-estimator/income-and-withholding/*.

¶1301.04   FILLED-IN FORM W-4

INFORMATION FOR FIGURE 13-2:

Jerry J. Page starts a new job in January, 2022. Jerry completes Form W-4 for his new employer. He expects to file a joint tax return for 2022 with his wife Belle. For 2022, Jerry expects to earn $64,000; Belle expects to earn $47,000. Jerry is paid biweekly. The Pages provide all the support for their three children, who have no income. All three are eligible children for purposes of claiming the child tax credit. The Pages decide that Jerry will claim all withholding allowances for the children. The Pages estimate that they will pay or receive the following amounts during 2022.

Deductible IRA payment for Belle	$5,000
Deductible IRA payment for Jerry	6,000
Taxable interest and dividend income	750
Itemized deductions (estimated)	32,000

In Step 1, he enters his basic information and filing status. He does not check the box in step 2, since he has only one job. Step 3 shows that he will claim three dependents, all of whom are eligible for him to claim the child credit.

Step 4(a) is the proper place to report his nonwage income of $750.

Step 4(b), detailed in the worksheet, shows his anticipated total deductions in excess of the standard deduction.

Step 4(c) is necessary since he and Belle both have wage income. In essence, Jerry is forgoing some of his benefit from the lower taxable income levels, and shifting the lower brackets to Belle. Using the calculations and the chart, he determines an extra amount per pay period so that his withholding will more accurately reflect the family income. The instructions are not well-articulated, since the result from the Step 2(b) worksheet goes to Step 4(c) on the form.

The Step 2(b) worksheet is:

Form W-4 (2022)		Page **3**

Step 2(b)—Multiple Jobs Worksheet *(Keep for your records.)*

If you choose the option in Step 2(b) on Form W-4, complete this worksheet (which calculates the total extra tax for all jobs) on **only ONE** Form W-4. Withholding will be most accurate if you complete the worksheet and enter the result on the Form W-4 for the highest paying job.

Note: If more than one job has annual wages of more than $120,000 or there are more than three jobs, see Pub. 505 for additional tables; or, you can use the online withholding estimator at *www.irs.gov/W4App*.

1   **Two jobs.** If you have two jobs or you're married filing jointly and you and your spouse each have one job, find the amount from the appropriate table on page 4. Using the "Higher Paying Job" row and the "Lower Paying Job" column, find the value at the intersection of the two household salaries and enter that value on line 1. Then, **skip** to line 3 . . . .   **1** $ **4,270**

2   **Three jobs.** If you and/or your spouse have three jobs at the same time, complete lines 2a, 2b, and 2c below. Otherwise, skip to line 3.

    a   Find the amount from the appropriate table on page 4 using the annual wages from the highest paying job in the "Higher Paying Job" row and the annual wages for your next highest paying job in the "Lower Paying Job" column. Find the value at the intersection of the two household salaries and enter that value on line 2a . . . .   **2a** $ _____

    b   Add the annual wages of the two highest paying jobs from line 2a together and use the total as the wages in the "Higher Paying Job" row and use the annual wages for your third job in the "Lower Paying Job" column to find the amount from the appropriate table on page 4 and enter this amount on line 2b . . . .   **2b** $ _____

    c   Add the amounts from lines 2a and 2b and enter the result on line 2c . . . .   **2c** $ _____

3   Enter the number of pay periods per year for the highest paying job. For example, if that job pays weekly, enter 52; if it pays every other week, enter 26; if it pays monthly, enter 12, etc. **3**   **26**

4   **Divide** the annual amount on line 1 or line 2c by the number of pay periods on line 3. Enter this amount here and in **Step 4(c)** of Form W-4 for the highest paying job (along with any other additional amount you want withheld) . . . .   **4** $ **164**

Line 2 is unnecessary since Jerry and Belle have only two jobs. For line 1 it is necessary to use a chart included with the Form W-4 instructions.

Form W-4 (2022)											Page **4**
Married Filing Jointly or Qualifying Widow(er)											
Higher Paying Job Annual Taxable Wage & Salary	**Lower Paying Job Annual Taxable Wage & Salary**										
	$0 - 9,999	$10,000 - 19,999	$20,000 - 29,999	$30,000 - 39,999	$40,000 - 49,999	$50,000 - 59,999	$60,000 - 69,999	$70,000 - 79,999	$80,000 - 89,999	$90,000 - 99,999	$100,000 - 109,999	$110,000 - 120,000
$0 - 9,999	$0	$110	$850	$860	$1,020	$1,020	$1,020	$1,020	$1,020	$1,020	$1,770	$1,870
$10,000 - 19,999	110	1,110	1,860	2,060	2,220	2,220	2,220	2,220	2,220	2,970	3,970	4,070
$20,000 - 29,999	850	1,860	2,800	3,000	3,160	3,160	3,160	3,160	3,910	4,910	5,910	6,010
$30,000 - 39,999	860	2,060	3,000	3,200	3,360	3,360	3,360	4,110	5,110	6,110	7,110	7,210
$40,000 - 49,999	1,020	2,220	3,160	3,360	3,520	3,520	4,270	5,270	6,270	7,270	8,270	8,370
$50,000 - 59,999	1,020	2,220	3,160	3,360	3,520	4,270	5,270	6,270	7,270	8,270	9,270	9,370
$60,000 - 69,999	1,020	2,220	3,160	3,360	4,270	5,270	6,270	7,270	8,270	9,270	10,270	10,370
$70,000 - 79,999	1,020	2,220	3,160	4,110	5,270	6,270	7,270	8,270	9,270	10,270	11,270	11,370
$80,000 - 99,999	1,020	2,820	4,760	5,960	7,120	8,120	9,120	10,120	11,120	12,120	13,150	13,450

Finding the intersection between Jerry's income, on the vertical axis, and Belle's income on the horizontal, it appears that they will be underwithheld by $4,490 if they claim no extra withholding. Thus, Jerry needs to have his employer withhold $173 per pay period.

The Step 4(b) worksheet is:

	Step 4(b)—Deductions Worksheet *(Keep for your records.)*			
1	Enter an estimate of your 2022 itemized deductions (from Schedule A (Form 1040)). Such deductions may include qualifying home mortgage interest, charitable contributions, state and local taxes (up to $10,000), and medical expenses in excess of 7.5% of your income	1	$	32,000
2	Enter: • $25,900 if you're married filing jointly or qualifying widow(er) • $19,400 if you're head of household • $12,950 if you're single or married filing separately	2	$	25,900
3	If line 1 is greater than line 2, subtract line 2 from line 1 and enter the result here. If line 2 is greater than line 1, enter "-0-"	3	$	6,100
4	Enter an estimate of your student loan interest, deductible IRA contributions, and certain other adjustments (from Part II of Schedule 1 (Form 1040)). See Pub. 505 for more information	4	$	11,000
5	**Add** lines 3 and 4. Enter the result here and in **Step 4(b)** of Form W-4	5	$	17,100

Figure 13-2: Filled-In Form W-4

Form **W-4**	**Employee's Withholding Certificate**	OMB No. 1545-0074
Department of the Treasury Internal Revenue Service	► Complete Form W-4 so that your employer can withhold the correct federal income tax from your pay. ► Give Form W-4 to your employer. ► Your withholding is subject to review by the IRS.	2022

Step 1:

Enter Personal Information

(a) First name and middle initial	Last name	(b) Social security number
Jerry J	Page	432-00-8410

Address

12220 West Center Street

City or town, state, and ZIP code

San Diego, CA 91444-8135

► **Does your name match the name on your social security card?** If not, to ensure you get credit for your earnings, contact SSA at 800-772-1213 or go to *www.ssa.gov*.

(c) ☐ Single or Married filing separately

☑ Married filing jointly or Qualifying widow(er)

☐ Head of household (Check only if you're unmarried and pay more than half the costs of keeping up a home for yourself and a qualifying individual.)

Complete Steps 2–4 ONLY if they apply to you; otherwise, skip to Step 5. See page 2 for more information on each step, who can claim exemption from withholding, when to use the estimator at *www.irs.gov/W4App*, and privacy.

Step 2:

Multiple Jobs or Spouse Works

Complete this step if you (1) hold more than one job at a time, or (2) are married filing jointly and your spouse also works. The correct amount of withholding depends on income earned from all of these jobs.

Do **only one** of the following.

(a) Use the estimator at *www.irs.gov/W4App* for most accurate withholding for this step (and Steps 3–4); **or**

(b) Use the Multiple Jobs Worksheet on page 3 and enter the result in Step 4(c) below for roughly accurate withholding; **or**

(c) If there are only two jobs total, you may check this box. Do the same on Form W-4 for the other job. This option is accurate for jobs with similar pay; otherwise, more tax than necessary may be withheld . . ► ☐

TIP: To be accurate, submit a 2022 Form W-4 for all other jobs. If you (or your spouse) have self-employment income, including as an independent contractor, use the estimator.

Complete Steps 3–4(b) on Form W-4 for only ONE of these jobs. Leave those steps blank for the other jobs. (Your withholding will be most accurate if you complete Steps 3–4(b) on the Form W-4 for the highest paying job.)

Step 3:

Claim Dependents

If your total income will be $200,000 or less ($400,000 or less if married filing jointly):

Multiply the number of qualifying children under age 17 by $2,000 ► $ 6,000

Multiply the number of other dependents by $500 . . . . ► $ _____

Add the amounts above and enter the total here . . . .   **3** $ 6,000

Step 4 (optional):

Other Adjustments

(a) **Other income (not from jobs).** If you want tax withheld for other income you expect this year that won't have withholding, enter the amount of other income here. This may include interest, dividends, and retirement income . . . . **4(a)** $ 750

(b) **Deductions.** If you expect to claim deductions other than the standard deduction and want to reduce your withholding, use the Deductions Worksheet on page 3 and enter the result here . . . . **4(b)** $ 17,100

(c) **Extra withholding.** Enter any additional tax you want withheld each **pay period** . . **4(c)** $ 164

Step 5:

Sign Here

Under penalties of perjury, I declare that this certificate, to the best of my knowledge and belief, is true, correct, and complete.

► _____   ► _____

Employee's signature (This form is not valid unless you sign it.)   **Date**

Employers Only

Employer's name and address	First date of employment	Employer identification number (EIN)
Metro Finance Company	01-02-2022	70-7654321

For Privacy Act and Paperwork Reduction Act Notice, see page 3.   Cat. No. 10220Q   Form **W-4** (2022)

¶1301.05   CHANGING WITHHOLDING ALLOWANCES

Employees are not required to submit a new Form W-4 to their employer each year. However, the employee should make sure that the form on file reflects the proper number of allowances for the year. While the IRS does not assess penalties for being overwithheld, it does assess a penalty for being underwithheld. Therefore, when an employee's withholding allowances decrease, the employee should give a new Form W-4 to the employer within ten days of the changing event (such as divorce). When an employee's withholding allowances increase, the employee can give the employer a new Form W-4 or leave the old Form W-4 in effect. When a continuing employee submits an updated Form W-4, the employer places it in effect no later than the start of the first payroll period ending on or after the 30th day from the date when the employer received the new Form W-4.

The death of a spouse or dependent in the current year does not change an employee's withholding allowances. However, an employee should submit a new Form W-4 by December 1 to ensure that it becomes effective at the start of the next tax year. For the two years after a spouse's death, qualifying widows(ers) who have a dependent child living with them can use the married filing jointly tax rates and standard deduction (¶112.03). However, the qualifying widow(er) cannot claim a withholding allowance for the deceased spouse. A qualifying widow(er) should take this into consideration when completing a new Form W-4.

¶1301.06   EXEMPTION FROM WITHHOLDING

Certain employees can claim exemption from federal income tax withholding on Form W-4. However, the employer must still withhold social security and Medicare taxes on the employee's wages. The provision to claim exemption from withholding of federal income taxes helps people who work for a short period of time or earn small amounts. Without this provision, employers would withhold taxes from employees with no tax liability. If an employer does withhold taxes, the employee would need to file a tax return just to get back the amounts withheld.

To claim exemption from withholding in 2022, an employee must have had no federal income tax liability in 2021. Furthermore, the employee must not expect to owe any federal income taxes for 2022. Also, dependents under the age of 65 who have income in excess of $1,150 that includes more than $400 of unearned income cannot claim an exemption from withholding for 2022.

The exemption from withholding for a given year expires on February 15 of the next year. Employees who wish to continue a withholding exemption for the next year must file a new Form W-4 by February 15. Also, employees must revoke their exemption within ten days of an event that causes them to no longer qualify as exempt.

EXAMPLE 1	Marisa's parents claim her as a dependent. She has never filed a tax return. Marisa is in the process of filling out her first W-4. She expects her wages for the year to be about $1,500. She has no other sources of taxable income. Thus, her standard deduction will reduce Marisa's taxable income to $0. Marisa can claim exemption from withholding for the current year. She can do this because (1) she has no unearned income, (2) she had no federal income tax liability in the previous year, and (3) she does not expect to owe taxes in the current year.

EXAMPLE 2	Same facts as in Example 1, except that Marisa will earn about $500 of taxable interest from bonds given to her by her parents. Because Marisa's income exceeds $1,050 and more than $400 of that amount comes from unearned sources, Marisa cannot claim exemption from withholding. Any amounts her employer withholds in excess of her tax liability can be refunded to her when she files her tax return.

¶1302   FICA Taxes

FICA is a payroll tax that consists of old age, survivors, and disability insurance (OASDI) and hospital insurance (HI). On Form W-2, the IRS calls the OASDI portion the **social security tax.** It calls the HI portion the **Medicare tax.** The government assesses FICA taxes on employers and employees. Each employer withholds the employee's share of FICA from the employee's wages. The employer then adds to this amount the employer's share of FICA taxes and remits both the employer and employee amounts to the government.

¶1302.01   SOCIAL SECURITY TAXES

The amount of FICA employers are required to withhold is set by law. In 2022, employers withhold 6.2% of the first $147,000 of each employee's social security (OASDI) wages. [I.R.C. §3101(a)] When an employee works for more than one employer during the year, it is possible that the employee may end up paying too much OASDI taxes. In 2022, the maximum OASDI tax an employee is required to pay is $9,114.00 ($147,000 × 6.2%). Employers match the amount of social security taxes they withhold from their employees' pay. They then deposit both their and their employees' shares to the IRS using the rules described later in the chapter at ¶1305.01.

If the employee ends up paying more than the maximum employee's share for the year because of FICA being withheld from multiple employers, the employee claims the excess amount withheld as an additional tax payment on his or her tax return. [I.R.C. §3503] However, when a single employer mistakenly withholds too much OASDI taxes, the employee asks the employer to return the excess. Employees cannot recover excess withholding on their tax returns when the overwithholding is due to employer error. On a joint return, each spouse determines their withheld OASDI taxes separately. Then, each spouse determines if too much withholding took place by subtracting the tax withheld from the OASDI maximum for the year.

EXAMPLE 3

Forms W-2 for Ellie and Morton Levy report the OASDI information shown below. Because Ellie works for only one employer, her withheld OASDI tax is limited to $9,114.00. The Levys enter Morton's excess OASDI withholdings of $186.00 ($9,300.00 – $9,114.00) on Schedule 3 (Form 1040), Additional Credits and Payments.

Employee	Total Social Security Wages Paid in 2022	OASDI Tax Withheld
Ellie Levy:		
Melville Dye Co.	$150,000	$9,114.00
Morton Levy:		
Step Mfg. Co.	$80,000	$4,960.00
United Corp.	70,000	4,340.00
	$150,000	$9,300.00

¶1302.02   MEDICARE TAXES

The second part of FICA is the Medicare tax. For unmarried taxpayers (including those who file as qualifying widow(er)), a 1.45% tax rate applies to the first $200,000 of Medicare earnings. [I.R.C. §3101(b)(1)] A 2.35% rate (1.45% + .9% additional Medicare tax) applies to Medicare earnings in excess of that amount. [I.R.C. §3101(b)(2)] For married taxpayers who file MFJ, the 2.35% tax rate applies once the couple's combined Medicare earnings exceed $250,000. For married taxpayers who file MFS, the higher tax rate applies to the taxpayer's Medicare earnings in excess of $125,000. Medicare earnings include an employee's Medicare wages. They also include net earnings from self-employment, which is 92.35% of a sole proprietor's profit reported on Schedule C (¶706). [However, recall that through the self-employment tax, sole proprietors have paid the 1.45% employee share of Medicare taxes. Thus, any excess Medicare earnings that come from net earnings from self- employment is subject to only the .9% additional Medicare tax.]

The tax laws require employers to withhold 1.45% of the first $200,000 of each employee's Medicare wages, and 2.35% on Medicare wages in excess of $200,000. This rule applies to all employees, regardless of whether the employee is married or employed elsewhere (or self-employed) during the year. Consequently, it is possible that an employee's Medicare taxes withheld will not be the same as the employee's actual Medicare tax liability.

Employees who end up having too much Medicare tax withheld report the excess as a tax payment when they file their income tax returns. Taxpayers whose Medicare tax liability exceeds the amount of Medicare tax withheld during the year complete Form 8959, Additional Medicare Tax, to compute the amount they owe. They then report this amount on Schedule 2 (Form 1040), Part II, Other Taxes.

EXAMPLE 4

Mark and Teresa Holm file a joint return. Mark's Medicare wages are $230,000; Teresa's are $90,000. Since Mark's employer will withhold 1.45% on the first $200,000 of wages, and 2.35% on the $30,000 in excess of $200,000, Mark's Medicare tax withheld for the year is $3,605 [($200,000 × 1.45%) + ($30,000 × 2.35%)]. Teresa's Medicare tax withheld equals $1,305 ($90,000 × 1.45%). As a couple, they have a total of $4,910 of Medicare taxes withheld for the year ($3,605 + $1,305).

The Holms' Medicare tax liability for the year is $5,270 [($250,000 × 1.45%) + ($70,000 Medicare wages in excess of $250,000 × 2.35%)]. Since this amount exceeds the $4,910 they had withheld from their pay, the Holms will need to attach a completed Form 8959 to their tax return and report the $360 difference ($5,270 – $4,910) on Schedule 2 (Form 1040), Additional Taxes. They also complete Form 8959 and attach it to their Form 1040.

EXAMPLE 5

Ryan and Rita Spaulding file a joint tax return. Both work full-time. Their Medicare wages are $212,000 and $22,000, respectively. Since Ryan's Medicare wages exceed $200,000, his employer will withhold 1.45% on his first $200,000 of Medicare wages and 2.35% on the $12,000 of Medicare wages in excess of $200,000. Rita's employer will withhold Medicare taxes at the 1.45% rate on her entire Medicare wages. The Spauldings' total Medicare tax withholdings for the year are $3,501 [(($200,000 + $22,000) × 1.45%) + ($12,000 × 2.35%)]. However, the Spauldings' combined Medicare wages do not exceed $250,000. Thus, their Medicare tax liability is only $3,393 ($234,000 × 1.45%). The Spauldings will report the $108 ($3,501 – $3,393) of overwithheld Medicare taxes on Schedule 21 of Form 1040, page 2. They also complete Form 8959 and attach it to their Form 1040.

The additional .9% Medicare tax only applies to employees. The employer's share is 1.45% on all wages. For each of their employees, the employer's share of the Medicare tax is 1.45% of the employee's Medicare wages. As with social security taxes, the employer deposits both the employer and employee shares of the Medicare taxes with the IRS in accordance with the rules described in ¶1305.01.

¶1302.03   SPECIAL FICA SITUATIONS

Not all wages nor are all employees subject to FICA taxes. For example, nontaxable fringe benefits are not subject to FICA taxes (see ¶401.05 for a discussion of fringe benefits). Section 15 of IRS Publication 15, *(Circular E), Employer's Tax Guide*, provides a list of how special types of services and payments are treated for FICA tax purposes. Table 2-1 of IRS Publication 15-B, *Employer's*

Tax Guide to Fringe Benefits, provides an overview of the employment tax treatment of various fringe benefits. Some of the more common types of wages exempt from FICA taxes are included in the discussion that follows.

Family Employees of a Business

Wages paid to a spouse who works for the taxpayer's business are subject to FICA taxes (and withholding). However, wages paid to the taxpayer's child who is under the age of 18 are not subject to FICA taxes if the taxpayer's business is operated as either a sole proprietorship or a partnership in which each partner is the child's parent. Once the child turns 18, the child's wages become subject to FICA tax withholding (and employer matching).

Household Employees

Household employees are workers who provide domestic services in the taxpayer's private home. These workers include housekeepers, babysitters, private nurses, gardeners, and nannies. Normally, household employees who are paid $2,400 or more during 2022 are subject to FICA tax withholding (and employer matching). [IRS Publication 926 (2022) Page 5] However, wages paid to any person who is under the age of 18 at any point during the year are generally exempt from FICA taxes (age 21 if the domestic worker is the taxpayer's child). Also, wages paid to the taxpayer's spouse or parent for domestic services are generally exempt from FICA taxes.

Employers of household workers whose wages are subject to FICA taxes report both the amounts they withheld from their employees' pay, plus their matching share of FICA taxes, on their Form 1040. Schedule H (Form 1040), Household Employment Taxes, supports the amount reported on Schedule 2 (Form 1040), Additional Taxes.

¶1302.04   PENALTY FOR FAILURE TO COLLECT OR DEPOSIT TAXES

The IRS can impose a penalty for FICA taxes (and withheld federal income taxes) that are not properly or timely deposited. The penalty amount depends on the number of days the deposit is late, whether it involves a direct payment, and whether electronic payment was required but not used. [I.R.C. §6656]

The IRS also has the power to assess a 100% penalty against employers who fail to collect or deposit FICA taxes (and withheld federal income taxes). [I.R.C. §6672(a)] The 100% penalty only applies to the employees' share of FICA taxes (amounts withheld from employees' pay). It does not apply to the employer's share of FICA taxes. The IRS can assess the penalty against employers who willfully try to avoid withholding income and payroll taxes by classifying employees as independent contractors. (Independent contractors are treated as self-employed workers, and as such, pay self-employment taxes on their net earnings from self-employment, as discussed in ¶706.) The IRS also can assess the penalty on any person responsible for an employer's tax withholdings when that person has the authority to decide which creditors receive payment when a shortage of funds exists.

¶1303   Reporting to Employees and the Government

In January, employers prepare a Form W-2, Wage and Tax Statement, for each employee. Thus, in January 2023, employers prepare a 2022 Form W-2 for each employee. Form W-2 shows an employee's taxable wages and tips; wages and tips subject to OASDI and tips subject to Medicare tax withholding; federal income taxes withheld; and amounts withheld for OASDI and Medicare taxes. Form W-2 also reports an employee's pension plan contributions, state and local income taxes withheld, as well as other items.

¶1303.01   DISTRIBUTION OF FORMS W-2

Employers prepare six copies of Form W-2 for each employee. These copies are named Copy A, B, C, D, 1, and 2. Employers send Copy A to the Social Security Administration by January 31. If applicable, they file Copy 1 with the proper state or local government agency. Employers send Copies B, C, and 2 to each employee by January 31. The employer holds on to Copy D.

When employment ends before the close of a calendar year, employers still send former employees their copies of Form W-2 by January 31 of the next year. Former employees can request a Form W-2 before this date. When requested, employers must give former employees their W-2 by the later of 30 days after the request or 30 days after the last wage payment. Employees attach a copy of their W-2s to each tax return they file. They keep one copy for their records.

¶1303.02   FORM W-2

Copy A of Form W-2 is read by a machine. Employers must use and prepare either an official printed IRS form (*not* the version downloaded from the IRS website) or an acceptable substitute form. Further, Form W-2 must be typed and free of erasures, whiteouts, and strikeovers. The employer should make all dollar entries without dollar signs or commas, but with decimal points (00000.00). The rest of this section describes the information reported on Form W-2. Not all boxes are covered since many are self-explanatory. For a full description of all boxes on Form W-2, see the *General Instructions for Forms W-2 and W-3,* which can be found on the IRS website.

Box 12

Employers complete this box to report up to four items of information. For each item, a code and the dollar amount are listed. Examples of items reported in this box include:

- Taxable amounts for providing the employee with more than $50,000 of group life insurance (Code C)
- Employee pre-tax contributions to a 401(k) or SIMPLE 401(k) plan (Code D)
- Employee pre-tax contributions to a SEP (Code F)
- Reimbursements received from a nonaccountable reimbursement plan (Code L)
- Nontaxable moving expense reimbursements paid to members of the U.S. Armed Forces on active duty who move pursuant to a military order and incident to a permanent change of station (Code P)
- Employee pre-tax contributions to a SIMPLE plan not part of a 401(k) plan (Code S)
- Amounts received under an adoption assistance program (Code T)

Statutory Employee, Retirement Plan, Third-Party Sick Pay (Box 13)

Employers place an **X** in the proper square (box 13) to identify one of three situations.

Statutory Employee. Employers withhold FICA taxes, but not federal income taxes, from statutory employees' wages. **Statutory employees** are independent contractors who are treated as employees by statute because they work in one of four occupation groups. Group 1 includes drivers who pick up and deliver laundry or dry cleaning, or who distribute non-milk beverages or certain food products, if the driver is the employer's agent or is paid on commission. Group 2 includes full-time life insurance salespersons. Group 3 includes workers who work from home using materials provided by and returned to the employer, if the employer furnishes specifications for the work. Group 4 includes full-time traveling or city salespersons who take orders on behalf of the employer from certain customers. To qualify as a statutory employee, group members must also meet other tests that are beyond the scope of this discussion.

Retirement Plan. Employers check this square to identify the employee as an active participant in the employer's retirement plan. Recall from Chapter 4 that limits may apply to the deduction for IRA contributions for taxpayers who are active participants in an employer's qualified retirement plan (¶402.10).

Third-Party Sick Pay. Employers check this square only if the payer is a third-party sick pay provider filing Form W-2 for an insured's employee, or is an employer reporting sick pay payments made by a third party.

Other (Box 14)

Employers use this box to provide any other information they feel is necessary to their employees. Each amount is labeled by its type. Items that may be listed include union dues, health insurance premiums paid by the employee, nontaxable income, after-tax contributions to retirement plans, and educational assistance payments.

¶1303.03   FILLED-IN FORM W-2

INFORMATION FOR FIGURE 13-3:

Harriett R. Shawver works for Anderson, Berger, and Green (ABG). From Harriett's **$43,500** of wages, ABG withheld **$7,356** for federal; **$2,039** for state; **$2,697** ($43,500 × 6.2%) for social security (OASDI); and **$630.75** ($43,500 × 1.45%) for Medicare taxes. These amounts (no dollar signs or commas) appear on Harriett's W-2.

Figure 13-3: Filled-In Form W-2

22222	**a** Employee's social security number 331-00-4821	OMB No. 1545-0008

b Employer identification number (EIN) 33-1004821	**1** Wages, tips, other compensation 43500.00 **2** Federal income tax withheld 7356.00
c Employer's name, address, and ZIP code	**3** Social security wages 43500.00 **4** Social security tax withheld 2697.00
	5 Medicare wages and tips 43500.00 **6** Medicare tax withheld 630.75
Anderson, Berger, and Green 2706 Seaview Pendleton, OR 97256	**7** Social security tips **8** Allocated tips .00
d Control number 999	**9** **10** Dependent care benefits .00
e Employee's first name and initial Last name Suff. Harriett R. Shawver	**11** Nonqualified plans **12a**
	13 Statutory employee ☐ Retirement plan ☐ Third-party sick pay ☐ **12b**
	14 Other **12c**
214 Emigrant Street Pendleton, OR 97256 02112-1415	**12d**
f Employee's address and ZIP code	

15 State Employer's state ID number	**16** State wages, tips, etc.	**17** State income tax	**18** Local wages, tips, etc.	**19** Local income tax	**20** Locality name
OR 25703	43500.00	2175.00	.00	.00	

Form **W-2** Wage and Tax Statement   **2022**   Department of the Treasury—Internal Revenue Service
Copy 1—For State, City, or Local Tax Department

¶1303.04   FORM W-3

Employers send to the Social Security Administration Copy A of Form W-2 for all employees along with Form W-3, Transmittal of Wage and Tax Statements. The due date is January 31, regardless of whether Forms W-3 and W-2 are filed electronically or in paper form. Electronic filing is required for those filing 250 or more Forms W-2. Employers must use and prepare either an official printed IRS Form W-3 (*not* the version downloaded from the IRS website) or an acceptable substitute form. When completing Form W-3, employers type all data entries, omitting dollar signs and commas, but using decimal points and zeros to show cents (00000.00). The amounts on Form W-3 represent the totals from all the amounts on all Copies A of Forms W-2 attached. The employer or payer must sign Form W-3. A transmitter or sender (e.g., a service bureau, paying agent, etc.) can sign Form W-3 (or use its PIN to e-file) for the employer or payer only if the sender (1) is authorized to sign by an agency agreement valid under state law, and (2) writes "For (name of payer)" next to the signature (for paper Forms W-3 only).

This section describes the data contained on Form W-3. However, it does not cover every box, since most boxes contain clear descriptive headings. The instructions for Form W-3 (available on the IRS website) describe the data needs for all boxes. (See Appendix A for instructions on how to use the IRS website.)

Control Number (Box a)

Employers can assign their own control number or leave the box blank.

Kind of Payer (Box b)

Employers check one of the following types of Form W-2 they are filing. Employers with more than one type of Form W-2 file a separate Form W-3 for each type.

1. *941.* Check this square when filing Form 941 and no other group applies.
2. *Military.* Check this square when sending Forms W-2 for members of the U.S. armed forces.
3. *943.* Check this square when filing Forms 943 for agricultural employees. Employers of agricultural and nonagricultural workers prepare and submit a separate Form W-3.
4. *944.* Check this square when filing Form 944, Employer's Annual Federal Tax Return, and no other category applies.
5. *CT-1.* Check this square when sending Forms W-2 for employees under the Railroad Retirement Tax Act.
6. *Hshld. emp.* Check this square when sending Forms W-2 for household employees if their taxes were not included on Forms 941, 943, or 944.
7. *Medicare gov't. emp.* Check this box if the employer is a U.S., state, or local agency filing Forms W-2 for employees subject only to the 1.45% Medicare tax.

Total Number of Forms W-2 (Box c)

Employers enter the number of Forms W-2 they are sending with Form W-3. However, voided forms are excluded from the count.

Establishment Number (Box d)

Employers can use this box to identify separate establishments in their business. They can file a separate Form W-3, with Forms W-2, for each establishment even if all the establishments have the same EIN. Alternatively, employers can use a single Form W-3 for all Forms W-2 of the same type.

Employer's State I.D. Number (Box 15)

A state in which an employer does business may assign a state I.D. number. Employers enter the two letter abbreviation for the state being reported on Form(s) W-2, and their state-assigned I.D. number in the space provided in box 15.

¶1303.05   FILLED-IN FORM W-3

INFORMATION FOR FIGURE 13-4:

Martinez Enterprises, Inc., sends two Forms W-2 (Copy A) to the Social Security Administration with Form W-3. The wages for the two employees total **$87,560**. For both employees, social security and Medicare wages were the same as overall wages. Federal income tax withheld for the two employees was **$13,518.40**. Social security and Medicare taxes withheld were **$5,428.72** and **$1,269.62**, respectively. Since Florida does not have a state income tax, lines 15–19 are blank.

Figure 13-4: Filled-In Form W-3

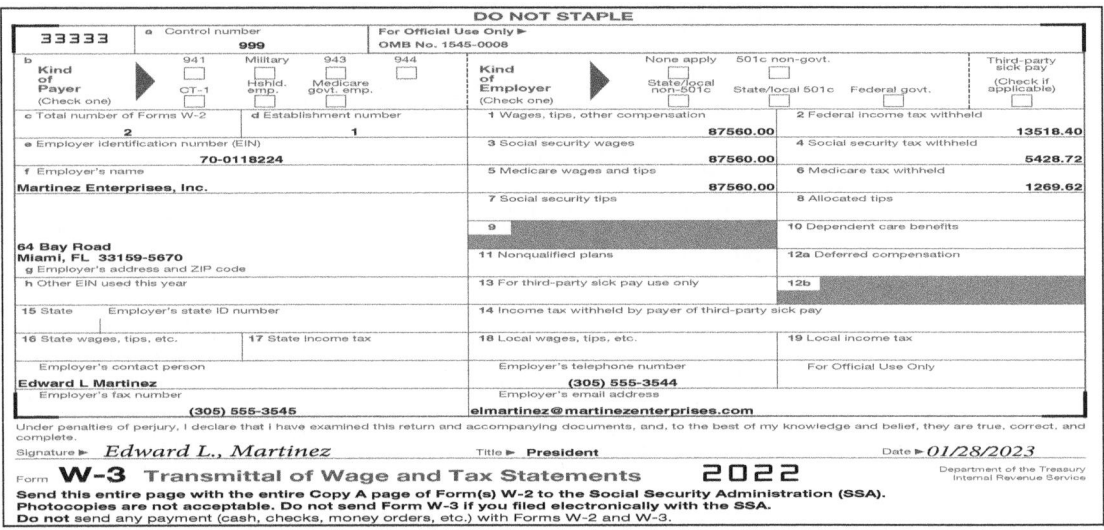

¶1304   Unemployment Taxes

In conjunction with state unemployment systems, the Federal Unemployment Tax Act (FUTA) makes payments to workers who have lost their jobs. The funding for the unemployment compensation comes solely from employers. Employers do not withhold any amounts from employees for this tax. Most employers pay taxes into both the state and federal unemployment systems.

¶1304.01   RATE AND BASE

Employers pay unemployment tax on the first $7,000 of each employee's taxable wages for the calendar year. For 2022, the FUTA tax rate is 6%. [I.R.C. §3301] However, employers who make timely deposits for the amounts owed to their state's unemployment fund may be able to reduce their FUTA rate to .6%. When computing the employer's FUTA taxes, wages paid to statutory employees or any wages paid to the taxpayer's spouse, parent, or child under the age of 21, are not included.

Employers normally must file their FUTA tax returns by January 31 of the next year. They do this by completing and filing Form 940, Employer's Annual Federal Unemployment (FUTA) Tax Return. However, employers that deposit their FUTA taxes on a timely basis during the year have until February 10th to file their FUTA tax return.

¶1304.02   DEPOSITING FUTA TAXES

Employers deposit FUTA taxes when their liability for the tax is more than $500 for a quarter. The FUTA tax is due on the last day of the month that follows the end of a quarter. When an employer's FUTA tax liability for any quarter does not exceed $500, the FUTA debt carries over to the next quarter. Employers with a fourth-quarter FUTA tax of $500 or less can either pay the tax when they file their FUTA return or make a deposit. If the fourth-quarter FUTA tax exceeds $500, they deposit the tax by January 31. Making a timely deposit extends the due date for filing Form 940 until February 10. When a deposit date falls on a Saturday, Sunday, or legal holiday, the deposit is timely if made by the next business day.

FUTA Tax Deposit Due Dates

Quarter Ending	Due Date
March 31	April 30
June 30	July 31
September 30	October 31
December 31	January 31

EXAMPLE 6

The Bucket Company's quarterly FUTA taxes for 2022 are: first, $235; second, $250; third, $245; and fourth, $200. No deposits are needed for the first and second quarters since the cumulative debt does not exceed $500 until the third quarter. Bucket must deposit $730 ($235 + $250 + $245) by October 31, 2022. For the fourth quarter, Bucket must deposit the tax by January 31, 2023. If Bucket makes timely deposits of its 2022 FUTA taxes, the due date for its FUTA tax return is extended to February 10, 2023.

¶1305   Federal Tax Deposit System

Most depositors of employment taxes must use the Treasury's electronic funds tax payment system to make their deposits.

Employment Taxes: What's Included?

- Federal income and FICA taxes withheld from employees
- Employer's share of FICA taxes
- Federal taxes withheld from pensions, annuities, and some deferred income
- Federal taxes withheld under the backup withholding rules

¶1305.01   DEPOSIT FREQUENCY

Employers make deposits using either a monthly or semiweekly deposit schedule. The required schedule depends on the total taxes the employer reported in the lookback period.

Lookback Period

The lookback period for an employer that files Form 941, Employer's QUARTERLY Federal Tax Return, is the 12-month period ending on June 30 of the prior year. For 2022, the lookback period runs from July 1, 2020, through June 30, 2021. The employment taxes reported on the four Forms 941 filed during the lookback period are used to determine the employer's deposit schedule. If an employer did not exist during the lookback period, the IRS treats the employer as having zero tax accumulations.

The deposit schedule for a calendar year for small employers that are allowed to file Form 944, Employer's ANNUAL Federal Tax Return, is determined from the total taxes reported during the second preceding calendar year. For Form 944 filers, the lookback period for 2022 is calendar year 2020.

Monthly Depositors

When total employment tax accumulations for an employer's lookback period are $50,000 or less, the employer deposits its employment taxes monthly. Monthly depositors deposit each month's employment taxes by the 15th day of the next month.

EXAMPLE 7	For the 12-month period ending June 30, 2021, Kirkwall Enterprises reported taxes on Form 941 totaling $47,000. Since this amount does not exceed $50,000, Kirkwall is a monthly schedule depositor for 2022. It deposits its monthly employment taxes on the 15th day of the following month. Thus, its payroll taxes for the month of January would be deposited on February 15. Its taxes for February would be due by March 15. By making timely deposits of its employment taxes, Kirkwall will be allowed to extend the deadline for filing Form 941 by ten days (see ¶1306.01).

Semiweekly Depositors

When total employment tax accumulations for an employer's lookback period exceed $50,000, the employer makes semiweekly deposits. Semiweekly depositors deposit their employment taxes on Wednesdays and Fridays. Wednesday tax deposits are for payrolls paid on the previous Wednesday, Thursday, and Friday. Friday tax deposits are for payrolls paid on the previous Saturday, Sunday, Monday, and Tuesday.

Semiweekly Depositors	
Deposit Day	**Deposit for Payrolls Paid**
Wednesday	Previous Wednesday - Friday
Friday	Previous Saturday - Tuesday

EXAMPLE 8	Continuing with Example 7, for the 12-month period ending on June 30, 2022, Kirkwall's taxes reported on Form 941 total $53,000. Since this amount exceeds $50,000, Kirkwall will be required to make semiweekly deposits during 2023. On Wednesdays, Kirkwall deposits the taxes related to the payrolls paid on Wednesday, Thursday or Friday of the previous week. Then on Fridays, Kirkwall deposits the taxes related to the payrolls paid on the previous Saturday - Tuesday.

Semiweekly depositors make two deposits when the end of a calendar quarter does not fall on the employer's payday. They make one deposit for the last day(s) in the quarter just ended. They make another deposit for the starting day(s) in the new quarter. Employers must make the deposits by the next regular deposit date.

EXAMPLE 9	Elite Corporation is a semiweekly depositor. Elite pays its employees every Friday. One of its payroll periods ends on June 24. The next payroll period ends on July 1 and the one after that ends on July 8. Elite normally deposits its payroll taxes on the Wednesday following its Friday payday. During the current year, the second quarter ends on Thursday, June 30. Thus, the end of the quarter does not coincide with the end of its payroll period. The taxes for the payroll period ending on Friday, June 24, would be deposited on Wednesday, June 29. Elite then must deposit the payroll taxes related to the period June 25 through June 30. It does this on the normal deposit date for Thursday payroll periods – the following Wednesday (July 6). It deposits the taxes for the short payroll period of July 1 on the following Wednesday (July 6).

EXAMPLE 10	Same facts as in Example 9, except that Elite pays its employees once a month on the last day of each month. Although Elite is a semiweekly depositor, it makes only one deposit for the month of June. If June 30 falls on Thursday, Elite makes the deposit the next Wednesday, July 6.

One-Day Rule

Whenever an employer's employment tax deposits reach $100,000 or more on any day of a deposit period, the one-day rule applies. This rule requires the employer to deposit employment taxes by the close of the next business day. This rule applies to both monthly and semiweekly depositors. Furthermore, once this event occurs for monthly depositors, they switch to being semiweekly depositors for the rest of the current calendar year and for the next calendar year. After that, the lookback period will determine whether the employer makes monthly or semiweekly deposits.

Semiweekly depositors determine whether they fall under the one-day rule by examining their employment tax accumulations since the last deposit date. They use Wednesday - Friday or Saturday - Tuesday for their examination period. On the day on which their accumulations reach $100,000, they meet the test for the one-day rule. Monthly depositors can determine if they fall under the one-day rule by examining their accumulations in the current month. They fall under the one-day rule on the day their accumulations reach $100,000. Once the employer deposits the employment taxes, the counting of accumulations starts over again at zero.

Weekends and Holidays

When a deposit date falls on a Saturday, Sunday, or a legal holiday, the deposit is timely if made by the close of the next business day. A "legal holiday" means any legal holiday in the District of Columbia.

| EXAMPLE 11 | RSV deposits employment taxes monthly. For April 20x1, RSV accumulates $10,000 of employment taxes. RSV normally would deposit these taxes by May 15, 20x1. However, in 20x1, May 15 falls on a Sunday. Thus, RSV must deposit the taxes by Monday, May 16, 20x1, the next business day. |

$2,500 Rule

A special deposit rule applies when the tax accumulations for a quarter do not reach $2,500. No deposits are necessary, and the employer may send the taxes in with Form 941.

| EXAMPLE 12 | A corporation's tax accumulations for the third quarter of 20x1 total $2,460. Since the total accumulations are less than $2,500, the corporation can send in the $2,460 when it files its third quarter Form 941. The due date for this return is October 31, 20x1 (or the next business day if October 31 falls on a weekend or holiday). |

Safe Harbor/*De Minimis* Rule

An employer satisfies its deposit requirement if the undeposited amount (shortfall) does not exceed the *larger of* (i) $100, or (ii) 2% of the required deposit. **Shortfall** means the required deposit amount less the amount deposited before the end of a deposit date. To use this rule, employers must deposit unplanned shortfalls before the end of their make-up date.

The shortfall make-up date for monthly depositors falls on the due date of the quarterly Form 941 for the period in which the shortfall occurs. The employer sends in the shortfall amount when it files its Form 941 or deposits the shortfall by the due date for filing Form 941.

A different shortfall make-up date applies to semiweekly and one-day depositors. For these employers, the shortfall must be deposited by the first Wednesday or Friday (whichever comes first) that falls on or after the 15th day of the month following the month of the shortfall. However, if the quarterly due date of the Form 941 for the return period of the tax liability falls before the shortfall make-up date, the shortfall deposit must take place by that earlier Form 941 due date.

| EXAMPLE 13 | Romano Company, a semiweekly depositor, has a shortfall for September 20x1. Romano's make-up period ends on the first Wednesday or Friday on or after October 15. Since October 15, 20x1, falls on a Saturday, the first Wednesday or Friday after that date would be Wednesday, October 19, 20x1. |

| EXAMPLE 14 | Same facts as in Example 13, except that Romano's shortfall occurs on Wednesday, October 5, 20x1, which is the normal deposit date for a Friday, September 30, 20x1, pay date. Normally, Romano would be required to deposit the shortfall by Wednesday, November 16 (the first Wednesday or Friday on or after the 15th of the month following the shortfall). However, Romano's third-quarter Form 941 is due on October 31. Thus, Romano must deposit the shortfall by October 31, 20x1. |

A flowchart of the employment tax deposit rules appears in Figure 13-5. It shows how the rules separate employment tax depositors by frequency of deposits.

¶1306   Employer's Quarterly Report

Most employers that withhold income taxes or owe FICA taxes file Form 941, Employer's QUARTERLY Federal Tax Return. Seasonal employers that do not pay wages in a quarter do not file a Form 941 for that quarter. On every Form 941 that seasonal employers file, they place an **X** in the seasonal employer box (line 18).

All depositors complete both pages of Form 941. Semiweekly depositors also complete Schedule B (Form 941), Report of Tax Liability for Semiweekly Schedule Depositors, and attach it to Form 941.

¶1306.01   FILING THE QUARTERLY REPORT

Employers must file Form 941 by the last day of the month that follows the close of a calendar quarter. For example, for the quarter ending September 30, 20x1, employers must file a Form 941 by October 31, 20x1. If the due date falls on a weekend or legal holiday, the return would be due the next business day. Employers that deposit all "941 taxes" by or before the required due dates get an additional ten days to file Form 941. Thus, if the employer deposits its 941 taxes for the quarter by the required due dates, Form 941 for the quarter ending December 31, 20x1, would be due by February 10, 20x2. Employers cannot use Form 941 to report taxes from more than one calendar quarter. Instead, each quarter must be reported separately.

Figure 13-5: Summary of the Employment Tax Deposit Rules

Are accumulated taxes on **any prior day** $100,000 or more for the period **since** the last required deposit?

YES   **NO**

FOR ONE DAY RULE

Semiweekly depositors use Wed–Fri or Sat–Tues period in which the day occurs.	Monthly depositors use calendar month in which the day occurs.

Deposit taxes by close of the next business day.

Are accumulated taxes ≤ $50,000 for the four quarters in the lookback period?

Any one-day depositor is treated as a semiweekly depositor for the rest of the year and for the next year.

NO   **YES**

Employer is a semi-weekly depositor and must make deposits
• by next Wedneday
or
• by next Friday.

Employer is a monthly depositor and must make deposits by the 15th day of the next month.

Does return period end on a day other than Wednesday or Friday?

YES   **NO**

Two separate deposits required

Taxes for the period just ended	Taxes for the new period

Only one deposit required

EXAMPLE 15	Betz, Inc., which uses the calendar year, withholds employment taxes from its employees' wages. Betz deposits its employees' withheld taxes plus Betz's share of employment taxes on a timely basis throughout 20x1. These actions allow Betz until May 10, 20x1 to file its first quarter Form 941 (the normal due date is April 30). It has until August 10, 20x1 to file Form 941 for the second quarter, and until November 10, 20x1 to file the third quarter Form 941. The due date for Betz's Form 941 for the fourth quarter is February 10, 20x2. If any of these days falls on a weekend or legal holiday, the return would be due the next business day.

EXAMPLE 16	Same facts as in Example 15, except that Betz fails to deposit its employment taxes on time. The due dates for filing Form 941 are the last day of the month that follows the close of the calendar quarter. This would be April 30, July 31, October 31 and January 31. If any of these days falls on a weekend or legal holiday, the return would be due the next business day.

Adjusting for Overwithholding or Underwithholding

Employers use Form 941-X, Adjusted Employer's QUARTERLY Federal Tax Return or Claim for Refund, to make a correction after they discover an error on a previously-filed Form 941. Similarly, Form 944-X is used to correct errors on a previously-filed Form 944. An employer will use the "adjustment process" if it (1) underreported employment taxes and is making a payment, or (2) overreported employment taxes and will be applying the credit to the Form 941 period during which the employer files Form 941-X. An employer will use the "claim process" if it overreported employment taxes and is requesting a refund or abatement of the overreported amount.

A chart on the back of Form 941-X (or Form 944-X) provides guidance on choosing whether to use the adjustment process or the claim process. The Instructions for Form 941-X (or the Instructions for Form 944-X) contain the details on how to make the adjustment or claim for refund or abatement.

Final Returns

When an employer goes out of business, the employer marks an **X** in the box on line 17 of Form 941 (line 14 of Form 944) and in the space provided, enters the final date wages were paid.

¶1306.02   SPECIAL RULES FOR 2020 AND 2021

In 2020, Congress and the President introduced several temporary measures to provide relief for the economic losses resulting from the COVID-19 pandemic. Among those were some relief provisions for employers' payroll tax liabilities. The provisions include:

> Qualified Sick Leave
> Qualified health plan expenses allocable to qualified family leave wages
> Qualified wages, and health plan expenses for purposes of the employee retention credit
> Deferred social security tax
> Deferred employee share of social security tax.

Most of these rules provided for a deferral for depositing taxes. The employers were required to deposit these taxes in 2022. Given that the penalties for failure to make timely deposits were so severe, most responsible tax advisers did not advocate deferring payment of employment taxes. However, there were probably some circumstances in which the deferral might be beneficial.

Some of these credits were extended into 2021. These credits offset payroll tax liabilities. See *https://www.irs.gov/coronavirus/employer-tax-credits*.

¶1306.03   FILLED-IN FORM 941

INFORMATION FOR FIGURE 13-6:

Martinez Enterprises, Inc. (a monthly depositor), reports combined wages for withholding and employment taxes of $22,396 for the first quarter ($6,172.61 in July, $6,714.90 in August, and $9,508.49 in September). Martinez withheld $3,369.49 in federal income taxes from its two employees ($928.31 in July, $1,010.41 in August, and $1,430.77 in September).

Line #

1: Number of employees, **2**
2: Wages, tips, and other compensation, **$22,396**
3: Federal income tax withheld from amounts reported on line 2, **$3,369.49**
16: Month 1 liability, **$1,872.71** [($6,172.61 × .124) + ($6,172.61 × .029) + $928.31]
    Month 2 liability, **$2,037.79** [($6,714.90 × .124) + ($6,714.90 × .029) + $1,010.41]
    Month 3 liability, **$2,885.57** [($9,508.49 × .124) + ($9,508.49 × .029) + $1,430.77]

Figure 13-6: Filled-In Form 941 (Page 1)

Form **941 for 2022:** Employer's QUARTERLY Federal Tax Return   950122
(Rev. June 2022)   Department of the Treasury — Internal Revenue Service
OMB No. 1545-0029

Employer identification number (EIN) 7 0 – 0 1 1 8 2 2 4

Name (not your trade name) Martinez Enterprises, Inc.

Trade name (if any)

Address 64 Bay Road
         Number   Street   Suite or room number

         Miami   FL   33139
         City   State   ZIP code

         Foreign country name   Foreign province/county   Foreign postal code

Report for this Quarter of 2022
(Check one.)

☐ 1: January, February, March
☐ 2: April, May, June
☒ 3: July, August, September
☐ 4: October, November, December

Go to *www.irs.gov/Form941* for instructions and the latest information.

Read the separate instructions before you complete Form 941. Type or print within the boxes.

Part 1: Answer these questions for this quarter.

1   Number of employees who received wages, tips, or other compensation for the pay period including: *June 12* (Quarter 2), *Sept. 12* (Quarter 3), or *Dec. 12* (Quarter 4) **1**   2

2   Wages, tips, and other compensation . . . .   **2**   22396 . 00

3   Federal income tax withheld from wages, tips, and other compensation . . . . . .   **3**   3369 . 49

4   If no wages, tips, and other compensation are subject to social security or Medicare tax   ☐ Check and go to line 6.

		Column 1		Column 2	
5a	Taxable social security wages* . .	22396 . 00	× 0.124 =	2777 . 10	
5a	(i) Qualified sick leave wages* .		.	× 0.062 =	.
5a	(ii) Qualified family leave wages* .		.	× 0.062 =	.
5b	Taxable social security tips . . .		.	× 0.124 =	.
5c	Taxable Medicare wages & tips. .	22396 . 00	× 0.029 =	649 . 48	
5d	Taxable wages & tips subject to Additional Medicare Tax withholding		.	× 0.009 =	.

*Include taxable qualified sick and family leave wages paid in this quarter of 2022 for leave taken after March 31, 2021, and before October 1, 2021, on line 5a. Use lines 5a(i) and 5a(ii) **only** for taxable qualified sick and family leave wages paid in this quarter of 2022 for leave taken after March 31, 2020, and before April 1, 2021.

5e Total social security and Medicare taxes. Add Column 2 from lines 5a, 5a(i), 5a(ii), 5b, 5c, and 5d   **5e**   649 . 48

5f Section 3121(q) Notice and Demand—Tax due on unreported tips (see instructions) . .   **5f**   .

6   Total taxes before adjustments. Add lines 3, 5e, and 5f . . . .   **6**   6796 . 07

7   Current quarter's adjustment for fractions of cents . . . .   **7**   .

8   Current quarter's adjustment for sick pay . . . .   **8**   .

9   Current quarter's adjustments for tips and group-term life insurance . . . .   **9**   .

10 Total taxes after adjustments. Combine lines 6 through 9 . . . .   **10**   6796 . 07

11a Qualified small business payroll tax credit for increasing research activities. Attach Form 8974   **11a**   .

11b Nonrefundable portion of credit for qualified sick and family leave wages for leave taken before April 1, 2021 . . . .   **11b**   .

11c Reserved for future use . . . .   **11c**   .

▶ You MUST complete all three pages of Form 941 and SIGN it.   Next ▶

For Privacy Act and Paperwork Reduction Act Notice, see the back of the Payment Voucher.   Cat. No. 17001Z   Form **941** (Rev. 6-2022)

Figure 13-6: Filled-In Form 941 (Page 2)

951222

Name *(not your trade name)*	Employer identification number (EIN)
Martinez Enterprises, Inc.	70 – 0118224

Part 1:   Answer these questions for this quarter. *(continued)*

11d Nonrefundable portion of credit for qualified sick and family leave wages for leave taken after March 31, 2021, and before October 1, 2021 . . . . **11d** [.   ]

11e Reserved for future use . . . . **11e** [.   ]

11f Reserved for future use . . . . [   ]

11g Total nonrefundable credits. Add lines 11a, 11b, and 11d . . . . **11g** [.   ]

12 Total taxes after adjustments and nonrefundable credits. Subtract line 11g from line 10 . **12** [6796 . 07]

13a Total deposits for this quarter, including overpayment applied from a prior quarter and overpayments applied from Form 941-X, 941-X (PR), 944-X, or 944-X (SP) filed in the current quarter **13a** [6796 . 07]

13b Reserved for future use . . . . **13b** [.   ]

13c Refundable portion of credit for qualified sick and family leave wages for leave taken before April 1, 2021 . . . . **13c** [.   ]

13d Reserved for future use . . . . **13d** [.   ]

13e Refundable portion of credit for qualified sick and family leave wages for leave taken after March 31, 2021, and before October 1, 2021 . . . . **13e** [.   ]

13f Reserved for future use . . . . **13f** [.   ]

13g Total deposits and refundable credits. Add lines 13a, 13c, and 13e . . . . **13g** [.   ]

13h Reserved for future use . . . . **13h** [.   ]

13i Reserved for future use . . . . **13i** [.   ]

14 Balance due. If line 12 is more than line 13g, enter the difference and see instructions . . . **14** [0 . 00]

15 Overpayment. If line 13g is more than line 12, enter the difference [0 . 00] Check one: ☐ Apply to next return. ☐ Send a refund.

Part 2:   Tell us about your deposit schedule and tax liability for this quarter.

If you're unsure about whether you're a monthly schedule depositor or a semiweekly schedule depositor, see section 11 of Pub. 15.

16 Check one: ☐ Line 12 on this return is less than $2,500 or line 12 on the return for the prior quarter was less than $2,500, and you didn't incur a $100,000 next-day deposit obligation during the current quarter. If line 12 for the prior quarter was less than $2,500 but line 12 on this return is $100,000 or more, you must provide a record of your federal tax liability. If you're a monthly schedule depositor, complete the deposit schedule below; if you're a semiweekly schedule depositor, attach Schedule B (Form 941). Go to Part 3.

☒ **You were a monthly schedule depositor for the entire quarter.** Enter your tax liability for each month and total liability for the quarter, then go to Part 3.

Tax liability: Month 1 [1872 . 71]

Month 2 [2037 . 79]

Month 3 [2885 . 57]

Total liability for quarter [6796 . 07] Total must equal line 12.

☐ **You were a semiweekly schedule depositor for any part of this quarter.** Complete Schedule B (Form 941), Report of Tax Liability for Semiweekly Schedule Depositors, and attach it to Form 941. Go to Part 3.

▶ **You MUST complete all three pages of Form 941 and SIGN it.**   Next ▶

Page **2**   Form **941** (Rev. 6-2022)

Figure 13-6: Filled-In Form 941 (Page 3)

950922

Name (not your trade name)	**Employer identification number (EIN)**
Martinez Enterprises, Inc.	70 – 0118224

Part 3: Tell us about your business. If a question does NOT apply to your business, leave it blank.

17 If your business has closed or you stopped paying wages . . . . ☐ Check here, and

enter the final date you paid wages [/   /   ] ; also attach a statement to your return. See instructions.

18 If you're a seasonal employer and you don't have to file a return for every quarter of the year . . . ☐ Check here.

19 Qualified health plan expenses allocable to qualified sick leave wages for leave taken before April 1, 2021   19 [▪]

20 Qualified health plan expenses allocable to qualified family leave wages for leave taken before April 1, 2021   20 [▪]

21 Reserved for future use . . . .   21 [▪]

22 Reserved for future use . . . .   22 [▪]

23 Qualified sick leave wages for leave taken after March 31, 2021, and before October 1, 2021   23 [▪]

24 Qualified health plan expenses allocable to qualified sick leave wages reported on line 23   24 [▪]

25 Amounts under certain collectively bargained agreements allocable to qualified sick leave wages reported on line 23 . . . .   25 [▪]

26 Qualified family leave wages for leave taken after March 31, 2021, and before October 1, 2021   26 [▪]

27 Qualified health plan expenses allocable to qualified family leave wages reported on line 26   27 [▪]

28 Amounts under certain collectively bargained agreements allocable to qualified family leave wages reported on line 26 . . . .   28 [▪]

Part 4: May we speak with your third-party designee?

Do you want to allow an employee, a paid tax preparer, or another person to discuss this return with the IRS? See the instructions for details.

☐ Yes. Designee's name and phone number [   ] [   ]

Select a 5-digit personal identification number (PIN) to use when talking to the IRS. ☐ ☐ ☐ ☐ ☐

☐ No.

Part 5: Sign here. You MUST complete all three pages of Form 941 and SIGN it.

Under penalties of perjury, I declare that I have examined this return, including accompanying schedules and statements, and to the best of my knowledge and belief, it is true, correct, and complete. Declaration of preparer (other than taxpayer) is based on all information of which preparer has any knowledge.

X Sign your name here   *Edward L. Martinez*

Print your name here Edward L. Martinez

Print your title here President

Date 10/04/2022

Best daytime phone (912) 003-4567

Paid Preparer Use Only   Check if you're self-employed . . . ☐

Preparer's name [ ]	PTIN [ ]
Preparer's signature [ ]	Date [/ /]
Firm's name (or yours if self-employed) [ ]	EIN [ ]
Address [ ]	Phone [ ]
City [ ] State [ ]	ZIP code [ ]

Page **3**   Form **941** (Rev. 6-2022)

¶1307   Estimated Taxes

Wage earners pay taxes on their wages through the payroll withholding system. Taxpayers with income from sources other than wages (self-employment profits, interest, dividends, etc.) estimate their taxes and make quarterly payments directly to the IRS. Quarterly due dates fall on April 15, June 15, September 15, and January 15.

 When any tax filing due date falls on a weekend or legal holiday, the filing deadline is extended to the next business day. Emancipation Day is a holiday in the District of Columbia, and is considered a legal holiday. When Emancipation Day (April 16) falls on a weekend, the observed holiday is moved to the nearest weekday.

¶1307.01   WHO MUST MAKE ESTIMATED PAYMENTS?

When individual taxpayers' estimated unpaid tax for the year equals or exceeds $1,000, they usually must make estimated tax payments. Unpaid taxes include income tax (which includes the alternative minimum tax) and self-employment taxes. It also includes any Medicare tax liability not covered through Medicare tax withholdings from employees' wages (see ¶1302.02). Employees do not need to make estimated payments in 2022 unless their tax withholdings and credits for 2022 fall below the *lesser of* (i) 90% of the tax to be shown on their 2022 tax return, or (ii) 100% of the tax on their 2021 tax return (110% for taxpayers whose 2021 AGI exceeded $150,000 ($75,000 for MFS)). Likewise, they do not need to make estimated payments in 2022 unless their tax withholdings and credits for 2023 fall below the *lesser of* (i) 90% of the tax to be shown on their 2023 tax return, or (ii) 100% of the tax on their 2022 tax return (110% for taxpayers whose 2022 AGI exceeded $150,000 ($75,000 for MFS)).

EXAMPLE 17   Tracy's AGI for 2022 was $62,500; her federal tax liability was $5,530. Tracy expects her 2023 tax liability to be $8,000. Tracy does not need to make estimated payments in 2023 unless her employer withholds less than $5,530 from her pay during the year. This amount is the *lesser of* (i) $7,200 ($8,000 × 90%), or (ii) $5,530 (100% of her 2022 tax liability).

EXAMPLE 18   Dora's AGI for 2022 was $162,500; her federal tax liability was $15,553. Dora expects her 2023 tax liability to be $18,000. Dora will not need to make estimated payments in 2023 unless her employer withholds less than $16,200 from her pay during the year. This amount is the *lesser of* (i) $16,200 ($18,000 × 90%), or (ii) $17,108 (110% of her $15,553 tax liability for 2022).

EXAMPLE 19   Same facts as in Example 18, except that Dora expects her 2023 tax liability to be $24,000. Dora will not need to make estimated payments in 2023 unless her employer withholds less than $17,108 from her pay during the year. This amount is the *lesser of* (i) $21,600 ($24,000 × 90%), or (ii) $17,108 (110% of her $15,553 tax liability for 2022).

Estimated Tax Worksheet

The IRS provides a worksheet to help taxpayers calculate their estimated tax. The difference between their total estimated tax, net of estimated credits and their employer's withholdings, represents the estimated unpaid tax. Taxpayers can pay this amount in four equal installments.

¶1307.02 FILLED-IN ESTIMATED TAX WORKSHEET

 ### INFORMATION FOR FIGURE 13-7:

Early in 2022, Audrey McGrath (single, age 25) estimates her 2022 withholdings will be $2,600 and her AGI will be $54,732, as shown below. Audrey has no dependents and uses the standard deduction. Her 2021 income taxes were $3,950. By completing the Estimated Tax Worksheet in Figure 13-7, Audrey determines she will need to make four quarterly payments of $338 in 2022.

Salary	$31,600
Net rentals from apartment building	19,600
Net income from business	3,800
Total income	$55,000
Less deduction for employer's share of self-employment tax	(268)
AGI	$54,732

Figure 13-7: Filled-In Estimated Tax Worksheet

2022 Estimated Tax Worksheet   *Keep for Your Records*

1	Adjusted gross income you expect in 2022 (see instructions)	**1**	54,732
2a	Deductions	**2a**	12,950
	• If you plan to itemize deductions, enter the estimated total of your itemized deductions.		
	• If you don't plan to itemize deductions, enter your standard deduction.		
b	If you can take the qualified business income deduction, enter the estimated amount of the deduction ▶	**2b**	4,680
c	Add lines 2a and 2b . . . . ▶	**2c**	17,630
3	Subtract line 2c from line 1	**3**	37,102
4	**Tax.** Figure your tax on the amount on line 3 by using the **2022 Tax Rate Schedules.**		
	Caution: *If you will have qualified dividends or a net capital gain, or expect to exclude or deduct foreign earned income or housing, see Worksheets 2-5 and 2-6 in Pub. 505 to figure the tax*	**4**	4,247
5	Alternative minimum tax from **Form 6251**	**5**	
6	Add lines 4 and 5. Add to this amount any other taxes you expect to include in the total on Form 1040 or 1040-SR, line 16	**6**	4,247
7	Credits (see instructions). **Do not** include any income tax withholding on this line	**7**	
8	Subtract line 7 from line 6. If zero or less, enter -0-	**8**	4,247
9	Self-employment tax (see instructions)	**9**	537
10	Other taxes (see instructions)	**10**	
11a	Add lines 8 through 10	**11a**	4,784
b	Earned income credit, refundable child tax credit* or additional child tax credit, fuel tax credit, net premium tax credit, refundable American opportunity credit, section 1341 credit, and refundable credit from Form 8885*	**11b**	
c	**Total 2022 estimated tax.** Subtract line 11b from line 11a. If zero or less, enter -0- . . . . ▶	**11c**	4,784

12a	Multiply line 11c by 90% (66²/₃% for farmers and fishermen)	**12a**	4,305	
b	Required annual payment based on prior year's tax (see instructions) . . .	**12b**	3,950	
c	**Required annual payment to avoid a penalty.** Enter the **smaller** of line 12a or 12b . . . . . ▶			**12c** 3,950

Caution: *Generally, if you do not prepay (through income tax withholding and estimated tax payments) at least the amount on line 12c, you may owe a penalty for not paying enough estimated tax. To avoid a penalty, make sure your estimate on line 11c is as accurate as possible. Even if you pay the required annual payment, you may still owe tax when you file your return. If you prefer, you can pay the amount shown on line 11c. For details, see chapter 2 of Pub. 505.*

13	Income tax withheld and estimated to be withheld during 2022 (including income tax withholding on pensions, annuities, certain deferred income, etc.)	**13**	2,600

14a	Subtract line 13 from line 12c	**14a** 1,350	
	Is the result zero or less?		
	☐ **Yes.** Stop here. You are not required to make estimated tax payments.		
	☑ **No.** Go to line 14b.		
b	Subtract line 13 from line 11c	**14b**	
	Is the result less than $1,000?		
	☐ **Yes.** Stop here. You are not required to make estimated tax payments.		
	☑ **No.** Go to line 15 to figure your required payment.		
15	If the first payment you are required to make is due April 18, 2022, enter ¼ of line 14a (minus any 2021 overpayment that you are applying to this installment) here, and on your estimated tax payment voucher(s) if you are paying by check or money order	**15**	338

* If applicable.

Joint Estimated Tax Payments

A husband and wife can make joint estimated tax payments. Making a joint payment or separate payments does not commit the couple to filing a joint tax return. When a husband and wife make joint payments but file separate income tax returns, they can divide the estimated taxes as they choose. A couple separated under a decree of divorce or separate maintenance cannot make joint estimated tax payments.

EXAMPLE 20

> Britney and Caleb Stonewell make joint estimated payments during 2022 that total $25,000. The Stonewells decide to file separate tax returns for 2022. They are free to split up the $25,000 amongst themselves. Thus, if Britney's tax withholdings are large enough to cover her tax liability, Caleb can apply the entire $25,000 against his 2022 tax liability. However, if it turns out that Britney's withholdings are less than her tax liability by $4,000, the couple can choose to apply $4,000 of their joint estimated payments against Britney's tax liability. The remaining $21,000 would then be taken on Caleb's separate tax return.

¶1307.03   PAYMENT OF ESTIMATED TAX

Taxpayers can pay estimated tax by:

1. crediting an overpayment on their prior year's tax return to their current year's estimated tax;
2. paying by direct transfer from their bank account, or by debit or credit card using a pay-by-phone system, mobile device, or online;
3. paying by cash with an in-person payment through retail partners; or
4. mailing their payment (by check or money order) with a Form 1040-ES payment voucher to the appropriate IRS Service Center listed in the Instructions for Form 1040-ES.

The vouchers and payments are due April 15, June 15, and September 15 of the current year, and January 15 of the next year. If the due date falls on a weekend or a legal holiday, the voucher and payment are due the next business day.

Prior-Year Overpayments

If a taxpayer's tax return for the year results in overpayment of taxes, the taxpayer can either choose to receive a refund, or apply the overpayment to any estimated tax due the next year. The taxpayer can use the overpayment either to reduce each subsequent installment until the overpayment is used up or to reduce each installment equally.

EXAMPLE 21

Betty overpaid her 2022 taxes by $1,600. Betty estimates her 2023 tax payments and withholding will be as follows.

Estimated tax for 2023	$ 18,200
Less projected income tax withholding during the year	(12,600)
Estimated unpaid tax	$ 5,600

   Because Betty's 2023 withholdings are expected to be less than her tax liability for the year, she should make estimated payments to avoid an underpayment penalty. Her quarterly installment payments are $1,400 ($5,600 ÷ 4). If Betty elects to apply her 2022 overpayment to her 2023 taxes, she will not need to pay the first installment, since the $1,400 first installment falls below last year's $1,600 overpayment. When the second installment comes due on June 15, 2023, Betty will pay $1,200 (second quarter installment of $1,400 less the remaining $200 from her last year's overpayment). Betty would then pay the full $1,400 quarterly estimate with her third and fourth installments.

   Alternatively, Betty could elect to apply the overpayment evenly against each installment. If she chooses to do this, Betty divides last year's overpayment by the number of installments ($1,600 ÷ 4) and applies this amount to each installment. Betty would pay four installments of $1,000 each ($1,400 – $400).

Underpayment of Estimated Tax

No underpayment penalty will be assessed when the amount of tax due after withholding is less than $1,000. Taxpayers who expect to owe $1,000 or more after withholdings should make timely estimated tax payments. As mentioned previously in the chapter, one way to avoid the underpayment penalty is to make four equal payments that total 90% of the taxpayer's current year tax liability. A second way to avoid the penalty is to make four equal payments that total 100% of the taxpayer's prior year tax liability (110% for taxpayers whose AGI in the previous year exceeded $150,000 [$75,000 for married filing separately]). A third way to avoid the underpayment penalty is to make estimated payments based on 90% of the current year's annualized tax liability. The calculations required in annualizing taxable income and tax liability are rather involved and beyond the scope of this textbook. Those interested in learning more about the annualized method for making estimated payments should refer to IRS Publication 505, *Tax Withholding and Estimated Tax*.

   Sometimes taxpayers need to make estimated payments, but also have wages subject to withholding. In calculating the amount of each estimated payment, wages are treated as occurring evenly throughout the year. Thus, taxpayers who work only part of the year and have $2,000 withheld from their wages will be treated as having had the $2,000 withheld evenly throughout the year.

EXAMPLE 22

On October 1, 2023, Wesley estimates that his tax liability for 2023 will be $15,000. In 2022, Wesley's AGI was $160,000 and his tax liability was $22,000. Thus, to avoid underpayment penalties, Wesley needs to have prepaid $13,500 for 2023. This amount is the *lesser of* (i) 90% of his 2023 tax liability ($15,000 × 90% = $13,500), or (ii) 110% of his 2022 tax liability ($22,000 × 110% = $24,200). Wesley's employer has been withholding $1,000 a month. Thus, Wesley is on target to have a total of $12,000 withheld during 2023. If Wesley does nothing, he will be subject to an underpayment penalty for the $1,500 deficiency ($13,500 required prepayments – $12,000 withheld from his wages). If Wesley decides to make an estimated payment for the fourth quarter to make up the $1,500 deficit, he will still be subject to penalties for not having paid enough during the first three quarters. However, if Wesley files a new W-4 with his employer and has an additional $1,500 withheld through the end of the year, he will avoid any underpayment penalties. His employer will have withheld a total of $13,500 during the year, which will be treated as having been paid evenly throughout the year.

Determining the Penalty Amount

Individual taxpayers determine the amount of their underpayment penalty on Form 2210, Underpayment of Estimated Tax by Individuals, Estates, and Trusts. Taxpayers enter their penalty for underpayment of estimated taxes on Form 1040, page 2, line 23. This penalty amount is then added to any other amounts due the government. Taxpayers may choose not to file Form 2210 and instead have the IRS calculate the penalty and bill them.

¶1308   Tax Penalties

When taxpayers fail to file a tax return or fail to pay the proper amount of tax, a penalty is assessed. Other actions may also invoke a penalty. Tax penalties are generally based on the amount of tax due on the tax return (tax liability in excess of credits and prepayments). Having a "reasonable cause" for not complying with the law may keep the taxpayer from owing a penalty (see ¶1308.01).

April 15th is the tax filing deadline for individual taxpayers. It is the deadline for both filing their income tax return as well as for paying any taxes owed. Taxpayers that file their tax returns on time but do not pay all the taxes they owe by April 15 will pay a late payment penalty. The **late payment penalty** is equal to one-half of 1% (.5%) of the taxes owed for each month, or part of a month, that the tax remains unpaid. The maximum late payment penalty is 25% of the taxes owed. For persons who file their tax returns by the due date, the one-half of 1% rate is reduced to one-quarter of 1% for any month in which an installment agreement is in effect.

Persons who owe taxes and do not file a tax return by the deadline (including extensions) will be charged a **late filing penalty**. This penalty is 5% of the taxes owed for each month, or part of a month, that the tax return is late. The maximum penalty is 25% of the taxes owed. [I.R.C. §6651] For 2022 tax returns required to be filed in 2023, and filed more than 60 days late, the minimum late filing penalty is the *lesser of* $435 or 100% of the taxes owed.

EXAMPLE 23	Agnes files her 2022 tax return on April 15, 2023. Agnes pays $500 of the $2,500 balance due when she files her return. She pays her tax balance on October 1, 5½ months after it was due. Agnes' late payment penalty is $60 ($2,000 × .5% × 6 months late).

EXAMPLE 24	Ike failed to file his 2022 tax return by the April 15 deadline and forgot to file for an extension. On June 3, 2023, he filed his tax return and paid the $500 taxes due with his return. Since Ike filed his return within 60 days of the deadline, his late filing penalty is $50 ($500 × 5% × 2 months late).

EXAMPLE 25	Same facts as in Example 24, except that Ike filed his 2022 tax return on July 3, 2023. Normally, Ike's late filing penalty would be $75 ($500 × 5% × 3 months late). However, since he filed his return more than 60 days late, his minimum late filing penalty is $435 (the *lesser of* (i) $435, or (ii) the $500 taxes owed). Since this amount exceeds what would normally be his late filing penalty ($75), Ike must pay the $435 minimum penalty.

Type of Penalty	Amount of Penalty
Failure to pay	.5% of the amount due for each full and partial month that the payment is late, up to 25%
Failure to file	5% of the amount due for each full and partial month that the return is late, up to 25%
Negligence or substantial understatement of income tax	20% of the tax due
Gross misstatement of valuation	40% of the tax due
Failure to file due to fraud	15% for each full and partial month, up to 75% of the tax due
Frivolous return filing	$5,000

¶1308.01   REASONABLE CAUSE

Taxpayers may avoid a penalty if failure to comply was due to reasonable cause and not willful neglect. The IRS lists the following circumstances which might be treated as reasonable causes for failing to comply with the tax laws. Other reasonable causes may exist. The IRS judges each case on its merits.

- Death or serious illness
- Unavoidable absence
- Destruction of certain facilities or records
- Timely mailing
- Wrong filing place
- Reliance on a competent tax adviser
- Unobtainable records
- IRS office visit in which an IRS employee was unable to be seen for reasons beyond the taxpayer's control
- Erroneous IRS information

¶1309   Information Returns

Information returns play an important part in the IRS computerized taxpayer compliance program. Persons and organizations making specific types of payments must report them to the IRS and the taxpayer. Taxpayers must then report these amounts on their income tax returns. This reporting process makes it possible for the IRS to determine whether taxpayers have reported the correct amounts on their tax returns. The taxpayer's identification number (social security number (SSN) for individuals; employer identification number (EIN) for businesses), shown on both the information return and the income tax return, is the basis for comparing reported data. Taxpayers do not attach information returns to the tax return unless federal income tax has been withheld by the payer. They should, however, retain copies for their records.

Common Information Returns

Form 1098, Mortgage Interest Statement

Form 1099-B, Proceeds from Broker and Barter Exchange Transactions

Form 1099-DIV, Dividends and Distributions

Form 1099-INT, Interest Income

Form 1099-G, Certain Government Payments

Form 1099-MISC, Miscellaneous Information

Form 1099-NEC, Nonemployee Compensation

Form 1099-R, Distributions From Pensions, Annuities, Retirement or Profit-Sharing Plans, IRAs, Insurance Contracts, etc.

Form 1099-S, Proceeds From Real Estate Transactions

Form 5498, IRA Contribution Information

Form 8027, Employer's Annual Information Return of Tip Income and Allocated Tips

¶1309.01   IRS COMPARISONS

The IRS routinely examines the amounts reported on information returns filed by the payers of interest, dividends, and other types of payments. It compares these amounts to those reported by taxpayers on their income tax returns. Taxpayers should report all amounts received on their returns as separate items. When taxpayers detect an error on an information return, they should ask the payer to correct the mistake and issue a corrected information return.

The computer may detect a difference between the amounts reported on the information returns and the amounts reported by the taxpayer. It may then generate a deficiency notice that will require an explanation by the taxpayer. The differences may be easily explained by the taxpayer with no penalty assessed. However, much time and effort can be saved if the taxpayer carefully reports the amounts as shown on the information returns.

¶1309.02   PENALTY FOR FAILURE TO FILE INFORMATION RETURNS

A penalty applies for filing late, incorrect, or incomplete information returns with the IRS. [I.R.C. §6721] Most information returns are due by February 28 (or 29). The deadline is extended to March 31 for returns filed electronically. The following penalty structure applies for 2022 information returns (to be filed in 2023):

1. Any reporting failure corrected within 30 days after the due date—$55 per return, with a yearly maximum of $588,500 ($206,000 for small businesses)
2. Any reporting failure corrected after the 30-day period but by August 1—$110 per return, with a yearly maximum of $1,177,500 ($588,500 for small businesses)
3. Any reporting failure corrected after August 1—$290 per return, with a yearly maximum of $3,532,500 ($1,172,500 for small businesses)

For purposes of these penalties, "small businesses" are those having average annual gross receipts of $5 million or less for the last three years.

A similar penalty applies for failure to timely furnish correct payee statements to payees.

EXAMPLE 26   On July 15, 2023, Kane Company realized it failed to file 300 Forms 1099-MISC for independent contractors who did work for the company during 2022. Kane corrected the error on July 20, 2023. Kane's penalty for filing a late information return is $33,000 (300 × $110 per return penalty because the error was corrected by August 1).

EXAMPLE 27   On March 31, 2023, Carnes, Inc. electronically filed 1,000 information returns. On August 20, 2023, Carnes realized that 600 of those returns contained incorrect information, and immediately corrected its mistake. Carnes's penalty for filing incorrect information returns is $174,000 (600 incorrect returns × $290 per return penalty because the error was not corrected by August 1).

    August 1 is approximately when the IRS begins processing information returns. Thus, filing a return after August 1 is the same as not filing one at all. For this reason, higher penalties are imposed on information returns filed after August 1.

The IRS imposes a penalty of $50 for each failure to provide certain required specified information, such as social security and other taxpayer identification numbers. [I.R.C. §6723] The maximum penalty is $100,000 a year. No penalty applies if it can be shown that the reporting failure was due to reasonable cause and not to willful neglect. Also, a *de minimis* correction rule limits the penalty for a certain number of timely-filed returns that contain incomplete or incorrect information, even if reasonable cause cannot be shown. To apply, correction of the errors must take place by August 1. Under the *de minimis* rule, the penalty for filing incorrect returns will not apply to the *greater of*:

1. 10 returns, or
2. One-half of 1% of the total number of information returns required to be filed.

There also is a safe harbor for certain *de minimis* dollar amount errors on information returns. If any dollar amounts are incorrect on an information return filed with the IRS or a payee statement furnished to a payee, the dollar amount(s) do not need to be corrected, and the return or statement will be treated as correct, if:

1. the difference between the dollar amount reported on the filed return or furnished payee statement, and the correct amount is no more than $100; and
2. the difference between the dollar amount reported for tax withheld, on the filed return or furnished payee statement, and the correct amount is no more than $25.

The safe harbor does not apply if the payee elects to receive a corrected statement.

¶1310   The Audit Process

When returns reach the IRS, a computer makes an initial check for math or clerical errors. The IRS corrects these errors and sends a notice of the correction to the taxpayer. It either requests payment for additional tax or encloses a refund for an overpayment. The types of errors include:

■ A math error shown on the return
■ Incorrect use of an IRS table
■ Inconsistent entries on the return

- Omission of information necessary to backup an amount shown on the return
- Entry of a deduction or credit item that exceeds a statutory limit based on information appearing on the return

Returns most in need of examination are identified by computer, using math formulas developed by the IRS to single out returns most likely to contain errors. The system focuses on those returns that stand the best chance of producing enough additional tax revenue to justify an audit. Examples of factors that could affect a return's selection for audit include:

- Large amounts of gross income
- Self-employed taxpayers with high incomes and large deductions
- Cash businesses (e.g., restaurants, businesses that provide services)
- Excessive itemized deductions relative to income level
- Claims for large refunds
- Disagreement between reported income and information returns (e.g., Form 1099, Form W-2)
- A large increase in dependents claimed
- A major decrease in rental income
- Informant information
- Prior tax deficiencies

Returns containing minor items that need clarification go to the audit division for correction by correspondence. Such returns may contain questionable charitable contributions or medical expenses, as an example.

Returns having the greatest audit possibility are sent to the district audit division to be examined. Within the district audit division, there are two types of audits. One is the **office audit**, which usually takes place in an IRS office and is limited in scope. A short discussion may be all that is needed to clear up any questions that arise during an office audit. The other is the **field audit**, which normally takes place on the taxpayer's premises. This is typically a much more extensive audit involving a number of major issues.

¶1310.01   BURDEN OF PROOF

Historically, the burden of proof for most tax disputes has rested with the taxpayer. During the mid-1980s, the IRS came under scrutiny for the way taxpayers were being treated during the audit process. Congress responded by enacting tax laws that shift the burden of proof to the IRS in court proceedings over factual issues when:

1. The taxpayer has provided the IRS with relevant, credible evidence,
2. The taxpayer has complied with the IRS's substantiation and record-keeping requirements, and
3. The taxpayer has maintained proper records and cooperates with any reasonable IRS request for witnesses, information, documents, meetings, and interviews.

To illustrate these rules, take a situation where the taxpayer uses the standard mileage method to deduct automobile expenses on Schedule C. As discussed in Chapter 7, the tax laws require that the taxpayer maintain written evidence to support the number of business miles driven during the year. Thus, if the taxpayer provides the IRS with the mileage log used to record the number of business miles driven during the tax year in question, the burden of proving that the deduction is not valid rests with the IRS.

In addition, the IRS has the burden of proof whenever it (1) uses statistics to reconstruct the taxpayer's income, (2) assesses the taxpayer with a penalty or other addition to tax, or (3) accuses the taxpayer of fraud with intent to evade taxes. The IRS also has the burden of proof in certain cases that involve hobby losses and in cases that involve the accumulated earnings tax for C corporations.

¶1310.02   **THE APPEALS PROCESS**

After the completion of an audit, the taxpayer will receive a report of the findings, along with a 30-day-letter describing the taxpayer's rights to appeal the findings. A taxpayer who does not agree with the findings may file an appeal. The taxpayer has a right to request a meeting with the examining officer to work out their differences. This request should be made within 15 days from the date of the letter. Taxpayers not wanting to meet with the examining officer have 30 days to either start the formal appeal process or make arrangements to pay the tax.

An *Appeals Office* headed by a Regional Director of Appeals is established in each Internal Revenue Service region. Each office has the authority to fully settle cases. When the amount involved does not exceed $2,500, the taxpayer will be granted an Appeals Office conference merely by requesting it. However, when the amount exceeds $2,500, an Appeals Office conference is available only to taxpayers who file a written protest stating the facts upon which the appeal is based.

If the taxpayer and the Appeals Office cannot agree on the issues in dispute, the taxpayer will receive a 90-*day deficiency notice*. This letter must be mailed to the taxpayer within three years of the date that the income tax return was filed. The taxpayer may petition for a judicial review with one of three trial courts. The taxpayer may file a petition with the Tax Court within 90 days after the deficiency notice is mailed. The taxpayer may also file a petition with the district court or U.S. Court of Claims to have the case heard. After 90 days have lapsed, the taxpayer's only avenues for a judicial review are with the district court or U.S. Court of Claims.

Either the taxpayer or the IRS can petition the Circuit Court of Appeals to review the trial court's decision. Final disposition of the case may be taken to the United States Supreme Court. The Supreme Court will hear only those cases it chooses to review. All of these steps may take years. However, final assessment of the tax due from a taxpayer may not be made until the case is closed. The IRS Commissioner then has 60 days from the final decision to make an assessment of the tax.

¶1311   **Taxpayer Rights**

Taxpayers have the right to plan their business and personal affairs so they will pay the least amount of tax due under the law. They also have the right to be treated fairly, professionally, promptly, and courteously by the IRS. The law entitles taxpayers to information and IRS assistance in complying with the tax laws. The IRS provides a wide variety of informational materials, educational programs, and tax assistance programs to aid people in understanding and complying with the tax laws.

Taxpayers who need a copy of a prior year tax return may receive it by completing Form 4506, Request for Copy of Tax Return. This form is sent to the IRS along with a small fee. If only certain information is needed, such as reported income from a prior year, the taxpayer may get this information for free. To receive this information, the taxpayer should write, visit, or call an IRS office. A taxpayer can also file Form 4506-T, Request for Transcript of Tax Return, to request tax return information free of charge.

Special assistance programs are available to people who cannot resolve their tax problems through normal channels. Help is also available to those whose tax problems cause significant hardship (that is, the inability to provide necessities).

People who have a complaint about the IRS may write to the district director or the service center director for their area. Additional information on taxpayer rights may be found in IRS Publication 1, *Your Rights as a Taxpayer*.

¶1312   **Tax Preparers' Responsibilities**

Many tax returns are prepared by someone other than the taxpayer. The tax laws consider anyone receiving pay in exchange for preparing an income tax return as an **income tax return preparer**. In the tax law, there are standards that must be adhered to by all income tax return preparers. Penalties that may be assessed for failing to adhere to these standards include the following. [I.R.C. §6695] For each of the first five penalties listed below, for a failure on a 2022 return or refund claim filed in 2023, the maximum annual penalty is $28,000.

1. A $55 penalty each time the tax preparer fails to sign the tax return as a paid preparer.
2. A $55 penalty each time the tax preparer fails to provide the taxpayer with a copy of his or her tax return.
3. A $55 penalty each time the tax preparer fails to keep a copy of the taxpayer's tax return.
4. A $55 penalty each time the tax preparer fails to furnish a required identification number.
5. A $55 penalty each time the tax preparer fails to file a correct information return.
6. A $560 penalty each time the tax preparer fails to exercise due diligence with respect to determining a taxpayer's eligibility for (or the amount of) the child, American Opportunity, lifetime learning, and earned income tax credits, or for head of household status.
7. A $560 penalty each time the tax preparer improperly endorses a taxpayer's refund check.

In addition, a tax preparer may be subject to the following penalties for understatements of a taxpayer's tax liability:

1. A penalty equal to the *greater of* (1) $1,000 or (ii) 50% of the income derived (or to be derived) from preparing the return will be assessed if the tax preparer prepares a return or refund claim in which any part of the tax liability understatement is due to an unreasonable position of which the preparer knew or reasonably should have known. An **unreasonable position** is one that does not have substantial authority. Substantial authority generally means that the likelihood that the taxpayer's position is correct is somewhere between 50% and the more lenient reasonable basis standard. Tax preparers can avoid this penalty if there is a reasonable basis for taking the position and the position is disclosed on the return. [I.R.C. §6694(a)]
2. A penalty equal to the *greater of* (1) $5,000 or (ii) 75% of the income derived (or to be derived) from preparing the return or refund claim will be assessed if the tax preparer willfully attempts to understate the tax liability, or recklessly or intentionally disregards the rules or regulations. [I.R.C. §6694(b)]

Attorneys and certified public accountants (CPAs) who prepare tax returns have met certain educational standards, passed a standardized exam, and met specific experience requirements that allow them to be licensed to practice in their respective professions. Enrolled agents, while not having met the level of education or experience that is required of CPAs and attorneys, have passed an IRS exam and have been granted the authority to represent taxpayers before the IRS. Other paid preparers can receive compensation for their services, but are not allowed to communicate with the IRS on behalf of their clients.

The IRS imposes additional standards for professional tax preparers. Failure to adhere to these standards may result in penalties being assessed, including disbarment from practicing before the IRS. Those interested in learning more about the additional standards for professional tax preparers should refer to IRS Circular 230, which can be obtained from the IRS website. (See Appendix A for instructions on how to access the IRS website.)

Paid tax preparers must provide the IRS with their preparer tax identification number (PTIN) in the designated area where they sign the tax return. Paid tax preparers include anyone who prepares all or substantially all of a federal tax return. There is a small fee to get a PTIN, and the IRS requires that PTINs be renewed each year. For 2022 returns filed in 2023, failing to provide a valid PTIN on the tax return will result in a $55 penalty per return, with a maximum $28,000 penalty for the calendar year.

¶1313   Amended Returns

Individuals file Form 1040-X, Amended U.S. Individual Income Tax Return, to correct mistakes made on their originally filed tax returns. Typical mistakes taxpayers may need to correct include incorrect use of filing status, or failing to report the correct amount of income, deductions, or tax credits. Taxpayers generally have three years from when they filed their original tax return to file an amended return. Taxpayers who file their tax return before the original due date are considered to have filed their tax return on April 15.

EXAMPLE 28	Joan filed an extension to file her 2022 tax return, giving her until October 15, 2023 (six months longer, see ¶208) to file her 2022 return. Joan files her return on July 16, 2023. Joan has until July 16, 2025 (three years after filing her return) to file an amended tax return for 2022.

EXAMPLE 29	Ami filed her 2019 return on March 29, 2020. For purpose of filing an amended return, Ami is considered to have filed her return on April 15, 2020. Thus, she has until April 15, 2023 to file an amended tax return for 2019.

¶1313.01   FILLED-IN FORM 1040-X

 INFORMATION FOR FIGURE 13-8:

Victor and Sharon Martin failed to claim a **$650** contribution made on July 15, 2021, to the General Hospital, Peoria, Illinois, a qualifying charity. Accordingly, they amend their Form 1040 for 2021 and claim a refund by filing a Form 1040-X on **March 2, 2022.** The Martins had no children or other dependents in 2021. Neither wants $3 to go to the presidential campaign fund, and they did not check the appropriate boxes on their original return. They enter the information shown in bold and follow the instructions on Form 1040-X to compute their refund due. The Martins provide the reason they are filing Form 1040-X in Part III of the form. They also attach both the originally filed and revised Schedule A to their amended return.

Line #
- 1: Adjusted gross income, **$91,094**
- 2A: Itemized deductions, originally reported, **$29,200**
- 2B: Net change, **$650**. Change explained in Part III.
- 2C: Itemized deductions, **$29,850** ($29,200 originally reported + $650)
- 6A: Tax on $61,894, **$7,027** (from the 2021 **Tax Table**)
- 6C: Tax on $61,244, **$6,949** (from the 2021 **Tax Table**)
- 10: Other taxes, **$4,177** (self-employment tax on net profits from Victor's business)
- 12: Federal income withheld, **$3,856**
- 13: Estimated payments, **$6,500**
- 16: Amount paid with original return, **$851**

Figure 13-8: Filled-In Form 1040-X (Page 1)

Form 1040-X
(Rev. July 2021)

Department of the Treasury—Internal Revenue Service
Amended U.S. Individual Income Tax Return
▶ Use this revision to amend 2019 or later tax returns.
▶ Go to *www.irs.gov/Form1040X* for instructions and the latest information.

OMB No. 1545-0074

This return is for calendar year (enter year) _____ **or fiscal year** (enter month and year ended) _____

Your first name and middle initial	Last name	Your social security number
Victor Z	Martin	4 7 1 0 0 0 4 1 9
If joint return, spouse's first name and middle initial	Last name	Spouse's social security number
Sharon O	Martin	9 1 6 0 0 2 1 2 4

Current home address (number and street). If you have a P.O. box, see instructions. — Apt. no. — Your phone number
2886 Linwood Court — (309) 555-0846

City, town or post office, state, and ZIP code. If you have a foreign address, also complete spaces below. See instructions.
Peoria, IL 61064-5414

Foreign country name — Foreign province/state/county — Foreign postal code

Amended return filing status. You must check one box even if you are not changing your filing status. **Caution:** In general, you can't change your filing status from married filing jointly to married filing separately after the return due date.

☐ Single ☑ Married filing jointly ☐ Married filing separately (MFS) ☐ Head of household (HOH) ☐ Qualifying widow(er) (QW)

If you checked the MFS box, enter the name of your spouse. If you checked the HOH or QW box, enter the child's name if the qualifying person is a child but not your dependent ▶

Enter on lines 1 through 23, columns A through C, the amounts for the return year entered above.
Use Part III on page 2 to explain any changes.

			A. Original amount reported or as previously adjusted (see instructions)	B. Net change— amount of increase or (decrease)— explain in Part III	C. Correct amount
Income and Deductions					
1	Adjusted gross income. If a net operating loss (NOL) carryback is included, check here ▶ ☐	1	91,094		91,094
2	Itemized deductions or standard deduction	2	29,200	650	29,850
3	Subtract line 2 from line 1	3	61,894	(650)	61,244
4a	Reserved for future use	4a			
b	Qualified business income deduction	4b			
5	Taxable income. Subtract line 4b from line 3. If the result is zero or less, enter -0-	5	61,894	(650)	61,244
Tax Liability					
6	Tax. Enter method(s) used to figure tax (see instructions): Tax Table	6	7,027	(78)	6,949
7	Nonrefundable credits. If a general business credit carryback is included, check here ▶ ☐	7			
8	Subtract line 7 from line 6. If the result is zero or less, enter -0-	8	7,027		6,949
9	Reserved for future use	9			
10	Other taxes	10	4,177		4,177
11	Total tax. Add lines 8 and 10	11	11,204		11,126
Payments					
12	Federal income tax withheld and excess social security and tier 1 RRTA tax withheld. (**If changing,** see instructions.)	12	3,856		3,856
13	Estimated tax payments, including amount applied from prior year's return	13	6,500		6,500
14	Earned income credit (EIC)	14			
15	Refundable credits from: ☐ Schedule 8812 Form(s) ☐ 2439 ☐ 4136 ☐ 8863 ☐ 8885 ☐ 8962 or ☐ other (specify): _____	15			
16	Total amount paid with request for extension of time to file, tax paid with original return, and additional tax paid after return was filed	16			848
17	Total payments. Add lines 12 through 15, column C, and line 16	17			11,204
Refund or Amount You Owe					
18	Overpayment, if any, as shown on original return or as previously adjusted by the IRS	18			
19	Subtract line 18 from line 17. (If less than zero, see instructions.)	19			11,204
20	**Amount you owe.** If line 11, column C, is more than line 19, enter the difference	20			
21	If line 11, column C, is less than line 19, enter the difference. This is the amount **overpaid** on this return	21			78
22	Amount of line 21 you want **refunded to you**	22			
23	Amount of line 21 you want **applied to your** (enter year): _____ estimated tax	23	78		

Complete and sign this form on page 2.

For Paperwork Reduction Act Notice, see separate instructions. — Cat. No. 11360L — Form **1040-X** (Rev. 7-2021)

¶1313.01

Figure 13-8: Filled-In Form 1040-X (Page 2)

Form 1040-X (Rev. 7-2021)   Page **2**

Part I   Dependents

Complete this part to change any information relating to your dependents.
This would include a change in the number of dependents.
Enter the information for the return year entered at the top of page 1.

		A. Original number of dependents reported or as previously adjusted	**B. Net change —** amount of increase or (decrease)	**C. Correct number**
24	Reserved for future use **24**			
25	Your dependent children who lived with you **25**			
26	Your dependent children who didn't live with you due to divorce or separation **26**			
27	Other dependents **27**			
28	Reserved for future use **28**			
29	Reserved for future use **29**			

30   List **ALL** dependents (children and others) claimed on this amended return.

Dependents (see instructions):

If more than four dependents, see instructions and check here ▶ ☐	**(a)** First name Last name	**(b)** Social security number	**(c)** Relationship to you	**(d)** ✓ if qualifies for (see instructions): Child tax credit	Credit for other dependents
				☐	☐
				☐	☐
				☐	☐
				☐	☐

Part II   Presidential Election Campaign Fund (for the return year entered at the top of page 1)

Checking below won't increase your tax or reduce your refund.

☐ Check here if you didn't previously want $3 to go to the fund, but now do.
☐ Check here if this is a joint return and your spouse did not previously want $3 to go to the fund, but now does.

Part III   Explanation of Changes. In the space provided below, tell us why you are filing Form 1040-X.

▶ Attach any supporting documents and new or changed forms and schedules.

A $650 contribution paid to Peoria General Hospital on July 15, 2021 was omitted in error from Schedule A line 16 for 2021. This amount is included on Form 1040X line 2 column B and is included in the correct itemized deduction amount for 2021. A copy of the originally filed 2021 Schedule A and revised 2021 schedule A are attached.

Remember to keep a copy of this form for your records.

Sign Here

Under penalties of perjury, I declare that I have filed an original return, and that I have examined this amended return, including accompanying schedules and statements, and to the best of my knowledge and belief, this amended return is true, correct, and complete. Declaration of preparer (other than taxpayer) is based on all information about which the preparer has any knowledge.

▶ _____   _____   Carpenter
Your signature   Date   Your occupation

▶ _____   _____   Secretary
Spouse's signature. If a joint return, **both** must sign.   Date   Spouse's occupation

Paid Preparer Use Only

Print/Type preparer's name	Preparer's signature	Date	Check ☐ if self-employed	PTIN
Firm's name ▶			Firm's EIN ▶	
Firm's address ▶			Phone no.	

For forms and publications, visit *www.irs.gov/Forms*.   Form **1040-X** (Rev. 7-2021)

13

QUESTIONS AND PROBLEMS

1. **Withholding Allowances.** (Obj. 1)

   a. How do employees claim withholding allowances?

   b. If employees do not give their employer a completed and signed Form W-4, Employee's Withholding Certificate, what withholding action must the employer take?

   c. If a taxpayer holds more than one job, can the taxpayer claim withholding allowances with more than one employer?

2. **Withholding Rules.** (Obj. 1) What tax withholding action, if any, must a taxpayer take for each of the following situations?

   a. Withholding allowances decrease.

   b. Withholding allowances increase.

3. **Withholding Rules.** (Obj. 1)

   a. An employee files a Form W-4 on June 10, 2022, claiming to be exempt from withholding. For what period does the exempt status apply?

   b. Does an exemption from withholding that an employee claims on Form W-4 apply to both FICA taxes and federal income taxes?

4. **Withholding Allowances.** (Obj. 1) On the basis of the information given, how many total withholding allowances can be claimed for 2022 by each of the following taxpayers A-D? Identify the type of each withholding allowance claimed.

   A: A single taxpayer, age 12, is claimed as a dependent on his parents' return. The taxpayer will earn $800 in wages during the year and receive dividends of $50.

   B: A single taxpayer, age 20, is not claimed as a dependent on another return. The taxpayer will have earned income of $18,500 and interest income of $150. The taxpayer uses the standard deduction and has no adjustments to income.

   C: A married couple files jointly. The couple claim four dependent children (ages 3 to 16). The taxpayer has two jobs, and the spouse has one job. The taxpayer's total wages are $79,500, and the spouse's wages are $20,500. Dividend income equals $400. No adjustments to income exist. Childcare expenses are $1,200, and expected itemized deductions are $17,200.

   D: A single taxpayer has one dependent (age 9) and files as head of household. The taxpayer will earn $44,600 from one job. Expected interest income is $200. The taxpayer has no adjustments to income. Childcare expenses are $3,200, and expected itemized deductions are $7,000.

Taxpayer	Number of Withholding Allowances	Type of Withholding Allowances
A	_____	_____
B	_____	_____
C	_____	_____
D	_____	_____

5. **Form W-4.** (Obj. 6) Married taxpayers, Ethel P. (SSN 448-00-4747) and Irving J. Mead, file a joint return. They reside at 1001 West Wind Plaza, Fox Lake, Wisconsin 53933-4611. Both are 42 years of age. They have one dependent child, Jean, age 14.

On November 15, 2022, the Meads became aware that their income tax for 2022 will be underpaid. Ethel decides to file a new Form W-4, Employee's Withholding Certificate, to change the number of withholding allowances to ensure more appropriate withholding in the future. Ethel will not claim an allowance for Irving but will claim Jean. The Meads' estimated income and deductions is as follows.

Wages:	Ethel: Axel Maintenance Company	$41,000
	Beta Corporation	8,000
	Total gross wages—Ethel	$49,000
	Irving: Readers' Specialty Store	24,500
Total gross wages		$73,500
Dividend income—Ethel		2,316
Interest income—Irving		1,034
Total		$76,850

The Meads estimate that their itemized deductions will be $32,650. In addition, they anticipate the following "deductions for AGI" and "other payments."

IRA contributions	$4,000
Fees for Mary Jean's school textbooks	216
Contributions to political party	320
Total	$4,536

Complete the 2022 Form W-4 that Ethel files with her employer, Axel Maintenance Company. Ethel signs and dates the form on November 18, 2022. Also prepare the necessary Form W-4 worksheets to determine the total number of withholding allowances. Use the form and worksheet provided on the pages that follow.

6. **FICA Taxes.** (Obj. 1) Discuss employers' FICA withholding responsibilities and how they differ (if at all) from employees' FICA tax liabilities.

(Use for Problem 5.)

Form **W-4** Department of the Treasury Internal Revenue Service	**Employee's Withholding Certificate** ▶ Complete Form W-4 so that your employer can withhold the correct federal income tax from your pay. ▶ Give Form W-4 to your employer. ▶ Your withholding is subject to review by the IRS.	OMB No. 1545-0074 20**22**

Step 1:

Enter Personal Information

(a) First name and middle initial Last name	(b) Social security number
Address	▶ **Does your name match the name on your social security card?** If not, to ensure you get credit for your earnings, contact SSA at 800-772-1213 or go to *www.ssa.gov*.
City or town, state, and ZIP code	

(c) ☐ **Single** or **Married filing separately**

☐ **Married filing jointly** or **Qualifying widow(er)**

☐ **Head of household** (Check only if you're unmarried and pay more than half the costs of keeping up a home for yourself and a qualifying individual.)

Complete Steps 2–4 ONLY if they apply to you; otherwise, skip to Step 5. See page 2 for more information on each step, who can claim exemption from withholding, when to use the estimator at *www.irs.gov/W4App*, and privacy.

Step 2:

Multiple Jobs or Spouse Works

Complete this step if you (1) hold more than one job at a time, or (2) are married filing jointly and your spouse also works. The correct amount of withholding depends on income earned from all of these jobs.

Do **only one** of the following.

(a) Use the estimator at *www.irs.gov/W4App* for most accurate withholding for this step (and Steps 3–4); **or**

(b) Use the Multiple Jobs Worksheet on page 3 and enter the result in Step 4(c) below for roughly accurate withholding; **or**

(c) If there are only two jobs total, you may check this box. Do the same on Form W-4 for the other job. This option is accurate for jobs with similar pay; otherwise, more tax than necessary may be withheld . . ▶ ☐

TIP: To be accurate, submit a 2022 Form W-4 for all other jobs. If you (or your spouse) have self-employment income, including as an independent contractor, use the estimator.

Complete Steps 3–4(b) on Form W-4 for only ONE of these jobs. Leave those steps blank for the other jobs. (Your withholding will be most accurate if you complete Steps 3–4(b) on the Form W-4 for the highest paying job.)

Step 3:

Claim Dependents

If your total income will be $200,000 or less ($400,000 or less if married filing jointly):

Multiply the number of qualifying children under age 17 by $2,000 ▶ $ _____

Multiply the number of other dependents by $500 . . . . ▶ $ _____

Add the amounts above and enter the total here . . . . **3** | $

Step 4 (optional):

Other Adjustments

(a) **Other income (not from jobs).** If you want tax withheld for other income you expect this year that won't have withholding, enter the amount of other income here. This may include interest, dividends, and retirement income . . . . **4(a)** | $

(b) **Deductions.** If you expect to claim deductions other than the standard deduction and want to reduce your withholding, use the Deductions Worksheet on page 3 and enter the result here . . . . **4(b)** | $

(c) **Extra withholding.** Enter any additional tax you want withheld each **pay period** . . **4(c)** | $

Step 5:

Sign Here

Under penalties of perjury, I declare that this certificate, to the best of my knowledge and belief, is true, correct, and complete.

▶ _____ ▶ _____
    Employee's signature (This form is not valid unless you sign it.)   Date

Employers Only	Employer's name and address	First date of employment	Employer identification number (EIN)

For Privacy Act and Paperwork Reduction Act Notice, see page 3.   Cat. No. 10220Q   Form **W-4** (2022)

(Use for Problem 5.)

General Instructions

Section references are to the Internal Revenue Code.

Future Developments

For the latest information about developments related to Form W-4, such as legislation enacted after it was published, go to *www.irs.gov/FormW4*.

Purpose of Form

Complete Form W-4 so that your employer can withhold the correct federal income tax from your pay. If too little is withheld, you will generally owe tax when you file your tax return and may owe a penalty. If too much is withheld, you will generally be due a refund. Complete a new Form W-4 when changes to your personal or financial situation would change the entries on the form. For more information on withholding and when you must furnish a new Form W-4, see Pub. 505, Tax Withholding and Estimated Tax.

Exemption from withholding. You may claim exemption from withholding for 2022 if you meet both of the following conditions: you had no federal income tax liability in 2021 **and** you expect to have no federal income tax liability in 2022. You had no federal income tax liability in 2021 if (1) your total tax on line 24 on your 2021 Form 1040 or 1040-SR is zero (or less than the sum of lines 27a, 28, 29, and 30), or (2) you were not required to file a return because your income was below the filing threshold for your correct filing status. If you claim exemption, you will have no income tax withheld from your paycheck and may owe taxes and penalties when you file your 2022 tax return. To claim exemption from withholding, certify that you meet both of the conditions above by writing "Exempt" on Form W-4 in the space below Step 4(c). Then, complete Steps 1(a), 1(b), and 5. Do not complete any other steps. You will need to submit a new Form W-4 by February 15, 2023.

Your privacy. If you prefer to limit information provided in Steps 2 through 4, use the online estimator, which will also increase accuracy.

As an alternative to the estimator: if you have concerns with Step 2(c), you may choose Step 2(b); if you have concerns with Step 4(a), you may enter an additional amount you want withheld per pay period in Step 4(c). If this is the only job in your household, you may instead check the box in Step 2(c), which will increase your withholding and significantly reduce your paycheck (often by thousands of dollars over the year).

When to use the estimator. Consider using the estimator at *www.irs.gov/W4App* if you:

1. Expect to work only part of the year;

2. Have dividend or capital gain income, or are subject to additional taxes, such as Additional Medicare Tax;

3. Have self-employment income (see below); or

4. Prefer the most accurate withholding for multiple job situations.

Self-employment. Generally, you will owe both income and self-employment taxes on any self-employment income you receive separate from the wages you receive as an employee. If you want to pay these taxes through withholding from your wages, use the estimator at *www.irs.gov/W4App* to figure the amount to have withheld.

Nonresident alien. If you're a nonresident alien, see Notice 1392, Supplemental Form W-4 Instructions for Nonresident Aliens, before completing this form.

Specific Instructions

Step 1(c). Check your anticipated filing status. This will determine the standard deduction and tax rates used to compute your withholding.

Step 2. Use this step if you (1) have more than one job at the same time, or (2) are married filing jointly and you and your spouse both work.

Option **(a)** most accurately calculates the additional tax you need to have withheld, while option **(b)** does so with a little less accuracy.

If you (and your spouse) have a total of only two jobs, you may instead check the box in option **(c)**. The box must also be checked on the Form W-4 for the other job. If the box is checked, the standard deduction and tax brackets will be cut in half for each job to calculate withholding. This option is roughly accurate for jobs with similar pay; otherwise, more tax than necessary may be withheld, and this extra amount will be larger the greater the difference in pay is between the two jobs.

 Multiple jobs. Complete Steps 3 through 4(b) on only one Form W-4. Withholding will be most accurate if you do this on the Form W-4 for the highest paying job.

Step 3. This step provides instructions for determining the amount of the child tax credit and the credit for other dependents that you may be able to claim when you file your tax return. To qualify for the child tax credit, the child must be under age 17 as of December 31, must be your dependent who generally lives with you for more than half the year, and must have the required social security number. You may be able to claim a credit for other dependents for whom a child tax credit can't be claimed, such as an older child or a qualifying relative. For additional eligibility requirements for these credits, see Pub. 501, Dependents, Standard Deduction, and Filing Information. You can also include **other tax credits** for which you are eligible in this step, such as the foreign tax credit and the education tax credits. To do so, add an estimate of the amount for the year to your credits for dependents and enter the total amount in Step 3. Including these credits will increase your paycheck and reduce the amount of any refund you may receive when you file your tax return.

Step 4 (optional).

Step 4(a). Enter in this step the total of your other estimated income for the year, if any. You shouldn't include income from any jobs or self-employment. If you complete Step 4(a), you likely won't have to make estimated tax payments for that income. If you prefer to pay estimated tax rather than having tax on other income withheld from your paycheck, see Form 1040-ES, Estimated Tax for Individuals.

Step 4(b). Enter in this step the amount from the Deductions Worksheet, line 5, if you expect to claim deductions other than the basic standard deduction on your 2022 tax return and want to reduce your withholding to account for these deductions. This includes both itemized deductions and other deductions such as for student loan interest and IRAs.

Step 4(c). Enter in this step any additional tax you want withheld from your pay **each pay period**, including any amounts from the Multiple Jobs Worksheet, line 4. Entering an amount here will reduce your paycheck and will either increase your refund or reduce any amount of tax that you owe.

(Use for Problem 5.)

Form W-4 (2022)   Page **3**

Step 2(b)—Multiple Jobs Worksheet *(Keep for your records.)*

If you choose the option in Step 2(b) on Form W-4, complete this worksheet (which calculates the total extra tax for all jobs) on **only ONE** Form W-4. Withholding will be most accurate if you complete the worksheet and enter the result on the Form W-4 for the highest paying job.

Note: If more than one job has annual wages of more than $120,000 or there are more than three jobs, see Pub. 505 for additional tables; or, you can use the online withholding estimator at *www.irs.gov/W4App.*

1	**Two jobs.** If you have two jobs or you're married filing jointly and you and your spouse each have one job, find the amount from the appropriate table on page 4. Using the "Higher Paying Job" row and the "Lower Paying Job" column, find the value at the intersection of the two household salaries and enter that value on line 1. Then, **skip** to line 3	**1** $ _____
2	**Three jobs.** If you and/or your spouse have three jobs at the same time, complete lines 2a, 2b, and 2c below. Otherwise, skip to line 3.	
	a Find the amount from the appropriate table on page 4 using the annual wages from the highest paying job in the "Higher Paying Job" row and the annual wages for your next highest paying job in the "Lower Paying Job" column. Find the value at the intersection of the two household salaries and enter that value on line 2a	**2a** $ _____
	b Add the annual wages of the two highest paying jobs from line 2a together and use the total as the wages in the "Higher Paying Job" row and use the annual wages for your third job in the "Lower Paying Job" column to find the amount from the appropriate table on page 4 and enter this amount on line 2b	**2b** $ _____
	c Add the amounts from lines 2a and 2b and enter the result on line 2c	**2c** $ _____
3	Enter the number of pay periods per year for the highest paying job. For example, if that job pays weekly, enter 52; if it pays every other week, enter 26; if it pays monthly, enter 12, etc.	**3** _____
4	**Divide** the annual amount on line 1 or line 2c by the number of pay periods on line 3. Enter this amount here and in **Step 4(c)** of Form W-4 for the highest paying job (along with any other additional amount you want withheld)	**4** $ _____

Step 4(b)—Deductions Worksheet *(Keep for your records.)*

1	Enter an estimate of your 2022 itemized deductions (from Schedule A (Form 1040)). Such deductions may include qualifying home mortgage interest, charitable contributions, state and local taxes (up to $10,000), and medical expenses in excess of 7.5% of your income	**1** $ _____
2	Enter: { • $25,900 if you're married filing jointly or qualifying widow(er) • $19,400 if you're head of household • $12,950 if you're single or married filing separately }	**2** $ _____
3	If line 1 is greater than line 2, subtract line 2 from line 1 and enter the result here. If line 2 is greater than line 1, enter "-0-"	**3** $ _____
4	Enter an estimate of your student loan interest, deductible IRA contributions, and certain other adjustments (from Part II of Schedule 1 (Form 1040)). See Pub. 505 for more information	**4** $ _____
5	**Add** lines 3 and 4. Enter the result here and in **Step 4(b)** of Form W-4	**5** $ _____

(Use for Problem 5.)

| Form W-4 (2022) | | | | | | | | | | | Page **4** |

Married Filing Jointly or Qualifying Widow(er)

Higher Paying Job Annual Taxable Wage & Salary	Lower Paying Job Annual Taxable Wage & Salary											
	$0 - 9,999	$10,000 - 19,999	$20,000 - 29,999	$30,000 - 39,999	$40,000 - 49,999	$50,000 - 59,999	$60,000 - 69,999	$70,000 - 79,999	$80,000 - 89,999	$90,000 - 99,999	$100,000 - 109,999	$110,000 - 120,000
$0 - 9,999	$0	$110	$850	$860	$1,020	$1,020	$1,020	$1,020	$1,020	$1,020	$1,770	$1,870
$10,000 - 19,999	110	1,110	1,860	2,060	2,220	2,220	2,220	2,220	2,220	2,970	3,970	4,070
$20,000 - 29,999	850	1,860	2,800	3,000	3,160	3,160	3,160	3,160	3,910	4,910	5,910	6,010
$30,000 - 39,999	860	2,060	3,000	3,200	3,360	3,360	3,360	4,110	5,110	6,110	7,110	7,210
$40,000 - 49,999	1,020	2,220	3,160	3,360	3,520	3,520	4,270	5,270	6,270	7,270	8,270	8,370
$50,000 - 59,999	1,020	2,220	3,160	3,360	3,520	4,270	5,270	6,270	7,270	8,270	9,270	9,370
$60,000 - 69,999	1,020	2,220	3,160	3,360	4,270	5,270	6,270	7,270	8,270	9,270	10,270	10,370
$70,000 - 79,999	1,020	2,220	3,160	4,110	5,270	6,270	7,270	8,270	9,270	10,270	11,270	11,370
$80,000 - 99,999	1,020	2,820	4,760	5,960	7,120	8,120	9,120	10,120	11,120	12,120	13,150	13,450
$100,000 - 149,999	1,870	4,070	6,010	7,210	8,370	9,370	10,510	11,710	12,910	14,110	15,310	15,600
$150,000 - 239,999	2,040	4,440	6,580	7,980	9,340	10,540	11,740	12,940	14,140	15,340	16,540	16,830
$240,000 - 259,999	2,040	4,440	6,580	7,980	9,340	10,540	11,740	12,940	14,140	15,340	16,540	17,590
$260,000 - 279,999	2,040	4,440	6,580	7,980	9,340	10,540	11,740	12,940	14,140	16,100	18,100	19,190
$280,000 - 299,999	2,040	4,440	6,580	7,980	9,340	10,540	11,740	13,700	15,700	17,700	19,700	20,790
$300,000 - 319,999	2,040	4,440	6,580	7,980	9,340	11,300	13,300	15,300	17,300	19,300	21,300	22,390
$320,000 - 364,999	2,100	5,300	8,240	10,440	12,600	14,600	16,600	18,600	20,600	22,600	24,870	26,260
$365,000 - 524,999	2,970	6,470	9,710	12,210	14,670	16,970	19,270	21,570	23,870	26,170	28,470	29,870
$525,000 and over	3,140	6,840	10,280	12,980	15,640	18,140	20,640	23,140	25,640	28,140	30,640	32,240

Single or Married Filing Separately

Higher Paying Job Annual Taxable Wage & Salary	Lower Paying Job Annual Taxable Wage & Salary											
	$0 - 9,999	$10,000 - 19,999	$20,000 - 29,999	$30,000 - 39,999	$40,000 - 49,999	$50,000 - 59,999	$60,000 - 69,999	$70,000 - 79,999	$80,000 - 89,999	$90,000 - 99,999	$100,000 - 109,999	$110,000 - 120,000
$0 - 9,999	$400	$930	$1,020	$1,020	$1,250	$1,870	$1,870	$1,870	$1,870	$1,970	$2,040	$2,040
$10,000 - 19,999	930	1,570	1,660	1,890	2,890	3,510	3,510	3,510	3,610	3,810	3,880	3,880
$20,000 - 29,999	1,020	1,660	1,990	2,990	3,990	4,610	4,610	4,710	4,910	5,110	5,180	5,180
$30,000 - 39,999	1,020	1,890	2,990	3,990	4,990	5,610	5,710	5,910	6,110	6,310	6,380	6,380
$40,000 - 59,999	1,870	3,510	4,610	5,610	6,680	7,500	7,700	7,900	8,100	8,300	8,370	8,370
$60,000 - 79,999	1,870	3,510	4,680	5,880	7,080	7,900	8,100	8,300	8,500	8,700	8,970	9,770
$80,000 - 99,999	1,940	3,780	5,080	6,280	7,480	8,300	8,500	8,700	9,100	10,100	10,970	11,770
$100,000 - 124,999	2,040	3,880	5,180	6,380	7,580	8,400	9,140	10,140	11,140	12,140	13,040	14,140
$125,000 - 149,999	2,040	3,880	5,180	6,520	8,520	10,140	11,140	12,140	13,320	14,620	15,790	16,890
$150,000 - 174,999	2,040	4,420	6,520	8,520	10,520	12,170	13,470	14,770	16,070	17,370	18,540	19,640
$175,000 - 199,999	2,720	5,360	7,460	9,630	11,930	13,860	15,160	16,460	17,760	19,060	20,230	21,330
$200,000 - 249,999	2,970	5,920	8,310	10,610	12,910	14,840	16,140	17,440	18,740	20,040	21,210	22,310
$250,000 - 399,999	2,970	5,920	8,310	10,610	12,910	14,840	16,140	17,440	18,740	20,040	21,210	22,310
$400,000 - 449,999	2,970	5,920	8,310	10,610	12,910	14,840	16,140	17,440	18,740	20,040	21,210	22,470
$450,000 and over	3,140	6,290	8,880	11,380	13,880	16,010	17,510	19,010	20,510	22,010	23,380	24,680

Head of Household

Higher Paying Job Annual Taxable Wage & Salary	Lower Paying Job Annual Taxable Wage & Salary											
	$0 - 9,999	$10,000 - 19,999	$20,000 - 29,999	$30,000 - 39,999	$40,000 - 49,999	$50,000 - 59,999	$60,000 - 69,999	$70,000 - 79,999	$80,000 - 89,999	$90,000 - 99,999	$100,000 - 109,999	$110,000 - 120,000
$0 - 9,999	$0	$760	$910	$1,020	$1,020	$1,020	$1,190	$1,870	$1,870	$1,870	$2,040	$2,040
$10,000 - 19,999	760	1,820	2,110	2,220	2,220	2,390	3,390	4,070	4,070	4,240	4,440	4,440
$20,000 - 29,999	910	2,110	2,400	2,510	2,680	3,680	4,680	5,360	5,530	5,730	5,930	5,930
$30,000 - 39,999	1,020	2,220	2,510	2,790	3,790	4,790	5,790	6,640	6,840	7,040	7,240	7,240
$40,000 - 59,999	1,020	2,240	3,530	4,640	5,640	6,780	7,980	8,860	9,060	9,260	9,460	9,460
$60,000 - 79,999	1,870	4,070	5,360	6,610	7,810	9,010	10,210	11,090	11,290	11,490	11,690	12,170
$80,000 - 99,999	1,870	4,210	5,700	7,010	8,210	9,410	10,610	11,490	11,690	12,380	13,370	14,170
$100,000 - 124,999	2,040	4,440	5,930	7,240	8,440	9,640	10,860	12,540	13,540	14,540	15,540	16,480
$125,000 - 149,999	2,040	4,440	5,930	7,240	8,860	10,860	12,860	14,540	15,540	16,830	18,130	19,230
$150,000 - 174,999	2,040	4,460	6,750	8,860	10,860	12,860	15,000	16,980	18,280	19,580	20,880	21,980
$175,000 - 199,999	2,720	5,920	8,210	10,320	12,600	14,900	17,200	19,180	20,480	21,780	23,080	24,180
$200,000 - 449,999	2,970	6,470	9,060	11,480	13,780	16,080	18,380	20,360	21,660	22,960	24,250	25,360
$450,000 and over	3,140	6,840	9,630	12,250	14,750	17,250	19,750	21,930	23,430	24,930	26,420	27,730

7. **FICA Taxes.** (Obj. 1) For each of the following scenarios, compute the amount of each employee's Medicare taxes owed (to be refunded) that they report on their respective tax returns.

    a. Mia, a single taxpayer, works for two employers during the year. Medicare wages at her jobs are $85,000 and $150,000, respectively.

    b. Shawn, a single taxpayer, works for two employers during the year. Medicare wages at his jobs are $215,000 and $35,000, respectively.

    c. Ron and Patty Simone file a joint tax return. Both Ron and Patty work full-time. Their Medicare wages are $210,000 and $120,000, respectively.

    d. Same as in Part c., except that Patty's wages are $20,000 (instead of $120,000).

8. **Form W-2.** (Obj. 6)

    a. By what date must an employer file Copy A of an employee's Form W-2 with the Social Security Administration?

    b. By what date must an employer give an employee Copies B and C of the employee's Form W-2?

9. **Form W-2.** (Obj. 6) Examine a Form W-2, Wage and Tax Statement. Explain the special meaning of *Statutory employee* in box 13.

10. **Form W-2.** (Obj. 6) Speedy Department Store (EIN is 33-1004821) is located at 2706 Bluff Drive, Boston, Massachusetts 02101-3214. Prepare the 2022 Form W-2, Wage and Tax Statement, for Susan W. Jenkins, a married employee with no dependents. The following data was taken from Speedy's payroll records:

> Susan W. Jenkins (SSN 331-00-4821)
>   214 Northup Street, Boston, Massachusetts 02112-1415

Total wages paid (before payroll deductions)	$45,000.00
Social security tax withheld	Calculate
Medicare tax withheld	Calculate
Federal income tax withheld	6,552.00
State income tax withheld	1,125.75
Employer's state I.D. number	25703

22222	VOID ☐	a Employee's social security number	For Official Use Only ▶ OMB No. 1545-0008	
b Employer identification number (EIN)			**1** Wages, tips, other compensation	**2** Federal income tax withheld
c Employer's name, address, and ZIP code			**3** Social security wages	**4** Social security tax withheld
			5 Medicare wages and tips	**6** Medicare tax withheld
			7 Social security tips	**8** Allocated tips
d Control number			**9**	**10** Dependent care benefits
e Employee's first name and initial / Last name / Suff.			**11** Nonqualified plans	**12a** See instructions for box 12
			13 Statutory employee ☐ / Retirement plan ☐ / Third-party sick pay ☐	**12b**
			14 Other	**12c**
				12d
f Employee's address and ZIP code				
15 State / Employer's state ID number	**16** State wages, tips, etc.	**17** State income tax	**18** Local wages, tips, etc.	**19** Local income tax / **20** Locality name

Form **W-2** Wage and Tax Statement   **2022**   Department of the Treasury—Internal Revenue Service
For Privacy Act and Paperwork Reduction Act Notice, see the separate instructions.

Copy A—For Social Security Administration. Send this entire page with Form W-3 to the Social Security Administration; photocopies are **not** acceptable.   Cat. No. 10134D

Do Not Cut, Fold, or Staple Forms on This Page

11. **Form W-3.** (Obj. 6)

   a. What documents does an employer transmit with Form W-3 when filing it with the Social Security Administration?

   b. By what date must an employer file these documents?

12. **Form W-3.** (Obj. 6) Golden Door Company (EIN 70– 0011822), 1906 North Avenue, Reno, Nevada 90234, withheld income and social security taxes from each of its 28 employees during 2022. Golden's telephone number is (619) 438–2444. In 2023, it prepared and sent to each employee a separate Form W-2 for 2022. All wages paid to employees total $225,250. Total federal income taxes withheld from employees were $36,250. Total social security and Medicare wages equaled $209,850. No employee's wages exceeded $147,000 during 2022. Prepare the company's Form W-3, Transmittal of Wage and Tax Statements. Golden Door is a 941 payer. If no entry applies to the box, leave it blank. Have Marsha A. Golden., president of Golden, sign the form on January 21, 2023.

DO NOT STAPLE

33333	a Control number	For Official Use Only ▶ OMB No. 1545-0008		

b Kind of Payer (Check one): 941 ☐ Military ☐ 943 ☐ 944 ☐ CT-1 ☐ Hshld. emp. ☐ Medicare govt. emp. ☐

Kind of Employer (Check one): None apply ☐ 501c non-govt. ☐ State/local non-501c ☐ State/local 501c ☐ Federal govt. ☐

Third-party sick pay (Check if applicable) ☐

c Total number of Forms W-2	d Establishment number	1 Wages, tips, other compensation	2 Federal income tax withheld
e Employer identification number (EIN)		3 Social security wages	4 Social security tax withheld
f Employer's name		5 Medicare wages and tips	6 Medicare tax withheld
		7 Social security tips	8 Allocated tips
		9	10 Dependent care benefits
		11 Nonqualified plans	12a Deferred compensation
g Employer's address and ZIP code			
h Other EIN used this year		13 For third-party sick pay use only	12b
15 State Employer's state ID number		14 Income tax withheld by payer of third-party sick pay	
16 State wages, tips, etc.	17 State income tax	18 Local wages, tips, etc.	19 Local income tax
Employer's contact person		Employer's telephone number	For Official Use Only
Employer's fax number		Employer's email address	

Under penalties of perjury, I declare that I have examined this return and accompanying documents, and, to the best of my knowledge and belief, they are true, correct, and complete.

Signature ▶   Title ▶   Date ▶

Form **W-3** Transmittal of Wage and Tax Statements   **2022**   Department of the Treasury Internal Revenue Service

Send this entire page with the entire Copy A page of Form(s) W-2 to the Social Security Administration (SSA). Photocopies are not acceptable. Do not send Form W-3 if you filed electronically with the SSA. **Do not** send any payment (cash, checks, money orders, etc.) with Forms W-2 and W-3.

13. **FUTA Withholdings.** (Obj. 1)

   a. Should employers withhold FUTA taxes from employees? Explain.

   b. When must an employer deposit FUTA taxes?

14. **Lookback Period.** (Obj. 2) Describe the lookback period and discuss its significance for purposes of determining an employer's deposit frequency.

15. **Deposit Dates.** (Obj. 2) For each of the following situations, determine the employer's required deposit date.

    a. A monthly depositor whose payroll period ends on Friday, October 28.

    b. A semiweekly depositor whose payroll period ends on Wednesday, April 12.

    c. A semiweekly depositor whose payroll period ends on Friday, December 28.

    d. A monthly depositor whose payroll period ends on Tuesday, May 15.

16. **Form 941.** (Obj. 6) During the third quarter of 2022, the Fillmore Restaurant (EIN 70-0530660) located at 244 North Second Street, Fillmore, New York 14735-0022, withheld income and social security taxes from its five employees. It withheld income taxes of $3,117 from employees' wages and tips of $15,570. In addition, Fillmore withheld $912.95 of social security taxes on $14,725 of social security wages, and $52.39 of social security taxes on $845 of social security tips. It also withheld $225.77 of Medicare taxes on $15,570 of Medicare wages. During the quarter, Fillmore electronically deposited income and employment taxes as follows: August 15, $1,833.52; September 15, $1,790.26; October 15, $1,875.43. Data for quarterly wages and reported tips of employees is as follows:

Name	Total Wages	Social Security Wages	Taxable Tips Reported
Barker, J. R.	$ 7,025	$ 7,025	$315
Duwe, H. K.	3,000	3,000	180
Miller, M. M.	2,000	2,000	120
Pressman, R. M.	1,200	1,200	125
Smathers, H. H.	1,500	1,500	105
	$14,725	$14,725	$845

Prepare the third quarter Form 941, Employer's QUARTERLY Federal Tax Return, for the Fillmore Restaurant, using the blank form provided on the pages that follow. Fillmore filed Form 941 and M. L. Wright, President, signed it on 10/03/2022. Fillmore's business did not suffer from the COVID-19 lockdown. Fillmore did not claim any employee retention credit, or any credit for family and sick leave.

(Use for Problem 16.)

Form 941 for 2022: Employer's QUARTERLY Federal Tax Return
(Rev. June 2022)
Department of the Treasury — Internal Revenue Service

950122

OMB No. 1545-0029

Employer identification number (EIN)

Name (not your trade name)

Trade name (if any)

Address

Number   Street   Suite or room number

City   State   ZIP code

Foreign country name   Foreign province/county   Foreign postal code

Report for this Quarter of 2022
(Check one.)

☐ **1:** January, February, March

☐ **2:** April, May, June

☐ **3:** July, August, September

☐ **4:** October, November, December

Go to *www.irs.gov/Form941* for instructions and the latest information.

Read the separate instructions before you complete Form 941. Type or print within the boxes.

Part 1:   Answer these questions for this quarter.

1   Number of employees who received wages, tips, or other compensation for the pay period including: *June 12* (Quarter 2), *Sept. 12* (Quarter 3), or *Dec. 12* (Quarter 4) **1**

2   Wages, tips, and other compensation **2**

3   Federal income tax withheld from wages, tips, and other compensation **3**

4   If no wages, tips, and other compensation are subject to social security or Medicare tax   ☐ Check and go to line 6.

	Column 1		Column 2	
5a Taxable social security wages* . .		× 0.124 =		
5a (i) Qualified sick leave wages* .		× 0.062 =		
5a (ii) Qualified family leave wages* .		× 0.062 =		
5b Taxable social security tips . . .		× 0.124 =		
5c Taxable Medicare wages & tips. .		× 0.029 =		
5d Taxable wages & tips subject to Additional Medicare Tax withholding		× 0.009 =		

*Include taxable qualified sick and family leave wages paid in this quarter of 2022 for leave taken after March 31, 2021, and before October 1, 2021, on line 5a. Use lines 5a(i) and 5a(ii) **only** for taxable qualified sick and family leave wages paid in this quarter of 2022 for leave taken after March 31, 2020, and before April 1, 2021.*

5e   Total social security and Medicare taxes. Add Column 2 from lines 5a, 5a(i), 5a(ii), 5b, 5c, and 5d   **5e**

5f   Section 3121(q) Notice and Demand—Tax due on unreported tips (see instructions) . .   **5f**

6   Total taxes before adjustments. Add lines 3, 5e, and 5f **6**

7   Current quarter's adjustment for fractions of cents **7**

8   Current quarter's adjustment for sick pay **8**

9   Current quarter's adjustments for tips and group-term life insurance **9**

10   Total taxes after adjustments. Combine lines 6 through 9 . . . .   **10**

11a   Qualified small business payroll tax credit for increasing research activities. Attach Form 8974   **11a**

11b   Nonrefundable portion of credit for qualified sick and family leave wages for leave taken before April 1, 2021 . . . .   **11b**

11c   Reserved for future use **11c**

▶ You MUST complete all three pages of Form 941 and SIGN it.   Next ▶

For Privacy Act and Paperwork Reduction Act Notice, see the back of the Payment Voucher.   Cat. No. 17001Z   Form **941** (Rev. 6-2022)

(Use for Problem 16.)

951222

Name *(not your trade name)*   **Employer identification number (EIN)**

___ — _____

| Part 1: | Answer these questions for this quarter. *(continued)* |

11d Nonrefundable portion of credit for qualified sick and family leave wages for leave taken
after March 31, 2021, and before October 1, 2021 . . . . **11d** ☐ ▪

11e Reserved for future use . . . . **11e** ▪

11f Reserved for future use . . . . ☐

11g Total nonrefundable credits. Add lines 11a, 11b, and 11d . . . . **11g** ☐ ▪

12 Total taxes after adjustments and nonrefundable credits. Subtract line 11g from line 10 . **12** ☐ ▪

13a Total deposits for this quarter, including overpayment applied from a prior quarter and
overpayments applied from Form 941-X, 941-X (PR), 944-X, or 944-X (SP) filed in the current quarter **13a** ☐ ▪

13b Reserved for future use . . . . **13b** ▪

13c Refundable portion of credit for qualified sick and family leave wages for leave taken
before April 1, 2021 . . . . **13c** ☐ ▪

13d Reserved for future use . . . . **13d** ▪

13e Refundable portion of credit for qualified sick and family leave wages for leave taken
after March 31, 2021, and before October 1, 2021 . . . . **13e** ☐ ▪

13f Reserved for future use . . . . **13f** ▪

13g Total deposits and refundable credits. Add lines 13a, 13c, and 13e . . . . **13g** ☐ ▪

13h Reserved for future use . . . . **13h** ▪

13i Reserved for future use . . . . **13i** ▪

14 Balance due. If line 12 is more than line 13g, enter the difference and see instructions . . . **14** ☐ ▪

15 Overpayment. If line 13g is more than line 12, enter the difference ☐ ▪ Check one: ☐ Apply to next return. ☐ Send a refund.

| Part 2: | Tell us about your deposit schedule and tax liability for this quarter. |

If you're unsure about whether you're a monthly schedule depositor or a semiweekly schedule depositor, see section 11 of Pub. 15.

16 Check one: ☐ **Line 12 on this return is less than $2,500 or line 12 on the return for the prior quarter was less than $2,500, and you didn't incur a $100,000 next-day deposit obligation during the current quarter.** If line 12 for the prior quarter was less than $2,500 but line 12 on this return is $100,000 or more, you must provide a record of your federal tax liability. If you're a monthly schedule depositor, complete the deposit schedule below; if you're a semiweekly schedule depositor, attach Schedule B (Form 941). Go to Part 3.

☐ **You were a monthly schedule depositor for the entire quarter.** Enter your tax liability for each month and total liability for the quarter, then go to Part 3.

Tax liability: Month 1 ☐ ▪

Month 2 ☐ ▪

Month 3 ☐ ▪

Total liability for quarter ☐ ▪   Total must equal line 12.

☐ **You were a semiweekly schedule depositor for any part of this quarter.** Complete Schedule B (Form 941), Report of Tax Liability for Semiweekly Schedule Depositors, and attach it to Form 941. Go to Part 3.

▶ **You MUST complete all three pages of Form 941 and SIGN it.** Next ▶

(Use for Problem 16.)

950922

Name *(not your trade name)*	Employer identification number (EIN)
	—

Part 3:   Tell us about your business. If a question does NOT apply to your business, leave it blank.

17 If your business has closed or you stopped paying wages . . . . ☐ Check here, and

enter the final date you paid wages [/ /] ; also attach a statement to your return. See instructions.

18 If you're a seasonal employer and you don't have to file a return for every quarter of the year . . . ☐ Check here.

19	Qualified health plan expenses allocable to qualified sick leave wages for leave taken before April 1, 2021	19	▪
20	Qualified health plan expenses allocable to qualified family leave wages for leave taken before April 1, 2021	20	▪
21	Reserved for future use	21	▪
22	Reserved for future use	22	▪
23	Qualified sick leave wages for leave taken after March 31, 2021, and before October 1, 2021	23	▪
24	Qualified health plan expenses allocable to qualified sick leave wages reported on line 23	24	▪
25	Amounts under certain collectively bargained agreements allocable to qualified sick leave wages reported on line 23	25	▪
26	Qualified family leave wages for leave taken after March 31, 2021, and before October 1, 2021	26	▪
27	Qualified health plan expenses allocable to qualified family leave wages reported on line 26	27	▪
28	Amounts under certain collectively bargained agreements allocable to qualified family leave wages reported on line 26	28	▪

Part 4:   May we speak with your third-party designee?

Do you want to allow an employee, a paid tax preparer, or another person to discuss this return with the IRS? See the instructions for details.

☐ **Yes.** Designee's name and phone number

Select a 5-digit personal identification number (PIN) to use when talking to the IRS. ☐ ☐ ☐ ☐ ☐

☐ **No.**

Part 5:   Sign here. You MUST complete all three pages of Form 941 and SIGN it.

Under penalties of perjury, I declare that I have examined this return, including accompanying schedules and statements, and to the best of my knowledge and belief, it is true, correct, and complete. Declaration of preparer (other than taxpayer) is based on all information of which preparer has any knowledge.

✗ **Sign your name here**

Print your name here

Print your title here

Date [/ /]

Best daytime phone

Paid Preparer Use Only   Check if you're self-employed . . . ☐

Preparer's name		PTIN	
Preparer's signature		Date	/ /
Firm's name (or yours if self-employed)		EIN	
Address		Phone	
City	State	ZIP code	

Page **3**   Form **941** (Rev. 6-2022)

17. **Form 941.** (Obj. 2)

   a. When must employers file Form 941?

   b. Can employers combine data from different quarters on one Form 941 as long as the combined period does not exceed three months?

18. **Estimated Taxes.** (Obj. 3) Indicate whether or not the following individuals are required to pay an estimated tax for 2022. (Check either the "*Yes*" or the "*No*" column.)

		Yes	*No*
a.	Single taxpayer with income derived solely from wages subject to withholding expected to equal $12,000. Estimated unpaid tax expected to be $250.	___	___
b.	Married couple with husband's income derived solely from wages subject to withholding expected to equal $21,500. Spouse does not receive wages. Estimated unpaid tax expected to be $400.	___	___
c.	Qualifying widower with income derived from wages subject to withholding expected to equal $24,500. Income from other sources not subject to withholding expected to total $5,000. Estimated unpaid tax expected to be $1,200.	___	___
d.	Married couple with husband's income derived solely from wages subject to withholding expected to equal $11,000. Spouse expects to receive dividend income totaling $22,000. Estimated unpaid tax expected to be $1,550.	___	___

19. **Estimated Taxes.** (Obj. 3) What steps can an unmarried taxpayer with AGI in 2022 of $75,000 take to avoid a penalty for underpayment of estimated taxes in 2023?

20. **Estimated Taxes.** (Obj. 3) What steps can a married couple with AGI of $200,000 in 2022 take to avoid the penalty for underpayment of estimated taxes in 2023?

21. **Estimated Taxes.** (Obj. 3) George Lewis works part-time and operates a business as a sole proprietorship on the side. For 2022, he estimates that his AGI (before consideration of the deduction for the employer's (½) share of the self-employment tax) will be $44,650. Included in this amount is wages of $19,250, net profits from his business of $25,000, and $400 of interest income. George is single and has no dependents. He estimates that his itemized deductions for the year will be $9,500, and that his employer will withhold $3,200 in federal income taxes. George's 2021 tax liability was $6,930. Using this information, complete the

Estimated Tax Worksheet below to compute the amount George will be required to make in quarterly estimated payments if he wants to avoid any underpayment penalty for 2022. At press time, the IRS had not issued the 2023 form.

2022 Self-Employment Tax and Deduction Worksheet for Lines 1 and 9 of the Estimated Tax Worksheet   *Keep for Your Records*

1a.	Enter your expected income and profits subject to self-employment tax*	1a.	
b.	If you will have farm income and also receive social security retirement or disability benefits, enter your expected Conservation Reserve Program payments that will be included on Schedule F (Form 1040) or listed on Schedule K-1 (Form 1065)	b.	
2.	Subtract line 1b from line 1a	2.	
3.	Multiply line 2 by 92.35% (0.9235)	3.	
4.	Multiply line 3 by 2.9% (0.029)	4.	
5.	Social security tax maximum income	5.	$147,000
6.	Enter your expected wages (if subject to social security tax or the 6.2% portion of tier 1 railroad retirement tax)	6.	
7.	Subtract line 6 from line 5	7.	
	Note. *If line 7 is zero or less, enter -0- on line 9 and skip to line 10.*		
8.	Enter the **smaller** of line 3 or line 7	8.	
9.	Multiply line 8 by 12.4% (0.124)	9.	
10.	Add lines 4 and 9. Enter the result here and on line 9 of your 2022 Estimated Tax Worksheet	10.	
11.	Multiply line 10 by 50% (0.50). This is your expected deduction for self-employment tax on Schedule 1 (Form 1040), line 15. Subtract this amount when figuring your expected AGI on line 1 of your 2022 Estimated Tax Worksheet	11.	

2022 Estimated Tax Worksheet   *Keep for Your Records*

1	Adjusted gross income you expect in 2022 (see instructions)	1	54,732
2a	Deductions	2a	12,950
	• If you plan to itemize deductions, enter the estimated total of your itemized deductions.		
	• If you don't plan to itemize deductions, enter your standard deduction.		
b	If you can take the qualified business income deduction, enter the estimated amount of the deduction	2b	4,680
c	Add lines 2a and 2b ▶	2c	17,630
3	Subtract line 2c from line 1	3	37,102
4	**Tax.** Figure your tax on the amount on line 3 by using the **2022 Tax Rate Schedules.** **Caution:** *If you will have qualified dividends or a net capital gain, or expect to exclude or deduct foreign earned income or housing, see Worksheets 2-5 and 2-6 in Pub. 505 to figure the tax.*	4	4,247
5	Alternative minimum tax from **Form 6251**	5	
6	Add lines 4 and 5. Add to this amount any other taxes you expect to include in the total on Form 1040 or 1040-SR, line 16	6	4,247
7	Credits (see instructions). **Do not** include any income tax withholding on this line	7	
8	Subtract line 7 from line 6. If zero or less, enter -0-	8	4,247
9	Self-employment tax (see instructions)	9	537
10	Other taxes (see instructions)	10	
11a	Add lines 8 through 10	11a	4,784
b	Earned income credit, refundable child tax credit* or additional child tax credit, fuel tax credit, net premium tax credit, refundable American opportunity credit, section 1341 credit, and refundable credit from Form 8885*	11b	
c	**Total 2022 estimated tax.** Subtract line 11b from line 11a. If zero or less, enter -0- ▶	11c	4,784

12a	Multiply line 11c by 90% (66⅔% for farmers and fishermen)	12a	4,305	
b	Required annual payment based on prior year's tax (see instructions)	12b	3,950	
c	**Required annual payment to avoid a penalty.** Enter the **smaller** of line 12a or 12b ▶	12c		3,950

Caution: *Generally, if you do not prepay (through income tax withholding and estimated tax payments) at least the amount on line 12c, you may owe a penalty for not paying enough estimated tax. To avoid a penalty, make sure your estimate on line 11c is as accurate as possible. Even if you pay the required annual payment, you may still owe tax when you file your return. If you prefer, you can pay the amount shown on line 11c. For details, see chapter 2 of Pub. 505.*

13	Income tax withheld and estimated to be withheld during 2022 (including income tax withholding on pensions, annuities, certain deferred income, etc.)	13	2,600

14a	Subtract line 13 from line 12c	14a	1,350
	Is the result zero or less?		
	☐ **Yes.** Stop here. You are not required to make estimated tax payments.		
	☑ **No.** Go to line 14b.		
b	Subtract line 13 from line 11c	14b	
	Is the result less than $1,000?		
	☐ **Yes.** Stop here. You are not required to make estimated tax payments.		
	☑ **No.** Go to line 15 to figure your required payment.		
15	If the first payment you are required to make is due April 18, 2022, enter ¼ of line 14a (minus any 2021 overpayment that you are applying to this installment) here, and on your estimated tax payment voucher(s) if you are paying by check or money order	15	338

* If applicable.

22. **Penalties.** (Obj. 5) Suzy files her tax return on April 1. Her return shows a balance due of $1,000. Suzy encloses a check payable to the Department of the Treasury in the amount of $700. Compute Suzy's late payment penalty if she pays the rest of the balance due ($300) on August 31.

23. **Penalties.** (Obj. 5) Tim failed to file his tax return on April 15 and forgot to file for an extension. He files his tax return on December 27 and encloses a check for the $11,000 balance due reported on his return.

    a.   Compute Tim's late filing penalty.

    b.   How, if at all, would your answer to part a. change if Tim were able to file his tax return (and pay the amount owed) by July 15?

24. **Audits and Penalties.** (Objs. 4 and 5) Answer each question in the space provided.

    a.   What is the monthly penalty for failure to file a tax return?   _____

    b.   What is the monthly penalty for late payment of taxes?   _____

    c.   What is the penalty for filing a frivolous return?   _____

    d.   What is the penalty for failing to provide an information return?   _____

    e.   What is the penalty assessed on a tax preparer for failing to
         provide a copy of the tax return to the taxpayer?   _____

    f.   Within the district audit division, there are two types of audits.
         One is the field audit. What is the other?   _____

    g.   After receiving a 30-day letter, how long does the taxpayer have
         to request a conference with the examining officer?   _____

    h.   After a tax return is filed, how many years does the IRS have to
         issue a 90-day deficiency notice?   _____

25. **Preparer Responsibilities.** (Obj. 4) What penalty does the IRS impose on a tax preparer that intentionally disregards the rules and regulations, or willfully understates the taxpayer's tax liability?

26. **Form 1040-X.** (Obj. 6) Eight months after filing their 2021 tax return with the IRS Center in Memphis, Tennessee, Jack L. (SSN 347-00-5784) and Judith K. (SSN 457-00-4758) Keith of 1618 Redford Lane, Kingsport, Tennessee 37664-3322, they realize they forgot to report their contribution of 20 shares of stock in the ABC Corporation that they made to Metropolitan Museum on November 5, 2021. The Keiths purchased the stock for $1,200 on August 6, 2004. Its FMV on November 7, 2021, was $2,000.

    The Keiths filed a joint return and claimed their son Darrell as a dependent. He was seven years old in 2021. His Social Security Number is 123-00-6789. Information from the 2021 Form 1040 that had been filed includes:

AGI (no qualified dividends or net capital gain)	$98,000
Itemized deductions	26,370
Taxable income	71,630
Total tax liability	8,213
Child tax credit	2,000
Federal income tax withheld	6,000
Amount paid with original return	213

    The Keiths have not been advised that their 2021 income tax return is under audit. Prepare an Amended U.S. Individual Income Tax Return, Form 1040-X, for the Keiths. They file the amended return on December 6, 2022.

27. **Internet Problem: Researching IRS Publication 926.** (Obj. 1)

    Brad and Carol Thomas made an agreement with a neighbor's child to care for their lawn. The neighbor's son, Tad, takes care of the lawns of others in the neighborhood. Tad provides all of his own machinery, tools and necessary supplies. During 2022, the Thomases pay Tad $2,400 for various lawn care services. Since this amount exceeds $2,000, they are worried that they might be required to report Tad as a household employee and be required to withhold employment taxes.

    Go to the IRS website. Locate IRS Publication 926, *Household Employer's Tax Guide*, and use it to answer the Thomases' question. Print out a copy of the page where you find the answer. Underline or highlight the pertinent information. Comment on what you believe to be the answer to the Thomases' question.

    See Appendix A for instructions on how to access the IRS website.

28. **Business Entity Problem.** (Obj. 3) This problem is designed for those using the "business entity" approach. **The solution may require information from Chapter 14.**

    a. Sunset Corporation had taxable income of $300,000 last year. To avoid underpayment penalties for the current year, what amount of estimated taxes must the company deposit during the year?

    b. If the corporation had taxable income of $3,000,000 last year, what amount of estimated taxes must be deposited in the current year to avoid an underpayment penalty?

(Use for Problem 26.)

Form 1040-X

(Rev. July 2021)

Department of the Treasury—Internal Revenue Service

Amended U.S. Individual Income Tax Return

▶ Use this revision to amend 2019 or later tax returns.
▶ Go to *www.irs.gov/Form1040X* for instructions and the latest information.

OMB No. 1545-0074

This return is for calendar year (enter year) _____ **or fiscal year (enter month and year ended)** _____

Your first name and middle initial	Last name	Your social security number

If joint return, spouse's first name and middle initial	Last name	Spouse's social security number

Current home address (number and street). If you have a P.O. box, see instructions.	Apt. no.	Your phone number

City, town or post office, state, and ZIP code. If you have a foreign address, also complete spaces below. See instructions.

Foreign country name	Foreign province/state/county	Foreign postal code

Amended return filing status. You must check one box even if you are not changing your filing status. Caution: In general, you can't change your filing status from married filing jointly to married filing separately after the return due date.

☐ Single ☐ Married filing jointly ☐ Married filing separately (MFS) ☐ Head of household (HOH) ☐ Qualifying widow(er) (QW)

If you checked the MFS box, enter the name of your spouse. If you checked the HOH or QW box, enter the child's name if the qualifying person is a child but not your dependent ▶

Enter on lines 1 through 23, columns A through C, the amounts for the return year entered above. Use Part III on page 2 to explain any changes.		**A. Original amount** reported or as previously adjusted (see instructions)	**B. Net change—** amount of increase or (decrease)— explain in Part III	**C. Correct amount**
Income and Deductions				
1	Adjusted gross income. If a net operating loss (NOL) carryback is included, check here . . . . ▶ ☐	**1**			
2	Itemized deductions or standard deduction	**2**			
3	Subtract line 2 from line 1	**3**			
4a	Reserved for future use	**4a**			
b	Qualified business income deduction	**4b**			
5	Taxable income. Subtract line 4b from line 3. If the result is zero or less, enter -0-	**5**			
Tax Liability				
6	Tax. Enter method(s) used to figure tax (see instructions): _____	**6**			
7	Nonrefundable credits. If a general business credit carryback is included, check here . . . . ▶ ☐	**7**			
8	Subtract line 7 from line 6. If the result is zero or less, enter -0- . . .	**8**			
9	Reserved for future use	**9**			
10	Other taxes	**10**			
11	Total tax. Add lines 8 and 10	**11**			
Payments				
12	Federal income tax withheld and excess social security and tier 1 RRTA tax withheld. (**If changing,** see instructions.)	**12**			
13	Estimated tax payments, including amount applied from prior year's return	**13**			
14	Earned income credit (EIC)	**14**			
15	Refundable credits from: ☐ Schedule 8812 Form(s) ☐ 2439 ☐ 4136 ☐ 8863 ☐ 8885 ☐ 8962 or ☐ other (specify): _____	**15**			
16	Total amount paid with request for extension of time to file, tax paid with original return, and additional tax paid after return was filed				**16**
17	Total payments. Add lines 12 through 15, column C, and line 16				**17**
Refund or Amount You Owe				
18	Overpayment, if any, as shown on original return or as previously adjusted by the IRS				**18**
19	Subtract line 18 from line 17. (If less than zero, see instructions.)				**19**
20	**Amount you owe.** If line 11, column C, is more than line 19, enter the difference				**20**
21	If line 11, column C, is less than line 19, enter the difference. This is the amount **overpaid** on this return				**21**
22	Amount of line 21 you want **refunded to you**				**22**
23	Amount of line 21 you want **applied to your** (enter year): _____ estimated tax	**23**			

Complete and sign this form on page 2.

For Paperwork Reduction Act Notice, see separate instructions.   Cat. No. 11360L   Form **1040-X** (Rev. 7-2021)

(Use for Problem 26.)

Form 1040-X (Rev. 7-2021)   Page **2**

Part I   Dependents

Complete this part to change any information relating to your dependents.
This would include a change in the number of dependents.
Enter the information for the return year entered at the top of page 1.

	A. Original number of dependents reported or as previously adjusted	**B. Net change — amount of increase or (decrease)**	**C. Correct number**
24 Reserved for future use	24		
25 Your dependent children who lived with you	25		
26 Your dependent children who didn't live with you due to divorce or separation	26		
27 Other dependents	27		
28 Reserved for future use	28		
29 Reserved for future use	29		

30   List **ALL** dependents (children and others) claimed on this amended return.

Dependents (see instructions):

If more than four dependents, see instructions and check here ▶ ☐	(a) First name Last name	(b) Social security number	(c) Relationship to you	(d) ✓ if qualifies for (see instructions): Child tax credit	Credit for other dependents
				☐	☐
				☐	☐
				☐	☐
				☐	☐

Part II   Presidential Election Campaign Fund (for the return year entered at the top of page 1)

Checking below won't increase your tax or reduce your refund.

☐ Check here if you didn't previously want $3 to go to the fund, but now do.

☐ Check here if this is a joint return and your spouse did not previously want $3 to go to the fund, but now does.

Part III   Explanation of Changes. In the space provided below, tell us why you are filing Form 1040-X.

▶ Attach any supporting documents and new or changed forms and schedules.

Remember to keep a copy of this form for your records.

Under penalties of perjury, I declare that I have filed an original return, and that I have examined this amended return, including accompanying schedules and statements, and to the best of my knowledge and belief, this amended return is true, correct, and complete. Declaration of preparer (other than taxpayer) is based on all information about which the preparer has any knowledge.

Sign Here

▶ Your signature   Date   Your occupation

▶ Spouse's signature. If a joint return, both must sign.   Date   Spouse's occupation

Paid Preparer Use Only

Print/Type preparer's name	Preparer's signature	Date	Check ☐ if self-employed	PTIN
Firm's name ▶			Firm's EIN ▶	
Firm's address ▶			Phone no.	

For forms and publications, visit *www.irs.gov/Forms*.   Form **1040-X** (Rev. 7-2021)

Chapter

14

C Corporations

CHAPTER CONTENTS

LEARNING OBJECTIVES

After completing Chapter 14, you should be able to:

1. Understand the tax consequences to both the shareholders and the corporation when shareholders contribute cash and noncash property to a corporation in exchange for stock in the corporation.
2. Calculate a corporation's taxable income.
3. Compute a corporation's tax liability.
4. Describe the tax consequences of distributions to both the corporation and the shareholders.
5. Prepare Form 1120.

CHAPTER OVERVIEW

The sole proprietorship is the most common form of business ownership. Chapter 7 focused on the taxation of income arising from sole proprietorship operations. Partnerships and corporations are also popular ownership structures that are available to carry out business activities. Business owners must weigh the advantages and disadvantages of each when choosing the best entity from which to conduct their business operations. The impact of income taxation on each of these business entities plays a major role in this important choice.

A business organized as a corporation is a separate legal and taxable entity. The corporation exists outside of its owners (shareholders), and it must pay a tax on its income. Such companies are called C corporations. The name comes from the location (Subchapter C) in the Internal Revenue Code where the tax rules specific to this type of entity can be found. However, Congress created another tax entity, called an S corporation, which has features of both a corporation and a partnership. As the name suggests, the tax laws specific to S corporations are located in Subchapter S of the Internal Revenue Code. The tax rules specific to C corporations are the focus of this chapter. Partnerships are the focus of Chapter 15. S corporations are covered in Chapter 16.

¶1401   The Nature of C Corporations

A business organized as a corporation qualifies as a separate tax entity and pays tax on corporate taxable income. Historically, a business was treated and taxed as a corporation if it had the following corporate traits:

1. Business associates
2. A purpose to carry on a business and divide the profits
3. Continuity of life
4. Centralized management
5. Limited liability
6. Free transferability of ownership interests

Since partnerships and corporations have these first two traits in common, the Internal Revenue Service (IRS) and the courts focused on the last four to distinguish entities. To help avoid disputes in this area, the tax laws now allow businesses to choose which type of entity they wish to be taxed as. This choice is commonly known as the "check-the-box" rules. Thus, when a business is formed, the owners can choose the business's tax status without regard to the extent of its corporate traits. However, certain business entities (such as entities formed as a corporation under state law) are treated as per-se corporations for federal tax purposes and cannot choose their tax classification. The IRS provides a list of domestic and foreign entities treated as per-se corporations for federal tax purposes. Corporations that pay tax on their taxable income are commonly called "C corporations" or "regular corporations." These corporations are the focus of this chapter. S corporations are a special type of corporation. They are discussed in Chapter 16.

¶1401.01   FORMING A CORPORATION

The owners of a corporation are called shareholders (or stockholders). The owners are called this because they possess shares of stock in the corporation. They get these shares in exchange for cash, property and/or services that they transfer to the corporation. This exchange can be done at the time the corporation is formed, or at a later date, when the corporation is in need of more funds (called capital). Once the transfer is complete, the investors and the corporation must determine their respective bases in the property they acquire. When investors exchange cash for shares of stock in the corporation, neither party realizes gain or loss on the exchange. Each investor's basis in the stock is the amount of cash they transfer to the corporation. These rules are the same as for any other cash purchase.

When investors transfer noncash property to a corporation solely in exchange for stock in the corporation, each investor realizes gain or loss equal to the difference between the fair market value (FMV) of the stock and the investor's adjusted basis in the property transferred to the corporation. However, if after the exchange, the transferring investors own (individually or as a group) at least 80% of the corporation's stock, then under the general rule, neither the investors nor the corporation recognize any gain or loss. [I.R.C. §351] Under these conditions, the investor's basis in the stock received is usually the amount of cash plus the investor's basis in the property transferred to the corporation. [I.R.C. §358] The investor's adjusted basis in the property becomes the corporation's basis in the property. [I.R.C. §362(a)]

If the adjusted basis of the transferred property exceeds its FMV in the hands of the corporation, the corporation's basis in the transferred property is limited to the property's FMV. [I.R.C. §362(e)] This rule is called the anti-loss duplication rule and requires the corporation to reduce its basis in the transferred property by the amount of the net built-in loss in the property.

Fair market value (FMV) is the price that a willing buyer will pay and a willing seller will accept. FMV assumes that neither the buyer nor the seller must buy or sell. It also assumes that the buyer and the seller have reasonable knowledge of all necessary facts. In the absence of an actual sale or exchange, FMV can be determined by an expert appraisal or other supporting evidence.

EXAMPLE 1

Dana and Penny form a DP corporation. Dana transfers land worth $160,000 (adjusted basis of $190,000) in exchange for 50% of the stock in DP. Penny transfers $40,000 cash and a building worth $120,000 (adjusted basis of $105,000) in exchange for 50% of the stock in DP. No other property was transferred. Both parties receive stock valued at $160,000 (same as the value of the property each party transferred to the corporation).

As a result of the exchange, Dana realizes a $30,000 loss ($160,000 FMV of the stock received – $190,000 adjusted basis in the land). Penny realizes a $15,000 gain ($160,000 amount realized – $40,000 cash – $105,000 adjusted basis in the building). Since after the transfer, Dana and Penny own at least 80% of DP's stock, neither Dana, Penny, nor DP recognize gain or loss from the exchange.

Dana's basis in her shares of DP stock equals $190,000 (same as her adjusted basis in the land). Penny's basis in her shares equals $145,000 ($40,000 cash + her $105,000 basis in the building). DP's basis in the land is the land's FMV, $160,000 ($190,000 basis, reduced by the amount of net built-in loss, $30,000). DP's basis in the building is $105,000, Penny's adjusted basis. The three parties' respective basis in the property received from the exchange is as follows:

Dana's basis in the stock	$190,000	DP's basis in the cash	$ 40,000
		DP's basis in the land	160,000
Penny's basis in the stock	$145,000	DP's basis in the building	105,000
			$305,000

 The formula for calculating realized gains and losses is the same as that discussed in ¶1001. Realized gain or loss reflects the economic tax consequences of the transfer. Recognized gain or loss is the amount of realized gain or loss taxpayers report on their tax returns (see ¶1003).

If the adjusted basis of the contributed property exceeds its FMV, the investor and the corporation can make an election to reduce the basis of the investor's stock, instead of reducing the corporation's basis in the contributed property to the property's FMV. [I.R.C. §362(e)(2)(C)] In this case, the corporation's basis in the property is equal to the investor's adjusted basis in the property, and the investor's basis in the stock is equal to the transferred property's FMV. If, in Example 1, Dana and DP make an election, Dana's basis in the received stock would be $160,000, and DP's basis in the land would be $190,000.

The general rule (nonrecognition of gain or loss, and carryover of basis) only applies when (1) after the transfer, the transferring investors own at least 80% of the corporation's stock, and (2) the only property the investors receive in return is stock in the corporation. If the corporation transfers other property (called "boot"), the investor recognizes gain equal to the lesser of (i) the realized gain, or (ii) the FMV of the boot received. When an investor receives boot from the corporation, the investor's basis in the stock is decreased by the value of the boot received, and increased by any recognized gain. Any gain recognized by the investor also increases the corporation's basis in the property it received from that investor. Realized losses are never recognized when a transferring investor receives boot from the corporation. However, the value of any boot received by an investor realizing a loss, still reduces the investor's basis in the stock received.

EXAMPLE 2

Tyler and Mike own 100% of TM stock. Tyler transfers equipment worth $100,000 (adjusted basis of $75,000) in exchange for $100,000 worth of TM stock. Mike transfers land worth $125,000 (adjusted basis of $105,000) in exchange for $25,000 cash and $100,000 worth of TM stock. Tyler realizes a $25,000 gain ($100,000 FMV of the stock received – $75,000 adjusted basis in the equipment). Mike realizes a $20,000 gain ($125,000 FMV of the stock and cash received – $105,000 adjusted basis in the land).

After the exchange, the transferring investors (Tyler and Mike) own at least 80% of TM's stock. Since Tyler did not receive any boot, he does not recognize gain. Thus, his basis in the stock he received is $75,000 (same as his adjusted basis in the equipment). Mike, however, received $25,000 of boot as part of the exchange. Therefore, Mike recognizes $20,000 gain (*lesser of* (i) $20,000 realized gain, or (ii) $25,000 boot received). Mike's basis in the stock he received equals $100,000 ($105,000 basis in the land – $25,000 FMV of the boot received + $20,000 recognized gain). TM's basis in the equipment is $75,000 (same as Tyler's basis in the equipment). Its basis in the land is $125,000 (Mike's $105,000 adjusted basis + $20,000 Mike's recognized gain). After the exchange, the basis of properties owned by the three parties is:

Tyler's basis in the stock	$ 75,000		TM's basis in the equipment	$ 75,000
			TM's basis in the land	125,000
Mike's basis in the cash	$ 25,000			$200,000
Mike's basis in the stock	100,000			
	$125,000			

EXAMPLE 3

Same facts as in Example 2, except that Mike's basis in the land was $140,000. In this scenario, nothing changes with respect to Tyler. However, Mike now realizes a $15,000 loss on the exchange ($125,000 FMV of property received – $140,000 adjusted basis in the land). Mike does not recognize any of this loss, since receipt of boot does not affect losses on these types of transfers. Thus, Mike's basis in the stock equals $115,000 ($140,000 basis in the land – $25,000 FMV of the boot received + $0 recognized gain). TM's basis in the land is now $125,000 (the FMV of the land). Thus, after the exchange, the basis of the property owned by the three parties is:

Tyler's basis in the stock	$ 75,000		TM's basis in the equipment	$ 75,000
			TM's basis in the land	125,000
Mike's basis in the cash	$ 25,000			$200,000
Mike's basis in the stock	115,000			
	$140,000			

Although boot used in the above example involved cash, boot can take on other forms. Any property transferred back to an investor that is not the corporation's stock is treated as boot. For example, if the corporation transfers back to the investor its holdings of stock in another corporation, the FMV of the other corporation's stock is treated as boot. Also, when an investor transfers mortgaged property to a corporation, the assumption of debt by the corporation is treated as boot given to the investor who transferred the property. In situations where the amount of debt assumed exceeds the investor's basis in the transferred property, the investor recognizes gain to the extent of the excess, even if the excess exceeds the investor's realized gain. As you can see, the tax consequences of transfers of boot that involve the assumption of debt can become quite complex, and thus, are beyond the scope of this introduction to corporate taxation.

When an investor(s) transfers property to a corporation solely in exchange for stock, and after the transfer, the transferring investors own less than 80% of the corporation's stock, then the investor(s) recognizes gain or loss on the transfer for the difference between the FMV of the stock and the adjusted basis of the property transferred to the corporation. The investor's basis in the stock and the corporation's basis in the property received is the FMV of the property (cost basis).

EXAMPLE 4	Stu transfers machinery worth $20,000 (adjusted basis of $0) in exchange for $20,000 of stock in a corporation. After the transfer, Stu owns 15% of the corporation's stock. Because Stu (the only transferring investor) owns less than 80% of the stock after the exchange, he realizes and recognizes a $20,000 gain ($20,000 FMV of the stock received – $0 adjusted basis in the machinery). His basis in the stock is $20,000 ($20,000 FMV of property transferred). Likewise, the corporation's basis in the machinery is $20,000.

When shareholders perform services in exchange for the corporation's stock, they recognize income equal to the FMV of the stock received. This amount also becomes their basis in the shares of the stock they receive.

EXAMPLE 5	Victor performs services in exchange for 1,000 shares of stock in a corporation. At the time the services were performed, the stock was worth $15 a share. Victor includes the $15,000 ($15 × 1,000 shares) in gross income. This becomes his basis in the 1,000 shares of stock.

	Stock basis is used to compute the shareholder's gain or loss when the stock is sold. It is also used to determine the tax consequences when the corporation makes distributions to its shareholders (discussed later in the chapter at ¶1405). Thus, it is important that shareholders understand how to compute their stock basis.

¶1402   Corporate Taxable Income

For the most part, corporations compute their taxable income the same as individuals compute their business profit or loss (Chapter 7). However, gains and loss from disposing of property are included in the calculation of a corporation's taxable income. (Recall that these items were not part of the calculation of profits on Schedule C, but were part of the calculation of AGI). Most of the rules governing income and business deductions apply to both individuals and corporations. One major difference between corporations and individuals concerns the treatment of nonbusiness deductions. Although individuals may deduct certain personal expenditures as itemized deductions, corporations have no personal expenses. Thus, corporations do not use the concept of adjusted gross income (AGI) because they have no deductions from AGI (no standard deduction or itemized deductions). Furthermore, corporations have different limits on capital losses and charitable contributions. They also are taxed on only a portion of the dividends that they receive. These differences are covered in more detail later in the chapter at ¶1402.04, ¶1402.05, and ¶1402.06.

¶1402.01   ACCOUNTING METHODS

A corporation must select an accounting method for determining its taxable income. Most corporations use the accrual method of accounting. With the **accrual method**, corporations report income when it is earned, regardless of when the cash is received. Also, they deduct expenses when they are incurred, regardless of when they are paid.

Besides the accrual method, the other accounting options available to certain corporations are the cash and hybrid methods. With the **cash method**, income is taxable when received, and expenses are deductible when paid. The **hybrid method** combines cash and accrual methods.

Here, the accrual method is used to compute gross profit from the sale of inventory and the cash method is used for all other income and deductions.

The types of corporations permitted to use the cash method are limited. Farming and personal service corporations may use the cash method. All other corporations must have average gross receipts for the last three years of $25 million (indexed) or less ($27 million in 2022). Even for these corporations, the tax law requires that they use the accrual method to compute gross profit from the sale of inventory. [I.R.C. §448(c)]

¶1402.02   ACCOUNTING PERIODS

Corporations normally use a 12-month year to report their taxable income. A C corporation may choose to use a calendar year or a fiscal year. A fiscal year is any 12-month period that ends on the last day of a month other than December. For example, a corporation may use a tax year of July 1 to June 30 as its fiscal tax year. [I.R.C. §441(b)]

Another tax year option that corporations may choose is a 52-53 week year. Corporations select this tax year when they want their tax year to end on the same day of the week each year. The day may be either the last one occurring in the last month of their tax year or the one occurring closest to their normal year-end.

EXAMPLE 6	Carolina Corporation closes its tax year on the last Friday in December each year. In 20x0, the last Friday falls on December 29. In 20x1, it falls on December 28, and in 20x2, it falls on December 26. Thus, Carolina's 52-53 week tax year for 20x1 runs from December 30, 20x0 to December 28, 20x1. Its tax year for 20x2 runs from December 29, 20x1 until December 26, 20x2.

Short Tax Year

Corporations can have a tax year shorter than 12 months in three situations. The first is in the year in which the corporation is formed. The second generally occurs in the last year of the corporation's operations. The third is when a corporation changes its tax year.

All taxpayers must get permission from the IRS to change their tax year. Corporations do this by filing Form 1128, Application to Adopt, Change, or Retain a Tax Year. [I.R.C. §442] When taxpayers change their tax year, they file a short-period return that covers the period between the close of their old tax year and the start of their new tax year.

EXAMPLE 7	A newly formed corporation selects a September 30 year-end. The corporation begins operations on May 16, 20x1. For the fiscal year ending September 30, 20x1, the corporation files a short period return for the period May 16, 20x1 – September 30, 20x1. Its fiscal year ending on September 30, 20x2 includes the activities of the corporation from October 1, 20x1 – September 30, 20x2.

EXAMPLE 8	A corporation that has a calendar year-end decides that an October 31 year-end more closely reflects the end of its annual business cycle. On June 1, 20x3, the corporation completes Form 1128 and files it with the IRS. The corporation receives permission from the IRS to change its tax year effective October 31, 20x3. The corporation files a tax return for the short period that runs from January 1, 20x3 – October 31, 20x3. Its next tax return will be for the fiscal year November 1, 20x3 – October 31, 20x4.

¶1402.03   CORPORATE TAXABLE INCOME FORMULA

Corporations compute their taxable income as gross income less business expenses. However, some specific deductions require special computations and therefore cannot be grouped with other business expenses. These include (1) the charitable contribution (CC) deduction, (2) the dividends received deduction (DRD), and (3) short-term capital loss (STCL) carrybacks. Corporations can no longer carry their net operating losses (NOLs) back but can carry forward NOLs indefinitely. NOLs from 2017 and earlier years are limited to a 20-year carryforward period. See ¶1402.06, subheading *Net Operating Loss (NOL)*. The formula for computing corporate taxable income is:

	Gross income
−	Deductions (all but CC, DRD, STCL carryback)
=	Taxable income used to compute CC deduction
−	Charitable contribution (CC) deduction
=	Taxable income used to compute DRD
−	Dividends received deduction (DRD)
=	Taxable income before STCL carrybacks
−	STCL carryback
=	Taxable income

¶1402.04   INCOME ITEMS

Typically, the same Code provisions determine the tax status of income items for individual taxpayers and corporations. However, in some cases additional rules apply.

Gross Profit from Sales

Net sales are gross sales less sales returns and allowances. Net sales minus cost of goods sold equals **gross profit from sales**. Corporations can deduct *sales discounts* directly from sales or treat them as a business expense.

For many businesses, inventories are a material factor in producing gross sales. Inventories include raw materials, supplies, work in process, and finished goods. Businesses that produce goods for sale include all production costs in inventories. These costs include direct materials, direct labor, as well as direct and indirect overhead. The term for this process is **full costing**. To compute **cost of goods sold**, the taxpayer adds beginning inventories, labor, and overhead. It then subtracts ending inventories, as shown below. This formula is the same one sole proprietors use to report their cost of goods sold on Schedule C (Part III), see ¶705.05.

Beginning inventories	$100,956
Add: Purchases	207,858
Labor	74,807
Other costs	30,529
Total inventory available for sale	$414,150
Less: Ending inventories	(90,283)
Cost of goods sold	$323,867

A corporation does not report cost of goods sold on Form 1120. Instead, it uses Form 1125-A to disclose this computation.

Capital Gains and Losses

Corporations report the sale of capital assets on Schedule D (Form 1120). Unlike individuals, corporations do not get a reduced tax rate on net capital gains. Corporations must include the full amount of capital gains in their regular taxable income. Corporations record capital gains separately from other income because their capital losses can be deducted only against capital gains. [I.R.C. §1211(a)] Any capital losses in excess of capital gains are carried back three years and forward five years to offset capital gains in those years. [I.R.C. §1212(a)]

Corporations treat all capital loss carryovers as short-term capital losses. They first use capital losses arising in the current year, followed by carryover capital losses in a first-created, first-used order. Corporations that cannot use their capital losses within the carryover period lose the tax benefit of the losses.

EXAMPLE 9	McCann, Inc. has the following capital gains and losses during the 20x3.

Short-term capital gain	$18,000
Short-term capital loss	(14,000)
Long-term capital gain	13,000
Long-term capital loss	(22,000)

McCann begins the process by offsetting short-term capital losses against short-term capital gains. It then offsets long-term capital losses against long-term capital gains. This results in a $4,000 net short-term gain and a $9,000 net long-term loss. McCann uses $4,000 of the net long-term capital loss to offset its net short-term capital gain. This is the same netting process that is described in ¶1101.03.

Short-Term	Long-Term
$18,000	$ 13,000
(14,000)	(22,000)
$ 4,000	($ 9,000)
(4,000) ←	
$0	

McCann must carry back $5,000 of its capital losses ($9,000 – $4,000 used in 20x3) to 20x0 (its third preceding tax year). These losses will be treated as short-term capital losses when the netting process for 20x0 is redone. Any losses not used in 20x0 are carried forward to 20x1 and then 20x2. If McCann cannot use up all of the capital losses in those carryback years, it carries forward any remaining amount as a short-term capital loss to 20x4 – 20x8 (for a total of five carryforward years).

| EXAMPLE 10 | Continuing with Example 9, assume that McCann, Inc. had the following capital gains and losses during 20x0. |

	Short-Term	Long-Term
	$12,000	$ 7,000
	(3,000)	(5,000)
	$ 9,000	$ 2,000

When the $5,000 excess capital loss from 20x3 is carried back to 20x0 as a short-term capital loss, the (redone) netting process from 20x0 looks like this.

	Short-Term	Long-Term
Carryback from 20x3	($ 5,000)	
	12,000	$ 7,000
	(3,000)	(5,000)
	$ 4,000	$ 2,000

When McCann adds the $5,000 short-term capital loss to the netting process, its taxable income is reduced by $5,000 ($11,000 overall net gain reported originally vs. $6,000 overall net gain as recomputed). McCann recomputes its tax for 20x0. McCann recomputes its tax for 20x0. McCann files for a refund of the taxes paid on the $5,000 of capital gain by filing Form 1139, Corporation Application for Tentative Refund. If McCann's marginal tax rate in 20x0 was 35%, then the IRS will refund McCann $1,750 ($5,000 × 35%), which represents the overpaid taxes for that year. [Currently, corporations are taxed at a flat 21% income tax rate.]

¶1402.05   BUSINESS DEDUCTIONS

Many corporate deductions are the same as those taken by sole proprietors (see Chapter 7). However, differences do exist. These differences are described in the discussions that follow.

Compensation

Corporations deduct payments for personal services as compensation when they pass three tests: (1) the payments represent an ordinary and necessary expense of the business, (2) the payments represent a reasonable amount for services received, and (3) the corporation pays or accrues the amount in the current tax year under its method of accounting. [I.R.C. §162(a)(1)] The deduction on the tax return for salaries and wages equals paid or accrued compensation less any tax credits (like the work opportunity tax credit, see ¶1203.06) taken on the return.

For publicly held corporations (those whose stock is publicly traded), a special rule limits the deduction for salaries paid to the Chief Executive Officer (CEO) or the Chief Financial Officer (CFO) and the other three most highly paid officers. Unless the corporation can justify paying a higher amount, the deduction for each of these officers cannot exceed $1 million, even though all compensation paid is taxable to the officer. [I.R.C. §162(m)] While there is no definite rule for determining reasonable compensation, guidelines do exist. The main guideline looks at what similar organizations pay for similar services. Other guidelines include local living costs, as well as the officer's skills and degree of responsibility.

| EXAMPLE 11 | Easton Corporation pays its CEO $1.5 million in 20x1. Easton cannot justify why the $1 million limit should not be imposed. Although Easton can pay its CEO $1.5 million, it can only deduct $1 million on its 20x1 tax return. The CEO is taxed on the full $1.5 million of compensation received. |

Bad Debts

Most taxpayers, including corporations, can only use the direct write-off method for bad debts. An exception exists for certain financial institutions. These institutions use the reserve method of accounting (the method used in financial reporting).

EXAMPLE 12	In August of 20x0, an accrual basis, calendar year corporation sold merchandise on account for $1,000. The corporation included the proceeds from the sale in its 20x0 gross income. On June 15, 20x1, the accounts receivable becomes worthless. Since the corporation recognized the income from the sale in 20x0, it takes a $1,000 bad debt deduction in 20x1. It is important to note that the corporation must be able to specifically identify which accounts receivable became worthless before it can take a bad debt deduction. This is known as the "direct write-off method."

Organizational and Start-Up Costs

The Internal Revenue Code (Code) allows corporations to deduct up to $5,000 of organizational costs for the tax year in which business operations begin. The $5,000 amount is reduced by $1 for each dollar of organizational costs that exceed $50,000. Thus, no current deduction is allowed to corporations that incur over $55,000 in organizational costs. Any costs not currently expensed may be written off (amortized) over a 180-month period using the straight-line method. The amortization period starts in the month in which the corporation begins operations.

Organizational costs include any costs related to the creation of the corporation that are chargeable to a capital account. These costs include (1) legal expenses for setting up the corporation, (2) costs of incorporation charged by the state government, (3) necessary accounting services, (4) expenses of temporary directors, and (5) costs of organizational meetings. Organizational expenditures do not include the costs of issuing or selling stocks or other securities, or costs associated with transferring assets to the corporation. Instead, these costs simply reduce the amount of paid-in capital. [I.R.C. §248]

EXAMPLE 13	Branis Corporation incurs $53,500 of organizational costs. Branis uses a calendar year-end and began its operations on November 1, 20x1. Since the organizational costs exceed $50,000, Branis can elect to expense only $1,500 ($5,000 – $3,500) in 20x1. It can then elect to amortize the remaining $52,000 ($53,500 – $1,500) over 180 months beginning on November 1, 20x1.

Start-up costs are costs that normally would be currently deductible if they had been incurred during the operations of an existing business. They often include costs incurred to investigate entering into or acquiring a new active trade or business. Like organizational costs, businesses can deduct up to $5,000 of start-up costs. However, the $5,000 is reduced by the amount by which the start-up costs exceed $50,000. The rest may be amortized evenly over 180 months starting with the month in which the business begins. The rules that apply to start-up costs are available to all types of businesses, including sole proprietorships, C corporations, partnerships, and S corporations. [I.R.C. §195]

EXAMPLE 14	Addison, Inc. uses a calendar year-end. During 20x1 it incurred $53,000 of start-up costs. Addison acquired the business on May 2, 20x1. Since the start-up costs exceed $50,000, Addison can elect to expense $2,000 in 20x1 ($5,000 – $3,000 excess over $50,000). Addison can amortize the remaining $51,000 over 180 months beginning in May 20x1.

Taxpayers can elect out of amortizing their organizational and start-up costs. These taxpayers would instead capitalize their costs to an asset account, which would be used to offset the amount realized on the sale of the business.

Passive Losses

The passive loss limitations rules (discussed at ¶905) do not apply to most corporations. However, closely-held corporations (over 50% of its stock owned by five or fewer individuals) and personal service corporations (discussed in ¶1403.03) are subject to the passive loss rules. Unlike an individual, a closely-held corporation may deduct passive losses against active business income, but not against portfolio income. [I.R.C. §469(c)(7)(D)(i)]

QBI Deduction

After 2017, individuals may claim a QBI deduction. A corporation may not claim this deduction (see Chapter 8).

¶1402.06   SPECIAL DEDUCTIONS

The deductions for corporations, for the most part, are treated the same as business deductions for other business entities. Nevertheless, some deductions for corporations receive special treatment. When introducing the corporation's taxable income formula in ¶1402.03, these special deductions were listed separately. The discussion that follows describes each of these special deductions.

Charitable Contributions

Like individuals, corporations can deduct contributions they make to charitable organizations. However, the deduction cannot exceed a specified percentage of the corporation's taxable income before certain items. For most years, the specified percentage is 10%. However, for 2020 and 2021 only, the law set the percentage at 25%. [This is an unusual law, which is not in the Internal Revenue Code. It appears in the CARES Act of 2020, P.L. 116-136 at §2205DivA and was then extended by the Consolidated Appropriations Act (CAA) of 2021, P.L. 116-260 at §213] For 2022, the limit returns to 10%. Any contributions made in excess of the 10% (or 25% for 2020 and 2021) taxable income limit are carried forward for five years. Like capital losses, amounts carried over are used on a first-made, first-used basis. If the corporation does not have enough taxable income in the carryover period to use the carried over contributions, the deduction is lost.

EXAMPLE 15

During 20x1, a corporation makes cash contributions of $20,000 to various charitable organizations. The corporation has taxable income of $180,000 before deducting any charitable contributions (CCs), dividends received deduction (DRD) or any capital loss carrybacks. The corporation's charitable deduction for 20x1 is $18,000.

Taxable income used to compute the CC deduction	$180,000
	× 10%
Maximum charitable contribution deduction	$ 18,000
Cash contributions made during 20x1	$20,000
Less corporate limitation	(18,000)
Charitable contribution carryover to 20x2	$ 2,000

If the year were 2020 or 2021, but no other tax year, the corporation could deduct up to $45,000 of a charitable contribution. In any other year, the corporation could deduct $18,000.

A corporation that donates appreciated property to a public charity computes the amount contributed in the same manner as individuals (see ¶506). Thus, when a corporation donates ordinary income property to a charity, it deducts its adjusted basis in the property.

An enhanced charitable contribution deduction is allowed for C corporations that donate inventory (like food, clothing, or medicine) to qualified charities that provide care for the ill, the needy, or infants. The enhanced deduction equals the taxpayer's basis in the inventory plus one-half of the excess of the inventory's FMV over the taxpayer's basis. However, the deduction is limited to twice the taxpayer's basis in the inventory. Thus, if a corporation with inventory having a basis of $650 and valued at $1,000, were to donate it to a qualified charity that cares for infants, the corporation's deduction would equal $825 ($650 + ½ × ($1,000 – $650)). For most years, the limit on this particular type of deduction is 15% of taxable income. However, for 2020 and 2021 only, this limit is 25%. [CARES Act of 2020, P.L. 116-136 at §2205DivA and CAA 2021, P.L. 116-260 at §213]

A corporation deducts a contribution in the year it transfers property or cash to a charity. A corporation using the accrual method of accounting, however, can choose to take the deduction in the year it makes the accrual (pledge). To take the deduction in the accrual year, the accrual basis corporation must pay the contribution within three months and 15 days after the close of its tax year. [I.R.C. §170(a)(2)]

Dividends Received Deduction

Corporations get a deduction for a certain amount of the dividends they receive. [I.R.C. §243] The deduction lessens or avoids triple taxation of the profits of corporations. Triple taxation occurs when a corporation distributes its after-tax profits to corporate shareholders. These corporate shareholders normally would pay taxes on the dividends before they distribute their profits to their shareholders (who also pay taxes on the dividends they receive). The amount of the dividends received deduction (DRD) depends on the corporation's percentage of stock ownership in the corporation paying the dividend.

Percentage Owned	DRD Percentage
Less than 20%	50%
From 20% to less than 80%	65%
From 80% to 100%	100%

EXAMPLE 16

Delta Corporation owns 60% of the total value and outstanding shares of stock in Epsilon Corporation. During the year, Epsilon pays a $100,000 dividend to Delta. Delta includes the $100,000 of dividends in income and takes a $65,000 DRD ($100,000 × 65%). Thus, the net amount of dividends taxed to Delta is $35,000 ($100,000 – $65,000).

For corporations whose ownership is at least 80%, the DRD is always 100% of the dividends received. A reduced DRD may apply to corporations whose ownership is less than 80%. Corporations with less than 80% ownership are required to apply the DRD percentage to taxable income (after deducting charitable contributions but before any capital loss carrybacks). Normally for these corporations, the DRD is computed as the *lesser of* (i) the DRD percentage times dividends received, or (ii) the DRD percentage times taxable income (as defined above). However, if deducting an amount equal to the DRD percentage times the dividends received results in an NOL for the year, then the rule limiting the deduction to the DRD times taxable income does not apply. In these situations, the corporation's DRD equals the DRD percentage times the dividends received.

Computing the DRD when ownership is less than 80%

Step 1	Multiply the appropriate DRD percentage times the dividends received.
Step 2	Multiply the DRD percentage by the corporation's taxable income after deducting charitable contributions.
Step 3	Subtract the result from Step 1 from the corporation's taxable income used in Step 2. If a loss results (NOL), then use the amount from Step 1 as the corporation's DRD. If the result is a positive amount, then use the *lesser of* Step 1 or Step 2 as the DRD.

EXAMPLE 17	Same facts as in Example 16, except that Delta's taxable income after the charitable contribution deduction but before any loss carrybacks is $90,000. If Delta were to deduct an $65,000 DRD based on dividends received ($100,000 × 65%), a positive amount results ($90,000 – $65,000 = $25,000 taxable income). Thus, Delta computes its DRD as the *lesser of* (i) $65,000 (65% of $100,000 dividends received), or (ii) $58,500 (65% × $90,000 taxable income). Delta's DRD is $58,500.

EXAMPLE 18	Same facts as in Example 16, except that Delta's taxable income after the charitable contribution deduction but before any loss carrybacks is $60,000. Now when Delta deducts a $65,000 DRD based on dividends received, an NOL results ($60,000 – $65,000 = $5,000 NOL). Thus, the DRD based on taxable income does not apply and Delta's DRD is $65,000 (65% × $100,000 dividends received).

EXAMPLE 19	Beta Corporation owns 80% of the total value and outstanding shares of stock in Alpha Corporation. During the year, Alpha pays a $50,000 dividend to Beta. Beta's taxable income after the charitable contribution deduction, but before any loss carrybacks is $60,000. (This amount includes the $50,000 of dividend income from Beta). Because Beta's ownership percentage is at least 80%, its DRD percentage is 100%. After subtracting the $50,000 DRD ($50,000 × 100%), Beta reports taxable income of $10,000. For corporations whose ownership is at least 80%, the DRD is always 100% of the dividends received, regardless of whether the DRD produces an NOL.

Net Operating Loss (NOL)

When a corporation's deductions exceed its income, the corporation may suffer a net loss for the year. A corporation needs to make only one adjustment to its taxable income in determining its NOL for the current year. It must add back any NOL carryovers from prior years that were deducted in computing the current year NOL. An NOL arising in a tax year beginning after 2017 is limited to 80% of taxable income, computed without regard to the NOL deduction allowed for the tax year.

The Tax Cuts and Jobs Act of 2017 amended the rules. Under the new rules, an NOL generated in a tax year ending after 2017 must be carried forward indefinitely, but may not be carried back. However, the CARES Act of 2020 modified these rules, so that they do not take full effect until 2021. For losses incurred in 2018, 2019 and 2020, there is a five-year carryback period. [I.R.C. §172(b)(1)(D)] See discussion at ¶1201.

EXAMPLE 20

Cougar Corporation has the following income and deductions in 2022.

Gross sales	$600,000
Long-term capital gains	25,000
Dividend income (18% ownership in the stock)	40,000
Interest income	10,000
Cost of goods sold	400,000
Other business expenses	60,000
Charitable contributions	22,000
Short-term capital loss carryforward from 2021	15,000

Cougar computes its 2022 taxable income as follows. The charitable contribution deduction is limited to 10% of the taxable income before the charitable contribution and DRD so Cougar carries forward a $2,000 charitable contribution to the next tax year ($22,000 − $20,000).

Gross income[1]	$260,000
Less deductions[2]	(60,000)
Taxable income for computing CC deduction	$200,000
Less charitable contribution deduction	(20,000)
Taxable income for figuring DRD	$180,000
Less DRD[3]	(20,000)
Taxable income	$160,000

[1] $600,000 − $400,000 COGS + ($25,000 capital gains − $15,000 capital losses) + $40,000 + $10,000.
[2] $60,000.
[3] *lesser of* (i) 50% × $40,000 dividends received or (ii) 50% × $180,000, since Cougar's 18% ownership in the stock is less than 80%.

¶1403 Corporate Tax Returns and Tax Rates

Every C corporation must file a tax return, regardless of the amount of its taxable income or loss. Once the corporation computes its taxable income, it applies the corporate tax rate. While individual tax rates are **progressive**, which means the rates increase as taxable income increases, corporate tax rate is flat. Further, the individual tax brackets are indexed for inflation each year. The next sections describe the corporate tax return and its tax rates.

¶1403.01 CORPORATE TAX RETURN

C corporations use Form 1120, U.S. Corporation Income Tax Return, to report their taxable income (loss). Form 1120 has six pages. A completed Form 1120 is shown in Figure 14-2 (¶1403.04).

Due Date

The due date for most C corporation income tax returns falls on the 15th of the fourth month after the corporation's year ends. This includes domestic corporations and foreign corporations with a U.S. place of business. The due date for C corporations with a June 30 year-end is one month earlier (the 15th day of their third month, or September 15th). Foreign corporations that do business in the U.S., but do not have a U.S. place of business have until the 15th day of the sixth month to file their U.S. tax returns. When a due date falls on a Saturday, Sunday, or legal holiday, the due date is the next business day.

A corporation that cannot file its tax return by the due date can request an automatic extension to file its return by filing Form 7004, Application for Automatic Extension of Time To File Certain Business Income Tax, Information, and Other Returns, by the due date of its tax return (¶208). The length of the extension is six months (seven months for corporations with a June 30 year-end). As with all extensions, filing this form only extends the due date for filing the tax return. It does not extend the payment of taxes owed. Taxpayers that do not pay the taxes they owe by the original due date of their tax return are subject to interest and penalties.

EXAMPLE 21	Amel, Inc. (a calendar year corporation) normally must file its tax return by April 15. If Amel is unable to file its return on time, it can file Form 7004 with the IRS by April 15. Amel will then have until October 15 (six more months) to file its tax return. Amel must, however, pay any taxes it owes when it files the extension, or else the unpaid taxes will be subject to interest and penalty. Should October 15 fall on a Saturday, Sunday or legal holiday, the deadline for filing a timely return with an extension would be the next business day.

EXAMPLE 22	Same facts as in Example 21, except that Amel uses a fiscal year that ends on March 31. Amel's due date for filing its tax return is July 15. This is 3½ months after the end of Amel's March 31 fiscal year-end. If Amel files a timely extension, its tax return deadline would be extended to January 15 (six months after July 15). If either of these deadlines falls on a weekend or legal holiday, the due date would be the next business day.

¶1403.02   CORPORATE TAX RATES

For tax years beginning after 2017, the graduated corporate income tax rate structure is eliminated and corporations are taxed at a flat 21% rate.

EXAMPLE 23	XYZ corporation, a calendar year corporation, has taxable income of $900,000. XYZ's income tax is computed by applying a flat rate of 21% (21% × $900,000 = $189,000).

¶1403.03   PERSONAL SERVICE CORPORATIONS

Personal service corporations (PSC) are corporations whose shareholders and employees provide professional services for a fee. Doctors, dentists, lawyers, architects, accountants, and other professionals organize as PSCs. These corporations provide the owners with several tax and nontax benefits. However, they also have some tax restrictions. For example, PSCs generally may only use a calendar year as a tax year. For tax years beginning after 2017, PSCs are taxed at a flat 21% rate similar to other corporations. A PSC usually pays out its net earnings to its shareholder-employees as salaries. These salaries are then deducted by the PSC, and taxed to the shareholder-employee using the individual tax rates.

¶1403.04 FILLED-IN FORM 1120

 INFORMATION FOR FIGURE 14-2:

Globe Manufacturing Company (EIN **70-0694770**, located at **2468 E. Van Buren, Phoenix, AZ 85019**) was incorporated on **January 3, 2000**. Its business activity code is 334419. Globe has always been on the accrual method of accounting and uses the cost method for valuing inventory of **electronic components** that it **manufactures**. Globe has over 100 shareholders. It made estimated payments of $4,000 during the year and paid out $16,446 in cash dividends.

The income and expense information for preparing Globe Manufacturing's Form 1120 comes from the Income Statement in Figure 14-1. The filled-in Form 1120 for Globe Manufacturing appears in Figure 14-2. The balance sheet information appears on Schedule L.

Figure 14-1: Income Statement for Globe Manufacturing

Globe Manufacturing Company
Income Statement
For Year Ended December 31, 2022

Revenue:		
Net sales (after subtracting $3,197 of goods returned)		$528,072
Interest income ($1,650 from municipal bonds)		2,559
Dividend income, 45% stock ownership ($1,750 domestic, $235 foreign)		1,985
Gross rent		500
Total revenues		$533,116
Less Expenses:		
Advertising	$ 17,500	
Bad debts written off during the year	1,960	
Charitable contributions	5,200	
Compensation of (sole) officer	80,000	
Cost of goods sold (COGS) other than depreciation[1]	293,338	
Depreciation ($30,529 related to COGS)[1]	36,744	
Insurance expense	2,270	
Interest expense	2,580	
Maintenance	3,140	
Other employee salaries	52,047	
Office supplies	163	
Taxes and licenses	8,200	
Utilities expense	1,087	(504,229)
Net income before federal income taxes		$ 28,887
Less income tax		(6,066)
Net income per books		$ 22,821

[1]From Form 1125-A (not included)

Line # (Form 1120, Page 1)

   D: Total assets, **$428,944** (source: Schedule L, line 15(d))

  1a: Gross receipts or sales, **$531,269** ($528,072 net sales + $3,197 returns)

  1b: Returns and allowances, **$3,197**

   2: Cost of goods sold (source: Form 1125-A), **$323,867** ($293,338 + $30,529 depreciation related to COGS)

   5: Interest, **$909** ($2,559 total interest – $1,650 tax-exempt interest)

  19: Charitable contributions, **$3,244**, limited to 10% of gross income - deductions on line 7 through 26 except for charitable ($207,599 - $175,162)

  20: Depreciation not claimed on Form 1125-A (COGS), **$6,215** ($36,744 – $30,529)

  26: Other deductions, **$3,520** ($2,270 insurance + $163 supplies + $1,087 utilities)

Line # (Form 1120, Schedule C)

  2(a): Dividends from 20%-or-more-owned domestic corporations, **$1,750**

 14(a): Dividends from foreign corporations, **$235**

Line # (Form 1120, Schedule J)

   2: Income tax, **$5,892** ($28,055 taxable income × 21% tax rate)

  14: 2022 estimated tax payments, **$6,000** (source: given)

Line # (Form 1120, Schedule K)

  1b: Check box for Accrual method of accounting

  2a: Business activity code no., **334419** (source: Instructions for Form 1120)

3 & 4: Mark **No**

   5: Charitable contribution difference-**$1,956**

  5a: Mark **Yes** and describe ownership of domestic and foreign corporations below

  5b: Mark **No**

6,7 & 8: Mark **No**

   9: Show tax exempt interest of **$1,650**

11-14: Mark **No**

15a & b: Mark **Yes**. This requirement is nearly universal for business taxpayers

16-26: Mark **No**

Line # (Form 1120, Schedule M-1)

   9: Tax-exempt interest recorded on books this year not included on this return, **$1,650**

Line # (Form 1120, Schedule M-2)

   1: Balance in unappropriated retained earnings at beginning of the year, **$44,708** (source: Schedule L, line 25(b))

  5a: Cash distributions, **$16,446** (source: given)

Figure 14-2: Filled-In Form 1120 (Page 1)

Form 1120

Department of the Treasury
Internal Revenue Service

U.S. Corporation Income Tax Return

For calendar year 2022 or tax year beginning _____, 2022, ending _____, 20 _____

Go to *www.irs.gov/Form1120* for instructions and the latest information.

OMB No. 1545-0123

2022

A Check if:
1a Consolidated return (attach Form 851) ☐
b Life/nonlife consolidated return . ☐
2 Personal holding co. (attach Sch. PH) . ☐
3 Personal service corp. (see instructions) . ☐
4 Schedule M-3 attached ☐

TYPE OR PRINT

Name
Globe Manufacturing Company

Number, street, and room or suite no. If a P.O. box, see instructions.
2468 E. Van Buren

City or town, state or province, country, and ZIP or foreign postal code
Phoenix, AZ 85019

B Employer identification number
70-0694770

C Date incorporated
01-03-2000

D Total assets (see instructions)
$ 426,531

E Check if: (1) ☐ Initial return (2) ☐ Final return (3) ☐ Name change (4) ☐ Address change

Income	1a	Gross receipts or sales	1a 531,269	
	b	Returns and allowances	1b 3,197	
	c	Balance. Subtract line 1b from line 1a	1c	528,072
	2	Cost of goods sold (attach Form 1125-A)	2	323,867
	3	Gross profit. Subtract line 2 from line 1c	3	204,205
	4	Dividends and inclusions (Schedule C, line 23)	4	1,985
	5	Interest	5	909
	6	Gross rents	6	500
	7	Gross royalties	7	
	8	Capital gain net income (attach Schedule D (Form 1120))	8	
	9	Net gain or (loss) from Form 4797, Part II, line 17 (attach Form 4797)	9	
	10	Other income (see instructions—attach statement)	10	
	11	**Total income.** Add lines 3 through 10	11	207,599
Deductions (See instructions for limitations on deductions.)	12	Compensation of officers (see instructions—attach Form 1125-E)	12	80,000
	13	Salaries and wages (less employment credits)	13	52,047
	14	Repairs and maintenance	14	3,140
	15	Bad debts	15	1,960
	16	Rents	16	
	17	Taxes and licenses	17	8,200
	18	Interest (see instructions)	18	2,580
	19	Charitable contributions	19	3,244
	20	Depreciation from Form 4562 not claimed on Form 1125-A or elsewhere on return (attach Form 4562)	20	6,215
	21	Depletion	21	
	22	Advertising	22	17,500
	23	Pension, profit-sharing, etc., plans	23	
	24	Employee benefit programs	24	
	25	Reserved for future use	25	
	26	Other deductions (attach statement)	26	3,520
	27	**Total deductions.** Add lines 12 through 26	27	178,406
	28	Taxable income before net operating loss deduction and special deductions. Subtract line 27 from line 11	28	29,193
	29a	Net operating loss deduction (see instructions)	29a 1,138	
	b	Special deductions (Schedule C, line 24)	29b	
	c	Add lines 29a and 29b	29c	1,138
Tax, Refundable Credits, and Payments	30	**Taxable income.** Subtract line 29c from line 28. See instructions	30	28,056
	31	Total tax (Schedule J, Part I, line 11)	31	5,892
	32	Reserved for future use	32	
	33	Total payments and credits (Schedule J, Part III, line 23)	33	6,000
	34	Estimated tax penalty. See instructions. Check if Form 2220 is attached ☐	34	
	35	**Amount owed.** If line 33 is smaller than the total of lines 31 and 34, enter amount owed	35	
	36	**Overpayment.** If line 33 is larger than the total of lines 31 and 34, enter amount overpaid	36	108
	37	Enter amount from line 36 you want: **Credited to 2023 estimated tax** 108 Refunded	37	

Sign Here

Under penalties of perjury, I declare that I have examined this return, including accompanying schedules and statements, and to the best of my knowledge and belief, it is true, correct, and complete. Declaration of preparer (other than taxpayer) is based on all information of which preparer has any knowledge.

Signature of officer _____ Date _____ Title _____

May the IRS discuss this return with the preparer shown below? See instructions. ☐ Yes ☐ No

Paid Preparer Use Only

Print/Type preparer's name	Preparer's signature	Date	Check ☐ if self-employed	PTIN
Firm's name			Firm's EIN	
Firm's address			Phone no.	

For Paperwork Reduction Act Notice, see separate instructions.

Cat. No. 11450Q

Form **1120** (2022)

Figure 14-2: Filled-In Form 1120 (Page 2)

	Form 1120 (2022)			Page **2**
	Schedule C Dividends, Inclusions, and Special Deductions (see instructions)	**(a)** Dividends and inclusions	**(b)** %	**(c)** Special deductions (a) × (b)
1	Dividends from less-than-20%-owned domestic corporations (other than debt-financed stock)		50	
2	Dividends from 20%-or-more-owned domestic corporations (other than debt-financed stock)	1,750	65	1,138
3	Dividends on certain debt-financed stock of domestic and foreign corporations		See instructions	
4	Dividends on certain preferred stock of less-than-20%-owned public utilities		23.3	
5	Dividends on certain preferred stock of 20%-or-more-owned public utilities		26.7	
6	Dividends from less-than-20%-owned foreign corporations and certain FSCs		50	
7	Dividends from 20%-or-more-owned foreign corporations and certain FSCs		65	
8	Dividends from wholly owned foreign subsidiaries		100	
9	**Subtotal.** Add lines 1 through 8. See instructions for limitations	1,750	See instructions	1,138
10	Dividends from domestic corporations received by a small business investment company operating under the Small Business Investment Act of 1958		100	
11	Dividends from affiliated group members		100	
12	Dividends from certain FSCs		100	
13	Foreign-source portion of dividends received from a specified 10%-owned foreign corporation (excluding hybrid dividends) (see instructions)		100	
14	Dividends from foreign corporations not included on line 3, 6, 7, 8, 11, 12, or 13 (including any hybrid dividends)	235		
15	Reserved for future use			
16a	Subpart F inclusions derived from the sale by a controlled foreign corporation (CFC) of the stock of a lower-tier foreign corporation treated as a dividend (attach Form(s) 5471) (see instructions)		100	
b	Subpart F inclusions derived from hybrid dividends of tiered corporations (attach Form(s) 5471) (see instructions)			
c	Other inclusions from CFCs under subpart F not included on line 16a, 16b, or 17 (attach Form(s) 5471) (see instructions)			
17	Global Intangible Low-Taxed Income (GILTI) (attach Form(s) 5471 and Form 8992)			
18	Gross-up for foreign taxes deemed paid			
19	IC-DISC and former DISC dividends not included on line 1, 2, or 3			
20	Other dividends			
21	Deduction for dividends paid on certain preferred stock of public utilities			
22	Section 250 deduction (attach Form 8993)			
23	**Total dividends and inclusions.** Add column (a), lines 9 through 20. Enter here and on page 1, line 4	1,985		
24	**Total special deductions.** Add column (c), lines 9 through 22. Enter here and on page 1, line 29b			1,138

Form **1120** (2022)

DRAFT AS OF October 3, 2022 DO NOT FILE

Figure 14-2: Filled-In Form 1120 (Page 3)

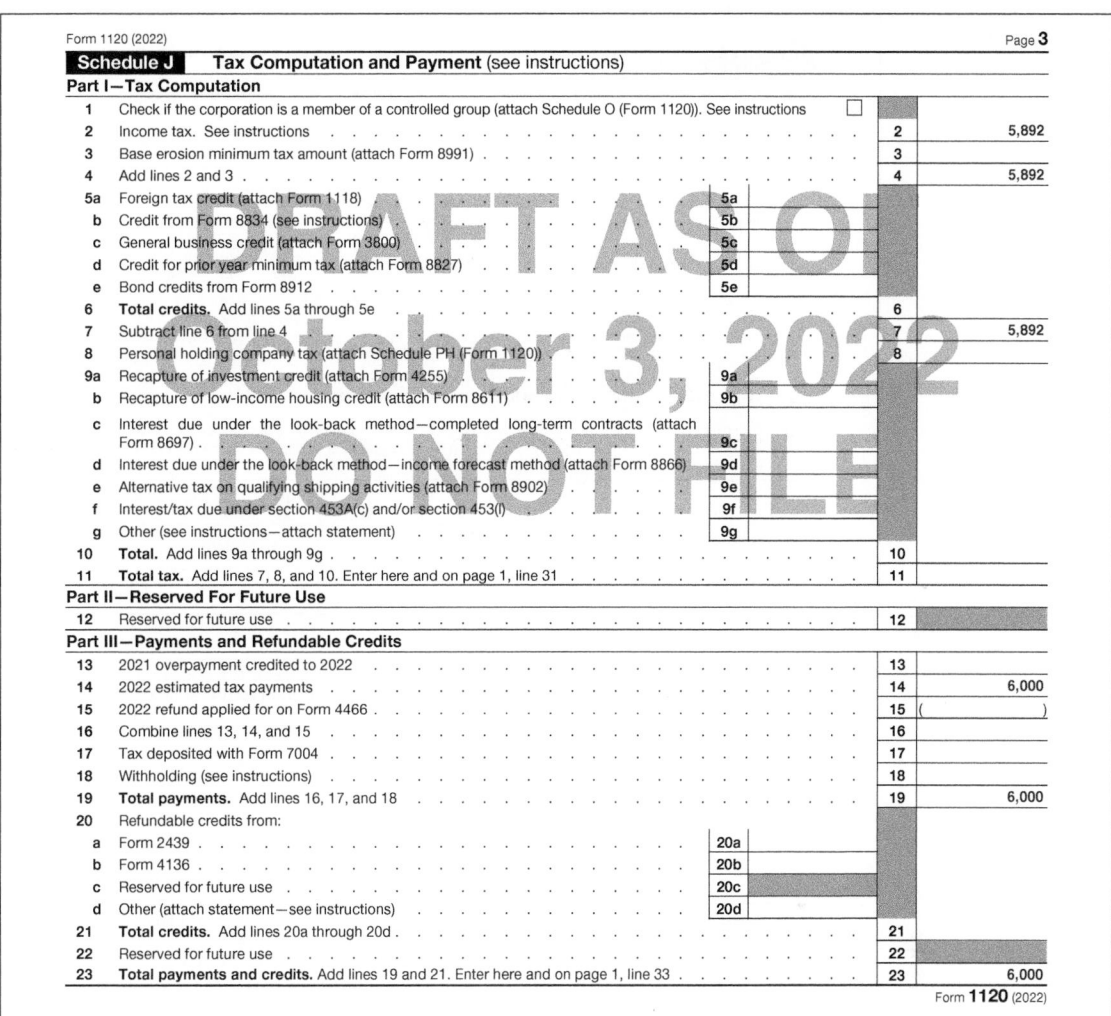

Figure 14-2: Filled-In Form 1120 (Page 4)

Form 1120 (2022)   Page **4**

Schedule K	**Other Information** (see instructions)		Yes	No

1 Check accounting method: **a** ☐ Cash   **b** ☑ Accrual   **c** ☐ Other (specify) _____

2 See the instructions and enter the:

a Business activity code no. _____ 334419

b Business activity **Manufacturing**

c Product or service **Electronic Components**

3 Is the corporation a subsidiary in an affiliated group or a parent–subsidiary controlled group? . . . . **No ✔**

If "Yes," enter name and EIN of the parent corporation _____

4 At the end of the tax year:

a Did any foreign or domestic corporation, partnership (including any entity treated as a partnership), trust, or tax-exempt organization own directly 20% or more, or own, directly or indirectly, 50% or more of the total voting power of all classes of the corporation's stock entitled to vote? If "Yes," complete Part I of Schedule G (Form 1120) (attach Schedule G) **No ✔**

b Did any individual or estate own directly 20% or more, or own, directly or indirectly, 50% or more of the total voting power of all classes of the corporation's stock entitled to vote? If "Yes," complete Part II of Schedule G (Form 1120) (attach Schedule G) **No ✔**

5 At the end of the tax year, did the corporation:

a Own directly 20% or more, or own, directly or indirectly, 50% or more of the total voting power of all classes of stock entitled to vote of any foreign or domestic corporation not included on **Form 851,** Affiliations Schedule? For rules of constructive ownership, see instructions. **Yes ✔**

If "Yes," complete (i) through (iv) below.

(i) Name of Corporation	**(ii)** Employer Identification Number (if any)	**(iii)** Country of Incorporation	**(iv)** Percentage Owned in Voting Stock
Electronic Components	70-0694407	USA	27.0
Canadian Widgets, Ltd		Canada	22.0

b Own directly an interest of 20% or more, or own, directly or indirectly, an interest of 50% or more in any foreign or domestic partnership (including an entity treated as a partnership) or in the beneficial interest of a trust? For rules of constructive ownership, see instructions. **No ✔**

If "Yes," complete (i) through (iv) below.

(i) Name of Entity	**(ii)** Employer Identification Number (if any)	**(iii)** Country of Organization	**(iv)** Maximum Percentage Owned in Profit, Loss, or Capital

6 During this tax year, did the corporation pay dividends (other than stock dividends and distributions in exchange for stock) in excess of the corporation's current and accumulated earnings and profits? See sections 301 and 316 . . . . **No ✔**

If "Yes," file **Form 5452,** Corporate Report of Nondividend Distributions. See the instructions for Form 5452.

If this is a consolidated return, answer here for the parent corporation and on Form 851 for each subsidiary.

7 At any time during the tax year, did one foreign person own, directly or indirectly, at least 25% of the total voting power of all classes of the corporation's stock entitled to vote or at least 25% of the total value of all classes of the corporation's stock? . **No ✔**

For rules of attribution, see section 318. If "Yes," enter:

(a) Percentage owned _____ and **(b)** Owner's country _____

(c) The corporation may have to file **Form 5472,** Information Return of a 25% Foreign-Owned U.S. Corporation or a Foreign Corporation Engaged in a U.S. Trade or Business. Enter the number of Forms 5472 attached _____

8 Check this box if the corporation issued publicly offered debt instruments with original issue discount . . . . ☐

If checked, the corporation may have to file **Form 8281,** Information Return for Publicly Offered Original Issue Discount Instruments.

9 Enter the amount of tax-exempt interest received or accrued during the tax year $ _____ 1,650

10 Enter the number of shareholders at the end of the tax year (if 100 or fewer) _____

11 If the corporation has an NOL for the tax year and is electing to forego the carryback period, check here (see instructions) . ☐

If the corporation is filing a consolidated return, the statement required by Regulations section 1.1502-21(b)(3) must be attached or the election will not be valid.

12 Enter the available NOL carryover from prior tax years (do not reduce it by any deduction reported on page 1, line 29a.) . . . . $ _____

Form **1120** (2022)

Figure 14-2: Filled-In Form 1120 (Page 5)

Form 1120 (2022) Page **5**

Schedule K   **Other Information** *(continued from page 4)*

		Yes	No
13	Are the corporation's total receipts (page 1, line 1a, plus lines 4 through 10) for the tax year **and** its total assets at the end of the tax year less than $250,000?		✔
	If "Yes," the corporation is not required to complete Schedules L, M-1, and M-2. Instead, enter the total amount of cash distributions and the book value of property distributions (other than cash) made during the tax year $ _____		
14	Is the corporation required to file Schedule UTP (Form 1120), Uncertain Tax Position Statement? See instructions		✔
	If "Yes," complete and attach Schedule UTP.		
15a	Did the corporation make any payments in 2022 that would require it to file Form(s) 1099?	✔	
b	If "Yes," did or will the corporation file required Form(s) 1099?	✔	
16	During this tax year, did the corporation have an 80%-or-more change in ownership, including a change due to redemption of its own stock?		✔
17	During or subsequent to this tax year, but before the filing of this return, did the corporation dispose of more than 65% (by value) of its assets in a taxable, non-taxable, or tax deferred transaction?		✔
18	Did the corporation receive assets in a section 351 transfer in which any of the transferred assets had a fair market basis or fair market value of more than $1 million?		✔
19	During the corporation's tax year, did the corporation make any payments that would require it to file Forms 1042 and 1042-S under chapter 3 (sections 1441 through 1464) or chapter 4 (sections 1471 through 1474) of the Code?		✔
20	Is the corporation operating on a cooperative basis?		✔
21	During the tax year, did the corporation pay or accrue any interest or royalty for which the deduction is not allowed under section 267A? See instructions		✔
	If "Yes," enter the total amount of the disallowed deductions $ _____		
22	Does the corporation have gross receipts of at least $500 million in any of the 3 preceding tax years? (See sections 59A(e)(2) and (3))		✔
	If "Yes," complete and attach Form 8991.		
23	Did the corporation have an election under section 163(j) for any real property trade or business or any farming business in effect during the tax year? See instructions		✔
24	Does the corporation satisfy one or more of the following? See instructions		✔
a	The corporation owns a pass-through entity with current, or prior year carryover, excess business interest expense.		
b	The corporation's aggregate average annual gross receipts (determined under section 448(c)) for the 3 tax years preceding the current tax year are more than $27 million and the corporation has business interest expense.		
c	The corporation is a tax shelter and the corporation has business interest expense.		
	If "Yes," complete and attach Form 8990.		
25	Is the corporation attaching Form 8996 to certify as a Qualified Opportunity Fund?		✔
	If "Yes," enter amount from Form 8996, line 15 . . . . . $		
26	Since December 22, 2017, did a foreign corporation directly or indirectly acquire substantially all of the properties held directly or indirectly by the corporation, and was the ownership percentage (by vote or value) for purposes of section 7874 greater than 50% (for example, the shareholders held more than 50% of the stock of the foreign corporation)? If "Yes," list the ownership percentage by vote and by value. See instructions		✔
	Percentage: By Vote _____ By Value _____		

Form **1120** (2022)

¶1403.04

Figure 14-2: Filled-In Form 1120 (Page 6)

Form 1120 (2022)   Page **6**

Schedule L — Balance Sheets per Books

		Beginning of tax year		End of tax year	
Assets		(a)	(b)	(c)	(d)
1	Cash		12,572		48,678
2a	Trade notes and accounts receivable	51,524		60,719	
b	Less allowance for bad debts	(4,589)	46,935	(4,589)	56,130
3	Inventories		100,956		90,283
4	U.S. government obligations		3,000		3,000
5	Tax-exempt securities (see instructions)		949		4,678
6	Other current assets (attach statement)				
7	Loans to shareholders				
8	Mortgage and real estate loans				
9	Other investments (attach statement)		18,100		30,000
10a	Buildings and other depreciable assets	200,001		220,500	
b	Less accumulated depreciation	(16,401)	183,600	(53,175)	167,325
11a	Depletable assets				
b	Less accumulated depletion	( )		( )	
12	Land (net of any amortization)		3,650		26,437
13a	Intangible assets (amortizable only)				
b	Less accumulated amortization	( )		( )	
14	Other assets (attach statement)				
15	Total assets		369,762		426,531
Liabilities and Shareholders' Equity					
16	Accounts payable		14,184		16,452
17	Mortgages, notes, bonds payable in less than 1 year		2,000		
18	Other current liabilities (attach statement)		10,640		1,840
19	Loans from shareholders				
20	Mortgages, notes, bonds payable in 1 year or more		100,000		100,000
21	Other liabilities (attach statement)		8,230		12,836
22	Capital stock: a Preferred stock	45,000		45,000	
	b Common stock	125,000	170,000	180,000	225,000
23	Additional paid-in capital		20,000		20,000
24	Retained earnings—Appropriated (attach statement)				
25	Retained earnings—Unappropriated		44,708		51,083
26	Adjustments to shareholders' equity (attach statement)				
27	Less cost of treasury stock		( )		( )
28	Total liabilities and shareholders' equity		369,762		426,531

Schedule M-1 — Reconciliation of Income (Loss) per Books With Income per Return

Note: The corporation may be required to file Schedule M-3. See instructions.

1	Net income (loss) per books	22,821	7	Income recorded on books this year not included on this return (itemize):	
2	Federal income tax per books	6,066		Tax-exempt interest $ 1,650	
3	Excess of capital losses over capital gains				
4	Income subject to tax not recorded on books this year (itemize):				1,650
			8	Deductions on this return not charged against book income this year (itemize):	
5	Expenses recorded on books this year not deducted on this return (itemize):		a	Depreciation . . $	
a	Depreciation . . . $		b	Charitable contributions $	
b	Charitable contributions . $ 1,956				
c	Travel and entertainment . $				
		1,956	9	Add lines 7 and 8	1,650
6	Add lines 1 through 5	30,843	10	Income (page 1, line 28)—line 6 less line 9	29,193

Schedule M-2 — Analysis of Unappropriated Retained Earnings per Books (Schedule L, Line 25)

1	Balance at beginning of year	44,708	5	Distributions: a Cash	16,446
2	Net income (loss) per books	22,821		b Stock	
3	Other increases (itemize):			c Property	
			6	Other decreases (itemize):	
			7	Add lines 5 and 6	16,446
4	Add lines 1, 2, and 3	67,529	8	Balance at end of year (line 4 less line 7)	51,083

Form **1120** (2022)

**SCHEDULE G
(Form 1120)**
(Rev. December 2011)
Department of the Treasury
Internal Revenue Service

**Information on Certain Persons Owning the
Corporation's Voting Stock**
► Attach to Form 1120.
► See instructions on page 2.

OMB No. 1545-0123

Name: Globe Manufacturing Company

Employer identification number (EIN): 70-0694770

Part I Certain Entities Owning the Corporation's Voting Stock. (Form 1120, Schedule K, Question 4a). Complete columns (i) through (v) below for any foreign or domestic corporation, partnership (including any entity treated as a partnership), trust, or tax-exempt organization that owns directly 20% or more, or owns, directly or indirectly, 50% or more of the total voting power of all classes of the corporation's stock entitled to vote (see instructions).

(i) Name of Entity	(ii) Employer Identification Number (if any)	(iii) Type of Entity	(iv) Country of Organization	(v) Percentage Owned in Voting Stock

Part II Certain Individuals and Estates Owning the Corporation's Voting Stock. (Form 1120, Schedule K, Question 4b). Complete columns (i) through (iv) below for any individual or estate that owns directly 20% or more, or owns, directly or indirectly, 50% or more of the total voting power of all classes of the corporation's stock entitled to vote (see instructions).

(i) Name of Individual or Estate	(ii) Identifying Number (if any)	(iii) Country of Citizenship (see instructions)	(iv) Percentage Owned in Voting Stock
Caroline A Simmonds	536-00-5089	U.S.	100.000

For Paperwork Reduction Act Notice, see the Instructions for Form 1120.

Cat. No. 52684S

Schedule G (Form 1120) (Rev. 12-2011)

¶1403.04

Form **1125-A**		**Cost of Goods Sold**	OMB No. 1545-0123

(Rev. November 2018)
Department of the Treasury
Internal Revenue Service

▶ Attach to Form 1120, 1120-C, 1120-F, 1120S, or 1065.
▶ Go to *www.irs.gov/Form1125A* for the latest information.

Name	Employer identification number
Globe Manufacturing Company	70-0694770

1	Inventory at beginning of year	1	100,956
2	Purchases	2	84,800
3	Cost of labor	3	155,466
4	Additional section 263A costs (attach schedule)	4	
5	Other costs (attach schedule)	5	72,929
6	**Total.** Add lines 1 through 5	6	414,150
7	Inventory at end of year	7	90,283
8	**Cost of goods sold.** Subtract line 7 from line 6. Enter here and on Form 1120, page 1, line 2 or the appropriate line of your tax return. See instructions	8	323,867

9a Check all methods used for valuing closing inventory:
   (i) ☑ Cost
   (ii) ☐ Lower of cost or market
   (iii) ☐ Other (Specify method used and attach explanation.) ▶ _____

b Check if there was a writedown of subnormal goods ▶ ☐
c Check if the LIFO inventory method was adopted this tax year for any goods (if checked, attach Form 970) ▶ ☐
d If the LIFO inventory method was used for this tax year, enter amount of closing inventory computed under LIFO . . . | 9d | |
e If property is produced or acquired for resale, do the rules of section 263A apply to the entity? See instructions ☐ Yes ☑ No
f Was there any change in determining quantities, cost, or valuations between opening and closing inventory? If "Yes," attach explanation ☐ Yes ☑ No

Section references are to the Internal Revenue Code unless otherwise noted.

What's New

Small business taxpayers. For tax years beginning after December 31, 2017, the following apply.

• A small business taxpayer (defined below), may use a method of accounting for inventories that either: (1) treats inventories as nonincidental materials and supplies, or (2) conforms to the taxpayer's financial accounting treatment of inventories.

• A small business taxpayer is not required to capitalize costs under section 263A.

General Instructions

Purpose of Form

Use Form 1125-A to calculate and deduct cost of goods sold for certain entities.

Who Must File

Filers of Form 1120, 1120-C, 1120-F, 1120S, or 1065, must complete and attach Form 1125-A if the applicable entity reports a deduction for cost of goods sold.

Inventories

Generally, inventories are required at the beginning and end of each tax year if the production, purchase, or sale of merchandise is an income-producing factor. See Regulations section 1.471-1. If inventories are required, you generally must use an accrual method of accounting for sales and purchases of inventory items.

Exception for certain taxpayers. A small business taxpayer (defined below), can adopt or change its accounting method to account for inventories in the same manner as material and supplies that are non-incidental, or conform to its treatment of inventories in an applicable financial statement (as defined in section 451(b)(3)), or if it does not have an applicable financial statement, the method of accounting used in its books and records prepared in accordance with its accounting procedures. See section 471(c)(3).

A small business taxpayer claiming exemption from the requirement to keep inventories is changing its method of accounting for purposes of section 481. For additional guidance on this method of accounting, see Pub. 538, Accounting Periods and Methods. For guidance on changing to this method of accounting, see Form 3115 and the Instructions for Form 3115.

Small business taxpayer. A small business taxpayer is a taxpayer that (a) has average annual gross receipts of $25 million or less (indexed for inflation) for the 3 prior tax years, and (b) is not a tax shelter (as defined in section 448(d)(3)). See Pub. 538.

Uniform capitalization rules. The uniform capitalization rules of section 263A generally require you to capitalize, or include in inventory, certain costs incurred in connection with the following.

• The production of real property and tangible personal property held in inventory or held for sale in the ordinary course of business.

• Real property or personal property (tangible and intangible) acquired for resale.

• The production of real property and tangible personal property for use in its trade or business or in an activity engaged in for profit.

A small business taxpayer (defined above) is not required to capitalize costs under section 263A. See section 263A(i).

See the discussion on section 263A uniform capitalization rules in the instructions for your tax return before completing Form 1125-A. Also see Regulations sections 1.263A-1 through 1.263A-3. See Regulations section 1.263A-4 for rules for property produced in a farming business.

For Paperwork Reduction Act Notice, see instructions.   Cat. No. 55988R   Form **1125-A** (Rev. 11-2018)

Form 1120 Schedules M-1 and M-2

Corporations with total receipts during the year and total assets at the end of the year of $250,000 or more must complete Schedules L, M-1 and M-2. (Total receipts are the sum of line 1c plus lines 4 through 10 on page 1, Form 1120.) The changes to retained earnings during the year are explained in Schedule M-2. On Schedule M-1, net income (loss) per books is reconciled with the amount reported on Form 1120, line 28 (taxable income before any NOL or DRD). For Globe Manufacturing in Figure 14-2, differences between book net income and taxable income before NOL and DRD include:

- The deduction for federal income taxes (deducted on the income statement, but not deductible in computing taxable income)
- Charitable contributions limited on the tax return by 10% of taxable income
- Tax-exempt interest (included on the income statement, but not taxable)

However, other differences may exist. For example, differences between net income and taxable income that may be reported on Schedule M-1 may result from:

- Differences in methods used to compute depreciation expense
- Amounts spent on travel, meals and entertainment that are not deductible on the tax return (for example, 50% of meals and entertainment)
- Differences in methods used to compute bad debt expense
- Charitable contributions carried over from a prior tax year that are deducted on the tax return in the current year

¶1404   Credits, Special Taxes, and Prepayments

¶1404.01   TAX CREDITS

Like individuals, corporations may offset their tax liabilities with available tax credits. Most of the credits available to corporations are also available to other businesses (see ¶1203). However, corporations cannot use the personal tax credits available to individuals, such as the earned income credit, child tax credit, or child and dependent care credit.

¶1404.02   SPECIAL TAXES

Besides the regular income tax, corporations may be subject to the accumulated earnings tax and the personal holding company tax. These taxes are penalty taxes on undistributed earnings. Careful tax planning can eliminate the need to pay these additional taxes. Corporations are no longer subject to the alternative minimum tax, which applied to tax years beginning before 2019. Discussion of these taxes is beyond the scope of this textbook.

¶1404.03   ESTIMATED TAX PAYMENTS

Corporations that expect their tax liability (after tax credits) to be $500 or more must make estimated tax payments. These payments are due in equal quarterly installments by the 15th day of the fourth, sixth, ninth, and twelfth months of the corporation's tax year. If the due date falls on a weekend or a legal holiday, the payment is due the next business day. For corporations using the calendar year, the payment due dates are April 15, June 15, September 15, and December 15.

Penalty for Underpayment of Estimated Tax: Small Corporations

Failure to pay the minimum amount due at each installment date results in an underpayment penalty. The IRS considers the estimated tax underpaid if a quarterly payment is less than 25% of the minimum amount due for the year. For small corporations, this amount is 25% of the *lesser of* (i) 100% of the total tax liability (after tax credits) shown on the current year's return or (ii) 100% of the total tax liability (after tax credits) for the preceding year. A small corporation is a corporation whose taxable income before any NOL carryover and capital loss carryover or carryback is less than $1 million for each of the last three tax years.

Estimated Payment Requirements: Large Corporations

For large corporations, the minimum amount due each quarter is 25% of the current year's total tax liability (after tax credits). Large corporations cannot avoid underpayment penalties by making their estimated payments based on last year's taxes. A large corporation has a taxable income before any NOL carryover and capital loss carryover or carrybacks of $1 million or more in any of its last three preceding tax years.

¶1405   Corporate Distributions

Shareholders receiving corporate distributions may have taxable dividends, tax-free returns of capital, or capital gain. A distribution may be subject to all three treatments. Determining the nature of a distribution takes place at the corporate level. However, the final taxability of a distribution may depend on shareholder circumstances.

¶1405.01   TAXABLE DIVIDENDS

Unless affected parties provide contrary evidence, corporate distributions receive ordinary dividend treatment. Shareholders include in gross income the full amount of any ordinary dividends received. [I.R.C. §61(a)(7)] When the distribution involves property, the property's FMV at the distribution date determines the amount of the dividend received. [I.R.C. §301(b)(1)] Technically, dividends receive ordinary income treatment only if the company has earnings and profits (E&P) to cover the distribution amount. [I.R.C. §301(c)(1)] Shareholders treat distributions in excess of E&P as a tax-free recovery of their basis in the stock. [I.R.C. §301(c)(2)] (See ¶1401.01 for discussion of how a shareholder's basis is determined). After shareholders recover their basis, any additional distribution is taxed as capital gain. [I.R.C. §301(c)(3)]

EXAMPLE 24

PDQ had $90,000 of E&P at the end of the current year. On the last day of the year, PDQ distributed $120,000 to its three shareholders Xandra, Yang, and Zack ($40,000 to each shareholder). It was PDQ's only distribution for the year. Immediately before the distribution, the shareholders had the following basis in their stock: Xandra—$0, Yang—$8,000, and Zack—$60,000. The tax consequences of the distribution are as follows:

	Xandra	Yang	Zack
Amount of the distribution	$40,000	$40,000	$40,000
From E&P (dividend income)	(30,000)	(30,000)	(30,000)
Not from E&P	$10,000	$10,000	$10,000
Return of capital (basis reduced)	(0)	(8,000)	(10,000)
Capital gain	$10,000	$2,000	$0

As this summary shows, each shareholder recognizes $30,000 of dividend income. In addition, Xandra and Yang recognize capital gain ($10,000 and $2,000, respectively). After the distribution, Xandra and Yang each have a $0 stock basis. Zack's basis in the stock is $50,000 ($60,000 – $10,000 return of capital).

¶1405.02   EARNINGS AND PROFITS

The Code does not specifically define earnings and profits (E&P). Consequently, many people compare E&P with retained earnings. While similarities exist, there are numerous differences, which causes much confusion. Corporate directors may think they can distribute cash or other property tax free when the corporation has zero retained earnings. However, this would be wrong.

If the corporation has E&P, some portion of the distribution will be a dividend. Basically, transactions that increase a corporation's ability to pay a dividend increase E&P. Transactions that decrease a corporation's ability to pay a dividend decrease E&P. Consider the following examples. When a corporation receives tax-exempt interest, the interest is not taxed. However, E&P is increased by the interest received because the interest can serve as a source for dividend distributions. In contrast, the deduction for charitable contributions is limited to 10% (or 25% in 2020 and 2021) of taxable income. When the actual contribution exceeds this limitation, E&P is decreased by the full contribution because the company has reduced its ability to pay a dividend by the full amount given to the charity. Also, while there is no definition of E&P, the law may require the use of certain accounting methods in some situations. For example, there are various acceptable methods by which to calculate depreciation expense for the tax return. However, the Alternative Depreciation System (¶602.04, ¶603.02) is required to calculate depreciation expense for purposes of E&P.

¶1405.03   DISTRIBUTIONS OF PROPERTY

Corporate distributions may involve either cash or property. For distributions of property, FMV determines the amount of the distribution. Corporations recognize a gain when they distribute appreciated property. [I.R.C. §311(b)] E&P increases as a result of the gain, and E&P decreases by the FMV of the property distributed. Corporations do not recognize a loss when they distribute property where the FMV is less than its basis. [I.R.C. §311(a)] The basis of the property shareholders receive is its FMV.

EXAMPLE 25

CQ corporation distributes appreciated land to its sole shareholder. The FMV of the land was $50,000. CQ's basis in the land was $10,000. Prior to the distribution, CQ's E&P was $100,000. CQ recognizes $40,000 gain on the distribution ($50,000 FMV – $10,000 basis). The gain increases CQ's E&P to $140,000 ($100,000 + $40,000). Thus, the entire $50,000 distribution is treated as a dividend (coming from E&P). After the distribution, CQ's E&P is $90,000 ($140,000 – $50,000), before considering the year's income tax.

EXAMPLE 26

At the end of the year, TLC distributes land (FMV of $10,000) with an adjusted basis of $4,000 to its only shareholder. TLC had no E&P before the distribution. As a result of the distribution, TLC reports gain of $6,000 ($10,000 – $4,000). This causes TLC's E&P to increase to $6,000 ($0 + $6,000). The shareholder receives a distribution equal to the FMV of the land. However, only $6,000 is a dividend (amount of E&P). The remaining portion of the distribution ($4,000) is a return of capital or capital gain, depending on the shareholder's basis in the stock. TLC's E&P is reduced to $0 after the distribution.

EXAMPLE 27

Same facts as in Example 26, except that the adjusted basis of the property is $24,000. As a result of the distribution, TLC reports no gain or loss. The shareholder still receives a distribution equal to the FMV of the land ($10,000). However, with no E&P, the entire $10,000 distribution is a return of capital or capital gain, depending on the shareholder's basis in the stock.

 As you can see from Example 27, C corporations should avoid distributing property where the FMV is less than the corporation's adjusted basis in the property.

14

Name:

Section:

Date:

QUESTIONS AND PROBLEMS

1. **Corporate Tax Status.** (Obj. 1) How do the tax laws determine whether a business should be taxed as a C corporation?

2. **Forming a Corporation.** (Obj. 1) Betty forms a corporation by transferring land worth $100,000 for 100% of the stock in the corporation. Betty paid $30,000 for the land.

   a. How much gain or loss do Betty and the corporation recognize on the transfer?

   b. What is Betty's basis in her shares of stock in the corporation?

   c. What is the corporation's basis in the land?

3. **Forming a Corporation.** (Obj. 1) Daniel forms a corporation by transferring land worth $50,000 for 100% of the stock in the corporation. Daniel paid $60,000 for the land.

   a. How much gain or loss do Daniel and the corporation recognize on the transfer?

   b. What is Daniel's basis in his shares of stock in the corporation?

   c. What is the corporation's basis in the land?

4. **Shareholder's Basis.** (Obj. 1) Jeannie is not currently a shareholder in ABC corporation. Jeannie contributes $20,000 cash and equipment worth $30,000 in exchange for 25% of the stock in ABC. Jeannie's basis in the equipment is $7,000. No other transfers were made at this time.

   a. How much gain or loss do Jeannie and the corporation recognize on the transfer?

   b. What is Jeannie's basis in the stock?

   c. What is the corporation's basis in the equipment?

5. **Forming a Corporation and Shareholder's Basis.** (Obj. 1) Toby contributes $60,000 cash in exchange for stock in the corporation. Keith contributes land worth $70,000 (basis of $55,000) in exchange for $10,000 cash and $60,000 worth of stock in the corporation. After the transfer, Toby and Keith own 100% of the corporation.

   a. How much gain or loss do Toby, Keith, and the corporation recognize on the transfer?

   b. What is Toby's basis in the stock?

   c. What is Keith's basis in the stock?

   d. What is the corporation's basis in the land?

   e. How, if at all, would your answers to parts a. through d. change if Keith's basis in the land were $66,000 (instead of $55,000)?

   f. How, if at all, would your answers to parts a. through d. change if Keith's basis in the land were $81,000 (instead of $55,000)?

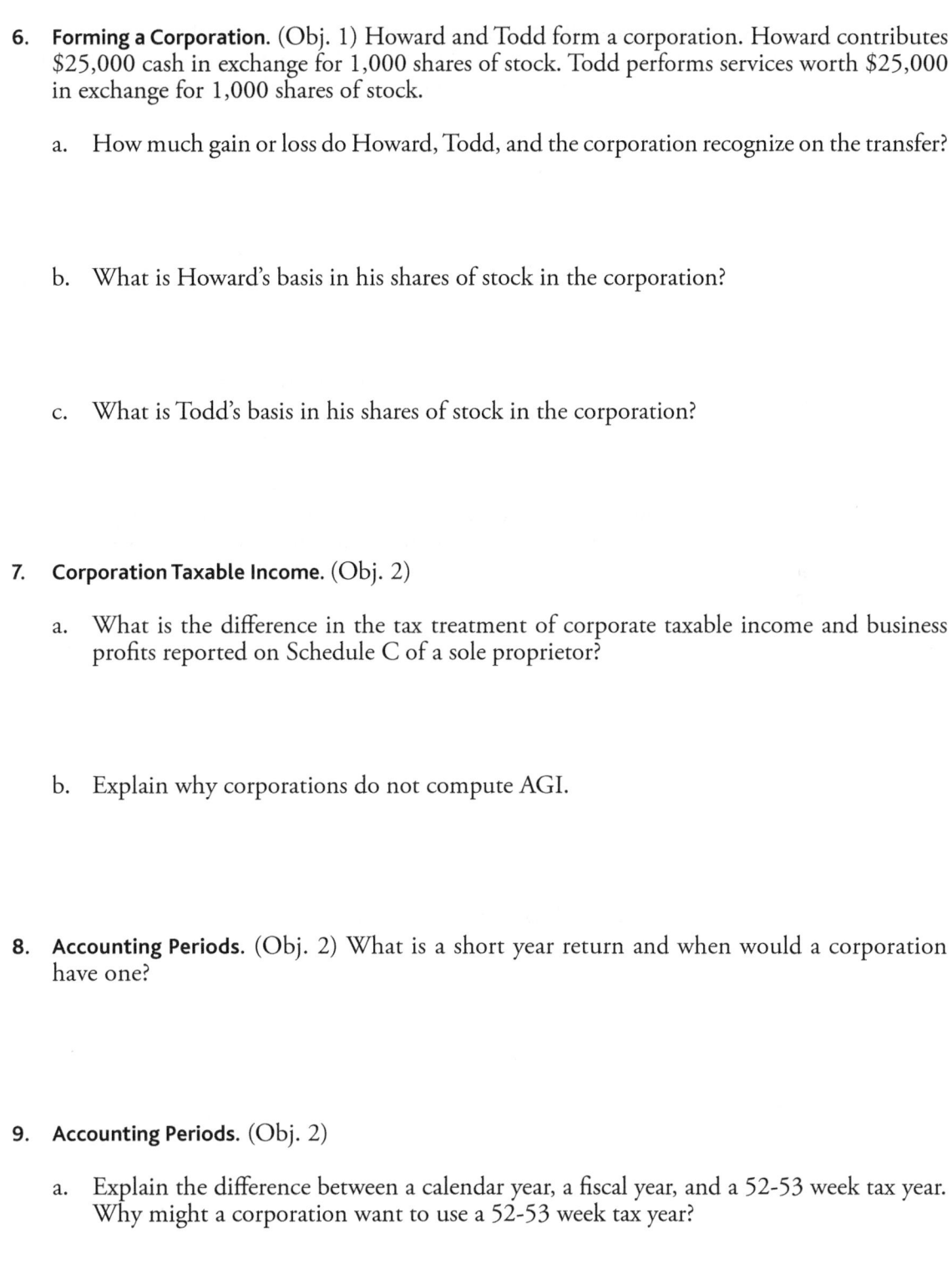

6. **Forming a Corporation.** (Obj. 1) Howard and Todd form a corporation. Howard contributes $25,000 cash in exchange for 1,000 shares of stock. Todd performs services worth $25,000 in exchange for 1,000 shares of stock.

    a. How much gain or loss do Howard, Todd, and the corporation recognize on the transfer?

    b. What is Howard's basis in his shares of stock in the corporation?

    c. What is Todd's basis in his shares of stock in the corporation?

7. **Corporation Taxable Income.** (Obj. 2)

    a. What is the difference in the tax treatment of corporate taxable income and business profits reported on Schedule C of a sole proprietor?

    b. Explain why corporations do not compute AGI.

8. **Accounting Periods.** (Obj. 2) What is a short year return and when would a corporation have one?

9. **Accounting Periods.** (Obj. 2)

    a. Explain the difference between a calendar year, a fiscal year, and a 52-53 week tax year. Why might a corporation want to use a 52-53 week tax year?

    b. If a corporation wants to change its tax year from October 31 to July 31, what must it do?

10. **Corporate Capital Gains and Losses.** (Obj. 2)

    a. How does the tax treatment of net capital gain differ between individual and corporate taxpayers?

    b. How does the tax treatment of net capital losses differ between individual and corporate taxpayers?

11. **Corporation Taxable Income.** (Obj. 2)

    a. For the current year, Wish Corporation had ordinary income from operations of $80,000, a net long-term capital gain of $17,000, and a net short-term capital loss of $7,000. Compute Wish's taxable income for the year.

    b. For the current year, BB Corporation had net income from operations of $65,000 and a net long-term capital loss of $9,000. It also had a net short-term capital gain of $7,000. Compute BB's taxable income for the year.

    c. For the current year, before considering capital loss carryovers, Adam Corporation had a net long-term capital loss of $8,000 and a net short-term capital loss of $3,000. Its net capital loss carryover from last year was $2,000. How much is Adam's capital loss carryover to the next tax year, and what is its nature (long-term or short-term)?

12. **Corporate Taxable Income.** (Obj. 2) A corporation pays its Chief Executive Officer (CEO) $2 million during the year. Discuss the tax implications of the CEO's salary both to the corporation and the CEO.

13. **Bad Debts.** (Obj. 2) A corporation properly uses the reserve method to deduct bad debts on the financial statements (as it is the only method allowed under Generally Accepted Accounting Principles). Does an accrual basis corporation use this method to deduct bad debts the corporate income tax return? Explain.

14. **Bad Debts.** (Obj. 2) HST uses the accrual method of reporting for income taxes. It is a retail hardware store. On average, 1% of its gross sales on account ($500,000 for the current year) become uncollectible. During the year, HST actually wrote off $4,700 of accounts receivable that were uncollectible. What is HST's deduction for bad debts on its tax return?

15. **Organizational Costs.** (Obj. 2) At formation, a corporation incurs the following costs: legal services to obtain a corporate charter, $1,000; state incorporation fees, $700; and costs related to issuing common stock, $3,000. How quickly will the corporation be allowed to deduct these costs?

16. **Organizational Costs.** (Obj. 2) In the process of incorporating a business, ABC corporation incurs organizational costs. ABC was incorporated on June 8, 2022. It officially began business on September 2, 2022. It uses a calendar year-end. The officers have asked that ABC take the maximum deduction as allowed under the tax law.

    a. How much can ABC deduct in 2022 if the total organizational costs are $45,000?

    b. How much can ABC deduct in 2022 if the total organizational costs are $52,000?

    c. How much can ABC deduct in 2022 if the total organizational costs are $75,000?

17. **Start-Up Costs.** (Obj. 2) DEF corporation uses a calendar year-end. DEF incurs start-up costs prior to the beginning of its business operations. DEF's business began on March 1, 2022.

    a. How much can DEF deduct in 2022 and 2023 if the total start-up costs are $35,000?

    b. How much can DEF deduct in 2022 and 2023 if the total start-up costs are $51,200?

    c. How much can DEF deduct in 2022 and 2023 if the total start-up costs are $85,000?

18. **Charitable Contributions.** (Obj. 2) How is the charitable contribution limitation for a C corporation computed and how are excess charitable contributions treated?

19. **Charitable Contributions.** (Obj. 2) Regal, Inc. reported the following for the year.

Gross income includable on the tax return	$115,000
Allowable business deductions, not including charitable contributions	90,000
Contributions to qualified charitable organizations	2,750
Dividends received from domestic corporations	
(30% ownership and included in the $115,000 gross income amount)	2,000

a. What is Regal's charitable contribution deduction for the current year, if the current year is not 2020 or 2021?

b. What is the amount of taxable income for the current year, if the current year is not 2020 or 2021?

c. What is Regal's charitable contribution deduction carryover, if any, if the current year is not 2020 or 2021?

20. **Charitable Contributions.** (Obj. 2) A corporation has taxable income of $107,000 after all deductions except the charitable contribution deduction, dividends received deduction, and loss carryforwards. The corporation contributed $30,000 to a qualified charity during the year. Compute the current year charitable contribution deduction and discuss what happens to any excess contribution, if the year is not 2020 or 2021.

21. **Charitable Contributions.** (Obj. 2) A calendar year corporation donates food inventory to a qualified charity that cares for the needy. The inventory is valued at $70,000; the corporation's basis in the inventory is $55,000. Compute the corporation's charitable contribution for this donation, if the year is not 2020 or 2021.

22. **Charitable Contributions.** (Obj. 2) An accrual basis corporation reports the following income and expenses for 2022.

Gross sales and receipts	$700,000
Returns and allowances	12,000
Cost of goods sold	330,000
Interest received	20,000
Rent expense	55,000
Wage expense	140,000
Charitable contributions	12,000
Other operating expenses	75,000
Depreciation expense	15,000

    a. Compute the corporation's taxable income for the year.

    b. What is the amount of the corporation's charitable contribution carryover (if any)? To which tax years can the corporation carry over this excess?

23. **Dividends Received Deduction.** (Obj. 2) Treeline Industries receives a $50,000 dividend from a corporation in which it owns 35% of the stock. Treeline's revenues (not including the dividends) and operating expenses for the year are $400,000 and $375,000, respectively. Other than the dividends received deduction, these are the only items of revenue and expense.

    a. Compute Treeline's taxable income.

    b. How, if at all, would your answer to Part a. change if Treeline owned 10% of the stock in the corporation?

    c. How, if at all, would your answer to Part a. change if Treeline's revenues were $370,000 (instead of $400,000), but it continued to own 35% of the corporation's stock?

24. **Dividends Received Deduction.** (Obj. 2) Express Corporation receives a $120,000 dividend from a corporation in which it owns 55% of the stock. Express's revenues (not including the dividends) and operating expenses for the year are $370,000 and $390,000, respectively. These are the only items of revenue and expense.

   a. Compute Express's taxable income.

   b. How, if at all, would your answer to Part a. change if Express owned 90% of the stock in the corporation?

25. **Filing Deadlines.** (Obj. 3) For each of the following corporations, determine the deadline for filing the corporate income tax return.

   a. The original due date for a corporation with a calendar year-end.

   b. The extended due date for a calendar year corporation that files Form 7004 prior to the original filing deadline.

   c. The original due date for a corporation with a June 30 year-end.

   d. The extended due date for corporation with a June 30 year-end that files Form 7004 prior to the original filing deadline.

   e. The original due date for a corporation with an August 31 year-end.

   f. The extended due date for a corporation with an October 31 year-end that files Form 7004 prior to the original filing deadline.

26. **Tax Liability.** (Obj. 3) Compute the corporate income tax liability for each of the following corporations.

    a. A corporation with taxable income of $25,000.

    b. A corporation with taxable income of $1,500,000.

    c. A corporation with taxable income of $33,750,000.

27. **Tax Liability.** (Obj. 3) Sanford Corporation had gross income from business operations of $150,000 for the current year. In addition, the company received dividends from domestic corporations (less than 20% owned) in the amount of $10,000. Allowable business expenses were $40,000. What is Sanford's tax liability for the year?

28. **Distributions.** (Obj. 4) A C corporation began the year with E&P of $12,000. During the year it added $8,000 of E&P before making any distributions for the year. The corporation has one shareholder, whose basis in the stock prior to any distributions for the year was $9,000.

    a. Describe the tax consequences to both the corporation and the shareholder if the corporation distributes $24,000 cash during the year.

    b. Same as in Part a., except that the corporation distributes $34,000 cash.

c. Same as Part a., except that the corporation distributes land worth $24,000 ($17,000 adjusted basis to the corporation).

d. Same as in Part c., except that the adjusted basis in the land is $30,000.

COMPREHENSIVE PROBLEMS

29. (Objs. 2 and 3) A corporation has the following income and deductions in 2022. Included in these amounts are $290,000 of income and $42,000 of taxable wages reported on Form W-2. Compute the corporation's taxable income, tax liability, and any carryovers to other tax years.

Gross sales	$830,000
Long-term capital gains	15,000
Dividend income (33% ownership in the stock)	60,000
Interest income	70,000
Cost of goods sold	444,000
Other business expenses	260,000
Charitable contributions	72,000
Long-term capital losses	35,000

30. (Obj. 5) Randolph Manufacturing Company, EIN (70-7299870) was organized on February 1, 1998. Randolph manufactures electronic components. Its business activity code is 310000. The offices of the company are located at 350 Mission Street, San Jose, CA 95107-4311. Randolph's financial statements are reproduced on the pages that follow.

During the year Randolph made estimated federal income tax payments totaling $15,800. If there is any overpayment of taxes, the accounting department has requested that it be applied toward next year's estimated tax. Randolph paid a total of $46,600 of dividends to its shareholders during the year. Randolph preferred stock is held by 17 different shareholders, none of whom own more than 10% of the stock in the company. Randolph's two officers each own 50% of the company's common stock. June Randolph-Rivers is President of the company. Her compensation is $75,000. June's husband, Travis Rivers is Vice-President. His compensation is $66,350.

During the year Randolph sold two investments. Orange County bonds purchased on July 6, 2004 were sold on November 16, 2022, for $3,215. Randolph's adjusted basis in the bonds was $3,740. Randolph sold 100 shares of National Acme common stock on March 14, 2022, for $26,300. The stock was purchased for $18,200 on May 9, 2000.

The bad debt expense reported on the income statement is based on the reserve method of accounting. Actual bad debts written off during the year were $7,950. The difference between these two amounts needs to be reported on Schedule M-1 when net income (loss) per books is reconciled with the amount reported on Form 1120, line 28.

Prepare Randolph's Form 1120 for the calendar year ended December 31, 2022. June Randolph-Rivers signs the return on April 15, 2022. Assume Form 4562 has been correctly filled out and that $6,068 of depreciation expense reported on the income statement is also the amount of tax depreciation. Also assume Schedule D, Capital Gains and Losses, and Form 1125-E, Compensation of Officers, have been correctly prepared.

RANDOLPH MANUFACTURING COMPANY
Comparative Balance Sheets
Beginning and End of 2022

ASSETS	As of January 1, 2022	As of December 31, 2022
Cash	$ 40,320	$ 63,600
Notes receivable	40,400	32,680
Accounts receivable	245,790	217,270
Allowance for doubtful accounts	(9,400)	(8,580)
Inventories at the lower of cost or market:		
Raw materials	46,980	77,616
Finished goods	108,756	140,625
Investment in municipal bonds—Orange County, CA	27,900	24,160

Investment in common stock—National Acme Co.	45,000	49,005
Land	98,700	98,700
Buildings	182,432	206,379
Machinery and equipment	207,450	207,450
Accumulated depreciation	(89,988)	(128,045)
Total assets	$944,340	$980,860

LIABILITIES AND STOCKHOLDERS' EQUITY	As of January 1, 2022	As of December 31, 2022
Bank loans	$ 67,500	$ 56,250
Accounts payable	187,646	164,882
Accrued expenses	11,054	12,894
Bonds payable	200,000	200,000
Preferred stock	160,000	160,000
Common stock	180,000	200,000
Paid-in surplus	54,000	83,000
Retained earnings (unappropriated)	84,140	103,834
Total liabilities and stockholders' equity	$944,340	$980,860

RANDOLPH MANUFACTURING COMPANY
Income Statement
For Year Ended December 31, 2022

Sales (after subtracting out $224,054 for returns)		$1,704,201
Less cost of goods sold (see COGS schedule below)		(1,351,371)
Gross profit on sales		$ 352,830
Operating expenses:		
Officers' salaries	$141,350	
Salaries and wage expense	29,583	
Repairs	2,214	
Property taxes	4,200	
Payroll taxes	11,398	
Depreciation of buildings	6,068	
Bad debts expense	7,130	
Advertising	29,033	
Travel expenses (includes $2,000 for meals)	20,180	
Other administration expenses	10,300	(261,456)
Net operating income		$ 91,374
Other income:		
Dividends from domestic corporations (15% ownership)	$ 3,600	
Interest income ($950 from municipal bonds)	3,033	
Gain on sale of National Acme stock	8,100	14,733
		$ 106,107

Other deductions:

Loss on sale of Orange County bonds	$ 525	
Interest expense	11,588	
Contributions to qualified charities	11,000	
Legal fees	900	(24,013)
Net income before federal income taxes		$ 82,094
Less estimated federal income taxes		(15,800)
Net income		$ 66,294

COST OF GOODS SOLD SCHEDULE

Inventories at beginning of year	$ 155,736
Materials bought for manufacture	1,224,000
Salaries and wages	112,860
Other costs (utilities, depreciation of machinery)	77,016
Total goods available for sale	$1,569,612
Less inventories at end of year	(218,241)
Cost of goods sold	$ 1,351,371

(Use for Problem 30.)

Form **1120**	**U.S. Corporation Income Tax Return**	OMB No. 1545-0123
Department of the Treasury Internal Revenue Service	For calendar year 2022 or tax year beginning _____, 2022, ending _____, 20 ____ Go to *www.irs.gov/Form1120* for instructions and the latest information.	**2022**

A Check if:			B Employer identification number
1a Consolidated return (attach Form 851) ☐	**TYPE OR PRINT**	Name	
b Life/nonlife consolidated return . . ☐		Number, street, and room or suite no. If a P.O. box, see instructions.	C Date incorporated
2 Personal holding co. (attach Sch. PH) . ☐		City or town, state or province, country, and ZIP or foreign postal code	D Total assets (see instructions) $
3 Personal service corp. (see instructions) . ☐			
4 Schedule M-3 attached ☐	E Check if: (1) ☐ Initial return (2) ☐ Final return (3) ☐ Name change (4) ☐ Address change	

Income

1a	Gross receipts or sales	1a	
b	Returns and allowances	1b	
c	Balance. Subtract line 1b from line 1a	1c	
2	Cost of goods sold (attach Form 1125-A)	2	
3	Gross profit. Subtract line 2 from line 1c	3	
4	Dividends and inclusions (Schedule C, line 23)	4	
5	Interest	5	
6	Gross rents	6	
7	Gross royalties	7	
8	Capital gain net income (attach Schedule D (Form 1120))	8	
9	Net gain or (loss) from Form 4797, Part II, line 17 (attach Form 4797)	9	
10	Other income (see instructions—attach statement)	10	
11	**Total income.** Add lines 3 through 10	11	

Deductions (See instructions for limitations on deductions.)

12	Compensation of officers (see instructions—attach Form 1125-E)	12	
13	Salaries and wages (less employment credits)	13	
14	Repairs and maintenance	14	
15	Bad debts	15	
16	Rents	16	
17	Taxes and licenses	17	
18	Interest (see instructions)	18	
19	Charitable contributions	19	
20	Depreciation from Form 4562 not claimed on Form 1125-A or elsewhere on return (attach Form 4562)	20	
21	Depletion	21	
22	Advertising	22	
23	Pension, profit-sharing, etc., plans	23	
24	Employee benefit programs	24	
25	Reserved for future use	25	
26	Other deductions (attach statement)	26	
27	**Total deductions.** Add lines 12 through 26	27	
28	Taxable income before net operating loss deduction and special deductions. Subtract line 27 from line 11.	28	
29a	Net operating loss deduction (see instructions)	29a	
b	Special deductions (Schedule C, line 24)	29b	
c	Add lines 29a and 29b	29c	

Tax, Refundable Credits, and Payments

30	**Taxable income.** Subtract line 29c from line 28. See instructions	30	
31	Total tax (Schedule J, Part I, line 11)	31	
32	Reserved for future use	32	
33	Total payments and credits (Schedule J, Part III, line 23)	33	
34	Estimated tax penalty. See instructions. Check if Form 2220 is attached . . . ☐	34	
35	**Amount owed.** If line 33 is smaller than the total of lines 31 and 34, enter amount owed	35	
36	**Overpayment.** If line 33 is larger than the total of lines 31 and 34, enter amount overpaid	36	
37	Enter amount from line 36 you want: **Credited to 2023 estimated tax** _____ Refunded	37	

Sign Here	Under penalties of perjury, I declare that I have examined this return, including accompanying schedules and statements, and to the best of my knowledge and belief, it is true, correct, and complete. Declaration of preparer (other than taxpayer) is based on all information of which preparer has any knowledge.		May the IRS discuss this return with the preparer shown below? See instructions. ☐ Yes ☐ No
	_____ Signature of officer	_____ Date _____ Title	

Paid Preparer Use Only	Print/Type preparer's name	Preparer's signature	Date	Check ☐ if self-employed	PTIN
	Firm's name			Firm's EIN	
	Firm's address			Phone no.	

For Paperwork Reduction Act Notice, see separate instructions.   Cat. No. 11450Q   Form **1120** (2022)

(Use for Problem 30.)

Form 1120 (2022) Page **2**

Schedule C	Dividends, Inclusions, and Special Deductions (see instructions)	(a) Dividends and inclusions	(b) %	(c) Special deductions (a) × (b)
1	Dividends from less-than-20%-owned domestic corporations (other than debt-financed stock)		50	
2	Dividends from 20%-or-more-owned domestic corporations (other than debt-financed stock)		65	
3	Dividends on certain debt-financed stock of domestic and foreign corporations		See instructions	
4	Dividends on certain preferred stock of less-than-20%-owned public utilities		23.3	
5	Dividends on certain preferred stock of 20%-or-more-owned public utilities		26.7	
6	Dividends from less-than-20%-owned foreign corporations and certain FSCs		50	
7	Dividends from 20%-or-more-owned foreign corporations and certain FSCs		65	
8	Dividends from wholly owned foreign subsidiaries		100	
9	**Subtotal.** Add lines 1 through 8. See instructions for limitations		See instructions	
10	Dividends from domestic corporations received by a small business investment company operating under the Small Business Investment Act of 1958		100	
11	Dividends from affiliated group members		100	
12	Dividends from certain FSCs		100	
13	Foreign-source portion of dividends received from a specified 10%-owned foreign corporation (excluding hybrid dividends) (see instructions)		100	
14	Dividends from foreign corporations not included on line 3, 6, 7, 8, 11, 12, or 13 (including any hybrid dividends)			
15	Reserved for future use			
16a	Subpart F inclusions derived from the sale by a controlled foreign corporation (CFC) of the stock of a lower-tier foreign corporation treated as a dividend (attach Form(s) 5471) (see instructions)		100	
b	Subpart F inclusions derived from hybrid dividends of tiered corporations (attach Form(s) 5471) (see instructions)			
c	Other inclusions from CFCs under subpart F not included on line 16a, 16b, or 17 (attach Form(s) 5471) (see instructions)			
17	Global Intangible Low-Taxed Income (GILTI) (attach Form(s) 5471 and Form 8992)			
18	Gross-up for foreign taxes deemed paid			
19	IC-DISC and former DISC dividends not included on line 1, 2, or 3			
20	Other dividends			
21	Deduction for dividends paid on certain preferred stock of public utilities			
22	Section 250 deduction (attach Form 8993)			
23	**Total dividends and inclusions.** Add column (a), lines 9 through 20. Enter here and on page 1, line 4			
24	**Total special deductions.** Add column (c), lines 9 through 22. Enter here and on page 1, line 29b			

Form **1120** (2022)

(Use for Problem 30.)

Form 1120 (2022)   Page **3**

Schedule J	Tax Computation and Payment (see instructions)	

Part I—Tax Computation

1	Check if the corporation is a member of a controlled group (attach Schedule O (Form 1120)). See instructions ☐	
2	Income tax. See instructions	2
3	Base erosion minimum tax amount (attach Form 8991)	3
4	Add lines 2 and 3	4
5a	Foreign tax credit (attach Form 1118)	5a
b	Credit from Form 8834 (see instructions)	5b
c	General business credit (attach Form 3800)	5c
d	Credit for prior year minimum tax (attach Form 8827)	5d
e	Bond credits from Form 8912	5e
6	**Total credits.** Add lines 5a through 5e	6
7	Subtract line 6 from line 4	7
8	Personal holding company tax (attach Schedule PH (Form 1120))	8
9a	Recapture of investment credit (attach Form 4255)	9a
b	Recapture of low-income housing credit (attach Form 8611)	9b
c	Interest due under the look-back method—completed long-term contracts (attach Form 8697)	9c
d	Interest due under the look-back method—income forecast method (attach Form 8866)	9d
e	Alternative tax on qualifying shipping activities (attach Form 8902)	9e
f	Interest/tax due under section 453A(c) and/or section 453(l)	9f
g	Other (see instructions—attach statement)	9g
10	**Total.** Add lines 9a through 9g	10
11	**Total tax.** Add lines 7, 8, and 10. Enter here and on page 1, line 31	11

Part II—Reserved For Future Use

12	Reserved for future use	12

Part III—Payments and Refundable Credits

13	2021 overpayment credited to 2022	13
14	2022 estimated tax payments	14
15	2022 refund applied for on Form 4466	15 ( )
16	Combine lines 13, 14, and 15	16
17	Tax deposited with Form 7004	17
18	Withholding (see instructions)	18
19	**Total payments.** Add lines 16, 17, and 18	19
20	Refundable credits from:	
a	Form 2439	20a
b	Form 4136	20b
c	Reserved for future use	20c
d	Other (attach statement—see instructions)	20d
21	**Total credits.** Add lines 20a through 20d	21
22	Reserved for future use	22
23	**Total payments and credits.** Add lines 19 and 21. Enter here and on page 1, line 33	23

Form **1120** (2022)

(Use for Problem 30.)

Form 1120 (2022)   Page **4**

Schedule K **Other Information** (see instructions)

		Yes	No
1	Check accounting method: **a** ☐ Cash **b** ☐ Accrual **c** ☐ Other (specify) _____		
2	See the instructions and enter the:		
a	Business activity code no. _____		
b	Business activity _____		
c	Product or service _____		
3	Is the corporation a subsidiary in an affiliated group or a parent–subsidiary controlled group? . . .		
	If "Yes," enter name and EIN of the parent corporation _____		
4	At the end of the tax year:		
a	Did any foreign or domestic corporation, partnership (including any entity treated as a partnership), trust, or tax-exempt organization own directly 20% or more, or own, directly or indirectly, 50% or more of the total voting power of all classes of the corporation's stock entitled to vote? If "Yes," complete Part I of Schedule G (Form 1120) (attach Schedule G) .		
b	Did any individual or estate own directly 20% or more, or own, directly or indirectly, 50% or more of the total voting power of all classes of the corporation's stock entitled to vote? If "Yes," complete Part II of Schedule G (Form 1120) (attach Schedule G) .		
5	At the end of the tax year, did the corporation:		
a	Own directly 20% or more, or own, directly or indirectly, 50% or more of the total voting power of all classes of stock entitled to vote of any foreign or domestic corporation not included on **Form 851**, Affiliations Schedule? For rules of constructive ownership, see instructions. If "Yes," complete (i) through (iv) below.		

(i) Name of Corporation	**(ii)** Employer Identification Number (if any)	**(iii)** Country of Incorporation	**(iv)** Percentage Owned in Voting Stock

b Own directly an interest of 20% or more, or own, directly or indirectly, an interest of 50% or more in any foreign or domestic partnership (including an entity treated as a partnership) or in the beneficial interest of a trust? For rules of constructive ownership, see instructions. If "Yes," complete (i) through (iv) below.

(i) Name of Entity	**(ii)** Employer Identification Number (if any)	**(iii)** Country of Organization	**(iv)** Maximum Percentage Owned in Profit, Loss, or Capital

		Yes	No
6	During this tax year, did the corporation pay dividends (other than stock dividends and distributions in exchange for stock) in excess of the corporation's current and accumulated earnings and profits? See sections 301 and 316		
	If "Yes," file **Form 5452**, Corporate Report of Nondividend Distributions. See the instructions for Form 5452.		
	If this is a consolidated return, answer here for the parent corporation and on Form 851 for each subsidiary.		
7	At any time during the tax year, did one foreign person own, directly or indirectly, at least 25% of the total voting power of all classes of the corporation's stock entitled to vote or at least 25% of the total value of all classes of the corporation's stock? .		
	For rules of attribution, see section 318. If "Yes," enter:		
	(a) Percentage owned _____ and **(b)** Owner's country _____		
	(c) The corporation may have to file **Form 5472**, Information Return of a 25% Foreign-Owned U.S. Corporation or a Foreign Corporation Engaged in a U.S. Trade or Business. Enter the number of Forms 5472 attached _____		
8	Check this box if the corporation issued publicly offered debt instruments with original issue discount . . . . ☐		
	If checked, the corporation may have to file **Form 8281**, Information Return for Publicly Offered Original Issue Discount Instruments.		
9	Enter the amount of tax-exempt interest received or accrued during the tax year $ _____		
10	Enter the number of shareholders at the end of the tax year (if 100 or fewer) _____		
11	If the corporation has an NOL for the tax year and is electing to forego the carryback period, check here (see instructions) ☐		
	If the corporation is filing a consolidated return, the statement required by Regulations section 1.1502-21(b)(3) must be attached or the election will not be valid.		
12	Enter the available NOL carryover from prior tax years (do not reduce it by any deduction reported on page 1, line 29a.) . . . . $ _____		

Form **1120** (2022)

(Use for Problem 30.)

Form 1120 (2022)   Page **5**

Schedule K   **Other Information** *(continued from page 4)*

		Yes	No
13	Are the corporation's total receipts (page 1, line 1a, plus lines 4 through 10) for the tax year **and** its total assets at the end of the tax year less than $250,000?		
	If "Yes," the corporation is not required to complete Schedules L, M-1, and M-2. Instead, enter the total amount of cash distributions and the book value of property distributions (other than cash) made during the tax year $ _____		
14	Is the corporation required to file Schedule UTP (Form 1120), Uncertain Tax Position Statement? See instructions		
	If "Yes," complete and attach Schedule UTP.		
15a	Did the corporation make any payments in 2022 that would require it to file Form(s) 1099?		
b	If "Yes," did or will the corporation file required Form(s) 1099?		
16	During this tax year, did the corporation have an 80%-or-more change in ownership, including a change due to redemption of its own stock?		
17	During or subsequent to this tax year, but before the filing of this return, did the corporation dispose of more than 65% (by value) of its assets in a taxable, non-taxable, or tax deferred transaction?		
18	Did the corporation receive assets in a section 351 transfer in which any of the transferred assets had a fair market basis or fair market value of more than $1 million?		
19	During the corporation's tax year, did the corporation make any payments that would require it to file Forms 1042 and 1042-S under chapter 3 (sections 1441 through 1464) or chapter 4 (sections 1471 through 1474) of the Code?		
20	Is the corporation operating on a cooperative basis?		
21	During the tax year, did the corporation pay or accrue any interest or royalty for which the deduction is not allowed under section 267A? See instructions		
	If "Yes," enter the total amount of the disallowed deductions $ _____		
22	Does the corporation have gross receipts of at least $500 million in any of the 3 preceding tax years? (See sections 59A(e)(2) and (3))		
	If "Yes," complete and attach Form 8991.		
23	Did the corporation have an election under section 163(j) for any real property trade or business or any farming business in effect during the tax year? See instructions		
24	Does the corporation satisfy one or more of the following? See instructions		
a	The corporation owns a pass-through entity with current, or prior year carryover, excess business interest expense.		
b	The corporation's aggregate average annual gross receipts (determined under section 448(c)) for the 3 tax years preceding the current tax year are more than $27 million and the corporation has business interest expense.		
c	The corporation is a tax shelter and the corporation has business interest expense.		
	If "Yes," complete and attach Form 8990.		
25	Is the corporation attaching Form 8996 to certify as a Qualified Opportunity Fund?		
	If "Yes," enter amount from Form 8996, line 15 . . . . . $		
26	Since December 22, 2017, did a foreign corporation directly or indirectly acquire substantially all of the properties held directly or indirectly by the corporation, and was the ownership percentage (by vote or value) for purposes of section 7874 greater than 50% (for example, the shareholders held more than 50% of the stock of the foreign corporation)? If "Yes," list the ownership percentage by vote and by value. See instructions		
	Percentage: By Vote _____ By Value _____		

Form **1120** (2022)

(Use for Problem 30.)

Form 1120 (2022)

Page **6**

Schedule L — Balance Sheets per Books

	Assets	Beginning of tax year (a)	(b)	End of tax year (c)	(d)
1	Cash				
2a	Trade notes and accounts receivable				
b	Less allowance for bad debts	( )		( )	
3	Inventories				
4	U.S. government obligations				
5	Tax-exempt securities (see instructions)				
6	Other current assets (attach statement)				
7	Loans to shareholders				
8	Mortgage and real estate loans				
9	Other investments (attach statement)				
10a	Buildings and other depreciable assets				
b	Less accumulated depreciation	( )		( )	
11a	Depletable assets				
b	Less accumulated depletion	( )		( )	
12	Land (net of any amortization)				
13a	Intangible assets (amortizable only)				
b	Less accumulated amortization	( )		( )	
14	Other assets (attach statement)				
15	Total assets				

	Liabilities and Shareholders' Equity				
16	Accounts payable				
17	Mortgages, notes, bonds payable in less than 1 year				
18	Other current liabilities (attach statement)				
19	Loans from shareholders				
20	Mortgages, notes, bonds payable in 1 year or more				
21	Other liabilities (attach statement)				
22	Capital stock: **a** Preferred stock				
	b Common stock				
23	Additional paid-in capital				
24	Retained earnings—Appropriated (attach statement)				
25	Retained earnings—Unappropriated				
26	Adjustments to shareholders' equity (attach statement)				
27	Less cost of treasury stock		( )		( )
28	Total liabilities and shareholders' equity				

Schedule M-1 — Reconciliation of Income (Loss) per Books With Income per Return

Note: The corporation may be required to file Schedule M-3. See instructions.

1	Net income (loss) per books		7	Income recorded on books this year not included on this return (itemize):	
2	Federal income tax per books			Tax-exempt interest $ _____	
3	Excess of capital losses over capital gains			_____	
4	Income subject to tax not recorded on books this year (itemize): _____		8	Deductions on this return not charged against book income this year (itemize):	
	_____		a	Depreciation . . $ _____	
5	Expenses recorded on books this year not deducted on this return (itemize):		b	Charitable contributions $ _____	
a	Depreciation . . . . $ _____			_____	
b	Charitable contributions . $ _____				
c	Travel and entertainment . $ _____		9	Add lines 7 and 8	
	_____		10	Income (page 1, line 28)—line 6 less line 9	
6	Add lines 1 through 5				

Schedule M-2 — Analysis of Unappropriated Retained Earnings per Books (Schedule L, Line 25)

1	Balance at beginning of year		5	Distributions: **a** Cash	
2	Net income (loss) per books			**b** Stock	
3	Other increases (itemize): _____			**c** Property	
	_____		6	Other decreases (itemize): _____	
	_____		7	Add lines 5 and 6	
4	Add lines 1, 2, and 3		8	Balance at end of year (line 4 less line 7)	

Form **1120** (2022)

Chapter

15

Partnerships

CHAPTER CONTENTS

LEARNING OBJECTIVES

After completing Chapter 15, you should be able to:

1. Understand the tax characteristics of partnerships and how they are formed, including the selection of a year-end (along with the tax consequences).
2. Distinguish between ordinary income and separately stated items, explain the need for separately stated items, and compute ordinary income.
3. Compute a partner's distributive share of partnership items, including how partners treat payments made to them from the partnership for services rendered.
4. Compute a partner's basis and understand its impact on the partner's ability to deduct losses and its impact on how distributions are treated.
5. Prepare the tax forms introduced in this chapter, including Form 1065 and Schedule K-1 (Form 1065).

CHAPTER OVERVIEW

Partnerships and S corporations are separate legal entities. However, neither is responsible for the income taxes on the business's profits. Instead, the results of all of the business's activities belong to the owners, who report their respective shares of the business activities on their own income tax returns. This results in only one level of tax being levied on the entity's profits. Partnerships and S corporations file informational tax returns at the end of each tax year. These returns tell the IRS the total income, deductions, gains, losses and credits generated by the business during the year. These returns also tell the IRS and each owner the share of each item that belongs to each of the owners. For this reason, partnerships and S corporations are often called flow-through entities.

This chapter focuses on partnership taxation. It looks at the tax aspects from the standpoint of the partnership and its partners. S corporations are the focus of Chapter 16.

¶1501   The Nature of Partnerships

A partnership is an association of two or more persons (or other entities) that conducts business with an intent to share profits or losses. A partnership does not include a joint undertaking merely to share expenses. Thus, if two neighbors dig a ditch merely to drain surface water from their respective properties, they do not create a partnership. However, if they actively carry on a business and divide the profits, they have created a partnership and become partners. [I.R.C. §761(a)]

Each person contributing property or services to the partnership receives an ownership interest. Each person then becomes a partner. Partners can be individuals, corporations, estates, other partnerships, or trusts.

A partner's interest in a partnership can be a profits-only interest or a capital and profits interest. The distinction lies in whether the partner will share in the partnership assets should the partnership go out of business. When a partner contributes property or services to the partnership in exchange for the right to share future profits and losses and to receive assets from the partnership should the entity go out of business, the partner is said to acquire a **capital and profits interest** in the partnership. If, on the other hand, the partner renders services to the partnership in exchange solely for the right to share in future profits and losses of the partnership, the partner's interest is a **profits-only interest**, also termed a **carried interest**.

> A typical carried interest arrangement allows a person to treat his or her compensation income from the partnership as a capital gain. This special rule has attracted considerable attention. The Tax Cuts and Jobs Act of 2017 enacted a limitation whereby the holder of a carried interest can only treat income as a capital gain if the partnership's holding period in the property is more than three years at the time of sale. However, attention still persists. Changes may be coming after this book goes to print.

Partnerships can be formed as either general or limited partnerships. In a general partnership, all of the partners are general partners. A **general partner** is fully liable for the debts and actions of the partnership. A limited partnership has limited partner(s) and at least one general partner. A **limited partner** is liable for the debts and actions of the partnership only to the extent of the partner's basis in the partnership interest plus any amounts the partnership owes the limited partner.

¶1502   Partnership Tax Returns

In a partnership, the partners, not the partnership, are responsible for the income taxes on the partnership's profits. All items of partnership income and loss pass through to the partners, where they appear on the partners' own tax returns. Partners must pay taxes on their respective shares of partnership income regardless of whether they receive distributions from the partnership. [I.R.C. §701]

Every partnership doing business within the United States files the informational return Form 1065, U.S. Return of Partnership Income. The return reports the partnership's revenues and expenses. It also reports each partner's share of all partnership items. The return is due by the 15th day of the third month after the end of the partnership's tax year. For a calendar year partnership, the due date is March 15. A partnership may receive an automatic six-month extension for filing its return by submitting Form 7004, Application for Automatic Extension of Time To File Certain Business Income Tax, Information, and Other Returns. This form must be filed by the due date for the original return. The Internal Revenue Code (Code) imposes a penalty on the partnership (not the partners) when it fails to file Form 1065 in a timely manner. For each month that the failure continues (not to exceed 12 months), the penalty equals $210 times the number of persons who were partners at any time during the year. [I.R.C. §6698]

Form 1065 consists of five pages. Page 1 provides general information about the partnership and shows the calculation of ordinary business income (loss). Schedule B appears on pages 2 and It is here that other information about the partnership is provided. Schedule K is found on page All items that must be separately stated are listed on Schedule K. Finally, page 5 contains the book balance sheet (Schedule L), reconciliation of book and tax income (Schedule M-1) and an analysis of the partners' capital accounts (Schedule M-2). A partnership whose business included manufacturing or resale must use Form 1125-A to report its calculation of cost of goods sold. This is the same form used by C corporations and S corporations.

A Schedule K-1 (Form 1065), Partner's Share of Income, Deductions, Credits, etc., is completed for each person who was a partner at any time during the year. All Schedules K-1 are attached to and filed with Form 1065, and the partnership furnishes the partners with a copy of their respective Schedule K-1. Failure to furnish a timely Schedule K-1 to a partner may result in a penalty up to $270 for each failure. Thus, if a partnership with 150 partners fails to timely furnish Schedules K-1 to its partners, the partnership may be assessed up to a $40,000 penalty ($270 penalty × 150 partners). A reduced penalty applies if the error is corrected within 30 days ($50) or by August 1 ($100) (see ¶1309.02).

 A partnership does not need to be taxed as a flow through entity. Instead, it can choose to be taxed as a corporation. This is done by having the business "check the box" to be taxed as a corporation on Form 8832 (see discussion at ¶1401). When this election is made, the rules discussed in Chapter 14 apply to both the business and its owners.

¶1502.01   YEAR TO REPORT PARTNERSHIP INCOME

Partners are taxed on their shares of partnership items in their tax year that includes the last day of the partnership's tax year. Partners include these partnership items on their tax returns in that year. [I.R.C. §706(a)]

EXAMPLE 1   Amber uses a calendar tax year. Amber is a partner in ABC partnership that uses a January 31 fiscal tax year. Amber reports her share of partnership items for the fiscal year February 1, 20x1 – January 31, 20x2 on her 20x2 tax return (Amber's tax year that includes January 31, 20x2). Because of this rule, the income ABC earns for the 11 months from February 1, 20x1 – December 31, 20x1 is not taxed until Amber files her 20x2 tax return. This is known as an 11-month deferral.

¶1502.02   REQUIRED TAX YEAR

To prevent partners from deferring partnership income into the next year (like Amber did for 11 months in Example 1), the tax laws limit a partnership's choice of tax years it can use. The partnership must select the same tax year as the majority of its partners. Majority partners own, in total, more than 50% of capital and profits. Because most individual partners use a calendar year, most partnerships also use the calendar year. However, if there is not a majority of partners with the same tax year, the partnership must select the same tax year as all of its principal partners. A principal partner is a partner that owns at least 5% of capital or profits. Partnerships unable to determine a tax year using these rules must adopt a tax year that results in the least aggregate deferral of income. The method used to determine the tax year with the least aggregate deferral of income is complex, and beyond the scope of this discussion.

EXAMPLE 2   Partners A and B contribute property to form AB partnership in exchange for a 70% and 30% interest in capital and profits, respectively. Partner A uses a June 30 year-end; Partner B uses the calendar year-end. Since Partner A is a majority partner, AB's required tax year is a June 30 fiscal year.

EXAMPLE 3   ABC partnership is formed when partners A, B and C contribute property in exchange for a 40%, 30%, and 30% interest in capital and profits, respectively. Partner A uses a June 30 year-end. Partners B and C use a calendar year-end. Since Partners B and C together own a majority interest in the partnership, ABC's required tax year is the calendar year.

| EXAMPLE 4 | Same facts as in Example 3, except that Partner C's year-end is October 31. Since no group of partners owns a majority interest in the partnership, and the principal partners do not all have the same year-end, ABC's required tax year must be determined using the least aggregate deferral of income method. |

| EXAMPLE 5 | D and E each own 25% of DE partnership. The remaining 50% is owned by 20 other partners, each of whom has less than a 5% partnership interest. D and E both have a June 30 year-end. The other 20 partners all use a calendar year-end. Since no group of partners having the same year-end owns more than a 50% interest in capital and profits, the partnership's required tax year is not determined by the majority interest rule. However, D and E are the only principal partners, and since all principal partners share the same tax year, DE's required tax year is June 30. |

Exceptions to the Required Tax Year Rule

Two exceptions allow a partnership to use a tax year other than its required tax year. The first permits a partnership to select a tax year based on the partnership's natural business year. A natural business year is one in which at least 25% of gross receipts are received in the last two months of a 12-month period for three consecutive years. [I.R.C. §444] Thus, the natural business year exception may be adopted only by partnerships that have been in existence for at least three years. The second exception allows partnerships to select a tax year that provides no more than a three-month deferral for its partners. Thus, a partnership with a calendar year as its required tax year could select a tax year ending the last day of September, October, or November. The partnership makes the election by filing Form 8716, Election To Have a Tax Year Other Than a Required Tax Year. This election requires partnerships to make tax deposits approximating the amount of tax deferral caused by the difference in the partnership and the partners' tax years. [I.R.C. §7519] These tax deposits eliminate any tax benefits the partners get by being able to defer reporting the income from the partnership. Treasury Regulations provide details regarding the computation of the required tax deposits.

| EXAMPLE 6 | Continuing with Example 5, DE's required tax year is June 30. The partnership can elect to use a March 31, April 30 or May 31 year-end as long as it agrees to make tax deposits equal to the estimated taxes the partners would owe on the profits generated during the deferral months. |

Change in Tax Year

A partnership wanting to change its tax year must first get permission from the IRS. Partnerships make the request on Form 1128, Application To Adopt, Change, or Retain a Tax Year. A partnership receiving permission to change its tax year files a short-year tax return in the year of change. This return covers the period from its prior year-end to its new year-end.

| EXAMPLE 7 | A change from a fiscal year ending March 31 to the calendar year ending December 31 requires a short-year return. The short-year return covers the nine-month period of April 1 to December 31. |

The partnership tax year closes when the partnership ceases to carry on any business. When a partnership tax year closes, all of the partners must recognize their shares of income/loss items at the time of closing.

Normally, the death of a partner or the addition of a partner will not terminate the partnership tax year. Rather, the partnership tax year closes with respect to a partner whose entire partnership interest terminates, but it does not close the tax year for the other partners.

¶1502.03   REPORTING PARTNERSHIP INCOME AND DEDUCTIONS

A partnership is not a taxable entity. A partnership *passes through* income and expenses to each of its partners. This pass-through treatment is an application of the **conduit principle**. Many partnership income and expense items receive special tax treatment on the partners' own tax returns. For example, net capital gain is taxed differently to individual and corporate taxpayers (compare discussions at ¶1101.03 and ¶1402.04). Also, different limitations on charitable contributions apply to these two types of taxpayers (compare discussions at ¶506.04 and ¶1402.06). Accordingly, the partnership must report these types of items separately on its tax return. [I.R.C. §702] Any items that do not require separate reporting are passed through to the partners as ordinary income or loss from partnership operations.

¶1502.04   QUALIFIED BUSINESS INCOME DEDUCTION

Noncorporate partners may deduct up to 20% of domestic qualified business income from a partnership. [I.R.C. §199A] The deduction is generally limited to the greater of (1) 50% of the partner's share of W-2 wages paid by the business, or (2) the sum of 25% of the partner's share of W-2 wages paid plus 2.5% of the partner's share of unadjusted basis of certain property the business uses to produce qualified business income. This limit may be phased-in or eliminated if the taxpayer's tax-able income meets certain threshold requirements. The qualified business income deduction, also known as the Section 199A deduction, applies to tax years 2018 through 2025. See Chapter 7.

Each partner must take into account his or her allocable share of each qualified item of income, gain, deduction, and loss. Further, each partner is treated as having W-2 wages and unadjusted basis immediately after acquisition of qualified property for the tax year, in an amount equal to his or her allocable or pro rata share of the partnership's W-2 wages and unadjusted basis for the tax year as determined in the regulations. The share of W-2 wages is determined in the same manner as the partner's share of wage expenses. The share of the unadjusted basis of qualified property is determined in the same manner as the partner's allocable share of depreciation.

EXAMPLE 8	Sue is a partner in the QRS Partnership. If Sue is allocated a deductible amount of 10% of wages paid by the partnership to employees for the tax year, she must be allocated 10% of the W-2 wages of the partnership for purposes of calculating the wage limit for the Code Sec. 199A deduction.

¶1502.05   BUSINESS INTEREST DEDUCTION LIMITATION

For businesses with average gross receipts of more than $27 million in 2022 ($25 million, adjusted for inflation after 2018), the deduction of business interest is limited for tax years beginning after 2017. The deductible amount is the sum of the taxpayer's business interest income, floor plan financing, and 30% of adjusted taxable income. However, the CARES Act of 2020 amended this rule so that taxpayers other than partnerships had a limit of 50% of adjusted taxable income for 2019 and 2020. Partnerships were subject to the 30% limit in 2019 and the 50% limit in 2020.

For partnerships, the limitation on the deduction of business interest is applied at the entity level. The partnership takes a deduction for business interest account in determining its non-separately stated taxable income or loss.

The partner's adjusted taxable income is determined without regard to the partner's distributive share of any partnership item of income, gain, deduction, or loss.

A partnership passes through to partners any excess taxable income for purposes of the deduction limit. The partnership's excess taxable income is a percentage of its adjusted taxable income for the year. The percentage is: 30% of the entity's adjusted taxable income, over its net excess business interest (the excess of business interest of the entity, reduced by floor plan financing interest, over business interest income), over 30% of the entity's adjusted taxable income.

Each partner's adjusted taxable income is increased by the partner's pro rata share of the partnership's excess taxable income. A partner's pro rata share of partnership excess taxable income is determined in the same manner as the partner's pro rata share of the partnership's non-separately stated taxable income or loss.

This addition to a partner's adjusted taxable income allows the partner to deduct more interest than the partner may have paid or incurred during the year, to the extent the partnership could have deducted more business interest.

Generally, business interest that is not deductible due to the limitation may be carried forward indefinitely. However, for a partnership a disallowed interest deduction is not carried forward to the succeeding tax year. Instead, the partnership's disallowed interest is treated as excess business interest that is allocated to each partner in the same manner as any non-separately stated taxable income or loss.

The partner treats the allocated excess business interest for the current tax year as business interest that the partner paid or accrued in the next succeeding year. In other words, the partner carries forward the allocated excess business interest to the next succeeding tax year, but only to the extent partner is allocated excess taxable income from the partnership in the succeeding year.

Excess taxable income allocated to a partner for any tax year must be used against excess business interest from the partnership from all tax years before it may be used against any other business interest.

If the partner does not have enough excess taxable income from the partnership to offset the carried forward excess business interest, the interest must continue to be carried forward to succeeding tax years. In all subsequent tax years, the excess business interest carried forward by the partner is treated as paid or accrued in the next subsequent tax year that may only be used against excess taxable income allocated by partnership to the partner for that tax year.

The partner's adjusted basis in the partner's interest in the partnership is reduced (but not below zero) by the amount of excess business interest allocated by the partnership to the partner. However, if the partner sells or otherwise disposes of the interest in the partnership, the partner's adjusted basis is increased immediately before the disposition by the excess (if any) of: the amount of the basis reduction due to the excess business interest allocated by the partnership to the partner, over any portion of the excess business interest allocated to the partner that has previously been treated as interest paid or accrued by the partner.

A disposition for purposes of an increase in the adjusted basis of a partnership interest includes any transactions in which gain is not recognized in whole or part (including in the case of the death of the partner). Also, no deduction is allowed to the transferor or transferee for any excess business interest that increases the adjusted basis in the partnership.

¶1502.06   SEPARATELY STATED ITEMS

Form 1065, Schedule K, is where separately stated items are listed. Each partner receives a Schedule K-1 (Form 1065), which shows that partner's share of ordinary income and each separately stated item. The following sections present the more common separately stated items.

Examples of Separately Stated Items

■ Rental income	■ Section 179 deductions
■ Interest income from investments	■ Investment expenses
■ Dividend income	■ Credits and recaptures of the credits
■ Royalty income	■ Guaranteed payments*
■ Net short-term capital gains and losses	■ AMT adjustments and preferences
■ Net long-term capital gains and losses	■ Foreign taxes
■ Other investment income	■ Tax-exempt income
■ Net Section 1231 gains and losses	■ Nondeductible expenses
■ Charitable contributions	■ Personal expenses paid for the partners

*Deducted in total in computing ordinary income but separately stated for each partner (see ¶1502.07)

Income Items

Rental income, interest, dividends, royalties, and gains (losses) from the sale of capital assets or business properties (Section 1231 assets) are separately stated on Schedules K and K-1. The partnership files Form 4797 to report and summarize any gains (losses) from the sale of business properties. Schedule D (Form 1065) supports the calculation of the partnership's long-term or short-term capital gains and losses. Partners add each separately stated item reported on their Schedule K-1 to other similar items they have personally. For example, an individual partner's share of partnership capital gains and losses is reported on the partner's own Schedule D (Form 1040). Similarly, partners report their shares of gains and losses from the sale of partnership business properties with their other business gains and losses on their own Form 4797.

Even though state and local (municipal) bond interest is exempt from federal income taxes, it may be subject to state income tax. Also, individuals must report tax-exempt interest on their tax returns. For these reasons, tax-exempt interest is reported on Schedules K and K-1 as a separately stated item.

Deduction Items

Relatively few deductions are separately stated on Schedules K and K-1. The partnership deducts most expenses in the calculation of ordinary income (¶1502.06). Three more common separately stated deductions include Section 179 expense, deductions related to portfolio (investment) income, and charitable contributions.

You may recall from Chapter 6 that Section 179 allows the immediate expensing of certain property purchased in the current year. The partnership decides whether or not to take the Section 179 deduction. The dollar amount and placed-in-service limits (¶602.05) apply at both the partnership level and again at the partner level. The partners add their distributive shares of this deduction to the amounts they have from other businesses in determining their own Section 179 deduction amount.

Individual taxpayers deduct investment interest expense to the extent of their net investment income (¶505.03). In addition, higher-income taxpayers may be subject to a 3.8% net investment income (NII) tax (¶315). Net investment income equals taxable investment income less deductible investment expenses. Individual taxpayers deduct investment expenses as itemized deductions. Thus, any partnership item affecting the calculation of NII must be separately stated. Charitable contributions are not business expenses for individual taxpayers. Therefore, the partnership does not claim them as a deduction in computing ordinary income. Instead, the partnership lists the total amount of charitable contributions on Schedule K. Individual partners add their shares of each contribution to their personal contributions and show the total as an itemized deduction on Schedule A (¶506). In 2020 only, a partner who does not itemize deductions may claim a $300 deduction for AGI. In 2021 only, a partner who does not itemize deductions may claim a $300 deduction from AGI. See Chapter 5.

When a partnership allocates a loss to a partner, there are several limits that may preclude the partner from claiming the deduction in the year of allocation. First, and probably the most restrictive limit, is that a partner cannot deduct any loss that exceeds basis in the partnership interest. [I.R.C. §704(d)] After this limit, a partner may be subject to more restrictions, in this order:

1. The partner's amount at-risk [I.R.C. §465]
2. The passive activity loss limit on rental activities and businesses in which the partner is not a material participant. [I.R.C. §469]
3. The excess business loss limit, when the partner's overall business losses exceed business income by more than $250,000 ($500,000 if married filing jointly). [I.R.C. §461(l)] The CARES Act of 2020 postponed the effective date of this limit until 2021. The limits are indexed for inflation. For 2022, the limit is $270,000 ($540,000 for married taxpayers filing jointly).

The basis limitation on partner losses takes into account a partner's distributive share of partnership charitable contributions, and taxes paid or accrued to foreign countries and U.S. possessions.

The amount of the basis limitation on partner losses is decreased by the partner's distributive share of the adjusted basis of the property contributed by the partnership. A special rule provides that if the partnership makes a charitable contribution of property whose fair market value is greater than its adjusted basis, the basis limitation on partner losses does not account for the partner's distributive share of the excess.

Net Operating Losses (NOLs)

A net operating loss (NOL) generally equals the excess of allowable deductions over taxable gross income in any tax year. A partnership does not carry over its losses to other partnership tax years. Instead, the partners report their shares of the partnership's losses on their own returns as deductions from gross income. The partnership allocates income and losses to partners only for that portion of the year that the partner is a member of the partnership. Partners cannot be allocated losses for the period before they joined the partnership.

When partners deduct losses, they reduce their basis in the partnership interest. However, basis cannot be reduced below zero. Any disallowed losses remain available to the partners in future years. When the basis increases, they can then deduct some or all of the suspended loss. Partners' basis is discussed in greater detail later in the chapter at ¶1503.01.

EXAMPLE 9	At the beginning of 20x1, Monroe has a 40% partnership interest with a basis of $16,000. During 20x1, the partnership has an ordinary loss of $60,000. Monroe's share of the loss is $24,000 ($60,000 × 40%). However, Monroe can only deduct $16,000 (to the extent of his basis). His basis in the partnership interest is reduced to $0. The $8,000 ($24,000 – $16,000) of the loss not deductible in 20x1 carries forward to future tax years. Monroe will be able to deduct his suspended loss when he establishes a positive partnership basis.

Foreign Taxes

Partnerships engaging in business activities outside the United States may pay income taxes to foreign countries. Such taxes receive special treatment on the tax return of an individual, and therefore are separately stated. Individual partners report their shares of these foreign income taxes on their own tax returns, either as an itemized deduction (¶504.04), or as a tax credit (¶204.01).

Credits

Since partnerships do not pay income tax, they do not take tax credits. The benefits of any credits pass through to the partners as separately stated items. The partnership makes any elections necessary to qualify for the credits. The partners claim the benefits on their own returns to the extent they meet the limitations that apply to the credits.

¶1502.07   PARTNERSHIP ORDINARY INCOME

When completing the partnership tax return, all income and expense items must be divided between separately stated items and ordinary items. The items not requiring separate statement are combined on Form 1065, page 1 and result in the ordinary income or loss for the partnership. Ordinary income generally consists of the receipts from the partnership's principal business activity. Thus, the gross profits from the sales of products or services are ordinary income. Any other income that is ordinary when passed through to the partners is ordinary income for this purpose. Items such as gains from the sale of business property held short-term, depreciation recapture (¶1102.02), and interest received on accounts receivables fall into this category.

From total (ordinary) income, the partnership subtracts out all non-separately stated deductions. The partnership reports this difference on its tax return as ordinary business income (loss).

Calculating Ordinary Income		
Gross receipts or gross sales		$xx
Less: Returns and allowances		(xx)
Less: Cost of goods sold from Form 1125-A		(xx)
Gross profit		$xx
Ordinary income (loss) from other entities		xx
Net ordinary gain (loss) from Form 4797		xx
Other income (loss)		xx
Total income (loss)		$xx
Less: Nonseparately stated expenses	$xx	
Guaranteed payments to partners	xx	(xx)
Ordinary business income (loss)		$xx

Guaranteed Payments to Partners

Partnership agreements frequently provide that some or all partners receive payments as compensation. These payments recognize the varying skills and amounts of time partners devote to partnership business. Also, partners may receive a stated rate of interest on the amount of capital that each has invested in the partnership.

The partnership generally deducts these guaranteed payments in computing partnership ordinary income. To be deductible, the payments must be reasonable in amount and determined without regard to partnership income. Guaranteed payments to partners are deducted to arrive at ordinary income and are taxable to the partner that receives them. [I.R.C. §707(b)] The partnership reports guaranteed payments separately on Schedule K-1s for the partners that receive them.

Although partners may receive payments for providing services, they are not considered employees. Therefore, the guaranteed payments are not subject to withholding of social security (OASDI), Medicare, or income taxes. Instead, guaranteed payments are subject to self-employment taxes. [I.R.C. §1402] The partners report guaranteed payments they receive as nonpassive income on Form 1040, Schedule E, Supplemental Income and Loss. The partnership can deduct salaries and wages paid to spouses or other members of a partner's family, provided they are reasonable in amount. Any unreasonable portion is considered a payment to the related partner.

EXAMPLE 10

Dave and Bob are equal general partners in a law firm that uses a calendar year. Dave and Bob receive monthly guaranteed payments of $3,000 and $2,500, respectively. Prior to deducting the guaranteed payments, the partnership has ordinary income of $146,000. After deducting the guaranteed payments ($36,000 to Dave ($3,000 × 12); $30,000 to Bob ($2,500 × 12)), the partnership's ordinary income is $80,000 ($146,000 – $36,000 – $30,000).

On his tax return, Dave will report $76,000 in income from the partnership. This includes $36,000 for his guaranteed payments and $40,000 for his share of partnership income ($80,000 × 50%). Both of these amounts will be subject to self-employment tax (as well as income tax). On his tax return, Bob will report $70,000 of income from the partnership ($30,000 guaranteed payments + $40,000 partnership ordinary income). Again, the entire $70,000 will be subject to self-employment tax (as well as income tax).

Partners are not employees of the partnership. Thus, there are no taxes withheld on their earnings. Instead, partners must make estimated payments large enough to cover both income and self-employment taxes on their shares of partnership income. See ¶1307 for a discussion of estimated tax payments.

¶1502.08   DEDUCTIONS NOT APPLICABLE TO PARTNERSHIPS

Partnerships do not include any nonbusiness deductions in the computation of ordinary income. There is no exemption deduction, standard deduction, or deduction for any personal expenses. [I.R.C. §703] These deductions apply solely to individuals. Personal expenses of a partner paid directly by the partnership are treated as withdrawals by the partner. They are not included in the calculation of partnership income. Withdrawals (distributions) are generally treated as tax-free reductions in the partner's investment. Usually, partners only pay taxes on partnership income, not distributions. The tax consequences of partnership distributions are discussed later in the chapter at ¶1503.02.

¶1502.09   FILLED-IN FORM 1065

INFORMATION FOR FIGURE 15-2:

Sarah Morton (SSN 294-00-8321) and Doug Baker are both active partners in **M&B Partnership (EIN 70-0464077)**. M&B is a general partnership that has been in existence since **July 1, 2000**. The offices of M&B are located at **524 Southside, Raleigh, NC 27604-1470**. M&B uses the **accrual method** of reporting for its **sporting goods business** (business code number 451110). Sarah is the designated partnership representative. She lives at **1609 Amber Way, Charlotte, NC 28201**. Under their partnership agreement, each partner is paid guaranteed payments of $1,600 per month. They share the remaining profits and losses equally. Of these profits, $7,000 was distributed in cash to Sarah. No distributions (other than his guaranteed payments) were made to Doug during the year.

The primary information for preparing Form 1065 comes from the information shown in Figure 15-1. The filled-in Form 1065 for M&B Partnership appears in Figure 15-2. On March 15, 2023, Sarah Morton signs and dates Form 1065 as a general partner of M&B. Although total assets and total gross receipts are not large enough to require completion of Item F on page 1, or Schedules L, M-1 and M-2, these schedules are completed in Figure 15-2 for illustration purposes. Depreciation expense is the same for book and tax purposes.

Figure 15-1: M&B Partnership Financial Statements

M&B Partnership
Income Statement
For Year Ended December 31, 2022

Sales	$216,410
Less: Sales returns and allowances	(3,502)
Net sales	$212,908
Less: Cost of goods sold (see schedule)	(106,754)
Gross profit on sales	$106,154
Less: Operating expenses (see schedule)	(87,622)
Operating income	$ 18,532
Interest income (business, $145; investment $1,100; tax-exempt, $50)	1,295
Qualified dividend income	1,700
Less: Interest expense	(253)
Less: Charitable contributions	(426)
Net income	$ 20,848

Schedule of Cost of Goods Sold

Inventory at beginning of year		$ 34,969
Purchases	$105,867	
Less: Purchases returns and allowances	(775)	
Less: Purchase discounts	(1,003)	
Net purchases		104,089
Merchandise available for sale		$139,058
Less: Inventory at end of year		(32,304)
Cost of goods sold		$106,754

Schedule of Operating Expenses
For Year Ended December 31, 2022

General and Administrative Expenses:		Selling Expenses:	
Sarah Morton, salary	$19,200	Sales salaries	$20,000
Doug Baker, salary	19,200	Advertising	1,164
Payroll taxes	4,378	Depreciation	1,400
Rent	5,400	Store supplies	492
Automobile	999	Miscellaneous	242
Utilities	1,345	Total selling expenses	$23,298
Bad debts (direct write-off method)	750		
Insurance	571	Total operating expenses	$87,622
Travel	673		
Office supplies	408		
Office salaries	11,250		
Depreciation	150		
Total G&A expenses	$64,324		

Line # (Form 1065, page 1)
- F: Total assets, **$78,340** (source: Schedule L, line 14(d))
  Because M&B answers "Yes" to Question 4 on Schedule B (Form 1065), it is not required to complete Item F on page 1 of Form 1065. Item F is completed here for illustration purposes.
- H: Accounting method, mark box **(2)**
- I: Number of Schedules K-1, **2** (Sarah Morton, Doug Baker)
- 7: Other income, **$145** (business interest)
- 9: Salaries and wages, **$31,250** ($20,000 sales salaries + $11,250 office salaries)
- 10: Guaranteed payments to partners, **$38,400** ($19,200 + $19,200)
- 16a: Depreciation, **$1,550** ($1,400 + $150)
- 20: Other deductions, **$5,894** ($1,164 advertising expense + $999 automobile expense + $1,345 utilities expense + $571 insurance expense + $673 travel expense + $492 store supplies + $408 office supplies + $242 miscellaneous selling expense)

Line # (Form 1065, pages 2 and 3, Schedule B)
- 1: Type of entity, mark box **(a)** for Domestic general partnership
- 2a-3b: mark **No**
- 4: mark **Yes**
- 5-10c: mark **No**
- 11: Leave blank
- 12-14: mark **No**
- 15: Leave blank or enter -0-
- 16a & b: mark **Yes**
- 17-18: Leave blank or enter -0-
- 19-29: mark **No**

Line # (Form 1065, page 4, Schedule K)
- 1: Ordinary business income (loss), **$18,424** (source: Form 1065 (page 1), line 22)
- 4: Guaranteed payments to partners, **$38,400** ($19,200 + $19,200)
- 5: Interest income, **$1,100** (taxable portfolio interest income)
- 13a: Contributions, **$426**
- 14a: Net earnings from self-employment, **$56,824** ($18,424 ordinary income + $38,400 guaranteed payments)
- 14c: Gross nonfarm income: **$106,154**
- 18a: Tax-exempt interest income **$50** (source: Income Statement, included as part of Interest income)
- 20a: Investment income **$2,800** ($1,100 taxable interest income + $1,700 dividend income)

Line # (Analysis of Net Income (Loss), Form 1065, page 5)
- 1: Net income (loss), **$59,198** (following the instructions on line 1, this amount is $18,424 + $38,400 + $1,100 + $1,700 − $426)

Line # (Form 1065, Schedule M-2)
- 1: Beginning partners' capital account balance, **$55,472** (source: Schedule L, line 21(b))
- 3: Net income (loss) per books, **$20,848** (source: Income Statement and Schedule M-1, line 1)
- 6a: Cash distributions, **$7,000** (source: given)

Figure 15-2: Filled-In Form 1065 (Page 1)

Form 1065

Department of the Treasury
Internal Revenue Service

U.S. Return of Partnership Income

For calendar year 2022, or tax year beginning _____, 2022, ending _____, 20 ____.

Go to *www.irs.gov/Form1065* for instructions and the latest information.

OMB No. 1545-0123

2022

A Principal business activity **Sales**	
B Principal product or service **General merchandise**	Type **or** Print
C Business code number **451110**	

Name of partnership: **M & B Partnership**

Number, street, and room or suite no. If a P.O. box, see instructions.
524 Southside

City or town, state or province, country, and ZIP or foreign postal code
Raleigh, NC 27604-1470

D Employer identification number: **70-0464077**

E Date business started: **07-01-2000**

F Total assets (see instructions): $ **78,340**

G Check applicable boxes: **(1)** ☐ Initial return **(2)** ☐ Final return **(3)** ☐ Name change **(4)** ☐ Address change **(5)** ☐ Amended return

H Check accounting method: **(1)** ☐ Cash **(2)** ☑ Accrual **(3)** ☐ Other (specify): _____

I Number of Schedules K-1. Attach one for each person who was a partner at any time during the tax year:

J Check if Schedules C and M-3 are attached ☐

K Check if partnership: **(1)** ☐ Aggregated activities for section 465 at-risk purposes **(2)** ☐ Grouped activities for section 469 passive activity purposes

Caution: Include **only** trade or business income and expenses on lines 1a through 22 below. See instructions for more information.

Income

1a	Gross receipts or sales	**1a** 216,410	
b	Returns and allowances	**1b** 3,502	
c	Balance. Subtract line 1b from line 1a	**1c**	212,908
2	Cost of goods sold (attach Form 1125-A)	**2**	106,754
3	Gross profit. Subtract line 2 from line 1c	**3**	106,154
4	Ordinary income (loss) from other partnerships, estates, and trusts (attach statement)	**4**	
5	Net farm profit (loss) (attach Schedule F (Form 1040))	**5**	
6	Net gain (loss) from Form 4797, Part II, line 17 (attach Form 4797)	**6**	
7	Other income (loss) (attach statement)	**7**	145
8	**Total income (loss).** Combine lines 3 through 7	**8**	106,299

Deductions (see instructions for limitations)

9	Salaries and wages (other than to partners) (less employment credits)	**9**	31,250
10	Guaranteed payments to partners	**10**	38,400
11	Repairs and maintenance	**11**	
12	Bad debts	**12**	750
13	Rent	**13**	5,400
14	Taxes and licenses	**14**	4,378
15	Interest (see instructions)	**15**	253
16a	Depreciation (if required, attach Form 4562)	**16a** 1,550	
b	Less depreciation reported on Form 1125-A and elsewhere on return	**16b**	**16c**
17	Depletion **(Do not deduct oil and gas depletion.)**	**17**	
18	Retirement plans, etc.	**18**	
19	Employee benefit programs	**19**	
20	Other deductions (attach statement)	**20**	5,894
21	**Total deductions.** Add the amounts shown in the far right column for lines 9 through 20	**21**	87,875
22	**Ordinary business income (loss).** Subtract line 21 from line 8	**22**	18,424

Tax and Payment

23	Interest due under the look-back method—completed long-term contracts (attach Form 8697)	**23**	
24	Interest due under the look-back method—income forecast method (attach Form 8866)	**24**	
25	BBA AAR imputed underpayment (see instructions)	**25**	
26	Other taxes (see instructions)	**26**	
27	**Total balance due.** Add lines 23 through 26	**27**	
28	Payment (see instructions)	**28**	
29	**Amount owed.** If line 28 is smaller than line 27, enter amount owed	**29**	
30	**Overpayment.** If line 28 is larger than line 27, enter overpayment	**30**	

Sign Here

Under penalties of perjury, I declare that I have examined this return, including accompanying schedules and statements, and to the best of my knowledge and belief, it is true, correct, and complete. Declaration of preparer (other than partner or limited liability company member) is based on all information of which preparer has any knowledge.

Signature of partner or limited liability company member _____ Date _____

May the IRS discuss this return with the preparer shown below? See instructions. ☐ Yes ☐ No

Paid Preparer Use Only

Print/Type preparer's name	Preparer's signature	Date	Check ☐ if self-employed	PTIN
Firm's name			Firm's EIN	
Firm's address			Phone no.	

For Paperwork Reduction Act Notice, see separate instructions.   Cat. No. 11390Z   Form **1065** (2022)

Figure 15-2: Filled-In Form 1065 (Page 2)

Form 1065 (2022)   Page **2**

Schedule B   **Other Information**

		Yes	No
1	What type of entity is filing this return? Check the applicable box:		
a	☑ Domestic general partnership **b** ☐ Domestic limited partnership		
c	☐ Domestic limited liability company **d** ☐ Domestic limited liability partnership		
e	☐ Foreign partnership **f** ☐ Other: _____		

2 At the end of the tax year:

a Did any foreign or domestic corporation, partnership (including any entity treated as a partnership), trust, or tax-exempt organization, or any foreign government own, directly or indirectly, an interest of 50% or more in the profit, loss, or capital of the partnership? For rules of constructive ownership, see instructions. If "Yes," attach Schedule B-1, Information on Partners Owning 50% or More of the Partnership   ✔

b Did any individual or estate own, directly or indirectly, an interest of 50% or more in the profit, loss, or capital of the partnership? For rules of constructive ownership, see instructions. If "Yes," attach Schedule B-1, Information on Partners Owning 50% or More of the Partnership   ✔

3 At the end of the tax year, did the partnership:

a Own directly 20% or more, or own, directly or indirectly, 50% or more of the total voting power of all classes of stock entitled to vote of any foreign or domestic corporation? For rules of constructive ownership, see instructions. If "Yes," complete (i) through (iv) below   ✔

(i) Name of Corporation	(ii) Employer Identification Number (if any)	(iii) Country of Incorporation	(iv) Percentage Owned in Voting Stock

b Own directly an interest of 20% or more, or own, directly or indirectly, an interest of 50% or more in the profit, loss, or capital in any foreign or domestic partnership (including an entity treated as a partnership) or in the beneficial interest of a trust? For rules of constructive ownership, see instructions. If "Yes," complete (i) through (v) below   ✔

(i) Name of Entity	(ii) Employer Identification Number (if any)	(iii) Type of Entity	(iv) Country of Organization	(v) Maximum Percentage Owned in Profit, Loss, or Capital

		Yes	No
4	Does the partnership satisfy **all four** of the following conditions?		
a	The partnership's total receipts for the tax year were less than $250,000.		
b	The partnership's total assets at the end of the tax year were less than $1 million.		
c	Schedules K-1 are filed with the return and furnished to the partners on or before the due date (including extensions) for the partnership return.		
d	The partnership is not filing and is not required to file Schedule M-3	✔	

If "Yes," the partnership is not required to complete Schedules L, M-1, and M-2; item F on page 1 of Form 1065; or item L on Schedule K-1.

		Yes	No
5	Is this partnership a publicly traded partnership, as defined in section 469(k)(2)?		✔
6	During the tax year, did the partnership have any debt that was canceled, was forgiven, or had the terms modified so as to reduce the principal amount of the debt?		✔
7	Has this partnership filed, or is it required to file, Form 8918, Material Advisor Disclosure Statement, to provide information on any reportable transaction?		✔
8	At any time during calendar year 2022, did the partnership have an interest in or a signature or other authority over a financial account in a foreign country (such as a bank account, securities account, or other financial account)? See instructions for exceptions and filing requirements for FinCEN Form 114, Report of Foreign Bank and Financial Accounts (FBAR). If "Yes," enter the name of the foreign country _____		✔
9	At any time during the tax year, did the partnership receive a distribution from, or was it the grantor of, or transferor to, a foreign trust? If "Yes," the partnership may have to file Form 3520, Annual Return To Report Transactions With Foreign Trusts and Receipt of Certain Foreign Gifts. See instructions		✔
10a	Is the partnership making, or had it previously made (and not revoked), a section 754 election? See instructions for details regarding a section 754 election.		✔
b	Did the partnership make for this tax year an optional basis adjustment under section 743(b) or 734(b)? If "Yes," attach a statement showing the computation and allocation of the basis adjustment. See instructions		✔
c	Is the partnership required to adjust the basis of partnership assets under section 743(b) or 734(b) because of a substantial built-in loss (as defined under section 743(d)) or substantial basis reduction (as defined under section 734(d))? If "Yes," attach a statement showing the computation and allocation of the basis adjustment. See instructions		✔

Form **1065** (2022)

Figure 15-2: Filled-In Form 1065 (Page 3)

Form 1065 (2022)   Page **3**

Schedule B	**Other Information** *(continued)*	Yes	No

11 Check this box if, during the current or prior tax year, the partnership distributed any property received in a like-kind exchange or contributed such property to another entity (other than disregarded entities wholly owned by the partnership throughout the tax year) . . . . □

12 At any time during the tax year, did the partnership distribute to any partner a tenancy-in-common or other undivided interest in partnership property? . . . . | | ✔

13 If the partnership is required to file Form 8858, Information Return of U.S. Persons With Respect to Foreign Disregarded Entities (FDEs) and Foreign Branches (FBs), enter the number of Forms 8858 attached. See instructions

14 Does the partnership have any foreign partners? If "Yes," enter the number of Forms 8805, Foreign Partner's Information Statement of Section 1446 Withholding Tax, filed for this partnership . . . . . . | | ✔

15 Enter the number of Forms 8865, Return of U.S. Persons With Respect to Certain Foreign Partnerships, attached to this return 0

16a Did you make any payments in 2022 that would require you to file Form(s) 1099? See instructions . . . . | ✔ |
  b If "Yes," did you or will you file required Form(s) 1099? . . . . | ✔ |

17 Enter the number of Forms 5471, Information Return of U.S. Persons With Respect to Certain Foreign Corporations, attached to this return 0

18 Enter the number of partners that are foreign governments under section 892 0

19 During the partnership's tax year, did the partnership make any payments that would require it to file Forms 1042 and 1042-S under chapter 3 (sections 1441 through 1464) or chapter 4 (sections 1471 through 1474)? . . . . | | ✔

20 Was the partnership a specified domestic entity required to file Form 8938 for the tax year? See the Instructions for Form 8938 . . . . | | ✔

21 Is the partnership a section 721(c) partnership, as defined in Regulations section 1.721(c)-1(b)(14)? . . . . . | | ✔

22 During the tax year, did the partnership pay or accrue any interest or royalty for which one or more partners are not allowed a deduction under section 267A? See instructions . . . . | | ✔
  If "Yes," enter the total amount of the disallowed deductions . . . . $

23 Did the partnership have an election under section 163(j) for any real property trade or business or any farming business in effect during the tax year? See instructions . . . . | | ✔

24 Does the partnership satisfy one or more of the following? See instructions . . . . | | ✔
  a The partnership owns a pass-through entity with current, or prior year carryover, excess business interest expense.
  b The partnership's aggregate average annual gross receipts (determined under section 448(c)) for the 3 tax years preceding the current tax year are more than $27 million and the partnership has business interest.
  c The partnership is a tax shelter (see instructions) and the partnership has business interest expense.
  If "Yes" to any, complete and attach Form 8990.

25 Is the partnership attaching Form 8996 to certify as a Qualified Opportunity Fund? . . . . | | ✔
  If "Yes," enter the amount from Form 8996, line 15 . . . . $

26 Enter the number of foreign partners subject to section 864(c)(8) as a result of transferring all or a portion of an interest in the partnership or of receiving a distribution from the partnership 0
  Complete Schedule K-3 (Form 1065), Part XIII, for each foreign partner subject to section 864(c)(8) on a transfer or distribution.

27 At any time during the tax year, were there any transfers between the partnership and its partners subject to the disclosure requirements of Regulations section 1.707-8? . . . . | | ✔

28 Since December 22, 2017, did a foreign corporation directly or indirectly acquire substantially all of the properties constituting a trade or business of your partnership, and was the ownership percentage (by vote or value) for purposes of section 7874 greater than 50% (for example, the partners held more than 50% of the stock of the foreign corporation)? If "Yes," list the ownership percentage by vote and by value. See instructions.
  Percentage: By vote: _____   By value: _____ | | ✔

29 How many Schedules K-1 and Schedules K-3 were not furnished or will not be furnished timely? _____ 0

30 Is the partnership electing out of the centralized partnership audit regime under section 6221(b)? See instructions. | | ✔
  If "Yes," the partnership must complete Schedule B-2 (Form 1065). Enter the total from Schedule B-2, Part III, line 3 . . . . _____
  If "No," complete Designation of Partnership Representative below.

Designation of Partnership Representative (see instructions)
Enter below the information for the partnership representative (PR) for the tax year covered by this return.

Name of PR   **Sarah Morton**

U.S. address of PR	**1609 Amber Way** **Charlotte, NC 28201**	U.S. phone number of PR	

If the PR is an entity, name of the designated individual for the PR

U.S. address of designated individual		U.S. phone number of designated individual	

Form **1065** (2022)

Figure 15-2: Filled-In Form 1065 (Page 4)

Form 1065 (2022)   Page **4**

		Schedule K	Partners' Distributive Share Items				Total amount
Income (Loss)	**1**	Ordinary business income (loss) (page 1, line 22)			**1**		18,424
	2	Net rental real estate income (loss) (attach Form 8825)			**2**		
	3a	Other gross rental income (loss)		**3a**			
	b	Expenses from other rental activities (attach statement)		**3b**			
	c	Other net rental income (loss). Subtract line 3b from line 3a			**3c**		
	4	Guaranteed payments: **a** Services **4a** 38,400 **b** Capital **4b**					
	c	Total. Add lines 4a and 4b			**4c**		38,400
	5	Interest income			**5**		1,100
	6	Dividends and dividend equivalents: **a** Ordinary dividends			**6a**		1,700
	b	Qualified dividends **6b** 1,700 **c** Dividend equivalents **6c**					
	7	Royalties			**7**		
	8	Net short-term capital gain (loss) (attach Schedule D (Form 1065))			**8**		
	9a	Net long-term capital gain (loss) (attach Schedule D (Form 1065))			**9a**		
	b	Collectibles (28%) gain (loss)		**9b**			
	c	Unrecaptured section 1250 gain (attach statement)		**9c**			
	10	Net section 1231 gain (loss) (attach Form 4797)			**10**		
	11	Other income (loss) (see instructions) Type:			**11**		
Deductions	**12**	Section 179 deduction (attach Form 4562)			**12**		
	13a	Contributions			**13a**		426
	b	Investment interest expense			**13b**		
	c	Section 59(e)(2) expenditures: **(1)** Type:_____ **(2)** Amount:			**13c(2)**		
	d	Other deductions (see instructions) Type:			**13d**		
Self-Employ-ment	**14a**	Net earnings (loss) from self-employment			**14a**		56,824
	b	Gross farming or fishing income			**14b**		
	c	Gross nonfarm income			**14c**		106,154
Credits	**15a**	Low-income housing credit (section 42(j)(5))			**15a**		
	b	Low-income housing credit (other)			**15b**		
	c	Qualified rehabilitation expenditures (rental real estate) (attach Form 3468, if applicable)			**15c**		
	d	Other rental real estate credits (see instructions) Type:			**15d**		
	e	Other rental credits (see instructions) Type:			**15e**		
	f	Other credits (see instructions) Type:			**15f**		
Inter-national	**16**	Attach Schedule K-2 (Form 1065), Partners' Distributive Share Items—International, and check this box to indicate that you are reporting items of international tax relevance . . . . . ☐					
Alternative Minimum Tax (AMT) Items	**17a**	Post-1986 depreciation adjustment			**17a**		
	b	Adjusted gain or loss			**17b**		
	c	Depletion (other than oil and gas)			**17c**		
	d	Oil, gas, and geothermal properties—gross income			**17d**		
	e	Oil, gas, and geothermal properties—deductions			**17e**		
	f	Other AMT items (attach statement)			**17f**		
Other Information	**18a**	Tax-exempt interest income			**18a**		50
	b	Other tax-exempt income			**18b**		
	c	Nondeductible expenses			**18c**		
	19a	Distributions of cash and marketable securities			**19a**		7,000
	b	Distributions of other property			**19b**		
	20a	Investment income			**20a**		2,800
	b	Investment expenses			**20b**		
	c	Other items and amounts (attach statement)					
	21	Total foreign taxes paid or accrued			**21**		

Form **1065** (2022)

Figure 15-2: Filled-In Form 1065 (Page 5)

Form 1065 (2022)   Page **5**

Analysis of Net Income (Loss) per Return

1	Net income (loss). Combine Schedule K, lines 1 through 11. From the result, subtract the sum of Schedule K, lines 12 through 13d, and 21				**1**	59,198

2	Analysis by partner type:	**(i)** Corporate	**(ii)** Individual (active)	**(iii)** Individual (passive)	**(iv)** Partnership	**(v)** Exempt Organization	**(vi)** Nominee/Other
a	General partners		59,198				
b	Limited partners						

Schedule L — Balance Sheets per Books

	Assets	Beginning of tax year (a)	(b)	End of tax year (c)	(d)
1	Cash		4,616		17,347
2a	Trade notes and accounts receivable	10,615		11,918	
b	Less allowance for bad debts	600	10,015	720	11,198
3	Inventories		34,969		32,304
4	U.S. Government obligations				
5	Tax-exempt securities				
6	Other current assets (attach statement) . . .				
7a	Loans to partners (or persons related to partners) .				
b	Mortgage and real estate loans . . .				
8	Other investments (attach statement) . . .		9,465		9,465
9a	Buildings and other depreciable assets . . .	11,900		11,900	
b	Less accumulated depreciation . . .	3,850	8,050	5,400	6,500
10a	Depletable assets				
b	Less accumulated depletion . . .				
11	Land (net of any amortization)				
12a	Intangible assets (amortizable only)				
b	Less accumulated amortization . . .				
13	Other assets (attach statement)		1,475		
14	Total assets		68,590		78,340
	Liabilities and Capital				
15	Accounts payable		7,639		8,623
16	Mortgages, notes, bonds payable in less than 1 year		5,000		
17	Other current liabilities (attach statement)		479		397
18	All nonrecourse loans				
19a	Loans from partners (or persons related to partners) .				
b	Mortgages, notes, bonds payable in 1 year or more .				
20	Other liabilities (attach statement)				
21	Partners' capital accounts		55,472		69,320
22	Total liabilities and capital		68,590		78,340

Schedule M-1 — Reconciliation of Income (Loss) per Books With Analysis of Net Income (Loss) per Return

Note: The partnership may be required to file Schedule M-3. See instructions.

1	Net income (loss) per books	20,848	**6**	Income recorded on books this year not included on Schedule K, lines 1 through 11 (itemize):	
2	Income included on Schedule K, lines 1, 2, 3c, 5, 6a, 7, 8, 9a, 10, and 11, not recorded on books this year (itemize): _____		**a**	Tax-exempt interest $ _____ 50	50
3	Guaranteed payments (other than health insurance)	38,400	**7**	Deductions included on Schedule K, lines 1 through 13d, and 21, not charged against book income this year (itemize):	
4	Expenses recorded on books this year not included on Schedule K, lines 1 through 13d, and 21 (itemize):		**a**	Depreciation $ _____	
a	Depreciation $ _____		**8**	Add lines 6 and 7	50
b	Travel and entertainment $ _____		**9**	Income (loss) (Analysis of Net Income (Loss), line 1). Subtract line 8 from line 5	59,198
5	Add lines 1 through 4	59,248			

Schedule M-2 — Analysis of Partners' Capital Accounts

1	Balance at beginning of year . . .	55,472	**6**	Distributions: **a** Cash	7,000
2	Capital contributed: **a** Cash . . .			**b** Property	
	b Property . .		**7**	Other decreases (itemize): _____	
3	Net income (loss) (see instructions) .	20,848			
4	Other increases (itemize): _____		**8**	Add lines 6 and 7	7,000
5	Add lines 1 through 4	76,320	**9**	Balance at end of year. Subtract line 8 from line 5	69,320

Form **1065** (2022)

¶1502.10   SCHEDULE K ITEMS

Those items of partnership income and expense not included in the calculation of ordinary income are separately stated items. Since the partnership is not a tax-paying entity, its credits are also separately stated. Schedule K provides a summary of these items as well as the partnership's ordinary income or loss.

Income Items

The income items requiring separate statement are those that receive special treatment or have limitations imposed at the partner level (see ¶1502.05). The partners combine their shares of the partnership income items with their own income items and then apply the special treatment or limitations. The resulting amounts appear on the partner's tax return.

Deductions

Most partnership expenses are incurred in the production of ordinary income. Therefore, there are only a few separately stated deductions. The expense items that must be separately stated on Schedule K include:

1. Section 179 deduction
2. Deductions related to portfolio income
3. AMT adjustments and preferences
4. Nondeductible expenses
5. Charitable contributions

As previously noted, charitable contributions are not deductible by the partnership in computing ordinary income. Rather, the partnership informs each partner on Schedule K-1 of the partner's share of contributions subject to the 60%, 30%, and 20% limitations. (See Chapter 5 for some temporary rules that apply only to 2020 and 2021.) Individual partners combine their shares with their personal contributions and claim these as itemized deductions (¶506.04). Corporate partners combine their shares of the partnership contributions with their own and apply the 10% taxable income limit (¶1402.06).

¶1502.11   OTHER SCHEDULES

A partnership is required to complete Schedules L, M-1, and M-2 only if it answers "No" to question 4 on Schedule B. This question asks whether each of the following four conditions have been met. Thus, if any of the following conditions are not met, the partnership must complete Schedules L, M-1, and M-2, as well as Item F (total assets) on page 1 of Form 1065:

1. The partnership's total receipts for the year were less than $250,000;
2. The partnership's total assets at the end of the year were less than $1 million;
3. Schedules K-1 are filed with the return and given to the partners on or before the due date (including extensions) for the partnership return; and
4. The partnership is not filing and is not required to file Schedule M-3.

Schedule L

Schedule L shows the balance sheet at the beginning and end of the tax year. Some items require supporting schedules, such as other assets and other liabilities. The amounts on Schedule L should agree with the books of the partnership, regardless of whether the accounts are kept in accordance with income tax law. Figure 15-2 shows the balance sheet for M&B Partnership:

Schedule M-1

Schedule M-1, Reconciliation of Income (Loss) per Books With Income (Loss) per Return, reconciles the financial net income (loss) with the income (loss) reported on the Analysis of Net Income (Loss), line 1 (found at the top of Form 1065, page 5). This amount includes ordinary income from page 1 plus separately stated income and deductions reported on Schedule K. Income and expenses appearing on the books but not on the tax return are disclosed in Schedule M-1. Also, income and expenses appearing on Form 1065 but not included in financial net income (loss) are reconciling items shown on Schedule M-1. The amount on Schedule M-1 (line 9) is also the amount on line 1 in the "Analysis of Net Income (Loss)" section found at the top of page 5 (Form 1065).

Most Schedule M-1 reconciliations tend to be more complex than the one in Figure 15-2. Other reconciling items include differences in book and tax depreciation, and differences in computing bad debt expense.

Schedule M-2

Schedule M-2, Analysis of Partners' Capital Accounts, reconciles the beginning capital accounts balance to the ending balance. The beginning and ending balances appear on the balance sheets in Schedule L (line 21). The amounts in Schedule M-2 should agree with the partnership's books. The partnership attaches a statement to Form 1065 to explain any differences.

Schedule K-1 (Form 1065)

The partnership prepares a Schedule K-1, Partner's Share of Income, Deductions, Credits, etc., for each partner. This schedule informs the partners of their respective share of the items reported on Schedule K. The line numbers on the Schedule K and Schedule K-1 are coordinated to make transferring the information easier. For example, guaranteed payments appear on line 4 of both Schedule K and Schedule K-1.

Schedule K-2 and Schedule K-3 (Form 1065)

In 2021, the IRS introduced draft versions of Schedule K-2 and Schedule K-3, for inclusion with Form 1065. Initially it appeared that these forms, which are massive and in length and detail, would apply only to partnerships with international dealings. However, in early 2022, when the final schedules arrived, it appeared that all partnerships would need to file these forms. For each Form 1065, the partnership would need to file Schedule K-2, which is 19 pages in length. Moreover, the partnership must include with its return and provide each partner with a copy of Schedule K-3. Schedule K-3 is 20 pages long.

Before 2022, Form 1065 Schedule K and Schedule K-1 each provided a line for reporting international tax information, and the partnership was obliged to provide a plain paper statement to each partner with the relevant information. Such information includes:

1. Gross income from sales;
2. Gross income from services;
3. Gross income from real estate rents;
4. Other gross rental income;
5. Interest income;
6. Nonqualified dividend income;
7. Qualified dividend income;
8. Gross income from royalties and license fees;
9. Gains, further segregated into net short-term capital gain, net long-term capital gain, gains from collectibles, unrecaptured Section 1250 gain and net Section 1231 gain;
10. Expenses allocable to sales;
11. Expenses allocable to service;

12. Losses, further segregated into net short-term capital loss, net long-term capital loss, loss from collectibles, and net Section 1231 loss;
13. Other gains;
14. Other losses;
15. Rental expenses, other than depreciation;
16. Depreciation allocable to rents;
17. Royalty expenses, other than depreciation;
18. Depreciation allocable to royalties;
19. Other depreciation;
20. Charitable contributions;
21. Various categories of allocable interest; and
22. Special international items, under Sections 986, 987, 988, 951, 951A, etc.

Even if the partnership has no foreign-source income, it must categorize each of its sources of income and allocable deductions. If the partnership has any income from foreign sources, it must fill each of the above categories into a matrix, and segregate each category by:

1. U.S. source;
2. Foreign branch category;
3. Foreign passive category;
4. Foreign general category; and,
5. Other foreign category.

There are also special rules for research and experimentation expenditure, which are no longer deductible under U.S. tax laws. The partnership must separate the gross receipts of the activities associated with research and experimentation by SIC Code. The partnership must also apportion interest expenses, payments to some related parties, payments associated with business interest expense, investment interest expense, etc. To comply with interest allocation rules, the partnership must determine the average value of assets associated with these categories of income.

For 2021 returns, a partnership is excused from filing these schedules, if it meets all of these conditions:

• In tax year 2021, the partnership has no foreign activity, including foreign taxes paid or accrued or ownership of assets that generate, have generated or may reasonably be expected to generate foreign-source income;
• In tax year 2020, the partnership did not provide to its partners nor did the partners request the information regarding Schedules K and K-1 line; and
• The partnership has no knowledge that the partners are requesting such information for tax year 2021.

However, even if the partnership meets all of these qualifications, it must provide this information to any partner who requests it, even if the partnership has already filed its return. At the time of publication of this book, the IRS has not announced any exemption from Schedules K-2 and K-3 for the 2022 taxable year.

¶1502.12   FILLED-IN SCHEDULE K-2 (FORM 1065)

Although M&B has no international assets or income, it must fill out certain parts of Schedule K-2. The rationale is that the Foreign Tax Credit requires each individual or corporation to segregate gross receipts, deductions and other items by country of origin, including the U.S. Therefore, page 1 contains a checklist that indicates which of the 11 parts apply. Most of these are relevant only to partnerships with foreign-source income or assets. However, Parts II and III apply to U.S. partnerships with no international dealings. Part III covers research and experimentation expenditures, which are no longer currently deductible under U.S. tax laws, but are deductible in many other countries.

If a partner has more than $600 in foreign-source income, that partner must attach Form 1116 to his or her or its tax return. Form 1116 is a matrix of various income and deduction items by type and by source country. Schedule K-2 is designed to feed directly into that form.

NFORMATION FOR FIGURE 15-3:

Line # (Form 1065 Schedule K-2, page 1)
Line or Box   (Form 1065 Schedule K-2 , page 1, Part I)   M&B Checks

A	Foreign partnership	No
B	Qualified derivatives dealer	No
C	Description	
1	Part applies only to certain international transactions	No
2	Foreign Tax Credit Limitation (All sources of gross income and deductions)	Yes
3	Other Information for Preparation of Form 1116 or 1118	No
4	Information on Partners' Section 250 Deduction With Respect to Foreign-Derived Intangible Income (FDII)	No
5	Distributions From Foreign Corporations to Partnership	No
6	Information on Partners' Section 951(a)(1) and Section 951A Inclusions	No
7	Information To Complete Form 8621	No
8	Partnership's Interest in Foreign Corporation Income (Section 960)	No
9	Partners' Information for Base Erosion and Anti-Abuse Tax (Section 59A)	No
10	Foreign Partners' Character and Source of Income and Deductions	No
11	Section 871(m) Covered Partnerships	No

Lines A, B and C are country codes

Wherever M&B reports income, gain, loss or deduction it enters "US"

Line	(Form 1065 Schedule K-2, page 1 Part II)	Column (a)	Column (g)	Sourc
1A	Sales	106,299	106,299	Page 1 Line 8

Figure 15-3: Filled-In Schedule K-2 (Form 1065) (Page 1)

SCHEDULE K-2 (Form 1065)	Partners' Distributive Share Items—International	OMB No. 1545-0123
Department of the Treasury Internal Revenue Service	Attach to Form 1065. Go to *www.irs.gov/Form1065* for instructions and the latest information.	2022

DRAFT AS OF September 29, 2022 DO NOT (watermark)

Name of partnership	Employer identification number (EIN)
M & B Partnership	70-0464077

A Is the partnership a withholding foreign partnership?   ☐ Yes ☐ No   If "Yes," enter your WP-EIN:

B Is the partnership (including the home office or any branch) a qualified derivatives dealer?   ☐ Yes ☑ No   If "Yes," enter your QI-EIN:

C Check to indicate the parts of Schedule K-2 that apply.

		Yes	No			Yes	No
1	Does Part I apply? If "Yes," complete and attach Part I . . . **1**			7	Does Part VII apply? If "Yes," complete and attach Part VII . . . **7**		
2	Does Part II apply? If "Yes," complete and attach Part II . . . **2**			8	Does Part VIII apply? If "Yes," complete and attach Part VIII . . . **8**		
3	Does Part III apply? If "Yes," complete and attach Part III . . . **3**			9	Does Part IX apply? If "Yes," complete and attach Part IX . . . **9**		
4	Does Part IV apply? If "Yes," complete and attach Part IV . . . **4**			10	Does Part X apply? If "Yes," complete and attach Part X . . . **10**		
5	Does Part V apply? If "Yes," complete and attach Part V . . . **5**			11	Does Part XI apply? If "Yes," complete and attach Part XI . . . **11**		
6	Does Part VI apply? If "Yes," complete and attach Part VI . . . **6**			12	Reserved for future use **12**		

Part I   Partnership's Other Current Year International Information

Check box(es) for additional specified attachments. See instructions.

☐ 1. Gain on personal property sale	☐ 5. High-taxed income	☐ 8. Form 5471 information
☐ 2. Foreign oil and gas taxes	☐ 6. Section 267A disallowed deduction	☐ 9. Other forms
☐ 3. Splitter arrangements	☐ 7. Form 8858 information	☐ 10. Partner loan transactions
☐ 4. Foreign tax translation		

☐ 11. Dual consolidated loss
☐ 12. Reserved for future use
☐ 13. Other international items (attach description and statement)

Part II   Foreign Tax Credit Limitation

Section 1—Gross Income

Description	(a) U.S. source	Foreign Source				(f) Sourced by partner	(g) Total
		(b) Foreign branch category income	(c) Passive category income	(d) General category income	(e) Other (category code)		
1 Sales							
A US	106,299						106,299
B							
C							
2 Gross income from performance of services							
A							
B							
C							
3 Gross rental real estate income							
A							
B							
C							
4 Other gross rental income							
A							
B							
C							

For Paperwork Reduction Act Notice, see the Instructions for Form 1065.   Cat. No. 73927C   Schedule K-2 (Form 1065) 2022

Figure 15-3: Filled-In Schedule K-2 (Form 1065) (Page 2)

Line	(Form 1065 Schedule K-2, page 2 Part II)	Column (a)	Column (g)	Source
5	Guaranteed payments	38,400	38,400	Schedule K line 4c
6A	Interest Income	1,100	1,100	Schedule K line 5
7A	Dividends (not qualified dividends	1,700	1,700	Schedule K line 6a

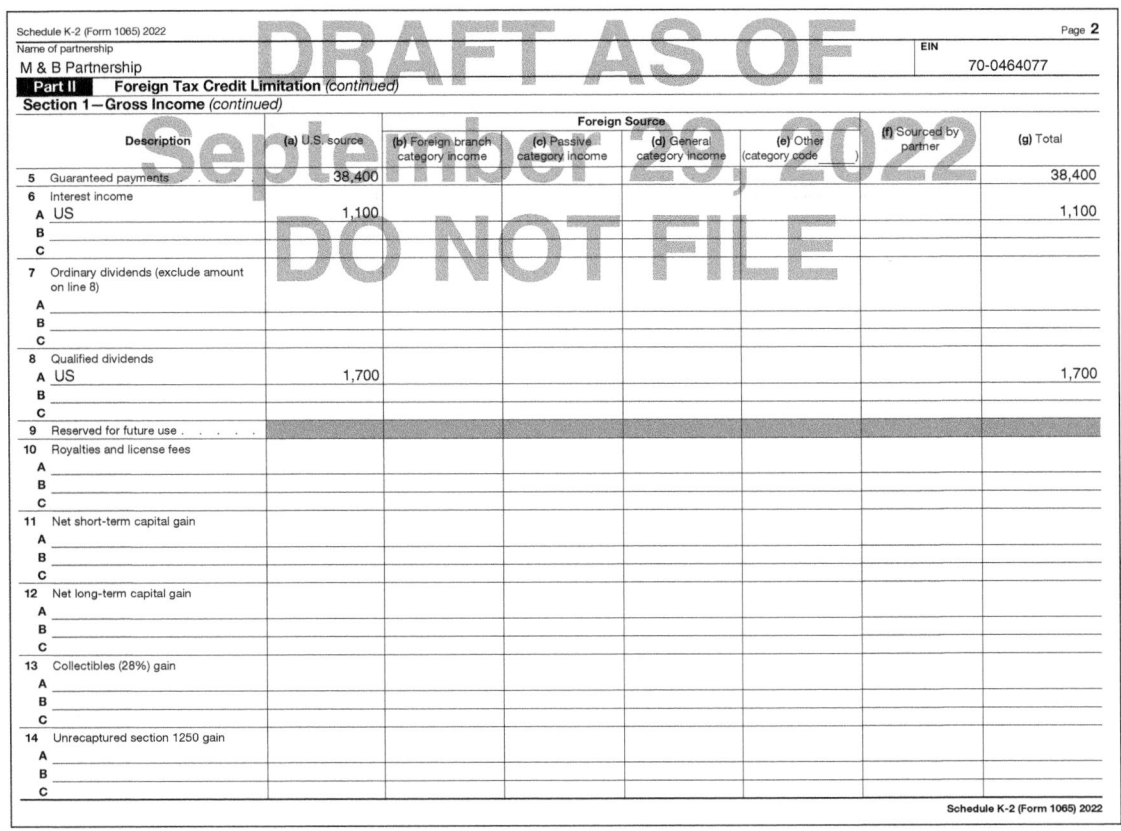

Figure 15-3: Filled-In Schedule K-2 (Form 1065) (Page 3)

Line	(Form 1065 Schedule K-2, page 3 Part III)	Column (a)	Column (g)	Source
24	Total gross income	147,499	147,499	Sum of lines 1 through 23

Schedule K-2 (Form 1065) 2022   Page 3

Name of partnership: M & B Partnership

EIN: 70-0464077

Part II Foreign Tax Credit Limitation (continued)

Section 1—Gross Income (continued)

| Description | (a) U.S. source | Foreign Source | | | | (f) Sourced by partner | (g) Total |
		(b) Foreign branch category income	(c) Passive category income	(d) General category income	(e) Other (category code)		
15 Net section 1231 gain							
A							
B							
C							
16 Section 986(c) gain							
17 Section 987 gain							
18 Section 988 gain							
19 Section 951(a) inclusions							
A							
B							
C							
20 Other income (see instructions)							
A							
B							
C							
21 Reserved for future use							
A							
B							
C							
22 Reserved for future use							
A							
B							
C							
23 Reserved for future use							
A							
B							
C							
24 Total gross income (combine lines 1 through 23)	147,499						147,499
A US	147,499						147,499
B							
C							

Schedule K-2 (Form 1065) 2022

Figure 15-3: Filled-In Schedule K-2 (Form 1065) (Page 4)

Line	(Form 1065 Schedule K-2, page 4 Part II)	Column (a)	Column (g)	Source
25	Expenses allocable to sales income	86,072	86,072	Deductions on page 1, except for lines 15 and 16
37	Depreciation	1,550	1,550	Page 1 line 16a
38	Charitable contributions	425	425	Schedule K line 13a
41	Interest expense – business	N/A	253/2	Page 1 line 15

Schedule K-2 (Form 1065) 2022   Page **4**

Name of partnership		EIN
M & B Partnership		70-0464077

Part II   Foreign Tax Credit Limitation *(continued)*

Section 2—Deductions

	Description	(a) U.S. source	Foreign Source (b) Foreign branch category income	(c) Passive category income	(d) General category income	(e) Other (category code____)	(f) Sourced by partner	(g) Total
25	Expenses allocable to sales income	86,072						86,072
26	Expenses allocable to gross income from performances of services							
27	Net short-term capital loss							
28	Net long-term capital loss							
29	Collectibles loss							
30	Net section 1231 loss							
31	Other losses							
32	Research & experimental (R&E) expenses							
A	SIC code:							
B	SIC code:							
C	SIC code:							
33	Allocable rental expenses—depreciation, depletion, and amortization							
34	Allocable rental expenses—other than depreciation, depletion, and amortization							
35	Allocable royalty and licensing expenses—depreciation, depletion, and amortization							
36	Allocable royalty and licensing expenses—other than depreciation, depletion, and amortization							
37	Depreciation not included on line 33 or 35	1,550						1,550
38	Charitable contributions	426						426
39	Interest expense specifically allocable under Regulations section 1.861-10(e)							
40	Other interest expense specifically allocable under Regulations section 1.861-10T							
41	Other interest expense—business							253
42	Other interest expense—investment							
43	Other interest expense—passive activity							
44	Section 59(e)(2) expenditures, excluding R&E expenses on line 32							
45	Foreign taxes not creditable but deductible							

Schedule K-2 (Form 1065) 2022

Figure 15-3: Filled-In Schedule K-2 (Form 1065) (Page 5)

Line	(Form 1065 Schedule K-2, page 5 Part II)	Column (a)	Column (g)	Source
54	Total deductions	88,047	88,300	Lines 25 through 53 (interest is not reported in column a)
55	Net income	59,452	59,199	Line 24 less line 54. Column (g) reconciles to analysis of net income, page 5, line 1

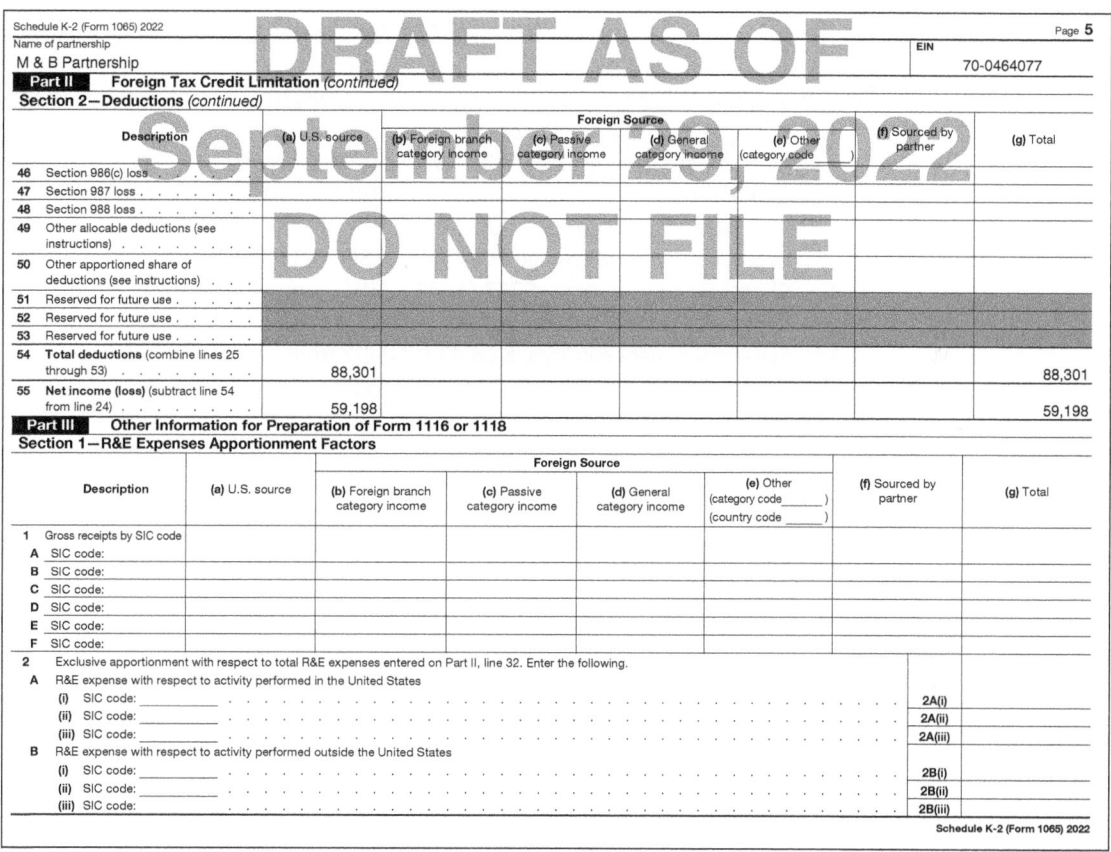

Figure 15-3: Form 1065 Schedule K-2: Pages 6 through 19 do not apply to any of the problems in *Essentials of Federal Income Taxation*. This chapter does not include them in any examples or problems.

¶1502.13   FILLED-IN SCHEDULE K-1 (FORM 1065)

 ### INFORMATION FOR FIGURE 15-4:

Figure 15-4 shows Schedule K-1 for one partner of M&B Partnership. Since Doug's Schedule K-1 would resemble Sarah's, only Sarah's K-1 is shown here.

Line #

K: Partner's share of recourse liabilities at the end of the year, **$4,510** (as a general partner, Sarah is responsible for 50% of the partnership's $9,020 of total liabilities)

L: Beginning capital account balance, **$27,736** (source: last year's ending balance) Current year increase or decrease, **$10,424** ($20,848 book net income × 50%) *Because M&B answered "Yes" to Question 4 on Schedule B of Form 1065, M&B is not required to complete Item L on Schedule K-1. Item L is completed here for illustration purposes.*

1: Ordinary business income (loss), **$9,212** ($18,424 × 50%)

4: Guaranteed payments to partners, **$19,200** ($1,600 × 12 months)

5: Interest income, **$550** ($1,100 × 50%)

6: Dividends (both ordinary and qualified), **$850** ($1,700 × 50%)

13: Charitable contributions, **$213** ($426 × 50%; contributions subject to the 50% AGI limit are designated Code "A" according to the instructions for Schedule K-1)

14: Self-employment earnings, **$28,412** ($9,212 from line 1 + $19,200 from line 4)

18: Code A, Tax-exempt income, **$25** ($50 × 50%)

19: Distributions, **$7,000** (provided) – Cash distributions are designated Code "A"

20: Code V, QBI, 50% of Form 1065, page 1, line 22, **$9,212**
Code V, W-2 wages, 50$ of Form 1065, page 1, line 9, **$15,625**
Code V, Unadjusted basis of property, 50% of Form 1065, Schedule L, line 9a, column c, **$5,950**
Code A, Investment Income, 50% of $2,800, **$1,400**

Figure 15-4: Filled-In Schedule K-1 (Form 1065)

651121

☐ Final K-1	☐ Amended K-1

OMB No. 1545-0123

Schedule K-1 (Form 1065)
Department of the Treasury
Internal Revenue Service

2022

For calendar year 2022, or tax year

beginning / / 2022 ending / /

Partner's Share of Income, Deductions, Credits, etc. See separate instructions.

Part I Information About the Partnership

A Partnership's employer identification number
70-0464077

B Partnership's name, address, city, state, and ZIP code

M & B Partnership
524 Southside
Charlotte, NC 28201

C IRS center where partnership filed return: Kansas City

D ☐ Check if this is a publicly traded partnership (PTP)

Part II Information About the Partner

E Partner's SSN or TIN (Do not use TIN of a disregarded entity. See instructions.)
294-00-8321

F Name, address, city, state, and ZIP code for partner entered in E. See instructions.

Sarah Morton
1609 Amber Way
Charlotte, NC 28201

G ☐ General partner or LLC member-manager ☐ Limited partner or other LLC member

H1 ☐ Domestic partner ☐ Foreign partner

H2 ☐ If the partner is a disregarded entity (DE), enter the partner's:
TIN _____ Name _____

I1 What type of entity is this partner? _____

I2 If this partner is a retirement plan (IRA/SEP/Keogh/etc.), check here ☐

J Partner's share of profit, loss, and capital (see instructions):

	Beginning	Ending
Profit	50 %	50 %
Loss	50 %	50 %
Capital	50 %	50 %

Check if decrease is due to sale or exchange of partnership interest ☐

K Partner's share of liabilities:

	Beginning	Ending
Nonrecourse	$ 0	$ 0
Qualified nonrecourse financing	$ 0	$ 0
Recourse	$ 6,559	$ 4,510

Check this box if item K includes liability amounts from lower-tier partnerships ☐

L Partner's Capital Account Analysis

Beginning capital account	$ 27,736
Capital contributed during the year	$
Current year net income (loss)	$ 10,424
Other increase (decrease) (attach explanation)	$
Withdrawals and distributions	$ (7,000)
Ending capital account	$ 31,160

M Did the partner contribute property with a built-in gain (loss)?
☐ Yes ☐ No If "Yes," attach statement. See instructions.

N Partner's Share of Net Unrecognized Section 704(c) Gain or (Loss)
Beginning $ 0
Ending $ 0

Part III Partner's Share of Current Year Income, Deductions, Credits, and Other Items

1	Ordinary business income (loss)	9,212
2	Net rental real estate income (loss)	
3	Other net rental income (loss)	
4a	Guaranteed payments for services	19,200
4b	Guaranteed payments for capital	
4c	Total guaranteed payments	19,200
5	Interest income	550
6a	Ordinary dividends	850
6b	Qualified dividends	850
6c	Dividend equivalents	
7	Royalties	
8	Net short-term capital gain (loss)	
9a	Net long-term capital gain (loss)	
9b	Collectibles (28%) gain (loss)	
9c	Unrecaptured section 1250 gain	
10	Net section 1231 gain (loss)	
11	Other income (loss)	
12	Section 179 deduction	
13	Other deductions	213

14	Self-employment earnings (loss)	A 28,412
15	Credits	
16	Schedule K-3 is attached if checked ☐	
17	Alternative minimum tax (AMT) items	
18	Tax-exempt income and nondeductible expenses	A 25
19	Distributions	A 7,000
20	Other information	V QB Income 9,212
		V W-2 Wages 15,625
		V UBIA 5,950
		A 1,400
21	Foreign taxes paid or accrued	
22	☐ More than one activity for at-risk purposes*	
23	☐ More than one activity for passive activity purposes*	

*See attached statement for additional information.

For IRS Use Only

For Paperwork Reduction Act Notice, see the Instructions for Form 1065. www.irs.gov/Form1065 Cat. No. 11394R Schedule K-1 (Form 1065) 2022

¶1502.13

¶1502.14   FILLED-IN SCHEDULE K-3 (FORM 1065)

Schedule K-3 follows the same format as the Schedule K-2. There are a few differences, where an item is relevant to the partnership but not to a partner, and vice versa. However, for a partnership with no international dealings, Schedule K-3 merely allocates each item reported on the Schedule K-2 to each partner. In essence the relationship between Schedule K-2 and Schedule K-3 is analogous to the relationship between Schedule K and Schedule K-1. In the M&B examples, the partnership allocated each pass through item 50% to each partner. The guaranteed payments were also equal between each partner. Therefore , the Schedule K-3 for this example is easy to follow, and only one is necessary for this text. However, this is not always the case. In realistic situations, there may be several items that are allocated in different proportions.

 ## INFORMATION FOR FIGURE 15-5:

Figure 15-5: Filled-In Schedule K-3 (Form 1065) (Page 1)

Line or Box	(Form 1065 Schedule K-3 , page 1, Part I)	
A	Partnership Employer Identification Number	
B	Partnership Name & address	
C	Partner Social Security Number or TIN	
D	Partnership Name & address	
E		M&B Checks
1	Part applies only to certain international transactions,	No
2	Foreign Tax Credit Limitation (All sources of gross income and deductions),	Yes
3	Other Information for Preparation of Form 1116 or 1118	No
4	Information on Partners' Section 250 Deduction With Respect to Foreign-Derived Intangible Income (FDII)	No
5	Distributions From Foreign Corporations to Partnership	No
6	Information on Partners' Section 951(a)(1) and Section 951A Inclusions	No
7	Information To Complete Form 8621	No
8	Partnership's Interest in Foreign Corporation Income (Section 960)	No
9	Partners' Information for Base Erosion and Anti-Abuse Tax (Section 59A)	No
10	Foreign Partners' Character and Source of Income and Deductions	No
11	Section 871(m) Covered Partnerships	No
12	Reserved	
13	Foreign Partner's Distributive Share of Deemed Sale Items on Transfer of Partnership Interest	No

Figure 15-5: Filled-In Schedule K-3 (Form 1065) (Page 1)

☐ Final K-3	☐ Amended K-3

Schedule K-3
(Form 1065)

Department of the Treasury
Internal Revenue Service

Partner's Share of Income, Deductions, Credits, etc.—International

For calendar year 2022, or tax year beginning / / 2022 , ending / /
See separate instructions.

OMB No. 1545-0123

2022

Information About the Partnership

A Partnership's employer identification number (EIN)

70-0464077

B Partnership's name, address, city, state, and ZIP code

M & B Partnership
524 Southside
Raleigh, NC 27604-1470

Information About the Partner

C Partner's SSN or Taxpayer Identification Number (TIN) (Do not use TIN of a disregarded entity. See instructions.)

294-00-8321

D Name, address, city, state, and ZIP code for partner entered in C. See instructions.

Sarah Morton
1609 Amber Way
Charlotte, NC 28201

E Check to indicate the parts of Schedule K-3 that apply.

			Yes	No
1	Does Part I apply? If "Yes," complete and attach Part I	1		✔
2	Does Part II apply? If "Yes," complete and attach Part II	2	✔	
3	Does Part III apply? If "Yes," complete and attach Part III	3		✔
4	Does Part IV apply? If "Yes," complete and attach Part IV	4		✔
5	Does Part V apply? If "Yes," complete and attach Part V	5		✔
6	Does Part VI apply? If "Yes," complete and attach Part VI	6		✔
7	Does Part VII apply? If "Yes," complete and attach Part VII	7		✔
8	Does Part VIII apply? If "Yes," complete and attach Part VIII	8		✔
9	Does Part IX apply? If "Yes," complete and attach Part IX	9		✔
10	Does Part X apply? If "Yes," complete and attach Part X	10		✔
11	Does Part XI apply? If "Yes," complete and attach Part XI	11		✔
12	Reserved for future use	12		
13	Does Part XIII apply? If "Yes," complete and attach Part XIII	13		✔

For IRS Use Only

For Paperwork Reduction Act Notice, see the Instructions for Form 1065. www.irs.gov/Form1065   Cat. No. 74715S   **Schedule K-3 (Form 1065) 2022**

¶1502.14

FIGURE 15-5: Filled-In Schedule K-3 (Form 1065) (Page 2)

Wherever M&B reports income, gain, loss or deduction, it enters "US"

Line	(Form 1065 Schedule K-3, page 2 Part II)	Column (a)	Column (g)	Source Schedule K-2 x partner's distributive share
1A	Sales	53,149.5	53,149.5	Page 1 line 1A
5	Guaranteed payments	19,200	19,200	Page 2 line 5
6A	Interest Income	550	550	Page 2 line 6A
7A	Dividends (not qualified dividends	850	850	

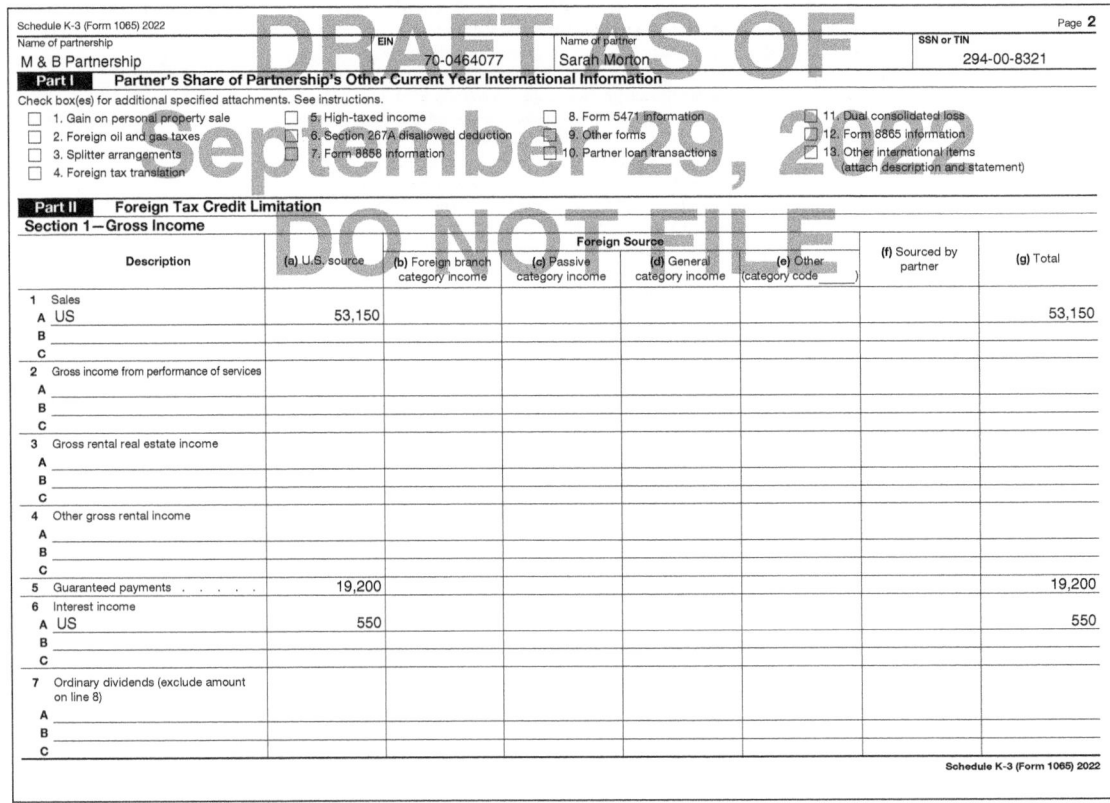

FIGURE 15-5: Filled-In Schedule K-3 (Form 1065) (Page 3)

Schedule K-3 (Form 1065) 2022

Page **3**

Name of partnership		EIN		Name of partner		SSN or TIN
M & B Partnership		70-0464077		Sarah Morton		

Part II   **Foreign Tax Credit Limitation** *(continued)*

Section 1—Gross Income *(continued)*

Description	(a) U.S. source	Foreign Source				(f) Sourced by partner	(g) Total
		(b) Foreign branch category income	(c) Passive category income	(d) General category income	(e) Other (category code___)		
8 Qualified dividends							
A US	850						850
B							
C							
9 Reserved for future use							
10 Royalties and license fees							
A							
B							
C							
11 Net short-term capital gain							
A							
B							
C							
12 Net long-term capital gain							
A							
B							
C							
13 Collectibles (28%) gain							
A							
B							
C							
14 Unrecaptured section 1250 gain							
A							
B							
C							
15 Net section 1231 gain							
A							
B							
C							

Schedule K-3 (Form 1065) 2022

¶1502.14

FIGURE 15-5: Filled-In Schedule K-3 (Form 1065) (Page 4)

Wherever M&B reports income, gain, loss or deduction, it enters "US"

Line	(Form 1065 Schedule K-3, page 4 Part II)	Column (a)	Column (g)	Source
24	Total gross income	147,499	73,749.5	Sum of line 1 through 23

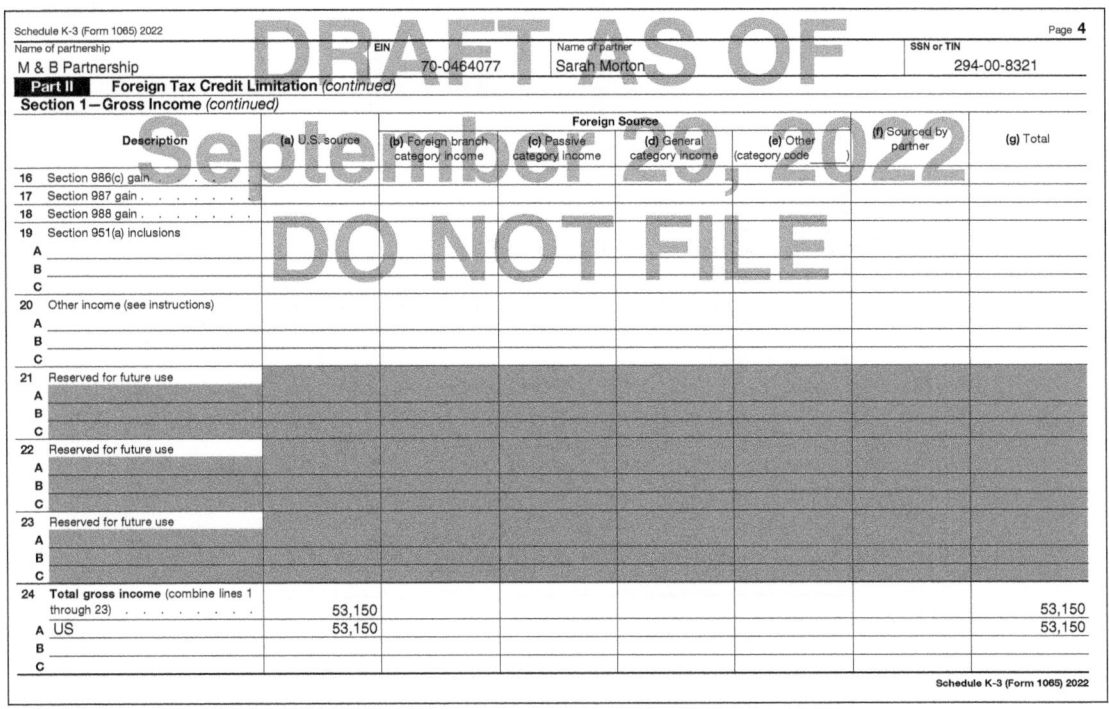

Figure 15-5: Filled-In Schedule K-3 (Form 1065) (Page 5)

Wherever M&B reports income, gain, loss or deduction, it enters "US"

Line	(Form 1065 Schedule K-2, page 4 Part II)	Column (a)	Column (g)	Source Schedule K-2 x partner's distributive share
25	Expenses allocable to sales income	86,072	43,036	Page 4 line 25
37	Depreciation	1,550	775	Page 4 line 37
38	Charitable contributions	425	212.5	Page 4 line 38
41	Interest expense—business	N/A	126.5	Page 4 line 41

Schedule K-3 (Form 1065) 2022 — Page 5

Name of partnership: M & B Partnership EIN: 70-0464077 Name of partner: Sarah Morton SSN or TIN: 294-00-8321

Part II — Foreign Tax Credit Limitation *(continued)*

Section 2—Deductions

	Description	(a) U.S. source	Foreign Source				(f) Sourced by partner	(g) Total
			(b) Foreign branch category income	(c) Passive category income	(d) General category income	(e) Other (category code)		
25	Expenses allocable to sales income	43,036						43,036
26	Expenses allocable to gross income from performances of services							
27	Net short-term capital loss							
28	Net long-term capital loss							
29	Collectibles loss							
30	Net section 1231 loss							
31	Other losses							
32	Research & experimental (R&E) expenses							
A	SIC code:							
B	SIC code:							
C	SIC code:							
33	Allocable rental expenses—depreciation, depletion, and amortization							
34	Allocable rental expenses—other than depreciation, depletion, and amortization							
35	Allocable royalty and licensing expenses—depreciation, depletion, and amortization							
36	Allocable royalty and licensing expenses—other than depreciation, depletion, and amortization							
37	Depreciation not included on line 33 or 35	775						775
38	Charitable contributions	213						213
39	Interest expense specifically allocable under Regulations section 1.861-10(e)							
40	Other interest expense specifically allocable under Regulations section 1.861-10T							
41	Other interest expense—business							
42	Other interest expense—investment							
43	Other interest expense—passive activity							
44	Section 59(e)(2) expenditures, excluding R&E expenses on line 32							
45	Foreign taxes not creditable but deductible							

Schedule K-3 (Form 1065) 2022

Figure 15-5: Filled-In Schedule K-3 (Form 1065) (Page 6)

Wherever M&B reports income, gain, loss or deduction, it enters "US"

Line	(Form 1065 Schedule K-2, page 5 Part II)	Column (a)	Column (g)	Source
54	Total deductions	44,023.5	44,150	Lines 25 through 53 (interest is not reported in column a)
55	Net income	29,726	29,599.5	Line 24 less line 54

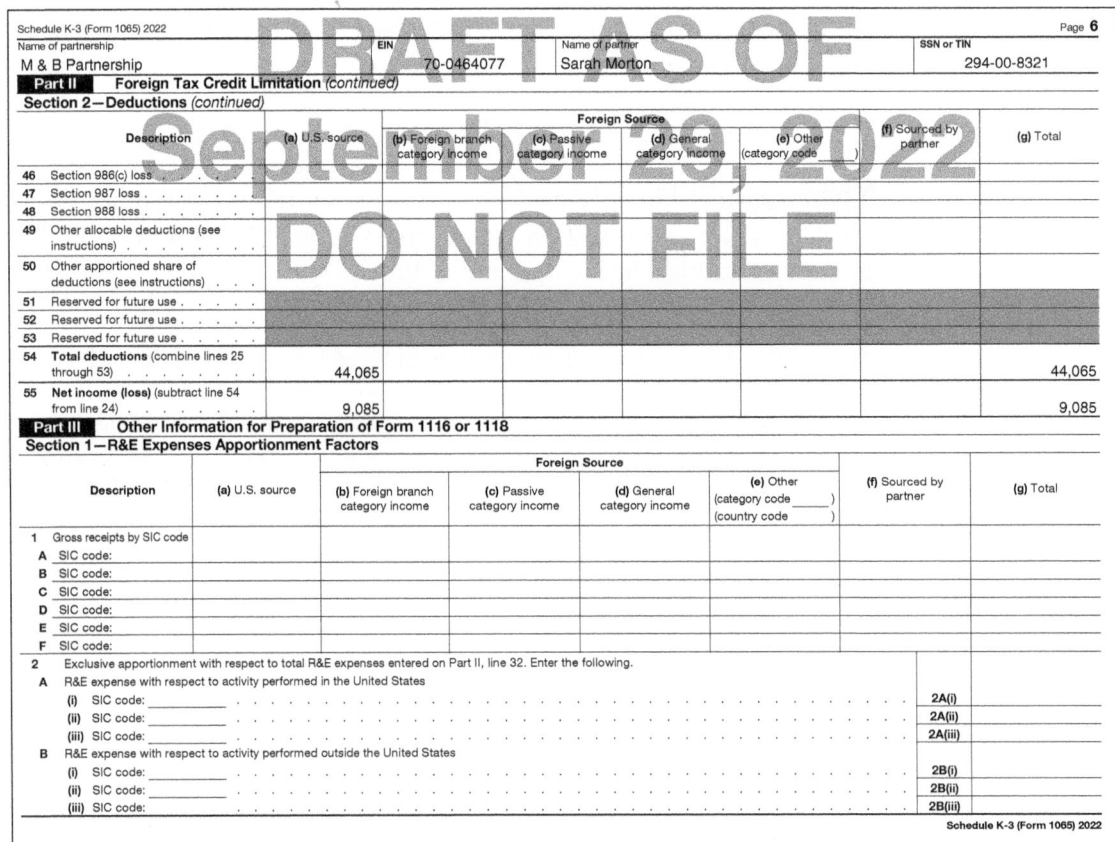

¶1503   Transactions Between Partnerships and Partners

A unique aspect to operating a business as a partnership versus a C corporation is that the profits of a partnership are only taxed once. This is accomplished, in part, by having the partnership file informational tax return, Form 1065, to report the activities of the business and allocate those activities amongst the partners (on Schedule K-1). These allocated amounts are then reported on the partners' income tax returns. Keeping with the concept of a single level of taxation, the tax laws allow partners to make tax-free withdrawals of both the contributions they made to the partnership plus their shares of previously taxed profits. However, if the partnership distributes cash to a partner in excess of these amounts, the partner is taxed on the excess. Thus, it is important to understand how partners keep track of their basis in a partnership interest to ensure a single layer of taxation of partnership profits.

¶1503.01   FACTORS AFFECTING BASIS

When a partnership is formed, the partners contribute cash, other property, or services to the partnership. Under the general rule, neither the partners nor the partnership recognize gain or loss on the transfer of property to a partnership in exchange for an interest in the partnership. [I.R.C. §721(a)] This rule applies both upon formation of a partnership, as well as to later transfers. The tax law does not require an 80% or more collective ownership for partnership transfers, like it does for C corporations (see discussion at ¶1401.01). The partner's basis includes the amount of cash plus the partner's basis in assets contributed to the partnership. However, when personal-use property is contributed to the partnership, the partner's basis is increased by the lesser of (i) the partner's adjusted basis in the property, or (ii) the fair market value of the property. The partnership's basis in contributed property is the same as that of the contributing partner.

EXAMPLE 11	Fran and Meg form FM partnership. Fran contributes land worth $50,000 ($65,000 basis) in exchange for a 50% partnership interest. Meg contributes $30,000 cash and equipment worth $20,000 ($3,000 basis) in exchange for a 50% partnership interest. Fran's basis in FM is $65,000 (same as her basis in the land). Meg's basis in FM is $33,000 ($30,000 cash + her $3,000 basis in the equipment). FM's basis in the assets it acquires is cash, $30,000; land, $65,000; equipment, $3,000.

When a partner performs services to a partnership in exchange for a partnership interest, the partner recognizes ordinary income equal to the fair market value (FMV) of the partnership interest. [Reg. §1.721-1(b)] This amount becomes the partner's initial basis in the partnership interest received.

EXAMPLE 12	Mel performs services for EFO partnership. In return, Mel acquires a 10% partnership interest in EFO, valued at $12,000. Mel includes the $12,000 in gross income. This amount becomes his initial basis in EFO partnership.

Although the partnership does not recognize gain or loss, per se, on the issuance of the partnership interest in exchange for services, it may be able to claim a compensation deduction for the value of the capital interest awarded to the recipient.

The above discussion involved transfers of cash, other property, or services to a partnership in exchange for an interest in the partnership. The tax consequences of transfers involving mortgaged property (where the debt attached to the property is assumed by the partnership); as well as transfers from the partnership of property other than an interest in the partnership can be more complex. Hence, the scope of this discussion is limited to transfers to a partnership of cash, other property, or services solely in exchange for a partnership interest.

To ensure a single level of taxation on partnership activities, partners adjust their basis to reflect their respective shares of partnership activities reported to them on Schedule K-1 (Form 1065). Partners increase their partnership basis by their allocated shares of ordinary income and separately stated income. [I.R.C. §705(a)(1)] This includes tax-exempt income, which is reported separately on Schedule K-1. Making these adjustments ensures that the taxable activities of the partnership are taxed only one time, and that tax-exempt income is never taxed. Examples 13 and 14 show how the adjustments to a partner's basis work to ensure income from the partnership is only taxed once.

EXAMPLE 13	Bree and Kate form BK partnership by each contributing $50,000 cash in exchange for a 50% interest in BK. Each partner's initial basis in BK is $50,000. BK uses the cash to invest in taxable bonds (face value of $100,000). During the first year, the bonds pay $6,000 of interest. BK reports $6,000 as taxable interest on Form 1065 (Schedule K). BK then reports $3,000 of interest income on each partner's Schedule K-1. Bree and Kate each report the $3,000 of taxable interest on their respective income tax returns.
	At the end of the first year, BK's only assets are the $6,000 of cash plus the $100,000 bond. The value of BK to a third party should be $106,000 (assuming the value of the bonds is still $100,000). Thus, the value of each partner's interest in BK is one-half of this amount, or $53,000. If the partners do not increase their basis by the $3,000 of taxable interest, then should a partner sell her interest in BK, she would recognize a $3,000 capital gain ($53,000 FMV − $50,000 basis). Accordingly, the partner would be taxed a second time on the interest from the bonds — once when the interest income is reported on the partner's return, and a second time when the gain is taxed to the partner. To keep this from happening, a partner's basis is increased for the partner's share of ordinary income and separately stated income items.

EXAMPLE 14	Same facts as in Example 13, except that BK invests the $100,000 in tax-exempt bonds that pay $6,000 of interest during the first year. BK reports the $6,000 as tax-exempt interest on Schedule K. Each partner is allocated $3,000 of tax-exempt interest on Schedule K-1, but neither is taxed on this income. However, as in Example 13, at the end of the first year, BK still has assets valued at $106,000 ($6,000 cash + $100,000 bond). Once again, if the partners do not increase their basis by the tax-exempt interest allocated to them, they will be taxed on this amount when they go to sell their partnership interests ($53,000 FMV − $50,000 basis = $3,000 gain). Accordingly, each partner's basis also must be adjusted upwards for the nontaxable income allocated to the partner. This ensures that the partner is never taxed on tax-exempt income.

Partners decrease their basis by their allocated share of ordinary loss, as well as any separately stated items of expense or loss (including nondeductible expenditures). [I.R.C. §705(a)(2)] These adjustments ensure that the partners only get a tax break for tax deductions one time, and that no tax benefit comes from nondeductible expenditures the partnership makes. Example 15 shows how the adjustments to a partner's basis work to ensure the partners only benefit one time from deductions and losses generated by partnership activities.

EXAMPLE 15	Karl and Joey form KJ partnership by each contributing $50,000 in exchange for a 50% interest in KJ. Each partner's initial basis in KJ is $50,000. During the first year of operations, KJ incurs a $20,000 ordinary loss, which is allocated to the partners on Schedule K-1. Thus, each partner deducts one-half of the loss, or $10,000, on his personal income tax return. This, in turn, reduces each partner's AGI by $10,000.
	At the end of the first year, KJ's value should be less due to the loss incurred during the first year of operations. Assuming the decline in value is the same as the $20,000 ordinary loss, KJ's value at the end of the first year would be $80,000. If Karl and Joey do not adjust their basis downward for their allocated losses, when they go to sell their respective partnership interests, the higher basis will result in each partner recognizing a $10,000 loss ($40,000 FMV − $50,000 basis). This loss would allow the partner to benefit twice from the partnership's first year operating loss. To keep this from happening, the tax laws require that a partner's basis be reduced for the partner's share of all losses and expense items. This includes both deductible and nondeductible expenditures.

Another aspect of partnerships that distinguish them from corporations is that general partners are personally liable for the debts of the partnership (¶1501). In contrast, shareholders are only liable to the extent of their stock basis. Because the general partners are personally liable for the debts of the partnership, they are at-risk to the extent of their share of partnership debt. For example, if a partnership's debt increases by $20,000 during the year, a 15% general partner's amount at-risk would increase by $3,000 (15% × $20,000). Likewise, if a partnership's debt decreases by $5,000, a 50% general partner's amount at risk would decrease by $2,500 (50% × $5,000). Adjusting a partner's basis at the end of the year by the change in the partner's share of partnership debt during the year ensures that the partner's basis reflects the partner's amount at-risk with respect to their investment in the partnership. For more on the at-risk rules, see ¶904.

Limited partners are not liable for the general debts of the partnership. Instead, they are only at-risk to the extent of their investment (basis) in their partnership interest. They do, however, increase their partnership basis by amounts owed to them by the partnership. Moreover, members of limited liability partnerships are usually protected from most debts of the partnership, except for those caused by the specific partner's tort liability (e.g., malpractice). Limited liability company members have similar protection. Nevertheless, these persons are still treated as having basis for partnership liabilities, to the extent that a partner's personal guarantee creates a risk.

EXAMPLE 16

Leon and Joyce are partners in LJ general partnership. They share profits and losses 40% and 60%, respectively. Leon's basis is $20,000; Joyce's basis is $30,000. LJ takes on $10,000 more of debt. Leon's basis increases to $24,000 [$20,000 + ($10,000 × 40%)]. Joyce's basis increases to $36,000 [$30,000 + ($10,000 × 60%)].

In the 21st century, the unlimited personal liability concept is largely a relic. Many, if not most, "partnerships" are limited liability partnerships and limited liability companies. These entities provide liability protection to the owners, in the same manner as corporations. However, the traditional rules that partners share in the liabilities of the entities remain in effect.

Although it no longer makes any sense from a nontax perspective, a shareholder in an S corporation does not claim a portion of the entity's liabilities. When a limited liability company or limited liability partnership elects to be treated as an S corporation for tax purposes, the S corporation rules govern.

Adjustments to Partner's Basis

In summary, partners adjust their basis in the partnership by the following:

1. Their allocated share of ordinary income (loss)
2. Their allocated share of all separately stated items
3. Contributions they make to the partnership
4. Distributions (withdrawals) from the partnership
5. Their proper share of changes to the partnership's debt

A partner's basis can never be reduced below zero. Any losses allocated to a partner that are in excess of a partner's basis carry over to the future when the partner gets a positive basis. This can be done when the partner makes another contribution to the partnership, or when the partner is allocated income (either taxable or tax-exempt) from the partnership. When computing a partner's basis, all items that increase basis are taken into account before taking into account items that decrease the partner's basis.

EXAMPLE 17

At the beginning of the year, Marshall's basis in his 20% interest in L&M partnership is $23,000. During the year, L&M reports an ordinary loss of $61,000, tax-exempt interest of $5,000, and $25,000 of Section 179 expense. Also during the year, L&M's debt increased by $14,000. Marshall first increases his basis in L&M by $3,800 for his share of L&M's income and increase in partnership debt (($5,000 + $14,000) × 20%). After this adjustment, Marshall's basis in his L&M partnership interest is $26,800 ($23,000 + $3,800 positive adjustments). Marshall's negative adjustments for the year total $17,200 (($61,000 + $25,000) × 20%). Since Marshall has enough basis to cover his negative adjustments, he can deduct the entire amount of his share of the partnership loss and Section 179 expense on his personal tax return. Marshall's basis in his L&M partnership interest at the end of the year is $9,600 ($26,800 − $17,200).

EXAMPLE 18	At the beginning of the year, Eve's basis in her 35% interest in DEF partnership is $6,000. During the year, DEF reports an ordinary loss of $40,000 and dividend income of $6,000. Also during the year, DEF's debt increased by $10,000. Eve first increases her basis in DEF by $5,600 for her share of DEF income and increase in partnership debt (($6,000 + $10,000) × 35%). After this adjustment, Eve's basis in her partnership interest is $11,600 ($6,000 + $5,600). Eve's negative adjustments for the year are $14,000 ($40,000 × 35%). Since this amount is greater than Eve's basis in DEF, she will only be able to deduct $11,600 of the partnership losses on her tax return. She carries over the $2,400 excess ($14,000 – $11,600 allowed under the basis rules). Eve will deduct this loss in the year she produces enough positive basis in her partnership interest to absorb the loss. Eve's basis in DEF at the end of the year is $0 ($11,600 – $11,600 of allowed losses).

¶1503.02   PARTNERSHIP DISTRIBUTIONS

Partnerships can make current or liquidating distributions. A **liquidating distribution** is one made to a partner who is exiting (being bought out of) the partnership. In a liquidating distribution, it is possible for the exiting partner to recognize gain or loss. A **current distribution** is any distribution that is not a liquidating distribution. Most distributions are current distributions, and are the focus of the discussion in this textbook.

Most distributions are tax free to the partners. In a current distribution, partners are simply withdrawing their contributions or previously taxed profits from the partnership. Distributions of money or property decrease partners' bases in their partnership interests, but never below zero. Distributions of cash in excess of the partner's basis result in capital gain to the partner. [I.R.C. §731(a)] The partner's basis in the partnership interest decreases by the adjusted basis of the property distributed. [I.R.C. §732] The basis of the property received by the partner is usually the same as it was in the hands of the partnership. [I.R.C. §733]

EXAMPLE 19	A partnership buys land in 20x1 for $5,000. In 20x3, the partnership distributes the land (now worth $23,000) to the partners. Although a 50% partner with a partnership basis of $50,000 receives land with a market value of $11,500 ($23,000 × 50%), he takes a $2,500 basis in the land ($5,000 × 50%). His partnership basis is reduced to $47,500 ($50,000 – $2,500). No gain is recognized until the partner sells his land.

When a partnership distributes both cash and property to one of its partners, the tax laws treat the cash as having been distributed first, followed by the property (at its adjusted basis to the partnership). If the partner's basis in the partnership is less than the partnership's basis in the property distributed, then the partner's basis in the partnership (after reducing it for any cash distributions) becomes the partner's basis in the distributed property.

EXAMPLE 20	M&M partnership distributes $10,000 cash and land worth $20,000 (adjusted basis of $5,000) to one of its partners, Marcia. Marcia's basis in her interest in M&M is $18,000 immediately before the distribution. In determining the tax consequences of the distribution, the cash is distributed first. Since Marcia's $18,000 basis in M&M is greater than the $10,000 cash distributed, Marcia is not taxed on the cash distribution, and she reduces her basis in M&M to $8,000 ($18,000 – $10,000). Next, the land is distributed at its adjusted basis to M&M. Since Marcia's remaining basis exceeds M&M's $5,000 basis in the land, Marcia takes a $5,000 basis in the land, and reduces her basis in M&M to $3,000 ($8,000 – $5,000).

EXAMPLE 21	Same facts as in Example 20, except that M&M's basis in the land is $15,000. Once again, the cash is distributed first (tax-free), and Marcia's basis in M&M is reduced to $8,000. However, now M&M's $15,000 basis in the land is greater than Marcia's remaining basis. Since Marcia's basis in M&M cannot be reduced below zero, her $8,000 remaining basis in M&M becomes her basis in the land. Marcia's basis in M&M is reduced to $0, and neither Marcia nor M&M recognize gain or loss on the distribution.

EXAMPLE 22	Same facts as in Example 20, except that M&M's cash distribution is $25,000. Since the cash distributed exceeds Marcia's basis in M&M, Marcia is taxed on the $7,000 excess ($25,000 – $18,000), and her basis in M&M is reduced to $0. When the land is distributed, Marcia's $0 basis in the partnership becomes her basis in the land. Neither party recognizes gain or loss on the distribution of the land (Marcia still recognizes $7,000 capital gain from the cash distribution).

Cash distributions in excess of a partner's basis are taxable to the partner. In contrast, property distributions are tax-free to the partner, even when the partner's basis in the partnership is less than the partnership's adjusted basis in the property distributed (as shown in Examples 21 and 22). Hence, the tax laws that consider cash distributions as having been distributed prior to any property reduces the chance that the partner will recognize gain on the distribution.

¶1504 Limited Liability Companies and Partnerships

Limited liability companies (LLCs) are a popular form of business ownership. All states have laws recognizing this form of business. LLCs provide the owners with the limited personal liability features of a corporation, but the flow through aspects of a partnership for tax purposes. Form 1065, Schedule B, now recognizes limited liability companies as one of the partnership forms along with general partnerships and limited partnerships. The major advantage of the LLC form of partnership over the general and limited partnerships is the limited liability. With a general partnership, all partners become personally liable for the debts of the partnership. Even with a limited partnership, there must be at least one general partner personally liable for the debts of the partnership. For limited partners to retain their limited liability, they cannot participate in the management of the partnership. The LLC grants personal limited liability for **all** of its owners and still allows each owner to participate in the management of the business. Thus, the LLC combines the corporate legal benefits of limited liability with the partnership tax benefits of a single level of tax.

While an LLC is a unique business entity for state legal purposes, a limited liability partnership (LLP) is a partnership for state legal and income tax purposes. Therefore, most LLPs avoid state taxes placed on corporations, such as franchise taxes. Yet the most important difference between LLCs and LLPs is in the owners' liability. LLC owners have the corporate benefit of limited liability. LLP owners, on the other hand, are liable for commercial debt and for their own malpractice and torts. However, they are not liable for the malpractice or torts of their partners. For this reason, most of the national and regional CPA firms have reorganized as LLPs. Changing from a general partnership to a LLP is not a taxable event. It is considered a continuation of the same partnership in most cases. Nevertheless, an LLP must register with the state to place the liability limitation on public record. The benefits of limited liability with the tax treatment as partnerships make LLCs and LLPs very popular forms for doing business today.

15

Name: _____

Section: _____

Date: _____

QUESTIONS AND PROBLEMS

1. **Partnership Characteristics.** (Obj. 1)

    a. Which tax form do partnerships use?

    b. Do partnerships withhold income taxes on guaranteed payments made to partners?

    c. An LLC is what type of tax entity?

    d. What is the extended due date for a calendar year partnership?

    e. What is the original due date for the tax return of a fiscal year partnership with an April 30 year-end?

2. **Partnership Tax Year.** (Obj. 1) ABCD partnership consists of four partners, A, B, C, and D. Each partner's year-end along with their ownership percentage of capital and profits is shown below. Determine ABCD's required tax year.

Partner	Year-End	Percentage
A	June 30	47%
B	May 31	3%
C	May 31	3%
D	June 30	47%
		100%

3. **Partnership Tax Year.** (Obj. 1) EFGH partnership consists of four partners, E, F, G, and H. Each partner's year-end along with their ownership percentage of capital and profits is shown below. Determine EFGH's required tax year.

Partner	Year-End	Percentage
E	June 30	48%
F	October 31	4%
G	December 31	24%
H	December 31	24%
		100%

4. **Partnership Activities.** (Obj. 2) Indicate how each of the following items is reported on the partnership tax return by placing a check mark in the appropriate column.

Item	Ordinary Income	Separately Stated
a. Rent received from rental property	_____	_____
b. Short-term loss on the sale of a capital asset	_____	_____
c. Dividends received from a U.S. corporation	_____	_____
d. Contribution to the Red Cross	_____	_____
e. Guaranteed payments to partners	_____	_____
f. Section 179 expense	_____	_____
g. Interest expense on a business loan	_____	_____
h. Annual business license	_____	_____
i. Interest income from a municipal bond	_____	_____
j. Property taxes on partnership assets	_____	_____

5. **Partner's Distributive Share.** (Obj. 3) Helen is a member of a partnership that reports ordinary income of $68,000 for the current taxable year. Helen's distributive share of the partnership income is $34,000, of which she withdrew $18,000 during the year. Compute the amount Helen should report as income from the partnership when preparing her personal income tax return for the year.

6. **Partnership Income.** (Obj. 2) Which of the following are separately stated partnership items?

    a. Business bad debts
    b. Foreign taxes paid
    c. Tax-exempt interest
    d. Guaranteed payments
    e. Net Section 1231 loss
    f. Depreciation recapture
    g. Interest income from business activities

7. **Partnership Charitable Contributions.** (Obj. 2) Leona and Calley operate a placement service as partners, sharing profits and losses equally. During the current calendar year, the partnership contributes $3,000 to Calley's alma mater, State University. The partnership treats this contribution as an expense in computing its $47,500 profit from operations.

    a. Is the partnership entitled to treat the contribution to State University as a deduction from ordinary income in the partnership return?

    b. What is each partner's distributive share of ordinary income from the partnership?

    c. Can each partner claim a deduction on her personal income tax return for the contribution the partnership made to State University? If so, how much?

8. **Guaranteed Payments.** (Obj. 2) What are guaranteed payments to partners and how are they treated by the partnership and the partner?

9. **Guaranteed Payments and Allocation of Partnership Income.** (Obj. 3) ABC partnership provides for "salaries" (guaranteed payments) of $70,000, $64,000, and $60,000 for partners A, B, and C, respectively. After the guaranteed payments are deducted, the partnership agreement calls for sharing of profits and losses as follows: A – 40%; B – 35%; and C – 25%.

    a. If partnership profits before the guaranteed payments are $120,000, what amount of income from the partnership should each partner report on his or her own personal income tax return?

    b. How would your answer to Part a. change if partnership profits before guaranteed payments were $220,000 (instead of $120,000)?

10. **Partnership Income.** (Obj. 3) Fred and Ken are general partners in a business sharing profits and losses 60% and 40%, respectively. The partnership uses a calendar year. Ken files his individual return on the basis of the calendar year. The partnership's ordinary income for the year is $140,000 (after deducting partners' guaranteed payments). During the year, each partner received a guaranteed payment of $8,000 per month. Compute the amount of partnership income Ken should report on his personal income tax return. How much of this amount is subject to self-employment tax?

11. **Partner's Basis.** (Objs. 1 and 4) Nikki and Nancy form N&N partnership. Nikki contributes $40,000 cash and a building worth $70,000 ($58,000 adjusted basis) in exchange for a 50% interest in N&N. Nancy contributes $10,000 and land worth $100,000 (basis of $120,000) in exchange for a 50% interest in N&N.

    a. How much gain or loss do Nikki, Nancy, and N&N recognize from the transfer?

    b. What is Nikki's basis in her partnership interest?

    c. What is Nancy's basis in her partnership interest?

    d. What is N&N's basis in the assets it acquired on the transfer?

12. **Partner's Basis.** (Objs. 1 and 4) Paul and Kyle form PK partnership. Paul contributes land worth $100,000 (basis of $75,000) in exchange for a 50% interest in PK. Kyle contributes $23,000 cash, his personal automobile worth $17,000 (basis of $32,000), and machinery worth $60,000 (adjusted basis of $37,000) in exchange for a 50% interest in PK.

    a. How much gain or loss do Paul, Kyle, and PK recognize from the transfer?

    b. What is Paul's basis in his partnership interest?

    c. What is Kyle's basis in his partnership interest?

    d. What is PK's basis in the assets it acquired on the transfer?

13. **Partner's Basis.** (Objs. 1 and 4) Brett performs services for ABC partnership. In return, Brett receives a 25% interest in ABC. At the time of the transfer, the assets of ABC are valued at $200,000.

    a. How much gain or loss do Brett and ABC recognize from the transfer?

    b. What is Brett's basis in his partnership interest?

14. **Partner's Basis.** (Obj. 4) At the beginning of the year, Robin's basis in her 25% interest in R&B partnership is $4,000. That year, on Schedule K, R&B reports an ordinary loss of $36,000, taxable interest of $4,500, tax-exempt interest of $3,000, and Section 179 expense of $25,000. During the year, R&B's debt increased by $42,000. Discuss the tax consequences of these partnership activities on Robin's personal income tax return, and compute her basis in R&B partnership at the end of the year.

15. **Partner's Basis.** (Obj. 4) At the beginning of the year, Bruce's basis in his 40% interest in B&R partnership is $11,000. That year, on Schedule K, B&R reports ordinary income of $6,000, dividend income of $12,400, and charitable contributions of $16,000. During the year, B&R's debt decreased by $25,000. Discuss the tax consequences of these partnership activities on Bruce's personal income tax return, and compute his basis in B&R partnership at the end of the year.

16. **Distributions.** (Obj. 4) AB partnership distributes $52,000 in cash to one of its partners, Alice.

    a. What are the tax consequences of the distribution if Alice's basis in AB partnership is $45,000 immediately before the distribution?

    b. How, if at all, would your answer to Part a. change if Alice's basis was $60,000 (instead of $45,000)?

17. **Distributions.** (Obj. 4) AJ partnership distributes $10,000 cash and a building worth $80,000 (adjusted basis of $66,000) to one of its partners, Joe.

    a. What are the tax consequences of the distribution if Joe's basis in AJ partnership is $46,000 immediately before the distribution?

    b. How, if at all, would your answer to Part a. change if Joe's basis in AJ partnership was $90,000 (instead of $46,000)?

    c. How, if at all, would your answer to Part a. change if the cash distribution was $50,000 (instead of $10,000)?

18. **Distributions.** (Obj. 4) PJ partnership distributes $6,000 cash and land worth $50,000 (adjusted basis of $56,000) to one of its partners, Patrick.

   a. What are the tax consequences of the distribution if Patrick's basis in PJ partnership is $80,000 immediately before the distribution?

   b. How, if at all, would your answer to Part a. change if the cash distribution was $60,000 (instead of $6,000)?

   c. How, if at all, would your answer to Part a. change if the cash distribution was $85,000 (instead of $6,000)?

19. **Form 1065.** (Obj. 5) On January 3, 2022, Ellen Elvers (SSN 299-00-1945) and Jack Ford form Elvers and Ford general partnership (EIN 70-0960341). Elvers and Ford operate a business that sells various types of merchandise (business code 452000) at 1425 Tyron Street, Charlotte, North Carolina 28201. To form the partnership, Ellen contributes $24,000; Jack contributes $16,000. The agreement provides that Ellen will participate in the partnership on a full-time basis and Jack on a part-time basis. The agreement further provides that Ellen and Jack will receive guaranteed annual payments of $34,000 and $18,000, respectively. The remaining profits go 60% to Ellen and 40% to Jack.

   Prepare Form 1065 and Schedule K-1 (Form 1065) for Ellen Elvers. Ellen is the designated Partnership Representative. Her address is 1609 Amber Way, Charlotte, NC 28201. Ellen signs the partnership return on March 10, 2023. The partnership tax return will be filed with the IRS Center in Kansas City, Missouri. Although the partnership is not required to complete Schedules L, M-1, M-2, or Item F on Form 1065 (page 1), complete these items for Elvers and Ford partnership. Also complete Schedule B-1, But not Schedule B-2. Complete the required pages on Schedule K-2 and Schedule K-3.

   The trial balance that follows was prepared as of December 31 after all necessary adjustments. Merchandise inventory is an exception. Total purchases of inventory during the year were $162,700. The ending balance in inventory was $22,000. Also, the partners' capital accounts do not reflect the partners' distributive shares of income and loss for the year. The accounts for the partners' "Drawings" represent withdrawals in addition to their respective guaranteed payments. Net income per books (Schedule M-1, line 1) is $23,990.

   The partnership uses the accrual method of accounting. Worthless accounts of $800 were written off directly to bad debt expense during the year. The equipment was purchased used. The partnership calculates depreciation using (accelerated) MACRS. The equipment was the only personal property purchased during 2022. The partnership does not elect Section 179. Book depreciation is reported on the trial balance. Book depreciation is based on a different method than MACRS. Charitable contributions are subject to the 50% limitation. On October 3, 2022, 50 shares of common stock in ZMT Corporation were sold for $2,900. The stock was purchased for $1,700 on March 29, 2022. For purposes of preparing Form

1065, assume that Form 4562 and Schedule D have been properly prepared.

ELVERS AND FORD
Trial Balance
December 31, 2022

Account	Debit	Credit
Cash	$ 11,017	
Accounts and notes receivable	17,550	
Equipment (purchased January 4, 2022)	28,000	
Accumulated depreciation-equipment		$ 5,000
Prepaid assets	900	
Long-term notes payable (to banks)		5,000
Accounts payable		8,797
Other accrued current liabilities		1,880
Ellen Elvers, Capital		24,000
Ellen Elvers, Drawing	3,120	
Jack Ford, Capital		16,000
Jack Ford, Drawing	2,080	
Sales		260,500
Sales returns and allowances	3,000	
Gain on sale of stock		1,200
Purchases	162,700	
Interest expense (business related)	300	
Partners' salaries	52,000	
Office and store salaries	14,300	
Rent expense	6,500	
Office expense	3,000	
Depreciation expense	5,000	
Property taxes on business property	383	
Payroll taxes	4,052	
Delivery expense	2,010	
Bad debt expense	800	
Store expenses	2,600	
Advertising expense	2,705	
Taxable interest income		200
Charitable contributions	560	
Total	$322,577	$322,577

(Use for Problem 19.)

Form **1065**		**U.S. Return of Partnership Income**		OMB No. 1545-0123
Department of the Treasury Internal Revenue Service		For calendar year 2022, or tax year beginning _____ , 2022, ending _____ , 20 ___ . Go to *www.irs.gov/Form1065* for instructions and the latest information.		**2022**

A Principal business activity		Name of partnership	**D** Employer identification number
B Principal product or service	Type or Print	Number, street, and room or suite no. If a P.O. box, see instructions.	**E** Date business started
C Business code number		City or town, state or province, country, and ZIP or foreign postal code	**F** Total assets (see instructions) $

G Check applicable boxes: **(1)** ☐ Initial return **(2)** ☐ Final return **(3)** ☐ Name change **(4)** ☐ Address change **(5)** ☐ Amended return
H Check accounting method: **(1)** ☐ Cash **(2)** ☐ Accrual **(3)** ☐ Other (specify): _____
I Number of Schedules K-1. Attach one for each person who was a partner at any time during the tax year: _____
J Check if Schedules C and M-3 are attached . . . . ☐
K Check if partnership: **(1)** ☐ Aggregated activities for section 465 at-risk purposes **(2)** ☐ Grouped activities for section 469 passive activity purposes

Caution: Include **only** trade or business income and expenses on lines 1a through 22 below. See instructions for more information.

Income	**1a**	Gross receipts or sales	**1a**		
	b	Returns and allowances	**1b**		
	c	Balance. Subtract line 1b from line 1a		**1c**	
	2	Cost of goods sold (attach Form 1125-A)		**2**	
	3	Gross profit. Subtract line 2 from line 1c		**3**	
	4	Ordinary income (loss) from other partnerships, estates, and trusts (attach statement)		**4**	
	5	Net farm profit (loss) (attach Schedule F (Form 1040))		**5**	
	6	Net gain (loss) from Form 4797, Part II, line 17 (attach Form 4797)		**6**	
	7	Other income (loss) (attach statement)		**7**	
	8	**Total income (loss).** Combine lines 3 through 7		**8**	

Deductions (see instructions for limitations)	**9**	Salaries and wages (other than to partners) (less employment credits)	**9**	
	10	Guaranteed payments to partners	**10**	
	11	Repairs and maintenance	**11**	
	12	Bad debts	**12**	
	13	Rent	**13**	
	14	Taxes and licenses	**14**	
	15	Interest (see instructions)	**15**	
	16a	Depreciation (if required, attach Form 4562)	**16a**	
	b	Less depreciation reported on Form 1125-A and elsewhere on return .	**16b**	**16c**
	17	Depletion **(Do not deduct oil and gas depletion.)**	**17**	
	18	Retirement plans, etc.	**18**	
	19	Employee benefit programs	**19**	
	20	Other deductions (attach statement)	**20**	
	21	**Total deductions.** Add the amounts shown in the far right column for lines 9 through 20 . . .	**21**	
	22	**Ordinary business income (loss).** Subtract line 21 from line 8	**22**	

Tax and Payment	**23**	Interest due under the look-back method—completed long-term contracts (attach Form 8697) . .	**23**	
	24	Interest due under the look-back method—income forecast method (attach Form 8866) . . .	**24**	
	25	BBA AAR imputed underpayment (see instructions)	**25**	
	26	Other taxes (see instructions)	**26**	
	27	**Total balance due.** Add lines 23 through 26	**27**	
	28	Payment (see instructions)	**28**	
	29	**Amount owed.** If line 28 is smaller than line 27, enter amount owed	**29**	
	30	**Overpayment.** If line 28 is larger than line 27, enter overpayment	**30**	

Sign Here

Under penalties of perjury, I declare that I have examined this return, including accompanying schedules and statements, and to the best of my knowledge and belief, it is true, correct, and complete. Declaration of preparer (other than partner or limited liability company member) is based on all information of which preparer has any knowledge.

_____   _____
Signature of partner or limited liability company member   Date

May the IRS discuss this return with the preparer shown below? See instructions. ☐ Yes ☐ No

Paid Preparer Use Only	Print/Type preparer's name	Preparer's signature	Date	Check ☐ if self-employed	PTIN
	Firm's name			Firm's EIN	
	Firm's address			Phone no.	

For Paperwork Reduction Act Notice, see separate instructions.   Cat. No. 11390Z   Form **1065** (2022)

(Use for Problem 19.)

Form 1065 (2022)   Page **2**

Schedule B	**Other Information**		

		Yes	No
1	What type of entity is filing this return? Check the applicable box:		

a ☐ Domestic general partnership   **b** ☐ Domestic limited partnership
c ☐ Domestic limited liability company   **d** ☐ Domestic limited liability partnership
e ☐ Foreign partnership   **f** ☐ Other: _____

2 At the end of the tax year:

a Did any foreign or domestic corporation, partnership (including any entity treated as a partnership), trust, or tax-exempt organization, or any foreign government own, directly or indirectly, an interest of 50% or more in the profit, loss, or capital of the partnership? For rules of constructive ownership, see instructions. If "Yes," attach Schedule B-1, Information on Partners Owning 50% or More of the Partnership . . . .

b Did any individual or estate own, directly or indirectly, an interest of 50% or more in the profit, loss, or capital of the partnership? For rules of constructive ownership, see instructions. If "Yes," attach Schedule B-1, Information on Partners Owning 50% or More of the Partnership . . . .

3 At the end of the tax year, did the partnership:

a Own directly 20% or more, or own, directly or indirectly, 50% or more of the total voting power of all classes of stock entitled to vote of any foreign or domestic corporation? For rules of constructive ownership, see instructions. If "Yes," complete (i) through (iv) below . . . .

(i) Name of Corporation	**(ii)** Employer Identification Number (if any)	**(iii)** Country of Incorporation	**(iv)** Percentage Owned in Voting Stock

b Own directly an interest of 20% or more, or own, directly or indirectly, an interest of 50% or more in the profit, loss, or capital in any foreign or domestic partnership (including an entity treated as a partnership) or in the beneficial interest of a trust? For rules of constructive ownership, see instructions. If "Yes," complete (i) through (v) below . .

(i) Name of Entity	**(ii)** Employer Identification Number (if any)	**(iii)** Type of Entity	**(iv)** Country of Organization	**(v)** Maximum Percentage Owned in Profit, Loss, or Capital

		Yes	No
4	Does the partnership satisfy **all four** of the following conditions?		

a The partnership's total receipts for the tax year were less than $250,000.
b The partnership's total assets at the end of the tax year were less than $1 million.
c Schedules K-1 are filed with the return and furnished to the partners on or before the due date (including extensions) for the partnership return.
d The partnership is not filing and is not required to file Schedule M-3 . . . .

If "Yes," the partnership is not required to complete Schedules L, M-1, and M-2; item F on page 1 of Form 1065; or item L on Schedule K-1.

5 Is this partnership a publicly traded partnership, as defined in section 469(k)(2)? . . . .

6 During the tax year, did the partnership have any debt that was canceled, was forgiven, or had the terms modified so as to reduce the principal amount of the debt? . . . .

7 Has this partnership filed, or is it required to file, Form 8918, Material Advisor Disclosure Statement, to provide information on any reportable transaction? . . . .

8 At any time during calendar year 2022, did the partnership have an interest in or a signature or other authority over a financial account in a foreign country (such as a bank account, securities account, or other financial account)? See instructions for exceptions and filing requirements for FinCEN Form 114, Report of Foreign Bank and Financial Accounts (FBAR). If "Yes," enter the name of the foreign country _____

9 At any time during the tax year, did the partnership receive a distribution from, or was it the grantor of, or transferor to, a foreign trust? If "Yes," the partnership may have to file Form 3520, Annual Return To Report Transactions With Foreign Trusts and Receipt of Certain Foreign Gifts. See instructions . . . .

10a Is the partnership making, or had it previously made (and not revoked), a section 754 election? . . . . . .
See instructions for details regarding a section 754 election.

b Did the partnership make for this tax year an optional basis adjustment under section 743(b) or 734(b)? If "Yes," attach a statement showing the computation and allocation of the basis adjustment. See instructions . . . . .

c Is the partnership required to adjust the basis of partnership assets under section 743(b) or 734(b) because of a substantial built-in loss (as defined under section 743(d)) or substantial basis reduction (as defined under section 734(d))? If "Yes," attach a statement showing the computation and allocation of the basis adjustment. See instructions

Form **1065** (2022)

(Use for Problem 19.)

Form 1065 (2022) Page **3**

Schedule B Other Information *(continued)*

		Yes	No
11	Check this box if, during the current or prior tax year, the partnership distributed any property received in a like-kind exchange or contributed such property to another entity (other than disregarded entities wholly owned by the partnership throughout the tax year) . . . . ☐		
12	At any time during the tax year, did the partnership distribute to any partner a tenancy-in-common or other undivided interest in partnership property?		
13	If the partnership is required to file Form 8858, Information Return of U.S. Persons With Respect to Foreign Disregarded Entities (FDEs) and Foreign Branches (FBs), enter the number of Forms 8858 attached. See instructions		
14	Does the partnership have any foreign partners? If "Yes," enter the number of Forms 8805, Foreign Partner's Information Statement of Section 1446 Withholding Tax, filed for this partnership		
15	Enter the number of Forms 8865, Return of U.S. Persons With Respect to Certain Foreign Partnerships, attached to this return		
16a	Did you make any payments in 2022 that would require you to file Form(s) 1099? See instructions		
b	If "Yes," did you or will you file required Form(s) 1099?		
17	Enter the number of Forms 5471, Information Return of U.S. Persons With Respect to Certain Foreign Corporations, attached to this return		
18	Enter the number of partners that are foreign governments under section 892		
19	During the partnership's tax year, did the partnership make any payments that would require it to file Forms 1042 and 1042-S under chapter 3 (sections 1441 through 1464) or chapter 4 (sections 1471 through 1474)?		
20	Was the partnership a specified domestic entity required to file Form 8938 for the tax year? See the Instructions for Form 8938		
21	Is the partnership a section 721(c) partnership, as defined in Regulations section 1.721(c)-1(b)(14)?		
22	During the tax year, did the partnership pay or accrue any interest or royalty for which one or more partners are not allowed a deduction under section 267A? See instructions . . . . If "Yes," enter the total amount of the disallowed deductions . . . . $		
23	Did the partnership have an election under section 163(j) for any real property trade or business or any farming business in effect during the tax year? See instructions		
24	Does the partnership satisfy one or more of the following? See instructions		
a	The partnership owns a pass-through entity with current, or prior year carryover, excess business interest expense.		
b	The partnership's aggregate average annual gross receipts (determined under section 448(c)) for the 3 tax years preceding the current tax year are more than $27 million and the partnership has business interest.		
c	The partnership is a tax shelter (see instructions) and the partnership has business interest expense. If "Yes" to any, complete and attach Form 8990.		
25	Is the partnership attaching Form 8996 to certify as a Qualified Opportunity Fund? . . . . If "Yes," enter the amount from Form 8996, line 15 . . . . $		
26	Enter the number of foreign partners subject to section 864(c)(8) as a result of transferring all or a portion of an interest in the partnership or of receiving a distribution from the partnership . . . . Complete Schedule K-3 (Form 1065), Part XIII, for each foreign partner subject to section 864(c)(8) on a transfer or distribution.		
27	At any time during the tax year, were there any transfers between the partnership and its partners subject to the disclosure requirements of Regulations section 1.707-8?		
28	Since December 22, 2017, did a foreign corporation directly or indirectly acquire substantially all of the properties constituting a trade or business of your partnership, and was the ownership percentage (by vote or value) for purposes of section 7874 greater than 50% (for example, the partners held more than 50% of the stock of the foreign corporation)? If "Yes," list the ownership percentage by vote and by value. See instructions. Percentage: By vote: By value:		
29	How many Schedules K-1 and Schedules K-3 were not furnished or will not be furnished timely?		
30	Is the partnership electing out of the centralized partnership audit regime under section 6221(b)? See instructions. If "Yes," the partnership must complete Schedule B-2 (Form 1065). Enter the total from Schedule B-2, Part III, line 3 . . . . If "No," complete Designation of Partnership Representative below.		

Designation of Partnership Representative (see instructions)
Enter below the information for the partnership representative (PR) for the tax year covered by this return.

Name of PR

U.S. address of PR	U.S. phone number of PR

If the PR is an entity, name of the designated individual for the PR

U.S. address of designated individual	U.S. phone number of designated individual

Form **1065** (2022)

(Use for Problem 19.)

Form 1065 (2022)						Page **4**
Schedule K		**Partners' Distributive Share Items**				**Total amount**
Income (Loss)	**1**	Ordinary business income (loss) (page 1, line 22)			**1**	
	2	Net rental real estate income (loss) (attach Form 8825)			**2**	
	3a	Other gross rental income (loss)	**3a**			
	b	Expenses from other rental activities (attach statement)	**3b**			
	c	Other net rental income (loss). Subtract line 3b from line 3a			**3c**	
	4	Guaranteed payments: **a** Services	**4a**	**b** Capital	**4b**	
		c Total. Add lines 4a and 4b			**4c**	
	5	Interest income			**5**	
	6	Dividends and dividend equivalents: **a** Ordinary dividends			**6a**	
	b	Qualified dividends	**6b**	**c** Dividend equivalents	**6c**	
	7	Royalties			**7**	
	8	Net short-term capital gain (loss) (attach Schedule D (Form 1065)) . .			**8**	
	9a	Net long-term capital gain (loss) (attach Schedule D (Form 1065)) . .			**9a**	
	b	Collectibles (28%) gain (loss)	**9b**			
	c	Unrecaptured section 1250 gain (attach statement) . . .	**9c**			
	10	Net section 1231 gain (loss) (attach Form 4797)			**10**	
	11	Other income (loss) (see instructions) Type:			**11**	
Deductions	**12**	Section 179 deduction (attach Form 4562)			**12**	
	13a	Contributions			**13a**	
	b	Investment interest expense			**13b**	
	c	Section 59(e)(2) expenditures: **(1)** Type:		**(2)** Amount:	**13c(2)**	
	d	Other deductions (see instructions) Type:			**13d**	
Self-Employ-ment	**14a**	Net earnings (loss) from self-employment			**14a**	
	b	Gross farming or fishing income			**14b**	
	c	Gross nonfarm income			**14c**	
Credits	**15a**	Low-income housing credit (section 42(j)(5))			**15a**	
	b	Low-income housing credit (other)			**15b**	
	c	Qualified rehabilitation expenditures (rental real estate) (attach Form 3468, if applicable) . .			**15c**	
	d	Other rental real estate credits (see instructions) Type:			**15d**	
	e	Other rental credits (see instructions) Type:			**15e**	
	f	Other credits (see instructions) Type:			**15f**	
Inter-national	**16**	Attach Schedule K-2 (Form 1065), Partners' Distributive Share Items—International, and check this box to indicate that you are reporting items of international tax relevance . . . . . ☐				
Alternative Minimum Tax (AMT) Items	**17a**	Post-1986 depreciation adjustment			**17a**	
	b	Adjusted gain or loss			**17b**	
	c	Depletion (other than oil and gas)			**17c**	
	d	Oil, gas, and geothermal properties—gross income			**17d**	
	e	Oil, gas, and geothermal properties—deductions			**17e**	
	f	Other AMT items (attach statement)			**17f**	
Other Information	**18a**	Tax-exempt interest income			**18a**	
	b	Other tax-exempt income			**18b**	
	c	Nondeductible expenses			**18c**	
	19a	Distributions of cash and marketable securities			**19a**	
	b	Distributions of other property			**19b**	
	20a	Investment income			**20a**	
	b	Investment expenses			**20b**	
	c	Other items and amounts (attach statement)				
	21	Total foreign taxes paid or accrued			**21**	

Form **1065** (2022)

(Use for Problem 19.)

Form 1065 (2022)   Page **5**

Analysis of Net Income (Loss) per Return

1	Net income (loss). Combine Schedule K, lines 1 through 11. From the result, subtract the sum of Schedule K, lines 12 through 13d, and 21 . . . . **1**					
2	Analysis by partner type:	**(i)** Corporate	**(ii)** Individual (active)	**(iii)** Individual (passive)	**(iv)** Partnership	**(v)** Exempt Organization	**(vi)** Nominee/Other
a	General partners						
b	Limited partners						

Schedule L   Balance Sheets per Books

	Assets	Beginning of tax year		End of tax year	
		(a)	**(b)**	**(c)**	**(d)**
1	Cash				
2a	Trade notes and accounts receivable				
b	Less allowance for bad debts				
3	Inventories				
4	U.S. Government obligations				
5	Tax-exempt securities				
6	Other current assets (attach statement)				
7a	Loans to partners (or persons related to partners) .				
b	Mortgage and real estate loans				
8	Other investments (attach statement)				
9a	Buildings and other depreciable assets				
b	Less accumulated depreciation				
10a	Depletable assets				
b	Less accumulated depletion				
11	Land (net of any amortization)				
12a	Intangible assets (amortizable only)				
b	Less accumulated amortization				
13	Other assets (attach statement)				
14	Total assets				
	Liabilities and Capital				
15	Accounts payable				
16	Mortgages, notes, bonds payable in less than 1 year				
17	Other current liabilities (attach statement)				
18	All nonrecourse loans				
19a	Loans from partners (or persons related to partners) .				
b	Mortgages, notes, bonds payable in 1 year or more .				
20	Other liabilities (attach statement)				
21	Partners' capital accounts				
22	Total liabilities and capital				

Schedule M-1   Reconciliation of Income (Loss) per Books With Analysis of Net Income (Loss) per Return

Note: The partnership may be required to file Schedule M-3. See instructions.

1	Net income (loss) per books		6	Income recorded on books this year not included on Schedule K, lines 1 through 11 (itemize):	
2	Income included on Schedule K, lines 1, 2, 3c, 5, 6a, 7, 8, 9a, 10, and 11, not recorded on books this year (itemize): _____		a	Tax-exempt interest $_____	
3	Guaranteed payments (other than health insurance)		7	Deductions included on Schedule K, lines 1 through 13d, and 21, not charged against book income this year (itemize):	
4	Expenses recorded on books this year not included on Schedule K, lines 1 through 13d, and 21 (itemize):		a	Depreciation $_____	
a	Depreciation $_____		8	Add lines 6 and 7	
b	Travel and entertainment $_____		9	Income (loss) (Analysis of Net Income (Loss), line 1). Subtract line 8 from line 5	
5	Add lines 1 through 4				

Schedule M-2   Analysis of Partners' Capital Accounts

1	Balance at beginning of year . . .		6	Distributions: **a** Cash	
2	Capital contributed: **a** Cash . . .			**b** Property	
	b Property . .		7	Other decreases (itemize): _____	
3	Net income (loss) (see instructions) .				
4	Other increases (itemize): _____		8	Add lines 6 and 7	
5	Add lines 1 through 4		9	Balance at end of year. Subtract line 8 from line 5	

Form **1065** (2022)

(Use for Problem 19.)

SCHEDULE B-1 (Form 1065) (Rev. August 2019) Department of the Treasury Internal Revenue Service	Information on Partners Owning 50% or More of the Partnership ▶ Attach to Form 1065. ▶ Go to www.irs.gov/Form1065 for the latest information.	OMB No. 1545-0123
Name of partnership		Employer identification number (EIN)

Part I **Entities Owning 50% or More of the Partnership** (Form 1065, Schedule B, Question 2a (Question 3a for 2009 through 2017))

Complete columns (i) through (v) below for any foreign or domestic corporation, partnership (including any entity treated as a partnership), trust, tax-exempt organization, or any foreign government that owns, directly or indirectly, an interest of 50% or more in the profit, loss, or capital of the partnership (see instructions).

(i) Name of Entity	(ii) Employer Identification Number (if any)	(iii) Type of Entity	(iv) Country of Organization	(v) Maximum Percentage Owned in Profit, Loss, or Capital

Part II **Individuals or Estates Owning 50% or More of the Partnership** (Form 1065, Schedule B, Question 2b (Question 3b for 2009 through 2017))

Complete columns (i) through (iv) below for any individual or estate that owns, directly or indirectly, an interest of 50% or more in the profit, loss, or capital of the partnership (see instructions).

(i) Name of Individual or Estate	(ii) Identifying Number (if any)	(iii) Country of Citizenship (see instructions)	(iv) Maximum Percentage Owned in Profit, Loss, or Capital

For Paperwork Reduction Act Notice, see the Instructions for Form 1065.   Cat. No. 49842K   Schedule B-1 (Form 1065) (Rev. 8-2019)

(Use for Problem 19.)

651121

Schedule K-1 (Form 1065)	2022			Part III Partner's Share of Current Year Income, Deductions, Credits, and Other Items

☐ Final K-1 ☐ Amended K-1 OMB No. 1545-0123

Schedule K-1
(Form 1065)
Department of the Treasury
Internal Revenue Service

2022

For calendar year 2022, or tax year

beginning ___ / ___ / 2022 ending ___ / ___ /

Partner's Share of Income, Deductions, Credits, etc. See separate instructions.

Part I Information About the Partnership

A Partnership's employer identification number

B Partnership's name, address, city, state, and ZIP code

C IRS center where partnership filed return:

D ☐ Check if this is a publicly traded partnership (PTP)

Part II Information About the Partner

E Partner's SSN or TIN (Do not use TIN of a disregarded entity. See instructions.)

F Name, address, city, state, and ZIP code for partner entered in E. See instructions.

G ☐ General partner or LLC member-manager ☐ Limited partner or other LLC member

H1 ☐ Domestic partner ☐ Foreign partner

H2 ☐ If the partner is a disregarded entity (DE), enter the partner's:
TIN _____ Name _____

I1 What type of entity is this partner? _____

I2 If this partner is a retirement plan (IRA/SEP/Keogh/etc.), check here . ☐

J Partner's share of profit, loss, and capital (see instructions):

	Beginning	Ending
Profit	%	%
Loss	%	%
Capital	%	%

Check if decrease is due to sale or exchange of partnership interest . . ☐

K Partner's share of liabilities:

	Beginning	Ending
Nonrecourse . .	$	$
Qualified nonrecourse financing . . .	$	$
Recourse . . .	$	$

Check this box if item K includes liability amounts from lower-tier partnerships ☐

L **Partner's Capital Account Analysis**

Beginning capital account . . . $ _____
Capital contributed during the year . . $ _____
Current year net income (loss) . . . $ _____
Other increase (decrease) (attach explanation) $ _____
Withdrawals and distributions . . . $ (_____)
Ending capital account . . . . . $ _____

M Did the partner contribute property with a built-in gain (loss)?
☐ Yes ☐ No If "Yes," attach statement. See instructions.

N **Partner's Share of Net Unrecognized Section 704(c) Gain or (Loss)**
Beginning . . . . $ _____
Ending . . . . $ _____

1	Ordinary business income (loss)	14	Self-employment earnings (loss)
2	Net rental real estate income (loss)		
3	Other net rental income (loss)	15	Credits
4a	Guaranteed payments for services		
4b	Guaranteed payments for capital	16	Schedule K-3 is attached if checked . . . . . . ☐
4c	Total guaranteed payments	17	Alternative minimum tax (AMT) items
5	Interest income		
6a	Ordinary dividends		
6b	Qualified dividends	18	Tax-exempt income and nondeductible expenses
6c	Dividend equivalents		
7	Royalties		
8	Net short-term capital gain (loss)		
9a	Net long-term capital gain (loss)	19	Distributions
9b	Collectibles (28%) gain (loss)		
9c	Unrecaptured section 1250 gain	20	Other information
10	Net section 1231 gain (loss)		
11	Other income (loss)		
12	Section 179 deduction	21	Foreign taxes paid or accrued
13	Other deductions		

22 ☐ More than one activity for at-risk purposes*
23 ☐ More than one activity for passive activity purposes*
*See attached statement for additional information.

For IRS Use Only

For Paperwork Reduction Act Notice, see the Instructions for Form 1065. www.irs.gov/Form1065 Cat. No. 11394R **Schedule K-1 (Form 1065) 2022**

(Use for Problem 19.)

SCHEDULE K-2 (Form 1065)	Partners' Distributive Share Items—International	OMB No. 1545-0123
Department of the Treasury Internal Revenue Service	Attach to Form 1065. Go to www.irs.gov/Form1065 for instructions and the latest information.	2022

Name of partnership

Employer identification number (EIN)

A Is the partnership a withholding foreign partnership?
☐ Yes ☐ No   If "Yes," enter your WP-EIN:

B Is the partnership (including the home office or any branch) a qualified derivatives dealer?
☐ Yes ☑ No   If "Yes," enter your QI-EIN:

C Check to indicate the parts of Schedule K-2 that apply.

		Yes	No			Yes	No
1	Does Part I apply? If "Yes," complete and attach Part I . . . **1**			7	Does Part VII apply? If "Yes," complete and attach Part VII . . **7**		
2	Does Part II apply? If "Yes," complete and attach Part II . . . **2**			8	Does Part VIII apply? If "Yes," complete and attach Part VIII . . **8**		
3	Does Part III apply? If "Yes," complete and attach Part III . . **3**			9	Does Part IX apply? If "Yes," complete and attach Part IX . . . **9**		
4	Does Part IV apply? If "Yes," complete and attach Part IV . . **4**			10	Does Part X apply? If "Yes," complete and attach Part X . . . **10**		
5	Does Part V apply? If "Yes," complete and attach Part V . . . **5**			11	Does Part XI apply? If "Yes," complete and attach Part XI . . . **11**		
6	Does Part VI apply? If "Yes," complete and attach Part VI . . . **6**			12	Reserved for future use **12**		

Part I   Partnership's Other Current Year International Information

Check box(es) for additional specified attachments. See instructions.

☐ 1. Gain on personal property sale
☐ 2. Foreign oil and gas taxes
☐ 3. Splitter arrangements
☐ 4. Foreign tax translation

☐ 5. High-taxed income
☐ 6. Section 267A disallowed deduction
☐ 7. Form 8858 information

☐ 8. Form 5471 information
☐ 9. Other forms
☐ 10. Partner loan transactions

☐ 11. Dual consolidated loss
☐ 12. Reserved for future use
☐ 13. Other international items
(attach description and statement)

Part II   Foreign Tax Credit Limitation

Section 1—Gross Income

Description	(a) U.S. source	Foreign Source				(f) Sourced by partner	(g) Total
		(b) Foreign branch category income	(c) Passive category income	(d) General category income	(e) Other (category code____)		
1 Sales							
A ___							
B ___							
C ___							
2 Gross income from performance of services							
A ___							
B ___							
C ___							
3 Gross rental real estate income							
A ___							
B ___							
C ___							
4 Other gross rental income							
A ___							
B ___							
C ___							

For Paperwork Reduction Act Notice, see the Instructions for Form 1065.   Cat. No. 73927C   Schedule K-2 (Form 1065) 2022

(Use for Problem 19.)

Schedule K-2 (Form 1065) 2022							Page **2**
Name of partnership						EIN	

Part II   Foreign Tax Credit Limitation (continued)

Section 1—Gross Income (continued)

Description	(a) U.S. source	Foreign Source				(f) Sourced by partner	(g) Total
		(b) Foreign branch category income	(c) Passive category income	(d) General category income	(e) Other (category code ___)		
5 Guaranteed payments . . .							
6 Interest income							
A _____							
B _____							
C _____							
7 Ordinary dividends (exclude amount on line 8)							
A _____							
B _____							
C _____							
8 Qualified dividends							
A _____							
B _____							
C _____							
9 Reserved for future use							
10 Royalties and license fees							
A _____							
B _____							
C _____							
11 Net short-term capital gain							
A _____							
B _____							
C _____							
12 Net long-term capital gain							
A _____							
B _____							
C _____							
13 Collectibles (28%) gain							
A _____							
B _____							
C _____							
14 Unrecaptured section 1250 gain							
A _____							
B _____							
C _____							

Schedule K-2 (Form 1065) 2022

(Use for Problem 19.)

| Schedule K-2 (Form 1065) 2022 | | | | | | Page **3** |

Name of partnership   EIN

Part II   Foreign Tax Credit Limitation *(continued)*

Section 1—Gross Income *(continued)*

Description	(a) U.S. source	Foreign Source				(f) Sourced by partner	(g) Total
		(b) Foreign branch category income	(c) Passive category income	(d) General category income	(e) Other (category code ___)		
15 Net section 1231 gain							
A							
B							
C							
16 Section 986(c) gain							
17 Section 987 gain							
18 Section 988 gain							
19 Section 951(a) inclusions							
A							
B							
C							
20 Other income (see instructions)							
A							
B							
C							
21 Reserved for future use							
A							
B							
C							
22 Reserved for future use							
A							
B							
C							
23 Reserved for future use							
A							
B							
C							
24 **Total gross income** (combine lines 1 through 23)							
A							
B							
C							

Schedule K-2 (Form 1065) 2022

(Use for Problem 19.)

Schedule K-2 (Form 1065) 2022 — Page **4**

Name of partnership | EIN

Part II Foreign Tax Credit Limitation *(continued)*

Section 2—Deductions

	Description	(a) U.S. source	(b) Foreign branch category income	(c) Passive category income	(d) General category income	(e) Other (category code ___)	(f) Sourced by partner	(g) Total
25	Expenses allocable to sales income							
26	Expenses allocable to gross income from performances of services							
27	Net short-term capital loss							
28	Net long-term capital loss							
29	Collectibles loss							
30	Net section 1231 loss							
31	Other losses							
32	Research & experimental (R&E) expenses							
A	SIC code:							
B	SIC code:							
C	SIC code:							
33	Allocable rental expenses—depreciation, depletion, and amortization							
34	Allocable rental expenses—other than depreciation, depletion, and amortization							
35	Allocable royalty and licensing expenses—depreciation, depletion, and amortization							
36	Allocable royalty and licensing expenses—other than depreciation, depletion, and amortization							
37	Depreciation not included on line 33 or 35							
38	Charitable contributions							
39	Interest expense specifically allocable under Regulations section 1.861-10(e)							
40	Other interest expense specifically allocable under Regulations section 1.861-10T							
41	Other interest expense—business							
42	Other interest expense—investment							
43	Other interest expense—passive activity							
44	Section 59(e)(2) expenditures, excluding R&E expenses on line 32							
45	Foreign taxes not creditable but deductible							

Schedule K-2 (Form 1065) 2022

(Use for Problem 19.)

Schedule K-2 (Form 1065) 2022   Page **5**

Name of partnership   EIN

Part II   Foreign Tax Credit Limitation *(continued)*

Section 2—Deductions *(continued)*

Description	(a) U.S. source	Foreign Source				(f) Sourced by partner	(g) Total
		(b) Foreign branch category income	(c) Passive category income	(d) General category income	(e) Other (category code____)		
46 Section 986(c) loss							
47 Section 987 loss							
48 Section 988 loss							
49 Other allocable deductions (see instructions)							
50 Other apportioned share of deductions (see instructions)							
51 Reserved for future use							
52 Reserved for future use							
53 Reserved for future use							
54 **Total deductions** (combine lines 25 through 53)							
55 **Net income (loss)** (subtract line 54 from line 24)							

Part III   Other Information for Preparation of Form 1116 or 1118

Section 1—R&E Expenses Apportionment Factors

Description	(a) U.S. source	Foreign Source				(f) Sourced by partner	(g) Total
		(b) Foreign branch category income	(c) Passive category income	(d) General category income	(e) Other (category code____) (country code____)		
1 Gross receipts by SIC code							
A SIC code:							
B SIC code:							
C SIC code:							
D SIC code:							
E SIC code:							
F SIC code:							

2   Exclusive apportionment with respect to total R&E expenses entered on Part II, line 32. Enter the following.

A   R&E expense with respect to activity performed in the United States

    (i)   SIC code: _____ ....   2A(i)

    (ii)   SIC code: _____ ....   2A(ii)

    (iii)   SIC code: _____ ....   2A(iii)

B   R&E expense with respect to activity performed outside the United States

    (i)   SIC code: _____ ....   2B(i)

    (ii)   SIC code: _____ ....   2B(ii)

    (iii)   SIC code: _____ ....   2B(iii)

Schedule K-2 (Form 1065) 2022

(Use for Problem 19.)

Schedule K-3 (Form 1065) Department of the Treasury Internal Revenue Service	☐ Final K-3 ☐ Amended K-3		
	Partner's Share of Income, Deductions, Credits, etc.—International For calendar year 2022, or tax year beginning ___ / ___ / 2022 , ending ___ / ___ / See separate instructions.	OMB No. 1545-0123 **2022**	

Information About the Partnership	**Information About the Partner**
A Partnership's employer identification number (EIN)	**C** Partner's SSN or Taxpayer Identification Number (TIN) (Do not use TIN of a disregarded entity. See instructions.)
B Partnership's name, address, city, state, and ZIP code	**D** Name, address, city, state, and ZIP code for partner entered in C. See instructions.

E Check to indicate the parts of Schedule K-3 that apply.

			Yes	No
1	Does Part I apply? If "Yes," complete and attach Part I	1		
2	Does Part II apply? If "Yes," complete and attach Part II	2		
3	Does Part III apply? If "Yes," complete and attach Part III	3		
4	Does Part IV apply? If "Yes," complete and attach Part IV	4		
5	Does Part V apply? If "Yes," complete and attach Part V	5		
6	Does Part VI apply? If "Yes," complete and attach Part VI	6		
7	Does Part VII apply? If "Yes," complete and attach Part VII	7		
8	Does Part VIII apply? If "Yes," complete and attach Part VIII	8		
9	Does Part IX apply? If "Yes," complete and attach Part IX	9		
10	Does Part X apply? If "Yes," complete and attach Part X	10		
11	Does Part XI apply? If "Yes," complete and attach Part XI	11		
12	Reserved for future use	12		
13	Does Part XIII apply? If "Yes," complete and attach Part XIII	13		

For IRS Use Only

For Paperwork Reduction Act Notice, see the Instructions for Form 1065.   www.irs.gov/Form1065   Cat. No. 74715S   Schedule K-3 (Form 1065) 2022

(Use for Problem 19.)

Schedule K-3 (Form 1065) 2022   Page **2**

Name of partnership		EIN		Name of partner			SSN or TIN

Part I   Partner's Share of Partnership's Other Current Year International Information

Check box(es) for additional specified attachments. See instructions.

☐ 1. Gain on personal property sale   ☐ 5. High-taxed income   ☐ 8. Form 5471 information   ☐ 11. Dual consolidated loss
☐ 2. Foreign oil and gas taxes   ☐ 6. Section 267A disallowed deduction ☐ 9. Other forms   ☐ 12. Form 8865 information
☐ 3. Splitter arrangements   ☐ 7. Form 8858 information   ☐ 10. Partner loan transactions   ☐ 13. Other international items
☐ 4. Foreign tax translation   (attach description and statement)

Part II   Foreign Tax Credit Limitation

Section 1—Gross Income

Description	(a) U.S. source	Foreign Source				(f) Sourced by partner	(g) Total
		(b) Foreign branch category income	(c) Passive category income	(d) General category income	(e) Other (category code ____)		
1 Sales							
A _____							
B _____							
C _____							
2 Gross income from performance of services							
A _____							
B _____							
C _____							
3 Gross rental real estate income							
A _____							
B _____							
C _____							
4 Other gross rental income							
A _____							
B _____							
C _____							
5 Guaranteed payments							
6 Interest income							
A _____							
B _____							
C _____							
7 Ordinary dividends (exclude amount on line 8)							
A _____							
B _____							
C _____							

Schedule K-3 (Form 1065) 2022

(Use for Problem 19.)

Schedule K-3 (Form 1065) 2022

Page **3**

| Name of partnership | | EIN | | Name of partner | | | | SSN or TIN | |

| **Part II** | **Foreign Tax Credit Limitation** *(continued)* |

Section 1—Gross Income *(continued)*

| Description | (a) U.S. source | Foreign Source | | | | (f) Sourced by partner | (g) Total |
		(b) Foreign branch category income	(c) Passive category income	(d) General category income	(e) Other (category code ___)		
8 Qualified dividends							
A							
B							
C							
9 Reserved for future use							
10 Royalties and license fees							
A							
B							
C							
11 Net short-term capital gain							
A							
B							
C							
12 Net long-term capital gain							
A							
B							
C							
13 Collectibles (28%) gain							
A							
B							
C							
14 Unrecaptured section 1250 gain							
A							
B							
C							
15 Net section 1231 gain							
A							
B							
C							

Schedule K-3 (Form 1065) 2022

(Use for Problem 19.)

Schedule K-3 (Form 1065) 2022							Page **4**
Name of partnership		EIN		Name of partner		SSN or TIN	

Part II	**Foreign Tax Credit Limitation** *(continued)*						

Section 1—Gross Income *(continued)*

Description	(a) U.S. source	Foreign Source				(f) Sourced by partner	(g) Total
		(b) Foreign branch category income	(c) Passive category income	(d) General category income	(e) Other (category code)		
16 Section 986(c) gain							
17 Section 987 gain							
18 Section 988 gain							
19 Section 951(a) inclusions							
A							
B							
C							
20 Other income (see instructions)							
A							
B							
C							
21 Reserved for future use							
A							
B							
C							
22 Reserved for future use							
A							
B							
C							
23 Reserved for future use							
A							
B							
C							
24 **Total gross income** (combine lines 1 through 23)							
A							
B							
C							

Schedule K-3 (Form 1065) 2022

(Use for Problem 19.)

Schedule K-3 (Form 1065) 2022 — Page **5**

| Name of partnership | | EIN | | Name of partner | | SSN or TIN |

Part II   Foreign Tax Credit Limitation *(continued)*

Section 2—Deductions

	Description	(a) U.S. source	(b) Foreign branch category income	(c) Passive category income	(d) General category income	(e) Other (category code ___)	(f) Sourced by partner	(g) Total
25	Expenses allocable to sales income							
26	Expenses allocable to gross income from performances of services							
27	Net short-term capital loss							
28	Net long-term capital loss							
29	Collectibles loss							
30	Net section 1231 loss							
31	Other losses							
32	Research & experimental (R&E) expenses							
A	SIC code:							
B	SIC code:							
C	SIC code:							
33	Allocable rental expenses—depreciation, depletion, and amortization							
34	Allocable rental expenses—other than depreciation, depletion, and amortization							
35	Allocable royalty and licensing expenses—depreciation, depletion, and amortization							
36	Allocable royalty and licensing expenses—other than depreciation, depletion, and amortization							
37	Depreciation not included on line 33 or 35							
38	Charitable contributions							
39	Interest expense specifically allocable under Regulations section 1.861-10(e)							
40	Other interest expense specifically allocable under Regulations section 1.861-10T							
41	Other interest expense—business							
42	Other interest expense—investment							
43	Other interest expense—passive activity							
44	Section 59(e)(2) expenditures, excluding R&E expenses on line 32							
45	Foreign taxes not creditable but deductible							

Schedule K-3 (Form 1065) 2022

(Use for Problem 19.)

Schedule K-3 (Form 1065) 2022   Page **6**

| Name of partnership | | EIN | | Name of partner | | SSN or TIN | |

Part II   Foreign Tax Credit Limitation *(continued)*

Section 2—Deductions *(continued)*

	Description	(a) U.S. source	Foreign Source				(f) Sourced by partner	(g) Total
			(b) Foreign branch category income	(c) Passive category income	(d) General category income	(e) Other (category code ____)		
46	Section 986(c) loss							
47	Section 987 loss							
48	Section 988 loss							
49	Other allocable deductions (see instructions)							
50	Other apportioned share of deductions (see instructions)							
51	Reserved for future use							
52	Reserved for future use							
53	Reserved for future use							
54	**Total deductions** (combine lines 25 through 53)							
55	**Net income (loss)** (subtract line 54 from line 24)							

Part III   Other Information for Preparation of Form 1116 or 1118

Section 1—R&E Expenses Apportionment Factors

	Description	(a) U.S. source	Foreign Source				(f) Sourced by partner	(g) Total
			(b) Foreign branch category income	(c) Passive category income	(d) General category income	(e) Other (category code ____) (country code ____)		
1	Gross receipts by SIC code							
A	SIC code:							
B	SIC code:							
C	SIC code:							
D	SIC code:							
E	SIC code:							
F	SIC code:							

2   Exclusive apportionment with respect to total R&E expenses entered on Part II, line 32. Enter the following.

A   R&E expense with respect to activity performed in the United States

(i) SIC code: _____	2A(i)	
(ii) SIC code: _____	2A(ii)	
(iii) SIC code: _____	2A(iii)	

B   R&E expense with respect to activity performed outside the United States

(i) SIC code: _____	2B(i)	
(ii) SIC code: _____	2B(ii)	
(iii) SIC code: _____	2B(iii)	

Schedule K-3 (Form 1065) 2022

Chapter

16

S Corporations

CHAPTER CONTENTS

LEARNING OBJECTIVES

After completing Chapter 16, you should be able to:

1. Understand the tax characteristics of S corporations, including the selection of a year-end, how they are formed and terminated (along with the tax consequences), and the eligibility requirements.
2. Distinguish between ordinary income and separately stated items, explain the need for separately stated items, and compute ordinary income.
3. Compute a shareholder's pro rata share of S corporation items, including how owners should treat payments made to them from the business for services rendered.
4. Compute an S corporation shareholder's basis and understand its impact on the shareholder's ability to deduct losses and its impact on how distributions are treated.
5. Prepare the tax forms introduced in this chapter, including Form 1120-S and Schedule K-1 (Form 1120-S).

CHAPTER OVERVIEW

Partnerships and S corporations are both flow-through entities. Although partnerships and S corporations share some common traits, S corporations have some corporate traits as well. For one, like a (regular) C corporation, the owners of an S corporation are shareholders. In contrast, the owners of a partnership are partners. Thus, shareholders of an S corporation have the same protection from the debts of the corporation that shareholders in a C corporation have. This chapter examines the tax aspects of S corporations both from the standpoint of the corporation and its shareholders.

¶1601   The Nature of S Corporations

When a corporation elects S corporation status, the shareholders, not the corporation, are responsible for the income taxes. The shareholders include their pro rata shares of the corporation's taxable income on their personal tax returns. This happens regardless of whether the corporation makes cash distributions to the shareholders. The corporation files an information return similar to a partnership's tax return. Hence, the conduit concept of passing through income, deductions, and credits to the owners applies to S corporations and partnerships. There are a few S corporations that pay a corporate-level income tax on certain items. The built-in gains tax [I.R.C. §1375] and the passive investment income tax [I.R.C. §1375] apply to a few S corporations and are beyond the scope of this book.

Even though an S corporation generally pays no income tax, it is in all other respects a corporation under state law and must act accordingly. This means that the owners can choose the S corporation form of organization for nontax reasons (like limited liability) and still benefit from the single level of taxing income. It should be noted that some states do not recognize S corporation status in filing a corporate tax return. In these states, the corporation must file a state corporate tax return and pay a state corporate income tax.

¶1602   S Corporation Status

A corporation must qualify as a small business corporation before it can elect S corporation status. The term **"small business corporation"** may seem misleading because the law does not limit the size of the corporation. Rather, it limits the types of corporations that qualify for S status, as well as the types and number of shareholders an S corporation can have.

¶1602.01   REQUIREMENTS

A corporation must have certain traits to qualify as a small business corporation. First, it must be a domestic corporation. Second, it can only have one class of stock. Third, it cannot have more than 100 shareholders; and finally, it can only have certain types of shareholders.

Domestic Corporation

An S corporation must be a U.S. or U.S. territory corporation. Certain U.S. corporations cannot elect S corporation status. These corporations include Domestic International Sales Corporations, financial institutions, insurance companies, and corporations taking the Puerto Rico or possessions tax credit. [I.R.C. §1361(b)(1)]

One Class of Stock

A small business corporation can only have one class of stock outstanding. [I.R.C. §1361(b)(1)(D)] One class of stock means that the outstanding shares of the corporation must have identical rights in both the distribution of profits and the liquidation of corporate assets. The articles of incorporation, other binding agreements, and state law determine whether all outstanding shares have identical rights. The tax laws, however, allow for differences in the voting rights within the one class of stock.

EXAMPLE 1   A corporation's articles of incorporation allow the corporation to issue both common and preferred stock. However, the corporation currently only has common shares outstanding. The preferred shares had been issued in the past, but no shares are outstanding at this time. The corporation currently has only one class of stock outstanding. Thus, it passes the one class of stock test.

EXAMPLE 2	All of the outstanding shares of common stock in a corporation give the owners the same rights to distribution and liquidation proceeds. However, some shares give the owner the right to vote on corporate matters, while others do not. Because all shares have the same distribution and liquidation rights, the corporation will be considered to have only one class of stock, even though some shares are voting and others are nonvoting.

Number of Shareholders

A small business corporation may have up to 100 shareholders. [I.R.C. §1361(b)(1)(A)] Family members are treated as one shareholder for purposes of counting the number of shareholders. "Family members" include a common ancestor and all lineal descendants within six generations of that common ancestor, as well as the spouses and former spouses of these individuals. The six-generation rule applies on the date that the first family member acquires the stock, or the date the corporation files its S election, whichever is later. Thereafter, there is no limit on the number of generations included in the family group. Thus, the S corporation can actually have more than 100 shareholders when some of the shareholders are family members. [I.R.C. §1361(c)(1)(B)] All other shareholders (i.e., those who are not family members) are counted separately, even if they own the stock jointly with someone else. Finally, when a voting trust holds stock in an S corporation, each "non-family" beneficiary of the trust, not the trust itself, counts as a shareholder for purposes of the 100-shareholder limit.

EXAMPLE 3	Lou and Marge Carter own stock in an S corporation. Lou's father, as well as the Carters' six children and nine grandchildren also own stock in the S corporation. These 18 individuals are treated as one shareholder for purposes of the 100-shareholder limit because they all have a common ancestor (Lou's father).

EXAMPLE 4	Jan Jansen and her best friend own stock in an S corporation as joint tenants. Jan and her friend are treated as two shareholders for purposes the 100-shareholder limit.

EXAMPLE 5	John and Mary Williams, a married couple, each own shares in an S corporation. The corporation has 100 shareholders, counting John and Mary as one shareholder under the "family member" rule. If John and Mary divorce and each retain shares in the S corporation, the corporation would still have 100 shareholders, since former spouses count as family members.

Eligible Shareholder Category Limitation

Shareholders in an S corporation must be individuals (other than nonresident aliens), estates, and certain trusts. [I.R.C. §1361(b)(1)(B)] Partnerships, C corporations, and other S corporations cannot be shareholders in an S corporation.

Estates of decedents may be shareholders. They are not subject to any special elections or restrictions. Bankruptcy estates of individuals may also be shareholders.

Unless a trust is within a specifically-defined category, it is ineligible to be a shareholder. If a trust holds shares and is not an eligible shareholder, the corporation faces one of two problems:

1. If the trust was a shareholder when the corporation filed its S election, the election is invalid.
2. If the trust acquired the shares after a valid S election was in effect, the corporation became a C corporation when the trust acquired the shares.

The specific categories of trusts permitted as S corporation shareholders are:

- *Voting Trusts.* [I.R.C. §1361(c)(2)(A)(iv)] All ownership aspects, other than the vote, are with the beneficial owners, who must include their portions of the S corporation's income and other items on their returns. [Reg. §1.1361-1(h)(3)(i)(E)]
- *Grantor Trusts.* [I.R.C. §1361(c)(2)(A)(i)] A grantor trust is one in which the grantor retains certain powers to control trust property. [I.R.C. §§673–677] The grantor is treated as the shareholder. If the grantor is a U.S. citizen or resident, the trust is a permitted shareholder. A revocable living trust is one example of a grantor trust. A grantor trust is a transparent, or disregarded entity for tax purposes. The grantor (person who established the trust and placed property into the trust) is treated as the owner of the trust property. When a grantor trust owns S corporation stock, the grantor must be a U.S. citizen or resident for the trust to be eligible. All of the S corporation's income and other items pass through to the grantor.
- *Deemed Grantor Trusts, also termed "Beneficiary Controlled Trusts."* [I.R.C. §1361(c)(2)(A)(i)] This category of trust is one in which a person other than the grantor retains certain powers to control trust property. [I.R.C. §§673–677] The deemed owner is treated as the shareholder. If the deemed owner is a U.S. citizen or resident, the trust is a permitted shareholder.
- *Grantor trusts and deemed grantor trusts after the death of the deemed owner.* [I.R.C. §1361(c)(2)(A)(ii)] This eligibility lasts for two years following the deemed owner's death. The estate is treated as the owner of the S corporation's stock during the two-year period. [Reg. §1.1361-1(h)(3)(i)(B)]
- *Testamentary trusts.* [I.R.C. §1361(c)(2)(A)(iii)] These trusts, created by a decedent's will, may hold shares for up to two years. During this two-year period, the trust may qualify as one of the other permitted trust types. However, it will need to divest its shares within the two-year period, or the corporation will lose its S election. The estate is treated as the owner of the S corporation's stock during the two-year period. [Reg. §1.1361-1(h)(3)(i)(D)]
- *Qualified Subchapter S Trusts (QSSTs).* [I.R.C. §1361(d)] The trust instrument must contain some important restrictions on the powers of the trustee, and the governing trust instrument. The trust instrument must provide that there is only one current income beneficiary, all distributions of trust property may be made only to the income beneficiary, and the income beneficiary's interest in the trust cannot terminate during his or her lifetime. The trust instrument must provide that all trust property must be distributed to the income beneficiary if the trust terminates during his or her lifetime. The trust instrument may require that all trust income is distributed annually, or the trustee must make annual distributions of income if the trust instrument does not require these distributions. The beneficiary elects to treat the trust as a QSST, and this election obligates the beneficiary to include the income and other items from the S corporation allocated to the trust on his or her personal income tax return.
- *Electing Small Business Trusts (ESBTs).* [I.R.C. §1361(e)] An ESBT reports all of the income and other items allocated from the S corporation. It is taxed at the highest individual rates on ordinary income and capital gains. [I.R.C. §641(c)(2)(A)] The trust cannot claim a deduction for distributions to beneficiaries and the beneficiaries do not claim any of the trust's portion of the S corporation income on their personal returns. This trust can have more than one potential current income beneficiary, and the trustee can have discretion in accumulating or sprinkling income. Among other restrictions, each beneficiary must be a natural person, an estate, or a permitted charitable organization. [I.R.C. §1361(e)(1)(A)(i)] An additional requirement is that no beneficiary may have acquired the interest by purchase, including any transaction in which the basis of the interest is its cost, in whole or in part. [Reg. §1.1361-1(m)(1)(iii)] In addition, the trustee must file an election to treat the trust as an ESBT. [Reg. §1.1361-1(m)(2)]
- *Tax-Exempt Organizations and Pension Trusts.* [I.R.C. §1361(c)(6)] These organizations are also permitted shareholders. However, all exempt organizations other than governmental entities and Employee Stock Ownership Plans (ESOPs) must treat their portions of income from the S corporation as unrelated business taxable income. The ESOP rules are restrictive and generally are beneficial only where there is broad participation in the ESOP.

¶1602.02   ELECTION

A corporation meeting the four requirements discussed in ¶1602.01 may make an S election with the consent of all its shareholders. [I.R.C. §1362] The corporation makes the election by filing Form 2553, Election by a Small Business Corporation.

Timing of Election

An election to become an S corporation always becomes effective at the beginning of the corporation's tax year. To have the election apply to the corporation's current tax year, the corporation must file Form 2553 during the prior tax year or within the first 2 months and 15 days of the current year. [I.R.C. §1362(b)(1)] Also, the corporation must meet the requirements for S status from the beginning of the current year and must continue meeting the requirements in order to maintain its S election. An election filed after the 15th day of the third month applies to the following tax year. However, the IRS grants relief for a late election if there is reasonable cause. [I.R.C. §1362(b)(5)]

EXAMPLE 6	On March 1, 2022, a calendar year C corporation files Form 2553 with the IRS to elect S corporation status. Because the election is filed by March 15, it normally would be effective retroactive to January 1, 2022. However, if during any time from January 1, 2022 and March 1, 2022, the corporation failed to qualify as a small business corporation, then its election would not be effective until January 1, 2022.

Only existing corporations can elect S status. Thus, deciding when a corporation comes into existence is important. This is especially true when determining the 2½-month election period. The election period begins in the month the corporation comes into existence. A corporation begins to exist when it (1) begins conducting business transactions, (2) acquires assets, or (3) first issues stock. An unincorporated entity that checks the box (see Chapter 15) to become a corporation may be an S corporation if its owners would all qualify as shareholders, and its equity interests are equivalent to a single class of stock. In this case, the corporation's existence begins on the day the entity elects to be a corporation.

EXAMPLE 7	On November 11, 2022, a corporation comes into existence. The corporation has until 2 months and 15 days after November 11, 2022 to file its S election if it wants to file as an S corporation in its first tax year (assuming it qualifies as a small business corporation).

Shareholder Consent

All shareholders must consent to the S corporation election. [I.R.C. §1362(a)(2)] This includes any former shareholders who owned stock in the year the election is effective, but prior to the filing of Form 2553. If a former shareholder will not agree to the election (but all current shareholders will), then the election will become effective on the first day of the next tax year. A shareholder's consent is binding and may be withdrawn only by following certain prescribed procedures.

EXAMPLE 8	On January 1, 2022, Karen Kelley owned stock in Angelo Corporation (a calendar year taxpayer). She sells all of her stock to Leo Lewis on February 10, 2022. On March 1, 2022, all current Angelo Corporation shareholders elect to be an S corporation effective January 1, 2022. In order for the election to be valid, Karen must consent to the election, even though she is no longer a shareholder on March 1, 2022. Karen's consent is necessary because she will report on her 2022 tax return her share of income from January 1, 2022, to February 10, 2022, while she owned stock in Angelo Corporation. If Karen does not consent to the S election, the election will become effective on January 1, 2022.

Shareholders execute a consent by providing all of the required information on Form 2553. Shareholders may also consent by signing a separate consent statement, which should be attached to Form 2553. The separate consent should furnish the following information:

1. The name, address, and taxpayer identification number of the corporation,
2. The name, address, and taxpayer identification number of the shareholder,
3. The number of shares owned by the shareholder and the dates on which the stock was acquired, and
4. The day and month of the end of the shareholder's tax year.

Each co-owner, tenant by entirety, tenant in common, and joint tenant must consent to the S election. This means that each family member must consent, even though they are treated as one shareholder. The legal representative or guardian may consent for a minor shareholder. The executor or administrator of an estate makes the consent for the estate. The consent of a qualified trust holding stock must be made by each person who is treated as a shareholder. Extensions of time to file a consent may be granted under certain circumstances.

Form 2553 is the only permitted election form. Plain paper statements or attachments to the corporation's tax returns are not permitted options. The corporation must file the form with the Internal Revenue Service Center where the corporation files its tax returns. [Form 2553 shows the fax numbers, depending upon the location of the corporation.] There is no electronic filing option, although the IRS accepts faxed elections and consents. Returns filed within the first two months and 15 days of the beginning of the desired tax year are timely and need no explanation.

Policies for acceptance of late returns depend on when the corporation files Form 2553:

1. If the corporation files Form 2553 within three years and 75 days of the intended effective date, it files the form with the Internal Revenue Service Center and includes an explanation of its reasonable cause for delinquency, "Reasonable cause" is not a difficult standard to meet. A typical statement would be that the shareholders and officers were unaware of the filing requirements. All shareholders from the intended effective date to the date of actual filing must attach their consents. This includes any persons who were shareholders on the intended effective date but have sold or otherwise transferred shares in the intervening period. [Rev. Proc. 2013-30, 2013-36 IRB 173] The corporation can file Form 2553 along with its first Form 1120-S, or it may file the election separately.

EXAMPLE 9

On January 1, 2023, Angelo's shareholders were Karen Kelley, Mike Miller and Norma Newman. Karen sold stock to Leo on February 10, 2023. On November 5, 2023, Angelo issued new shares to Caroline Chandler. On April 16, 2024, Norma sold half of her shares to Paul Phillips. On October 17, 2025, Mike gave half of his stock to his daughter Sally Stone.

Angelo missed the March 15, 2023 deadline for filing a timely Form 2553. The required consents depend on when the corporation files the form:

- If the corporation files Form 2553 before November 5, 2023, Karen, Mike, Norma and Leo must consent.
- If the corporation files after November 4, 2023 but before April 16, 2024, Karen, Mike, Norma, Leo and Caroline must consent.
- If the corporation files after April 16, 2024 but before October 17, 2025, Karen, Mike, Norma, Leo, Caroline and Paul must consent.
- If the corporation files Form 2553 after October 16, 2025, Karen, Mike, Norma, Leo, Caroline, Paul and Sally must consent.

All of these dates are within the three-year-and-75-day period during which the Internal Revenue Service Center may accept a late election. If the corporation files Form 2553 within this period, it sends the form to the service center, with the required consents and a statement of reasonable cause.

2. After three years and 75 days, the IRS might still accept a late Form 2553. However, the process is more complicated. The corporation must request a private letter ruling, which requires considerable preparation and a user fee ($12,600 for 2023). Preparation of a request is time-consuming and detailed. If the IRS approves the request, the corporation attaches the ruling to Form 2553 and sends it to the service center. Each shareholder, including every person who owned stock from the intended effective date of the election to the actual date of filing the ruling request, must consent. A ruling may take anywhere between three and six months.

Regardless of the time period, each one of these persons must attest, under penalties of perjury, that they have filed, and will continue to file, their tax returns consistent with the required inclusions from the S corporation.

¶1602.03   FORM 2553

Form 2553 is a tax election, not a tax return. Since the form, per se, does not include any information relating to the tax liability of the corporation or of any person, it is not subject to any statute of limitations. The IRS can request this form, and proof of filing, from the corporation in any year beginning with the first S corporation year. Accordingly, it is critical to retain evidence of filing. Accepted evidence includes:

- A registered or certified mail receipt.
- A receipt from a designated private delivery service.
- A fax receipt acknowledging Form 2553.

Normally the IRS sends CP261, Notice of Acceptance as an S Corporation, within 60 days after an S corporation files Form 2553. If the corporation does not receive this notice, it should contact the IRS and be prepared to offer evidence that it filed Form 2553.

EXAMPLE 10

On April 15, 2022, James Roberts, Stephanie Terry and Polly Barber incorporated Taxpub, Inc. James and Stephanie each owned 40% of the stock and Polly owned 20%. All shareholders were married. James lived in Washington, Stephanie in Alaska and Polly in New Jersey. Washington is a community property state, and the other two are separate property states. James's wife Jennifer must consent to the election since she is a co-owner of James's shares under Washington law. Since the other shareholders are residents of separate property states, spousal consent is unnecessary.

In early 2024, James, the president, delivered the financial records to his tax preparer. The preparer asked for Notice CP261, and then discovered that Taxpub had never filed Form 2553. Since less than three years and 75 days from the intended effective date of April 15, 2023 had elapsed, the preparer filled out Form 2553 and obtained the required signatures. The preparer faxed the form to the IRS on March 10, 2024.

Page 1 contains the basic information about the corporation.

- Item E is important, especially if the corporation does not file a timely election. In Example 10, the corporation files Form 2553 within the first two months and 15 days of its 2024 taxable year. However, it is seeking permission to have an effective election date of April 15, 2022. Failure to specify the desired 2022 effective date at this point could leave uncertainty and future delays in processing.
- Item F selects the taxable year. Most S corporations use the calendar year, so Taxpub checks box (1).
- Item G applies only if there are more than 100 shareholders at the time of filing. Only a few corporations are concerned with this rule.
- Item H notifies the IRS of an appropriate officer, who is empowered to sign the corporation's tax returns.

- Item I is necessary if the corporation misses the timely filing deadline. Without this information, the IRS might treat the election as being valid for 2023 or 2024.
- The last part of the first page is critical. Without the signature of an appropriate officer, who is empowered to sign the corporation's tax returns, the election is invalid.

Figure 16-1: Filled-In Form 2553 (Page 1)

Form 2553
(Rev. December 2017)

Department of the Treasury
Internal Revenue Service

Election by a Small Business Corporation
(Under section 1362 of the Internal Revenue Code)
(Including a late election filed pursuant to Rev. Proc. 2013-30)

► You can fax this form to the IRS. See separate instructions.
► Go to *www.irs.gov/Form2553* for instructions and the latest information.

OMB No. 1545-0123

Note: This election to be an S corporation can be accepted only if all the tests are met under *Who May Elect* in the instructions, all shareholders have signed the consent statement, an officer has signed below, and the exact name and address of the corporation (entity) and other required form information have been provided.

Part I   Election Information

Type or Print

Name (see instructions)	A Employer identification number
Taxpub, Inc.	70-1234567
Number, street, and room or suite no. If a P.O. box, see instructions.	B Date incorporated
9522 Broad St.	04-15-2022
City or town, state or province, country, and ZIP or foreign postal code	C State of incorporation
Umatilla, OR 97456	Oregon

D Check the applicable box(es) if the corporation (entity), after applying for the EIN shown in **A** above, changed its ☐ name or ☐ address

E Election is to be effective for tax year beginning (month, day, year) (see instructions) . . . . . . ► 04-15-2022

Caution: A corporation (entity) making the election for its first tax year in existence will usually enter the beginning date of a short tax year that begins on a date other than January 1.

F Selected tax year:
(1) ☑ Calendar year
(2) ☐ Fiscal year ending (month and day) ►
(3) ☐ 52-53-week year ending with reference to the month of December
(4) ☐ 52-53-week year ending with reference to the month of ►
If box (2) or (4) is checked, complete Part II.

G If more than 100 shareholders are listed for item J (see page 2), check this box if treating members of a family as one shareholder results in no more than 100 shareholders (see test 2 under *Who May Elect* in the instructions) ► ☐

H Name and title of officer or legal representative whom the IRS may call for more information

James Roberts, President

Telephone number of officer or legal representative

(509) 525-5124

I If this S corporation election is being filed late, I declare I had reasonable cause for not filing Form 2553 timely. If this late election is being made by an entity eligible to elect to be treated as a corporation, I declare I also had reasonable cause for not filing an entity classification election timely and the representations listed in Part IV are true. See below for my explanation of the reasons the election or elections were not made on time and a description of my diligent actions to correct the mistake upon its discovery. See instructions.

Taxpub, Inc., was incorporated under the laws of Oregon on April 15, 2022.

The shareholders assumed that it would be an S corporation, and instructed

corporate counsel to make sure the corporation qualified for S corporation status.

However, the parties were unaware of the necessity to file Form 2553.

On February 25, 2023, the tax preparer received the financial information

and discovered that the corporation had not filed Form 2553. This election

is within the three year and 75 day window period in Rev. Proc. 2013-30.

By signing consent to the election each shareholder agrees to report income and other

items from the corporation consistently with an S election effective April 15, 2022.

Sign Here

Under penalties of perjury, I declare that I have examined this election, including accompanying documents, and, to the best of my knowledge and belief, the election contains all the relevant facts relating to the election, and such facts are true, correct, and complete.

► *James Roberts*
Signature of officer

President
Title

03/06/2023
Date

For Paperwork Reduction Act Notice, see separate instructions.

Cat. No. 18629R

Form **2553** (Rev. 12-2017)

Page 2 lists up to seven shareholders and provides certain information about each.

- Column J shows the name and address of each. If there are more than seven, the corporation attaches a schedule with the same information.
- Column K contains a place for the signature and date thereof. A corporation may provide the signatures on separate plain paper statements.
- Column L indicates the number of shares and dates acquired for each shareholder. If any shareholder owns more than one block of stock, this column should show the number and acquisition dates of each block. If the entity is not formally incorporated but has elected, or is electing, to be a corporation for tax purposes, each owner lists the percentage ownership.
- Column M shows the identification number of each. Individuals use social security numbers. Estates, trusts and exempt organizations use employer identification numbers.
- Column N shows the month in which each shareholder's taxable year ends.

Figure 16-1: Filled-In Form 2553 (Page 2)

Form 2553 (Rev. 12-2017)						Page **2**
Name Taxpub, Inc.					Employer identification number 70-1234567	

Part I — Election Information *(continued)* **Note:** If you need more rows, use additional copies of page 2.

J Name and address of each shareholder or former shareholder required to consent to the election. (see instructions)	K Shareholder's Consent Statement Under penalties of perjury, I declare that I consent to the election of the above-named corporation (entity) to be an S corporation under section 1362(a) and that I have examined this consent statement, including accompanying documents, and, to the best of my knowledge and belief, the election contains all the relevant facts relating to the election, and such facts are true, correct, and complete. I understand my consent is binding and may not be withdrawn after the corporation (entity) has made a valid election. If seeking relief for a late filed election, I also declare under penalties of perjury that I have reported my income on all affected returns consistent with the S corporation election for the year for which the election should have been filed (see beginning date entered on line E) and for all subsequent years.		L Stock owned or percentage of ownership (see instructions)		M Social security number or employer identification number (see instructions)	N Shareholder's tax year ends (month and day)
	Signature	Date	Number of shares or percentage of ownership	Date(s) acquired		
James Roberts 21 Division St Walla Walla WA 99362	*James Roberts*	03-04-2023	40	04-15-2022	425-00-1234	12/31
Stephanie Terry 3402 Sliver Lake Dr. NE Eagle River, AK 99017	*Stephanie Terry*	03-05-2023	40	04-15-2022	518-00-3214	12/31
Polly Barber 64 Affluent Lane East Egg, NJ 02134	*Polly Barber*	03-06-2023	20	04-15-2022	709-87-6543	12/31
Jennifer Roberts, community interest in shares of James Roberts 21 Division St Walla Walla WA 99362	*Jennifer Roberts*	03-04-2023		04-15-2022	52-5005089	12/31

Form **2553** (Rev. 12-2017)

Part II of Form 2553 is dedicated to selection of a taxable year. Most S corporations use the calendar year. A few use a 52-53-week year so that the accounting period ends on a consistent weekday. See Chapter 14, at ¶1402.02, for discussion. The next portion of this chapter describes the natural business year-end and the Section 444 year. Also see Chapter 15, at ¶1502.02, for discussion of the Section 444 year.

Taxpub, Inc. plans to use the calendar year. It checks Item O box 1 and leaves the other boxes blank.

Figure 16-1: Filled-In Form 2553 (Pages 3 and 4)

Form 2553 (Rev. 12-2017)   Page **3**

Name	Employer identification number
Taxpub, Inc.	70-1234567

Part II   Selection of Fiscal Tax Year (see instructions)

Note: All corporations using this part must complete item O and item P, Q, or R.

O   Check the applicable box to indicate whether the corporation is:

    1. ☑ A new corporation **adopting** the tax year entered in item F, Part I.

    2. ☐ An existing corporation **retaining** the tax year entered in item F, Part I.

    3. ☐ An existing corporation **changing** to the tax year entered in item F, Part I.

P   Complete item P if the corporation is using the automatic approval provisions of Rev. Proc. 2006-46, 2006-45 I.R.B. 859, to request (1) a natural business year (as defined in section 5.07 of Rev. Proc. 2006-46) or (2) a year that satisfies the ownership tax year test (as defined in section 5.08 of Rev. Proc. 2006-46). Check the applicable box below to indicate the representation statement the corporation is making.

    1. Natural Business Year ▶ ☐   I represent that the corporation is adopting, retaining, or changing to a tax year that qualifies as its natural business year (as defined in section 5.07 of Rev. Proc. 2006-46) and has attached a statement showing separately for each month the gross receipts for the most recent 47 months. See instructions. I also represent that the corporation is not precluded by section 4.02 of Rev. Proc. 2006-46 from obtaining automatic approval of such adoption, retention, or change in tax year.

    2. Ownership Tax Year ▶ ☐   I represent that shareholders (as described in section 5.08 of Rev. Proc. 2006-46) holding more than half of the shares of the stock (as of the first day of the tax year to which the request relates) of the corporation have the same tax year or are concurrently changing to the tax year that the corporation adopts, retains, or changes to per item F, Part I, and that such tax year satisfies the requirement of section 4.01(3) of Rev. Proc. 2006-46. I also represent that the corporation is not precluded by section 4.02 of Rev. Proc. 2006-46 from obtaining automatic approval of such adoption, retention, or change in tax year.

Note: If you do not use item P and the corporation wants a fiscal tax year, complete either item Q or R below. Item Q is used to request a fiscal tax year based on a business purpose and to make a back-up section 444 election. Item R is used to make a regular section 444 election.

Q   Business Purpose—To request a fiscal tax year based on a business purpose, check box Q1. See instructions for details including payment of a user fee. You may also check box Q2 and/or box Q3.

    1. Check here ▶ ☐ if the fiscal year entered in item F, Part I, is requested under the prior approval provisions of Rev. Proc. 2002-39, 2002-22 I.R.B. 1046. Attach to Form 2553 a statement describing the relevant facts and circumstances and, if applicable, the gross receipts from sales and services necessary to establish a business purpose. See the instructions for details regarding the gross receipts from sales and services. If the IRS proposes to disapprove the requested fiscal year, do you want a conference with the IRS National Office?

    ☐ Yes   ☐ No

    2. Check here ▶ ☐ to show that the corporation intends to make a back-up section 444 election in the event the corporation's business purpose request is not approved by the IRS. See instructions for more information.

    3. Check here ▶ ☐ to show that the corporation agrees to adopt or change to a tax year ending December 31 if necessary for the IRS to accept this election for S corporation status in the event (1) the corporation's business purpose request is not approved and the corporation makes a back-up section 444 election, but is ultimately not qualified to make a section 444 election, or (2) the corporation's business purpose request is not approved and the corporation did not make a back-up section 444 election.

R   Section 444 Election—To make a section 444 election, check box R1. You may also check box R2.

    1. Check here ▶ ☐ to show that the corporation will make, if qualified, a section 444 election to have the fiscal tax year shown in item F, Part I. To make the election, you must complete **Form 8716**, Election To Have a Tax Year Other Than a Required Tax Year, and either attach it to Form 2553 or file it separately.

    2. Check here ▶ ☐ to show that the corporation agrees to adopt or change to a tax year ending December 31 if necessary for the IRS to accept this election for S corporation status in the event the corporation is ultimately not qualified to make a section 444 election.

Form **2553** (Rev. 12-2017)

Form 2553 (Rev. 12-2017)   Page **4**

Name	Employer identification number
Taxpub, Inc.	70-1234567

Part III **Qualified Subchapter S Trust (QSST) Election Under Section 1361(d)(2)*** **Note:** If you are making more than one QSST election, use additional copies of page 4.

Income beneficiary's name and address	Social security number

Trust's name and address	Employer identification number

Date on which stock of the corporation was transferred to the trust (month, day, year) . . . . ▶

In order for the trust named above to be a QSST and thus a qualifying shareholder of the S corporation for which this Form 2553 is filed, I hereby make the election under section 1361(d)(2). Under penalties of perjury, I certify that the trust meets the definitional requirements of section 1361(d)(3) and that all other information provided in Part III is true, correct, and complete.

Signature of income beneficiary or signature and title of legal representative or other qualified person making the election   Date

* Use Part III to make the QSST election only if stock of the corporation has been transferred to the trust on or before the date on which the corporation makes its election to be an S corporation. The QSST election must be made and filed separately if stock of the corporation is transferred to the trust **after** the date on which the corporation makes the S election.

Part IV **Late Corporate Classification Election Representations** (see instructions)

If a late entity classification election was intended to be effective on the same date that the S corporation election was intended to be effective, relief for a late S corporation election must also include the following representations.

1   The requesting entity is an eligible entity as defined in Regulations section 301.7701-3(a);

2   The requesting entity intended to be classified as a corporation as of the effective date of the S corporation status;

3   The requesting entity fails to qualify as a corporation solely because Form 8832, Entity Classification Election, was not timely filed under Regulations section 301.7701-3(c)(1)(i), or Form 8832 was not deemed to have been filed under Regulations section 301.7701-3(c)(1)(v)(C);

4   The requesting entity fails to qualify as an S corporation on the effective date of the S corporation status solely because the S corporation election was not timely filed pursuant to section 1362(b); **and**

5a   The requesting entity timely filed all required federal tax returns and information returns consistent with its requested classification as an S corporation for all of the years the entity intended to be an S corporation and no inconsistent tax or information returns have been filed by or with respect to the entity during any of the tax years, **or**

b   The requesting entity has not filed a federal tax or information return for the first year in which the election was intended to be effective because the due date has not passed for that year's federal tax or information return.

Form **2553** (Rev. 12-2017)

The final pages of the form serve two purposes:
1. If one of the shareholders is a Qualified Subchapter S Trust, the beneficiary may use this form to file the appropriate election for the trust. If there are more than one of these trusts, they may use duplicates of this form or plain paper statements. Taxpub, Inc. does not have any trusts as shareholders, so this part of the form is blank.
2. If the entity electing S status is not a corporation, *per se*, and has not field a timely election to be treated as an association, Part IV contains the language necessary for the IRS to accept the late classification election, along with the late S election. The signature on page 1 is sufficient to complete this part of the form. Since Taxpub, Inc. is a corporation, this part of the form has no relevance.

¶1602.04   TERMINATION OF S CORPORATION STATUS

An S corporation election may be terminated either voluntarily or automatically upon the occurrence of certain events.

Voluntary Termination

To voluntarily terminate S corporation status, shareholders owning more than 50% of the shares must consent to end the S status. [I.R.C. §1362(d)(1)] The corporation then files a statement to this effect with the IRS office where it had previously filed its election. If a timely filed revocation specifies an effective date, the revocation will be effective on that date. From that date forward, the corporation is taxed as a (regular) C corporation. Thus, even though an election to become an S corporation must be effective on the first day of a tax year, a termination may be effective before the end of the regular tax year. When no specific termination date is given, a revocation filed within the first two months and 15 days of the corporation's tax year is retroactive to the first day of the tax year. When filed after the first two months and 15 days, the revocation is effective on the first day of the following tax year.

EXAMPLE 11	On March 15, 2022, a calendar year S corporation files a statement with the IRS to revoke its S election. If the statement does not specify a future date on which the revocation is to take effect, the corporation's S status will be revoked retroactively to January 1, 2022.

EXAMPLE 12	Same facts as in Example 11, except that the corporation files the statement to revoke its S election on March 18, 2022. If the statement does not specify a future date on which the revocation is to take effect, the corporation's S status will be revoked effective January 1, 2023.

 To elect S status, the tax law requires that all affected shareholders consent to the election. To revoke an S election, only a majority of the corporation's shareholders must provide their consent.

Automatic Termination

S corporation status automatically terminates upon the occurrence of one of the following events:

1. The corporation fails to remain a small business corporation. [I.R.C. §1362(d)(2)]
2. The corporation that has earnings and profits (E&P) carried over from when it was a regular C corporation generates passive investment income in excess of 25% of its gross receipts for three consecutive years. (Thus, if the corporation was always an S corporation or was once a C corporation but has no E&P, passive investment income cannot trigger automatic termination). [I.R.C. §1362(d)(3)]

When an S corporation no longer qualifies as a small business corporation, the S status terminates as of the date on which the disqualifying event occurs. As a result, the day before the terminating event is the last day for the S corporation, and the day of termination becomes the first day of C corporation status. When the S status terminates because of prolonged excessive passive income, the termination is effective beginning with the first day of the next tax year.

EXAMPLE 13	An S corporation has been operating on a calendar year basis for the last few years with 100 shareholders. On July 21, 2022, one of the shareholders dies, with his shares passing equally to his wife and best friend on that date. Having no common ancestor, the wife and best friend count as two shareholders. Thus, the status as an S corporation automatically terminates on July 21, 2022. The S corporation must file a return for the period January 1, 2022, through July 20, 2022. On July 21, 2022, the corporation becomes a C corporation for the remainder of the year ending December 31, 2022. All income (loss) and separately stated items are prorated between the S corporation tax return and the C corporation tax return on a daily basis.

Reelection

Generally, if an election terminates (either voluntarily or automatically), the corporation may not reelect S status for five years. [I.R.C. §1362(g)] However, the IRS may allow an earlier election when there is a change of ownership of more than 50% of the shares. If the S corporation election was inadvertently terminated, the IRS may even waive termination when the corporation promptly corrects the violation. [I.R.C. §1362(f)]

¶1603   S Corporation Tax Income, Losses and Distributions

An S corporation files an annual informational tax return, Form 1120-S, U.S. Income Tax Return for an S Corporation. It is due on the 15th day of the third month after the end of the corporation's tax year. For a calendar year S corporation, the return is due March 15. An S corporation receives an automatic six-month extension of time to file its return when it completes and files Form 7004 by the due date for the original return. The Internal Revenue Code (Code) imposes a penalty on the S corporation (not the shareholders) when it fails to file Form 1120-S in a timely manner. The monthly penalty (imposed for up to 12 months) is $220 times the number of persons who were shareholders at any time during the year. [I.R.C. §6699] This is the same penalty that is imposed on partnerships that fail to file a timely tax return (¶1502).

The character of all items of income, deductions, losses, and credits passes through from the corporation to the shareholders in a manner similar to partnerships. The shareholders receive a Schedule K-1 (Form 1120-S) that reports their shares of the ordinary income and each separately stated item. The tax law requires companies to furnish this information to owners no later than the filing due date for Form 1120-S. The S corporation may be assessed a penalty of up to $270 for each Schedule K-1 not provided to its shareholders in a timely manner. A reduced penalty applies if the error is corrected within 30 days ($50) or by August 1 ($100). This penalty is the same penalty imposed on a partnership that fails to furnish timely Schedules K-1 (Form 1065) to each of its partners (¶1502). The information reported on Form 1120-S and Schedule K-1 (Form 1120-S) is explained in greater detail later in the chapter.

¶1603.01   TAX YEAR

Most S corporations must have the same tax year as the shareholders owning more than 50% of the stock. Since most S corporation shareholders are individuals, this is generally a calendar year. [I.R.C. §1378] However, exceptions may apply. One exception involves the natural business year. In a natural business year, 25% of gross receipts are received in the last two months of the fiscal year for three years in a row. A second exception allows an S corporation to elect a tax year that provides no more than a three-month deferral for its shareholders. This is known as a *Section 444* election. These two exceptions are the same two exceptions to the required tax year rule for partnerships. See ¶1502.02 for further discussion of these exceptions and for more on the Section 444 election.

EXAMPLE 14	The shareholders of an S corporation have a calendar tax year. If allowed, they would prefer the S corporation to have a January 31 year-end. This would allow the income earned from February 1, 2022, to January 31, 2023, to be taxable on the shareholders' 2023 tax returns. This would result in an 11-month tax deferral. The tax law, however, requires S corporations have a calendar year-end unless they can meet requirements for one of the exceptions to the required tax year rule.

¶1603.02   REPORTING INCOME AND DEDUCTIONS

When completing Form 1120-S, it is necessary to divide the S corporation's tax items into two categories: (1) separately stated items and (2) ordinary items. The ordinary items not separately stated comprise ordinary income or loss. As with partnerships, the separately stated items and ordinary income (loss) pass through to the shareholders, who report them on their personal income tax returns.

Separately Stated Items

As discussed in Chapter 15 in the context of partnership taxable income, separately stated items are income, deductions, and tax credits that have the possibility of affecting shareholders' tax returns differently. The most common separately stated items for S corporations are the same as the items separately stated for partnerships (see discussion at ¶1502.05). However, there are no special allocations of gains, losses or depreciation on contributed property for an S corporation. Moreover, an S corporation cannot allocate any type of income, gain, loss or deduction among the shareholders other than on a per-day, per-share basis. The separately stated items appear on Form 1120-S, Schedule K, Shareholders' Pro Rata Share Items. Schedule K-1 (Form 1120-S) provides each shareholder's share of separately stated items. Beginning with the 2022 returns, each S corporation must prepare Schedule K-3 for each shareholder. The corporation must attach one copy per shareholder to its Form 1120-S and send it to the IRS, and must also send a copy to each shareholder.

Examples of Separately Stated Items

- Charitable contributions
- Net short-term and long-term capital gains (losses)
- Tax-exempt income
- Investment income (interest, dividends)
- Nondeductible expenses
- Section 179 expense deduction
- Investment expenses
- Net Section 1231 gains (losses)
- Personal expenses paid for the shareholder's benefit
- Foreign taxes
- Tax credits
- Tax preferences and adjustments related to AMT activities
- Net income (loss) from rental real estate activities

Ordinary Income or Loss

Ordinary income (loss) is generally the net result of the S corporation's trade or business activities. It includes all items of income or deductions that are not separately stated. These tend to be the same items used in determining partnership ordinary income (see discussion at ¶1502.06). The resulting amount of ordinary income (loss) passes through to the shareholders along with the separately stated items on the Schedule K-1 (Form 1120-S). [I.R.C. §1363(a)] A copy of each shareholder's Schedule K-1 is attached to the S corporation's Form 1120-S. A copy is also given to the shareholder. The shareholders include taxable items from their Schedules K-1 on their own income tax returns. For example, the shareholder's pro rata share of an S corporation's ordinary income (loss) appears on the shareholder's Form 1040, Schedule E.

 In general partnerships, limited liability companies, and sole proprietorships, FICA taxes (self-employment taxes) apply to all ordinary income passing to the owners. However, in S corporations, FICA taxes apply only to designated salaries, and the corporation is responsible for sending in the FICA taxes to the government. Recall that FICA is shared by the employee and the employer (¶1302). No FICA taxes are paid on the S corporation's ordinary income, which flows through to the owners.

Deductions Not Allowed

Like partnerships, certain individual deductions are not available to S corporations, such as the standard deduction, itemized deductions, and the deduction for personal and dependency exemptions. S corporations also cannot take certain deductions available to regular taxable C corporations. The most notable of these deductions is the dividends received deduction.

¶1603.03   ALLOCATION OF TAX ITEMS TO SHAREHOLDERS

A shareholder's share of S corporation income, deductions, losses, and credits is determined on a per-share-per-day basis. [I.R.C. §1377(a)(1)] The S corporation allocates an equal amount of each item to each share on a per-day basis for the corporation's tax year. The per-share-per-day amount is multiplied by the number of shares the shareholder owned each day of the year. The shareholders' personal tax returns include their allocated yearly totals for each of the S corporation tax items.

EXAMPLE 15

On January 1, 2022, the 30,000 shares of stock outstanding in Shades, Inc., a calendar year S corporation, are owned equally by George Greene, Wilma White, and Betty Brown. On October 19, 2022, Brown sells his 10,000 shares to Burl Black. During 2022, Shades earns $150,000 of ordinary taxable income and $90,000 of long-term capital gains. Since George and Wilma own their respective one-third interests for the entire year, each reports one-third of the ordinary income ($50,000) and one-third of the capital gains ($30,000) on their 2022 tax returns. However, because neither Betty nor Burl owned their shares for the entire tax year, their pro rata share of Shades's ordinary income and long-term capital gain must be determined on a per-share, per-day basis.

Betty owned 10,000 shares from January 1 through October 19, a total of 292 days (in a nonleap year). Burl owned 10,000 shares for 73 days (from October 20 through December 31). Betty's pro rata share of ordinary income and capital gain equal $40,000 ($50,000 × 292/365) and $24,000 ($30,000 × 292/365), respectively. Similarly, Burl's pro rata share of these items equals $10,000 ($50,000 × 73/365) and $6,000 ($30,000 × 73/365), respectively. These prorated amounts are reported on each shareholder's respective Schedule K-1.

When a shareholder disposes of all of his or her stock in the S corporation, the corporation may elect to allocate income, loss and separately stated items to each portion of the year, and then allocate to the shareholders based on their proportionate ownership in that part of the year. [I.R.C. §1377(a)(2)] The corporation must make that election. Shareholders are deemed to consent.

EXAMPLE 16	Shades, in Example 15, could separately account for the portion of the year ending October 19 and allocate 1/3 of all of the January 1 through October 19 pass-through items to Betty. It would then measure its pass-through items from October 20 through December 31 and allocate 1/3 of these amounts to Burl. George and Wilma would not be affected by the different allocation methods, since they owned the same percentages in both portions of the year.

¶1603.04　SHAREHOLDER'S INVESTMENT (BASIS) IN STOCK

Shareholders compute their initial basis in S corporation stock using the same rules used when forming a regular C corporation (see discussion at ¶1401.01). If the requirements are met, their basis in the assets contributed to the corporation becomes the basis of their investment (stock) in the corporation. Thus, shareholders can avoid the taxation of gains or losses on forming an S corporation. When shareholders purchase their shares, their basis in the stock is its cost. Shareholders adjust their initial basis in S corporation stock by the following:

1. Ordinary income (loss)
2. Separately stated items
3. Additional contributions to the S corporation
4. Distributions from the S corporation

Ordinary income, separately stated income [I.R.C. §1367(a)(1)], and additional contributions to capital increase the shareholder's basis in the stock. Ordinary loss, separately stated deductions or losses, and distributions reduce the shareholder's basis. [I.R.C. §1367(a)(2)] Corporate liabilities generally do not affect a shareholder's basis unless the shareholder personally loans money to the corporation.

EXAMPLE 17	Jody Yoerger pays $7,500 for 100 shares of LTB corporation stock at the beginning of the corporation's 2023 calendar tax year. LTB is an S corporation. Her share of income and separately stated items of the S corporation are $1,500 of ordinary income and $300 of long-term capital gains. The corporation distributed $1,000 cash to Jody during the year. Jody's $8,300 basis in her stock on December 31, 2023 is calculated as follows:

Amount paid for S shares	$7,500
Add: Share of ordinary income	1,500
Share of capital gains	300
Less: Distributions received	(1,000)
Basis at December 31, 20x1	$8,300

Starting with the 2019 returns, the IRS required shareholders to file a basis schedule with their tax returns for any year in which:

- The corporation reported a loss;
- The shareholder received a distribution; or,
- The corporation repaid a loan from the shareholder.

There were few instances where shareholders were not required to include this schedule. For the 2022 and future tax years, the IRS introduced Form 7203, which is required under those same circumstances.

EXAMPLE 18

Jody, from Example 17, received a distribution from LTB in 2023. She completes Form 7203 and attaches it to her Form 1040. Since she does not make any loans to the corporation and does not report losses for this year, she does not need to fill out Parts II and III. However, this material shows these parts of the form for educational purposes.

Figure 16-2: Filled-In Form 7203 (Page 1)

Form 7203
(Rev. December 2022)
Department of the Treasury
Internal Revenue Service

S Corporation Shareholder Stock and Debt Basis Limitations

Attach to your tax return.
Go to *www.irs.gov/Form7203* for instructions and the latest information.

OMB No. 1545-2302

Attachment Sequence No. **203**

Name of shareholder
Virginia Kendall

Identifying number
421-00-8045

A Name of S corporation
Kendall Management Company

B Employer identification number
70-1739257

C Stock block (see instructions):

D Check applicable box(es) to indicate how stock was acquired:
(1) ☑ Original shareholder **(2)** ☐ Purchased **(3)** ☐ Inherited **(4)** ☐ Gift **(5)** ☐ Other:

E Check if you have a Regulations section 1.1367-1(g) election in effect during the tax year for this S corporation . . . . . ☐

Part I   Shareholder Stock Basis

1	Stock basis at the beginning of the corporation's tax year	1	0
2	Basis from any capital contributions made or additional stock acquired during the tax year . . .	2	38,000
3a	Ordinary business income (enter losses in Part III)	3a	12,000
b	Net rental real estate income (enter losses in Part III)	3b	
c	Other net rental income (enter losses in Part III)	3c	
d	Interest income	3d	216
e	Ordinary dividends	3e	600
f	Royalties	3f	
g	Net capital gains (enter losses in Part III)	3g	
h	Net section 1231 gain (enter losses in Part III)	3h	3,144
i	Other income (enter losses in Part III)	3i	
j	Excess depletion adjustment	3j	
k	Tax-exempt income	3k	330
l	Recapture of business credits	3l	
m	Other items that increase stock basis	3m	
4	Add lines 3a through 3m	4	16,290
5	Stock basis before distributions. Add lines 1, 2, and 4	5	54,290
6	Distributions (excluding dividend distributions)	6	9,000

Note: If line 6 is larger than line 5, subtract line 5 from line 6 and report the result as a capital gain on Form 8949 and Schedule D. See instructions.

7	Stock basis after distributions. Subtract line 6 from line 5. If the result is zero or less, enter -0-, skip lines 8 through 14, and enter -0- on line 15	7	45,290
8a	Nondeductible expenses	8a	
b	Depletion for oil and gas	8b	
c	Business credits (sections 50(c)(1) and (5))	8c	
9	Add lines 8a through 8c	9	
10	Stock basis before loss and deduction items. Subtract line 9 from line 7. If the result is zero or less, enter -0-, skip lines 11 through 14, and enter -0- on line 15	10	45,290
11	Allowable loss and deduction items. Enter the amount from line 47, column (c)	11	2,100
12	Debt basis restoration (see net increase in instructions for line 23)	12	
13	Other items that decrease stock basis	13	
14	Add lines 11, 12, and 13	14	2,100
15	**Stock basis at the end of the corporation's tax year.** Subtract line 14 from line 10. If the result is zero or less, enter -0-	15	43,190

Part II   Shareholder Debt Basis

Section A—Amount of Debt (If more than three debts, see instructions.)

Description	(a) Debt 1 ☐ Formal note ☐ Open account	(b) Debt 2 ☐ Formal note ☐ Open account	(c) Debt 3 ☐ Formal note ☐ Open account	(d) Total
16 Loan balance at the beginning of the corporation's tax year				
17 Additional loans (see instructions)				
18 Loan balance before repayment. Add lines 16 and 17				
19 Principal portion of debt repayment (this line doesn't include interest)				
20 Loan balance at the end of the corporation's tax year. Subtract line 19 from line 18				

For Paperwork Reduction Act Notice, see separate instructions.   Cat. No. 56396V   Form **7203** (Rev. 12-2022)

Figure 16-2: Filled-In Form 7203 (Page 2)

Form 7203 (Rev. 12-2022)   Page **2**

Part II   Shareholder Debt Basis *(continued)*

Section B—Adjustments to Debt Basis

	Description	(a) Debt 1	(b) Debt 2	(c) Debt 3	(d) Total
21	Debt basis at the beginning of the corporation's tax year				
22	Enter the amount, if any, from line 17				
23	Debt basis restoration (see instructions)				
24	Debt basis before repayment. Add lines 21, 22, and 23				
25	Divide line 24 by line 18				
26	Nontaxable debt repayment. Multiply line 25 by line 19				
27	Debt basis before nondeductible expenses and losses. Subtract line 26 from line 24				
28	Nondeductible expenses and oil and gas depletion deductions in excess of stock basis				
29	Debt basis before losses and deductions. Subtract line 28 from line 27. If the result is zero or less, enter -0-				
30	Allowable losses in excess of stock basis. Enter the amount from line 47, column (d)				
31	**Debt basis at the end of the corporation's tax year.** Subtract line 30 from line 29. If the result is zero or less, enter -0-				

Section C—Gain on Loan Repayment

32	Repayment. Enter the amount from line 19				
33	Nontaxable repayments. Enter the amount from line 26				
34	**Reportable gain.** Subtract line 33 from line 32				

Part III   Shareholder Allowable Loss and Deduction Items

	Description	(a) Current year losses and deductions	(b) Carryover amounts (column (e)) from the previous year	(c) Allowable loss from stock basis	(d) Allowable loss from debt basis	(e) Carryover amounts
35	Ordinary business loss					
36	Net rental real estate loss					
37	Other net rental loss					
38	Net capital loss					
39	Net section 1231 loss					
40	Other loss					
41	Section 179 deductions					
42	Charitable contributions	2,100		2,100		
43	Investment interest expense					
44	Section 59(e)(2) expenditures					
45	Other deductions					
46	Foreign taxes paid or accrued					
47	**Total loss.** Add lines 35 through 46 for each column. Enter the total loss in column (c) on line 11 and enter the total loss in column (d) on line 30	2,100		2,100		

Form **7203** (Rev. 12-2022)

When S corporation shareholders sell stock, the taxable gain or loss cannot be determined until after the end of the corporation's tax year. The shareholders who sell shares must adjust their stock bases by their share of the S corporation's ordinary income or loss and separately stated items. This information will not be known until after the S corporation's year-end. The unknown effect at the time of sale can be lessened if the seller and the buyer agree to an adjustment of the selling price based on the year-end profit or loss results. As an alternative, the affected shareholders can agree to divide the tax year into two parts for accounting purposes. One part would be from the beginning of the year through the day of sale; the second part would be the remainder of the year. This agreement limits the income or loss of the selling shareholder to the corporation's results up to the date of sale. The shareholders who remain will share income or losses occurring after the date of sale. Even though the tax year is split into two parts for shareholder income (loss) computations, the S corporation files only one tax return for the year.

¶1603.05   DISTRIBUTIONS TO SHAREHOLDERS

Distributions from S corporations formed after 1982 are generally tax free to the shareholder. The distributions reduce the shareholder's basis in the stock, but not below zero. If the distributions exceed the shareholder's stock basis, the excess is treated as a capital gain. The tax consequences of distributions from an S corporation formed before 1983 are more complex and beyond the scope of this discussion.

The S corporation keeps track of all its income and losses in a special account called the accumulated adjustments account, or AAA. [I.R.C. §1368(e)] The account can have a positive or negative balance, depending on the income and losses the corporation has sustained. Distributions to shareholders reduce the AAA balance. However, distributions themselves cannot reduce the balance below zero. The distributions from AAA can be thought of as disbursing income that has already been taxed on the shareholders' personal income tax returns. When an S election terminates, shareholders can still receive tax-free distributions. The payments cannot exceed the balance of AAA and must be made within an acceptable period (about one year after termination).

EXAMPLE 19	JL Corporation, formed on January 1, 2023, elected S corporation status. Shareholders Jill Jones and Lisa Lyons each invested $30,000, and each received 50% of the stock. JL's taxable income for 2023 was $20,000, all ordinary income. The shareholders each received $12,000 in cash distributions during 2023, from a total distribution of $24,000.
	In 2023, Jill and Lisa each report $10,000 of income on their individual income tax returns. The $12,000 distribution to each shareholder is tax free. The basis of the stock to each shareholder at the end of 2023 is $28,000 ($30,000 + $10,000 − $12,000). The balance in the AAA account is zero ($20,000 income − $20,000 distribution). The distribution cannot reduce AAA below zero. Thus, $2,000 of each shareholder's distribution in 2023 is treated as a tax-free return of capital.

Distributions from an S corporation that was previously a regular C corporation may be taxable. This occurs when an S corporation has earnings and profits (E&P) carried over from C corporation years. [I.R.C. §1368(c)] (See ¶1405.02 for a discussion of E&P.) Distributions are first payments out of AAA, which are tax free and reduce the shareholder's basis in the stock. To the extent that the distributions exceed AAA, they are considered to be payments out of E&P and taxed as dividends. The corporation's E&P is reduced but shareholders do not reduce their stock basis for these taxable distributions. Any distributions in excess of AAA and E&P are not taxable as long as they do not exceed the shareholder's remaining basis in the stock. Such distributions, however, reduce the shareholder's basis in the stock. Any amount of the distribution in excess of AAA, E&P, and the shareholder's basis is taxed as capital gain to the shareholder.

EXAMPLE 20	KK Corporation was a regular corporation until 2023, when an S election was made. KK carried over $5,000 of E&P from its C corporation years. In 2023, KK has $16,000 of ordinary income, which is added to KK's AAA balance. KK distributes $30,000 to its sole shareholder, Ken, whose stock basis prior to the distribution was $40,000.
	The first $16,000 of distributions comes out of AAA and is not taxable. Both Ken's basis in his stock and KK's AAA balance are reduced by $16,000. The next $5,000 comes from E&P and is a taxable dividend. No stock basis reduction results from the $5,000. The last $9,000 distributed is not taxable. Ken reduces his stock basis by the nontaxable distributions. His stock basis at the end of 2023 is $15,000 ($40,000 − $16,000 − $9,000).

S corporations can elect to have distributions come from E&P first, thus bypassing AAA. [I.R.C. §1368(e)(3)] The election requires the consent of all shareholders and is irrevocable. The reason S corporations may want to make this election is to remove all prior C corporation E&P at a time when its shareholders can most afford to pay tax on the income. Further, corporations benefit from this election by removing the possibility of being subject to a special tax on excess passive investment income (beyond the scope of this discussion). Along those same lines, an S corporation with E&P and too much passive investment income runs the risk of terminating its S corporation status (see ¶1602.04).

Distributions of Property

Distributions to shareholders may be in cash or property. As with C corporations, the fair market value (FMV) of the property determines the amount of the distribution. [I.R.C. §301(b)] This is the amount by which the AAA balance and the shareholder's stock basis are reduced. The shareholder's basis in the property is its FMV. If an S corporation distributes appreciated property to shareholders, the corporation recognizes gain. The amount of gain recognized is the same as if the property had been sold for its FMV. This gain then passes through to the shareholders. Both the S corporation's AAA balance and the shareholder's stock basis increase accordingly. However, the S corporation does not recognize a loss when the FMV of the property distributed is less than its corporate basis. The shareholder's basis in the property is its FMV.

EXAMPLE 21

Freda receives a distribution of property from Flint, an S corporation. Freda is the sole shareholder. Her basis in the Flint stock (prior to the distribution) is $75,000. The property Freda receives has an FMV of $30,000 and an adjusted basis to Flint of $50,000. Freda's basis in the property received is $30,000. Her basis in the Flint stock is reduced to $45,000 ($75,000 – $30,000). Flint does not recognize the $20,000 loss ($50,000 – $30,000). Flint's AAA is reduced by $30,000.

EXAMPLE 22

Same facts as in Example 21, except that the FMV of the property is $70,000 (instead of $30,000). Flint recognizes gain of $20,000 ($70,000 – $50,000) when it distributes appreciated property to its shareholder. This causes Flint's AAA to increase by $20,000. Freda reports the $20,000 of gain on her tax return when it flows through to her on the Schedule K-1 she receives from Flint. This increases her basis in the S corporation stock by $20,000. The distribution of the property will then reduce her basis in the stock by $70,000 (its FMV). After the distribution, Freda's basis in her Flint stock will be $25,000 ($75,000 + $20,000 – $70,000). Her basis in the property is $70,000.

 Since neither the corporation nor the shareholder recognizes the loss, S corporations should avoid distributing property that has declined in value.

¶1603.06 UTILIZING LOSSES

S corporation shareholders may deduct their pro rata share of losses to the extent of their basis in the S corporation stock. [I.R.C. §1366(d)(1)] Thus, losses cannot reduce the owner's basis below zero. A partner's basis includes the partner's share of all partnership liabilities. In contrast, the S corporation's general liabilities are not part of the S shareholder's basis because of the limited liability feature that comes with having corporate status. The only time the corporation's debt increases an S corporation shareholder's basis is when the shareholder has loaned amounts directly to the corporation. [I.R.C. §1366(d)(2)] Thus, a partner generally has a larger basis for utilizing losses than would an S shareholder. Disallowed losses carry forward and are deductible when the shareholder has sufficient basis to cover the losses.

EXAMPLE 23	Swift (an S corporation) has five shareholders, each owning 100 shares and each having a $25,000 basis in the stock. Each shareholder materially participates in the operations of Swift. For 2022, Swift reports an operating loss of $75,000. Each shareholder's pro rata share of the loss ($15,000) is deductible on the shareholder's individual tax return because it does not reduce any shareholder's basis below zero. After the $15,000 loss, each shareholder's basis in his or her Swift shares is $10,000 ($25,000 – $15,000).

EXAMPLE 24	Chelsea Chang owns a 30% interest in Inco, an S corporation. At the end of 2022, Chelsea's basis in Inco stock is $15,000 and she has $12,000 of loans outstanding to Inco. The corporation reports an operating loss for 2022 of $120,000, of which Chelsea's 30% share is $36,000. Chelsea deducts $27,000 of the total loss ($15,000 stock basis + $12,000 loan basis) on her personal tax return. The remaining $9,000 loss ($36,000–$27,000) carries over to 2023 and later years to be offset against future positive stock basis. Chelsea reduces her stock and debt basis to zero at the end of 2022.

When the lack of basis limits the shareholder's deductibility of losses, an allocation of the allowed loss among the various items is necessary. The allocation percentage equals each loss item divided by the shareholder's total losses for the year. The portion of each item disallowed carries forward.

EXAMPLE 25	Ike Ingmann has a $20,000 basis in his 40% ownership in an S corporation. Ike's 40% share of the corporation's ordinary loss and capital loss is $24,000 and $8,000, respectively. His pro rata share of total losses equal $32,000 ($24,000 + $8,000). Ike can deduct $20,000 of losses (an amount equal to his basis). More specifically, he deducts $15,000 of ordinary income ($20,000 × $24,000/$32,000) on his tax return and includes $5,000 of capital loss in his netting process ($20,000 × $8,000/$32,000). Ike carries forward to future years a total loss of $12,000. The carryover loss consists of an ordinary loss deduction of $9,000 ($24,000 – $15,000) and a capital loss deduction of $3,000 ($8,000 – $5,000)

 In addition to the basis loss limitation rules described above, S corporation shareholders are also subject to the at-risk (¶904) and passive loss (¶905) rules.

When an S corporation allocates a loss to a shareholder, there are several limits that may preclude the shareholder from claiming the deduction in the year of allocation. After a loss clears the basis rule, a shareholder may be subject to more restrictions, in this order:

1. The shareholder's amount at-risk [I.R.C. §465]
2. The passive activity loss limit on rental activities and businesses in which the shareholder is not a material participant. [I.R.C. §469]
3. The excess business loss limit, when the shareholder's overall business losses exceed business income by more than $250,000 ($500,000 if married filing jointly). [I.R.C. §461(l)] The limits are indexed for inflation. For 2022, the limits are $270,000, or $540,000 for married taxpayers filing jointly. [Rev. Proc. 2021-45, 2021-48 I.R.B. 764]

When an S corporation election terminates, any disallowed loss can be deducted as long as the shareholders restore their stock basis sufficiently to cover their losses. The basis must be restored by the *later of* the following two dates:

1. One year after the effective date of termination or the due date of the last S corporation tax return, whichever is later, or
2. 120 days after a determination that the corporation's election had terminated for a previous year.

Excess Business Losses

Noncorporate taxpayers are not allowed "excess business losses" for tax years beginning after December 31, 2021, and before January 1, 2026. Any excess business loss that is disallowed is treated as a net operating loss (NOL) carryforward to the following tax year. Taxpayers must apply the passive activity loss rules before applying the excess business loss rules. [I.R.C. §461(l)] The limits are indexed for inflation.

An excess business loss is the excess, if any, of:

1. the taxpayer's aggregate deductions for the tax year from the taxpayer's trades or businesses, determined without regard to whether or not such deductions are disallowed for such tax year under the excess business loss limitation; over
2. the sum of:
    a. the taxpayer's aggregate gross income or gain for the tax year from such trades or businesses, plus
    b. $250,000, adjusted annually for inflation (for a joint return, 200% of the $250,000 amount). For 2022, the limits are $540,000 for married taxpayers filing jointly and $270,000 for all others. As this edition goes to press, the 2023 limits are not yet available.

For S corporations, the limit on excess business losses is applied at the shareholder level. A shareholder takes into account his or her pro rata share of each of the S corporation's items of income, gain, deduction, or loss in applying the excess business loss rules to the shareholder's tax year with or within which the S corporation's tax year ends.

¶1603.07   BUSINESS INTEREST DEDUCTION LIMITATION

For businesses with average gross receipts of more than $27 million in 2022 ($25 million, adjusted for inflation after 2018), the deduction of business interest is limited for tax years beginning after 2017. The deductible amount is the sum of the taxpayer's business interest income, floor plan financing, and 30% of adjusted taxable income. However, the CARES Act of 2020 amended this rule so that taxpayers other than partnerships had a limit of 50% of adjusted taxable income for 2019 and 2020.

For S corporations, the limitation on the deduction of business interest is applied at the entity level. The S corporation takes a deduction for business interest account in determining its non-separately stated taxable income or loss.

The shareholder's adjusted taxable income is determined without regard to the shareholder's distributive share of any S corporation item of income, gain, deduction, or loss.

An S corporation passes through to shareholders any excess taxable income for purposes of the deduction limit. The S corporation's excess taxable income is a percentage of its adjusted taxable income for the year. The percentage is: 30% (or 50% for 2019 and 2020) of the entity's adjusted taxable income, over its net excess business interest (the excess of business interest of the entity, reduced by floor plan financing interest, over business interest income); over 30% (or 50%) of the entity's adjusted taxable income.

Each shareholder's adjusted taxable income is increased by the shareholder's pro rata share of the S corporation's excess taxable income. A shareholder's pro rata share of partnership excess taxable income is determined in the same manner as the shareholder's pro rata share of the S corporation's non-separately stated taxable income or loss.

This addition to a shareholder's adjusted taxable income, allows the shareholder to deduct more interest than the shareholder may have paid or incurred during the year, to the extent the S corporation could have deducted more business interest.

Generally business interest that is not deductible due to the limitation may be carried forward indefinitely. For S corporations, a disallowed interest deduction is carried forward to the succeeding tax year.

The shareholder's adjusted basis in the shareholder's interest in the S corporation is unaffected by the amount of excess business interest allocated by the corporation to the partner or shareholder.

¶1603.08   FORM 1120-S

Form 1120-S resembles the partnership tax return. Form 1120-S consists of five pages. On page 1, the S corporation provides general information about itself and computes its ordinary business income (loss). On page 2 of Form 1120-S, the corporation provides other information about itself on Schedule B. Schedule K begins on page 3 and concludes at the top of page 4. Like with the partnership tax return, Schedule K reports the corporation's ordinary income (or loss) plus all separately stated items. Page 4 also reports the corporation's balance sheet on Schedule L. Finally, page 5 concludes with Schedules M-1 (reconciliation of book income and tax income), and M-2 (analysis of the accumulated adjustment account and other capital accounts).

As with partnerships, the calculation of ordinary business income (loss) on page 1 includes all items of income and expense that are treated and taxed the same for all taxpayers. These items are not subject to any limitations that would be unique to any one taxpayer. The calculation of ordinary business income (loss) for S corporations is essentially the same as that for partnerships, with one important exception. Chapter 15, stated that partners could not be employees of the partnership. Thus, payments that resemble "salaries" paid to partners are called guaranteed payments (see ¶1502.06). These amounts are deducted in the calculation of the partnership's ordinary business income (loss). With respect to an S corporation, all shareholders working for the S corporation are considered employees, and payments to shareholders in exchange for services they perform are deducted as wages. Thus, an S corporation does not make guaranteed payments.

Another difference between partnerships and S corporations is the characterization of self-employment income. An individual partner's share of business income, as well as guaranteed payments for services, are subject to self-employment tax. In contrast, an S corporation's income is not self-employment income to any shareholder. However, an S corporation and any shareholder-employee are subject to FICA tax on the compensation. The corporation must observe all of the payroll tax and reporting procedures required for all employers. S corporations that do not observe these rules have often been subject to the penalties for failure to withhold and failure to deposit payroll taxes. See Chapter 13.

Schedule K Items

The S corporation's ordinary business income (loss) from Form 1120-S, page 1 (line 21) is also reported on Schedule K, Shareholders' Pro Rata Share Items. Income and expense items not part of ordinary income as well as tax credits, are separately stated and reported on Schedule K. The S corporation uses the amounts found on the Schedule K to make its per-share-per-day allocations to its shareholders. These are reported to each shareholder on a separate Schedule K-1. The shareholders combine their Schedule K-1 items with their other income, expense, and credit items. The resulting amounts appear on the shareholders' own income tax returns.

Schedule L

Schedule L, Balance Sheets per Books, contains a beginning and ending balance sheet for the S corporation. The amounts shown should agree with the corporation's regular books or records. Thus, they typically are not reported on a tax basis. An S corporation is required to complete Schedule L only when its total assets at the end of the year or total receipts for the year are $250,000 or more (see items a and b below question 11 on Form 1120-S, page 2, Section B).

Schedule M-1

Schedule M-1, Reconciliation of Income (Loss) per Books With Income (Loss) per Return, is completed if total assets at year-end or total receipts for the year are $250,000 or more (see items a and b below question 11 on Form 1120-S, page 2, Section B). This schedule accounts for all differences between book (financial) income and the income reported on the tax return. The tax return income includes ordinary income (loss) plus the separately stated items found on Schedule K. Any items included in book income, but not on Form 1120-S or vice versa, are reconciling items on Schedule M-1. The most common reconciling items on Schedule M-1 are depreciation; travel and entertainment expenses; and tax-exempt items.

Schedule M-2

Schedule M-2, Analysis of Accumulated Adjustments Account, Shareholders' Undistributed Taxable Income Previously Taxed, Accumulated Earnings and Profits, and Other Adjustments Account, shows the changes in the equity accounts for the income and deductions reported on Form 1120-S. Column (a) provides the changes in the accumulated adjustments account (AAA) for the year (described in the chapter at ¶1603.05). The ending balance becomes the beginning balance of Schedule M-2 (line 1), column (a) for the next year. Column (b) on Schedule M-2 lists the amount of undistributed taxable income previously included in shareholders' income tax returns. Only corporations electing S status before 1983 use column (b). Column (c), Accumulated earnings and profits, is used to enter the amount of any accumulated earnings and profits (E&P) at the close of its prior tax year, if the corporation was a C corporation in a prior year, or if it engaged in a tax-free reorganization with a C corporation. Column (d), other adjustments account, is for an analysis of other items, such as tax-exempt income and related expenses, not used in computing AAA.

Schedule M-3

An S corporation with assets of $10,000,000 or more files Schedule M-3 instead of Schedule M-1. Schedule M-3 is a detailed, line-by-line reconciliation of book-tax differences. This form separates permanent differences, such as tax-exempt income, into one category and timing differences, such as depreciation, into another category.

Schedule K-2

Beginning with returns required for the 2021 taxable year, many S corporations must include Schedule K-2 with their returns. This is a lengthy (up to 14 page) schedule that classifies financial details so that shareholders can properly calculate their Foreign Tax Credit limitations.

For 2021 returns, an S corporation is excused from filing these schedules, if it meets all of these conditions:

- In tax year 2021, the S corporation has no foreign activity, including foreign taxes paid or accrued or ownership of assets that generate, have generated or may reasonably expected to generate foreign-source income;
- In tax year 2020, the S corporation did not provide to its shareholders nor did the shareholders request the information regarding Schedules K and K-1 line; and
- The S corporation has no knowledge that the shareholders are requesting such information for tax year 2021.

However, all S corporations must file this schedule (as well as Schedule K-3, discussed below), for 2022 returns, unless the IRS changes policy.

¶1603.08

FILLED-IN FORM 1120-S

 ## INFORMATION FOR FIGURE 16-4:

Kendall Management Company (EIN **70-1739257**) is a cash basis management service business that provides consulting services to its clients. The company was incorporated on **January 15, 2004**, and elected S corporation status that same day. Kendall's business activity code number is **541610**. Kendall is located at **731 Delhi Road, Atlanta, GA 30307. Tax Consultants, Inc.** prepares Kendall's Form 1120-S. **Virginia Kendall, President**, signs the tax return for the corporation on **March 1, 2023**.

During the year, Kendall distributed a total of $30,000 to its shareholders out of AAA. Kendall had six shareholders during the year. The remaining information for preparing Form 1120-S comes from the income statement found in Figure 16-3.

Line # (Form 1120-S, page 1)
   F: Total assets, **$225,650** (source: Schedule L, line 15, column d)
   I: Number of shareholders, **6** (source: given)
  18: Employee benefits program, **$7,300** (employee health insurance)
  19: Other deductions, **$4,900** ($1,400 insurance + $800 supplies + $2,700 utilities)

Line # (Form 1120-S, Schedule B)
   1: Accounting method, check box **a** (source: cash basis taxpayer)
  2a: Business activity, **Management services** (source: given)
  2b: Product or service, **Consulting** (source: given)
  11: Check box for Yes, since both total receipts and total assets are less than $250,000
       Kendall is not required to complete schedules L and M -1. However, it is a good practice to complete these schedules, which are shown in the solution

Line # (Form 1120-S, Schedule K)
   4: Interest income, **$720** (source: taxable interest reported on the Income Statement)
  5a: Ordinary dividends, **$2,000** (source: total dividends reported on the Income Statement)
  5b: Qualified dividends, **$1,250** (source: Income Statement)
  8a: Net long-term capital gain, **$10,480** (source: Schedule D (Form 1120-S), line 13)
 12a: Charitable contributions, **$7,000** (source: Income Statement)
 16a: Tax-exempt interest, **$1,100** (source: Income Statement)
 17a: Investment income, **$2,720** ($720 taxable interest + $2,000 dividend income)
  18: Income/loss reconciliation, **$46,200** ($40,000 + $720 + $2,000 + $10,480 − $7,000)

Line # (Form 1120-S, Schedule M-2)
 1(a): Beginning balance Accumulated adjustments account, **$74,900** (source: last year's ending balance)
 1(b): $0. This account only applies to corporations that were S corporations before 1983
 1(c): Accumulated earnings and profits at the end of the year, **$0** (never a C corporation, thus no E&P)
 1(d): Beginning balance Other adjustments account, **$15,100** (source: last year's ending balance)
 3(a): Other additions to AAA, **$13,200** ($720 taxable interest + $2,000 ordinary dividends + $10,480 capital gain)
 3(d): Other additions to Other adjustments account, **$1,100** (tax-exempt interest)
 5(a): Other reductions, **$7,000** (charitable contributions)
 7(a): Distributions, **$30,000** (source: given)

Figure 16-3: Kendall Management 2022 Income Statement

Income:

Receipts from services	$165,350
Interest income (taxable, $720; tax-exempt, $1,100)	1,820
Dividend income (qualified dividends, $1,250)	2,000
Gain on sale of stock	10,480
Total income	$179,650

Expenses:

Advertising	$ 7,700
Charitable contributions	7,000
Depreciation (book and tax depreciation)	1,700
Employee health insurance	7,300
Insurance expense	1,400
Maintenance and repairs	1,200
Officers' salaries	70,000
Other employee salaries	21,550
Office supplies	800
Payroll taxes	5,000
Retirement plan contributions	6,000
Utilities	2,700
Total expenses	$132,350
Net Income	$ 47,300

Figure 16-4: Filled-In Form 1120-S (Page 1)

Form **1120-S**	**U.S. Income Tax Return for an S Corporation**	OMB No. 1545-0123
Department of the Treasury Internal Revenue Service	Do not file this form unless the corporation has filed or is attaching Form 2553 to elect to be an S corporation. Go to *www.irs.gov/Form1120S* for instructions and the latest information.	20**22**

For calendar year 2022 or tax year beginning _____, 2022, ending _____, 20 ____

A S election effective date	01/15/2004	TYPE OR PRINT	Name Kendall Management Company	D Employer identification number 70-1739257
B Business activity code number (see instructions)	541610		Number, street, and room or suite no. If a P.O. box, see instructions. 731 Delhi Road	E Date incorporated 01/15/2004
C Check if Sch. M-3 attached ☐			City or town, state or province, country, and ZIP or foreign postal code Atlanta, GA 30307	F Total assets (see instructions) $ 225,650

G Is the corporation electing to be an S corporation beginning with this tax year? See instructions. ☐ Yes ☑ No
H Check if: (1) ☐ Final return (2) ☐ Name change (3) ☐ Address change (4) ☐ Amended return (5) ☐ S election termination
I Enter the number of shareholders who were shareholders during any part of the tax year ... 6
J Check if corporation: (1) ☐ Aggregated activities for section 465 at-risk purposes (2) ☐ Grouped activities for section 469 passive activity purposes

Caution: Include **only** trade or business income and expenses on lines 1a through 21. See the instructions for more information.

Income

1a	Gross receipts or sales	1a	165,350	
b	Returns and allowances	1b		
c	Balance. Subtract line 1b from line 1a		1c	165,350
2	Cost of goods sold (attach Form 1125-A)		2	
3	Gross profit. Subtract line 2 from line 1c		3	165,350
4	Net gain (loss) from Form 4797, line 17 (attach Form 4797)		4	
5	Other income (loss) (see instructions—attach statement)		5	
6	**Total income (loss).** Add lines 3 through 5		6	165,350

Deductions (see instructions for limitations)

7	Compensation of officers (see instructions—attach Form 1125-E)	7	70,000
8	Salaries and wages (less employment credits)	8	21,550
9	Repairs and maintenance	9	1,200
10	Bad debts	10	
11	Rents	11	
12	Taxes and licenses	12	5,000
13	Interest (see instructions)	13	
14	Depreciation from Form 4562 not claimed on Form 1125-A or elsewhere on return (attach Form 4562)	14	1,700
15	Depletion (**Do not deduct oil and gas depletion.**)	15	
16	Advertising	16	7,700
17	Pension, profit-sharing, etc., plans	17	6,000
18	Employee benefit programs	18	7,300
19	Other deductions (attach statement)	19	4,900
20	**Total deductions.** Add lines 7 through 19	20	125,350
21	**Ordinary business income (loss).** Subtract line 20 from line 6	21	40,000

Tax and Payments

22a	Excess net passive income or LIFO recapture tax (see instructions)	22a		
b	Tax from Schedule D (Form 1120-S)	22b		
c	Add lines 22a and 22b (see instructions for additional taxes)		22c	
23a	2022 estimated tax payments and 2021 overpayment credited to 2022	23a		
b	Tax deposited with Form 7004	23b		
c	Credit for federal tax paid on fuels (attach Form 4136)	23c		
d	Add lines 23a through 23c		23d	
24	Estimated tax penalty (see instructions). Check if Form 2220 is attached ☐		24	
25	**Amount owed.** If line 23d is smaller than the total of lines 22c and 24, enter amount owed		25	
26	**Overpayment.** If line 23d is larger than the total of lines 22c and 24, enter amount overpaid		26	
27	Enter amount from line 26: Credited to 2023 estimated tax _____ Refunded		27	

Sign Here
Under penalties of perjury, I declare that I have examined this return, including accompanying schedules and statements, and to the best of my knowledge and belief, it is true, correct, and complete. Declaration of preparer (other than taxpayer) is based on all information of which preparer has any knowledge.

Signature of officer _____ Date _____ Title _____

May the IRS discuss this return with the preparer shown below? See instructions. ☐ Yes ☐ No

Paid Preparer Use Only

Print/Type preparer's name	Preparer's signature	Date	Check ☐ if self-employed	PTIN
Firm's name			Firm's EIN	
Firm's address			Phone no.	

For Paperwork Reduction Act Notice, see separate instructions.   Cat. No. 11510H   Form **1120-S** (2022)

Figure 16-4: Filled-In Form 1120-S (Page 2)

Form 1120-S (2022)   Page **2**

Schedule B   Other Information (see instructions)

		Yes	No
1	Check accounting method: **a** ☑ Cash **b** ☐ Accrual		
	c ☐ Other (specify) _____		
2	See the instructions and enter the:		
	a Business activity **Service** **b** Product or service **Management**		
3	At any time during the tax year, was any shareholder of the corporation a disregarded entity, a trust, an estate, or a nominee or similar person? If "Yes," attach Schedule B-1, Information on Certain Shareholders of an S Corporation . .		✔
4	At the end of the tax year, did the corporation:		
a	Own directly 20% or more, or own, directly or indirectly, 50% or more of the total stock issued and outstanding of any foreign or domestic corporation? For rules of constructive ownership, see instructions. If "Yes," complete (i) through (v) below		✔

(i) Name of Corporation	(ii) Employer Identification Number (if any)	(iii) Country of Incorporation	(iv) Percentage of Stock Owned	(v) If Percentage in (iv) Is 100%, Enter the Date (if applicable) a Qualified Subchapter S Subsidiary Election Was Made

		Yes	No
b	Own directly an interest of 20% or more, or own, directly or indirectly, an interest of 50% or more in the profit, loss, or capital in any foreign or domestic partnership (including an entity treated as a partnership) or in the beneficial interest of a trust? For rules of constructive ownership, see instructions. If "Yes," complete (i) through (v) below		✔

(i) Name of Entity	(ii) Employer Identification Number (if any)	(iii) Type of Entity	(iv) Country of Organization	(v) Maximum Percentage Owned in Profit, Loss, or Capital

		Yes	No
5a	At the end of the tax year, did the corporation have any outstanding shares of restricted stock?		✔
	If "Yes," complete lines (i) and (ii) below.		
	(i) Total shares of restricted stock _____		
	(ii) Total shares of non-restricted stock . . . . _____		
b	At the end of the tax year, did the corporation have any outstanding stock options, warrants, or similar instruments? .		✔
	If "Yes," complete lines (i) and (ii) below.		
	(i) Total shares of stock outstanding at the end of the tax year . _____		
	(ii) Total shares of stock outstanding if all instruments were executed _____		
6	Has this corporation filed, or is it required to file, **Form 8918,** Material Advisor Disclosure Statement, to provide information on any reportable transaction?		✔
7	Check this box if the corporation issued publicly offered debt instruments with original issue discount . . . . . ☐		
	If checked, the corporation may have to file **Form 8281,** Information Return for Publicly Offered Original Issue Discount Instruments.		
8	If the corporation **(a)** was a C corporation before it elected to be an S corporation **or** the corporation acquired an asset with a basis determined by reference to the basis of the asset (or the basis of any other property) in the hands of a C corporation, **and (b)** has net unrealized built-in gain in excess of the net recognized built-in gain from prior years, enter the net unrealized built-in gain reduced by net recognized built-in gain from prior years. See instructions . . . . $		
9	Did the corporation have an election under section 163(j) for any real property trade or business or any farming business in effect during the tax year? See instructions		✔
10	Does the corporation satisfy one or more of the following? See instructions		
a	The corporation owns a pass-through entity with current, or prior year carryover, excess business interest expense.		
b	The corporation's aggregate average annual gross receipts (determined under section 448(c)) for the 3 tax years preceding the current tax year are more than $27 million and the corporation has business interest expense.		
c	The corporation is a tax shelter and the corporation has business interest expense.		
	If "Yes," complete and attach **Form 8990,** Limitation on Business Interest Expense Under Section 163(j).		
11	Does the corporation satisfy **both** of the following conditions?	✔	
a	The corporation's total receipts (see instructions) for the tax year were less than $250,000.		
b	The corporation's total assets at the end of the tax year were less than $250,000.		
	If "Yes," the corporation is not required to complete Schedules L and M-1.		

Form **1120-S** (2022)

¶1603.08

Figure 16-4: Filled-In Form 1120-S (Page 3)

Form 1120-S (2022)					Page **3**

Schedule B	Other Information (see instructions) *(continued)*		Yes	No
12	During the tax year, did the corporation have any non-shareholder debt that was canceled, was forgiven, or had the terms modified so as to reduce the principal amount of the debt?			✔
	If "Yes," enter the amount of principal reduction . . . . $			
13	During the tax year, was a qualified subchapter S subsidiary election terminated or revoked? If "Yes," see instructions .			✔
14a	Did the corporation make any payments in 2022 that would require it to file Form(s) 1099?		✔	
b	If "Yes," did or will the corporation file required Form(s) 1099?		✔	
15	Is the corporation attaching Form 8996 to certify as a Qualified Opportunity Fund?			✔
	If "Yes," enter the amount from Form 8996, line 15 . . . . $			

Schedule K		Shareholders' Pro Rata Share Items			Total amount
Income (Loss)	1	Ordinary business income (loss) (page 1, line 21)		1	40,000
	2	Net rental real estate income (loss) (attach Form 8825)		2	
	3a	Other gross rental income (loss)	3a		
	b	Expenses from other rental activities (attach statement) . . .	3b		
	c	Other net rental income (loss). Subtract line 3b from line 3a		3c	
	4	Interest income		4	720
	5	Dividends: **a** Ordinary dividends		5a	2,000
		b Qualified dividends	5b	1,250	
	6	Royalties		6	
	7	Net short-term capital gain (loss) (attach Schedule D (Form 1120-S)) . .		7	
	8a	Net long-term capital gain (loss) (attach Schedule D (Form 1120-S)) . .		8a	10,480
	b	Collectibles (28%) gain (loss)	8b		
	c	Unrecaptured section 1250 gain (attach statement)	8c		
	9	Net section 1231 gain (loss) (attach Form 4797)		9	
	10	Other income (loss) (see instructions) Type:		10	
Deductions	11	Section 179 deduction (attach Form 4562)		11	
	12a	Charitable contributions		12a	7,000
	b	Investment interest expense		12b	
	c	Section 59(e)(2) expenditures . . . . Type:		12c	
	d	Other deductions (see instructions) Type:		12d	
Credits	13a	Low-income housing credit (section 42(j)(5))		13a	
	b	Low-income housing credit (other)		13b	
	c	Qualified rehabilitation expenditures (rental real estate) (attach Form 3468, if applicable) . .		13c	
	d	Other rental real estate credits (see instructions) Type:		13d	
	e	Other rental credits (see instructions) . . . Type:		13e	
	f	Biofuel producer credit (attach Form 6478)		13f	
	g	Other credits (see instructions) . . . . . Type:		13g	
International	14	Attach Schedule K-2 (Form 1120-S), Shareholders' Pro Rata Share Items—International, and check this box to indicate you are reporting items of international tax relevance . . . . . ✔			
Alternative Minimum Tax (AMT) Items	15a	Post-1986 depreciation adjustment		15a	
	b	Adjusted gain or loss		15b	
	c	Depletion (other than oil and gas)		15c	
	d	Oil, gas, and geothermal properties—gross income		15d	
	e	Oil, gas, and geothermal properties—deductions		15e	
	f	Other AMT items (attach statement)		15f	
Items Affecting Shareholder Basis	16a	Tax-exempt interest income		16a	1,100
	b	Other tax-exempt income		16b	
	c	Nondeductible expenses		16c	
	d	Distributions (attach statement if required) (see instructions)		16d	30,000
	e	Repayment of loans from shareholders		16e	
	f	Foreign taxes paid or accrued		16f	

		Form **1120-S** (2022)

Figure 16-4: Filled-In Form 1120-S (Page 4)

Form 1120-S (2022)   Page **4**

Schedule K   **Shareholders' Pro Rata Share Items** *(continued)*   Total amount

Other Information

			Total amount
17a	Investment income	17a	2,720
b	Investment expenses	17b	
c	Dividend distributions paid from accumulated earnings and profits	17c	
d	Other items and amounts (attach statement)		

Reconciliation

18   **Income (loss) reconciliation.** Combine the amounts on lines 1 through 10 in the far right column. From the result, subtract the sum of the amounts on lines 11 through 12d and 16f   **18**   46,200

Schedule L   **Balance Sheets per Books**

	Assets	Beginning of tax year (a)	(b)	End of tax year (c)	(d)
1	Cash		14,000		18,000
2a	Trade notes and accounts receivable	18,000		21,600	
b	Less allowance for bad debts	( )	18,000	( )	
3	Inventories				
4	U.S. government obligations				
5	Tax-exempt securities (see instructions)				
6	Other current assets (attach statement)		25,650		33,000
7	Loans to shareholders				
8	Mortgage and real estate loans				
9	Other investments (attach statement)		100,000		
10a	Buildings and other depreciable assets	53,550		53,550	
b	Less accumulated depreciation	(10,200)	43,350	(11,900)	41,650
11a	Depletable assets				
b	Less accumulated depletion	( )		( )	
12	Land (net of any amortization)				
13a	Intangible assets (amortizable only)				
b	Less accumulated amortization	( )		( )	
14	Other assets (attach statement)				
15	Total assets		201,000		225,650
	Liabilities and Shareholders' Equity				
16	Accounts payable		11,000		18,350
17	Mortgages, notes, bonds payable in less than 1 year				
18	Other current liabilities (attach statement)				
19	Loans from shareholders				
20	Mortgages, notes, bonds payable in 1 year or more				
21	Other liabilities (attach statement)				
22	Capital stock		100,000		100,000
23	Additional paid-in capital				
24	Retained earnings		90,000		107,300
25	Adjustments to shareholders' equity (attach statement)				
26	Less cost of treasury stock	( )		( )	
27	Total liabilities and shareholders' equity		201,000		225,650

Form **1120-S** (2022)

¶1603.08

Figure 16-4: Filled-In Form 1120-S (Page 5)

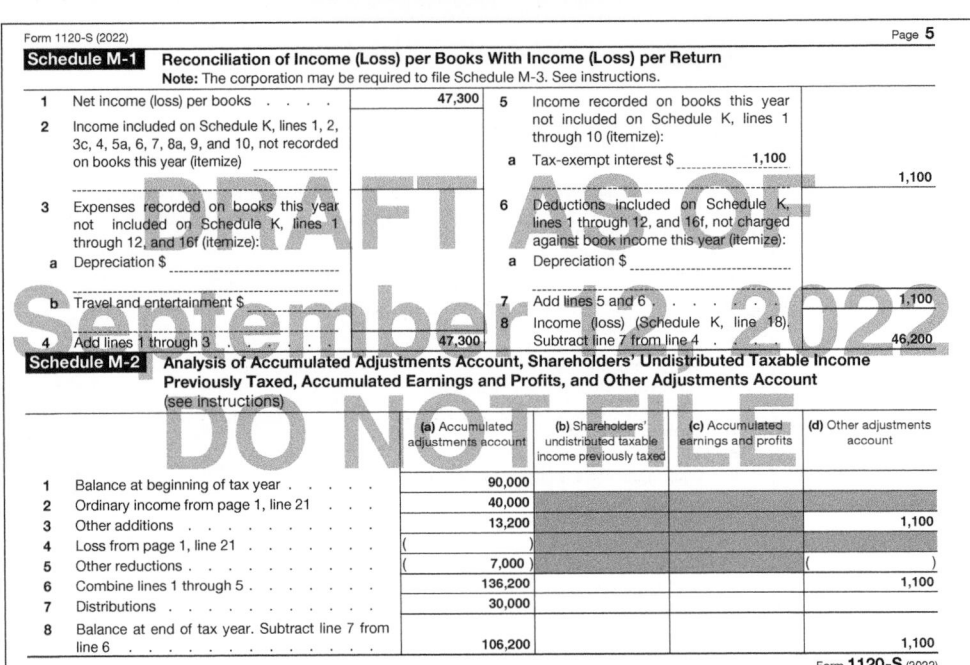

Beginning with the returns for the 2021 taxable year, most S corporations must also complete Form 1120-S Schedule K-2. This form provides shareholders with information for computing the Foreign Tax Credit.

- Page 1 contains the usual identification information and a checklist.
- Part I applies if the corporation has foreign-sourced sales of personal property. Kendall does not check this box.
- Part II applies to most, if not all, S corporations. It includes most types of gross income, gains, losses and deductions. Kendall checks this box.
- Part III contains details of research and experimentation expenditures. Kendall has none and leaves this box blank.
- Part IV discloses distributions from foreign corporations. Kendall has none and leaves this box blank.
- Part V applies when an S corporation owns 10% or more of certain foreign corporations. Kendall has none and leaves this box blank.
- Part VI provides information about investments in certain specialized categories of foreign corporations. Kendall has none and leaves this box blank.
- Part VII covers certain foreign taxes paid by foreign subsidiaries, which are attributed to U.S. shareholders. Kendall has none and leaves this box blank.

Page 1 is also the beginning of Part II, the details of gross income, gains, losses and deductions. Since the separate classification of these items might affect any shareholder's Foreign Tax Credit, Kendall must fill in the appropriate portions of this part. Since Kendall's business income is from services and is all within the U.S., it enters the appropriate information on line 2.

Figure 16-5: Filled-In Schedule K-2 (Form 1120-S) (Page 1)

SCHEDULE K-2 (Form 1120-S) Department of the Treasury Internal Revenue Service	Shareholders' Pro Rata Share Items—International Attach to Form 1120-S. Go to www.irs.gov/Form1120S for instructions and the latest information.	OMB No. 1545-0123 2022

Name of corporation: Kendall Management Company   Employer identification number (EIN): 70-1739257

A Check to indicate the parts of Schedule K-2 that apply.

		Yes	No
1	Does Part I apply? If "Yes," complete and attach Part I		✔
2	Does Part II apply? If "Yes," complete and attach Part II	✔	
3	Does Part III apply? If "Yes," complete and attach Part III		✔
4	Does Part IV apply? If "Yes," complete and attach Part IV		✔
5	Does Part V apply? If "Yes," complete and attach Part V		✔
6	Does Part VI apply? If "Yes," complete and attach Part VI		✔
7	Does Part VII apply? If "Yes," complete and attach Part VII		✔

Part I — Corporation's Other Current Year International Information

Check box(es) for additional specified attachments. See instructions.

- ☐ 1. Gain on personal property sale
- ☐ 2. Foreign oil and gas taxes
- ☐ 3. Splitter arrangements
- ☐ 4. Foreign tax translation
- ☐ 5. High-taxed income
- ☐ 6. Section 267A disallowed deduction
- ☐ 7. Form 8858 information
- ☐ 8. Form 5471 information
- ☐ 9. Other forms
- ☐ 10. Shareholder loan transactions
- ☐ 11. Entity treatment for certain S corporations
- ☐ 12. Reserved for future use
- ☐ 13. Other international items (attach description and statement)

Part II — Foreign Tax Credit Limitation
Section 1—Gross Income

Description	(a) U.S. source	(b) Foreign branch category income	(c) Passive category income	(d) General category income	(e) Other (category code)	(f) Sourced by shareholder	(g) Total
1 Sales							
A							
B							
C							
2 Gross income from performance of services							
A US	165,350						165,350
B							
C							
3 Gross rental real estate income							
A							
B							
C							
4 Other gross rental income							
A							
B							
C							

For Paperwork Reduction Act Notice, see the Instructions for Form 1120-S.   Cat. No. 73973Q   Schedule K-2 (Form 1120-S) 2022

Kendall reports its interest, ordinary dividend, qualified dividend and capital gains on page 2.

Figure 16-5: Filled-In Schedule K-2 (Form 1120-S) (Page 2)

Schedule K-2 (Form 1120-S) 2022   Page **2**

Name of corporation							EIN
Kendall Management Company							70-1739257

Part II   **Foreign Tax Credit Limitation** *(continued)*

Section 1—Gross Income *(continued)*

Description	(a) U.S. source	Foreign Source				(f) Sourced by shareholder	(g) Total
		(b) Foreign branch category income	(c) Passive category income	(d) General category income	(e) Other (category code____)		
5 Reserved for future use							
6 Interest income							
A US	720						720
B							
C							
7 Ordinary dividends (exclude amount on line 8)							
A US	750						750
B							
C							
8 Qualified dividends							
A US	1,250						1,250
B							
C							
9 Reserved for future use							
10 Royalties and license fees							
A							
B							
C							
11 Net short-term capital gain							
A							
B							
C							
12 Net long-term capital gain							
A US	10,480						10,480
B							
C							
13 Collectibles (28%) gain							
A							
B							
C							
14 Unrecaptured section 1250 gain							
A							
B							
C							

Schedule K-2 (Form 1120-S) 2022

On page 3, Kendall summarizes its gross income. It has no other items to report on this page.

Figure 16-5: Filled-In Schedule K-2 (Form 1120-S) (Page 3)

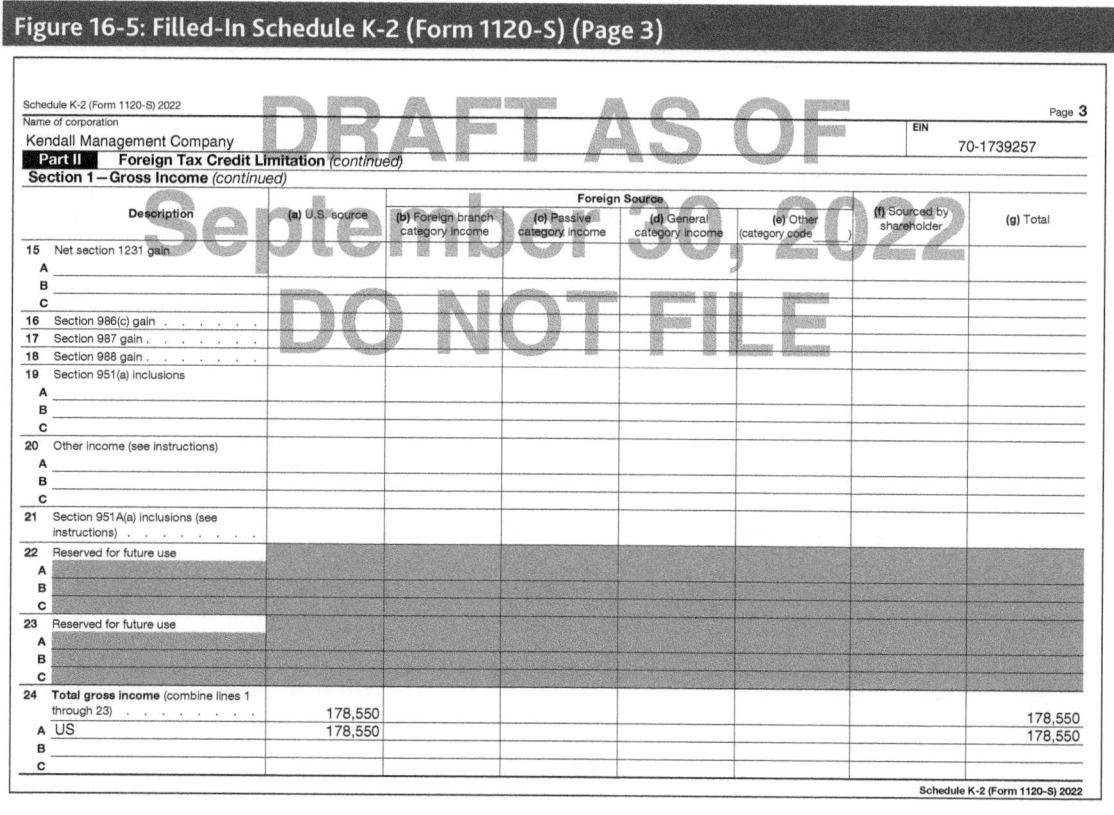

On page 4, Kendall reports expenses and other expenditures. The corporation needs to segregate depreciation and interest expense from other deductions. It also must report charitable contributions on this page.

Figure 16-5: Filled-In Schedule K-2 (Form 1120-S) (Page 4)

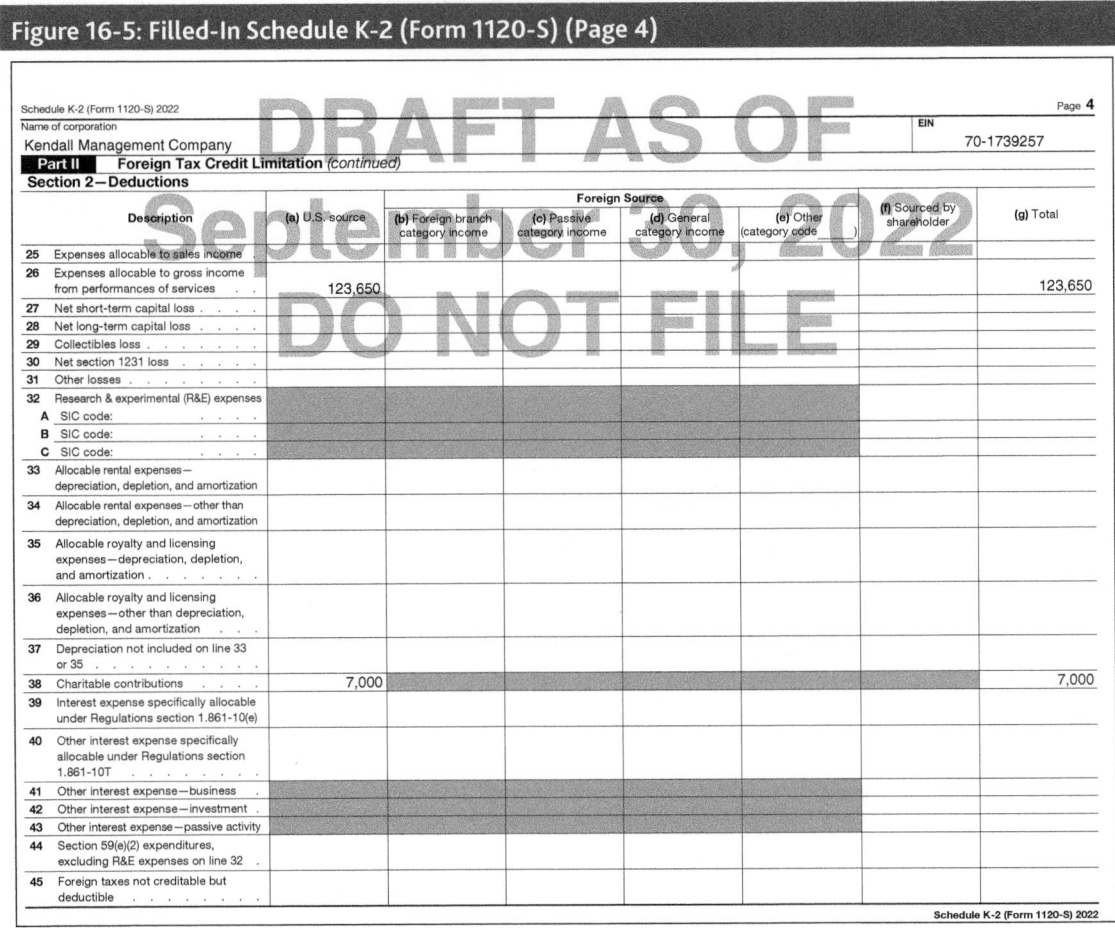

On page 5, Kendall would report certain foreign-source losses, if it had such items. The final lines of Part II summarize the deductions and report the net income or loss. The net income on line 55 is the same as the amount on Schedule K, line 18.

The remainder of page 5 deals with research and experimentation costs. Kendall has none of these costs this year so it is not necessary to complete this part, or attach it to the return. However, for educational purposes, this material presents the entire form.

Figure 16-5: Filled-In Schedule K-2 (Form 1120-S) (Page 5)

Schedule K-2 (Form 1120-S) 2022 | Page **5**

Name of corporation: Kendall Management Company | EIN: 70-1739257

Part II — Foreign Tax Credit Limitation *(continued)*
Section 2—Deductions *(continued)*

	Description	(a) U.S. source	(b) Foreign branch category income	(c) Passive category income	(d) General category income	(e) Other (category code)	(f) Sourced by shareholder	(g) Total
46	Section 986(c) loss							
47	Section 987 loss							
48	Section 988 loss							
49	Other allocable deductions (see instructions)							
50	Other apportioned share of deductions (see instructions)							
51	Reserved for future use							
52	Reserved for future use							
53	Reserved for future use							
54	Total deductions (combine lines 25 through 53)	130,650						130,650
55	Net income (loss) (subtract line 54 from line 24)	47,900						47,900

Part III — Other Information for Preparation of Form 1116
Section 1—R&E Expenses Apportionment Factors

	Description	(a) U.S. source	(b) Foreign branch category income	(c) Passive category income	(d) General category income	(e) Other (category code ___) (country code ___)	(f) Sourced by shareholder	(g) Total
1	Gross receipts by SIC code							
A	SIC code:							
B	SIC code:							
C	SIC code:							
D	SIC code:							
E	SIC code:							
F	SIC code:							

2 Exclusive apportionment with respect to total R&E expenses entered on Part II, line 32. Enter the following.
A R&E expense with respect to activity performed in the United States
  (i) SIC code: _____ .... 2A(i)
  (ii) SIC code: _____ .... 2A(ii)
  (iii) SIC code: _____ .... 2A(iii)
B R&E expense with respect to activity performed outside the United States
  (i) SIC code: _____ .... 2B(i)
  (ii) SIC code: _____ .... 2B(ii)
  (iii) SIC code: _____ .... 2B(iii)

Schedule K-2 (Form 1120-S) 2022

Figure 16 5: Filled-In Form 1120-S Schedule K-2 (Pages 6 through 14) Since Kendall Management Company has no international dealings, it is not required to include any of these pages with its return. This chapter does not include these pages in any examples or problems.

¶1603.09   FILLED-IN SCHEDULE K-1 (FORM 1120-S)

 ### INFORMATION FOR FIGURE 16-6:

Virginia Kendall (**SSN 421-00-8045**) owns 30 shares (30% of the corporation's stock). Her ownership did not change at any time this year. Virginia's address is **4524 Peachtree Drive, Atlanta, GA 30307**.

Line #

- C: IRS Center where corporation filed return, **Kansas City, MO**
- F: Shareholder's percentage of stock ownership for tax year, **30**
- G: Number of shares:
  - Beginning of tax year **30**
  - End of tax year   **30**
- 1: Ordinary income, **$12,000** (30% × $40,000)
- 4: Interest income, **$216** (30% × $720)
- 5a: Ordinary dividends, **$600** (30% × $2,000)
- 5b: Qualified dividends, **$375** (30% × $1,250)
- 8a: Net long-term capital gain, **$3,144** (30% × $10,480)
- 12: Charitable contributions, **$2,100** (30% × $7,000) – Designated with a code **A** from the instructions to Schedule K-1
- 16: Tax-exempt interest, **$330** (30% × $1,100) – Designated with a code **A** from the instructions to Schedule K-1
- 16: Distribution, **$9,000** (30% of $30,000) – Designated with a code **D** from the instructions to Schedule K-1
- 17: Investment income, **$816** (30% × ($720 + $2,000)) – Designated with a code **A** from the instructions to Schedule K-1
- 17: Code V for Qualified business income deduction
  - Consulting is a specified service trade or business, so all ordinary income is in this category. (30% × $40,000)
  - Officer compensation and other compensation both qualify as W-2 wages (30% × $91,550)
  - Unadjusted bases (given, $60,000)

Figure 16-6: Filled-In Schedule K-1 (Form 1120-S)

671121

☐ Final K-1 ☐ Amended K-1	OMB No. 1545-0123

Schedule K-1
(Form 1120-S)
2022

Department of the Treasury
Internal Revenue Service

For calendar year 2022, or tax year

beginning / / 2022   ending / /

Shareholder's Share of Income, Deductions, Credits, etc.   See separate instructions.

DRAFT AS OF July 7, 2022 DO NOT FILE

Part III	**Shareholder's Share of Current Year Income, Deductions, Credits, and Other Items**

Part I	Information About the Corporation

A Corporation's employer identification number
70-1739257

B Corporation's name, address, city, state, and ZIP code

Kendall Management Company
731 Delhi Road
Atlanta, GA 30307

C IRS Center where corporation filed return
Kansas City, MO

D Corporation's total number of shares

Beginning of tax year	100
End of tax year	100

Part II	Information About the Shareholder

E Shareholder's identifying number
421-00-8045

F Shareholder's name, address, city, state, and ZIP code

Virginia Kendall
1524 Peachtree Drive
Atlanta, GA 30307

G Current year allocation percentage . . . 030.0000 %

H Shareholder's number of shares

Beginning of tax year	30
End of tax year	30

I Loans from shareholder

Beginning of tax year	$
End of tax year	$

For IRS Use Only

#	Item		#	Item
1	Ordinary business income (loss) 12,000		13	Credits
2	Net rental real estate income (loss)			
3	Other net rental income (loss)			
4	Interest income 216			
5a	Ordinary dividends 600			
5b	Qualified dividends 375		14	Schedule K-3 is attached if checked . . . . . . ☒
6	Royalties		15	Alternative minimum tax (AMT) items
7	Net short-term capital gain (loss)			
8a	Net long-term capital gain (loss) 3,144			
8b	Collectibles (28%) gain (loss)			
8c	Unrecaptured section 1250 gain			
9	Net section 1231 gain (loss)		16	Items affecting shareholder basis 330
10	Other income (loss)			9,000
			17	Other information
			V	QB Income 12,000
11	Section 179 deduction			W-2 Wages 27,465
12 A	Other deductions 2,100		V	UBIA 16,065
			A	816
18	☐ More than one activity for at-risk purposes*			
19	☐ More than one activity for passive activity purposes*			

* See attached statement for additional information.

For Paperwork Reduction Act Notice, see the Instructions for Form 1120-S.   www.irs.gov/Form1120S   Cat. No. 11520D   **Schedule K-1 (Form 1120-S) 2022**

Form 1120-S Schedule K-3 allocates the items from Schedule K-2 to each shareholder. This example shows the Schedule K-3 for Virginia Kendall. This material contains only the necessary portions of this schedule. Each entry corresponds with an entry on Schedule K-2. Thus Kendall checks the box that Part II, but no other part, applies to Virginia.

¶1603.09

Figure 16-7: Filled-In Schedule K-3 (Form 1120-S) (Page 1)

	☐ Final K-3 ☐ Amended K-3	

Schedule K-3 (Form 1120-S)

Department of the Treasury
Internal Revenue Service

Shareholder's Share of Income, Deductions, Credits, etc.—International

OMB No. 1545-0123

2022

For calendar year 2022, or tax year beginning ___ / ___ / 2022 , ending ___ / ___ / ___
See separate instructions.

Information About the Corporation

A Corporation's employer identification number (EIN)

70-1739257

B Corporation's name, address, city, state, and ZIP code

Kendall Management Company
731 Delhi Road
Atlanta, GA 30307

Information About the Shareholder

C Shareholder's identifying number

421-00-8045

D Shareholder's name, address, city, state, and ZIP code

Virginia Kendall
1524 Peachtree Drive
Atlanta, GA 30307

E Check to indicate the parts of Schedule K-3 that apply.

		Yes	No
1	Does Part I apply? If "Yes," complete and attach Part I .	1	✓
2	Does Part II apply? If "Yes," complete and attach Part II	2 ✓	
3	Does Part III apply? If "Yes," complete and attach Part III	3	✓
4	Does Part IV apply? If "Yes," complete and attach Part IV	4	✓
5	Does Part V apply? If "Yes," complete and attach Part V	5	✓
6	Does Part VI apply? If "Yes," complete and attach Part VI	6	✓
7	Does Part VII apply? If "Yes," complete and attach Part VII	7	✓

For IRS Use Only

For Paperwork Reduction Act Notice, see the Instructions for Form 1120-S.   www.irs.gov/Form1120S   Cat. No. 74747C   **Schedule K-3 (Form 1120-S) 2022**

Figure 16-7: Filled-In Schedule K-3 (Form 1120-S) (Page 2)

Schedule K-3 (Form 1120-S) 2022

Page **2**

Corporation's name	EIN	Shareholder's name	Shareholder's identifying number
Kendall Management Company	70-1739257	Virginia Kendall	421-00-8045

Part I Shareholder's Share of Corporation's Other Current Year International Information

Check box(es) for additional specified attachments. See instructions.

- ☐ 1. Gain on personal property sale
- ☐ 2. Foreign oil and gas taxes
- ☐ 3. Splitter arrangements
- ☐ 4. Foreign tax translation
- ☐ 5. High-taxed income
- ☐ 6. Section 267A disallowed deduction
- ☐ 7. Form 8858 information
- ☐ 8. Form 5471 information
- ☐ 9. Other forms
- ☐ 10. Shareholder loan transactions
- ☐ 11. Entity treatment for certain S corporations
- ☐ 12. Form 8865 information
- ☐ 13. Other international items (attach description and statement)

Part II Foreign Tax Credit Limitation

Section 1—Gross Income

Description	(a) U.S. source	Foreign Source				(f) Sourced by shareholder	(g) Total
		(b) Foreign branch category income	(c) Passive category income	(d) General category income	(e) Other (category code ___)		
1 Sales							
A							
B							
C							
2 Gross income from performance of services							
A US	49,605						49,605
B							
C							
3 Gross rental real estate income							
A							
B							
C							
4 Other gross rental income							
A							
B							
C							
5 Reserved for future use							
6 Interest income							
A US	216						216
B							
C							
7 Ordinary dividends (exclude amount on line 8)							
A US	225						225
B							
C							

Schedule K-3 (Form 1120-S) 2022

This page show's Virginia's 30% share of gross receipts from services, interest and dividends (other than qualified dividends).

Figure 16-7: Filled-In Schedule K-3 (Form 1120-S) (Pages 3 and 4)

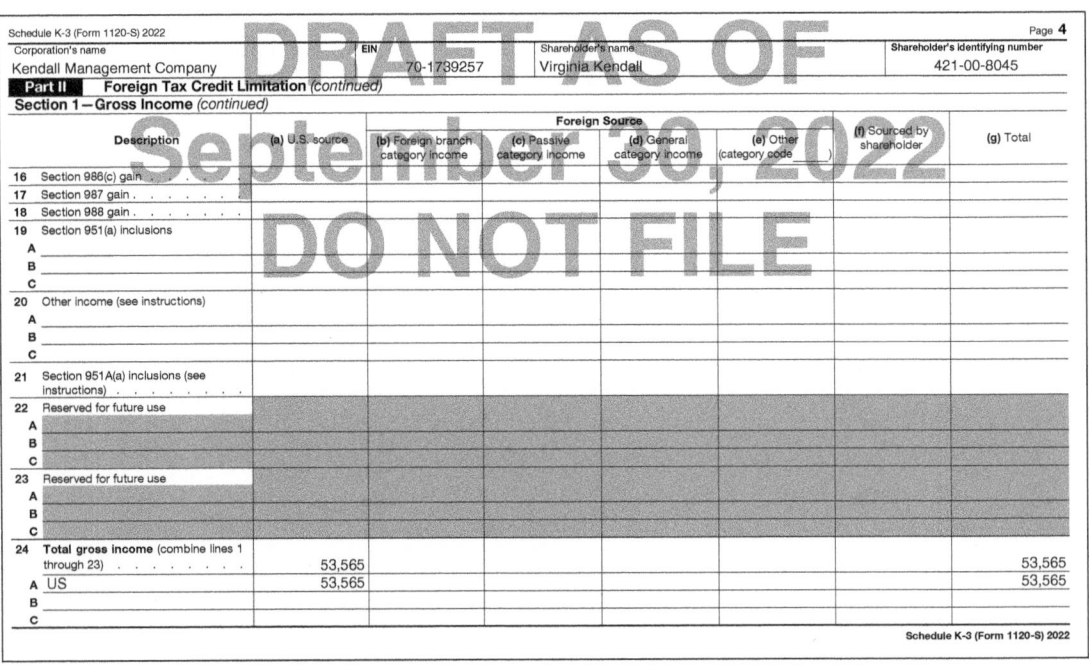

These pages show Virginia's shares of qualified dividends, long-term capital gains and total gross income, all of U.S. source.

Figure 16-7: Filled-In Schedule K-3 (Form 1120-S) (Pages 5 and 6)

Schedule K-3 (Form 1120-S) 2022 — Page **5**

Corporation's name	EIN	Shareholder's name	Shareholder's identifying number
Kendall Management Company	70-1739257	Virginia Kendall	421-00-8045

Part II Foreign Tax Credit Limitation *(continued)*

Section 2—Deductions

	Description	(a) U.S. source	(b) Foreign branch category income	(c) Passive category income	(d) General category income	(e) Other (category code)	(f) Sourced by shareholder	(g) Total
25	Expenses allocable to sales income							
26	Expenses allocable to gross income from performances of services	37,095						37,095
27	Net short-term capital loss							
28	Net long-term capital loss							
29	Collectibles loss							
30	Net section 1231 loss							
31	Other losses							
32	Research & experimental (R&E) expenses							
A	SIC code:							
B	SIC code:							
C	SIC code:							
33	Allocable rental expenses—depreciation, depletion, and amortization							
34	Allocable rental expenses—other than depreciation, depletion, and amortization							
35	Allocable royalty and licensing expenses—depreciation, depletion, and amortization							
36	Allocable royalty and licensing expenses—other than depreciation, depletion, and amortization							
37	Depreciation not included on line 33 or 35	510						510
38	Charitable contributions	2,100						2,100
39	Interest expense specifically allocable under Regulations section 1.861-10(e)							
40	Other interest expense specifically allocable under Regulations section 1.861-10T							
41	Other interest expense—business							
42	Other interest expense—investment							
43	Other interest expense—passive activity							
44	Section 59(e)(2) expenditures, excluding R&E expenses on line 32							
45	Foreign taxes not creditable but deductible							

Schedule K-3 (Form 1120-S) 2022

Schedule K-3 (Form 1120-S) 2022 — Page **6**

Corporation's name	EIN	Shareholder's name	Shareholder's identifying number
Kendall Management Company	70-1739257	Virginia Kendall	421-00-8045

Part II Foreign Tax Credit Limitation *(continued)*

Section 2—Deductions *(continued)*

	Description	(a) U.S. source	(b) Foreign branch category income	(c) Passive category income	(d) General category income	(e) Other (category code)	(f) Sourced by shareholder	(g) Total
46	Section 986(c) loss							
47	Section 987 loss							
48	Section 988 loss							
49	Other allocable deductions (see instructions)							
50	Other apportioned share of deductions (see instructions)							
51	Reserved for future use							
52	Reserved for future use							
53	Reserved for future use							
54	**Total deductions** (combine lines 25 through 53)	39,705						39,705
55	**Net income (loss)** (subtract line 54 from line 24)	13,860						13,860

These pages show Virginia's shares of expenses, depreciation contributions, total deductions and net income, all of U.S. source.

Since none of the other parts of Schedule K-3 apply to Virginia, Kendall does not file these parts with the IRS or send them to the shareholder.

¶1604   Transactions Between S Corporations and Shareholders

¶1604.01   QUALIFIED BUSINESS INCOME DEDUCTION (PASSTHROUGH DEDUCTION)

S corporation stockholders may deduct up to 20% of domestic qualified business income (QBI) from an S corporation. The deduction (a.k.a. Section 199A deduction) is generally limited to the greater of:

1. 50% of W-2 wages paid by the business, or
2. the sum of 25% of the W-2 wages paid plus 2.5% of the unadjusted basis of certain property the business uses to produce qualified business income.

This limit may be phased-in or eliminated if the taxpayer's taxable income meets certain threshold requirements. The deduction is generally not allowed for certain service trades or businesses, but this disallowance is phased-in for taxpayers whose taxable income meets certain threshold requirements. See Chapter 7 for discussion of this important deduction.

This deduction is applied at the shareholder level. Each shareholder must take into account his or her pro rata share, of each qualified item of income, gain, deduction, and loss. Further, each shareholder is treated as having W-2 wages and unadjusted basis immediately after the acquisition of qualified property for the tax year, in an amount equal to his or her allocable or pro rata share of the S corporation's W-2 wages and unadjusted basis for the tax year as determined in the regulations. The share of W-2 wages is determined in the same manner as the shareholder's share of wage expenses. The share of the unadjusted basis of qualified property is determined in the same manner as the shareholder's allocable share of depreciation.

EXAMPLE 26   Keith Kelso is a stockholder in the Keith Inc., an S corporation. If Keith is allocated a deductible amount of 10% of wages paid by the S corporation to employees for the tax year as a component of the corporation's income, he must be allocated 10% of the W-2 wages of the S corporation for purposes of calculating the wage limit for the Section 199A deduction.

16

Name:

Section:

Date:

QUESTIONS AND PROBLEMS

1. **Comparison of Business Entities.** (Obj. 1) How is an S corporation similar to, yet different from, a partnership?

2. **Comparison of Business Entities.** (Obj. 1) How is an S corporation similar to, yet different from, a C corporation?

3. **S Corporation Eligibility Requirements.** (Obj. 1) What corporations qualify as a small business corporation?

4. **S Corporation Eligibility Requirements.** (Obj. 1) When will a corporation be treated as having one class of stock?

5. **S Corporation Eligibility Requirements.** (Obj. 1) Can a corporation that has previously issued shares of preferred stock ever qualify as a small business corporation? Explain.

6. **S Corporation Eligibility Requirements.** (Obj. 1) Discuss how a corporation that currently has 102 shareholders, one of whom is a partnership, can pass the number of shareholders test and qualify as a small business corporation.

7. **S Corporation Eligibility Requirements.** (Obj. 1) The stock of an S corporation is owned by 105 different persons. Among its shareholders are Bob, Bob's mother and Bob's two children, Bob's brother and Bob's niece. Based on these facts, how many shareholders does the corporation have for purposes of determining whether it can elect S status?

8. **S Corporation Characteristics.** (Obj. 1) Answer each of the following questions.

   a. How many shareholders may an S corporation have?

   b. What types of shareholders can an S corporation have?

9. **S Corporation Characteristics.** (Obj. 1)

   a. What are the tax advantages of S corporation status over C corporation status?

   b. What are the advantages of S corporation status over being a general partnership?

10. **Electing and Terminating S Status.** (Obj. 1)

   a. What is the period during which the shareholders of a corporation may elect S corporation status?

   b. What events automatically terminate a corporation's S status?

   c. When is the termination of S corporation status effective under voluntary termination versus under automatic termination?

11. **Electing S Corporation Status.** (Obj. 1) Sherwin Corporation is a U.S. corporation owned by 12 shareholders. All of the stock outstanding is common stock. At a regular meeting of the shareholders, all shareholders except one agreed to have the corporation become an S corporation. Can Sherwin Corporation elect S corporation status? Explain.

12. **Electing S Corporation Status.** (Obj. 1) A newly formed corporation issues its first shares of stock on June 1. On July 15, it buys its first asset, and on August 1, it begins business operations. If the corporation wants to elect S status for its first tax year, by what date must it file a valid S election with the IRS?

13. **Electing S Corporation Status.** (Obj. 1) On February 21, 2022, Paul Kelso (SSN 421-00-9873) and Caroline Sims (SSN 536-00-5089) incorporate Carpaul, Inc. Carpaul sells and rents formal clothing. The state of incorporation is Indiana. Paul and his wife Mary (213-00-8320) are residents of Indiana. Caroline and her husband Robert (SSN 425-00-5361) are residents of Wisconsin. Indiana is a separate property state and Wisconsin is a community property state. Carpaul receives Employer Identification Number 70-6245329. Paul and Caroline each own 50 shares.

Paul and Caroline understand that an S corporation offers tax benefits for losses and for distributions. The inform their attorney that they intend to treat Carpaul as an S corporation. However, they do not instruct their attorney to prepare the form. On February 1, 2023, they bring their financial records to Homer Rath, CPA. When Homer asks for a copy of the Form 2553 and CP261 they have no idea what he means. Homer takes every necessary step to prepare Form 2553 to be valid for 2022. Prepare pages 1 and 2 of Form 2553, assuming that Carpaul uses the calendar year. Include all necessary consents, but no unnecessary consents. The corporation faxes the form, with all proper signatures and a statement of reasonable cause for failure to file timely, on February 12, 2023.

(Use for Problem 13.)

Form **2553** (Rev. December 2017) Department of the Treasury Internal Revenue Service	**Election by a Small Business Corporation** (Under section 1362 of the Internal Revenue Code) (Including a late election filed pursuant to Rev. Proc. 2013-30) ▶ You can fax this form to the IRS. See separate instructions. ▶ Go to *www.irs.gov/Form2553* for instructions and the latest information.	OMB No. 1545-0123

Note: This election to be an S corporation can be accepted only if all the tests are met under *Who May Elect* in the instructions, all shareholders have signed the consent statement, an officer has signed below, and the exact name and address of the corporation (entity) and other required form information have been provided.

Part I   Election Information

Type or Print	Name (see instructions)	**A** Employer identification number
	Number, street, and room or suite no. If a P.O. box, see instructions.	**B** Date incorporated
	City or town, state or province, country, and ZIP or foreign postal code	**C** State of incorporation

D   Check the applicable box(es) if the corporation (entity), after applying for the EIN shown in **A** above, changed its ☐ name or ☐ address

E   Election is to be effective for tax year beginning (month, day, year) (see instructions) . . . . . . ▶ _____

Caution: A corporation (entity) making the election for its first tax year in existence will usually enter the beginning date of a short tax year that begins on a date other than January 1.

F   Selected tax year:
(1) ☐ Calendar year
(2) ☐ Fiscal year ending (month and day) ▶ _____
(3) ☐ 52-53-week year ending with reference to the month of December
(4) ☐ 52-53-week year ending with reference to the month of ▶ _____
If box (2) or (4) is checked, complete Part II.

G   If more than 100 shareholders are listed for item J (see page 2), check this box if treating members of a family as one shareholder results in no more than 100 shareholders (see test 2 under *Who May Elect* in the instructions) ▶ ☐

H   Name and title of officer or legal representative whom the IRS may call for more information | Telephone number of officer or legal representative

I   If this S corporation election is being filed late, I declare I had reasonable cause for not filing Form 2553 timely. If this late election is being made by an entity eligible to elect to be treated as a corporation, I declare I also had reasonable cause for not filing an entity classification election timely and the representations listed in Part IV are true. See below for my explanation of the reasons the election or elections were not made on time and a description of my diligent actions to correct the mistake upon its discovery. See instructions.

Sign Here   Under penalties of perjury, I declare that I have examined this election, including accompanying documents, and, to the best of my knowledge and belief, the election contains all the relevant facts relating to the election, and such facts are true, correct, and complete.

▶ _____   _____   _____
Signature of officer   Title   Date

For Paperwork Reduction Act Notice, see separate instructions.	Cat. No. 18629R	Form **2553** (Rev. 12-2017)

(Use for Problem 13.)

Form 2553 (Rev. 12-2017)

Page **2**

Name

Employer identification number

Part I   **Election Information** *(continued)* **Note:** If you need more rows, use additional copies of page 2.

J Name and address of each shareholder or former shareholder required to consent to the election. (see instructions)	K **Shareholder's Consent Statement** Under penalties of perjury, I declare that I consent to the election of the above-named corporation (entity) to be an S corporation under section 1362(a) and that I have examined this consent statement, including accompanying documents, and, to the best of my knowledge and belief, the election contains all the relevant facts relating to the election, and such facts are true, correct, and complete. I understand my consent is binding and may not be withdrawn after the corporation (entity) has made a valid election. If seeking relief for a late filed election, I also declare under penalties of perjury that I have reported my income on all affected returns consistent with the S corporation election for the year for which the election should have been filed (see beginning date entered on line E) and for all subsequent years.		L Stock owned or percentage of ownership (see instructions)		M Social security number or employer identification number (see instructions)	N Shareholder's tax year ends (month and day)
	Signature	Date	Number of shares or percentage of ownership	Date(s) acquired		

Form **2553** (Rev. 12-2017)

14. **Terminating an S Election.** (Obj. 1) For each of the scenarios, determine whether the calendar year corporation's S status has terminated, and if so, the date the corporation starts being taxed as a C corporation.

   a. An S corporation currently has 63 shareholders. On April 4, 2022, one of its shareholders sells his shares of stock to a partnership that has ten partners.

   b. An S corporation currently has 100 shareholders. On October 14, 2022, one of its shareholders sells half of his shares of stock to his sister.

   c. An S corporation currently has 35 shareholders. On February 26, 2022, one of its shareholders dies, and his shares of stock are transferred to his estate.

   d. An S corporation currently has 97 shareholders. On August 11, 2022, one of the shareholders sells her shares to a voting trust that has 5 beneficiaries, none of whom are related.

15. **Terminating an S Election.** (Obj. 1) For each of the following scenarios, determine whether the calendar year corporation's S status has terminated, and if so, the date the corporation starts being taxed as a C corporation.

   a. An S corporation was previously a C corporation, but does not have any E&P carried over from its years as a C corporation. For the past three years, the corporation has generated passive investment income in excess of 25% of its gross receipts.

   b. Same as in Part a., except that the C corporation had $1,000 of E&P from when it was a C corporation.

   c. Same as in Part a., except that the corporation was never a C corporation.

16. **Terminating an S Election.** (Obj. 1) For each of the following scenarios, determine whether the calendar year corporation's S status has terminated, and if so, the date the corporation starts being taxed as a C corporation.

   a. On February 1, 2022, 75% of the shareholders consent to revoke the corporation's S election. No date specific termination date is provided.

   b. Same as in Part a., except that the shareholders specify July 1, 2022 as their desired termination date.

   c. Same as in Part a., except that only 50% of the shareholders provide their consent.

   d. Same as in Part a., except that the date the shareholders filed their consent is April 5, 2022.

17. **Sale of S Corporation Stock.** (Obj. 4) Jordan owned a 10% interest in an S corporation for several years. The basis of his stock on January 1, 2022, is $40,000. On April 30, 2022, Jordan sells his entire interest in the S corporation for $58,000. For the calendar year 2022, the S corporation estimated that its ordinary income would be $80,000. No distributions were made in 2022 prior to the sale of Jordan's stock.

   a. On April 30, 2022, the date of sale, what is the expected gain Jordan will report on his 2022 tax return as the result of the sale of his stock?

   b. At year-end, the S corporation determines that its actual ordinary income for 2022 is $100,000. On the basis of this year-end knowledge, does this additional information affect Jordan's 2022 tax return? If so, how is the 2022 tax return affected, and if it is not affected, why not?

18. **S Corporation Loss.** (Obj. 3) The Viking Corporation (70-1739257), a calendar year corporation, formed and immediately elected to become an S corporation as of January 2, 2020. Brendon Bates (521-00-3925) has owned 40% of the stock (40 shares) since the corporation's inception, with an original investment of $27,000. In 2020 and 2021, Viking had ordinary losses of $45,000 and $30,000, respectively. During 2022, Viking reported taxable income of $60,000, all ordinary income. During 2022, Viking made cash distributions of $40,000.

    a.   How does Brendon report his share of the 2020-2021 and 2021-2022 losses?

    b.   How does Brendon report his share of the 2022 ordinary income and cash distributions from Viking?

    c.   What is Brendon's basis in his shares of Viking stock on December 31, 2022?

    d.   Complete Brendon's Form 7203 for each of the three years.

(Use for Problem 18.)

Form **7203** (Rev. December 2022) Department of the Treasury Internal Revenue Service	**S Corporation Shareholder Stock and Debt Basis Limitations** **Attach to your tax return.** Go to *www.irs.gov/Form7203* for instructions and the latest information.

OMB No. 1545-2302

Attachment Sequence No. **203**

Name of shareholder

Identifying number

A Name of S corporation

B Employer identification number

C Stock block (see instructions):
D Check applicable box(es) to indicate how stock was acquired:
 (1) ☐ Original shareholder **(2)** ☐ Purchased **(3)** ☐ Inherited **(4)** ☐ Gift **(5)** ☐ Other:
E Check if you have a Regulations section 1.1367-1(g) election in effect during the tax year for this S corporation . . . . . ☐

Part I	Shareholder Stock Basis		
1	Stock basis at the beginning of the corporation's tax year	**1**	
2	Basis from any capital contributions made or additional stock acquired during the tax year . . .	**2**	
3a	Ordinary business income (enter losses in Part III)	**3a**		
b	Net rental real estate income (enter losses in Part III)	**3b**		
c	Other net rental income (enter losses in Part III)	**3c**		
d	Interest income	**3d**		
e	Ordinary dividends	**3e**		
f	Royalties	**3f**		
g	Net capital gains (enter losses in Part III)	**3g**		
h	Net section 1231 gain (enter losses in Part III)	**3h**		
i	Other income (enter losses in Part III)	**3i**		
j	Excess depletion adjustment	**3j**		
k	Tax-exempt income	**3k**		
l	Recapture of business credits	**3l**		
m	Other items that increase stock basis	**3m**		
4	Add lines 3a through 3m	**4**	
5	Stock basis before distributions. Add lines 1, 2, and 4	**5**	
6	Distributions (excluding dividend distributions)	**6**	
	Note: If line 6 is larger than line 5, subtract line 5 from line 6 and report the result as a capital gain on Form 8949 and Schedule D. See instructions.		
7	Stock basis after distributions. Subtract line 6 from line 5. If the result is zero or less, enter -0-, skip lines 8 through 14, and enter -0- on line 15	**7**	
8a	Nondeductible expenses	**8a**		
b	Depletion for oil and gas	**8b**		
c	Business credits (sections 50(c)(1) and (5))	**8c**		
9	Add lines 8a through 8c	**9**	
10	Stock basis before loss and deduction items. Subtract line 9 from line 7. If the result is zero or less, enter -0-, skip lines 11 through 14, and enter -0- on line 15	**10**	
11	Allowable loss and deduction items. Enter the amount from line 47, column (c)	**11**	
12	Debt basis restoration (see net increase in instructions for line 23)	**12**	
13	Other items that decrease stock basis	**13**	
14	Add lines 11, 12, and 13	**14**	
15	**Stock basis at the end of the corporation's tax year.** Subtract line 14 from line 10. If the result is zero or less, enter -0-	**15**	

Part II	Shareholder Debt Basis				
	Section A—Amount of Debt (If more than three debts, see instructions.)				
	Description	**(a)** Debt 1 ☐ Formal note ☐ Open account	**(b)** Debt 2 ☐ Formal note ☐ Open account	**(c)** Debt 3 ☐ Formal note ☐ Open account	**(d)** Total
16	Loan balance at the beginning of the corporation's tax year				
17	Additional loans (see instructions)				
18	Loan balance before repayment. Add lines 16 and 17				
19	Principal portion of debt repayment (this line doesn't include interest)				
20	Loan balance at the end of the corporation's tax year. Subtract line 19 from line 18				

For Paperwork Reduction Act Notice, see separate instructions. Cat. No. 56396V Form **7203** (Rev. 12-2022)

(Use for Problem 18.)

Form 7203 (Rev. 12-2022)   Page **2**

Part II   **Shareholder Debt Basis** *(continued)*

Section B—Adjustments to Debt Basis

	Description	(a) Debt 1	(b) Debt 2	(c) Debt 3	(d) Total
21	Debt basis at the beginning of the corporation's tax year				
22	Enter the amount, if any, from line 17				
23	Debt basis restoration (see instructions)				
24	Debt basis before repayment. Add lines 21, 22, and 23				
25	Divide line 24 by line 18				
26	Nontaxable debt repayment. Multiply line 25 by line 19				
27	Debt basis before nondeductible expenses and losses. Subtract line 26 from line 24				
28	Nondeductible expenses and oil and gas depletion deductions in excess of stock basis				
29	Debt basis before losses and deductions. Subtract line 28 from line 27. If the result is zero or less, enter -0-				
30	Allowable losses in excess of stock basis. Enter the amount from line 47, column (d)				
31	**Debt basis at the end of the corporation's tax year.** Subtract line 30 from line 29. If the result is zero or less, enter -0-				

Section C—Gain on Loan Repayment

32	Repayment. Enter the amount from line 19				
33	Nontaxable repayments. Enter the amount from line 26				
34	**Reportable gain.** Subtract line 33 from line 32				

Part III   **Shareholder Allowable Loss and Deduction Items**

	Description	(a) Current year losses and deductions	(b) Carryover amounts (column (e)) from the previous year	(c) Allowable loss from stock basis	(d) Allowable loss from debt basis	(e) Carryover amounts
35	Ordinary business loss					
36	Net rental real estate loss					
37	Other net rental loss					
38	Net capital loss					
39	Net section 1231 loss					
40	Other loss					
41	Section 179 deductions					
42	Charitable contributions					
43	Investment interest expense					
44	Section 59(e)(2) expenditures					
45	Other deductions					
46	Foreign taxes paid or accrued					
47	**Total loss.** Add lines 35 through 46 for each column. Enter the total loss in column (c) on line 11 and enter the total loss in column (d) on line 30					

Form **7203** (Rev. 12-2022)

19. **S Corporation Income.** (Obj. 3) Siegal Management Corporation has operated as an S corporation for the years 2020, 2021, and 2022. The shareholders of the corporation are Erica and Dina. They each own 200 shares of stock of the corporation, for which each paid $25,000 at the beginning of 2020. The corporation's ordinary income and cash distributions for the three years are as follows.

	2020	*2021*	*2022*
Ordinary income	$10,000	$11,000	$16,000
Cash distributions	6,000	11,000	24,000

   a. How much do Erica and Dina report as income on their individual income tax returns for 2022?

   b. Compute Erica and Dina's stock bases at the end of 2022.

20. **S Corporation Losses.** (Obj. 3) Melbourne Corporation is an S corporation with ten shareholders. Chris owns 100 shares of stock, which represents a 15% interest in the corporation. His basis for those 100 shares is $12,000. He also has loaned the corporation $4,000 to support the purchase of a special machine. For the year 2022, the corporation reports an operating loss of $120,000. In addition, the corporation made charitable contributions for the year of $10,000.

   a. Explain how Chris reports his share of the S corporation's operating loss and charitable contributions.

   b. What is Chris's basis in his S corporation stock at the end of 2022?

   c. Compute the amount for each type of carryover to 2023. Discuss what must happen in order for Chris to be able to deduct these amounts in 2023.

21. **Accumulated Adjustments Account.** (Obj. 4) What is the accumulated adjustments account and what purpose does it serve?

22. **Shareholder's Basis in S Corporation Stock.** (Obj. 4) An S corporation (with a $3,000 balance in its AAA and no E&P) distributes $9,000 to its sole shareholder. The shareholder's basis in his shares of stock was $5,000 prior to the distribution.

   a. Is the shareholder taxed on the distribution, and if so, how?

   b. Compute the shareholder's basis in the S stock after the distribution.

23. **Shareholder's Basis in S Corporation Stock.** (Obj. 4) An S corporation (with a $5,000 balance in its AAA and $8,000 of E&P) distributes $15,000 to its sole shareholder. The shareholder's adjusted basis in his shares of stock was $12,000 prior to the distribution.

   a. Is the shareholder taxed on the distribution, and if so, how?

   b. Compute the shareholder's basis in the S stock after the distribution.

24. **Form 1120-S.** (Obj. 5) Prince Corporation (EIN 70-2152973), an S corporation, operates as a small variety store on the accrual basis. It is located at 1701 Governors Drive, College Station, TX 77843. The company was incorporated on January 2, 1999, and elected S corporation status on the same day. The business code is 54. John R. Prince (SSN 201-00-5064) and his wife, Joyce B. Prince (SSN 265-00-8133) each own 35% of the corporation's 100 outstanding shares. Joyce was an original shareholder. Her stock basis was $12,000 at the beginning of the year. Together they manage the store. The remaining stock is owned by John's father. John is President; Joyce is VP and Treasurer.

At the end of the calendar year 2022, the income statement accounts, balance sheet accounts, and other information taken from the records are as follows.

Inventory, January 1, 2022 (at cost)	$ 29,500
Inventory, December 31, 2022 (at cost)	32,400
Purchases (net)	133,800
Sales revenue	246,500
Sales returns and allowances	15,900
Taxable interest income	4,650
Tax exempt interest	6,000
Depreciation expense ("book" depreciation was $6,000)	5,200
Bad debts expense ("book" bad debt expense was $1,000)	1,500
Repairs and maintenance	3,300
Interest expense (business related)	2,700
Payroll taxes	7,800
Compensation of officers	30,000
Salaries and wages	24,500
Rental of equipment	700
Charitable contributions	1,600
Advertising	1,400
Distributions made during the year	24,000
Total assets, December 31, 2022	108,700

The beginning and ending balance sheets for the year are:

Assets	January 1	December 31
Cash	$12,000	$15,000
Accounts Receivable	13,950	12,250
Inventory	29,500	32,400
Depreciable Assets	53,550	66,250
Less Accumulated Depreciation	(10,200)	(17,200)
	43,350	49,050
Total	$98,800	$108,700
Liabilities and Shareholders' Equity		
Accounts Payable	$18,320	$21,870
Capital Stock	23,000	23,000
Retained Earnings	57,480	63,830
Total	$98,800	$108,700

All of Prince Corporation's assets and liabilities are in the U.S. Prince Corporation had no foreign-source income for the year.

Based on this information, the Princes have asked you to prepare the 2022 Form 1120-S for Prince Corporation, along with the necessary forms for Schedule K-2. The return will be filed at the IRS Center in Ogden, Utah and will be signed by John Prince on March 10, 2023. Even though it is not required, prepare Schedules M-1 and M-2. On page 4, assume that the net income per books of Schedule M-1 (line 1) is $30,350 and the beginning balance of the AAA is $42,630 (Schedule M-2 (line 1a)). The beginning balance in the Other adjustments account (Schedule M-2 (line 1b)) is $14,850. Assume that Form 1125-A showing the calculation of Cost of Goods Sold (Form 1120-S, line 2) has been completed. Schedule K-1 and Schedule K-3 should be prepared for Joyce's 35% share of the S corporation's items of income and deductions. John and Joyce live at 1074 Bright Leaf Square, College Station, TX 77841. Also prepare Joyce's Form 7203.

(Use for Problem 24.)

Form **1120-S**	**U.S. Income Tax Return for an S Corporation**		OMB No. 1545-0123
Department of the Treasury Internal Revenue Service	Do not file this form unless the corporation has filed or is attaching Form 2553 to elect to be an S corporation. Go to *www.irs.gov/Form1120S* for instructions and the latest information.		2022

For calendar year 2022 or tax year beginning , 2022, ending , 20

A S election effective date	Name	**D** Employer identification number	
B Business activity code number (see instructions)	**TYPE OR PRINT** Number, street, and room or suite no. If a P.O. box, see instructions.	**E** Date incorporated	
C Check if Sch. M-3 attached ☐	City or town, state or province, country, and ZIP or foreign postal code	**F** Total assets (see instructions) $	

G Is the corporation electing to be an S corporation beginning with this tax year? See instructions. ☐ Yes ☐ No

H Check if: **(1)** ☐ Final return **(2)** ☐ Name change **(3)** ☐ Address change **(4)** ☐ Amended return **(5)** ☐ S election termination

I Enter the number of shareholders who were shareholders during any part of the tax year . . . .

J Check if corporation: **(1)** ☐ Aggregated activities for section 465 at-risk purposes **(2)** ☐ Grouped activities for section 469 passive activity purposes

Caution: Include **only** trade or business income and expenses on lines 1a through 21. See the instructions for more information.

Income	**1a**	Gross receipts or sales	**1a**	
	b	Returns and allowances	**1b**	
	c	Balance. Subtract line 1b from line 1a	**1c**	
	2	Cost of goods sold (attach Form 1125-A)	**2**	
	3	Gross profit. Subtract line 2 from line 1c	**3**	
	4	Net gain (loss) from Form 4797, line 17 (attach Form 4797)	**4**	
	5	Other income (loss) (see instructions—attach statement)	**5**	
	6	**Total income (loss).** Add lines 3 through 5	**6**	
Deductions (see instructions for limitations)	**7**	Compensation of officers (see instructions—attach Form 1125-E) . . .	**7**	
	8	Salaries and wages (less employment credits)	**8**	
	9	Repairs and maintenance	**9**	
	10	Bad debts	**10**	
	11	Rents	**11**	
	12	Taxes and licenses	**12**	
	13	Interest (see instructions)	**13**	
	14	Depreciation from Form 4562 not claimed on Form 1125-A or elsewhere on return (attach Form 4562)	**14**	
	15	Depletion **(Do not deduct oil and gas depletion.)**	**15**	
	16	Advertising	**16**	
	17	Pension, profit-sharing, etc., plans	**17**	
	18	Employee benefit programs	**18**	
	19	Other deductions (attach statement)	**19**	
	20	**Total deductions.** Add lines 7 through 19	**20**	
	21	**Ordinary business income (loss).** Subtract line 20 from line 6 . . .	**21**	
Tax and Payments	**22a**	Excess net passive income or LIFO recapture tax (see instructions) . . .	**22a**	
	b	Tax from Schedule D (Form 1120-S)	**22b**	
	c	Add lines 22a and 22b (see instructions for additional taxes)	**22c**	
	23a	2022 estimated tax payments and 2021 overpayment credited to 2022 .	**23a**	
	b	Tax deposited with Form 7004	**23b**	
	c	Credit for federal tax paid on fuels (attach Form 4136)	**23c**	
	d	Add lines 23a through 23c	**23d**	
	24	Estimated tax penalty (see instructions). Check if Form 2220 is attached . . . . . . ☐	**24**	
	25	**Amount owed.** If line 23d is smaller than the total of lines 22c and 24, enter amount owed . .	**25**	
	26	**Overpayment.** If line 23d is larger than the total of lines 22c and 24, enter amount overpaid . . .	**26**	
	27	Enter amount from line 26: **Credited to 2023 estimated tax** **Refunded** .	**27**	

Sign Here	Under penalties of perjury, I declare that I have examined this return, including accompanying schedules and statements, and to the best of my knowledge and belief, it is true, correct, and complete. Declaration of preparer (other than taxpayer) is based on all information of which preparer has any knowledge.

Signature of officer	Date	Title	May the IRS discuss this return with the preparer shown below? See instructions. ☐ Yes ☐ No

Paid Preparer Use Only	Print/Type preparer's name	Preparer's signature	Date	Check ☐ if self-employed	PTIN
	Firm's name			Firm's EIN	
	Firm's address			Phone no.	

For Paperwork Reduction Act Notice, see separate instructions.   Cat. No. 11510H   Form **1120-S** (2022)

(Use for Problem 24.)

Form 1120-S (2022)   Page **2**

Schedule B	Other Information (see instructions)					Yes	No

1 Check accounting method: **a** ☐ Cash   **b** ☐ Accrual
                                   c ☐ Other (specify) _____

2 See the instructions and enter the:
    a Business activity _____   **b** Product or service _____

3 At any time during the tax year, was any shareholder of the corporation a disregarded entity, a trust, an estate, or a nominee or similar person? If "Yes," attach Schedule B-1, Information on Certain Shareholders of an S Corporation . .

4 At the end of the tax year, did the corporation:

    a Own directly 20% or more, or own, directly or indirectly, 50% or more of the total stock issued and outstanding of any foreign or domestic corporation? For rules of constructive ownership, see instructions. If "Yes," complete (i) through (v) below . . . .

(i) Name of Corporation	(ii) Employer Identification Number (if any)	(iii) Country of Incorporation	(iv) Percentage of Stock Owned	(v) If Percentage in (iv) Is 100%, Enter the Date (if applicable) a Qualified Subchapter S Subsidiary Election Was Made

    b Own directly an interest of 20% or more, or own, directly or indirectly, an interest of 50% or more in the profit, loss, or capital in any foreign or domestic partnership (including an entity treated as a partnership) or in the beneficial interest of a trust? For rules of constructive ownership, see instructions. If "Yes," complete (i) through (v) below . . . . .

(i) Name of Entity	(ii) Employer Identification Number (if any)	(iii) Type of Entity	(iv) Country of Organization	(v) Maximum Percentage Owned in Profit, Loss, or Capital

5a At the end of the tax year, did the corporation have any outstanding shares of restricted stock? . . . .
    If "Yes," complete lines (i) and (ii) below.
    (i)   Total shares of restricted stock . . . . _____
    (ii)   Total shares of non-restricted stock . . . . _____

    b At the end of the tax year, did the corporation have any outstanding stock options, warrants, or similar instruments? .
    If "Yes," complete lines (i) and (ii) below.
    (i)   Total shares of stock outstanding at the end of the tax year . . _____
    (ii)   Total shares of stock outstanding if all instruments were executed _____

6 Has this corporation filed, or is it required to file, **Form 8918,** Material Advisor Disclosure Statement, to provide information on any reportable transaction? . . . .

7 Check this box if the corporation issued publicly offered debt instruments with original issue discount . . . . . ☐
    If checked, the corporation may have to file **Form 8281,** Information Return for Publicly Offered Original Issue Discount Instruments.

8 If the corporation **(a)** was a C corporation before it elected to be an S corporation **or** the corporation acquired an asset with a basis determined by reference to the basis of the asset (or the basis of any other property) in the hands of a C corporation, **and (b)** has net unrealized built-in gain in excess of the net recognized built-in gain from prior years, enter the net unrealized built-in gain reduced by net recognized built-in gain from prior years. See instructions . . . . . . $ _____

9 Did the corporation have an election under section 163(j) for any real property trade or business or any farming business in effect during the tax year? See instructions . . . .

10 Does the corporation satisfy one or more of the following? See instructions . . . .

    a The corporation owns a pass-through entity with current, or prior year carryover, excess business interest expense.

    b The corporation's aggregate average annual gross receipts (determined under section 448(c)) for the 3 tax years preceding the current tax year are more than $27 million and the corporation has business interest expense.

    c The corporation is a tax shelter and the corporation has business interest expense.
    If "Yes," complete and attach **Form 8990,** Limitation on Business Interest Expense Under Section 163(j).

11 Does the corporation satisfy **both** of the following conditions? . . . .

    a The corporation's total receipts (see instructions) for the tax year were less than $250,000.

    b The corporation's total assets at the end of the tax year were less than $250,000.
    If "Yes," the corporation is not required to complete Schedules L and M-1.

Form **1120-S** (2022)

(Use for Problem 24.)

Form 1120-S (2022)   Page **3**

Schedule B	Other Information (see instructions) (continued)	Yes	No
12	During the tax year, did the corporation have any non-shareholder debt that was canceled, was forgiven, or had the terms modified so as to reduce the principal amount of the debt?		
	If "Yes," enter the amount of principal reduction . . . . $		
13	During the tax year, was a qualified subchapter S subsidiary election terminated or revoked? If "Yes," see instructions .		
14a	Did the corporation make any payments in 2022 that would require it to file Form(s) 1099?		
b	If "Yes," did or will the corporation file required Form(s) 1099?		
15	Is the corporation attaching Form 8996 to certify as a Qualified Opportunity Fund?		
	If "Yes," enter the amount from Form 8996, line 15 . . . . $		

Schedule K		Shareholders' Pro Rata Share Items			Total amount
Income (Loss)	**1**	Ordinary business income (loss) (page 1, line 21)		**1**	
	2	Net rental real estate income (loss) (attach Form 8825)		**2**	
	3a	Other gross rental income (loss)	3a		
	b	Expenses from other rental activities (attach statement) . .	3b		
	c	Other net rental income (loss). Subtract line 3b from line 3a		**3c**	
	4	Interest income		**4**	
	5	Dividends: **a** Ordinary dividends		**5a**	
		b Qualified dividends	5b		
	6	Royalties		**6**	
	7	Net short-term capital gain (loss) (attach Schedule D (Form 1120-S)) . . .		**7**	
	8a	Net long-term capital gain (loss) (attach Schedule D (Form 1120-S)) . . .		**8a**	
	b	Collectibles (28%) gain (loss)	8b		
	c	Unrecaptured section 1250 gain (attach statement)	8c		
	9	Net section 1231 gain (loss) (attach Form 4797)		**9**	
	10	Other income (loss) (see instructions) Type:		**10**	
Deductions	**11**	Section 179 deduction (attach Form 4562)		**11**	
	12a	Charitable contributions		**12a**	
	b	Investment interest expense		**12b**	
	c	Section 59(e)(2) expenditures . . . . . Type:		**12c**	
	d	Other deductions (see instructions) . . . . Type:		**12d**	
Credits	**13a**	Low-income housing credit (section 42(j)(5))		**13a**	
	b	Low-income housing credit (other)		**13b**	
	c	Qualified rehabilitation expenditures (rental real estate) (attach Form 3468, if applicable) . .		**13c**	
	d	Other rental real estate credits (see instructions) Type:		**13d**	
	e	Other rental credits (see instructions) . . . . Type:		**13e**	
	f	Biofuel producer credit (attach Form 6478)		**13f**	
	g	Other credits (see instructions) . . . . . Type:		**13g**	
International	**14**	Attach Schedule K-2 (Form 1120-S), Shareholders' Pro Rata Share Items—International, and check this box to indicate you are reporting items of international tax relevance . . . . . ☐			
Alternative Minimum Tax (AMT) Items	**15a**	Post-1986 depreciation adjustment		**15a**	
	b	Adjusted gain or loss		**15b**	
	c	Depletion (other than oil and gas)		**15c**	
	d	Oil, gas, and geothermal properties—gross income		**15d**	
	e	Oil, gas, and geothermal properties—deductions		**15e**	
	f	Other AMT items (attach statement)		**15f**	
Items Affecting Shareholder Basis	**16a**	Tax-exempt interest income		**16a**	
	b	Other tax-exempt income		**16b**	
	c	Nondeductible expenses		**16c**	
	d	Distributions (attach statement if required) (see instructions)		**16d**	
	e	Repayment of loans from shareholders		**16e**	
	f	Foreign taxes paid or accrued		**16f**	

Form **1120-S** (2022)

(Use for Problem 24.)

Form 1120-S (2022)								Page **4**

Schedule K — Shareholders' Pro Rata Share Items *(continued)* — Total amount

			Total amount
Other Information	**17a**	Investment income	**17a**
	b	Investment expenses	**17b**
	c	Dividend distributions paid from accumulated earnings and profits	**17c**
	d	Other items and amounts (attach statement)	
Reconciliation	**18**	**Income (loss) reconciliation.** Combine the amounts on lines 1 through 10 in the far right column. From the result, subtract the sum of the amounts on lines 11 through 12d and 16f	**18**

Schedule L — Balance Sheets per Books

	Assets	Beginning of tax year (a)	(b)	End of tax year (c)	(d)
1	Cash				
2a	Trade notes and accounts receivable				
b	Less allowance for bad debts	( )		( )	
3	Inventories				
4	U.S. government obligations				
5	Tax-exempt securities (see instructions)				
6	Other current assets (attach statement)				
7	Loans to shareholders				
8	Mortgage and real estate loans				
9	Other investments (attach statement)				
10a	Buildings and other depreciable assets				
b	Less accumulated depreciation	( )		( )	
11a	Depletable assets				
b	Less accumulated depletion	( )		( )	
12	Land (net of any amortization)				
13a	Intangible assets (amortizable only)				
b	Less accumulated amortization	( )		( )	
14	Other assets (attach statement)				
15	Total assets				
	Liabilities and Shareholders' Equity				
16	Accounts payable				
17	Mortgages, notes, bonds payable in less than 1 year				
18	Other current liabilities (attach statement)				
19	Loans from shareholders				
20	Mortgages, notes, bonds payable in 1 year or more				
21	Other liabilities (attach statement)				
22	Capital stock				
23	Additional paid-in capital				
24	Retained earnings				
25	Adjustments to shareholders' equity (attach statement)				
26	Less cost of treasury stock		( )		( )
27	Total liabilities and shareholders' equity				

Form **1120-S** (2022)

(Use for Problem 24.)

Form 1120-S (2022)   Page **5**

Schedule M-1	Reconciliation of Income (Loss) per Books With Income (Loss) per Return

Note: The corporation may be required to file Schedule M-3. See instructions.

1	Net income (loss) per books		5	Income recorded on books this year not included on Schedule K, lines 1 through 10 (itemize):	
2	Income included on Schedule K, lines 1, 2, 3c, 4, 5a, 6, 7, 8a, 9, and 10, not recorded on books this year (itemize)		a	Tax-exempt interest $	
3	Expenses recorded on books this year not included on Schedule K, lines 1 through 12, and 16f (itemize):		6	Deductions included on Schedule K, lines 1 through 12, and 16f, not charged against book income this year (itemize):	
a	Depreciation $		a	Depreciation $	
b	Travel and entertainment $		7	Add lines 5 and 6	
			8	Income (loss) (Schedule K, line 18). Subtract line 7 from line 4 .	
4	Add lines 1 through 3 . . .				

Schedule M-2	Analysis of Accumulated Adjustments Account, Shareholders' Undistributed Taxable Income Previously Taxed, Accumulated Earnings and Profits, and Other Adjustments Account (see instructions)

		(a) Accumulated adjustments account	(b) Shareholders' undistributed taxable income previously taxed	(c) Accumulated earnings and profits	(d) Other adjustments account
1	Balance at beginning of tax year				
2	Ordinary income from page 1, line 21 . . .				
3	Other additions				
4	Loss from page 1, line 21	( )			
5	Other reductions	( )			( )
6	Combine lines 1 through 5				
7	Distributions				
8	Balance at end of tax year. Subtract line 7 from line 6				

Form **1120-S** (2022)

(Use for Problem 24.)

671121

| Final K-1 | Amended K-1 | OMB No. 1545-0123 |

**Schedule K-1
(Form 1120-S)**
Department of the Treasury
Internal Revenue Service

2022

For calendar year 2022, or tax year

beginning / / 2022 ending / /

Shareholder's Share of Income, Deductions, Credits, etc. See separate instructions.

DRAFT AS OF
July 7, 2022
DO NOT FILE

Part III	**Shareholder's Share of Current Year Income, Deductions, Credits, and Other Items**

Part I	**Information About the Corporation**

A Corporation's employer identification number

B Corporation's name, address, city, state, and ZIP code

C IRS Center where corporation filed return

D Corporation's total number of shares
    Beginning of tax year . . . . .
    End of tax year . . . .

Part II	**Information About the Shareholder**

E Shareholder's identifying number

F Shareholder's name, address, city, state, and ZIP code

G Current year allocation percentage . . . _____ %

H Shareholder's number of shares
    Beginning of tax year . . . . . . _____
    End of tax year . . . . _____

I Loans from shareholder
    Beginning of tax year . . . . . $ _____
    End of tax year . . . . $ _____

For IRS Use Only

#	Item	#	Item
1	Ordinary business income (loss)	13	Credits
2	Net rental real estate income (loss)		
3	Other net rental income (loss)		
4	Interest income		
5a	Ordinary dividends		
5b	Qualified dividends	14	Schedule K-3 is attached if checked . . . . . ☐
6	Royalties	15	Alternative minimum tax (AMT) items
7	Net short-term capital gain (loss)		
8a	Net long-term capital gain (loss)		
8b	Collectibles (28%) gain (loss)		
8c	Unrecaptured section 1250 gain		
9	Net section 1231 gain (loss)	16	Items affecting shareholder basis
10	Other income (loss)		
		17	Other information
11	Section 179 deduction		
12	Other deductions		
18	☐ More than one activity for at-risk purposes*		
19	☐ More than one activity for passive activity purposes*		

* See attached statement for additional information.

For Paperwork Reduction Act Notice, see the Instructions for Form 1120-S.   www.irs.gov/Form1120S   Cat. No. 11520D   **Schedule K-1 (Form 1120-S) 2022**

(Use for Problem 24.)

SCHEDULE K-2 (Form 1120-S) Department of the Treasury Internal Revenue Service	Shareholders' Pro Rata Share Items—International Attach to Form 1120-S. Go to www.irs.gov/Form1120S for instructions and the latest information.	OMB No. 1545-0123 2022

Name of corporation   Employer identification number (EIN)

A Check to indicate the parts of Schedule K-2 that apply.

		Yes	No
1	Does Part I apply? If "Yes," complete and attach Part I	1	
2	Does Part II apply? If "Yes," complete and attach Part II	2	
3	Does Part III apply? If "Yes," complete and attach Part III	3	
4	Does Part IV apply? If "Yes," complete and attach Part IV	4	
5	Does Part V apply? If "Yes," complete and attach Part V	5	
6	Does Part VI apply? If "Yes," complete and attach Part VI	6	
7	Does Part VII apply? If "Yes," complete and attach Part VII	7	

Part I **Corporation's Other Current Year International Information**

Check box(es) for additional specified attachments. See instructions.

☐ 1. Gain on personal property sale ☐ 5. High-taxed income ☐ 8. Form 5471 information ☐ 11. Entity treatment for certain S corporations
☐ 2. Foreign oil and gas taxes ☐ 6. Section 267A disallowed deduction ☐ 9. Other forms ☐ 12. Reserved for future use
☐ 3. Splitter arrangements ☐ 7. Form 8858 information ☐ 10. Shareholder loan transactions ☐ 13. Other international items
☐ 4. Foreign tax translation (attach description and statement)

Part II **Foreign Tax Credit Limitation**

Section 1—Gross Income

Description	(a) U.S. source	Foreign Source				(f) Sourced by shareholder	(g) Total
		(b) Foreign branch category income	(c) Passive category income	(d) General category income	(e) Other (category code ____)		
1 Sales							
A							
B							
C							
2 Gross income from performance of services							
A							
B							
C							
3 Gross rental real estate income							
A							
B							
C							
4 Other gross rental income							
A							
B							
C							

For Paperwork Reduction Act Notice, see the Instructions for Form 1120-S.   Cat. No. 73973Q   Schedule K-2 (Form 1120-S) 2022

(Use for Problem 24.)

Schedule K-2 (Form 1120-S) 2022							Page **2**
Name of corporation						EIN	

Part II   Foreign Tax Credit Limitation *(continued)*

Section 1—Gross Income *(continued)*

Description	(a) U.S. source	Foreign Source				(f) Sourced by shareholder	(g) Total
		(b) Foreign branch category income	(c) Passive category income	(d) General category income	(e) Other (category code)		
5 Reserved for future use . . .							
6 Interest income							
A							
B							
C							
7 Ordinary dividends (exclude amount on line 8)							
A							
B							
C							
8 Qualified dividends							
A							
B							
C							
9 Reserved for future use							
10 Royalties and license fees							
A							
B							
C							
11 Net short-term capital gain							
A							
B							
C							
12 Net long-term capital gain							
A							
B							
C							
13 Collectibles (28%) gain							
A							
B							
C							
14 Unrecaptured section 1250 gain							
A							
B							
C							

Schedule K-2 (Form 1120-S) 2022

(Use for Problem 24.)

Schedule K-2 (Form 1120-S) 2022

Page **3**

Name of corporation

EIN

DRAFT AS OF September 30, 2022 DO NOT FILE

Part II   **Foreign Tax Credit Limitation** *(continued)*

Section 1—Gross Income *(continued)*

Description	(a) U.S. source	Foreign Source				(f) Sourced by shareholder	(g) Total
		(b) Foreign branch category income	(c) Passive category income	(d) General category income	(e) Other (category code)		
15 Net section 1231 gain							
A							
B							
C							
16 Section 986(c) gain							
17 Section 987 gain							
18 Section 988 gain							
19 Section 951(a) inclusions							
A							
B							
C							
20 Other income (see instructions)							
A							
B							
C							
21 Section 951A(a) inclusions (see instructions)							
22 Reserved for future use							
A							
B							
C							
23 Reserved for future use							
A							
B							
C							
24 **Total gross income** (combine lines 1 through 23)							
A							
B							
C							

Schedule K-2 (Form 1120-S) 2022

(Use for Problem 24.)

Schedule K-2 (Form 1120-S) 2022							Page **4**
Name of corporation						EIN	

Part II   Foreign Tax Credit Limitation *(continued)*

Section 2—Deductions

Description	(a) U.S. source	Foreign Source				(f) Sourced by shareholder	(g) Total
		(b) Foreign branch category income	(c) Passive category income	(d) General category income	(e) Other (category code ___)		
25 Expenses allocable to sales income							
26 Expenses allocable to gross income from performances of services							
27 Net short-term capital loss							
28 Net long-term capital loss							
29 Collectibles loss							
30 Net section 1231 loss							
31 Other losses							
32 Research & experimental (R&E) expenses							
A SIC code:							
B SIC code:							
C SIC code:							
33 Allocable rental expenses—depreciation, depletion, and amortization							
34 Allocable rental expenses—other than depreciation, depletion, and amortization							
35 Allocable royalty and licensing expenses—depreciation, depletion, and amortization							
36 Allocable royalty and licensing expenses—other than depreciation, depletion, and amortization							
37 Depreciation not included on line 33 or 35							
38 Charitable contributions							
39 Interest expense specifically allocable under Regulations section 1.861-10(e)							
40 Other interest expense specifically allocable under Regulations section 1.861-10T							
41 Other interest expense—business							
42 Other interest expense—investment							
43 Other interest expense—passive activity							
44 Section 59(e)(2) expenditures, excluding R&E expenses on line 32							
45 Foreign taxes not creditable but deductible							

Schedule K-2 (Form 1120-S) 2022

(Use for Problem 24.)

Schedule K-2 (Form 1120-S) 2022

Page **5**

Name of corporation

EIN

Part II Foreign Tax Credit Limitation *(continued)*

Section 2—Deductions *(continued)*

| Description | (a) U.S. source | Foreign Source | | | | (f) Sourced by shareholder | (g) Total |
		(b) Foreign branch category income	(c) Passive category income	(d) General category income	(e) Other (category code __)		
46 Section 986(c) loss							
47 Section 987 loss							
48 Section 988 loss							
49 Other allocable deductions (see instructions)							
50 Other apportioned share of deductions (see instructions) . . .							
51 Reserved for future use							
52 Reserved for future use							
53 Reserved for future use							
54 **Total deductions** (combine lines 25 through 53)							
55 **Net income (loss)** (subtract line 54 from line 24)							

Part III Other Information for Preparation of Form 1116

Section 1—R&E Expenses Apportionment Factors

| Description | (a) U.S. source | Foreign Source | | | | (f) Sourced by shareholder | (g) Total |
		(b) Foreign branch category income	(c) Passive category income	(d) General category income	(e) Other (category code ____) (country code ____)		
1 Gross receipts by SIC code							
A SIC code:							
B SIC code:							
C SIC code:							
D SIC code:							
E SIC code:							
F SIC code:							

2	Exclusive apportionment with respect to total R&E expenses entered on Part II, line 32. Enter the following.	
A	R&E expense with respect to activity performed in the United States	
(i) SIC code: _____	**2A(i)**	
(ii) SIC code: _____	**2A(ii)**	
(iii) SIC code: _____	**2A(iii)**	
B	R&E expense with respect to activity performed outside the United States	
(i) SIC code: _____	**2B(i)**	
(ii) SIC code: _____	**2B(ii)**	
(iii) SIC code: _____	**2B(iii)**	

Schedule K-2 (Form 1120-S) 2022

(Use for Problem 24.)

Schedule K-2 (Form 1120-S) 2022   Page **6**

Name of corporation   EIN

Part III   Other Information for Preparation of Form 1116 *(continued)*

Section 2—Interest Expense Apportionment Factors

Description	(a) U.S. source	Foreign Source (b) Foreign branch category income	(c) Passive category income	(d) General category income	(e) Other (category code ___) (country code ___)	(f) Sourced by shareholder	(g) Total
1 Total average value of assets							
2 Reserved for future use							
3 Assets attracting directly allocable interest expense under Regulations section 1.861-10(e)							
4 Other assets attracting directly allocable interest expense under Regulations section 1.861-10T							
5 Assets excluded from apportionment formula							
6a Total assets used for apportionment (subtract the sum of lines 3, 4, and 5 from the sum of lines 1 and 2)							
b Assets attracting business interest expense							
c Assets attracting investment interest expense							
d Assets attracting passive activity interest expense							
7 Basis in stock of 10%-owned noncontrolled foreign corporations (see attachment)							
8 Basis in stock of CFCs (see attachment)							

Schedule K-2 (Form 1120-S) 2022

(Use for Problem 24.)

Schedule K-3 (Form 1120-S)	☐ Final K-3 ☐ Amended K-3	
	Shareholder's Share of Income, Deductions, Credits, etc.—International	OMB No. 1545-0123
Department of the Treasury Internal Revenue Service	For calendar year 2022, or tax year beginning / / 2022 , ending / / See separate instructions.	2022

Information About the Corporation

A Corporation's employer identification number (EIN)

B Corporation's name, address, city, state, and ZIP code

Information About the Shareholder

C Shareholder's identifying number

D Shareholder's name, address, city, state, and ZIP code

E Check to indicate the parts of Schedule K-3 that apply.

		Yes	No
1	Does Part I apply? If "Yes," complete and attach Part I .		
2	Does Part II apply? If "Yes," complete and attach Part II		
3	Does Part III apply? If "Yes," complete and attach Part III		
4	Does Part IV apply? If "Yes," complete and attach Part IV .		
5	Does Part V apply? If "Yes," complete and attach Part V		
6	Does Part VI apply? If "Yes," complete and attach Part VI .		
7	Does Part VII apply? If "Yes," complete and attach Part VII		

For IRS Use Only

For Paperwork Reduction Act Notice, see the Instructions for Form 1120-S.   www.irs.gov/Form1120S   Cat. No. 74747C   **Schedule K-3 (Form 1120-S) 2022**

(Use for Problem 24.)

Schedule K-3 (Form 1120-S) 2022 — Page 2

DRAFT AS OF September 30, 2022 DO NOT FILE

Corporation's name	EIN	Shareholder's name	Shareholder's identifying number

Part I   Shareholder's Share of Corporation's Other Current Year International Information

Check box(es) for additional specified attachments. See instructions.

- ☐ 1. Gain on personal property sale
- ☐ 2. Foreign oil and gas taxes
- ☐ 3. Splitter arrangements
- ☐ 4. Foreign tax translation
- ☐ 5. High-taxed income
- ☐ 6. Section 267A disallowed deduction
- ☐ 7. Form 8858 information
- ☐ 8. Form 5471 information
- ☐ 9. Other forms
- ☐ 10. Shareholder loan transactions
- ☐ 11. Entity treatment for certain S corporations
- ☐ 12. Form 8865 information
- ☐ 13. Other international items (attach description and statement)

Part II   Foreign Tax Credit Limitation

Section 1—Gross Income

Description	(a) U.S. source	(b) Foreign branch category income	(c) Passive category income	(d) General category income	(e) Other (category code ___)	(f) Sourced by shareholder	(g) Total
1 Sales							
A							
B							
C							
2 Gross income from performance of services							
A							
B							
C							
3 Gross rental real estate income							
A							
B							
C							
4 Other gross rental income							
A							
B							
C							
5 Reserved for future use							
6 Interest income							
A							
B							
C							
7 Ordinary dividends (exclude amount on line 8)							
A							
B							
C							

Schedule K-3 (Form 1120-S) 2022

(Use for Problem 24.)

Schedule K-3 (Form 1120-S) 2022   Page **3**

| Corporation's name | | EIN | Shareholder's name | | Shareholder's identifying number |

Part II **Foreign Tax Credit Limitation** *(continued)*

Section 1—Gross Income *(continued)*

Description	(a) U.S. source	Foreign Source				(g) Total
		(b) Foreign branch category income	(c) Passive category income	(d) General category income	(e) Other (category code)	(f) Sourced by shareholder	

Description	(a) U.S. source	(b) Foreign branch category income	(c) Passive category income	(d) General category income	(e) Other (category code)	(f) Sourced by shareholder	(g) Total
8 Qualified dividends							
A							
B							
C							
9 Reserved for future use							
10 Royalties and license fees							
A							
B							
C							
11 Net short-term capital gain							
A							
B							
C							
12 Net long-term capital gain							
A							
B							
C							
13 Collectibles (28%) gain							
A							
B							
C							
14 Unrecaptured section 1250 gain							
A							
B							
C							
15 Net section 1231 gain							
A							
B							
C							

Schedule K-3 (Form 1120-S) 2022

(Use for Problem 24.)

Schedule K-3 (Form 1120-S) 2022   Page **4**

| Corporation's name | | EIN | Shareholder's name | | | Shareholder's identifying number | |

Part II   Foreign Tax Credit Limitation *(continued)*

Section 1—Gross Income *(continued)*

Description	(a) U.S. source	Foreign Source				(f) Sourced by shareholder	(g) Total
		(b) Foreign branch category income	(c) Passive category income	(d) General category income	(e) Other (category code ____)		
16 Section 986(c) gain							
17 Section 987 gain							
18 Section 988 gain							
19 Section 951(a) inclusions							
A							
B							
C							
20 Other income (see instructions)							
A							
B							
C							
21 Section 951A(a) inclusions (see instructions)							
22 Reserved for future use							
A							
B							
C							
23 Reserved for future use							
A							
B							
C							
24 **Total gross income** (combine lines 1 through 23)							
A							
B							
C							

Schedule K-3 (Form 1120-S) 2022

(Use for Problem 24.)

Schedule K-3 (Form 1120-S) 2022

Page **5**

Corporation's name		EIN		Shareholder's name		Shareholder's identifying number	

Part II — Foreign Tax Credit Limitation (continued)

Section 2—Deductions

	Description	(a) U.S. source	(b) Foreign branch category income	(c) Passive category income	(d) General category income	(e) Other (category code ___)	(f) Sourced by shareholder	(g) Total
			Foreign Source					
25	Expenses allocable to sales income							
26	Expenses allocable to gross income from performances of services							
27	Net short-term capital loss							
28	Net long-term capital loss							
29	Collectibles loss							
30	Net section 1231 loss							
31	Other losses							
32	Research & experimental (R&E) expenses							
A	SIC code:							
B	SIC code:							
C	SIC code:							
33	Allocable rental expenses— depreciation, depletion, and amortization							
34	Allocable rental expenses—other than depreciation, depletion, and amortization							
35	Allocable royalty and licensing expenses—depreciation, depletion, and amortization							
36	Allocable royalty and licensing expenses—other than depreciation, depletion, and amortization							
37	Depreciation not included on line 33 or 35							
38	Charitable contributions							
39	Interest expense specifically allocable under Regulations section 1.861-10(e)							
40	Other interest expense specifically allocable under Regulations section 1.861-10T							
41	Other interest expense—business							
42	Other interest expense—investment							
43	Other interest expense—passive activity							
44	Section 59(e)(2) expenditures, excluding R&E expenses on line 32							
45	Foreign taxes not creditable but deductible							

Schedule K-3 (Form 1120-S) 2022

(Use for Problem 24.)

Schedule K-3 (Form 1120-S) 2022   Page **6**

| Corporation's name | | EIN | | Shareholder's name | | Shareholder's identifying number | |

Part II   Foreign Tax Credit Limitation *(continued)*

Section 2—Deductions *(continued)*

Description	(a) U.S. source	Foreign Source				(f) Sourced by shareholder	(g) Total
		(b) Foreign branch category income	(c) Passive category income	(d) General category income	(e) Other (category code ___)		
46 Section 986(c) loss							
47 Section 987 loss							
48 Section 988 loss							
49 Other allocable deductions (see instructions)							
50 Other apportioned share of deductions (see instructions)							
51 Reserved for future use							
52 Reserved for future use							
53 Reserved for future use							
54 **Total deductions** (combine lines 25 through 53)							
55 **Net income (loss)** (subtract line 54 from line 24)							

Part III   Other Information for Preparation of Form 1116

Section 1—R&E Expenses Apportionment Factors

Description	(a) U.S. source	Foreign Source				(f) Sourced by shareholder	(g) Total
		(b) Foreign branch category income	(c) Passive category income	(d) General category income	(e) Other (category code ___) (country code ___)		
1 Gross receipts by SIC code							
A SIC code:							
B SIC code:							
C SIC code:							
D SIC code:							
E SIC code:							
F SIC code:							

2   Exclusive apportionment with respect to total R&E expenses entered on Part II, line 32. Enter the following.

A   R&E expense with respect to activity performed in the United States

    (i)   SIC code: _____ ....   **2A(i)**

    (ii)   SIC code: _____ ....   **2A(ii)**

    (iii)   SIC code: _____ ....   **2A(iii)**

B   R&E expense with respect to activity performed outside the United States

    (i)   SIC code: _____ ....   **2B(i)**

    (ii)   SIC code: _____ ....   **2B(ii)**

    (iii)   SIC code: _____ ....   **2B(iii)**

Schedule K-3 (Form 1120-S) 2022

(Use for Problem 24.)

| **Form 7203** (Rev. December 2022)
Department of the Treasury
Internal Revenue Service | **S Corporation Shareholder Stock and Debt Basis Limitations**
Attach to your tax return.
Go to *www.irs.gov/Form7203* for instructions and the latest information. | OMB No. 1545-2302

Attachment
Sequence No. **203** |

Name of shareholder

Identifying number

A Name of S corporation

B Employer identification number

C Stock block (see instructions):

D Check applicable box(es) to indicate how stock was acquired:
(1) ☐ Original shareholder   **(2)** ☐ Purchased   **(3)** ☐ Inherited   **(4)** ☐ Gift   **(5)** ☐ Other:

E Check if you have a Regulations section 1.1367-1(g) election in effect during the tax year for this S corporation . . . . . ☐

Part I   Shareholder Stock Basis

1	Stock basis at the beginning of the corporation's tax year	**1**
2	Basis from any capital contributions made or additional stock acquired during the tax year . . .	**2**
3a	Ordinary business income (enter losses in Part III) **3a**	
b	Net rental real estate income (enter losses in Part III) **3b**	
c	Other net rental income (enter losses in Part III) **3c**	
d	Interest income **3d**	
e	Ordinary dividends **3e**	
f	Royalties **3f**	
g	Net capital gains (enter losses in Part III) **3g**	
h	Net section 1231 gain (enter losses in Part III) **3h**	
i	Other income (enter losses in Part III) **3i**	
j	Excess depletion adjustment **3j**	
k	Tax-exempt income **3k**	
l	Recapture of business credits **3l**	
m	Other items that increase stock basis **3m**	
4	Add lines 3a through 3m	**4**
5	Stock basis before distributions. Add lines 1, 2, and 4	**5**
6	Distributions (excluding dividend distributions)	**6**
	Note: If line 6 is larger than line 5, subtract line 5 from line 6 and report the result as a capital gain on Form 8949 and Schedule D. See instructions.	
7	Stock basis after distributions. Subtract line 6 from line 5. If the result is zero or less, enter -0-, skip lines 8 through 14, and enter -0- on line 15	**7**
8a	Nondeductible expenses **8a**	
b	Depletion for oil and gas **8b**	
c	Business credits (sections 50(c)(1) and (5)) **8c**	
9	Add lines 8a through 8c	**9**
10	Stock basis before loss and deduction items. Subtract line 9 from line 7. If the result is zero or less, enter -0-, skip lines 11 through 14, and enter -0- on line 15	**10**
11	Allowable loss and deduction items. Enter the amount from line 47, column (c)	**11**
12	Debt basis restoration (see net increase in instructions for line 23)	**12**
13	Other items that decrease stock basis	**13**
14	Add lines 11, 12, and 13	**14**
15	**Stock basis at the end of the corporation's tax year.** Subtract line 14 from line 10. If the result is zero or less, enter -0-	**15**

Part II   Shareholder Debt Basis

Section A—Amount of Debt (If more than three debts, see instructions.)

Description	(a) Debt 1 ☐ Formal note ☐ Open account	(b) Debt 2 ☐ Formal note ☐ Open account	(c) Debt 3 ☐ Formal note ☐ Open account	(d) Total
16	Loan balance at the beginning of the corporation's tax year				
17	Additional loans (see instructions)				
18	Loan balance before repayment. Add lines 16 and 17				
19	Principal portion of debt repayment (this line doesn't include interest)				
20	Loan balance at the end of the corporation's tax year. Subtract line 19 from line 18				

For Paperwork Reduction Act Notice, see separate instructions.   Cat. No. 56396V   Form **7203** (Rev. 12-2022)

(Use for Problem 24.)

Part II	Shareholder Debt Basis *(continued)*				
	Section B—Adjustments to Debt Basis				
	Description	**(a)** Debt 1	**(b)** Debt 2	**(c)** Debt 3	**(d)** Total
21	Debt basis at the beginning of the corporation's tax year				
22	Enter the amount, if any, from line 17				
23	Debt basis restoration (see instructions)				
24	Debt basis before repayment. Add lines 21, 22, and 23				
25	Divide line 24 by line 18				
26	Nontaxable debt repayment. Multiply line 25 by line 19				
27	Debt basis before nondeductible expenses and losses. Subtract line 26 from line 24				
28	Nondeductible expenses and oil and gas depletion deductions in excess of stock basis				
29	Debt basis before losses and deductions. Subtract line 28 from line 27. If the result is zero or less, enter -0-				
30	Allowable losses in excess of stock basis. Enter the amount from line 47, column (d)				
31	**Debt basis at the end of the corporation's tax year.** Subtract line 30 from line 29. If the result is zero or less, enter -0-				
	Section C—Gain on Loan Repayment				
32	Repayment. Enter the amount from line 19				
33	Nontaxable repayments. Enter the amount from line 26				
34	**Reportable gain.** Subtract line 33 from line 32				

Part III	Shareholder Allowable Loss and Deduction Items					
	Description	**(a)** Current year losses and deductions	**(b)** Carryover amounts (column (e)) from the previous year	**(c)** Allowable loss from stock basis	**(d)** Allowable loss from debt basis	**(e)** Carryover amounts
35	Ordinary business loss					
36	Net rental real estate loss					
37	Other net rental loss					
38	Net capital loss					
39	Net section 1231 loss					
40	Other loss					
41	Section 179 deductions					
42	Charitable contributions					
43	Investment interest expense					
44	Section 59(e)(2) expenditures					
45	Other deductions					
46	Foreign taxes paid or accrued					
47	**Total loss.** Add lines 35 through 46 for each column. Enter the total loss in column (c) on line 11 and enter the total loss in column (d) on line 30					

Form **7203** (Rev. 12-2022)

CUMULATIVE PROBLEM (CHAPTERS 14–16)

Bebop, Inc. distributes investment property to its shareholders. The property was acquired five years ago and has a basis of $50,000 and a market value of $80,000.

a. How will this distribution be treated for tax purposes at both the corporate and shareholder levels if Bebop is a C corporation?

b. If Bebop, Inc. was an S corporation, how would your answer to Part a. differ?

c. If the company was a partnership, how would the distribution be treated for tax purposes at the partnership and partner levels?

Appendix

Viewing and Downloading IRS Tax Forms and Publications

In order to view IRS tax forms and publications, you must have Adobe (Acrobat Reader) installed on your computer. If you do not have Adobe Acrobat Reader on your computer, you can download a copy free from the Adobe web site: *https://get.adobe.com/reader*

■ To access and download forms and IRS publications, you must first go to the IRS website: *https://www.irs.gov*

■ This will take you to the IRS web page, titled, **IRS**. On this page you will see a series of tabs across the top of the page (see sample below). Click on the tab, **Form & Instructions.** This will take you to the **Forms, Instructions & Publications** page.

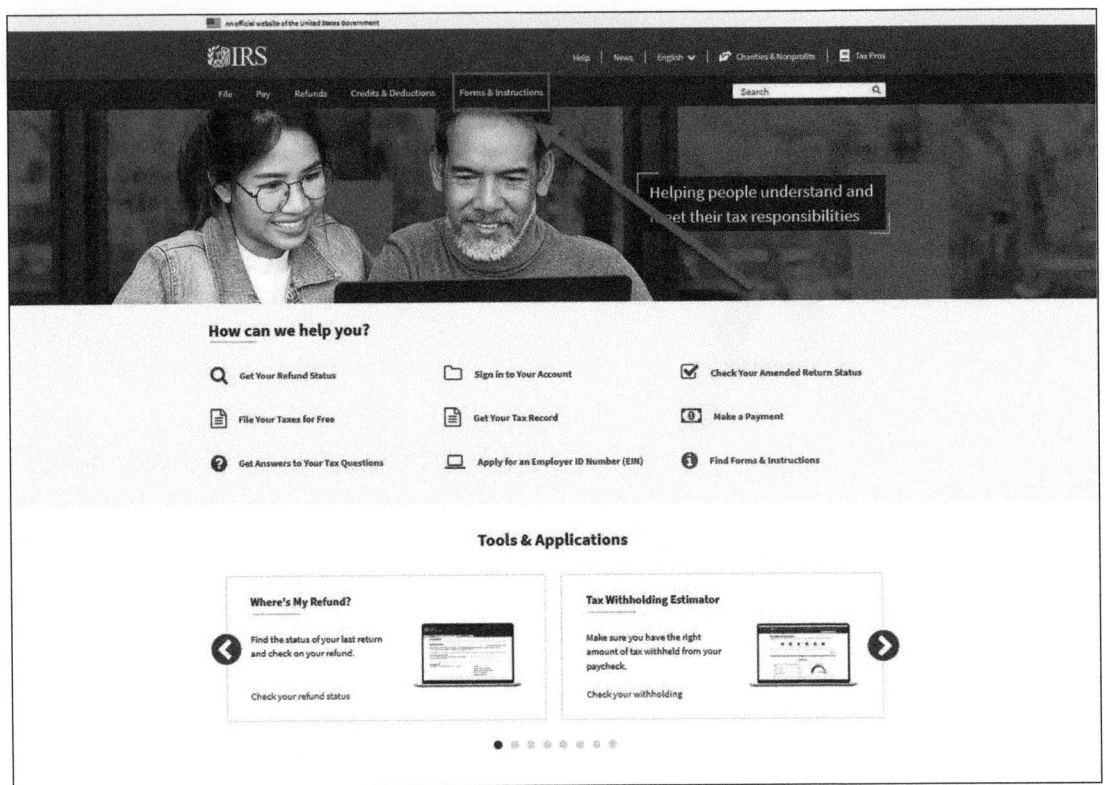

- On the **Forms, Instructions & Publications** page, you will find a list of options (see sample below). The first one, **Current Year**, shows "Popular Forms, Instructions & Publications" for individuals and businesses. Here you will find links to the forms and instructions for the more commonly requested forms and publications. If the form or publication you want is not listed, click on the button, "List All Current Forms & Instructions," and it will take you to a page where you can search for the form or publication you are looking to find.

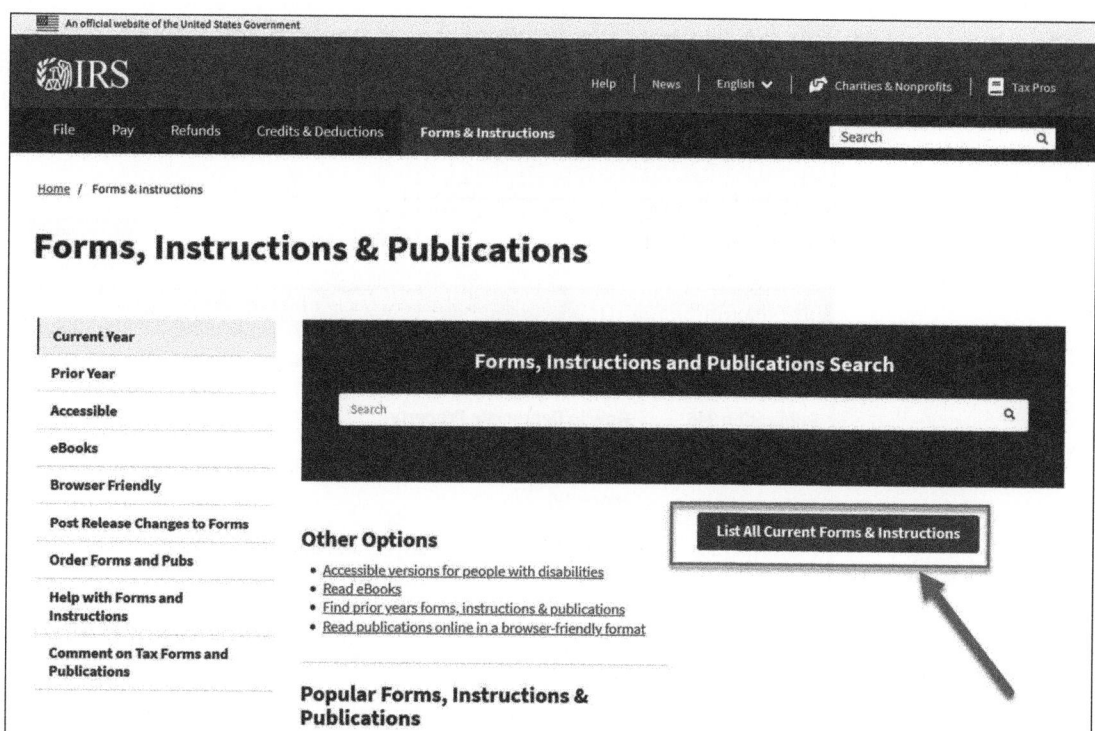

■ Once you are on the page with the list of forms and publications, you can locate a specific form or publication by entering the number in the box to the right of the word "**Find**." For example, if you are interested in locating Form 2441, you would enter 2441 in the search box (as shown below), choose **Product Number** from the menu in the box next to "in", and then click on the Search button. The following screen would then appear.

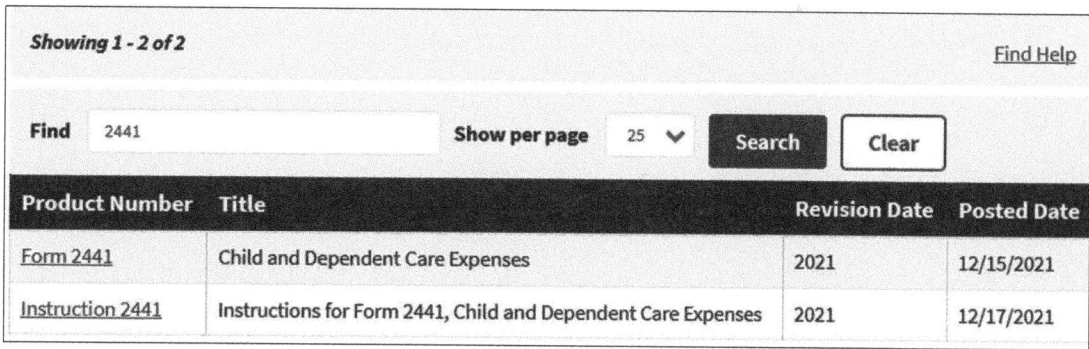

■ Clicking the Form 2441 link will download this form in PDF format. (Depending on your browser, you may need to follow some additional instructions to be allowed to open the .pdf file). Clicking on the Instruction 2441 link will download the instructions in PDF format. Many of the forms and schedules are available as fill-in forms, where you can type in the information you want on the form, print it out, and save it to your computer as a .pdf file for future reference. However, please note that this is not a computer program, so you still must type in the information correctly (no spell check or automatic calculations). Also be cautious about sending a fillable form to someone else as it doesn't always transmit correctly. Print a static copy of the form before trying to email it.

■ You can also search by keyword. For example, if you wanted to locate a form or publication on depreciation, you would enter **depreciation** in the search box and click the **Search** button. Below is the screen that would appear. Once again, you can then click on the appropriate link to download/view the item of interest.

| **Find** depreciation | **Show per page** 25 ∨ | **Search** | **Clear** |

Product Number	Title	Revision Date	Posted Date
Publication 534	Depreciating Property Placed In Service Before 1987	Nov 2016	11/07/2016
Publication 946	How to Depreciate Property	2021	03/07/2022
Form 4562	Depreciation and Amortization (Including Information on Listed Property)	2021	12/20/2021
Instruction 4562	Instructions for Form 4562, Depreciation and Amortization (Including Information on Listed Property)	2021	01/11/2022
Form 8866	Interest Computation Under the Look-Back Method for Property Depreciated Under the Income Forecast Method	Nov 2018	11/08/2018
Instruction 8866	Instructions for Form 8866, Interest Computation Under the Look-Back Method for Property Depreciated Under the Income Forecast Method	Nov 2018	11/09/2018

Appendix

B

Selected Forms and Schedules

On the following pages you will find blank copies of selected forms and schedules that you can use to help you visualize the flow of information through the tax return, Form 1040.

Form 1040

Department of the Treasury—Internal Revenue Service

U.S. Individual Income Tax Return **2022** OMB No. 1545-0074 | IRS Use Only—Do not write or staple in this space.

Filing Status
Check only one box.

☐ Single ☐ Married filing jointly ☐ Married filing separately (MFS) ☐ Head of household (HOH) ☐ Qualifying widow(er) (QW)

If you checked the MFS box, enter the name of your spouse. If you checked the HOH or QW box, enter the child's name if the qualifying person is a child but not your dependent:

Your first name and middle initial	Last name		Your social security number
If joint return, spouse's first name and middle initial	Last name		Spouse's social security number

Home address (number and street). If you have a P.O. box, see instructions.		Apt. no.	**Presidential Election Campaign**
City, town, or post office. If you have a foreign address, also complete spaces below.	State	ZIP code	Check here if you, or your spouse if filing jointly, want $3 to go to this fund. Checking a box below will not change your tax or refund.
Foreign country name	Foreign province/state/county	Foreign postal code	☐ You ☐ Spouse

At any time during 2022, did you: (a) receive (as a reward, award, or compensation); or (b) sell, exchange, gift, or otherwise dispose of a digital asset (or a financial interest in a digital asset)? (See instructions.) . . . ☐ Yes ☐ No

Standard Deduction

Someone can claim: ☐ You as a dependent ☐ Your spouse as a dependent
☐ Spouse itemizes on a separate return or you were a dual-status alien

Age/Blindness You: ☐ Were born before January 2, 1958 ☐ Are blind **Spouse:** ☐ Was born before January 2, 1958 ☐ Is blind

Dependents (see instructions):
If more than four dependents, see instructions and check here . . ☐

(1) First name　Last name	(2) Social security number	(3) Relationship to you	(4) Check the box if qualifies for (see instructions):	
			Child tax credit	Credit for other dependents
			☐	☐
			☐	☐
			☐	☐
			☐	☐

Income

Attach Form(s) W-2 here. Also attach Forms W-2G and 1099-R if tax was withheld.

If you did not get a Form W-2, see instructions.

1a	Total amount from Form(s) W-2, box 1 (see instructions)	1a
b	Household employee wages not reported on Form(s) W-2	1b
c	Tip income not reported on line 1a (see instructions)	1c
d	Medicaid waiver payments not reported on Form(s) W-2 (see instructions) .	1d
e	Taxable dependent care benefits from Form 2441, line 26	1e
f	Employer-provided adoption benefits from Form 8839, line 29	1f
g	Wages from Form 8919, line 6	1g
h	Other earned income (see instructions)	1h
i	Nontaxable combat pay election (see instructions) 1i	
z	Add lines 1a through 1h	1z

Attach Sch. B if required.

2a	Tax-exempt interest . . .	2a		b	Taxable interest	2b
3a	Qualified dividends . . .	3a		b	Ordinary dividends	3b
4a	IRA distributions . . .	4a		b	Taxable amount	4b
5a	Pensions and annuities . .	5a		b	Taxable amount	5b
6a	Social security benefits . .	6a		b	Taxable amount	6b
c	If you elect to use the lump-sum election method, check here (see instructions) . . . ☐					

Standard Deduction for—
• Single or Married filing separately, $12,950
• Married filing jointly or Qualifying widow(er), $25,900
• Head of household, $19,400
• If you checked any box under *Standard Deduction,* see instructions.

7	Capital gain or (loss). Attach Schedule D if required. If not required, check here . . . . . . ☐	7
8	Other income from Schedule 1, line 10	8
9	Add lines 1z, 2b, 3b, 4b, 5b, 6b, 7, and 8. This is your **total income** . . .	9
10	Adjustments to income from Schedule 1, line 26	10
11	Subtract line 10 from line 9. This is your **adjusted gross income** . . .	11
12	**Standard deduction or itemized deductions** (from Schedule A)	12
13	Qualified business income deduction from Form 8995 or Form 8995-A . . .	13
14	Add lines 12 and 13	14
15	Subtract line 14 from line 11. If zero or less, enter -0-. This is your **taxable income**	15

For Disclosure, Privacy Act, and Paperwork Reduction Act Notice, see separate instructions. Cat. No. 11320B Form **1040** (2022)

Version A, Cycle 7

Form 1040 (2022)

Page **2**

Tax and Credits	16	**Tax** (see instructions). Check if any from Form(s): 1 ☐ 8814 2 ☐ 4972 3 ☐ _____	16	
	17	Amount from Schedule 2, line 3	17	
	18	Add lines 16 and 17	18	
	19	Child tax credit or credit for other dependents from Schedule 8812	19	
	20	Amount from Schedule 3, line 8	20	
	21	Add lines 19 and 20	21	
	22	Subtract line 21 from line 18. If zero or less, enter -0-	22	
	23	Other taxes, including self-employment tax, from Schedule 2, line 21	23	
	24	Add lines 22 and 23. This is your **total tax**	24	

Payments	25	Federal income tax withheld from:		
	a	Form(s) W-2	25a	
	b	Form(s) 1099	25b	
	c	Other forms (see instructions)	25c	
	d	Add lines 25a through 25c	25d	
If you have a qualifying child, attach Sch. EIC.	26	2022 estimated tax payments and amount applied from 2021 return	26	
	27	Earned income credit (EIC)	27	
	28	Additional child tax credit from Schedule 8812	28	
	29	American opportunity credit from Form 8863, line 8	29	
	30	Reserved for future use	30	
	31	Amount from Schedule 3, line 15	31	
	32	Add lines 27, 28, 29, and 31. These are your **total other payments and refundable credits**	32	
	33	Add lines 25d, 26, and 32. These are your **total payments**	33	

Refund	34	If line 33 is more than line 24, subtract line 24 from line 33. This is the amount you **overpaid** . .	34	
	35a	Amount of line 34 you want **refunded to you.** If Form 8888 is attached, check here . . . . ☐	35a	
Direct deposit? See instructions.	b	Routing number		
	d	Account number	c Type: ☐ Checking ☐ Savings	
	36	Amount of line 34 you want **applied to your 2023 estimated tax** . . .	36	

| Amount You Owe | 37 | Subtract line 33 from line 24. This is the **amount you owe.** For details on how to pay, go to *www.irs.gov/Payments* or see instructions . . . . | 37 | |
| | 38 | Estimated tax penalty (see instructions) . . . . | 38 | |

Third Party Designee

Do you want to allow another person to discuss this return with the IRS? See instructions . . . . ☐ **Yes.** Complete below.   ☐ **No**

| Designee's name | | Phone no. | | Personal identification number (PIN) | |

Sign Here

Under penalties of perjury, I declare that I have examined this return and accompanying schedules and statements, and to the best of my knowledge and belief, they are true, correct, and complete. Declaration of preparer (other than taxpayer) is based on all information of which preparer has any knowledge.

Joint return? See instructions. Keep a copy for your records.

| Your signature | Date | Your occupation | If the IRS sent you an Identity Protection PIN, enter it here (see inst.) |
| Spouse's signature. If a joint return, **both** must sign. | Date | Spouse's occupation | If the IRS sent your spouse an Identity Protection PIN, enter it here (see inst.) |

| Phone no. | Email address |

Paid Preparer Use Only

Preparer's name	Preparer's signature		Date	PTIN	Check if: ☐ Self-employed
Firm's name				Phone no.	
Firm's address				Firm's EIN	

Go to *www.irs.gov/Form1040* for instructions and the latest information.

Form **1040** (2022)

SCHEDULE 1
(Form 1040)

Department of the Treasury
Internal Revenue Service

Additional Income and Adjustments to Income

Attach to Form 1040, 1040-SR, or 1040-NR.
Go to *www.irs.gov/Form1040* for instructions and the latest information.

OMB No. 1545-0074

2022

Attachment
Sequence No. **01**

Name(s) shown on Form 1040, 1040-SR, or 1040-NR

Your social security number

Part I　**Additional Income**

1	Taxable refunds, credits, or offsets of state and local income taxes	1
2a	Alimony received	2a
b	Date of original divorce or separation agreement (see instructions):	
3	Business income or (loss). Attach Schedule C	3
4	Other gains or (losses). Attach Form 4797	4
5	Rental real estate, royalties, partnerships, S corporations, trusts, etc. Attach Schedule E	5
6	Farm income or (loss). Attach Schedule F	6
7	Unemployment compensation	7
8	Other income:	
a	Net operating loss	8a ( )
b	Gambling	8b
c	Cancellation of debt	8c
d	Foreign earned income exclusion from Form 2555	8d ( )
e	Income from Form 8853	8e
f	Income from Form 8889	8f
g	Alaska Permanent Fund dividends	8g
h	Jury duty pay	8h
i	Prizes and awards	8i
j	Activity not engaged in for profit income	8j
k	Stock options	8k
l	Income from the rental of personal property if you engaged in the rental for profit but were not in the business of renting such property	8l
m	Olympic and Paralympic medals and USOC prize money (see instructions)	8m
n	Section 951(a) inclusion (see instructions)	8n
o	Section 951A(a) inclusion (see instructions)	8o
p	Section 461(l) excess business loss adjustment	8p
q	Taxable distributions from an ABLE account (see instructions)	8q
r	Scholarship and fellowship grants not reported on Form W-2	8r
s	Nontaxable amount of Medicaid waiver payments included on Form 1040, line 1a or 1d	8s ( )
t	Pension or annuity from a nonqualifed deferred compensation plan or a nongovernmental section 457 plan	8t
u	Wages earned while incarcerated	8u
z	Other income. List type and amount: _____	8z
9	Total other income. Add lines 8a through 8z	9
10	Combine lines 1 through 7 and 9. Enter here and on Form 1040, 1040-SR, or 1040-NR, line 8	10

For Paperwork Reduction Act Notice, see your tax return instructions.　　Cat. No. 71479F　　Schedule 1 (Form 1040) 2022

Schedule 1 (Form 1040) 2022   Page **2**

Part II Adjustments to Income

11	Educator expenses	**11**
12	Certain business expenses of reservists, performing artists, and fee-basis government officials. Attach Form 2106	**12**
13	Health savings account deduction. Attach Form 8889	**13**
14	Moving expenses for members of the Armed Forces. Attach Form 3903	**14**
15	Deductible part of self-employment tax. Attach Schedule SE	**15**
16	Self-employed SEP, SIMPLE, and qualified plans	**16**
17	Self-employed health insurance deduction	**17**
18	Penalty on early withdrawal of savings	**18**
19a	Alimony paid	**19a**
b	Recipient's SSN	
c	Date of original divorce or separation agreement (see instructions): _____	
20	IRA deduction	**20**
21	Student loan interest deduction	**21**
22	Reserved for future use	**22**
23	Archer MSA deduction	**23**
24	Other adjustments:	
a	Jury duty pay (see instructions) **24a**	
b	Deductible expenses related to income reported on line 8l from the rental of personal property engaged in for profit **24b**	
c	Nontaxable amount of the value of Olympic and Paralympic medals and USOC prize money reported on line 8m **24c**	
d	Reforestation amortization and expenses **24d**	
e	Repayment of supplemental unemployment benefits under the Trade Act of 1974 . . . . **24e**	
f	Contributions to section 501(c)(18)(D) pension plans **24f**	
g	Contributions by certain chaplains to section 403(b) plans **24g**	
h	Attorney fees and court costs for actions involving certain unlawful discrimination claims (see instructions) **24h**	
i	Attorney fees and court costs you paid in connection with an award from the IRS for information you provided that helped the IRS detect tax law violations **24i**	
j	Housing deduction from Form 2555 . . . . **24j**	
k	Excess deductions of section 67(e) expenses from Schedule K-1 (Form 1041) **24k**	
z	Other adjustments. List type and amount: _____ _____ **24z**	
25	Total other adjustments. Add lines 24a through 24z	**25**
26	Add lines 11 through 23 and 25. These are your **adjustments to income**. Enter here and on Form 1040 or 1040-SR, line 10, or Form 1040-NR, line 10a	**26**

Schedule 1 (Form 1040) 2022

SCHEDULE 2 (Form 1040) Department of the Treasury Internal Revenue Service	**Additional Taxes** Attach to Form 1040, 1040-SR, or 1040-NR. Go to *www.irs.gov/Form1040* for instructions and the latest information.	OMB No. 1545-0074 20**22** Attachment Sequence No. **02**
Name(s) shown on Form 1040, 1040-SR, or 1040-NR		Your social security number

Part I Tax

1	Alternative minimum tax. Attach Form 6251	**1**
2	Excess advance premium tax credit repayment. Attach Form 8962	**2**
3	Add lines 1 and 2. Enter here and on Form 1040, 1040-SR, or 1040-NR, line 17 . .	**3**

Part II Other Taxes

4	Self-employment tax. Attach Schedule SE	**4**
5	Social security and Medicare tax on unreported tip income. Attach Form 4137 . . . . **5**	
6	Uncollected social security and Medicare tax on wages. Attach Form 8919 . . . . **6**	
7	Total additional social security and Medicare tax. Add lines 5 and 6 .	**7**
8	Additional tax on IRAs or other tax-favored accounts. Attach Form 5329 if required. If not required, check here . . . . ☐	**8**
9	Household employment taxes. Attach Schedule H	**9**
10	Repayment of first-time homebuyer credit. Attach Form 5405 if required	**10**
11	Additional Medicare Tax. Attach Form 8959	**11**
12	Net investment income tax. Attach Form 8960	**12**
13	Uncollected social security and Medicare or RRTA tax on tips or group-term life insurance from Form W-2, box 12	**13**
14	Interest on tax due on installment income from the sale of certain residential lots and timeshares	**14**
15	Interest on the deferred tax on gain from certain installment sales with a sales price over $150,000	**15**
16	Recapture of low-income housing credit. Attach Form 8611	**16**

(continued on page 2)

For Paperwork Reduction Act Notice, see your tax return instructions.	Cat. No. 71478U	Schedule 2 (Form 1040) 2022

Schedule 2 (Form 1040) 2022   Page **2**

Part II **Other Taxes** *(continued)*

17 Other additional taxes:

a Recapture of other credits. List type, form number, and amount:

_____ **17a**

b Recapture of federal mortgage subsidy, if you sold your home
see instructions **17b**

c Additional tax on HSA distributions. Attach Form 8889 . . . **17c**

d Additional tax on an HSA because you didn't remain an eligible
individual. Attach Form 8889 . . . . **17d**

e Additional tax on Archer MSA distributions. Attach Form 8853 . **17e**

f Additional tax on Medicare Advantage MSA distributions. Attach
Form 8853 . . . . **17f**

g Recapture of a charitable contribution deduction related to a
fractional interest in tangible personal property **17g**

h Income you received from a nonqualified deferred compensation
plan that fails to meet the requirements of section 409A . . . **17h**

i Compensation you received from a nonqualified deferred
compensation plan described in section 457A **17i**

j Section 72(m)(5) excess benefits tax **17j**

k Golden parachute payments **17k**

l Tax on accumulation distribution of trusts **17l**

m Excise tax on insider stock compensation from an expatriated
corporation **17m**

n Look-back interest under section 167(g) or 460(b) from Form
8697 or 8866 . . . . **17n**

o Tax on non-effectively connected income for any part of the
year you were a nonresident alien from Form 1040-NR **17o**

p Any interest from Form 8621, line 16f, relating to distributions
from, and dispositions of, stock of a section 1291 fund **17p**

q Any interest from Form 8621, line 24 . . . . **17q**

z Any other taxes. List type and amount: _____

_____ **17z**

18 Total additional taxes. Add lines 17a through 17z **18**

19 Reserved for future use **19**

20 Section 965 net tax liability installment from Form 965-A . . . **20**

21 Add lines 4, 7 through 16, and 18. These are your **total other taxes.** Enter here and
on Form 1040 or 1040-SR, line 23, or Form 1040-NR, line 23b **21**

Schedule 2 (Form 1040) 2022

SCHEDULE 3
(Form 1040)

Department of the Treasury
Internal Revenue Service

Additional Credits and Payments

Attach to Form 1040, 1040-SR, or 1040-NR.
Go to *www.irs.gov/Form1040* for instructions and the latest information.

OMB No. 1545-0074

2022

Attachment
Sequence No. **03**

Name(s) shown on Form 1040, 1040-SR, or 1040-NR

Your social security number

Part I   **Nonrefundable Credits**

1	Foreign tax credit. Attach Form 1116 if required	**1**	
2	Credit for child and dependent care expenses from Form 2441, line 11. Attach Form 2441	**2**	
3	Education credits from Form 8863, line 19	**3**	
4	Retirement savings contributions credit. Attach Form 8880 . . .	**4**	
5	Residential energy credits. Attach Form 5695	**5**	
6	Other nonrefundable credits:		
a	General business credit. Attach Form 3800	**6a**	
b	Credit for prior year minimum tax. Attach Form 8801 . . .	**6b**	
c	Adoption credit. Attach Form 8839	**6c**	
d	Credit for the elderly or disabled. Attach Schedule R	**6d**	
e	Alternative motor vehicle credit. Attach Form 8910	**6e**	
f	Qualified plug-in motor vehicle credit. Attach Form 8936 . . .	**6f**	
g	Mortgage interest credit. Attach Form 8396	**6g**	
h	District of Columbia first-time homebuyer credit. Attach Form 8859	**6h**	
i	Qualified electric vehicle credit. Attach Form 8834	**6i**	
j	Reserved for future use	**6j**	
k	Credit to holders of tax credit bonds. Attach Form 8912 . . .	**6k**	
l	Amount on Form 8978, line 14. See instructions	**6l**	
z	Other nonrefundable credits. List type and amount: _____ _____	**6z**	
7	Total other nonrefundable credits. Add lines 6a through 6z	**7**	
8	Add lines 1 through 5 and 7. Enter here and on Form 1040, 1040-SR, or 1040-NR, line 20	**8**	

(continued on page 2)

For Paperwork Reduction Act Notice, see your tax return instructions.   Cat. No. 71480G   Schedule 3 (Form 1040) 2022

Part II	Other Payments and Refundable Credits		
9	Net premium tax credit. Attach Form 8962	**9**	
10	Amount paid with request for extension to file (see instructions)	**10**	
11	Excess social security and tier 1 RRTA tax withheld	**11**	
12	Credit for federal tax on fuels. Attach Form 4136	**12**	
13	Other payments or refundable credits:		
a	Form 2439	**13a**	
b	Credit for qualified sick and family leave wages paid in 2022 from Schedule(s) H for leave taken before April 1, 2021	**13b**	
c	Reserved for future use	**13c**	
d	Credit for repayment of amounts included in income in earlier years	**13d**	
e	Reserved for future use	**13e**	
f	Deferred amount of net 965 tax liability (see instructions) . . .	**13f**	
g	Reserved for future use	**13g**	
h	Credit for qualified sick and family leave wages paid in 2022 from Schedule(s) H for leave taken after March 31, 2021, and before October 1, 2021	**13h**	
z	Other payments or refundable credits. List type and amount: _____	**13z**	
14	Total other payments or refundable credits. Add lines 13a through 13z	**14**	
15	Add lines 9 through 12 and 14. Enter here and on Form 1040, 1040-SR, or 1040-NR, line 31	**15**	

SCHEDULE A (Form 1040)

Department of the Treasury
Internal Revenue Service

Itemized Deductions

Go to *www.irs.gov/ScheduleA* for instructions and the latest information.
Attach to Form 1040 or 1040-SR.

Caution: If you are claiming a net qualified disaster loss on Form 4684, see the instructions for line 16.

OMB No. 1545-0074

2022

Attachment Sequence No. **07**

Name(s) shown on Form 1040 or 1040-SR

Your social security number

DRAFT AS OF July 21, 2022 DO NOT FILE

Medical and Dental Expenses	**Caution:** Do not include expenses reimbursed or paid by others.	
	1 Medical and dental expenses (see instructions)	1
	2 Enter amount from Form 1040 or 1040-SR, line 11 2	
	3 Multiply line 2 by 7.5% (0.075)	3
	4 Subtract line 3 from line 1. If line 3 is more than line 1, enter -0-	4
Taxes You Paid	5 State and local taxes.	
	a State and local income taxes or general sales taxes. You may include either income taxes or general sales taxes on line 5a, but not both. If you elect to include general sales taxes instead of income taxes, check this box ☐	5a
	b State and local real estate taxes (see instructions)	5b
	c State and local personal property taxes	5c
	d Add lines 5a through 5c	5d
	e Enter the smaller of line 5d or $10,000 ($5,000 if married filing separately)	5e
	6 Other taxes. List type and amount: _____	6
	7 Add lines 5e and 6	7
Interest You Paid **Caution:** Your mortgage interest deduction may be limited. See instructions.	8 Home mortgage interest and points. If you didn't use all of your home mortgage loan(s) to buy, build, or improve your home, see instructions and check this box ☐	
	a Home mortgage interest and points reported to you on Form 1098. See instructions if limited	8a
	b Home mortgage interest not reported to you on Form 1098. See instructions if limited. If paid to the person from whom you bought the home, see instructions and show that person's name, identifying no., and address	8b
	c Points not reported to you on Form 1098. See instructions for special rules	8c
	d Reserved for future use	8d
	e Add lines 8a through 8c	8e
	9 Investment interest. Attach Form 4952 if required. See instructions	9
	10 Add lines 8e and 9	10
Gifts to Charity **Caution:** If you made a gift and got a benefit for it, see instructions.	11 Gifts by cash or check. If you made any gift of $250 or more, see instructions	11
	12 Other than by cash or check. If you made any gift of $250 or more, see instructions. You **must** attach Form 8283 if over $500	12
	13 Carryover from prior year	13
	14 Add lines 11 through 13	14
Casualty and Theft Losses	15 Casualty and theft loss(es) from a federally declared disaster (other than net qualified disaster losses). Attach Form 4684 and enter the amount from line 18 of that form. See instructions	15
Other Itemized Deductions	16 Other—from list in instructions. List type and amount: _____	16
Total Itemized Deductions	17 Add the amounts in the far right column for lines 4 through 16. Also, enter this amount on Form 1040 or 1040-SR, line 12	17
	18 If you elect to itemize deductions even though they are less than your standard deduction, check this box ☐	

For Paperwork Reduction Act Notice, see the Instructions for Form 1040.   Cat. No. 17145C   Schedule A (Form 1040) 2022

SCHEDULE B (Form 1040) Department of the Treasury Internal Revenue Service	Interest and Ordinary Dividends Go to *www.irs.gov/ScheduleB* for instructions and the latest information. Attach to Form 1040 or 1040-SR.	OMB No. 1545-0074 2022 Attachment Sequence No. 08

Name(s) shown on return   Your social security number

Part I

Interest

(See instructions
and the
Instructions for
Form 1040,
line 2b.)

Note: If you
received a
Form 1099-INT,
Form 1099-OID,
or substitute
statement from
a brokerage firm,
list the firm's
name as the
payer and enter
the total interest
shown on that
form.

		Amount
1	List name of payer. If any interest is from a seller-financed mortgage and the buyer used the property as a personal residence, see the instructions and list this interest first. Also, show that buyer's social security number and address:	**1**
2	Add the amounts on line 1	**2**
3	Excludable interest on series EE and I U.S. savings bonds issued after 1989. Attach Form 8815	**3**
4	Subtract line 3 from line 2. Enter the result here and on Form 1040 or 1040-SR, line 2b	**4**

Note: If line 4 is over $1,500, you must complete Part III.

Part II

Ordinary Dividends

(See instructions
and the
Instructions for
Form 1040,
line 3b.)

Note: If you
received a
Form 1099-DIV
or substitute
statement from
a brokerage firm,
list the firm's
name as the
payer and enter
the ordinary
dividends shown
on that form.

		Amount
5	List name of payer:	**5**
6	Add the amounts on line 5. Enter the total here and on Form 1040 or 1040-SR, line 3b	**6**

Note: If line 6 is over $1,500, you must complete Part III.

Part III

Foreign Accounts and Trusts

Caution: If
required, failure to
file FinCEN Form
114 may result in
substantial
penalties.
Additionally, you
may be required
to file Form 8938,
Statement of
Specified Foreign
Financial Assets.
See instructions.

You must complete this part if you (**a**) had over $1,500 of taxable interest or ordinary dividends; (**b**) had a foreign account; or (**c**) received a distribution from, or were a grantor of, or a transferor to, a foreign trust.

		Yes	No
7a	At any time during 2022, did you have a financial interest in or signature authority over a financial account (such as a bank account, securities account, or brokerage account) located in a foreign country? See instructions		
	If "Yes," are you required to file FinCEN Form 114, Report of Foreign Bank and Financial Accounts (FBAR), to report that financial interest or signature authority? See FinCEN Form 114 and its instructions for filing requirements and exceptions to those requirements		
b	If you are required to file FinCEN Form 114, list the name(s) of the foreign country(-ies) where the financial account(s) are located:		
8	During 2022, did you receive a distribution from, or were you the grantor of, or transferor to, a foreign trust? If "Yes," you may have to file Form 3520. See instructions		

For Paperwork Reduction Act Notice, see your tax return instructions.   Cat. No. 17146N   Schedule B (Form 1040) 2022

**SCHEDULE C
(Form 1040)**

Department of the Treasury
Internal Revenue Service

Profit or Loss From Business
(Sole Proprietorship)

Go to *www.irs.gov/ScheduleC* for instructions and the latest information.
Attach to Form 1040, 1040-SR, 1040-NR, or 1041; partnerships must generally file Form 1065.

OMB No. 1545-0074

2022

Attachment
Sequence No. **09**

Name of proprietor

Social security number (SSN)

A	Principal business or profession, including product or service (see instructions)	**B** Enter code from instructions
C	Business name. If no separate business name, leave blank.	**D** Employer ID number (EIN) (see instr.)
E	Business address (including suite or room no.)	
	City, town or post office, state, and ZIP code	

F Accounting method: **(1)** ☐ Cash **(2)** ☐ Accrual **(3)** ☐ Other (specify)

G Did you "materially participate" in the operation of this business during 2022? If "No," see instructions for limit on losses . ☐ Yes ☐ No

H If you started or acquired this business during 2022, check here . . . . ☐

I Did you make any payments in 2022 that would require you to file Form(s) 1099? See instructions . . . . ☐ Yes ☐ No

J If "Yes," did you or will you file required Form(s) 1099? . . . . ☐ Yes ☐ No

Part I   Income

1	Gross receipts or sales. See instructions for line 1 and check the box if this income was reported to you on Form W-2 and the "Statutory employee" box on that form was checked . . . . . ☐	**1**	
2	Returns and allowances	**2**	
3	Subtract line 2 from line 1	**3**	
4	Cost of goods sold (from line 42)	**4**	
5	**Gross profit.** Subtract line 4 from line 3	**5**	
6	Other income, including federal and state gasoline or fuel tax credit or refund (see instructions)	**6**	
7	**Gross income.** Add lines 5 and 6	**7**	

Part II   Expenses. Enter expenses for business use of your home **only** on line 30.

8	Advertising	**8**		18	Office expense (see instructions) .	**18**
9	Car and truck expenses (see instructions) . . .	**9**		19	Pension and profit-sharing plans .	**19**
				20	Rent or lease (see instructions):	
10	Commissions and fees .	**10**		a	Vehicles, machinery, and equipment	**20a**
11	Contract labor (see instructions)	**11**		b	Other business property . . .	**20b**
12	Depletion	**12**		21	Repairs and maintenance . .	**21**
13	Depreciation and section 179 expense deduction (not included in Part III) (see instructions)	**13**		22	Supplies (not included in Part III) .	**22**
				23	Taxes and licenses	**23**
				24	Travel and meals:	
14	Employee benefit programs (other than on line 19) .	**14**		a	Travel	**24a**
15	Insurance (other than health)	**15**		b	Deductible meals (see instructions)	**24b**
16	Interest (see instructions):			25	Utilities	**25**
a	Mortgage (paid to banks, etc.)	**16a**		26	Wages (less employment credits)	**26**
b	Other	**16b**		27a	Other expenses (from line 48) . .	**27a**
17	Legal and professional services	**17**		b	**Reserved for future use** . . .	**27b**

28	**Total expenses** before expenses for business use of home. Add lines 8 through 27a	**28**	
29	Tentative profit or (loss). Subtract line 28 from line 7	**29**	
30	Expenses for business use of your home. Do not report these expenses elsewhere. Attach Form 8829 unless using the simplified method. See instructions. **Simplified method filers only:** Enter the total square footage of (a) your home: _____ and (b) the part of your home used for business: _____ . Use the Simplified Method Worksheet in the instructions to figure the amount to enter on line 30	**30**	
31	**Net profit or (loss).** Subtract line 30 from line 29. • If a profit, enter on both **Schedule 1 (Form 1040), line 3,** and on **Schedule SE, line 2.** (If you checked the box on line 1, see instructions.) Estates and trusts, enter on **Form 1041, line 3.** • If a loss, you **must** go to line 32.	**31**	
32	If you have a loss, check the box that describes your investment in this activity. See instructions. • If you checked 32a, enter the loss on both **Schedule 1 (Form 1040), line 3,** and on **Schedule SE, line 2.** (If you checked the box on line 1, see the line 31 instructions.) Estates and trusts, enter on **Form 1041, line 3.** • If you checked 32b, you **must** attach **Form 6198.** Your loss may be limited.	**32a** ☐ All investment is at risk. **32b** ☐ Some investment is not at risk.	

For Paperwork Reduction Act Notice, see the separate instructions.   Cat. No. 11334P   Schedule C (Form 1040) 2022

Schedule C (Form 1040) 2022   Page **2**

Part III   Cost of Goods Sold (see instructions)

33   Method(s) used to
       value closing inventory: **a** ☐ Cost   **b** ☐ Lower of cost or market   **c** ☐ Other (attach explanation)

34   Was there any change in determining quantities, costs, or valuations between opening and closing inventory?
       If "Yes," attach explanation . . . . ☐ Yes   ☐ No

35   Inventory at beginning of year. If different from last year's closing inventory, attach explanation . | **35** |

36   Purchases less cost of items withdrawn for personal use . . . . | **36** |

37   Cost of labor. Do not include any amounts paid to yourself . . . . | **37** |

38   Materials and supplies . . . . | **38** |

39   Other costs . . . . | **39** |

40   Add lines 35 through 39 . . . . | **40** |

41   Inventory at end of year . . . . | **41** |

42   **Cost of goods sold.** Subtract line 41 from line 40. Enter the result here and on line 4 . . . . . . | **42** |

Part IV   Information on Your Vehicle. Complete this part **only** if you are claiming car or truck expenses on line 9 and are not required to file Form 4562 for this business. See the instructions for line 13 to find out if you must file Form 4562.

43   When did you place your vehicle in service for business purposes? (month/day/year) _____ / _____ / _____

44   Of the total number of miles you drove your vehicle during 2022, enter the number of miles you used your vehicle for:

a   Business _____ **b** Commuting (see instructions) _____ **c** Other _____

45   Was your vehicle available for personal use during off-duty hours? . . . . ☐ Yes   ☐ No

46   Do you (or your spouse) have another vehicle available for personal use?. . . . . ☐ Yes   ☐ No

47a Do you have evidence to support your deduction? . . . . ☐ Yes   ☐ No

b   If "Yes," is the evidence written? . . . . ☐ Yes   ☐ No

Part V   Other Expenses. List below business expenses not included on lines 8–26 or line 30.

-- | |

-- | |

-- | |

-- | |

-- | |

-- | |

-- | |

-- | |

48   **Total other expenses.** Enter here and on line 27a . . . . | **48** |

Schedule C (Form 1040) 2022

SCHEDULE D (Form 1040) Department of the Treasury Internal Revenue Service	Capital Gains and Losses Attach to Form 1040, 1040-SR, or 1040-NR. Go to *www.irs.gov/ScheduleD* for instructions and the latest information. Use Form 8949 to list your transactions for lines 1b, 2, 3, 8b, 9, and 10.	OMB No. 1545-0074 2022 Attachment Sequence No. **12**

Name(s) shown on return		Your social security number

Did you dispose of any investment(s) in a qualified opportunity fund during the tax year? ☐ **Yes** ☐ **No**
If "Yes," attach Form 8949 and see its instructions for additional requirements for reporting your gain or loss.

Part I   Short-Term Capital Gains and Losses—Generally Assets Held One Year or Less (see instructions)

See instructions for how to figure the amounts to enter on the lines below. This form may be easier to complete if you round off cents to whole dollars.	(d) Proceeds (sales price)	(e) Cost (or other basis)	(g) Adjustments to gain or loss from Form(s) 8949, Part I, line 2, column (g)	(h) Gain or (loss) Subtract column (e) from column (d) and combine the result with column (g)
1a Totals for all short-term transactions reported on Form 1099-B for which basis was reported to the IRS and for which you have no adjustments (see instructions). However, if you choose to report all these transactions on Form 8949, leave this line blank and go to line 1b				
1b Totals for all transactions reported on Form(s) 8949 with **Box A** checked				
2 Totals for all transactions reported on Form(s) 8949 with **Box B** checked				
3 Totals for all transactions reported on Form(s) 8949 with **Box C** checked				

4 Short-term gain from Form 6252 and short-term gain or (loss) from Forms 4684, 6781, and 8824 . .	**4**	
5 Net short-term gain or (loss) from partnerships, S corporations, estates, and trusts from Schedule(s) K-1	**5**	
6 Short-term capital loss carryover. Enter the amount, if any, from line 8 of your **Capital Loss Carryover Worksheet** in the instructions	**6** (	)
7 **Net short-term capital gain or (loss).** Combine lines 1a through 6 in column (h). If you have any long-term capital gains or losses, go to Part II below. Otherwise, go to Part III on the back	**7**	

Part II   Long-Term Capital Gains and Losses—Generally Assets Held More Than One Year (see instructions)

See instructions for how to figure the amounts to enter on the lines below. This form may be easier to complete if you round off cents to whole dollars.	(d) Proceeds (sales price)	(e) Cost (or other basis)	(g) Adjustments to gain or loss from Form(s) 8949, Part II, line 2, column (g)	(h) Gain or (loss) Subtract column (e) from column (d) and combine the result with column (g)
8a Totals for all long-term transactions reported on Form 1099-B for which basis was reported to the IRS and for which you have no adjustments (see instructions). However, if you choose to report all these transactions on Form 8949, leave this line blank and go to line 8b .				
8b Totals for all transactions reported on Form(s) 8949 with **Box D** checked				
9 Totals for all transactions reported on Form(s) 8949 with **Box E** checked				
10 Totals for all transactions reported on Form(s) 8949 with **Box F** checked.				

11 Gain from Form 4797, Part I; long-term gain from Forms 2439 and 6252; and long-term gain or (loss) from Forms 4684, 6781, and 8824	**11**	
12 Net long-term gain or (loss) from partnerships, S corporations, estates, and trusts from Schedule(s) K-1	**12**	
13 Capital gain distributions. See the instructions	**13**	
14 Long-term capital loss carryover. Enter the amount, if any, from line 13 of your **Capital Loss Carryover Worksheet** in the instructions	**14** (	)
15 **Net long-term capital gain or (loss).** Combine lines 8a through 14 in column (h). Then, go to Part III on the back	**15**	

For Paperwork Reduction Act Notice, see your tax return instructions.   Cat. No. 11338H   Schedule D (Form 1040) 2022

Schedule D (Form 1040) 2022

Page **2**

| **Part III** | Summary |

16 Combine lines 7 and 15 and enter the result . . . . | 16 |

- If line 16 is a **gain**, enter the amount from line 16 on Form 1040, 1040-SR, or 1040-NR, line 7. Then, go to line 17 below.
- If line 16 is a **loss**, skip lines 17 through 20 below. Then, go to line 21. Also be sure to complete line 22.
- If line 16 is **zero**, skip lines 17 through 21 below and enter -0- on Form 1040, 1040-SR, or 1040-NR, line 7. Then, go to line 22.

17 Are lines 15 and 16 **both** gains?
☐ **Yes.** Go to line 18.
☐ **No.** Skip lines 18 through 21, and go to line 22.

18 If you are required to complete the **28% Rate Gain Worksheet** (see instructions), enter the amount, if any, from line 7 of that worksheet . . . . | 18 |

19 If you are required to complete the **Unrecaptured Section 1250 Gain Worksheet** (see instructions), enter the amount, if any, from line 18 of that worksheet . . . . . . | 19 |

20 Are lines 18 and 19 both zero or blank and you are not filing Form 4952?
☐ **Yes.** Complete the **Qualified Dividends and Capital Gain Tax Worksheet** in the instructions for Form 1040, line 16. **Don't** complete lines 21 and 22 below.

☐ **No.** Complete the **Schedule D Tax Worksheet** in the instructions. **Don't** complete lines 21 and 22 below.

21 If line 16 is a loss, enter here and on Form 1040, 1040-SR, or 1040-NR, line 7, the **smaller** of:

- The loss on line 16; or
- ($3,000), or if married filing separately, ($1,500) } . . . . | 21 | ( ) |

Note: When figuring which amount is smaller, treat both amounts as positive numbers.

22 Do you have qualified dividends on Form 1040, 1040-SR, or 1040-NR, line 3a?

☐ **Yes.** Complete the **Qualified Dividends and Capital Gain Tax Worksheet** in the instructions for Form 1040, line 16.

☐ **No.** Complete the rest of Form 1040, 1040-SR, or 1040-NR.

Schedule D (Form 1040) 2022

SCHEDULE E
(Form 1040)

Department of the Treasury
Internal Revenue Service

Supplemental Income and Loss

(From rental real estate, royalties, partnerships, S corporations, estates, trusts, REMICs, etc.)

Attach to Form 1040, 1040-SR, 1040-NR, or 1041.
Go to www.irs.gov/ScheduleE for instructions and the latest information.

OMB No. 1545-0074

2022

Attachment Sequence No. **13**

Name(s) shown on return

Your social security number

Part I   **Income or Loss From Rental Real Estate and Royalties**

Note: If you are in the business of renting personal property, use **Schedule C**. See instructions. If you are an individual, report farm rental income or loss from **Form 4835** on page 2, line 40.

A Did you make any payments in 2022 that would require you to file Form(s) 1099? See instructions . . . ☐ Yes ☐ No

B If "Yes," did you or will you file required Form(s) 1099? . . . . ☐ Yes ☐ No

1a Physical address of each property (street, city, state, ZIP code)

A	
B	
C	

1b	Type of Property (from list below)	**2**	For each rental real estate property listed above, report the number of fair rental and personal use days. Check the QJV box only if you meet the requirements to file as a qualified joint venture. See instructions.		Fair Rental Days	Personal Use Days	QJV
A				**A**			☐
B				**B**			☐
C				**C**			☐

Type of Property:

1 Single Family Residence   3 Vacation/Short-Term Rental   5 Land   7 Self-Rental
2 Multi-Family Residence   4 Commercial   6 Royalties   8 Other (describe) _____

			Properties:		
			A	**B**	**C**
Income:					
3	Rents received	3			
4	Royalties received	4			
Expenses:					
5	Advertising	5			
6	Auto and travel (see instructions)	6			
7	Cleaning and maintenance	7			
8	Commissions	8			
9	Insurance	9			
10	Legal and other professional fees	10			
11	Management fees	11			
12	Mortgage interest paid to banks, etc. (see instructions)	12			
13	Other interest	13			
14	Repairs	14			
15	Supplies	15			
16	Taxes	16			
17	Utilities	17			
18	Depreciation expense or depletion	18			
19	Other (list) _____	19			
20	Total expenses. Add lines 5 through 19	20			
21	Subtract line 20 from line 3 (rents) and/or 4 (royalties). If result is a (loss), see instructions to find out if you must file **Form 6198**	21			
22	Deductible rental real estate loss after limitation, if any, on **Form 8582** (see instructions)	22	( )	( )	( )

23a	Total of all amounts reported on line 3 for all rental properties		23a		
b	Total of all amounts reported on line 4 for all royalty properties		23b		
c	Total of all amounts reported on line 12 for all properties		23c		
d	Total of all amounts reported on line 18 for all properties		23d		
e	Total of all amounts reported on line 20 for all properties		23e		
24	**Income.** Add positive amounts shown on line 21. **Do not** include any losses			24	
25	**Losses.** Add royalty losses from line 21 and rental real estate losses from line 22. Enter total losses here			25	( )
26	**Total rental real estate and royalty income or (loss).** Combine lines 24 and 25. Enter the result here. If Parts II, III, IV, and line 40 on page 2 do not apply to you, also enter this amount on Schedule 1 (Form 1040), line 5. Otherwise, include this amount in the total on line 41 on page 2			26	

For Paperwork Reduction Act Notice, see the separate instructions.   Cat. No. 11344L   Schedule E (Form 1040) 2022

Schedule E (Form 1040) 2022 | Attachment Sequence No. **13** | Page **2**

Name(s) shown on return. Do not enter name and social security number if shown on other side. | Your social security number

Caution: The IRS compares amounts reported on your tax return with amounts shown on Schedule(s) K-1.

Part II	Income or Loss From Partnerships and S Corporations

Note: If you report a loss, receive a distribution, dispose of stock, or receive a loan repayment from an S corporation, you **must** check the box in column **(e)** on line 28 and attach the required basis computation. If you report a loss from an at-risk activity for which **any** amount is **not** at risk, you **must** check the box in column **(f)** on line 28 and attach **Form 6198**. See instructions.

27 Are you reporting any loss not allowed in a prior year due to the at-risk or basis limitations, a prior year unallowed loss from a passive activity (if that loss was not reported on Form 8582), or unreimbursed partnership expenses? If you answered "Yes," see instructions before completing this section . . . . ☐ **Yes** ☐ **No**

28

	(a) Name	**(b)** Enter **P** for partnership; **S** for S corporation	**(c)** Check if foreign partnership	**(d)** Employer identification number	**(e)** Check if basis computation is required	**(f)** Check if any amount is not at risk
A			☐		☐	☐
B			☐		☐	☐
C			☐		☐	☐
D			☐		☐	☐

	Passive Income and Loss		Nonpassive Income and Loss		
	(g) Passive loss allowed (attach **Form 8582** if required)	**(h)** Passive income from **Schedule K-1**	**(i)** Nonpassive loss allowed (see **Schedule K-1**)	**(j)** Section 179 expense deduction from **Form 4562**	**(k)** Nonpassive income from **Schedule K-1**
A					
B					
C					
D					
29a Totals					
b Totals					

30 Add columns (h) and (k) of line 29a . . . . | **30** |
31 Add columns (g), (i), and (j) of line 29b . . . . | **31** ( )
32 **Total partnership and S corporation income or (loss).** Combine lines 30 and 31 . . . . | **32** |

Part III	Income or Loss From Estates and Trusts

33

	(a) Name	**(b)** Employer identification number
A		
B		

	Passive Income and Loss		Nonpassive Income and Loss	
	(c) Passive deduction or loss allowed (attach **Form 8582** if required)	**(d)** Passive income from **Schedule K-1**	**(e)** Deduction or loss from **Schedule K-1**	**(f)** Other income from **Schedule K-1**
A				
B				
34a Totals				
b Totals				

35 Add columns (d) and (f) of line 34a . . . . | **35** |
36 Add columns (c) and (e) of line 34b . . . . | **36** ( )
37 **Total estate and trust income or (loss).** Combine lines 35 and 36 . . . . . . | **37** |

Part IV	Income or Loss From Real Estate Mortgage Investment Conduits (REMICs)—Residual Holder

38

	(a) Name	**(b)** Employer identification number	**(c)** Excess inclusion from **Schedules Q**, line 2c (see instructions)	**(d)** Taxable income (net loss) from **Schedules Q**, line 1b	**(e)** Income from **Schedules Q**, line 3b

39 Combine columns (d) and (e) only. Enter the result here and include in the total on line 41 below . | **39** |

Part V	Summary

40 Net farm rental income or (loss) from **Form 4835**. Also, complete line 42 below . . . . . . | **40** |

41 **Total income or (loss).** Combine lines 26, 32, 37, 39, and 40. Enter the result here and on Schedule 1 (Form 1040), line 5 . . . . | **41** |

42 **Reconciliation of farming and fishing income.** Enter your **gross** farming and fishing income reported on Form 4835, line 7; Schedule K-1 (Form 1065), box 14, code B; Schedule K-1 (Form 1120-S), box 17, code AD; and Schedule K-1 (Form 1041), box 14, code F. See instructions . | **42** |

43 **Reconciliation for real estate professionals.** If you were a real estate professional (see instructions), enter the net income or (loss) you reported anywhere on Form 1040, Form 1040-SR, or Form 1040-NR from all rental real estate activities in which you materially participated under the passive activity loss rules . . . . | **43** |

Schedule E (Form 1040) 2022

SCHEDULE SE
(Form 1040)

Department of the Treasury
Internal Revenue Service

Self-Employment Tax

Go to *www.irs.gov/ScheduleSE* for instructions and the latest information.
Attach to Form 1040, 1040-SR, or 1040-NR.

OMB No. 1545-0074

2022

Attachment
Sequence No. **17**

Name of person with self-employment income (as shown on Form 1040, 1040-SR, or 1040-NR) | Social security number of person with **self-employment** income

DRAFT AS OF July 28, 2022 DO NOT FILE

Part I   Self-Employment Tax

Note: If your only income subject to self-employment tax is **church employee income,** see instructions for how to report your income and the definition of church employee income.

A   If you are a minister, member of a religious order, or Christian Science practitioner **and** you filed Form 4361, but you had $400 or more of **other** net earnings from self-employment, check here and continue with Part I . . . . ☐

Skip lines 1a and 1b if you use the farm optional method in Part II. See instructions.

1a	Net farm profit or (loss) from Schedule F, line 34, and farm partnerships, Schedule K-1 (Form 1065), box 14, code A	**1a**	
b	If you received social security retirement or disability benefits, enter the amount of Conservation Reserve Program payments included on Schedule F, line 4b, or listed on Schedule K-1 (Form 1065), box 20, code AH	**1b**	( )

Skip line 2 if you use the nonfarm optional method in Part II. See instructions.

2	Net profit or (loss) from Schedule C, line 31; and Schedule K-1 (Form 1065), box 14, code A (other than farming). See instructions for other income to report or if you are a minister or member of a religious order .	**2**	
3	Combine lines 1a, 1b, and 2	**3**	
4a	If line 3 is more than zero, multiply line 3 by 92.35% (0.9235). Otherwise, enter amount from line 3 .	**4a**	
	Note: If line 4a is less than $400 due to Conservation Reserve Program payments on line 1b, see instructions.		
b	If you elect one or both of the optional methods, enter the total of lines 15 and 17 here	**4b**	
c	Combine lines 4a and 4b. If less than $400, **stop;** you don't owe self-employment tax. **Exception:** If less than $400 and you had **church employee income,** enter -0- and continue	**4c**	
5a	Enter your **church employee income** from Form W-2. See instructions for definition of church employee income **5a**		
b	Multiply line 5a by 92.35% (0.9235). If less than $100, enter -0-	**5b**	
6	Add lines 4c and 5b	**6**	
7	Maximum amount of combined wages and self-employment earnings subject to social security tax or the 6.2% portion of the 7.65% railroad retirement (tier 1) tax for 2022	**7**	147,000
8a	Total social security wages and tips (total of boxes 3 and 7 on Form(s) W-2) and railroad retirement (tier 1) compensation. If $147,000 or more, skip lines 8b through 10, and go to line 11 . . . . **8a**		
b	Unreported tips subject to social security tax from Form 4137, line 10 . . . **8b**		
c	Wages subject to social security tax from Form 8919, line 10 . . . . . . **8c**		
d	Add lines 8a, 8b, and 8c	**8d**	
9	Subtract line 8d from line 7. If zero or less, enter -0- here and on line 10 and go to line 11	**9**	
10	Multiply the **smaller** of line 6 or line 9 by 12.4% (0.124)	**10**	
11	Multiply line 6 by 2.9% (0.029)	**11**	
12	**Self-employment tax.** Add lines 10 and 11. Enter here and on **Schedule 2 (Form 1040), line 4** . .	**12**	
13	**Deduction for one-half of self-employment tax.** Multiply line 12 by 50% (0.50). Enter here and on **Schedule 1 (Form 1040), line 15** **13**		

Part II   Optional Methods To Figure Net Earnings (see instructions)

Farm Optional Method. You may use this method **only** if **(a)** your gross farm income[1] wasn't more than $9,060, **or (b)** your net farm profits[2] were less than $6,540.

14	Maximum income for optional methods	**14**	6,040
15	Enter the **smaller** of: two-thirds (²/₃) of gross farm income[1] (not less than zero) **or** $6,040. Also, include this amount on line 4b above	**15**	

Nonfarm Optional Method. You may use this method **only** if **(a)** your net nonfarm profits[3] were less than $6,540 and also less than 72.189% of your gross nonfarm income,[4] **and (b)** you had net earnings from self-employment of at least $400 in 2 of the prior 3 years. **Caution:** You may use this method no more than five times.

16	Subtract line 15 from line 14	**16**	
17	Enter the **smaller** of: two-thirds (²/₃) of gross nonfarm income[4] (not less than zero) **or** the amount on line 16. Also, include this amount on line 4b above	**17**	

[1] From Sch. F, line 9; and Sch. K-1 (Form 1065), box 14, code B.
[2] From Sch. F, line 34; and Sch. K-1 (Form 1065), box 14, code A—minus the amount you would have entered on line 1b had you not used the optional method.
[3] From Sch. C, line 31; and Sch. K-1 (Form 1065), box 14, code A.
[4] From Sch. C, line 7; and Sch. K-1 (Form 1065), box 14, code C.

For Paperwork Reduction Act Notice, see your tax return instructions.   Cat. No. 11358Z   **Schedule SE (Form 1040) 2022**

Name(s) shown on tax return. Do not enter name and identifying number if shown on other side.

Identifying number

SECTION B—Business and Income-Producing Property

Part I   **Casualty or Theft Gain or Loss** (Use a separate Part I for each casualty or theft.)

19 Description of properties (show type, location, and date acquired for each property). Use a separate line for each property lost or damaged from the same casualty or theft. **See instructions if claiming a loss due to a Ponzi-type investment scheme and Section C is not completed.**

Property **A** _____

Property **B** _____

Property **C** _____

Property **D** _____

		Properties			
		A	**B**	**C**	**D**
20	Cost or adjusted basis of each property	**20**				
21	Insurance or other reimbursement (whether or not you filed a claim). See the instructions for line 3 . . . . **Note:** If line 20 is **more** than line 21, skip line 22.	**21**				
22	Gain from casualty or theft. If line 21 is **more** than line 20, enter the difference here and on line 29 or line 34, column (c), except as provided in the instructions for line 33. Also, skip lines 23 through 27 for that column. See the instructions for line 4 if line 21 includes insurance or other reimbursement you did not claim, or you received payment for your loss in a later tax year	**22**				
23	Fair market value **before** casualty or theft	**23**				
24	Fair market value **after** casualty or theft	**24**				
25	Subtract line 24 from line 23	**25**				
26	Enter the **smaller** of line 20 or line 25 . . . . . **Note:** If the property was totally destroyed by casualty or lost from theft, enter on line 26 the amount from line 20.	**26**				
27	Subtract line 21 from line 26. If zero or less, enter -0- .	**27**				
28	Casualty or theft loss. Add the amounts on line 27. Enter the total here and on line 29 **or** line 34. See instructions . .				**28**	

Part II   **Summary of Gains and Losses** (from separate Parts I)

	(b) Losses from casualties or thefts		**(c)** Gains from casualties or thefts includible in income
(a) Identify casualty or theft	**(i)** Trade, business, rental, or royalty property	**(ii)** Income-producing property	

Casualty or Theft of Property Held One Year or Less

29	_____	( )	( )	
	_____	( )	( )	
30	Totals. Add the amounts on line 29 . . . . **30**	( )	( )	

31 Combine line 30, columns (b)(i) and (c). Enter the net gain or (loss) here and on Form 4797, line 14. If Form 4797 is not otherwise required, see instructions **31**

32 Enter the amount from line 30, column (b)(ii), here. Individuals, enter the amount from income-producing property on Schedule A (Form 1040), line 16; or Schedule A (Form 1040-NR), line 7. (Do not include any loss on property used as an employee.) Estates and trusts, partnerships, and S corporations, see instructions **32**

Casualty or Theft of Property Held More Than One Year

33	Casualty or theft gains from Form 4797, line 32		**33**
34	_____	( )	( )
	_____	( )	( )
35	Total losses. Add amounts on line 34, columns (b)(i) and (b)(ii) **35**	( )	( )

36 Total gains. Add lines 33 and 34, column (c) **36**

37 Add amounts on line 35, columns (b)(i) and (b)(ii) **37**

38 If the loss on line 37 is **more** than the gain on line 36:

   a Combine line 35, column (b)(i), and line 36, and enter the net gain or (loss) here. Partnerships and S corporations, see the *Note* below. All others, enter this amount on Form 4797, line 14. If Form 4797 is not otherwise required, see instructions **38a**

   b Enter the amount from line 35, column (b)(ii), here. Individuals, enter the amount from income-producing property on Schedule A (Form 1040), line 16; or Schedule A (Form 1040-NR), line 7. (Do not include any loss on property used as an employee.) Estates and trusts, enter on the "Other deductions" line of your tax return. Partnerships and S corporations, see the *Note* below **38b**

39 If the loss on line 37 is **less** than or **equal** to the gain on line 36, combine lines 36 and 37 and enter here. Partnerships, see the *Note* below. All others, enter this amount on Form 4797, line 3 . . . . **39**

   Note: Partnerships, enter the amount from line 38a, 38b, or 39 on Form 1065, Schedule K, line 11.
   S corporations, enter the amount from line 38a or 38b on Form 1120-S, Schedule K, line 10.

Form **4684** (2022)

Form **4797**	**Sales of Business Property**	OMB No. 1545-0184
	(Also Involuntary Conversions and Recapture Amounts Under Sections 179 and 280F(b)(2))	**2022**
Department of the Treasury Internal Revenue Service	**Attach to your tax return.** Go to *www.irs.gov/Form4797* for instructions and the latest information.	Attachment Sequence No. **27**

Name(s) shown on return   Identifying number

1a	Enter the gross proceeds from sales or exchanges reported to you for 2022 on Form(s) 1099-B or 1099-S (or substitute statement) that you are including on line 2, 10, or 20. See instructions	**1a**	
b	Enter the total amount of gain that you are including on lines 2, 10, and 24 due to the partial dispositions of MACRS assets	**1b**	
c	Enter the total amount of loss that you are including on lines 2 and 10 due to the partial dispositions of MACRS assets	**1c**	

Part I   Sales or Exchanges of Property Used in a Trade or Business and Involuntary Conversions From Other Than Casualty or Theft—Most Property Held More Than 1 Year (see instructions)

2	(a) Description of property	(b) Date acquired (mo., day, yr.)	(c) Date sold (mo., day, yr.)	(d) Gross sales price	(e) Depreciation allowed or allowable since acquisition	(f) Cost or other basis, plus improvements and expense of sale	(g) Gain or (loss) Subtract (f) from the sum of (d) and (e)

3	Gain, if any, from Form 4684, line 39	**3**	
4	Section 1231 gain from installment sales from Form 6252, line 26 or 37	**4**	
5	Section 1231 gain or (loss) from like-kind exchanges from Form 8824	**5**	
6	Gain, if any, from line 32, from other than casualty or theft	**6**	
7	Combine lines 2 through 6. Enter the gain or (loss) here and on the appropriate line as follows	**7**	

Partnerships and S corporations. Report the gain or (loss) following the instructions for Form 1065, Schedule K, line 10, or Form 1120-S, Schedule K, line 9. Skip lines 8, 9, 11, and 12 below.

Individuals, partners, S corporation shareholders, and all others. If line 7 is zero or a loss, enter the amount from line 7 on line 11 below and skip lines 8 and 9. If line 7 is a gain and you didn't have any prior year section 1231 losses, or they were recaptured in an earlier year, enter the gain from line 7 as a long-term capital gain on the Schedule D filed with your return and skip lines 8, 9, 11, and 12 below.

8	Nonrecaptured net section 1231 losses from prior years. See instructions	**8**	
9	Subtract line 8 from line 7. If zero or less, enter -0-. If line 9 is zero, enter the gain from line 7 on line 12 below. If line 9 is more than zero, enter the amount from line 8 on line 12 below and enter the gain from line 9 as a long-term capital gain on the Schedule D filed with your return. See instructions	**9**	

Part II   Ordinary Gains and Losses (see instructions)

10	Ordinary gains and losses not included on lines 11 through 16 (include property held 1 year or less):

11	Loss, if any, from line 7	**11**	( )
12	Gain, if any, from line 7 or amount from line 8, if applicable	**12**	
13	Gain, if any, from line 31	**13**	
14	Net gain or (loss) from Form 4684, lines 31 and 38a	**14**	
15	Ordinary gain from installment sales from Form 6252, line 25 or 36	**15**	
16	Ordinary gain or (loss) from like-kind exchanges from Form 8824	**16**	
17	Combine lines 10 through 16	**17**	
18	For all except individual returns, enter the amount from line 17 on the appropriate line of your return and skip lines a and b below. For individual returns, complete lines a and b below.		
a	If the loss on line 11 includes a loss from Form 4684, line 35, column (b)(ii), enter that part of the loss here. Enter the loss from income-producing property on Schedule A (Form 1040), line 16. (Do not include any loss on property used as an employee.) Identify as from "Form 4797, line 18a." See instructions	**18a**	
b	Redetermine the gain or (loss) on line 17 excluding the loss, if any, on line 18a. Enter here and on Schedule 1 (Form 1040), Part I, line 4	**18b**	

For Paperwork Reduction Act Notice, see separate instructions.   Cat. No. 13086I   Form **4797** (2022)

Form 4797 (2022)   Page **2**

Part III Gain From Disposition of Property Under Sections 1245, 1250, 1252, 1254, and 1255
(see instructions)

19	(a) Description of section 1245, 1250, 1252, 1254, or 1255 property:		(b) Date acquired (mo., day, yr.)	(c) Date sold (mo., day, yr.)
A				
B				
C				
D				

	These columns relate to the properties on lines 19A through 19D.		Property A	Property B	Property C	Property D
20	Gross sales price (**Note:** *See line 1a before completing.*)	20				
21	Cost or other basis plus expense of sale	21				
22	Depreciation (or depletion) allowed or allowable	22				
23	Adjusted basis. Subtract line 22 from line 21	23				
24	Total gain. Subtract line 23 from line 20	24				
25	**If section 1245 property:**					
a	Depreciation allowed or allowable from line 22	25a				
b	Enter the **smaller** of line 24 or 25a	25b				
26	**If section 1250 property:** If straight line depreciation was used, enter -0- on line 26g, except for a corporation subject to section 291.					
a	Additional depreciation after 1975. See instructions	26a				
b	Applicable percentage multiplied by the **smaller** of line 24 or line 26a. See instructions	26b				
c	Subtract line 26a from line 24. If residential rental property **or** line 24 isn't more than line 26a, skip lines 26d and 26e	26c				
d	Additional depreciation after 1969 and before 1976	26d				
e	Enter the **smaller** of line 26c or 26d	26e				
f	Section 291 amount (corporations only)	26f				
g	Add lines 26b, 26e, and 26f	26g				
27	**If section 1252 property:** Skip this section if you didn't dispose of farmland or if this form is being completed for a partnership.					
a	Soil, water, and land clearing expenses	27a				
b	Line 27a multiplied by applicable percentage. See instructions	27b				
c	Enter the **smaller** of line 24 or 27b	27c				
28	**If section 1254 property:**					
a	Intangible drilling and development costs, expenditures for development of mines and other natural deposits, mining exploration costs, and depletion. See instructions	28a				
b	Enter the **smaller** of line 24 or 28a	28b				
29	**If section 1255 property:**					
a	Applicable percentage of payments excluded from income under section 126. See instructions	29a				
b	Enter the **smaller** of line 24 or 29a. See instructions	29b				

Summary of Part III Gains. Complete property columns A through D through line 29b before going to line 30.

30	Total gains for all properties. Add property columns A through D, line 24	30	
31	Add property columns A through D, lines 25b, 26g, 27c, 28b, and 29b. Enter here and on line 13	31	
32	Subtract line 31 from line 30. Enter the portion from casualty or theft on Form 4684, line 33. Enter the portion from other than casualty or theft on Form 4797, line 6	32	

Part IV Recapture Amounts Under Sections 179 and 280F(b)(2) When Business Use Drops to 50% or Less
(see instructions)

			(a) Section 179	(b) Section 280F(b)(2)
33	Section 179 expense deduction or depreciation allowable in prior years	33		
34	Recomputed depreciation. See instructions	34		
35	Recapture amount. Subtract line 34 from line 33. See the instructions for where to report	35		

Form **4797** (2022)

Form **8949**

Department of the Treasury
Internal Revenue Service

Sales and Other Dispositions of Capital Assets

Go to *www.irs.gov/Form8949* for instructions and the latest information.

File with your Schedule D to list your transactions for lines 1b, 2, 3, 8b, 9, and 10 of Schedule D.

OMB No. 1545-0074

2022

Attachment
Sequence No. **12A**

Name(s) shown on return

Social security number or taxpayer identification number

Before you check Box A, B, or C below, see whether you received any Form(s) 1099-B or substitute statement(s) from your broker. A substitute statement will have the same information as Form 1099-B. Either will show whether your basis (usually your cost) was reported to the IRS by your broker and may even tell you which box to check.

Part I   **Short-Term.** Transactions involving capital assets you held 1 year or less are generally short-term (see instructions). For long-term transactions, see page 2.

Note: You may aggregate all short-term transactions reported on Form(s) 1099-B showing basis was reported to the IRS and for which no adjustments or codes are required. Enter the totals directly on Schedule D, line 1a; you aren't required to report these transactions on Form 8949 (see instructions).

You *must* check Box A, B, or C below. Check only one box. If more than one box applies for your short-term transactions, complete a separate Form 8949, page 1, for each applicable box. If you have more short-term transactions than will fit on this page for one or more of the boxes, complete as many forms with the same box checked as you need.

- ☐ **(A)** Short-term transactions reported on Form(s) 1099-B showing basis was reported to the IRS (see **Note** above)
- ☐ **(B)** Short-term transactions reported on Form(s) 1099-B showing basis **wasn't** reported to the IRS
- ☐ **(C)** Short-term transactions not reported to you on Form 1099-B

1	(a) Description of property (Example: 100 sh. XYZ Co.)	(b) Date acquired (Mo., day, yr.)	(c) Date sold or disposed of (Mo., day, yr.)	(d) Proceeds (sales price) (see instructions)	(e) Cost or other basis See the **Note** below and see *Column (e)* in the separate instructions.	Adjustment, if any, to gain or loss If you enter an amount in column (g), enter a code in column (f). See the separate instructions.		(h) Gain or (loss) Subtract column (e) from column (d) and combine the result with column (g).
						(f) Code(s) from instructions	(g) Amount of adjustment	
2 Totals. Add the amounts in columns (d), (e), (g), and (h) (subtract negative amounts). Enter each total here and include on your Schedule D, **line 1b** (if **Box A** above is checked), **line 2** (if **Box B** above is checked), or **line 3** (if **Box C** above is checked) . .								

Note: If you checked Box A above but the basis reported to the IRS was incorrect, enter in column (e) the basis as reported to the IRS, and enter an adjustment in column (g) to correct the basis. See *Column (g)* in the separate instructions for how to figure the amount of the adjustment.

For Paperwork Reduction Act Notice, see your tax return instructions.   Cat. No. 37768Z   Form **8949** (2022)

Form 8949 (2022) Attachment Sequence No. **12A** Page **2**

Name(s) shown on return. Name and SSN or taxpayer identification no. not required if shown on other side	Social security number or taxpayer identification number

Before you check Box D, E, or F below, see whether you received any Form(s) 1099-B or substitute statement(s) from your broker. A substitute statement will have the same information as Form 1099-B. Either will show whether your basis (usually your cost) was reported to the IRS by your broker and may even tell you which box to check.

Part II **Long-Term.** Transactions involving capital assets you held more than 1 year are generally long-term (see instructions). For short-term transactions, see page 1.

Note: You may aggregate all long-term transactions reported on Form(s) 1099-B showing basis was reported to the IRS and for which no adjustments or codes are required. Enter the totals directly on Schedule D, line 8a; you aren't required to report these transactions on Form 8949 (see instructions).

You must check Box D, E, or F below. Check only one box. If more than one box applies for your long-term transactions, complete a separate Form 8949, page 2, for each applicable box. If you have more long-term transactions than will fit on this page for one or more of the boxes, complete as many forms with the same box checked as you need.

- ☐ **(D)** Long-term transactions reported on Form(s) 1099-B showing basis was reported to the IRS (see **Note** above)
- ☐ **(E)** Long-term transactions reported on Form(s) 1099-B showing basis **wasn't** reported to the IRS
- ☐ **(F)** Long-term transactions not reported to you on Form 1099-B

1 **(a)** Description of property (Example: 100 sh. XYZ Co.)	**(b)** Date acquired (Mo., day, yr.)	**(c)** Date sold or disposed of (Mo., day, yr.)	**(d)** Proceeds (sales price) (see instructions)	**(e)** Cost or other basis. See the **Note** below and see *Column (e)* in the separate instructions.	**(f)** Code(s) from instructions	**(g)** Amount of adjustment	**(h)** Gain or (loss) Subtract column (e) from column (d) and combine the result with column (g).
2 Totals. Add the amounts in columns (d), (e), (g), and (h) (subtract negative amounts). Enter each total here and include on your Schedule D, **line 8b** (if **Box D** above is checked), **line 9** (if **Box E** above is checked), or **line 10** (if **Box F** above is checked) .							

Note: If you checked Box D above but the basis reported to the IRS was incorrect, enter in column (e) the basis as reported to the IRS, and enter an adjustment in column (g) to correct the basis. See *Column (g)* in the separate instructions for how to figure the amount of the adjustment.

Form **8949** (2022)

Form 8582

Department of the Treasury
Internal Revenue Service

Passive Activity Loss Limitations

See separate instructions.
Attach to Form 1040, 1040-SR, or 1041.
Go to *www.irs.gov/Form8582* for instructions and the latest information.

OMB No. 1545-1008

2022

Attachment Sequence No. **858**

Name(s) shown on return

Identifying number

[DRAFT AS OF October 11, 2022 DO NOT FILE]

Part I   **2022 Passive Activity Loss**

Caution: Complete Parts IV and V before completing Part I.

Rental Real Estate Activities With Active Participation (For the definition of active participation, see *Special Allowance for Rental Real Estate Activities* in the instructions.)

1a	Activities with net income (enter the amount from Part IV, column (a))	1a
b	Activities with net loss (enter the amount from Part IV, column (b))	1b ( )
c	Prior years' unallowed losses (enter the amount from Part IV, column (c))	1c ( )
d	Combine lines 1a, 1b, and 1c	1d

All Other Passive Activities

2a	Activities with net income (enter the amount from Part V, column (a))	2a
b	Activities with net loss (enter the amount from Part V, column (b))	2b ( )
c	Prior years' unallowed losses (enter the amount from Part V, column (c))	2c ( )
d	Combine lines 2a, 2b, and 2c	2d

3 Combine lines 1d and 2d. If this line is zero or more, stop here and include this form with your return; all losses are allowed, including any prior year unallowed losses entered on line 1c or 2c. Report the losses on the forms and schedules normally used **3**

If line 3 is a loss and: • Line 1d is a loss, go to Part II.
                   • Line 2d is a loss (and line 1d is zero or more), skip Part II and go to line 10.

Caution: If your filing status is married filing separately and you lived with your spouse at any time during the year, **do not** complete Part II. Instead, go to line 10.

Part II   **Special Allowance for Rental Real Estate Activities With Active Participation**

Note: Enter all numbers in Part II as positive amounts. See instructions for an example.

4	Enter the **smaller** of the loss on line 1d or the loss on line 3	**4**
5	Enter $150,000. If married filing separately, see instructions	**5**
6	Enter modified adjusted gross income, but not less than zero. See instructions	**6**

Note: If line 6 is greater than or equal to line 5, skip lines 7 and 8 and enter -0- on line 9. Otherwise, go to line 7.

7	Subtract line 6 from line 5	**7**
8	Multiply line 7 by 50% (0.50). **Do not** enter more than $25,000. If married filing separately, see instructions	**8**
9	Enter the **smaller** of line 4 or line 8	**9**

Part III   **Total Losses Allowed**

10	Add the income, if any, on lines 1a and 2a and enter the total	**10**
11	**Total losses allowed from all passive activities for 2022.** Add lines 9 and 10. See instructions to find out how to report the losses on your tax return	**11**

Part IV   **Complete This Part Before Part I, Lines 1a, 1b, and 1c.** See instructions.

Name of activity	Current year		Prior years	Overall gain or loss	
	(a) Net income (line 1a)	**(b)** Net loss (line 1b)	**(c)** Unallowed loss (line 1c)	**(d)** Gain	**(e)** Loss
Total. Enter on Part I, lines 1a, 1b, and 1c					

For Paperwork Reduction Act Notice, see instructions.   Cat. No. 63704F   Form **8582** (2022)

Form 8582 (2022)   Page **2**

Part V	**Complete This Part Before Part I, Lines 2a, 2b, and 2c.** See instructions.				
Name of activity	Current year		Prior years	Overall gain or loss	
	(a) Net income (line 2a)	**(b)** Net loss (line 2b)	**(c)** Unallowed loss (line 2c)	**(d)** Gain	**(e)** Loss
Total. Enter on Part I, lines 2a, 2b, and 2c					

Part VI	**Use This Part if an Amount Is Shown on Part II, Line 9.** See instructions.				
Name of activity	Form or schedule and line number to be reported on (see instructions)	**(a)** Loss	**(b)** Ratio	**(c)** Special allowance	**(d)** Subtract column (c) from column (a).
Total			1.00		

Part VII	**Allocation of Unallowed Losses.** See instructions.			
Name of activity	Form or schedule and line number to be reported on (see instructions)	**(a)** Loss	**(b)** Ratio	**(c)** Unallowed loss
Total			1.00	

Part VIII	**Allowed Losses.** See instructions.			
Name of activity	Form or schedule and line number to be reported on (see instructions)	**(a)** Loss	**(b)** Unallowed loss	**(c)** Allowed loss
Total				

Form **8582** (2022)

Form 8582 (2022)   Page **3**

Part IX	Activities With Losses Reported on Two or More Forms or Schedules. See instructions.					

Name of activity:		**(a)**	**(b)**	**(c)** Ratio	**(d)** Unallowed loss	**(e)** Allowed loss
Form or schedule and line number to be reported on (see instructions):						
1a	Net loss plus prior year unallowed loss from form or schedule .					
b	Net income from form or schedule					
c	Subtract line 1b from line 1a. If zero or less, enter -0-					
Form or schedule and line number to be reported on (see instructions):						
1a	Net loss plus prior year unallowed loss from form or schedule . .					
b	Net income from form or schedule					
c	Subtract line 1b from line 1a. If zero or less, enter -0-					
Form or schedule and line number to be reported on (see instructions):						
1a	Net loss plus prior year unallowed loss from form or schedule . .					
b	Net income from form or schedule					
c	Subtract line 1b from line 1a. If zero or less, enter -0-					
Total				1.00		

Form **8582** (2022)

Form 8995

Department of the Treasury
Internal Revenue Service

**Qualified Business Income Deduction
Simplified Computation**

▶ Attach to your tax return.
▶ Go to *www.irs.gov/Form8995* for instructions and the latest information.

OMB No. 1545-2294

2021

Attachment
Sequence No. **55**

Name(s) shown on return

Your taxpayer identification number

Note. *You can claim the qualified business income deduction **only** if you have qualified business income from a qualified trade or business, real estate investment trust dividends, publicly traded partnership income, or a domestic production activities deduction passed through from an agricultural or horticultural cooperative. See instructions.*
Use this form if your taxable income, before your qualified business income deduction, is at or below $164,900 ($164,925 if married filing separately; $329,800 if married filing jointly), and you aren't a patron of an agricultural or horticultural cooperative.

1	(a) Trade, business, or aggregation name	(b) Taxpayer identification number	(c) Qualified business income or (loss)
i			
ii			
iii			
iv			
v			

2	Total qualified business income or (loss). Combine lines 1i through 1v, column (c)	2	
3	Qualified business net (loss) carryforward from the prior year	3 ( )	
4	Total qualified business income. Combine lines 2 and 3. If zero or less, enter -0-	4	
5	Qualified business income component. Multiply line 4 by 20% (0.20)		5
6	Qualified REIT dividends and publicly traded partnership (PTP) income or (loss) (see instructions)	6	
7	Qualified REIT dividends and qualified PTP (loss) carryforward from the prior year	7 ( )	
8	Total qualified REIT dividends and PTP income. Combine lines 6 and 7. If zero or less, enter -0-	8	
9	REIT and PTP component. Multiply line 8 by 20% (0.20)		9
10	Qualified business income deduction before the income limitation. Add lines 5 and 9		10
11	Taxable income before qualified business income deduction (see instructions)	11	
12	Net capital gain (see instructions)	12	
13	Subtract line 12 from line 11. If zero or less, enter -0-	13	
14	Income limitation. Multiply line 13 by 20% (0.20)		14
15	Qualified business income deduction. Enter the smaller of line 10 or line 14. Also enter this amount on the applicable line of your return (see instructions) ▶		15
16	Total qualified business (loss) carryforward. Combine lines 2 and 3. If greater than zero, enter -0-		16 ( )
17	Total qualified REIT dividends and PTP (loss) carryforward. Combine lines 6 and 7. If greater than zero, enter -0-		17 ( )

For Privacy Act and Paperwork Reduction Act Notice, see instructions.   Cat. No. 37806C   Form **8995** (2021)

Applicable Figures
(Used in Computing the Premium Tax Credit)

Table 2. Applicable Figure

TIP *If the amount on line 5 is 150 or less, your applicable figure is 0.0000. If the amount on line 5 is 400 or more, your applicable figure is 0.0850.*

IF Form 8962, line 5, is . . .	ENTER on Form 8962, line 7 . . .	IF Form 8962, line 5, is . . .	ENTER on Form 8962, line 7 . . .	IF Form 8962, line 5, is . . .	ENTER on Form 8962, line 7 . . .	IF Form 8962, line 5, is . . .	ENTER on Form 8962, line 7 . . .	IF Form 8962, line 5, is . . .	ENTER on Form 8962, line 7 . . .
less than 150	0.0000	200	0.0200	251	0.0404	302	0.0605	353	0.0733
150	0.0000	201	0.0204	252	0.0408	303	0.0608	354	0.0735
151	0.0004	202	0.0208	253	0.0412	304	0.0610	355	0.0738
152	0.0008	203	0.0212	254	0.0416	305	0.0613	356	0.0740
153	0.0012	204	0.0216	255	0.0420	306	0.0615	357	0.0743
154	0.0016	205	0.0220	256	0.0424	307	0.0618	358	0.0745
155	0.0020	206	0.0224	257	0.0428	308	0.0620	359	0.0748
156	0.0024	207	0.0228	258	0.0432	309	0.0623	360	0.0750
157	0.0028	208	0.0232	259	0.0436	310	0.0625	361	0.0753
158	0.0032	209	0.0236	260	0.0440	311	0.0628	362	0.0755
159	0.0036	210	0.0240	261	0.0444	312	0.0630	363	0.0758
160	0.0040	211	0.0244	262	0.0448	313	0.0633	364	0.0760
161	0.0044	212	0.0248	263	0.0452	314	0.0635	365	0.0763
162	0.0048	213	0.0252	264	0.0456	315	0.0638	366	0.0765
163	0.0052	214	0.0256	265	0.0460	316	0.0640	367	0.0768
164	0.0056	215	0.0260	266	0.0464	317	0.0643	368	0.0770
165	0.0060	216	0.0264	267	0.0468	318	0.0645	369	0.0773
166	0.0064	217	0.0268	268	0.0472	319	0.0648	370	0.0775
167	0.0068	218	0.0272	269	0.0476	320	0.0650	371	0.0778
168	0.0072	219	0.0276	270	0.0480	321	0.0653	372	0.0780
169	0.0076	220	0.0280	271	0.0484	322	0.0655	373	0.0783
170	0.0080	221	0.0284	272	0.0488	323	0.0658	374	0.0785
171	0.0084	222	0.0288	273	0.0492	324	0.0660	375	0.0788
172	0.0088	223	0.0292	274	0.0496	325	0.0663	376	0.0790
173	0.0092	224	0.0296	275	0.0500	326	0.0665	377	0.0793
174	0.0096	225	0.0300	276	0.0504	327	0.0668	378	0.0795
175	0.0100	226	0.0304	277	0.0508	328	0.0670	379	0.0798
176	0.0104	227	0.0308	278	0.0512	329	0.0673	380	0.0800
177	0.0108	228	0.0312	279	0.0516	330	0.0675	381	0.0803
178	0.0112	229	0.0316	280	0.0520	331	0.0678	382	0.0805
179	0.0116	230	0.0320	281	0.0524	332	0.0680	383	0.0808
180	0.0120	231	0.0324	282	0.0528	333	0.0683	384	0.0810
181	0.0124	232	0.0328	283	0.0532	334	0.0685	385	0.0813
182	0.0128	233	0.0332	284	0.0536	335	0.0688	386	0.0815
183	0.0132	234	0.0336	285	0.0540	336	0.0690	387	0.0818
184	0.0136	235	0.0340	286	0.0544	337	0.0693	388	0.0820
185	0.0140	236	0.0344	287	0.0548	338	0.0695	389	0.0823
186	0.0144	237	0.0348	288	0.0552	339	0.0698	390	0.0825
187	0.0148	238	0.0352	289	0.0556	340	0.0700	391	0.0828
188	0.0152	239	0.0356	290	0.0560	341	0.0703	392	0.0830
189	0.0156	240	0.0360	291	0.0564	342	0.0705	393	0.0833
190	0.0160	241	0.0364	292	0.0568	343	0.0708	394	0.0835
191	0.0164	242	0.0368	293	0.0572	344	0.0710	395	0.0838
192	0.0168	243	0.0372	294	0.0576	345	0.0713	396	0.0840
193	0.0172	244	0.0376	295	0.0580	346	0.0715	397	0.0843
194	0.0176	245	0.0380	296	0.0584	347	0.0718	398	0.0845
195	0.0180	246	0.0384	297	0.0588	348	0.0720	399	0.0848
196	0.0184	247	0.0388	298	0.0592	349	0.0723	400 or more	0.0850
197	0.0188	248	0.0392	299	0.0596	350	0.0725		
198	0.0192	249	0.0396	300	0.0600	351	0.0728		
199	0.0196	250	0.0400	301	0.0603	352	0.0730		

Appendix

Earned Income Credit Tables

2022 Earned Income Credit (EIC) Table

Caution. This is **not** a tax table.

1. To find your credit, read down the "At least - But less than" columns and find the line that includes the amount you were told to look up from your EIC Worksheet.

2. Then, go to the column that includes your filing status and the number of qualifying children you have who have valid SSNs as defined earlier. Enter the credit from that column on your EIC Worksheet.

Example. If your filing status is single, you have one qualifying child who has a valid SSN, and the amount you are looking up from your EIC Worksheet is $2,455, you would enter $842.

If the amount you are looking up from the worksheet is—		And your filing status is—			
		Single, head of household, or qualifying surviving spouse and the number of children you have is—			
		0	1	2	3
At least	But less than	Your credit is—			
2,400	2,450	186	825	970	1,091
2,450	2,500	189	842	990	1,114

If the amount you are looking up from the worksheet is—		Single, head of household, or qualifying surviving spouse★ and you have—				Married filing jointly and you have—			
		0	1	2	3	0	1	2	3
At least	But less than	Your credit is—				Your credit is—			
1	50	2	9	10	11	2	9	10	11
50	100	6	26	30	34	6	26	30	34
100	150	10	43	50	56	10	43	50	56
150	200	13	60	70	79	13	60	70	79
200	250	17	77	90	101	17	77	90	101
250	300	21	94	110	124	21	94	110	124
300	350	25	111	130	146	25	111	130	146
350	400	29	128	150	169	29	128	150	169
400	450	33	145	170	191	33	145	170	191
450	500	36	162	190	214	36	162	190	214
500	550	40	179	210	236	40	179	210	236
550	600	44	196	230	259	44	196	230	259
600	650	48	213	250	281	48	213	250	281
650	700	52	230	270	304	52	230	270	304
700	750	55	247	290	326	55	247	290	326
750	800	59	264	310	349	59	264	310	349
800	850	63	281	330	371	63	281	330	371
850	900	67	298	350	394	67	298	350	394
900	950	71	315	370	416	71	315	370	416
950	1,000	75	332	390	439	75	332	390	439
1,000	1,050	78	349	410	461	78	349	410	461
1,050	1,100	82	366	430	484	82	366	430	484
1,100	1,150	86	383	450	506	86	383	450	506
1,150	1,200	90	400	470	529	90	400	470	529
1,200	1,250	94	417	490	551	94	417	490	551
1,250	1,300	98	434	510	574	98	434	510	574
1,300	1,350	101	451	530	596	101	451	530	596
1,350	1,400	105	468	550	619	105	468	550	619
1,400	1,450	109	485	570	641	109	485	570	641
1,450	1,500	113	502	590	664	113	502	590	664
1,500	1,550	117	519	610	686	117	519	610	686
1,550	1,600	120	536	630	709	120	536	630	709
1,600	1,650	124	553	650	731	124	553	650	731
1,650	1,700	128	570	670	754	128	570	670	754
1,700	1,750	132	587	690	776	132	587	690	776
1,750	1,800	136	604	710	799	136	604	710	799
1,800	1,850	140	621	730	821	140	621	730	821
1,850	1,900	143	638	750	844	143	638	750	844
1,900	1,950	147	655	770	866	147	655	770	866
1,950	2,000	151	672	790	889	151	672	790	889
2,000	2,050	155	689	810	911	155	689	810	911
2,050	2,100	159	706	830	934	159	706	830	934
2,100	2,150	163	723	850	956	163	723	850	956
2,150	2,200	166	740	870	979	166	740	870	979
2,200	2,250	170	757	890	1,001	170	757	890	1,001
2,250	2,300	174	774	910	1,024	174	774	910	1,024
2,300	2,350	178	791	930	1,046	178	791	930	1,046
2,350	2,400	182	808	950	1,069	182	808	950	1,069
2,400	2,450	186	825	970	1,091	186	825	970	1,091
2,450	2,500	189	842	990	1,114	189	842	990	1,114
2,500	2,550	193	859	1,010	1,136	193	859	1,010	1,136
2,550	2,600	197	876	1,030	1,159	197	876	1,030	1,159
2,600	2,650	201	893	1,050	1,181	201	893	1,050	1,181
2,650	2,700	205	910	1,070	1,204	205	910	1,070	1,204
2,700	2,750	208	927	1,090	1,226	208	927	1,090	1,226
2,750	2,800	212	944	1,110	1,249	212	944	1,110	1,249
2,800	2,850	216	961	1,130	1,271	216	961	1,130	1,271
2,850	2,900	220	978	1,150	1,294	220	978	1,150	1,294
2,900	2,950	224	995	1,170	1,316	224	995	1,170	1,316
2,950	3,000	228	1,012	1,190	1,339	228	1,012	1,190	1,339
3,000	3,050	231	1,029	1,210	1,361	231	1,029	1,210	1,361
3,050	3,100	235	1,046	1,230	1,384	235	1,046	1,230	1,384
3,100	3,150	239	1,063	1,250	1,406	239	1,063	1,250	1,406
3,150	3,200	243	1,080	1,270	1,429	243	1,080	1,270	1,429
3,200	3,250	247	1,097	1,290	1,451	247	1,097	1,290	1,451
3,250	3,300	251	1,114	1,310	1,474	251	1,114	1,310	1,474
3,300	3,350	254	1,131	1,330	1,496	254	1,131	1,330	1,496
3,350	3,400	258	1,148	1,350	1,519	258	1,148	1,350	1,519
3,400	3,450	262	1,165	1,370	1,541	262	1,165	1,370	1,541
3,450	3,500	266	1,182	1,390	1,564	266	1,182	1,390	1,564
3,500	3,550	270	1,199	1,410	1,586	270	1,199	1,410	1,586
3,550	3,600	273	1,216	1,430	1,609	273	1,216	1,430	1,609
3,600	3,650	277	1,233	1,450	1,631	277	1,233	1,450	1,631
3,650	3,700	281	1,250	1,470	1,654	281	1,250	1,470	1,654
3,700	3,750	285	1,267	1,490	1,676	285	1,267	1,490	1,676
3,750	3,800	289	1,284	1,510	1,699	289	1,284	1,510	1,699
3,800	3,850	293	1,301	1,530	1,721	293	1,301	1,530	1,721
3,850	3,900	296	1,318	1,550	1,744	296	1,318	1,550	1,744
3,900	3,950	300	1,335	1,570	1,766	300	1,335	1,570	1,766
3,950	4,000	304	1,352	1,590	1,789	304	1,352	1,590	1,789
4,000	4,050	308	1,369	1,610	1,811	308	1,369	1,610	1,811
4,050	4,100	312	1,386	1,630	1,834	312	1,386	1,630	1,834
4,100	4,150	316	1,403	1,650	1,856	316	1,403	1,650	1,856
4,150	4,200	319	1,420	1,670	1,879	319	1,420	1,670	1,879
4,200	4,250	323	1,437	1,690	1,901	323	1,437	1,690	1,901
4,250	4,300	327	1,454	1,710	1,924	327	1,454	1,710	1,924
4,300	4,350	331	1,471	1,730	1,946	331	1,471	1,730	1,946
4,350	4,400	335	1,488	1,750	1,969	335	1,488	1,750	1,969
4,400	4,450	339	1,505	1,770	1,991	339	1,505	1,770	1,991
4,450	4,500	342	1,522	1,790	2,014	342	1,522	1,790	2,014
4,500	4,550	346	1,539	1,810	2,036	346	1,539	1,810	2,036
4,550	4,600	350	1,556	1,830	2,059	350	1,556	1,830	2,059
4,600	4,650	354	1,573	1,850	2,081	354	1,573	1,850	2,081
4,650	4,700	358	1,590	1,870	2,104	358	1,590	1,870	2,104
4,700	4,750	361	1,607	1,890	2,126	361	1,607	1,890	2,126
4,750	4,800	365	1,624	1,910	2,149	365	1,624	1,910	2,149
4,800	4,850	369	1,641	1,930	2,171	369	1,641	1,930	2,171
4,850	4,900	373	1,658	1,950	2,194	373	1,658	1,950	2,194
4,900	4,950	377	1,675	1,970	2,216	377	1,675	1,970	2,216
4,950	5,000	381	1,692	1,990	2,239	381	1,692	1,990	2,239
5,000	5,050	384	1,709	2,010	2,261	384	1,709	2,010	2,261
5,050	5,100	388	1,726	2,030	2,284	388	1,726	2,030	2,284
5,100	5,150	392	1,743	2,050	2,306	392	1,743	2,050	2,306
5,150	5,200	396	1,760	2,070	2,329	396	1,760	2,070	2,329
5,200	5,250	400	1,777	2,090	2,351	400	1,777	2,090	2,351
5,250	5,300	404	1,794	2,110	2,374	404	1,794	2,110	2,374
5,300	5,350	407	1,811	2,130	2,396	407	1,811	2,130	2,396
5,350	5,400	411	1,828	2,150	2,419	411	1,828	2,150	2,419
5,400	5,450	415	1,845	2,170	2,441	415	1,845	2,170	2,441
5,450	5,500	419	1,862	2,190	2,464	419	1,862	2,190	2,464
5,500	5,550	423	1,879	2,210	2,486	423	1,879	2,210	2,486
5,550	5,600	426	1,896	2,230	2,509	426	1,896	2,230	2,509

★   Use this column if your filing status is married filing separately and you qualify to claim the EIC. See the instructions for line 27.

(Continued)

Earned Income Credit (EIC) Table - Continued

(**Caution.** This is **not** a tax table.)

At least	But less than	Single, head of household, or qualifying surviving spouse★ and you have– 0	1	2	3	Married filing jointly and you have– 0	1	2	3	At least	But less than	Single, head of household, or qualifying surviving spouse★ and you have– 0	1	2	3	Married filing jointly and you have– 0	1	2	3
5,600	5,650	430	1,913	2,250	2,531	430	1,913	2,250	2,531	8,800	8,850	560	3,001	3,530	3,971	560	3,001	3,530	3,971
5,650	5,700	434	1,930	2,270	2,554	434	1,930	2,270	2,554	8,850	8,900	560	3,018	3,550	3,994	560	3,018	3,550	3,994
5,700	5,750	438	1,947	2,290	2,576	438	1,947	2,290	2,576	8,900	8,950	560	3,035	3,570	4,016	560	3,035	3,570	4,016
5,750	5,800	442	1,964	2,310	2,599	442	1,964	2,310	2,599	8,950	9,000	560	3,052	3,590	4,039	560	3,052	3,590	4,039
5,800	5,850	446	1,981	2,330	2,621	446	1,981	2,330	2,621	9,000	9,050	560	3,069	3,610	4,061	560	3,069	3,610	4,061
5,850	5,900	449	1,998	2,350	2,644	449	1,998	2,350	2,644	9,050	9,100	560	3,086	3,630	4,084	560	3,086	3,630	4,084
5,900	5,950	453	2,015	2,370	2,666	453	2,015	2,370	2,666	9,100	9,150	560	3,103	3,650	4,106	560	3,103	3,650	4,106
5,950	6,000	457	2,032	2,390	2,689	457	2,032	2,390	2,689	9,150	9,200	560	3,120	3,670	4,129	560	3,120	3,670	4,129
6,000	6,050	461	2,049	2,410	2,711	461	2,049	2,410	2,711	9,200	9,250	555	3,137	3,690	4,151	560	3,137	3,690	4,151
6,050	6,100	465	2,066	2,430	2,734	465	2,066	2,430	2,734	9,250	9,300	551	3,154	3,710	4,174	560	3,154	3,710	4,174
6,100	6,150	469	2,083	2,450	2,756	469	2,083	2,450	2,756	9,300	9,350	547	3,171	3,730	4,196	560	3,171	3,730	4,196
6,150	6,200	472	2,100	2,470	2,779	472	2,100	2,470	2,779	9,350	9,400	544	3,188	3,750	4,219	560	3,188	3,750	4,219
6,200	6,250	476	2,117	2,490	2,801	476	2,117	2,490	2,801	9,400	9,450	540	3,205	3,770	4,241	560	3,205	3,770	4,241
6,250	6,300	480	2,134	2,510	2,824	480	2,134	2,510	2,824	9,450	9,500	536	3,222	3,790	4,264	560	3,222	3,790	4,264
6,300	6,350	484	2,151	2,530	2,846	484	2,151	2,530	2,846	9,500	9,550	532	3,239	3,810	4,286	560	3,239	3,810	4,286
6,350	6,400	488	2,168	2,550	2,869	488	2,168	2,550	2,869	9,550	9,600	528	3,256	3,830	4,309	560	3,256	3,830	4,309
6,400	6,450	492	2,185	2,570	2,891	492	2,185	2,570	2,891	9,600	9,650	524	3,273	3,850	4,331	560	3,273	3,850	4,331
6,450	6,500	495	2,202	2,590	2,914	495	2,202	2,590	2,914	9,650	9,700	521	3,290	3,870	4,354	560	3,290	3,870	4,354
6,500	6,550	499	2,219	2,610	2,936	499	2,219	2,610	2,936	9,700	9,750	517	3,307	3,890	4,376	560	3,307	3,890	4,376
6,550	6,600	503	2,236	2,630	2,959	503	2,236	2,630	2,959	9,750	9,800	513	3,324	3,910	4,399	560	3,324	3,910	4,399
6,600	6,650	507	2,253	2,650	2,981	507	2,253	2,650	2,981	9,800	9,850	509	3,341	3,930	4,421	560	3,341	3,930	4,421
6,650	6,700	511	2,270	2,670	3,004	511	2,270	2,670	3,004	9,850	9,900	505	3,358	3,950	4,444	560	3,358	3,950	4,444
6,700	6,750	514	2,287	2,690	3,026	514	2,287	2,690	3,026	9,900	9,950	501	3,375	3,970	4,466	560	3,375	3,970	4,466
6,750	6,800	518	2,304	2,710	3,049	518	2,304	2,710	3,049	9,950	10,000	498	3,392	3,990	4,489	560	3,392	3,990	4,489
6,800	6,850	522	2,321	2,730	3,071	522	2,321	2,730	3,071	10,000	10,050	494	3,409	4,010	4,511	560	3,409	4,010	4,511
6,850	6,900	526	2,338	2,750	3,094	526	2,338	2,750	3,094	10,050	10,100	490	3,426	4,030	4,534	560	3,426	4,030	4,534
6,900	6,950	530	2,355	2,770	3,116	530	2,355	2,770	3,116	10,100	10,150	486	3,443	4,050	4,556	560	3,443	4,050	4,556
6,950	7,000	534	2,372	2,790	3,139	534	2,372	2,790	3,139	10,150	10,200	482	3,460	4,070	4,579	560	3,460	4,070	4,579
7,000	7,050	537	2,389	2,810	3,161	537	2,389	2,810	3,161	10,200	10,250	479	3,477	4,090	4,601	560	3,477	4,090	4,601
7,050	7,100	541	2,406	2,830	3,184	541	2,406	2,830	3,184	10,250	10,300	475	3,494	4,110	4,624	560	3,494	4,110	4,624
7,100	7,150	545	2,423	2,850	3,206	545	2,423	2,850	3,206	10,300	10,350	471	3,511	4,130	4,646	560	3,511	4,130	4,646
7,150	7,200	549	2,440	2,870	3,229	549	2,440	2,870	3,229	10,350	10,400	467	3,528	4,150	4,669	560	3,528	4,150	4,669
7,200	7,250	553	2,457	2,890	3,251	553	2,457	2,890	3,251	10,400	10,450	463	3,545	4,170	4,691	560	3,545	4,170	4,691
7,250	7,300	557	2,474	2,910	3,274	557	2,474	2,910	3,274	10,450	10,500	459	3,562	4,190	4,714	560	3,562	4,190	4,714
7,300	7,350	560	2,491	2,930	3,296	560	2,491	2,930	3,296	10,500	10,550	456	3,579	4,210	4,736	560	3,579	4,210	4,736
7,350	7,400	560	2,508	2,950	3,319	560	2,508	2,950	3,319	10,550	10,600	452	3,596	4,230	4,759	560	3,596	4,230	4,759
7,400	7,450	560	2,525	2,970	3,341	560	2,525	2,970	3,341	10,600	10,650	448	3,613	4,250	4,781	560	3,613	4,250	4,781
7,450	7,500	560	2,542	2,990	3,364	560	2,542	2,990	3,364	10,650	10,700	444	3,630	4,270	4,804	560	3,630	4,270	4,804
7,500	7,550	560	2,559	3,010	3,386	560	2,559	3,010	3,386	10,700	10,750	440	3,647	4,290	4,826	560	3,647	4,290	4,826
7,550	7,600	560	2,576	3,030	3,409	560	2,576	3,030	3,409	10,750	10,800	436	3,664	4,310	4,849	560	3,664	4,310	4,849
7,600	7,650	560	2,593	3,050	3,431	560	2,593	3,050	3,431	10,800	10,850	433	3,681	4,330	4,871	560	3,681	4,330	4,871
7,650	7,700	560	2,610	3,070	3,454	560	2,610	3,070	3,454	10,850	10,900	429	3,698	4,350	4,894	560	3,698	4,350	4,894
7,700	7,750	560	2,627	3,090	3,476	560	2,627	3,090	3,476	10,900	10,950	425	3,715	4,370	4,916	560	3,715	4,370	4,916
7,750	7,800	560	2,644	3,110	3,499	560	2,644	3,110	3,499	10,950	11,000	421	3,733	4,390	4,939	560	3,733	4,390	4,939
7,800	7,850	560	2,661	3,130	3,521	560	2,661	3,130	3,521	11,000	11,050	417	3,733	4,410	4,961	560	3,733	4,410	4,961
7,850	7,900	560	2,678	3,150	3,544	560	2,678	3,150	3,544	11,050	11,100	413	3,733	4,430	4,984	560	3,733	4,430	4,984
7,900	7,950	560	2,695	3,170	3,566	560	2,695	3,170	3,566	11,100	11,150	410	3,733	4,450	5,006	560	3,733	4,450	5,006
7,950	8,000	560	2,712	3,190	3,589	560	2,712	3,190	3,589	11,150	11,200	406	3,733	4,470	5,029	560	3,733	4,470	5,029
8,000	8,050	560	2,729	3,210	3,611	560	2,729	3,210	3,611	11,200	11,250	402	3,733	4,490	5,051	560	3,733	4,490	5,051
8,050	8,100	560	2,746	3,230	3,634	560	2,746	3,230	3,634	11,250	11,300	398	3,733	4,510	5,074	560	3,733	4,510	5,074
8,100	8,150	560	2,763	3,250	3,656	560	2,763	3,250	3,656	11,300	11,350	394	3,733	4,530	5,096	560	3,733	4,530	5,096
8,150	8,200	560	2,780	3,270	3,679	560	2,780	3,270	3,679	11,350	11,400	391	3,733	4,550	5,119	560	3,733	4,550	5,119
8,200	8,250	560	2,797	3,290	3,701	560	2,797	3,290	3,701	11,400	11,450	387	3,733	4,570	5,141	560	3,733	4,570	5,141
8,250	8,300	560	2,814	3,310	3,724	560	2,814	3,310	3,724	11,450	11,500	383	3,733	4,590	5,164	560	3,733	4,590	5,164
8,300	8,350	560	2,831	3,330	3,746	560	2,831	3,330	3,746	11,500	11,550	379	3,733	4,610	5,186	560	3,733	4,610	5,186
8,350	8,400	560	2,848	3,350	3,769	560	2,848	3,350	3,769	11,550	11,600	375	3,733	4,630	5,209	560	3,733	4,630	5,209
8,400	8,450	560	2,865	3,370	3,791	560	2,865	3,370	3,791	11,600	11,650	371	3,733	4,650	5,231	560	3,733	4,650	5,231
8,450	8,500	560	2,882	3,390	3,814	560	2,882	3,390	3,814	11,650	11,700	368	3,733	4,670	5,254	560	3,733	4,670	5,254
8,500	8,550	560	2,899	3,410	3,836	560	2,899	3,410	3,836	11,700	11,750	364	3,733	4,690	5,276	560	3,733	4,690	5,276
8,550	8,600	560	2,916	3,430	3,859	560	2,916	3,430	3,859	11,750	11,800	360	3,733	4,710	5,299	560	3,733	4,710	5,299
8,600	8,650	560	2,933	3,450	3,881	560	2,933	3,450	3,881	11,800	11,850	356	3,733	4,730	5,321	560	3,733	4,730	5,321
8,650	8,700	560	2,950	3,470	3,904	560	2,950	3,470	3,904	11,850	11,900	352	3,733	4,750	5,344	560	3,733	4,750	5,344
8,700	8,750	560	2,967	3,490	3,926	560	2,967	3,490	3,926	11,900	11,950	348	3,733	4,770	5,366	560	3,733	4,770	5,366
8,750	8,800	560	2,984	3,510	3,949	560	2,984	3,510	3,949	11,950	12,000	345	3,733	4,790	5,389	560	3,733	4,790	5,389

★ Use this column if your filing status is married filing separately and you qualify to claim the EIC. See the instructions for line 27.

(Continued)

Earned Income Credit (EIC) Table - *Continued*

(Caution. This is **not** a tax table.)

At least	But less than	Single, HoH, or QSS ★ — 0	1	2	3	MFJ — 0	1	2	3
12,000	12,050	341	3,733	4,810	5,411	560	3,733	4,810	5,411
12,050	12,100	337	3,733	4,830	5,434	560	3,733	4,830	5,434
12,100	12,150	333	3,733	4,850	5,456	560	3,733	4,850	5,456
12,150	12,200	329	3,733	4,870	5,479	560	3,733	4,870	5,479
12,200	12,250	326	3,733	4,890	5,501	560	3,733	4,890	5,501
12,250	12,300	322	3,733	4,910	5,524	560	3,733	4,910	5,524
12,300	12,350	318	3,733	4,930	5,546	560	3,733	4,930	5,546
12,350	12,400	314	3,733	4,950	5,569	560	3,733	4,950	5,569
12,400	12,450	310	3,733	4,970	5,591	560	3,733	4,970	5,591
12,450	12,500	306	3,733	4,990	5,614	560	3,733	4,990	5,614
12,500	12,550	303	3,733	5,010	5,636	560	3,733	5,010	5,636
12,550	12,600	299	3,733	5,030	5,659	560	3,733	5,030	5,659
12,600	12,650	295	3,733	5,050	5,681	560	3,733	5,050	5,681
12,650	12,700	291	3,733	5,070	5,704	560	3,733	5,070	5,704
12,700	12,750	287	3,733	5,090	5,726	560	3,733	5,090	5,726
12,750	12,800	283	3,733	5,110	5,749	560	3,733	5,110	5,749
12,800	12,850	280	3,733	5,130	5,771	560	3,733	5,130	5,771
12,850	12,900	276	3,733	5,150	5,794	560	3,733	5,150	5,794
12,900	12,950	272	3,733	5,170	5,816	560	3,733	5,170	5,816
12,950	13,000	268	3,733	5,190	5,839	560	3,733	5,190	5,839
13,000	13,050	264	3,733	5,210	5,861	560	3,733	5,210	5,861
13,050	13,100	260	3,733	5,230	5,884	560	3,733	5,230	5,884
13,100	13,150	257	3,733	5,250	5,906	560	3,733	5,250	5,906
13,150	13,200	253	3,733	5,270	5,929	560	3,733	5,270	5,929
13,200	13,250	249	3,733	5,290	5,951	560	3,733	5,290	5,951
13,250	13,300	245	3,733	5,310	5,974	560	3,733	5,310	5,974
13,300	13,350	241	3,733	5,330	5,996	560	3,733	5,330	5,996
13,350	13,400	238	3,733	5,350	6,019	560	3,733	5,350	6,019
13,400	13,450	234	3,733	5,370	6,041	560	3,733	5,370	6,041
13,450	13,500	230	3,733	5,390	6,064	560	3,733	5,390	6,064
13,500	13,550	226	3,733	5,410	6,086	560	3,733	5,410	6,086
13,550	13,600	222	3,733	5,430	6,109	560	3,733	5,430	6,109
13,600	13,650	218	3,733	5,450	6,131	560	3,733	5,450	6,131
13,650	13,700	215	3,733	5,470	6,154	560	3,733	5,470	6,154
13,700	13,750	211	3,733	5,490	6,176	560	3,733	5,490	6,176
13,750	13,800	207	3,733	5,510	6,199	560	3,733	5,510	6,199
13,800	13,850	203	3,733	5,530	6,221	560	3,733	5,530	6,221
13,850	13,900	199	3,733	5,550	6,244	560	3,733	5,550	6,244
13,900	13,950	195	3,733	5,570	6,266	560	3,733	5,570	6,266
13,950	14,000	192	3,733	5,590	6,289	560	3,733	5,590	6,289
14,000	14,050	188	3,733	5,610	6,311	560	3,733	5,610	6,311
14,050	14,100	184	3,733	5,630	6,334	560	3,733	5,630	6,334
14,100	14,150	180	3,733	5,650	6,356	560	3,733	5,650	6,356
14,150	14,200	176	3,733	5,670	6,379	560	3,733	5,670	6,379
14,200	14,250	173	3,733	5,690	6,401	560	3,733	5,690	6,401
14,250	14,300	169	3,733	5,710	6,424	560	3,733	5,710	6,424
14,300	14,350	165	3,733	5,730	6,446	560	3,733	5,730	6,446
14,350	14,400	161	3,733	5,750	6,469	560	3,733	5,750	6,469
14,400	14,450	157	3,733	5,770	6,491	560	3,733	5,770	6,491
14,450	14,500	153	3,733	5,790	6,514	560	3,733	5,790	6,514
14,500	14,550	150	3,733	5,810	6,536	560	3,733	5,810	6,536
14,550	14,600	146	3,733	5,830	6,559	560	3,733	5,830	6,559
14,600	14,650	142	3,733	5,850	6,581	560	3,733	5,850	6,581
14,650	14,700	138	3,733	5,870	6,604	560	3,733	5,870	6,604
14,700	14,750	134	3,733	5,890	6,626	560	3,733	5,890	6,626
14,750	14,800	130	3,733	5,910	6,649	560	3,733	5,910	6,649
14,800	14,850	127	3,733	5,930	6,671	560	3,733	5,930	6,671
14,850	14,900	123	3,733	5,950	6,694	560	3,733	5,950	6,694
14,900	14,950	119	3,733	5,970	6,716	560	3,733	5,970	6,716
14,950	15,000	115	3,733	5,990	6,739	560	3,733	5,990	6,739
15,000	15,050	111	3,733	6,010	6,761	560	3,733	6,010	6,761
15,050	15,100	107	3,733	6,030	6,784	560	3,733	6,030	6,784
15,100	15,150	104	3,733	6,050	6,806	560	3,733	6,050	6,806
15,150	15,200	100	3,733	6,070	6,829	560	3,733	6,070	6,829
15,200	15,250	96	3,733	6,090	6,851	560	3,733	6,090	6,851
15,250	15,300	92	3,733	6,110	6,874	560	3,733	6,110	6,874
15,300	15,350	88	3,733	6,130	6,896	557	3,733	6,130	6,896
15,350	15,400	85	3,733	6,150	6,919	553	3,733	6,150	6,919
15,400	15,450	81	3,733	6,164	6,935	550	3,733	6,164	6,935
15,450	15,500	77	3,733	6,164	6,935	546	3,733	6,164	6,935
15,500	15,550	73	3,733	6,164	6,935	542	3,733	6,164	6,935
15,550	15,600	69	3,733	6,164	6,935	538	3,733	6,164	6,935
15,600	15,650	65	3,733	6,164	6,935	534	3,733	6,164	6,935
15,650	15,700	62	3,733	6,164	6,935	531	3,733	6,164	6,935
15,700	15,750	58	3,733	6,164	6,935	527	3,733	6,164	6,935
15,750	15,800	54	3,733	6,164	6,935	523	3,733	6,164	6,935
15,800	15,850	50	3,733	6,164	6,935	519	3,733	6,164	6,935
15,850	15,900	46	3,733	6,164	6,935	515	3,733	6,164	6,935
15,900	15,950	42	3,733	6,164	6,935	511	3,733	6,164	6,935
15,950	16,000	39	3,733	6,164	6,935	508	3,733	6,164	6,935
16,000	16,050	35	3,733	6,164	6,935	504	3,733	6,164	6,935
16,050	16,100	31	3,733	6,164	6,935	500	3,733	6,164	6,935
16,100	16,150	27	3,733	6,164	6,935	496	3,733	6,164	6,935
16,150	16,200	23	3,733	6,164	6,935	492	3,733	6,164	6,935
16,200	16,250	20	3,733	6,164	6,935	488	3,733	6,164	6,935
16,250	16,300	16	3,733	6,164	6,935	485	3,733	6,164	6,935
16,300	16,350	12	3,733	6,164	6,935	481	3,733	6,164	6,935
16,350	16,400	8	3,733	6,164	6,935	477	3,733	6,164	6,935
16,400	16,450	4	3,733	6,164	6,935	473	3,733	6,164	6,935
16,450	16,500	*	3,733	6,164	6,935	469	3,733	6,164	6,935
16,500	16,550	0	3,733	6,164	6,935	466	3,733	6,164	6,935
16,550	16,600	0	3,733	6,164	6,935	462	3,733	6,164	6,935
16,600	16,650	0	3,733	6,164	6,935	458	3,733	6,164	6,935
16,650	16,700	0	3,733	6,164	6,935	454	3,733	6,164	6,935
16,700	16,750	0	3,733	6,164	6,935	450	3,733	6,164	6,935
16,750	16,800	0	3,733	6,164	6,935	446	3,733	6,164	6,935
16,800	16,850	0	3,733	6,164	6,935	443	3,733	6,164	6,935
16,850	16,900	0	3,733	6,164	6,935	439	3,733	6,164	6,935
16,900	16,950	0	3,733	6,164	6,935	435	3,733	6,164	6,935
16,950	17,000	0	3,733	6,164	6,935	431	3,733	6,164	6,935
17,000	17,050	0	3,733	6,164	6,935	427	3,733	6,164	6,935
17,050	17,100	0	3,733	6,164	6,935	423	3,733	6,164	6,935
17,100	17,150	0	3,733	6,164	6,935	420	3,733	6,164	6,935
17,150	17,200	0	3,733	6,164	6,935	416	3,733	6,164	6,935
17,200	17,250	0	3,733	6,164	6,935	412	3,733	6,164	6,935
17,250	17,300	0	3,733	6,164	6,935	408	3,733	6,164	6,935
17,300	17,350	0	3,733	6,164	6,935	404	3,733	6,164	6,935
17,350	17,400	0	3,733	6,164	6,935	400	3,733	6,164	6,935
17,400	17,450	0	3,733	6,164	6,935	397	3,733	6,164	6,935
17,450	17,500	0	3,733	6,164	6,935	393	3,733	6,164	6,935
17,500	17,550	0	3,733	6,164	6,935	389	3,733	6,164	6,935
17,550	17,600	0	3,733	6,164	6,935	385	3,733	6,164	6,935
17,600	17,650	0	3,733	6,164	6,935	381	3,733	6,164	6,935
17,650	17,700	0	3,733	6,164	6,935	378	3,733	6,164	6,935
17,700	17,750	0	3,733	6,164	6,935	374	3,733	6,164	6,935
17,750	17,800	0	3,733	6,164	6,935	370	3,733	6,164	6,935
17,800	17,850	0	3,733	6,164	6,935	366	3,733	6,164	6,935
17,850	17,900	0	3,733	6,164	6,935	362	3,733	6,164	6,935
17,900	17,950	0	3,733	6,164	6,935	358	3,733	6,164	6,935
17,950	18,000	0	3,733	6,164	6,935	355	3,733	6,164	6,935
18,000	18,050	0	3,733	6,164	6,935	351	3,733	6,164	6,935
18,050	18,100	0	3,733	6,164	6,935	347	3,733	6,164	6,935
18,100	18,150	0	3,733	6,164	6,935	343	3,733	6,164	6,935
18,150	18,200	0	3,733	6,164	6,935	339	3,733	6,164	6,935
18,200	18,250	0	3,733	6,164	6,935	335	3,733	6,164	6,935
18,250	18,300	0	3,733	6,164	6,935	332	3,733	6,164	6,935
18,300	18,350	0	3,733	6,164	6,935	328	3,733	6,164	6,935
18,350	18,400	0	3,733	6,164	6,935	324	3,733	6,164	6,935

★ Use this column if your filing status is married filing separately and you qualify to claim the EIC. See the instructions for line 27.

* If the amount you are looking up from the worksheet is at least $16,450 but less than $16,480, and you have no qualifying children who have valid SSNs, your credit is $1.

If the amount you are looking up from the worksheet is $16,480 or more, and you have no qualifying children who have valid SSNs, you can't take the credit.

(Continued)

Earned Income Credit (EIC) Table - *Continued*

(Caution. This is not a tax table.)

If the amount you are looking up from the worksheet is—		Single, head of household, or qualifying surviving spouse★ and you have—				Married filing jointly and you have—			
At least	But less than	0	1	2	3	0	1	2	3
		Your credit is—				Your credit is—			
18,400	18,450	0	3,733	6,164	6,935	320	3,733	6,164	6,935
18,450	18,500	0	3,733	6,164	6,935	316	3,733	6,164	6,935
18,500	18,550	0	3,733	6,164	6,935	313	3,733	6,164	6,935
18,550	18,600	0	3,733	6,164	6,935	309	3,733	6,164	6,935
18,600	18,650	0	3,733	6,164	6,935	305	3,733	6,164	6,935
18,650	18,700	0	3,733	6,164	6,935	301	3,733	6,164	6,935
18,700	18,750	0	3,733	6,164	6,935	297	3,733	6,164	6,935
18,750	18,800	0	3,733	6,164	6,935	293	3,733	6,164	6,935
18,800	18,850	0	3,733	6,164	6,935	290	3,733	6,164	6,935
18,850	18,900	0	3,733	6,164	6,935	286	3,733	6,164	6,935
18,900	18,950	0	3,733	6,164	6,935	282	3,733	6,164	6,935
18,950	19,000	0	3,733	6,164	6,935	278	3,733	6,164	6,935
19,000	19,050	0	3,733	6,164	6,935	274	3,733	6,164	6,935
19,050	19,100	0	3,733	6,164	6,935	270	3,733	6,164	6,935
19,100	19,150	0	3,733	6,164	6,935	267	3,733	6,164	6,935
19,150	19,200	0	3,733	6,164	6,935	263	3,733	6,164	6,935
19,200	19,250	0	3,733	6,164	6,935	259	3,733	6,164	6,935
19,250	19,300	0	3,733	6,164	6,935	255	3,733	6,164	6,935
19,300	19,350	0	3,733	6,164	6,935	251	3,733	6,164	6,935
19,350	19,400	0	3,733	6,164	6,935	247	3,733	6,164	6,935
19,400	19,450	0	3,733	6,164	6,935	244	3,733	6,164	6,935
19,450	19,500	0	3,733	6,164	6,935	240	3,733	6,164	6,935
19,500	19,550	0	3,733	6,164	6,935	236	3,733	6,164	6,935
19,550	19,600	0	3,733	6,164	6,935	232	3,733	6,164	6,935
19,600	19,650	0	3,733	6,164	6,935	228	3,733	6,164	6,935
19,650	19,700	0	3,733	6,164	6,935	225	3,733	6,164	6,935
19,700	19,750	0	3,733	6,164	6,935	221	3,733	6,164	6,935
19,750	19,800	0	3,733	6,164	6,935	217	3,733	6,164	6,935
19,800	19,850	0	3,733	6,164	6,935	213	3,733	6,164	6,935
19,850	19,900	0	3,733	6,164	6,935	209	3,733	6,164	6,935
19,900	19,950	0	3,733	6,164	6,935	205	3,733	6,164	6,935
19,950	20,000	0	3,733	6,164	6,935	202	3,733	6,164	6,935
20,000	20,050	0	3,733	6,164	6,935	198	3,733	6,164	6,935
20,050	20,100	0	3,733	6,164	6,935	194	3,733	6,164	6,935
20,100	20,150	0	3,733	6,164	6,935	190	3,733	6,164	6,935
20,150	20,200	0	3,726	6,155	6,925	186	3,733	6,164	6,935
20,200	20,250	0	3,718	6,144	6,914	182	3,733	6,164	6,935
20,250	20,300	0	3,710	6,133	6,904	179	3,733	6,164	6,935
20,300	20,350	0	3,702	6,123	6,893	175	3,733	6,164	6,935
20,350	20,400	0	3,694	6,112	6,883	171	3,733	6,164	6,935
20,400	20,450	0	3,686	6,102	6,872	167	3,733	6,164	6,935
20,450	20,500	0	3,678	6,091	6,862	163	3,733	6,164	6,935
20,500	20,550	0	3,670	6,081	6,851	160	3,733	6,164	6,935
20,550	20,600	0	3,662	6,070	6,841	156	3,733	6,164	6,935
20,600	20,650	0	3,654	6,060	6,830	152	3,733	6,164	6,935
20,650	20,700	0	3,646	6,049	6,820	148	3,733	6,164	6,935
20,700	20,750	0	3,638	6,039	6,809	144	3,733	6,164	6,935
20,750	20,800	0	3,630	6,028	6,799	140	3,733	6,164	6,935
20,800	20,850	0	3,622	6,018	6,788	137	3,733	6,164	6,935
20,850	20,900	0	3,614	6,007	6,778	133	3,733	6,164	6,935
20,900	20,950	0	3,606	5,997	6,767	129	3,733	6,164	6,935
20,950	21,000	0	3,598	5,986	6,757	125	3,733	6,164	6,935
21,000	21,050	0	3,590	5,976	6,746	121	3,733	6,164	6,935
21,050	21,100	0	3,582	5,965	6,735	117	3,733	6,164	6,935
21,100	21,150	0	3,574	5,954	6,725	114	3,733	6,164	6,935
21,150	21,200	0	3,566	5,944	6,714	110	3,733	6,164	6,935
21,200	21,250	0	3,558	5,933	6,704	106	3,733	6,164	6,935
21,250	21,300	0	3,550	5,923	6,693	102	3,733	6,164	6,935
21,300	21,350	0	3,542	5,912	6,683	98	3,733	6,164	6,935
21,350	21,400	0	3,534	5,902	6,672	94	3,733	6,164	6,935
21,400	21,450	0	3,526	5,891	6,662	91	3,733	6,164	6,935
21,450	21,500	0	3,518	5,881	6,651	87	3,733	6,164	6,935
21,500	21,550	0	3,510	5,870	6,641	83	3,733	6,164	6,935
21,550	21,600	0	3,502	5,860	6,630	79	3,733	6,164	6,935
21,600	21,650	0	3,494	5,849	6,620	75	3,733	6,164	6,935
21,650	21,700	0	3,486	5,839	6,609	72	3,733	6,164	6,935
21,700	21,750	0	3,478	5,828	6,599	68	3,733	6,164	6,935
21,750	21,800	0	3,470	5,818	6,588	64	3,733	6,164	6,935
21,800	21,850	0	3,462	5,807	6,578	60	3,733	6,164	6,935
21,850	21,900	0	3,454	5,797	6,567	56	3,733	6,164	6,935
21,900	21,950	0	3,446	5,786	6,556	52	3,733	6,164	6,935
21,950	22,000	0	3,438	5,775	6,546	49	3,733	6,164	6,935
22,000	22,050	0	3,430	5,765	6,535	45	3,733	6,164	6,935
22,050	22,100	0	3,422	5,754	6,525	41	3,733	6,164	6,935
22,100	22,150	0	3,414	5,744	6,514	37	3,733	6,164	6,935
22,150	22,200	0	3,406	5,733	6,504	33	3,733	6,164	6,935
22,200	22,250	0	3,398	5,723	6,493	29	3,733	6,164	6,935
22,250	22,300	0	3,390	5,712	6,483	26	3,733	6,164	6,935
22,300	22,350	0	3,382	5,702	6,472	22	3,733	6,164	6,935
22,350	22,400	0	3,374	5,691	6,462	18	3,733	6,164	6,935
22,400	22,450	0	3,366	5,681	6,451	14	3,733	6,164	6,935
22,450	22,500	0	3,358	5,670	6,441	10	3,733	6,164	6,935
22,500	22,550	0	3,350	5,660	6,430	7	3,733	6,164	6,935
22,550	22,600	0	3,342	5,649	6,420	3	3,733	6,164	6,935
22,600	22,650	0	3,334	5,639	6,409	*	3,733	6,164	6,935
22,650	22,700	0	3,327	5,628	6,399	0	3,733	6,164	6,935
22,700	22,750	0	3,319	5,617	6,388	0	3,733	6,164	6,935
22,750	22,800	0	3,311	5,607	6,377	0	3,733	6,164	6,935
22,800	22,850	0	3,303	5,596	6,367	0	3,733	6,164	6,935
22,850	22,900	0	3,295	5,586	6,356	0	3,733	6,164	6,935
22,900	22,950	0	3,287	5,575	6,346	0	3,733	6,164	6,935
22,950	23,000	0	3,279	5,565	6,335	0	3,733	6,164	6,935
23,000	23,050	0	3,271	5,554	6,325	0	3,733	6,164	6,935
23,050	23,100	0	3,263	5,544	6,314	0	3,733	6,164	6,935
23,100	23,150	0	3,255	5,533	6,304	0	3,733	6,164	6,935
23,150	23,200	0	3,247	5,523	6,293	0	3,733	6,164	6,935
23,200	23,250	0	3,239	5,512	6,283	0	3,733	6,164	6,935
23,250	23,300	0	3,231	5,502	6,272	0	3,733	6,164	6,935
23,300	23,350	0	3,223	5,491	6,262	0	3,733	6,164	6,935
23,350	23,400	0	3,215	5,481	6,251	0	3,733	6,164	6,935
23,400	23,450	0	3,207	5,470	6,241	0	3,733	6,164	6,935
23,450	23,500	0	3,199	5,460	6,230	0	3,733	6,164	6,935
23,500	23,550	0	3,191	5,449	6,220	0	3,733	6,164	6,935
23,550	23,600	0	3,183	5,438	6,209	0	3,733	6,164	6,935
23,600	23,650	0	3,175	5,428	6,198	0	3,733	6,164	6,935
23,650	23,700	0	3,167	5,417	6,188	0	3,733	6,164	6,935
23,700	23,750	0	3,159	5,407	6,177	0	3,733	6,164	6,935
23,750	23,800	0	3,151	5,396	6,167	0	3,733	6,164	6,935
23,800	23,850	0	3,143	5,386	6,156	0	3,733	6,164	6,935
23,850	23,900	0	3,135	5,375	6,146	0	3,733	6,164	6,935
23,900	23,950	0	3,127	5,365	6,135	0	3,733	6,164	6,935
23,950	24,000	0	3,119	5,354	6,125	0	3,733	6,164	6,935
24,000	24,050	0	3,111	5,344	6,114	0	3,733	6,164	6,935
24,050	24,100	0	3,103	5,333	6,104	0	3,733	6,164	6,935
24,100	24,150	0	3,095	5,323	6,093	0	3,733	6,164	6,935
24,150	24,200	0	3,087	5,312	6,083	0	3,733	6,164	6,935
24,200	24,250	0	3,079	5,302	6,072	0	3,733	6,164	6,935
24,250	24,300	0	3,071	5,291	6,062	0	3,733	6,164	6,935
24,300	24,350	0	3,063	5,281	6,051	0	3,733	6,164	6,935
24,350	24,400	0	3,055	5,270	6,041	0	3,733	6,164	6,935
24,400	24,450	0	3,047	5,259	6,030	0	3,733	6,164	6,935
24,450	24,500	0	3,039	5,249	6,019	0	3,733	6,164	6,935
24,500	24,550	0	3,031	5,238	6,009	0	3,733	6,164	6,935
24,550	24,600	0	3,023	5,228	5,998	0	3,733	6,164	6,935
24,600	24,650	0	3,015	5,217	5,988	0	3,733	6,164	6,935
24,650	24,700	0	3,007	5,207	5,977	0	3,733	6,164	6,935
24,700	24,750	0	2,999	5,196	5,967	0	3,733	6,164	6,935
24,750	24,800	0	2,991	5,186	5,956	0	3,733	6,164	6,935

★ Use this column if your filing status is married filing separately and you qualify to claim the EIC. See the instructions for line 27.

* If the amount you are looking up from the worksheet is at least $22,600 but less than $22,610, and you have no qualifying children who have valid SSNs, your credit is $0.

If the amount you are looking up from the worksheet is $22,610 or more, and you have no qualifying children who have valid SSNs, you can't take the credit.

(Continued)

Earned Income Credit (EIC) Table - Continued   (Caution. This is **not** a tax table.)

If the amount you are looking up from the worksheet is—		Single, head of household, or qualifying surviving spouse★ and you have—				Married filing jointly and you have—			
At least	But less than	0	1	2	3	0	1	2	3
		Your credit is—				Your credit is—			
24,800	24,850	0	2,983	5,175	5,946	0	3,733	6,164	6,935
24,850	24,900	0	2,975	5,165	5,935	0	3,733	6,164	6,935
24,900	24,950	0	2,967	5,154	5,925	0	3,733	6,164	6,935
24,950	25,000	0	2,959	5,144	5,914	0	3,733	6,164	6,935
25,000	25,050	0	2,951	5,133	5,904	0	3,733	6,164	6,935
25,050	25,100	0	2,943	5,123	5,893	0	3,733	6,164	6,935
25,100	25,150	0	2,935	5,112	5,883	0	3,733	6,164	6,935
25,150	25,200	0	2,927	5,102	5,872	0	3,733	6,164	6,935
25,200	25,250	0	2,919	5,091	5,861	0	3,733	6,164	6,935
25,250	25,300	0	2,911	5,080	5,851	0	3,733	6,164	6,935
25,300	25,350	0	2,903	5,070	5,840	0	3,733	6,164	6,935
25,350	25,400	0	2,895	5,059	5,830	0	3,733	6,164	6,935
25,400	25,450	0	2,887	5,049	5,819	0	3,733	6,164	6,935
25,450	25,500	0	2,879	5,038	5,809	0	3,733	6,164	6,935
25,500	25,550	0	2,871	5,028	5,798	0	3,733	6,164	6,935
25,550	25,600	0	2,863	5,017	5,788	0	3,733	6,164	6,935
25,600	25,650	0	2,855	5,007	5,777	0	3,733	6,164	6,935
25,650	25,700	0	2,847	4,996	5,767	0	3,733	6,164	6,935
25,700	25,750	0	2,839	4,986	5,756	0	3,733	6,164	6,935
25,750	25,800	0	2,831	4,975	5,746	0	3,733	6,164	6,935
25,800	25,850	0	2,823	4,965	5,735	0	3,733	6,164	6,935
25,850	25,900	0	2,815	4,954	5,725	0	3,733	6,164	6,935
25,900	25,950	0	2,807	4,944	5,714	0	3,733	6,164	6,935
25,950	26,000	0	2,799	4,933	5,704	0	3,733	6,164	6,935
26,000	26,050	0	2,791	4,923	5,693	0	3,733	6,164	6,935
26,050	26,100	0	2,783	4,912	5,682	0	3,733	6,164	6,935
26,100	26,150	0	2,775	4,901	5,672	0	3,733	6,164	6,935
26,150	26,200	0	2,767	4,891	5,661	0	3,733	6,164	6,935
26,200	26,250	0	2,759	4,880	5,651	0	3,733	6,164	6,935
26,250	26,300	0	2,751	4,870	5,640	0	3,733	6,164	6,935
26,300	26,350	0	2,743	4,859	5,630	0	3,723	6,150	6,921
26,350	26,400	0	2,735	4,849	5,619	0	3,715	6,140	6,910
26,400	26,450	0	2,727	4,838	5,609	0	3,707	6,129	6,900
26,450	26,500	0	2,719	4,828	5,598	0	3,699	6,119	6,889
26,500	26,550	0	2,711	4,817	5,588	0	3,691	6,108	6,879
26,550	26,600	0	2,703	4,807	5,577	0	3,683	6,098	6,868
26,600	26,650	0	2,695	4,796	5,567	0	3,675	6,087	6,858
26,650	26,700	0	2,687	4,786	5,556	0	3,667	6,077	6,847
26,700	26,750	0	2,679	4,775	5,546	0	3,659	6,066	6,837
26,750	26,800	0	2,671	4,765	5,535	0	3,651	6,056	6,826
26,800	26,850	0	2,663	4,754	5,525	0	3,643	6,045	6,816
26,850	26,900	0	2,655	4,744	5,514	0	3,635	6,034	6,805
26,900	26,950	0	2,647	4,733	5,503	0	3,627	6,024	6,794
26,950	27,000	0	2,639	4,722	5,493	0	3,619	6,013	6,784
27,000	27,050	0	2,631	4,712	5,482	0	3,611	6,003	6,773
27,050	27,100	0	2,623	4,701	5,472	0	3,603	5,992	6,763
27,100	27,150	0	2,615	4,691	5,461	0	3,595	5,982	6,752
27,150	27,200	0	2,607	4,680	5,451	0	3,587	5,971	6,742
27,200	27,250	0	2,599	4,670	5,440	0	3,579	5,961	6,731
27,250	27,300	0	2,591	4,659	5,430	0	3,571	5,950	6,721
27,300	27,350	0	2,583	4,649	5,419	0	3,563	5,940	6,710
27,350	27,400	0	2,575	4,638	5,409	0	3,555	5,929	6,700
27,400	27,450	0	2,567	4,628	5,398	0	3,547	5,919	6,689
27,450	27,500	0	2,559	4,617	5,388	0	3,539	5,908	6,679
27,500	27,550	0	2,551	4,607	5,377	0	3,531	5,898	6,668
27,550	27,600	0	2,543	4,596	5,367	0	3,523	5,887	6,658
27,600	27,650	0	2,535	4,586	5,356	0	3,515	5,877	6,647
27,650	27,700	0	2,528	4,575	5,346	0	3,507	5,866	6,637
27,700	27,750	0	2,520	4,564	5,335	0	3,499	5,855	6,626
27,750	27,800	0	2,512	4,554	5,324	0	3,491	5,845	6,615
27,800	27,850	0	2,504	4,543	5,314	0	3,483	5,834	6,605
27,850	27,900	0	2,496	4,533	5,303	0	3,475	5,824	6,594
27,900	27,950	0	2,488	4,522	5,293	0	3,467	5,813	6,584
27,950	28,000	0	2,480	4,512	5,282	0	3,459	5,803	6,573

If the amount you are looking up from the worksheet is—		Single, head of household, or qualifying surviving spouse★ and you have—				Married filing jointly and you have—			
At least	But less than	0	1	2	3	0	1	2	3
		Your credit is—				Your credit is—			
28,000	28,050	0	2,472	4,501	5,272	0	3,451	5,792	6,563
28,050	28,100	0	2,464	4,491	5,261	0	3,443	5,782	6,552
28,100	28,150	0	2,456	4,480	5,251	0	3,435	5,771	6,542
28,150	28,200	0	2,448	4,470	5,240	0	3,427	5,761	6,531
28,200	28,250	0	2,440	4,459	5,230	0	3,419	5,750	6,521
28,250	28,300	0	2,432	4,449	5,219	0	3,411	5,740	6,510
28,300	28,350	0	2,424	4,438	5,209	0	3,403	5,729	6,500
28,350	28,400	0	2,416	4,428	5,198	0	3,395	5,719	6,489
28,400	28,450	0	2,408	4,417	5,188	0	3,387	5,708	6,479
28,450	28,500	0	2,400	4,407	5,177	0	3,379	5,698	6,468
28,500	28,550	0	2,392	4,396	5,167	0	3,371	5,687	6,457
28,550	28,600	0	2,384	4,385	5,156	0	3,363	5,676	6,447
28,600	28,650	0	2,376	4,375	5,145	0	3,355	5,666	6,436
28,650	28,700	0	2,368	4,364	5,135	0	3,347	5,655	6,426
28,700	28,750	0	2,360	4,354	5,124	0	3,339	5,645	6,415
28,750	28,800	0	2,352	4,343	5,114	0	3,331	5,634	6,405
28,800	28,850	0	2,344	4,333	5,103	0	3,323	5,624	6,394
28,850	28,900	0	2,336	4,322	5,093	0	3,315	5,613	6,384
28,900	28,950	0	2,328	4,312	5,082	0	3,307	5,603	6,373
28,950	29,000	0	2,320	4,301	5,072	0	3,299	5,592	6,363
29,000	29,050	0	2,312	4,291	5,061	0	3,291	5,582	6,352
29,050	29,100	0	2,304	4,280	5,051	0	3,283	5,571	6,342
29,100	29,150	0	2,296	4,270	5,040	0	3,275	5,561	6,331
29,150	29,200	0	2,288	4,259	5,030	0	3,267	5,550	6,321
29,200	29,250	0	2,280	4,249	5,019	0	3,259	5,540	6,310
29,250	29,300	0	2,272	4,238	5,009	0	3,251	5,529	6,300
29,300	29,350	0	2,264	4,228	4,998	0	3,243	5,519	6,289
29,350	29,400	0	2,256	4,217	4,988	0	3,235	5,508	6,278
29,400	29,450	0	2,248	4,206	4,977	0	3,227	5,497	6,268
29,450	29,500	0	2,240	4,196	4,966	0	3,219	5,487	6,257
29,500	29,550	0	2,232	4,185	4,956	0	3,211	5,476	6,247
29,550	29,600	0	2,224	4,175	4,945	0	3,203	5,466	6,236
29,600	29,650	0	2,216	4,164	4,935	0	3,195	5,455	6,226
29,650	29,700	0	2,208	4,154	4,924	0	3,187	5,445	6,215
29,700	29,750	0	2,200	4,143	4,914	0	3,179	5,434	6,205
29,750	29,800	0	2,192	4,133	4,903	0	3,172	5,424	6,194
29,800	29,850	0	2,184	4,122	4,893	0	3,164	5,413	6,184
29,850	29,900	0	2,176	4,112	4,882	0	3,156	5,403	6,173
29,900	29,950	0	2,168	4,101	4,872	0	3,148	5,392	6,163
29,950	30,000	0	2,160	4,091	4,861	0	3,140	5,382	6,152
30,000	30,050	0	2,152	4,080	4,851	0	3,132	5,371	6,142
30,050	30,100	0	2,144	4,070	4,840	0	3,124	5,361	6,131
30,100	30,150	0	2,136	4,059	4,830	0	3,116	5,350	6,121
30,150	30,200	0	2,128	4,049	4,819	0	3,108	5,340	6,110
30,200	30,250	0	2,120	4,038	4,808	0	3,100	5,329	6,099
30,250	30,300	0	2,112	4,027	4,798	0	3,092	5,318	6,089
30,300	30,350	0	2,104	4,017	4,787	0	3,084	5,308	6,078
30,350	30,400	0	2,096	4,006	4,777	0	3,076	5,297	6,068
30,400	30,450	0	2,088	3,996	4,766	0	3,068	5,287	6,057
30,450	30,500	0	2,080	3,985	4,756	0	3,060	5,276	6,047
30,500	30,550	0	2,072	3,975	4,745	0	3,052	5,266	6,036
30,550	30,600	0	2,064	3,964	4,735	0	3,044	5,255	6,026
30,600	30,650	0	2,056	3,954	4,724	0	3,036	5,245	6,015
30,650	30,700	0	2,048	3,943	4,714	0	3,028	5,234	6,005
30,700	30,750	0	2,040	3,933	4,703	0	3,020	5,224	5,994
30,750	30,800	0	2,032	3,922	4,693	0	3,012	5,213	5,984
30,800	30,850	0	2,024	3,912	4,682	0	3,004	5,203	5,973
30,850	30,900	0	2,016	3,901	4,672	0	2,996	5,192	5,963
30,900	30,950	0	2,008	3,891	4,661	0	2,988	5,182	5,952
30,950	31,000	0	2,000	3,880	4,651	0	2,980	5,171	5,942
31,000	31,050	0	1,992	3,870	4,640	0	2,972	5,160	5,931
31,050	31,100	0	1,984	3,859	4,629	0	2,964	5,150	5,920
31,100	31,150	0	1,976	3,848	4,619	0	2,956	5,139	5,910
31,150	31,200	0	1,968	3,838	4,608	0	2,948	5,129	5,899

★ Use this column if your filing status is married filing separately and you qualify to claim the EIC. See the instructions for line 27.

(Continued)

Earned Income Credit (EIC) Table - *Continued*
(Caution. This is not a tax table.)

At least	But less than	Single, head of household, or qualifying surviving spouse★ and you have– 0	1	2	3	Married filing jointly and you have– 0	1	2	3
31,200	31,250	0	1,960	3,827	4,598	0	2,940	5,118	5,889
31,250	31,300	0	1,952	3,817	4,587	0	2,932	5,108	5,878
31,300	31,350	0	1,944	3,806	4,577	0	2,924	5,097	5,868
31,350	31,400	0	1,936	3,796	4,566	0	2,916	5,087	5,857
31,400	31,450	0	1,928	3,785	4,556	0	2,908	5,076	5,847
31,450	31,500	0	1,920	3,775	4,545	0	2,900	5,066	5,836
31,500	31,550	0	1,912	3,764	4,535	0	2,892	5,055	5,826
31,550	31,600	0	1,904	3,754	4,524	0	2,884	5,045	5,815
31,600	31,650	0	1,896	3,743	4,514	0	2,876	5,034	5,805
31,650	31,700	0	1,888	3,733	4,503	0	2,868	5,024	5,794
31,700	31,750	0	1,880	3,722	4,493	0	2,860	5,013	5,784
31,750	31,800	0	1,872	3,712	4,482	0	2,852	5,003	5,773
31,800	31,850	0	1,864	3,701	4,472	0	2,844	4,992	5,763
31,850	31,900	0	1,856	3,691	4,461	0	2,836	4,981	5,752
31,900	31,950	0	1,848	3,680	4,450	0	2,828	4,971	5,741
31,950	32,000	0	1,840	3,669	4,440	0	2,820	4,960	5,731
32,000	32,050	0	1,832	3,659	4,429	0	2,812	4,950	5,720
32,050	32,100	0	1,824	3,648	4,419	0	2,804	4,939	5,710
32,100	32,150	0	1,816	3,638	4,408	0	2,796	4,929	5,699
32,150	32,200	0	1,808	3,627	4,398	0	2,788	4,918	5,689
32,200	32,250	0	1,800	3,617	4,387	0	2,780	4,908	5,678
32,250	32,300	0	1,792	3,606	4,377	0	2,772	4,897	5,668
32,300	32,350	0	1,784	3,596	4,366	0	2,764	4,887	5,657
32,350	32,400	0	1,776	3,585	4,356	0	2,756	4,876	5,647
32,400	32,450	0	1,768	3,575	4,345	0	2,748	4,866	5,636
32,450	32,500	0	1,760	3,564	4,335	0	2,740	4,855	5,626
32,500	32,550	0	1,752	3,554	4,324	0	2,732	4,845	5,615
32,550	32,600	0	1,744	3,543	4,314	0	2,724	4,834	5,605
32,600	32,650	0	1,736	3,533	4,303	0	2,716	4,824	5,594
32,650	32,700	0	1,729	3,522	4,293	0	2,708	4,813	5,584
32,700	32,750	0	1,721	3,511	4,282	0	2,700	4,802	5,573
32,750	32,800	0	1,713	3,501	4,271	0	2,692	4,792	5,562
32,800	32,850	0	1,705	3,490	4,261	0	2,684	4,781	5,552
32,850	32,900	0	1,697	3,480	4,250	0	2,676	4,771	5,541
32,900	32,950	0	1,689	3,469	4,240	0	2,668	4,760	5,531
32,950	33,000	0	1,681	3,459	4,229	0	2,660	4,750	5,520
33,000	33,050	0	1,673	3,448	4,219	0	2,652	4,739	5,510
33,050	33,100	0	1,665	3,438	4,208	0	2,644	4,729	5,499
33,100	33,150	0	1,657	3,427	4,198	0	2,636	4,718	5,489
33,150	33,200	0	1,649	3,417	4,187	0	2,628	4,708	5,478
33,200	33,250	0	1,641	3,406	4,177	0	2,620	4,697	5,468
33,250	33,300	0	1,633	3,396	4,166	0	2,612	4,687	5,457
33,300	33,350	0	1,625	3,385	4,156	0	2,604	4,676	5,447
33,350	33,400	0	1,617	3,375	4,145	0	2,596	4,666	5,436
33,400	33,450	0	1,609	3,364	4,135	0	2,588	4,655	5,426
33,450	33,500	0	1,601	3,354	4,124	0	2,580	4,645	5,415
33,500	33,550	0	1,593	3,343	4,114	0	2,572	4,634	5,404
33,550	33,600	0	1,585	3,332	4,103	0	2,564	4,623	5,394
33,600	33,650	0	1,577	3,322	4,092	0	2,556	4,613	5,383
33,650	33,700	0	1,569	3,311	4,082	0	2,548	4,602	5,373
33,700	33,750	0	1,561	3,301	4,071	0	2,540	4,592	5,362
33,750	33,800	0	1,553	3,290	4,061	0	2,532	4,581	5,352
33,800	33,850	0	1,545	3,280	4,050	0	2,524	4,571	5,341
33,850	33,900	0	1,537	3,269	4,040	0	2,516	4,560	5,331
33,900	33,950	0	1,529	3,259	4,029	0	2,508	4,550	5,320
33,950	34,000	0	1,521	3,248	4,019	0	2,500	4,539	5,310
34,000	34,050	0	1,513	3,238	4,008	0	2,492	4,529	5,299
34,050	34,100	0	1,505	3,227	3,998	0	2,484	4,518	5,289
34,100	34,150	0	1,497	3,217	3,987	0	2,476	4,508	5,278
34,150	34,200	0	1,489	3,206	3,977	0	2,468	4,497	5,268
34,200	34,250	0	1,481	3,196	3,966	0	2,460	4,487	5,257
34,250	34,300	0	1,473	3,185	3,956	0	2,452	4,476	5,247
34,300	34,350	0	1,465	3,175	3,945	0	2,444	4,466	5,236
34,350	34,400	0	1,457	3,164	3,935	0	2,436	4,455	5,225
34,400	34,450	0	1,449	3,153	3,924	0	2,428	4,444	5,215
34,450	34,500	0	1,441	3,143	3,913	0	2,420	4,434	5,204
34,500	34,550	0	1,433	3,132	3,903	0	2,412	4,423	5,194
34,550	34,600	0	1,425	3,122	3,892	0	2,404	4,413	5,183
34,600	34,650	0	1,417	3,111	3,882	0	2,396	4,402	5,173
34,650	34,700	0	1,409	3,101	3,871	0	2,388	4,392	5,162
34,700	34,750	0	1,401	3,090	3,861	0	2,380	4,381	5,152
34,750	34,800	0	1,393	3,080	3,850	0	2,373	4,371	5,141
34,800	34,850	0	1,385	3,069	3,840	0	2,365	4,360	5,131
34,850	34,900	0	1,377	3,059	3,829	0	2,357	4,350	5,120
34,900	34,950	0	1,369	3,048	3,819	0	2,349	4,339	5,110
34,950	35,000	0	1,361	3,038	3,808	0	2,341	4,329	5,099
35,000	35,050	0	1,353	3,027	3,798	0	2,333	4,318	5,089
35,050	35,100	0	1,345	3,017	3,787	0	2,325	4,308	5,078
35,100	35,150	0	1,337	3,006	3,777	0	2,317	4,297	5,068
35,150	35,200	0	1,329	2,996	3,766	0	2,309	4,287	5,057
35,200	35,250	0	1,321	2,985	3,755	0	2,301	4,276	5,046
35,250	35,300	0	1,313	2,974	3,745	0	2,293	4,265	5,036
35,300	35,350	0	1,305	2,964	3,734	0	2,285	4,255	5,025
35,350	35,400	0	1,297	2,953	3,724	0	2,277	4,244	5,015
35,400	35,450	0	1,289	2,943	3,713	0	2,269	4,234	5,004
35,450	35,500	0	1,281	2,932	3,703	0	2,261	4,223	4,994
35,500	35,550	0	1,273	2,922	3,692	0	2,253	4,213	4,983
35,550	35,600	0	1,265	2,911	3,682	0	2,245	4,202	4,973
35,600	35,650	0	1,257	2,901	3,671	0	2,237	4,192	4,962
35,650	35,700	0	1,249	2,890	3,661	0	2,229	4,181	4,952
35,700	35,750	0	1,241	2,880	3,650	0	2,221	4,171	4,941
35,750	35,800	0	1,233	2,869	3,640	0	2,213	4,160	4,931
35,800	35,850	0	1,225	2,859	3,629	0	2,205	4,150	4,920
35,850	35,900	0	1,217	2,848	3,619	0	2,197	4,139	4,910
35,900	35,950	0	1,209	2,838	3,608	0	2,189	4,129	4,899
35,950	36,000	0	1,201	2,827	3,598	0	2,181	4,118	4,889
36,000	36,050	0	1,193	2,817	3,587	0	2,173	4,107	4,878
36,050	36,100	0	1,185	2,806	3,576	0	2,165	4,097	4,867
36,100	36,150	0	1,177	2,795	3,566	0	2,157	4,086	4,857
36,150	36,200	0	1,169	2,785	3,555	0	2,149	4,076	4,846
36,200	36,250	0	1,161	2,774	3,545	0	2,141	4,065	4,836
36,250	36,300	0	1,153	2,764	3,534	0	2,133	4,055	4,825
36,300	36,350	0	1,145	2,753	3,524	0	2,125	4,044	4,815
36,350	36,400	0	1,137	2,743	3,513	0	2,117	4,034	4,804
36,400	36,450	0	1,129	2,732	3,503	0	2,109	4,023	4,794
36,450	36,500	0	1,121	2,722	3,492	0	2,101	4,013	4,783
36,500	36,550	0	1,113	2,711	3,482	0	2,093	4,002	4,773
36,550	36,600	0	1,105	2,701	3,471	0	2,085	3,992	4,762
36,600	36,650	0	1,097	2,690	3,461	0	2,077	3,981	4,752
36,650	36,700	0	1,089	2,680	3,450	0	2,069	3,971	4,741
36,700	36,750	0	1,081	2,669	3,440	0	2,061	3,960	4,731
36,750	36,800	0	1,073	2,659	3,429	0	2,053	3,950	4,720
36,800	36,850	0	1,065	2,648	3,419	0	2,045	3,939	4,710
36,850	36,900	0	1,057	2,638	3,408	0	2,037	3,928	4,699
36,900	36,950	0	1,049	2,627	3,397	0	2,029	3,918	4,688
36,950	37,000	0	1,041	2,616	3,387	0	2,021	3,907	4,678
37,000	37,050	0	1,033	2,606	3,376	0	2,013	3,897	4,667
37,050	37,100	0	1,025	2,595	3,366	0	2,005	3,886	4,657
37,100	37,150	0	1,017	2,585	3,355	0	1,997	3,876	4,646
37,150	37,200	0	1,009	2,574	3,345	0	1,989	3,865	4,636
37,200	37,250	0	1,001	2,564	3,334	0	1,981	3,855	4,625
37,250	37,300	0	993	2,553	3,324	0	1,973	3,844	4,615
37,300	37,350	0	985	2,543	3,313	0	1,965	3,834	4,604
37,350	37,400	0	977	2,532	3,303	0	1,957	3,823	4,594
37,400	37,450	0	969	2,522	3,292	0	1,949	3,813	4,583
37,450	37,500	0	961	2,511	3,282	0	1,941	3,802	4,573
37,500	37,550	0	953	2,501	3,271	0	1,933	3,792	4,562
37,550	37,600	0	945	2,490	3,261	0	1,925	3,781	4,552

★ Use this column if your filing status is married filing separately and you qualify to claim the EIC. See the instructions for line 27.

(Continued)

Earned Income Credit (EIC) Table - *Continued*   (**Caution.** This is **not** a tax table.)

If the amount you are looking up from the worksheet is—		Single, head of household, or qualifying surviving spouse★ and you have—				Married filing jointly and you have—			
At least	But less than	0	1	2	3	0	1	2	3
		Your credit is—				Your credit is—			
37,600	37,650	0	937	2,480	3,250	0	1,917	3,771	4,541
37,650	37,700	0	930	2,469	3,240	0	1,909	3,760	4,531
37,700	37,750	0	922	2,458	3,229	0	1,901	3,749	4,520
37,750	37,800	0	914	2,448	3,218	0	1,893	3,739	4,509
37,800	37,850	0	906	2,437	3,208	0	1,885	3,728	4,499
37,850	37,900	0	898	2,427	3,197	0	1,877	3,718	4,488
37,900	37,950	0	890	2,416	3,187	0	1,869	3,707	4,478
37,950	38,000	0	882	2,406	3,176	0	1,861	3,697	4,467
38,000	38,050	0	874	2,395	3,166	0	1,853	3,686	4,457
38,050	38,100	0	866	2,385	3,155	0	1,845	3,676	4,446
38,100	38,150	0	858	2,374	3,145	0	1,837	3,665	4,436
38,150	38,200	0	850	2,364	3,134	0	1,829	3,655	4,425
38,200	38,250	0	842	2,353	3,124	0	1,821	3,644	4,415
38,250	38,300	0	834	2,343	3,113	0	1,813	3,634	4,404
38,300	38,350	0	826	2,332	3,103	0	1,805	3,623	4,394
38,350	38,400	0	818	2,322	3,092	0	1,797	3,613	4,383
38,400	38,450	0	810	2,311	3,082	0	1,789	3,602	4,373
38,450	38,500	0	802	2,301	3,071	0	1,781	3,592	4,362
38,500	38,550	0	794	2,290	3,061	0	1,773	3,581	4,351
38,550	38,600	0	786	2,279	3,050	0	1,765	3,570	4,341
38,600	38,650	0	778	2,269	3,039	0	1,757	3,560	4,330
38,650	38,700	0	770	2,258	3,029	0	1,749	3,549	4,320
38,700	38,750	0	762	2,248	3,018	0	1,741	3,539	4,309
38,750	38,800	0	754	2,237	3,008	0	1,733	3,528	4,299
38,800	38,850	0	746	2,227	2,997	0	1,725	3,518	4,288
38,850	38,900	0	738	2,216	2,987	0	1,717	3,507	4,278
38,900	38,950	0	730	2,206	2,976	0	1,709	3,497	4,267
38,950	39,000	0	722	2,195	2,966	0	1,701	3,486	4,257
39,000	39,050	0	714	2,185	2,955	0	1,693	3,476	4,246
39,050	39,100	0	706	2,174	2,945	0	1,685	3,465	4,236
39,100	39,150	0	698	2,164	2,934	0	1,677	3,455	4,225
39,150	39,200	0	690	2,153	2,924	0	1,669	3,444	4,215
39,200	39,250	0	682	2,143	2,913	0	1,661	3,434	4,204
39,250	39,300	0	674	2,132	2,903	0	1,653	3,423	4,194
39,300	39,350	0	666	2,122	2,892	0	1,645	3,413	4,183
39,350	39,400	0	658	2,111	2,882	0	1,637	3,402	4,172
39,400	39,450	0	650	2,100	2,871	0	1,629	3,391	4,162
39,450	39,500	0	642	2,090	2,860	0	1,621	3,381	4,151
39,500	39,550	0	634	2,079	2,850	0	1,613	3,370	4,141
39,550	39,600	0	626	2,069	2,839	0	1,605	3,360	4,130
39,600	39,650	0	618	2,058	2,829	0	1,597	3,349	4,120
39,650	39,700	0	610	2,048	2,818	0	1,589	3,339	4,109
39,700	39,750	0	602	2,037	2,808	0	1,581	3,328	4,099
39,750	39,800	0	594	2,027	2,797	0	1,574	3,318	4,088
39,800	39,850	0	586	2,016	2,787	0	1,566	3,307	4,078
39,850	39,900	0	578	2,006	2,776	0	1,558	3,297	4,067
39,900	39,950	0	570	1,995	2,766	0	1,550	3,286	4,057
39,950	40,000	0	562	1,985	2,755	0	1,542	3,276	4,046
40,000	40,050	0	554	1,974	2,745	0	1,534	3,265	4,036
40,050	40,100	0	546	1,964	2,734	0	1,526	3,255	4,025
40,100	40,150	0	538	1,953	2,724	0	1,518	3,244	4,015
40,150	40,200	0	530	1,943	2,713	0	1,510	3,234	4,004
40,200	40,250	0	522	1,932	2,702	0	1,502	3,223	3,993
40,250	40,300	0	514	1,921	2,692	0	1,494	3,212	3,983
40,300	40,350	0	506	1,911	2,681	0	1,486	3,202	3,972
40,350	40,400	0	498	1,900	2,671	0	1,478	3,191	3,962
40,400	40,450	0	490	1,890	2,660	0	1,470	3,181	3,951
40,450	40,500	0	482	1,879	2,650	0	1,462	3,170	3,941
40,500	40,550	0	474	1,869	2,639	0	1,454	3,160	3,930
40,550	40,600	0	466	1,858	2,629	0	1,446	3,149	3,920
40,600	40,650	0	458	1,848	2,618	0	1,438	3,139	3,909
40,650	40,700	0	450	1,837	2,608	0	1,430	3,128	3,899
40,700	40,750	0	442	1,827	2,597	0	1,422	3,118	3,888
40,750	40,800	0	434	1,816	2,587	0	1,414	3,107	3,878
40,800	40,850	0	426	1,806	2,576	0	1,406	3,097	3,867
40,850	40,900	0	418	1,795	2,566	0	1,398	3,086	3,857
40,900	40,950	0	410	1,785	2,555	0	1,390	3,076	3,846
40,950	41,000	0	402	1,774	2,545	0	1,382	3,065	3,836
41,000	41,050	0	394	1,764	2,534	0	1,374	3,054	3,825
41,050	41,100	0	386	1,753	2,523	0	1,366	3,044	3,814
41,100	41,150	0	378	1,742	2,513	0	1,358	3,033	3,804
41,150	41,200	0	370	1,732	2,502	0	1,350	3,023	3,793
41,200	41,250	0	362	1,721	2,492	0	1,342	3,012	3,783
41,250	41,300	0	354	1,711	2,481	0	1,334	3,002	3,772
41,300	41,350	0	346	1,700	2,471	0	1,326	2,991	3,762
41,350	41,400	0	338	1,690	2,460	0	1,318	2,981	3,751
41,400	41,450	0	330	1,679	2,450	0	1,310	2,970	3,741
41,450	41,500	0	322	1,669	2,439	0	1,302	2,960	3,730
41,500	41,550	0	314	1,658	2,429	0	1,294	2,949	3,720
41,550	41,600	0	306	1,648	2,418	0	1,286	2,939	3,709
41,600	41,650	0	298	1,637	2,408	0	1,278	2,928	3,699
41,650	41,700	0	290	1,627	2,397	0	1,270	2,918	3,688
41,700	41,750	0	282	1,616	2,387	0	1,262	2,907	3,678
41,750	41,800	0	274	1,606	2,376	0	1,254	2,897	3,667
41,800	41,850	0	266	1,595	2,366	0	1,246	2,886	3,657
41,850	41,900	0	258	1,585	2,355	0	1,238	2,875	3,646
41,900	41,950	0	250	1,574	2,344	0	1,230	2,865	3,635
41,950	42,000	0	242	1,563	2,334	0	1,222	2,854	3,625
42,000	42,050	0	234	1,553	2,323	0	1,214	2,844	3,614
42,050	42,100	0	226	1,542	2,313	0	1,206	2,833	3,604
42,100	42,150	0	218	1,532	2,302	0	1,198	2,823	3,593
42,150	42,200	0	210	1,521	2,292	0	1,190	2,812	3,583
42,200	42,250	0	202	1,511	2,281	0	1,182	2,802	3,572
42,250	42,300	0	194	1,500	2,271	0	1,174	2,791	3,562
42,300	42,350	0	186	1,490	2,260	0	1,166	2,781	3,551
42,350	42,400	0	178	1,479	2,250	0	1,158	2,770	3,541
42,400	42,450	0	170	1,469	2,239	0	1,150	2,760	3,530
42,450	42,500	0	162	1,458	2,229	0	1,142	2,749	3,520
42,500	42,550	0	154	1,448	2,218	0	1,134	2,739	3,509
42,550	42,600	0	146	1,437	2,208	0	1,126	2,728	3,499
42,600	42,650	0	138	1,427	2,197	0	1,118	2,718	3,488
42,650	42,700	0	131	1,416	2,187	0	1,110	2,707	3,478
42,700	42,750	0	123	1,405	2,176	0	1,102	2,696	3,467
42,750	42,800	0	115	1,395	2,165	0	1,094	2,686	3,456
42,800	42,850	0	107	1,384	2,155	0	1,086	2,675	3,446
42,850	42,900	0	99	1,374	2,144	0	1,078	2,665	3,435
42,900	42,950	0	91	1,363	2,134	0	1,070	2,654	3,425
42,950	43,000	0	83	1,353	2,123	0	1,062	2,644	3,414
43,000	43,050	0	75	1,342	2,113	0	1,054	2,633	3,404
43,050	43,100	0	67	1,332	2,102	0	1,046	2,623	3,393
43,100	43,150	0	59	1,321	2,092	0	1,038	2,612	3,383
43,150	43,200	0	51	1,311	2,081	0	1,030	2,602	3,372
43,200	43,250	0	43	1,300	2,071	0	1,022	2,591	3,362
43,250	43,300	0	35	1,290	2,060	0	1,014	2,581	3,351
43,300	43,350	0	27	1,279	2,050	0	1,006	2,570	3,341
43,350	43,400	0	19	1,269	2,039	0	998	2,560	3,330
43,400	43,450	0	11	1,258	2,029	0	990	2,549	3,320
43,450	43,500	0	*	1,248	2,018	0	982	2,539	3,309
43,500	43,550	0	0	1,237	2,008	0	974	2,528	3,298
43,550	43,600	0	0	1,226	1,997	0	966	2,517	3,288
43,600	43,650	0	0	1,216	1,986	0	958	2,507	3,277
43,650	43,700	0	0	1,205	1,976	0	950	2,496	3,267
43,700	43,750	0	0	1,195	1,965	0	942	2,486	3,256
43,750	43,800	0	0	1,184	1,955	0	934	2,475	3,246
43,800	43,850	0	0	1,174	1,944	0	926	2,465	3,235
43,850	43,900	0	0	1,163	1,934	0	918	2,454	3,225
43,900	43,950	0	0	1,153	1,923	0	910	2,444	3,214
43,950	44,000	0	0	1,142	1,913	0	902	2,433	3,204

★   Use this column if your filing status is married filing separately and you qualify to claim the EIC. See the instructions for line 27.

*   If the amount you are looking up from the worksheet is at least $43,450 but less than $43,492, and you have one qualifying child who has a valid SSN, your credit is $3.

    If the amount you are looking up from the worksheet is $43,492 or more, and you have one qualifying child who has a valid SSN, you can't take the credit.

(Continued)

Earned Income Credit (EIC) Table - *Continued*

(Caution. This is not a tax table.)

If the amount you are looking up from the worksheet is—		Single, head of household, or qualifying surviving spouse★ and you have—				Married filing jointly and you have—			
At least	But less than	0	1	2	3	0	1	2	3
		Your credit is—				Your credit is—			
44,000	44,050	0	0	1,132	1,902	0	894	2,423	3,193
44,050	44,100	0	0	1,121	1,892	0	886	2,412	3,183
44,100	44,150	0	0	1,111	1,881	0	878	2,402	3,172
44,150	44,200	0	0	1,100	1,871	0	870	2,391	3,162
44,200	44,250	0	0	1,090	1,860	0	862	2,381	3,151
44,250	44,300	0	0	1,079	1,850	0	854	2,370	3,141
44,300	44,350	0	0	1,069	1,839	0	846	2,360	3,130
44,350	44,400	0	0	1,058	1,829	0	838	2,349	3,119
44,400	44,450	0	0	1,047	1,818	0	830	2,338	3,109
44,450	44,500	0	0	1,037	1,807	0	822	2,328	3,098
44,500	44,550	0	0	1,026	1,797	0	814	2,317	3,088
44,550	44,600	0	0	1,016	1,786	0	806	2,307	3,077
44,600	44,650	0	0	1,005	1,776	0	798	2,296	3,067
44,650	44,700	0	0	995	1,765	0	790	2,286	3,056
44,700	44,750	0	0	984	1,755	0	782	2,275	3,046
44,750	44,800	0	0	974	1,744	0	775	2,265	3,035
44,800	44,850	0	0	963	1,734	0	767	2,254	3,025
44,850	44,900	0	0	953	1,723	0	759	2,244	3,014
44,900	44,950	0	0	942	1,713	0	751	2,233	3,004
44,950	45,000	0	0	932	1,702	0	743	2,223	2,993
45,000	45,050	0	0	921	1,692	0	735	2,212	2,983
45,050	45,100	0	0	911	1,681	0	727	2,202	2,972
45,100	45,150	0	0	900	1,671	0	719	2,191	2,962
45,150	45,200	0	0	890	1,660	0	711	2,181	2,951
45,200	45,250	0	0	879	1,649	0	703	2,170	2,940
45,250	45,300	0	0	868	1,639	0	695	2,159	2,930
45,300	45,350	0	0	858	1,628	0	687	2,149	2,919
45,350	45,400	0	0	847	1,618	0	679	2,138	2,909
45,400	45,450	0	0	837	1,607	0	671	2,128	2,898
45,450	45,500	0	0	826	1,597	0	663	2,117	2,888
45,500	45,550	0	0	816	1,586	0	655	2,107	2,877
45,550	45,600	0	0	805	1,576	0	647	2,096	2,867
45,600	45,650	0	0	795	1,565	0	639	2,086	2,856
45,650	45,700	0	0	784	1,555	0	631	2,075	2,846
45,700	45,750	0	0	774	1,544	0	623	2,065	2,835
45,750	45,800	0	0	763	1,534	0	615	2,054	2,825
45,800	45,850	0	0	753	1,523	0	607	2,044	2,814
45,850	45,900	0	0	742	1,513	0	599	2,033	2,804
45,900	45,950	0	0	732	1,502	0	591	2,023	2,793
45,950	46,000	0	0	721	1,492	0	583	2,012	2,783
46,000	46,050	0	0	711	1,481	0	575	2,001	2,772
46,050	46,100	0	0	700	1,470	0	567	1,991	2,761
46,100	46,150	0	0	689	1,460	0	559	1,980	2,751
46,150	46,200	0	0	679	1,449	0	551	1,970	2,740
46,200	46,250	0	0	668	1,439	0	543	1,959	2,730
46,250	46,300	0	0	658	1,428	0	535	1,949	2,719
46,300	46,350	0	0	647	1,418	0	527	1,938	2,709
46,350	46,400	0	0	637	1,407	0	519	1,928	2,698
46,400	46,450	0	0	626	1,397	0	511	1,917	2,688
46,450	46,500	0	0	616	1,386	0	503	1,907	2,677
46,500	46,550	0	0	605	1,376	0	495	1,896	2,667
46,550	46,600	0	0	595	1,365	0	487	1,886	2,656
46,600	46,650	0	0	584	1,355	0	479	1,875	2,646
46,650	46,700	0	0	574	1,344	0	471	1,865	2,635
46,700	46,750	0	0	563	1,334	0	463	1,854	2,625
46,750	46,800	0	0	553	1,323	0	455	1,844	2,614

If the amount you are looking up from the worksheet is—		Single, head of household, or qualifying surviving spouse★ and you have—				Married filing jointly and you have—			
At least	But less than	0	1	2	3	0	1	2	3
		Your credit is—				Your credit is—			
46,800	46,850	0	0	542	1,313	0	447	1,833	2,604
46,850	46,900	0	0	532	1,302	0	439	1,822	2,593
46,900	46,950	0	0	521	1,291	0	431	1,812	2,582
46,950	47,000	0	0	510	1,281	0	423	1,801	2,572
47,000	47,050	0	0	500	1,270	0	415	1,791	2,561
47,050	47,100	0	0	489	1,260	0	407	1,780	2,551
47,100	47,150	0	0	479	1,249	0	399	1,770	2,540
47,150	47,200	0	0	468	1,239	0	391	1,759	2,530
47,200	47,250	0	0	458	1,228	0	383	1,749	2,519
47,250	47,300	0	0	447	1,218	0	375	1,738	2,509
47,300	47,350	0	0	437	1,207	0	367	1,728	2,498
47,350	47,400	0	0	426	1,197	0	359	1,717	2,488
47,400	47,450	0	0	416	1,186	0	351	1,707	2,477
47,450	47,500	0	0	405	1,176	0	343	1,696	2,467
47,500	47,550	0	0	395	1,165	0	335	1,686	2,456
47,550	47,600	0	0	384	1,155	0	327	1,675	2,446
47,600	47,650	0	0	374	1,144	0	319	1,665	2,435
47,650	47,700	0	0	363	1,134	0	311	1,654	2,425
47,700	47,750	0	0	352	1,123	0	303	1,643	2,414
47,750	47,800	0	0	342	1,112	0	295	1,633	2,403
47,800	47,850	0	0	331	1,102	0	287	1,622	2,393
47,850	47,900	0	0	321	1,091	0	279	1,612	2,382
47,900	47,950	0	0	310	1,081	0	271	1,601	2,372
47,950	48,000	0	0	300	1,070	0	263	1,591	2,361
48,000	48,050	0	0	289	1,060	0	255	1,580	2,351
48,050	48,100	0	0	279	1,049	0	247	1,570	2,340
48,100	48,150	0	0	268	1,039	0	239	1,559	2,330
48,150	48,200	0	0	258	1,028	0	231	1,549	2,319
48,200	48,250	0	0	247	1,018	0	223	1,538	2,309
48,250	48,300	0	0	237	1,007	0	215	1,528	2,298
48,300	48,350	0	0	226	997	0	207	1,517	2,288
48,350	48,400	0	0	216	986	0	199	1,507	2,277
48,400	48,450	0	0	205	976	0	191	1,496	2,267
48,450	48,500	0	0	195	965	0	183	1,486	2,256
48,500	48,550	0	0	184	955	0	175	1,475	2,245
48,550	48,600	0	0	173	944	0	167	1,464	2,235
48,600	48,650	0	0	163	933	0	159	1,454	2,224
48,650	48,700	0	0	152	923	0	151	1,443	2,214
48,700	48,750	0	0	142	912	0	143	1,433	2,203
48,750	48,800	0	0	131	902	0	135	1,422	2,193
48,800	48,850	0	0	121	891	0	127	1,412	2,182
48,850	48,900	0	0	110	881	0	119	1,401	2,172
48,900	48,950	0	0	100	870	0	111	1,391	2,161
48,950	49,000	0	0	89	860	0	103	1,380	2,151
49,000	49,050	0	0	79	849	0	95	1,370	2,140
49,050	49,100	0	0	68	839	0	87	1,359	2,130
49,100	49,150	0	0	58	828	0	79	1,349	2,119
49,150	49,200	0	0	47	818	0	71	1,338	2,109
49,200	49,250	0	0	37	807	0	63	1,328	2,098
49,250	49,300	0	0	26	797	0	55	1,317	2,088
49,300	49,350	0	0	16	786	0	47	1,307	2,077
49,350	49,400	0	0	*	776	0	39	1,296	2,066
49,400	49,450	0	0	0	765	0	31	1,285	2,056
49,450	49,500	0	0	0	754	0	23	1,275	2,045
49,500	49,550	0	0	0	744	0	15	1,264	2,035
49,550	49,600	0	0	0	733	0	7	1,254	2,024

★ Use this column if your filing status is married filing separately and you qualify to claim the EIC. See the instructions for line 27.

* If the amount you are looking up from the worksheet is at least $49,350 but less than $49,399, and you have two qualifying children who have valid SSNs, your credit is $5.

If the amount you are looking up from the worksheet is $49,399 or more, and you have two qualifying children who have valid SSNs, you can't take the credit.

(Continued)

Earned Income Credit (EIC) Table - *Continued*

(Caution. This is **not** a tax table.)

If the amount you are looking up from the worksheet is—		Single, head of household, or qualifying surviving spouse★ and you have—				Married filing jointly and you have—				If the amount you are looking up from the worksheet is—		Single, head of household, or qualifying surviving spouse★ and you have—				Married filing jointly and you have—			
At least	But less than	0	1	2	3	0	1	2	3	At least	But less than	0	1	2	3	0	1	2	3
		Your credit is—				Your credit is—						Your credit is—				Your credit is—			
49,600	49,650	0	0	0	723	0	*	1,243	2,014	52,000	52,050	0	0	0	217	0	0	738	1,508
49,650	49,700	0	0	0	712	0	0	1,233	2,003	52,050	52,100	0	0	0	207	0	0	727	1,498
49,700	49,750	0	0	0	702	0	0	1,222	1,993	52,100	52,150	0	0	0	196	0	0	717	1,487
49,750	49,800	0	0	0	691	0	0	1,212	1,982	52,150	52,200	0	0	0	186	0	0	706	1,477
49,800	49,850	0	0	0	681	0	0	1,201	1,972	52,200	52,250	0	0	0	175	0	0	696	1,466
49,850	49,900	0	0	0	670	0	0	1,191	1,961	52,250	52,300	0	0	0	165	0	0	685	1,456
49,900	49,950	0	0	0	660	0	0	1,180	1,951	52,300	52,350	0	0	0	154	0	0	675	1,445
49,950	50,000	0	0	0	649	0	0	1,170	1,940	52,350	52,400	0	0	0	144	0	0	664	1,435
50,000	50,050	0	0	0	639	0	0	1,159	1,930	52,400	52,450	0	0	0	133	0	0	654	1,424
50,050	50,100	0	0	0	628	0	0	1,149	1,919	52,450	52,500	0	0	0	123	0	0	643	1,414
50,100	50,150	0	0	0	618	0	0	1,138	1,909	52,500	52,550	0	0	0	112	0	0	633	1,403
50,150	50,200	0	0	0	607	0	0	1,128	1,898	52,550	52,600	0	0	0	102	0	0	622	1,393
50,200	50,250	0	0	0	596	0	0	1,117	1,887	52,600	52,650	0	0	0	91	0	0	612	1,382
50,250	50,300	0	0	0	586	0	0	1,106	1,877	52,650	52,700	0	0	0	81	0	0	601	1,372
50,300	50,350	0	0	0	575	0	0	1,096	1,866	52,700	52,750	0	0	0	70	0	0	590	1,361
50,350	50,400	0	0	0	565	0	0	1,085	1,856	52,750	52,800	0	0	0	59	0	0	580	1,350
50,400	50,450	0	0	0	554	0	0	1,075	1,845	52,800	52,850	0	0	0	49	0	0	569	1,340
50,450	50,500	0	0	0	544	0	0	1,064	1,835	52,850	52,900	0	0	0	38	0	0	559	1,329
50,500	50,550	0	0	0	533	0	0	1,054	1,824	52,900	52,950	0	0	0	28	0	0	548	1,319
50,550	50,600	0	0	0	523	0	0	1,043	1,814	52,950	53,000	0	0	0	17	0	0	538	1,308
50,600	50,650	0	0	0	512	0	0	1,033	1,803	53,000	53,050	0	0	0	7	0	0	527	1,298
50,650	50,700	0	0	0	502	0	0	1,022	1,793	53,050	53,100	0	0	0	**	0	0	517	1,287
50,700	50,750	0	0	0	491	0	0	1,012	1,782	53,100	53,150	0	0	0	0	0	0	506	1,277
50,750	50,800	0	0	0	481	0	0	1,001	1,772	53,150	53,200	0	0	0	0	0	0	496	1,266
50,800	50,850	0	0	0	470	0	0	991	1,761	53,200	53,250	0	0	0	0	0	0	485	1,256
50,850	50,900	0	0	0	460	0	0	980	1,751	53,250	53,300	0	0	0	0	0	0	475	1,245
50,900	50,950	0	0	0	449	0	0	970	1,740	53,300	53,350	0	0	0	0	0	0	464	1,235
50,950	51,000	0	0	0	439	0	0	959	1,730	53,350	53,400	0	0	0	0	0	0	454	1,224
51,000	51,050	0	0	0	428	0	0	948	1,719	53,400	53,450	0	0	0	0	0	0	443	1,214
51,050	51,100	0	0	0	417	0	0	938	1,708	53,450	53,500	0	0	0	0	0	0	433	1,203
51,100	51,150	0	0	0	407	0	0	927	1,698	53,500	53,550	0	0	0	0	0	0	422	1,192
51,150	51,200	0	0	0	396	0	0	917	1,687	53,550	53,600	0	0	0	0	0	0	411	1,182
51,200	51,250	0	0	0	386	0	0	906	1,677	53,600	53,650	0	0	0	0	0	0	401	1,171
51,250	51,300	0	0	0	375	0	0	896	1,666	53,650	53,700	0	0	0	0	0	0	390	1,161
51,300	51,350	0	0	0	365	0	0	885	1,656	53,700	53,750	0	0	0	0	0	0	380	1,150
51,350	51,400	0	0	0	354	0	0	875	1,645	53,750	53,800	0	0	0	0	0	0	369	1,140
51,400	51,450	0	0	0	344	0	0	864	1,635	53,800	53,850	0	0	0	0	0	0	359	1,129
51,450	51,500	0	0	0	333	0	0	854	1,624	53,850	53,900	0	0	0	0	0	0	348	1,119
51,500	51,550	0	0	0	323	0	0	843	1,614	53,900	53,950	0	0	0	0	0	0	338	1,108
51,550	51,600	0	0	0	312	0	0	833	1,603	53,950	54,000	0	0	0	0	0	0	327	1,098
51,600	51,650	0	0	0	302	0	0	822	1,593	54,000	54,050	0	0	0	0	0	0	317	1,087
51,650	51,700	0	0	0	291	0	0	812	1,582	54,050	54,100	0	0	0	0	0	0	306	1,077
51,700	51,750	0	0	0	281	0	0	801	1,572	54,100	54,150	0	0	0	0	0	0	296	1,066
51,750	51,800	0	0	0	270	0	0	791	1,561	54,150	54,200	0	0	0	0	0	0	285	1,056
51,800	51,850	0	0	0	260	0	0	780	1,551	54,200	54,250	0	0	0	0	0	0	275	1,045
51,850	51,900	0	0	0	249	0	0	769	1,540	54,250	54,300	0	0	0	0	0	0	264	1,035
51,900	51,950	0	0	0	238	0	0	759	1,529	54,300	54,350	0	0	0	0	0	0	254	1,024
51,950	52,000	0	0	0	228	0	0	748	1,519	54,350	54,400	0	0	0	0	0	0	243	1,013

★   Use this column if your filing status is married filing separately and you qualify to claim the EIC. See the instructions for line 27.

*   If the amount you are looking up from the worksheet is at least $49,600 but less than $49,622, and you have one qualifying child who has a valid SSN, your credit is $2.

If the amount you are looking up from the worksheet is $49,622 or more, and you have one qualifying child who has a valid SSN, you can't take the credit.

**   If the amount you are looking up from the worksheet is at least $53,050 but less than $53,057, and you have three qualifying children who have valid SSNs, your credit is $1.

If the amount you are looking up from the worksheet is $53,057 or more, and you have three qualifying children who have valid SSNs, you can't take the credit.

(Continued)

Earned Income Credit (EIC) Table - *Continued*

(Caution. This is not a tax table.)

If the amount you are looking up from the worksheet is—		Single, head of household, or qualifying surviving spouse★ and you have—				Married filing jointly and you have—			
At least	But less than	0	1	2	3	0	1	2	3
		Your credit is—				Your credit is—			
54,400	54,450	0	0	0	0	0	0	232	1,003
54,450	54,500	0	0	0	0	0	0	222	992
54,500	54,550	0	0	0	0	0	0	211	982
54,550	54,600	0	0	0	0	0	0	201	971
54,600	54,650	0	0	0	0	0	0	190	961
54,650	54,700	0	0	0	0	0	0	180	950
54,700	54,750	0	0	0	0	0	0	169	940
54,750	54,800	0	0	0	0	0	0	159	929
54,800	54,850	0	0	0	0	0	0	148	919
54,850	54,900	0	0	0	0	0	0	138	908
54,900	54,950	0	0	0	0	0	0	127	898
54,950	55,000	0	0	0	0	0	0	117	887
55,000	55,050	0	0	0	0	0	0	106	877
55,050	55,100	0	0	0	0	0	0	96	866
55,100	55,150	0	0	0	0	0	0	85	856
55,150	55,200	0	0	0	0	0	0	75	845
55,200	55,250	0	0	0	0	0	0	64	834
55,250	55,300	0	0	0	0	0	0	53	824
55,300	55,350	0	0	0	0	0	0	43	813
55,350	55,400	0	0	0	0	0	0	32	803
55,400	55,450	0	0	0	0	0	0	22	792
55,450	55,500	0	0	0	0	0	0	11	782
55,500	55,550	0	0	0	0	0	0	*	771
55,550	55,600	0	0	0	0	0	0	0	761
55,600	55,650	0	0	0	0	0	0	0	750
55,650	55,700	0	0	0	0	0	0	0	740
55,700	55,750	0	0	0	0	0	0	0	729
55,750	55,800	0	0	0	0	0	0	0	719
55,800	55,850	0	0	0	0	0	0	0	708
55,850	55,900	0	0	0	0	0	0	0	698
55,900	55,950	0	0	0	0	0	0	0	687
55,950	56,000	0	0	0	0	0	0	0	677
56,000	56,050	0	0	0	0	0	0	0	666
56,050	56,100	0	0	0	0	0	0	0	655
56,100	56,150	0	0	0	0	0	0	0	645
56,150	56,200	0	0	0	0	0	0	0	634
56,200	56,250	0	0	0	0	0	0	0	624
56,250	56,300	0	0	0	0	0	0	0	613
56,300	56,350	0	0	0	0	0	0	0	603
56,350	56,400	0	0	0	0	0	0	0	592
56,400	56,450	0	0	0	0	0	0	0	582
56,450	56,500	0	0	0	0	0	0	0	571
56,500	56,550	0	0	0	0	0	0	0	561
56,550	56,600	0	0	0	0	0	0	0	550
56,600	56,650	0	0	0	0	0	0	0	540
56,650	56,700	0	0	0	0	0	0	0	529
56,700	56,750	0	0	0	0	0	0	0	519
56,750	56,800	0	0	0	0	0	0	0	508
56,800	56,850	0	0	0	0	0	0	0	498
56,850	56,900	0	0	0	0	0	0	0	487
56,900	56,950	0	0	0	0	0	0	0	476
56,950	57,000	0	0	0	0	0	0	0	466
57,000	57,050	0	0	0	0	0	0	0	455
57,050	57,100	0	0	0	0	0	0	0	445
57,100	57,150	0	0	0	0	0	0	0	434
57,150	57,200	0	0	0	0	0	0	0	424
57,200	57,250	0	0	0	0	0	0	0	413
57,250	57,300	0	0	0	0	0	0	0	403
57,300	57,350	0	0	0	0	0	0	0	392
57,350	57,400	0	0	0	0	0	0	0	382
57,400	57,450	0	0	0	0	0	0	0	371
57,450	57,500	0	0	0	0	0	0	0	361
57,500	57,550	0	0	0	0	0	0	0	350
57,550	57,600	0	0	0	0	0	0	0	340
57,600	57,650	0	0	0	0	0	0	0	329
57,650	57,700	0	0	0	0	0	0	0	319
57,700	57,750	0	0	0	0	0	0	0	308
57,750	57,800	0	0	0	0	0	0	0	297
57,800	57,850	0	0	0	0	0	0	0	287
57,850	57,900	0	0	0	0	0	0	0	276
57,900	57,950	0	0	0	0	0	0	0	266
57,950	58,000	0	0	0	0	0	0	0	255
58,000	58,050	0	0	0	0	0	0	0	245
58,050	58,100	0	0	0	0	0	0	0	234
58,100	58,150	0	0	0	0	0	0	0	224
58,150	58,200	0	0	0	0	0	0	0	213
58,200	58,250	0	0	0	0	0	0	0	203
58,250	58,300	0	0	0	0	0	0	0	192
58,300	58,350	0	0	0	0	0	0	0	182
58,350	58,400	0	0	0	0	0	0	0	171
58,400	58,450	0	0	0	0	0	0	0	161
58,450	58,500	0	0	0	0	0	0	0	150
58,500	58,550	0	0	0	0	0	0	0	139
58,550	58,600	0	0	0	0	0	0	0	129
58,600	58,650	0	0	0	0	0	0	0	118
58,650	58,700	0	0	0	0	0	0	0	108
58,700	58,750	0	0	0	0	0	0	0	97
58,750	58,800	0	0	0	0	0	0	0	87
58,800	58,850	0	0	0	0	0	0	0	76
58,850	58,900	0	0	0	0	0	0	0	66
58,900	58,950	0	0	0	0	0	0	0	55
58,950	59,000	0	0	0	0	0	0	0	45
59,000	59,050	0	0	0	0	0	0	0	34
59,050	59,100	0	0	0	0	0	0	0	24
59,100	59,150	0	0	0	0	0	0	0	13
59,150	59,187	0	0	0	0	0	0	0	**

★ Use this column if your filing status is married filing separately and you qualify to claim the EIC. See the instructions for line 27.

* If the amount you are looking up from the worksheet is at least $55,500 but less than $55,529, and you have two qualifying children who have valid SSNs, your credit is $3.

If the amount you are looking up from the worksheet is $55,529 or more, and you have two qualifying children who have valid SSNs, you can't take the credit.

** If the amount you are looking up from the worksheet is at least $59,150 but less than $59,187, and you have three qualifying children who have valid SSNs, your credit is $4.

If the amount you are looking up from the worksheet is $59,187 or more, and you have three qualifying children who have valid SSNs, you can't take the credit.

Appendix

T

Tax Tables

2022 Tax Table

See the instructions for line 16 to see if you must use the Tax Table below to figure your tax.

Example. A married couple are filing a joint return. Their taxable income on Form 1040, line 15, is $25,300. First, they find the $25,300-25,350 taxable income line. Next, they find the column for married filing jointly and read down the column. The amount shown where the taxable income line and filing status column meet is $2,628. This is the tax amount they should enter in the entry space on Form 1040, line 16.

Sample Table

At Least	But Less Than	Single	Married filing jointly*	Married filing separately	Head of a household
			Your tax is—		
25,200	25,250	2,822	2,616	2,822	2,734
25,250	25,300	2,828	2,622	2,828	2,740
25,300	25,350	2,834	(2,628)	2,834	2,746
25,350	25,400	2,840	2,634	2,840	2,752

If line 15 (taxable income) is— At least	But less than	Single	Married filing jointly*	Married filing separately	Head of a house-hold
			Your tax is—		
0	5	0	0	0	0
5	15	1	1	1	1
15	25	2	2	2	2
25	50	4	4	4	4
50	75	6	6	6	6
75	100	9	9	9	9
100	125	11	11	11	11
125	150	14	14	14	14
150	175	16	16	16	16
175	200	19	19	19	19
200	225	21	21	21	21
225	250	24	24	24	24
250	275	26	26	26	26
275	300	29	29	29	29
300	325	31	31	31	31
325	350	34	34	34	34
350	375	36	36	36	36
375	400	39	39	39	39
400	425	41	41	41	41
425	450	44	44	44	44
450	475	46	46	46	46
475	500	49	49	49	49
500	525	51	51	51	51
525	550	54	54	54	54
550	575	56	56	56	56
575	600	59	59	59	59
600	625	61	61	61	61
625	650	64	64	64	64
650	675	66	66	66	66
675	700	69	69	69	69
700	725	71	71	71	71
725	750	74	74	74	74
750	775	76	76	76	76
775	800	79	79	79	79
800	825	81	81	81	81
825	850	84	84	84	84
850	875	86	86	86	86
875	900	89	89	89	89
900	925	91	91	91	91
925	950	94	94	94	94
950	975	96	96	96	96
975	1,000	99	99	99	99

1,000

At least	But less than	Single	Married filing jointly*	Married filing separately	Head of a house-hold
			Your tax is—		
1,000	1,025	101	101	101	101
1,025	1,050	104	104	104	104
1,050	1,075	106	106	106	106
1,075	1,100	109	109	109	109
1,100	1,125	111	111	111	111
1,125	1,150	114	114	114	114
1,150	1,175	116	116	116	116
1,175	1,200	119	119	119	119
1,200	1,225	121	121	121	121
1,225	1,250	124	124	124	124
1,250	1,275	126	126	126	126
1,275	1,300	129	129	129	129
1,300	1,325	131	131	131	131
1,325	1,350	134	134	134	134
1,350	1,375	136	136	136	136
1,375	1,400	139	139	139	139
1,400	1,425	141	141	141	141
1,425	1,450	144	144	144	144
1,450	1,475	146	146	146	146
1,475	1,500	149	149	149	149
1,500	1,525	151	151	151	151
1,525	1,550	154	154	154	154
1,550	1,575	156	156	156	156
1,575	1,600	159	159	159	159
1,600	1,625	161	161	161	161
1,625	1,650	164	164	164	164
1,650	1,675	166	166	166	166
1,675	1,700	169	169	169	169
1,700	1,725	171	171	171	171
1,725	1,750	174	174	174	174
1,750	1,775	176	176	176	176
1,775	1,800	179	179	179	179
1,800	1,825	181	181	181	181
1,825	1,850	184	184	184	184
1,850	1,875	186	186	186	186
1,875	1,900	189	189	189	189
1,900	1,925	191	191	191	191
1,925	1,950	194	194	194	194
1,950	1,975	196	196	196	196
1,975	2,000	199	199	199	199

2,000

At least	But less than	Single	Married filing jointly*	Married filing separately	Head of a house-hold
			Your tax is—		
2,000	2,025	201	201	201	201
2,025	2,050	204	204	204	204
2,050	2,075	206	206	206	206
2,075	2,100	209	209	209	209
2,100	2,125	211	211	211	211
2,125	2,150	214	214	214	214
2,150	2,175	216	216	216	216
2,175	2,200	219	219	219	219
2,200	2,225	221	221	221	221
2,225	2,250	224	224	224	224
2,250	2,275	226	226	226	226
2,275	2,300	229	229	229	229
2,300	2,325	231	231	231	231
2,325	2,350	234	234	234	234
2,350	2,375	236	236	236	236
2,375	2,400	239	239	239	239
2,400	2,425	241	241	241	241
2,425	2,450	244	244	244	244
2,450	2,475	246	246	246	246
2,475	2,500	249	249	249	249
2,500	2,525	251	251	251	251
2,525	2,550	254	254	254	254
2,550	2,575	256	256	256	256
2,575	2,600	259	259	259	259
2,600	2,625	261	261	261	261
2,625	2,650	264	264	264	264
2,650	2,675	266	266	266	266
2,675	2,700	269	269	269	269
2,700	2,725	271	271	271	271
2,725	2,750	274	274	274	274
2,750	2,775	276	276	276	276
2,775	2,800	279	279	279	279
2,800	2,825	281	281	281	281
2,825	2,850	284	284	284	284
2,850	2,875	286	286	286	286
2,875	2,900	289	289	289	289
2,900	2,925	291	291	291	291
2,925	2,950	294	294	294	294
2,950	2,975	296	296	296	296
2,975	3,000	299	299	299	299

(Continued)

* This column must also be used by a qualifying surviving spouse.

3,000

At least	But less than	Single	Married filing jointly *	Married filing separately	Head of a household
3,000	3,050	303	303	303	303
3,050	3,100	308	308	308	308
3,100	3,150	313	313	313	313
3,150	3,200	318	318	318	318
3,200	3,250	323	323	323	323
3,250	3,300	328	328	328	328
3,300	3,350	333	333	333	333
3,350	3,400	338	338	338	338
3,400	3,450	343	343	343	343
3,450	3,500	348	348	348	348
3,500	3,550	353	353	353	353
3,550	3,600	358	358	358	358
3,600	3,650	363	363	363	363
3,650	3,700	368	368	368	368
3,700	3,750	373	373	373	373
3,750	3,800	378	378	378	378
3,800	3,850	383	383	383	383
3,850	3,900	388	388	388	388
3,900	3,950	393	393	393	393
3,950	4,000	398	398	398	398

4,000

At least	But less than	Single	Married filing jointly *	Married filing separately	Head of a household
4,000	4,050	403	403	403	403
4,050	4,100	408	408	408	408
4,100	4,150	413	413	413	413
4,150	4,200	418	418	418	418
4,200	4,250	423	423	423	423
4,250	4,300	428	428	428	428
4,300	4,350	433	433	433	433
4,350	4,400	438	438	438	438
4,400	4,450	443	443	443	443
4,450	4,500	448	448	448	448
4,500	4,550	453	453	453	453
4,550	4,600	458	458	458	458
4,600	4,650	463	463	463	463
4,650	4,700	468	468	468	468
4,700	4,750	473	473	473	473
4,750	4,800	478	478	478	478
4,800	4,850	483	483	483	483
4,850	4,900	488	488	488	488
4,900	4,950	493	493	493	493
4,950	5,000	498	498	498	498

5,000

At least	But less than	Single	Married filing jointly *	Married filing separately	Head of a household
5,000	5,050	503	503	503	503
5,050	5,100	508	508	508	508
5,100	5,150	513	513	513	513
5,150	5,200	518	518	518	518
5,200	5,250	523	523	523	523
5,250	5,300	528	528	528	528
5,300	5,350	533	533	533	533
5,350	5,400	538	538	538	538
5,400	5,450	543	543	543	543
5,450	5,500	548	548	548	548
5,500	5,550	553	553	553	553
5,550	5,600	558	558	558	558
5,600	5,650	563	563	563	563
5,650	5,700	568	568	568	568
5,700	5,750	573	573	573	573
5,750	5,800	578	578	578	578
5,800	5,850	583	583	583	583
5,850	5,900	588	588	588	588
5,900	5,950	593	593	593	593
5,950	6,000	598	598	598	598

6,000

At least	But less than	Single	Married filing jointly *	Married filing separately	Head of a household
6,000	6,050	603	603	603	603
6,050	6,100	608	608	608	608
6,100	6,150	613	613	613	613
6,150	6,200	618	618	618	618
6,200	6,250	623	623	623	623
6,250	6,300	628	628	628	628
6,300	6,350	633	633	633	633
6,350	6,400	638	638	638	638
6,400	6,450	643	643	643	643
6,450	6,500	648	648	648	648
6,500	6,550	653	653	653	653
6,550	6,600	658	658	658	658
6,600	6,650	663	663	663	663
6,650	6,700	668	668	668	668
6,700	6,750	673	673	673	673
6,750	6,800	678	678	678	678
6,800	6,850	683	683	683	683
6,850	6,900	688	688	688	688
6,900	6,950	693	693	693	693
6,950	7,000	698	698	698	698

7,000

At least	But less than	Single	Married filing jointly *	Married filing separately	Head of a household
7,000	7,050	703	703	703	703
7,050	7,100	708	708	708	708
7,100	7,150	713	713	713	713
7,150	7,200	718	718	718	718
7,200	7,250	723	723	723	723
7,250	7,300	728	728	728	728
7,300	7,350	733	733	733	733
7,350	7,400	738	738	738	738
7,400	7,450	743	743	743	743
7,450	7,500	748	748	748	748
7,500	7,550	753	753	753	753
7,550	7,600	758	758	758	758
7,600	7,650	763	763	763	763
7,650	7,700	768	768	768	768
7,700	7,750	773	773	773	773
7,750	7,800	778	778	778	778
7,800	7,850	783	783	783	783
7,850	7,900	788	788	788	788
7,900	7,950	793	793	793	793
7,950	8,000	798	798	798	798

8,000

At least	But less than	Single	Married filing jointly *	Married filing separately	Head of a household
8,000	8,050	803	803	803	803
8,050	8,100	808	808	808	808
8,100	8,150	813	813	813	813
8,150	8,200	818	818	818	818
8,200	8,250	823	823	823	823
8,250	8,300	828	828	828	828
8,300	8,350	833	833	833	833
8,350	8,400	838	838	838	838
8,400	8,450	843	843	843	843
8,450	8,500	848	848	848	848
8,500	8,550	853	853	853	853
8,550	8,600	858	858	858	858
8,600	8,650	863	863	863	863
8,650	8,700	868	868	868	868
8,700	8,750	873	873	873	873
8,750	8,800	878	878	878	878
8,800	8,850	883	883	883	883
8,850	8,900	888	888	888	888
8,900	8,950	893	893	893	893
8,950	9,000	898	898	898	898

9,000

At least	But less than	Single	Married filing jointly *	Married filing separately	Head of a household
9,000	9,050	903	903	903	903
9,050	9,100	908	908	908	908
9,100	9,150	913	913	913	913
9,150	9,200	918	918	918	918
9,200	9,250	923	923	923	923
9,250	9,300	928	928	928	928
9,300	9,350	933	933	933	933
9,350	9,400	938	938	938	938
9,400	9,450	943	943	943	943
9,450	9,500	948	948	948	948
9,500	9,550	953	953	953	953
9,550	9,600	958	958	958	958
9,600	9,650	963	963	963	963
9,650	9,700	968	968	968	968
9,700	9,750	973	973	973	973
9,750	9,800	978	978	978	978
9,800	9,850	983	983	983	983
9,850	9,900	988	988	988	988
9,900	9,950	993	993	993	993
9,950	10,000	998	998	998	998

10,000

At least	But less than	Single	Married filing jointly *	Married filing separately	Head of a household
10,000	10,050	1,003	1,003	1,003	1,003
10,050	10,100	1,008	1,008	1,008	1,008
10,100	10,150	1,013	1,013	1,013	1,013
10,150	10,200	1,018	1,018	1,018	1,018
10,200	10,250	1,023	1,023	1,023	1,023
10,250	10,300	1,028	1,028	1,028	1,028
10,300	10,350	1,034	1,033	1,034	1,033
10,350	10,400	1,040	1,038	1,040	1,038
10,400	10,450	1,046	1,043	1,046	1,043
10,450	10,500	1,052	1,048	1,052	1,048
10,500	10,550	1,058	1,053	1,058	1,053
10,550	10,600	1,064	1,058	1,064	1,058
10,600	10,650	1,070	1,063	1,070	1,063
10,650	10,700	1,076	1,068	1,076	1,068
10,700	10,750	1,082	1,073	1,082	1,073
10,750	10,800	1,088	1,078	1,088	1,078
10,800	10,850	1,094	1,083	1,094	1,083
10,850	10,900	1,100	1,088	1,100	1,088
10,900	10,950	1,106	1,093	1,106	1,093
10,950	11,000	1,112	1,098	1,112	1,098

11,000

At least	But less than	Single	Married filing jointly *	Married filing separately	Head of a household
11,000	11,050	1,118	1,103	1,118	1,103
11,050	11,100	1,124	1,108	1,124	1,108
11,100	11,150	1,130	1,113	1,130	1,113
11,150	11,200	1,136	1,118	1,136	1,118
11,200	11,250	1,142	1,123	1,142	1,123
11,250	11,300	1,148	1,128	1,148	1,128
11,300	11,350	1,154	1,133	1,154	1,133
11,350	11,400	1,160	1,138	1,160	1,138
11,400	11,450	1,166	1,143	1,166	1,143
11,450	11,500	1,172	1,148	1,172	1,148
11,500	11,550	1,178	1,153	1,178	1,153
11,550	11,600	1,184	1,158	1,184	1,158
11,600	11,650	1,190	1,163	1,190	1,163
11,650	11,700	1,196	1,168	1,196	1,168
11,700	11,750	1,202	1,173	1,202	1,173
11,750	11,800	1,208	1,178	1,208	1,178
11,800	11,850	1,214	1,183	1,214	1,183
11,850	11,900	1,220	1,188	1,220	1,188
11,900	11,950	1,226	1,193	1,226	1,193
11,950	12,000	1,232	1,198	1,232	1,198

* This column must also be used by a qualifying surviving spouse.

(Continued)

2022 Tax Table — *Continued*

12,000

At least	But less than	Single	Married filing jointly *	Married filing separately	Head of a household
12,000	12,050	1,238	1,203	1,238	1,203
12,050	12,100	1,244	1,208	1,244	1,208
12,100	12,150	1,250	1,213	1,250	1,213
12,150	12,200	1,256	1,218	1,256	1,218
12,200	12,250	1,262	1,223	1,262	1,223
12,250	12,300	1,268	1,228	1,268	1,228
12,300	12,350	1,274	1,233	1,274	1,233
12,350	12,400	1,280	1,238	1,280	1,238
12,400	12,450	1,286	1,243	1,286	1,243
12,450	12,500	1,292	1,248	1,292	1,248
12,500	12,550	1,298	1,253	1,298	1,253
12,550	12,600	1,304	1,258	1,304	1,258
12,600	12,650	1,310	1,263	1,310	1,263
12,650	12,700	1,316	1,268	1,316	1,268
12,700	12,750	1,322	1,273	1,322	1,273
12,750	12,800	1,328	1,278	1,328	1,278
12,800	12,850	1,334	1,283	1,334	1,283
12,850	12,900	1,340	1,288	1,340	1,288
12,900	12,950	1,346	1,293	1,346	1,293
12,950	13,000	1,352	1,298	1,352	1,298

13,000

At least	But less than	Single	Married filing jointly *	Married filing separately	Head of a household
13,000	13,050	1,358	1,303	1,358	1,303
13,050	13,100	1,364	1,308	1,364	1,308
13,100	13,150	1,370	1,313	1,370	1,313
13,150	13,200	1,376	1,318	1,376	1,318
13,200	13,250	1,382	1,323	1,382	1,323
13,250	13,300	1,388	1,328	1,388	1,328
13,300	13,350	1,394	1,333	1,394	1,333
13,350	13,400	1,400	1,338	1,400	1,338
13,400	13,450	1,406	1,343	1,406	1,343
13,450	13,500	1,412	1,348	1,412	1,348
13,500	13,550	1,418	1,353	1,418	1,353
13,550	13,600	1,424	1,358	1,424	1,358
13,600	13,650	1,430	1,363	1,430	1,363
13,650	13,700	1,436	1,368	1,436	1,368
13,700	13,750	1,442	1,373	1,442	1,373
13,750	13,800	1,448	1,378	1,448	1,378
13,800	13,850	1,454	1,383	1,454	1,383
13,850	13,900	1,460	1,388	1,460	1,388
13,900	13,950	1,466	1,393	1,466	1,393
13,950	14,000	1,472	1,398	1,472	1,398

14,000

At least	But less than	Single	Married filing jointly *	Married filing separately	Head of a household
14,000	14,050	1,478	1,403	1,478	1,403
14,050	14,100	1,484	1,408	1,484	1,408
14,100	14,150	1,490	1,413	1,490	1,413
14,150	14,200	1,496	1,418	1,496	1,418
14,200	14,250	1,502	1,423	1,502	1,423
14,250	14,300	1,508	1,428	1,508	1,428
14,300	14,350	1,514	1,433	1,514	1,433
14,350	14,400	1,520	1,438	1,520	1,438
14,400	14,450	1,526	1,443	1,526	1,443
14,450	14,500	1,532	1,448	1,532	1,448
14,500	14,550	1,538	1,453	1,538	1,453
14,550	14,600	1,544	1,458	1,544	1,458
14,600	14,650	1,550	1,463	1,550	1,463
14,650	14,700	1,556	1,468	1,556	1,468
14,700	14,750	1,562	1,473	1,562	1,474
14,750	14,800	1,568	1,478	1,568	1,480
14,800	14,850	1,574	1,483	1,574	1,486
14,850	14,900	1,580	1,488	1,580	1,492
14,900	14,950	1,586	1,493	1,586	1,498
14,950	15,000	1,592	1,498	1,592	1,504

15,000

At least	But less than	Single	Married filing jointly *	Married filing separately	Head of a household
15,000	15,050	1,598	1,503	1,598	1,510
15,050	15,100	1,604	1,508	1,604	1,516
15,100	15,150	1,610	1,513	1,610	1,522
15,150	15,200	1,616	1,518	1,616	1,528
15,200	15,250	1,622	1,523	1,622	1,534
15,250	15,300	1,628	1,528	1,628	1,540
15,300	15,350	1,634	1,533	1,634	1,546
15,350	15,400	1,640	1,538	1,640	1,552
15,400	15,450	1,646	1,543	1,646	1,558
15,450	15,500	1,652	1,548	1,652	1,564
15,500	15,550	1,658	1,553	1,658	1,570
15,550	15,600	1,664	1,558	1,664	1,576
15,600	15,650	1,670	1,563	1,670	1,582
15,650	15,700	1,676	1,568	1,676	1,588
15,700	15,750	1,682	1,573	1,682	1,594
15,750	15,800	1,688	1,578	1,688	1,600
15,800	15,850	1,694	1,583	1,694	1,606
15,850	15,900	1,700	1,588	1,700	1,612
15,900	15,950	1,706	1,593	1,706	1,618
15,950	16,000	1,712	1,598	1,712	1,624

16,000

At least	But less than	Single	Married filing jointly *	Married filing separately	Head of a household
16,000	16,050	1,718	1,603	1,718	1,630
16,050	16,100	1,724	1,608	1,724	1,636
16,100	16,150	1,730	1,613	1,730	1,642
16,150	16,200	1,736	1,618	1,736	1,648
16,200	16,250	1,742	1,623	1,742	1,654
16,250	16,300	1,748	1,628	1,748	1,660
16,300	16,350	1,754	1,633	1,754	1,666
16,350	16,400	1,760	1,638	1,760	1,672
16,400	16,450	1,766	1,643	1,766	1,678
16,450	16,500	1,772	1,648	1,772	1,684
16,500	16,550	1,778	1,653	1,778	1,690
16,550	16,600	1,784	1,658	1,784	1,696
16,600	16,650	1,790	1,663	1,790	1,702
16,650	16,700	1,796	1,668	1,796	1,708
16,700	16,750	1,802	1,673	1,802	1,714
16,750	16,800	1,808	1,678	1,808	1,720
16,800	16,850	1,814	1,683	1,814	1,726
16,850	16,900	1,820	1,688	1,820	1,732
16,900	16,950	1,826	1,693	1,826	1,738
16,950	17,000	1,832	1,698	1,832	1,744

17,000

At least	But less than	Single	Married filing jointly *	Married filing separately	Head of a household
17,000	17,050	1,838	1,703	1,838	1,750
17,050	17,100	1,844	1,708	1,844	1,756
17,100	17,150	1,850	1,713	1,850	1,762
17,150	17,200	1,856	1,718	1,856	1,768
17,200	17,250	1,862	1,723	1,862	1,774
17,250	17,300	1,868	1,728	1,868	1,780
17,300	17,350	1,874	1,733	1,874	1,786
17,350	17,400	1,880	1,738	1,880	1,792
17,400	17,450	1,886	1,743	1,886	1,798
17,450	17,500	1,892	1,748	1,892	1,804
17,500	17,550	1,898	1,753	1,898	1,810
17,550	17,600	1,904	1,758	1,904	1,816
17,600	17,650	1,910	1,763	1,910	1,822
17,650	17,700	1,916	1,768	1,916	1,828
17,700	17,750	1,922	1,773	1,922	1,834
17,750	17,800	1,928	1,778	1,928	1,840
17,800	17,850	1,934	1,783	1,934	1,846
17,850	17,900	1,940	1,788	1,940	1,852
17,900	17,950	1,946	1,793	1,946	1,858
17,950	18,000	1,952	1,798	1,952	1,864

18,000

At least	But less than	Single	Married filing jointly *	Married filing separately	Head of a household
18,000	18,050	1,958	1,803	1,958	1,870
18,050	18,100	1,964	1,808	1,964	1,876
18,100	18,150	1,970	1,813	1,970	1,882
18,150	18,200	1,976	1,818	1,976	1,888
18,200	18,250	1,982	1,823	1,982	1,894
18,250	18,300	1,988	1,828	1,988	1,900
18,300	18,350	1,994	1,833	1,994	1,906
18,350	18,400	2,000	1,838	2,000	1,912
18,400	18,450	2,006	1,843	2,006	1,918
18,450	18,500	2,012	1,848	2,012	1,924
18,500	18,550	2,018	1,853	2,018	1,930
18,550	18,600	2,024	1,858	2,024	1,936
18,600	18,650	2,030	1,863	2,030	1,942
18,650	18,700	2,036	1,868	2,036	1,948
18,700	18,750	2,042	1,873	2,042	1,954
18,750	18,800	2,048	1,878	2,048	1,960
18,800	18,850	2,054	1,883	2,054	1,966
18,850	18,900	2,060	1,888	2,060	1,972
18,900	18,950	2,066	1,893	2,066	1,978
18,950	19,000	2,072	1,898	2,072	1,984

19,000

At least	But less than	Single	Married filing jointly *	Married filing separately	Head of a household
19,000	19,050	2,078	1,903	2,078	1,990
19,050	19,100	2,084	1,908	2,084	1,996
19,100	19,150	2,090	1,913	2,090	2,002
19,150	19,200	2,096	1,918	2,096	2,008
19,200	19,250	2,102	1,923	2,102	2,014
19,250	19,300	2,108	1,928	2,108	2,020
19,300	19,350	2,114	1,933	2,114	2,026
19,350	19,400	2,120	1,938	2,120	2,032
19,400	19,450	2,126	1,943	2,126	2,038
19,450	19,500	2,132	1,948	2,132	2,044
19,500	19,550	2,138	1,953	2,138	2,050
19,550	19,600	2,144	1,958	2,144	2,056
19,600	19,650	2,150	1,963	2,150	2,062
19,650	19,700	2,156	1,968	2,156	2,068
19,700	19,750	2,162	1,973	2,162	2,074
19,750	19,800	2,168	1,978	2,168	2,080
19,800	19,850	2,174	1,983	2,174	2,086
19,850	19,900	2,180	1,988	2,180	2,092
19,900	19,950	2,186	1,993	2,186	2,098
19,950	20,000	2,192	1,998	2,192	2,104

20,000

At least	But less than	Single	Married filing jointly *	Married filing separately	Head of a household
20,000	20,050	2,198	2,003	2,198	2,110
20,050	20,100	2,204	2,008	2,204	2,116
20,100	20,150	2,210	2,013	2,210	2,122
20,150	20,200	2,216	2,018	2,216	2,128
20,200	20,250	2,222	2,023	2,222	2,134
20,250	20,300	2,228	2,028	2,228	2,140
20,300	20,350	2,234	2,033	2,234	2,146
20,350	20,400	2,240	2,038	2,240	2,152
20,400	20,450	2,246	2,043	2,246	2,158
20,450	20,500	2,252	2,048	2,252	2,164
20,500	20,550	2,258	2,053	2,258	2,170
20,550	20,600	2,264	2,058	2,264	2,176
20,600	20,650	2,270	2,064	2,270	2,182
20,650	20,700	2,276	2,070	2,276	2,188
20,700	20,750	2,282	2,076	2,282	2,194
20,750	20,800	2,288	2,082	2,288	2,200
20,800	20,850	2,294	2,088	2,294	2,206
20,850	20,900	2,300	2,094	2,300	2,212
20,900	20,950	2,306	2,100	2,306	2,218
20,950	21,000	2,312	2,106	2,312	2,224

(Continued)

* This column must also be used by a qualifying surviving spouse.

2022 **Tax Table** — *Continued*

If line 15 (taxable income) is—		And you are—				If line 15 (taxable income) is—		And you are—				If line 15 (taxable income) is—		And you are—			
At least	But less than	Single	Married filing jointly *	Married filing separately	Head of a household	At least	But less than	Single	Married filing jointly *	Married filing separately	Head of a household	At least	But less than	Single	Married filing jointly *	Married filing separately	Head of a household
		Your tax is—						Your tax is—						Your tax is—			
21,000						**24,000**						**27,000**					
21,000	21,050	2,318	2,112	2,318	2,230	24,000	24,050	2,678	2,472	2,678	2,590	27,000	27,050	3,038	2,832	3,038	2,950
21,050	21,100	2,324	2,118	2,324	2,236	24,050	24,100	2,684	2,478	2,684	2,596	27,050	27,100	3,044	2,838	3,044	2,956
21,100	21,150	2,330	2,124	2,330	2,242	24,100	24,150	2,690	2,484	2,690	2,602	27,100	27,150	3,050	2,844	3,050	2,962
21,150	21,200	2,336	2,130	2,336	2,248	24,150	24,200	2,696	2,490	2,696	2,608	27,150	27,200	3,056	2,850	3,056	2,968
21,200	21,250	2,342	2,136	2,342	2,254	24,200	24,250	2,702	2,496	2,702	2,614	27,200	27,250	3,062	2,856	3,062	2,974
21,250	21,300	2,348	2,142	2,348	2,260	24,250	24,300	2,708	2,502	2,708	2,620	27,250	27,300	3,068	2,862	3,068	2,980
21,300	21,350	2,354	2,148	2,354	2,266	24,300	24,350	2,714	2,508	2,714	2,626	27,300	27,350	3,074	2,868	3,074	2,986
21,350	21,400	2,360	2,154	2,360	2,272	24,350	24,400	2,720	2,514	2,720	2,632	27,350	27,400	3,080	2,874	3,080	2,992
21,400	21,450	2,366	2,160	2,366	2,278	24,400	24,450	2,726	2,520	2,726	2,638	27,400	27,450	3,086	2,880	3,086	2,998
21,450	21,500	2,372	2,166	2,372	2,284	24,450	24,500	2,732	2,526	2,732	2,644	27,450	27,500	3,092	2,886	3,092	3,004
21,500	21,550	2,378	2,172	2,378	2,290	24,500	24,550	2,738	2,532	2,738	2,650	27,500	27,550	3,098	2,892	3,098	3,010
21,550	21,600	2,384	2,178	2,384	2,296	24,550	24,600	2,744	2,538	2,744	2,656	27,550	27,600	3,104	2,898	3,104	3,016
21,600	21,650	2,390	2,184	2,390	2,302	24,600	24,650	2,750	2,544	2,750	2,662	27,600	27,650	3,110	2,904	3,110	3,022
21,650	21,700	2,396	2,190	2,396	2,308	24,650	24,700	2,756	2,550	2,756	2,668	27,650	27,700	3,116	2,910	3,116	3,028
21,700	21,750	2,402	2,196	2,402	2,314	24,700	24,750	2,762	2,556	2,762	2,674	27,700	27,750	3,122	2,916	3,122	3,034
21,750	21,800	2,408	2,202	2,408	2,320	24,750	24,800	2,768	2,562	2,768	2,680	27,750	27,800	3,128	2,922	3,128	3,040
21,800	21,850	2,414	2,208	2,414	2,326	24,800	24,850	2,774	2,568	2,774	2,686	27,800	27,850	3,134	2,928	3,134	3,046
21,850	21,900	2,420	2,214	2,420	2,332	24,850	24,900	2,780	2,574	2,780	2,692	27,850	27,900	3,140	2,934	3,140	3,052
21,900	21,950	2,426	2,220	2,426	2,338	24,900	24,950	2,786	2,580	2,786	2,698	27,900	27,950	3,146	2,940	3,146	3,058
21,950	22,000	2,432	2,226	2,432	2,344	24,950	25,000	2,792	2,586	2,792	2,704	27,950	28,000	3,152	2,946	3,152	3,064
22,000						**25,000**						**28,000**					
22,000	22,050	2,438	2,232	2,438	2,350	25,000	25,050	2,798	2,592	2,798	2,710	28,000	28,050	3,158	2,952	3,158	3,070
22,050	22,100	2,444	2,238	2,444	2,356	25,050	25,100	2,804	2,598	2,804	2,716	28,050	28,100	3,164	2,958	3,164	3,076
22,100	22,150	2,450	2,244	2,450	2,362	25,100	25,150	2,810	2,604	2,810	2,722	28,100	28,150	3,170	2,964	3,170	3,082
22,150	22,200	2,456	2,250	2,456	2,368	25,150	25,200	2,816	2,610	2,816	2,728	28,150	28,200	3,176	2,970	3,176	3,088
22,200	22,250	2,462	2,256	2,462	2,374	25,200	25,250	2,822	2,616	2,822	2,734	28,200	28,250	3,182	2,976	3,182	3,094
22,250	22,300	2,468	2,262	2,468	2,380	25,250	25,300	2,828	2,622	2,828	2,740	28,250	28,300	3,188	2,982	3,188	3,100
22,300	22,350	2,474	2,268	2,474	2,386	25,300	25,350	2,834	2,628	2,834	2,746	28,300	28,350	3,194	2,988	3,194	3,106
22,350	22,400	2,480	2,274	2,480	2,392	25,350	25,400	2,840	2,634	2,840	2,752	28,350	28,400	3,200	2,994	3,200	3,112
22,400	22,450	2,486	2,280	2,486	2,398	25,400	25,450	2,846	2,640	2,846	2,758	28,400	28,450	3,206	3,000	3,206	3,118
22,450	22,500	2,492	2,286	2,492	2,404	25,450	25,500	2,852	2,646	2,852	2,764	28,450	28,500	3,212	3,006	3,212	3,124
22,500	22,550	2,498	2,292	2,498	2,410	25,500	25,550	2,858	2,652	2,858	2,770	28,500	28,550	3,218	3,012	3,218	3,130
22,550	22,600	2,504	2,298	2,504	2,416	25,550	25,600	2,864	2,658	2,864	2,776	28,550	28,600	3,224	3,018	3,224	3,136
22,600	22,650	2,510	2,304	2,510	2,422	25,600	25,650	2,870	2,664	2,870	2,782	28,600	28,650	3,230	3,024	3,230	3,142
22,650	22,700	2,516	2,310	2,516	2,428	25,650	25,700	2,876	2,670	2,876	2,788	28,650	28,700	3,236	3,030	3,236	3,148
22,700	22,750	2,522	2,316	2,522	2,434	25,700	25,750	2,882	2,676	2,882	2,794	28,700	28,750	3,242	3,036	3,242	3,154
22,750	22,800	2,528	2,322	2,528	2,440	25,750	25,800	2,888	2,682	2,888	2,800	28,750	28,800	3,248	3,042	3,248	3,160
22,800	22,850	2,534	2,328	2,534	2,446	25,800	25,850	2,894	2,688	2,894	2,806	28,800	28,850	3,254	3,048	3,254	3,166
22,850	22,900	2,540	2,334	2,540	2,452	25,850	25,900	2,900	2,694	2,900	2,812	28,850	28,900	3,260	3,054	3,260	3,172
22,900	22,950	2,546	2,340	2,546	2,458	25,900	25,950	2,906	2,700	2,906	2,818	28,900	28,950	3,266	3,060	3,266	3,178
22,950	23,000	2,552	2,346	2,552	2,464	25,950	26,000	2,912	2,706	2,912	2,824	28,950	29,000	3,272	3,066	3,272	3,184
23,000						**26,000**						**29,000**					
23,000	23,050	2,558	2,352	2,558	2,470	26,000	26,050	2,918	2,712	2,918	2,830	29,000	29,050	3,278	3,072	3,278	3,190
23,050	23,100	2,564	2,358	2,564	2,476	26,050	26,100	2,924	2,718	2,924	2,836	29,050	29,100	3,284	3,078	3,284	3,196
23,100	23,150	2,570	2,364	2,570	2,482	26,100	26,150	2,930	2,724	2,930	2,842	29,100	29,150	3,290	3,084	3,290	3,202
23,150	23,200	2,576	2,370	2,576	2,488	26,150	26,200	2,936	2,730	2,936	2,848	29,150	29,200	3,296	3,090	3,296	3,208
23,200	23,250	2,582	2,376	2,582	2,494	26,200	26,250	2,942	2,736	2,942	2,854	29,200	29,250	3,302	3,096	3,302	3,214
23,250	23,300	2,588	2,382	2,588	2,500	26,250	26,300	2,948	2,742	2,948	2,860	29,250	29,300	3,308	3,102	3,308	3,220
23,300	23,350	2,594	2,388	2,594	2,506	26,300	26,350	2,954	2,748	2,954	2,866	29,300	29,350	3,314	3,108	3,314	3,226
23,350	23,400	2,600	2,394	2,600	2,512	26,350	26,400	2,960	2,754	2,960	2,872	29,350	29,400	3,320	3,114	3,320	3,232
23,400	23,450	2,606	2,400	2,606	2,518	26,400	26,450	2,966	2,760	2,966	2,878	29,400	29,450	3,326	3,120	3,326	3,238
23,450	23,500	2,612	2,406	2,612	2,524	26,450	26,500	2,972	2,766	2,972	2,884	29,450	29,500	3,332	3,126	3,332	3,244
23,500	23,550	2,618	2,412	2,618	2,530	26,500	26,550	2,978	2,772	2,978	2,890	29,500	29,550	3,338	3,132	3,338	3,250
23,550	23,600	2,624	2,418	2,624	2,536	26,550	26,600	2,984	2,778	2,984	2,896	29,550	29,600	3,344	3,138	3,344	3,256
23,600	23,650	2,630	2,424	2,630	2,542	26,600	26,650	2,990	2,784	2,990	2,902	29,600	29,650	3,350	3,144	3,350	3,262
23,650	23,700	2,636	2,430	2,636	2,548	26,650	26,700	2,996	2,790	2,996	2,908	29,650	29,700	3,356	3,150	3,356	3,268
23,700	23,750	2,642	2,436	2,642	2,554	26,700	26,750	3,002	2,796	3,002	2,914	29,700	29,750	3,362	3,156	3,362	3,274
23,750	23,800	2,648	2,442	2,648	2,560	26,750	26,800	3,008	2,802	3,008	2,920	29,750	29,800	3,368	3,162	3,368	3,280
23,800	23,850	2,654	2,448	2,654	2,566	26,800	26,850	3,014	2,808	3,014	2,926	29,800	29,850	3,374	3,168	3,374	3,286
23,850	23,900	2,660	2,454	2,660	2,572	26,850	26,900	3,020	2,814	3,020	2,932	29,850	29,900	3,380	3,174	3,380	3,292
23,900	23,950	2,666	2,460	2,666	2,578	26,900	26,950	3,026	2,820	3,026	2,938	29,900	29,950	3,386	3,180	3,386	3,298
23,950	24,000	2,672	2,466	2,672	2,584	26,950	27,000	3,032	2,826	3,032	2,944	29,950	30,000	3,392	3,186	3,392	3,304

* This column must also be used by a qualifying surviving spouse.

(Continued)

2022 Tax Table — *Continued*

30,000

At least	But less than	Single	Married filing jointly *	Married filing separately	Head of a household
30,000	30,050	3,398	3,192	3,398	3,310
30,050	30,100	3,404	3,198	3,404	3,316
30,100	30,150	3,410	3,204	3,410	3,322
30,150	30,200	3,416	3,210	3,416	3,328
30,200	30,250	3,422	3,216	3,422	3,334
30,250	30,300	3,428	3,222	3,428	3,340
30,300	30,350	3,434	3,228	3,434	3,346
30,350	30,400	3,440	3,234	3,440	3,352
30,400	30,450	3,446	3,240	3,446	3,358
30,450	30,500	3,452	3,246	3,452	3,364
30,500	30,550	3,458	3,252	3,458	3,370
30,550	30,600	3,464	3,258	3,464	3,376
30,600	30,650	3,470	3,264	3,470	3,382
30,650	30,700	3,476	3,270	3,476	3,388
30,700	30,750	3,482	3,276	3,482	3,394
30,750	30,800	3,488	3,282	3,488	3,400
30,800	30,850	3,494	3,288	3,494	3,406
30,850	30,900	3,500	3,294	3,500	3,412
30,900	30,950	3,506	3,300	3,506	3,418
30,950	31,000	3,512	3,306	3,512	3,424

31,000

At least	But less than	Single	Married filing jointly *	Married filing separately	Head of a household
31,000	31,050	3,518	3,312	3,518	3,430
31,050	31,100	3,524	3,318	3,524	3,436
31,100	31,150	3,530	3,324	3,530	3,442
31,150	31,200	3,536	3,330	3,536	3,448
31,200	31,250	3,542	3,336	3,542	3,454
31,250	31,300	3,548	3,342	3,548	3,460
31,300	31,350	3,554	3,348	3,554	3,466
31,350	31,400	3,560	3,354	3,560	3,472
31,400	31,450	3,566	3,360	3,566	3,478
31,450	31,500	3,572	3,366	3,572	3,484
31,500	31,550	3,578	3,372	3,578	3,490
31,550	31,600	3,584	3,378	3,584	3,496
31,600	31,650	3,590	3,384	3,590	3,502
31,650	31,700	3,596	3,390	3,596	3,508
31,700	31,750	3,602	3,396	3,602	3,514
31,750	31,800	3,608	3,402	3,608	3,520
31,800	31,850	3,614	3,408	3,614	3,526
31,850	31,900	3,620	3,414	3,620	3,532
31,900	31,950	3,626	3,420	3,626	3,538
31,950	32,000	3,632	3,426	3,632	3,544

32,000

At least	But less than	Single	Married filing jointly *	Married filing separately	Head of a household
32,000	32,050	3,638	3,432	3,638	3,550
32,050	32,100	3,644	3,438	3,644	3,556
32,100	32,150	3,650	3,444	3,650	3,562
32,150	32,200	3,656	3,450	3,656	3,568
32,200	32,250	3,662	3,456	3,662	3,574
32,250	32,300	3,668	3,462	3,668	3,580
32,300	32,350	3,674	3,468	3,674	3,586
32,350	32,400	3,680	3,474	3,680	3,592
32,400	32,450	3,686	3,480	3,686	3,598
32,450	32,500	3,692	3,486	3,692	3,604
32,500	32,550	3,698	3,492	3,698	3,610
32,550	32,600	3,704	3,498	3,704	3,616
32,600	32,650	3,710	3,504	3,710	3,622
32,650	32,700	3,716	3,510	3,716	3,628
32,700	32,750	3,722	3,516	3,722	3,634
32,750	32,800	3,728	3,522	3,728	3,640
32,800	32,850	3,734	3,528	3,734	3,646
32,850	32,900	3,740	3,534	3,740	3,652
32,900	32,950	3,746	3,540	3,746	3,658
32,950	33,000	3,752	3,546	3,752	3,664

33,000

At least	But less than	Single	Married filing jointly *	Married filing separately	Head of a household
33,000	33,050	3,758	3,552	3,758	3,670
33,050	33,100	3,764	3,558	3,764	3,676
33,100	33,150	3,770	3,564	3,770	3,682
33,150	33,200	3,776	3,570	3,776	3,688
33,200	33,250	3,782	3,576	3,782	3,694
33,250	33,300	3,788	3,582	3,788	3,700
33,300	33,350	3,794	3,588	3,794	3,706
33,350	33,400	3,800	3,594	3,800	3,712
33,400	33,450	3,806	3,600	3,806	3,718
33,450	33,500	3,812	3,606	3,812	3,724
33,500	33,550	3,818	3,612	3,818	3,730
33,550	33,600	3,824	3,618	3,824	3,736
33,600	33,650	3,830	3,624	3,830	3,742
33,650	33,700	3,836	3,630	3,836	3,748
33,700	33,750	3,842	3,636	3,842	3,754
33,750	33,800	3,848	3,642	3,848	3,760
33,800	33,850	3,854	3,648	3,854	3,766
33,850	33,900	3,860	3,654	3,860	3,772
33,900	33,950	3,866	3,660	3,866	3,778
33,950	34,000	3,872	3,666	3,872	3,784

34,000

At least	But less than	Single	Married filing jointly *	Married filing separately	Head of a household
34,000	34,050	3,878	3,672	3,878	3,790
34,050	34,100	3,884	3,678	3,884	3,796
34,100	34,150	3,890	3,684	3,890	3,802
34,150	34,200	3,896	3,690	3,896	3,808
34,200	34,250	3,902	3,696	3,902	3,814
34,250	34,300	3,908	3,702	3,908	3,820
34,300	34,350	3,914	3,708	3,914	3,826
34,350	34,400	3,920	3,714	3,920	3,832
34,400	34,450	3,926	3,720	3,926	3,838
34,450	34,500	3,932	3,726	3,932	3,844
34,500	34,550	3,938	3,732	3,938	3,850
34,550	34,600	3,944	3,738	3,944	3,856
34,600	34,650	3,950	3,744	3,950	3,862
34,650	34,700	3,956	3,750	3,956	3,868
34,700	34,750	3,962	3,756	3,962	3,874
34,750	34,800	3,968	3,762	3,968	3,880
34,800	34,850	3,974	3,768	3,974	3,886
34,850	34,900	3,980	3,774	3,980	3,892
34,900	34,950	3,986	3,780	3,986	3,898
34,950	35,000	3,992	3,786	3,992	3,904

35,000

At least	But less than	Single	Married filing jointly *	Married filing separately	Head of a household
35,000	35,050	3,998	3,792	3,998	3,910
35,050	35,100	4,004	3,798	4,004	3,916
35,100	35,150	4,010	3,804	4,010	3,922
35,150	35,200	4,016	3,810	4,016	3,928
35,200	35,250	4,022	3,816	4,022	3,934
35,250	35,300	4,028	3,822	4,028	3,940
35,300	35,350	4,034	3,828	4,034	3,946
35,350	35,400	4,040	3,834	4,040	3,952
35,400	35,450	4,046	3,840	4,046	3,958
35,450	35,500	4,052	3,846	4,052	3,964
35,500	35,550	4,058	3,852	4,058	3,970
35,550	35,600	4,064	3,858	4,064	3,976
35,600	35,650	4,070	3,864	4,070	3,982
35,650	35,700	4,076	3,870	4,076	3,988
35,700	35,750	4,082	3,876	4,082	3,994
35,750	35,800	4,088	3,882	4,088	4,000
35,800	35,850	4,094	3,888	4,094	4,006
35,850	35,900	4,100	3,894	4,100	4,012
35,900	35,950	4,106	3,900	4,106	4,018
35,950	36,000	4,112	3,906	4,112	4,024

36,000

At least	But less than	Single	Married filing jointly *	Married filing separately	Head of a household
36,000	36,050	4,118	3,912	4,118	4,030
36,050	36,100	4,124	3,918	4,124	4,036
36,100	36,150	4,130	3,924	4,130	4,042
36,150	36,200	4,136	3,930	4,136	4,048
36,200	36,250	4,142	3,936	4,142	4,054
36,250	36,300	4,148	3,942	4,148	4,060
36,300	36,350	4,154	3,948	4,154	4,066
36,350	36,400	4,160	3,954	4,160	4,072
36,400	36,450	4,166	3,960	4,166	4,078
36,450	36,500	4,172	3,966	4,172	4,084
36,500	36,550	4,178	3,972	4,178	4,090
36,550	36,600	4,184	3,978	4,184	4,096
36,600	36,650	4,190	3,984	4,190	4,102
36,650	36,700	4,196	3,990	4,196	4,108
36,700	36,750	4,202	3,996	4,202	4,114
36,750	36,800	4,208	4,002	4,208	4,120
36,800	36,850	4,214	4,008	4,214	4,126
36,850	36,900	4,220	4,014	4,220	4,132
36,900	36,950	4,226	4,020	4,226	4,138
36,950	37,000	4,232	4,026	4,232	4,144

37,000

At least	But less than	Single	Married filing jointly *	Married filing separately	Head of a household
37,000	37,050	4,238	4,032	4,238	4,150
37,050	37,100	4,244	4,038	4,244	4,156
37,100	37,150	4,250	4,044	4,250	4,162
37,150	37,200	4,256	4,050	4,256	4,168
37,200	37,250	4,262	4,056	4,262	4,174
37,250	37,300	4,268	4,062	4,268	4,180
37,300	37,350	4,274	4,068	4,274	4,186
37,350	37,400	4,280	4,074	4,280	4,192
37,400	37,450	4,286	4,080	4,286	4,198
37,450	37,500	4,292	4,086	4,292	4,204
37,500	37,550	4,298	4,092	4,298	4,210
37,550	37,600	4,304	4,098	4,304	4,216
37,600	37,650	4,310	4,104	4,310	4,222
37,650	37,700	4,316	4,110	4,316	4,228
37,700	37,750	4,322	4,116	4,322	4,234
37,750	37,800	4,328	4,122	4,328	4,240
37,800	37,850	4,334	4,128	4,334	4,246
37,850	37,900	4,340	4,134	4,340	4,252
37,900	37,950	4,346	4,140	4,346	4,258
37,950	38,000	4,352	4,146	4,352	4,264

38,000

At least	But less than	Single	Married filing jointly *	Married filing separately	Head of a household
38,000	38,050	4,358	4,152	4,358	4,270
38,050	38,100	4,364	4,158	4,364	4,276
38,100	38,150	4,370	4,164	4,370	4,282
38,150	38,200	4,376	4,170	4,376	4,288
38,200	38,250	4,382	4,176	4,382	4,294
38,250	38,300	4,388	4,182	4,388	4,300
38,300	38,350	4,394	4,188	4,394	4,306
38,350	38,400	4,400	4,194	4,400	4,312
38,400	38,450	4,406	4,200	4,406	4,318
38,450	38,500	4,412	4,206	4,412	4,324
38,500	38,550	4,418	4,212	4,418	4,330
38,550	38,600	4,424	4,218	4,424	4,336
38,600	38,650	4,430	4,224	4,430	4,342
38,650	38,700	4,436	4,230	4,436	4,348
38,700	38,750	4,442	4,236	4,442	4,354
38,750	38,800	4,448	4,242	4,448	4,360
38,800	38,850	4,454	4,248	4,454	4,366
38,850	38,900	4,460	4,254	4,460	4,372
38,900	38,950	4,466	4,260	4,466	4,378
38,950	39,000	4,472	4,266	4,472	4,384

(Continued)

* This column must also be used by a qualifying surviving spouse.

2022 Tax Table — *Continued*

If line 15 (taxable income) is—		And you are—			
At least	But less than	Single	Married filing jointly *	Married filing separately	Head of a household
		Your tax is—			

39,000

At least	But less than	Single	Married filing jointly *	Married filing separately	Head of a household
39,000	39,050	4,478	4,272	4,478	4,390
39,050	39,100	4,484	4,278	4,484	4,396
39,100	39,150	4,490	4,284	4,490	4,402
39,150	39,200	4,496	4,290	4,496	4,408
39,200	39,250	4,502	4,296	4,502	4,414
39,250	39,300	4,508	4,302	4,508	4,420
39,300	39,350	4,514	4,308	4,514	4,426
39,350	39,400	4,520	4,314	4,520	4,432
39,400	39,450	4,526	4,320	4,526	4,438
39,450	39,500	4,532	4,326	4,532	4,444
39,500	39,550	4,538	4,332	4,538	4,450
39,550	39,600	4,544	4,338	4,544	4,456
39,600	39,650	4,550	4,344	4,550	4,462
39,650	39,700	4,556	4,350	4,556	4,468
39,700	39,750	4,562	4,356	4,562	4,474
39,750	39,800	4,568	4,362	4,568	4,480
39,800	39,850	4,574	4,368	4,574	4,486
39,850	39,900	4,580	4,374	4,580	4,492
39,900	39,950	4,586	4,380	4,586	4,498
39,950	40,000	4,592	4,386	4,592	4,504

40,000

At least	But less than	Single	Married filing jointly *	Married filing separately	Head of a household
40,000	40,050	4,598	4,392	4,598	4,510
40,050	40,100	4,604	4,398	4,604	4,516
40,100	40,150	4,610	4,404	4,610	4,522
40,150	40,200	4,616	4,410	4,616	4,528
40,200	40,250	4,622	4,416	4,622	4,534
40,250	40,300	4,628	4,422	4,628	4,540
40,300	40,350	4,634	4,428	4,634	4,546
40,350	40,400	4,640	4,434	4,640	4,552
40,400	40,450	4,646	4,440	4,646	4,558
40,450	40,500	4,652	4,446	4,652	4,564
40,500	40,550	4,658	4,452	4,658	4,570
40,550	40,600	4,664	4,458	4,664	4,576
40,600	40,650	4,670	4,464	4,670	4,582
40,650	40,700	4,676	4,470	4,676	4,588
40,700	40,750	4,682	4,476	4,682	4,594
40,750	40,800	4,688	4,482	4,688	4,600
40,800	40,850	4,694	4,488	4,694	4,606
40,850	40,900	4,700	4,494	4,700	4,612
40,900	40,950	4,706	4,500	4,706	4,618
40,950	41,000	4,712	4,506	4,712	4,624

41,000

At least	But less than	Single	Married filing jointly *	Married filing separately	Head of a household
41,000	41,050	4,718	4,512	4,718	4,630
41,050	41,100	4,724	4,518	4,724	4,636
41,100	41,150	4,730	4,524	4,730	4,642
41,150	41,200	4,736	4,530	4,736	4,648
41,200	41,250	4,742	4,536	4,742	4,654
41,250	41,300	4,748	4,542	4,748	4,660
41,300	41,350	4,754	4,548	4,754	4,666
41,350	41,400	4,760	4,554	4,760	4,672
41,400	41,450	4,766	4,560	4,766	4,678
41,450	41,500	4,772	4,566	4,772	4,684
41,500	41,550	4,778	4,572	4,778	4,690
41,550	41,600	4,784	4,578	4,784	4,696
41,600	41,650	4,790	4,584	4,790	4,702
41,650	41,700	4,796	4,590	4,796	4,708
41,700	41,750	4,802	4,596	4,802	4,714
41,750	41,800	4,808	4,602	4,808	4,720
41,800	41,850	4,819	4,608	4,819	4,726
41,850	41,900	4,830	4,614	4,830	4,732
41,900	41,950	4,841	4,620	4,841	4,738
41,950	42,000	4,852	4,626	4,852	4,744

42,000

At least	But less than	Single	Married filing jointly *	Married filing separately	Head of a household
42,000	42,050	4,863	4,632	4,863	4,750
42,050	42,100	4,874	4,638	4,874	4,756
42,100	42,150	4,885	4,644	4,885	4,762
42,150	42,200	4,896	4,650	4,896	4,768
42,200	42,250	4,907	4,656	4,907	4,774
42,250	42,300	4,918	4,662	4,918	4,780
42,300	42,350	4,929	4,668	4,929	4,786
42,350	42,400	4,940	4,674	4,940	4,792
42,400	42,450	4,951	4,680	4,951	4,798
42,450	42,500	4,962	4,686	4,962	4,804
42,500	42,550	4,973	4,692	4,973	4,810
42,550	42,600	4,984	4,698	4,984	4,816
42,600	42,650	4,995	4,704	4,995	4,822
42,650	42,700	5,006	4,710	5,006	4,828
42,700	42,750	5,017	4,716	5,017	4,834
42,750	42,800	5,028	4,722	5,028	4,840
42,800	42,850	5,039	4,728	5,039	4,846
42,850	42,900	5,050	4,734	5,050	4,852
42,900	42,950	5,061	4,740	5,061	4,858
42,950	43,000	5,072	4,746	5,072	4,864

43,000

At least	But less than	Single	Married filing jointly *	Married filing separately	Head of a household
43,000	43,050	5,083	4,752	5,083	4,870
43,050	43,100	5,094	4,758	5,094	4,876
43,100	43,150	5,105	4,764	5,105	4,882
43,150	43,200	5,116	4,770	5,116	4,888
43,200	43,250	5,127	4,776	5,127	4,894
43,250	43,300	5,138	4,782	5,138	4,900
43,300	43,350	5,149	4,788	5,149	4,906
43,350	43,400	5,160	4,794	5,160	4,912
43,400	43,450	5,171	4,800	5,171	4,918
43,450	43,500	5,182	4,806	5,182	4,924
43,500	43,550	5,193	4,812	5,193	4,930
43,550	43,600	5,204	4,818	5,204	4,936
43,600	43,650	5,215	4,824	5,215	4,942
43,650	43,700	5,226	4,830	5,226	4,948
43,700	43,750	5,237	4,836	5,237	4,954
43,750	43,800	5,248	4,842	5,248	4,960
43,800	43,850	5,259	4,848	5,259	4,966
43,850	43,900	5,270	4,854	5,270	4,972
43,900	43,950	5,281	4,860	5,281	4,978
43,950	44,000	5,292	4,866	5,292	4,984

44,000

At least	But less than	Single	Married filing jointly *	Married filing separately	Head of a household
44,000	44,050	5,303	4,872	5,303	4,990
44,050	44,100	5,314	4,878	5,314	4,996
44,100	44,150	5,325	4,884	5,325	5,002
44,150	44,200	5,336	4,890	5,336	5,008
44,200	44,250	5,347	4,896	5,347	5,014
44,250	44,300	5,358	4,902	5,358	5,020
44,300	44,350	5,369	4,908	5,369	5,026
44,350	44,400	5,380	4,914	5,380	5,032
44,400	44,450	5,391	4,920	5,391	5,038
44,450	44,500	5,402	4,926	5,402	5,044
44,500	44,550	5,413	4,932	5,413	5,050
44,550	44,600	5,424	4,938	5,424	5,056
44,600	44,650	5,435	4,944	5,435	5,062
44,650	44,700	5,446	4,950	5,446	5,068
44,700	44,750	5,457	4,956	5,457	5,074
44,750	44,800	5,468	4,962	5,468	5,080
44,800	44,850	5,479	4,968	5,479	5,086
44,850	44,900	5,490	4,974	5,490	5,092
44,900	44,950	5,501	4,980	5,501	5,098
44,950	45,000	5,512	4,986	5,512	5,104

45,000

At least	But less than	Single	Married filing jointly *	Married filing separately	Head of a household
45,000	45,050	5,523	4,992	5,523	5,110
45,050	45,100	5,534	4,998	5,534	5,116
45,100	45,150	5,545	5,004	5,545	5,122
45,150	45,200	5,556	5,010	5,556	5,128
45,200	45,250	5,567	5,016	5,567	5,134
45,250	45,300	5,578	5,022	5,578	5,140
45,300	45,350	5,589	5,028	5,589	5,146
45,350	45,400	5,600	5,034	5,600	5,152
45,400	45,450	5,611	5,040	5,611	5,158
45,450	45,500	5,622	5,046	5,622	5,164
45,500	45,550	5,633	5,052	5,633	5,170
45,550	45,600	5,644	5,058	5,644	5,176
45,600	45,650	5,655	5,064	5,655	5,182
45,650	45,700	5,666	5,070	5,666	5,188
45,700	45,750	5,677	5,076	5,677	5,194
45,750	45,800	5,688	5,082	5,688	5,200
45,800	45,850	5,699	5,088	5,699	5,206
45,850	45,900	5,710	5,094	5,710	5,212
45,900	45,950	5,721	5,100	5,721	5,218
45,950	46,000	5,732	5,106	5,732	5,224

46,000

At least	But less than	Single	Married filing jointly *	Married filing separately	Head of a household
46,000	46,050	5,743	5,112	5,743	5,230
46,050	46,100	5,754	5,118	5,754	5,236
46,100	46,150	5,765	5,124	5,765	5,242
46,150	46,200	5,776	5,130	5,776	5,248
46,200	46,250	5,787	5,136	5,787	5,254
46,250	46,300	5,798	5,142	5,798	5,260
46,300	46,350	5,809	5,148	5,809	5,266
46,350	46,400	5,820	5,154	5,820	5,272
46,400	46,450	5,831	5,160	5,831	5,278
46,450	46,500	5,842	5,166	5,842	5,284
46,500	46,550	5,853	5,172	5,853	5,290
46,550	46,600	5,864	5,178	5,864	5,296
46,600	46,650	5,875	5,184	5,875	5,302
46,650	46,700	5,886	5,190	5,886	5,308
46,700	46,750	5,897	5,196	5,897	5,314
46,750	46,800	5,908	5,202	5,908	5,320
46,800	46,850	5,919	5,208	5,919	5,326
46,850	46,900	5,930	5,214	5,930	5,332
46,900	46,950	5,941	5,220	5,941	5,338
46,950	47,000	5,952	5,226	5,952	5,344

47,000

At least	But less than	Single	Married filing jointly *	Married filing separately	Head of a household
47,000	47,050	5,963	5,232	5,963	5,350
47,050	47,100	5,974	5,238	5,974	5,356
47,100	47,150	5,985	5,244	5,985	5,362
47,150	47,200	5,996	5,250	5,996	5,368
47,200	47,250	6,007	5,256	6,007	5,374
47,250	47,300	6,018	5,262	6,018	5,380
47,300	47,350	6,029	5,268	6,029	5,386
47,350	47,400	6,040	5,274	6,040	5,392
47,400	47,450	6,051	5,280	6,051	5,398
47,450	47,500	6,062	5,286	6,062	5,404
47,500	47,550	6,073	5,292	6,073	5,410
47,550	47,600	6,084	5,298	6,084	5,416
47,600	47,650	6,095	5,304	6,095	5,422
47,650	47,700	6,106	5,310	6,106	5,428
47,700	47,750	6,117	5,316	6,117	5,434
47,750	47,800	6,128	5,322	6,128	5,440
47,800	47,850	6,139	5,328	6,139	5,446
47,850	47,900	6,150	5,334	6,150	5,452
47,900	47,950	6,161	5,340	6,161	5,458
47,950	48,000	6,172	5,346	6,172	5,464

* This column must also be used by a qualifying surviving spouse.

(Continued)

2022 Tax Table — *Continued*

48,000 / 49,000 / 50,000

At least	But less than	Single	Married filing jointly *	Married filing separately	Head of a household
48,000					
48,000	48,050	6,183	5,352	6,183	5,470
48,050	48,100	6,194	5,358	6,194	5,476
48,100	48,150	6,205	5,364	6,205	5,482
48,150	48,200	6,216	5,370	6,216	5,488
48,200	48,250	6,227	5,376	6,227	5,494
48,250	48,300	6,238	5,382	6,238	5,500
48,300	48,350	6,249	5,388	6,249	5,506
48,350	48,400	6,260	5,394	6,260	5,512
48,400	48,450	6,271	5,400	6,271	5,518
48,450	48,500	6,282	5,406	6,282	5,524
48,500	48,550	6,293	5,412	6,293	5,530
48,550	48,600	6,304	5,418	6,304	5,536
48,600	48,650	6,315	5,424	6,315	5,542
48,650	48,700	6,326	5,430	6,326	5,548
48,700	48,750	6,337	5,436	6,337	5,554
48,750	48,800	6,348	5,442	6,348	5,560
48,800	48,850	6,359	5,448	6,359	5,566
48,850	48,900	6,370	5,454	6,370	5,572
48,900	48,950	6,381	5,460	6,381	5,578
48,950	49,000	6,392	5,466	6,392	5,584
49,000					
49,000	49,050	6,403	5,472	6,403	5,590
49,050	49,100	6,414	5,478	6,414	5,596
49,100	49,150	6,425	5,484	6,425	5,602
49,150	49,200	6,436	5,490	6,436	5,608
49,200	49,250	6,447	5,496	6,447	5,614
49,250	49,300	6,458	5,502	6,458	5,620
49,300	49,350	6,469	5,508	6,469	5,626
49,350	49,400	6,480	5,514	6,480	5,632
49,400	49,450	6,491	5,520	6,491	5,638
49,450	49,500	6,502	5,526	6,502	5,644
49,500	49,550	6,513	5,532	6,513	5,650
49,550	49,600	6,524	5,538	6,524	5,656
49,600	49,650	6,535	5,544	6,535	5,662
49,650	49,700	6,546	5,550	6,546	5,668
49,700	49,750	6,557	5,556	6,557	5,674
49,750	49,800	6,568	5,562	6,568	5,680
49,800	49,850	6,579	5,568	6,579	5,686
49,850	49,900	6,590	5,574	6,590	5,692
49,900	49,950	6,601	5,580	6,601	5,698
49,950	50,000	6,612	5,586	6,612	5,704
50,000					
50,000	50,050	6,623	5,592	6,623	5,710
50,050	50,100	6,634	5,598	6,634	5,716
50,100	50,150	6,645	5,604	6,645	5,722
50,150	50,200	6,656	5,610	6,656	5,728
50,200	50,250	6,667	5,616	6,667	5,734
50,250	50,300	6,678	5,622	6,678	5,740
50,300	50,350	6,689	5,628	6,689	5,746
50,350	50,400	6,700	5,634	6,700	5,752
50,400	50,450	6,711	5,640	6,711	5,758
50,450	50,500	6,722	5,646	6,722	5,764
50,500	50,550	6,733	5,652	6,733	5,770
50,550	50,600	6,744	5,658	6,744	5,776
50,600	50,650	6,755	5,664	6,755	5,782
50,650	50,700	6,766	5,670	6,766	5,788
50,700	50,750	6,777	5,676	6,777	5,794
50,750	50,800	6,788	5,682	6,788	5,800
50,800	50,850	6,799	5,688	6,799	5,806
50,850	50,900	6,810	5,694	6,810	5,812
50,900	50,950	6,821	5,700	6,821	5,818
50,950	51,000	6,832	5,706	6,832	5,824

51,000 / 52,000 / 53,000

At least	But less than	Single	Married filing jointly *	Married filing separately	Head of a household
51,000					
51,000	51,050	6,843	5,712	6,843	5,830
51,050	51,100	6,854	5,718	6,854	5,836
51,100	51,150	6,865	5,724	6,865	5,842
51,150	51,200	6,876	5,730	6,876	5,848
51,200	51,250	6,887	5,736	6,887	5,854
51,250	51,300	6,898	5,742	6,898	5,860
51,300	51,350	6,909	5,748	6,909	5,866
51,350	51,400	6,920	5,754	6,920	5,872
51,400	51,450	6,931	5,760	6,931	5,878
51,450	51,500	6,942	5,766	6,942	5,884
51,500	51,550	6,953	5,772	6,953	5,890
51,550	51,600	6,964	5,778	6,964	5,896
51,600	51,650	6,975	5,784	6,975	5,902
51,650	51,700	6,986	5,790	6,986	5,908
51,700	51,750	6,997	5,796	6,997	5,914
51,750	51,800	7,008	5,802	7,008	5,920
51,800	51,850	7,019	5,808	7,019	5,926
51,850	51,900	7,030	5,814	7,030	5,932
51,900	51,950	7,041	5,820	7,041	5,938
51,950	52,000	7,052	5,826	7,052	5,944
52,000					
52,000	52,050	7,063	5,832	7,063	5,950
52,050	52,100	7,074	5,838	7,074	5,956
52,100	52,150	7,085	5,844	7,085	5,962
52,150	52,200	7,096	5,850	7,096	5,968
52,200	52,250	7,107	5,856	7,107	5,974
52,250	52,300	7,118	5,862	7,118	5,980
52,300	52,350	7,129	5,868	7,129	5,986
52,350	52,400	7,140	5,874	7,140	5,992
52,400	52,450	7,151	5,880	7,151	5,998
52,450	52,500	7,162	5,886	7,162	6,004
52,500	52,550	7,173	5,892	7,173	6,010
52,550	52,600	7,184	5,898	7,184	6,016
52,600	52,650	7,195	5,904	7,195	6,022
52,650	52,700	7,206	5,910	7,206	6,028
52,700	52,750	7,217	5,916	7,217	6,034
52,750	52,800	7,228	5,922	7,228	6,040
52,800	52,850	7,239	5,928	7,239	6,046
52,850	52,900	7,250	5,934	7,250	6,052
52,900	52,950	7,261	5,940	7,261	6,058
52,950	53,000	7,272	5,946	7,272	6,064
53,000					
53,000	53,050	7,283	5,952	7,283	6,070
53,050	53,100	7,294	5,958	7,294	6,076
53,100	53,150	7,305	5,964	7,305	6,082
53,150	53,200	7,316	5,970	7,316	6,088
53,200	53,250	7,327	5,976	7,327	6,094
53,250	53,300	7,338	5,982	7,338	6,100
53,300	53,350	7,349	5,988	7,349	6,106
53,350	53,400	7,360	5,994	7,360	6,112
53,400	53,450	7,371	6,000	7,371	6,118
53,450	53,500	7,382	6,006	7,382	6,124
53,500	53,550	7,393	6,012	7,393	6,130
53,550	53,600	7,404	6,018	7,404	6,136
53,600	53,650	7,415	6,024	7,415	6,142
53,650	53,700	7,426	6,030	7,426	6,148
53,700	53,750	7,437	6,036	7,437	6,154
53,750	53,800	7,448	6,042	7,448	6,160
53,800	53,850	7,459	6,048	7,459	6,166
53,850	53,900	7,470	6,054	7,470	6,172
53,900	53,950	7,481	6,060	7,481	6,178
53,950	54,000	7,492	6,066	7,492	6,184

54,000 / 55,000 / 56,000

At least	But less than	Single	Married filing jointly *	Married filing separately	Head of a household
54,000					
54,000	54,050	7,503	6,072	7,503	6,190
54,050	54,100	7,514	6,078	7,514	6,196
54,100	54,150	7,525	6,084	7,525	6,202
54,150	54,200	7,536	6,090	7,536	6,208
54,200	54,250	7,547	6,096	7,547	6,214
54,250	54,300	7,558	6,102	7,558	6,220
54,300	54,350	7,569	6,108	7,569	6,226
54,350	54,400	7,580	6,114	7,580	6,232
54,400	54,450	7,591	6,120	7,591	6,238
54,450	54,500	7,602	6,126	7,602	6,244
54,500	54,550	7,613	6,132	7,613	6,250
54,550	54,600	7,624	6,138	7,624	6,256
54,600	54,650	7,635	6,144	7,635	6,262
54,650	54,700	7,646	6,150	7,646	6,268
54,700	54,750	7,657	6,156	7,657	6,274
54,750	54,800	7,668	6,162	7,668	6,280
54,800	54,850	7,679	6,168	7,679	6,286
54,850	54,900	7,690	6,174	7,690	6,292
54,900	54,950	7,701	6,180	7,701	6,298
54,950	55,000	7,712	6,186	7,712	6,304
55,000					
55,000	55,050	7,723	6,192	7,723	6,310
55,050	55,100	7,734	6,198	7,734	6,316
55,100	55,150	7,745	6,204	7,745	6,322
55,150	55,200	7,756	6,210	7,756	6,328
55,200	55,250	7,767	6,216	7,767	6,334
55,250	55,300	7,778	6,222	7,778	6,340
55,300	55,350	7,789	6,228	7,789	6,346
55,350	55,400	7,800	6,234	7,800	6,352
55,400	55,450	7,811	6,240	7,811	6,358
55,450	55,500	7,822	6,246	7,822	6,364
55,500	55,550	7,833	6,252	7,833	6,370
55,550	55,600	7,844	6,258	7,844	6,376
55,600	55,650	7,855	6,264	7,855	6,382
55,650	55,700	7,866	6,270	7,866	6,388
55,700	55,750	7,877	6,276	7,877	6,394
55,750	55,800	7,888	6,282	7,888	6,400
55,800	55,850	7,899	6,288	7,899	6,406
55,850	55,900	7,910	6,294	7,910	6,412
55,900	55,950	7,921	6,300	7,921	6,421
55,950	56,000	7,932	6,306	7,932	6,432
56,000					
56,000	56,050	7,943	6,312	7,943	6,443
56,050	56,100	7,954	6,318	7,954	6,454
56,100	56,150	7,965	6,324	7,965	6,465
56,150	56,200	7,976	6,330	7,976	6,476
56,200	56,250	7,987	6,336	7,987	6,487
56,250	56,300	7,998	6,342	7,998	6,498
56,300	56,350	8,009	6,348	8,009	6,509
56,350	56,400	8,020	6,354	8,020	6,520
56,400	56,450	8,031	6,360	8,031	6,531
56,450	56,500	8,042	6,366	8,042	6,542
56,500	56,550	8,053	6,372	8,053	6,553
56,550	56,600	8,064	6,378	8,064	6,564
56,600	56,650	8,075	6,384	8,075	6,575
56,650	56,700	8,086	6,390	8,086	6,586
56,700	56,750	8,097	6,396	8,097	6,597
56,750	56,800	8,108	6,402	8,108	6,608
56,800	56,850	8,119	6,408	8,119	6,619
56,850	56,900	8,130	6,414	8,130	6,630
56,900	56,950	8,141	6,420	8,141	6,641
56,950	57,000	8,152	6,426	8,152	6,652

(Continued)

* This column must also be used by a qualifying surviving spouse.

DRAFT AS OF

If line 15 (taxable income) is—		And you are—			
At least	But less than	Single	Married filing jointly *	Married filing separately	Head of a household
		Your tax is—			

57,000

At least	But less than	Single	Married filing jointly *	Married filing separately	Head of a household
57,000	57,050	8,163	6,432	8,163	6,663
57,050	57,100	8,174	6,438	8,174	6,674
57,100	57,150	8,185	6,444	8,185	6,685
57,150	57,200	8,196	6,450	8,196	6,696
57,200	57,250	8,207	6,456	8,207	6,707
57,250	57,300	8,218	6,462	8,218	6,718
57,300	57,350	8,229	6,468	8,229	6,729
57,350	57,400	8,240	6,474	8,240	6,740
57,400	57,450	8,251	6,480	8,251	6,751
57,450	57,500	8,262	6,486	8,262	6,762
57,500	57,550	8,273	6,492	8,273	6,773
57,550	57,600	8,284	6,498	8,284	6,784
57,600	57,650	8,295	6,504	8,295	6,795
57,650	57,700	8,306	6,510	8,306	6,806
57,700	57,750	8,317	6,516	8,317	6,817
57,750	57,800	8,328	6,522	8,328	6,828
57,800	57,850	8,339	6,528	8,339	6,839
57,850	57,900	8,350	6,534	8,350	6,850
57,900	57,950	8,361	6,540	8,361	6,861
57,950	58,000	8,372	6,546	8,372	6,872

58,000

At least	But less than	Single	Married filing jointly *	Married filing separately	Head of a household
58,000	58,050	8,383	6,552	8,383	6,883
58,050	58,100	8,394	6,558	8,394	6,894
58,100	58,150	8,405	6,564	8,405	6,905
58,150	58,200	8,416	6,570	8,416	6,916
58,200	58,250	8,427	6,576	8,427	6,927
58,250	58,300	8,438	6,582	8,438	6,938
58,300	58,350	8,449	6,588	8,449	6,949
58,350	58,400	8,460	6,594	8,460	6,960
58,400	58,450	8,471	6,600	8,471	6,971
58,450	58,500	8,482	6,606	8,482	6,982
58,500	58,550	8,493	6,612	8,493	6,993
58,550	58,600	8,504	6,618	8,504	7,004
58,600	58,650	8,515	6,624	8,515	7,015
58,650	58,700	8,526	6,630	8,526	7,026
58,700	58,750	8,537	6,636	8,537	7,037
58,750	58,800	8,548	6,642	8,548	7,048
58,800	58,850	8,559	6,648	8,559	7,059
58,850	58,900	8,570	6,654	8,570	7,070
58,900	58,950	8,581	6,660	8,581	7,081
58,950	59,000	8,592	6,666	8,592	7,092

59,000

At least	But less than	Single	Married filing jointly *	Married filing separately	Head of a household
59,000	59,050	8,603	6,672	8,603	7,103
59,050	59,100	8,614	6,678	8,614	7,114
59,100	59,150	8,625	6,684	8,625	7,125
59,150	59,200	8,636	6,690	8,636	7,136
59,200	59,250	8,647	6,696	8,647	7,147
59,250	59,300	8,658	6,702	8,658	7,158
59,300	59,350	8,669	6,708	8,669	7,169
59,350	59,400	8,680	6,714	8,680	7,180
59,400	59,450	8,691	6,720	8,691	7,191
59,450	59,500	8,702	6,726	8,702	7,202
59,500	59,550	8,713	6,732	8,713	7,213
59,550	59,600	8,724	6,738	8,724	7,224
59,600	59,650	8,735	6,744	8,735	7,235
59,650	59,700	8,746	6,750	8,746	7,246
59,700	59,750	8,757	6,756	8,757	7,257
59,750	59,800	8,768	6,762	8,768	7,268
59,800	59,850	8,779	6,768	8,779	7,279
59,850	59,900	8,790	6,774	8,790	7,290
59,900	59,950	8,801	6,780	8,801	7,301
59,950	60,000	8,812	6,786	8,812	7,312

60,000

At least	But less than	Single	Married filing jointly *	Married filing separately	Head of a household
60,000	60,050	8,823	6,792	8,823	7,323
60,050	60,100	8,834	6,798	8,834	7,334
60,100	60,150	8,845	6,804	8,845	7,345
60,150	60,200	8,856	6,810	8,856	7,356
60,200	60,250	8,867	6,816	8,867	7,367
60,250	60,300	8,878	6,822	8,878	7,378
60,300	60,350	8,889	6,828	8,889	7,389
60,350	60,400	8,900	6,834	8,900	7,400
60,400	60,450	8,911	6,840	8,911	7,411
60,450	60,500	8,922	6,846	8,922	7,422
60,500	60,550	8,933	6,852	8,933	7,433
60,550	60,600	8,944	6,858	8,944	7,444
60,600	60,650	8,955	6,864	8,955	7,455
60,650	60,700	8,966	6,870	8,966	7,466
60,700	60,750	8,977	6,876	8,977	7,477
60,750	60,800	8,988	6,882	8,988	7,488
60,800	60,850	8,999	6,888	8,999	7,499
60,850	60,900	9,010	6,894	9,010	7,510
60,900	60,950	9,021	6,900	9,021	7,521
60,950	61,000	9,032	6,906	9,032	7,532

61,000

At least	But less than	Single	Married filing jointly *	Married filing separately	Head of a household
61,000	61,050	9,043	6,912	9,043	7,543
61,050	61,100	9,054	6,918	9,054	7,554
61,100	61,150	9,065	6,924	9,065	7,565
61,150	61,200	9,076	6,930	9,076	7,576
61,200	61,250	9,087	6,936	9,087	7,587
61,250	61,300	9,098	6,942	9,098	7,598
61,300	61,350	9,109	6,948	9,109	7,609
61,350	61,400	9,120	6,954	9,120	7,620
61,400	61,450	9,131	6,960	9,131	7,631
61,450	61,500	9,142	6,966	9,142	7,642
61,500	61,550	9,153	6,972	9,153	7,653
61,550	61,600	9,164	6,978	9,164	7,664
61,600	61,650	9,175	6,984	9,175	7,675
61,650	61,700	9,186	6,990	9,186	7,686
61,700	61,750	9,197	6,996	9,197	7,697
61,750	61,800	9,208	7,002	9,208	7,708
61,800	61,850	9,219	7,008	9,219	7,719
61,850	61,900	9,230	7,014	9,230	7,730
61,900	61,950	9,241	7,020	9,241	7,741
61,950	62,000	9,252	7,026	9,252	7,752

62,000

At least	But less than	Single	Married filing jointly *	Married filing separately	Head of a household
62,000	62,050	9,263	7,032	9,263	7,763
62,050	62,100	9,274	7,038	9,274	7,774
62,100	62,150	9,285	7,044	9,285	7,785
62,150	62,200	9,296	7,050	9,296	7,796
62,200	62,250	9,307	7,056	9,307	7,807
62,250	62,300	9,318	7,062	9,318	7,818
62,300	62,350	9,329	7,068	9,329	7,829
62,350	62,400	9,340	7,074	9,340	7,840
62,400	62,450	9,351	7,080	9,351	7,851
62,450	62,500	9,362	7,086	9,362	7,862
62,500	62,550	9,373	7,092	9,373	7,873
62,550	62,600	9,384	7,098	9,384	7,884
62,600	62,650	9,395	7,104	9,395	7,895
62,650	62,700	9,406	7,110	9,406	7,906
62,700	62,750	9,417	7,116	9,417	7,917
62,750	62,800	9,428	7,122	9,428	7,928
62,800	62,850	9,439	7,128	9,439	7,939
62,850	62,900	9,450	7,134	9,450	7,950
62,900	62,950	9,461	7,140	9,461	7,961
62,950	63,000	9,472	7,146	9,472	7,972

63,000

At least	But less than	Single	Married filing jointly *	Married filing separately	Head of a household
63,000	63,050	9,483	7,152	9,483	7,983
63,050	63,100	9,494	7,158	9,494	7,994
63,100	63,150	9,505	7,164	9,505	8,005
63,150	63,200	9,516	7,170	9,516	8,016
63,200	63,250	9,527	7,176	9,527	8,027
63,250	63,300	9,538	7,182	9,538	8,038
63,300	63,350	9,549	7,188	9,549	8,049
63,350	63,400	9,560	7,194	9,560	8,060
63,400	63,450	9,571	7,200	9,571	8,071
63,450	63,500	9,582	7,206	9,582	8,082
63,500	63,550	9,593	7,212	9,593	8,093
63,550	63,600	9,604	7,218	9,604	8,104
63,600	63,650	9,615	7,224	9,615	8,115
63,650	63,700	9,626	7,230	9,626	8,126
63,700	63,750	9,637	7,236	9,637	8,137
63,750	63,800	9,648	7,242	9,648	8,148
63,800	63,850	9,659	7,248	9,659	8,159
63,850	63,900	9,670	7,254	9,670	8,170
63,900	63,950	9,681	7,260	9,681	8,181
63,950	64,000	9,692	7,266	9,692	8,192

64,000

At least	But less than	Single	Married filing jointly *	Married filing separately	Head of a household
64,000	64,050	9,703	7,272	9,703	8,203
64,050	64,100	9,714	7,278	9,714	8,214
64,100	64,150	9,725	7,284	9,725	8,225
64,150	64,200	9,736	7,290	9,736	8,236
64,200	64,250	9,747	7,296	9,747	8,247
64,250	64,300	9,758	7,302	9,758	8,258
64,300	64,350	9,769	7,308	9,769	8,269
64,350	64,400	9,780	7,314	9,780	8,280
64,400	64,450	9,791	7,320	9,791	8,291
64,450	64,500	9,802	7,326	9,802	8,302
64,500	64,550	9,813	7,332	9,813	8,313
64,550	64,600	9,824	7,338	9,824	8,324
64,600	64,650	9,835	7,344	9,835	8,335
64,650	64,700	9,846	7,350	9,846	8,346
64,700	64,750	9,857	7,356	9,857	8,357
64,750	64,800	9,868	7,362	9,868	8,368
64,800	64,850	9,879	7,368	9,879	8,379
64,850	64,900	9,890	7,374	9,890	8,390
64,900	64,950	9,901	7,380	9,901	8,401
64,950	65,000	9,912	7,386	9,912	8,412

65,000

At least	But less than	Single	Married filing jointly *	Married filing separately	Head of a household
65,000	65,050	9,923	7,392	9,923	8,423
65,050	65,100	9,934	7,398	9,934	8,434
65,100	65,150	9,945	7,404	9,945	8,445
65,150	65,200	9,956	7,410	9,956	8,456
65,200	65,250	9,967	7,416	9,967	8,467
65,250	65,300	9,978	7,422	9,978	8,478
65,300	65,350	9,989	7,428	9,989	8,489
65,350	65,400	10,000	7,434	10,000	8,500
65,400	65,450	10,011	7,440	10,011	8,511
65,450	65,500	10,022	7,446	10,022	8,522
65,500	65,550	10,033	7,452	10,033	8,533
65,550	65,600	10,044	7,458	10,044	8,544
65,600	65,650	10,055	7,464	10,055	8,555
65,650	65,700	10,066	7,470	10,066	8,566
65,700	65,750	10,077	7,476	10,077	8,577
65,750	65,800	10,088	7,482	10,088	8,588
65,800	65,850	10,099	7,488	10,099	8,599
65,850	65,900	10,110	7,494	10,110	8,610
65,900	65,950	10,121	7,500	10,121	8,621
65,950	66,000	10,132	7,506	10,132	8,632

* This column must also be used by a qualifying surviving spouse.

(Continued)

2022 Tax Table — *Continued*

66,000

At least	But less than	Single	Married filing jointly *	Married filing separately	Head of a household
66,000	66,050	10,143	7,512	10,143	8,643
66,050	66,100	10,154	7,518	10,154	8,654
66,100	66,150	10,165	7,524	10,165	8,665
66,150	66,200	10,176	7,530	10,176	8,676
66,200	66,250	10,187	7,536	10,187	8,687
66,250	66,300	10,198	7,542	10,198	8,698
66,300	66,350	10,209	7,548	10,209	8,709
66,350	66,400	10,220	7,554	10,220	8,720
66,400	66,450	10,231	7,560	10,231	8,731
66,450	66,500	10,242	7,566	10,242	8,742
66,500	66,550	10,253	7,572	10,253	8,753
66,550	66,600	10,264	7,578	10,264	8,764
66,600	66,650	10,275	7,584	10,275	8,775
66,650	66,700	10,286	7,590	10,286	8,786
66,700	66,750	10,297	7,596	10,297	8,797
66,750	66,800	10,308	7,602	10,308	8,808
66,800	66,850	10,319	7,608	10,319	8,819
66,850	66,900	10,330	7,614	10,330	8,830
66,900	66,950	10,341	7,620	10,341	8,841
66,950	67,000	10,352	7,626	10,352	8,852

67,000

At least	But less than	Single	Married filing jointly *	Married filing separately	Head of a household
67,000	67,050	10,363	7,632	10,363	8,863
67,050	67,100	10,374	7,638	10,374	8,874
67,100	67,150	10,385	7,644	10,385	8,885
67,150	67,200	10,396	7,650	10,396	8,896
67,200	67,250	10,407	7,656	10,407	8,907
67,250	67,300	10,418	7,662	10,418	8,918
67,300	67,350	10,429	7,668	10,429	8,929
67,350	67,400	10,440	7,674	10,440	8,940
67,400	67,450	10,451	7,680	10,451	8,951
67,450	67,500	10,462	7,686	10,462	8,962
67,500	67,550	10,473	7,692	10,473	8,973
67,550	67,600	10,484	7,698	10,484	8,984
67,600	67,650	10,495	7,704	10,495	8,995
67,650	67,700	10,506	7,710	10,506	9,006
67,700	67,750	10,517	7,716	10,517	9,017
67,750	67,800	10,528	7,722	10,528	9,028
67,800	67,850	10,539	7,728	10,539	9,039
67,850	67,900	10,550	7,734	10,550	9,050
67,900	67,950	10,561	7,740	10,561	9,061
67,950	68,000	10,572	7,746	10,572	9,072

68,000

At least	But less than	Single	Married filing jointly *	Married filing separately	Head of a household
68,000	68,050	10,583	7,752	10,583	9,083
68,050	68,100	10,594	7,758	10,594	9,094
68,100	68,150	10,605	7,764	10,605	9,105
68,150	68,200	10,616	7,770	10,616	9,116
68,200	68,250	10,627	7,776	10,627	9,127
68,250	68,300	10,638	7,782	10,638	9,138
68,300	68,350	10,649	7,788	10,649	9,149
68,350	68,400	10,660	7,794	10,660	9,160
68,400	68,450	10,671	7,800	10,671	9,171
68,450	68,500	10,682	7,806	10,682	9,182
68,500	68,550	10,693	7,812	10,693	9,193
68,550	68,600	10,704	7,818	10,704	9,204
68,600	68,650	10,715	7,824	10,715	9,215
68,650	68,700	10,726	7,830	10,726	9,226
68,700	68,750	10,737	7,836	10,737	9,237
68,750	68,800	10,748	7,842	10,748	9,248
68,800	68,850	10,759	7,848	10,759	9,259
68,850	68,900	10,770	7,854	10,770	9,270
68,900	68,950	10,781	7,860	10,781	9,281
68,950	69,000	10,792	7,866	10,792	9,292

69,000

At least	But less than	Single	Married filing jointly *	Married filing separately	Head of a household
69,000	69,050	10,803	7,872	10,803	9,303
69,050	69,100	10,814	7,878	10,814	9,314
69,100	69,150	10,825	7,884	10,825	9,325
69,150	69,200	10,836	7,890	10,836	9,336
69,200	69,250	10,847	7,896	10,847	9,347
69,250	69,300	10,858	7,902	10,858	9,358
69,300	69,350	10,869	7,908	10,869	9,369
69,350	69,400	10,880	7,914	10,880	9,380
69,400	69,450	10,891	7,920	10,891	9,391
69,450	69,500	10,902	7,926	10,902	9,402
69,500	69,550	10,913	7,932	10,913	9,413
69,550	69,600	10,924	7,938	10,924	9,424
69,600	69,650	10,935	7,944	10,935	9,435
69,650	69,700	10,946	7,950	10,946	9,446
69,700	69,750	10,957	7,956	10,957	9,457
69,750	69,800	10,968	7,962	10,968	9,468
69,800	69,850	10,979	7,968	10,979	9,479
69,850	69,900	10,990	7,974	10,990	9,490
69,900	69,950	11,001	7,980	11,001	9,501
69,950	70,000	11,012	7,986	11,012	9,512

70,000

At least	But less than	Single	Married filing jointly *	Married filing separately	Head of a household
70,000	70,050	11,023	7,992	11,023	9,523
70,050	70,100	11,034	7,998	11,034	9,534
70,100	70,150	11,045	8,004	11,045	9,545
70,150	70,200	11,056	8,010	11,056	9,556
70,200	70,250	11,067	8,016	11,067	9,567
70,250	70,300	11,078	8,022	11,078	9,578
70,300	70,350	11,089	8,028	11,089	9,589
70,350	70,400	11,100	8,034	11,100	9,600
70,400	70,450	11,111	8,040	11,111	9,611
70,450	70,500	11,122	8,046	11,122	9,622
70,500	70,550	11,133	8,052	11,133	9,633
70,550	70,600	11,144	8,058	11,144	9,644
70,600	70,650	11,155	8,064	11,155	9,655
70,650	70,700	11,166	8,070	11,166	9,666
70,700	70,750	11,177	8,076	11,177	9,677
70,750	70,800	11,188	8,082	11,188	9,688
70,800	70,850	11,199	8,088	11,199	9,699
70,850	70,900	11,210	8,094	11,210	9,710
70,900	70,950	11,221	8,100	11,221	9,721
70,950	71,000	11,232	8,106	11,232	9,732

71,000

At least	But less than	Single	Married filing jointly *	Married filing separately	Head of a household
71,000	71,050	11,243	8,112	11,243	9,743
71,050	71,100	11,254	8,118	11,254	9,754
71,100	71,150	11,265	8,124	11,265	9,765
71,150	71,200	11,276	8,130	11,276	9,776
71,200	71,250	11,287	8,136	11,287	9,787
71,250	71,300	11,298	8,142	11,298	9,798
71,300	71,350	11,309	8,148	11,309	9,809
71,350	71,400	11,320	8,154	11,320	9,820
71,400	71,450	11,331	8,160	11,331	9,831
71,450	71,500	11,342	8,166	11,342	9,842
71,500	71,550	11,353	8,172	11,353	9,853
71,550	71,600	11,364	8,178	11,364	9,864
71,600	71,650	11,375	8,184	11,375	9,875
71,650	71,700	11,386	8,190	11,386	9,886
71,700	71,750	11,397	8,196	11,397	9,897
71,750	71,800	11,408	8,202	11,408	9,908
71,800	71,850	11,419	8,208	11,419	9,919
71,850	71,900	11,430	8,214	11,430	9,930
71,900	71,950	11,441	8,220	11,441	9,941
71,950	72,000	11,452	8,226	11,452	9,952

72,000

At least	But less than	Single	Married filing jointly *	Married filing separately	Head of a household
72,000	72,050	11,463	8,232	11,463	9,963
72,050	72,100	11,474	8,238	11,474	9,974
72,100	72,150	11,485	8,244	11,485	9,985
72,150	72,200	11,496	8,250	11,496	9,996
72,200	72,250	11,507	8,256	11,507	10,007
72,250	72,300	11,518	8,262	11,518	10,018
72,300	72,350	11,529	8,268	11,529	10,029
72,350	72,400	11,540	8,274	11,540	10,040
72,400	72,450	11,551	8,280	11,551	10,051
72,450	72,500	11,562	8,286	11,562	10,062
72,500	72,550	11,573	8,292	11,573	10,073
72,550	72,600	11,584	8,298	11,584	10,084
72,600	72,650	11,595	8,304	11,595	10,095
72,650	72,700	11,606	8,310	11,606	10,106
72,700	72,750	11,617	8,316	11,617	10,117
72,750	72,800	11,628	8,322	11,628	10,128
72,800	72,850	11,639	8,328	11,639	10,139
72,850	72,900	11,650	8,334	11,650	10,150
72,900	72,950	11,661	8,340	11,661	10,161
72,950	73,000	11,672	8,346	11,672	10,172

73,000

At least	But less than	Single	Married filing jointly *	Married filing separately	Head of a household
73,000	73,050	11,683	8,352	11,683	10,183
73,050	73,100	11,694	8,358	11,694	10,194
73,100	73,150	11,705	8,364	11,705	10,205
73,150	73,200	11,716	8,370	11,716	10,216
73,200	73,250	11,727	8,376	11,727	10,227
73,250	73,300	11,738	8,382	11,738	10,238
73,300	73,350	11,749	8,388	11,749	10,249
73,350	73,400	11,760	8,394	11,760	10,260
73,400	73,450	11,771	8,400	11,771	10,271
73,450	73,500	11,782	8,406	11,782	10,282
73,500	73,550	11,793	8,412	11,793	10,293
73,550	73,600	11,804	8,418	11,804	10,304
73,600	73,650	11,815	8,424	11,815	10,315
73,650	73,700	11,826	8,430	11,826	10,326
73,700	73,750	11,837	8,436	11,837	10,337
73,750	73,800	11,848	8,442	11,848	10,348
73,800	73,850	11,859	8,448	11,859	10,359
73,850	73,900	11,870	8,454	11,870	10,370
73,900	73,950	11,881	8,460	11,881	10,381
73,950	74,000	11,892	8,466	11,892	10,392

74,000

At least	But less than	Single	Married filing jointly *	Married filing separately	Head of a household
74,000	74,050	11,903	8,472	11,903	10,403
74,050	74,100	11,914	8,478	11,914	10,414
74,100	74,150	11,925	8,484	11,925	10,425
74,150	74,200	11,936	8,490	11,936	10,436
74,200	74,250	11,947	8,496	11,947	10,447
74,250	74,300	11,958	8,502	11,958	10,458
74,300	74,350	11,969	8,508	11,969	10,469
74,350	74,400	11,980	8,514	11,980	10,480
74,400	74,450	11,991	8,520	11,991	10,491
74,450	74,500	12,002	8,526	12,002	10,502
74,500	74,550	12,013	8,532	12,013	10,513
74,550	74,600	12,024	8,538	12,024	10,524
74,600	74,650	12,035	8,544	12,035	10,535
74,650	74,700	12,046	8,550	12,046	10,546
74,700	74,750	12,057	8,556	12,057	10,557
74,750	74,800	12,068	8,562	12,068	10,568
74,800	74,850	12,079	8,568	12,079	10,579
74,850	74,900	12,090	8,574	12,090	10,590
74,900	74,950	12,101	8,580	12,101	10,601
74,950	75,000	12,112	8,586	12,112	10,612

(Continued)

* This column must also be used by a qualifying surviving spouse.

2022 Tax Table — *Continued*

75,000

At least	But less than	Single	Married filing jointly *	Married filing separately	Head of a household
75,000	75,050	12,123	8,592	12,123	10,623
75,050	75,100	12,134	8,598	12,134	10,634
75,100	75,150	12,145	8,604	12,145	10,645
75,150	75,200	12,156	8,610	12,156	10,656
75,200	75,250	12,167	8,616	12,167	10,667
75,250	75,300	12,178	8,622	12,178	10,678
75,300	75,350	12,189	8,628	12,189	10,689
75,350	75,400	12,200	8,634	12,200	10,700
75,400	75,450	12,211	8,640	12,211	10,711
75,450	75,500	12,222	8,646	12,222	10,722
75,500	75,550	12,233	8,652	12,233	10,733
75,550	75,600	12,244	8,658	12,244	10,744
75,600	75,650	12,255	8,664	12,255	10,755
75,650	75,700	12,266	8,670	12,266	10,766
75,700	75,750	12,277	8,676	12,277	10,777
75,750	75,800	12,288	8,682	12,288	10,788
75,800	75,850	12,299	8,688	12,299	10,799
75,850	75,900	12,310	8,694	12,310	10,810
75,900	75,950	12,321	8,700	12,321	10,821
75,950	76,000	12,332	8,706	12,332	10,832

76,000

At least	But less than	Single	Married filing jointly *	Married filing separately	Head of a household
76,000	76,050	12,343	8,712	12,343	10,843
76,050	76,100	12,354	8,718	12,354	10,854
76,100	76,150	12,365	8,724	12,365	10,865
76,150	76,200	12,376	8,730	12,376	10,876
76,200	76,250	12,387	8,736	12,387	10,887
76,250	76,300	12,398	8,742	12,398	10,898
76,300	76,350	12,409	8,748	12,409	10,909
76,350	76,400	12,420	8,754	12,420	10,920
76,400	76,450	12,431	8,760	12,431	10,931
76,450	76,500	12,442	8,766	12,442	10,942
76,500	76,550	12,453	8,772	12,453	10,953
76,550	76,600	12,464	8,778	12,464	10,964
76,600	76,650	12,475	8,784	12,475	10,975
76,650	76,700	12,486	8,790	12,486	10,986
76,700	76,750	12,497	8,796	12,497	10,997
76,750	76,800	12,508	8,802	12,508	11,008
76,800	76,850	12,519	8,808	12,519	11,019
76,850	76,900	12,530	8,814	12,530	11,030
76,900	76,950	12,541	8,820	12,541	11,041
76,950	77,000	12,552	8,826	12,552	11,052

77,000

At least	But less than	Single	Married filing jointly *	Married filing separately	Head of a household
77,000	77,050	12,563	8,832	12,563	11,063
77,050	77,100	12,574	8,838	12,574	11,074
77,100	77,150	12,585	8,844	12,585	11,085
77,150	77,200	12,596	8,850	12,596	11,096
77,200	77,250	12,607	8,856	12,607	11,107
77,250	77,300	12,618	8,862	12,618	11,118
77,300	77,350	12,629	8,868	12,629	11,129
77,350	77,400	12,640	8,874	12,640	11,140
77,400	77,450	12,651	8,880	12,651	11,151
77,450	77,500	12,662	8,886	12,662	11,162
77,500	77,550	12,673	8,892	12,673	11,173
77,550	77,600	12,684	8,898	12,684	11,184
77,600	77,650	12,695	8,904	12,695	11,195
77,650	77,700	12,706	8,910	12,706	11,206
77,700	77,750	12,717	8,916	12,717	11,217
77,750	77,800	12,728	8,922	12,728	11,228
77,800	77,850	12,739	8,928	12,739	11,239
77,850	77,900	12,750	8,934	12,750	11,250
77,900	77,950	12,761	8,940	12,761	11,261
77,950	78,000	12,772	8,946	12,772	11,272

78,000

At least	But less than	Single	Married filing jointly *	Married filing separately	Head of a household
78,000	78,050	12,783	8,952	12,783	11,283
78,050	78,100	12,794	8,958	12,794	11,294
78,100	78,150	12,805	8,964	12,805	11,305
78,150	78,200	12,816	8,970	12,816	11,316
78,200	78,250	12,827	8,976	12,827	11,327
78,250	78,300	12,838	8,982	12,838	11,338
78,300	78,350	12,849	8,988	12,849	11,349
78,350	78,400	12,860	8,994	12,860	11,360
78,400	78,450	12,871	9,000	12,871	11,371
78,450	78,500	12,882	9,006	12,882	11,382
78,500	78,550	12,893	9,012	12,893	11,393
78,550	78,600	12,904	9,018	12,904	11,404
78,600	78,650	12,915	9,024	12,915	11,415
78,650	78,700	12,926	9,030	12,926	11,426
78,700	78,750	12,937	9,036	12,937	11,437
78,750	78,800	12,948	9,042	12,948	11,448
78,800	78,850	12,959	9,048	12,959	11,459
78,850	78,900	12,970	9,054	12,970	11,470
78,900	78,950	12,981	9,060	12,981	11,481
78,950	79,000	12,992	9,066	12,992	11,492

79,000

At least	But less than	Single	Married filing jointly *	Married filing separately	Head of a household
79,000	79,050	13,003	9,072	13,003	11,503
79,050	79,100	13,014	9,078	13,014	11,514
79,100	79,150	13,025	9,084	13,025	11,525
79,150	79,200	13,036	9,090	13,036	11,536
79,200	79,250	13,047	9,096	13,047	11,547
79,250	79,300	13,058	9,102	13,058	11,558
79,300	79,350	13,069	9,108	13,069	11,569
79,350	79,400	13,080	9,114	13,080	11,580
79,400	79,450	13,091	9,120	13,091	11,591
79,450	79,500	13,102	9,126	13,102	11,602
79,500	79,550	13,113	9,132	13,113	11,613
79,550	79,600	13,124	9,138	13,124	11,624
79,600	79,650	13,135	9,144	13,135	11,635
79,650	79,700	13,146	9,150	13,146	11,646
79,700	79,750	13,157	9,156	13,157	11,657
79,750	79,800	13,168	9,162	13,168	11,668
79,800	79,850	13,179	9,168	13,179	11,679
79,850	79,900	13,190	9,174	13,190	11,690
79,900	79,950	13,201	9,180	13,201	11,701
79,950	80,000	13,212	9,186	13,212	11,712

80,000

At least	But less than	Single	Married filing jointly *	Married filing separately	Head of a household
80,000	80,050	13,223	9,192	13,223	11,723
80,050	80,100	13,234	9,198	13,234	11,734
80,100	80,150	13,245	9,204	13,245	11,745
80,150	80,200	13,256	9,210	13,256	11,756
80,200	80,250	13,267	9,216	13,267	11,767
80,250	80,300	13,278	9,222	13,278	11,778
80,300	80,350	13,289	9,228	13,289	11,789
80,350	80,400	13,300	9,234	13,300	11,800
80,400	80,450	13,311	9,240	13,311	11,811
80,450	80,500	13,322	9,246	13,322	11,822
80,500	80,550	13,333	9,252	13,333	11,833
80,550	80,600	13,344	9,258	13,344	11,844
80,600	80,650	13,355	9,264	13,355	11,855
80,650	80,700	13,366	9,270	13,366	11,866
80,700	80,750	13,377	9,276	13,377	11,877
80,750	80,800	13,388	9,282	13,388	11,888
80,800	80,850	13,399	9,288	13,399	11,899
80,850	80,900	13,410	9,294	13,410	11,910
80,900	80,950	13,421	9,300	13,421	11,921
80,950	81,000	13,432	9,306	13,432	11,932

81,000

At least	But less than	Single	Married filing jointly *	Married filing separately	Head of a household
81,000	81,050	13,443	9,312	13,443	11,943
81,050	81,100	13,454	9,318	13,454	11,954
81,100	81,150	13,465	9,324	13,465	11,965
81,150	81,200	13,476	9,330	13,476	11,976
81,200	81,250	13,487	9,336	13,487	11,987
81,250	81,300	13,498	9,342	13,498	11,998
81,300	81,350	13,509	9,348	13,509	12,009
81,350	81,400	13,520	9,354	13,520	12,020
81,400	81,450	13,531	9,360	13,531	12,031
81,450	81,500	13,542	9,366	13,542	12,042
81,500	81,550	13,553	9,372	13,553	12,053
81,550	81,600	13,564	9,378	13,564	12,064
81,600	81,650	13,575	9,384	13,575	12,075
81,650	81,700	13,586	9,390	13,586	12,086
81,700	81,750	13,597	9,396	13,597	12,097
81,750	81,800	13,608	9,402	13,608	12,108
81,800	81,850	13,619	9,408	13,619	12,119
81,850	81,900	13,630	9,414	13,630	12,130
81,900	81,950	13,641	9,420	13,641	12,141
81,950	82,000	13,652	9,426	13,652	12,152

82,000

At least	But less than	Single	Married filing jointly *	Married filing separately	Head of a household
82,000	82,050	13,663	9,432	13,663	12,163
82,050	82,100	13,674	9,438	13,674	12,174
82,100	82,150	13,685	9,444	13,685	12,185
82,150	82,200	13,696	9,450	13,696	12,196
82,200	82,250	13,707	9,456	13,707	12,207
82,250	82,300	13,718	9,462	13,718	12,218
82,300	82,350	13,729	9,468	13,729	12,229
82,350	82,400	13,740	9,474	13,740	12,240
82,400	82,450	13,751	9,480	13,751	12,251
82,450	82,500	13,762	9,486	13,762	12,262
82,500	82,550	13,773	9,492	13,773	12,273
82,550	82,600	13,784	9,498	13,784	12,284
82,600	82,650	13,795	9,504	13,795	12,295
82,650	82,700	13,806	9,510	13,806	12,306
82,700	82,750	13,817	9,516	13,817	12,317
82,750	82,800	13,828	9,522	13,828	12,328
82,800	82,850	13,839	9,528	13,839	12,339
82,850	82,900	13,850	9,534	13,850	12,350
82,900	82,950	13,861	9,540	13,861	12,361
82,950	83,000	13,872	9,546	13,872	12,372

83,000

At least	But less than	Single	Married filing jointly *	Married filing separately	Head of a household
83,000	83,050	13,883	9,552	13,883	12,383
83,050	83,100	13,894	9,558	13,894	12,394
83,100	83,150	13,905	9,564	13,905	12,405
83,150	83,200	13,916	9,570	13,916	12,416
83,200	83,250	13,927	9,576	13,927	12,427
83,250	83,300	13,938	9,582	13,938	12,438
83,300	83,350	13,949	9,588	13,949	12,449
83,350	83,400	13,960	9,594	13,960	12,460
83,400	83,450	13,971	9,600	13,971	12,471
83,450	83,500	13,982	9,606	13,982	12,482
83,500	83,550	13,993	9,612	13,993	12,493
83,550	83,600	14,004	9,621	14,004	12,504
83,600	83,650	14,015	9,632	14,015	12,515
83,650	83,700	14,026	9,643	14,026	12,526
83,700	83,750	14,037	9,654	14,037	12,537
83,750	83,800	14,048	9,665	14,048	12,548
83,800	83,850	14,059	9,676	14,059	12,559
83,850	83,900	14,070	9,687	14,070	12,570
83,900	83,950	14,081	9,698	14,081	12,581
83,950	84,000	14,092	9,709	14,092	12,592

* This column must also be used by a qualifying surviving spouse.

(Continued)

2022 Tax Table — *Continued*

84,000

At least	But less than	Single	Married filing jointly *	Married filing separately	Head of a household
84,000	84,050	14,103	9,720	14,103	12,603
84,050	84,100	14,114	9,731	14,114	12,614
84,100	84,150	14,125	9,742	14,125	12,625
84,150	84,200	14,136	9,753	14,136	12,636
84,200	84,250	14,147	9,764	14,147	12,647
84,250	84,300	14,158	9,775	14,158	12,658
84,300	84,350	14,169	9,786	14,169	12,669
84,350	84,400	14,180	9,797	14,180	12,680
84,400	84,450	14,191	9,808	14,191	12,691
84,450	84,500	14,202	9,819	14,202	12,702
84,500	84,550	14,213	9,830	14,213	12,713
84,550	84,600	14,224	9,841	14,224	12,724
84,600	84,650	14,235	9,852	14,235	12,735
84,650	84,700	14,246	9,863	14,246	12,746
84,700	84,750	14,257	9,874	14,257	12,757
84,750	84,800	14,268	9,885	14,268	12,768
84,800	84,850	14,279	9,896	14,279	12,779
84,850	84,900	14,290	9,907	14,290	12,790
84,900	84,950	14,301	9,918	14,301	12,801
84,950	85,000	14,312	9,929	14,312	12,812

85,000

At least	But less than	Single	Married filing jointly *	Married filing separately	Head of a household
85,000	85,050	14,323	9,940	14,323	12,823
85,050	85,100	14,334	9,951	14,334	12,834
85,100	85,150	14,345	9,962	14,345	12,845
85,150	85,200	14,356	9,973	14,356	12,856
85,200	85,250	14,367	9,984	14,367	12,867
85,250	85,300	14,378	9,995	14,378	12,878
85,300	85,350	14,389	10,006	14,389	12,889
85,350	85,400	14,400	10,017	14,400	12,900
85,400	85,450	14,411	10,028	14,411	12,911
85,450	85,500	14,422	10,039	14,422	12,922
85,500	85,550	14,433	10,050	14,433	12,933
85,550	85,600	14,444	10,061	14,444	12,944
85,600	85,650	14,455	10,072	14,455	12,955
85,650	85,700	14,466	10,083	14,466	12,966
85,700	85,750	14,477	10,094	14,477	12,977
85,750	85,800	14,488	10,105	14,488	12,988
85,800	85,850	14,499	10,116	14,499	12,999
85,850	85,900	14,510	10,127	14,510	13,010
85,900	85,950	14,521	10,138	14,521	13,021
85,950	86,000	14,532	10,149	14,532	13,032

86,000

At least	But less than	Single	Married filing jointly *	Married filing separately	Head of a household
86,000	86,050	14,543	10,160	14,543	13,043
86,050	86,100	14,554	10,171	14,554	13,054
86,100	86,150	14,565	10,182	14,565	13,065
86,150	86,200	14,576	10,193	14,576	13,076
86,200	86,250	14,587	10,204	14,587	13,087
86,250	86,300	14,598	10,215	14,598	13,098
86,300	86,350	14,609	10,226	14,609	13,109
86,350	86,400	14,620	10,237	14,620	13,120
86,400	86,450	14,631	10,248	14,631	13,131
86,450	86,500	14,642	10,259	14,642	13,142
86,500	86,550	14,653	10,270	14,653	13,153
86,550	86,600	14,664	10,281	14,664	13,164
86,600	86,650	14,675	10,292	14,675	13,175
86,650	86,700	14,686	10,303	14,686	13,186
86,700	86,750	14,697	10,314	14,697	13,197
86,750	86,800	14,708	10,325	14,708	13,208
86,800	86,850	14,719	10,336	14,719	13,219
86,850	86,900	14,730	10,347	14,730	13,230
86,900	86,950	14,741	10,358	14,741	13,241
86,950	87,000	14,752	10,369	14,752	13,252

87,000

At least	But less than	Single	Married filing jointly *	Married filing separately	Head of a household
87,000	87,050	14,763	10,380	14,763	13,263
87,050	87,100	14,774	10,391	14,774	13,274
87,100	87,150	14,785	10,402	14,785	13,285
87,150	87,200	14,796	10,413	14,796	13,296
87,200	87,250	14,807	10,424	14,807	13,307
87,250	87,300	14,818	10,435	14,818	13,318
87,300	87,350	14,829	10,446	14,829	13,329
87,350	87,400	14,840	10,457	14,840	13,340
87,400	87,450	14,851	10,468	14,851	13,351
87,450	87,500	14,862	10,479	14,862	13,362
87,500	87,550	14,873	10,490	14,873	13,373
87,550	87,600	14,884	10,501	14,884	13,384
87,600	87,650	14,895	10,512	14,895	13,395
87,650	87,700	14,906	10,523	14,906	13,406
87,700	87,750	14,917	10,534	14,917	13,417
87,750	87,800	14,928	10,545	14,928	13,428
87,800	87,850	14,939	10,556	14,939	13,439
87,850	87,900	14,950	10,567	14,950	13,450
87,900	87,950	14,961	10,578	14,961	13,461
87,950	88,000	14,972	10,589	14,972	13,472

88,000

At least	But less than	Single	Married filing jointly *	Married filing separately	Head of a household
88,000	88,050	14,983	10,600	14,983	13,483
88,050	88,100	14,994	10,611	14,994	13,494
88,100	88,150	15,005	10,622	15,005	13,505
88,150	88,200	15,016	10,633	15,016	13,516
88,200	88,250	15,027	10,644	15,027	13,527
88,250	88,300	15,038	10,655	15,038	13,538
88,300	88,350	15,049	10,666	15,049	13,549
88,350	88,400	15,060	10,677	15,060	13,560
88,400	88,450	15,071	10,688	15,071	13,571
88,450	88,500	15,082	10,699	15,082	13,582
88,500	88,550	15,093	10,710	15,093	13,593
88,550	88,600	15,104	10,721	15,104	13,604
88,600	88,650	15,115	10,732	15,115	13,615
88,650	88,700	15,126	10,743	15,126	13,626
88,700	88,750	15,137	10,754	15,137	13,637
88,750	88,800	15,148	10,765	15,148	13,648
88,800	88,850	15,159	10,776	15,159	13,659
88,850	88,900	15,170	10,787	15,170	13,670
88,900	88,950	15,181	10,798	15,181	13,681
88,950	89,000	15,192	10,809	15,192	13,692

89,000

At least	But less than	Single	Married filing jointly *	Married filing separately	Head of a household
89,000	89,050	15,203	10,820	15,203	13,703
89,050	89,100	15,214	10,831	15,214	13,714
89,100	89,150	15,226	10,842	15,226	13,726
89,150	89,200	15,238	10,853	15,238	13,738
89,200	89,250	15,250	10,864	15,250	13,750
89,250	89,300	15,262	10,875	15,262	13,762
89,300	89,350	15,274	10,886	15,274	13,774
89,350	89,400	15,286	10,897	15,286	13,786
89,400	89,450	15,298	10,908	15,298	13,798
89,450	89,500	15,310	10,919	15,310	13,810
89,500	89,550	15,322	10,930	15,322	13,822
89,550	89,600	15,334	10,941	15,334	13,834
89,600	89,650	15,346	10,952	15,346	13,846
89,650	89,700	15,358	10,963	15,358	13,858
89,700	89,750	15,370	10,974	15,370	13,870
89,750	89,800	15,382	10,985	15,382	13,882
89,800	89,850	15,394	10,996	15,394	13,894
89,850	89,900	15,406	11,007	15,406	13,906
89,900	89,950	15,418	11,018	15,418	13,918
89,950	90,000	15,430	11,029	15,430	13,930

90,000

At least	But less than	Single	Married filing jointly *	Married filing separately	Head of a household
90,000	90,050	15,442	11,040	15,442	13,942
90,050	90,100	15,454	11,051	15,454	13,954
90,100	90,150	15,466	11,062	15,466	13,966
90,150	90,200	15,478	11,073	15,478	13,978
90,200	90,250	15,490	11,084	15,490	13,990
90,250	90,300	15,502	11,095	15,502	14,002
90,300	90,350	15,514	11,106	15,514	14,014
90,350	90,400	15,526	11,117	15,526	14,026
90,400	90,450	15,538	11,128	15,538	14,038
90,450	90,500	15,550	11,139	15,550	14,050
90,500	90,550	15,562	11,150	15,562	14,062
90,550	90,600	15,574	11,161	15,574	14,074
90,600	90,650	15,586	11,172	15,586	14,086
90,650	90,700	15,598	11,183	15,598	14,098
90,700	90,750	15,610	11,194	15,610	14,110
90,750	90,800	15,622	11,205	15,622	14,122
90,800	90,850	15,634	11,216	15,634	14,134
90,850	90,900	15,646	11,227	15,646	14,146
90,900	90,950	15,658	11,238	15,658	14,158
90,950	91,000	15,670	11,249	15,670	14,170

91,000

At least	But less than	Single	Married filing jointly *	Married filing separately	Head of a household
91,000	91,050	15,682	11,260	15,682	14,182
91,050	91,100	15,694	11,271	15,694	14,194
91,100	91,150	15,706	11,282	15,706	14,206
91,150	91,200	15,718	11,293	15,718	14,218
91,200	91,250	15,730	11,304	15,730	14,230
91,250	91,300	15,742	11,315	15,742	14,242
91,300	91,350	15,754	11,326	15,754	14,254
91,350	91,400	15,766	11,337	15,766	14,266
91,400	91,450	15,778	11,348	15,778	14,278
91,450	91,500	15,790	11,359	15,790	14,290
91,500	91,550	15,802	11,370	15,802	14,302
91,550	91,600	15,814	11,381	15,814	14,314
91,600	91,650	15,826	11,392	15,826	14,326
91,650	91,700	15,838	11,403	15,838	14,338
91,700	91,750	15,850	11,414	15,850	14,350
91,750	91,800	15,862	11,425	15,862	14,362
91,800	91,850	15,874	11,436	15,874	14,374
91,850	91,900	15,886	11,447	15,886	14,386
91,900	91,950	15,898	11,458	15,898	14,398
91,950	92,000	15,910	11,469	15,910	14,410

92,000

At least	But less than	Single	Married filing jointly *	Married filing separately	Head of a household
92,000	92,050	15,922	11,480	15,922	14,422
92,050	92,100	15,934	11,491	15,934	14,434
92,100	92,150	15,946	11,502	15,946	14,446
92,150	92,200	15,958	11,513	15,958	14,458
92,200	92,250	15,970	11,524	15,970	14,470
92,250	92,300	15,982	11,535	15,982	14,482
92,300	92,350	15,994	11,546	15,994	14,494
92,350	92,400	16,006	11,557	16,006	14,506
92,400	92,450	16,018	11,568	16,018	14,518
92,450	92,500	16,030	11,579	16,030	14,530
92,500	92,550	16,042	11,590	16,042	14,542
92,550	92,600	16,054	11,601	16,054	14,554
92,600	92,650	16,066	11,612	16,066	14,566
92,650	92,700	16,078	11,623	16,078	14,578
92,700	92,750	16,090	11,634	16,090	14,590
92,750	92,800	16,102	11,645	16,102	14,602
92,800	92,850	16,114	11,656	16,114	14,614
92,850	92,900	16,126	11,667	16,126	14,626
92,900	92,950	16,138	11,678	16,138	14,638
92,950	93,000	16,150	11,689	16,150	14,650

* This column must also be used by a qualifying surviving spouse.

(Continued)

If line 15 (taxable income) is—		And you are—				If line 15 (taxable income) is—		And you are—				If line 15 (taxable income) is—		And you are—			
At least	But less than	Single	Married filing jointly *	Married filing separately	Head of a household	At least	But less than	Single	Married filing jointly *	Married filing separately	Head of a household	At least	But less than	Single	Married filing jointly *	Married filing separately	Head of a household
		Your tax is—						Your tax is—						Your tax is—			

93,000 / 96,000 / 99,000

At least	But less than	Single	MFJ	MFS	HoH	At least	But less than	Single	MFJ	MFS	HoH	At least	But less than	Single	MFJ	MFS	HoH
93,000	93,050	16,162	11,700	16,162	14,662	96,000	96,050	16,882	12,360	16,882	15,382	99,000	99,050	17,602	13,020	17,602	16,102
93,050	93,100	16,174	11,711	16,174	14,674	96,050	96,100	16,894	12,371	16,894	15,394	99,050	99,100	17,614	13,031	17,614	16,114
93,100	93,150	16,186	11,722	16,186	14,686	96,100	96,150	16,906	12,382	16,906	15,406	99,100	99,150	17,626	13,042	17,626	16,126
93,150	93,200	16,198	11,733	16,198	14,698	96,150	96,200	16,918	12,393	16,918	15,418	99,150	99,200	17,638	13,053	17,638	16,138
93,200	93,250	16,210	11,744	16,210	14,710	96,200	96,250	16,930	12,404	16,930	15,430	99,200	99,250	17,650	13,064	17,650	16,150
93,250	93,300	16,222	11,755	16,222	14,722	96,250	96,300	16,942	12,415	16,942	15,442	99,250	99,300	17,662	13,075	17,662	16,162
93,300	93,350	16,234	11,766	16,234	14,734	96,300	96,350	16,954	12,426	16,954	15,454	99,300	99,350	17,674	13,086	17,674	16,174
93,350	93,400	16,246	11,777	16,246	14,746	96,350	96,400	16,966	12,437	16,966	15,466	99,350	99,400	17,686	13,097	17,686	16,186
93,400	93,450	16,258	11,788	16,258	14,758	96,400	96,450	16,978	12,448	16,978	15,478	99,400	99,450	17,698	13,108	17,698	16,198
93,450	93,500	16,270	11,799	16,270	14,770	96,450	96,500	16,990	12,459	16,990	15,490	99,450	99,500	17,710	13,119	17,710	16,210
93,500	93,550	16,282	11,810	16,282	14,782	96,500	96,550	17,002	12,470	17,002	15,502	99,500	99,550	17,722	13,130	17,722	16,222
93,550	93,600	16,294	11,821	16,294	14,794	96,550	96,600	17,014	12,481	17,014	15,514	99,550	99,600	17,734	13,141	17,734	16,234
93,600	93,650	16,306	11,832	16,306	14,806	96,600	96,650	17,026	12,492	17,026	15,526	99,600	99,650	17,746	13,152	17,746	16,246
93,650	93,700	16,318	11,843	16,318	14,818	96,650	96,700	17,038	12,503	17,038	15,538	99,650	99,700	17,758	13,163	17,758	16,258
93,700	93,750	16,330	11,854	16,330	14,830	96,700	96,750	17,050	12,514	17,050	15,550	99,700	99,750	17,770	13,174	17,770	16,270
93,750	93,800	16,342	11,865	16,342	14,842	96,750	96,800	17,062	12,525	17,062	15,562	99,750	99,800	17,782	13,185	17,782	16,282
93,800	93,850	16,354	11,876	16,354	14,854	96,800	96,850	17,074	12,536	17,074	15,574	99,800	99,850	17,794	13,196	17,794	16,294
93,850	93,900	16,366	11,887	16,366	14,866	96,850	96,900	17,086	12,547	17,086	15,586	99,850	99,900	17,806	13,207	17,806	16,306
93,900	93,950	16,378	11,898	16,378	14,878	96,900	96,950	17,098	12,558	17,098	15,598	99,900	99,950	17,818	13,218	17,818	16,318
93,950	94,000	16,390	11,909	16,390	14,890	96,950	97,000	17,110	12,569	17,110	15,610	99,950	100,000	17,830	13,229	17,830	16,330

94,000 / 97,000

$100,000 or over use the Tax Computation Worksheet

At least	But less than	Single	MFJ	MFS	HoH	At least	But less than	Single	MFJ	MFS	HoH
94,000	94,050	16,402	11,920	16,402	14,902	97,000	97,050	17,122	12,580	17,122	15,622
94,050	94,100	16,414	11,931	16,414	14,914	97,050	97,100	17,134	12,591	17,134	15,634
94,100	94,150	16,426	11,942	16,426	14,926	97,100	97,150	17,146	12,602	17,146	15,646
94,150	94,200	16,438	11,953	16,438	14,938	97,150	97,200	17,158	12,613	17,158	15,658
94,200	94,250	16,450	11,964	16,450	14,950	97,200	97,250	17,170	12,624	17,170	15,670
94,250	94,300	16,462	11,975	16,462	14,962	97,250	97,300	17,182	12,635	17,182	15,682
94,300	94,350	16,474	11,986	16,474	14,974	97,300	97,350	17,194	12,646	17,194	15,694
94,350	94,400	16,486	11,997	16,486	14,986	97,350	97,400	17,206	12,657	17,206	15,706
94,400	94,450	16,498	12,008	16,498	14,998	97,400	97,450	17,218	12,668	17,218	15,718
94,450	94,500	16,510	12,019	16,510	15,010	97,450	97,500	17,230	12,679	17,230	15,730
94,500	94,550	16,522	12,030	16,522	15,022	97,500	97,550	17,242	12,690	17,242	15,742
94,550	94,600	16,534	12,041	16,534	15,034	97,550	97,600	17,254	12,701	17,254	15,754
94,600	94,650	16,546	12,052	16,546	15,046	97,600	97,650	17,266	12,712	17,266	15,766
94,650	94,700	16,558	12,063	16,558	15,058	97,650	97,700	17,278	12,723	17,278	15,778
94,700	94,750	16,570	12,074	16,570	15,070	97,700	97,750	17,290	12,734	17,290	15,790
94,750	94,800	16,582	12,085	16,582	15,082	97,750	97,800	17,302	12,745	17,302	15,802
94,800	94,850	16,594	12,096	16,594	15,094	97,800	97,850	17,314	12,756	17,314	15,814
94,850	94,900	16,606	12,107	16,606	15,106	97,850	97,900	17,326	12,767	17,326	15,826
94,900	94,950	16,618	12,118	16,618	15,118	97,900	97,950	17,338	12,778	17,338	15,838
94,950	95,000	16,630	12,129	16,630	15,130	97,950	98,000	17,350	12,789	17,350	15,850

95,000 / 98,000

At least	But less than	Single	MFJ	MFS	HoH	At least	But less than	Single	MFJ	MFS	HoH
95,000	95,050	16,642	12,140	16,642	15,142	98,000	98,050	17,362	12,800	17,362	15,862
95,050	95,100	16,654	12,151	16,654	15,154	98,050	98,100	17,374	12,811	17,374	15,874
95,100	95,150	16,666	12,162	16,666	15,166	98,100	98,150	17,386	12,822	17,386	15,886
95,150	95,200	16,678	12,173	16,678	15,178	98,150	98,200	17,398	12,833	17,398	15,898
95,200	95,250	16,690	12,184	16,690	15,190	98,200	98,250	17,410	12,844	17,410	15,910
95,250	95,300	16,702	12,195	16,702	15,202	98,250	98,300	17,422	12,855	17,422	15,922
95,300	95,350	16,714	12,206	16,714	15,214	98,300	98,350	17,434	12,866	17,434	15,934
95,350	95,400	16,726	12,217	16,726	15,226	98,350	98,400	17,446	12,877	17,446	15,946
95,400	95,450	16,738	12,228	16,738	15,238	98,400	98,450	17,458	12,888	17,458	15,958
95,450	95,500	16,750	12,239	16,750	15,250	98,450	98,500	17,470	12,899	17,470	15,970
95,500	95,550	16,762	12,250	16,762	15,262	98,500	98,550	17,482	12,910	17,482	15,982
95,550	95,600	16,774	12,261	16,774	15,274	98,550	98,600	17,494	12,921	17,494	15,994
95,600	95,650	16,786	12,272	16,786	15,286	98,600	98,650	17,506	12,932	17,506	16,006
95,650	95,700	16,798	12,283	16,798	15,298	98,650	98,700	17,518	12,943	17,518	16,018
95,700	95,750	16,810	12,294	16,810	15,310	98,700	98,750	17,530	12,954	17,530	16,030
95,750	95,800	16,822	12,305	16,822	15,322	98,750	98,800	17,542	12,965	17,542	16,042
95,800	95,850	16,834	12,316	16,834	15,334	98,800	98,850	17,554	12,976	17,554	16,054
95,850	95,900	16,846	12,327	16,846	15,346	98,850	98,900	17,566	12,987	17,566	16,066
95,900	95,950	16,858	12,338	16,858	15,358	98,900	98,950	17,578	12,998	17,578	16,078
95,950	96,000	16,870	12,349	16,870	15,370	98,950	99,000	17,590	13,009	17,590	16,090

* This column must also be used by a qualifying surviving spouse.

2022 Tax Computation Worksheet—Line 16

 See the instructions for line 16 to see if you must use the worksheet below to figure your tax.

Note. If you are required to use this worksheet to figure the tax on an amount from another form or worksheet, such as the Qualified Dividends and Capital Gain Tax Worksheet, the Schedule D Tax Worksheet, Schedule J, Form 8615, or the Foreign Earned Income Tax Worksheet, enter the amount from that form or worksheet in column (a) of the row that applies to the amount you are looking up. Enter the result on the appropriate line of the form or worksheet that you are completing.

Section A—Use if your filing status is Single. Complete the row below that applies to you.

Taxable income. If line 15 is—	(a) Enter the amount from line 15	(b) Multiplication amount	(c) Multiply (a) by (b)	(d) Subtraction amount	Tax. Subtract (d) from (c). Enter the result here and on the entry space on line 16.
At least $100,000 but not over $170,050	$	× 24% (0.24)	$	$ 6,164.50	$
Over $170,050 but not over $215,950	$	× 32% (0.32)	$	$ 19,768.50	$
Over $215,950 but not over $539,900	$	× 35% (0.35)	$	$ 26,247.00	$
Over $539,900	$	× 37% (0.37)	$	$ 37,045.00	$

Section B—Use if your filing status is Married filing jointly or Qualifying surviving spouse. Complete the row below that applies to you.

Taxable income. If line 15 is—	(a) Enter the amount from line 15	(b) Multiplication amount	(c) Multiply (a) by (b)	(d) Subtraction amount	Tax. Subtract (d) from (c). Enter the result here and on the entry space on line 16.
At least $100,000 but not over $178,150	$	× 22% (0.22)	$	$ 8,766.00	$
Over $178,150 but not over $340,100	$	× 24% (0.24)	$	$ 12,329.00	$
Over $340,100 but not over $431,900	$	× 32% (0.32)	$	$ 39,537.00	$
Over $431,900 but not over $647,850	$	× 35% (0.35)	$	$ 52,494.00	$
Over $647,850	$	× 37% (0.37)	$	$ 65,451.00	$

Section C—Use if your filing status is Married filing separately. Complete the row below that applies to you.

Taxable income. If line 15 is—	(a) Enter the amount from line 15	(b) Multiplication amount	(c) Multiply (a) by (b)	(d) Subtraction amount	Tax. Subtract (d) from (c). Enter the result here and on the entry space on line 16.
At least $100,000 but not over $170,050	$	× 24% (0.24)	$	$ 6,164.50	$
Over $170,050 but not over $215,950	$	× 32% (0.32)	$	$ 19,768.50	$
Over $215,950 but not over $323,925	$	× 35% (0.35)	$	$ 26,247.00	$
Over $323,925	$	× 37% (0.37)	$	$ 32,725.50	$

Section D—Use if your filing status is Head of household. Complete the row below that applies to you.

Taxable income. If line 15 is—	(a) Enter the amount from line 15	(b) Multiplication amount	(c) Multiply (a) by (b)	(d) Subtraction amount	Tax. Subtract (d) from (c). Enter the result here and on the entry space on line 16.
At least $100,000 but not over $170,050	$	× 24% (0.24)	$	$ 7,664.00	$
Over $170,050 but not over $215,950	$	× 32% (0.32)	$	$ 21,268.00	$
Over $215,950 but not over $539,900	$	× 35% (0.35)	$	$ 27,746.50	$
Over $539,900	$	× 37% (0.37)	$	$ 38,544.50	$

Topical Index

References are to paragraph (¶) numbers

FOR

FOR

SEC

WOR